Footprint Handbook

Arg

CALGARY PUBLIC LIBRARY

OCT   2017

CHRIS WALLACE

This is
Argentina

Few countries confront you with their sheer immensity quite like Argentina. It is an intense, dramatic place offering breathtaking contrasts in every corner of the nation. From the arid deserts of the north to the sprawling ice fields of the south, Argentina has something for any intrepid traveller itching for things remote, and every 'blighted wanderer' looking for an escape.

The capital, Buenos Aires, is a star on the global stage, a potent blend of modern European metropolis and throwback Latin American port city. Its residents tolerate the day only to come alive at night, and life races past the grand baroque buildings at a dizzying speed. However, step into a *milonga* and the pace slows as the unmistakable strings and accordion notes of the tango transport you to a previous century, where poor men killed each other with knives and prostitutes died of broken hearts.

In the north of the country the muscular Iguazú Falls thunder through impenetrable jungle filled with electric-blue butterflies and rainbow-billed toucans. Greedy capuchin monkeys snatch berries over the heads of tourists while crumbling mission ruins lie undisturbed among the trees. In the south, world-class ski resorts overlook lakes of cobalt blue fading in colour from the centre until crystalline waters lap at the shores. Further towards the end of the world, silent glaciers stretch endlessly until they shatter with a roar into a milky turquoise lagoon.

And in between? Infinite space. Drive the desolate Ruta 40 through the lonely expanse of Patagonia and the only sign of life will be a couple of condors and a thousand prehistoric handprints on a cave wall; wander the pampas and you'll find nothing other than cattle and the occasional solitary ombu tree. Yet throughout the country, from colonial Salta to wild Ushuaia, you'll find that the Argentine people are welcoming, boisterous and always at the ready with *mate* and conversation.

Chris Wallace

Best of
Argentina

❷ Córdoba

A metropolitan experience as vibrant as Buenos Aires but operating at a more relaxed pace. The second largest city in Argentina boasts the country's oldest university and is famous for its colonial centre. But the real stars are the outlying areas, which include Jesuit estancias, Che Guevara's childhood home, and the Germanic town of Villa General Belgrano. Page 129.

❸ Aconcagua

Bordering the sleepy college town of Mendoza is the Andes mountain range. And amid this mighty backbone of South America sits Aconcagua, the highest peak on the continent and second-highest in the world outside the Himalaya. Beckoning adventurers from across the globe, only the fittest and most serious of mountaineers need apply. Page 199.

❶ San Telmo

The oldest barrio in Buenos Aires, colonial San Telmo is destination number one for an authentic tango experience. But it's more than antique shops, bustling street fairs, poetic cafés and fish-netted dancers twirling in *milongas*. Here tourists, artists, vagabonds and businesspeople mingle, strolling the cobbled streets and frequenting the dive bars, artisanal beer houses and buzzworthy restaurants. Page 53.

❸

❹

❺ Esteros del Iberá

Those who are willing to travel outside the capital and into Corrientes Province will discover a treasure unlike any other in the country. This system of bogs, lagoons and floating islands is a paradise for wildlife enthusiasts and birdwatchers. These are the second-largest wetlands in the world after Brazil's Pantanal. Page 347.

❺

❹ Quebrada de Humahuaca

The northwest of Argentina is home to many natural wonders, like these stunning terracotta gorges just outside Jujuy. Mother Nature went wild with the paint box, coating the rock strata in shades of red, a backdrop for the idyllic oasis villages in the area. Be sure to come for the raucous Easter and Carnival celebrations. Page 295.

❻ San Ignacio

On the surface, the town of San Ignacio is a quiet, unassuming place. Pay a visit, though, and you'll discover its colonial heart: the Jesuit ruins of San Ignacio Miní, a mission founded in the 1600s. This crumbling UNESCO World Heritage Site is a great remnant of a time when South America as we know it was only just beginning to take shape. Page 359.

❼ Iguazú Falls

As you twist and turn along wooden walkways, you're met with a sheer drop to one side and thundering falls spraying you with mist on the other. Brave the Garganta del Diablo Circuit and you'll reach a harrowing view straight down the Devil's Throat. Look up for the spectacular sight of 275 converging waterfalls. Page 367.

❽ Parque Nacional Los Alerces

There are few better vantage points in which to enjoy the Patagonian Andes in all their splendour than Los Alerces. Christened after the superlatively thick tree of the same name, this national park boasts virgin forest, hanging glaciers and perfect hikes. It's also a short jaunt from the pristine Patagonian town of Esquel. Page 473.

❾ Península Valdés

This little rock jutting out to sea is home to some of the best wildlife spotting on the Atlantic Coast of Patagonia. A conservation site for marine mammals, the peninsula is a natural habitat for threatened species, such as the southern right whale. Highlights include ravenous orcas, penguin colonies and glorious beaches. Page 493.

⑩ Glaciar Perito Moreno

A living monolith, tourists flock to experience the awe of being dwarfed by this glacier's presence. An expanse of white stretches away until a wall of jagged blue ice, millions of years old, rumbles and fractures, crashing into the turquoise waters below. This is the world's only advancing and retreating glacier. Page 541.

⑪ Parque Nacional Torres del Paine

Quite simply one of the world's greatest national parks. When trekkers dream, they dream of Torres del Paine. Those with iron wills can put themselves to the ultimate test and attempt the full circuit, a seven-to eight-day trek that showcases all the splendour the park has to offer. Page 579.

⑫ Estancia Harberton

Over a century before Ushuaia was a tourist destination, there was Estancia Harberton. The missionary Thomas Bridges founded it in 1886 as an outpost where he hoped to learn about the indigenous peoples of Tierra del Fuego. The result was a national landmark sitting on the serene Beagle Channel that is still run by Bridges' descendants today. Page 617.

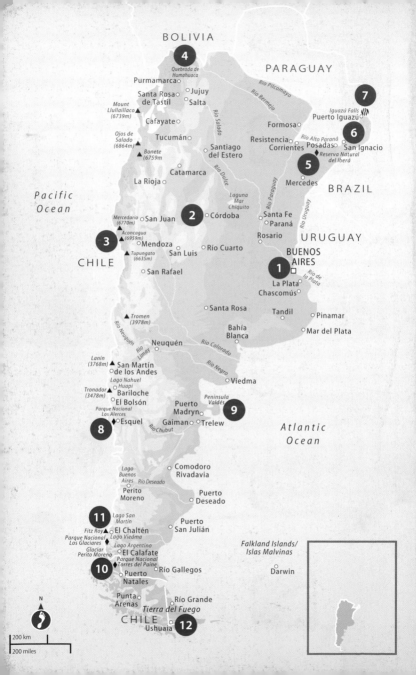

Route
planner

One week
city nightlife and mighty waterfalls

The essentials for any trip are the bright lights of Buenos Aires and the stunning Iguazú Falls. Buenos Aires is a great first port of call, whether you want to see the football, try tango or shop till you drop, and to get any sense of the city you need a minimum of three days. Then take an overnight bus (16 hours), or a more expensive but much quicker flight, to Iguazú Falls. These are the country's star attraction and should not be missed. Two days is sufficient to see both the Argentine and Brazilian sides of the falls, or better still allow two days to explore the larger Argentine park in more detail. Then return to Buenos Aires. Alternatively, if you've money to spare, spend the weekend at one of the grandiose estancias close to the capital, where you can ride horses, play sports, swim or just relax in the sun.

Two weeks
world-class trekking, rich indigenous culture and stunning landscape

This itinerary is best suited to the warmer months (November to March). Start by enjoying fast-paced Buenos Aires in all its glory for three packed days and spend a couple of days at the Iguazú Falls. Then fly, via Buenos Aires, to El Calafate in Patagonia for breathtaking views of the southern ice field. Spend at least a day staring at the 60-m-high ice walls of the immense Perito Moreno Glacier from the wooden walkways on the peninsula, then catch the four-hour bus to El Chaltén to enjoy the relatively easy four-day hikes into the mountains. Otherwise, skip

Right: La Boca, Buenos Aires
Opposite page: Cerro Fitz Roy

El Chaltén and head across the border to Puerto Natales in Chile. From there, hire your camping equipment and head off on the 'W' Circuit of the spectacular Parque Nacional Torres del Paine. You could also visit the Parque Nacional Bernardo O'Higgins. Return to Buenos Aires for a night before your journey home.

An alternative itinerary heads northwest from Buenos Aires to Salta. The city's colonial splendour contrasts perfectly with the culture of the *puna*, where Pachamama festivities are a glimpse of another time. Hire a car here or catch a local bus to Quebrada de Humahuaca, a vast red gorge dotted with ancient rock formations in astounding colours, connecting a string of little villages, including Tilcara, Humahuaca and Purmamarca. From Salta you can also visit the timeless Valles Calchaquíes, where high-altitude wine is grown in dramatic rugged landscapes. Fly back to Buenos Aires for one last night.

One month

lose yourself in BA's barrios, then discover the jewels of north and south

A month is the ideal amount of time to spend in Argentina, giving you a feel for the country's extraordinary contrasts. Start in Buenos Aires, where you'll have time to explore chic Palermo Viejo and old San Telmo with its cobbled streets. You could also visit the delta river system just north of the city. Heading north, your trip to the Iguazú Falls should be combined with a visit to the Jesuit mission ruins hidden by the thick jungle, or time in a lodge in the Esteros del Iberá wetlands.

After Iguazú, fly south to El Calafate to experience the immensity of the Perito Moreno Glacier. From November to March head over to El Chaltén for a few days' hiking, or cross the border into Chile to trek in the Torres del Paine National Park. From El Calafate you have time to drive the lonely Ruta 40 north to Bariloche in Ernesto 'Che'

Guevara's tyre tracks. Stop off at the Cueva de las Manos to see incredibly preserved prehistoric cave paintings. Alternatively, fly south from El Calafate to Ushuaia to see the 'End of the World'. Tierra del Fuego offers the ultimate wilderness and, as you take a boat trip along the Beagle Channel, you'll feel like a true explorer.

From Ushuaia, take a flight to picturesque Bariloche, where you'll find chalet-style hotels, chocolate shops and a backdrop of peaks. The next few days should be spent exploring the Lake District on foot and by car: enjoy the serene lakeside setting of San Martín de Los Andes; discover quiet Villa Pehuenia, surrounded by monkey puzzle trees, or fish for giant trout at Junín de los Andes. Then head south to laid-back El Bolsón for superb hiking in the 2000-year-old forests of Los Alerces National Park or ride the *Old Patagonian Express* train into the hills.

Moving on, head north by bus to Mendoza to visit the nearby vineyards and do a winery tour, before travelling to Córdoba to marvel at the colonial architecture and the restored Jesuit missions. Finally, make your way up to Salta in the northwest. This is another Argentina, of rich indigenous culture and ancient civilizations. Visit the Valles Calchaquíes and the Quebrada de Humahuaca, before heading back to Buenos Aires for your final night.

Right: Cueva de las Manos
Below: Vineyards, Mendoza
Opposite page: Salta church

Best
treks

La Cumbrecita

Located in the heart of Córdoba province, La Cumbrecita is a small town best accessed on foot. No cars or motorcycles are allowed into the village, and this simple rule creates a peaceful getaway. What you will see is lots of thirsty trekkers looking for some of the locally brewed beers. You can walk here from the German-style town of Villa General Belgrano and from some of the other little towns nearby as well. This is an easy to intermediate trek. The village's website has lots of useful information: www.lacumbrecita.gov.ar. Page 159.

Above: Aconcagua
Opposite page top: Parque
Nacional Perito Moreno
Opposite page bottom: El Chaltén

Aconcagua

Less than 200 km from Mendoza, Aconcagua National Park is home to the highest peak in the world outside the Himalaya. The mighty Aconcagua scrapes the sky at 6959 m and should only be attempted by experienced climbers with a guide. Allow at least eight days to acclimatize to the altitude before you attempt this trek, and speak to the park rangers about a permit. For more information, see www.aconcagua.mendoza.gov.ar. Page 199.

Sendero Chorro de los Loros

Only a short distance from Salta is El Rey National Park, located in a horseshoe-shaped valley, surrounded by the peaks of the Sierra del Piquete mountain range. Few people make it here due to its remote location, ensuring clean trails, more wildlife and the chance to be alone in the wild. There are eight trails, with the most interesting being the Sendero Chorro de los Loros, which takes you through the jungle for 10 km and brings you up close and personal with the local wildlife. This is an intermediate trek. See www.welcomeargentina.com/parques/elrey.html. Page 312.

Volcán Lanín

One of the world's most beautiful mountains, Lanín (3776 m) is geologically

one of the youngest volcanoes (though now extinct) of the Andes. To reach the summit is a challenging three-day climb, with two [italic]refugios at 2400 m. The views are spectacular but the climb will keep you out of breath. Because of its relative accessibility, the risks are often underestimated: crampons and ice axe are essential. Page 408.

Parque Nacional Perito Moreno

If you are a lover of all things remote and inaccessible, head to the Perito Moreno

National Park, just off the Ruta 40. Tours to the park are increasing, but it may be easiest to rent a car. The best trek to do is to Lago Burmeister, which is easy, relatively short and offers stunning views of the lake as well as the pristine surrounds. You will be the only person here. Camp by the lake and watch the shadows of the mountains dance in the moonlight. Check out www.losglaciares.com. Page 528.

El Chaltén

Nestled in between jagged peaks and snow-laden valleys, El Chaltén is the perfect base for treks in the area. Follow the signs from the edge of town, and in less than 30 minutes you'll be all alone on a mountain pass overlooking deep blue lakes and fertile valleys. Return to your hostel and relax in one of the lively restaurants in town. The routes range from easy two-hour walks to challenging multi-day treks. A helpful website is www.elchalten.com. Page 543.

Palace of the Argentine National Congress, Buenos Aires

When to go

Climate

Argentina is an appealing destination for warm, sunny holidays in the middle of the northern hemisphere winter. However, since the country covers such a vast area, there is somewhere to visit at any time of year. The southern hemisphere summer is from December to March, spring is from mid-September to November, autumn is from March to May and winter from June to August.

Before you look at when to go, start thinking about what you would like to see. Generally speaking, November to April is the best time for travelling to Mendoza, San Juan, Córdoba, Patagonia and Ushuaia. Trekking trails are open and national parks are at their prettiest. For the rest of the country, namely Salta, Jujuy, Tucumán, Corrientes and Iguazú Falls, May to October is best, as temperatures tend to be cooler and there is less rain. Exceptions are the marine reserve at Península Valdés, which has different seasons for different animals, and also the ski resorts, whose season runs from about June to mid-October, depending on the climate.

Buenos Aires city is wonderful any time of year but is at its best in spring and autumn, when the weather is sunny and mild. The city can be hot and humid in the height of summer, with temperatures over 40°C and humidity at 80%. If you come in summer, consider spending a night in the delta or on an estancia to cool down.

See also weather charts at the beginning of chapters.

Festivals

It is worth planning your trip to coincide with certain festivals but book transport and accommodation well in advance. The main holiday period is January to March when all Argentine schoolchildren are on holiday and most families go away for a few weeks up to two months. All popular tourist destinations become extremely busy at this time, with foreign visitors adding to the crowds, particularly in Bariloche, El Calafate and Ushuaia. You'll find that most of Buenos Aires' residents leave town for the whole of January. The richest go to Punta del Este in Uruguay and the beaches in Brazil, everyone else heads to Mar del Plata and the rest of the coast.

During Easter week, and the winter school holidays throughout July, hotels may also fill up fast, particularly in the ski resorts.

No one works on the national holidays, and these are often long weekends, with a resulting surge of people to popular holiday places. See also public holidays, page 679.

Best festivals

Empanada festival

Each September the *empanada* festival in Tucumán brings together the best *empanada* chefs in the country. There are cooking displays, music and the fiercely contested 'best *empanada*' competition. The region produces spicy *empanadas* with golden pastry. Don't eat for a week beforehand so you'll have room to fit in as many as you can. Book bus tickets and accommodation early.

Festival de la Luz

Festival de la Luz (Festival of Light), each August and September in Buenos Aires, is a collaboration of dozens of photography festivals around the world. All over the city free exhibitions, events, conferences and workshops are held, and even the smallest of art galleries participate. Look in newspapers for free events.

Fiesta de la Tradición

To celebrate the culture and lifestyle of the Argentine gauchos, each November the population of San Antonio de Areco, a small town near Buenos Aires, swells as people arrive from far afield to attend the Fiesta de la Tradición. There are horse-riding displays, live music, stalls selling gaucho clothes and metal work, and gaucho-inspired artwork is on show. The festival concludes on 10 November with the Día de la Tradición, which pays homage to José Hernández who wrote the epic gaucho poem *Martín Fierro*.

Fiesta Nacional de la Cereza

Situated just off the Ruta 40 in an oasis on the shores of Lago Buenos Aires, Los Antiguos is usually a sleepy country town. But come January and the Fiesta Nacional de la Cereza (cherry festival), now running for over a quarter-century, the hotels fill up, the streets crowd with cars, and people from all over Argentina come to enjoy the regional produce. There are stalls selling local fruit, including cherries, and crafts. Each night there are fireworks and at the end of the festival a Cherry Queen is chosen, attracting crowds of up to 30,000 people.

Oktoberfest

Attractive Villa General Belgrano in Córdoba keeps up the Oktoberfest tradition every year when the small German-style village turns into a mosh pit of beer lovers. Local beer halls fill up quickly and accommodation is really hard to find. Come for the party atmosphere and the mix of people, not for a peaceful weekend away. The locally brewed beers are always a favourite.

Vendimia wine festival

The Vendimia wine festival in Mendoza lasts from January right through to the first weeks of March and involves huge flamboyant parades day and night, featuring floats carrying the 17 candidates for Harvest Queen. The festival also promotes local growers and their products, as well as national musicians and artists. It has been celebrated for nearly 70 years and it attracts more and more people every year.

What to do

from climbing the Andes to cross-country skiing

Birdwatching

It comes as no surprise in a country so rich in untouched natural habitats that the birdlife is extraordinary and extremely varied. From the wealth of seabirds at Península Valdés to the colourful species in the subtropical rainforest near the Iguazú Falls, from the marshlands of Esteros del Iberá or the Chaco savannah to the Lake District and the mountainous interior of Tierra del Fuego, there are marvellous opportunities to spot birds. At least 980 of the 2926 species of bird registered in South America exist in Argentina, and many birdwatching hotspots have easy access. There are specialist tours led by expert guides in most areas; see the travelling text for details.

All Patagonia, www.allpatagonia.com, runs birdwatching trips in Patagonia and Tierra del Fuego. In the northeast, contact Daniel Samay of **Explorador Expediciones**, www.rainforest. iguazuargentina.com. An excellent British-based tour operator that can arrange birdwatching trips is **Select Latin America**, T020-7407 1478, www.selectlatinamerica.co.uk.

Climbing

The Andes offer great climbing opportunities. The most popular peaks include Aconcagua in Mendoza province, Pissis in Catamarca, and Lanín and Tronador, reached from the Lake District. The northern part of Los Glaciares National Park, around El Chaltén, has some spectacular peaks with very difficult mountaineering. Climbing clubs can be found in Mendoza, Bariloche, Esquel, Junín de los Andes, Ushuaia and other cities, and in some places equipment can be hired. Also contact **Club Andino**, www.caba.org.ar.

Fishing

Argentina offers some of the world's finest fishing, in beautiful virgin landscape, and with good accommodation. In the Lake District, there's world-renowned fly-fishing for trout (rainbow, brown and brook) and for chinook or landlocked salmon. The centre is around Junín de los Andes and Bariloche, in rivers Quilquihue, Chimehuín, Collón-Curá, Meliquina and Caleufú, and lakes Traful, Gutiérrez, Mascardi, Cholila, Futalaufquén (in Los Alerces National Park), Falkner, Villarino; Huechulafquén, Paimún, Epulafquén, Tromen (all in Lanín National Park); and, in the far north, Quillén. In the

Lake District, the season lasts usually from November to April.

In Tierra del Fuego, huge brown trout can be fished from Río Grande and Lago Fagnano, while over the border in Chilean Tierra del Fuego, Lago Blanco is fast becoming popular. In the northeast, *sorubim* and giant *pacu* can be fished at the confluence of rivers Paraná and Paraguay, as well as *dorado*, known for its challenging fight. The closed season in this area is November to January.

On the Atlantic coast, San Blas is famous for shark fishing, for bacota shark and bull shark weighing up to 130 kg, while all along the coast, there's good sea fishing. Fishing can also be found in other parts of the country and is offered by many estancias. *Pejerrey*, *corvina* and *pescadilla* can be found in large quantities along the coast of Buenos Aires province, and many of the reservoirs of the Central Sierras, the West and Northwest are well stocked. All rivers are 'catch and release' and to fish anywhere in Argentina, you need a permit.

For fishing licences, contact the **Fly Fishing Association of Argentina**, T011-4773 0821, www.aapm.org.ar. In Patagonia, there's assistance from the **National Parks Administration**, T011-4311 8853/0303, www.parquesnacionales.gob.ar.

Horse riding

In a country that, in any given year, boasts the top five or 10 polo players in the world, the tradition of horse treks and horse riding is alive and strong. Offered all through the country, from Salta in the north to El Calafate in the south, horse-riding tours, or *cabalgatas*, vary in length and in quality. Generally speaking, if you visit an estancia or working farm that offers horse riding you'll find healthy horses, huge expanses of land and the wind whistling through your hair. If you go with adventure tourism agencies, you may have an English-speaking guide more suited to beginners. Choose the best option to suit your level of experience.

One of the most challenging and spectacular horse treks traces the path that General San Martín and his soldiers took across the Andes near San Juan. Reaching up to 4000 m, and scaling the cliff edge, the five-day ride uses donkeys due to the harsh terrain.

See **www.estanciasargentinas.com** for estancias that offer horse riding.

Skiing

The ski season runs from mid-June to mid-October, but dates vary between resorts. The country's best and deservedly most famous is Las Leñas, south of Mendoza, due to its long, varied and challenging pistes, its spectacular setting, superb accommodation, and also for having a dedicated snowboarding area. It's also the most expensive place, so if you're looking for a cheaper option in the same area, consider Los Penitentes, a more modest but friendly resort. There's good skiing all along the Lake District, with the biggest centre at Cerro Catedral, near Bariloche. This is a huge resort with scope for cross-country skiing and snowboarding, and the advantages of a major town with excellent hotels and services. Nearby, the smaller but upmarket resorts of Cerro Bayo at Villa la Angostura and Cerro Chapelco at

Tango

What was once the dance of immigrants from the Buenos Aires dockyards is now one of the most internationally recognizable aspects of Argentine culture. At the turn of the 19th century, the tango was seen as a dance practised by the lower classes in the streets and in brothels. And it wasn't until Argentine sailors brought it to Europe through French ports that it started to become acceptable in polite society in Buenos Aires. A little later, in 1913, Europe was officially in the grips of a tango craze. In London, the Waldorf Hotel introduced Tango Teas in the same vein as the French *Thés Dansants*, and Selfridges held a successful Tango Ball. In Paris, women's fashion was influenced by the dance, and shops sold tango stockings, tango hats and tango shoes. Even silent film star Rudolph Valentino danced it on-screen in 1921. Around this time, famous tango singer Carlos Gardel (whose name and face you'll see throughout Buenos Aires; see also box, page 48) toured South America as well as Paris, Barcelona, Madrid and New York.

The so-called Golden Era for tango was from the 1930s to 1955 when a military coup ousted the president. From then onwards until the early 1980s, tango was in decline. It was ignored and even persecuted during the military dictatorship. Young people no longer wanted to dance it, and nearly two generations of Argentines grew up without learning it.

However, after years of neglect, the Argentine people have re-embraced the dance at all levels. One more influence is fuelling this vibrant resurgence: the hundreds of tourists from around the world who arrive every year anxious to learn, practise and live the dance. A recent movement, which is causing a small sensation, is gay tango, known as Tango Queer. Several gay *milongas* have started up and there is a constant stream of dancers eager to learn the sexy steps. Each year in August, Buenos Aires hosts a tango festival, which boasts the best international and local dancers, free displays, classes and the sale of all things tango.

Useful websites

www.welcomeargentina.com/tango/lugares.html For an overview of tango shows available.
www.festivales.buenosaires.gob.ar/en/tango Government website listing tango festivals.

www.festivaltangoqueer.com.ar Tango Queer festival in Buenos Aires.
www.history-of-tango.com Looks at the history of the dance.
www.buenosaires.gob.ar/la2x4 Website for tango radio station.

San Martín de los Andes have even more beautiful settings and cater for families. La Hoya, near Esquel, is much cheaper with a laid-back family feel. And at the end of the world, in Ushuaia, there's great cross-country and downhill skiing at Cerro Castor. Details of all of these resorts are given in the text, together with websites.

For general information on all resorts see www.welcomeargentina.com/ski and www.allaboutar.com/sports_skiing.htm.

Trekking

The whole of the west of the country, along the mountains of the Andes, offers superb opportunities for trekking. The Lake District in summer is the most rewarding because there are so many spectacular landscapes to explore within easy reach of the centres of Bariloche, El Bolsón and San Martín de los Andes. The national parks here are well set up for walkers, with good information and basic maps available, and *refugios* and campsites that provide convenient accommodation on longer hikes. However, it's worth exploring the lesser-known extremes of the lakes, at Pehuenia in the north, with wonderful walks among the araucaria trees, and at Parque Nacional Los Alerces, with trekking into the virgin forest. All these walks are described in detail in the relevant areas. The season for walking is December to April.

The mountainous region to the west of Mendoza, around Aconcagua, offers good and challenging trekking, as well as further north in the Cordón del Plata in San Juan, where oasis villages in the valley are good bases for several peaks around Mercedario. Altitude sickness (see Health, page 674) can be a problem in these areas, and you should allow time in your schedule for adjustment.

Further north, in Salta and Jujuy, there's a complete contrast of landscape. The *puna* to the west is dramatic desert, dropping to the arid and rocky mountainous landscape in the Quebrada de Humahuaca and, continuing east, there are cloudforests. It's possible to

walk through all three zones in a single extended expedition, though you'd need to go with a guide. Throughout the area there are attractive villages to use as bases for day walks. In the northeast, there are a few good walks in the national park of the Iguazú Falls, and many more good places to walk in the provinces to the south.

The centre of the country, in the sierras around Córdoba, are good for day walks, especially in the Traslasierra. In Patagonia, there are petrified forests and caves with prehistoric handprints to walk to, as well as the remoter reaches of Parque Nacional Perito Moreno. The most dramatic trekking is in the south of Patagonia, whether in the mountains around Cerro Fitz Roy or ice trekking on the glaciers themselves in Parque Nacional Los Glaciares. And near Ushuaia, there are unforgettable views from peaks in the Parque Nacional Tierra del Fuego, along the shores of the Beagle Channel and from wilder peaks in mountains behind the town.

These are the highlights, but wherever you go in Argentina, you can find somewhere to trek. The spaces are wide open and there really are no limits.

Shops in large towns in Argentina stock clothes and camping supplies, but the following are things to consider taking. **Clothing**: a warm hat (wool or man-made fibre), wicking thermal underwear, T-shirts/shirts, trousers (quick-drying and preferably windproof), warm (wool or fleece) jumper/jacket (preferably two), gloves, waterproof jacket and overtrousers (preferably Gore-Tex), shorts, walking boots and socks, change of footwear or flip-flops. **Camping gear**: tent (capable of withstanding high winds), sleeping mat (closed cell, Karrimat, or inflatable, Thermarest), sleeping bag (three-season minimum), sleeping bag liner, stove and spare parts, fuel, matches and lighter, cooking and eating utensils, pan scrubber, survival bag. **Food**: take supplies for at least two days more than you plan to use; tea, coffee, sugar, dried milk, porridge, dried fruit, honey, soup, pasta, rice, soya (TVP), fresh fruit and vegetables, bread, cheese, crackers, biscuits, chocolate, salt, pepper, other herbs and spices, cooking oil. **Miscellaneous**: map and compass, torch and spare batteries, pen and notebook, Swiss army knife, sunglasses, sun cream, lip salve and insect repellent, first-aid kit, water bottle and towel.

Hikers have little to fear from the animal kingdom apart from insects, and robbery

Shopping tips

Best buys

Argentine fashion and leather goods are good value; shoes, sunglasses and outdoor gear too are reasonably priced, and if you have a free afternoon in Buenos Aires, it might be worth considering buying your holiday clothes here when you arrive: head straight for Palermo Viejo.

Tax free shopping is relatively easy and it's worth following this simple procedure to get the IVA (VAT) returned to you at the airport as you leave the country: shop at places displaying the Global Blue TAX FREE sign. Before you pay, ask for the tax free refund form. The shop must fill this out for you as you pay. Keep this form, in the envelope they'll give you, together with your receipt. At the airport, after security, and before passport control, look out for the tax free kiosk. Hand them all your tax free envelopes, with the receipts, and they will give them the customs stamp. Then once you've gone through passport control, look for the Refund Desk displaying the Global Blue logo, where your stamped forms will be taken, and the tax will be refunded either in cash or to your credit card (you can also mail in the forms and have the refund applied to your credit card). Not all shops offer this service; the ones that do usually have a sign up. See www.globalblue.com for more information.

Argentine specialities

In Buenos Aires, leather is the best buy, with many shops selling fine leather jackets, coats and trousers, as well as beautifully made bags and shoes. With a mixture of Italian-influenced design, and a flavour of the old gaucho leather-working traditions, there's a strong emerging Argentine style.

and assault are very rare. You are more of a threat to the environment than vice versa.

Note It's best not to go hiking alone, as hiking areas in Argentina are generally far less visited than those in Europe, and if you twist an ankle, it might be a long time before someone finds you. So try to join up with other people, and always register with *guardaparques* (rangers) before you set off.

Visit **www.parquesnacionales.gov.ar** for more detailed information.

Whitewater rafting

There are some good whitewater-rafting runs in Mendoza province, near the provincial capital and near San Rafael and Malargüe. In the Lake District there are possibilities in the Lanín, Nahuel Huapi and Los Alerces national parks.

Handicrafts, *artesanía*, are available all over the country, but vary from region to region. Traditional gaucho handicrafts include woven or plaited leather belts of excellent quality, as well as key rings and other pieces made of silver. These are small and distinctive and make excellent gifts. Look out, too, for the traditional baggy gaucho trousers, *bombachas*, comfortable for days in the saddle, and ranging from cheap sturdy cotton to smart versions with elaborate tucks.

Take home a *mate*, the hollowed gourd, often decorated, and the silver *bombilla* that goes with it, for drinking the national drink (see box, page 36). In the northwest there are beautifully made woven items: brightly coloured rugs, or saddle mats, and the country's best ponchos. Look out for the hand-dyed and woven ponchos, instead of the mass-produced variety, available in smaller rural areas, or in the fine handicrafts market at Salta or Catamarca. There are the deep red Guemes versions or soft fine ponchos made of *vicuña* (a local cousin of the llama), usually in natural colours. In markets all over the northwest, you'll find llama wool jumpers, hats and socks, and brightly coloured woven bags, Bolivian-influenced, but typical of the *puna* region. There are also fine carved wooden pieces.

In the Lake District too, there's lots of woodwork, and weavings of a different kind, from the Mapuche peoples, with distinctive black and white patterns. Smoked fish and meat, and delicious home-made jams from *sauco* (elderberry) or *frambuesa* (raspberry) are among the local delicacies.

In the northeast, there are Guaraní handicrafts such as bows and arrows. Argentina's national stone, the fleshy pink and marbled rhodochrosite, is mined in the northwest, but available all over Buenos Aires too, worked into fine jewellery, and less subtle paperweights and ashtrays.

Improve your travel photography

Taking pictures is a highlight for many travellers, yet too often the results turn out to be disappointing. Steve Davey, author of Footprint's *Travel Photography*, sets out his top rules for coming home with pictures you can be proud of.

Before you go

Don't waste precious travelling time and do your research before you leave. Find out what festivals or events might be happening or which day the weekly market takes place, and search online image sites such as Flickr to see whether places are best shot at the beginning or end of the day, and what vantage points you should consider.

Get up early

The quality of the light will be better in the few hours after sunrise and again before sunset – especially in the tropics when the sun will be harsh and unforgiving in the middle of the day. Sometimes seeing the sunrise is a part of the whole travel experience: sleep in and you will miss more than just photographs.

Stop and think

Don't just click away without any thought. Pause for a few seconds before raising the camera and ask yourself what you are trying to show with your photograph. Think about what things you need to include in the frame to convey this meaning. Be prepared to move around your subject to get the best angle. Knowing the point of your picture is the first step to making sure that the person looking at the picture will know it too.

Compose your picture

Avoid simply dumping your subject in the centre of the frame every time you take a picture. If you compose with it to one side, then your picture can look more balanced. This will also allow you to show a significant background and make the picture more meaningful. A good rule of thumb is to place your subject or any significant detail a third of the way into the frame; facing into the frame not out of it.

This rule also works for landscapes. Compose with the horizon two-thirds of the way up the frame if the fore-ground is the most interesting part of the picture; one-third of the way up if the sky is more striking.

Don't get hung up with this so-called Rule of Thirds, though. Exaggerate it by pushing your subject out to the edge of the frame if it makes a more interesting picture; or if the sky is dull in a landscape, try cropping with the horizon near the very top of the frame.

Fill the frame

If you are going to focus on a detail or even a person's face in a close-up portrait, then be bold and make sure that you fill the frame. This is often a case of physically getting in close. You can use a telephoto setting on a zoom lens but this can lead to pictures looking quite flat; moving in close is a lot more fun!

Interact with people

If you want to shoot evocative portraits then it is vital to approach people and seek permission in some way, even if it is just by smiling at someone. Spend a little time with them and they are likely to relax and look less stiff and formal. Action portraits where people are doing something, or environmental portraits, where they are set against a significant background, are a good way to achieve relaxed portraits. Interacting is a good way to find out more about people and their lives, creating memories as well as photographs.

Focus carefully

Your camera can focus quicker than you, but it doesn't know which part of the picture you want to be in focus. If your camera is using the centre focus sensor then move the camera so it is over the subject and half press the button, then, holding it down, recompose the picture. This will lock the focus. Take the now correctly focused picture when you are ready.

Another technique for accurate focusing is to move the active sensor over your subject. Some cameras with touch-sensitive screens allow you to do this by simply clicking on the subject.

Leave light in the sky

Most good night photography is actually taken at dusk when there is some light and colour left in the sky; any lit portions of the picture will balance with the sky and any ambient lighting. There is only a very small window when this will happen, so get into position early, be prepared and keep shooting and reviewing the results. You can take pictures after this time, but avoid shots of tall towers in an inky black sky; crop in close on lit areas to fill the frame.

Bring it home safely

Digital images are inherently ephemeral: they can be deleted or corrupted in a heartbeat. The good news though is they can be copied just as easily. Wherever you travel, you should have a backup strategy. Cloud backups are popular, but make sure that you will have access to fast enough Wi-Fi. If you use RAW format, then you will need some sort of physical back-up. If you don't travel with a laptop or tablet, then you can buy a backup drive that will copy directly from memory cards.

Recently updated and available in both digital and print formats, Footprint's Travel Photography by Steve Davey covers everything you need to know about travelling with a camera, including simple post-processing. More information is available at www.footprinttravelguides.com

Where to stay

from self-catering cabañas to sheep estancias

Hotels and guesthouses may display a star rating, but this doesn't necessarily match international standards. Many more expensive hotels charge different prices for *extranjeros* (non-Argentines) in US dollars, which is unavoidable since a passport is required as proof of residency. If you pay in cash (pesos) you may get a reduction. Room tax (VAT) is 21% and is not always included in the price (ask when you check in). All hotels will store luggage for a day, and most of the bigger hotels in cities have English-speaking staff.

For upmarket chain hotels throughout Argentina contact **N/A Town & Country Hotels** ⓘ *www.newage-hotels.com*. For hostels, see **Hostelling International Argentina** ⓘ *Florida 835, T011-4511-8723, www.hostels.org.ar, Mon-Fri 0900-1900*. HI no longer has a major presence in Argentina, but their website does provide a list of hostels, and a few of them still offer a discount to cardholders. For a complete listing of sleeping options, see www.welcomeargentina.com.

Hotels, hosterías, residenciales and hospedajes

The standard of accommodation in Argentina is generally good, and although prices have risen in the last few years, decent hotels are generally excellent value for visitors. You'll find that most cities and tourist towns list hotels and *hosterías* as separate: this is no reflection on quality or comfort, but simply on size: a *hostería* has fewer than 20 rooms. Both hotels and *hosterías* will have rooms

---

Price codes

Where to stay	Restaurants
$$$$ over US$150	$$$ over US$12
$$$ US$66-150	$$ US$7-12
$$ US$30-65	$ US$6 and under
$ under US$30	Price for a two-course meal for one person, excluding drinks or service charge.
Price of a double room in high season, including taxes.	

---

with private bathrooms (usually showers rather than bath tubs, which you'll find only in the more expensive establishments). Note that most Argentine hotels, even the five-star ones, do not provide tea and coffee-making services, nor do they always have minibars.

Prices often rise in high summer (January to February), at Easter and in July. During public holidays or high season you should always book ahead. A few of the more expensive hotels in Buenos Aires and major tourist centres such as Puerto Madryn, Bariloche and El Calafate charge foreigners higher prices than Argentines, which can be very frustrating, though there's little you can do about it. If you're given a price, ask if there's a reduction if you pay in cash (as opposed to your card). Sometimes hotels offer cheaper deals through their websites: always check there first.

Most places now accept credit cards, but check before you come. It's worth booking your first few nights' accommodation before you arrive. Check where the hotel is located before you book. In El Calafate, for instance, some fabulous hotels are situated quite a distance out of town; unless you have a car, they might not be the right option for you.

Estancias

These are the large farms and cattle ranches found all over the country, many of them now open to tourists, which offer a marvellous insight into Argentine life. There's a whole spectrum of estancias from a simple dwelling on the edge of a pristine lake in the Patagonian wilderness to a Loire-style chateau in the Pampas. In the province of Buenos Aires you will find estancias covering thousands of hectares of flat grassland with large herds of cattle and wind pumps to extract water; horse riding will certainly be offered and perhaps cattle-mustering. Some of the finest buildings are in this area, such as **Dos Talas** and **La Porteña**. In Patagonia there are giant sheep estancias overlooking glaciers, mountains and lakes, such as **Helsingfors**. There are estancias on Tierra del Fuego that are full of the history of the early pioneers who built them (like **Harberton**), while on the mainland nearby **Estancia Monte Dinero** has a colony of Magellanic penguins on its doorstep. There's more wildlife close at hand in the estancias on Península Valdés. And in Salta, there are colonial-style fincas, whose land includes cloudforest with marvellous horse riding.

The most distinctive or representative estancias are mentioned in the text, but for more information see www.turismo.gob.ar (in English), the national tourist website with all estancias listed, and www.estanciasdesantacruz.com, a helpful agency which arranges estancia stays in Santa Cruz and the south, including transport. A useful book, *Turismo en Estancias y Hosterías,* is produced by **Tierra Buena**. You can, of course, contact estancias directly and reserve your stay, ideally with a couple of weeks' notice. See also box, page 83.

Cabañas

These are a great option if you have transport and there are at least two of you. They are self-catering cottages, cabins or apartments, usually in rural areas, and often in superb locations, such as the Lake District. They're tremendously popular among Argentine holidaymakers, who tend to travel in large groups of friends, or of several families together, and as a result the best *cabañas* are well-equipped and comfortable. They can be very economical too, especially for groups of four or more, but are feasible even for two, with considerable reductions off-season. If you're travelling by public transport, *cabañas* are generally more difficult to get to, but ask the tourist office if there are any within walking or taxi distance. Throughout the Lake District, *cabañas* are plentiful and competitively priced.

Camping

Organized campsites are referred to in the text after the hotel listings for each town. Camping is very popular in Argentina (except in Buenos Aires) and there are many superbly situated sites, most with good services, whether municipal or private. There are many quieter, family-orientated places, but if you want a livelier time, look for a campsite (often by the beaches) with younger people, where there's likely to be partying until the small hours. Camping is allowed at the side of major highways and in all national parks (except at Iguazú Falls), but in Patagonia strong winds can make camping very difficult. Wherever you camp, pack your rubbish and put out fires with earth and water. Fires are not allowed in many national parks because of the serious risk of forest fires. It's a good idea to carry insect repellent.

If taking a cooker, the most frequent recommendation is a multi-fuel stove that will burn unleaded petrol or, if that is not available, kerosene or white fuel. Alcohol-burning stoves are reliable but slow and you have to carry a lot of fuel. Fuel can usually be found at chemists/pharmacies. Gas cylinders and bottles are usually exchangeable, but if not can be refilled; specify whether you use butane or propane. Gas canisters are not always available. White gas (*bencina blanca*) is readily available in hardware shops (*ferreterías*).

Food
& drink
meat parrilladas, Italian pizzas and traditional empanadas

Asados and parrillas

Not for vegetarians! The great classic meal throughout the country is the *asado* – beef or lamb cooked expertly over an open fire. This ritual is far more than a barbecue, and with luck you'll be invited to sample an *asado* at a friend's home or estancia to see how it's done traditionally. *Al asador* is the way meat is cooked in the countryside, with a whole cow splayed out on a cross-shaped stick, stuck into the ground at an angle over the fire beneath. And in the *parrilla* restaurants, found all over Argentina, cuts of meat are grilled over an open fire in much the same way.

You can order any cuts from the range as individual meals, but if you order *parrillada* (usually for two or more people), you'll be brought a selection; see box, page 33, for a list. You can ask for '*cocido*' to have your meat well-done, '*a punto*' for medium, and '*jugoso*' for rare. Typical accompaniments are *papas fritas* (chips), salad and the spicy *chimichurri* sauce made from oil, chilli pepper, salt, garlic and vinegar.

For more on Argentine beef, see box, page 35.

Italian influences

It might seem that when Argentines aren't eating meat, they're eating pizza. Italian immigration has left a fine legacy in thick and crispy pizzas available from even the humblest pizza joint, adapted to the Argentine palate with some unusual toppings. *Palmitos* are tasty, slightly crunchy hearts of palm, usually tinned, and a popular Argentine delicacy, though they're in short supply and the whole plant has to be sacrificed for one heart. They're often accompanied on a pizza with the truly unspeakable *salsa golf*, a lurid mixture of tomato ketchup and mayonnaise. You'll probably prefer excellent provolone or roquefort cheeses on your pizza – both Argentine and delicious.

Fresh pasta is widely available, bought ready to cook from dedicated shops. Raviolis are filled with ricotta, *verduras* (spinach), or *cuatro quesos* (four cheeses), and with a variety of sauces. These are a good option for vegetarians, who need

Menu reader

The basics

ají/pimiento chilli or green pepper
ajo garlic
arroz blanco boiled rice
bocadillo sandwich
calabaza squash
caldo clear soup, stock
camote yam
carne meat
carne picada minced meat
cebolla onion
cerdo pork
chicle chewing gum
chivo goat
cocido cooked
comer to eat
comida meal
cuchara spoon
cuchillo knife
dulce sweet
empanada/pastelito pasty, turnover
ensalada salad
frijoles/habichuelas beans
frito fried
guayaba guava
helado ice cream
horno baked
huevo egg
huevos revueltos scrambled eggs
jamón ham
legumbres/vegetales vegetables
limón lemon
longaniza/chorizo sausage
manteca butter
mermelada jam
naranja orange
palta avocado
pan bread

panadería bakery
papa potato
pavo turkey
picante hot, spicy
pimiento pepper
plancha grilled/griddled
pollo chicken
sal salt
salsa sauce
sin carne without meat
sopa soup
tenedor fork
torta cake
tostado toasted

Fish and seafood

albacore swordfish
camarones prawns
cangrejo crab
cazuela de marisco seafood stew
centolla king crab
ceviche raw fish marinated in lemon juice, is either made with *corvina* or salmon
congrio ling or kingclip; *caldillo de congrio*, a soup containing a large *congrio* steak
corvina bass
lenguado sole
manduví river fish with pale flesh
mariscos shellfish
merluza hake
pacú river fish with firm meaty flesh
pejerrey inland water fish
surubí a kind of catfish, tender flesh

Puddings (postre), cakes and pastries

alfajores soft maize-flour biscuits filled with jam

not go hungry in this land of meat. Most restaurants have *pasta casero* – home-made pasta – and sauces without meat, such as *fileto* (tomato sauce) or pesto.

Ñoquis (gnocchi), potato dumplings normally served with tomato sauce, are cheap and delicious (traditionally eaten on the 29th of the month).

budín de pan a gooey dense bread pudding, often with dried fruit

dulce de batata a hard, dense, sweet potato jam, so thick you can carve it

dulce de leche the Argentine obsession – a sweet caramel made from boiling milk spread on toast, cakes and inside pastries

dulce de membrillo quince preserve

dulce de zapallo pumpkin in syrup

facturas pastries in general, bought by the dozen

flan crème caramel, an Argentine favourite

helados ice cream, served piled high in tiny cones

media luna croissant (dulce or salado – sweet or savoury)

torta cake (not to be confused with tarte: vegetable pie)

tortilla dry crumbly layered breakfast pastry (in northwest)

Parrilla and asado

The most important vocabulary is for the various cuts of meat in the *asado*, or barbecue, which you can eat at any *parrilla* or steakhouse.

achuras offal

bife ancho entrecôte steak

bife angosto sirloin

bife de chorizo or cuadril rumpsteak

cerdo pork

chinchulines entrails

chivito kid

chorizos beef sausages

cordero lamb

costilla pork chop

lomo fillet steak

molleja sweetbread

morcilla blood sausage

pollo chicken

riñón kidney

tira de asado ribs

vacío flank

Argentine specialities

bife a caballo steak with a fried egg on top

choripán hot dog, made with meat sausage

ciervo venison

cocina criolla typical Argentine food

empanadas small pasties, traditionally meat, but often made with cheese or other fillings

fiambre cold meats, hams, salami

guiso meat and vegetable stew

humitas a puree of sweetcorn, onions and cheese, wrapped in corn cob husks, steamed

jabalí wild boar

locro stew made with corn, onions, beans, and various cuts of meat, chicken or sausage

lomito sandwich of thin slice of steak in a bread roll, *lomito completo* comes with tomato, cheese, ham and egg

matambre stuffed flank steak with vegetables and hard-boiled eggs

milanesas breaded, boneless chicken or veal, found everywhere and good value

picada a selection of fiambre, cheeses and olives to accompany a drink

puchero meat stew; *puchero de gallina* is chicken, sausage, maize, potatoes and squash cooked together

tamales cornflour balls with meat and onion, wrapped in corn cob husks and boiled

tostados delicate toasted cheese and tomato sandwiches, often made from the soft crustless *pan de miga*

Vegetarian

Vegetables in Argentina are cheap, of excellent quality, many of them organic, and available fresh in *verdulerías* (vegetable shops) all over towns. Look out for *acelga*, a large-leafed chard with a strong flavour, often used to fill pasta, or *tarta de verduras*, vegetable pies, which you can buy everywhere, fresh and very good. Butternut squash, *zapallo*, is used to good effect in *tartas* and in filled pasta. Salads are quite safe to eat in restaurants, and fresh, although not wildly imaginative. Only in remote areas in the northwest of the country should you be wary of salads, since the water here is not reliable. In most large towns there are vegetarian restaurants and don't forget the wonderful vegetarian *empanadas* such as cheese and onion, spinach or mushroom (see below).

Vegetarians must specify: *'No como carne, ni jamón, ni pollo'* ('I don't eat meat, or ham, or chicken'), since many Argentines think that vegetarians will eat chicken or ham, and will certainly not take it seriously that you want to avoid all meat products.

Regional specialities

The Argentine speciality *empanadas* are tasty small semi-circular pies traditionally filled with meat, but now widely available filled with cheese, *acelga* (chard) or corn. They originate in Salta and Tucumán, where you'll still find the best examples, but can be found all over the country as a starter in a *parrilla*, or ordered by the dozen to be delivered at home with drinks among friends.

Northwest Around Salta and Jujuy you'll find superb *humitas*, parcels of sweetcorn and onions, steamed in the corn husk, and *tamales*, balls of cornflour filled with beef and onion, and similarly wrapped in corn husk leaves to be steamed. The other speciality of the region is *locro* – a thick stew made of maize, white beans, beef, sausages, pumpkin and herbs. Good fish is served in many areas of the country and along the east coast you'll always be offered *merluza* (hake), *lenguado* (sole) and often salmon as well.

Atlantic coast If you go to Puerto Madryn or the Atlantic coast near Mar del Plata, then seafood is a must: *arroz con mariscos* is similar to paella and absolutely delicious. There will often be *ostras* (oysters) and *centolla* (king crab) on the menu too.

Lake District The *trucha* (trout) is very good and is best served grilled, but as with all Argentine fish you'll be offered a bewildering range of sauces, such as roquefort, which rather drown the flavour. Also try the smoked trout and the wild boar. Berries are very good here in summer, with raspberries and strawberries abundant and flavoursome, particularly around El Bolsón. And in Puehuenia, you must try the pine nuts of the monkey puzzle trees: sacred food to the Mapuche people.

ON THE ROAD
Argentine beef

So how did Argentina come to be synonymous with great beef? Cattle certainly aren't indigenous to the Pampas. But after Juan de Garay's expedition in 1580 brought cattle from Paraguay, the animals roamed wild on the fertile plains, reproducing so quickly that by the time the Spanish returned in 1780, there were 40 million of them. But by then, local indigenous groups were making a roaring trade, driving herds of cattle through the Andean passes to sell in southern Chile. Gauchos, meanwhile, were hunting cattle with the use of *boleadoras* (a lasso with three stone balls), and slaughtering them by the thousand for their hides alone, sometimes leaving the meat to rot. When salting plants – *saladeros* – arrived in 1810, the hides were transported to Europe, together with tallow for candles. The meat was turned into *charqui*, cut into strips, dried and salted, and sold to feed slaves in Brazil and Cuba. It was only with the invention of refrigerated ships that Argentina's produce was exported to meet the growing demand for beef in an expanding Europe. Cattle farmers introduced new breeds to replace the scrawny Pampas cattle, and sowed alfalfa as richer fodder than Pampas grasses. Today Herefords and Aberdeen Angus are still bred for meat.

And why is Argentine beef so good? Because these cows are healthy! With such vast expanses of land to roam, the cattle burn off any fat, are well-toned and lean: the meat is even high in omega 3. So head straight for the best *parrilla* in town, and, unless you're vegetarian, try a few different cuts. Better still, stay at an estancia to try home-reared beef cooked on the *asado*, the traditional way over an open wood fire. A word of warning: learn some of the names for the parts of a cow so you don't end up eating hoof, intestines or glands. See the Menu reader, page 33.

Northeast In the northeast, there are some superb river fish to try: *pacú* is a large, firm fleshed fish with lots of bones, but very tasty. The other great speciality is *surubí*, a kind of catfish, particularly good cooked delicately in banana leaves.

Desserts
Argentines have a sweet tooth, and are passionate about *dulce de leche* – milk and sugar evaporated to a pale, soft caramel, and found on all cakes, pastries, and even for breakfast. If you like this, you'll be delighted by *facturas* and other pastries, stuffed with *dulce de leche*, jams of various kinds, and sweet cream fillings. *Helado* (ice cream) is really excellent in Argentina, and for US$2-3 in any *heladería*, you'll get two flavours, from a huge range, piled up high on a tiny cone; an unmissable treat. Jauja (El Bolsón) and Persicco (Buenos Aires) are the best makes, and there are many great options in Rosario, a city renowned for its ice cream.

Other popular desserts are *dulce de batata* (sweet potato jam), *dulce de membrillo* (quince preserve) and *dulce de zapallo* (pumpkin in syrup). All are eaten with

The mate ritual

Mate (pronounced mattay) is the essential Argentine drink. All over the country, whenever groups of Argentines get together, they share a *mate*. It's an essential part of your trip to Argentina that you give it a go, at least once. It's a bitter green tea made from the leaves of the *yerba mate* plant, *Ilex paraguaiensis*, and is mildly stimulating, less so than caffeine, and effective at ridding the body of toxins as well as being mildly laxative and diuretic. It was encouraged by the Jesuits as an alternative to alcohol and grown in their plantations in the northeast of Argentina.

The *mate* container is traditionally made from a hollowed gourd, but can be made of wood or tin. There are also ornate varieties made to traditional gaucho patterns by the best silversmiths.

Dried yerba leaves are placed in the *mate* to just over half full and then the whole container is shaken upside down using a hand to prevent spillage. This makes sure that any excess powder is removed from the leaves before drinking. Hot water is added to create the infusion, which is then sipped through the *bombilla*, a perforated metal straw. One person in the group acts as *cebador*, trickling fresh hot water into the *mate*, having the first sip (which is the most bitter) and passing it to each person in turn to sip. The water must be at 80-82°C (just as the kettle starts to 'sing') and generally *mate* is drunk *amargo* (bitter) – without sugar. But add a little if it's your first time, as the drink is slightly bitter. When you've had enough, simply say *gracias* as you hand the *mate* back to the *cebador*, and you'll be missed out on the next round.

If you're invited to drink *mate* on your visit to Argentina, always accept, as it's rude not to, and then keep trying: it might take a few attempts before you actually like the stuff. To share a *mate* is to be part of a very special Argentine custom and you'll delight your hosts by giving it a go.

cheese. The most loved of all is *flan*, which is not a flan at all but crème caramel, often served on a pool of caramelized sugar, and *dulce de leche*. Every Argentine loves *alfajores*, soft maize-flour biscuits filled with *dulce de leche* or apricot jam, and then coated with chocolate, especially if they're the Havanna brand.

Croissants (*media lunas*) come in two varieties: *de grasa* (savoury, made with beef fat) and *dulce* (sweet and fluffy). These will often be your only breakfast since Argentines are not keen on eating first thing in the morning (maybe because they've only just had dinner!), and only supply the huge buffet-style 'American breakfast' in international hotels to please tourists.

Drink

The great Argentine drink, which you must try if invited, is *mate* (see box, above). A kind of green tea made from dried *yerba* leaves, drunk from a cup or seasoned

Argentine wine

Wine is grown in Argentina along the length of the Andean foothills, from Cafayate in Salta to the Río Negro valley in Neuquén, with the oldest and most famous wine-producing areas in Mendoza and San Juan provinces, where the climate is ideal: warm, almost consistently sunny days, and cold nights, with a 'thermal amplitude' of 15°C which gives grapes such a rich flavour. Water is the other magical ingredient: wine was made in Argentina long before the Jesuits planted their first vines here in the 1550s, and irrigation canals made by pre-Incan cultures still carry pure, mineral-rich snow-melt from the Andes today, compensating for the low rainfall.

Modern grapes were introduced when Argentina was flooded with Spanish and Italian immigrants in the late 19th century, so that today the main grapes grown are Cabernet Sauvignon, Merlot, Malbec and Syrah; Chardonnay, Chenin and Sauvignon Blanc. 'High-altitude wine' is a tiny, but fast-growing industry in Salta's Calchaquí Valley, with superb boutique wineries Colomé and El Estecco producing wines of extraordinary intensity. Cafayate is the only place on earth where the white Torrontés grape thrives, producing a deliciously dry, fruity wine with an aromatic bouquet.

Argentina was among the five biggest wine producers of the world in the early 20th century, but exported very little, since home consumption used up all that was produced. However, in the 1970s wine drinking slumped. But in the last decade the Argentine wine industry has started producing far more sophisticated premium wines, resulting in a boom of wine drinking at home and internationally. Look out for the famous names in Argentine restaurants: Valentín Bianchi, Trapiche, Flichman, Navarro Correas, Senetiner and Norton. In Argentine supermarkets, wines can be bought for US$1.50-10 a bottle, but go to a *vinoteca* (specialist wine shop) where US$15 will buy you a superb bottle, you'll get expert advice, and can try smaller labels.

See also www.argentinewines.com; www.vinosdeargentina.com; www.turismo.mendoza.gov.ar; www.welcomeargentina.com/vino; and the magazine *El Conocedor* (www.elconocedor.com), as well as the wonderful free English-language magazine *Wine Republic* (www.wine-republic.com), distributed in cafés and shops. Learn more about Argentine wines at **Mente Argentina** (Santa Fe 3192 4 to B, T011-3968 7861, www.menteargentina.com) a comprehensive institute that offers a number of programmes, from wine tasting and Spanish classes.

gourd through a silver perforated straw, it is shared by a group of friends, family or work colleagues as a daily social ritual.

The local **beers**, mainly lager-type, are passable: Quilmes is the best seller, but microbreweries producing good-quality beer are popping up more and more throughout the country. **Antares** is one such chain, offering tasty brews and good food. **Spirits** are relatively cheap, other than those that are imported; there are cheap drinkable Argentine gins and whiskeys. **Clericó** is a white-wine **sangria** drunk in summer and you'll see lots of young Argentines drink the liquor

Fernet with cola. It tastes like medicine but is very popular. Many Argentines mix soda water with their wine (even red wine) as a refreshing drink.

It is best not to drink the **tap water**; in the main cities it's safe, but often heavily chlorinated. Never drink tap water in the northwest, where it is notoriously poor.

Wines Argentine wines are excellent and drinkable throughout the price range, which starts at US$1.50 or US$2 a bottle. Red grape varieties of Malbec, Merlot, Syrah, Cabernet Sauvignon, and the white Torrontés are particularly recommended; try brands **Lurton**, **Norton**, **Bianchi**, **Trapiche** or **Etchart** in any restaurant. Good sparkling wines include the *brut nature* of **Navarro Correas**, whose Los Arboles Cabernet Sauvignon is an excellent red wine, and **Norton**'s Cosecha Especial. See Mendoza, page 190, and Salta, page 270, for more details.

For more on Argentine wine, see box, page 37.

Eating out

The siesta is observed nearly everywhere but Buenos Aires and some of the larger cities. At around 1700, many people go to a *confitería* (café) for *merienda* – tea, sandwiches and cakes.

Restaurants rarely open before 2100 and most people turn up at around 2230, often later. Dinner usually begins at 2200 or 2230; Argentines like to eat out, and usually bring babies and children along, however late it is. If you're invited to someone's house for dinner, don't expect to eat before 2300, so have a few *facturas* (pastries) at 1700, the Argentine *merienda*, to keep you going.

If you're on a tight budget, ask for the *menú fijo* (set-price menu), which is usually good value (especially during lunchtime). Also try *tenedor libre* restaurants, where you can eat all you want for a fixed price. Markets usually have cheap food. Food in supermarkets is cheap and good quality.

Buenos Aires

birthplace of the tango, people of the port

Often viewed by visitors as 'Paris of the south' due to its baroque architecture and fashion-conscious inhabitants, Buenos Aires exists in two worlds.

Those looking for a prototypical metropolitan experience will find it in the expansive boulevards, neat plazas, leafy parks and ornate theatres. It can be touched and tasted in the city's chic shops, convivial restaurants and breezy cafés. However, it's in the enormous steaks, passionate tango and 24/7 *boliches* where you'll discover the distinctly Argentine voice of the city, one which echoes throughout the entire country.

Buenos Aires has been virtually rebuilt since the beginning of the 20th century and its oldest buildings mostly date from the early 1900s, with some elegant examples from the 1920s and 1930s. The centre has maintained the original layout since its foundation and so the streets are often narrow and mostly one way.

Its original name, 'Santa María del Buen Ayre' referred to the favourable winds which brought sailors across the ocean.

South and west of Buenos Aires the flat, fertile lands of the *pampa húmeda* stretch seemingly without end, the horizon broken only by a lonely wind pump or a line of poplar trees. This is home to the gaucho, whose traditions of horsemanship, music, hunting and craftsmanship remain alive to this day.

Best for
Culture ▪ Nightlife ▪ Shopping

Footprint
picks

★ **Café Tortoni**, page 45

Stop in at the city's oldest café and enjoy a coffee amid opulent surroundings, a throwback to another era.

★ **Cementerio Recoleta**, page 49

See Evita's final resting place among the rows of ornate tombs in this famous cemetery.

★ **Palermo Viejo**, page 51

Shop and dine in the trendiest enclave in the city.

★ **San Telmo**, page 53

Cobbled streets, corner cafés and outdoor markets make this neighbourhood a must-see.

★ **Tigre and the delta**, page 73

A riverside weekend retreat where the streets are waterways.

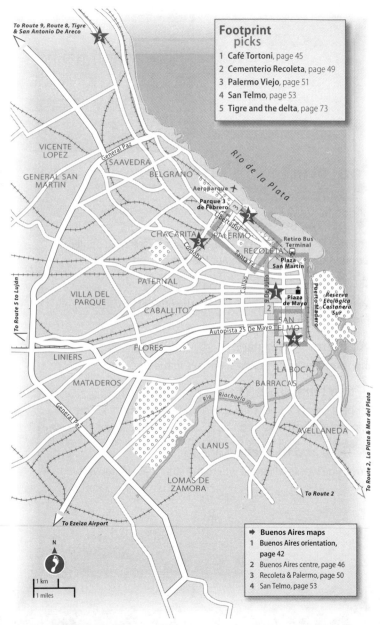

To Route 9, Route 8, Tigre
& San Antonio De Areco

Río de la Plata

VICENTE
LOPEZ

SAAVEDRA

GENERAL SAN
MARTIN

BELGRANO

General Paz

Aeroparque

Parque 3
de Febrero

Libertador

CHACARITA

PALERMO

Córdoba

Santa Fe

Retiro Bus
Terminal

RECOLETA

Plaza
San Martín

PATERNAL

Callao

Quintana

VILLA DEL
PARQUE

Plaza
de Mayo

Puerto Madero

Reserva
Ecológica
Costanera
Sur

To Route 5 to Luján

CABALLITO

Autopista 25 De Mayo

SAN
TELMO

FLORES

LINIERS

LA BOCA

BARRACAS

MATADEROS

General Paz

Río Riachuelo

AVELLANEDA

To Route 2, La Plata & Mar del Plata

LANUS

LOMAS DE
ZAMORA

To Route 2

To Ezeiza Airport

N

1 km
1 miles

Around Plaza de Mayo

The heart of the city is the **Plaza de Mayo**. On the east side is the **Casa de Gobierno**. Called the Casa Rosada because it is pink, it contains the presidential offices. It is notable for its statuary and the rich furnishing of its halls. The **Museo Casa Rosada** ① *Paseo Colón 100, T011-4344 3802, www.casarosada.gob.ar, Wed-Sun and holidays 1000-1800, free*, in the Fuerte de Buenos Aires and Aduana Taylor, covers the period 1810-2010 with historical exhibits and art exhibitions, permanent and temporary. The **Antiguo Congreso Nacional** (Old Congress Hall, 1864-1905) ① *Balcarce 139, guided tours every Mon, Tue, Thu and Fri at 1230 and 1700, closed Jan, free*, on the south of the Plaza, is a national monument. The **Cathedral** ① *San Martín 27, T011-4331 2845, www.catedralbuenosaires.org.ar, Mon-Fri 0800-1900, Sat-Sun 0900-1930; guided visits to San Martín's Mausoleum and Crypt, religious artefacts, and Temple and Crypt; Mass is held daily, check times*, on the north of Plaza, stands on the site of the first **church** in Buenos Aires. The current structure dates from 1753-1822 (its portico built in 1827), but the 18th-century towers were never rebuilt.

The imposing **tomb** (1880) ① *Mon-Fri 0900-1900*, of the Liberator, General José de San Martín, is guarded by soldiers in fancy uniforms. A small exhibition to the left of the main nave displays items related to Pope Francis, former archbishop of Buenos Aires. The **Museo del Cabildo y la Revolución de Mayo** ① *Bolívar 65, T011-4334 1782, www. cabildonacional.cultura.gob.ar, Tue, Wed, Fri 1030-1700, Thu 1030-2000, Sat-Sun and holidays 1030-1800, guided visits in English Oct-Mar, free*, is in the old Cabildo where the movement for Independence from Spain was first planned. It's worth a visit for the paintings of old Buenos Aires, the documents and maps recording the May 1810 Revolution, and memorabilia of the 1806 British attack; also Jesuit art. There are booklets in English in each of the rooms. In the patio is a café and restaurant and stalls selling handicrafts (Thursday-Friday 1100-1800). Also on the Plaza is the Palacio de Gobierno de la Ciudad (City Hall). Within a few blocks north of the Plaza are the main banks and business houses, such as the **Banco de la Nación**, opposite the Casa Rosada (see above), with an impressively huge main hall and topped by a massive marble dome 50 m in diameter.

On the Plaza de Mayo, the **Mothers of the Plaza de Mayo** ① *H Yrigoyen 1584, T011-4383 0377, www.madres.org, and Piedras 153, T011-4343 1926, www.madresfundadoras.blogspot. com.ar*, march in remembrance of their children who disappeared during the 'dirty war' of the 1970s. The Mothers march anti-clockwise round the central monument every Thursday at 1530, with photos of their disappeared loved ones pinned to their chests.

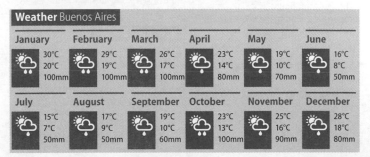

Weather Buenos Aires

January 30°C 20°C 100mm	**February** 29°C 19°C 100mm	**March** 26°C 17°C 100mm
April 23°C 14°C 80mm	**May** 19°C 10°C 70mm	**June** 16°C 8°C 50mm
July 15°C 7°C 50mm	**August** 17°C 9°C 50mm	**September** 19°C 10°C 60mm
October 23°C 13°C 100mm	**November** 25°C 16°C 90mm	**December** 28°C 18°C 80mm

Essential Buenos Aires

Finding your feet

Buenos Aires has two **airports**, **Ezeiza**, for international and few domestic flights, and **Aeroparque**, for domestic flights, most services to Uruguay and some to Brazil and Chile. Ezeiza is 35 km southwest of the centre, while Aeroparque is 4 km north of the city centre on the riverside.

A display in immigration in **Ezeiza** airport details transport options. The safest way between the airport and the city is by an airport bus service (every 30 minutes 0500-2100, one way US$13 to Puerto Madero, US$13.50 to Aeroparque airport; pay in pesos, dollars, euros or credit card) operated by **Manuel Tienda León** (T0818-888-5366, www.tiendaleon.com); the office is in front of you as you arrive. *Remise* taxis for up to four (**Manuel Tienda León**, **Taxi Ezeiza**, www.taxiezeiza.com.ar, and other counters at Ezeiza) charge between US$30-40 but less from city to airport. Radio taxis charge a minimum US$40 (make sure you pay for your taxi at the booth and then wait in the queue), see Taxi, page 72. **Manuel Tienda León** operates buses between Ezeiza and Aeroparque airports, US$14. On no account take an unmarked car at Ezeiza, no matter how low the fare. Always ask to see the taxi driver's licence. If you take an ordinary taxi the Policía de Seguridad Aeroportuaria on duty notes down the car's licence and time of departure.

Local bus No 45 runs from outside **Aeroparque** airport to the Retiro railway station. No 37 goes to Palermo and Recoleta and No 160 to Palermo and Almagro. *Remise* taxis to Ezeiza, operated by **Manuel Tienda León**, cost around US$50; to the city centre US$18. Taxi to centre US$10.

All international and interprovincial buses use the Retiro **bus terminal** at Ramos Mejía y Antártida Argentina, next to the Retiro **railway station**. See Transport, page 70.

Orientation

The commercial heart of the city runs from Retiro station and Plaza San Martín through Plaza de Mayo to San Telmo, east of Avenida 9 de Julio. Street numbers start from the dock side rising from east to west, but north/south streets are numbered from Avenida Rivadavia, one block north of Avenida de Mayo rising in both directions. Avenida Roque Sáenz Peña and Avenida Julio A Roca are commonly referred to as Diagonal Norte and Diagonal Sur respectively.

Getting around

The commercial centre can be explored on foot, but you'll probably want to take a couple of days to explore its museums, shops and markets. Many places of interest lie outside this zone, so you will need to use public transport. City **buses** (*colectivos*) are plentiful. See What to do, page 69, for city guides. The **metro**, or Subte, is fast and clean; see Transport, page 72, for fares. Yellow and black **taxis** can be hailed on the street, but if possible, book a radio or a *remise* taxi by phone. Again, see Transport for details.

Useful addresses

Central Police Station, Moreno 1550, Virrey Cevallos 362, T011-4346 5700 (emergency, T101 or 911 from any phone, free). **Immigration (Migración)**, Antártida Argentina 1355, edif 4, T011-4317 0234, www.migraciones.gov.ar. Monday-Friday 0830-1330.

Best parrillas

Don Julio, page 62
La Brigada, page 63
Cabaña Las Lilas, page 64

West of Plaza de Mayo

Running west from the Plaza, the Avenida de Mayo leads 1.5 km to the **Palacio del Congreso** (Congress Hall) ⓘ *Plaza del Congreso, Av Rivadavia 1864, T011-6310 7222 for 1-hr guided visits, Sat at 1600 and 1700, Sun at 1100 and 1600, www.congreso.gob.ar; passport essential.* This huge Greco-Roman building houses the seat of the legislature. Avenida de Mayo has several examples of fine architecture of the early 20th century, such as the sumptuous La Prensa building (No 575, free guided visits at weekends), the traditional ★ Café Tortoni ⓘ *No 825, www.cafetortoni.com.ar,* or the eclectic **Palacio Barolo** ⓘ *No 1370, www.pbarolo.com.ar,* and many others of faded grandeur. Avenida de Mayo crosses **Avenida 9 de Julio**, one of the widest avenues in the world, which consists of three major carriageways with heavy traffic over 140 m wide, separated in some parts by wide grass borders.

Five blocks north of Avenida de Mayo the great **Plaza de la República**, with a 67-m obelisk commemorating the 400th anniversary of the city's founding, is at the junction of Avenida 9 de Julio with Avenidas Roque Sáenz Peña and Corrientes.

Teatro Colón ⓘ *Cerrito 628, entrance for guided visits Tucumán 1171, T011-4378 7109, www.teatrocolon.org.ar,* is one of the world's great opera houses. The interior is resplendent with red plush and gilt; the stage is huge and salons, dressing rooms and banquet halls are equally sumptuous. Consult the website for details of performances, tickets and guided visits. Close by is the **Museo Judío** ⓘ *Libertad 769, T011-4123 0832, www.judaica.org.ar; for visits make an appointment with the rabbi (take identification),* which has religious objects relating to Jewish presence in Argentina in a 19th-century synagogue. Not far away is the **Museo del Holocausto (Shoah Museum)** ⓘ *Montevideo 919, T011-4811 3588, www.museodelholocausto.org.ar, Mon-Thu 1000-1900, Fri 1000-1600, US$4.50 (ID required),* a permanent exhibition of pictures, personal and religious items with texts in Spanish on the Holocaust, antisemitism in Argentina and the lives of many Argentine Jews in the pre- and post-war periods.

La Chacarita ⓘ *Guzmán 670, daily 0730-1700, take Subte Line B to the Federico Lacroze station,* is a well-known cemetery with the lovingly tended tomb of **Carlos Gardel**, the tango singer. See box, page 48, and the unofficial website: www.cementeriochacarita.com.ar.

North of Plaza de Mayo

The city's traditional shopping centre, Calle Florida, is reserved for pedestrians, with clothes and souvenir shops, restaurants and the elegant **Galerías Pacífico** ⓘ *Florida entre Córdoba y Viamonte, www.galeriaspacifico.com.ar, guided visits from the fountain on lower ground floor on Mon-Fri at 1130 and 1630,* a beautiful mall with fine murals and architecture, many exclusive shops and good food outlets. More shops are to be found on Avenida Santa Fe, which crosses Florida at Plaza San Martín. Avenida Corrientes, a street of theatres, bookshops, restaurants and cafés, and nearby Calle Lavalle (partly reserved for pedestrians), used to be the entertainment centre, but both are now regarded as faded. Recoleta, Palermo and Puerto Madero have become much more fashionable (see below).

The **Basílica Nuestra Señora de La Merced** ⓘ *J D Perón y Reconquista 207, Mass times, Wed 1730, Sun 11300,* founded 1604, rebuilt for the third time in the 18th century, has a beautiful interior with baroque and rococo features. In 1807 it was a command post against the invading British. **Museo y Biblioteca Mitre** ⓘ *San Martín 336, T011-4394 8240, www.museomitre.gob.ar, Mon-Fri 1300-1730 (library archives Wed 1400-1730), US$1.30,* preserves intact the household of President Bartolomé Mitre and has a coin and map collection and historical archives.

② Buenos Aires centre

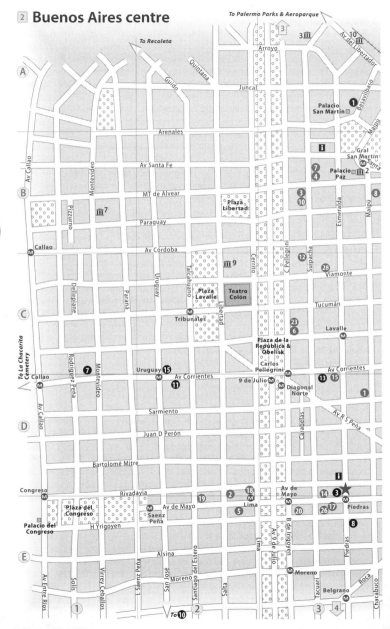

To Palermo Parks & Aeroparque

To Recoleta

46 · Buenos Aires Sights

➡ **Buenos Aires maps**
1 Buenos Aires orientation, page 42
2 Buenos Aires centre, page 46
3 Recoleta & Palermo, page 50
4 San Telmo, page 53

N

200 metres
200 yards

Where to stay 🛏

1 06 Central *D3*
2 BA Stop *D2*
3 Bisonte Palace *B3*
4 Casa Calma *B3*
5 Castelar *E2*
6 Colón *C3*
7 Dolmen *B3*
8 Dorá *B3*
10 El Conquistador *B3*
11 Faena *C5*
12 Goya *C3*
14 Hispano *D3*
15 Hostel Suites Obelisco *D3*
17 La Argentina *E3*
18 Limehouse Hostel *D2*
19 Marbella *E2*
20 Milhouse Hostel *E3*
21 Moreno *E4*
23 Panamericano & Tomo 1 restaurant *C3*
26 Portal del Sur *E3*
28 V&S *C3*
29 Waldorf *B4*

Restaurants 🍴

1 BASA *A3*
2 Cabañá Las Lilas *D5*
3 Café Tortoni *D3*
6 Dadá *B4*
7 El Gato Negro *C1*
8 Fikä *E3*
9 Florida Garden *B4*
12 Gianni's *B4/C4*
10 Gijón *E2*
11 Güerrín *D2*
13 Las Cuartetas *D3*
14 Le Grill *D5*
15 Los Inmortales *C2*
16 Sam Bucherié *C4*
17 Sorrento *C4*
18 Tancat *B3*

Bars & clubs 🎵

19 Bahrein *C4*
20 Druid In *B4*

Museums 🏛

2 Museo de Armas *B3*
3 Museo de Arte Hispanoamericano Isaac Fernández Blanco *A3*
4 Museo de la Ciudad *E4*
5 Museo Casa Rosada *E5*
6 Museo del Cabildo y la Revolución de Mayo *E4*
7 Museo del Holocausto *B1*
8 Museo Etnográfico JB Ambrosetti *E4*
9 Museo Judío *C2*
10 Museo Nacional Ferroviario *A3*
11 Museo y Biblioteca Mitre *D4*

Carlos Gardel

To this day there is still a lot of controversy about the origins of Argentina's favourite performer. Most people argue that Gardel, the legendary singer whose name is virtually synonymous with tango, was born in 1890 in Toulouse, France, to Berthe Gardès and an unknown father. To avoid social stigma, his mother decided to emigrate to the Abasto market area of Buenos Aires when her son was just two years old, and it was partly these humble beginnings that helped him to become an icon for poor Porteños.

Just as the exact origin of tango itself is something of a mystery, Gardel's formative years around the city are obscure, until around 1912 when he began his artistic career in earnest, performing as one half of the duo Gardel-Razzano. He began his recording career with Columbia with a recording of 15 traditional songs, but it was with his rendition of *Mi Noche Triste* (My Sorrowful Night) in 1917, that his mellifluous voice became known. As *tango-canción* became popular – the song rather than just a musical accompaniment to the dance – Gardel's career took off, and by the early 1920s he was singing entirely within this new genre, and achieving success as far afield as Madrid.

Gardel became a solo artist in 1925 and with his charm and natural machismo was the very epitome of tango both in Argentina and, following his tours to Europe, around the world. Between 1933 and 1935, he was based in New York, starring in numerous Spanish-speaking films, and the English-language *The Tango on Broadway* in 1934. On 24 June 1935, while on a tour of South America, his plane from Medellin, Colombia, crashed into another on the ground while taking off. Gardel was killed instantly; he was only 45 years old.

Gardel had recorded some 900 songs during his relatively short career, and the brilliance of his voice, the way he represented the spirit of the Río de la Plata to his fans at home, and the untimely nature of his death ensured his enduring popularity.

The **Plaza San Martín** has a monument to San Martín at the western corner of the main park and, at the north end, a memorial with an eternal flame to those who fell in the Falklands/Malvinas War of 1982. On the plaza is **Palacio San Martín** ① *Arenales 761, T011-4819 7297, www.mrecic.gov.ar, Tue and Thu 1500 free tours in Spanish and English*. Built 1905-1909, it is three houses linked together, now the Foreign Ministry. It has collections of pre-Hispanic and 20th-century art. On the opposite side of the plaza is the opulent **Palacio Paz (Círculo Militar)** ① *Av Santa Fe 750, T011-4311 1071, www.circulomilitar.org, guided tours Tue-Fri 1100, 1500 (1100 only on Wed), tours in English on Thu at 1530, US$10*. The Círculo Militar includes **Museo de Armas** ① *Av Santa Fe 702, Mon-Fri 1300-1900, US$2.60*, which has all kinds of weaponry related to Argentine history, including the 1982 Falklands/Malvinas War, plus Oriental weapons.

Plaza Fuerza Aérea Argentina (formerly Plaza Británica) has the clock tower presented by British and Anglo-Argentine residents, while in the **Plaza Canadá** (in front of the Retiro Station) there is a Pacific Northwest Indian totem pole, donated by the Canadian government. Behind Retiro station is the **Museo Nacional Ferroviario** ① *Av del Libertador 405, T011-4318 3343, daily 1000-1800 (closed on holidays), free*. For railway fans, it has locomotives, machinery, documents of the Argentine system's history; the building is in very poor condition. In a warehouse beside is the workshop of the sculptor Carlos Regazzoni (**Regazzoni Arts**, see Facebook) who recycles refuse material from railways.

The **Museo de Arte Hispanoamericano Isaac Fernández Blanco** ⓘ *Suipacha 1422 (3 blocks west of Retiro), T011-4327 0228, www.museos.buenosaires.gob.ar/mifb.htm, Tue-Fri, 1300-1900, Sat, Sun and holidays 1100-1900, Wed free, US$0.65*, is one of the city's best museums. It contains a fascinating collection of colonial art, especially paintings and silver, as well as temporary exhibitions of Latin American art, in a beautiful neocolonial mansion, the **Palacio Noel**, dating from the 1920s, with Spanish gardens. Weekend concerts are also held here.

Recoleta

Nuestra Señora del Pilar ⓘ *Junín 1898*, is a jewel of colonial architecture dating from 1732 (renovated in later centuries), facing onto the public gardens of Recoleta. A fine wooden image of San Pedro de Alcántara, attributed to the famous 17th-century Spanish sculptor Alonso Cano, is preserved in a side chapel on the left, and there are stunning gold altars. Upstairs is an interesting museum of religious art.

Next to it, the ★ **Cementerio Recoleta** ⓘ *entrance at Junín 1760, near Museo de Bellas Artes (see below), www.cementeriorecoleta.com.ar, 0700-1745, tours in Spanish and English are available Tue-Fri at 1100, Sat-Sun at 1100 and 1500 (visitasguiadasrecoleta@buenosaires. gob.ar)*, is one of the must-see sights of Buenos Aires. With its streets and alleys separating family mausoleums built in every imaginable architectural style, La Recoleta cemetery is often compared to a miniature city. Among the famous names from Argentine history is Evita Perón who lies in the Duarte family mausoleum: to find it from the entrance go to the first tree-filled plaza; turn left and where this avenue meets a main avenue (go just beyond the Turriaca tomb), turn right; then take the third passage on the left. On Saturday and Sunday there is a good craft market in the park on Plaza Francia outside the cemetery (1000-1800/1900), with street artists and performers. Next to the cemetery, the **Centro Cultural Recoleta** ⓘ *Junín 1930, T011-4803 1040, www.centroculturalrecoleta.org, Tue-Fri 1330-2030, Sat, Sun, holidays 1130-2030*, specializes in contemporary local art.

The excellent **Museo de Bellas Artes** (National Gallery) ⓘ *Av del Libertador 1473, T011-5288 9900, www.mnba.gob.ar, Tue-Fri 1130-1930, Sat-Sun 0930-1930, free*, gives a taste of Argentine art, as well as having a fine collection of European works, particularly post-Impressionist. It has superb Argentine 19th- and 20th-century paintings, sculpture and wooden carvings; it also hosts films, classical music concerts and art courses. The **Biblioteca Nacional** (National Library) ⓘ *Av del Libertador 1600 y Agüero 2502, T011-4808 6000, www.bn.gov.ar, Mon-Fri 0900-2100, Sat and Sun 1200-1900, closed Jan*, is housed in a modern building and contains an art gallery and periodical archives (only a fraction of the extensive stock can be seen); cultural events are held here too. Next to it is the **Museo del Libro y de la Lengua** ⓘ *Av Las Heras 2555, T011-4808 0090, Tue-Sun 1400-1900, free*, whose exhibitions illustrate singularities of the Spanish (Castellano) spoken in Argentina and the local publishing industry. The **Museo Nacional de Arte Decorativo** ⓘ *Av del Libertador 1902, T011-4802 6606, www.mnad.org, Tue-Sun 1400-1900 (closed Sun in Jan), US$1.30, Tue free, guided visits in English Tue-Fri at 1430, US$4*, contains collections of painting, furniture, porcelain, crystal and sculpture exhibited in sumptuous halls, once a family residence.

Palermo

Palermo Chico is a delightful residential area with several houses of once-wealthy families, dating from the early 20th century. The predominant French style of the district was broken in 1929 by the rationalist lines of the **Casa de la Cultura** ⓘ *Rufino de Elizalde 2831,*

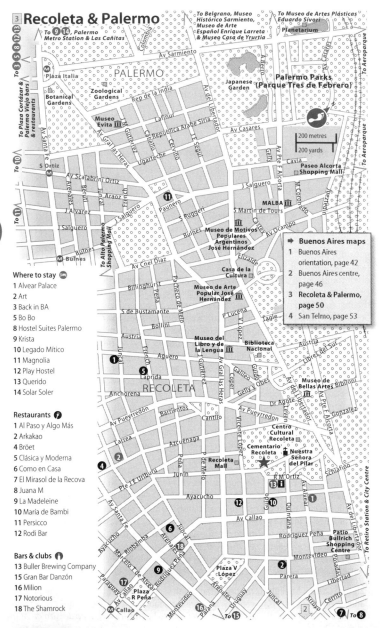

3 Recoleta & Palermo

To Belgrano, Museo
Histórico Sarmiento,
Museo de Arte
Español Enrique Larreta
& Museo Casa de Yrrutia

To Museo de Artes Plásticas
Eduardo Sívori
Planetarium

To 9 14, Palermo
Metro Station & Las Cañitas

Av Sarmiento

PALERMO

Plaza Italia

Japanese
Garden

Palermo Parks
(Parque Tres de Febrero)

To Plaza Cortázar &
Palermo Viejo bars
& restaurants

Botanical
Gardens

Zoological
Gardens

Rep de la India

Museo
Evita

Lafinur

República Árabe Siria

Av del Libertador

Av Casares

200 metres
200 yards

To 10

S Ortiz

Av Scalabrini Ortiz

Ugarteche

Cevirá

J Salguero

Paseo Alcorta
Shopping Mall

Cavia

To 11

Arenales
Berutti
French

Araoz

J Álvarez

J Salguero

Salguero

Paunero

R Ruggeri

S Martín de Tours

MALBA

Av Pte F Alcorta

J Salguero

Bulnes

Museo de Motivos
Populares
Argentinos
José Hernández

Av Ocampo

Av Corrientes

To Alto Palermo Shopping Mall

Bulnes

Av Cnel Díaz

Casa de la
Cultura

Enzalde

Buenos Aires maps

1 Buenos Aires
   orientation, page 42
2 Buenos Aires centre,
   page 46
3 Recoleta & Palermo,
   page 50
4 San Telmo, page 53

Billinghurst

Pacheco de Melo

Peña

Museo de Arte
Popular José
Hernández

P Lucena

Tagle

Where to stay

1 Alvear Palace
2 Art
3 Back in BA
5 Bo Bo
8 Hostel Suites Palermo
9 Krista
10 Legado Mítico
11 Magnolia
12 Play Hostel
13 Querido
14 Solar Soler

S de Bustamante

Austria

Bollini

French

Museo del
Libro y de
la Lengua

Av Gral las Heras

López

Biblioteca
Nacional

Austria

Libertador del Sur

Aguero

Gutierrez

Galileo

Gelly y Obes

Museo de
Bellas Artes

Av del Libertador

González

RECOLETA

Laprida

Anchorena

Barrientos

Av Pueyrredón

Cantilo

Dr Agote

Av Pueyrredón

Av Pte Alcorta

Restaurants

1 Al Paso y Algo Más
2 Arkakao
4 Bröet
5 Clásica y Moderna
6 Como en Casa
7 El Mirasol de la Recova
8 Juana M
9 La Madeleine
10 María de Bambi
11 Persicco
12 Rodi Bar

Larrea

Azcuénaga

Vicente López

Schiafino

Centro
Cultural
Recoleta

Cementerio
Recoleta

Nuestra
Señora
del Pilar

To Retiro Station & City Centre

Pte E Uriburu

Recoleta
Mall

R M Ortiz

Junín

Quintana

Ayacucho

Av Callao

Bars & clubs

13 Buller Brewing Company
15 Gran Bar Danzón
16 Milion
17 Notorious
18 The Shamrock

Paraguay

Av Callao

Marcelo T de Alvear

Arenales

Rodríguez Peña

Juncal

Patio
Bullrich
Shopping
Centre

Montevideo

Paraná

Riobamba

Plaza V
López

Parera

Plaza
R Peña

Av Callao

Montevideo

Uruguay

Arroyo

Cerrito

Libertad

Posadas

M Callao

Paraná

To 15

To 2

7 To 8

T011-4808 0553, www.fnartes.gov.ar, Tue-Sun 1500-2000 (Jan closed). The original residence of the writer Victoria Ocampo, this was a gathering place for artists and intellectuals and is now an attractive cultural centre with art exhibitions and occasional concerts.

The **Museo de Arte Popular José Hernández** ① *Av del Libertador 2373, T011-4803 2384, www.buenosaires.gob.ar/museojosehernandez, Tue-Fri 1300-1900, Sat-Sun and holidays 1000-1800, US$0.65, free Wed; see website for exhibitions, events and workshops,* has a wide collection of Argentine folkloric art, with rooms dedicated to indigenous, colonial and gaucho artefacts; there's a handicraft shop and library. The **Museo de Arte Latinoamericano (MALBA)** ① *Av Figueroa Alcorta 3415, T011-4808 6500, www.malba. org.ar, Thu-Mon and holidays 1200-2000, US$5.50, students and seniors US$3 (Wed half price, students free, open till 2100); Tue closed,* one of the most important museums in the city, houses renowned Latin American artists' works: powerful, moving and highly recommended. It's not a vast collection, but representative of the best from the continent. It also has a good library, cinema (showing art house films as well as Argentine classics), seminars and a shop, as well as an elegant café, serving delicious food and cakes.

Of the fine Palermo parks, the largest is **Parque Tres de Febrero**, famous for its extensive rose garden, Andalusian Patio, and the delightful **Jardín Japonés** (with café) ① *T011-4804 4922, www.jardinjapones.org.ar, daily 1000-1800, US$4.50, seniors free.* It is a charming place for a walk, delightful for children, and with a good café serving some Japanese dishes. Close by is the **Hipódromo Argentino** (Palermo racecourse) ① *T011-4778 2800, www.palermo.com.ar, races 10 days per month, free.* Opposite the parks are the Botanical and Zoological Gardens. At the entrance to the **Planetarium** ① *just off Belisario Roldán, in Palermo Park, T011-4771 6629, www.planetario.gob.ar, 2 presentations Tue-Fri, 6 at weekends, US$4; small museum,* are several large meteorites from Campo del Cielo. The **Museo de Artes Plásticas Eduardo Sívori** ① *Av Infanta Isabel 555 (Parque Tres de Febrero), T011-4774 9452, www.buenosaires.gob.ar/museosivori, Tue-Fri 1200-1900, Sat-Sun and holidays 1000-1900 (1800 in winter), US$1.60, Wed and Fri free,* emphasizes 19th- and 20th-century Argentine art, sculpture and tapestry.

The **Botanical Gardens** ① *Santa Fe 3951, T011-4831 4527, entrance from Plaza Italia (take Subte, line D) or from C República Arabe Siria, Tue-Fri 0800-17450, Sat-Sun 0930-1745 (closes at 1845 in summer), free guided visits Sat-Sun and holidays 1030, 1500,* contain characteristic specimens of the world's vegetation. The trees native to the different provinces of Argentina are brought together in one section; see also the *yerba mate* section. One block beyond is **Museo Evita** ① *Lafinur 2988, T011-4807 0306, www.museoevita.org, Tue-Sun 1100-1900, US$5.* In a former women's shelter run by Fundación Eva Perón, the exhibition of dresses, paintings and other items is quite interesting though lacks the expected passion; there's also a library and a café-restaurant.

Southwest of here, around Plaza Cortázar, is ★ **Palermo Viejo**, the most atmospheric part of Palermo. It's a very seductive place, characterized by leafy, cobbled streets, bohemian houses and chic eateries and shops.

Belgrano

In Belgrano is the **Museo de Arte Español Enrique Larreta** ① *Juramento 2291, T011-4784 4040, www.buenosaires.gob.ar/museolarreta Mon-Fri, 1200-1900, Sat-Sun 1000-2000, guided visits Mon-Fri 1430, Sat-Sun 1600, 1800, US$0.65, Thu free.* The home of the writer Larreta, with paintings and religious art from the 14th to the 20th century, it also has a beautiful garden. Also in Belgrano is the **Museo Histórico Sarmiento** ① *Juramento 2180, T011-4782 2354, www.museosarmiento.cultura.gob.ar, Mon-Fri 1300-1800, Sat-Sun 1400-1900,*

The Greatest Gardener in Buenos Aires

Next time you look up at the trees along Buenos Aires' streets, or the next time you enjoy the parks in some of Argentina's most important towns, spare a thought for French architect and landscaper Jean Charles Thays. Known as the 'greatest gardener in Buenos Aires', Thays played a large role in 'greening' Argentina by designing botanical gardens, parks and the odd estancia all around the country.

Born in France in 1849, he had a successful career as principal assistant to leading landscape architect Édouard André until, on his master's advice, he set sail for Argentina for a short visit at the age of 40. He never left and spent the rest of his life designing and remodelling most of Argentina's green spaces, including the botanical gardens and most of the parks. He also built stylized gardens in local hospitals and other public buildings, and planted over 150,000 trees in the streets of Buenos Aires. Not satisfied with just the capital, Thays worked throughout Argentina, and you will see his name all over the place.

He is remembered for combining romantic English informality with the French formal garden, as well as his use of open and closed curved roads, lakes with islands, ornamental buildings, sculptures and monuments. He received several awards, including the Légion d'Honneur in France, and when he died in 1934 he was revered for his life's work throughout Argentina and Europe.

and **Museo Casa de Yrurtia** ① *O'Higgins 2390, T011-4781 0385, www.museoyrurtia.cultura. gob.ar, closed for restoration in 2016.*

South of Plaza de Mayo

The church of **San Ignacio de Loyola**, begun in 1664, is the oldest colonial building in Buenos Aires (renovated in the 18th and 19th centuries). It stands in a block of Jesuit origin, called the **Manzana de las Luces** (Block of Enlightenment – Moreno, Alsina, Perú and Bolívar). Also in this block are the **Colegio Nacional de Buenos Aires** ① *Bolívar 263, T011-4331 0734 www.cnba.uba.ar,* formerly the site of the Jesuits' Colegio Máximo, the Procuraduría de las Misiones (today the **Mercado de las Luces**, a crafts market) and 18th-century **tunnels**. For centuries the whole block was the centre of intellectual activity, though little remains today but a small **cultural centre** ① *T011-4343 3260, www.manzanadelasluces.gov.ar, guided tours from Perú 272, Mon-Fri 1500, Sat and Sun 1500, 1630, 1800 in Spanish (in English by prior arrangement), arrive 15 mins before tour, US$3.25; the tours explore the tunnels and visit the buildings on C Perú,* with art courses, concerts, plays and film shows. The **Museo de la Ciudad** ① *Alsina 412, T011-4343 2123, www.buenosaires.gob.ar/museodelaciudad, daily 1100-1800, US$0.30, free on Mon and Wed,* has a permanent exhibition covering social history and popular culture, and special exhibitions on daily life in Buenos Aires that are changed every two months. There's also a reference library open to the public.

Santo Domingo ① *Defensa y Belgrano, T011-4331 1668, www.op.org.armass, Mon-Fri 0700-1800, Sat afternoon only, Sun 1000-1300, Mass held Mon-Fri at 1230, Sat 1830, Sun 1100,* was founded in 1751. During the British attack on Buenos Aires in 1806 some of Whitelocke's soldiers took refuge in the church. The local forces bombarded it, the British capitulated and their regimental colours were preserved in the church. General Belgrano is buried here. The church holds occasional concerts.

Museo Etnográfico JB Ambrosetti ① *Moreno 350, T011-4345 8196, see Facebook, Tue-Fri 1300-1900, Sat-Sun 1500-1900 (closed Jan), US$2, guided visits Sat-Sun 1600*, contains anthropological and ethnographic collections from Patagonian and Argentina's northwest cultures (the latter a rich collection displayed on the first floor). There's also a small international room with a magnificent Japanese Buddhist altar.

★ San Telmo
One of the few places which still has late colonial and Rosista buildings (mostly renovated in the 20th century) is the barrio of San Telmo, south of Plaza de Mayo. It's a place rich in culture, with lots of cafés, antique shops and little art galleries. On Sundays, it has a great atmosphere, with an antiques market at the Plaza Dorrego (see page 68), with the occasional free tango show and live music. The **Museo de Arte Moderno de Buenos Aires (MAMBA)** ① *Av San Juan 350, T011-4361 6919, Tue-Fri 1100-1900, Sat, Sun and holidays 1100-2000, US$1.31, Tue free*, has temporary art exhibitions from local and foreign artists.

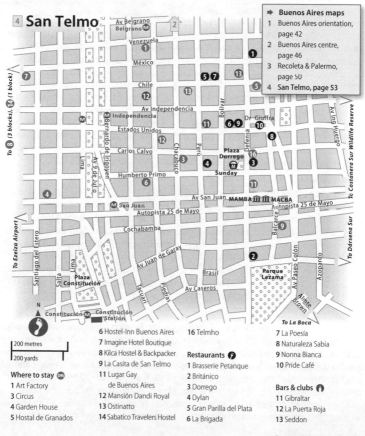

➡ **Buenos Aires maps**
1 Buenos Aires orientation, page 42
2 Buenos Aires centre, page 46
3 Recoleta & Palermo, page 50
4 San Telmo, page 53

Where to stay 🛏
1 Art Factory
3 Circus
4 Garden House
5 Hostal de Granados
6 Hostel-Inn Buenos Aires
7 Imagine Hotel Boutique
8 Kilca Hostel & Backpacker
9 La Casita de San Telmo
11 Lugar Gay de Buenos Aires
12 Mansión Dandi Royal
13 Ostinatto
14 Sabatico Travelers Hostel
16 Telmho

Restaurants 🍴
1 Brasserie Petanque
2 Británico
3 Dorrego
4 Dylan
5 Gran Parilla del Plata
6 La Brigada
7 La Poesía
8 Naturaleza Sabia
9 Nonna Bianca
10 Pride Café

Bars & clubs 🍸
11 Gibraltar
12 La Puerta Roja
13 Seddon

Next door is the **Museo de Arte Contemporáneo de Buenos Aires (MACBA)** ① *T011-5299 2010, www.macba.com.ar, Mon-Fri (closed Tue) 1100-1900, Sat, Sun 1100-1930, US$3.90 (Wed US$2.60)*, focusing on geometric abstraction.

La Boca

East of the Plaza de Mayo, behind the Casa Rosada, a broad avenue, Paseo Colón, runs south towards San Telmo and, as Avenida Almirante Brown, on to the old port district of La Boca, where the Riachuelo flows into the Plata. The much-photographed, brightly painted tin and wooden houses cover one block of the pedestrianized Caminito. As La Boca is the poorest and roughest area within central Buenos Aires, tourists are limited to this little street running from the Plaza La Vuelta de Rocha.

> **Tip...**
> La Boca is reportedly up-and-coming and less dangerous than in recent years, but always ask about safety, especially if you're thinking of going at night. Travel by radio taxi (US$5 one way from the centre or San Telmo); to return, call for a taxi from any café.

You can also visit **Fundación Proa** ① *Av Pedro de Mendoza 1929, T011-4104 1000, www.proa.org, Tue-Sun 1100-1900*, for varied art exhibitions, cultural events and for its café-restaurant with a view, and the **Museo de Bellas Artes Benito Quinquela Martín** ① *Av Pedro de Mendoza 1835, T011-4301 1080, www.buenosaires.gob.ar/museoquinquelamartin, Tue-Fri 1000-1800, Sat, Sun and holidays 1115-1800, US$2*, with over 1000 works by Argentine artists, particularly Benito Quinquela Martín (1890-1977), who painted La Boca port life. It also houses sculptures and figureheads rescued from ships. Do not go anywhere else in La Boca and avoid it at night. The area is especially rowdy when the Boca Juniors football club is playing at home. At Boca Juniors stadium is **Museo de la Pasión Boquense** ① *Brandsen 805, T011-4362 1100, www.museoboquense.com, daily 1000-1800, US$9, guided tour of the stadium in Spanish or English, daily 1000-1800, plus ticket to the museum, US$12*.

Puerto Madero

The Puerto Madero dock area has been renovated; the 19th-century warehouses are restaurants and bars, an attractive place for a stroll and popular nightspot. **Fragata Presidente Sarmiento** ① *dock 3, Av Alicia Moreau de Justo 980, Puerto Madero, T011-4334 9386, daily 1000-1900, entry by donation*, was a naval training ship until 1961; now it's a museum. Nearby, in dock 4, is the **Corbeta Uruguay** ① *T011-4314 1090, for both ships see www.ara.mil.ar, daily 1000-1900, entry by donation*, the ship that rescued Otto Nordenskjold's Antarctic expedition in 1903. In dock 4 there is also **Colección Fortabat** ① *Olga Cossettini 141, T011-4310 6600, www.coleccionfortabat.org.ar, Tue-Sun 1200-2000, US$4.50*, which houses a great art collection.

Costanera Sur

East of San Telmo on the far side of the docks, the Avenida Costanera runs as a long, spacious boulevard. A stretch of marshland reclaimed from the river forms the interesting **Costanera Sur Wildlife Reserve** ① *entrances at Av Tristán Achával Rodríguez 1550 (take Estados Unidos east from San Telmo) or next to the Buquebús ferry terminal (take Av Córdoba east), T0800 444 5343; for pedestrians and bikers only, Tue-Sun 0800-1800 (in summer, closes at 1900), free*, where over 150 bird species have been spotted over the past few years.

There are free guided tours at weekends and holidays 0930, 1600 (1030-1530 in winter), from the administration next to the southern entrance, but much can be seen from the road before then (binoculars useful). Also free nocturnal visits operate every month on the Friday closest to the full moon (book Monday before, visitasguiadas_recs@buenosaires.gob.ar). To get there take *colectivos* 4, 130 or 152. It's a 30-minute walk from the entrance to the river shore and it takes about three hours to walk the whole perimeter. In summer it's very hot with little shade. For details (particularly birdwatching) contact **Aves Argentinas/AOP** (see Birdwatching, page 68), or see www.reservacostanera.com.ar (English version).

Listings Buenos Aires *maps pages 42, 46, 50 and 53.*

Tourist information

A good guide to bus and subway routes is *Guía T*, available at newsstands. There is also the interactive map at www.mapa.buenosaires.gob.ar. Other useful maps found at newsstands include Mapa-Guía's pocket map of Buenos Aires (US$3.50), the more detailed city map (US$6.75) and the robust GBA Gran Buenos Aires map, which includes outlying neighbourhoods. Otherwise it is easy to get free maps of the centre from tourist kiosks and most hotels. The daily press has useful supplements, such as the Sunday tourism section in *La Nación* (www.lanacion.com.ar), *Sí* in *Clarín* (www.si.clarin.com) and the equivalent *No* of *Página 12* (www.pagina12.com.ar). The *Buenos Aires Herald* also has information on what's on at www.buenosairesherald.com, or see www.agendacultural.buenosaires.gob.ar, www.vuenosairez.com and www.wipe.com.ar. Also very useful are www.gringoinbuenosaires.com and www.discoverbuenosaires.com. Blogs worth exploring include www.baexpats.com and www.goodmorningba.com.

City information
www.turismo.buenosaires.gob.ar, in Spanish only.
There are tourist kiosks open daily (0900-1800) downtown at Florida 50, in Recoleta (Av Quintana 596, junction with Ortiz), in Puerto Madero (JM Gorriti 200), and at Retiro bus station (ground floor, daily 0730-1630).

Defensoría del Turista
Defensa 1302 (San Telmo), T011-4307 5102, turistasantelmo@defensoria.org.ar. Mon-Fri 1000-1800, Sat-Sun and holidays 1100-1800.
To report being overcharged or cheated.

National office
Av Santa Fe 883, T011-4312 2232 or T0800-555 0016, info@turismo.gov.ar. Mon-Fri 0900-1900.
Has maps and literature covering the whole country. There are kiosks at Aeroparque and Ezeiza airports (Mon-Fri 0900-1700, Sat-Sun 0900-1800).

Where to stay

Shop around for hotels offering discounts on multi-night stays. The tourist offices at Ezeiza and Aeroparque airports book rooms. A/c is a must in high summer. Finding hotels for Fri, Sat, Sun nights can be difficult and hostels can get very busy, resulting in pressure on staff. A bed in a hostel dorm costs US$11-21. The range of 'boutique' hotels and hostels is impressive, especially in Palermo and San Telmo. The same applies to restaurants, bars and clubs. There are far more than we can list here. There are fine examples of the **Four Seasons** (www.fourseasons.com/buenosaires), **Hilton** (www.hilton.com), **Hyatt** (www.buenosaires.park.hyatt.com), **Marriott** (www.marriott.com), **NH** (www.nh-hoteles.com), **Pestana** (www.pestana.com/en), **Sofitel** (www.sofitel.com) and **Unique Hotels** (www.uniquehotels.com.ar). Hotels will store luggage, and most have English-speaking staff.

$$$$ Alvear Palace
Av Alvear 1891, T011-4808 2100,
www.alvearpalace.com.
The height of elegance, an impeccably
preserved 1920s Recoleta palace, sumptuous
marble foyer, with Louis XV-style chairs, and
a charming orangery where you can take
tea with superb patisseries. Antique-filled
bedrooms. Recommended.

$$$$ Casa Calma
Suipacha 1015, T011-4312 5000,
www.casacalmahotel.com.
A relaxing haven in a downtown setting,
homely yet luxurious, with a wellness centre
and honesty bar.

$$$$ Faena
Martha Salotti 445 (Puerto Madero),
T011-4010 9000, www.faena.com.
Set in a 100-year-old silo, renovated by
Philippe Starck, this is not for all budgets
or tastes. Eclectic decoration, staff trained
to be perfect.

$$$$-$$$ Castelar
Av de Mayo 1152, T011-4383 5000,
www.castelarhotel.com.ar.
A wonderfully elegant 1920s hotel which
retains all the original features in the
grand entrance and bar. Cosy bedrooms,
charming staff, and excellent value. Also
a spa with Turkish baths and massage.
Highly recommended.

$$$$-$$$ Dolmen
Suipacha 1079, T011-4315 7117,
www.hoteldolmen.com.ar.
Good location, smart spacious entrance
lobby, with a calm relaxing atmosphere, good
professional service, modern, comfortable
well-designed rooms, small pool.

$$$$-$$$ El Conquistador
Suipacha 948, T011-4328 3012,
www.elconquistador.com.ar.
Stylish 1970s hotel, which retains the wood
and chrome foyer, but has bright modern
rooms, and a lovely light restaurant on the

10th floor with great views. Well situated,
good value.

$$$$-$$$ Panamericano
Carlos Pellegrini 551, T011-4348 5000,
www.panamericano.us.
Very smart and modern hotel, with luxurious
and tasteful rooms, covered rooftop pool,
Celtic Bar pub with a cigar club, and the
superb restaurant, **Tomo 1**. Excellent service
too. Also has properties in Bariloche (www.
panamericanobariloche.com) and El Calafate
(www.casalossauces.com).

$$$ Art
Azcuénaga 1268, T011-4821 6248,
www.ahotel.com.ar.
Charming boutique hotel on a quiet
residential street, only a few blocks from
Recoleta or Av Santa Fe, simple but warmly
decorated, good service, solarium, compact
standard rooms.

$$$ Bisonte Palace
MT de Alvear 902, T011-4390 7830,
www.bisontepalace.com.
Charming, with calm entrance foyer, which
remains gracious thanks to courteous staff.
Plain but spacious rooms, ample breakfast,
good location. Very good value.

$$$ Colón
Carlos Pellegrini 507, T011-4320 3500,
www.exehotelcolon.com.
Splendid location overlooking Av 9 de
Julio and Teatro Colón, extremely good
value. Charming bedrooms, comfortable,
gym, great breakfasts, and perfect service.
Highly recommended.

$$$ Dorá
Maipú 963, T011-4312 7391,
www.dorahotel.com.ar.
Charming and old-fashioned with
comfortable rooms, good service,
attractive lounge with paintings.
Warmly recommended.

$$$ Goya
Suipacha 748, T011-4322 9269,
www.goyahotel.com.ar.

Welcoming and central, worth paying more for superior rooms, though all are comfortable. Good breakfast, English spoken.

$$$ Hispano
Av de Mayo 861, T011-4345 2020, www.hhispano.com.ar.
Plain but comfortable rooms in this hotel which has been welcoming travellers since the 1950s, courtyard and small garden, central.

$$$ Marbella
Av de Mayo 1261, T011-4383 3573, www.hotelmarbella.com.ar.
Modernized, and central, though quiet, multilingual. Recommended.

$$$ Moreno
Moreno 376, T011-4831 6831, www.morenobuenosaires.com.
150 m from the Plaza de Mayo, decorated in dark, rich tones, large rooms, good value, jacuzzi, gym and chic bar, winery and restaurant.

$$$ Waldorf
Paraguay 450, T011-4312 2071, www.waldorf-hotel.com.ar.
Welcoming staff and a comfortable mixture of traditional and modern in this centrally located hotel. Good value, with safe boxes in all rooms and a buffet breakfast, English spoken. Recommended.

$ La Argentina
Av de Mayo 860, T011-4342 0078.
Cheap, central and rickety, but it stands the test of time. Amazing old building, bringing new meaning to the term 'high-ceilinged'; can be noisy if your room is near the 'slam-the-door-shut' elevator. Good, cheap and cheerful restaurant attached, doing very affordable *menú del día*. Recommended.

Youth hostels

$ pp 06 Central
Maipú 306, T011-5219 0052, www.06centralhostel.com.
A few metres from the Obelisco and Av Corrientes, simple, spacious dorms,

attractively decorated doubles ($$), cosy communal area.

$ pp BA Stop
Rivadavia 1194, T011-6091 2156, www.bastop.com.
In a lovely converted 1900s corner block, dorms for 4-8 people, 11 private rooms ($$ double), TV, table tennis, English spoken, safe, very helpful staff can organize tours, Spanish classes. Repeatedly recommended; the best hostel in the centre.

$ pp Hostel Suites Obelisco
Av Corrientes 830, T011-4328 4040, www.hostelsuites.com.
Elegant hostel built in a completely restored old building in the heart of the city. Dorms, doubles and private apartments ($$), DVD room, laundry service. Free transfer from Ezeiza airport.

$ pp Limehouse Hostel
Lima 11, T011-4383 4561, www.limehouse.com.ar.
Dorms for up to 8 and doubles with and without bath ($$), popular, typical city hostel with bar, roof terrace, 'chilled', great if you like the party atmosphere, efficient staff. Recommended.

$ pp Milhouse Hostel
Hipólito Yrigoyen 959, T011-4345 9604, www.milhousehostel.com.
In an 1890 house, lovely rooms ($$$ in double) and dorms, comfortable, laundry, tango lessons, very popular so reconfirm bookings at all times. Also at Av De Mayo 1245.

$ pp Portal del Sur
Hipólito Yrigoyen 855, T011-4342 8788, www.portaldelsurba.com.ar.
Good dorms and especially lovely doubles ($$) and singles in a converted 19th-century building. Recommended for single travellers.

$ pp V&S
Viamonte 887, T011-4322 0994, www.hostelclub.com.
Central popular hostel ($$ in attractive double room, bath), café, tango classes,

tours, warm atmosphere, welcoming. Recommended.

Palermo *map page 50.*

$$$$ Legado Mítico
Gurruchaga 1848, T011-4833 1300, www.legadomitico.com.
Stylish small hotel with 11 rooms named after Argentine cultural legends. They use local designs and products. Luxurious and recommended.

$$$$ Magnolia
Julián Alvarez 1746, T011-4867 4900, www.magnoliahotelboutique.com.
Lovely boutique hotel in a quiet area. This refurbished early 20th-century house has attractively designed rooms opening onto the street or to inner courtyards and a perfect retreat on its rooftop terrace.

$$$$ Querido
Juan Ramírez de Velazco 934, T011-4854 6297, www.queridobuenosaires.com.
Purpose-built, designed and cared for by a Brazilian/English couple. 7 rooms, 4 of which have balconies, for a comfortable stay in Villa Crespo area, a few blocks from Palermo Soho and from the subway.

$$$$-$$$ Bo Bo
Guatemala 4870, T011-4774 0505, www.bobohotel.com.
On a leafy street, 15 rooms decorated in contemporary style, some with private balconies, excellent restaurant.

$$$$-$$$ Krista
Bonpland 1665, T011-4771 4697, www.kristahotel.com.ar.
Intimate, hidden behind the plain façade of an elegant townhouse, well placed for restaurants. Good value, comfortable, individually designed spacious rooms, wheelchair access.

$$$ Solar Soler
Soler 5676, T011-4776 7494, www.solarsoler.com.ar.

Welcoming B&B in Palermo Hollywood, excellent service. Recommended.

Youth hostels

$ pp Back in BA
El Salvador 5115, T011-4774 2859, www.backinba.com.
Small hostel with dorms for up to 6 and private rooms ($$), lockers with charging points, patio, bar, Netflix, information, tours, apartment rentals, and classes can be arranged, good Palermo Soho location.

$ pp Hostel Suites Palermo
Charcas 4752, T011-4773 0806, www.palermo.hostelsuites.com.
A beautiful century-old residence with the original grandeur partially preserved and a quiet atmosphere. Comfortable renovated dorms and private rooms with bath ($$ doubles), good service, small travel agency, Wi-Fi, cooking and laundry facilities, DVD room and breakfast included. Free transfer from Ezeiza airport.

$ Play Hostel
Guatemala 3646, T011-4832 4257, www.playhostel.com.
Popular option with dorms for 4-10 people. Wi-Fi, laundry service, bike hire, tourist info and tango classes.

San Telmo and around *map page 53.*

$$$$ Mansión Dandi Royal
Piedras 922, T011-4361 3537, www. hotelmansiondandiroyal.com.
A wonderfully restored 1903 residence, small upmarket hotel with an elegant tango atmosphere, small pool, good value. Daily tango lessons and *milonga* every Fri at 2130.

$$$$-$$$ Imagine Hotel Boutique
México 1330, T011-4383 2230, www.imaginehotelboutique.com.
9 suites in a beautifully restored 1820s house, each room individually designed, quiet, buffet breakfast, parking. Recommended.

$$$ La Casita de San Telmo
Cochabamba 286, T011-4307 5073,
www.lacasitadesantelmo.com.
7 rooms in restored 1840s house, most
open onto a garden with a beautiful fig tree,
owners are tango fans; rooms rented by day,
week or month.

$$$ Lugar Gay de Buenos Aires
Defensa 1120 (no sign), T011-4300 4747,
www.lugargay.com.ar.
A men-only gay B&B with 8 comfortable
rooms, video room and jacuzzi. A stone's
throw from Plaza Dorrego.

$$$ Telmho
Defensa 1086, T011-4307 9898,
www.telmho-hotel.com.ar.
Smart rooms overlooking Plaza Dorrego,
huge beds, modern bathrooms, lovely roof
garden, helpful staff.

Youth hostels

$ pp Art Factory
Piedras 545, T011-4343 1463,
www.artfactoryba.com.ar.
Large, early 1900s house converted into a
hostel, informal atmosphere with individually
designed and brightly painted private
rooms (some with bath, **$$**), dorms, halfway
between the centre and San Telmo.

$ pp Circus
Chacabuco 1020, T011-4300 4983,
www.hostelcircus.com.
Stylish rooms for 2 (**$$**) to 4 people,
tastefully renovated building, small
heated swimming pool.

$ pp Garden House
Av San Juan 1271, T011-4304 1824,
www.gardenhouseba.com.ar.
Small, welcoming independent hostel for
those who don't want a party atmosphere;
good barbecues on the terrace. Dorms and
some doubles (**$$**). Recommended.

$ pp Hostal de Granados
Chile 374, T011-4362 5600,
www.hostaldegranados.com.ar.

Small, light, well-equipped rooms in an
interesting building on a popular street,
rooms for 2 (**$$**), dorms for 4 to 8, laundry.

$ pp Hostel-Inn Buenos Aires
Humberto Primo 820, T011-4300 7992,
www.hibuenosaires.com.
An old 2-storey mansion with dorms for
up to 8 people and also private rooms (**$$**),
activities, loud parties and individual lockers
in every room.

$ pp Kilca Hostel & Backpacker
México 1545, between Sáenz Peña
and Virrey Cevallos, T011-4381 1166,
www.kilcabackpacker.com.
In a restored 19th-century house with
attractive landscaped patios. A variety of
rooms from dorms to doubles; all bathrooms
shared, but 1 double with bath (**$$**). Offers a
host of guest services including bike rental,
pub crawl, tango classes, Spanish lessons,
football tickets and more.

$ pp Ostinatto
Chile 680, T011-4362 9639,
www.ostinatto.com.
Minimalist contemporary design in a 1920s
building, promotes the arts, music, piano bar,
movie room, tango lessons, arranges events,
rooftop terrace. Shared rooms, also has
double rooms with and without bath (**$$**),
and apartments for rent.

$ pp Sabatico Travelers Hostel
México 1410, T011-4381 1138,
www.sabaticohostel.com.ar.
Hostel in a good location, with dorms and
double rooms with and without bath (**$$**). It
offers a full range of services and information,
a rooftop barbecue, mini pool and bar.

Apartments/self-catering/homestays

Argenhomes
T011-4044 5978, www.argenhomes.com.
For those who like attentive, personalized
service, this is the best apartment-rental
option. A limited selection of charming flats
in San Telmo, Recoleta, Belgrano, Palermo

and even Tigre. Accepts dollars, euros, pounds and pesos; no credit cards.

B&T Argentina
T011-4876 5000, www.bytargentina.com.
Accommodation in student residences and host families; also furnished flats. Reputable.

Bahouse
T011 5811 3832, www.bahouse.com.ar.
Very good flats, by the week or month, all furnished and well located in San Telmo, Retiro, Recoleta, Belgrano, Palermo and the centre.

Casa 34
Nicaragua 6045, T011-4775 0207, www.casa34.com.
Helpful, with a big range of options.

Restaurants

Eating out in Buenos Aires is one of the city's great pleasures, with a huge variety of restaurants from the chic to the cheap. To try some of Argentina's excellent steaks, choose from one of the many *parrillas*, where your huge slab of lean meat will be expertly cooked over fiery *carbón* (charcoal).

If in doubt about where to eat, head for Puerto Madero, the revamped docks area, an attractive place to stroll along the waterfront before dinner. There are good places here, generally in stylish interiors, serving international as well as local cuisine, with good service if a little overpriced. Less expensive yet just as delicious and longer-standing *parrillas* can be found in San Telmo. Take a radio taxi to Palermo or Las Cañitas for a wide range of excellent restaurants all within strolling distance. For more information on the gastronomy of Buenos Aires see: www.guiaoleo.com.ar, a restaurant guide in Spanish.

There is a growing interest in less conventional eating out, from secret, or *puerta cerrada*, restaurants, to local eateries off the normal restaurant circuit, exploring local markets and so on. 3 solid food-oriented blogs in English are: www.salt shaker.net, by chef Dan Perlman who also runs a highly recommended private restaurant in his house, see website for details; www.buenosairesfoodies.com; and the *Yanqui* expat-penned www.pickupthe fork.com. Another highly regarded closed-door option can be found at **The Argentine Experience** (www.theargentineexperience. com), while tours are run by **Parrilla Tour Buenos Aires** (www.parrillatour.com).

Some restaurants are *tenedor libre*: eat as much as you like for a fixed price. Most cafés serve tea or coffee plus *facturas* (pastries) for breakfast.

Centre *map page 46.*

$$$ Dadá
San Martín 941.
A restaurant and bar with eclectic decoration. Good for gourmet lunches.

$$$ Sorrento
Av Corrientes 668 (just off Florida), www.sorrentorestaurant.com.ar.
Intimate, elegant atmosphere, one of the most traditional places in the centre for very good pastas and seafood.

$$$ Tancat
Paraguay 645, www.tancatrestaurante.com.
Delicious Spanish food, very popular at lunchtime.

$$$-$$ Gijón
Chile y San José.
Very good-value *parrilla* at this popular *bodegón*, south of Congreso district.

$$ Fikä
Hipólito Yrigoyen 782, see Facebook. Mon-Fri open till 1700.
Popular at lunchtime with a varied menu, this place is also attractive for a coffee break or a drink.

$$ Gianni's
Reconquista 1028, www.giannisonline.com.ar. Open till 1700.

The set menu with the meal-of-the-day makes an ideal lunch. Good risottos and salads. Slow service.

$$ Güerrín
Av Corrientes 1368,
www.pizzeriaguerrin.com.
A Buenos Aires institution. Serves filling pizza and *faina* (chickpea polenta) which you eat standing up at a bar, or at tables, though you miss out on the colourful local life that way. For an extra service fee, upstairs room is less crowded or noisy. Try the chicken *empanadas al horno* (baked pies).

$$ Las Cuartetas
Av Corrientes 838, www.lascuartetas.com.
Another local institution open early to very late for fantastic pizza, can be busy and noisy as it's so popular.

$$ Los Inmortales
Corrientes 1369, www.losinmortales.com.
Opposite **Güerrín**, this does some of the city's other best pizza (with a thinner crust). It's also a *parrilla*.

$$ Sam Bucherie
25 de Mayo 562. Open till 1800.
The most imaginative sandwiches and salads downtown.

Cafés

Café Tortoni
Av de Mayo 825-9.
This most famous Buenos Aires café has been the elegant haunt of artists and writers for over 100 years, with marble columns, stained-glass ceilings, old leather chairs, and photographs of its famous clientele on the walls. Live tango. Packed with tourists, pricey, but still worth a visit.

El Gato Negro
Av Corrientes 1669, see Facebook.
A beautiful tearoom, serving a choice of coffees and teas, and good cakes. Delightfully scented from the wide range of spices on sale.

Florida Garden
Florida y Paraguay,
www.floridagarden.com.ar.
Another well-known café, popular for lunch, and tea.

Ice cream
The Italian ice cream tradition has been marked for decades by *'heladerías'* such as **Cadore** (Av Corrientes 1695, www.heladeriacadore.com.ar), or **El Vesuvio** (Av Corrientes 1181), the oldest of all.

North of Plaza de Mayo
maps pages 46 and 50.
3 blocks west of Plaza San Martín, under the flyover at the northern end of Av 9 de Julio, between Arroyo and Av del Libertador in La Recova, are several recommended restaurants.

$$$ BASA
Basavilbaso 1328, www.basabar.com.ar.
Great food and smart cocktails in ultra-chic surroundings. Same owners as other upscale hangout **Gran Bar Danzón**, see Bars and clubs, page 64.

$$$ El Mirasol de la Recova
Posadas 1032, elmirasol.com.ar.
Serves top-quality *parrilla* in an elegant atmosphere.

$$$ Juana M
Carlos Pellegrini 1535 (downstairs),
www.juanam.com.
Excellent choice, popular with locals for its good range of dishes, and its excellent salad bar.

Recoleta *map page 50.*

$$$ Rodi Bar
Vicente López 1900.
Excellent *bife* and other dishes in this typical *bodegón*, welcoming and unpretentious.

$$$-$$ La Madeleine
Av Santa Fe 1726.
Bright and cheerful choice, quite good pastas.

$$$-$$ María de Bambi
Ayacucho 1821 (with a small branch at Arenales 920). Open till 2200 (2300 Fri and Sat), closed on Sun.
This small, quiet place is probably the best value in the area, serving very good and simple meals, also *salón de té* and patisserie.

$$ Al Paso y Algo Más
Juncal 2684, www.alpasoyalgomas.com.
Recommended choice for *choripán* and *churrasquito* sandwiches plus other meat dishes.

Tea rooms, café/bars and ice cream

Arkakao
Av Quintana 188, www.arkakao.com.ar.
Great ice creams at this elegant tea room.

Bröet
Azcuénaga 1144, see Facebook.
Austrian-owned artisanal bakery with traditionally made bread from around the world.

Clásica y Moderna
Av Callao 892, T011-4812 8707, www.clasicaymoderna.com.
One of the city's most welcoming cafés, with a bookshop, great atmosphere, good breakfast through to drinks at night, daily live music and varied shows.

Como en Casa
Av Quintana 2, Riobamba 1239, Laprida 1782 and at Céspedes 2647 (Belgrano), www.tortascomoencasa.com.
In the former convent of Santa Catalina, this place is very popular in the afternoon for its varied and delicious cakes and fruit pies.

Freddo and Un'Altra Volta
Ice cream parlours, both with several branches in the city.

Palermo *map page 50.*
This area of Buenos Aires is very popular with tourists and expats (on the streets you're more likely to hear English spoken than Spanish). There are many chic restaurants and bars in Palermo Viejo (referred to as 'Palermo Soho' for the area next to Plaza Cortázar and 'Palermo Hollywood' for the area beyond the railways and Av Juan B Justo) and the Las Cañitas district. It's a sprawling district, so you could take a taxi to one of these restaurants, and walk around before deciding where to eat. It's also a great place to stop for lunch, with cobbled streets, and 1900s buildings, now housing chic clothes shops. The Las Cañitas area is fashionable, with a wide range of interesting restaurants mostly along Báez.

$$$ Bio
Humboldt 2192, T011-4774 3880, www.biorestaurant.com.ar. Daily.
Delicious gourmet organic food, on a sunny corner.

$$$ Campobravo
Báez y Arévalo and Honduras y Fitz Roy, www.campobravo.com.ar.
Stylish, minimalist, superb steaks and vegetables on the *parrilla*. Popular, can be noisy. Recommended.

$$$ Don Julio
Guatemala 4691, www.parrilladonjulio.com.ar.
Regarded, along with **La Brigada** in San Telmo, as one of the best *parrillas* in the city. The *entraña* (skirt steak) has a sterling reputation.

$$$ El Manto
Costa Rica 5801, T011-4774 2409, www.elmanto.com.
Genuine Armenian dishes, relaxed, good for a quiet evening.

$$$ El Preferido de Palermo
Borges y Guatemala, T011-4774 6585.
Very popular *bodegón* serving both Argentine and Spanish-style dishes.

$$$ Janio
Malabia 1805, T011-4833 6540. Open for breakfast through to the early hours.
One of Palermo's first restaurants, sophisticated Argentine cuisine in the evening.

$$$ Morelia
Baez 260 and Humboldt 2005,
http://morelia.com.ar.
Cooks superb pizzas on the *parrilla*, and
has a lovely roof terrace for summer.

$$$ Siamo nel forno
Costa Rica 5886, see Facebook.
Excellent true Italian pizzas. The tiramisu
is recommended.

$$$ Social Paraíso
Honduras 5182, see Facebook.
Closed Sun evening and Mon.
Simple delicious dishes in a relaxed chic
atmosphere, with a lovely patio at the back.
Good fish and tasty salads.

$$$-$$ El Tejano
Honduras 4416, T011-4833 3545,
www.eltejanoba.com.ar.
A delight for those who like to compare
and contrast traditional Argentine *asado*
with authentic US barbecue. This small
eatery showcases expat owner Larry's
hot sauces and smoked meats, a model
of Texas hospitality.

$$$-$$ La Fábrica del Taco
Gorriti 5062, www.lafabricadeltaco.com.
While not on par with the Real McCoy, it's
some of the most authentic Mexican food
in South America.

$$ Krishna
Malabia 1833, www.krishnaveggie.com.
A small, intimate place serving Indian-
flavoured vegetarian dishes.

Tea rooms, café/bars and ice cream
Palermo has good cafés opposite the park
on Av del Libertador.

Persicco
Honduras 4900 and multiple other locations,
www.persicco.com.
The grandsons of **Freddo**'s founders also
offer excellent ice cream.

San Telmo *map page 53.*

$$$ Brasserie Petanque
Defensa y México,
www.brasseriepetanque.com.
Very attractive, informal French restaurant
offering a varied menu with very good,
creative dishes. Excellent value for their
set lunch menus.

$$$ Gran Parrilla del Plata
Chile 594, T011-4300 8858,
www.parrilladelplata.com.
Popular, good value *parrilla* on a
historic corner.

$$$ La Brigada
Estados Unidos 465, T011-4361 5557,
www.parrillalabrigada.com.ar.
Excellent *parrilla*, serving Argentine cuisine
and wines. The *asado de tira* (grilled short
rib, order it *jugoso*) is consistently ranked
one of the best cuts of meat in the city.
Very popular, always reserve.

$$$-$$ Naturaleza Sabia
Balcarce 958, www.naturalezasabia.com.ar.
Tasty vegetarian and vegan dishes in an
attractive ambience.

Tea rooms, café/bars and ice cream

Británico
Brasil y Defensa 399.
Historic 24-hr place with a good atmosphere
at lunchtime.

Dorrego
Humberto Primo y Defensa.
Bar/café with great atmosphere, seating outside
on plaza, good for late-night coffee or drinks.

Dylan
Perú 1086, see Facebook.
Very good ice cream.

La Poesía
Chile y Bolívar, www.cafelapoesia.com.ar.
More character than you can shake a stick at.
Ideal for a coffee break on the sunny sidewalk.

Nonna Bianca
Estados Unidos 425.
For ice cream in an internet café.

Pride Café
Balcarce y Giuffra, see Facebook.
Wonderful sandwiches, juices, salads and brownies, with lots of magazines to read.

Puerto Madero *map page 46.*

$$$ Cabaña Las Lilas
Av Moreau de Justo 516, T011-4313 1336, www.restaurantlaslilas.com.ar.
A solid upscale *parrilla* with a good reputation, pricey and popular with foreigners and business people.

$$$ Le Grill
Av Moreau de Justo 876, T011-4331 0454, www.legrill.com.ar/esp.
A gourmet touch at a sophisticated *parrilla* which includes dry-aged beef, pork and lamb on its menu.

Bars and clubs

Generally it is not worth going to clubs before 0230 at weekends. Dress is usually smart. Entry can be from US$10-15, sometimes including a drink. A good way to visit some of the best bars is to join a pub crawl, eg **The Buenos Aires Pub Crawl**, www.buenosairespubcrawl.com, whose daily crawls are a safe night out.

Bars

The corner of Reconquista and Marcelo T de Alvear in Retiro is the centre of the small 'Irish' pub district, overcrowded on St Patrick's Day, 17 Mar. **Druid In** (Reconquista 1040, Centre), is by far the most attractive choice there, open for lunch and with live music weekly. **The Shamrock** (Rodríguez Peña 1220, in Recoleta, www.theshamrock.com.ar), is another Irish-run, popular bar, happy hour until 0000.

Buller Brewing Company
Roberto M Ortiz 1827, Recoleta, www.bullerpub.com.
Brew pub which also serves international food.

Chez Juanito
Cabrera 5083, Palermo Soho, next to La Cabrera west of Palermo Viejo.
Cheerful, popular bar serving drinks, snacks and pizzas. Good for a relaxed evening.

Gibraltar
Perú 895, www.thegibraltarbar.com.
An inauthentic British pub that somehow does everything right. Popular San Telmo option and a great place to shoot pool.

Gran Bar Danzón
Libertad 1161, www.granbardanzon.com.ar.
Original BA swank and a good dark ambience for a cocktail and romance. Same owners as **BASA** (see Restaurants, page 61).

La Puerta Roja
Chacabuco 733 (upstairs).
The 'Red Door' is San Telmo's best dive.

Milion
Paraná 1048.
In a beautifully restored mansion with unique (almost unsettling) art on the walls, supposedly once a favourite haunt of Borges' widow. Great bartenders, also serves tapas. Recommended Fri after midnight.

Mundo Bizarro
Serrano 1222, Palermo Viejo, see Facebook.
Famous for its weird films, cocktails, American-style food, electronic and pop music. A solid dive bar.

Seddon
Defensa y Chile, hbarseddon.blogspot.com.ar.
Traditional bar open till late with live music on Fri.

Sugar
Costa Rica 4619, Palermo Viejo, www.sugarbuenosaires.com.
Welcoming bar with cheap beer and drinks, happy hour nightly, shows international sports.

Clubs

Bahrein
Lavalle 345, Centre, www.bahreinba.com.
Funky and electronic.

El Living
Marcelo T de Alvear 1540 (upstairs).
Smaller intimate club good for dancing to
80s and Britpop.

L'Arc
Niceto Vega 5452, Palermo Viejo.
Hosts **The X Club** weekly, with a cocktail bar
and live bands.

Niceto Club
*Niceto Vega 5510, Palermo Viejo, T011-4779
9396, www.nicetoclub.com.*
Early live shows and dancing afterwards.
Club 69 weekly parties for house, electronic,
hip hop and funk music.

Gay clubs Most gay clubs charge from
US$10 entry. **Amerika** (Gascón 1040,
Almagro, www.ameri-k.com.ar, Fri-Sun),
attracting more than 2000 party-goers over
3 floors; **Bach Bar** (Cabrera 4390, www.bach-
bar.com.ar, Fri-Sun), a friendly lesbian bar
in Palermo Viejo; **Sitges** (Av Córdoba 4119,
Palermo Viejo, T011-4861 3763, see Facebook,
Thu-Sun), a gay and lesbian bar.

Jazz clubs Notorious (Av Callao 966, T011-
4813 6888, www.notorious.com.ar). Live
jazz at a music shop with bar and restaurant.
Thelonious (Salguero 1884, T011-4829 1562,
www.thelonious.com.ar), for live jazz and
DJs; **Virasoro Bar** (Guatemala 4328, T011-
4831 8918, www.virasorobar.com.ar), for
live jazz in a 1920s art deco house.

Salsa clubs La Salsera (Yatay 961, Palermo
Viejo, T011-4866 1829, www.lasalsera.com),
is highly regarded.

Entertainment

At carnival time, look for the **Programa
Carnaval Porteño** (it's on Facebook).

Cinema
The selection of films is excellent, ranging
from new Hollywood releases to Argentine
and world cinema; details are listed daily
in main newspapers. Films are shown
uncensored and most foreign films (other
than animated films) are subtitled. Tickets
best booked early afternoon to ensure good
seats (average price US$10, some chains offer
discounts on Wed or with members' card).

Independent foreign and national films
are shown during the **Festival de Cine
Independiente** (BAFICI), www.festivales.
buenosaires.gob.ar, held every Apr.

Cultural events
Centro Cultural Borges, *Galerías Pacífico,
Viamonte y San Martín, p 1, T011-5555 5359,
www.ccborges.org.ar.* Art exhibitions,
concerts, film shows and ballet; some
student discounts.
Ciudad Cultural Konex, *Sarmiento
3131 (Abasto), T011-4864 3200, www.
ciudadculturalkonex.org.* A converted oil
factory hosts this huge complex holding
plays, live music shows, summer film
projections under the stars, modern ballet,
puppet theatre and, occasionally, massive
parties, including the must-visit drum
extravaganza, La Bomba de Tiempo.
Fototeca Latinoamericana, *Godoy Cruz
2626, Arcos (near Palermo metro station),
http://fola.com.ar. Thu-Tue 1200-2000.*
With a permanent collection of photography
from the continent, plus temporary
exhibitions. US$4.50.
Usina del Arte, *Caffarena y Av Pedro de
Mendoza (La Boca), www.usinadelarte.org.*
Temporary art exhibitions, plays, live music,
film shows at an impressive 1910s converted
power station which also offers guided visits.
Villa Ocampo, *Elortondo 1837, Beccar,
Partido de San Isidro, T011-4732 4988, www.
villaocampo.org.* Former residence of writer
and founder of Revista Sur Victoria Ocampo,
now owned by UNESCO, in northern
suburbs, Wed-Fri 1230-1800, Sat-Sun and
holidays, 1230-1900, US$3.25 entry, open for

visits, courses, exhibitions and meals at its café/restaurant.

See also the programmes of the **Alliance Française** (www.alianzafrancesa.org.ar), **British Arts Centre** (www.britishartscentre.org.ar), **Goethe Institut** (www.goethe.de), and **Instituto Cultural Argentino Norteamericano** (www.icana.org.ar).

Tango shows

There are 2 ways to enjoy tango: you can watch the dancing at a tango show. Most pride themselves on very high standards and, although they are not cheap (show only US$50-90, show and dinner US$75-150), this is tango at its best. Most prices include drinks and hotel transfers. Or you can learn to dance at a class and try your steps at a *milonga* (tango club). The Tango page on www. turismo.buenosaires.gob.ar lists *tanguerías* for tango shows, classes and *milongas*.

See also the websites www.tangocity.com and www.todotango.com.

Every Aug there is a tango dancing competition, **Festival y Mundial de Baile**, open to both locals and foreigners.
Bar Sur, *Estados Unidos 299, T011-4362 6086, www.bar-sur.com.ar. Open 2000-0200.* Price with or without dinner. Good fun, the public sometimes join the professional dancers.
El Querandí, *Perú 302, T011-5199 1770, www.querandi.com.ar. Daily shows, with or without dinner, also open for lunch.* Tango show restaurant, dating back to 1920s.
El Viejo Almacén, *Independencia y Balcarce, T011-4307 7388, www.viejoalmacen.com.ar. Daily, dinner from 2000, show 2200.* Impressive dancing and singing. Recommended.
Esquina Carlos Gardel, *Carlos Gardel 3200 y Anchorena, T011-4867 6363, www.esquinacarlosgardel.com.ar.* Opposite the former Mercado del Abasto, this is the most popular venue in Gardel's own neighbourhood; dinner at 2100, show at 2200. Recommended.
Esquina Homero Manzi, *Av San Juan 3601 (Subte Boedo), T011-4957 8488, www.esquinahomeromanzi.com.ar.* Traditional

show at 2200 with excellent musicians and dancers, dinner (2100) and show available, tango school. Recommended.
Piazzolla Tango, *Florida 165 (basement), Galería Güemes, T011-4344 8201, www.piazzollatango.com.* A beautifully restored belle époque hall hosts a smart tango show; dinner at 2045, show at 2215.

Milongas These are very popular with younger Porteños. You can take a class and get a feel for the music before the dancing starts a couple of hours later. Both tango and *milonga* (the music that contributed to the origins of tango and is more cheerful) are played. It costs from around US$8; even beginners are welcome.
Centro Cultural Torquato Tasso, *Defensa 1575, T011-4307 6506, www.torquatotasso.com.ar.* See web for programme and prices (daily lessons), English spoken.
La Viruta *(at Centro Armenio), Armenia 1366, Palermo Viejo, T011-4774 6357, www.lavirutatango.com.* Very popular, classes every day except Mon, entry US$5.50 Mon and Tue, US$6.50 Wed and Sun (check website for times), also salsa, zumba, and rock dancing classes, with restaurant.

Theatre

About 20 commercial theatres play all year and there are many amateur theatres. The main theatre street is Av Corrientes.
Complejo Teatral de Buenos Aires, *Corrientes 1530, T011-4371 0111/8, www.complejoteatral.gob.ar.* A group of 5 theatres with many cultural activities. Book seats for theatre, ballet and opera as early as possible. Tickets for most popular shows (including rock and pop concerts) are sold also through **Ticketek** (T011-5237 7200, www.ticketek.com.ar). See also www.alternativateatral.com and www.mundoteatral.com.ar. For live Argentine and Latin American bands, best venues are: **La Trastienda** (Balcarce 460, San Telmo, www.latrastienda.com), theatre/café with lots of live events, also serving meals and drinks from breakfast to dinner, great

music; or **ND Teatro** (Paraguay 918, www.ndteatro.com.ar).

Shopping

The main, fashionable shopping streets are Florida and Santa Fe (from Av 9 de Julio to Av Pueyrredón). Palermo is the best area for chic boutiques, and well-known international fashion labels; head for C Honduras and C El Salvador, between Malabia and Serrano. C Defensa in San Telmo is known for its antique shops. It also has a few craft stalls around C Alsina, Fri 1000-1700. **Pasaje de la Defensa** (Defensa 1179) is a beautifully restored 1880s house containing small shops.

Bookshops

Buenos Aires is renowned for its bookshops and was UNESCO's World Book Capital in 2011. Many shops are along Florida, Av Corrientes (from Av 9 de Julio to Callao) or Av Santa Fe, and in shopping malls. Second-hand and discount bookshops are mostly along Av Corrientes and Av de Mayo. Rare books are sold in several specialized stores in the Microcentro (the area enclosed by Suipacha, Esmeralda, Tucumán and Paraguay). The main chains of bookshops, usually selling a small selection of foreign books are: **Cúspide** (www.cuspide.com); **Distal** (www.distalnet.com); **Kel** (www.distalnet.com), imported books, mostly in English; and **Yenny-El Ateneo** (www.yenny-elateneo.com), whose biggest store is on Av Santa Fe 1860, in an old theatre; there is café where the stage used to be.
Eterna Cadencia, *Honduras 5574, T011-4774 4100, www.eternacadencia.com*. Has an excellent selection and a good café.
Walrus Books, *Estados Unidos 617, San Telmo, T011-4300 7135, www.walrus-books.com.ar*. Sells second-hand books in English, including Latin American authors, good children's section.

Handicrafts

Arte y Esperanza, *Balcarce 234 and Suipacha 892, www.arteyesperanza.com.ar*. Crafts made by indigenous communities, sold by a Fair Trade organization.
Artesanías Argentinas, *Montevideo 1386*. Aboriginal crafts and other traditional items sold by a Fairtrade organization.
El Boyero, *Florida 753 (Galerías Pacífico) and 953, T011-4312 3564, www.elboyero.com*. High-quality silver, leather, woodwork and other typical Argentine handicrafts.
Martín Fierro, *Santa Fe 992*. Good handicrafts, stonework, etc. Recommended.
Plata Nativa, *Galería del Sol, Florida 860, local 41, www.platanativa.com*. For Latin American folk handicrafts and high-quality jewellery.

In Dec there is a **Feria Internacional de Artesanías** (see Facebook).

Leather goods

Several shops are concentrated along Florida next to Plaza San Martín and also in Suipacha (900 block).
Aida, *Galería de la Flor, local 30, Florida 670*. Quality, inexpensive leather products, can make a leather jacket to measure in the same day.
Casa López, *MT de Alvear 640/658, www.casalopez.com.ar*. The most traditional and finest leather shop, expensive but worth it.
Dalla Fontana, *Reconquista 735, see Facebook*. Leather factory, fast, efficient and reasonably priced for made-to-measure clothes.
Galería del Caminante, *Florida 844*. Has a variety of good shops with leather goods, arts and crafts, souvenirs, etc.
Prüne, *Santa Fe 3253 and in many shopping centres, www.prune.com.ar*. Fashionable designs for women, many options in leather and not very expensive.

Markets and malls

Markets can be found in many of the city's parks and plazas, which hold weekend fairs. You will find they all sell pretty much the same sort of handicrafts. The following offer something different:
Feria de Mataderos, *Lisandro de la Torre y Av de los Corrales, T011-4342 9629, www.feriademataderos.com.ar, subte E to end of line*

then taxi, or buses 36, 55, 63, 80, 92, 103, 117, 126, 141, 155, 180, 185. Sat from 1800 (Jan-Feb), Sun 1100-2000 (Mar-Dec). Long way but few tourists, fair of Argentine handicrafts and traditions, music and dance festivals, gaucho horsemanship skills; nearby **Museo Criollo de los Corrales** (Av de los Corrales 6436, T011-4687 1949, Sun 1200-1830, US$0.10).
Mercado de las Luces, *Manzana de las Luces, Perú y Alsina. Mon-Fri 1030-1930, Sun 1400-1930.* Handicrafts, second-hand books, plastic arts.
Parque Centenario, *Av Díaz Vélez y L Marechal, see Facebook. Sat-Sun and holidays 1100-2000.* Local crafts, cheap handmade clothes, used items of all sorts.
Parque Rivadavia, *Av Rivadavia 4900, see Facebook. Daily 1100-2000.* Second-hand books, stamps, coins, records, tapes, CDs and magazines.
Plaza Dorrego, *San Telmo, www. feriadesantelmo.com. Sun 1000-1700.* For souvenirs, antiques, etc, with free tango performances and live music, wonderfully atmospheric, and an array of 'antiques'.
Plaza Italia, *Santa Fe y Uriarte (Palermo). Sat-Sun 1200-2030.* Second-hand textbooks and magazines (daily), handicrafts market.

The city has many fine shopping malls, including **Alto Palermo** (Santa Fe 3253, www.altopalermo.com.ar, Subte line D at Bulnes), the most popular and fashionable mall in the city. There's also **Abasto de Buenos Aires** (Av Corrientes 3247, www. abasto-shopping.com.ar, nearest Subte: Carlos Gardel, line B), in the city's impressive, art deco former fruit and vegetable market building, and **Patio Bullrich** (Av del Libertador 750 and Posadas 1245, www. shoppingbullrich.com.ar, nearest Subte: 8 blocks from Plaza San Martín, line C).

What to do

Birdwatching
Aves Argentinas/AOP, *Matheu 1246, T011-4943 7216, www.avesargentinas.org.ar.* For information on birdwatching and specialist

tours. Also has a good library Mon-Fri 1030-1330 and 1430-2030 (closed Jan). A BirdLife International partner.

Cricket
Asociación Argentina de Cricket, *Juan María Gutiérrez 3829, T011-3974 9593, www.cricketargentina.com.* Cricket is played Sep-Apr.

Cycle hire and tours
La Bicicleta Naranja, *Pasaje Giuffra 308, San Telmo and Nicaragua 4817, Palermo, T011-4362 1104, www.labicicletanaranja. com.ar.* Bike hire and tours to all parts of the city, 3-4 hrs and Tigre, 7-8 hrs.
Lan&Kramer Bike Tours, *San Martín 910 p 6, T011-4311 5199, www.biketours.com.ar. Daily at 0930 and 1400.* Next to the monument of San Martín (Plaza San Martín), 3½- to 4-hr cycle tours to the south or the north of the city; also to San Isidro and Tigre, 4½-5 hrs and full day tours, plus summer evening tours downtown; also bike rental.
Urban biking, *Esmeralda 1084, T011-4314 2325, www.urbanbiking.com.* 4½-hr tours either to the south or to the north of the centre, starting daily 0900 and 1400 from Av Santa Fe y Esmeralda. Full day tours (7 hrs) and tours to Tigre (including kayaking in the Delta (8 hrs), or occasionally to the Pampas. Also rents bikes.

Football and rugby
Football fans should see **Boca Juniors**, matches every other Sun at their stadium (**La Bombonera**, Brandsen 805, La Boca, www.bocajuniors.com.ar, tickets for non-members only through tour operators, or the museum – see the murals), or their arch-rivals, **River Plate** (Av Figueroa Alcorta 7597, T011-4789 1200, www.cariverplate.com.ar). The football season is Feb-Jun, and Aug-Dec, most matches are on Sun. Buy tickets from stadiums, sports stores near the grounds, ticket agencies or hostels and hotels, which may arrange guide/transport (don't take a bus if travelling alone, phone a radio taxi; see

also **Tangol**, page 70). Rugby season Apr-Oct/Nov. For more information, **Unión de Rugby de Buenos Aires** (www.urba.org.ar), or **Unión Argentina de Rugby** (T011-4898 8500, www.uar.com.ar).

Language schools
Academia Buenos Aires, *Hipólito Yrigoyen 571, p 4, T011-4345 5954, www.academiabuenosaires.com.*
All-Spanish, *Talcahuano 77 p 1, T011-4832 7794, www.all-spanish.com.ar.* One-to-one classes.
Amauta Spanish School, *Av de Mayo 1370, T011-4383 7706, www.amautaspanish.com.* Spanish classes, one-to-one or small groups, centres in Buenos Aires, Bariloche and at an estancia in the Pampas. Also has a location in Cusco, Peru.
Argentina ILEE, *T011-4782 7173, www.argentinailee.com.* Recommended by individuals and organizations alike, with a school in Bariloche.
Cedic, *Reconquista 715, p 11 E, T011-4312 1016, www.cedic.com.ar.* Recommended.
Elebaires, *Av de Mayo 1370, of 10, p 3, T011-4383 7706, www.elebaires.com.ar.* Small school with focused classes, also offers one-to-one lessons and trips. Recommended.
Expanish, *Av 25 de Mayo 457 p 4, T011-5252 3040, www.expanish.com.* Well-organized courses which can involve trips and accommodation. Highly recommended.
IBL (Argentina Spanish School), *Florida 165, p 3, of 328, T011-4331 4250, www.ibl.com.ar.* Intensive lessons, group and private, all levels, recommended. Also offers accommodation.
Laboratorio de Idiomas (Universidad de Buenos Aires), *25 de Mayo 221 (also other branches), T011-4343 5981, www.idiomas.filo.uba.ar.* Offers cheap, coherent courses, including summer intensive courses. For other schools teaching Spanish and for private tutors look in *Buenos Aires Herald* in the classified advertisements. Enquire also at **Almundo** (see Transport, below).

Polo
The high handicap season is Sep-Dec, but it is played all year round. Argentina has the top polo players in the world. A visit to the national finals at Palermo in Nov and Dec is recommended. For information, **Asociación Argentina de Polo** (T011-4777 6444, www.aapolo.com).

Tour operators and travel agents
Guided tours are organized by the city authorities, including a Pope Francis tour (0900 and 1500) throughout the city and bike tours in Palermo parks, both on weekends and holidays only: free leaflet from city-run offices and other suggested circuits on city website.

An excellent way of seeing Buenos Aires is on a 3-hr tour. Longer tours may include dinner and a tango show, or a boat trip in the Delta, or a gaucho fiesta at a ranch (great food and dancing). Bookable through most travel agents. See also **BA Free Tour** (www.bafreetour.com, www.buenosaireslocaltours.com), and **City Walkers** (www.buenosaires freewalks.com), for free walking tours. For another type of walking tour, see **BA Street Art** (www.buenosairesstreetart.com), and **Graffitimundo** (www.graffitimundo.com), who offer tours of the city's best graffiti, see websites for prices and times.
Anda, *T011-3221 0833, www.andatravel.com.ar.* Operator specializing in socially and environmentally responsible tourism in Buenos Aires and around the country, including volunteering opportunities.
Argentina Excepción, *Sinclair 3244 p 9, T011-4772 6620, www.argentina-excepcion.com.* French/Argentine agency offering tailor-made, upper-end tours, self-drives, themed trips and other services. Also has a Santiago branch, www.chile-excepcion.com.
Buenos Aires Bus (Bus Turístico), *www.buenosairesbus.com.* Open yellow double-decker buses follow 2 routes every 20 mins, 3½ hrs covering main sights from La Boca to Núñez with multilingual recorded tours. 1-day pass (US$24) and 2-day pass (US$32)

hop-on/hop-off tickets can be purchased online or on board. Find bus stops on website or on map provided at city's tourist offices.

Buenos Aires Vision, *Esmeralda 356, p 8, T011-4394 4682, www.buenosaires-vision.com. ar.* City tours, Tigre and Delta, Tango (cheaper without dinner) and Fiesta Gaucha.

Cultour, *T011-5624 7368 (mob), www.cultour. com.ar.* A highly recommended walking tour of the city, 3-4 hrs led by a group of Argentine history/tourism graduates. In English and Spanish.

Eternautas, *Av Julio A Roca 584 p 7, T011-5031 9916, www.eternautas.com.* Historical, cultural and artistic tours of the city and Pampas guided in English, French or Spanish by academics from the University of Buenos Aires, flexible.

Kallpa, *Tucumán 861, p 2, T011-5278 8010, www.kallpatour.com.* Tailor-made tours to natural and cultural destinations throughout the country, with an emphasis on adventure, conservation and golf.

Mai10, *Av Córdoba 657, p 3, T011-4314 3390, www.mai10.com.ar.* High-end, personalized tours for groups and individuals, covers the whole country, special interests include art, cuisine, estancias, photo safaris, fishing and many more.

Say Hueque, *branches in Palermo at Thames 2062, T011-5258 8740, and in San Telmo at Chile 557, T011-4307 3451, www.sayhueque.com.* Recommended travel agency offering good-value tours aimed at independent travellers, friendly English-speaking staff.

Tangol, *Florida 971, PB local 31, Centro, and Defensa 831, San Telmo, T011-4363 6000, www.tangol.com.* Friendly, independent agency specializing in football and tango, plus various other sports, such as polo and paragliding. Can arrange tours, plane and bus tickets, accommodation. English spoken. Discounts for students. Overland tours in Patagonia Oct-Apr. Also offers tours to Brazil, Peru and Chile.

Transport

Air

Ezeiza (officially Ministro Pistarini, T011-5480 6111, www.aa2000.com.ar), the international airport, is 35 km southwest of the centre (also handles some domestic flights). The airport has 3 terminals: 'A', 'B' and 'C'. There are duty free shops (expensive), ATM and exchange facilities at **Banco Nación** (terminal 'A') (only change the very minimum to get you into the city), a **Ministerio de Turismo** desk, and a post office (Mon-Fri 1000-1800, Sat 1000-1300). No hotels nearby, but there is an attractive B&B 5 mins away with transfer included: **$$$ Bernie's**, Estrada 186, Barrio Uno, T011-4480 0420, www.posadabernies. com, book in advance.

There is a **Devolución IVA/Tax Free** desk (return of VAT) for purchases over the value of AR$70 (ask for a Global Refund check plus the invoice from the shop when you buy). A hotel booking service is at the Tourist Information desk; staff are helpful, but prices are higher if booked in this way.

For Transport from **Ezeiza** and **Aeroparque** airports, see Finding your feet, page 44. For transport to Ezeiza airport, take a **Manuel Tienda León** bus (office and terminal at Av Madero 1299 y San Martín, behind the **Sheraton Hotel** in Retiro; take a taxi from the terminal; do not walk outside, T0818-888-5366, www.tiendaleon. com). **Manuel Tienda León** will also collect passengers from addresses in centre for a small extra fee, book the previous day.

Aeroparque (officially Jorge Newbery Airport, T011-5480 6111, www.aa2000. com.ar) handles all internal flights, and some flights to neighbouring countries. On the 1st floor there is a *patio de comidas* (food hall) and many shops. At the airport there is also tourist information, car rental, bus companies, ATM, public phones and luggage deposit (ask at information desk in sector B). **Manuel Tienda León** buses run to Aeroparque (see above for address) from Puerto Madero, more or less hourly, 24 hrs a day, a 20-min journey, US$6. If going to the airport, make sure it goes to Aeroparque by asking the driver.

The helpful **Argentine Youth and Student Travel Organization** (**Almundo**) runs a Student Flight Centre, Florida 835, p 3, oficina 320, T0810-4328 7907, www.almundo.com.ar, Mon-Fri 0900-2000, Sat 0900-1500 (with many branches in BA and around the country). Booking for flights, hotels and travel; information for all South America, noticeboard for travellers, English and French spoken. Cheap fares also at **TIJE**, San Martín 601, T011-5272 8453 or branches at Av Santa Fe 898, T011-5272 8450, and elsewhere in the city, Argentina, Uruguay and Chile, www.tije.com.

Bus

Local City buses are called *colectivos* and cover a very wide radius. They are clean, frequent, efficient and very fast. *Colectivo* fares are calculated in 3-km sections, US$0.50, but fares are cheaper if you have a pre-paid smart card called *Sube* (see www.xcolectivo.com.ar for details). If not using a smart card, have coins ready for ticket machine as drivers do not sell tickets, but may give change. The bus number is not always sufficient indication of destination, as each number may have a variety of routes, but bus stops display routes of buses stopping there and little plaques are displayed in the driver's window. A rapid transit system, **Metrobús**, incorporating existing bus routes, runs along Av 9 de Julio. See www.omnilineas.com.ar for city guides listing bus routes.

Long distance The bus terminal for all international and interprovincial buses is at Ramos Mejía y Antártida Argentina (Subte Line C), behind Retiro station, T011-4310 0700, www.tebasa.com.ar. The terminal is on 3 floors.

Bus information is at the Ramos Mejía entrance on the middle floor. Ticket offices are on the upper floor, but there are hundreds of them so you'll need to consult the list of companies and their office numbers at the top of the escalator. They are organized by region and are colour coded. The Buenos Aires city information desk is on the upper floor. It is advisable to go to the bus station the day before you travel to get to know where the platforms are so that when you are fully laden you know exactly where to go. At the basement and ground levels there are left-luggage lockers; tokens are sold in kiosks; for large baggage, there's a *guarda equipaje* on the lower floor. For further details of bus services and fares, look under proposed destinations. There are no direct buses to either of the airports.

International buses International services are run by both local and foreign companies; they are heavily booked Dec-Mar (especially at weekends), when most fares rise sharply. To **Uruguay**: Do not buy Uruguayan bus tickets in Buenos Aires; wait till you get to Colonia or Montevideo. To **Montevideo**, **Cita** (www.cita.com.uy), **Cauvi** (cauvibue@hotmail.com) and **Cóndor Estrella** (www.condorestrella.com.ar), US$45-50, 8 hrs; see Ferry, below.

Car

Driving in Buenos Aires is no problem, provided you have eyes in the back of your head and good nerves. Traffic fines are high and police look out for drivers without the correct papers. Car hire is cheaper if you arrange it when you arrive rather than from home. Companies include **Localiza**, Cerrito 1575, T0800-999 2999, www.localiza.com/argentina/es-ar; **Ruta Sur**, T011-5238 4071, www.rutasur.eu, rents 4WDs and motorhomes; and **Sixt**, Cerrito 1314, www.sixt.com.ar.

Ferry

To **Montevideo** and **Colonia** from Terminal Dársena Norte, Av Antártida Argentina 821 (2 blocks from Av Córdoba y Alem). **Buquebus**, T011-4316 6530, www.buquebus.com (tickets from Terminal, Retiro bus station, from offices at Av Córdoba 867 and Posadas 1452, by phone or online): **1)** Direct to **Montevideo**, 1-2 a day, 2½ hrs, from US$105 tourist class, one way, also carries vehicles and motorcycles. **2)** To **Colonia**, services by 3 companies: **Buquebus**: minimum 3 crossings a day, from 1-3 hrs, US$34 tourist class/US$46 business class (if booked in advance) one way, with bus connection to **Montevideo**. (**Buquebus** also offers international flights booked through www.buquebusturismo.com.) **Colonia Express**, www.coloniaexpress.com, makes 2-3 crossings a day between Buenos Aires and Colonia in a fast catamaran (no vehicles carried), 50 mins, prices range from US$33 to US$68 one way, depending on type of service and where bought. Office is at Av Córdoba 753, T011-4317 4100; Terminal Fluvial is at Av Pedro de Mendoza 330. You must go there by taxi (around US$6 from Retiro). **Seacat**, www.seacatcolonia.com, 3 fast ferries to Colonia, 1 hr, US$44-71 one way, from the same terminal as Buquebus, with bus to **Montevideo** (US$46-78) and **Punta del Este** (US$65, Fri-Sat only) on most crossings. Office: Av Córdoba 772, T011-4314 5100.

Metro (Subte)

7 lines link the outer parts of the city to the centre. **Line 'A'** runs under Av Rivadavia, from Plaza de Mayo to San Pedrito (Flores). **Line 'B'** from central Post Office, on Av L N Alem, under Av Corrientes to Federico Lacroze railway station at Chacarita, ending at Juan Manuel de Rosas (Villa Urquiza). **Line 'C'** links Plaza Constitución with the Retiro railway station, and provides connections with all the other lines but 'H'. **Line 'D'** runs from Plaza de Mayo (Catedral), under Av Roque Sáenz Peña (Diagonal Norte), Córdoba, Santa Fe and Palermo to Congreso de Tucumán (Belgrano). **Line 'E'** runs from Plaza de Mayo (Cabildo, on C Bolívar) through San Juan to Plaza de los Virreyes (connection to Line 'P' or Premetro train service to the southwest end of the city). **Line 'H'** runs from Corrientes,

via Once to Hospitales (Parque Patricios), under Av Jujuy and Av Almafuerte. Note that 3 stations, 9 de Julio (Line 'D'), Diagonal Norte (Line 'C') and Carlos Pellegrini (Line 'B') are linked by pedestrian tunnels. The fare is US$0.30, the same for any direct trip or combination between lines; magnetic cards (for 1, 2, 5, 10, or 30 journeys) must be bought at the station before boarding; only pesos accepted. Trains are operated by **Metrovías**, T0800-555 1616, www.metrovias. com.ar, and run Mon-Sat 0500-2200/2300 (Sun 0800-2230). Line A, the oldest was built in 1913, the earliest in South America. Backpacks and luggage allowed. Free map (if available) from stations and tourist office.

Taxi

Taxis are painted yellow and black, and carry Taxi flags. Fares are shown in pesos. The meter starts at US$1.40 when the flag goes down; make sure it isn't running when you get in. A fixed rate of US$0.15 for every 200 m or 1-min wait is charged thereafter. The fare from 2200 to 0600 starts at US$1.70, plus US$0.18 for every 200 m or 1-min wait. A charge is sometimes made for each piece of hand baggage (ask first). Tipping isn't mandatory, but rounding the change up is appreciated. For security, take a *remise* or radio taxi booked by phone or at the company's office. Check that the driver's licence is displayed. Lock doors on the inside. The 2 airports and Retiro bus station are notorious for unlicensed taxi crime; use the airport buses and *remises* listed on page 44, and taxis from the official rank in the bus terminal which are registered with police and safe.

Radio taxis are managed by several different companies. Phone a radio taxi from your hotel (they can make recommendations), a phone box or *locutorio*, giving the address where you are, and you'll usually be collected within 10 mins. **City**, T011-4585 5544; **Porteño**, T011-4566 5777, www.radiotaxiportenio.com; **Premium**, T011-5238 0000, www.taxipremium.com;

Tiempo, T011-4854 3838, www.radiotaxi tiemposrl.com.ar.

Remise taxis operate all over the city, run from an office and have no meter. The companies are identified by signs on the pavement. Fares are fixed and can be cheaper than regular taxis, verifiable by phoning the office, and items left in the car can easily be reclaimed. **Universal**, T011-4105 5555, www.remisesuniversal.com.

Train

There are 4 main terminals:

1) Retiro (3 lines: **Mitre**, **Belgrano** and **San Martín** in separate buildings). The state of services changes all the time, owing largely to poor maintenance. The independent website, www.satelite ferroviario.com.ar, is a good source of information on all services. Urban and suburban services include: Mitre line (T0800-222 8736) to **Belgrano** (connection to Tren de la Costa, see page 75), **Olivos**, **San Isidro**, and **Tigre** (see below); daily long-distance services to **Rosario Norte**, 7½ hrs, US$14-18; to **Tucumán** via Rosario, Mon 0930 and Thu 1810 (return Wed 0920, Sat 1445), 26½ hrs, US$88 sleeper (for 2, breakfast included), US$30 pullman, US$25 To **Córdoba** via Rosario, Mon and Fri 2105 (return Wed and Sun 1530), 17 hrs, US$72 sleeper (for 2, breakfast included), US$24.50

pullman, US$20.50 1st class, Belgrano line to northwestern suburbs, including Villa Rosa, run by **Ferrovías**, T0800-777 3377, www.ferrovias.com.ar. San Martín line for services to **Pilar** and long-distance services to **Junín** and **Alberdi** (see www. ferrobaires.gba.gov.ar).

2) Constitución, Roca line urban and suburban services to La Plata, Ezeiza, Ranelagh and Quilmes. Long-distance services are run by **Ferrobaires**, T011-4304 0028, www.ferrobaires.gba.gov.ar.

3) Federico Lacroze, Urquiza line and Metro headquarters (run by **Metrovías**, T0800-555 1616, www.metrovias.com.ar). Suburban services: to General Lemos.

4) Once, Sarmiento line, urban and suburban services to Moreno and Luján. Long distance services to Lincoln (run by **Ferrobaires**).

Tram

Old-fashioned trams operate Mar-Nov on Sat and holidays 1600-1930 and Sun 1000-1300, 1600-1930 and Dec-Feb on Sat and holidays 1700-2030, Sun 1000-1300, 1700-2030, free, and depart every 20 mins on a circular route along the streets of Caballito district, from C Emilio Mitre 500, Subte Primera Junta (Line A) or Emilio Mitre (Line E), no stops en route. Operated by **Asociación Amigos del Tranvía**, T011-4431 1073, www.tranvia.org.ar.

Around Buenos Aires

perfect destinations for a weekend getaway

★ Tigre

Just over 30 km northwest of Buenos Aires, the touristy little town of Tigre (population 42,000) is a popular weekend destination lying on the lush jungle-clad banks of the Río Luján, with a funfair and an excellent fruit and handicrafts market, **Puerto de Frutos** ⓘ *Mon-Fri 1000-1800, Sat, Sun and holidays 1000-1900 with access from C Sarmiento or Perú*. There are restaurants on the waterfront in Tigre across the Río Tigre from the railway line, along Lavalle and Paseo Victorica; cheaper places can be found on Italia and Cazón on the near side, or at the Puerto de Frutos.

The **Museo Naval** ⓘ *Paseo Victorica 602, T011-4749 0608, Tue-Fri 0830-1730, Sat-Sun and holidays 1030-1830, (voluntary fee)*, is worth a visit to see the displays on the Argentine navy. There are also relics of the 1982 Falklands/Malvinas War. The **Museo de Arte** ⓘ *Paseo Victorica 972, T011-4512 4528, www.mat.gov.ar, Wed-Fri 0900-1900, Sat-Sun 1200-1900,*

US$2.75, hosts a collection of Argentine figurative art in the former Tigre Club Casino, a beautiful belle epoque building. **Museo del Mate** ① *Lavalle 289, T011-4506 9594, www.elmuseodelmate.com, Wed-Sun 1100-1800 (1100-1900 in spring and summer), US$3*, tells the history of *mate* and has an interesting collection of the associated paraphernalia.

North of the town is the delta of the Río Paraná, with innumerable canals and rivulets which have holiday homes and restaurants on the banks, and a fruit-growing centre. The fishing is excellent and the peace is only disturbed by motorboats at weekends. Regattas are held in November. Take a trip on one of the regular launch services (*lanchas colectivas*) which run to all parts of the delta, including taxi launches – watch prices for these – from the wharf (Estación Fluvial); see What to do, below.

Isla Martín García

This island in the Río de la Plata (Juan Díaz de Solís' landfall in 1516) used to be a military base. Now it is an ecological/historical centre and an ideal excursion from the capital, with many trails through the cane brakes, trees and rocky outcrops and interesting birds and flowers. Boat trips from Tigre leave at Lavalle 520 at 0830, returning 1730, four times a week. It's a three-hour journey, US$28 return including lunch, *asado* and guide; two-day/one-night package, including weekend overnight at inn, full board, US$65 per person. Reservations only through **Cacciola** (see Transport, opposite), who also handle bookings for the inn and restaurant on the island. There is also a campsite.

Listings Around Buenos Aires

Tourist information

Tigre

Tourist office
By the Estación Fluvial, Mitre 305, T0800-888 84473, www.tigre.gov.ar/turismo, also at Juncal 1600 and the Puerto de Frutos.
They have a full list of houses to rent, activities, etc.

Where to stay

Tigre

$$$$ La Becasina
Arroyo Las Cañas (Delta islands second section), T011-4328 2687, www.labecasina.com.
One of Argentina's most delightful places to stay, an hour by launch from Tigre, buried deep from the outside world, with 15 individual lodges on stilts in the water, connected by wooden walkways, all comforts and luxuries provided and tasteful decor, with an intimate dining room, jacuzzi and pool amidst the trees. Full board, excellent food and service. Recommended.

$$$$ Villa Julia
Paseo Victorica 800, in Tigre itself, T011-4749 0642, www.villajuliaresort.com.ar.
A 1906 villa converted into a chic hotel, beautifully restored fittings, comfortable, good restaurant open to non-residents.

$$$ Los Pecanes
On Arroyo Felicaria, T011-4728 1932, www.hosterialospecanes.com.
On a secluded island visited regularly by hummingbirds. Ana and Richard offer a few comfortable rooms and delicious food. Ideal base for boat trips and birdwatching. Cheaper Mon-Fri.

$$$-$ Posada de 1860
Av Libertador 190, T011-4749 4034, www.tigrehostel.com.ar.
A beautiful stylish villa with suites and an associated Hostel Tigre at No 137 (same phone and website) with dorms for up to 6 (**$** pp), and private rooms (**$$$** double).

$$ TAMET

Río Carapachay Km 24, T011-4728 0055,
www.tamet.com.ar.

For a relaxing stay on an island with sandy
beaches and quite comfortable premises,
with breakfast, games and canoes. Also has
camping with hot water showers.

What to do

Tigre

Many companies run daily services on
tourist catamarans. Trips of 1-2 hrs costing
US$10-14 and full-day group tours (minimum
20 passengers) depart from Lavalle 499
on Río Tigre, T011-4731 0261/63, www.
tigreencatamaran.com.ar. 1½-hr trips (3 trips
a day Mon-Fri, 2 a day Sat-Sun), US$13, from
Puerto de Frutos, **Río Tur** (T011-4731 0280,
www.rioturcatamaranes.com.ar). **Sturla**
(Estación Fluvial, oficina 10, T011-4731 1300,
www.sturlaviajes.com.ar) runs 4 1-hr trips a
day, US$10 (includes a ride on **Bus Turístico**);
they also have trips with lunch, night-time
boat trips and full-day trips from the centre
of Buenos Aires, commuting services to
Puerto Madero, and more.

You can also hire kayaks, canoes or rowing
boats, rent houses, or visit *recreos*, little
resorts with swimming pools, tennis courts,
bar and restaurant. **Bus Turístico** (T011-4731
1300, www.busturisticotigre.com.ar) runs
1-hr tours, US$4, every hour on an open-top
bus with 10 stops, starting at 1040 at the
railway station.

Centro de Guías de Tigre y Delta,
Estación Fluvial de 2, T011-4731 3555, www.
guiastigreydelta.com.ar. Organizes guided
walks and launch trips.

Transport

Tigre
Bus

From central **Buenos Aires**: take No 60 from
Constitución: the 60 'bajo' is a little longer
than the 60 'alto' but is better for sightseeing.

Ferry

To **Carmelo** (Uruguay) from Terminal
Internacional, Lavalle 520, Tigre with
Cacciola, T011-4749 0931, www.cacciola
viajes.com (in Buenos Aires at Córdoba 755,
T5353 9005), 2 a day, 2½ hrs, US$33; US$23
if booked online. To **Montevideo** (bus
from Carmelo), 5½ hrs, US$39; US$27
if booked online. To **Nueva Palmira**
(Uruguay) from Terminal Internacional.
Líneas Delta Argentino, oficina 6 at
Estación Fluvial, T011-4731 1236, www.
lineasdelta.com.ar. Daily at 0730, 3 hrs,
US$34, US$48 return. **Note** Argentine
port taxes are generally included in the
fares for Argentine departures.

Train

From **Buenos Aires**: Mitre line from Retiro.
Alternatively, **Tren de la Costa**, T011-3220
6300, US$1.30 one way from Maipú station
(reached by Mitre line from Retiro) to Delta
station (Tigre) every 30 mins from 0725 to
2055. (Buses to Tren de la Costa are No 60
from Constitución, No 19 or 71 from Once,
No 152 from centre.) Terminus, Estación
Delta, has the huge funfair, El Parque de la
Costa, and a casino.

Buenos Aires province

lose yourself in the land of the gaucho

The Pampas are the perfect antidote to the frenzied pace of Buenos Aires. These peaceful flatlands, stretching towards dramatic mountains in the south and the unspoiled Atlantic coast to the east, are relaxing places a few hours' drive of the capital.

Staying in one of Argentina's estancias is a quintessential part of Argentine life, complete with gauchos (cowboys) and *asados* (much more than a barbecue). Whether you choose a grand colonial mansion, or a simple working farm, you'll be welcomed as part of the family, and will gain a real insight into the culture. Ride your horse across the plains, and then tuck into a meal of succulent home-grown beef cooked on an open fire under the stars. Gauchos are still very much part of Argentine rural life and you can enjoy their music and fine horsemanship in quaint Pampas towns such as San Antonio de Areco and Chascomús, virtually unchanged since the early 1900s.

The Atlantic beaches are a great way to cool down in the summer. Avoid the tawdry casinos of famous Mar del Plata and head instead for the chic resorts of Mar de los Pampas and Cariló, or escape to Pinamar where in summer you can party with the young Porteños of Buenos Aires.

Two of the oldest mountain ranges in the world pop up from the flat Pampas at Tandil and Sierra de la Ventana, attracting climbers, hikers and anyone looking for a relaxing weekend in beautiful countryside.

Best for
Asados ▪ Horse riding ▪ Visiting estancias

Footprint picks

★ Gaucho towns: San Antonio de Areco and Chascomús, pages 81 and 91

Escape city life and spend an afternoon mingling with locals in a well-preserved gaucho town.

★ Estancias, page 83

Visit some of the oldest family-owned estancias and working cattle ranches in the country.

★ Mar del Plata, page 104

Beat the summer heat in this coastal metropolis and playground for Argentines.

★ Sierra de la Ventana, page 119

These rolling hills mark the highest point in the Pampas.

★ Tandil, page 120

The perfect base for exploring the surrounding Sierra mountain range.

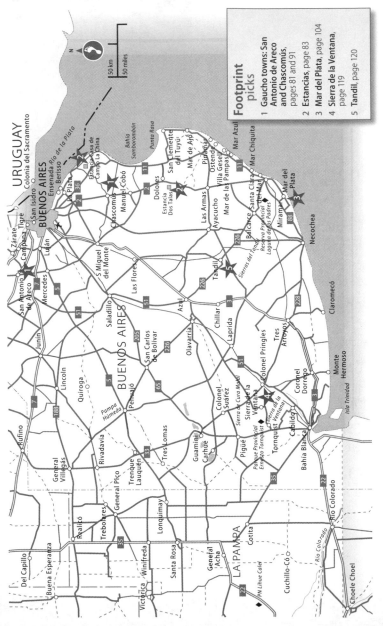

Footprint picks

1 Gaucho towns: San Antonio de Areco and Chascomús, pages 81 and 91

2 Estancias, page 83

3 Mar del Plata, page 104

4 Sierra de la Ventana, page 119

5 Tandil, page 120

50 km
50 miles

URUGUAY

Colonia del Sacramento

BUENOS AIRES

Ensenada

Río de la Plata

Berisso

La Plata

San Isidro

Tigre

Zárate

Campana

Luján

Mercedes

San Antonio de Areco

Junín

Lincoln

Rufino

Quiroga

General Villegas

Realicó

Del Capillo

Buena Esperanza

Trebolares

Victorica

PN Lihue Calel

Santa Rosa

General Acha

La Pampa

Cuchillo-Co

Cotita

Río Colorado

Choele Choel

Río Colorado

Winifreda

Lonquimay

General Pico

Trenque Lauquén

Rivadavia

Tres Lomas

Pampa Humeda

Carhué

Guaminí

Piqué

Parque Provincial Ernesto Tornquist

Sierra de la Ventana

Cabildo

Bahía Blanca

Monte Hermoso

Isla Trinidad

Coronel Dorrego

Coronel Pringles

Tres Arroyos

Claromecó

Necochea

Miramar

Mar del Plata

Santa Clara del Mar

Mar Chiquita

Mar Azul

Villa Gesell

Ostende

Pinamar

Mar de Ajó

San Clemente del Tuyú

Punta Rasa

Bahía Samborombón

Dolores

Estancia Dos Talas

Las Armas

Mar de la Plata

Ayacucho

Balcarce

Reserva Provincial Laguna de los Padres

Sierras del Tandil

Tandil

Azul

Chillar

Laprida

Olavarría

San Carlos de Bolívar

Saladillo

Las Flores

S Miguel del Monte

Chascomús

Manuel Cobo

Estancia Casa de Campo La China

Coronel Suárez

Sierra de Cura Malal

Pehuajó

Coronel Dorrego

Cabildo

General Acha

78 • Buenos Aires province

The Pampas

The Pampas are home to one of the most enduring images of Argentina: the gaucho on horseback, roaming the plains. All over the Pampas there are quiet, unspoiled towns where gaucho culture is still very much alive.

Two impeccably preserved gaucho towns very much worth visiting are San Antonio de Areco and Chascomús. The former is home to expert craftsmen, working silver and leather in the traditional gaucho way. Near here there are many of the finest and most historical estancias: two are recommended, El Ombú and La Bamba. Further southeast, Chascomús is similarly charming, a traditional cowboy town come to life, with pristine examples of 1870s architecture, a good museum of the Pampas and gauchos, and a lake for watersports in summer. There are fine estancias here too: friendly, relaxed La Fe, and best of all, Dos Talas, with its extraordinary history and beautiful grounds. Whether you stay the night or just visit for an afternoon to eat lunch and ride, you'll get an unforgettable taste of life on the land.

The Pampas are also rich in wildlife, and on lakes and *lagunas* you're likely to spot Chilean flamingos and herons, maguari storks, white-faced ibis and black-necked swans. Ostrich-like greater rheas can also be seen in many parts.

Luján (population 102,000) is a place of pilgrimage for devout Catholics throughout Argentina. In 1630 an image of the Virgin brought by ship from Brazil was being transported to its new owner in Santiago del Estero by ox cart, when the cart got stuck, despite strenuous efforts by men and oxen to move it. This was taken as a sign that the Virgin willed she should stay there. A chapel was built for the image, and around it grew Luján. The chapel has long since been superseded by an impressive neo-Gothic basilica and the Virgin now stands on the High Altar. Luján is a very popular spot at weekends, and during pilgrimages (see Festivals, below).

Complejo Museográfico Provincial Enrique Udaondo ① *T02323-420245, www.gba.gob. ar/cultura/museos, Wed 1300-1630, Thu-Fri 1130-1630, Sat-Sun 1030-1730, US$0.70*, in the old Cabildo building, is one of the most interesting museums in the country. Exhibits illustrate its historical and political development. General Beresford, the commander of the British troops which seized Buenos Aires in 1806, was a prisoner here, as were Generals Mitre, Paz and Belgrano in later years. Next to it are museums devoted to transport and to motor vehicles. Behind the Cabildo is the river, with river walks, cruises and restaurants.

Some 20 km before Luján, near General Rodríguez, is **Eco Yoga Park** ① *T011-6507 0577, www.ecoyogapark.com.ar,* a spiritual centre and farm with volunteering opportunities, yoga, meditation, organic gardens and vegetarian food. See the website for day and weekend packages. Take the Luján bus from Buenos Aires (see Transport, below), get off at La Serenísima, then take taxi US$8-10.

Essential The Pampas

Getting around

It's easy to get around the province with a network of buses to and from Buenos Aires, and between towns. Train services to Mar del Plata, Chascomús and Tandil, and many coastal towns on the way, were suspended in 2016. You'll need to hire a car to reach the more remote estancias, and there are good, fast toll roads radiating out from the capital to Mar del Plata, via Chascomús, San Antonio de Areco and Lobos. For further details, see Transport, page 85.

When to go

The coastal areas can be pleasantly warm from December to March, although accommodation can be hard to find December to January. It can be windy and cold the rest of the year. Inland, May to August is cold and can be unpleasant.

Tourist information

For information on the province, see www.turismo.gba.gov.ar (in Spanish). For more on the Pampas, see www. lapampa.tur.ar (in Spanish).

Listings Luján

Festivals

The town is completely packed during the following festivals.
8 May Día de la Virgen de Luján, the town's saint's day, with a religious procession.
Last weekend in Sep La Peregrinación Gaucho, a huge pilgrimage.
Last weekend of Sep Peregrinación Juvenil, another massive pilgrimage.
8 Dec Fiesta de la Inmaculada Concepción.

BACKGROUND

The Pampas

Travelling through these calm lands you wouldn't think they'd had such a violent past, but these are the rich fertile plains that justified conquering the indigenous people in the bloody 19th-century Campaign of the Desert (see box, page 88). Once the Spanish newcomers had gained control, their produce made Argentina the 'breadbasket of the world', and the sixth richest nation on Earth, exporting beef, lamb, wheat and wool when a growing Europe demanded cheap food and clothing.

When you see these huge, perfect wheat fields, and superbly healthy Aberdeen Angus cattle roaming vast plains, you might wonder how a country with such riches can possibly have suffered an economic crisis. It's one of the great enigmas of Argentina. To get an idea of Argentina's former wealth, visit an estancia with history, like Dos Talas (see page 93), and ask their owners what went wrong. Some blame Perón, and then the Kirchners, for taxing the farmers too harshly, or Menem for resorting to desperate measures to keep up with the US dollar by selling the nationalized industries. Many farmers complained the Kirchner government imposed impossible taxes for those who produce from the land.

The fields of Buenos Aires province provide more than half of Argentina's cereal production, and over a third of her livestock, but many estancia owners have had to turn to tourism in order to maintain the homes built by their ancestors in more affluent times. Still, staying in an estancia is a rare privilege, to be wholeheartedly enjoyed.

Transport

Bus From **Buenos Aires** Bus 57 **Empresa Atlántida**, either from Plaza Once, route O (the fastest), or from Plaza Italia, routes C and D, US$2-3. To **San Antonio de Areco**, several a day, US$4, Empresa Argentina, 1 hr.

★ San Antonio de Areco *Colour map 4, B5.*

where tradition and history are alive

San Antonio de Areco (population 25,000), 113 km northwest of Buenos Aires, is *the* original gaucho town and makes a perfect escape from the capital. Built in the late 19th century, much of its charm lies in the authenticity of its crumbling buildings surrounding an atmospheric plaza filled with palms and plane trees, and the streets lined with orange trees. The attractive *costanera* along the riverbank is a great place to swim and picnic. There are several estancias nearby, and the town itself has several historical *boliches* (combined bar and provisions stores), where you can lap up the atmosphere, listen to live music and meet locals. Gaucho traditions are on display in the many weekend activities, and the town's craftsmen produce wonderful silverwork, textiles and traditional worked leather handicrafts.

The **Museo Gauchesco Ricardo Güiraldes** ① *Camino Güiraldes, T02326-455839, www. museoguiraldes.com.ar, Mon-Fri 1100-1700, free*, is a replica of a typical estancia of the late 19th century and is dedicated to the life of the writer, who was a sophisticated member of Parisian literary circles and an Argentine nationalist who romanticized gaucho life.

ON THE ROAD
Gaucho life

The gaucho is the cowboy of Argentina, found all over the country, and one of Argentina's most important cultural icons. Gauchos emerged as a distinct social group in the early 18th century. Brought over by the Spanish to tend cattle, they combined their Moorish roots with Argentine Criollo stock, adopting aspects of the indigenous peoples' lifestyle, but creating their own particular style and dress. The gaucho lived on horseback, dressing in a poncho, *bombachas* (baggy trousers) held up by a *tirador* (broad leather belt) and home-made boots with leather spurs. He was armed with a *facón* or large knife, and *boleadoras*, a lasso made from three stones tied with leather thongs, which when expertly thrown would wrap around the legs of animals to bring them swiftly to the ground. Gauchos roamed the Pampas, hunting the seemingly inexhaustible herds of wild cattle and horses in the long period before fencing protected private property. The gaucho's wild reputation derived from his resistance to government officials who tried to exert their control by the use of anti-vagrancy laws and military conscription. Much of the urban population of the time regarded the gaucho as a savage, on a par with the 'indians'.

The gaucho's lifestyle was doomed in the advent of railways, fencing and the redistribution of land that followed the massacre of indigenous peoples. Increasingly the term gaucho came to mean an estancia worker who made a living on horseback tending cattle. As the real gaucho disappeared from the Pampas, he became a major subject of Argentine folklore and literature, most famously in José Hernández' epic poem of 1872, *Martín Fierro*, and in Güiraldes' later novel *Don Segundo Sombra*. But you can still see gauchos in their traditional dress at work today in any estancia. Visit Mataderos, Chascomús or San Antonio de Areco for displays of traditional gaucho horsemanship, music, silversmithing and leatherwork.

Güiraldes spent much of his early life on **Estancia La Porteña** ① *8 km from town, T011-15-5626 7347, www.laporteniadeareco.com*, which dates from 1823. It is a national historic monument and offers day visits and accommodation (see Where to stay, page 84). He settled there to write his best-known book, *Don Segundo Sombra* (1926), which was set in San Antonio. The estancia and sights in the town, such as the old bridge and the Pulpería La Blanqueada (at the entrance to the museum), became famous through its pages.

Superb gaucho silverwork is for sale at the workshop and **Centro Cultural y Museo Taller Draghi** ① *Lavalle 387, T02326-454219, www.draghiplaterosorfebres.com, Mon-Thu 0930-1300 and 1600-1900, Fri-Sat 1000-1300 and 1600-1900, Sun 1000-1230, US$5 for a guided visit*. You can get a further idea of the life of the gauchos at the **Museo Las Lilas** ① *Moreno 279, T02326-456425, www.museolaslilas.org, Thu-Sun 1000-2000 (until 1800 in winter), US$6.80*, which houses a collection of paintings by famous Argentine artist Florencio Molina Campos, who dedicated his life to the display of the gaucho way of life.

Excellent chocolates are made at **La Olla de Cobre** ① *Matheu 433, T02326-453105, www.laolladecobre.com.ar*, with a charming little café for drinking chocolate and trying the most amazing home-made *alfajores*. There is a large park, **Parque San Martín**, spanning the river to the north of the town near the tourist information centre. While you're here, you should visit one of the old traditional bars, or *pulperías*, many of which

ON THE ROAD

★ Estancias

Argentina's estancias vary enormously from ostentatious mansions to simple colonial-style ranches that still work as cattle farms. Many now open their doors to tourists as paying guests, enabling you to experience traditional Argentine rural life. There are two main types of estancia: those that function as rural hotels, and those where you're welcomed as a guest of the family. The latter are particularly recommended as a great way to meet Argentine people. You dine with the owners and they'll often tell you about their family's history and talk about life on the farm, turning a tourist experience into a meeting of friends. Some estancias offer splendid rooms filled with family antiques. Others are simple affairs where you'll stay in an old farmhouse, and the focus is on peace and quiet. They can be the perfect place to retreat and unwind for a few days or to try an activity such as horse riding or birdwatching. Whichever kind you choose, a good estancia will give you an unparalleled taste of traditional hospitality: welcoming strangers is one of the things Argentines do best.

Activities These depend on the estancia, but almost all provide horse riding, which is highly recommended even if you've no experience. Galloping across the plains on a *criollo* horse has to be one of the biggest thrills of visiting the country. If you're a beginner, let your hosts know beforehand so that they can arrange for you to ride an especially docile creature. The horse-shy might be offered a ride in a *sulky*, the traditional open horse-drawn carriage, more relaxing, but just as much fun. Cattle mustering, meanwhile, may sound daunting but is the best way to get into life on the *campo*. You'll help your hosts move cattle while sitting astride your trusty steed. Gauchos will be on hand to guide you and by the end of the day you'll be whooping and hollering with the best of them.

Access As estancias are inevitably located in the country you'll need to hire a car, although many will pick you up from the nearest town if you don't have one. If you're visiting for a few days ask your hosts to arrange a *remise* taxi; some estancias will arrange transfers on request. There are many estancias within easy access of Ezeiza International Airport in Buenos Aires, so it can be an ideal way to relax after a long flight at the start of your trip, or to spend your last couple of nights, allowing you to return home feeling refreshed and with vivid memories of Argentine hospitality.

Recommended estancias in Buenos Aires province include Dos Talas (pages 93 and 93), Casa de Campo La China (page 90) and Palantelén (page 97).

---

have been lovingly restored to recreate the 1900s ambience and are brought to life by a genuine local clientele every night. Try La Vieja Sodería, on General Paz and Bolívar, or El Almacén de Ramos Generales Parrilla, at Zapiola 143. At Alsina 66 is the city museum, Centro Cultural y Museo Usina Vieja ① T02326-454722, www.sanantoniodeareco.com/centro-cultural-y-museo-usina-vieja, Tue-Sun 1100-1700, free. There are ATMs on the plaza, and at the country club you can play golf or watch a polo match in restful surroundings; ask at the tourist office for directions.

Some of the province's finest estancias are within easy reach of San Antonio for day visits, offering an *asado* lunch, horse riding and other activities. One such place is La Cinacina

ⓘ *T02326-452045, www.lacinacina.com.ar*, which offers day visits to groups of 24 or more. For a list of those estancias offering accommodation, see Where to stay, below.

Listings San Antonio de Areco

Tourist information

Tourist information centre
Parque San Martín, Zerboni y Arellano, T02326-453165, www.sanantoniodeareco.com.
Friendly, helpful, English-speaking staff who can advise on gaucho activities in the town, as well as accommodation and transport. Other useful websites include www.areco.gob.ar, www.portaldeareco.com and www.turismo.gba.gov.ar.

Where to stay

Most hotels offer discounts Mon-Fri.

$$$ Antigua Casona
Segundo Sombra 495, T02325-15-416030, www.antiguacasona.com.
Charmingly restored 1897 house with 6 rooms opening onto a delightful patio and exuberant garden, relaxing and romantic. Bikes to borrow.

$$$ Paradores Draghi
Matheu 380, T02326-455583, www.paradoresdraghi.com.ar.
Traditional-style, comfortable rooms face a manicured lawn with a pool. Just metres away Draghi family has its silversmith workshop. Recommended.

$$$ Patio de Moreno
Moreno 251, T02326-455197, www.patiodemoreno.com.
The top hotel in town is a stylish place with spacious, minimalist rooms, a large patio with a pool and great service.

$$ Hostal de Areco
Zapiola 25, T02326-456118, www.hostaldeareco.com.ar.
Popular, with a warm welcome, good value.

$$ Los Abuelos
Zerboni y Zapiola T02326-456390, see Facebook.
Welcoming, small pool, plain but comfortable rooms, facing riverside park.

Estancias
Some of the province's finest estancias are within easy reach for day visits, offering horse riding, an *asado* lunch and other activities. Stay overnight to really appreciate the peace and beauty of these historical places. Look online at: www.sanantoniodeareco.com/turismo/estancias/index.htm.

$$$$ El Ombú
T02326-492080, office T011-4737 0436, www.estanciaelombu.com.
Fine house with magnificent terrace dating from 1890, comfortable rooms, horse riding, English-speaking owners; price includes full board and activities but not transfer. Recommended.

$$$$ La Bamba
T02326-454895, www.labambadeareco.com.
Dating from 1830, in grand parkland, charming rooms, English-speaking owners who have lived here for generations, superb meals, price is for full board. Recommended.

$$$$ La Porteña
Ruta 8, Km 110, T011-15-5626 7347, www.laporteniadeareco.com.
One of Argentina's most famous estancias was once host to writers Ricardo Güiraldes and Antoine de Saint Exupéry. Stunning traditional building built in 1822, with original features, large grounds with 150-year-old trees and working horses. There are 3 lovely houses where you can stay, including huge banquets of food (lots of meat), or you can spend a day here, enjoying the grounds.

Camping

Club River Plate
Camino de la Ribera, T02326 453590,
www.sanantoniodeareco.com/
club-atletico-river-plate-areco.
The best of 3 sites in the park by the river.
It's an attractive sports club offering shady
sites with all facilities, a pool and sports of
all kinds, US$20 per tent.

Restaurants

There are many *parrillas* on the bank of the
Río Areco.

$$ Almacén de Ramos Generales
Zapiola 143, T02326-456376
(best to book ahead).
Perfect place, popular with locals,
very atmospheric, superb meat, very
good pastas and a long wine list.

$$ Café de las Artes
Bolívar 70, T02326-456398
(better to book ahead; see Facebook).
In a hidden spot, this cosy place serves
delicious pastas with a large wine selection.

$$ La Costa
Zerboni y Belgrano, T02326-452481
(on the riverside park).
A very good traditional *parrilla* with an
attractive terrace.

$$ La Ochava de Cocota
T02326-454852, Alsina y Alem.
Relaxing, attractive, excellent service,
superb *empanadas* and vegetable pies.
It is also a café.

$ La Esquina de Merti
T02326-456705 Arellano y Segundo Sombra.
The ideal place for a beer on the main plaza.
Go early to get a table outside.

Bars and clubs

Boliche de Bessonart
Segundo Sombra y Zapiola.
A long-standing landmark dripping with
history and character. Perfect for an
afternoon beer; a must-visit.

Festivals

Jan *Pato* competition, Argentina's national
game, a mix of polo and basketball.
Mar Fiesta Criolla, with traditional local
music, dance and other cultural events.
2nd week of Nov Día de la Tradición,
www.sanantoniodeareco.travel. The
most important festival of the year, with
traditional parades, gaucho games, events
on horseback, music and dance. Book
accommodation in advance.

What to do

All estancias offer horse riding. Other
operators can be contacted from the hotels
in the Pampas towns.
Country Club, *R8, Km 11, www.sanantonio
deareco.com/country-club.* Play golf or watch
a polo match in restful surroundings. Good
food is also served. Ask at the tourist office
for directions.

Transport

Bus
From **Buenos Aires** (Retiro bus terminal),
1½-2 hrs, US$7-8, every hour with **Chevallier**
or **Autotransportes San Juan**.

Remise taxis
Sol, San Martín y Alsina, T02326-455444.

The capital of Buenos Aires province is La Plata (population 732,000), a modern university city with a lively student population, and consequently good nightlife, with lots of restaurants and bars. There's no particular reason to visit as a tourist, but if you're passing through or on a day trip from Buenos Aires (only 60 minutes by bus), you'll appreciate the broad avenues, leafy plazas and elaborate public buildings. It's a young and vibrant place, where football and rugby are major passions. At the east of the city there's a beautiful park, Paseo del Bosque, popular at weekends with families for *asados*, with its famous science museum, the magnificent but slightly run-down Museo de Ciencias Naturales.

Sights

The major public buildings are centred around two parallel north–south streets, 51 and 53, which run north from the Plaza Moreno to the Plaza San Martín, and from there to the Paseo del Bosque at the north of the city centre. On the west side of Plaza Moreno is the enormous brick neo-Gothic **cathedral** ⓘ *www.catedraldelaplata.com, Mon-Sat 0900-1900, Sun 0900-2000*, built between 1885 and 1936, and inspired by Cologne and Amiens. It has a beautiful and inspiring interior, and is definitely worth a visit. Opposite is the large, white building of the **Municipalidad** in German Renaissance style, with a striking clock tower. Plaza San Martín, six blocks east, is bounded by the **Legislature**, with its huge neoclassical façade and, opposite, the **Casa de Gobierno** is a mixture of French and Flemish Renaissance styles. On the north side of the plaza is the lovely **Pasaje Dardo Rocha**, designed as the main railway station in Italian Renaissance style. It now houses a tourist information office (see Tourist information, below) and the **Museo de Arte Contemporáneo** ⓘ *C 50 entre 6 y 7, T0221-427 1843, www.macla. com.ar, Tue-Fri 1000-2000, Sat-Sun 1400-2100 (1600-2200 in summer), free*, with a gallery of contemporary Latin American art, a café and two theatres. East of the Municipalidad, **Teatro Argentino** ⓘ *www.gba.gob.ar/ teatroargentino*, has its own orchestra and ballet company. Nearby on streets 6 and 7 are the imposing **Universidad Nacional** and the **Banco Provincial**. The main shopping streets are 8 and 12. A good market selling handicrafts and local *artesanía* is in Plaza Italia at weekends.

If you do find yourself in La Plata at the weekend, or on a sunny evening, head straight for **Paseo del Bosque**, a pretty public park of woodlands and an artificial

---

Essential La Plata

Finding your feet

La Plata Terminal, is north of the centre at Calle 41 entre 3 y 4, at Diagonal 74. Long-distance buses arrive here from all major cities. Trains arrive at the station on Avenida 1 also north of the centre.

Orientation

Streets have numbers, rather than names, and diagonal streets cross the entire city, which can be very confusing. When you approach one of these crossroads with six choices, make sure you remember the number of the street you're on.

Getting around

The city is easy to get around. There's an efficient network of buses all over the city, and taxis are safe, cheap and plentiful.

---

lake, where all the locals head for *asados* and picnics. Also here are the **Zoological Gardens,** with giraffes, elephants and pumas amongst others, an astronomical observatory and the Hipodromo, dating from the 1930s and one of the most important racecourses in the country.

The **Museo de La Plata** ① *Av 122 y 60, T0221-425 7744, www.fcnym.unlp.edu.ar, Tue-Sun and holiday Mon 1000-1800, closed 1 Jan, 1 May, 24, 25, 31 Dec, US$2,* is one of the

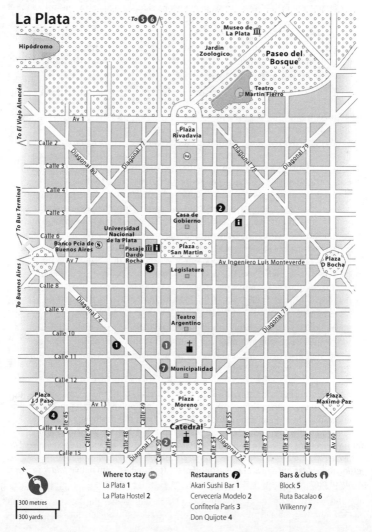

La Plata

Where to stay 🛏	Restaurants 🍴	Bars & clubs 🍸
La Plata **1**	Akari Sushi Bar **1**	Block **5**
La Plata Hostel **2**	Cervecería Modelo **2**	Ruta Bacalao **6**
	Confitería París **3**	Wilkenny **7**
	Don Quijote **4**	

300 metres

300 yards

BACKGROUND
The Conquest of the Desert

Until the 1870s, the Pampas, and indeed most of Argentina, was inhabited by indigenous tribes. After independence, President Rosas (see page 629) launched the first attempt to claim territory in Buenos Aires province in his 1833 Campaign of the Desert. But in the 1870s, pressure grew for a campaign to defeat the indigenous people, since the withdrawal of Argentine troops to fight in the War of Triple Alliance had led to a series of increasingly audacious raids by *malones*, the indigenous armies. War minister Alsina planned a series of forts and ramparts to contain the indigenous peoples, and defend the territory won from them. But his successor General Julio Roca found these plans too defensive, and called for a war of extermination, aiming to make the whole of Patagonia available for settlement.

Roca's Conquest of the Desert was launched in 1879, with 8000 troops in five divisions, one of them led by Roca himself. Five important indigenous chiefs were captured, along with 1300 warriors. A further 2300 were killed or wounded. Roca's view was that "it is a law of human nature that the Indian succumb to the impact of civilized man". He destroyed villages and forced the inhabitants to choose between exile in Chile, or life in a reservation. After the campaign, mountain passes to Chile were closed, and any remaining indigenous groups were cruelly forced onto reservations.

Although Roca claimed victory in the Conquest of the Desert as a personal triumph, he was aided by technological advances: the telegraph gave commanders intelligence reports to offset the indigenous peoples' knowledge of the terrain and enabled them to co-ordinate their efforts. Railways moved troops swiftly, and Remington repeating rifles enabled any one soldier to take on five indigenous people and murder them all.

Roca was hailed as a hero, elected president in 1880, and dominated Argentine politics until his death in 1904. The land he conquered was handed out mainly to Roca's friends, since the campaign had been funded by mortgaging plots in advance, with bonds worth 25,000 acres being bought by only 500 people. Argentina has yet to come to terms with this shameful part of its history. But you can see that most statues of Roca throughout the country have been defaced with red paint symbolizing the blood he spilt. There is no attempt made by the authorities to stop this. In Buenos Aires the statue of Roca is on the corner of Perú and Roca, and it is covered in graffiti which is neither removed nor cleaned, unlike other public monuments.

most famous museums in Latin America. It is particularly outstanding on anthropology and archaeology, with a huge collection of pre-Columbian artefacts including pre-Incan ceramics from Peru and beautiful ceramics from the northwest of Argentina. It is slightly run down and some exhibits need replacing, but the preserved animal and dinosaur sections are worth visiting. The **Parque Ecológico** ① *Camino Centenario y San Luis, Villa Elisa, T0221-473 2449, www.parquecologico.laplata.gov.ar, daily 0900-1900, free, getting there: take bus 273 D or 6,* is a good place for families, with native *tala* forest and plenty of birds.

Tourist information

The provincial tourism website is
www.turismo.gba.gov.ar (in English).

Camino del Gaucho
57 No 393, T011 15-3282 4661,
www.caminodelgaucho.com.ar.
A helpful website and information point for
exploring estancias, stables and for visiting
craftsmen in the Pampas. The English-
speaking staff are extremely informative and
will help you arrange your own itinerary.

Dirección de Turismo
Diagonal 79 entre 5 y 56, Palacio
Campodónico, T0221-422 9764,
www.laplata.gov.ar. Mon-Fri 0900-1700.
The main tourist office. There is also
a small **tourist booth** (C 50 entre 6 y 7,
T0221-427 1535, daily 1000-2000) at
Pasaje Dardo Rocha.

Where to stay

$$$ La Plata Hotel
Av 51 No 783, T0221-422 9090,
www.weblaplatahotel.com.ar.
Modern, well furnished, comfortable,
spacious rooms and good bathrooms.
Price includes continental breakfast.

$ pp La Plata Hostel
C 50 No 1066, T0221-457 1424,
www.laplata-hostel.com.ar.
Well-organized, convenient hostel in a
historic house, high ceilings, small garden,
simple but comfortable dorms for 4, 5 or 8.

Restaurants

$$ Akari Sushi Bar
Diagonal 74 No 1531, T0221-422 7549,
www.akari-sushi.com.ar.
The most popular sushi spot in the city.
Makes a nice change from so much beef.

$$ Cervecería Modelo
C 54 y C5, T0221-421 1321,
www.cerveceriamodelo.com.ar.
Traditional German-style *cervecería*,
with good menu and beer.

$$ Don Quijote
Plaza Paso 146, T0221-483 3653,
www.rdonquijote.com.ar.
A well-known restaurant serving delicious
food in lovely surroundings.

Cafés

Confitería París
T0221-482 8840, C 7 y 48.
The best croissants, and a lovely place
for coffee.

Bars and clubs

The following bars are popular and lively:
Block (corner of Calles 122 and 50), and
Ruta Bacalao (see Facebook, in Gonnet),
a pleasant residential area to the north of
the city.

Wilkenny
www.wilkenny.com.ar, Calle 50 corner of 11.
Hugely popular Irish-style pub.

Entertainment

El Viejo Almacén, *Calle 13 at 71, www.viejo*
almacen.com.ar. Tango and tropical music.
Teatro Martín Fierro, *Paseo del Bosque.*
Free concerts during the summer.

Transport

La Plata is 56 km southeast of Buenos Aires,
45 mins by car.

Bus
Buses to La Plata from Buenos Aires leave
every 20-30 mins and take about 1½ hrs.
They leave from the Retiro bus terminal
(every 20 mins) and Once (every 30 mins).

To **Buenos Aires** from La Plata Terminal (C 42 entre 3 y 4, T0221-427 3198, www.laplataterminal.com), every 20 mins from 0430-0000 (less frequent between 2200-0000), **Costera Metropolitana** and **Plaza**, 1 hr 10 mins either to Retiro terminal in Buenos Aires or to Centro (stops along Av 9 de Julio), US$2.60. To **Mar del Plata,** US$30 with **El Rápido Argentina** and **El Aguila**.

Train
There are frequent trains, to/from **Buenos Aires** (Constitución), US$0.70, 1 hr 20 mins.

Around La Plata

Evita's fantasy come to life

Eight kilometres northwest of the city, the **República de los Niños** (Colonel General Belgrano and Calle 500, T0221-484 1409, www.republica.laplata.gov.ar, Monday-Friday 1000-1800, Saturday-Sunday 0900-1900, US$1.40, children under seven free, parking US$0.70), is Eva Perón's legacy and was built under the first Perón administration. It is a delightful children's village, with scaled-down castles, oriental palaces, boating lake, cafés and even a little train. It's a fun place for families to picnic.

This area of the country has some lovely rural accommodation. A delightful option close to La Plata is the **Casa de Campo La China**, see Where to stay, below.

Parque Costero Sur Reserve
This is a large nature reserve 110 km south of La Plata, and 160 km south of Buenos Aires – just two hours' drive away. Declared a UNESCO Biosphere Site in 1997, it extends along 70 km of the coastline of Bahía Samborombón and was created to protect a wide range of birds that come here to breed. There are several estancias inside the reserve.

Listings Around La Plata

Where to stay

Estancias

$$$$ Casa de Campo La China
60 km from La Plata on Ruta 11, T0221-421 2931, www.casadecampolachina.com.ar.
A charming 1930s adobe house set in eucalyptus woods, with far-reaching views.

The beautifully decorated spacious rooms are set around an open gallery. Day visits (US$80) for groups (minimum 15 people) to ride horses, or in carriages, eat *asado*, or stay the night, guests of the lovely Cecilia and Marcelo, who speak perfect English. There's delicious food; meals are included in the price. Highly recommended.

where cowboys still roam the prairie

Around 125 km south of Buenos Aires, the quaint historical town of Chascomús (population 40,000) is worth visiting to enjoy the vibrant combination of gaucho culture and fine 19th-century architecture, creating an atmosphere of colonial refinement with a Wild West feel. Its streets are full of well-preserved buildings dating from the mid-1800s, and lined with mature trees. The town has a lively feel and its position along the eastern edge of the huge Laguna Chascomús gives it an attractive *costanera*, which comes to life in summer. You can take a boat out on the *laguna*, or head to a couple of fine estancias nearby.

Chascomús has a strong historical significance. It was founded in 1779, when a fort was built as protection against the indigenous tribes. In 1839, it was the site of the Battle of the Libres del Sur (the Free of the South).

Sights

Around the quiet Plaza Independencia are the fudge-coloured colonial-style **Palacio Municipal** and **Iglesia Catedral**. Southeast of the plaza is the extraordinary **Capilla de los Negros** (1862) ① *Tue-Fri 0900-1500 and Sat-Sun 1100-1700*, a small brick chapel with earth floor, built as a place of worship for African slaves who were bought by wealthy families in the early 1800s; it's an atmospheric place that still holds the slaves' offerings. A highly recommended museum for an insight into gaucho culture is the **Museo Pampeano** ① *Av Lastra and Muñiz, T02241-430982, Mon-Fri 0900-1900, US$1*, which has lots of information on gaucho traditions, fabulous maps of the Spanish conquest, furniture and all the evident wealth of the early pioneers.

To the south of the town lies the **Laguna Chascomús**, one of a chain of seven connected lakes; the *costanera* is a pleasant place to stroll, you can sail and windsurf in the summer, and there are frequent regattas. It's also an important breeding site for *pejerrey* fish, with amateur fishing competitions held from November to March. The delightful **Estancia La Fe** ① *www.estancialafe.com.ar*, is nearby (see page 92).

Listings Chascomús

Tourist information

The website www.turismo.gba.gov.ar also has links to this small town.

Tourist office
Av Costanera España y Espigón de Pesca, T02241-430405, www.chascomus.com.ar, and www.chascomus.net. Mon-Fri 0800-1700, Sat-Sun 0900-1700.
4 blocks from the main avenue, Las Astras.

Where to stay

For a full list see www.chascomus.com.ar.

$$$ Chascomús
Av Lastra 367, T02241-422968, www.chascomus.com.ar (under 'hoteles').
The town's most comfortable hotel, atmospheric, welcoming, with stylish turn-of-the-century public rooms and lovely terrace.

$$$ La Posada
Costanera España 18, T02241-423503, www.acechascomus.com.ar/ace-la_posada.
On the *laguna*, delightful and comfortable *cabañas* with cooking facilities.

$$$ Roble Blanco
Mazzini 130, T02241-436235,
www.robleblanco.com.ar.
A very good choice in a refurbished
100-year-old house, modern comfortable
rooms, a large heated pool with attractive
deck and welcoming common areas. Also
has a spa. Recommended.

$$ Laguna
Libres del Sur y Maipú, T02241-426113,
www.lagunahotel.com.ar.
Old-fashioned, sleepy hotel by the station.
Pleasant, quiet rooms.

Estancias
Estancias will collect you from Chascomús.

$$$$ Estancia La Fe
R2, Km 116, T02241-154 42222,
www.estancialafe.com.ar.
A charming and typical place to come for
a few days to get a feel for life on the land.
Activities include horse riding, riding in
carriages and walking in the grounds.
Simple, comfortable rooms, wide views
from the grounds, great *asado*.

$$$ La Horqueta
3 km from Chascomús on Ruta 20,
T011-4777 0150, www.lahorqueta.com.
Full board, mansion in lovely grounds with

laguna for fishing, horse riding, bikes to
borrow, English-speaking hosts, safe gardens
especially good for children, plain food.

Camping
There are multiple sites around the *laguna*,
all with good facilities; **Mutual 6 de
Septiembre**, 8 km away, T011-155 182 3836,
see Facebook, has a pool.

Restaurants

$$ Colonial
T02241-430322, Estados Unidos y Artigas.
Great food, pastas and cakes
are recommended.

Transport

Bus
Frequent service, several per day to **Buenos
Aires** (2 hrs, US$10), **La Plata**, **Mar del Plata**,
and daily to **Bahía Blanca** and **Villa Gesell**;
terminal T02241-426300, see Facebook.

Train
Ferrobaires, T02241-422220, www.
ferrobaires.gba.gov.ar. Trains to **Buenos
Aires** (Constitución) and to **Mar del Plata**
were suspended in 2016.

Dolores *Colour map 4, C6.*

sleepy town in the Pampas

Dolores (population 30,000) is a pretty, peaceful little town, 204 km south of
Buenos Aires. Founded in 1818, it was the first town in independent Argentina, and
its attractive old buildings would be perfect as a film set for a 19th-century drama.

There's an interesting little museum, **Museo Libres del Sur** ⓘ *Parque Libres del Sur, Wed-
Sun 1000-1700*, with good displays on local history, in particular about the Campaign of
the Desert (see box, page 88) and the subsequent revolt against Rosas. It also contains
lots of gaucho silver, plaited leather *tableros*, branding irons and a huge cart from 1868.
There's a charming plaza at the heart of the town, with a central obelisk and impressive
classical-style church, the **Iglesia Nuestra Señora de Dolores**.

Estancia Dos Talas
See Where to stay, below.

The main reason to visit Dolores is its proximity to one of the oldest and most beautiful estancias in the Pampas, Dos Talas. The fabulously elegant house is set in grand parkland designed by Charles Thays, with a lovely chapel copied from Notre Dame de Passy and a fascinating history. Come for the day or, even better, stay. You'll be warmly welcomed by the owners, who are descendants of the estancia's original owner, Pedro Luro.

Listings Dolores

Tourist information

Tourist office
*T02245-441925, www.dolores.gov.ar.
Mon-Fri 0730-1830.*

Where to stay

$$$$ Estancia Dos Talas
10 km from Dolores, 2 hrs' drive from Buenos Aires, T02245-443020, www.dostalas.com.ar. Nov to early Apr.
This beautifully decorated home is one of Argentina's really special places to stay. One of the oldest estancias, owner Luis makes you feel like a member of the family. The rooms and the service are impeccable, the food exquisite; stay for days, and completely relax. Pool, riding, English spoken. See also above.

$$ Hotel Plaza
Castelli 75, T02245-442362.
Comfortable and welcoming old place on the plaza, all rooms with bath and TV, breakfast extra, good *confitería* downstairs. There's another good café next door.

Camping

Camping del Náutico
Lago Parque Náutico.

Restaurants

$$ La Donosa
Avellaneda 298.
This popular *parrilla* comes highly recommended by locals.

$$ Moebius
Buenos Aires 342, see Facebook.
Good Argentine fare; the place to be on weekend nights.

$ Parrilla Don Pedro
Av del Valle and Crámer.
Ignore the unimaginative decor; order steak.

$ Pizzería Cristal
Buenos Aires 226.
Pizzas.

Festivals

Mid- to late Feb Fiesta de la Guitarra, with performances from internationally famous musicians, dancing and processions. This is a good time to visit, but book ahead.

Transport

Bus
To **Buenos Aires**, 3 hrs, US$17-19, and to **La Plata**, US$12-14, **El Rápido Argentino**, T0800-333 1970, www.rapido-argentino.com.

Taxi
There is a stand at Belgrano and Rico, 1 block from the plaza.

Atlantic Coast

There are 500 km of beautiful beaches and some splendid resorts spread out along the great sweeping curve of coastline between La Plata and Bahía Blanca. Closest to Buenos Aires, there's a string of sleepy seaside towns known collectively as the Partido de la Costa, popular with older retired Argentines and better for sea fishing than beachcombing.

For more beautiful beaches, head further southwest to party town Pinamar, the jewel of the whole coast with its excellent hotels and fine restaurants. Its neighbour, smarter still, is chic Cariló, where the *balnearios* (swimming beaches) are exclusive and the *cabañas* luxurious. Nearby Villa Gesell is more of an ugly working town and best avoided. Also close is a quieter resort becoming known for its natural beauty and complete peace: Mar de las Pampas, where you can find *cabañas* set in idyllic woodland right by to the sea.

Argentina's most famous resort, Mar del Plata was the very height of chic in the 1920s, but it's now a busy seaside city, with packed beaches and casinos – not the best place to relax but still interesting. To the west, two old-fashioned resorts are rather more appealing: Miramar is quiet and low-key, good for young families; and larger Necochea has an appealing woodland park along its coastline, with a vast area of unspoilt dunes, perfect for exploring on horseback. The southern stretch of beaches ends in the major port of Bahía Blanca, a useful transport hub if you're heading south, with an attractive town inland from the sea.

Essential Atlantic Coast

Access

All resorts on the coast are linked to each other and to Buenos Aires by frequent bus services. Train services to the coast were mostly suspended in 2016. If you're combining beaches and estancias, it's best to hire a car.

The main artery south is the fast, privately run toll road Route Provincial 2 (with US$2-3 tolls every 100 km), which runs from Buenos Aires to Mar del Plata, via Chascomús and Dolores, with another fast road branching off to Pinamar from Dolores: take Route 63 and then 56. Alternatively, head along the coast from La Plata on Route Provincial 11, also fast and with tolls, to San Clemente del Tuyú and then parallel to the coast to Mar del Plata. Route Provincial 88 links Mar del Plata and Necochea, further southwest. Remember to have small change for the tolls as they will not give change for large bills, and do not take credit cards.

Mar del Plata also has a domestic airport with flights from Buenos Aires. For further information see Transport, page 103.

When to go

Avoid January if you can, when the whole coast is packed out with hordes of tourists from Buenos Aires. December and late February are ideal for hot weather and fewer crowds. Many resorts are very pleasant in spring and autumn, but out of season (and the season is from December to March) most resorts apart from busy Mar del Plata are ghost towns. The winter wind can be harsh, but if you want a quiet weekend away to read books and relax, then it can be a good time to travel, with good deals to be had at resorts.

Tourist information

There are well-organized tourist information offices in all resorts with complete lists of places to stay; see Tourist information in Listings, page 99. There's plenty of accommodation along the coast, so only a small selection is listed. There's a useful provincial website, www. gba.gov.ar (in Spanish) and each town also has its own website: **Partido de la Costa**, http://lacosta.tur.ar/; **Pinamar**, www.pinamar.gov.ar and www.pinamar turismo.com.ar; **Mar de las Pampas** and **Mar Azul**, www.mardelaspampas.com.ar; **Mar del Plata**, www.mardelplata.gov.ar and www.turismomardelplata.gov.ar; **Miramar**, www.miramarense.com.ar; **Necochea**, http://necochea.gov.ar and www.necocheanet.com.ar; **Bahía Blanca**, www.bahiablanca.gov.ar.

seaside towns along the Atlantic coast

Heading south from Buenos Aires, San Clemente del Tuyú is the first of a string of 14 small towns on the coast, known as Partido de la Costa, stretching down to Mar de Ajó. First built in the 1930s, they lost popularity when the more glamorous resorts were built further south. It's not the best part of the coast and can't be recommended as most of the resorts are slightly run down with peeling 1950s seafront hotels and tacky attractions, though they're also rather cheaper than the more upmarket resorts. The beaches are crowded in January but absolutely deserted at other times and particularly forlorn in winter. However, there is an interesting nature reserve and excellent sea fishing. The Río de la Plata has gained international recognition as the widest freshwater river in the world, and here at its mouth you can fish for shark, *pejerrey* and *brótola* from piers or from boats. Fish can often be bought on the beach from local fishermen.

San Clemente del Tuyú *Colour map 4, C6.*

Some 320 km south of Buenos Aires, the main attraction in San Clemente (population 12,126) is **Mundo Marino** ① *Av Décima No 157, signposted from the main road into town, T02252-430300, www.mundomarino.com.ar, Jan-Feb daily 1000-2000, Mar-Dec daily 1000-1800, off season Sat-Sun only, US$26, children US$17.* This is the biggest sea life centre in South America, where you can watch performing seals, dolphins, whales and penguins go through their completely unnatural routines; it's fun for children. There's also a smaller, far less spectacular theme park, **Termas Marinas** ① *take the road to Faro San Antonio at the far south of Bahía Samborombón, T02252-423000, www.termasmarinas.com.ar, daily 1000-2000 in Jan-Feb, closing earlier in winter, US$19, children US$13.50 (cheaper online),* where children can swim in thermal pools, identify birds and, for a small extra fee, ascend to the top of a historical lighthouse, which has impressive views.

Even more appealing is the unspoilt wildness of **Reserva Natural Punta Rasa** ① *2 km from San Clemente, take the road to Faro San Antonio and follow signs, free, managed by the Fundación Vida Silvestre, www.vidasilvestre.org.ar.* This is a private reserve protecting a special area at the southernmost point of the Bahía de Samborombón, where a long tongue of dense sand stretches into the bay where the Río de la Plata meets the sea. Vast numbers of migrating birds and a resident population of crabs and shellfish make this an interesting place to spend an afternoon. It's a great place for a walk, with a short, self-guided trail and a lighthouse to visit. It's also a world-famous sea fishing site; the water around the peninsula can be up to 20 m deep, attracting large specimens of *corvina negra* (black sea bass) weighing over 20 kg. It's possible to drive along the 5-km peninsula but watch out for the tides. Information is available from *guardaparques* at the entrance and at the tip of the peninsula.

San Clemente has a busy fishing port, with yolk-yellow boats characteristic of the area, and the **Club Náutico**, at Tapera de López, offering all kinds of watersports.

South of the centre, there's an attractive area of woodland, **Vivero Cosme Argerich** ① *T02252-421103 (see Facebook), daily 0800-2000 in summer (daylight hours off season), free, guided visits offered,* a 37-ha park with woodlands, a plant nursery and sports centre.

Tip...
Avoid visiting towns in Partido de la Costa during January when the whole coast is packed out.

Santa Teresita

From San Clemente, drive through Las Toninas and Costa Chica to reach Santa Teresita (population 18,000), where the biggest attraction is fishing, though there's also a good golf course, tennis and horse riding on offer. The **pier** is one of the largest on the coast and is lit for night fishing.

Mar del Tuyú

Approximately 20 km south of San Clemente del Tuyú, Mar del Tuyú (population 7000) is the administrative centre of Partido de las Costa. It's a tranquil place to visit in February, with a little more life than the other resorts nearby in winter. Boat trips are organized along the coast in summer, all the way to **Faro San Antonio**, where you can see whales basking at close proximity in August and September. Fishing is also a big attraction (see What to do, page 103).

Mar de Ajó and around *Colour map 4, C6.*

Another quiet, old-fashioned resort, 40 km south of San Clemente del Tuyú, Mar de Ajó (population 13,800) has a couple of natural attractions as well as motor racing, a shipwreck and a casino. The **Autódromo Regional** ① *follow signs from the access roundabout for Mar de Ajó*, holds important motor-racing championships every summer. You can dive or snorkel at the *Naufragio Margarita*, a large German ship, wrecked off the coast here in 1880, and one of the oldest in the region. Mar de Ajó has one of the largest fleets of small fishing boats on the coast, as well as the largest pier.

The most spectacular part of this area of coastline is **Altos Médanos**, a long stretch of high sand dunes that are, apparently, constantly changing shape. It's one of the wildest and most unspoilt areas of the coast, bordered along the shore by a wide flat beach, perfect for walking, horse riding or 4WD.

The best way to enjoy this area is by visiting one of the few estancias near the coast. Estancia Palantelén ① *15 km south of Mar de Ajó, T011-15-5577 8075, see Facebook, or book on Air BnB*, is owned by descendants of a pioneering Pampas family, whose atmospheric old house has views of the sea and is beautifully furnished and lined with mahogany panels salvaged from a shipwreck. Walk on to the sands, birdwatch or gallop across the miles of beaches, either on horseback or in a *sulky* (open horse-drawn carriage). Spend a few days here and absorb the complete peace; the estancia is available for rent by the weekends, week or month.

Pinamar *Colour map 4, C6.*

The two most desirable resorts on the coast are right next to each other, with the quieter old-fashioned **Ostende** in between (see below). Both party-town Pinamar (population 28,400) and forested Cariló are upmarket places to stay, attracting wealthy Argentines, and have far smarter hotels than elsewhere on the coast, not to mention fine restaurants and, in Pinamar, plenty of trendy beach bars and nightclubs. Pinamar is perfect for young people and families, with live bands playing at its beach clubs in the evenings in high season; these are also quiet and elegant places to dine on superb seafood.

Access to the beach is mostly by day membership to a *balneario* (beach club). You pay a fee of US$20-50 per family or group of friends per day, and then you can make use of all the *balneario's* facilities. You can rent a *carpa* – one of the little wooden beach huts built in tightly packed rows perpendicular to the sea, and furnished with tables and chairs to use when you retreat from the hot sun. Alternatively, you can rent a big beach umbrella and stake a claim on an area closer to the sea. Renting either will allow you to use the *balneario*'s showers, toilets, restaurants and even beach games. Pinamar's *balnearios* range from exclusive, quiet places with superb restaurants, to party spots with loud music, beach parties and live bands at night. There is free public access to the beach between the *balnearios*, but it's worth visiting one for a day to enjoy beach life. Their restaurants are also open to those not renting *carpas*.

Tip...
It's best to visit in December, February or March. During the rest of the year, especially in June and July, the town virtually shuts down, and few hotels and restaurants are open.

The town also has golf courses and tennis courts, and there are lots of hotels and smart restaurants along the main street, Avenida Bunge, running perpendicular to the sea. Explore the dunes at **Reserva Dunícola**, 13 km north, by horse or 4WD. The **tourist office** ⓘ *Av Shaw 18, T02254-491680, www.pinamar.gov.ar, www.pinamarturismo.com.ar, Mon-Fri 0800-2000, Sat-Sun 1000-1700, English spoken*, is helpful and can arrange accommodation. During the peak month of January, Pinamar is packed with Argentines, accommodation is extremely hard to get and very expensive.

Cariló

Cariló is the most exclusive, and expensive, beach resort in Argentina, and you'll soon see why. There's a large and lovely area of mature woodland right on the beach, where luxury apart hotels and very chic *cabañas* are all tastefully concealed, so that its visitors have complete privacy, something that inevitably appeals to the many celebrities, sports stars and politicians who visit. The *balnearios* are neat and exclusive; **Hemingway** (T02254-570585, www.paradorhemingway.com) is *the* place to be seen for wealthy Porteños.

Around the tiny centre, on Cerezo and Carpintero, there are good restaurants and chi-chi arcades with upmarket clothing shops where you can browse for top Argentine fashion labels among the usual international designers. You might find Cariló less friendly than Pinamar if you're in search of nightlife, since the emphasis is on exclusivity, but it's a good place for couples or for a quiet solo retreat.

Around Pinamar and Cariló

In between Pinamar and Cariló is **Ostende**, a small town founded in 1908 but largely abandoned on the outbreak of the First World War. This is a wilder part of the coast and there are plenty of campsites.

Inland, **General Madariaga** is a quaint 1900s town that is definitely worth visiting for December's **Fiesta Nacional del Gaucho**; see Festivals, below. From General Madariaga, fishing enthusiasts could visit the **Laguna Salada Grande**, the largest lake in the province with a nature reserve and excellent *pejerrey* fishing.

Villa Gesell *Colour map 4, C6.*

In complete contrast to overdeveloped Mar del Plata and upmarket Pinamar, Villa Gesell (population 40,000), 22 km north, was planned by German inventor, Carlos Gesell, as an eco-resort. He came to live here in 1931 with the aim of growing trees for wood on the barren sand dunes. His project then evolved into an ecological holiday retreat and the first guests were invited in the 1940s. He planned and built the town in harmony with nature, planting thousands of shady trees that would draw water to the surface and constructing roads around the sand dunes. Today, however, it bears no resemblance to his idea. It is crammed full of decaying 1970s holiday homes and apartment blocks, broken cars and tacky shops. Gesell would be aghast at the commercial feel of the main street, Avenida 3, which is filled with games arcades, fast-food shops and noisy cafés. It is best to avoid staying here, although it can be much cheaper than Pinamar only 10 minutes away.

The **Reserva Forestal and Parque Cultural Pinar del Norte**, at the eastern end of Avenida 3, is where Carlos Gesell built his first house in the woods. It's now a museum, the **Museo Casa Histórica** ① *T02255-468624, Tue-Sat 1000-1600, Sun 1400-1700; guided visits Sat at 1100 after 18 April*, with inspiring biographical information (in English) and an interesting daily tour. Gesell's second house, **Chalet Don Carlos Gesell**, is now a cultural centre for exhibitions and concerts.

Mar de las Pampas and Mar Azul

Just 5 km south of Villa Gesell, two quiet resorts are developing: the pine forests and dirt roads of **Mar de las Pampas** and the more commercial, less pretty **Mar Azul** are wilder and quieter than anywhere else on this coast and have some appealing accommodation in more natural surroundings. There are lots of *cabañas* for rent and an increasing number of hotels, but most people rent a house for the weekend; this is especially good if you are in a group. The beach here is broad and uncrowded, so although there is less to do than in Pinamar or Mar del Plata and no nightlife to speak of, you can completely relax and enjoy the sea in peace. It's a perfect retreat for writing or reflecting, or a cosy hideaway for couples, although in January you'll find traffic jams and queues at restaurants.

Listings Partido de la Costa

Tourist information

San Clemente del Tuyú

Tourist office
Calle 2 Sur and 63 Sur, San Clemente, T02252-423249, also at the bus terminal, T02252-430718, turismocentrosc@lacosta.gob.ar.

Santa Teresita

Tourist office
Costanera between C 39 and 40 (next to the Caravel Santa Maria), T02246-4211383, www.santateresita.com.ar. Daily 1000-1900.
Staff can advise on accommodation.

Mar del Tuyú

Tourist office
Municipalidad, Costanera 8001.
Helpful.

Cariló

Tourist office
Boyero and Castaño, T02254-570773, www.carilo.com and www.parquecarilo.com (both in Spanish).

General Madariaga

Tourist office
Rivadavia No 1086, T02267-421058, www.madariaga.gob.ar.
Can provide accommodation information.

Villa Gesell

There's a good website with lots of accommodation and other information, www.gesell.gob.ar.

Tourist office
Av 3 Nro 820, T02255-478042, www.gesell.gov.ar. Daily 0800-2000.
The main tourist office is on the right-hand side of the road as you enter the town. There's another office in the bus terminal and 3 other locations.

Mar de las Pampas
See www.mardelaspampas.com.ar
for more information.

Tourist office
Mercedes Sosa y El Lucero, T02255-452823.
Summer daily 0800-2000.

Where to stay

Since accommodation is plentiful all
along the coast, only a small selection
is listed here. All the resorts also have a
wide selection of campsites; most are
well-equipped and many have *cabañas*
as well as tent sites. Most resorts have
balnearios, private beaches, where you pay
US$20-50 per day for family/group use of
a sunshade or beach hut, showers, toilets
and restaurants.

San Clemente del Tuyú
See www.portaldesanclemente.com
for a complete list.

$$$-$$ Altair Hotel
Calle 3, 2283, T02252-421429,
www.altairhotel.com.ar.
A 3-star hotel with decent, simple rooms,
some with balconies with sea views, in a
modern block.

$$$-$$ Fontainebleau
Calle 3, 2294, T02252-421187,
www.fontainebleau.com.ar.
Dated but comfortable 4-star hotel on
the coast, good value, with an elegant
entrance and light airy rooms. There is
a pool and a restaurant.

$$ Morales
Calle 1, 1856, T02252-430357,
www.hotelmorales.com.ar.
A welcoming option that also has a large
pool and a restaurant. Rooms are plain
but comfortable.

$$ Sun Shine
Av Talas del Tuyú 3025, T02252-430316,
www.sunshinehotel.com.ar.

The most recommendable of the cheaper
places to stay.

$$ Sur
Calle 3, 2194, T02252-521137,
www.hotelsur.com.ar.
A central location with
simple accommodation.

Campsites

Los Tres Pinos
T02252-430151, www.los3pinos.com.ar.
Attractive, well-organized campsite (US$14
for 2 people) as well as basic wooden cabins
(US$31 for up to 4 people). Good option for
budget travellers.

Santa Teresita
See www.santateresita.com.ar
for a complete list.

$$$-$$ Sorrento
Calle 37, 235, between Calles 2 and 3,
T02246-420 0298, www.santateresita.com.
ar/sorrento.
Dated 3-star hotel with pleasant rooms,
though somewhat on the kitsch side.

$$ Hostería Santa Teresita
Av Costanera 747, between Calles 34 and 35,
T02246-420202, www.hosteriast.com.ar.
A nicely maintained, simple, family chalet-
type hotel by the sea.

$ Turista
Av 32, 464, T02246-526093,
www.santateresita.com.ar/turista/.
Rather basic, with simple rooms around a
central courtyard, but clean and friendly.

Campsites

Estancia El Carmen
Calle 23 and Playa, T02246-420220,
www.estanciaelcarmen.com.ar.
A really excellent site on the beach, with
grassy shaded areas and all facilities.
Camping US$20.50 per tent for 2;
cabañas for rent. Recommended.

Mar del Tuyú

There's little on offer in Mar del Tuyú itself, but Costa del Este next door has a couple of places, both comfortable; see www.mardeltuyu.com for a complete list.

Campsites

El Refugio
Calle 94 between 2 and 3, T02246-435529.

Mar de Ajó and around

This town has a couple of good places to stay, but there is better accommodation offered at San Bernardo, the next resort along; see www.sanbernardo.com.ar for a complete list.

$$$ Gran Playa Hotel
Costanera Sur 195, Mar de Ajó, T02257-420001, www.hotelgranplaya.com.
The best choice in town and also the oldest, still in the family of the original owners. A comfortable beachfront place. All rooms have bathrooms and sea views, some have jacuzzis too. Good buffet breakfast.

$$$-$$ Neptuno Plaza
Hernández 313, San Bernardo, T02257-461789, www.neptunoplaza.com.ar.
A well-equipped 4-star place with good service.

$$ Hostería Mar de Ajó
Av Costanera Norte 205, Mar de Ajó, T02257-420023, www.hosteriamardeajo.com.ar.
A modest but comfortable beachfront *hostería*.

Camping

ACA
Avellaneda 147, T02257-420230, www.aca.org.ar.

Pinamar

There are plenty of hotels of a high standard in Pinamar; all 4-stars have a pool but some hotels are a long way from the beach. Book ahead in Jan and Feb. All those listed are recommended.

$$$$-$$$ Del Bosque
Av Bunge 1550 y Júpiter, T011-4394 9605, www.hotel-delbosque.com.
Very attractive, in woods, not on the beach, a smart 4-star with a wide range of rooms and seasonal prices, pool, tennis courts, nice restaurant, good service.

$$$ La Posada
Del Tuyú y Del Odiseo, T02254-482267, www.laposadapinamar.com.ar.
Very comfortable, small, quiet, with spacious rooms, next to sea and town centre, pretty gardens where breakfast is served. An excellent choice.

$$$ Viejo Hotel Ostende
Biarritz y El Cairo, T02254-486081, www.viejohotelostende.com.ar. Summer only.
Attractive, smallish hotel, open since 1913. Although it has been renovated, it retains some historic flavour in the old wing, comfortable in a simple way, excellent service. There's a pool and private *balneario*. Breakfast, dinner and a beach hut are all included.

Estancias

$$$ Rincón de Cobo
Access on R91, 30 km north of Pinamar, T02257-15-580448, www.rincondecobo.com.ar.
3 secluded houses by the sea offering rustic comfort and the kind of service you'd expect in a hotel, with all the usual calm of the Pampas. It has its own airstrip in case you're tempted to fly here yourself.

Cariló

Most of the accommodation is in apart hotels and timeshares; see www.carilo.com for more options.

$$$$ Cariló Village
Carpintero and Divisadero, T02254-470244, www.carilovillage.com.ar.
Well-designed, cottage-style, attractive but not luxurious rooms and apartments; there is an excellent restaurant and a spa with 2 pools.

$$$$ Marcín
Laurel (on the oceanfront), T02254-570888,
www.hotelmarcin.com.ar.
Modern and large, very swish complex, right
on the beach, with a spa and a restaurant.

Around Pinamar and Cariló
There are several well-equipped campsites
(around US$26 per day for 4 people in
2 tents) near the beach at Ostende,
between Pinamar and Cariló;
try www.campingostende.com.ar.

Villa Gesell

$$$ De la Plaza
Av 2 entre 103 y 104, T02255-468793,
www.delaplazahotel.com. All year round.
Small, spotless, with excellent service. Rooms
are plain but very comfortable, good value.

$$ Hostería Gran Chalet
Paseo 105 No 447 entre Av 4-5, T02255-
462913, www.gesell.com.ar/granchalet.
Closed off season.
Warm welcome, comfortable large rooms,
good breakfast. Recommended.

$ pp Hostel El Galeón
Av 5 No 834 (entre Paseos 108 y 109),
T02255-453785, www.galeongesell.com.ar.
Summer only.
Popular hostel, can accommodate from
singles to groups of 8 but no dorms;
some rooms have kitchen. DVDs, laundry
service, cooking facilities, good communal
areas, convenient.

Mar de las Pampas and Mar Azul
See www.mardelaspampas.com.ar
for a complete list of accommodation.

$$$$ La Mansión del Bosque
Juez Repetto y R Peñaloza, T02255-479555,
www.lamansiondelbosque.com.ar.
Open all year round.
Just 150 m away from the sea, this attractive
large house is beautifully decorated
in minimalist style and has extremely
comfortable rooms. It's one of the area's

more pricey options, but there's a great
spa that attracts affluent, stressed young
Porteños from Buenos Aires.

$$$$-$$$ Posada Piñen
Juan de Garay y R Payró, T02255-479974,
www.posadapinen.com.
A very comfortable *hostería*, with a
wonderfully rustic atmosphere. Breakfasts
are gorgeous and include delicious home-
made pies.

$$$ Posada La Casona
Hudson entre Mercedes Sosa y
JV González, T02255-479693,
www.posadalacasona.com.ar.
A really stylish, comfortable place with
a great restaurant. Excellent value.

Apart hotels
There are many apart hotels in the woods;
the following is recommended:

Village de las Pampas
Corvina y Mercedes Sosa, T02255-454244,
www.villagedelaspampas.com.ar.
There are several apartments of
different sizes, all very comfortable
and attractively designed, and only
a few metres from the sea.

Cabañas
There are many attractive, well-equipped
cabañas, including **Arco Iris** (Victoria
Ocampo between Los Alamos and
Ombú, T02255-479535, www.
mardelaspampas.com.ar/arcoiris).

Restaurants

Mar de Ajó
If you're self-catering, buy fresh fish on the
beach from the fishermen.
  El Quincho Bodegón ($) (Francisco de
las Carreras 800), and **Parrilla San Rafael ($)**
(Av Libertador 817), are both recommended.

Pinamar
The restaurants listed here are the best
options in town.

$$ Tante
De las Artes 35, T02254-494949,
www.tante.com.ar.
A small, elegant place – and one of the
most expensive – serving a good variety
of dishes. Often recommended. Fantastic
hot chocolate.

$ Tulumei
Av Bunge 64.
A nautical theme in the decor goes with
the excellent fish served in this small and
popular place.

Cariló

$$ Divisadero del Mar
Acacia and the beach, T02254-572010.
Wonderful location overlooking the
beach. Try the Caribbean salad and
the grilled salmon.

$$ El Totem
Av Divisadero and Cerezo, T02254-571936.
Local favourite for pizzas and quick meals.

Mar de las Pampas and Mar Azul

$$ Amorinda
Lucero and Gerchunoff, T02255-479750,
www.amorinda.com.ar.
Wildly popular, family-run Italian restaurant
with a homely ambience. Great for pasta.

$$ Viejos Tiempos
Leoncio Paiva between Cruz del Sur y
Peñaloza, T02255-479524.
This is owned by local pioneers, who also
serve some Mexican and German specialities
together with more refined meals. Homely
surroundings. This is *the* place to come for
tea – worth a detour for the gorgeous cakes.

Festivals

General Madariaga
**2nd weekend in Dec Festival Nacional
del Gaucho**, with processions, singing
and dancing.

What to do

Mar del Tuyú
Fishing
Excellent fishing either from the pier or on a
boat trip.
El Pescador II, *Calle 2, between 67 and 68,
T02246-430733.* Organizes day trips to Laguna
La Salada, as well as the usual sea excursions.
Tiburon II, *Calle 1 BIS No 7503 and Calle 75,
T02246-434698.* 3-hr boat trips, leaving daily
at 0700.

Villa Gesell
Horse riding
Tante Puppi, *Alameda 205 E/Calle 307 y 308,
T02255-455533, see Facebook.* Offers horse rides
in the dunes daily on summer afternoons
and also moonlit rides on the beach.

Transport

San Clemente del Tuyú
Bus
To **Mar del Plata** (and to resorts in between)
services are frequent with **El Rápido Argentino**.
To **Buenos Aires**, US$25-28, several companies.

Pinamar
Bus
The **bus terminal** (Av Bunge and Intermédanos,
T02254-403500) is near the access road into
town, a 20-min walk to the beach. To **Buenos
Aires**, US$27-31, 4-5 hrs, several companies.

Train
The railway station is a few kilometres from
town, but there are free bus transfers. To
Buenos Aires (Constitución), check with
Ferrobaires (www.ferrobaires.gba.gov.ar)
to see if the Fri train to Pinamar (return Sun)
is running. It was suspended in 2016.

Villa Gesell
Bus
The **bus terminal** (Av 3 and Paseo 140, T02255-
477253) is at the southern end of town. Direct
to **Buenos Aires**, many companies, 5 hrs,
US$29-36. To **Mar del Plata** see page 111.

The oldest and most famous Argentine resort – built in 1874 – has lost much of its charm since its heyday in the 1930s but it is still an interesting place to stay. It's now a big city of 650,000 with plenty of entertainment, but unless you're a lover of crowds or casinos, there are better beaches elsewhere. There are some good bars and cafés along Güemes and Alem, near the cemetery, and superb fish restaurants by the port and on the pier. There are hundreds of hotels, all busy and overpriced even in low season (although prices double in January and February), as this is a popular conference city.

Sights

The city centre is around **Playa Bristol**, where a broad promenade, the Rambla, runs past the fine casino (upper floor open to the public) and the luxury refurbished **Gran Hotel Provincial**, both of which were designed by famous Argentine architect Bustillo, and date from the late 1930s. Six blocks north along San Martín is the Plaza San Martín, a good place for shopping, flanked by an attractive **cathedral**. Ten blocks southwest, at the end of Avenida Colón there are some impressive and attractive mansions dating from Mar del Plata's heyday, from mock-Tudor **Villa Blaquier** to **Villa Ortiz Basualdo** (1909), inspired by a Loire chateaux, now the **Museo Municipal de Arte** ① *Av Colón 1189, T0223-486 1636, Mon, Wed, Thu, Fri 1400-2000, Sat-Sun 1500-2000, US$0.70, including tour*, with rooms furnished in period style. The **Centro Cultural Victoria Ocampo** ① *Matheu 1851, T0223-494 2878, Wed-Mon 1200-1800, US$2*, is in a beautiful 1900s wooden house in lovely gardens, where the famous author entertained illustrious literary figures. In summer,

Essential Mar del Plata

Finding your feet

Astor Piazzola International Airport is 7 km north of town. Regular buses (bus No 542, US$0.50, payable with a magnetic card) run from the airport into town, or it's US$10 in a *remise* taxi.

The **bus terminal** and **railway station** are combined in the **Terminal Ferroautomotora** about 13 blocks northwest of the centre. Bus No 541 runs to the centre. Buses Nos 511, 512 and 512B continue to the lighthouse, south to the beaches and to the port, with buses running every 10 minutes or so (less frequently at night). Single trips cost US$0.50. Buses can only be used with a top-up card available from any kiosk, US$0.35. In general, buses are quick and comfortable.

When to go

Winter is the best time to visit if you want to see the town itself and the sea lion colony, although the wind is relentless. There are several festivals throughout the summer, with live music shows, parades and the coronation of all kinds of carnival queens. For more details, see Festivals, page 110. If you're coming for the beaches, January is best avoided because of overcrowding; December or late February are much more pleasant and it's still warm.

Useful addresses

Immigration office, San Lorenzo 3449, T0223-475 5707, www.migraciones.gov.ar/conare. Monday-Friday 0800-1400.

concerts are held in the grounds. Nearby is the **Museo Roberto T Barili Villa Mitre** ① *Lamadrid 3870, T0223-495 1200, Mon-Fri 0900-1500, Sat-Sun 1400-1800, US$2, free Tue*, owned by a son of Bartolomé Mitre, with an eclectic collection of artefacts including old photos of the city. There's no shortage of events going on in the city, with lots of theatres and cinemas, live music and the casino. See Entertainment, page 110.

Beaches and port area

There are several beaches along this stretch of coast, each with a different feel. Fashionable **Playa Grande** has the best hotels and shops, as well as the famous golf course, with private *balnearios* attracting wealthy Porteños, and a small area open to the public. **Playa La Perla** is packed in summer and far from relaxing, while **Playa Punta Mogotes**, further west, is by far the most appealing beach. However, a short bus ride (Nos 511 or 221) further south will take you to some other quieter beaches, including La Morocha and La Arena, where it is also possible to park the car on the beach close to the sea for a small fee.

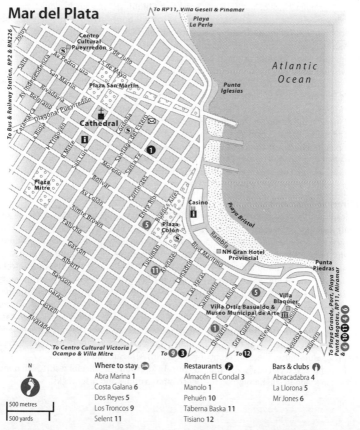

Mar del Plata

N		
500 metres		
500 yards		

Where to stay ⊜	Restaurants ❼	Bars & clubs ❶
Abra Marina 1	Almacén El Condal 3	Abracadabra 4
Costa Galana 6	Manolo 1	La Llorona 5
Dos Reyes 5	Pehuén 10	Mr Jones 6
Los Troncos 9	Taberna Baska 11	
Selent 11	Tisiano 12	

The **port area**, south of Playa Grande, is interesting when the old orange fishing boats come in, and this is the place to come at night, as there are many seafood restaurants gathered in one place; be selective as some are very touristy. A sea lion colony basks on rusting wrecks by the **Escollera Sur**, the southern breakwater that stretches out into the sea. Fishing for *pejerrey*, *corvina* and *pescadilla* is good all along the coast.

Beyond the port are the **Punta Mogotes lighthouse**, built in 1891, and the **Bosque Peralta Ramos**, a 400-ha forest of eucalyptus and conifers, which is an excellent place to take a stroll. Also here is a local restaurant, **El Descanso del Marino**, which serves tasty food.

If you want sea and sand, rather than bars and entertainment, the best beaches are further southwest of the city, along the road to Miramar. Here you'll find several fine broad beaches interrupted by high cliffs; all are easily reached by regular buses from the terminal.

Around Mar del Plata

Santa Clara del Mar is a low-key family resort 18 km north of Mar del Plata that has *balnearios* and a relaxed feel. Though it's far from chic, it's a welcoming place. Beyond, some 34 km northeast of Mar del Plata, is the **Mar Chiquita** ① *www.marchiquita.gov.ar*, a lagoon joined to the sea by a narrow channel, with huge dunes in between, offering good beaches, sailing, fishing and boating, and rich bird life.

Balcarce, 68 km northwest and inland from Mar del Plata, is an attractive small town, with some splendid art deco buildings and a leafy central plaza. The main reason for visiting, though, is to see the famous **Museo Juan Manuel Fangio** ① *Dardo Rocha y Mitre, T02266-425540, www.museofangio.com, Tue-Sun 1000-1700, US$6.50, children US$4.50, seniors US$4.80*. Argentina's most beloved racing driver was born here, and the Municipalidad on the plaza has been turned into a great museum, housing all his trophies and many of the racing cars he drove. It's recommended for car enthusiasts.

Laguna La Brava, 38 km away, at the foot of the Balcarce hills, offers *pejerrey* fishing and plentiful birdlife in lovely wooded surroundings. For further information on fishing, see What to do, page 111. Visit **Estancia Antiguo Casca La Brava** ① *R226, Km 36.5, T0223-4608062, groups only, see Facebook*, for horse riding, trekking, mountain biking and water sports on the lake with fine views of Sierra Brava.

Miramar *Colour map 4, C6.*

A delightful, low-key alternative to Mar del Plata, Miramar (population 33,000) lies 47 km southwest along the coast road and is an old-fashioned little resort, known as the 'city of bicycles' and orientated towards families. It has a big leafy plaza at its centre, a good stretch of beach with soft sand, and a pleasant atmosphere. The most attractive area of the town is away from the high-rise buildings on the seafront, at the **Vivero Dunícola Florentino Ameghino**, a 502-ha forest park on the beach, with lots of walks, restaurants and picnic places for *asado* among the mature trees. There's also a small **Museo Municipal** ① *www.museodemiramar.blogspot.com.ar, Mon-Fri (closed Wed) 1500-1800 and Sat-Sun 1000-1800*, with displays of animal fossils and indigenous Querandí artefacts. Further east is the dense wood of the **Bosque Energético**, possessed of an allegedly magical magnetic energy, which attracts large twigs to hang from tree trunks and groups of meditators to sit in hopeful silence. There are plenty of banks with ATMs around the plaza.

From here, you can easily visit **Mar del Sur**, 14 km south, a peaceful resort with good fishing in a lagoon and bathing on the beach among dunes and black rocks.

Necochea *Colour map 4, C5.*

One hundred kilometres west of Miramar is the well-established town of Necochea (population 90,000). It's one of the most surprising resorts on the whole Atlantic coast, famous for its enormously long (74 km) beach. While the central area is built up and busy in summer months, further west is a spectacular expanse of sand with high dunes, perfect for exploring on foot, horseback or 4WD. There's also a huge forest park, a golf club and rafting on the river Quequén. A number of banks with ATMs and *locutorios* are located along the pedestrianized shopping street, Calle 83.

The town lies on the west bank of the Río Quequén and is in two parts, with its administrative centre 2 km inland from the seafront area. On the opposite bank of the river, Quequén (population 15,000) is mostly a residential area, with one of the most important grain-exporting ports in the country. The two towns are linked by three bridges; one of them, Puente Colgante, is a 270-m suspension bridge built in Cherbourg and opened here in 1929.

The **Parque Miguel Lillo** (named after the Argentine botanist) is a wonderful dense forest of over 500 ha with more than a million trees, open to the public for all kinds of activities. It starts three blocks west of Plaza San Martín, and stretches along the seafront. There are lovely walks, many campsites and picnic spots, a swan lake with paddle boats, an amphitheatre, lots of restaurants, a couple of tiny museums and places to practise various sports.

West of Necochea, there's a natural arch of rock at the **Cueva del Tigre**, and beyond it stretches a vast empty beach, separated from the land by sand dunes up to 100 m high, the **Médano Blanco**. This is an exhilarating area for walking or horse riding, and the dunes are popular for 4WD, riding and sand boarding. East of Quequén harbour there are equally tranquil beaches, particularly **Balneario La Virazón**, and a lighthouse built in 1921, with a good 18-hole golf course.

Around Necochea

You can go rafting on the **Río Quequén** and visit the **Cascadas de Quequén**, small waterfalls 13 km north. The forested **Parque Cura-Meucó** is 70 km north, on the river. There's also diving off the coast at **Parque Subacuático Kabryl**, just 1500 m from the coast. For more on scuba diving, contact **Paradiso Buceo** ⓘ *T02262-550207, paradisobuceo@ hotmail.com, and see Facebook.*

Listings Mar del Plata and around *map page 105.*

Tourist information

Mar del Plata
For what's on, see www.todomardelplata.com.

Tourist offices
Belgrano 2740, T0223-494 4140 (ext 130 or 131) or, more conveniently, next to Casino Central, on Blv Marítimo 2270, T0223-495 1777, www.turismomardelplata.gov.ar. Daily 0800-2000.

Very helpful and can provide good leaflets on events, information on bus routes and lists of hotels and apartment/chalet letting agents, including family homes (when everywhere else is full). There are also tourist offices at the airport and the bus station.

Santa Clara del Mar

Tourist office
T0223-460 2433, www.santaclaradelmar.com.

Balcarce

Tourist office
Calle 17 No 671, T02266-422394,
www.balcarce.mun.gba.gov.ar.

Miramar

Tourist office
Av Costanera y 21, T02291-420190,
www.miramar.tur.ar. Daily 0800-2200
in summer, 0800-1900 in winter.
Has helpful accommodation lists and maps.

Necochea

Tourist office
Av 79 y Av 2, T02262-438333,
www.necochea.tur.ar. Daily 0900-2100.
On the seafront, with useful information
on accommodation and entertainment.

Where to stay

Mar del Plata
Busy traffic makes it impossible to move
along the coast in summer, so choose a
hotel near your preferred beach.

$$$$ Costa Galana
Blv Peralta Ramos 5725, T0223-410 5000,
www.hotelcostagalana.com.
The best by far, a 5-star modern tower,
all luxury facilities, at Playa Grande.

$$$ Dos Reyes
Av Colón 2129, T0223-491 0383,
www.dosreyes.com.ar.
Long-established but modernized town
centre hotel with smart, well-equipped
rooms. Guests have access to a *balneario*.
Good value off season, big breakfast.

$$$-$$ Selent
Arenales 2347, T0223-494 0878,
www.hotelselent.com.ar. Open all year.
Quiet with neat rooms, warm welcome,
great value. Recommended.

$$ Abra Marina
Alsina 2444, T0223-486 4646, http://users.
copetel.com.ar/abramarinacafehotel.
Open all year.
A good budget choice, simple rooms,
all services, café/bar, central.

$$ Los Troncos
Rodríguez Peña 1561, T0223-451 8882,
www.hotellostroncos.com.ar.
Small, chalet-style hotel in quiet
residential area, handy for Güemes
bars and restaurants, garden.

Apartment rental
Prices vary a lot, with higher rates in Jan,
slightly lower in Feb and even lower in
Dec and Mar. Prices rise again at Easter
and over long weekends; cheap deals off
season. The tourist office has a list of agents
and a helpful section in English on their
website, www.mardelplata.gob.ar. Try
Gonnet (Corrientes 1987 (y Moreno),
T0223-495 2171, www.gonnet.com.ar).

Camping
Many on the road south of the city,
but far better sites at Villa Gesell.

Balcarce

$$$ Balcarce
Calle 16 646, T02266-422055,
www.hotelbalcarce.com.
Next to the museum, on the main plaza, the
most comfortable option, with breakfast, spa.

Camping
Campsites are plentiful, and include:

Club de Pesca Balcarce
At Laguna La Brava, R226, Km 39.4,
T0223-460 8029.
Well-organized site, with all facilities and
good fishing.

Municipal
R55, Km 63.5, south of the centre in Parque
Cerro El Triunfo.
Pools and good facilities, all kinds of sports too.

Miramar

Dozens of hotels and apartments between Av 26 and the sea. For a full list see www.miramar-digital.com.ar.

$$ Brisas del Mar
Calle 29, 557, T02291-420334, www.brisas delmarhotel.com.ar. Summer only.
Family-run seafront hotel with neat rooms, cheery restaurant and attentive service; good value.

Camping
There are lots of campsites, including:

$ pp El Durazno
R91, T02291-431984, www. campingeldurazno.com.ar.
Campsite 2 km from town with good facilities, shops, restaurant and *cabañas*. Take bus No 501 marked 'Playas'.

Necochea

Most hotels are in the seafront area just north of Av 2. There are at least 100 within 700 m of the beach. Many close off season, when you can bargain with those still open.

$$$ Hostería del Bosque
Calle 89, 350, T02262-420002, www.hosteria-delbosque.com.ar.
5 blocks from beach, quiet, comfortable, lovely atmosphere in this renovated former residence of an exiled Russian princess, great restaurant. Recommended.

$$$ Presidente
Calle 4, 4040, T02262-423800, www.presinec.com.ar. Mostly closed in winter; open some weekends.
A large 4-star hotel recommended for excellent service, comfortable rooms and pool, price depends on room category and season.

$$ Bahía
Diagonal San Martín 731, T02262-423353, hotelbahia@necocheanet.com.ar.
Very kind owners, comfortable rooms, pool in neat gardens. Recommended.

$$ San Miguel
C 85 No 301, T02262-521433, www.hotel-sanmiguel.com.ar. Open all year.
Good service and value, comfortable.

Camping
The following are recommended:

Camping UATRE
Av 10 y 187, T02262-438278.
The best site, a few kilometres west of town towards Médano Blanco, with great facilities, and beautifully situated *cabañas* too.

Río Quequén
Calle 22 y Ribera Río Quequén, T02262-428068, www.cabaniasrioquequen.com.ar.
Lovely area, cabins available. Sports facilities, pool, bar and cycle hire. Well-maintained in attractive setting on the river.

Restaurants

Mar del Plata
2 areas have become popular thanks to their smaller shops, bars and restaurants.

Around Calle Güemes

$$ Almacén El Condal
Alsina y Garay.
Charming old street-corner bar, serving *picadas* and drinks, popular with young crowd.

$$ Tisiano
San Lorenzo 1332.
Good pasta restaurant in leafy patio.

Around Alem
There are lots of pubs and bars next to the cemetery, including traditional favourites.

$$ Manolo
Rivadavia 2371 and on the coast at Blv Marítimo y Castelli, as well as Leandro N Alem y Almafuerte, www.churrosmanolo.com.
Famous for *churros* and hot chocolate in the early hours, popular with post-party people.

$$ Pehuén
Bernardo de Irigoyen 3666, see Facebook.
Very good and popular *parrilla*.

Centro Comercial Puerto
Many of the seafood restaurants at the port
are brightly lit and not atmospheric.

$$ Taberna Baska
12 de Octubre 3301.
Seafood and Basque country dishes, next to
the port.

Miramar
There are lots of restaurants along Calle 21
and at the *balnearios* on the seafront.

$ Cantina Italiana
Calle 19, 1461.
As its name suggests, this is recommended
for good pasta and seafood; also offers a
delivery service.

$ El Pescador Romano
Calle 19, 1058.
Excellent fish in a popular family restaurant.

$ Mickey
Calle 21 No 686.
A lively long-established *confitería* serving
cheap meals.

Necochea
There are some excellent seafood restaurants.

$$ Chimichurri
C 83 No 345, T02262-420642.
Recommended for *parrilla*.

$$ Parrilla El Loco
Av 10 y 65, T02262-422761.
A classic *parrilla*, deservedly popular
for superb steaks.

$$ Sotavento
7630 Necochea.
On the beach, varied menu, can get
very busy but good value.

$ Pizzería Tempo
Calle 83 No 310, T02262-425100.
A lively traditional place serving good pizzas.

Bars and clubs

Mar del Plata
Many bars and nightclubs are on Alem or its
surroundings and start at around 0200.
Abracadabra (Ruta 11 Km 3.5); and **Mr Jones**
(Alem 3738, www.mrjonesbar.com), are for
the hip under-25 crowd, while **La Llorona**
(on Olavarría, near Blv Marítimo and the
Torreón del Monje), is the place for over-25s.

Entertainment

Mar del Plata
On Wed there is a discount at most cinemas.
Cinemas and shows are listed in the free
leaflet *Guía de Actividades* from the city tourist
office, www.turismomardelplata.gov.ar.
Casino Central, *Blv Marítimo Patricio Peralta
Ramos 2100, www.casinodelacosta.com/
casino-central. Sun-Thu 1100-0230, Fri-Sat
1100-0330, free.* There are others that operate
nearby in summer.
Centro Cultural Osvaldo Soriano, *25 de
Mayo 3108, T0223-499 7877.* Daily screenings,
music shows, plays or conferences, mostly
free or for a small fee.

Festivals

Mar del Plata
Jan National Fishing Festival.
Nov International Film Festival, www.
mardelplatafilmfest.com. This famous festival
showcases new Argentine films and attracts
some good premières from all over the world.
Dec Fiesta del Mar. One of the biggest
festivals, it takes place mid-month.

What to do

Mar del Plata
There are lots of tour operators at the port
and in the town centre along the promenade
where you can find information about city
tours or tours to the surrounding areas.

Boat trips
Anamora, *T0223-496 2000, www.crucero
anamora.com.ar.* Boat trips along the city

coast, several times daily in summer, Sat-Sun only in winter. Departs from from Dársena B, Muelle de Guardacostas in the port, US$19.50, children US$11.

Cycling
Bicicletería Madrid, *Hipólito Yrigoyen 2249, on Plaza Mitre, T0223-494 1932*. Hires bikes for 1 and 2 people.

Fishing
There is good fishing all year along the coast from the shore and off shore in hired boats. *Pejerrey* and *corvina* abound or you can charter a private launch for shark fishing. Offshore fishing is best in Nov and Dec, when *pescadilla* are plentiful; winter is ideal for *pejerrey*. Deep-sea fishing yields salmon and sea bass. Contact the tourist office for advice, see Tourist information, above.

Fishing licences are available from **Dirección de Fiscalización Pesquera** (Mitre 2853, T0223-493 2528), and fishing gear shops.

Golf
Mar del Plata Golf Club, *Aristóbulo del Valle 3940 (near Playa Grande), T0223-486 2221, www.mardelplatagolfclub.com.ar*. This is a great course and deservedly famous, in a wonderful elevated position by the beach.

Tour operators
City tours leave from Plaza España and Plaza Colón. There are tours also to Miramar and the sierras.
Almundo, *Guemes 2416, T0223-451 3497. Mon-Fri 0900-2000, Sat 1000-1300*.

Balcarce
Fishing
Club de Pesca Balcarce, *Villa Laguna Brava, T0223-460 8029, www.irapescar.com (in Spanish)*.

Necochea
Cycling
There are several options for bike hire in the park, Av Pinolandia between 2 and 10.

Fishing
There's splendid *pejerrey* fishing at Laguna Loma Danesa, near La Dulce (60 km northwest of Necochea), T02262-1550 6504, www.irapescar.com/lomadanesa. Tackle can be bought from **Gómez Pesca** (Av 59, 1168, T02262-427494).

Golf
Golf club, *Armada Argentina S/N, Quequén, T02262-450684, www.necocheagolfclub.com.ar*.

Transport

Mar del Plata
Air
Airport, T0223-478 5811. Several flights daily to **Buenos Aires**. LADE flies to many Patagonian towns once or twice a week.

Bus
Local El Rápido del Sud line 212 from the Terminal goes south along the coast from Mar del Plata to **Miramar**.

Long distance The **Terminal Ferroauto-motora** is at Av Luro y San Juan, T0223-561 3743, www.nuevaterminalmardel.com.ar. **El Rápido del Sud** (T0223-154 562059) runs several services a day to most coastal towns: to **San Clemente del Tuyú**, 4 hrs 45 mins, US$18.50; **Villa Gesell**, 1½ hrs, US$10.50; to **Pinamar**, 2 hrs, US$11.50; to **Necochea**, 3 hrs, US$12; to **Bahía Blanca**, 8 hrs, US$42. The same company also goes to **Balcarce**, 1½ hrs, US$5.

To **Buenos Aires**, 5-6 hrs, US$29-41, many companies. To **Bariloche**, **Vía Bariloche**, 18-20 hrs, US$118. To all Patagonian towns along RN 3, ending at **Comodoro Rivadavia**, 23 hrs, US$123-136, with **Transportadora Patagónica**. To **Mendoza**, **Andesmar**, daily, 19-22 hrs, US$72-104.

Train
The service was suspended in 2016.

Balcarce
Bus
Frequent services to **Buenos Aires**, US$29-36.

Miramar
Bus
There are **bus terminals** at Calle 34 and Avenida 23, and at Fortunato de la Plaza and Calle 19, and a few others. To **Buenos Aires**, 6½-7 hrs, US$39-45.

Train
The service was suspended in 2016.

Necochea
Bus
Necochea's **bus terminal** (Av 58 y Jesuita Cardiel, T02262-422470) is rather inconveniently northeast of the centre (3 km from the beach). Take local buses Nos 511 and 512 from the terminal to Quequén Beach, or No 513 to Necochea Beach. You can also catch a taxi for around US$5. There's a good bus network all over the city. To **Buenos Aires**, daily, 6½-8½ hrs, US$32-44. There are also several buses daily to **Mar del Plata** and **Bahía Blanca**.

Bahía Blanca and around *Colour map 4, C4.*

big city, small-town vibe

The province's most important port and a big naval base, Bahía Blanca (population 300,500) is a busy city, and yet it's a relaxed and attractive place with some fine early 20th-century architecture around its large plaza. There's not much to attract tourists, but it's a useful stopping point on the route south, or a base for exploring the beautiful mountains 100 km north at Sierra de la Ventana. It's a city with the feel of a small town, where people are friendly and everyone knows everyone else.

Sights
Bahía Blanca is pleasant to walk around, with well-preserved architecture from the early 20th century. At the city's heart is the large **Plaza Rivadavia**, a broad, well-kept leafy space, with a striking sculpture. On the west side is the Italianate **Municipalidad** (1904), and to the south the impressive French-style **Banco de la Nación** (1927); it's worth popping in to see its perfectly preserved interior. Three blocks north is the classical **Teatro Municipal** (1922) ⓘ *T0291-456 3973, see Facebook*, which hosts regular theatre, live music and dance. At the side of the theatre, the **Museo Histórico** ⓘ *Dorrego 116, T0291-456 3117, mhistorico. bahiablanca.gov.ar, Mon-Fri 0800-1300,* has interesting displays on the city's history.

To the northwest of the centre, along the attractive Avenida Além, the **Parque de Mayo** is filled with eucalyptus trees, children's play areas and bars. Nearby there's a golf course, sports centre and a long area for walking by the river through a sculpture park.

Not to be missed is the **Museo del Puerto** ⓘ *7 km away at the port area Ingeniero White, Torres 4180, T0291-457 3006, www.museodelpuerto.blogspot.com.ar, Mon-Fri 0830-1230, Sat-Sun 1530-1930, free, bus No 500A or 504 from the plaza, or a taxi; free.* Set in a former customs building, this has entertaining and imaginative displays on immigrant life in the early 20th century, with witty photographs, evocative music and sound. And there's a great café in one of the exhibition spaces on Sundays. Highly recommended. The port also has a couple of fine fish restaurants in its red light district; take a taxi.

Around Bahía Blanca

Bahía Blanca has both mountains and beach within an hour's drive. At **Pehuén-Có**, 84 km east, there's a long stretch of sandy beaches and dunes, all relatively empty and unspoilt (beware of jellyfish when the wind is in the south). It's signposted from the main road 24 km from Bahía Blanca. It has a wild and un-touristy feel, with a single hotel, apartment rentals, *cabañas* and several campsites well shaded by pine trees. There are also a couple of places to eat.

There's a more established resort at **Monte Hermoso**, 106 km east, with good hotels and better organized campsites, but still retaining a quiet, family feel, and with wonderful beaches for bathing. Its claim to fame is that it's one of the few places where the sun rises and sets over the sea (here too, don't swim when the wind is in the south because of jellyfish – ask a local if in doubt).

Santa Rosa de la Pampa *Colour map 4, C2.*

Santa Rosa (population 130,000) is the capital of La Pampa province. Founded in 1892, it's an important administrative centre 663 km from Buenos Aires, and though it's not a wildly exciting destination, it's a friendly place. There aren't really any tourist sights, though the **Teatro Español** ① *Lagos 44, T02954-455325, see Facebook*, dates from 1908, and 10 blocks west of the Plaza San Martín is **Laguna Don Tomás** and a park with sports facilities.

The main reason to stop here is to visit the Parque Nacional Lihue Calel (see below). Closer however, is the **Parque Luro** ① *32 km south of Santa Rosa, T02954-15590606, www.parqueluro.tur.ar, reached by bus*, which covers over 6500 ha. This provincial park occupies the former estate of Pedro Luro, who created his own hunting grounds for aristocratic friends visiting from Europe, introducing red deer and wild boar to run wild in the park, with many species of bird. Luro's mansion, a French-style chateau, has been turned into a museum, and opposite is a **Centro de Interpretación Ecológico**, with displays on the flora and fauna of the Pampas.

Parque Nacional Lihue Calel

T02952-436595, www.lihuecalel.com.ar and www.parquesnacionales.gov.ar. There's a camping area and toilets at the administration centre.

The Lihue Calel National Park is situated 240 km southwest of Santa Rosa and 120 km from General Acha, and is reached by paved Route 152. The name derives from the Mapuche for 'place of life', and you can understand why when you see its low vegetated hills rising out

Essential Bahía Blanca

Finding your feet

The **Airport Comandante Espora** is 11 km northeast of town, US$8-10 in a taxi. The **bus terminal** is at Estados Unidos and Brown 1700, 2 km east of the centre. Buses Nos 512 and 514 run to the centre, or it's US$4-5 in a taxi; there are no hotels nearby. There are trains from Buenos Aires; the **railway station** is at Avenida General Cerri 750, six blocks east of the plaza.

Getting around

The city is pleasant to walk around, with a small centre and most things you'll need on streets Alsina or San Martín north/east of the plaza. There's a good network of local buses, taking *Urbana* cards rather than cash (available from shops and kiosks), which you'll need to catch if you want to get to the shopping mall 20 blocks north. Taxis are cheap and plentiful.

Useful addresses

Immigration office, Brown 963, T0291-456 1529. Monday-Friday 0900-1300.

BACKGROUND
Bahía Blanca

Bahía Blanca was founded in 1828 as a fort, the Fortaleza Protectora Argentina, both to control cattle-rustling by the indigenous population and to protect the coast from Brazil, whose navy had landed in the area in 1827. Though the indigenous people of the area were defeated in the campaigns of Rosas, the fortress was attacked several times, notably by 3000 Calfucurá warriors in 1859. An important centre of European immigration, it became a major port with the building of the railways connecting it to grain-producing areas in the Pampas. The biggest industry now is a huge petrochemicals plant 8 km from town at the port.

of rather arid desert. Its microclimate allows it to support a wide variety of plant species, including a number of unique species of cactus in its rocky terrain. Wildlife includes pumas, but you're more likely to spot *maras* (Patagonian hare), vizcachas, guanacos and rheas as well as a wide variety of birds. The area was home to various groups of indigenous people 2000 years ago; there are geometric cave paintings in the **Valle de las Pinturas** and the **Valle de Namuncurá**, seen on one of two self-guided trails through the park. The other trail, **El Huitru**, climbs the highest hill in the park and explores some of its amazing flora. The park is best visited in spring.

Listings Bahía Blanca and around

Tourist information

Bahía Blanca

Tourist office
Alsina 63, T0291-481 8944, www.turismo.bahiablanca.gov.ar. Mon-Fri 0800-1900, Sat 1000-1300 and 1500-1900.
Very helpful.

Monte Hermoso

Tourist office
Faro Recalada y Pedro de Mendoza, T02921-481123, www.montehermoso.porinternet.com.ar.

Santa Rosa de la Pampa

Tourist office
Luro y Corrientes, T02954-436555, www.santarosa.gov.ar.
In the bus terminal, 7 blocks east of Plaza San Martín.

Where to stay

Bahía Blanca

$$$ Argos
España 149, T0291-455 0404, www.hotelargos.com.
3 blocks from plaza, 4-star business hotel, smart, Wi-Fi, good breakfast, restaurant.

$$ Bahía Blanca
Chiclana 227, T0291-455 3050, www.bahia-hotel.com.ar.
Business hotel, good value, well-equipped comfortable rooms, bright bar and *confitería*. Recommended.

$$ Barne
H Yrigoyen 270, T0291-453 0294, www.hotelbarne.bvconline.com.ar.
Family-run, low-key, good value, welcoming.

$ Hostel Bahía Blanca
Soler 701, T0291-452 6802, www.hostelbahiablanca.com.

Light, spacious dorms from US$11 and
doubles with and without bath in this
old building. Close to town, offers lots
of travel advice.

Camping
Best to head for Pehuen Có or Monte
Hermoso – both lovely beach places
with plentiful campsites 1 hr away by bus;
see below.

Monte Hermoso

$$ Petit Hotel
Av Argentina 244, T0291-481818,
www.petitfrentealmar.com.ar.
Simple, modernized 1950s style, family-run,
on the beach, restaurant, breakfast extra,
cooking facilities. Recommended.

Camping
See http://campingpehuen-co.com.ar/.
There are many sites around Monte
Hermoso with good facilities.

Camping Americano
T0291-456 4939, www.campingamericano.
com.ar, signposted from main road 5 km
before town (bus or taxi from town).
A lovely, sprawling, shady site by a quiet
stretch of beach, with excellent facilities,
hot showers, pool, electricity, restaurant,
fireplaces, food shop and *locutorio*. US$20-
25 (depending on season) for 2 per day.
Recommended.

Santa Rosa de la Pampa
See www.santarosa.gov.ar for a complete list.

$$$ Club de Campiña
R5, Km 604, T02954-456800,
www.lacampina.com.
A rather more appealing option than below
if you have transport. Wonderful old
building, cosy rooms with high ceilings,
attractive gardens, pool, gym and spa.

$$$-$$ Calfucura
San Martín 695, T02954-433 303,
www.hotelcalfucura.com.

A 4-star, business-oriented place with
comfortable rooms. Pool, restaurants
and a few apartments to rent.

Camping
There is a municipal site near the Laguna
Don Tomás.

Bahía Blanca

$$ Micho
Guillermo Torres 3875, T0291-457 0346.
A superb chic fish restaurant at the port (take
bus 500 or 501, but go there by taxi at night,
as it's in an insalubrious area).

$$ Santino
Dorrego 38, see Facebook.
Italian-influenced, quiet, sophisticated
atmosphere, good value. Recommended.

$ El Mundo de la Pizza
Dorrego 55, see Facebook.
Fabulous pizzas, lots of choice,
the city's favourite.

Cafés

Café del Angel
Paseo del Angel, entrances at
O'Higgins 71 and Drago 63.
Good-value lunches, friendly place.

Muñoz
O'Higgins y Drago.
Sophisticated café, good for reading
the papers.

Piazza
On the corner of the plaza at
O'Higgins y Chiclana.
Great coffee, buzzing atmosphere,
good salads, and cakes too.

Monte Hermoso

$$ Marfil
Valle Encantado 91.
The smartest, serving delicious fish
and pastas.

$ Pizza Jet

Valle Encantado e Int Majluf, see Facebook.
Hugely popular for all kinds of food, arrive before 2130 to get a table.

Bars and clubs

Bahía Blanca

Lots of discos on Fuerte Argentino (along the stream leading to the park) mainly catering for under 25s, including **Chocolate** (www.chocolatedisco.com.ar), and **Toovaks**. The best place for the over 25s is **La Barraca** (see Facebook).

Shopping

Bahía Blanca

There's a smart, modern shopping mall, **Bahía Blanca Plaza Shopping** (www.bahia blancaplazashopping.com), 2 km north of town on Sarmiento, with a cheap food hall, cinema and supermarket. There's also the supermarket, **Cooperativa** (www. cooperativaobrera.coop), on Donado and other locations, and plenty of clothes and shoe shops on Alsina and San Martín within a couple of blocks of the plaza.

Transport

Bahía Blanca
Air

Bahia Blanca airport, T0291-486 0300. Daily flights to **Buenos Aires** with **Aerolíneas Argentinas**.

Bus

Bus terminal information, T0291-481 9615, Mon-Fri 0600-1200.

Long distance To **Buenos Aires** frequent, several companies, 8-10 hrs, US$52-59, shop around. Most comfortable by far is **Plusmar** suite bus (T0291-456 0616), with flat beds. To **Mar del Plata**, see above. To **Córdoba**, 13-15 hrs, US$65-75. To **Bariloche**, **Andesmar**, **El Valle** and **Via Bariloche**, 11-13 hrs, US$69-79. To **Mendoza**, **Andesmar** (T0810-122 1122), 16 hrs, US$76-91. To **Puerto Madryn**, **Andesmar** and **Tramat** (www. tramatweb.com) 8½-10½ hrs, US$46-61. To **Tornquist**, US$5, **Cóndor Estrella**, 1 hr 20 mins; to **Sierra de la Ventana** (town) **Cóndor Estrella** and **Marilao**, 2 hrs 20 mins, US$7.50. Also minibus to Tornquist with **Meli Bus**, T0291-154 616596. Other bus companies: **Ceferino** (www.empresaceferino.com.ar) and **Rápido del Sur** (T0291-481 3118).

Taxi

Taxi Universitario, T0291-452 0000, T0291-454 0000.

Train

Services were suspended in 2016.

Around Bahía Blanca
Bus

From Monte Hermoso either to **Buenos Aires** or **Bahía Blanca** (US$6-7) with **Cóndor Estrella** and **Marilau**. Several combis or minibuses also to **Bahía Blanca**, including **Empresa Fuertes** (T02921-481611) and **Norte Bus** (T02921-481524).

Santa Rosa de la Pampa
Bus

To **Buenos Aires**, 8 hrs, US$43-49; to **Neuquén**, 8 hrs, US$44-49, with **Andesmar** (T02954-432841), **El Valle** or **Vía Bariloche** (T02954-432694).

Southern
Sierras

The south of Buenos Aires province has two ranges of ancient mountains rising suddenly from the flat Pampas; both are easily accessible and offer great opportunities for a weekend escape. The Sierra de Tandil range, due south from Buenos Aires, is 340 km long and 2000 million years old – among the oldest in the world. The beautiful, curved hills of granite and basalt offer wonderful walking and riding, with the pleasant airy town of Tandil as a base. There are plenty of small hotels, though nearby estancias offer the best way to explore the hills.

Further west, the magnificent Sierra de la Ventana is the highest range of hills in the Pampas and so called because craggy Cerro de la Ventana has a natural hole near its summit. Located next to the Parque Provincial Ernesto Tornquist, it is within easy reach of Bahía Blanca for a day or weekend visit, and the attractive villages of Villa Ventana and Sierra de la Ventana nearby are appealing places to stay, with plenty of accommodation options. These mountains are not quite as old as those in Tandil but offer more demanding hikes in wilder terrain, with stunning views from their summits. There are daily buses and combis from Bahía Blanca, but you could break the journey at the quaint sleepy town of Tornquist.

off the tourist trail

Seventy kilometres north of Bahía Blanca, Tornquist (population 12,000) is a pretty, sleepy, rural town that you will pass through if travelling to Sierra de la Ventana via Route 33. It has an attractive church on the large central plaza (which is more like a tidy park), a strangely green artificial lake, and a big children's play area. It's not a touristy place, but that's precisely its appeal, and it's a good starting point for trips into the sierras.

About 11 km east of town is the Tornquist family mansion (not open to tourism), built in a mixture of French styles. The town is named after Ernesto Tornquist (1842-1908), the son of a Buenos Aires merchant of Swedish origin. Under his leadership the family established an important industrial investment bank and Tornquist helped to set up the country's first sugar refinery, meat-packing plant and several chemical plants.

Listings Tornquist

Tourist information

Tourist office
Plaza Ernesto Tornquist, 9 de Julio and Alem, T0291-494 0081, www.tornquist.gob.ar. Daily 0800-1800.

Where to stay

$ La Casona
Rawson 232, T0291-494 0693, http://com-tur.com.ar/lacasona.
A renovated house with plain rooms.

$ San José
Güemes 138, T0291-494 0152, www. hotelsanjose1.wix.com/hotelsanjose.
Small, central, with plain, faded rooms.

Parque Provincial Ernesto Tornquist

where the Pampas meet the mountains

The sierras are accessed from the Parque Provincial Ernesto Tornquist which is 25 km east of Tornquist on Route 76. There are two main access points, one at the foot of Cerro Ventana (no ascents after 1100) and the other one, further east, at the foot of Cerro Bahía Blanca. Other than the Campamento Base (see below), the nearest places for accommodation are the two towns of Sierra de la Ventana and Villa Ventana. For details on getting to the park, see Transport, page 120.

Cerro Ventana

Cerro de la Ventana (1136 m) has fantastic views from the 'window' (*ventana*) in the summit ridge. To enter this section of the park, turn left after the massive ornate gates at the entrance to the Tornquist family home. There are showers, a food kiosk and an **information point** ① *Dec-Easter daily 0900-1700*, and *guardaparques* who you can ask for advice and register with for the longer walks. Nearby is the hospitable **Campamento Base** ① *T0291-156 495304, www.haciafuera.com.ar/campamentobase.htm*, with hot showers, dormitory accommodation and an attractive campsite. From this entrance, it's a three-hour walk, clearly marked, but with no shade, up **Cerro de la Ventana**. Register with *guardaparques* and set off no later than midday.

Alternative hikes are a gentle stroll to **Garganta Olvidada** (one hour each way), where you can set off up to the **Piletones**, small pools (two hours each way), and **Garganta del Diablo** (six hours return), a wonderful narrow gorge with waterfalls. Guides are available for the walk to Garganta Olvidada, for a minimum of 10 people.

Cerro Bahía Blanca
The entrance to this section of the park is 4 km further east along Route 76. There's a car park and **interpretation centre** ① *T0291-491 0039, Dec-Easter 0900-1700*, with *guardaparques* who can advise on walks. From here you can go on a guided visit to **Cueva del Toro** (only with your own vehicle, four to five hours), natural caves and the **Cueva de las Pinturas Rupestres** which contains petroglyphs. There are also good walks, including up **Cerro Bahía Blanca** (two hours return), a gentle climb rewarded with panoramic views; highly recommended. There's lots of wildlife to spot, but you're most likely to see grey foxes, guanacos, wild horses and red deer.

Villa Ventana
Some 10 km beyond from the park's second entrance at Cerro Bahía Blanca is an attractive laid-back wooded settlement with weekend homes, *cabañas* for rent and a municipal campsite by the river with all facilities. There's an excellent tea shop, **Casa de Heidi**, and good food served in rustic surroundings at **Las Golondrinas**. The pretty village is the base for climbing **Cerro Tres Picos** (1239 m), to the south of the park, which is the highest peak in the province. The ruins of the **Hotel Club Casino** (1911) can still be seen; once the most luxurious hotel in Argentina, it burned down in 1983.

★ Sierra de la Ventana *Colour map 4, C4.*
Continuing east, the town of Sierra de la Ventana (population 2200) is a good base for exploring the hills, with a greater choice of hotels than Villa Ventana and wonderful open landscapes all around. There is an 18-hole golf course and good trout fishing in the Río Sauce Grande. There's also a wonderful tea shop, **La Angelita**, in the leafy lanes of Villa Arcadia (across the river), and several places on the river to bathe.

Listings Parque Provincial Ernesto Tornquist

Tourist information

Villa Ventana

Tourist office
T0291-491 0001, www.villaventana.com.
Friendly office at the entrance to the village.

Sierra de la Ventana

Tourist office
Av Roca 19, just before railway track, T0291-491 5303, www.sierradelaventana.org.ar.
Helpful office with a complete list of

all hotels, *cabañas* and campsites with availability and prices.

Where to stay

Villa Ventana
Lots of accommodation in *cabañas*; municipal campsite by river with all facilities. See www.sierradelaventana.org.ar.

$$$ El Mirador
On RP 76 Km 226, T0291-494 1338, www.complejoelmirador.com.ar.

Great location right at the foot of Cerro de la Ventana, comfortable rooms, some with tremendous views, very peaceful, good restaurant.

Sierra de la Ventana

$$$ Cabañas La Caledonia
Los Robles y Ombúes in Villa Arcadia, a couple of blocks over the railway track, T0291-491 5268, www.lacaledonia.com.ar.
Well-equipped, comfortable small cabins in pretty gardens with a pool. Price is for a cabin for up to 4 people.

$$$ Las Vertientes
RP 76, Km 221, signposted just west of the turning to Villa Ventana, T011-4773 6647, http://com-tur.com.ar/lasvertientes.
Very welcoming ranch with a house for rent (price is for 6 people; breakfast extra) in lovely relaxing surroundings, with horse riding, mountain biking, trekking, day visits.

$$ Alihuen
Tornquist y Balneario, T0291-491 5074, http://com-tur.com.ar/alihuen.
A delightful old place near the river, dining room, garden, pool, good value.

Camping

Yamila
Access on C Tornquist, T0291-15-418 9266, www.campingyamila.8m.com.
Camping and small cabins with bunks ($). Lovely shady site by river, hot showers, food shop.

Transport

Parque Provincial Ernesto Tornquist
Bus
La Estrella/El Cóndor has daily services connecting Tornquist and Sierra de la Ventana with Buenos Aires and **Bahía Blanca**. To **Bahía Blanca** also **Expreso Cabildo** and a few minibus companies.

★ Tandil   *Colour map 4, C5.*

from the pueblo to the sierras

Tandil (population 111,000) is an attractive town, with a light breezy feel, and is a centre for outdoor activities, making it a good base for exploring the nearby sierras. There are a couple of marvellous estancias in the area and a clutch of restaurants, cafés and bars within the town.

Sights

On the south side of the main Plaza Independencia are the neoclassical **Municipalidad** (1923), the former **Banco Hipotecario Nacional** (1924) and the **Iglesia del Santísimo Sacramento** (1878), inspired (apparently) by the Sacre Coeur in Paris. Six blocks south of the plaza, up on a hill, is the **Parque Independencia**, with a granite entrance in Italianate style, built by the local Italian community to celebrate the town's centenary. Inside the park, the road winds up to a vantage point, where there's a Moorish-style **castle**, built by the Spanish community to mark the same event, with marvellous views over the surrounding sierras. At the base of the hill is an amphitheatre, where a famous community theatre event takes place during Easter week (book accommodation ahead). South of the park is the **Lago del Fuerte**, a popular place for water sports; bathing is possible at the Balneario del Sol in a complex of several swimming pools.

West of the plaza on the outskirts of town is **Cerro Calvario**, an easy walk leading to the **Capilla Santa Gemma** at the top. Further away, 5 km from town, **Cerro El Centinela** has a large, attractive, family-oriented tourist complex that includes a 1200-m cable car ride, a good restaurant (book your table in advance) and swimming pools.

It's easy to get out of the city to explore the hilly countryside on foot or by bike. Heading south past the lake, follow Avenida Don Bosco or one of the nearby tree-lined roads into the beautiful surroundings. Note that you should not enter any private land without permission. Instead, contact local tour operators who have arranged exclusive access with the land owners.

Six kilometres south is the 140-ha **Reserva Natural Sierra del Tigre**, with good views over Tandil from **Cerro Venado**. Wild foxes and guanacos can be seen occasionally, as well as llamas.

Tandil

Where to stay 🛏
Ave María **6**
Cabañas Brisas Serranas **2**
Casa Chango **10**
Chacra Bliss **11**
El Solar de las Magnolias **12**
Hermitage **3**
Hostal de la Sierra
  del Tandil **5**
Jazmines en la Sierra **7**
Las Acacias **9**
Plaza de las Carretas **4**
Tanta Pacha Hostel **13**

Restaurants 🍴
1905 **11**
El Molino **2**
El Viejo Sauce **9**
Epoca de Quesos **3**
Parador del Sol **7**
Taberna Pizuela **10**

Bars & clubs 🍸
Antares **12**
Liverpool **6**

200 metres
200 yards

Tourist information

Tourist office
At the access to town (next to R226),
Av Cte Espora 1120, T0249-4432073,
www.tandil.com.ar.
Mon-Sat 0800-2000, Sun 0900-1300.
Very well organized, with good brochures
and urban maps. There are other offices
in the main plaza near the corner of General
Rodríguez NS Pinto, and at the bus terminal
(Av Buzón 650, T0249-4432092, 12 blocks
northeast of the centre).

Where to stay

The real joy of Tandil lies in the beauty
of its surroundings, best explored by
staying in an estancia. Ask at the tourist
offices for suggestions. Otherwise, there
are some good options around town;
see www.tandil.com for a complete list.

$$$$ Ave María
Paraje la Portena, T0249-442 2843,
www.avemariatandil.com.ar.
One of the most exquisite small hotels in
the whole province, this may call itself a
hostería, but the splendid Norman-style
building set in beautiful gardens overlooking
the rocky summits of the sierras is much
more like an estancia. Charming owner
Asunti encourages you to feel completely at
home and ramble around the place as you
please. There are 10 rooms, all impeccably
designed with everything you could possibly
need, some with doors opening directly
onto the gardens. Many of the discreet staff
speak English. A great place to relax and
swim in the pool or walk in the grounds,
hills and woodland. Prices are half-board
and discounts apply Mon-Thu. Highly
recommended, not to be missed.

$$$$-$$$ Chacra Bliss
Paraje La Porteña, T011-15-3179 8000,
www.chacrabliss.com.ar.

Charmingly decorated rooms with simple
but comfortable furniture, a welcoming
pool and a long veranda that catches the
afternoon sun. Very relaxing.

$$$$-$$$ Las Acacias
Av Brasil 642, T0249-442 3373,
www.posadalasacacias.com.ar.
Hostería in a restored 1890s dairy farm in
the Golf Club area, with very comfortable
rooms looking out on to large gardens with
a splendid pool. Friendly owners, who speak
English and Italian, and excellent staff help to
create a welcoming and homely atmosphere
for a delightful stay. Recommended.

$$$$-$$ Cabañas Brisas Serranas
Scavini y Los Corales, T0249-440 6110,
www.brisasserranas.com.ar.
Very comfortable and well-furnished
cabañas, pool, lovely views and
welcoming owners.

$$$$-$$ El Solar de las Magnolias
Ituzaingo 941, T0249-442 8618,
www.solarmagnolias.com.ar.
Apartment complex of lovely, roomy
traditional single-storey buildings, with
a mix of antique and modern furniture.
Parking and breakfast included.

$$$ Hostal de la Sierra del Tandil
Av Avellaneda 909/41, T0249-442 2330,
www.hostaldeltandil.com.ar.
Spanish-style building, with boldly designed
rooms with bath, appealing areas to sit, a
good restaurant for residents only and a pool.

$$$-$$ Hermitage
Av Avellaneda and Rondeau, T0249-442 3987,
www.hermitagetandil.com.ar.
Good value in this quiet, old-fashioned
hotel next to the park. There are some smart
modernized rooms, though these aren't
very different to the standard ones, all very
simple, but the service is welcoming.

$$$-$$ Jazmines en la Sierra
Libertad 316, T0249-442 2873,
www.jazminesenlasierra.com.ar.
6 attractive rooms with a colour theme,
a lovely cottage garden and slightly less
appealing common areas with fireplace.

$$$-$$ Plaza de las Carretas
Av Santamarina 728, T0249-444 7850.
An early 20th-century family house, now a
homely and quiet place to stay, with good
rooms with eclectic decor and an attractive
garden at the back.

$ pp Casa Chango
25 de Mayo 451, T0249-442 2260,
www.casa-chango.com.ar.
Bright, colourful hostel set in an old house
with lovely communal areas. Central and
friendly. Also room for camping.

$ pp Tanta Pacha Hostel
Dabidos 1263,T0249-447 7575,
www.tantapacha.com.
Lovely, spacious hostel set in an old country
house in attractive grounds. Rustic wooden
furniture, dorms only.

Restaurants

Local produce here traditionally includes
cheese and sausages, both excellent and
served as part of the *picadas* (nibbles with
drinks) offered in local bars and restaurants,
or available to take away in several good
delis in town, such as **Syquet** (General
Rodríguez and Mitre, www.syquet.com.ar).

$$ 1905
Av Santamarina and San Martín.
A minimalist setting in a charming old house
that serves excellent, finely elaborate meals.

$ El Molino
Curupaytí 95, see Facebook.
A small, simple place with a little windmill.
It specializes in different cuts of meat cooked
traditionally *al disco* – in an open pan on
the fire.

$ El Viejo Sauce
Av Don Bosco and Suiza (see Facebook).
Next to the Reserva Sierra del Tigre, in
attractive natural surroundings, this is an
ideal stopover at tea time for its cakes and
home-made jams.

$ Epoca de Quesos
San Martín and 14 de Julio, T0249-444 8750,
www.epocadequesos.com.
An atmospheric 1860s house serving
delicious local produce, wines, home-
brewed beers and memorable *picadas*
to share, which include a great range of
cheeses, salami, sausages and traditional
Pampas bread. Recommended.

$ Parador del Sol
Zarini s/n, T0249-443 5697.
Located in the attractive *balneario* by Lago
del Fuerte, serving great pastas and salads
in a smart beach-style trattoria.

$ Taberna Pizuela
Paz and Pinto.
Attractive old place serving a broad range of
very good simple dishes, including pizzas –
the speciality.

Bars and clubs

Antares
9 de Julio 758, www.cerveza
antares.com.ar.
A popular brewpub, lively in the
late evening with excellent beers,
good meals and live music every Mon.

Liverpool
9 de Julio and San Martín.
Pictures of the Beatles in this relaxed and
friendly bar.

What to do

Golf
Tandil Golf Club, *Av Fleming s/n,*
www.tandilgolfclub.com.

Horse riding
Cabalgatas Tandil, *Avellaneda 673, T0249-15-450 9609, cabalgatasbarletta@yahoo.com.ar, see also Facebook*. Recommended rides with Gabriel Barletta, expert on native flora, who might end your tour with an informal acoustic guitar session.

Trekking
To find an approved guide who will take you to otherwise inaccessible land for trekking, see www.guiasturismotandil.com.ar.
Eco de las Sierras, *Maipú 714, www.ecodelasierras.com*. Run by Lucrecia Ballesteros, a highly recommended guide who is young, friendly and knowledgeable. Day trips from US$27.

Kumbre, *T0249-443 4313, www.kumbre.com*. Trekking, mountain biking and some climbing guided by experienced Carlos Centineo.

Transport

Bus
To **Buenos Aires**, 5-6 hrs, US$30, with **La Estrella/El Cóndor**, **El Rápido** and **Río Paraná**. **Río Paraná** also goes daily to **Bahía Blanca**, 6 hrs, US$29, and to **Mar del Plata**, 4 hrs, US$15.

Train
Services were suspended in 2016.

Córdoba & Central Sierras

a world away from Buenos Aires

Córdoba, Argentina's second biggest city, has an entirely different character from Buenos Aires. Cordobeses are known for their quick wit and warm welcome.

The Jesuits established magnificent estancias in the Sierras Chicas, which are now the province's main tourist attraction. North are the remote reaches of Cerro Colorado, with amazing displays of art in a bizarre rocky landscape.

South of the city in Alta Gracia is Che Guevara's childhood home and the best Jesuit museum inside a spectacular estancia. Nearby, Villa General Belgrano remains a German stronghold, with chalet-style architecture, microbreweries and *apfelstrudel*.

Córdoba's most stunning scenery is high along the Camino de las Altas Cumbres into the Valle de Traslasierra, with condors wheeling overhead in the Parque Nacional Quebrada del Condorito.

To the southwest, the sleepy provincial capital of San Luis lies at the foot of its own magnificent sierra and the Parque Nacional Sierra de las Quijadas, with its dramatic red sandstone canyon. At El Trapiche and Carolina you can even mine for gold.

Best for
Estancias ▪ Hiking ▪ Horse riding ▪ Museums

Footprint picks

★ **The Jesuit estancia trail**, page 138

Stroll the corridors of the first residences the Jesuits constructed upon their arrival in Argentina.

★ **Estancia Los Potreros**, page 145

Horse riding and birdwatching are just some of the activities on offer at this famous estancia.

★ **Paragliding in Cuchi Corral near La Cumbre**, page 146

Take to the skies and soar over the fabulous Sierras de Córdoba mountain range.

★ **Villa General Belgrano**, page 155

Celebrate Oktoberfest in this quaint mountain town bursting with German heritage.

★ **Cerro Champaquí**, page 159

Climb to the top of the highest peak in Córdoba province.

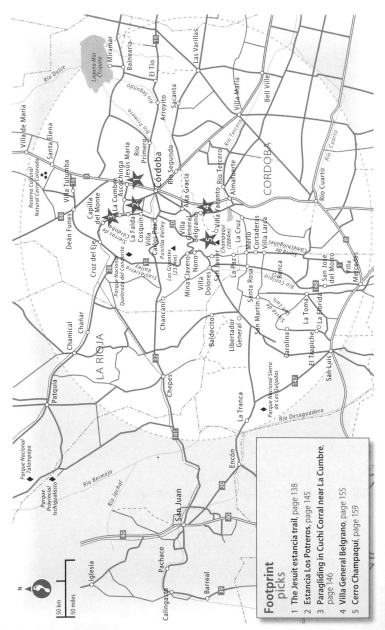

Footprint picks

Córdoba
city

At the centre of an area of great natural beauty lies a modern city with a fascinating past. Córdoba is the capital of one of the country's most densely populated and wealthy provinces, with a lively student population and buzzing atmosphere. It lies on the Río Suquía, extending over a wide valley, with the sierras visible in the west.

The city has been an important trade centre since the area was colonized in the 16th century, and it retains an unusually fine set of colonial buildings at its heart, the astonishing Manzana de los Jesuitas, complete with its temple still intact.

Cordobeses are renowned throughout the country for their sharp sense of humour, defiant attitude and a lilting accent that other regions delight in imitating. However, along with their strong sense of civic pride, the locals' warm welcome makes Córdoba one of the most hospitable areas in the country.

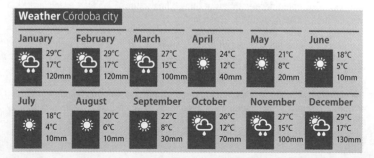

Weather Córdoba city

January	February	March	April	May	June
29°C	29°C	27°C	24°C	21°C	18°C
17°C	17°C	15°C	12°C	8°C	5°C
120mm	120mm	100mm	40mm	20mm	10mm

July	August	September	October	November	December
18°C	20°C	22°C	26°C	27°C	29°C
4°C	6°C	8°C	12°C	15°C	17°C
10mm	10mm	30mm	70mm	100mm	130mm

Essential Córdoba city

Finding your feet

The Aeropuerto Internacional Ingeneiro Ambrosio Taravella, more commonly known as **Pajas Blancas,** is 12 km northwest of the centre. The best way to get to the city from the **airport** is by taxi (US$12-14), as the bus service is unreliable.

Long-distance buses arrive at the central **bus terminal** on Blv Perón 380, eight blocks east of the main plaza. To leave the terminal, go upstairs and cross the bridges towards the city centre. A taxi to Plaza San Martín costs US$4. Minibuses that travel to nearby towns stop at the main terminal and then stop at the **minibus terminal** on Boulevard Illia. See Transport, page 136.

Getting around

Most of the city's sights can easily be visited on foot within a day or so. There's a leafy pedestrian shopping area to the north of the Plaza San Martín, and the historical Manzana de los Jesuitas is two blocks southwest of here. Buses share the main roads with trolleybuses. Neither accepts cash; instead you have to buy **Red Bus** cards (www. red-bus.com.ar; US$2 per card, normal fare US$0.60) from kiosks. Ordinary yellow taxis are usually more convenient for short distances than green *remise* taxis, which are better value for longer journeys.

When to go

Avoid the hot and stormy summer months from December to February, when daytime temperatures are around 30°C. The dry season is April to September, with clear skies and cooler, but still pleasantly warm, temperatures.

Useful addresses

Immigration office, **Dirección Nacional de Migraciones**, Caseros 676, T0351-422 2740. Monday-Friday 0800-1600.

Sights *Colour map 4, A2.*

Old Córdoba

Old City

Córdoba's centre comes as a pleasant surprise. Its most interesting buildings are grouped around a pedestrianized area, enabling you to gaze up at the magnificent architecture without being mown down by traffic. Most of the older buildings lie within a few blocks of the **Plaza San Martín**, which dates from 1577 when it was the site for the odd bullfight. Now it's a wide open space, with lots of cafés, a fine statue of San Martín, and jacaranda trees creating a mass of purple in late spring.

On the west side, the former **Cabildo**, built in 1610, with characteristic arches and two interior patios, has a colourful history. It has served as a prison, courthouse and clandestine detention centre during the last military dictatorship. Next to it, the **cathedral** ⓘ *T0351-422 3446, daily 0800-1300 and 1630-2000*, is the oldest in Argentina, an extraordinary confection of 17th- and 18th-century styles from successive renovations. The marvellous neo-baroque interior has wooden doors from a Jesuit temple and statues of angels resembling the indigenous peoples, with a silver tabernacle and lavishly decorated ceiling.

Just south of the cathedral is the 16th-century **Carmelo Convent** and chapel of **Santa Teresa** ⓘ *Independencia 122, Mon-Sat, 0700-1430 and 1730-1930*, whose rooms and beautiful patio form the **Museo de Arte Religioso Juan de Tejeda** ① *Mon-Fri 0900-1600, Sat 1000-1330, US$1, US$1.25 on Sat, under 12s free, guided visits also in English and French, www.museotejeda.com*. This houses one of the finest collections of religious art in the country and is not to be missed.

One block west, on the west side of pleasant Plaza del Fundador, is the convent and church of **Santa Catalina de Siena**. It was founded in 1613 but rebuilt in the late 19th century and contains a splendid collection of paintings from Peru as well as colonial Spanish tapestries and carpets. For more contemporary art, the **Museo Municipal de Bellas Artes** ① *Av General Paz 33, T0351-434 1636, Tue-Sun 1000-2000, free*, has a permanent collection by celebrated Argentine artists in an early 20th-century French-style mansion.

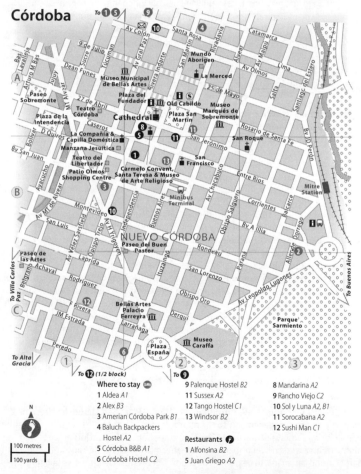

Córdoba

Where to stay 🛏
1 Aldea *A1*
2 Alex *B3*
3 Amerian Córdoba Park *B1*
4 Baluch Backpackers Hostel *A2*
5 Córdoba B&B *A1*
6 Córdoba Hostel *C2*
9 Palenque Hostel *B2*
11 Sussex *A2*
12 Tango Hostel *C1*
13 Windsor *B2*

Restaurants 🍴
1 Alfonsina *B2*
5 Juan Griego *A2*
8 Mandarina *A2*
9 Rancho Viejo *C2*
10 Sol y Luna *A2, B1*
11 Sorocabana *A2*
12 Sushi Man *C1*

BACKGROUND
Córdoba city

Founded in 1573 by an expedition from Santiago del Estero led by Jerónimo Luis de Cabrera, Córdoba was the most important city in the country in colonial times. During the late 16th and 17th centuries, the Jesuit Order made the city their headquarters for the southern part of the continent and founded the first university in the country here, giving the city its nickname, 'La Doctora' (the Learned). In 1810, when Buenos Aires backed independence, the leading figures of Córdoba voted to remain loyal to Spain, and after independence the city was a stronghold of opposition to Buenos Aires. It has remained fiercely independent ever since, supporting many Radical party governments, and in May 1969 disturbances in the city ignited opposition to military rule throughout the country.

Since the 1940s Córdoba has grown from a cultural, administrative and communications centre into a large industrial city of 1.5 million people, though more recently the recession has resulted in growing unemployment. However, the city has an upbeat feel and fabulous nightlife.

The **Manzana Jesuítica (Jesuit Block)**, contained within the streets Avenida Vélez Sarsfield, Caseros, Duarte Quirós and Obispo Trejo, has been declared a World Heritage Site by UNESCO. The **Iglesia de la Compañía**, at the corner of Obispo Trejo and Caseros, was originally built between 1640 and 1676, and its curious vaulted ceiling is a ship's hull, created by a Jesuit trained in the Dutch shipyards. Behind the church, on Caseros, is the smaller, more beautiful **Capilla Doméstica**, a private 17th-century Jesuit chapel, accessible only on the guided tour (see below) and worth seeing for the indigenous painting on the altar. To the south is the main building of the **Universidad Nacional de Córdoba** ① *T0351-433 2075, Mon-Sat 0900-1830, US$2 by guided tour only, guided visits in English to the church, chapel, university and school leave from Obispo Trejo 242 daily at 1000 and 1700*, originally the Jesuit Colegio Máximo. It now houses one of the most valuable libraries in the country, as well as the Colegio Nacional de Montserrat, the most traditional high school in the province.

Other fine examples of religious architecture are the **Iglesia de San Francisco**, Buenos Aires and Entre Ríos, on a leafy plaza, and the **Iglesia de San Roque** at Obispo Salguero 84. One block east of Plaza San Martín is the **Museo Histórico Provincial Marqués de Sobremonte** ① *Rosario de Santa Fe 218, T0351-433 1661, Mon-Fri 0900-1200, 1800-2000, US$1*, the only surviving colonial family residence in the city, dating from 1760. It has a labyrinth of patios and simply decorated rooms with texts in English and German. The **Basílica de La Merced** at 25 de Mayo 83 has a fine gilded wooden pulpit dating from the colonial period and beautifully carved wooden doors, with fine ceramic murals revealing Córdoba's history on the outside by the local artist Armando Sica.

Nueva Córdoba

Over the past few years Nueva Córdoba (south of the Plaza San Martín) has become the hippest part of town, due in part to the numbers of students that frequent the area (the university is a short walk from here). There are cute shops, cafés and lots of hostels, and, at night, the area is taken over by bars and clubs; head to Rondeau and Cañada, or Boulevard San Juan and Larrañaga, to be part of the action. There is an eclectic mix of building styles along Avenida Hipólito Yrigoyen. The **Paseo del Buen Pastor** ⓘ *Av Hipólito Yrigoyen 325, T0351-434 2727*, has a cultural centre at its heart with an **art gallery** ⓘ *daily 1000-2000, free*, a book shop, cafés (**Colores Santos**), bars (**Black Sheep**) and a beautifully presented **chapel** ⓘ *Tue-Sun 0900-1800*. Next door the neo-Gothic **Iglesia de los Capuchinos** ⓘ *T0351-468 1922 Tue-Sat 0800-1900, Sun Mass at 1030, 1200, 1930 and 2100*, displays the night skies for every month of the year.

Further up towards the park are two worthwhile art galleries. Set in an amazing turn-of-the-century palace, the **Museo Superior de Bellas Artes Evita-Palacio Ferreyra** ⓘ *Av Hipólito Yrigoyen 511, T0351-434 3636, Tue-Sun 1000-2000 (in Jan 1000-1300 and 1800-2100), US$1, Wed free*, has 12 salons spread out over three floors and shows a range of Argentine and international artists. Opposite, in front of Plaza España, is the modern **Museo de Bellas Artes Emilio Caraffa** ⓘ *Av Poeta Lugones 411, T0351-434 3348, www.museocaraffa.org.ar, Tue-Sun 1000-2000 (in Jan 1000-1300 and 1800-2100), US$1, Wed free (near 50% discount when buying tickets for both Bellas Artes and Museo Caraffa)*, which is dedicated to presenting the best of Cordobese visual arts.

Parque Sarmiento is the largest green area of the city, laid out by French architect Charles Thays in 1889 with small lakes, a neat rose garden and a **zoo** ⓘ *T0351-421 7648, www.zoo-cordoba.com.ar, daily 1000-1730, US$8.50*, set among steep hills.

Other sights

The magnificent **Mitre railway station**, near the bus terminal, has a beautifully tiled *confitería*. The lively, crowded market, **Mercado de la Ciudad**, provides a taste of local urban culture.

Listings Córdoba city *map page 131.*

Tourist information

Agencia Córdoba Turismo
Cabildo viejo, Pasaje Santa Catalina, T0351-434 1200, www.turismo.cordoba.gov.ar and www.cordobaturismo.gov.ar. Daily 0800-2000.
Also at the bus terminal (T0351-433 1982, daily 0700-2100), and at the airport (T0351-434 8390, daily 0800-2000). All have useful city maps and information on guided walks and cycle tours.

Where to stay

$$$ Amerian Córdoba Park
Blv San Juan 165, T0351-526 6600, www.amerian.com.
Swish, modern hotel with marbled foyer and professional service. Comfortable, superb breakfast, convenient and reliable. Also has a business centre, gym, spa and pool.

$$$ Windsor
Buenos Aires 214, T0351-422 4012, www.windsortower.com.
Small, smart and warm hotel, with a sauna, gym and pool. There's excellent white tablecloth dining at the expensive **Sibaris** restaurant. Large breakfasts.

$$ Alex
Blv Illia 742, T0351-421 4350, www.alexhotel.com.ar.
Good value, modern, cosy despite a slightly off-putting exterior. All rooms include a *mate* kit, and there are helpful staff. Close to the bus station.

$$ Córdoba B&B
Tucumán 440, T0351-423 0973, www.cordobabyb.com.ar.
Central, good-value place with sparsely decorated but pleasant doubles and triples. Parking.

$$ Sussex
San Jerónimo 125, T0351-422 9070,
www.hotelsussexcba.com.ar.
Well-kept hotel, with a small pool.
Families welcome, buffet breakfast.

$ pp Aldea
Santa Rosa 447, T0351-426 1312,
www.aldeahostel.com.
Reasonably central hostel which is
attractively designed and decorated, and
has welcoming staff. There's a terrace with
sofas and games. Dorm prices depend on
the number sharing.

$ pp Baluch Backpackers Hostel
San Martin 338, T0351-422 3977,
www.baluchbackpackers.com.
Inviting dorms for 4-6 (US$10-12) and good
doubles (**$$**) at this central hostel, which
is owned and run by backpackers. Offers
information, bus tickets and many services,
and organizes various activities.

$ pp Córdoba Hostel
Ituzaingó 1070, T0351-468 7359,
www.cordobahostel.com.ar.
In Nueva Córdoba district, this hostel has
small rooms (US$12.50 in dorms, US$30 in
double), and is quite noisy. There are private
lockers in the rooms.

$ pp Palenque Hostel
Av Gral Paz 371, T0351-423 7588,
see Facebook.
Lovely hostel in a 100-year-old building,
with spacious common areas, small dorms
(US$12-15), and doubles with TV (**$**).

$ pp Tango Hostel
Bolívar 613, T0351-425 6023,
www.tangohostelcordoba.com.
Good hostel in the Nueva Córdoba student
district, with clubs and bars all around.
Dorms for 4-11 (US$10.50-13.50), doubles
(US$40), a library and free coffee/*mate*.
Local trips arranged.

Restaurants

$$$-$$ Juan Griego
Obispo Trejo 104, T0351-570 6577,
www.juangriegorestobar.com. Mon-Fri
0800-1600, open for breakfast and lunch.
On the 7th floor of the Colegio de Escribanos
with a view of the Manzana Jesuítica, this
modern Argentine restaurant is unmissable.

$$ Rancho Viejo
Martínez 1900, Parque Sarmiento,
T0351-468 3685.
Popular *parrilla* in rustic surroundings
in the park.

$$-$ Sol y Luna
Gral Paz 278, T0351-425 1189, www.soly
lunaonline.com.ar. Mon-Sat 1200-1530.
Vegetarian fresh food with a change of menu
daily, lunchtime specials and good desserts.
There's a 2nd branch at Montevideo 66,
Nuevo Córdoba, T0351-421 1863.

$$-$ Sushi Man
Independencia 1181, T0351-460 3586,
www.sushimanweb.com.
Those who have had their fill of meat and
would like to order in can opt for this chain
restaurant offering decent, if not spectacular,
sushi options.

$ Alfonsina
Duarte Quirós 66j, T0351-427 2847,
see Facebook. Daily 0800-0300.
Rural style in an old house, simple meals,
pizzas and *empanadas*, or breakfasts
with home-made bread, piano and guitar
music, popular.

Cafés

Mandarina
Obispo Trejo 171, T0351-426 4909,
www.mandarinaresto.com.ar.
Central, welcoming, leafy, lots of great
breakfasts, good for lunch and dinner.
Highly recommended.

Sorocabana
San Jerónimo 91, T0351-422 7872, Facebook. Daily 24 hrs.
Great breakfasts, popular, good views of Plaza San Martín.

Bars and clubs

Córdoba has plenty of bars and *boliches* in which to drink and dance the night away; see www.nochecordobacapital.com.ar. In **Nuevo Córdoba** head to calles Rondeau, Larrañaga and Cañada. Also try Calle Buenos Aires between Centro and Nuevo Córdoba for trendy nightspots and **El Abasto** district on the river (about 8 blocks north of Plaza San Martín) for several good, cheap places. Another popular nightlife area lies further northwest in **Chateau Carreras**.

Entertainment

See free listings in the local newspaper *La Voz del Interior* (www.vos.com.ar) for events.

Cinema
Many, including **Cineclub Municipal** (Blv San Juna 49) and **Teatro Córdoba** (27 de Abril 275), both showing independent and foreign-language films. The **Hoyts Cinema** in **Shopping Patio Olmos** (see below) shows new releases.

Music and dance
Cuarteto is a Cordobés music style with an enthusiastic following; see www.kuarteto.com for groups, news and shows. There is a free **tango** show every Sat at 2100 in Plaza San Martin and in Shopping Patio Olmos on Sun at 2000.

Theatre
Teatro del Libertador, *Av Vélez Sarsfield 365, T0351-433 2323*. A traditional and sumptuous building, with a rich history. There are several other smaller theatres.

Shopping

The main shopping area is along the pedestrian streets north of the plaza. **Shopping Patio Olmos** (Av Vélez Sarsfield and Blv San Juan, www.patioolmos.com) is the city's best mall, located in a wonderful old palace with a stylish food area. There's a weekend handicraft market at **Paseo de las Artes** (Achával Rodríguez y Belgrano, Sat-Sun 1700-2200), selling ceramics, leather, wood and metalware. At other times visit **Mundo Aborigen** (Rivadavia 155, see Facebook), an NGO promoting indigenous communities.

What to do

Language schools
Able Spanish, *Tucumán 443, T0351-422 4692*. One-on-one and group classes, daily or weekly, can help with accommodation. Also has offices in Santiago, Chile.

Tour operators
City tours
The city tourist office (see Tourist information, page 133) offers city tours on foot or bike, and recommendations for cheap guided visits to the Jesuit estancias in Jesús María and Alta Gracia. The **Municipality** (Rosario de Santa Fe 39, T0351-434 1200, www2.cordoba.gov.ar/turismo/visitas-guiadas), also runs good daily tours of religious buildings and of Córdoba Misteriosa; most are free although a charge may be made for an English-speaking guide. **Córdoba City Tour**, *T0351-15-537 8687, www2.cordoba.gov.ar/turismo/city-tour. Thu-Tue 1100, 1400, 1630, US$10 (US$7.50 for students)*. The big red sightseeing bus departs from outside the cathedral.

Provincial tours
The main destinations are in the Punilla, Calamuchita and Traslasierra valleys and all Jesuit-related places.
Explorando, *T03543-645601, www.explorandosierras.com.ar*. Tours include

birdwatching, mountain biking, horse riding and local trips.

Itatí, *27 de Abril 220, T0351-422 5020, www.itati.com.ar.* Good local company with tours throughout the province.
Nativo, *Independencia 174, T0351-424 5341, www.cordobanativoviajes.com.ar.* Huge range of tours, very professional and reliable.

Transport

Air
The airport (T0351-475 0877) has shops, post office, a good restaurant and a *casa de cambio* (Mon-Fri 1000-1500). **AR** and **LAN** have services several times a day between Córdoba's Pajas Blancas airport and **Buenos Aires** (2 hrs); **AR** also flies to **Rosario** 6 days a week. Most other major Argentine cities are served, usually via Buenos Aires, and there are direct international flights to **Peru, Brazil, Uruguay** and **Chile**, and to other countries via Buenos Aires.

Bus
The bus terminal (T0351-434 1692, www. terminaldecordoba.com) has restaurants, internet facilities, a supermarket, left-luggage lockers, a *remise* taxi desk, an ATM and a tourist office on the lower level, where the ticket offices are located. To **Buenos Aires**, several companies, 9-11 hrs, US$53-60, (*semi-cama* and *ejecutivo*). To **Salta,** 12 hrs, US$77-102. To **Mendoza**, 9-12 hrs, frequent, US$46-66. To **La Rioja**, 6-7 hrs, US$30-40. To **Catamarca**, 6 hrs, US$30. **TAC** and **Andesmar** have connecting services to several destinations in **Patagonia**. See towns below for buses to the **Sierras de Córdoba**.

Northern
Córdoba province

North from Córdoba city are two parallel chains of mountains known as the Sierras Chicas, with wonderfully wild landscapes. There are two main routes.

Head up Route 9, named by the tourist board as the Camino de la Historia, to visit Jesús María and the Jesuit estancias, the cultural highlights of Córdoba province. Stop off at the more attractive villages in the hills and stay at rural estancias, such as luxurious La Paz in Ascochinga. North of Jesús head to Laguna Mar Chiquita, a lake the size of a small sea that attracts migratory birds. Route 9, meanwhile, continues to the Reserva Natural Cerro Colorado, where there are extraordinary pre-Hispanic paintings in red rocky landscapes. Or you could follow the old Camino Real, now Route 60, northwest to quaint unspoiled villages and the remote Estancia San Pedro Viejo.

The alternative route north along the Punilla valley (Route 38) takes you through depressing built-up tourist towns, so keep going until you reach the pretty little mountain town of La Cumbre, which offers spectacular paragliding and golf. The region's most interesting rural landscapes lie to the east of Route 38 in the Sierras Chicas; explore the beautiful rolling mountains on horseback.

The real jewel in the crown of Córdoba province is the collection of fine 17th-century Jesuit estancias in the hilly, rural areas to the north of the provincial capital. Three of the oldest estancias – Estancia Jesús María, 40 km north of Córdoba, Estancia Caroya, nearby, and Santa Catalina, 20 km further northwest – lie close to what used to be the Camino Real (the 'royal road'), used by the Spanish to link Córdoba with Lima and the Alto Perú mines. Jesuit missionaries established huge, enterprising estancias in the countryside here in order to finance their educational and artistic work in Córdoba city. The elegant residences and beautiful chapels built for the priests still remain, complete with some wonderful art and walled gardens.

You could visit all three Jesuit estancias in a day's drive from Córdoba, but part of the charm of exploring the sierras is to enjoy a night or two in the area's modern-day estancias – the kind where you're offered fine wine and horse riding, rather than religious instruction. For more information, visit www.sierraschicas.net and www.cordobaciudad.com/estanciasjesuiticas.

Jesús María *Colour map 4, A3.*
The sleepy town of Jesús María (population 31,602), its avenues lined with trees, is a good base for exploring two of Córdoba's oldest Jesuit estancias. It's typical of a number of towns that developed in the late 19th century, following a wave of immigration from Friuli in the north of Italy, starting with 60 families in 1878. There's a distinctly Italian influence to the food, with some superb salamis to be found in the cafés and shops. Jesús María itself has little to offer tourists, but during the first half of January it hosts the **Festival de Doma y Folclore**; see Festivals, below. From the main road into town, Estancia Jesús María and Estancia Caroya are clearly signposted.

Estancia Jesús María
1 km northeast of the centre of Jesús María, T03525-420126, see Facebook. Tue-Fri 0900-1900, Sat-Sun, 1000-1200 and 1400-1800, US$1.75.

This is a well-conserved example of a Jesuit-built estancia, whose produce supported the schools in Córdoba. Argentina's first vineyards were created here and wine from Jesús María was reputed to have been the first American wine served to the Spanish royal family. The residence and church, built mainly in 1618, form three sides of a square enclosing a neat garden, with pleasing cloisters on two sides. The imposing façade of the church is in good condition, with tall, plaster-covered pillars contrasting with the stonework of the main building, but it's a sober affair compared with the opulent interior of the church and its finely decorated cupola. In the adjoining **Museo Jesuítico**, beautiful Cuzco-style paintings, religious objects and a curious collection of plates are on display, together with early winemaking artefacts. There are no remains of the housing for slaves and indigenous workers, or of the cultivation areas, but, with its lovely pond underneath mature trees and a small graveyard to the left of the church, the whole place is very attractive and peaceful. It's highly recommended for a few hours' visit.

You can get there by taxi, or it's an easy 15-minute walk from the Jesús María bus station: take Avenida Juan B Justo, north, turn left at Avenida Cleto Peña, cross the bridge over the river and follow a dirt road right about 300 m.

Estancia de Caroya

In the southern suburbs of Jesús María, T03525-426701. Tue-Fri 0900-1900, Sat-Sun 0900-1200 and 1700-2000, US$1.

Estancia de Caroya, dating from 1616, was the first of the Jesuit establishments to be built in the area and has an interesting history. It was acquired in 1661 by the Jesuit founder of the Colegio Convictorio de Montserrat (in Córdoba city). While its agricultural activities funded the college, it was also a holiday home for the students. Between 1814 and 1816, it was used as a weapons factory for the Army of the North fighting in the Wars of Independence, and then in 1878 the first Italian immigrants stayed here. A simpler construction than Jesús María, Estancia de Caroya consists of single-storey cloisters around a central patio, with access to kitchens, dining rooms and a simple stone chapel. The fascinating history is well presented in the displays here, including a room with artefacts from the Italian immigration. (Note that, although the tour is informative, your guide may not speak English.) Ruins of a dam and a mill can be seen in the surrounding gardens.

You can go by taxi or it's a 20-minute walk from the bus station: take Avenida Juan B Justo, south, and turn right at Avenida 28 de Julio. After 500 m, the gates of the estancia are on the left side of the road. Ask the staff at the estancia to call you a taxi to get back into town; they are very helpful.

Around Jesús María

Just south of Jesús María, **Colonia Caroya** was the heart of Italian immigration to the area, and you can taste delicious salami at any of the local restaurants. The long access road is beautifully lined by an uninterrupted avenue of mature sycamore trees, where you'll find **Bodega La Caroyense** ① *Av San Martín 2281, T03525-466270, www.lacaroyense-sa.com.ar, Mon-Fri 0700-1200 and 1500-1900, Sat-Sun 1000-1900, free,* a winery offering guided visits.

Set picturesquely among hills, 22 km west of Route 9, the attractive village of **Villa Tulumba** has hardly changed since colonial times. It's worth visiting for the beautiful 17th-century baroque tabernacle in its church, crafted in the Jesuit missions.

Estancia Santa Catalina

70 km northwest of Jesús María, T0351-15-550 3752, www.santacatalina.info. Tue-Sun 1000-1300, 1430-1900 in summer, 1000-1300 1400-1800 in winter, US$0.75.

This is the largest of the estancias, beautifully located in rolling fertile countryside northwest of Jesús María, and not to be missed. It is also the best preserved of all the estancias and the only one that remains in private hands, having the added advantage of being close to Ascochinga (see below), which has some good accommodation.

The house is still in use by the extended Díaz family as their weekend and summer home, but the church and all the outbuildings are open to the public. The guided tour (Spanish only) is included in the entrance price and provides lots of information on the way of life here, as well as allowing you to visit the seminary buildings and the second and third patios (not during January, February, July and Easter), which are rich in architectural detail.

Built in 1622, the church has the most wonderful baroque façade, with swooping curves and scrolls in white plaster, and twin bell towers. The beautifully maintained interior has a fabulous gold pulpit and retable, brought from Alto Perú, with religious figures made by indigenous craftsmen betraying certain anatomical details of their makers, such as their big knees and robust workmen's thighs. There are superb Cuzco-school paintings representing the Passion and, opposite the retable, an intriguing articulated sculpture of Jesus on the cross. This was used by the Jesuit priests as a teaching device to evangelize the indigenous peoples, and unlike most such figures, this Jesus has his eyes open: his arms could be lowered to enact scenes from his life, pre-crucifixion, and then raised, as he was mounted on the cross. It's a moving and fascinating figure.

The house has a beautiful central patio, where just three priests lived in spacious splendour, organizing a staff of 600 and a workforce of thousands of African slaves and local indigenous peoples. Santa Catalina was the most important of the estancias economically, with its 25,000 head of cattle and extensive agriculture. To the right of the church is a huge vegetable garden and, further out, a little brick building with six tiny rooms where novice priests were trained. The slaves' quarters were even more miserable and can be found on the road leading to the estancia, now converted into a restaurant. The servants for the main house were housed in the second patio, and in the third patio were wood and metal workshops. In the lovely surrounding parkland, you can see the *tajamar*, a reservoir used for the sophisticated watering system for crops.

Access to the estancia is along a 14-km dirt road branching off Route E66 to Ascochinga, 6 km west of Jesús María (signposted, 20 km in total). From Jesús María bus station, *remise* taxis make a return trip, including two hours' waiting time at the estancia. Good lunches are available at **La Ranchería de Santa Catalina** ⓘ *T03525-15-431558*, a simple rustic restaurant on the right as you approach the estancia. It also has two small guest rooms with a shared bathroom.

Ascochinga and Estancia La Paz

The upmarket little village of **Ascochinga**, 13 km west of Santa Catalina, is full of second homes for rich *Córdobes* and has a couple of shops, a part-time *locutorio*, an ACA petrol station and plenty of accommodation options. A fabulously opulent place to stay is the historical **Estancia La Paz** ⓘ *see Where to stay, below*, which was owned by President Roca from 1872 until his death in 1914, and remains almost untouched. Just try not to think about him planning the massacre of the indigenous peoples in the Conquest of the Desert when he stayed here.

Roca added the neoclassical Italianate touches to the building, and commissioned a splendid 100-ha park from Argentina's most famous landscape architect Charles Thays, whose work includes the parks at Palermo, Tucumán and Mendoza. There are grand bedrooms, with enormously high ceilings, coming directly off a long terrace with wonderful views across the huge ornamental lake where you can go rowing if the mood takes you. In the immense groves filled with exotic trees are blissful, private places to sit on the 1930s garden furniture while you order tea from the impeccable staff.

Asochinga to La Cumbre

From Asochinga a spectacular route heads over the mountains to **La Cumbre** (see page 146). The road courses through wonderful landscapes of rounded mountain ridges and deep valleys and is much loved by rally drivers and cyclists in training. This winding dirt road, full of hairpin bends, is probably best not attempted in the dark or in bad weather. Keep your speed below 40 kph, watch out for hares and perdis crossing the road, and allow at least two hours for the journey. The vegetation varies from lush subtropical woodlands to lush scrub on the summits, and there are consistently great views on a fine day.

Northeast of Córdoba *Colour map 4, A3.*

From Route 9 north of Ascochinga you can head east to Argentina's largest inland sea, the **Laguna Mar Chiquita** ('Lagoon of the Small Sea'), set on the borders of the Pampas and the Chaco, 192 km northeast of Córdoba. The lake is very shallow (maximum depth 12 m) and has no outlet into any rivers, so its size varies (from 65 km by 80 km, to 30 km by 40 km) according to rainfall patterns. At times, the water is apparently so salty you can float in it.

A reserve, called the **Reserva Natural Bañados del Río Dulce y Laguna Mar Chiquita** ⓘ *www.promarmarchiquita.com.ar*, has been created to protect the huge numbers of migratory birds that flock here in summer from the northern hemisphere. So far, over 300 species of bird have been spotted here, returning to different parts of the lagoon each year. There are also large resident populations of flamingos representing all three species extant in South America. It's the site of greatest biodiversity in the province, and is also popular for fishing *pejerrey* all year round. During the summer, human visitors flock here too, since the salty waters are used in the treatment of rheumatic ailments and skin diseases. It's a singular and spectacular landscape and, although you may feel it's not worth a big detour, if you're spending some time in the area, it would make a good relaxing day out. Park administration is in **Miramar** on the southern shore, the only settlement nearby, where there are a few hotels and campsites.

Listings Camino de la Historia and the Jesuit estancias

Tourist information

Jesús María

Tourist offices
At the bus station on Belgrano 580, T03525-443773, and on the way into town on R9, T03525-465700, www.jesusmaria.gov.ar.
Provide useful information. Ask for the leaflet *Caminos de las Estancias Jesuíticas*, which includes a handy map of the estancias in relation to Córdoba and some information on each estancia (in Spanish).

Miramar

Tourist office
Libertad 351, T03563-493777, www.turismomiramar.com.

Where to stay

Jesús María

$$$ Hotel Jesús María
Calle Almafuerte 177, T03252-445888, www.hoteljesusmaria.com.ar.

Modern hotel with rooftop pool, a small gym and spacious rooms.

$$$ La Cabaña del Tío Juan
R9, Km 755, T03525-420563, www.lacabanadeltiojuan.com.ar.
Estancia-style building with basic but appealing doubles, a small, slightly old-fashioned restaurant and a lovely pool in the gardens.

$$$-$$ Napoleón
Ameghino 211, T03525-401700, www.napoleononline.com.ar.
Modern tower block with a/c and a rooftop pool.

$$ La Gringa II
Tucumán 658, T03525-425249, 1 block across the railway lines from the bus station.
A/c, breakfast included.

Estancia Santa Catalina

$$ La Ranchería de Santa Catalina
10 m before the entrance to the estancia, on the right-hand side, T03525-15-431558.

Basic, but convenient for visiting the Jesuit estancia. 2 small rooms in the former slaves' quarters. Separate bathroom.

Ascochinga and Estancia La Paz

$$$$ Estancia La Paz
Route E66, Km 14, a few kilometres from Ascochinga, signposted, but ring for directions, T03525-492600, www.puebloestancialapaz.com.
Luxurious splendour in presidential style, but this is a warmly welcoming estancia with impeccable service and beautiful parkland. Old-fashioned opulence is combined with modern facilities such as an Olympic-sized pool, tennis courts, a spa with expert masseuse and a superb restaurant (open to the non-guests), making this a real treat. It also offers golf and horse riding. Bilingual reception staff. Recommended.

Restaurants

Jesús María

$ Fertilia
Signposted from Av San Martín 5200, Colonia Caroya, T03525-467031, www.fertilia.com.ar.
Welcoming farmers serve excellent quality salamis and ham accompanied by delicious local red wine. An unmissable treat. Buses stop on the main road, from where it's a 15-min walk along a dirt road to the farm.

$ Viejo Comedor
Tucumán 360, T03525-421601.
Popular for cheap meals.

Festivals

Jesús María
Jan **Festival de Doma y Folclore**, a popular *folclore* music and gaucho event during the 1st half of Jan, US$5. Profits benefit local schools. For more information, see www.festival.org.ar.

Transport

Jesús María
Bus
To **Córdoba** direct, 1 hr, US$3, with **Ciudad de Córdoba**, **Colonia Tirolesa**, or minibus **Fono Bus**. To **Córdoba** via Ascochinga, 2½ hrs, US$3, **Ciudad de Córdoba**. To **Colonia Caroya**, US$0.75, with **Ciudad de Córdoba** or **Colonia Tirolesa**.

Northeast of Córdoba
Bus
Laguna Mar Chiquita to **Córdoba**, **Expreso Ciudad de San Francisco** (from **Miramar**), 3½ hrs, US$3; and **Transportes Morteros** (from **Balnearia**), 3 hrs, US$4.

Córdoba Norteña

nature and tranquility at the edge of the province

If you're enjoying getting off the beaten track and want to see where the Camino Real leads, keep going northwest from Jesús María along Route 60 into the northernmost extreme of the province. In Deán Funes (118 km from Córdoba), you'll find a couple of decent hotels and plenty of places to eat.

From Deán Funes head east on provincial road 16 to find **San Pedro Viejo** ① *www.sanpedroviejo.com.ar*. This tiny hamlet has a beautiful little church, built in adobe with a squat square bell tower, and an estancia, where you can stay for a few nights to completely unwind and explore the rolling land on foot or horseback. San Pedro Viejo has a history: it was an important staging post on the royal road between the Río de la Plata and Perú, and such illustrious figures as General San Martín and President Belgrano stayed in the building which is now a chic and rustic boutique hotel.

Reserva Cultural y Natural Cerro Colorado

www.cba.gov.ar/reserva-cultural-y-natural-cerro-colorado. Tue-Sun 0900-1300 and 1600-2000. The park can only be visited as part of a guided tour which lasts 1½ hrs and is included in the entry.

Some 104 km north of Jesús María, reached by an unpaved road (12 km) that branches off Route 9 at Santa Elena (see Transport, page 144), is this provincial park covering 3000 ha of rocky hills and woodlands protecting some 35,000 rock paintings in around 200 sites, some of them underground. It's thought that they were painted by the indigenous Comechingones people sometime between the 10th century and the arrival of the Spanish roughly 600 years later. The strikingly bold paintings, in red, black and white, portray animals and plants, hunting scenes, magic rituals and dancing; even battles against the Spanish, mounted on horseback. There are lots of more enigmatic paintings with geometric patterns, open to wildly imaginative interpretations.

There are also two small museums. **Museo Arqueológico** ① *daily 1000-1700 (closes early on Mon)*, at the foot of Cerro Intihuasi, has information on the site itself. **Museo Atahualpa and Yupanqui** ① *T0351-15-6685 3900, www.fundacionyupanqui.com.ar, daily 0900-1300 and 1600-2000, US$2.75,* at the end of the winding road to Agua Escondida, also offers guided tours. The vegetation is interesting with lots of ancient algarrobo trees, molles and a rare *mato* forest in the park, where you can also spot small armadillos.

There's a hotel and a few *cabaña* complexes nearby in the sprawling villages at the foot of the Cerro, and plenty of handicrafts for sale. A useful website is www.cerrocolorado. infoturis.com.ar (in Spanish).

Listings Córdoba Norteña

Tourist information

Deán Funes

Tourist office
Sáenz Peña 466, T03521-420020.

Where to stay

San Pedro Viejo

$$$$ Estancia San Pedro Viejo
Ruta Provincial 18, San Pedro Norte, San Pedro Viejo, T0351-15-543 1797, www.sanpedroviejo.com.ar.
A quaint, historical post house converted into a chic boutique hotel with 1-m-thick walls, old fireplaces, and ancient trees near a charming lake. The 6 bedrooms are furnished with antiques, and some have a jacuzzi. There's great food and wines, relaxing walks and horse riding in the nearby hills. A lovely retreat. Price is for full board.

Reserva Cultural y Natural Cerro Colorado

There are several places to stay in the hamlets around the foot of the *cerro*, and you can also stay with local families if the hotel is full. The tourist office produces a helpful free leaflet, *El Chasqui de Cerro Colorado*, available in Córdoba city before you set off. A few to try (all **$$**) are **Cerro Colorado** (T03522-1564 8990, www.hotelcerrocolorado.com); **Complejo Argañaraz** (T0351-15-697 7193); and **La Italiana** (T0351-15-687 0445, www. cab-laitaliana.neositios.com).

Restaurants

Reserva Cultural y Natural Cerro Colorado

$ Inti Huasi
In the visitor centre for Córdoba Ambiente agency.
More of a café with food.

**Reserva Cultural y Natural Cerro
Colorado**
Bus
Ciudad de Córdoba, T0351-424 0048, and
Fonobus go to **Córdoba** (Ciudad de

Córdoba leaves from Córdoba for Cerro
Colorado on Sat at 0730 and returns on Sun at
1945, 3½ hrs, US$5.50. There are also combis
to **Santa Elena** with **El Tatú**, T0351-423 6335.

Punilla Valley to La Cumbre

weekend retreats, folklore … and alien spotting

The Punilla Valley, situated between the Sierras Chicas to the east and the Sierra
Grande to the west, was the first area of the sierras to become populated by
weekend and summer visitors from the cities of Córdoba and Buenos Aires back in
the 1920s. Sadly, these once-idyllic weekend retreats have now developed into one
long string of built-up urban areas alongside Route 38: Villa Carlos Paz, Cosquín,
Valle Hermoso and La Falda. There's no real reason to stop, unless you're keen to
visit Cosquín's famous *folclore* music festival, which is held every year in January
and attracts the country's best musicians and budding talent.

Any time of the year, it is preferable to head
straight for **La Cumbre** further north (see
page 146), where there's a more civilized
pace of life and plenty of appealing places
to stay in this pretty hillside town. A brief
description of the main Punilla Valley
towns is followed by a more complete
description of La Cumbre.

Tip...

Avoid the Argentine holiday periods of
January, February and Easter, when the
whole of Punilla Valley is unbearably busy.

Villa Carlos Paz and around *Colour map 4, A2.*
Thirty-five kilometres west of Córdoba, ghastly Villa Carlos Paz (population 75,315) is
a large and overpopulated resort, crammed with hotels and brimming with Argentine
tourists in summer. There are lots of activities on offer and a chairlift runs from the
Complejo Aerosilla to the summit of the Cerro de la Cruz, but your only reason to come
here would be if everywhere else is full, or to use it as a base for the area's superb trekking.
There are plenty of hotels, and some quieter places to bathe and hang out, such as the
balnearios along Río San Antonio, and **Villa Las Jarillas**, 15 km south of town.
    Villa Carlos Paz is on the road to Traslasierra further west (see page 161), but if you're not
going that far and are into hiking or climbing, it's worth heading for **Cerro Los Gigantes**
(2374 m), 39 km west of Villa Carlos Paz, with its spectacular views and challenging walks.
To get there take the unpaved Route 28 via **Tanti** over the Pampa de San Luis towards
Salsacate. Los Gigantes is signposted at Km 30, where you turn off left; here you'll find the
nearest base for climbing the granite massif. By public transport, you'll need to get a local
bus from Villa Carlos Paz to Tanti, and from there to Los Gigantes. Daily buses to Salsacate
stop at Los Gigantes.

Cosquín *Colour map 4, A2.*
Twenty kilometres north of Carlos Paz, Cosquín (population 40,685) is not an attractive
town, but its setting on the banks of the wide Río Cosquín gives it several *balnearios*

ON THE ROAD
★ Sierras Chicas and Estancia Los Potreros

To really get into the wild, remote country that is the Sierras Chicas, you need to spend a few nights away from civilization, and the best way to do this is to stay at an estancia such as Estancia Los Potreros, an exclusive 2500-ha working cattle farm in the wild and scenic Córdoba hills. One of Argentina's finest riding estancias, it is situated in the middle of its own range of peaks, but is easily accessible, and is just an hour from Córdoba airport. It is owned and run by the Anglo-Argentine Begg family, who were brought up on this land and breed fine horses. They offer a wonderful mixture of real gaucho Argentine ranch culture and British hospitality in keeping with a time past. If you're not a rider, you can walk, birdwatch, swim or simply relax, and enjoy the peace and immense vistas. If you'd like to learn to ride, the Beggs are the most patient teachers and the horses are very tame, impeccably trained and sure-footed.

There's a three-night minimum stay which allows you to get a feel for the place, with delicious food and wine all included; for those with more time, a riding tour of the sierras taking several days can be arranged. As well as enjoying spectacular scenery, a longer tour allows you to explore remote mountain villages with their tiny churches and schools, and stay at other mountain estancias in the region, gaining invaluable insights into the local culture and communities that you could never otherwise access. This is an unique way to experience the Sierras de Córdoba.

Estancia Los Potreros, Sierras Chicas, Casilla de Correo 64, 5111 Río Ceballos, T011-6091 2692, www.estancialospotreros.com. To get there, either take a bus to the nearest town, Río Ceballos, or the managers, Kevin and Louisa, will arrange a taxi from Córdoba city or airport (one hour).

ESTANCIA LOS POTREROS, CÓRDOBA, ARGENTINA
A TRUE ESTANCIA EXPERIENCE

WWW.ESTANCIALOSPOTREROS.COM

(swimming areas), of which **Pan de Azúcar** is the quietest option. Cosquín is also known as the national *folclore* capital, and Argentina's most important *folclore* festival is held here in the last two weeks of January. Also, an increasingly popular rock festival is held here in early February, so accommodation is almost impossible to find between 10 January and 10 February. See Festivals, page 149.

The country's most famous bands and singers play every night on **Plaza Próspero Molina**, and there are plentiful food and handicrafts stalls.

La Falda and around *Colour map 4, A2.*

La Falda (population 16,000), 20 km north of Cosquín, is another seething and tawdry tourist town, once the destination of Argentina's wealthy and influential who all stayed at the magnificent **Hotel Edén**. The hotel is now sadly in ruins but the bar gives you a flavour of its former grandeur, with an exhibition of old photographs. The town is known for its nightlife – bars and casinos abound – but it's really a place to avoid unless you want to use it as a base for hiking in the surrounding hills and Pampas.

The sierras to the east of La Falda are a good place for hiking. **Cerro La Banderita** (1350 m), which is also popular with paragliders, is a 1½-hour walk from the town centre and provides panoramic views of the valley: leave from the left side of Hotel Edén and take the street called Austria. Ask at tourist office for a map and directions. From La Falda you could also head out west to the Pampas: an 80-km rough, winding road goes to La Higuera, on the west side of the Cumbres de Gaspar. It crosses the vast **Pampa de Olaén**, a grass-covered plateau at 1100 m, where you'll find the tiny Capilla de Santa Bárbara (1750), 20 km from La Falda, and waterfalls Cascadas de Olaén, 2 km south of the chapel. There are more beautiful rivers and waterfalls at **Río Pintos** (26 km from La Falda) and **Characato** (36 km from La Falda). Jesuit **Estancia La Candelaria** lies further along this road, 53 km west of La Falda.

> **Tip...**
> The mountains east of La Falda are great for cycling, but make sure you take water with you.

La Cumbre and around *Colour map 4, A2.*

By far the most attractive town in this whole area, La Cumbre (population 9500) sits at the highest point of the Punilla Valley at 1141 m and is only 1½-hour's drive from Córdoba, if you head straight here without stopping on the way. Unlike the rest of the valley, this friendly little town still feels authentic and the town centre bustles busily just before midday. There are some classy shops, as well as lots of places to eat and a couple of tea rooms selling superb cakes. It was founded by the British engineers and workers who built the railway here in 1900 and who have given the place its distinctive flavour, with trees lining the avenues in the attractive residential area to the east of town, where you'll find the best hotels.

Golf Club La Cumbre ① *T03548-452283, www.lacumbregolf.com.ar, US$18-20 for a round,* to the southeast of town, was built 90 years ago and is beautifully landscaped with mature trees and a quaint Tudor-style clubhouse. Further east you'll find lots of craftsmen selling their wares.

For the more adventurous, there's excellent paragliding nearby in the world-renowned paragliding site of ★ **Cuchi Corral** 9 km southwest of the town on an unpaved road (see What to do, page 149). There are also plenty of places to walk in the mountains, with access from residential areas **Cruz Chica** and **Cruz Grande**, on the road to **Los Cocos**.

As a visitor to Argentina, you may have noticed the national obsession with *alfajores*, the soft cakey biscuits made of a double layer of cornflour sponge, and sandwiched with *dulce de leche*. The chocolate-covered ones from **Havanna** *alfajores* shops in any town centre are particularly recommended. While you're in La Cumbre, you could visit the famous *alfajores* factory, **Estancia El Rosario** ⓘ *R66, 5 km east of town, T03548-451257, www.estanciaelrosario.com.ar, Mon-Fri 1000-1900*, to see them being made and try a fine specimen or three. The factory has been operating since 1924 and was, for many years, a major tourist attraction. These days there are still free guided visits to the small factory where fruit preserves and other sweet delicacies are also made.

Located 11 km from La Cumbre is the **Centro de Rescate Rehabilitación y Conservación de Primates (Center for Rescue, Rehabilitacion and Care of Primates)** ⓘ *www. proyectocaraya.com.ar, daily 1000-1630, US$10 (US$3.50 for children)*, where visitors can see a wide array of howler monkeys in their natural environment. Guided tours are available. To get there take a taxi from La Cumbre (US$14).

Head east from the golf course along Route 66 for the spectacular mountain crossing that leads to Ascochinga (for a route description, see page 140). North of La Cumbre, there are more hotels in the lovely leafy residential areas of Cruz Chica, Cruz Grande and Los Cocos. Further along this picturesque road are two popular places for families: **El Descanso**, with its well-designed garden and maze, and **Complejo Aerosilla** (www. aerosilla.com), with a chairlift to the nearby hills (US$8), an aquarium and toboggans.

Capilla del Monte and around *Colour map 4, A2.*
Capilla del Monte (population 17,000) is a quiet town which offers a base for good trekking and paragliding, and for exploring nearby rock formations at Agua de los Palos. The landscape is hilly and scrubby, with places rather reminiscent of the lunar landscapes in Ischigualasto: the Valle de la Luna in San Juan (see page 218). The town is overlooked by dramatic **Cerro Uritorco** (1979 m), which you can climb: head 3 km east of town and it's another 5 km to the summit, though be warned that this is a four-hour climb each way with no shade (US$13.50 entry).

UFO-spotters flock to the amazing landscape of **Quebrada de la Luna**, **Los Terrones** and **Parque Natural Ongamira**, where there are curious rock formations. Ask in the tourist office for more information and for a *remise* to take you there. The area is popular for 'mystical tourism' and holds an annual Festival Alienígena; see Festivals, page 149.

Listings Punilla Valley to La Cumbre

Tourist information

Villa Carlos Paz
See www.villacarlospaz.com and www. villacarlospaz.gov.ar (both in Spanish) for more information on the area.

Municipal tourist office
Av San Martín 400, T0810-888 2729, www.villacarlospaz.gov.ar.

Cosquín

Tourist office
Av San Martín 590, Plaza Nacional del Folclore, T03541-454644, www.cosquinturismo.gob.ar.

La Falda

Tourist office
Av Edén 93, T03548-423007, www.turismolafalda.gob.ar.

La Cumbre

See also www.lacumbre.gob.ar (in English) and www.alacumbre.com.ar and (in Spanish).

Tourist office

Av Caraffa 300, in the old train station, T03548-452966. Daily from early morning until late in the evening.
Many of the friendly staff speak English. They'll give you a very helpful map listing all the hotels and restaurants.

Capilla del Monte

Tourist office

RN 38 y F Alcorta, at the end of the Diagonal Buenos Aires, T482200, www. capilladelmonte.gov.ar. Daily 0830-2030.

Where to stay

Cosquín

$$$ La Puerta del Sol
Perón 820, T03541-452045, www. lapuertadelsolhotel.com.ar.
A decent choice, pool, car hire, half board available. **$$$$** in high season.

$$ Siempreverde
Santa Fe 525, behind Plaza Molina, T03541-450093, www.hosteriasiempreverde.com.
Spotless, comfortable place, with a welcoming and informative owner. Some rooms are small. There's a gorgeous garden.

La Falda and around

All hotels are full in Dec-Feb.

$$$ L'Hirondelle
Av Edén 861, T03548-422825, www.lhirondellehostal.com.
Lovely building, some rooms retain their original parquet floor and there's a large garden with a pool. Welcoming owners.

$$ La Asturiana
Av Edén 835, T03548-422923.
Simple, comfortable rooms.
Pool and a superb breakfast.

La Cumbre and around

There are plenty of hotels, and *cabañas* here are high quality and in attractive settings, ideal for larger groups who want the flexibility of self-catering. **Cruz Chica** is a lovely area to stay, but you'll need a car or taxi to get there.

$$ Hotel La Viña
Caraffa 48, T03548-451388, www.hotellavina.com.ar.
A good budget option, with cosy flowery rooms, a large pool and pleasant gardens.

$ pp Hostel La Cumbre
Av San Martín 282, T03548-451368, www.hostellacumbre.com.
Dorms, rooms for up to 6 and doubles (**$$**). Family-owned, historic building with garden and pool, occasional *asados*, laundry, information and activities. Recommended.

Capilla del Monte and around

See www.capilladelmonte.gov.ar for more listings.

$$$ Montecassino
La Pampa 107, T03548-482572, www.hotelmontecassino.com.ar.
Beautiful building from 1901, with lovely rooms, cable TV, jacuzzi and pool with stunning views.

$$ Petit Sierras
Pueyrredón y Salta, T03548-481667, www.hotelpetitsierras.com.
Renovated hotel with comfortable rooms. The owners run the restaurant **Zarzamora** (**$$**), at the access to town (discounts and free transport for guests).

Restaurants

Cosquín

$$ La Encrucijada del Supaj-Ñuñú
On the way to the Cerro Pan de Azúcar, T03541-15-606033, www.laencrucijada.com.ar.
Pleasant restaurant, tea house and brewery, serving meals, fondue, cakes or sandwiches at moderate prices.

La Falda and around

$ Pachamama
Av Edén 127.
If you're tired of eating beef, there is a health food shop with a few neat tables at the back where you can have cheap organic vegetable pies, or wholemeal pizzas and *empanadas*.

La Cumbre and around

$$ La Casona del Toboso
Belgrano 349, T03548-451436.
Also highly recommended for excellent food across a wide menu, including *parrilla*.

$ Dani Cheff
Opposite the tourist office, Av Caraffa and Belgrano, T03548-451379.
The best place for afternoon tea, serves delicious pastries and cakes, and there's a lively buzz mid-morning when locals flock there.

Festivals

Cosquín
Jan Festival Nacional del Folclore, www.aquicosquin.org (in Spanish). Cosquín's famous music festival attracts the country's best musicians and budding talent. In the last 2 weeks of Jan, the country's most famous bands and singers play every night on Plaza Próspero Molina.
Feb Cosquín Rock, www.cosquinrock.net. Showcases national rock singers and groups, as well as international rock bands from Spanish-speaking countries.

Capilla del Monte
Feb Festival Alienígena, a celebration of all things extra-terrestrial, with a dressing-up competition and other events.

What to do

La Falda and around
Tour operators
Turismo Talampaya, *T03548-470412, turismotalampaya@yahoo.com.ar*. Run by Teresa Pagni who guides 4WD full-day trips to the Pampa de Olaen and Jesuit estancia La Candelaria.

La Cumbre and around
Golf
Golf Club La Cumbre, *Belgrano 1091, T03548-452284, www.lacumbregolf.com.ar*. Follow Belgrano from the town centre, opposite the tourist office, to reach the corner of the golf course, then turn left onto Posadas. Attractive 18-hole golf course, with caddies and coaching. There's also a putting green and an Olympic-sized pool.

Horse riding
Chachito Silva, *T03548-451703*. Hires horses and offers half-day, 1- and 2-day guided horse riding trips to the sierras and Candonga.
La Granja de los Gringos, *R38, T03548-566389, www.cordobaserrana.com.ar/lacumbre/cabalgatas.htm*. Guided horse rides by the hour, day or for multiple days.

Paragliding
Escuela de Parapentes, *Ruta 38, Km 65, T03548-15 637130, www.cordobaserrana.com.ar/parapente.htm*. Several local companies offer flights, which start at US$100 for your first flight, the *Vuelo Bautismo*, 20 mins, accompanied by a trained paragliding instructor in tandem.

Tour operators
Estancia Puesto Viejo, *T03548-15-566504, www.estanciapuestoviejo.com*. Lots of outdoor activities (including trekking, riding, parapenting and birdwatching), at a remote estancia northwest of La Cumbre.

Trekking
Escuela de Montaña y Escalada, *T03548-451393, jorgemallory@yahoo.com*. Run by Jorge González, for parapenting, but also climbing and mountain trekking courses and trips, eg to the Cascada de los 70 Pies in Cruz Grande. Equipment hire.

Capilla del Monte and around
Cycling
Claudio, *Deán Funes 567*. Mountain bike hire.

Transport

Cosquín
Bus
The bus terminal is at Perón and Salta.
Ciudad de Córdoba, **Sarmiento** and **TAC**
run frequent buses to **Córdoba**, 1-1½ hrs,
US$3.75, and along the **Punilla Valley** to
La Falda, US$1.75; to **La Cumbre** US$2.50;
to **Capilla del Monte** US$3.50. Several
minibuses do the same route.

Train
A tourist **Tren de las Sierras** runs 52 km
between Cosquín and **Alta Córdoba**,
via **La Calera**, 2 a day Mon-Fri, 3 a day
Sat, Sun, 2¼ hrs, US$0.50. See www.
ferrocentralsa.com.ar.

La Falda
Bus
The bus terminal is at Av Buenos Aires y
Chubut, a 5-min walk north of Av Edén.
Chevallier, **General Urquiza** and **Sierras
de Córdoba** go daily to **Buenos Aires**
(US$57-64) and to several other domestic
destinations. **Ciudad de Córdoba** and
Sarmiento run frequent buses to **Córdoba**,
US$5, and along the **Punilla Valley** to
Cosquín, US$1.75; to **La Cumbre**, US$2.50;
to **Capilla del Monte**, US$1.50. Several
minibuses also travel the same route.

Remise taxis
Casa Blanca, 9 de Julio 541, T03548-422 912.

La Cumbre and around
Bus
The bus terminal is at Juan José Valle and
Ruznak, around the corner from the tourist
office (see Tourist information, page 148).
 Daily buses to **Buenos Aires** with **General
Urquiza/Sierras de Córdoba**, T03548-
452400, and others, 11 hrs, US$58-82. To
Córdoba, Ciudad de Córdoba, T03548-
452442, and **La Calera**, T03548-452300, US$7.

Car hire
Reynas, 25 de Mayo 448, T03548-452107,
gustavobecker2003@hotmail.com. Ask for
a discount if you hire for several days. Bring
credit card and passport.

Taxis
Auto Remis, López and Planes 321, T03548-
451800, T0800-444 7040; **Remis Victoria**,
25 de Mayo 272, T03548-452150.

Capilla del Monte and around
Bus
Daily buses to **Buenos Aires**, 12 hrs, US$58-
86, and to **Córdoba**, US$8.50. **Ciudad de
Córdoba** and **La Calera** and minibuses
El Serra run services along the **Punilla
valley**. Twice a day, **Ciudad de Córdoba** goes
to **Traslasierra Valley** via Cruz del Eje.

Remise taxis
El Cerro, Pueyrredón 426, T03548-482300.

Southern Córdoba province:
Calamuchita Valley

South of Córdoba, there's another fascinating and well-preserved Jesuit estancia in the unprepossessing town of Alta Gracia, which is the gateway to a picturesque hilly area between the high peaks of the Sierra Grande and Sierra de Comechingones. Fans of that great 20th-century icon Ernesto 'Che' Guevara will also want to visit his childhood home. Further south still, there's superb walking in the wooded countryside near the quaint Germanic town of Villa General Belgrano and, prettier still, the mountain town, La Cumbrecita. It's well worth spending two or three days combining the Jesuit heritage with some walking or relaxing in the hills to understand the essence of Córdoba's history and landscapes.

The great attraction of Alta Gracia (population 48,335) is the wonderful 17th-century Estancia Jesuítica Alta Gracia (see below), whose church, residential buildings and small lake make a splendid hilltop centre to the town, around the scrappy Plaza Solares. The rather tawdry main commercial area spills down Belgrano, with everything you need, but no charm whatsoever. Head instead to the pretty residential area west of centre El Alto, where the most appealing restaurants are to be found. El Alto was built when the British came here to build the housing which the locals describe as typically 'British': two stories with corrugated-iron roofs.

The rather grand **Hotel Sierras** (www.hojoar.com), stylishly built in 1907 as Argentina's first casino, was made popular by the rich upper classes who flocked to the area for the summer in the 1920s when Alta Gracia was in its heyday. It has been restored and now is a four-star hotel and casino. There's also an attractive golf course in this area, whose club has one of the town's best restaurants, open to non-members (see page 154). All this aristocratic pleasure might sound an unlikely environment for Ernesto 'Che' Guevara to have grown up in, but his family house can now be visited; see the **Museo Casa de Ernesto 'Che' Guevara**, below.

Estancia Jesuítica Alta Gracia and Museo Casa de Virrey Liniers

Plaza Solares, Av Padre Viera 41, T03547-421303, www.museoliniers.org.ar. Summer Tue-Fri 0900-1300 and 1500-1900, Sat-Sun 0930-1230 and 1530-1830. Closed 1 Jan, 1 May and 25 Dec. US$1.25, free Wed, excellent guided visits included in the price but phone in advance for English tours. There are also informative laminated cards in several languages in each room.

Part of the same development of Jesuit establishments as Jesús María and Santa Catalina (see pages 138 and 139), Alta Gracia is a fascinating testimony to the Jesuits' culture, and the entire estancia is now an excellent museum. If you visit only one Jesuit estancia in Córdoba, make it this one. There's added interest in the life of Viceroy Liniers, who owned the house from 1810.

Alta Gracia dates from 1643, when Córdoba was the capital of the Jesuit province of Paraguay, and this estancia – one of their most prosperous rural establishments – was built to fund the religious education of their young men in the Colegio Maximo in Córdoba city. The centre comprised a **Residence** (now a museum), the **Obraje** (industrial workshops), the **Ranchería** (where the slaves lived), the **Tajamar** (built by the Jesuits as a water reservoir), the **watermill** and the **church** (open only for Mass). This latter was started in 1659 and completed only in 1723. It has a splendid baroque façade and a grand cupola, which is the only part that has been renovated. The rest is all now sadly a little dilapidated, but it's the only Jesuit church that still functions today as the parish church.

The Jesuits built their ambitious project in two stages: first they lived in an adobe building while the main house was constructed of brick. This first building then became the *herrería* (smithy), where iron was smelted with the aid of bellows, and workers made all the tools they needed for construction. There are impressive locks, keys and nails on display, testimony to their fine metalworking skills. Just three Jesuit priests lived in the Residence, which was built on two floors around an enclosed patio; the lower floor was used only for storage. All the workers lived outside the estancia, but 310 African slaves lived on the premises in the Ranchería. They were of great importance to the Jesuits, as they were used as overseers in the ranches, and did carpentry, brickwork, and blacksmithing. In the Obraje, African women and girls learned to spin and knit. The Jesuits built canals to bring water here to the Tajamar, a large reservoir outside the estancia, which supplied them with the power to run a flour mill (*molino*), which was built in the wall of the reservoir; it's now ruined, but there is a good model upstairs in the Residence. There are also some original clay tiles on display here that were moulded on the thighs of the slaves.

Part of the Jesuits' evangelizing technique included using music, and their exquisite little organ can be seen here, made in the Guaraní missions further northeast. There are some fine paintings and sculptures on display, made by the local population under the supervision of the Jesuit priests – beautiful in their simplicity. Even the toilets are impressive, complete with running water to wash the waste away, half of it channelled to be used in the kitchen garden. All the wooden doors and windows are original, and the overall impression is of sophisticated organization and pleasing aesthetics. A couple of rooms are filled with 18th- and 19th-century original furniture from Liniers' family, less interesting, but evocative of the life of a Spanish Viceroy of the Río de la Plata from 1807 to 1809.

Museo Casa de Ernesto 'Che' Guevara

Avellaneda 501, T03547 428579. Tue-Sun 0900-1845, Mon 1400-1845, US$5 (US$3 for students). A triple pass is available for US$6 for entry to Casa de 'Che' Guevara, Museo de Falla (see below) and the Museo de Arte Gabriel Dubois, the famed French sculptor who lived in Alta Gracia from 1932 until his death in 1968. To get to the Casa de 'Che' Guevara, from the Sierras Hotel go north along Vélez Sarsfield, which becomes Quintana, and turn left on to Avellaneda.

Guevara's parents moved to Alta Gracia when the young revolutionary was four years old, hoping that the dry climate here would help the boy's asthma. They lived in this pleasant middle-class neighbourhood for 12 years. Unfortunately, the museum inside his old family home is utterly disappointing and retains few relics of Guevara's upbringing. The biographical information is scant, the photographs are all photocopies and there is no intelligent thesis behind the displays. Cheap quality T-shirts are on sale. For more information on 'Che', see box, page 327.

Among the limited details about his early years, you will learn that his mother educated him at home, and that asthma should have prevented him from being too athletic, but he played rugby and golf, was a keen cyclist and had a wide group of friends, among whom he was known

> **Tip...**
> It's best to bring a biography of Guevara with you, since the books on sale are in Spanish only.

as being fair-minded and kind to the poor. His motorcycle trips around Argentina in 1951-1952 and 1953-1956 are well documented in his own book *The Motorcycle Diaries*, which is recommended reading. There are two videos shown here, a 10-minute extract of a longer documentary, which is almost unintelligible, in Spanish with English subtitles, and a short introductory documentary, with interviews of some friends and teachers from his childhood and the family's former maid. The best photos are in the video room, unfortunately, so you'll have to scoot around them fast between screenings of the videos.

Around Alta Gracia

If you've time and energy for more museums, you might be interested in **Museo Manuel de Falla** ⓘ *Carlos Pellegrini 1011, T03547-429292, museomanueldefalla@altagracia.gov.ar, Mon 1400-1830, Tue-Sun 0900-1845, US$1.25, see under Museo Casa de 'Che' Guevara, above,* the charming home of the famous Spanish composer for the last four years of his life from 1942 to 1946. It's an attractive Spanish-style house with great views from its beautiful garden. There are concerts from April to November, and the **Festival de Falla** in November attracts some fine musicians.

There's an easy 5-km walk to **Los Paredones**, with the remains of a Jesuit mill in a rocky section of the river. To get there, follow Avenida Sarmiento to the west and cross the river, passing the bus station on your left. On the way is the **Gruta de Lourdes**, where, every 11 February, hundreds of pilgrims arrive on foot from Córdoba city. Nearby lies the **Laguna Azul**, a small lake surrounded by impressive cliffs. From Alta Gracia take Avenida Sarmiento, turn right at Vélez Sarsfield and left at Carlos Pellegrini until the end of the road, where you turn right and follow the road, passing Parque García Lorca on your left.

Some 21 km northwest of Alta Gracia is the **Observatorio Bosque Alegre** ⓘ *www.oac. uncor.edu, summer Sat-Sun 1100-1300 and 1500-1800 (Fri visits to the observatory from 1900-2200), US$2,* built in 1942 for astrophysics research. At 1250 m, it offers good views over Alta Gracia, Córdoba and the Sierra Grande. Visits are guided by astronomers.

Listings Alta Gracia and around

Tourist information

Alta Gracia

Tourist information
El Molino y Av del Tajamar, T03547-428128, www.altagracia.gov.ar. Mon-Fri 0700-2000, Sat-Sun 0800-2000.
At the base of the clock tower on the corner of the Jesuit reservoir, the *tajamar*. Staff don't speak much English but are helpful and will give you a map and a useful *Guía Turística*. There's also a tourist information point in the bus terminal (Mon-Fri 0800-1400).

Where to stay

Alta Gracia

$$$$-$$$ El Potrerillo de Larreta
On the road to Los Paredones, 3 km from Alta Gracia, T03547-439033, www.potrerillodelarreta.com.
Old-fashioned, fabulous 1918 resort and country club in gorgeous gardens with wonderful views. There are tennis courts,

an 18-hole golf course and a swimming pool. Great service.

$$$ 279 Boutique Bed + Breakfast
Giorello 279, T03547-15459493, www.279altagracia.com.
This small, immaculate bed and breakfast is the best place to stay in town. A short stroll to the centre of town, in a quiet location. Recommended.

$ pp Alta Gracia Hostel
Paraguay 218, T03547-428810, www.altagraciahostel.com.ar.
Family-run hostel, with dorm beds (US$13, breakfast extra), good bathrooms and kitchen. 3 blocks from the main street. Highly recommended.

Restaurants

Alta Gracia

$$ Alta Gracia Golf Club
Av Carlos Pellegrini 1000, T03547-422922, www.altagraciagolf.com.ar.

Superb food in elegant surroundings in this charming neighbourhood golf club (see What to, below), with the added advantage that you can watch the machinations of small town upper echelons social life unfold around you. Recommended.

$ Hispania
Urquiza y Mateo Beres, T03547-426772.
Excellent restaurant serving fish and seafood, including paella and *fideuba*, with sangría and occasionally gazpacho. Desserts such as *crema catalana* are fabulous. It gets busy, so try to make a reservation.

$ Leyendas
Blv Pellegrini 797, T03547-429042.
This American-style, sport-inspired bar has cosy nooks to sit in, and really good hamburgers and snacks. A buzzing atmosphere and friendly, welcoming staff. Recommended.

Festivals

Alta Gracia
Dec Festival de Falla.

What to do

Alta Gracia
Golf
Alta Gracia Golf Club, *see Restaurants, above.*
Beautifully landscaped 9-hole golf course, with a fine restaurant.

Sky diving
Paracaidismo, *Aero Club de Alta Gracia, Route C45, T0351-15-348 7628, www. paracaidismo-ag.com.* Sky diving in tandem and courses.

Transport

Alta Gracia
Bus
For **Villa General Belgrano** and other towns in Calamuchita valley, buses stop at the bus terminal (T03547-428127, 10 blocks from the centre on the river at Butori and Perón 1977) and at the El Crucero roundabout, a 30-min walk from centre. To **Córdoba**, buses leave every 15 mins, 1 hr, US$2, **Empresa La Serranita** T03547-432588; **Sarmiento** T03547-432588; **Sierras de Calamuchita**, T800-555 3928, www.sierrasdecalamuchita.com. To **Villa Carlos Paz**, 1 hr, US$2, **Sarmiento**. To **Villa General Belgrano**, 1 hr, US$2, **Sierras de Calamuchita**. To **Buenos Aires**, 10-11 hrs, US$49-58, **TUS**, T03547-429370, www.tus. com.ar; **San Juan Mar del Plata**, T0800 999 7272, www.sanjuanmardelplata.com.ar.

Car hire
Rodar Rent a Car, T03547-427164, www.autosrodar.com.ar.

★ Villa General Belgrano *Colour map 4, A2.*

a slice of Germany in Argentina

Imagine a German theme park, Disneyland-style, with *bierkellers* and chocolate shops, carved wooden signposts and cute Alpine architecture, and you get an idea of what the centre of Villa General Belgrano (population 6500) is like. It's a pretty mountain town, with wooded avenues and wonderful views of the sierras beyond. It's a lovely place to spend a few days.

The town was founded in 1932 when two German immigrants bought land and sold it off through advertisements in the German newspapers, with the intention of

Tip...
You can go to the top of the tower above the tourist office for amazing views of the surrounding hills.

ON THE ROAD

Graf Spee

The famous *Graf Spee* was a German 'pocket' battleship, successful because she was of cruiser size and speed, but with the fire power of a battleship. Early in the Second World War, in 1939, the *Graf Spee* sank nine merchant ships in the Atlantic before being cornered outside Uruguay on 13 December by three Allied cruisers sent to find and destroy her. After the 14-hour Battle of the River Plate, in which one British ship was badly damaged, the *Graf Spee's* commander, Captain Hans Langsdorff, retreated into the neutral port of Montevideo, where he landed most of his crew, and the 36 dead German crewmen were buried. Under British pressure, the Uruguayan government, which operated the neutral harbour, granted Langsdorff just two days to repair his ship, and on 17 December the *Graf Spee* sailed out to sea. Crowds lined the shore expecting to see another battle, but watched the vessel sink within minutes. All the remaining crew and 50 captured British seamen on board were rescued. Langsdorff had been trapped into believing that a superior British force was waiting for him over the horizon, and Hitler had given him the order to scuttle the vessel rather than allow it to be captured. Two days later in Buenos Aires, Langsdorff wrapped himself in the flag of the Imperial German Navy and committed suicide.

Most of the crew were interned in Argentina and warmly welcomed by the German community of Buenos Aires, but British pressure forced the Argentine government to disperse them. In Mendoza, they were stoned by the locals and beaten up by the police. In Córdoba they were welcomed by the governor, while the German embassy tried to enforce military discipline and prevent the men from getting too friendly with local women.

In 1944, the US and British governments demanded the repatriation of all the men to Germany. Nearly 200 managed to avoid this by marrying Argentine women, and another 75 escaped: after six years in Argentina, many had no wish to return to a country shattered by defeat. German communities created a distinctive culture in many areas, none more so than Villa General Belgrano in Córdoba, with its German architecture, beer festival and superb chocolate and pastries, where many members of the *Graf Spee* crew made their homes. Meanwhile the carcass of the *Graf Spee*, once visible above the sea line, has been lying on the sea floor for some six decades.

starting a German colony. Its German character was boosted by the arrival of 155 sailors from the *Graf Spee* in 1939 (see box, above), many of whom later settled here. Plagues of locusts and heavy rainfall meant that the colony grew slowly at first, and so children from German schools in Buenos Aires were encouraged to come here for holidays, bringing the very first influx of tourists to the town. German is still spoken by older inhabitants, and the architecture along the main street, Avenida Julio Roca, is dominated by Swiss chalet-style buildings and German beer-houses. (Note that the street of Julio Roca changes its name to San Martín at the oval plaza, halfway along.)

You can find genuine German smoked sausages and a wide variety of German breads, delicious Viennese cakes and locally brewed beer. You can even celebrate **Oktoberfest** ⓘ *www.elsitiodelavilla.com/oktoberfest*, when the town is brimming with thousands of tourists. This is not the best time of year to appreciate the town, but the **Viennese Pastry**

Festival in Easter week and the **Alpine Chocolate Festival** during the July holidays are certainly worth a visit. Book accommodation in advance at these times.

The town makes a great centre for hikes in the nearby hills, with plenty of places to stay and good restaurants. The souvenir shops along the main street are crammed with Tirolean hats, beer mugs and *Graf Spee* memorabilia; however there are also fine chocolates for sale and a handicrafts market near the small oval plaza on Sundays and during the holidays.

Walks around Villa General Belgrano

There are plenty of walks in and around the town itself; a map is available from the tourist office (see Tourist information below), ask for directions before setting off. Two rivers run through the town, **La Toma** and **El Sauce**, and a lovely shaded area for walking has been created along their banks. You could also hike up the **Cerro de la Virgen** (one hour), the hill to the east of town. Start at Ojo de Agua, 200 m east of Avenida Julio Roca. Walk along Ojo del Agua, turn right onto the main road, Route 5, then left where signposted. It's a steep walk, but there are rewarding views. Alternatively, a lower and easier hike is up to **Cerro Mirador**, northeast of town. To get here, walk along Avenida las Magnolias, turn left on the main road and then right along Pozo Verde (one hour). From the top there are great views of the valley and the town.

Listings Villa General Belgrano

Tourist information

Villa General Belgrano

For more help with planning your visit, see www.elsitiodelavilla.com (in Spanish and German).

Tourist office

Av Roca 168, T03546-461215, or call T125 free from inside the town, www.vgb.com.ar. Daily 0900-2100.
Friendly English- and German-speaking staff, who'll give you a great map, accommodation list and a free booklet with loads of tourist information.

Where to stay

There are many *cabaña* complexes, chalet-style hotels, which are often family-oriented. Book ahead Jan-Feb, Jul and Easter.

$$ La Posada de Akasha
Los Manantiales 60, T03546-462440, www.laposadadeakasha.com.
Extremely comfortable, spotless chalet-style house, with a small pool, welcoming.

$ pp El Rincón
Fleming 347, T03546-461323, www.hostelelrincon.com.ar.
The only hostel in town is beautifully set in dense forests and green clearings a 10-min walk from the bus terminal. Dorms (US$10-12), doubles or singles with bath (**$$** pp) and camping (US$6-8 pp). US$3.50 for superb breakfasts. Half price for children under 16. In high season rates are higher and the hostel is usually full. Recommended.

Restaurants

$$ Bierkeller
Av Las Magnolias and R5, T03546-461425.
Look for the giant beer bottle outside. A chalet-style building with a welcoming family feel. Goulash and *spatzle* recommended, trout too. Slow service but the staff wear jolly Tyrolean outfits. Recommended.

$$ Blumen Haus
Roca and Bolivia, where Roca divides, T03546-462568.

Touristy but with attractive gardens.
Pretty place to sit outside.

$ El Viejo Munich
Av San Martín 362, T03546-463122,
www.cervezaartesanal.com.
The first brewery in the town, serving superb
beer. There are 8 different kinds of the stuff
on draft (ask for 'Chopp') and legendary
cold cuts of meat (*fiambres*), superb smoked
meats, hams and trout, in a charming rustic
Bavarian-style interior. Recommended.

$ La Casa de Dina
Los Incas 463, T03546-461040,
www.lacasadedina.com.
Superb cakes and fondues in this cheery
and welcoming place.

$ La Posta del Arroyo
Ojo de Agua 174, T03546-461767.
Smart *parrilla* that also serves such
delicacies as kid and frogs. Good pastas,
welcoming atmosphere.

$ Ottilia
Av San Martín y Strauss.
A traditional cosy Austrian tea room.
Delicious *apfelstrudel* and *kirschtorte*.

Festivals

Easter week Viennese Pastry Festival.
Jul Alpine Chocolate Festival.
Oct Oktoberfest, www.elsitiodelavilla.
com/oktoberfest.

What to do

Cycling
Fly Machine, *Av Roca 50, T03546-462425.*
Bike hire.

Tour operators
Alto Rumbo, *www.champaqui.com.ar.*
Frequently recommended tour company
that specializes in alternative tours.

They run trips for beginners and also
experienced climbers.
DAPA, *Av Roca 74, T03546-463417,*
www.dapaturismo.com.ar. Day trips to
La Cumbrecita and guided walks in the
surroundings: Cerro Champaquí in 4WD
and a 40-min walk to the summit;
El Durazno or San Miguel de los Ríos.
Diego Caliari, *T03546-461510, www.*
champaquiadventure.com. An excellent,
trained, friendly young guide who has
worked extensively in Traslasierra, and
who can take you hiking up Champaquí
or on other walks, or arrange horse-riding
trips in the area.
Friedrich, *Av Roca 224, T03546-461372, www.*
dusseldorf.com.ar. Reliable company offering
adventure tourism, 4WD hire and day trips to
La Cumbrecita or Yacanto de Calamuchita.
Also a 10-hr walk across Sierras Chicas along
Camino de los Chilenos.
Peperina Tur, *Av Roca 235, T03546-461800,*
www.peperina.tur.ar. Great company
organizing treks to Champaquí and
Traslasierra and trips in 4WD.

Transport

To reach Villa General Belgrano from
Alta Gracia, take the faster route via
Portrero de Garay.

Bus
To **Córdoba**, 1½-2hrs, US$6.50, **Sierras de
Calamuchita**. To **Buenos Aires**, 10-11 hrs,
US$51-55, **Chevallier, TUS, San Juan Mar
del Plata**; to **La Cumbrecita**, every 2-4 hrs,
1 hr 20 mins, US$5.50, **Pájaro Blanco,** Av San
Martín 105, T03546-461709; also goes to the
nearby villages of **Los Reartes, Villa Berna,
Villa Alpina** and **Yacanto de Calamuchita**.

Remise taxi
Central de Remises, Ojo de Agua 33,
T03546-462000.

To get right into the mountain scenery, head west from Villa General Belgrano via the tiny hamlet of Los Reartes with its old chapel to La Cumbrecita, a charming, Alpine-style village hidden away in the forested hills, where there are no cars permitted. Although crowded in summer, life here is very tranquil indeed and if you visit during spring or autumn to walk in the surrounding mountains, you'll probably have them all to yourself.

It's an excellent centre for trekking or horse riding, with walks from half a day to three days, including to **Cerro Champaquí**, though this peak is better accessed from Villa Alpina (see below). There are short walks to a 14-m-high waterfall **La Cascada**, and to a small lake of crystalline water, **La Olla**, a natural pool with sandy beaches that is good for swimming. Longer walks or horse rides follow footpaths or 4WD vehicle tracks to the **Cerro Cristal**, the pools along **Río del Medio**, or for spectacular panoramic views, hike up **Cerro Wank** (1715 m), two hours return. A footpath leads south to another quaint village, Villa Alpina, but it's a six-hour walk (return) and you should take a guide. You can also go horse riding, try rappelling, or explore the area with 4WDs. Many summer visitors just come for the day, but there are plenty of places to stay and eat including *cabañas* for hire, and tasty food in chalet-style restaurants with lovely settings and great views.

Villa Alpina and Cerro Champaquí
South of La Cumbrecita is another quaint mountain village, **Villa Alpina**, a small remote resort set in the forested upper valley of **Río de los Reartes**. On the map it looks close to La Cumbrecita, but there's no road connecting the two so the only direct way to get there is to walk, which takes three hours. By vehicle, you'll need to head back to pretty wooded Villa Berna, and from there it's 38 km west, along a poor gravel road. See www.turismocordoba.com.ar/losreartes (in Spanish), or contact Villa Alpina's tourist office; see Tourist information, below.

Villa Alpina is the best base for the three-day trek to ★ **Cerro Champaquí** (2790 m), 19 km from the village. It's possible to take a 4WD almost to the summit, but the longer walk is much more rewarding for the superb mountainous scenery and the chance to meet local inhabitants as you stop at the *puestos* on the way. You'll need an all-season sleeping bag to stay in the *puestos*, and be aware that it can snow even in summer. Take a local guide to avoid getting lost. Information is available from Villa General Belgrano tourist office (see page 157), or in La Cumbrecita (see Tourist information, below).

There are more picturesque hilly landscapes with streams and falls close to **Yacanto de Calamuchita**, a village in the mountains, reached via Santa Rosa de Calamuchita, the largest town in this part of the valley, and a very popular, but drab resort. From Yacanto de Calamuchita you can drive almost to the summit of Cerro Champaquí, thanks to a dirt road climbing up to Cerro de los Linderos, leaving you with only a 40-minute walk. See www.villayacanto.gob.ar for planning information or call T03546-485007 (Spanish only). For access to Champaquí from the west, see page 164.

Tourist information

La Cumbrecita
For general information, see
www.calamuchita.com, and www.
lacumbrecita.gov.ar (in Spanish).

Tourist office
*T03546-481088. Mon-Fri 0900-1800
(until 1900 in summer).*
Staff can advise on walking guides
and where to get information on
riding and other activities.

Villa Alpina

Tourist office
*T03547-15-595163, www.villaalpina
cordoba.com.ar.*

Where to stay

There are various hotels and *cabañas*,
prices **$$$-$$**.

La Cumbrecita

$$ El Ceibo
T03546-481060, www.hosteriaelceibo.com.
Neat rooms for 2-4, near the entrance to the
town, great views, access to the river.

What to do

Villa Alpina and Cerro Champaquí Climbing
For Cerro Champaquí (2790 m), near Villa
General Belgrano, see operators like **Alto
Rumbo** in Córdoba (see page 158), or ask
at the information offices in Villa Alpina,
or Villa Yacanto.
Club Andino Córdoba, *27 de Abril 2050,
Barrio Alto Alberdi, Córdoba, T0351-480 5126,
www.clubandinocordoba.com.ar.* Information
on climbing and trekking throughout the
region. It has *refugios* in the Tanti area,
northwest of Villa Carlos Paz.

Transport

La Cumbrecita and the sierra villages
Bus
Reliable daily bus service to **Córdoba
city**, 2½ hrs, US$6.50; from **Villa General
Belgrano**, 1½ hrs, US$5.50. There are also
regular minibuses between Los Reartes, Villa
Berna, La Cumbrecita, Villa Alpina, Santa Rosa
and Yacanto de Calamuchita.

Traslasierra
Valley

Situated west of the Sierra Grande, Traslasierra (literally, 'across the mountains') is far less developed for tourism than neighbouring valleys, but ideal for those looking for an adventure. With its drier climate and generally slower pace of life, it's also a perfect place to relax for a few days. It can be accessed from Córdoba city by the Camino de las Altas Cumbres ('Route of the high peaks'; see below); from the north, via the long but not uninteresting Route 15 across the Pampa de Pocho; or from San Luis province in the south, via Villa Dolores. See www.valledetraslasierra.com.ar and www.turismotraslasierra.com.ar (in Spanish).

The main road (Route 20) to the Traslasierra Valley from Córdoba is the most spectacular route in the sierras. Running southwest from Villa Carlos Paz, the road passes Villa Icho Cruz before climbing into the Sierra Grande and crossing the Pampa de Achala, a huge granite plateau at 2000 m, and descending into the Traslasierra valley near Mina Clavero. This road provides access to the Parque Nacional Quebrada del Condorito, where condors can be seen circling in a spectacular gorge (see box, opposite).

If you've come to escape the crowds, Mina Clavero is probably too busy but it is really picturesque. Further south lie Nono, Los Hornillos and San Javier which are quieter and just as pretty. They all make great bases for hiking.

Mina Clavero *Colour map 4, A2.*
Mina Clavero (population 10,000, altitude 915 m) has the best nightlife and most raucous atmosphere in the entire valley (during school holidays), with nightclubs, theatres, a casino and dozens of hotels, restaurants and small shops. It's a good base for trips into the surrounding area of natural beauty. It lies at the foot of the **Camino de las Altas Cumbres** and at the confluence of the Río Panaholma and Río Mina Clavero, which form many small falls among impressive rocks right in the town centre, and there are attractive views along the riverside.

On the other side of the rivers is the quieter **Villa Cura Brochero**, named after Father Brochero who built schools, roads and aqueducts here at the end of the 19th century. Every March, he is remembered with the **Cabalgatas Brocherianas**; see Festivals, page 165.

Around Mina Clavero
Nearby rivers offer several attractive places for swimming among huge rocks and waterfalls, all busy in high season. About 5 km north of Villa Cura Brochero, a dirt road passing San Lorenzo branches east to the **Cascada de Toro Muerto**, where icy water falls into a 7-m-deep pool. The *balneario* (bathing area) serves very good meals.

Las Maravillas, a *balneario* set in a deep ravine, is 4 km north of San Lorenzo, and it's another 7 km to the hamlet of Panaholma with its old chapel. The **Camino de los Artesanos** is an 18-km stretch of road from Mina Clavero to Villa Benegas along which a dozen families offer hand-woven handicrafts and distinctive black ceramics.

North of Villa Cura Brochero, Route 15 crosses the vast **Pampa de Pocho**, a strange landscape covered by palm trees, with small inactive volcanoes in the background. At Taninga, Route 28 branches off east across the Sierra Grande and the northern edge of Reserva Hídrica Pampa de Achala to Villa Carlos Paz.

Nono and around *Colour map 4, A2.*
Nono (altitude 900 m), 8 km south of Mina Clavero, is an attractive little town. On the plaza there is a handicraft market in summer and a lovely little church. Among other well-preserved houses is the historic **Casa Uez**, which serves as a shop, café and basic hotel, and has been the lively meeting point for locals since 1931.

The most visited sight is the extraordinary **Museo Rocsen** ⓘ *5 km east, following Av Los Porteños, T03544-498065, www.museorocsen.org, daily 0900 till sunset, US$6.50.* This eclectic selection of fabulously bizarre objects spanning archaeology, anthropology and human history is the personal vision of Frenchman Juan Santiago Bouchon. Not to be missed.

ON THE ROAD
Parque Nacional Quebrada del Condorito

Covering 37,000 ha of the Pampa de Achala and the surrounding sierras slopes at altitudes of between 1900 and 2300 m, the park was created in 1996 to protect the central section of Córdoba's sierras, including the spectacular Quebrada del Condorito. This 800-m-deep gorge is the easternmost habitat of the condor. Since you're at the same level as the top of the gorge, it's possible to see fledgling birds taking their first flying lessons. Though condors are elusive and sightings are not guaranteed, you may be lucky enough to see them take a bath under the waterfalls. There's great trekking on the *pastizal de altura* (high-altitude grassland), which is the most southerly habitat of rare tabaquillo trees. The landscapes are superb and the climate is subtropical but you should take a warm jacket.

The only accessible section of the park is its northeast corner, reached by a short walk from La Pampilla (well signposted), on Route 34, 55 km southwest of Villa Carlos Paz (see page 144). It takes about three hours to get to the first vantage point (Balcón Norte) and two more hours to the Balcón Sur, by crossing the Río de los Condoritos. Tours are available from Villa Carlos Paz.

There are three camping areas with no facilities, along the path to Balcón Norte and Balcón Sur.

Transport Ciudad de Córdoba and TAC buses will both stop at La Pampilla on their way from Villa Carlos Paz to Mina Clavero (one hour). If you go with your own vehicle, you can park in front of the visitor centre.

Park information There's a national park administration office in Villa Carlos Paz at Resistencia 30, office 2, T3541-486287. For an excellent guide for trekking and horse riding, contact Diego Caliari T03546-461510, dfcaliari@yahoo.com.ar. For further information, see www.condoritoapn.com.ar (in Spanish).

A network of minor roads east and southeast link the town with the foot of the mountains across a pretty landscape of rivers and hamlets, such as **Paso de las Tropas** and and **El Huayco**. To the west, a dusty road leads from the church to the sandy beaches of **Río Los Sauces** and 11 km beyond to the village of **Piedras Blancas**. Cerro Champaquí is accessible from Nono (via San Javier) but you need to take a guide.

Nono to Villa Dolores
South of Nono, the road skirts the base of some imposing mountains amid lush vegetation and there are scattered villages offering some accommodation. At Los Hornillos (15 km from Nono) there are good walks 500 m east of the road (left of the campsite), along Río Los Hornillos. From there, footpaths lead to the nearby summits, such as the five-hour trek to **La Ventana** (2300 m) passing a 50-m fall halfway. A 1½-hour walk upstream along the riverbed takes you to **Piedra Encajada**, a huge rock with waterfalls. Ten kilometres northwest is **Dique La Viña** with a large reservoir and an impressive 106-m-high dam, not recommended for vertigo sufferers.

West of the sierras the main town is **Villa Dolores**, a useful transport hub, with a couple of banks and a few hotels, though there's no reason to stop here, unless you're keen to see the potato festival in January.

San Javier and Yacanto

These neighbouring villages lie at the foot of the **Cerro Champaquí** (2790 m), the highest peak in the sierras. They are both very pleasant, peaceful places to stay, with old houses under mature trees. Even if you're not keen to climb the peak itself, you could relax by the streams or stroll around the picturesque area. The ascent of Champaquí takes about seven hours from San Javier along the Quebrada del Tigre, but take a guide, as many people get lost. For more information, contact the **Municipalidad** ① *T03544-482041, www.sanjavieronline.com.ar.* For access to Champaquí from the east, see page 159.

Further south there are more small resort towns where tourism is developing, such as **La Población**, **Luyaba**, **La Paz**, **Luyaba**, **La Paz** and nearby **Loma Bola**, which lie along the road to Merlo, 42 km of San Javier.

Listings Camino de las Altas Cumbres

Tourist information

Mina Clavero

Tourist office
Next to the intersection of Av San Martín and Av Mitre at Plazoleta Merlo, T03544-470171, www.minaclavero.gov.ar. Daily 0800-2000.
Large office with ATMs.

Nono

See also www.traslasierra.com/nono and www.nono-cordoba.com (in Spanish) for planning advice.

Tourist office
T03544-498332, www.nonoturismo.gob.ar. Daily 0900-2030.

Villa Dolores

See also www.villadolores.gov.ar.

Tourist office
San Martín 650, T03544-15 408841. Mon-Fri 0800-1400 and 1500-2000, Sat-Sun 0900-1300 and 1600-2000.

Where to stay

Mina Clavero

Several places close in low season.

$ pp Hostel Andamundos
San Martín 554, T03544-470249, www.andamundoshostel.com.ar.

Doubles **$$**, dorms US$10-13.50. Centrally located, well-maintained hostel with a bright, great atmosphere. Unlike many other hostels in Argentina, it still offers HI discounts. They also organize local trips.

$ pp Oh La La!! Hostel
Villanueva 1192, T03544-472634, www.ohlalahostel.com.ar.
Youth hostel (dorms US$10-15; double rooms **$$**), with shared bathrooms. They offer tourist information, and have a pool and gardens.

Nono and around

Several family houses next to the plaza have signs offering rooms for rent by the day. See www.traslasierra-nono.com.ar for a full list.

$$$ Gran Hotel Nono
Vicente Castro 289, T03544-498022, www.granhotelnono.com.ar.
On the riverside with views of the sierras and surrounded by a large and leafy park with a pool and tennis courts, this is a comfortable and welcoming place with rustic decor. It has a restaurant, and breakfast (with lots of fruit) is included. Rates are for half-board in high season (**$$$$**).

$$$ La Lejanía
T03544-15585476, www.lalejania.com.
Lovely little house surrounded by 1000 ha of wilderness. Great swimming pool, tennis courts and a fantastic breakfast.

$$$-$$ La Gloria
On the way to Museo Rocsen, 800 m
from Calle Sarmiento, T03544-15465185,
www.hostal-lagloria.com.ar.
On the rural outskirts set in 5 ha of park,
this old house has comfortable though not
luxurious rooms in a relaxed atmosphere.
It also has *cabañas*, a pool and access to
the river. Delicious breakfast included.

Camping
A road to the left of the church goes west
to the river where there are 3 sites. Next to
the *cabañas* of **Los Canadienses** (T03544-
498861, www.loscanadienses.com.ar), is
La Rueda (www.campinglarueda.com.ar),
a shady place with bathrooms and electricity
supply. Open high season only.

Nono to Villa Dolores

$$$ Alta Montaña
Los Hornillos, 300 m east of road to the
mountains (signposted), T03544-499009,
www.hosteriaaltamontania.com.
The Von Ledebur family has run this lovely
hotel on 8 ha of virgin land by the river since
1947. Neat, comfortable rooms have splendid
views of the grounds and the sierras. Pool
and restaurant; rates are for half board in
high season. Recommended.

San Javier and Yacanto

$$$-$$ Yacanto
T03544-482002, www.hotelyacanto.com.ar.
A traditional 1920s hotel with comfortable
rooms and a beautifully situated 9-hole golf
course. Price depends on season; only half-
board offered.

Restaurants

Mina Clavero

$$ Rincón Suizo
Down by the river, on Calle Recalde, 1 block
off Av San Martín, www.rinconsuizo.com.ar.

This is an unmissable treat. It's basically
a cosy tea room serving rich strudel or
chocolate cakes.

Nono and around

$$ La Casona de Nono
Sarmiento 302.
Not a particularly attractive place, but it
offers *pollo al disco* (grilled chicken) and
humita as its specialities.

$$ La Pulpería de Gonzalo
On the plaza, opposite the church.
Alfresco dining in the wonderful,
romantically lit patio. *Parrilla* dishes are the
speciality, but fish is also recommended.

Festivals

Mina Clavero
20 Mar Cabalgatas Brocherianas, a
celebration of Father Brochero, who helped
with community projects in Mina Clavero
in the late 19th century. The Cabalgata is
a gaucho procession on horses and mules
that follows a section of the former road he
helped to build across the mountains. See
also www.cabalgatabrocheriana.net.

What to do

Nono and around
Traslahuella, *Sarmiento 392, T03544-498084,*
traslahuella@yahoo.com.ar. Local guide
Martín Zalazar runs half-day guided treks
and mountain-bike tours along the river and
to the nearby mountains. Also available is a
day walk to the summit of Cerro Champaquí.
Mountain bikes can be hired.

Transport

Mina Clavero
Bus
The bus terminal is in the centre at Av Mitre
1191. To **Córdoba**, Ciudad de Córdoba via
Altas Cumbres, 3 hrs, US$9, **Coata Córdoba**,
T0810 555 0102, www.coata-cordoba.com.ar.
To **Buenos Aires**, 12 hrs, US$59-66, **Chevallier**,

Expreso del Oeste, **TAC**; to **Mendoza**, 9 hrs, US$40-50, **Andesmar**; to **Merlo**, 2 hrs, US$8.50, **Expreso del Oeste**. Minibuses go to **Villa Cura Brochero** and south to **Nono** and **Villa Dolores**, calling at villages in between, including Los Hornillos. To **Villa Dolores** with **Chevallier** and **Coata Córdoba**, 45 mins, US$3.50; **TAC** buses go to **Panaholma** and some villages in the **Pampa de Pocho**. Other nearby places are only accessible with own vehicle or with a *remise* taxi. No buses go along the Camino de los Túneles, only tour operators.

Nono and around
Bus
Expreso del Oeste to **Villa Dolores**, 50 mins, US$3.50; or up to **Villa Cura Brochero**, 15 mins, US$2.

San Luis
province

The province of San Luis has always been considered Córdoba's poorer sister: it's further from Buenos Aires, its provincial capital lacks the grandeur of its neighbour, and it's not popular with tourists, apart from the overvisited resort town of Merlo on the border. However, it has a spectacular national park, Sierra de las Quijadas, with a great red sandstone canyon and fossil-strewn lunar landscape, and you can still find remote places where rural life is sleepy and traditional.

civilization encroaching on nature

The city of San Luis (population 250,947) was founded in 1594, but it wasn't until the late 19th century that it really started to grow, with a flood of European immigration. There was further development in the 1980s when tax incentives encouraged industry to the area. The result is a modern city with a few colonial buildings, but little to attract visitors. However, it is a friendly place with decent accommodation and food, and is a good starting point for exploring the Sierras de San Luis and the Parque Nacional Sierra de las Quijadas; see box, opposite.

Sights

The centre of the city is the attractive, leafy **Plaza Pringles**, filled with beautiful jacarandas and palm trees and thronging with young crowds after sunset. It's worth popping into the **cathedral** ⓘ *daily 0730-1300, 1830-2130*, with its slender towers and sumptuous interior, to see replicas of famous Murillo paintings and an extraordinary *pesebre electrónico*, a personal vision of the birth of Christ, with moving figures to the accompaniment of Beethoven's *Ninth Symphony* and Scottish pipes: kitsch and marvellous. Northwest of the plaza, there's a magnificent, decaying former railway station.

For hotels and bars, stroll along Avenida Illia, which becomes very lively at night. There's a tiny **Museo de Historia Natural** ⓘ *university campus, Italia y Ejército de los Andes, T02652-426744 (ext 290), museo.unsl. edu.ar, Tue-Sun 0900-1300, US$0.10,* which traces the evolution of San Luis, including the fossil of an alarming giant spider and a dinosaur footprint. The main commercial heart of the city is on Rivadavia, and three blocks away there's the quieter Plaza Independencia, with its extraordinary Moorish Dominican temple, with a Moorish façade. There is a handicraft market: **Centro Artesanal San Martín de Porres** ⓘ *25 de Mayo 955, T02652-424222, Mon-Fri 0800-1300.*

Essential San Luis city

Finding your feet

The **airport** is 3 km northwest from town. Ordinary and *remise* taxis charge about US$3 to the centre. The **bus terminal** is at Avenida España 990 in a triangular-shaped building with offices and bus stops on all sides. To reach the city centre, take Rivadavia. There is left luggage at **Kiosko Portos** (facing the University), which is open 24 hours.

Listings San Luis city

Tourist information

See www.sanluisturismo.com.ar and www.infosanluis.com for more information.

Tourist office
At the corner of Av Illia and Junín, T02652-4423957.
Large office but offers little information.

Where to stay

For more listings, see www.sanluisturismo.com.ar.

$$$ Hotel Quitana
Av Pte Illia 546, T0266-443 8400, www.hotelquintana.com.ar.
6 floors and 84 rooms make this hotel one of San Luis' biggest. The rooms are a little

ON THE ROAD
Parque Nacional Sierra de Las Quijadas

Situated 125 km northwest of San Luis in the northwestern corner of the province, the park covers 150,000 ha of wonderful scenery in one of the hottest and most arid areas of Argentina. Its only accessible area, **Potrero de la Aguada**, is an immense natural amphitheatre of nearly 4000 ha, surrounded by steep red sandstone walls, eroded into strange shapes. There's a small archaeological site next to the access road, and the fossil-rich field of Loma del Pterodaustro shows intriguing evidence of dinosaurs and pterosaurs (winged reptiles). The vegetation is largely scrub; *jarillas* are very common, though there are also trees, such as the *quebracho blanco*. Wildlife includes guanaco, collared peccaries, pumas, tortoises, crowned eagles, peregrine falcons and condors.

Near the park warden's office is **Mirador de Elda**, the first of the two vantage points on the Potrero. From here two optional footpaths go to **Mirador Superior** (an easy 45-minute return) or down to the *huella* (a more demanding two-hour return walk to a dinosaur footprint). This path also leads to the impressive cliffs of **Farallones**, reached by a five-hour return walk and only advisable well after midday. **Tours and access** Open from dawn till dusk. Visit early in the morning or late afternoon for the best views and to avoid the heat. To get there, take the 8-km unpaved road that turns off from Route 147 (San Luis to San Juan) at Hualtarán. There are a few companies with daily services that link San Luis and San Juan, the two main ones are **Autotransportes San Juan** and **Del Sur y Media Agua** both stop at Hualtarán.

Tour operators in San Luis and Merlo (see What to do, pages 170 and 174) run half- or full-day tours to the park. Entry costs US$10.
Accommodation There are luxury cottages at **Complejo La Aguada**, T011-2184-0515, www.laaguada.com. Prices ($$$$) include all meals and activities. The only site for camping (free) is 100 m from the park warden's office, next to a basic canteen.
Further information T0266 444 5141, www.parquesnacionales.gov.ar (in Spanish).

dated but the staff are friendly and the location is great.

$$$ Vista Suites & Spa
Av Pte Illia 526, T0266-444 6380,
www.vistasuites.com.ar.
Stunning hotel with a lovely view from the rooftop pool. Stylish, modern rooms (suites cost up to **$$$$**). Great bar and restaurant.

$$ Belgrano
Belgrano 1440, T0266-443 5923,
www.belgranohotel.com.ar.
This is probably the best budget hotel, with welcoming staff, renovated rooms with fan and bath, and breakfast included.

Restaurants

Chivito (kid) is the main local dish. Its usual accompaniment is *chanfaina* (a stew whose main ingredients are the goat's entrails).

$$ La Porteña
Junín y General Paz, T02652-443 1722.
Simple meals such as the *plato del día*. Prepare for enormous portions in the enjoyable atmosphere of this popular place.

$ Crocantes
San Martín 630.
A bakery where cheap and superb sandwiches are prepared at your request and with your chosen bread.

$ La Pulpería del Arriero
9 de Julio 753, T0266-443 2446.
With tasty regional specialities and live folk music in the evenings, this is the place for trying *empanadas* or *asado* during a lively night out. The set menus are good value.

$ Los Robles
9 de Julio 745, T0266-443 6767,
www.losroblesresto.com.ar.
Formal atmosphere and excellent food, you can eat at moderate prices at this smart *parrilla*. There is a wide choice of dishes (*bife de chorizo* is great), including *chivito* and trout. Recommended.

Cafés and bars
There's a cluster spread along Av Illia and Rivadavia between blocks 0800 and 1000. During the day, an enjoyable café on the plaza is **Aranjuez** (www.cafearanjuez.com).

What to do

All agencies offer similar tours at standard rates (rates in leaflets usually do not include fees to national parks). A half-day tour to Sierra de las Quijadas is the most popular and includes a walk to Los Miradores (1-1½ hrs) and to La Huella (2-2½ hrs). Weather permitting (usually not in summer), a more demanding walk to Los Farallones (4-5 hrs) is organized. The Circuito Serrano Chico is a short walk around El Volcán, Potrero de los Funes and the town itself, while the Circuito Serrano Grande adds El Trapiche and La Florida. Circuito de Oro goes up to Carolina and Intihuasi and may include the Circuitos Serranos. There are also tours to religious sites in Suyuque and Villa de la Quebrada, and to the hot springs of Balde and the salt flats in Salinas del Bebedero. A day trip to Merlo via La Toma is also available.

Bruno Aliberti, *T02652-426021, T02652-15-502971, Bruno_aliberti@hotmail.com.* Guide only, for those with their own vehicle.
Dasso, *Rivadavia 540, T02652-421017, www.dassoviajes.com.ar.*
Gimatur, *Av Illia y Caseros, T02652-435751, www.gimatur.com.* English spoken.
Luciano Franchi, *Chile 1430, T02652-420345.*

Transport

Air
Access to San Luis airport (T0266-442 2427) is via Colón, Av Justo Daract and Sargento Baigorria. For transport from the airport, see box, page 168. There's 1 flight per day (2 on Fri) to **Buenos Aires**, 1¼ hrs, with **Aerolíneas Argentinas**, Av Illia 472, T0266-4425671.

Bus
Check at the office at the bus terminal (T02652-424021) where your bus leaves from. To **Buenos Aires**, 10-11 hrs, US$60-87, several companies. To **Mendoza**, 3-4 hrs, US$20-25, several companies. To **Córdoba**, 6-7 hrs, US$37-42, several companies. To **San Juan**, 4 hrs, US$25-31, several companies. To **Santa Rosa** (La Pampa), 10 hrs, US$38, **Dumas**, **Andesmar**; also to destinations in southern San Luis. To **Merlo**, 3 hrs, US$9, Chevallier, **Automotores Merlo** (packed minibuses). To **Balde** and **Salinas del Bebedero** 45 mins, US$2-4; and 1 hr, US$1, with **El Rápido** and **San Juan**. To **El Trapiche**, US$1, **María del Rosario**, **San José**; same services go to La Florida and Río Grande. To **Carolina** and **Intihuasi**, Polos, 3 daily (unreliable timetable), US$2-3.

Car hire
Alamo, Belgrano 1440, T02652-440288;
Travel, Chacabuco 649, T0810-333 2763, www.travelrentacar.com.ar.

Remise taxis
Cosmos, Chacabuco 1151, T02652-440000.

Northeast of the city, the Sierras de San Luis are a beautiful range of hills that remain little known to travellers, with just two frequently visited resorts, the small town of El Trapiche and the reservoir in La Florida. The rest of this vast hilly region is sparsely inhabited, with quiet villages that maintain old rural traditions and a simple way of life. The eastern edge of the sierras and the upper valleys and high Pampas around Carolina can be visited by taking Route 9 north from San Luis. Regular buses go up to Carolina and Intihuasi.

El Trapiche
At Km 40, El Trapiche is an attractive village set on the Río Trapiche in wooded hills. There are summer homes, hotels and picnic sites, and some good easy walks to **Los Siete Cajones**, on the sparkling waters of Río Grande, and 6 km west, to the pleasant surroundings of the rivers **Virorco** and **Virorco** and **De las Aguilas**.

Carolina *Colour map 4, A2.*
Carolina is a former gold-mining village (population 250) founded in 1792 at the foot of Cerro Tomolasta (2018 m), which offers great views from its summit. It's a picturesque place with stone houses and a gold mine, which can be visited through San Luis tour operators (see What to do, opposite). The local **Huellas agency** ⓘ *16 de Julio and El Minero, T0266-490224, www.huellasturismo.com.ar*, dresses you up as a miner and guides you along a 300-m tunnel for about 1½ hours (English spoken), and provides tools in case you suddenly feel the desire to dig.

From Carolina a rough track leads north over the Cuesta Larga to San Francisco del Monte de Oro, on Route 146. Two other roads in better condition cross attractive scenery of undulating Pampas and volcanic peaks to Libertador General San Martín or to La Toma.

Listings Sierras de San Luis

Tourist information

Carolina

Municipalidad
16 de Julio s/n, T0266-490214.

Where to stay

$$$$-$$$ Hotel Potrero de los Funes
R18, Km 16, T0266-444 0038,
www.hotelpotrero.sanluis.gov.ar.
Set in a mountainous area, this impressive lakeside resort offers affordable rooms, some with splendid views (slightly pricier). A pool and sport facilities are included, as well as a large breakfast.

$$$-$$ Campo La Sierra
19 km east of San Luis (access via R20), T0266-449 4171, www.campolasierra.com.ar.
A warm welcome at this 70-ha farm with native flora (cacti experts visit annually). Self-contained units, German-style cooking, breakfast, pool, archery, German and Spanish lessons, English also spoken.

El Trapiche

$$$ Villa Alinor
T0266-449 3038. Price is per house.
A group of small houses at a most attractive location on a natural rocky balcony next to the river. Each house sleeps 4-6 with

kitchen, fridge and phone; bedlinen and towels are extra.

$ pp Hotel Class
Av San Martin s/n, T0266-348402.
A family-orientated hotel with full- or half-board accommodation.

Estancias

$$$ Estancia Altos del Durazno
10 km west of El Trapiche, Ruta Provincial 18, El Durazno Alto, Estancia Grande, T0266-15-426 5151, http://altosdeldurazno.tripod.com.
A peaceful place in lovely countryside, with individual stone cottages that sleep 2-5 and have wooden furniture and kitchen. Breakfast is brought to your cottage, and airport or bus station transfer is available. There is horse riding and trekking.

Carolina

$$$ Hostería Las Verbenas
10 km south of Carolina, T0266-4430918, www.lasverbenas.com.ar.
Situated in the beautiful Pancanta Valley, this is an ideal base for walking and horse riding or for enjoying a relaxing stay. Price is for full board.

$$ La Posta del Caminante
R9, Km 0.83, T0266-445 2000, www.lapostadelcaminante.jimdo.com.
Housed in a former residence for mining engineers. Offers comfortable rooms with bath and breakfast (cheaper with shared bath), pool in natural setting, and has a small restaurant next door. Walks to the mines and horse riding trips are also arranged.

Eastern San Luis

attractive villages, mountain walks and paragliding

Villa Mercedes *Colour map 4, B2.*
Founded in 1856 as a fortress, Villa Mercedes (population 118,000) is an important intersection and alternative transport hub, though it's of little of interest to the tourist. It lies on Route 7, 100 km southeast of San Luis. Accommodation is mainly found along Avenida Mitre (six blocks east of the bus terminal).

Villa Mercedes is also the gateway to the southern plains, which are dotted with dozens of small lakes that are attractive for anglers. *Pejerrey* is the main catch and the fishing season runs from November to August. Accommodation is available at local estancias (ask at the tourist office, see below). For more, see www.villamercedes.gov.ar (in Spanish).

Conlara Valley
Lying east of the Sierra de San Luis and west of the Sierra de Comechingones, the broad Conlara Valley (population 90,000) runs into the Traslasierra Valley to the north, with a number of attractive places to visit and stay. **San José del Morro** has an 18th-century chapel in its blissfully traditional village. Nearby, the **Sierra del Morro** (1639 m) is the remains of a collapsed volcano; inside its crater are small volcanic cones, and lots of rose quartz can be found here (access through Estancia La Morena). In May, at tiny **Renca**, El Señor de Renca is celebrated; see Festivals, below.

Santa Rosa del Conlara is a pleasant small town by a river, a good alternative for accommodation when Merlo is packed (reached by bus or *combi* from San Luis). A more scenic journey is via Provincial Route 1, which runs parallel to the east of Route 148 along the base of the Sierra de Comechingones through a string of pretty villages: **Papagayos**, surrounded by natural palm tree groves of *Trithrinax campestris*; **Villa Larca**, where the waterfall **Chorro de San Ignacio** and upper natural pools offer lovely walks; **Cortaderas**; **Carpintería,** and up to the well-promoted Merlo.

Merlo *Colour map 4, A2.*

Situated almost at the San Luis-Córdoba border, Merlo (population 17,084) is a popular holiday centre on the steep western slopes of the Sierra de Comechingones. It has lost much of its charm in recent years, due to mass tourism, which has made it busy and overpriced. It claims to have a special microclimate, and sunny days can certainly be enjoyed throughout the year. The town was founded in 1797, but the **church** on the plaza, said to be of Jesuit origin, dates from the early 18th century, and is soon to be replaced by the huge new red-brick church behind.

Merlo's surroundings at the foot of the mountains are pleasant for walking or you can hike to their summits (the **Circuito de Damiana Vega** takes three to four hours). The slopes are covered with woods and scrub and there are numerous refreshing streams with falls. Higher up there are some excellent sites for paragliding; an experienced pilot reached heights of 5000 m. A paved road (15 km long) leads to the top of the sierras at **Mirador del Sol**, where there are wonderful panoramic views, best at sunrise or sunset. The mirador is accessible by bus and is the starting point for a rough track leading across 82 km of Pampas and Sierras de Córdoba to Embalse del Río Tercero.

Quieter places to stay are spread in the neighbouring small settlements of **Piedra Blanca** (1 km north) or **Rincón del Este** (4 km east), but book ahead in high season.

Listings Eastern San Luis

Tourist information

Villa Mercedes

Tourist office
Av 25 de Mayo 1500.

Merlo

Tourist offices
At the roundabout on R5 and R1, and next to the plaza at Coronel Mercau 605, T02656-476078, www.lavillademerlo.com.ar.

Where to stay

Conlara Valley

$$ Hotel Río Conlara
Rivadavia and San José, T02656-492012, www.hotelrioconlara.com.ar.
Next to a well-maintained *balneario*, where the river was dammed, this place has clean, comfortable rooms. Breakfast included.

Merlo
Book in advance for high season: Jan and Feb, Easter, Jul and Aug. See www.turismo-

merlo.com.ar and www.lavillademerlo.com.ar for more listings.

$$$$-$$$ Altos del Sol
Andrada and Borges, T02656-478399, www.altosdelsol.com.
Charming *cabañas* set above town with endless views. For 2-7 people, good rooms and a pool.

$$$ Colonial Villa de Merlo
Pedernera and Av del Sol, T02656-470157, www.hotelvillademerlo.com.ar.
Comfortable rooms with splendid views of the sierras and a large garden with pool. There are sport facilities, though the quiet atmosphere of this rather exclusive 3-star hotel is more appealing for a relaxing holiday. There's a moderately priced restaurant.

$$$ La Quinta Resorts
Román Gonzáles s/n, Piedra Blanca, T02656-479598, www.laquintaresort.net.
Huge complex just outside town with lovely stylishly decorated cabins. There's a jacuzzi, pool and tennis courts.

$$$ Rincón de los Troncos
Av José Percau 164, T02656-476768,
www.rincondelostroncos.com.ar.
Huge rustic but comfortable cabins for
2-6 people. Wonderful alpine wood and
stone building within tranquil grounds and
2 large pools, only a short distance to the
centre of town. Often recommended.

$$$-$$ Colonial
Av Dos Venados y P Tisera, T02656-475388,
www.hchosteriacolonial.com.ar.
Probably the best value, in a quiet residential
area not far from the centre. This attractive,
neocolonial building has simple rooms on a
patio with an incredibly small pool. Breakfast
is included, and there's Wi-Fi.

Camping

Las Violetas
*Chumamaya and Av Dos Venados, T02656-
475730, lasvioletas@merlo-sl.com.ar.*
The closest site to the centre has a small
shady area for tents, a pool, canteen, grocery
shop and clean but not spotless bathrooms,
US$12.50.

Restaurants

Merlo

$$ El Ciprés
Av del Ciprés 381.
Popular with the locals. Good, filling
meals are guaranteed though the menu
is pretty standard.

$$ El Establo
Av del Sol 450.
Handsome *parrilla*, where the grill or *asador*
is strangely trapped in a glass enclosure.
Try *chivito* here.

Festivals

Renca
3 May El Señor de Renca, one of the most
popular religious festivities in the region.

What to do

Merlo
Tour operators
Trips to local sights and provincial attractions
are provided, including full-day tours to
Sierra de las Quijadas. Closer destinations
include half-day trips to Mina Los Cóndores
and to Bajo de Véliz, an over-promoted
palaeontological site, where giant
spiders used to live millions of years ago.
Surrounding villages may also be explored
for a few hours. More unusual activities
such as visiting a remote ghost mining
town, sleeping in caves or crossing rivers are
offered by **Cimarrón Turismo** (Av del Sol
300, T0266-478290).

Transport

Merlo
Air
There's a modern **airport** on Route 148,
23 km west of Merlo.

Bus
The **bus terminal is** on Route 1, next to
the roundabout (10 mins' walk from the
plaza). Frequent services to **San Luis**, 3 hrs,
US$9, several companies. To **Buenos Aires**,
US$52-58, 10-12 hrs, several companies. To
Córdoba, 5 hrs, US$16, **Chevallier, El Rápido**;
To **Mina Clavero**, 2 hrs, US$7, **Expreso del
Oeste, Chevallier**. To **Villa Dolores**, 2 hrs,
US$3-4. **La Costa** goes daily along R1 to
Cortaderas, Villa Larca and Papagayos. **STU**
runs frequent services to **Mirador del Sol**,
stopping there for 10 mins, US$2.50 return.

Remise taxis
Avenida, Becerra 575, T02656-476031; **Unión**,
Videla 114, T02656-478444.

Mendoza &
the West

the heart of Argentina's wine country

Argentina's west is wild and largely unvisited, despite having one of the country's most stylish and vibrant cities at its heart.

Mendoza is the centre of the biggest wine-producing region in Argentina, and with plenty of fine restaurants and a beautiful setting at the foothills of the Andes, it's a great base for exploring the surrounding vineyards for a few days.

You could happily spend a week visiting bodegas, before heading west to climb Mount Aconcagua, South America's highest mountain. There are many other dramatic peaks to hike up in summer, or ski down in winter, such as the country's most famous ski and snowboarding resort, Las Leñas.

South of Mendoza, you can find sparkling wine producers in San Rafael, or set off for adventures in the wild landscapes beyond. Go rafting in the eerie ravine of Cañón del Atuel; see thousands of flamingos rising from the Prussian-blue waters at Llancanelo; or ride a horse through the starkly beautiful volcanic landscape of La Payunia. You'll need a spirit of adventure to explore the San Juan and La Rioja provinces, but you'll be rewarded with forgotten valleys offering perfect peace and natural beauty.

The undoubted stars of the region are two national parks. The 'Valley of the Moon' at Ischigualasto is an otherworldly landscape: a 200-million-year-old lake bed, strewn with fossils. And Talampaya's vast canyons of terracotta rock have been eroded by wind into gigantic sculptures.

Best for
Adventure sports ▪ Fine dining ▪ Wine tours

Footprint picks

★ **Mendoza's fine wineries**, page 190

Take a bodega tour and discover some of the finest wines in the world.

★ **Parque Provincial Aconcagua**, page 199

This protected area in the Andes has the tallest mountain in the western hemisphere.

★ **Las Leñas**, page 210

Hit the slopes at this expansive jewel of an Andean ski resort.

★ **La Payunia Reserve**, page 211

Extinct volcanoes and roaming guanacos pepper the landscape at this nature reserve.

★ **Parque Provincial Ischigualasto**, page 218

The 'Valley of the Moon' is home to some stunning landscapes dating back to the Triassic Period.

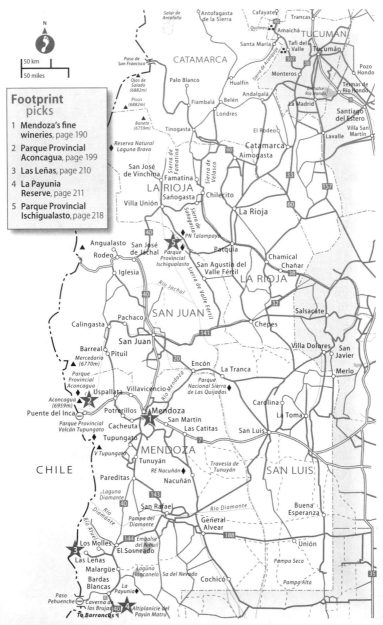

Footprint picks

1 Mendoza's fine wineries, page 190
2 Parque Provincial Aconcagua, page 199
3 Las Leñas, page 210
4 La Payunia Reserve, page 211
5 Parque Provincial Ischigualasto, page 218

Mendoza
city

Mendoza is undoubtedly the tourism hub of the west of Argentina, and is a good place to spend a few days, with its pretty plazas, wide boulevards and sophisticated nightlife. Its flourishing economy is based entirely around wine, as it is the centre of Argentina's wine industry.

Any trip to the city should include a tour of some of the vineyards at Maipú and Luján de Cuyo to the south. There are large flashy commercial bodegas and smaller family wineries, and after seeing the process of winemaking, you'll be treated to a generous tasting to appreciate why Argentina's wine is receiving such worldwide acclaim. Wine is part of the city's culture too: there's a profusion of wonderful *vinotecas* where you can taste fine wines, and a spectacular festival held to celebrate the wine harvest every March in Mendoza's splendid Parque San Martín.

The city has some small interesting museums and a lively nightlife, with sophisticated restaurants serving all kinds of fine food. It's also a good place to plan a trip into the mountains to the west; the snow-capped peaks form a dramatic backdrop to the city. You can hire ski gear, get expert advice on climbing Aconcagua or find specialist adventure tour operators for climbing or rafting elsewhere in the region. The city is well set up for tourism, with a huge range of comfortable hotels, and plentiful bilingual tour operators.

Essential Mendoza city

Finding your feet

Governor Francisco Gabrielli Airport is 8 km northeast of the city. To get to Plaza Independencia in the centre catch bus No 6 (line 63 'Mosconi'), hourly, a 50-minute journey. *Remise* taxi to/from centre US$8-10. The long-distance bus terminal is on Avenida Videla, 15 minutes' walk from the centre (go via Avenida Alem, which has pedestrian tunnel to gates opposite platforms 38-39). A taxi to the centre costs US$2-3; prepare for long queues. See Transport, page 189.

Getting around

Mendoza's city centre is easy to find your way around on foot, with the large leafy Plaza Independencia occupying four blocks at its centre. Pedestrianized Sarmiento runs between the plaza and the main shopping street, San Martín, which runs north to south.

You're unlikely to need transport in the centre, but if you do, there are plentiful buses (single fares from US$0.40), six trolley bus routes, a tram 'Metrotranvía' that runs along Avenida Belgrano in the centre from Mendoza station to Gutiérrez station in Maipú (30 minutes, US$0.40) and a tourist bus decorated as a tram that runs along the main commercial avenues (US$0.40). In addition, taxis are plentiful and safe. The bodegas (wineries) in the nearby towns of Luján de Cuyo and Maipú, just to the south, can be reached by bus, but if you're keen to see more than one, it's better to hire a car. See Transport, page 189.

Best bodegas (wineries)

Tapiz, page 192
Renacer, page 192
Achával Ferrer, page 192
El Lagar de Carmelo Patti, page 193

When to go

The biggest festival of the year, **Fiesta de la Vendimia**, is held from mid-February to mid-March to celebrate the start of the wine harvest; see Festivals, page 187. A parallel event is the less-promoted but equally entertaining **Gay Vendimia**. Bodegas can be visited all year round, and at harvest time (March and April) you'll see the machinery in action. If you're heading beyond Mendoza to explore the landscape, note that trekking in the mountains is only possible from November to April, when the snow has melted. The most pleasant time for trekking is December to February, which is also the only feasible season for trekking at higher altitudes. Skiing at Los Penitentes (on the road to Chile) is from July to October, though Las Leñas further south is open from mid-June.

Useful addresses

Migraciones, San Juan 211, T0261-424 3510. Monday-Friday 0700-1400. Immigration office. **Unidad Policial de Asistencia al Turista**, Avenida San Martín 1143, T0261-413 2135. Open 24 hours. Tourist police.

Weather Mendoza city

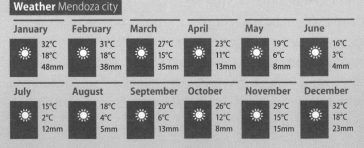

January	February	March	April	May	June
32°C 18°C 48mm	31°C 18°C 38mm	27°C 15°C 35mm	23°C 11°C 13mm	19°C 6°C 8mm	16°C 3°C 4mm

July	August	September	October	November	December
15°C 2°C 12mm	18°C 4°C 5mm	20°C 6°C 13mm	26°C 12°C 8mm	29°C 15°C 15mm	32°C 18°C 23mm

BACKGROUND
Mendoza city

Mendoza was founded by Pedro del Castillo in 1561, who was sent from the Spanish colony in Chile by Captain General García Hurtado de Mendoza to cross the 4000-m pass over the Andes and start a new city. Mediterranean fruits were introduced to the region soon afterwards and thrived in its sunny climate, aided by pre-Hispanic irrigation channels that are still used today to water the dry lands with abundant snow-melt from the Andes. The city's wealth grew, although it remained largely isolated throughout the colonial period, being governed from Chile and having little contact with modern-day Argentina.

The city's greatest blow came on Easter Saturday in 1861 when it was completely destroyed in a devastating earthquake which killed some 4000 of its 12,000 inhabitants. Very quickly, a new centre was built by the French architect Ballofet, several blocks to the southwest of the original. This modern city was designed with low, quake-proof buildings, broad avenues and many plazas to aid evacuation in case of further tremors. Plane trees were planted on all the streets, watered by a network of irrigation channels which still gush with water every spring.

Nowadays, Mendoza is a city of 115,000, with the main industry being wine, though a busy university and, increasingly, tourism help to sustain its wealth and lively character.

Sights Colour map 3, A2.

wide boulevards and leafy plazas

Plaza Independencia and around

The large **Plaza Independencia** is a popular meeting place for Mendocinos, with its shady acacia and plane trees and pretty fountains. In the middle is the small **Museo de Arte Moderno** ⓘ *T0261-425 7279, see Facebook, Tue-Fri 0900-2000 (free guided visits), Sat, Sun and holidays 1400-2000, US$1 (valid also for 24 hrs for Museo del Area Fundacional and Acuario Municipal, see below), closed for renovation in 2016.* Originally designed to be an emergency bunker for victims of earthquakes, it now houses temporary exhibitions. On the western side is the luxurious **Park Hyatt Hotel** ⓘ *www.mendoza.park.hyatt.com*, which was once a splendid 1920s palace where Juan Perón and Evita stayed. The eastern side of the plaza is filled with a handicrafts market at weekends, where Sarmiento runs to San Martín.

One block out from the four corners of Plaza Independencia are four smaller plazas. The most attractive is the **Plaza España**, to the southeast. Its floor and benches are beautifully tiled and it's a lovely place to sit under the trees and gaze at the rather sentimental mural displaying historical episodes as well as scenes from *Don Quijote* and the famous gaucho poem, *Martín Fierro*.

Four blocks west along Montevideo, with its pretty Italianate and colonial-style buildings, is **Plaza Italia**, with wonderful mature tipa trees. Nearby it's worth visiting the small **Museo del Pasado Cuyano** ⓘ *Montevideo 544, T0261-423 6031, Mon-Fri 0900-1300 US$1.25,* housed in a beautiful 1873 mansion owned by the Civit family. There's a lot of San Martín memorabilia, and an exquisite Spanish 15th-century carved altarpiece. The director will give you an excellent tour and insights into the city's history.

Area Fundacional

Getting there: buses 5 (line 54) and 3 (line 112) from C Chile; the Bus Turístico also stops here.

The original city centre, destroyed by the earthquake in 1861, was located 12 blocks to the northeast of today's Plaza Independencia and is now known as the Area Fundacional. Here there is a broad tranquil plaza and a beautifully designed **Museo del Area Fundacional** ⓘ *Beltrán and Videla Castillo, T0261-425 6927, Tue-Sat 0900-2000, Sun 1200-2000, holidays 1000-1900, US$2 (valid also 24 hrs for Museo de Arte Moderno, see above, and Acuario Municipal, see below),* whose glass floor reveals the continuing excavation of the foundations of the old Cabildo and the buildings that followed, with an array of objects

Where to stay 🛏
1 Alamo Hostel & Suites *B1*
2 Campo Base *B1*
3 Chimbas Hostel *C3*
4 Confluencia *A2*

5 Damajuana *C1*
6 Hostel Internacional Mendoza *C2*
8 InterContinental *C3*
9 Mendoza Backpackers *C2*
10 Mendoza Inn *C1*
11 NH *B1*
12 Nutibara *C1*
13 Park Hyatt *B1*
14 Sheraton *B2*

Restaurants 🍴
1 Anna Bistro *A1*
2 Azafrán *B1*
3 Facundo *B1*
4 Ferruccio Soppelsa *A2*
5 Francesco Barbera *B1*
6 Gio Bar *B1*
7 La Marchigiana *A2*
9 Las Tinajas *B2*
11 Mesón Español *C2*
13 Montecatini *A1*

15 Por Acá *C1*
16 Quinta Norte *B1*
17 Vía Civit *B1*

Bars & clubs 🍸
18 Antares *C1*
19 Iskara *C2*
20 Liverpool *B2*

ON THE ROAD
San Martín El Libertador

If you learn about only one Argentine hero on your trip, make it San Martín, one of the greatest independence heroes of South America. Celebrated by statues in every town in the country, José Francisco de San Martín hoped to unite Spanish America after independence, and though he failed to achieve this aim, his military genius played a major role in securing independence. He possessed a tremendous organizational ability, even when leading troops scattered over large distances and mountainous terrain, and his epic crossing of the Andes in 1817 was a turning point in the Wars of Independence, and the bloody campaigns that followed in Chile and Peru ended Spanish rule in South America.

Born in Yapeyú, Corrientes, in 1778 and educated in Spain, San Martín served in the Spanish army in North Africa, Spain and France from the age of 15. In 1811 he resigned from the army and made contact with Francisco de Miranda and other supporters of South American independence, returning to Buenos Aires in 1812 to train the new cavalry regiment. The following year, he replaced Belgrano as commander of the northern armies and, once appointed governor of Cuyo province, spent the next two years preparing to capture Peru from his base in Mendoza by means of a giant flanking movement through Chile and up through the coast to Lima. His 'Army of the Andes' was drawn from regular troops sent by Buenos Aires, but San Martín personally reconnoitred the mountain passes to plan the crossing to Chile himself. He also planned a brilliant deception, calling a meeting of Pehuenche chiefs to ask their permission to cross their territory to invade Chile via mountain passes south of Mendoza. As he'd expected, spies carried this news across the Andes, leaving San Martín free to use a more northerly route, with the main force crossing by Los Patos and Uspallata passes. Some 3778 men set out on 19 January 1817, with equipment and 10,791 horses and mules, and they crossed the Andes in 21 days, arriving on time at their intended destinations. Within days, the army defeated the Spanish at Chacabuco and entered Santiago, Chile, in triumph, though the conclusive victory was at the Battle of Maipú in April 1818.

With Chilean independence secure, San Martín led his forces by sea to Peru in 1820. Avoiding battle against the larger Spanish forces, he negotiated a truce. Finally entering Lima in triumph in July 1821, he assumed political and military command of the new republic of Peru. Afterwards, San Martín resigned his post and returned to his small farm in Mendoza, before travelling to Europe in 1824 to settle in Brussels and then Grand Bourg, France. He died in Boulogne-sur-Mer in 1850, and his remains now lie in the Buenos Aires cathedral. Symbolizing to many Argentines the virtues of sacrifice, bravery and the lack of personal gain, he's remembered by street names in even the smallest towns.

salvaged from the rubble. The informative free tour is highly recommended to give you a picture of Mendoza's history. Under the plaza you can see the first fountain to bring running water to the city, and nearby, at the corner of Ituzaingó and Beltrán, are the ruins of the Jesuit **Iglesia de San Francisco**. **Plaza Pellegrini** is another attractive little plaza, at Avenida Alem and Avenida San Juan, where wedding photos are taken on Friday and Saturday nights, and there's a small antiques market on Friday at lunchtime.

Not far from the Area Fundacional, at the southern end of Parque O'Higgins, kids might enjoy the small aquarium **Acuario Municipal** ① *Ituzaingó and Buenos Aires, daily 0900-1930, US$2 (free with ticket for Museo de Arte Moderno and Museo del Area Fundacional)*. Across the street is a small **Serpentario** ① *daily 0900-1930, US$2*, with plenty of snakes and lizards.

Parque General San Martín and around

Ten blocks west of Plaza Independencia, wrought-iron gates mark the entrance to the great Parque General San Martín, 350 ha of lavishly planted parkland designed by famous Argentine landscape architect Charles Thays, with sports facilities, a big lake where regattas are held, a sports stadium and an amphitheatre. There's also a helpful **tourist information office** next to the main gates. Within the park is the **Cerro de la Gloria**, popular with paragliders, which gives splendid views of the Andes to the west. There's a monument here to San Martín, showing him leading his army across the Andes to liberate Argentina and Chile from the Spanish. **Bus Turístico** and **El Oro Negro** tourist buses run to the top of the Cerro de la Gloria from the city centre, otherwise it's a 45-minute walk from park's gates.

At the south end of the lake is the **Museo de Ciencias Naturales y Antropológicas** ① *T0261-428 7666, Tue-Fri 0900-1845, Sat-Sun 1500-1845*, with an ancient female mummy and stuffed animals among its collections.

The city's best art gallery is in the nearby suburb of **Luján de Cuyo**, in the house where Fernando Fader painted his beautiful murals. The **Museo Provincial de Bellas Artes** ① *Casa de Fader, Carril San Martín 3651, Mayor Drummond, T0261-496 0224, Tue-Fri 0830-1800, Sat-Sun 1400-1900, closed for remodelling in 2016*, has a small, charming collection of Argentine paintings. There are also sculptures in the lovely gardens. To get there catch bus No 1 (line 19) from Calle La Rioja, between Catamarca and Garibaldi (40 minutes).

Listings Mendoza city *map page 182.*

Tourist information

Mendoza has a well-developed tourism infrastructure, with tourist offices all over the city. Also see www.mendoza.com and www.welcometomendoza.com (both in English).

Provincial tourist office
Av San Martín 1143, T0261-413 2101, www.turismo.mendoza.gov.ar.
For regional information.

Tourist office
Garibaldi y San Martín, T0261-420 1333, www. ciudaddemendoza.gov.ar. Daily 0900-2100.
The main tourist office, which provides tourist and cultural information for the city. There's a useful booth on the street outside. There is also a tourist office at the

Municipalidad (9 de Julio 500, 7th floor, T0261-449 5185, Mon-Fri 0800-1400). There are 2 small but very helpful kiosks at the airport and at the bus terminal, and another extremely helpful office at the entrance to **Parque San Martín** (daily 0800-1800). All hand out maps and accommodation lists, lists of private lodgings in high season, information on bodegas and buses. The city also runs free walking tours and the **Bus Turístico** (see What to do, page 187).

Where to stay

Breakfast is included, unless specified otherwise. Hostels advertise themselves outside the tourist office in town, offering free transfers and lots of extras; don't be pressured into something you don't want. Hostels cost about US$11-18 pp. Hotels fill up fast and prices rise during the Vendimia (wine-harvesting) festival, Easter, Jul (the ski season) and around mid-Sep (the Chilean holidays).

The **Hyatt** (www.mendoza.park.hyatt.com), **InterContinental** (www.ihg.com), **Sheraton** (www.starwoodhotels.com) and **NH** (www.nh-hotels.com) chains have good hotels in the city; for something more unusual stay at one of the bodegas (see below).

$$$ Nutibara
Mitre 867, T0261-429 5428,
www.nutibara.com.ar.
Its small rooms are in need of renovation, but it's still a good choice due to its central and quiet location and its pool.

$ pp Alamo Hostel & Suites
Necochea 740, T0261-429 5565,
www.hostelalamo.com.
Beautiful hostel in a very well-kept 1940s residence with dorms for 4 to 8 and doubles with or without bath (**$$**). Bike rental and tiny pool in a pleasant patio. Recommended for a quiet, yet sociable stay.

$ pp Campo Base
Mitre 946, T0261-429 0707,
www.hostelcampobase.com.ar.
A lively place, cramped rooms and private doubles (**$$**), lots of parties and barbecues, popular with mountain climbers, tours run by **BackPackers Travel & Adventure** agency.

$ pp Chimbas Hostel
Cobos 92 y Acceso Este, T0261-431 4191,
www.chimbashostel.com.ar.
Pleasant hostel with a quiet atmosphere, 20 mins' walk to the centre and near the bus station (phone in advance for pick up). Rooms are cheaper without bath and in triples, also private doubles with bath (**$$**). There's a swimming pool and a gym.

$ pp Confluencia
España 1512, T0261-429 0430,
www.hostalconfluencia.com.ar.

Slightly more expensive than rest of hostels, this is a convenient choice though for groups who care for tidiness and a central location. Rooms for 2 to 4 (private doubles (**$$**), all with bath, some en suite. Offers lots of adventure activities as well as wine tours, cycling and riding.

$ pp Damajuana
Arístides Villanueva 282, T0261-425 5858,
www.damajuanahostel.com.ar.
A great hostel, comfortable stylish dorms with bath, also double rooms (**$$**), pool and garden. Recommended.

$ pp Hostel Internacional Mendoza
España 343, T0261-424 0018,
www.hostelmendoza.net.
A comfortable hostel with a warm atmosphere, 15 mins' walk south of Plaza Independencia. Small rooms for 4 and 6 with bath (cheaper without a/c), doubles with bath (**$$**), good value dinners on offer, barbecues on Fri, bike rental, and a huge range of tours run by **BackPackers Travel & Adventure** agency. Warmly recommended.

$ pp Mendoza Backpackers
San Lorenzo 19, T0261-429 4941,
www.mendozabackpackers.com.
Well-run central hostel with an attractive lounge and terrace bar, dorms for 4 and 6, some with bath. Tours run by **BackPackers Travel & Adventure** agency.

$ pp Mendoza Inn
Arístides Villanueva 470, T0261-420 2486,
www.mendozahostel.com.
In the lively bar area, small dorms for 4 to 8, some with bath, and a private double (**$$**), large garden with a tiny pool, dinners offered extra. Tours run by **BackPackers Travel & Adventure** agency.

Camping

Camping Suizo
Av Champagnat, El Challao, 8 km from city,
www.campingsuizo.com.ar.

Modern, shady, with pool, barbecues, hot showers and *cabañas* for 4 and 6. Recommended.

Restaurants

There are many open-air cafés for lunch on Peatonal Sarmiento and restaurants around Las Heras. The atmospheric indoor market on Las Heras, Mon-Sat 0830-1300 and 1600-1900, has cheap pizza, *parrilla* and pasta. A few food stalls remain open 0830-2300. Calle Arístides Villanueva, the extension of Colón heading west, has good restaurants (as well as hostels). See also Bars and clubs, below.

\$\$\$ Anna Bistró
Av Juan B Justo 161, T0261-425 1818, www.annabistro.com. Open from breakfast to a late dinner.
One of the most attractive restaurants in town, informal, French-owned, very welcoming, good food and drink, French and Italian flavours, excellent value. Recommended

\$\$\$ Azafrán
Sarmiento 765, T0261-429 4200, http://azafranresto.com.
A fine-wine lover's heaven, with an extensive range from all the best bodegas, expert advice on wines and a fabulous delicatessen where you can enjoy superb *picadas*. Its menu changes with the season. Recommended.

\$\$\$ Facundo
Sarmiento 641, T0261-420 2866.
Good modern *parrilla*, lots of other choices including Italian, good salad bar.

\$\$\$ Francesco Barbera
Chile 1268, T0261-425 3912, www.francescoristorante.com.ar.
Smart old town house with a wonderful garden, excellent Italian food, choose from over 200 different wines.

\$\$\$ La Marchigiana
Patricias Mendocinas 1550, T0261-429 1590, www.marchigiana.com.ar.
One of Mendoza's best restaurants and great value. Italian food served

in spacious surroundings with charming old-fashioned service.

\$\$\$ Mesón Español
Montevideo 244, T0261-429 6175, see Facebook.
Spanish food, including great paella, live music and flamenco shows Fri-Sat.

\$\$\$ Montecatini
Gral Paz 370, T0261-425 2111, http://montecatiniristo.com.ar.
Good Italian food, seafood and *parrilla*, more tourist oriented, popular with families.

\$\$ Gio Bar
Chile 1288, T0261 420 4107, http://giobar.com.ar.
Attractively set and casual, a good choice for Italian-style sandwiches, pizzas and salads.

\$\$ Las Tinajas
Lavalle 38, T0261-429 1174, www.lastinajas.com.
Large buffet-style/all-you-can-eat at very reasonable prices, wide selection of pastas, grills, Chinese, desserts and so on. Cheap wine, too.

\$\$ Por Acá
Arístides Villanueva 577, see Facebook. Open 2100 till 0500.
Bar for pizzas and drinks, popular, noisy.

\$\$ Quinta Norte
Mitre 1206, see Facebook.
Cheap deals and generous portions in an elegant mansion on Plaza Independencia.

\$\$ Vía Civit
Emilio Civit 277. Breakfast (0630) onwards.
For first-class sandwiches, tarts and pastries in a relaxed, elegant traditional bakery.

Ice cream parlours

Ferruccio Soppelsa
Espejo y Patricias Mendocinas, with several branches, www.soppelsahelados.com.
The best place for ice cream (even wine flavours!). Recommended.

Bars and clubs

Av Arístedes Villanueva, just 10 mins' walk southwest of the main plaza, is the area for an evening stroll and has exciting bars and restaurants that are popular with a younger crowd. (Note that this street changes its name to Colón at Belgrano.) You'll find it quiet if you're heading out for an early dinner, but it livens up after 2400 when the bars are full. La Alameda (Av San Martín, north of C Córdoba) is another pleasant bar area with some basic restaurants that are also open at lunchtime. For other suggestions, see www.mendozanoduerme.com.ar (in Spanish).

Antares
Av Villanueva 153, www.cervezaantares.com. Popular place to hang out Fri nights, try the microbrewery beer.

Iskra
Av San Martín Sur 905, see Facebook. Late-night club, with live music.

Liverpool
San Martín y Rivadavia, www.publiverpool.net. Pub food, sandwiches, burgers, Beatles memorabilia and European football matches on the screen.

Festivals

Early Mar Fiesta de la Vendimia, a riotous wine harvesting festival, which includes a carnival queen, a procession of floats and outdoor extravaganzas in the park – but little wine tasting. It's held in the amphitheatre of the Parque San Martín. See www.vendimia2017.mendoza.gov.ar. Local wine festivals start in Dec.
   A parallel event is the less-promoted but equally entertaining **Gay Vendimia Festival**, featuring parties, shows and the crowning of the Festival Queen. See www.vendimiaparatodos.com.ar. **Mid-Mar Vendimia Obrera**, a much more modest affair when vineyard workers, many of whom are of Bolivian origin, recover the

roots of the original celebration with live music, wine and food in Cordón del Plata, a village in the Uco valley.

Shopping

The main shopping area is along San Martín and Las Heras, with good clothes, souvenir, leather and handicraft shops as well as vast sports emporia. There's a **Mercado Artesanal** (San Martín 1133, Mon-Fri 0800-1800, Sat 0900-1300), for traditional leather, baskets, weaving; also a weekend market on Plaza Independencia. Cheap shops include: **El Turista** (Las Heras 351), and **Las Viñas** (Las Heras 399, www.lasvinas.com.ar). For higher quality head to **Raíces** (Peatonal Sarmiento 162), or **Alpataco** (www.alpatacoweb.com.ar) next door. *Vinotecas* offer a good choice of wines; try **Winery** (Chile 898, T0261-420 2840).

What to do

The sight of distant purple mountains is bound to draw you from the city up into the dramatic Andes to the west. This area, known as Alta Montaña (see page 194), is the undoubted highlight of the region and shouldn't be missed, but if you're thinking of taking a day trip from Mendoza city, bear in mind that you'll get very little chance to explore; you're better off hiring a car and spending a few days staying up in the mountains. For water sports, Embalse El Carrizal, an artificial lake 60 km south of Mendoza, has yachting and fishing, campsites and picnic areas.

Bus tours
Bus Turístico, *www.mendozacitytour.com.* Open-top sightseeing bus with 18 stops, including Cerro de la Gloria. Hourly departures from Peatonal Sarmiento y Av San Martín, Tickets (US$10, hop on/hop off) sold at city's tourist offices.
Bus Vitivinícola, *www.busvitivinicola.com.* 4 departures each week from top hotels and Av San Martín y Garibaldi to Luján de Cuyo's

Visiting bodegas

Transport

There are plenty of tours on offer from agencies in Mendoza city, allowing you to visit a couple of bodegas in an afternoon. These are fine if you haven't got a car, but it's much more interesting to go independently, so that you can choose where you'd like to visit, and take your time. Touring wineries by bus really isn't an option, since almost all the bodegas are some way out of any town and you might waste a lot of time waiting for buses. Cycle tours are an appealing alternative to exploring one limited area, such as Mapiú, with a couple of specialized agencies based in the wine regions, and reasonable distances to cover: you could put together a tour of bodegas that are a five- to 20-minute ride from each other.

Reserve in advance

Remember always to ring and book your tour first, and if you don't speak Spanish, ask if they have an English-speaking guide. You'll be able to get a vague idea of the process but it will be far more interesting if you understand the detail.

Map

Get hold of a map of the wine region: there are lots of maps available in free tourist brochures, but the best is the *Winemap Turístico*, www.winemapturistico.com, sold in some restaurants and wine stores: it's very good and informative. There is also a good free wine magazine in English called *Wine Republic* (www.wine-republic.com).

Variety

Limit yourself to four or five bodegas in a day, especially if you're driving. It's worth trying to see both a big modern winery and smaller and more intimate places, since their processes are quite different, and often a smaller winery will take even more time and trouble to share their produce with you.

Try it at home

One of the great things about visiting these bodegas is that often you'll be trying wines that are available in your own country, so that even if you can't carry a crate home with you, you can buy the same wine at home wine supplier.

---

main wineries in 2 alternative circuits, half- or full-day tours, hop on/hop off, US$17. **El Oro Negro**, *T0261-498 0510, www. bateatour.com.ar.* Open-top bus offering 2½-hr bilingual city tours (US$8) including Cerro de la Gloria, 3 daily departures from Plaza Independencia (on C Chile); also 90-min bilingual tours of Parque San Martín and Cerro de la Gloria (US$5), 3 to 4 daily departures from same point.

Climbing

Club Andinista Mendoza, *FL Beltrán 357, Guaymallén, T0261-431 9870, see Facebook.* Treks and climbs are also organized by the famous climber Sr Fernando Grajales, T1-310-402 2388 (US toll free), www.grajales.net.

Cycling

For bike tours and rentals, try **Internacional Mendoza** (Pedro Molina 63, T0261-423 2103, www.intermza.com). See also **BackPackers**

Travel & Adventure (see below) for bike tours and rentals, or shop around the handful of agencies along C Urquiza in the wine region of Coquimbito, Maipú, such as **Mr Hugo** (Urquiza 2288, Coquimbito, Maipú, T0261-497 4067, www.mrhugobikes.com). Good.

Language schools
Intercultural, *República de Siria 241, T0261-429 0269, www.spanishcourses.com.ar.*

Skiing
There are 3 resorts within striking distance of Mendoza: Los Penitentes, Los Puquios and Vallecitos; for all, see the Alta Montaña section, below.

Tour operators
Many agencies, especially on Peatonal Sarmiento, run trekking, riding and rafting expeditions, as well as traditional tours to Alta Montaña and the bodegas.
Aconcagua Spirit, *Colón 165 T0261-464 9111, www.aconcaguaspirit.com.ar.* Recommended for their 11-day horse riding expeditions across the Andes.
BackPackers Travel & Adventure, *Peatonal Sarmiento 231, T0261-425 5511 see Facebook.* Bilingual trips and bike rides through vineyards (US$27 pp). Occasional treks in Aconcagua area. Discounts for hostel network guests. Make sure about extra costs.
Huentata, *Perú 1485, T0261-425 8950, www.huentata.com.ar.* Conventional tours including Villavicencio and Cañón del Atuel. Recommended.
Inka Expediciones, *Juan B Justo 345, Ciudad, T0261-425 0871, www.inka.com.ar.* Climbing expeditions, including Aconcagua, highly professional, fixed departure dates, mules for hire.
Kahuak, *Rivadavia 234, T0261-423 8409, www.kahuak.com.ar.* Mainly focused on a wide range of wine tours. Recommended.
Mendoza Viajes, *Peatonal Sarmiento 129, T0261-461 0210, www.mendozaviajes.com.* Imaginative tours in comfortable coaches, professional, cheap deals available.

Trekking Travel, *Adolfo Calle 4171, Villa Nueva, Guaymallén, T0261-421 0450, www.trekking-travel.com.ar.* From easy horse riding to the Andes crossing; trekking in the Aconcagua and Cordón del Plata.

Whitewater rafting
Popular on the Río Mendoza; ask agencies for details.
Argentina Rafting, *Amigorena 86, T0261-429 6325, www.argentinarafting.com.* Offers varied activities from its base camp in Potrerillos (see page 197).

Transport

Mendoza is 1060 km west of Buenos Aires.

Air
El Plumerillo airport (T0261-520 6000) has money exchange, tourist information, shops, a restaurant and a *locutorio*, but no left luggage. Daily flights to **Buenos Aires** and **Santiago de Chile**. Also to **Córdoba**, **Bariloche**, **Iguazú** and a few other national destinations.

Bus
Local Most local buses have 2 numbers: the big number painted onto the bus in the top front corner is the bus company or *grupo*, while the smaller number (*subnúmero*) shown on a card propped in the window is the actual route (*recorrido* or *línea*). For example, if you're going to the bodega **La Rural** in Maipú, you'll need bus No 10, *subnúmero* 173; don't be tempted to get on all the other 10s that go past. Bus fares within and near the city start from US$0.40 and are paid with *Red Bus* magnetic cards (US$0.75-1), which are sold and topped up at designated outlets.

Long distance Buses depart from the huge terminal on the east side of Av Videla. It has shops, a *locutorio*, tourist information, ATMs, a good café, left luggage (opposite platform 53) and toilets. Beware of thieves at all times in the bus station and note that it's not a place to linger at night. Mendoza is a good stopping point for routes in and out of Chile with frequent services to Santiago, and at least one bus a day stopping at Uspallata and the mountainous region on the way to the Chilean border for those wanting to trek or ski.

To **Buenos Aires**, 13-17 hrs, US$79-113, many companies. To **Bariloche**, 17 hrs, US$95-107, with **Cata** and **Andesmar**. To **Córdoba**, 9-12 hrs, US$45-65, several companies. To **San Juan**, US$14, 2-2½ hrs. To **La Rioja**, US$40-55, 8-9½ hrs. To **Catamarca** 10-11½ hrs, US$50-73. To **Tucumán**, 13-20 hrs, US$65-89. To **Salta**, 18 hrs, US$64-106, with **Andesmar**. To **Potrerillos**, 1 hr, US$2.50 with **Buttini** (opposite platform 56), which goes on to **Uspallata**, US$5, 2¼ hrs, and up to **Las Cuevas** (Chilean border), twice a day, US$8, 4 hrs. To **Tupungato**, US$4, 1½-2 hrs, with **Cata**. To **San Rafael**, US$8, 3-3½ hrs, with **Buttini** and **Cata**. To **Malargüe**, direct with **Viento Sur** minibuses, US$13, 5 hrs, or with **Cata**, 5-6½ hrs, for connection in San Rafael.

International buses To **Santiago**, Chile (US$26-42, 6-7 hrs) with **Cata Internacional**, **Andesmar**, **El Rápido** and **Coitram**. Most buses and minibuses are comfortable enough, but it's worth paying for a good service as waiting time at the border can be several hours. Buses also go daily to **Viña del Mar** and **Valparaíso**; enquire at Mendoza bus terminal and shop around. For all services to Chile, book at least 1 day ahead; passport required, tourist cards given on bus. The ride is spectacular.

There are also direct services, though not daily, to **Lima** (Perú) with **Cata Internacional**, US$167-215 and **El Rápido Internacional**; and to **Montevideo** (Uruguay), with **El Rápido Internacional**, US$74.

Car hire
Most companies have their offices along C P de la Reta (900 block), next to Plaza Pellegrini.

★ Wineries in Zona Alta del Río Mendoza

bodega tours and famous vineyards

There are three main wine-producing areas in Mendoza province. The Zona Alta del Río Mendoza, the oldest wine-producing area, is immediately to the south of Mendoza city with bodegas sprinkled among two towns, Maipú and Luján de Cuyo. Wineries in this region are described in more detail below. The second region is the Uco Valley, to the south of the small town of Tupungato which lies southwest of Mendoza in the foothills of the Andes. And the third region is around San Rafael (286 km south of Mendoza city). Both Tupungato and San Rafael are described in the Southern Mendoza section (see page 203).

Argentina's wine industry has grown considerably in recent years (see box, page 37). Now it's being shaken up by the arrival of foreign investors who have bought extensive vineyards in the region. As well as wine growers, other enthusiasts have settled here and started up related businesses, running bodega tours, wine clubs, wine magazines and opening restaurants. This area of tourism is bound to change dramatically in the next few years, so check for new information if you're serious about your wine. For more information on the Mendoza wine-growing region in general, see the following websites: www. turismo.mendoza.gov.ar (with maps and information on the Camino del Vino); www. mendoza.com (in English with lots of information); www.vendimia2016.mendoza.gov.ar (covering the annual wine harvest festival in Mendoza); www.welcometomendoza.com (another very useful site, designed in English by expats with a good general overview). For tips on visiting bodegas, see box, page 188.

The area immediately to the south of Mendoza city, around the sprawling centres of Maipú and Luján de Cuyo, contains the oldest and some of the most famous vineyards in the province, producing wines with a high concentration of fruit. Malbec, particularly, thrives here, in altitudes between 650 m and 1050 m. Although the grape was brought from France, many experts argue that it is in Argentina that Malbec has found its real home, and in Zona Alta del Río Mendoza that it is at its best. Winegrowing styles are eclectic in the various vineyards here, but this area produces premium wines, thanks to the unique combination of soil and climate. Other grape varieties grown here are Cabernet Sauvignon, Merlot, Chardonnay, Syrah and Tempranillo.

> **Tip...**
> Take a map because the wineries are spread out along pretty country roads, with few signs to guide you. It's also worth contacting bodegas ahead of your visit.

This is the closest region to the city of Mendoza and easily visited in a few hours.

Bodega Escorihuela
Belgrano 1188, Godoy Cruz, T0261-424 2744, www.escorihuela.com.ar. Getting there: the winery is easily reached by all buses going south along Av San Martín in Mendoza (Belgrano runs parallel to San Martín, one block east) or by 5-min taxi ride.

Before you reach Maipú or Luján de Cuyo, it's worth stopping to visit one of the most famous bodegas in the country, in the suburb of Godoy Cruz. This is the closest winery to the city and was founded in 1884 by Spanish immigrants; it retains its traditional atmosphere in the original buildings. Escorihuela exports wine to the UK under the Gascón label and still produces Pont L'Eveque, which was Perón's favourite brand. The stunning centrepiece of your tour is in the cellars, where there's an ornately carved barrel from Nancy, France. If your Spanish isn't good, you might like to visit this bodega before the others for its helpful brochure explaining the whole wine production process in pictures. Escorihuela also has an excellent and expensive restaurant, **1884 Francis Mallman** (see Restaurants, page 193) with a superb menu, the perfect complement to the bodegas' fine wines.

Maipú
From Mendoza take bus No 10 (173), at Rioja y Garibaldi.

The satellite town of Maipú sprawls immediately southeast of Mendoza. You may find it useful to collect information from the local tourist office (see Tourist information, page 193), where bus No 10 (173) stops. There are many famous brands in this area, and some more intimate bodegas described here. There are also several wineries in Coquimbito district, immediately east of Maipú. The two smaller family-owned wineries, **Tempus Alba** and **Viña El Cerno**, are both delightful for a visit and lie very close to each other.

Familia Zuccardi winery ① *R33, Las Margaritas, Km 7.5, San Roque, T0261-441 0000, www.familiazuccardi.com, Mon-Sat 0900-1630, Sun 1000-1530.* Quite a long way east of Maipú town centre, and 35 km east of Mendoza, is this large and highly developed winery, whichs is exceptionally welcoming. There's a good restaurant, extensive wine tasting, a tea room, and occasional music concerts on offer. Anyone wanting to pick grapes during the harvest is always welcome, and cookery lessons are available with the restaurant's chef. Their wines are easily found abroad, where they're known as Q and Santa Julia.

Tempus Alba ⓘ *Perito Moreno 572, Coquimbito, T0261-481 3501, www.tempusalba.com.* A modern bodega where the Biondolillo family takes great pride in their attention to detail and are happy to share it with you.

Viña El Cerno ⓘ *Perito Moreno 631, Coquimbito, T0261-481 1567, www.elcerno-wines.com.ar.* This winery has a lovely country house, a restaurant and olive groves.

Carinae ⓘ *Videla Aranda 2899, Cruz de Piedra, south of Maipú town centre, T0261-499 0470, www.carinaevinos.com, daily 1000-1700.* This is another charming, small and welcoming winery. As the name might suggest, wines aren't the only passion of Philippe and Brigitte, the French owners, but astronomy too. They have an interesting collection of telescopes, which you can use. They produce Malbec, Syrah and Cabernet Sauvignon under the Carinae name (for export), and Octans and El Galgo labels (within Argentina).

Luján de Cuyo

Southwest of Maipú, Luján de Cuyo is another wine-producing area, with restaurants and small hotels in the leafy suburb of Chacras de Coria. There are now several wineries that offer accommodation, but the most famous and deservedly popular is **Tapiz** (see below).

Catena Zapata ⓘ *Cobos, Agrelo, T0261-413 1100, www.catenawines.com.* This large and impressively modern pyramid-like bodega is in one of the most beautiful settings in the region. It's owned by a traditional family who produce outstanding wines that are exported under the names Catena Alta, Alamos, Nicolás Catena Zapata and Catena. There is a restaurant too.

Carlos Pulenta-Vistalba ⓘ *Roque Sáenz Peña 3531, Vistalba (west of Luján de Cuyo town centre), T0261-498 9400, www.carlospulentawines.com.* This smaller but highly developed winery is renowned for its marvellous Vistalba wines and for having an exclusive lodge, **La Posada**, on its ultra-modern premises.

Séptima ⓘ *R7, Km 6.5, Agrelo, T0261-498 9550, www.bodegaseptima.com, Mon-Fri 1000-1800, Sat 1000-1400, with sunset tastings on Thu in summer.* Further west is another large, modern bodega with fantastic mountain views.

Tapiz ⓘ *Pedro Molina Russell, T0261-490 0202, www.tapiz.com.ar.* A small, exquisite winery that owns a finca in Luján de Cuyo. The restored 1890s house is the region's most exclusive hotel: Club Tapiz, see Where to stay, below. It also has one of the finest restaurants in Mendoza: **El Terruño**, see Restaurants, below.

Renacer ⓘ *Brandsen 1863, Perdriel (south of Luján de Cuyo town centre), T0261-524 4416, www.bodegarenacer.com.ar.* The Malbec grape flourishes wonderfully at this winery, which produces Punto Final Reserva, one of the top Argentine Malbec wines.

Achával Ferrer ⓘ *C Cobos 2601, by the Mendoza river, Perdriel (southwest of Luján de Cuyo town centre), T0261-481 9205, www.achaval-ferrer.com.* Near **Renacer** is this young, modern and repeatedly prize-winning boutique bodega which produces the finest quality red wines, including the great Finca Altamira.

El Lagar de Carmelo Patti ① *Av San Martín 2614, Mayor Drummond (north of Luján de Cuyo town centre), T0261-498 1379.* Highly recommended for its welcoming owner, who personally leads the tours (or his daughters, if he's busy), and takes pride in serving his excellent Cabernet Sauvignon or his Gran Assemblage for tasting, even straight from the barrel (Spanish only).

Listings Wineries in Zona Alta del Río Mendoza

Tourist information

Maipú

Tourist office
Pablo Pescara 190, T0261-497 2448, www.maipu.gob.ar.

Luján de Cuyo

Tourist office
Roque Sáenz Peña 1000, T0261-498 1912, www.lujandecuyo.gov.ar.

Where to stay

Maipú

$$$ Club Tapiz
C Pedro Molina Russell, T0261-496 3433, www.tapiz.com.
Surrounded by vineyards, Tapiz is a small, beautifully restored Italianate villa, where the minimalist style helps you unwind in comfort. A spa and the superb cuisine in its **Terruño** restaurant make this unquestionably one of the top hotels in Mendoza, see below.

$$$ Tikay Killa Lodge & Wines
Montecaseros 3543, Coquimbito, T0261-15 368 5170, www.tikaykilla.com.ar.
Small lodge in the Ruta del Vino, white rooms, parking, garden, wine tours and other activities organized, helpful English-speaking manager.

Luján de Cuyo

$$$$ Cavas Wine Lodge
Costaflores, Alto Agrelo, T0261-456 1748, www.cavaswinelodge.com.
A pricey but heavenly experience, ideal for a romantic and wonderfully relaxing stay. Spacious rooms in a beautifully restored rural mansion, surrounded by vineyards, with a restaurant and spa. Each room has a fireplace and terrace, swimming pool, wonderful views. Highly recommended.

$$$ Parador del Angel
Jorge Newbery 5418, 100 m from main plaza, Chacras de Coria, T0261-496 2201, www.paradordelangel.com.ar.
Restored 100-year-old house, tastefully decorated, very relaxing, gardens, pool. The owner is an experienced mountain climber.

Restaurants

Bodega Escorihuela

$$$ 1884 Francis Mallman
Belgrano 1188, Godoy Cruz, T0261-424 2698, http://1884restaurante.com.ar. Dinner only, reservations advisable.
The place to go for a really special dinner. Mallman is one of the country's great chefs, exotic and imaginative menu. Highly recommended.

Maipú

$$$ Terruño
Bodega Tapiz, Pedro Molina Russell, T0261-496 0131, www.club-tapiz.com.ar.
Refined minimalist decor in the beautifully restored rooms of an Italianate residence. Exquisite dishes made from local produce match Mediterranean flavours with a dash of Asian style. Recommended.

Alta
Montaña

The high Andes to the west of Mendoza city are the world's highest mountains outside the Himalayas and offer some of the country's most amazing scenery. This spectacular landscape is the setting for hiking, mountain climbing and adventures of all kinds, and is easily accessible from the Route Nacional 7 to Chile; simply driving west along Route 7 is an unforgettable experience.

Alta Montaña is an essential part of any trip to the province, even if you're not crossing the border, or planning to climb Aconcagua. From the pretty oasis town of Uspallata, the road to Chile climbs up between the jagged snow-capped mountains, with staggering views of Volcán Tupungato in the distance to the south and Aconcagua closer at hand to the north. In winter, you'll quickly reach the snowline and the charming small ski resort of Los Penitentes; beyond it is the natural wonder of the bridge at Puente del Inca, near the base for climbing Aconcagua. The road climbs finally to the border, crossing at Túnel Cristo Redentor, and if you continue to Chile, the steep descent on the other side offers yet more superb views.

There are two ways to reach Uspallata from Mendoza, both offering great views. Most dramatic is the climb north via many hairpin bends past the (abandoned) spa resort of Villavicencio (104 km, of which 52 km is on unpaved roads); alternatively, you can head south from Mendoza to pleasant Potrerillos (102 km, all paved roads) and take a short detour to the thermal springs at Cacheuta.

Villavicencio *Colour map 3, A2.*

Famous to all Argentines from the image of its Alpine-style 1940s hotel seen on bottles of ubiquitous mineral water, Villavicencio (altitude 1800 m, Km 47) is reached by a wonderful drive. From Mendoza, head north along Route 52, across flat plains growing nothing but scrubby *jarilla* bushes, following the *pre-cordillera* mountains on your left.

The road rises steeply to climb through thickly forested mountains to the **Reserva Natural Villavicencio** ① *www.rnvillavicencio.com.ar*, a beautiful former spa resort, now the centre of its own little nature reserve and a good place for a picnic and a stroll. The reserve protects the sources of mineral water and the whole area is owned by the French company **Danone**, who run a smart information centre on the local wildlife and employ *guardaparques* who can direct you to nearby walks. You can also stroll around the splendid grounds of the old hotel, visit its chapel and eat at the **Hostería Villavicencio** ① *T0261-424 6482*, run by a friendly local family who offer good value lunches and teas with fine local produce such as *jamón crudo* (prosciutto) and *chivo* (goat), which you can enjoy at tables outside.

Beyond Villavicencio the *ripio* road climbs up over the spectacular **Cruz de Paramillo**, via the ridiculously twisting hairpin bends of the Caracoles de Villavicencio. In total, there are allegedly 365 hairpin bends along the route, which give the road its name *La Ruta del Año* (Route of the Year).

Tip...
If cycling, carry plenty of water. Be aware that this is a high-altitude area with little shade; take your time.

At an altitude of 3050 m, there are breathtaking views all around, and this is a marvellous introduction to the vast peaks of Aconcagua, Tupungato and Mercedario. Descending to the fertile valley of Uspallata, there are rocks popping up like jagged teeth through the earth, in extraordinary colours from aubergine through to oxidized copper green, orange and creamy white. There are no bus services, but many tour operators include this trip. With your own transport, this makes for a great route to Uspallata.

Cacheuta

An alternative route to Uspallata and into the Andes is via the pretty villages of Cacheuta and Portrerillos, offering thermal spa and watersports respectively. If you're driving, note that since the river has been dammed there is no direct road between Cacheuta (altitude 1245 m) and Potrerillos, so you need to take a detour to get to Cacheuta. From Mendoza, head south out of the city by Avenida J Vicente Zapata, access Route 7, leading to Ruta 40. Follow signs to Cacheuta, passing the area's biggest petrochemical plant, before you climb up into the hills.

Cacheuta's pretty setting in a narrow valley merits the extra journey to reach it. There's a huge complex of several thermal pools where you can spend a day, and next to this, a fine hotel in attractive gardens with a good restaurant. It's better to stay at least a night to really enjoy the mountain scenery. See Where to stay, page 197.

Potrerillos *Colour map 3, B1.*
Potrerillos (altitude 1354 m, Km 68), just 10 km further on from Cacheuta, is a charming, laid-back village sprawling among the foothills of the Cordón del Plata mountains. In the summer it's a popular retreat among Mendocinos, but it's excellent for a weekend's walking or horse riding at any time of year, though particularly lovely in spring, or in autumn, when the avenues of *álamo* (poplar) trees are a rich yellow against the mauve haze of mountains beyond. From December to February, you can go rafting and kayaking on Río Mendoza, which runs through the valley below the village. The water level depends on the time of year and the amount of snow melt swelling the river, so that the high season varies from year to year. In summer you can hike from Potrerillos to Vallecitos over two days. There's also a lovely walk to Cascada del Salto, but the path isn't marked, so take a guide.

From Potrerillos' centre – where there's little more than a hotel, campsite and YPF station on a crossroads – you could take the road south up to Vallecitos via the little hamlets of El Salto, Las Vegas and San Jorge, with its small *cervecería* (microbrewery). There are *parrilla* restaurants, tea rooms and lots of *cabañas* for hire around these areas, and the views are wonderful.

Vallecitos
This tiny hamlet (altitude 2900 m) is 27 km west of Potrerillos along a madly winding *ripio* road, certainly not to be attempted in poor weather conditions. There's little here apart from a couple of *refugios* with hostel accommodation and a rather basic family ski resort, but it's popular as a day trip from Mendoza. The **ski centre**, Valles del Plata Centro de Esqui, has 4.7 km of pistes, mostly intermediate standard, seven ski lifts and a ski school. Vallecitos is used as a base camp by climbers for training in the nearby peaks, before attempting Aconcagua. The beautiful summits of the Cordón del Plata range are less well known than Aconcagua, but also spectacular.

Uspallata *Colour map 3, A2.*
Some 120 km from Mendoza and 52 km from Potrerillos, the picturesque village of Uspallata (population 3400, altitude 1751 m) lies in its own wide valley, very close to the high Andes, and so it's become a popular stopping point on the road to Chile. All routes pass through it, and yet it has retained a rather charming unspoilt atmosphere, out of peak season at least. With distant mountains glimpsed through a frame of *álamo* (poplar) trees, it is reminiscent of the Himalayas and was the setting for *Seven Years in Tibet*. Stay for a day at least to explore the mysterious white egg-shaped domes of **Las Bóvedas** ① *2 km on RN 149 north,* built in the early 19th century by the indigenous Huarpes people, under instruction by the Jesuits, to melt silver. There is an interesting small museum.

From Uspallata, the Route Provincial 39 leads north to **Calingasta** and **Barreal** (see page 221), unpaved for its first part and tricky when the snow-melt floods it in summer. Here you'll find the remains of the Inca road, one of the most important archaeological sites in the region, with foundations of an Inca Tambo (post house) too; look for signs on the left-hand side of the road. Uspallata has a few hotels, a hostel, food shops, bakeries, a post office and a YPF station with restaurant, shop and *locutorio*s.

Tourist information

Upsallata
The tourist office keeps unreliable hours.
For information, see www.lasheras.gob.ar.

Where to stay

Cacheuta

$$$$-$$$ Hotel & Spa Termas Cacheuta
R82, Km 38, T02624-490152,
www.termascacheuta.com.
A warm and inviting place with comfortable
rustic-style rooms and thermal water piped
into the private bathrooms. There's a large
swimming pool, a good restaurant and
access to the lovely spa included. Prices
are full board and are cheaper Sun-Thu.
Entry into the Thermal Spa Park is US$46
(slightly cheaper on weekdays) for a full day.
Recommended.

Potrerillos

$$$ Silver Cord B&B
Valle del Sol, T02624-481083,
www.silvercordbb.com.ar.
With breakfast, internet, laundry service,
lots of outdoor activities and 4WD trips,
guides speak English.

Camping
Excellent ACA site (T02624-482013).
Shady, hot water after 1800, pool, clean.

Uspallata

$$$ Gran Hotel Uspallata
On RN 7, Km 1149, towards Chile, T02624-
420003, www.granhoteluspallata.com.ar.
Lovely location, spacious and modern in big
gardens away from the centre, pool, good
value, restaurant.

$$$ Los Cóndores
Las Heras s/n, T02624-420002,
www.loscondoreshotel.com.ar.

Low season prices, bright, neat rooms,
good restaurant, heated pool.

$$$ Valle Andino
Ruta 7, T02624-420095,
www.hotelvalleandino.com.
Modern airy place, good rooms, heated
pool and restaurant. Breakfast included.

$ pp Hostel Internacional Uspallata
RN 7, Km 1141.5, T0261-575 9204,
www.hosteluspallata.com.ar.
Attractive surroundings offering dorms for 4
to 6 with or without bath, private rooms sleep
1-6, with bath ($$$-$$), also comfortable
cabins for up to 5. There's also a bar and
restaurant. Tours arranged, bike and ski rental.

Restaurants

Potrerillos

$$$-$$ Tomillo
Av Los Cóndores, El Salto, T02624-483072,
www.tomillorestaurant.com.ar. Open all day
(closed Tue and Wed in low season).
Excellent home cooking, including trout.
Also simple and warm accommodation
in private doubles ($$).

Uspallata

$$$ La Estancia de Elías
Km 1146.
Opposite petrol station, a good and
crowded *parrilla*.

$$$-$$ Lo de Pato
RN7 Km 1148.
A popular *parrilla*; also pasta; takeaway food
and bakery.

What to do

Potrerillos
Argentina Rafting, *base camp at Ruta Perilago,*
T02624-482037, www.argentinarafting.com.
Reliable company, organizes good trips
with climbing, hiking, kayaking and other

adventure sports. Office in Mendoza city at Amigorena 86, T0261-429 6325.

Uspallata
Desnivel Aventura, *RN 7 by the YPF petrol station, T0261-15-554 8872, www.desnivel aventura.com.* Offers rafting, riding, mountain biking, trekking, climbing and skiing.

Transport

Bus
Buttini (www.abuttini.com) has daily services to and from **Mendoza** with stops at all towns along RN 7; there are fewer services in winter, when roads can be blocked by snow, west of **Uspallata**. To **Mendoza**: from **Uspallata**, several services daily, 2-2½ hrs, US$5; from **Cacheuta**, daily; from **Potrerillos**, 1 hr, US$2.50; Uspallata to **Puente del Inca**, US$3.25. Buttini continues twice a day from Puente del Inca to **Las Cuevas**, US$3.75 (from Uspallata), US$0.65 (from Puente de Inca). Note that buses going to Chile do not pick up passengers on their way. See also box, page 201, for more on the border crossing at Las Cuevas.

Uspallata to Chile via Parque Provincial Aconcagua
high-altitude peaks and ski resorts on the road to Chile

This dramatic road, which runs past the foothills of Aconcagua, is one of Mendoza's most memorable sights and not to be missed. From Uspallata, a good paved road to Chile crosses a broad plain, with maroon and chalk-white rocks sticking up from the rolling land. The road winds alongside a ravine with a thread of turquoise water below, before climbing up into a mountain pass with amazing terracotta rock formations and a heart-stopping glimpse of Volcán Tupungato, one of the giants of the Andes, rising to 6600 m. The first tiny village you come to, Punta de Vacas, has a large *gendarmería* (police station) but little accommodation.

In the mountains, the road may blocked by snow and ice from June to October; if travelling by car at these times, enquire about road conditions and requirements for snow chains and a shovel in Mendoza before setting out. See also www.vialidad.mendoza.gov.ar and www.gendarmeria.gov.ar.

Ski resorts
The road continues, climbing quickly beyond the snowline in winter, to the charming small ski resort of **Los Penitentes** (altitude 2580 m) ⓘ *Km 183, www.penitentesweb.com, May-Sep, daily ski hire US$35-45.* The resort is named after the mass of pinnacled rocks on its mountainside, which you might think looks vaguely like a group of cowled monks climbing upwards. It is a low-key family resort and is surprisingly quiet. There is good skiing on the 28 pistes (total length of 25 km, with 10 lifts); most of them are graded difficult but there are a couple of long descents of medium difficulty and three beginners' slopes. It's good value and uncrowded.

Another low-key ski resort in the area is **Los Puquios** ⓘ *www.puquios.com,* 5 km west. It's small, ideal for beginners and good value. It's also used as a base camp for climbers for acclimatization to the high altitudes, and as a departure point for mule caravans to higher base camps closer to Aconcagua. On the southern side

Tip...
Bring warm clothing, even if you're just coming for a day trip, because there can be snow as late as September and October.

of Route 7, opposite, you'll find a cemetery for climbers who have died on Aconcagua's slopes; a reminder that this summit is not to be undertaken lightly.

Puente del Inca *Colour map 3, B1.*

Seven kilometres further on, Puente del Inca (altitude 2718 m, Km 190) is set among breathtaking mountains and is a great base for exploring the peaks on foot or on horseback, with access to the Parque Provincial Aconcagua. The naturally formed bridge, after which the village is named, is said to be one of the Great Wonders of South America. Crossing a tributary of the Río Mendoza at a height of 19 m, the natural bridge is 21 m long and 27 m wide and seems to have been formed by sulphur-bearing hot springs below which have stained the whole ravine an incredible ochre yellow, and left the bridge an eerie orange colour. Underneath the bridge are the ruins of a 1940s spa hotel, destroyed by an avalanche and now mostly washed away by the river, but a torrent of hot sulphurous water still gushes from its walls. (Watch your footing on the steps as they are extremely slippery.) The old baths, to the side of the river, between the bridge and the small church, have basic facilities and are good for a soak amidst magnificent scenery.

West of the village is the access road for Laguna Horcones in the Parque Provincial Aconcagua; see box, page 200. Route 7 continues west, with fine views of Aconcagua sharply silhouetted against the sky, to the customs post at Los Horcones, the settlement of Las Cuevas (16 km beyond Puente del Inca) and on through the Cristo Redentor tunnel to Chile (see box, page 201).

★ Parque Provincial Aconcagua

The Aconcagua Provincial Park is 190 km west of Mendoza city, and apart from Aconcagua itself – the highest peak in the world outside the Himalayas, at 6959 m – it includes 30 other peaks over 4000 m, nine of them over 5000 m, making it a great centre for hiking and climbing. Mount Aconcagua gets its name from the Quechua for 'stone sentry', and it is indeed a majestic peak with five great glaciers hanging from its slopes.

It's a demanding climb even for the experienced, and it's absolutely essential to take at least eight to 10 days just to adapt to the altitude before you ascend. Pulmonary and cerebral oedema are serious risks and the dangers should not be underestimated: climbers die on the mountain every year. If you're planning to climb Aconcagua, it's essential to seek expert advice and plan your trip carefully. See the official website, www.aconcagua. mendoza.gov.ar, for more details. For emergencies only, use the *guardaparques'* radio frequency 142.8 Mhz.

Trekking and climbing routes There are two access routes to Aconcagua's summit, Río Horcones and Río de las Vacas, which lead to the two main base camps, Plaza de Mulas and Plaza Argentina respectively. For climbing Aconcagua, allow two weeks for the complete trip. Getting to the summit is not technically difficult: the problem is in taking sufficient time for your body to adjust to the high altitude. Most people fail simply because they take it too fast. All climbers should allow at least one week for acclimatization at lower altitudes before attempting the summit. Allow another few days for the weather.

Day permits allow you to walk from Horcones four hours up to Confluencia Base Camp (3390 m) and then two hours back, all along the Quebrada del Río Horcones. The walk presents no difficulties, except for the high altitude – don't be surprised that some people in your group will be affected more than others. Altitude sickness affects everyone differently.

Essential Parque Provincial Aconcagua

Access

Valle de los Horcones (2950 m), 2 km west of Puente del Inca and another 2 km off R7: *guardaparque* and free camping, open in the climbing season. This is the last accessible point for vehicles.

Entry fee

There is an entrance fee of US$1.25 for the short walk to the mirador on Laguna Horcones, where you have excellent views of Aconcagua's southern face.

What to take

Tents must be able to withstand 160-kph winds. Clothing and sleeping gear need to be suitable for temperatures below -40°C. Always carry plenty of water, as there are very few sources. Take all your rubbish out with you: no litter is to be thrown away in the park, and bags are handed out at the park entrance to be collected when you leave. Bring a stove and sufficient fuel; no wood is to be used for lighting fires.

Services and tours

Mules are available from Puente del Inca: about US$240 for 60 kg of gear one way to Plaza de Mulas or US$480 for 60 kg one way to Plaza Argentina; arrange return before setting out for a reduced two-way price. Organized trekking expeditions and tours can be booked in Mendoza (see Tour operators, page 189; and the official website).

Permits

It's essential to obtain a permit for trekking or climbing at any time of year: pay a fee (much cheaper for Argentine nationals) and fill in a form. You'll need to submit certain other documents for some specific activities. The rules and prices vary according to time of year and activity. For climbing in the high season (15 December-31 January) you must obtain a permit in person in Mendoza, at the **Subsecretaría de Turismo**, Avenida San Martín 1143, T0261-425 8751, Monday-Friday 0800-1300. In the winter season (1 April-14 November) you must enlist the services of an official mountain guide (see www.aconcagua.mendoza.gov.ar, under 'services' then 'guides') and the guide will obtain the proper permits.

An ascent permit lasts for 20 consecutive days from the moment it is stamped at the park entrance, and prices vary from US$440 in high season to US$237 in winter. Be warned that places selling the permits, and fees, may change, so it's vital to check the official website (www.aconcagua.mendoza.gov.ar).

Trekking permits are needed for all walks up to any of the base camps (excluding Plaza Guanacos camp, at the end of the only ascent trek) and are sold near the park itself at Horcones ranger station. These cost US$142 for seven consecutive days; US$61 for three consecutive days in high season; and US$78 the rest of the year.

When to go

The best time to climb is from the end of December to end of February.

BORDER CROSSING
Argentina–Chile

Las Cuevas

The paved road to the border goes through the 3.2-km **Cristo Redentor tunnel**, open 0800-2000 in winter and 24 hours in summer, US$2 for cars (no cyclists), into Chile. The last settlement before the tunnel is tiny forlorn Las Cuevas, 16 km from Puente del Inca, offering only a *kiosko*, café and hostel accommodation. In summer you can take the old road over La Cumbre pass to El Cristo Redentor (Christ the Redeemer), an 8-m-high statue erected jointly by Chile and Argentina in 1904 to celebrate the settlement of their boundary dispute. If you want to see this, take an all-day trip from Mendoza, or drive up in a 4WD, after the snow has melted, or walk from Las Cuevas (4½ hours up, two hours down; only to be attempted by the fit, in good weather). Expreso Uspallata runs buses to here from Mendoza.

Accommodation Arco de las Cuevas ($ per person, doubles $$), T0261-426 5273. Set right above the old road to Cristo Redentor on a picturesque old Alpine-like stone and wooden arch, this has spartan though comfortable dorms, a restaurant and a bar that mostly attracts climbers, some skiers and mountain guides. They can also organize adventure trips into Chile. Transfer for access to Aconcagua Provincial Park.

Precautions There are many dangerous bends on this route so drive slowly, and at Km 1097 the 13-m bridge over Río Blanco is only 4.70 m wide, so there is only one car allowed past at any one time. Due to fog, snow, mud or falling rocks, this route is sometimes closed. For up-to-date information, contact Escuadrón 27, Punta de Vacas, T0261-4205 275, esc27p_vacas@fullzero.com.ar. For information on the curves and lookouts, see www.gendarmeria.gov.ar/pasos-chile/cristo-redentor.html (in Spanish).

Chilean customs The Chilean border is beyond Las Cuevas, but customs is back near Los Horcones, 2 km west of Puente del Inca.

Confluencia Base Camp can get horribly crowded in summer with dozens of climbers and many more mules. There is a ranger station, public showers and medical services (in high season). From here you can either take the North Face route, used by 80% of climbers, to Plaza de Mulas (4365 m), in eight hours, or the South Face route to Plaza Francia (4250 m), in five hours. It's a tiring, rather monotonous walk up to Plaza de Mulas, another busy camp, with a ranger station, medical services and the highest hotel in the world another 20-minute walk away.

South Face route leads from Confluencia to Plaza Francia base camp (five hours), with a mirador after about four hours looking over the lower Horcones glacier, with an outstanding view of the 3000-m high rock and ice walls of Aconcagua's south face. Plaza Francia Camp is less crowded, but has no services at all.

Route via the Polish Glacier: This little-used route starts at Punta de Vacas (2400 m), 16 km east of Puente del Inca. Plaza Argentina (4200 m) is the base camp with intermediate camps at Pampa de Leñas (2900 m), with ranger station, reached after four hours of easy walking from Punta de Vacas, and Casa de Piedra (3240 m), reached after a further moderate six-hour walk along the same Quebrada del río de las Vacas, also with ranger station. From here, it's a steep seven-hour walk to Plaza Argentina (ranger station and medical services).

Where to stay

Ski resorts
There is also camping at Los Puquios.

$$$ Hostería Puente del Inca
RN7, Km 175, T0810-220 0031, www.
hosteriapuentedelinca.onlinetravel.com.ar.
Next to the small ski centre at Los Puquios.
Huge cosy dining room, advice on
Aconcagua, helpful owners and a great
atmosphere. Full board available.

$$ pp Hostería Penitentes
Villa Los Penitentes, T0261-524 4708.
Cheery place near ski slopes, with breakfast
and a good café. It's cheaper for several
nights. Recommended.

$ pp Campo Base Penitentes
T0261-425 5511, www.penitentes.com.ar.
Open all year.
A lively place and a cheap ski resort option,
with slightly cramped dorms, shared bath,

restaurant, bar and minibus service to
Mendoza. Offers ski programmes in season.

Parque Provincial Aconcagua

$$$ Hotel Plaza de Mulas
Book through www.aconcaguaspirit.com.ar/
pmulas.htm. Open high season only.
Full board or cheaper without meals. Good
food, information, medical treatment, also
camping area. Recommended.

Transport

Puente del Inca
Bus
To **Mendoza**, 3 a day, 4 hrs, US$6, with
Buttini (www.abuttini.com). **Buttini**
continues twice a day from Puente del Inca
to **Las Cuevas**.

Southern
Mendoza province

The southern half of the province is wilder and less visited by tourists than the area around Mendoza city. There are two main centres, the closest of which, and most appealing, is the charming town of San Rafael, the centre of its own wine-growing region, with tree-lined streets and excellent bodegas. Near here, there's rafting heaven in the extraordinary Cañón del Atuel, a canyon of weird rock formations with a wonderful fast-flowing river running through it. The other centre, much further south, is the fledgling tourist town of Malargüe, which you could use as a base for skiing at Las Leñas, or for visiting remote areas of natural beauty at La Payunia and Llancanelo.

There are two possible routes to the south of the province: you can take the fast Ruta 40 directly to San Rafael or the picturesque route from Potrerillos along the Cordón del Plata to Tupungato, a sleepy place with superb wineries and the starting point for long trips into Tupungato Provincial Park. An appealing detour here is to scenic Manzano Histórico, right in the foothills of the Andes.

To reach the quiet little town of Tupungato (population 13,218, altitude 1050 m), take the picturesque road (Route 89) from Potrerillos, descending along the Cordón del Plata mountain range, with splendid views of the mountains, and through the fertile fruit- and vine-growing Uco Valley. (Otherwise, take Route 86 from Route Nacional 40, south of Mendoza.) Nearby are the stunningly wild mountain landscapes of Tupungato Provincial Park, named after the imposing peak of its volcano, 6600 m, which is inaccessible to the public unless you go with an approved guide; Rómulo Nieto's company (see Tour operators, below) is recommended.

There are also superb wild landscapes on the upper Río de Las Tunas, to the west of town; contact the tourist office at Tupungato to stay overnight at the nearby Refugio Santa Clara (they'll direct you to the army for the key).

There are many vineyards around Tupungato; one of the most famous is **Bodega Salentein** ① *Los Arboles, 15 km south, T02622-429500, www.bodegasalentein.com, tours of the bodega daily*, whose fine wines you may have noticed in many restaurants. With a beautiful setting against the foothills of the Andes, the bodega produces some of the country's finest wine (the Malbec is exquisite) and you can stay in **Posada Salentein**, which has comfortable rooms and extremely welcoming hosts; there's perfect peace in which to walk, ride and relax. Recommended.

A much newer winery also worth visiting is the Spanish-owned **O Fournier** ① *Los Indios, La Consulta, west of San Carlos, T02622-451579, www.ofournier.com*. Its output is dedicated mainly to Tempranillo grapes, and here you can admire both the vines and the avant-garde architecture of the winery building, which is strictly functional and state of the art.

Continue south from Salentein to **Manzano Histórico**, a tiny hamlet in fabulous scenery, where a statue of San Martín marks his victorious return via this route from Chile. A *hostería* and campsite make this a good base for trekking, and there's a little shop and bar for provisions.

Listings Tupungato and around

Tourist information

Tupungato
Information on Tupungato and the surrounding area is available from the foyer of **Hotel Turismo** (see Where to stay, below). Ask them about nearby bodegas and estancia visits for horse riding. See also www.tupungato.gov.ar (in Spanish).

Where to stay

Tupungato

$$$$ Chateau d'Ancon
R89, San José, Tupungato, T0261-4235843, www.estanciancon.com.ar. Mid-Oct to Apr.
At the foot of the mighty Tupungato volcano, a 1933 French-style rural mansion is at the heart of a traditional estancia owned by the Bombal family, who were originally French, but have been living in Mendoza since 1760. The magnificent park was designed by famous Argentine landscape architect Charles Thays, and all the fruit and vegetables

used for meals here are grown in nearby orchards and kitchen gardens. A wonderfully comfortable place to stay, with elegant decor inside the house, and excellent service.

$$$-$$ Hostería Don Romulo
Almirante Brown 1200, T02622-489020, www.donromulo.com.ar.
This *hostería* is owned by Rómulo Nieto, who runs his own tour company (see Tour operators, below). There are simple rooms with TV and bath for 2-4 with a cosy lounge to relax in and decent, inexpensive food from the restaurant.

$$ Hotel Turismo
Belgrano 1060, T02622-488007.
A slightly modernized 1940s place, basic but comfortable rooms with wonderful kingfisher-blue tiles in the bathrooms, some family rooms, a pool and a good restaurant. Tourist information in the foyer.

Camping

Camping San Antonio
R94, Km 27.5, T0261-15-535 4888, www.campingsanantonio.com.ar.
There are various attractive spots in the Manzano Histórico, but this one is particularly recommended for its good, well-kept facilities, including a large pool. They also rent out small *cabañas*.

Patios de Correa
Calle La Costa, El Peral, 4.3 km northwest of Tupungato.
A good site in woods of willow and walnut trees, on the riverbank, also a good picnic spot.

Restaurants

Tupungato
Apart from hotel restaurants, there are a few pizzerias and cafés to choose from on the main street, Belgrano.

$$ La Posada del Jamón
R92, Km 14, Vista Flores, Tunuyán, T02622-492053, www.laposadadeljamon.com.ar.
Pork rules on the menu here, in this charmingly rustic and popular roadside restaurant. There are other tasty dishes on offer though, and excellent local wines.

What to do

Tupungato
Tour operators
Rómulo Nieto, *www.donromulo.com.ar.*
A highly recommended guide who organizes trekking and horse riding into the provincial park. He also runs the base camp **Refugio El Cóndor**. In summer, Rómulo offers trekking to the summit and horse riding along the old path to Chile from Manzano Histórico to Portezuelo de los Piuquenes.
Tupungato Expedición, *Liniers 1139, T02622-489791, www.tupungatoexpedicion.com.ar.*
Run by 2 professional guides, 1- and 2-day treks or 18-day adventures.

Transport

Tupungato
Bus
To **Mendoza** and **Las Heras**, daily, 1½-2 hrs, US$4.

San Rafael (population 200,000, altitude 688 m) is a charming, quiet, airy town 236 km south of Mendoza in the heart of fertile land that produces wine, fruit and olives in abundance. It's a relaxed place, smaller and less sophisticated than Mendoza but trim and well maintained, with a good range of accommodation. It makes an ideal base for exploring the vineyards and for trying adventure sports at nearby Cañón del Atuel (see page 208) or more challenging activities further west.

Sights
There are lovely, leafy boulevards of French-influenced buildings in the city centre, thanks to the arrival of a significant French community here in the early 1900s. There are ATMs and *locutorios* all along Yrigoyen.

Río Diamante runs just south of the town, with a lovely park, **Parque Mariano Moreno**, situated on an island in the middle of the stream. Among its attractions are a zoo and a small museum, the **Museo Municipal de Historia Natural** ① *6 km southwest of town, daily 0800-1900, US$0.25; Iselín bus along Av JA Balloffet.*

San Rafael is at the heart of an important wine-producing region, whose wines are at least as excellent as those around Mendoza. One of the country's most important wineries is **Bianchi** ① *Ruta 143, 9 km west of the centre, T0260-444 9600, www.casabianchi.com,* whose vineyard and champagne house can be visited on a commercialized tour. It's worth

Essential San Rafael

Finding your feet

The airport is at Las Paredes, 7 km west of town, with access from Route 143. A bus to the centre costs US$0.75 with Buttini bus; US$0.45 with **Iselín Urbano**; *remise* taxis charge US$5-7. The central bus terminal is at General Paz y Paunero, a 10-minute walk to the centre.

Getting around

Most people cycle around the city, so you'll see more bikes than cars on the streets.

Orientation

The main thoroughfare, Avenida Hipólito Yrigoyen, runs northwest to southeast through the city, changing names at Avenida San Martín/El Libertador to become Avenida Mitre.

seeing for the fascinating process and rather over-the-top pseudo-classical building (take a taxi as buses are infrequent). They also have a traditional bodega in town, at the corner of Comandante Torres and Ortiz de Rosas, which offers an excellent and detailed tour, and sells the top wines at reduced prices after a generous tasting. (Look for their exported wines abroad under the names Elsa, Elsa's vineyard or Valentín Bianchi Premium.) **Jean Rivier** ① *H Yrigoyen 2385, T0260-443 2675, www.jeanrivier.com,* is a smaller, more intimate bodega in town which also produces excellent wine.

Within walking distance from town is San Rafael's oldest winery, **La Abeja** ① *Av H Yrigoyen 1900, T0260-443 9804, www.bodegalaabeja.com.ar,* while on the way to Malargüe, around 20 km southwest of San Rafael, is **Algodón Wine Estates** ① *Ruta 144, Cuadro Benegas, T866 960 7700, www.algodonwineestates.com.* This is a state-of-the-art winery with pricey accommodation, restaurant, tennis courts and a golf course.

Tourist information

See also www.sanrafael.gov.ar and www.sanrafael-tour.com (both in Spanish).

Tourist office
Av H Yrigoyen 775 y Balloffet, T0260-443 7860, www.sanrafaelturismo.gov.ar.
Friendly and helpful staff. There's also an office in the bus terminal (mornings only).

Where to stay

$$$ Nuevo Mundo
Av Balloffet 725, T0260-444 5666, www.hnmsanrafael.com.
Small business hotel, a little out of town, with pool, restaurant and spa.

$$ Francia
Francia 248, T0260-442 9351, www.alojamientofrancia.com.ar.
A lovely place on a quiet street in town with simple, functional rooms on a manicured garden; excellent value.

$$ Regine
Independencia 623, T0260-442 1470, www.hotelregine.com.ar.
Some 8 blocks away from centre, this is a comfortable choice with good rooms, a restaurant and a large pool in an attractive garden. Very good value.

$$ San Rafael
Calle Day 30, T0260-443 0127, www.hotelsanrafael.com.ar.
A decent and reasonably priced option with plain rooms in need of some renovation.

$ pp Tierrasoles Hostel
Pellegrini 248, T0260-443 3449, www.tierrasoles.com.ar.
5 blocks from bus station, it has small dorms for 6 to 8 and doubles (**$$**) in a pleasant residence with a courtyard.

$ pp Trotamundos Hostel
Barcala 298, T0260-443 2795, www.trotamundoshostel.com.ar.
In a quiet area next to the main street. A lively hostel with a good patio, small dorms for 3 to 6 and a private double (**$$**).

Restaurants

An area of attractive open-air cafés and small restaurants lies along C Pellegrini between Chile and Day in town.

$$$ El Rey del Chivo
Av H Yrigoyen 651.
A good and basic place for trying the regional speciality, *chivito*, or kid.

$$$ Pettra
Av H Yrigoyen 1750.
Very good choice for a great range of meals in an area full of restaurants.

$$ Las Duelas
Pellegrini 190.
For tasty sandwiches and salads.

$$ Nina
Av San Martín y Olascoaga. Open till late.
A casual, open-air place on a central corner, good for a light meal, including fine salads.

Ice cream parlours

La Delicia del Boulevard
Av H Yrigoyen 1594, www.ladelicia boulevard.com.ar.
Very good ice cream on the way to wineries.

What to do

Tour operators charge similar prices for standard trips, including the most popular day tour to Cañón del Atuel for about US$25-30 pp (lunch and extra activities are not included). Ask in advance for tours in English.

Atuel Travel, *Buenos Aires 31, T0260-442 9282, www.atueltravel.com.ar*. A recommended agency.
Raffeish, *Valle Grande, T0260-443 6996, www.raffeish.com.ar*. Recommended as the most professional rafting company.
Renta Bike, *Day 487, T0260-440 1236, www.renta-bike.com.ar*. Bike rental, wine tours and trips along Cañón del Atuel.

Transport

Air
To/from **Buenos Aires** with **Aerolíneas Argentinas**/Austral.

Bus
To/from **Mendoza**, 3-3½ hrs, many daily, US$7; **Neuquén**, US$44-57, 7-9½ hrs. To **Buenos Aires**, 12½-14 hrs, US$75-80. To **Valle Grande**, US$2.75, with **Iselín**. To **Las Leñas**, 3 hrs, US$7, with **Iselín** and **Cata**. To **Malargüe**, 2½-3 hrs, US$7.

For wineries west of town, take **Buttini** bus (destination 25 de Mayo) along C Avellaneda and then Av H Yrigoyen, and tell the driver which bodega you want to visit.

Around San Rafael

whitewater rafting, horse riding and remote lakes

The countryside surrounding San Rafael offers great opportunities for all kinds of activities, including rafting, horse riding, trekking, climbing and fishing.

Valle Grande and Cañón del Atuel
The most spectacular place for adventure is the nearby **Cañón del Atuel**, 35 km southwest. The gorge lies between two lakes 46 km apart, Valle Grande (508 ha) and El Nihuil (9600 ha). It's an atmospheric drive along the *ripio* road, which winds through the 20-km-long ravine of extraordinary rock formations in vibrant hues of cream, pink, metallic green and vivid terracotta. There are constantly changing views and an eerie atmosphere in the darker recesses of the canyon, where birds of prey wheel overhead. The best place for rafting is near **Valle Grande**, 2 km down the river from the Valle Grande Dam (about 40 km from San Rafael). On the south side of the river, near the bridge, you'll see plenty of adventure tour operators (see San Rafael What to do, above, for the most reliable ones). Many offer river rafting (Grade II for beginners), horse riding and trips for more challenging rafting, such as the upper Atuel or Diamante river (up to Grade V, experience required). There are plenty of hotels and campsites lining the pretty riverbanks on the north side of the river, in a 13-km stretch from this bridge back in the direction of San Rafael.

From San Rafael, **Iselín** runs daily buses to the Valle Grande dam at the near end of the canyon, returning in the evening, US$2.75. *Remise* taxis from San Rafael to Valle Grande charge about US$20. The only public transport through the entire gorge up to El Nihuil is the Iselín bus at weekends in summer.

Other trips
Lago Los Reyunos is another popular trip, 35 km west of San Rafael, a lake set in a barren rocky landscape, which can only be reached on a tour, as there are no buses. But far more spectacular is the **Laguna Diamante**, 200 km northwest of San Rafael, an ultramarine blue expanse of water, whipped by perpetual winds, set against the craggy backdrop of the Andes and the perfectly conical Volcán Maipo. Only 4WD vehicles will make it over

the last 60 km or so of track, and it's best to go on a tour from San Rafael with **Taiel Viajes** ⓘ *www.sierrapintada.com.*

There is some superb horse riding in the region into the Andes. You could leave from El Sosneado (see below) or Tupungato (see page 204) to the place where the Uruguayan plane crashed into the mountains, subject of the book and film *Alive!*. This is less gruesome than you might think, since the landscapes are amazing: stark and very beautiful. **Laguna del Atuel**, 200 km west of San Rafael, has incredible turquoise water lapping against ochre mountains, and makes for another fabulous five-day horse-riding trip.

Listings Around San Rafael

Where to stay

Cañón del Atuel

$$$-$$ Finca El Maitén
Mercado 1405, T0260-15-471 7946,
www.fincaelmaiten.com.ar.
A charming B&B 10 km from town in the wine-growing region. Spacious, rustic-style double bedroom and a lovely garden to relax in.

$$$-$$ Valle Grande Hotel & Resort
T0260-15-458 0660,
www.hotelvallegrande.com.
Well situated on the banks of the river in the Cañón del Atuel, with a big terrace and good views from its restaurant, this has smart rooms, a pool and friendly service. It's popular with families and very lively in summer. There are lots of activities laid on for guests. Also has *cabañas* for hire (**$$$**).

San Rafael to Las Leñas

thermal pools and powdery slopes

The greatest attraction west of San Rafael is the superb ski resort of Las Leñas. A good paved road (Ruta 144 and then Ruta 40) leads west from San Rafael across the vast plain of the Río Atuel, passing salt flats and marshland as you head towards stark snow-dusted mountains rising steeply out of the ochre-coloured land. If you're heading southwest this way to ski or hike, or south to explore the area around Malargüe, you might like to stop off at El Sosneado, at Km 138.

El Sosneado

El Sosneado is the only settlement in this area, with a service station and a small shop for fine home-cured hams and olives, where you can also take away delicious sandwiches. The **YPF** station sells snacks and hot drinks. El Sosneado is also the starting point for good rafting and treks into the mountains, but there is little infrastructure in the village itself, and most visitors prefer to arrange their trips before coming here, in San Rafael or Malargüe.

Nearby there's a good lake for trout fishing, **Laguna El Sosneado**, 42 km away, reached by a *ripio* side road following the valley of the Río Atuel northwest. Some 13 km or so beyond the lake are natural thermal pools, the **Termas el Sosneado**, where you can bathe in the sulphurous waters for free, since there's no organization here, and the **Hotel Termas El Sosneado** is in ruins. Ahead, you'll see the Overo volcano (4619 m).

Los Molles *Colour map 3, B1.*

Twenty-one kilometres southwest of El Sosneado and 156 km southwest of San Rafael a road branches off RN 40 towards Las Leñas, following the Río Salado west into the Andes.

After 30 km, the road passes through the tiny hamlet of Los Molles, a small, faded old thermal resort, now little more than a cluster of hotels, the oldest of which has access to thermal springs. None of these establishments is luxurious but they offer an alternative to expensive Las Leñas hotels, plus some adventure tourism trips in the summer that mainly include horse riding to nearby sites.

Opposite Los Molles a *ripio* road leads to the *refugio* of the **Club Andino Pehuenche** and, 8 km further on, to the **Laguna de la Niña Encantada**, a beautiful little lake and shrine to the Virgin. Continuing towards Las Leñas, there are the strange **Pozo de las Animas** (Well of the Spirits), two natural circular pits filled with water (the larger is 80 m deep), where wind blowing across the holes makes a ghostly wail, hence the name. They're a curious sight if you happen to be passing, but don't quite merit a special trip.

★ **Las Leñas** *Colour map 3, B1.*
T011-4819 6060, or T0800-222 5362, www.laslenas.com, lift pass in high season US$68 per day, equipment hire from US$26 daily.

Las Leñas (altitude 2250 m), 49 km off the San Rafael–Malargüe road, is internationally renowned for its excellent skiing and snowboarding. As a result, it's one of the most expensive resorts in the country, full of wealthy Argentine families and beautiful people in trendy bars. Set at the end of a spectacular valley, in the middle of five snow-capped peaks, it has powder snow throughout the season on 29 pistes with a total length of 64 km, and, despite the frequent bad weather and lack of tree cover, it's the best resort in South America, thanks to its steep slopes, with a vertical drop of some 1230 m, and the fact that you can walk straight out of your hotel onto the pistes. A constantly circulating free bus service picks up guests from further-flung hotels in the resort.

The resort also has a ski school, a special snowboard park, many cafés, bars and restaurants (several right on the pistes) and a useful information point where there are lockers. There are also banks, doctors and tourist information. There are also ski patrol units all over the pistes, so you're in safe hands here.

The season runs from mid-June to early October but the busiest and most expensive time is July and August, when prices are at least 50% higher. In summer, Las Leñas operates as a resort for adventure sports, such as trekking and climbing.

Beyond Las Leñas the road continues into **Valle Hermoso**, a beautiful valley accessible only from December to March.

Listings San Rafael to Las Leñas

Where to stay

Los Molles
There are cheaper options here than Las Leñas.

$$$ Complejo Los Molles
T0260-15-459 1654,
www.complejolosmolles.com.
Wood and stone detached houses, plain and comfortable, for 4-6 people with breakfast. Restaurant and ski rental.

$$$ Hotel Termas Lahuen-Có
T0260-449 9700, www.hotellahuenco.com.
Dating from 1930s and now rather kitsch, with thermal baths and meals.

$$$ La Valtellina
T0260-15-440 2761, www.lavaltellina.com.ar.
Attractively rustic Alpine cottages, Italian owned and run, with an excellent restaurant and tea house.

Las Leñas
There are several plush hotels, all **$$$$-$$$**, most with pool, plus a disco, ski rental shop and several restaurants (see www.laslenas. com). For cheaper accommodation stay in Los Molles (see above) or Malargüe (see below).

El Sosneado and around
Bus
Daily buses to/from **Malargüe**, **Las Leñas** and **San Rafae**l all stop at El Sosneado.

Malargüe and around   *Colour map 3, B2.*
outdoor activities amid snow-capped peaks

Situated 186 km southwest of San Rafael in reach of really spectacular unspoilt landscapes, Malargüe (population 35,000, altitude 1426 m) is slowly developing as a centre for hiking and horse riding, although its self-promotion as the national centre for adventure tourism is probably over-blown. In ski season it serves as a cheap alternative to Las Leñas, with frequent minibus services between the two. Malargüe has a broad main street, San Martín, with an assortment of small shops, *locutorios*, cafés and the odd run-down hotel, but the best accommodation is in the outskirts, north of the centre.

Sights
Malargüe has gained the interest of astrophysicists by hosting the world's largest **Pierre Auger Cosmic Ray Observatory** ① *Av San Martín (Norte) 304, T0260-447 1562, www.auger.org, Mon-Fri 0900-1230, 1530-1830, Sat-Sun 1530-1830 (ask in advance for English presentations).* A

Tip...
The best time to come is from spring to autumn, when you can make the most of the landscape for walking and riding.

visit here should be combined with the excellent **Planetarium** ① *Comandante Rodríguez (Oeste) 207, T0260-447 2116, www.planetariomalargue.com.ar,* which offers free guided visits and daily shows.

Around Malargüe
The wild untouched landscape around Malargüe is surprising and extraordinarily beautiful. There are three main places to visit, all pretty remote and with little or no public transport, so unless you have your own vehicle, they can only be visited on a tour. Even if you do have your own transport, you must be accompanied by an authorized guide, which must be arranged in advance and requires a certain amount of planning.

★ **La Payunia Reserve**, 208 km south, is the most remarkable of the three, and dominated by the majestic peaks of several snow-capped volcanoes. The vast expanse of seductive altiplano grasslands is studded with volcanic peaks and deep red and black crags of extraordinary sculpted lava. The appearance of hundreds of guanaco running wild across your path adds to the magic. The entrance is 100 km south of Malargüe on sandy *ripio* roads. You can bring your own vehicle here and the *guardaparques* will show you around in their 4WD. Ask at the tourist office in Malargüe for directions; they will also radio the *guardaparques* and tell them to expect you. The best way to enjoy the reserve is on horseback, on a three-day expedition, or you can take a tour from Malargüe with **Karen Travel** ① *www.karentravel.com.ar.*

Argentina–Chile

Paso Pehuenche

Paso Pehuenche (2553 m) is reached by a *ripio* road that branches off Ruta 40, 66 km south of Malargüe. On the Chilean side the road continues down the valley of the Río Maule to Talca.

Opening hours The border is open from 0900-1900 (in Chile 0800-1800). See www. gendarmeria.gov.ar/pasos-chile/pehuenche.html for detailed information (in Spanish).

The **Laguna Llancanelo** (pronounced *shancannello*), 65 km southeast, is filled with hugely varied birdlife in spring, when 150 species come to nest on its lakes. At any time of year you'll see Chilean flamingos, rising in a pink cloud from pale turquoise waters where volcanic peaks are perfectly reflected. You may also see tern, curlews, grebes, teal and black-necked swans, among others. To get there, contact the Llancanelo *guardaparques* via the tourist office, or go on a trip from Malargüe.

At **Caverna de las Brujas** ① *1 hr's drive away, 2-hr guided tours, lights and helmets provided, children over 7 welcome*, there are 5 km of underground caves to explore, taking you through the Earth's development from the Jurassic period onwards; enjoy the fantastic variety of elaborate stalactites and stalagmites. There is no independent access to the caves and all visits must be arranged with one of the authorized tour operators in Malargüe (see What to do, below); the tourist office in Malargüe can make recommendations (see Tourist information, below).

Listings Malargüe and around

Tourist information

Malargüe

Tourist office
Ruta 40 Norte, T0260-447 1659, www. malargue.gov.ar. Mon-Fri 0900-1600-2000.
Also at the bus station. Can arrange visits to the nearby provincial parks.

Where to stay

Malargüe

$$$ Malargüe
Av San Martín (Norte) 1230, T0260-447 2300, www.hotelmalarguesuite.com.
On the northern access to town, this comfortable 4-star hotel has a newer wing with slightly bigger rooms, an indoor pool, restaurant and spa.

$$ Rioma
Fray Inalicán (Oeste) 127, T0260-447 1065, www.hotelrioma.com.ar.
Small, family-run and spotless place with basic facilities and a pool. Convenient for the bus station.

$ pp Eco Hostel Malargüe
Prolongación Constitución Nacional (Finca No 65), Colonia Pehuenche, 5 km from centre, T0260-447 0391, www.hostelmalargue.com.
Eco-hostel built with an enhanced traditional *quincha* method, in rural surroundings on a dairy farm with organic fruit and veg, and good meals. Basic, comfortable dorms and rooms (**$$**), cheaper without bath. **Choique** travel agency.

Restaurants

Malargüe

$$$ La Cima
Av San Martín (Norte) 886.
Parrilla and more elaborate meals,
including fish. Good value dishes.

$$$-$$ El Chuma
Illescas (Oeste) 155.
The place for sampling *chivo* (kid),
the local speciality.

$$ Bonafide
Av San Martín (Sur) 364, see Facebook.
Open till late.
Excellent café serving simple meals,
including good pizza.

$$ La Posta
Av Roca (Este) 174, see Facebook.
Popular *parrilla*, offering pastas and
pizza too.

Festivals

Malargüe
**First 2 weeks of Jan Fiesta Nacional del
Chivo**, featuring locally produced kid (*chivo*),
a delicacy, with live music and partying.
It attracts national *folclore* stars, as well as
Chilean performers and public from across
the Andes.

What to do

Malargüe
Tour operators charge similar rates for
standard trips (eg Payunia for about US$80-
90 pp), which take a full day in most cases
and may include a light meal. 2-day treks in
Payunia, fly-fishing, rafting and several-day
horse rides in the Andes, including the
approach to the remains of the crashed
Uruguayan airplane (described in the film
Alive!) are also available, though some
activities are in summer only. Ask in advance
for tours in English.

A recommended range of tours is offered
by **Choique** (Av San Martín (Sur) 33, T0260-
447 0391, www.choique.com), and **Karen
Travel** (Av San Martín (Sur) 54, T0260-447
2226, www.karentravel.com.ar).

Some 30 km south of Malargüe, in the
Cuesta del Chihuido area on route 40, is
Manqui Malal (T0260-447 2567) and **Turcará**
(T0260-15-453 5908, www.turcara.com),
which offers trekking, zip-lining, camping
and meals.

Transport

Malargüe
Air
The airport (T0260-447 1600) is on the
southern edge of town. Chartered flights
from **Buenos Aires** and **São Paulo** (Brazil)
in the skiing season.

Bus
The bus terminal is at Aldao y Beltrán. To
Mendoza, direct daily with **Viento Sur**
minibuses, 5 hrs, or with **Cata**, 6½ hrs, US$13;
alternatively change buses in San Rafael.
To **San Rafael**, 2½-3 hrs, US$7, with **Buttini**,
Cata or **Iselin**. There are **Cata** buses and
several transfer services to **Las Leñas** in ski
season. **Cata** leaves twice weekly across
La Payunia to **Agua Escondida** on the border
with La Pampa province, and also heads
south along route 40 to Barrancas, on the
border with Neuquén province. Otherwise,
to **Neuquén** (via route 40 and Rincón de los
Sauces), Sun-Fri 2200, with **Leader/Rincón**
from Los Amigos bar, Av San Martín (Sur) 765,
by the clock tower.

San Juan
province

The province of San Juan extends north and west from the capital, San Juan city, which lies in the broad valley of the Río San Juan, and is the centre of a wine-producing area as big as Mendoza's but not of the same quality. The city itself is sleepy and not wildly interesting for visitors, but there are two areas in the province that might lure you here. San Juan's jewel is the little-visited west of the province, where the foothills of the Andes rise in ranges separated by beautiful, lush valleys such as the lovely Calingasta. There is great climbing and trekking here, with several Andean peaks to explore, including the mighty Mercedario (6770 m), and incredibly peaceful ancient hamlets provide charming places to completely unwind.

The northeast of the province, near the border with La Rioja, is the site of the Ischigualasto Provincial Park, often known as the Valle de la Luna (Valley of the Moon), where millions of years of the planet's history and dinosaur fossils are on display in dried-out lagoons, Talampaya National Park, just over the border in La Rioja, has fabulous dramatic canyons and eroded rocks. This northern region is inhospitably hot and dry almost all year round, but the landscapes are impressive: empty and starkly beautiful.

The provincial city of San Juan (population 119,423, altitude 650 m), located 177 km north of Mendoza, is much less inviting than the marvellous landscapes all around and you're most likely to arrive here on the way to the Calingasta Valley or the parks further north. However, it's a good base for organizing those trips as there are several good places to stay and eat, and some good bodegas for wine tasting. There's also one sight of fascinating cultural interest in the shrine to pagan saint La Difunta Correa.

Although the city was founded on its present site in 1593, little of the original settlement remains, since the most powerful earthquake in Argentine history struck in 1944, killing over 10,000 inhabitants. Though it's been rebuilt in modern style, San Juan has not yet recovered, unlike Mendoza. It was at a fundraising event at Luna Park in Buenos Aires for the victims of the tragedy that Juan Perón met Eva Duarte, the radio actress who became his second wife. Note that the main street, Avenida San Martín, is often called Libertador.

Sights
This is an important wine-producing area and there are lots of bodegas to visit, if you haven't seen those in Mendoza. See www.travelsanjuan.com.ar/vino.html for some suggestions of bodegas to visit. Those offering tours include **Santiago Graffigna** ① *Colón 1342 N, Desamparados, northwest of centre, T0264-421 4227, www.graffignawines.com, Mon-Sat 0915-1715, Sun 1015-1515*, the oldest in San Juan, with an interesting museum displaying winemaking machinery and old photos, and a wine bar. **Fabril Alto Verde** ① *R40, between Calle 13 and 14, Pocito, south of centre, T0264-421 2683, www.fabril-altoverde.com.ar, Mon, Fri, Sat, 0900-1800*, is an organic winery with a smart showroom and small bar. **Antigua Bodega** ① *Salta 782 N, near the ring road, northwest of centre, T0261-459 7777, www.antiguabodega.com*, has a museum, below which the sparkling wine is made. **Viñas de Segisa** ① *Aberastain and Calle 15, La Rinconada, Pocito, south of centre, T0264-492 2000, www.saxsegisa.com.ar*, is a small boutique bodega with attractively renovated buildings. Not far from here is the charming, family-run bodega **Las Marianas** ① *Nueva, La Rinconada, Pocito, south of centre, T0264-15-463 9136, www.bodegalasmarianas.com.ar, Tue-Sun 1000-1700.* **Cavas de Zonda** ① *R12 Km 15, Rivadavia, west of centre, T0264-494 5144*, has an interesting setting right inside a mountain and a champagne house at the end of a tunnel carved into the rocky hills, where wines are made following traditional Spanish and French methods.

Opposite Plaza 25 de Mayo, take the lift 53 m up to the top of cathedral's **campanile** ① *daily 0930-1300 and 1700-2100, US$1*, for city views. San Juan's museums are mostly rather dry, but if you're interested in Argentine history, pop into **Museo Casa Natal de Sarmiento** ① *Sarmiento 21 Sur, T0264-422 4603, www.casanatalsarmiento.com.ar, Mon-Fri and Sun 0900-2030, Sat Sun 1030-1600, US$1.35*, dedicated to the important Argentine president and educator, Domingo Sarmiento. **Museo Histórico Celda de San Martín** ① *Laprida 57 Este, Mon-Sat 0930-1330, US$1.25*, includes the restored cloisters and two cells of the Convent of Santo Domingo. San Martín slept in one of these cells on his way to lead the crossing of the Andes. The **Museo de Ciencias Naturales** ① *Predio Ferial, España and Maipú, T0264-421 6774, daily 1100-1900*, has some of the fossils from Ischigualasto Provincial Park, which you won't see at the site itself. There's a wonderful collection of pre-

Hispanic indigenous artefacts including several well-preserved mummies, at the **Museo Arqueológico** ⓘ *University of San Juan, Acceso Sur entre Calle 5 and Progreso, Rawson, a few kilometres south of centre, T0264-424 1424, Mon-Fri 0800-2000, Sat-Sun 1000-1800, US$2, buses 15, 49, 50 run from the centre.* The museum offers fascinating insights into the culture of the indigenous Huarpe peoples and into the Inca practice of mountain-top sacrifices.

Listings San Juan city

Tourist information

See also www.sanjuanla estrelladelosandes.com.

Tourist office
Sarmiento Sur 24 and San Martín, T0264-421 0004, www.sanjuan.gov.ar (in Spanish). Daily 0800-2000.
Basic tourist office. There's also a tourist office at the bus station.

Where to stay

$$$ Alkázar
Laprida 82 Este, T0264-421 4965, www.alkazarhotel.com.ar.
Central, well-run hotel with comfortable rooms, sauna, pool, gym and an excellent restaurant.

$$$ América
9 de Julio 1052 Este, T0264-427 2701, www.hotel-america.com.ar.
A good, quite comfortable choice if you need to be next to bus station.

$$$ Gran Hotel Provincial
Av J I de la Roza 132 Este, T0264-430 9999, www.granhotelprovincial.com.
Large, central hotel, with good rooms, pool, gym and restaurant.

$$$-$$ Albertina
Mitre 31 Este, T0264-421 4222, www.hotelalbertina.com.
Next to the cinema on the plaza is this small hotel with comfortable rooms and a restaurant. Junior suites have a jacuzzi. No parking. Very good value.

$ pp San Juan Hostel
Av Córdoba 317 Este, T0264-420 1835, www.sanjuan hostel.com.
Kind owner, central, with dorms for 4 to 10, and private rooms with and without bath (**$$-$**), barbecues on rooftop, bike rental, tours arranged.

$ pp Zonda
Caseros 486 Sur, T0264-420 1009, www.zondahostel.com.ar.
Simple, light rooms for 2-6, shared bath, room for 4 with bath (**$$**). Trips and Spanish lessons arranged. HI member discount.

Restaurants

A lively area of bars and restaurants lies along Av San Martín Oeste (west of 1500 block).

$$$ Club Sirio Libanés 'Restaurant Palito'
Entre Ríos 33 Sur, see Facebook.
Pleasant and long-established, serving tasty food, some Middle Eastern dishes, including an 'arab potpourri', and a buffet. Recommended.

$$ Remolacha
Av de la Roza y Sarmiento, T0264-422 7070.
Stylish, warm atmosphere, great terrace on C Sarmiento, superb Italian-inspired menu, delicious steaks and pastas. Recommended.

$$ Soychú
Av de la Roza 223 Oeste, T0264-422 1939.
Great-value vegetarian food. Highly recommended.

$$ Tagore
Av San Martín 1556 T0264-426 2702, see Facebook.
Vegetarian meals to take away.

Shopping

San Juan is known for its fine bedspreads, blankets, saddle cloths and other items made from sheep and llama wool, fine leather, wooden plates and mortars and, of course, its wines. The **Mercado Artesanal Tradicional** (España and San Luis, T0264-421 4189), sells woven blankets/saddlebags, knives and ponchos. If you haven't time for a bodega tour, there are a few wine stores where you can buy the local produce, such as **La Bodega** (25 de Mayo 957 Este), or **La Reja** (Jujuy 424 Sur).

What to do

Tour operators
CH Travel, *General Acha 714 Sur, T0264-427 4160, www.chtraveltur.com*. Recommended for its tours to Barreal, Valle de la Luna and 4-day expeditions to Parque Nacional San Guillermo, in the remote north of San Juan's high plateau. All great experiences.
Nerja Tours, *Mendoza 353 Sur, T0264-421 5214, www.nerja-tours.com.ar*. Good for local day trips and adventure tourism inside the national parks.

Transport

Air
Chacritas Airport is 11 km southeast of the city on Route 20. There are no regular buses, but there are *remise* taxis to the centre, about US$10. Daily flights to/from **Buenos Aires** with **Aerolíneas Argentinas/Austral**.

Bus
The **bus terminal** (Estados Unidos 492, T0264-422 1604) is 9 blocks east of the city centre, with almost all buses going through the centre. A taxi to the centre costs US$2-3.
  La Rioja, 5½-7 hrs, US$29-40, many daily. **Chilecito**, 8 hrs, US$29, daily with **Vallecito**. **Tucumán**, many daily, 11-14 hrs, US$54-74. **Córdoba**, many daily, 8-14 hrs, US$39-50. **Buenos Aires**, 14-17 hrs, US$84-104 (**Autotransportes San Juan, Mar del Plata**, US$128). **San Agustín**, with **Vallecito**, 3 a day (2 on Sun), 4 hrs, US$11. To **Mendoza**, US$13-14, 2-2½ hrs. Also to **Barreal**, 3½ hrs, US$12, and **Calingasta**, 3 hrs, US$12, 2 a day with **El Triunfo**, T0265-421 4532 (tell the driver your accommodation is in Barreal, as the bus stops en route).

Car hire
Trébol, Laprida 82 Este, T0264-422 5935, trebolrentacar@live.com.ar.

San Juan to Valle de la Luna

pagan saints and unspoilt landscapes

The Parque Provincial Ischigualasto (or Valle de la Luna) is one of the highlights of San Juan province. From San Juan it can be reached by taking Route 20 and Route 141 east via Vallecito, then turning north onto Route 510 via San Agustín del Valle Fértil.

La Difunta Correa
At **Vallecito**, 64 km east of San Juan city, the famous shrine to Argentina's most beloved pagan saint, **La Difunta Correa** has to be seen to be believed and will give you far more insight into the Argentine character than any cathedral. By now, you'll have noticed piles of bottles at roadside shrines all over Argentina.
  The legend goes that the beautiful young Correa was making the long walk to reclaim the body of her young husband, killed in the wars of independence, when she fell by the roadside dying of thirst. No one would help her, but, by some miracle, the baby she was

carrying suckled at her breast and survived, and thus La Difunta Correa became the pagan patron saint of all travellers.

People leave bottles of water by her shrine to quench her thirst and to thank her for her protection on their journey. During Holy Week, 100,000 pilgrims visit this extraordinary series of shrines at Vallecito, to make offerings to splendidly florid effigies of Difunta and her child. Testimony to their faith is a remarkable collection of personal items left in tribute, filling several buildings, including cars, number plates from all over the world, photographs, stuffed animals, tea sets, hair (in plaits), plastic flowers, trophies, tennis rackets and guitars – and vast numbers of bottles of water (which are used for the plants, and the plastic recycled).

There are cafés, toilets, a hotel and souvenir stalls. It's bizarre and fascinating. Buses from San Juan to La Rioja stop here for five minutes, or Vallecito runs a couple of services a day.

San Agustín del Valle Fértil

San Agustín (population 3900) is a charming little town, 250 km northeast of San Juan, and is definitely the best base for exploring the Ischigualasto park, with several good places to stay and eat. You could also fish in the Dique San Agustín, and buy ponchos and blankets from the local weavers here.

★ Parque Provincial Ischigualasto (Valle de la Luna)

Popularly known as the Valle de la Luna (Valley of the Moon), this protected area covers 62,000 ha of spectacular desert landforms, and is the site of important palaeontological discoveries. Named after a Huarpe chief, the site occupies an immense basin, which was once filled by a lake, lying, at an average altitude of 1200 m, between the scarlet red Barrancas Coloradas to the east and the green, black and grey rocks of Los Rastros to the west. The vegetation is arid scrub and bushes; you may be lucky enough to see guanacos, vizcachas, Patagonian hares or red foxes and rheas.

For many visitors, the attraction lies in the bizarre shapes of massive hunks of rock eroded into fantastical shapes, dotted throughout the park's otherworldly terrain. With the Argentines' charming penchant for naming all natural structures after things that they resemble, these are signposted accordingly: 'The Submarine', 'The Kiosk', 'Gusanos' (Worms), and 'La Cancha de Bochas' (the Bowling Green); extraordinary spheres of fine compacted sand. Sadly, 'El Hongo' (the Mushroom) has fallen over.

However, the park's real fascination lies in the 250 million years of strata that you can see in the eroded cliffs of the rocks where fossils from all the geological periods have been found, among them fossils of the oldest dinosaurs known, including Eoraptor, 225 million years old and discovered in 1993. Your tour guide will show you the extraordinary strata, but you'll be disappointed to discover that there's no evidence of the dinosaur fossils here: you'll have to go to the **Museo de Ciencias Naturales** in San Juan (see page 184). The views throughout the park are impressive though, and the span of time you can witness here is mind-blowing. Highly recommended.

Essential Parque Provincial Ischigualasto (Valle de la Luna)

Access

There are no regular buses that reach the park, so your only alternative is to take a tour, either from San Juan, La Rioja or San Agustín. From San Juan, tours cost around US$80 (including breakfast and lunch) and take 14 hours. In San Agustín, there are a couple of small agencies that offer day trips combining Ischigualasto with Talampaya Park. Talampaya Park (in La Rioja province; see box, page 238) lies only 94 km away from Ischigualasto, and some agencies organize a combined visit to both parks in one intense day: explore this option before you set off, and plan accordingly. For around five days every full moon, the park runs Full Moon tours, for US$20 plus entrance fee.

A taxi to the park costs around US$40 from San Agustín (recommended if there are four or five people), but is more expensive out of season. If you are travelling in your own transport, plan to stay overnight at San Agustín or the less lovely Villa Unión, as the drive is long, hot and tiring. From San Juan, both Ischigualasto and Talampaya can be reached by taking Route 20 east through Caucete and joining Route 141, via Difunta Correa to Marayes, then turning north onto Route 510 for 174 km northwest up to Los Baldecitos, from where it's 17 km to the entrance to Ischigualasto. If you're driving, beware of the donkeys and goats wandering across the roads.

Entry fee

Entrance costs US$14, including a tour. The tour route is about 40 km long, lasting three hours, visiting only a part of the park but encompassing the most interesting sites. If you're in your own vehicle, you'll be accompanied by one of the rangers, whose knowledge and interest vary greatly: with luck you'll get a knowledgeable one. There's no fee but a tip is appreciated.

When to go

It can be crowded at holiday times, January, Easter and July.

Where to stay

You can camp opposite the ranger station in the park (US$4), which has a small museum, but bring all food and water as there's only an expensive *confitería* here, and nothing else for miles.

Listings San Juan to Valle de la Luna

Tourist information

San Agustín del Valle Fértil

Tourist information office
Municipalidad, General Acha 1065, T02646-420192, www.vallefertilsanjuan.com. Mon-Fri 0900-1300 and 1700-2100, Sat 0900-1300.
Very helpful staff who can give you a map and advice on accommodation.

Parque Provincial Ischigualasto
See www.ischigualasto.gob.ar, an excellent website full of comprehensive information (in Spanish) about the park, and well worth a look before you come.

Where to stay

San Agustín del Valle Fértil
At Easter all accommodation is fully booked. There are a couple of good hotels and lots of *cabañas*; the following are recommended:

$$$-$$ Cabañas Valle Pintado
Tucumán y Mitre, T0264-434 5737, www.vallepintado.com.ar.
Incredibly good-value option with cabins for up to 6 people also available. Basic,

clean rooms, with a large swimming pool surrounded by trees.

$$$-$$ Finca La Media Luna
La Majadita, T0264-404 1038,
www.fincalamedialuna.com.ar.
Only 12 km from the centre of San Agustín, each room in this hotel has a private outdoor area, with views over the trees to the mountains. A lovely good-sized pool adds to the attraction. Cabins for up to 4 (**$$$**) available.

$$ Hostería Valle Fértil
Rivadavia s/n, T02646-420015,
www.hosteriavallefertil.com.
Smart, comfortable hotel with fine views from its elevated position above town (though it's an ugly building), also has *cabañas* and a good restaurant open to non-residents.

Hostels

$ pp Campo Base
Tucumán between San Luis and Libertador, T02646-420063, www.hostelvalledelaluna. com.ar.
Lively, cheerful hostel with basic dorms, shared bath and small kitchen. Discounts to HI members. Tours arranged to Ischigualasto.

$ pp Los Olivos
Santa Fe and Tucumán, T02646-420115.

Welcoming and simple, with hostel accommodation and a good restaurant.

Camping
There are several campsites, of which the most highly recommended is **La Majadita** in a lovely spot on the river 8 km to the west of town with hot showers and great views. There's a municipal campsite in the town on Calle Rivadavia, 5 blocks from the plaza, T0264-15 520 1185 (municipal office for information on both sites).

San Agustín del Valle Fértil

$ El Astiqueño
Tucumán next to the Dique.
Good regional specialities.

$ Noche Azul
General Acha s/n, off the plaza.
Parrilla offering local *chivito* (kid).

San Agustín del Valle Fértil
Bus
Empresa Vallecito runs daily to **San Juan**, 4 hrs, US$11; there are also 3 buses a week to **La Rioja**, 3 hrs, US$9.

Calingasta Valley

a long fertile valley bordered by jagged peaks

The most beautiful part of the province, Calingasta Valley lies 100 km west of San Juan between the snow-capped Andes and the stark crinkled range of the Sierra del Tontal, west of San Juan city. Inhabited since at least 10,000 BC, the Calingasta Valley was once the route of the Camino del Inca, and though little of this history remains today, it still carries a compelling attraction. Its few oasis villages are charming places to stay to explore the hills, utterly tranquil and unspoilt.

The valley is reached from San Juan by the scenic paved Route Provincial 12. About halfway between Calingasta and Barreal, this passes the Cerros Pintados, to the east, a range of red, white and grey stratified hills, striped like toothpaste. There are beautiful views of the whole valley here, with its meandering river, a ribbon of green running through the dusty plain between the *cordillera* and Sierra del Tigre.

Cyclists should note that there is no shade on these roads; fill up with water at every opportunity and consult the police before cycling between Calingasta and San Juan.

Calingasta

The road from Pachaco to Calingasta follows the winding course of the Río San Juan through a steep-sided gorge of astonishingly coloured and stratified rock. After Pachaco the landscape opens out, and Calingasta village (population 2100, altitude 1430 m) lies at the confluence of the Ríos de los Patos and Calingasta, a vivid green splash on the otherwise arid landscape. This idyllic, secluded little village (135 km west of San Juan) is a delightful place to rest for a few days or plan a trek into the mountains. The Jesuit chapel, **Capilla de Nuestra Señora del Carmen**, is worth seeing: a simple adobe building dating from the 1600s, with the original bells.

Barreal and around *Colour map 3, A2.*

Another peaceful oasis, Barreal (population 2400, altitude 1650 m) offers more accommodation and services than Calingasta and is the best base if you plan to trek into the Andes. However, it's still small and quiet enough to feel like a village and offers spectacular views of the peaks all around. From here you can explore the mountains of **Sierra del Tontal**, which rise to 4000 m and give superb views over San Juan, Mercedario and Aconcagua, or climb the mighty **Cerro Mercedario** (6770 m) itself, one of the Andes' greatest peaks. For information, contact the **tourist office** in Barreal; see Tourist information, below.

Barreal is famous for *carrovelismo* (wind-car racing), thanks to its vast expanse of flat land known as Barreal del Leoncito, parallel to the main road, south of town. A more tranquil attraction are the two observatories at nearby **Parque Nacional El Leoncito** (2348 m), 26 km from Barreal: **CESCO** ① *T02648-441087, centrohugomira@yahoo.com.ar, daily visits 1000-1200, 1600-1800 (US$3)* and nocturnal visits with small telescopes from sunset (US$6); and **CASLEO** ① *T02648-441088, www.casleo.gov.ar, mid-Sep to mid-Mar daily 1000-1200, 1430-1700 (1500-1730 in summer), US$1*; phone in advance for three-hour night visits with small telescopes, US$16, also with dinner and accommodation (US$58 pp). There's a ranger post at the observatory entrance but no facilities, so if you if you want to camp, take all supplies. The observatories were built here because of the climate, with 320 clear nights a year, making it a perfect place for observing the stars and planets. The observatories are set within an immense **nature reserve** ① *office: Cordillera de Ansilta s/n, Barreal, T02648-441240, www.elleoncito.gob.ar, free*, covering 76,000 ha of the western slopes of the Sierra del Tontal and rising to over 4000 m. To the west there are fine views of Mercedario and other peaks in the *cordillera* with the flat plain and lush valley between. But hiking in the reserve is limited to one short walk to a small waterfall, near the entrance. Fauna includes suris (rheas), guanacos, red and grey foxes and peregrine falcons.

There's no public transport to the park except *remise* taxis from Barreal; take the partly paved road (17 km) that turns off Route 412, 22 km south of Barreal or take a tour from Barreal or San Juan.

Cerro Mercedario

Known in Chile as El Ligua and rising to 6770 m, the mighty peak of Mercedario, southwest of Calingasta, is considered by many mountaineers to be a more interesting climb than Aconcagua. It was first climbed in 1934 by a Polish expedition,

> **Tip...**
> The best time to climb Cerro Mercedario is from mid-December to the end of February.

which went on to climb the nearby peaks of Pico Polaco (6050 m), La Mesa (6200 m), Alma Negra (6120 m) and Ramada (6410 m). This is a serious climb and requires the same time to adjust to the altitude and the careful preparation as Aconcagua. You must not consider this expedition without hiring an experienced mountain guide (*baqueano*), who can provide mules if necessary, as there are no facilities and no rescue service. No authorization is required to climb, but it is advisable to inform the Gendarmería Nacional at Barreal. Note that the mountain passes to Chile here are not officially open, making the crossing illegal.

Listings Calingasta Valley

Tourist information

Calingasta

Tourist office
Av Argentina s/n, T02648-441066,
www.calingastaturismo.gob.ar,
or at the Municipalidad in Tamberías,
Lavalle and Sarmiento, T02648-492005.

Barreal

Tourist office
Calle Las Heras s/n, T02648-441066.

Where to stay

Calingasta

$$ Hotel de Campo Calingasta
Take the left fork from the gendarmería, cross the river and continue 2 km, hotel is up a hill on your right, T02648-421220, see Facebook.
A restored colonial-style building with airy rooms off a colonnaded patio, with open views to the mountains and a pool in the garden. Very tranquil. Meals also available. Recommended.

Barreal

$$$ Eco Posada El Mercedario
Av Roca y C de los Enamorados (Las Tres Esquinas), T0264-15-509 0907 or T02648-441167, www.elmercedario.com.ar.
Built in 1928 on the northern edge of town, this lovely adobe building preserves a traditional atmosphere with renovated comfort in its good rooms; solar-heated

water, good-value restaurant, a tiny pool in a large garden, bicycles and excursions arranged through their own agency **Ruta Sur**. Recommended.

$$$ El Alemán
Los Huarpes s/n, T02648-441193,
www.elalemanbarreal.com.
Run by Perla, Bernhard and their daughter, functional apartments for 2 to 4 (with solar-heated water) facing a neat garden in a rural area next to the river. Restaurant with some German specialities.

$$$ Posada de Campo La Querencia
T0264-15-436 4699, www.laquerencia posada.com.
A few spotless comfortable rooms in a homely place south of town run by very attentive owners. Delicious breakfast, manicured park with a pool and magnificent views of the Andes.

$$$ Posada Paso de los Patos
Patricias Mendocinas y Gualino, T0264-463 4727, www.posadapasolospatos.com.ar.
In a lovely location south of town with grand views, a stylish building with 10 well-equipped rooms facing the Andes, restaurant, pool, many activities including horse riding, rafting and mountain biking to the nearby mountains.

$$$-$$ Posada San Eduardo
Av San Martín s/n, T02648-441046,
www.posada-saneduardo.com.
Charming colonial-style house, simple rooms around a courtyard, superior rooms with

fireplace, relaxing, beautiful park with a large pool, restaurant, horse rides.

$ pp Hostel Barreal
Av San Martín s/n, T0264-15 415 7147, www.hostelbarreal.com.
A neat place with rooms with bath and a lovely garden. Rafting, kayaks and tours organized.

$ pp Hostel Don Lisandro
Av San Martín s/n, T0264-15-505 9122, www.donlisandro.com.ar.
In a house built in 1908, a few dorms in rustic style for 3 and 4 and doubles with or without bath (**$$-$**). Its table football is a gem. Trekking and trips organized, including fabulous blokarting.

Camping

Municipal site
At C Belgrano, T0264-15-672 3914.
Open all year. Shady, well-maintained site with a pool.

Barreal
Tour operators
Don Lisandro Expediciones, *Av San Martín s/n, T0264-15-505 9122, www.donlisandro. com.ar.* Full-day to several-day high-altitude treks in the Andes, including Laguna Blanca and Balcón de los Seis Mil. Combined visit to astronomical observatories and blokarting on Pampa del Leoncito. Check available activities in winter. Recommended.
Fortuna, *Viajes, Av Roca s/n (at Posada Don Ramón, northern outskirts), T0264-15-404 0913.* 1-week horse ride crossing of the Andes led by expert Ramón Ossa. Also trekking in the Andes and 4WD trips in the Precordillera.

Transport

Barreal
Bus
To **San Juan**, **El Triunfo** departs Tue-Fri at 1400, Sat-Sun 1600, 3½ hrs, US$13; bus stops en route along main road (Av Roca); tickets sold at YPF station.

La Rioja &
Catamarca

La Rioja is usually visited for the wonderful Parque Nacional Talampaya, a vast canyon of rock sculpted by wind and water into fantastic shapes, declared a World Heritage Site by UNESCO. However, there's also stunning scenery beyond the national park and places where you can find perfect tranquility, since the area is sparsely populated and little visited. Between the mountain ranges of the west are the extended Famatina and Vinchina valleys with verdant oasis villages at the foot of colourful eroded hills. The city of La Rioja itself has two fine museums of indigenous art.

Most of the population of Catamarca province live in the hot, sleepy capital, leaving the stunning countryside virtually empty of people. The province has one really impressive archaeological find: the ruined Inca town of El Shincal, close to Londres, but accessible on a tour from Belén. West are remote outposts on the road to Chile, while to the north, a lonely road leads across the *puna* to Antofagasta de la Sierra, surrounded by a vast expanse of salt flats. Catamarca's most appealing place to stay is the charming hilltop town of El Rodeo; a popular weekend retreat for Catamarqueños, with its refreshing microclimate and good walks.

Beyond the main towns, the infrastructure in La Rioja and Catamarca provinces can be frustratingly basic, but you'll be warmly welcomed in the remotest reaches.

Though not obviously touristy, the provincial capital of La Rioja (population 180,995, altitude 498 m) does offer decent accommodation and is a good starting point for a trip to more remote parts. Founded in 1591 at the edge of the plains, with views of Sierra de Velasco, La Rioja has a few interesting museums, some neo-colonial houses and the oldest building in the country. Sleepy and oppressively hot from November to March, the town becomes lively every day after siesta time and during the local carnivals, such as Chaya and the Tinkunaco.

Sights

The centre of the city is **Plaza 25 de Mayo** with its shady tipas, sycamores, araucarias and pine trees. Here, in 1637, the head of the native leader of an insurrection was exhibited as a trophy by the Spaniards. On the plaza is the early 20th-century **cathedral** with the image of San Nicolás de Bari and a room full of silver offerings. Other interesting sights on the plaza are the neocolonial government buildings, the **Casa de Gobierno** and the **Poder Judicial**, together with the pink building of the **Club Social**.

The oldest surviving church in Argentina is one block northeast, the **Church of Santo Domingo** ① *Pelagio B Luna y Lamadrid*. It's a quaint stone temple, sparsely decorated inside but with magnificent carved wooden doors, dating from 1623 and renovated in later centuries. There is a lovely patio in the adjacent convent.

The **Church and Convent of San Francisco** ① *25 de Mayo y Bazán y Bustos, Tue-Sun 0700-1300, 1700-2100, free*, contains the Niño Alcalde, a remarkable image of the infant Jesus. You can also see the cell (*celda*) in which San Francisco Solano lived and the orange tree, now dead, which he planted in 1592 (25 de Mayo 218). San Francisco helped to bring peace between the Spaniards and the indigenous people in 1593, an event celebrated at the Tinkunaco festival; see Festivals, below.

By far the most interesting sight in the town is the **Museo Arqueológico Inca Huasi** ① *JB Alberdi 650, T0380-443 9268, Tue-Fri 0900-1300 and 1800-2100, open some weekends, call beforehand, US$1*, which houses one of the most important collections of pre-Hispanic ceramics in Argentina. These beautiful pieces were made by the ancient cultures that originally inhabited the region and include a remarkable funerary urn from the Aguada culture which existed 1500 years ago.

The **Mercado Artesanal** ① *Luna 782, Tue-Sun 1000-1200 and 1600-2000*, has expensive handicrafts. In a beautiful and well-kept house, the **Museo Folklórico** ① *Luna 802, T0380-442 8500, Tue-Sun 1000-1200 and 1600-2000*, gives a fascinating insight into traditional La Rioja life, with a superb collection of native deities, rustic wine-making machinery and delicate silver *mates*. It's well worth a visit for its leafy patio.

Essential La Rioja city

Finding your feet

The city airport, **VA Almonacid**, is 5 km northeast of La Rioja city, and taxis charge US$4-5 to the centre. The **bus terminal** is a few kilometres out of town at Avenida Circunvalación and Ortiz de Ocampo. To get into town, take either the **San Francisco** or **Minube** bus, US$0.50, 15 minutes, taxi US$4-5, or you could walk, 45 minutes to one hour. Minibuses are useful for journeys within the province; they have their own terminal at Artigas y España.

Around La Rioja city

Seven kilometres west of La Rioja is **Las Padercitas**, where there is a large stone temple protecting the adobe remains of what is supposed to have been a Spanish fortress in the 16th century. Route 75 passes Las Padercitas before following the **Quebrada del Río Los Sauce**s for 4 km to the reservoir of Dique Los Sauces. Just 10 km west of La Rioja, this is the fastest escape from the heat of the city. There's a shaded river with campsites and a reservoir amidst lovely mountain scenery. From the reservoir, a 13-km dirt track (no shade) leads to the summit of the **Cerro de la Cruz** (1648 m) with great panoramic views; it's popular with hang gliders.

Regular minibuses, or *diferenciales* as they're called here, depart from Rivadavia 519 to Villa Sanagasta via the Quebrada and **Dique Los Sauces**, US$2. *Remise* taxis charge US$10. Some tour operators also run trips.

Listings La Rioja city and around

Tourist information

For information on the region, see www.lariojaturismo.com (in English) and www.catamarcaguia.com.ar (in Spanish).

Municipalidad
Av Santa Fe 950, T0380-447 0001,
and on the plaza opposite the cathedral.
Daily 0800-2100.
Both offices have information on the city, including a map, and are friendly and helpful. Ask here about accommodation, including rooms with families (*casas de familia*).

Provincial tourist office
Av Ortiz de Ocampo y Av Félix de la Colina (opposite bus terminal), T0380-442 6345, www.turismolarioja.gov.ar. Daily 0800-2100.

Where to stay

La Rioja city
A/c or fan are essential for summer nights. High season is during the Jul winter holidays.

$$$ Plaza
San Nicolás de Bari y 9 de Julio (on Plaza 25 de Mayo), T0380-443 6290, www.plazahotel-larioja.com.
Functional 4-star, pool on top floor, breakfast included, a/c. Superior rooms have balconies on the plaza.

$$$ Vincent Apart Hotel
Santiago del Estero 10, T0380-443 2326, www.vincentaparthotel.com.ar.
Spotless flats for up to 4, a/c, dining room, kitchen and fridge, excellent value. Breakfast included.

$$ Savoy
San Nicolás de Bari y Roque A Luna, T0380-442 6894, www.hotelsavoylarioja.com.ar.
This tidy, comfortable hotel with a/c is in a quiet residential area. Rooms on the 2nd floor are best.

$ pp Apacheta Hostel
San Nicolás de Bari 669, T0380-15-444 5445, see Facebook.
Cheerfully decorated, this is a well-run central hostel with dorms for 5 to 8 and a private double (**$$**).

Restaurants

La Rioja city

$$$ El Nuevo Corral
Av Quiroga y Rivadavia.
Traditional rustic *comidas de campo* and good local wines.

$$$ La Vieja Casona
Rivadavia 457, www.lacasonalunch.com.ar.
Smart *parrilla*, offering *chivito* (kid).

$$ La Aldea de la Virgen de Luján
Rivadavia 756.
Cheap and popular small place with a lively atmosphere, serving some Middle Eastern dishes.

Festivals

La Rioja city
It's worth planning your visit to coincide with one of La Rioja's 2 lively festivals.
Jan Tinkunaco. Beginning on New Year's Eve and lasting 4 days, this festival is a vestige of the peacemaking efforts of San Francisco Solano. A colourful procession accompanies the meeting of the images of San Nicolás de Bari and the Niño Alcalde in front of the cathedral.
Feb Chaya. At this very popular festival, flour and basil are thrown, and percussion music is played for 4 nights at the Estadio del Centro.

What to do

La Rioja city
The most common destination, Talampaya, is usually offered together with Valle de la Luna (see box, page 219) in a long day tour, plus occasionally Cuesta de Miranda

in 1 or 2 days. Check if park entry, IVA (VAT) and meals are included. Trips to the high mountains and plateaux in the west are restricted to good weather, Sep-Apr.
Corona del Inca, *PB Luna 914, T0380-445 0054, www.coronadelinca.com.ar.* Wide range of tours to Talampaya, Valle de la Luna, Laguna Brava, Corona del Inca crater, horse riding in Velasco mountains and further afield, English spoken.

Transport

La Rioja city
Air
Airport, T0380-446 2160. To **Buenos Aires** daily with **Austral**.

Bus
Bus terminal, T0380-442 5453. To **Buenos Aires**, **Urquiza** and **Chevallier** US$80-115, 13½-17 hrs. To **Mendoza**, US$41-60, 8-9½ hrs, many companies. To **San Juan**, 5½-7 hrs, US$29-51, many daily. To **Tucumán**, US$31-43, 5-7 hrs. To **Villa Unión**, 5 companies daily, 4 hrs, US$12. To **Chilecito**, several daily, 3 hrs, US$8. Minibuses run provincial services; they are faster and more frequent than buses but cost a little more.

La Rioja to Catamarca

thermal springs, fishing lakes and mountain retreats

Two roads head north from La Rioja: Route 75 to Aimogasta (see page 231) and Route 38 to Catamarca. From Route 38, you could take a detour to visit thermal baths at Termas Santa Teresita, Km 33 take R9 (later 10) to Villa Mazán, Km 99. The *termas* are some 7 km north and there's a budget Hostería Termas Santa Teresita, T03827-420445, www.termasantateresita.com.ar, which has an open-air thermal pool, thermal baths in all rooms and breakfast included.

Catamarca city *Colour map 1, C3.*
The real name of this sleepy and traditional provincial capital (population 172,000) is the rather lengthy San Fernando del Valle de Catamarca. Unless you're here for the Poncho festival in mid-July (see Festivals, page 230), there's little to draw you to the city. The summers are unbearably hot with temperatures up to 45°C; very sensibly, the siesta is strictly observed here and everything closes down between 1230 and 1700. El Rodeo, an hour away by regular minibus, makes a far more appealing alternative base.

Sights The central, leafy **Plaza 25 de Mayo** was designed by the illustrious architect Charles Thays (see box, page 52) and contains tall trees that provide much-needed shade from the scorching summer heat. Around the plaza are the white stuccoed **Casa de Gobierno** (1891), designed by Caravati, and the faded red bulk of his neoclassical **cathedral** (1878). In a chapel high above and behind the altar, you can visit the much-worshipped Virgen del Valle, surrounded by plaques and cases crammed with thousands of offerings. One block north of the plaza, the **Iglesia de San Francisco** (1882) has an impressive colonial-style façade.

The must-see of the city is the incredible **Museo Arqueológico 'Adán Quiroga'** ① *Sarmiento 450, T0383-443 7413, daily 0830-2000, free,* containing an enormous collection of artefacts from the sophisticated pre-Hispanic cultures who inhabited the area from around 1000 BC. There are carved stone vessels with animal figures leaping off their sides, beautifully painted funerary urns, deliberately flattened skulls (compressed by the owners by wearing wooden boards), and quite a shocking mummified baby, naturally conserved above 5000 m. Allow at least an hour to discover the many fascinating finds. Highly recommended.

Around Catamarca city
Some 25 km north of Catamarca, the **Dique Las Pirquitas** has good fishing and water sports, as well as trekking and mountain biking. To get to the lake, take bus No 1A from the bus terminal to the **Hostería de Turismo** at Villa Pirquitas, from where it is about 45-minute walk. An alternative trip is to visit a series of attractive churches in the **Valle de Catamarca**. The oldest of these is **La Señora del Rosario**, 2 km east of the city, a simple white building dating from 1715. Others are at **San Isidro**, 5 km east; **Villa Dolores**, 1 km further north, and at **San José**, a further 4 km north, which dates from 1780.

Northeast of Catamarca, there are fine panoramic views over the Valle de Catamarca and the city at the **Cuesta del Portezuelo**, along the road snaking up the Sierra de Ancasti. Over 20 km, the Cuesta rises through 13 hairpin bends to 1680 m then descends via El Alto (950 m). There's a reservoir nearby, **Dique Ipizca**, that's good for *pejerrey* fishing.

The best place to head to escape from the city is the pretty weekend retreat of **El Rodeo**, some 37 km north of Catamarca in a lovely mountain setting with a cool microclimate and lots of good walks and horse riding. There's a great two-day hike to Cerro el Manchao 4550 m, and trout fishing in the Río Ambato. Ask for advice at the **tourist office**; see Tourist information, below. It's easy to get here by bus or hire car, and there are plenty of delightful *hosterías*, but if you plan to stay overnight, make sure you book beforehand, especially at weekends. **Las Juntas**, 20 km away on the same road, is another attractive mountain retreat from the city.

Listings La Rioja to Catamarca

Tourist information

Catamarca city

Provincial tourist office
Roca and Virgen del Valle, T0383-455 5308.

Tourist office
Rivadavia 598, T0810-777 4321, www. turismocatamarca.gob.ar. Daily 0900-2100.

Helpful staff. There's also an information point at the airport.

El Rodeo

Tourist office
T0383-449 0043, www.municipiodeelrodeo.com.

Where to stay

Catamarca city

See also www.turismocatamarca.gob.ar.

$$$ Amerian Park
República 347, T0383-442 5444,
www.amerian.com.
A modern but expensive business hotel,
with spacious, attractively decorated and
very comfortable rooms. Large restaurant
and pool.

$$$ Ancasti
Sarmiento 520, T0383-443 5951,
www.hotelancasti.com.ar.
Aspiring to be a business hotel. The rooms
are comfortable but the bathrooms are
tiny. Deals include dinner in the pleasant
airy restaurant.

$$$ Hostel Casino Catamarca
Esquiú 151, corner Ayachuco, T0383-443 2928,
www.hotelcasinocatamarca.com.
Large and surprisingly inviting hotel with
comfy beds, a good pool and a spa.

$$$ La Aguada
*16 km from the city along Ruta 38, T0383-
15-436 5723, www.la-aguada.com.*
This wonderful boutique hotel has
5 beautifully decorated rooms. The friendly
owners also offer trekking, horse riding
and abseiling. Breakfast, local phone calls,
laundry and bicycle hire are included in
the price.

$$$-$$ Arenales
Sarmiento 542, T0383-443 1329,
www.hotel-arenales.com.ar.
Welcoming, but slightly institutional in feel.
Plain rooms with well-equipped bathrooms,
minimalist though not exactly stylish. The
most comfy in this price range.

$$ Grand Hotel
Camilo Melet 41, T0383-4426715,
www.grandhotelcatamarca.com.ar.
You'll get the friendliest welcome here and
they have spacious and comfortable rooms,
all with bath, TV and a/c.

Hostels

$ pp Hostel San Pedro
Sarmiento 341, T0383-445 4708,
www.hostelsanpedro.com.ar.
Cheapest option in town, this new hostel
offers brightly coloured dorms, a large
garden, small pool and lively bar.

El Rodeo

$$$-$$ Hostería El Rodeo
R4, T0383-449044, see Facebook.
Lovely spacious rooms, pool, good restaurant
and great views. Climbing, 4WD trips and
trips for children. Highly recommended.

$$ Hostería La Casa de Chicha
Los Gladiolos s/n, T0384-4490082.
With fewer facilities than **El Rodeo**, but with
a more idyllic setting right in the mountains,
and rooms with antique furniture. Try the
excellent restaurant for lunch and dinner, or
have tea in the beautiful garden filled with
pear trees.

$ pp Hostel El Rodeo
Las Maravillas and Las Aljabas,
T0383-438 8204.
Although the dorms are basic and the
double is small, this hostel has a nice,
relaxed atmosphere. Bicycles for hire.

Restaurants

Catamarca city
There are many cheap restaurants around
the Plaza 25 de Agosto, and also at the bus
terminal but this area is not safe at night.

$$$-$$ La Tinaja
Sarmiento 533, T0383-443 5853.
The best eating choice by far, this delicious
parrilla does excellent pasta. Slightly pricey,
but worth it. Deservedly popular.

$$ Salsa Criolla
República 546, on the plaza, T0383-443 3584.
Traditional and popular *parrilla*. Sloppy
service, but the beef is recommended.

$$ Sociedad Española
Av Virgen del Valle 725, T0383-443 1896.
Recommended for its quality and variety,
serving paella, seafood and other Spanish
specialities, with friendly service. Worth
the 5-block walk from the main plaza.

Festivals

Catamarca city
Mar-Apr Virgen del Valle pilgrimage.
In the week following Easter, there are
pilgrimages to the Virgen del Valle. Hotel
rooms are hard to find.
Jul Festival Nacional del Poncho. The
city's major festival. It includes a huge *feria
artesanal* with the best of the province's
handicrafts, as well as those from other parts
of the country, and 10 nights of excellent
folclore music.
29 Nov-8 Dec Virgen del Valle pilgrimage.
A crowded pilgrimage in which thousands
of people show their devotion to the Virgin.
Hotel rooms are hard to find.

Shopping

Catamarca city
Catamarca specialities are available from
Cuesta del Portezuelo (Sarmiento 571,
T0383-445 2675); and **Fábrica Valdez**
(Sarmiento 578, T0383-442 5175). There's a
range of handicrafts and you can see carpets
being woven at the **Mercado Artesanal**
(Av Virgen del Valle 945, see www.facebook.
com/PaginaArtesaniasCatamarca, Mon-Fri
0700-1300, 1500-2000, Sat-Sun 0800-2000).

What to do

Catamarca city
Tours are offered to El Rodeo, and there are
opportunities for adventure sports.

Alta Catamarca, *Esquiú 433, T0383-443 0333,
www.altacatamarca.tur.ar.* Adventure-style
trips into the mountains, visits to local
villages and spa packages.
Catamarca Viajes y Turismo, *Sarmiento 581,
T0383-442 9450, www.catamarcaviajesytur.
com.ar.* Conventional tours to main sights in
eastern Catamarca.
La Lunita, *T011-6054 3442, www.lalunita.
com.ar.* Great trekking company that runs
tours throughout the region.

Transport

Catamarca city
Air
Aeropuerto Felipe Varela is 20 km south,
T0383-445 3684. **Aerolíneas Argentinas**,
Sarmiento 589, T0383-442 4460, fly to
Buenos Aires, Mon-Sat.

Bus
The bus terminal (Av Güemes 881 and
Tucumán, T0383-443 7578) is 7 blocks
southeast of the main plaza. It has shops,
a café, an ATM and a *locutorio*. The
entrance is through a car park.
  To **Tucumán**, 4 hrs, US$19-26, several
companies. To **Buenos Aires**, daily, 16-18 hrs,
US$79-87, 4 companies. To **Córdoba**, daily,
5 hrs, US$30. To **Santiago del Estero**, 2 buses
a day (0420, 0605), 4½-6 hrs, US$19-31. To
Mendoza, daily, 10 hrs, US$51-89, several
companies. To **La Rioja**, daily, 2 hrs, US$12-18,
several companies. To **Tinogasta**, 5 hrs,
US$16, **Gutiérrez** or **Robledo**. To **Belén**,
via Aimogasta and Londres, 4-6 hrs, US$16,
Gutiérrez. To **Andalgalá**, 4½-6 hrs, US$14,
4 companies including **Marín** (via Aconquija).
El Rodeo Bus runs *combis* (minibuses) a day
to El Rodeo and **Las Juntas** from the car park
half a block east of the plaza on San Martín,
returning the same day.

La Costa

If you have time and want a tranquil place to hang out or retreat to for a few days, with no distractions, head north from La Rioja for the long narrow strip of land known as La Costa, lying at the edge of the plains at the foot of the Sierra de Velasco mountains. There are delightful small villages with old chapels dotted all along Route 75, surrounded by vineyards, orchards and olive groves.

The first town you'll come across on Route 75 to La Costa is **Villa Sanagasta**, attractively set among orchards. On the last Friday in September a big religious procession takes place from here to La Rioja. At Santa Vera Cruz, near Anillaco, look out for the **Castillo de Dionisio,** a house built on a rock and surrounded by cacti that looks like something from a fairy tale or horror story (depending on your mood). In the desert 30 km east of Anillaco is the massive **Señor de la Peña**, a naturally shaped rock and very popular religious sanctuary during Holy Week. Also near Anillaco is the 18th-century **chapel of Udpinango**.

The largest town in the area and centre of olive production is **Aimogasta**, which serves as a good transport hub, with links to several towns in the province of Catamarca.

Londres

From Aimogasta, Ruta 60 goes 41 km north to the provincial border, where it joins Ruta 40. The latter continues north for 70 km to Londres (population 2100, altitude 1300 m), a pretty and quiet village with a remote feel. Founded in 1558, it is the second oldest town in Argentina (though its site was moved several times) and was named in honour of the marriage of Mary Tudor and Philip II. The Municipalidad displays a glass coat-of-arms of the city of London and a copy of the marriage proposal. There are important Inca ruins at **El Shincal** (see below), signposted from the second plaza you come to after entering the village from Belén. Londres celebrates its walnut festival in January. There are no hotels here, but there are several *hospedajes*, **Estancia La Casona** and a campsite (T03835-491019) on the route to Shincal. Food can be bought from the few shops around the plaza.

El Shincal

7 km from Londres, daily 0700-1900. Cóndor buses between Belén and Londres stop 100 m from the ruins, US$2. Taxi from Belén about US$20 with wait. The site is quite small and you will only need around 2 hrs there.

This ruined town is one of the most astonishing remains of the Incas' occupation of Argentina from the 1470s to their demise in 1532. The setting is superb, in a flat area between a crown of mountains and the river – a place the Incas clearly recognized as having sacred significance. Their religious beliefs were deeply entwined with their worship of mountains and their modification of natural forms – the most extreme example of which is Machu Picchu in Peru. Cuzco, too, follows strict conventions that ensure the town lines up auspiciously with sacred hills, water sources and the home of the ancestors. According to expert Ian Farrington, El Shincal is a 'little Cuzco', following precisely the same rules of orientation to mountains and water sources. There are large *kallankas* (thought to be either grain stores or military barracks), sleeping areas and a central plaza, lined up between two artificially shaped hills and perfectly aligned with the rising and setting sun at the solstice. In the middle of the plaza is a sacred platform with a specially designed trough for sacrifices.

It's best to visit El Shincal with a guide, but you'll be lucky to find one in Londres so take a tour from Belén. It's a remarkable site, well worth visiting.

Belén *Colour map 1, B2.*

From whichever direction you approach Belén – whether west from Andagalá on Route 46, north along Ruta 40 from La Rioja or south from Santa María – you'll be very relieved to arrive. Ruta 40 is a better road than Route 46, but still should not be attempted in the rainy season (February to March) when the rivers crossing the roads are high. Both roads are easier and safer in a 4WD.

Belén is an intimate little town (population 12,256, altitude 1240 m), famous for its ponchos, saddlebags and rugs, which you can see being woven. The museum, **Cóndor Huasi** ⓘ *San Martín y Belgrano, 1st floor, Mon-Fri 0800-1200*, contains fascinating Diaguita artefacts. There are good views from the **Cerro de Nuestra Señora de Belén**, a hill above the town, where a relatively new statue of the Virgin (the last one was struck by lightning) watches over the place.

North of Belén

There are two routes north from Belén. Ruta 40 runs northeast across vast open plains fringed with chocolate-coloured flaking mountains and through the desolate little village of **Hualfin**. (There are thermal baths in summer at **Pozo Verde**, to the north.) The road continues to Santa María (176 km, see page 252) and Cafayate (page 257). The alternative is Ruta 43, which branches west off Ruta 40 at a point 52 km north of Belén and runs across the high *puna* to Antofagasta de la Sierra and San Antonio de los Cobres (see page 285). This route is challenging at the best of times and impassable for ordinary cars after heavy rains. The stretch just after the junction with Ruta 40 is very difficult, with 37 km of fords. At Km 87 is Cerro Compo (3125 m), from which the descent is magnificent. At Km 99 the road turns right to Laguna Blanca, where there is a museum and a small vicuña farm (don't go straight ahead at the junction). There are thermal springs along this road at **Villavil**, 13 km further north, open from January to April.

Drivers should note that you'll need enough fuel for 600 km on unmaintained roads, with fuel consumption being double at high altitudes. Fill up at Hualfín and San Antonio de los Cobres, and possibly carry extra.

Antofagasta de la Sierra *Colour map 1, B2.*
Buses from Belén and Catamarca arrive Wed and Fri evening, or hire a car.

Antofagasta de la Sierra (population 1600, altitude 3365 m) is the main settlement in the sparsely populated northwest corner of Catamarca province, situated on the Río Punilla, 260 km north of Belén and 557 km northwest of the provincial capital. With its low pinkish adobe buildings, surrounded by vast empty lunar landscapes and massive volcanoes, it's an impressively remote place.

To the west are the salt flats of the **Salar de Antofalla**, though these are pretty much inaccessible. The **Salar del Hombre Muerto** on Ruta 43 can be visited, but it's best to hire a guide. It's a wonderful journey. There's nothing at all to do here and that's just the point. There are few places on earth that remain so wild and untouched, and these otherworldly landscapes are a paradise for photographers. If you're attracted to wild, immense open spaces and long roads leading apparently to nowhere, you'll love it.

Within reach of Antofagasta de la Sierra are several interesting archaeological sites including the ruins at **Campo Alumbreras**, in the shadow of the volcano of the same name. There's a pre-Columbian *pucará* (fort) and some nearby petroglyphs. Guides can be found at the small but wonderful museum **Museo del Hombre** ⓘ *Fiambalá Abaucán s/n, T03835-496250, Mon-Fri 0900-1200, 1500-1900*, which contains incredibly well preserved pre-Hispanic textiles and a 2000-year-old mummified baby. There's no petrol station, but fuel can be bought from the *intendencia*.

Listings North of La Rioja

Tourist information

Belén

Dirección de Turismo
At the bus terminal, a block from the plaza on Rivadavia and Lavalle, T03835-461304. Daily 0800-1300 and 1500-2200.
Small tourist office.

Where to stay

La Costa

$ Hostería Anillaco (ACA)
T03827-494064.
The best place to stay in the area. Breakfast included, a pool and also a decent restaurant.

Londres

$$$-$$ Estancia La Casona
Ruta 38, T03835-491061.
With a capacity of 10 people, this estancia has basic rooms and can organize a trip to El Shincal. In your free time you can help harvest nuts and herbs.

Belén

$$$ Hotel Belén
Belgrano y Cubas, T03835-461501, www.belen cat.com.ar.
Comfortable, with restaurant. Prices depend on day of arrival and tours taken.

$$ Samai
Urquiza 349, T03835-461320, see Facebook.
Old fashioned but welcoming, homely little rooms with bath and fan.

Antofagasta de la Sierra

Several family houses have cheap, basic but very welcoming accommodation, including private bath and breakfast. Ask the tourist office for details, T03833-422300.

$$-$ Hostería Municipal de Antofagasta
T03835-410679, see Facebook.
This is the only really comfortable accommodation, and though its 18 rooms are simple, they're perfectly decent, and the owners also have a restaurant and offer travel advice.

Restaurants

Belén

$$ 1900
Belgrano 391.
Laid-back restaurant with affordable food. Popular with locals.

$$ El Unico
Corner of General Roca and Sarmiento.
Great *parrilla* for a light meal.

Festivals

Belén

Feb Carnival. Celebrated in style.
Mar/Apr Easter. There are processions for the Virgin.
20 Dec-6 Jan Fiesta de Nuestra Señora de Belén. The town's most important fiesta.

What to do

Belén

For 4WD tours, go to the friendly and extremely helpful **Ampujaco Tur** (see below) or ask at **Hotel Belén** (see Where to stay, above) in town.
Ampujaco Tur, *General Roca 190, T03835-461189*. Organizes interesting Spanish-only tours to El Shincal for US$18 per person for 4, with tour guides and possibly an archaeologist (if requested in advance).

Belén
Bus

To **Santa María**, **San Cayetano** and **Parra** (connection there with other companies to Cafayate and Salta), daily, 5 hrs, US$11-15. To **Tinogasta**, daily except Mon and Wed, 2-3 hrs, US$8, with **Robledo**. To **Antofagasta de la Sierra**, El Antofagasteño, T03837-461152, Wed and Fri at 1200, 8-9 hrs, US$19. Buses

to **Catamarca** leave at 0430, US$16, 4-6 hrs; check with **Gutiérrez**, **El Antofagasteño** and **Robledo** bus companies. For more frequent services to **Catamarca** or **La Rioja**, take bus to **Aimogasta**, 2½ hrs, US$4.

Antofagasta de la Sierra
Bus

Buses to **Belén**, Mon and Fri 0900, with **El Antofagasteño**.

charming border towns

Chilecito

The second biggest town in La Rioja province and certainly the most attractive, Chilecito (population 37,000, altitude 1074 m) lies at the foot of the snow-capped Famatina Mountains in an area of vineyards and olive groves, and is the best base for exploring the hills and nearby villages. Founded in 1715, its name derives from the influx of Chilean miners in the 19th century. The town centre, with lots of cafés and a modern church, is centred on Plaza de los Caudillos, which is beautifully shaded with mature pine and red gum trees, and two pergolas covered with grapevines. Each February the plaza is the focus of the *chaya* celebrations and the anniversary of the town's foundation.

There is good local wine to sample at the **Cooperativa La Riojana** ① *La Plata 646, T03825-423150, www.lariojana.com.ar, free 45-min guided visits and a smart wine shop open in the morning*, where you can watch local grapes being processed to make a wide variety of red and white wines, including organic products, many of which are exported to Europe under the labels Inti, 7 Days, Pircas Negras or Santa Florentina.

For an easy five-minute walk from the plaza, head along El Maestro, past the pleasant Parque Municipal and up to the **Mirador El Portezuelo** where there are splendid panoramic views of the town and the Velasco and Famatina mountains. Another delightful nearby attraction is the botanical garden at **Chirau Mita** ① *Av Primera Junta, Km 0.25, take Arturo Marasso northwards, turning right at Primera Junta; it's on the way to La Puntilla*. The beautiful private garden has a rich collection of over 1500 cacti and succulent plants (native and non-native species) growing on terraces on the rocky slopes, and using the same techniques ancient Andes people used for cultivation. Not to be missed. **Finca Samay Huasi** ① *San Miguel, 3 km southeast of town, T03825-422629, Mon-Fri 0800-1900, Sat-Sun 0800-1200, 1400-1800 (closed 22 Dec-6 Jan), US$0.35*, is an attractive place to come and relax for a day, or stay overnight. The estate was once the summer residence of Joaquín V González, founder of La Plata University, who designed the gardens using native trees and strange stone monoliths expressing his love of ancient cultures. There's also a small natural history museum here.

Around Chilecito: the Famatina Valley

One of the richest areas of the province and only a few hours west of the capital, the immense Famatina valley is attractively flanked to the west by the magnificent Famatina Mountains, 6000 m high, and to the east by the Sierra de Velasco, rising to 4000 m. Once an important mining area, it's now famous for its tasty wines, olives and walnuts. You can combine the most challenging treks in the region with a relaxing stay in a calm, rural finca. While

BORDER CROSSING
Argentina–Chile

Paso San Francisco
The border is open 0700-1900, T03837-4200031. On the Chilean side roads run to
El Salvador and Copiapó. This route is closed by snow June to October; take enough
fuel for at least 400 km as there are no service stations from Fiambalá to just before
Copiapó. See also www.gendarmeria.gov.ar/pasos-fronterizos/sanfrancisco.html.

the mountains are best explored on a guided tour, you can amble to the villages around
Chilecito, with their old adobe houses and historical chapels, quite easily on your own. In
Famatina, Good Friday and Christmas Day are celebrated with fabulous processions, and
there's also a good site for paragliding. At **Santa Florentina** (8 km northwest of Chilecito),
the impressive remains of a huge early-20th-century foundry can be reached by cable car.

Western Catamarca
From Chilecito it's 126 km to the junction with Ruta 60 at the Catamarca/La Rioja border.
The desert here is spectacular, with a distinct culture and remote untouristy towns. In this
region the *Zonda*, a strong, dry mountain wind, can cause dramatic temperature increases.

The small settlement of **Tinogasta** is set in an oasis of vineyards, olive groves and
poplars. It is the starting point for expeditions to Ojos del Salado (6891 m) and **Pissis**
(6795 m), the second and third highest mountains in the Western hemisphere. Ruta 3
goes northeast from Tinogasta to Londres (see above).

Fiambalá lies 49 km north of Tinogasta, a peaceful place in a vine-filled valley, with the
Termas de Fiambalá hot springs situated 16 km east (take a taxi; make sure fare includes
wait and return). 4WD vehicles may be hired for approaching the Pissis-Ojos del Salado
region; ask at the Intendencia. **Fiambalá** is also the starting point for the crossing to Chile
via Paso San Francisco (4726 m), 203 km northwest along a paved road. See also box, above.

Listings Chilecito to Chile

Tourist information

Chilecito

Tourist office
Castro and Bazán 52, T03825-429665.
Daily 0800-2200.
There's another office at the bus station.

Where to stay

Chilecito

$$$ Chilecito (ACA)
T Gordillo y A G Ocampo, T03825-422201,
www.aca.tur.ar.
Comfortable place, with renovated rooms,
parking, a pool and cheap set menus.

$$$ Hotel Ruta 40
Libertad 68, T03825-422804.
Family-run hotel with all services, including
kitchen and laundry, bicycles, and local
produce for breakfast.

$$$ Posada del Sendero
Pasaje Spilimbergo, San Miguel, T03825-
414041, www.posadadelsendero.com.ar.
In peaceful Chilecito's rural suburbs, a
pleasant family-run place offering simple
rooms with a/c on a lovely park with pool.
Tours with their own **Salir del Cráter** agency;
see What to do, below.

$$ Hostal Mary Pérez
Florencio Dávila 280, T03825-423156,
hostal_mp@hotmail.com.
Good value, comfortable *hostal*, with a
welcoming atmosphere and a good breakfast.

Western Catamarca

$$$ Hotel de Adobe Casagrande
Moreno 801, Tinogasta, T0387-421140,
www.casagrandetour.com.
Hotel offering individually designed rooms,
bar, restaurant, pool and jacuzzi. They can
also arrange tours and activities.

$$ Hostería Municipal
Almagro s/n, Fiambalá, T03837-496291.
Good value, also has a restaurant.

$$ Hotel Nicolás
Perón 231, Tinogasta, T0387-420028.
Small hotel with breakfast, a/c, Wi-Fi,
laundry service and parking.

$ pp Complejo Turístico
At the Termas, Fiambalá, bookings at the
tourist office T03837-496250.
With cabins, a restaurant and camping.

Restaurants

Chilecito

$$$-$$ El Rancho de Ferrito
PB Luna 647, T03825-422481.
Popular *parrilla*, with local wines.

$$ La Rosa
Ocampo 149, T03825-424693.
Relaxing atmosphere, huge variety of pizzas,
more extensive menu Fri and Sat.

What to do

Chilecito
This is an excellent base for amazing treks
in the Famatina mountains and 1-day trips
to Talampaya and Valle de la Luna.
Salir del Cráter, *T03825-15 679620,*
www.salirdelcrater.com.ar. Trekking and
4WD trips around Chilecito, plus tours
to neighbouring provinces.

Transport

Chilecito
Bus
Terminal on Av Perón, on southern access
road to town. To **San Juan** with **Vallecito**,
8 hrs, US$29; to **La Rioja**, several times
daily, US$8, 3 hrs. To **Córdoba**, US$35,
7-8 hrs, and **Buenos Aires**, US$85-91, 17 hrs,
with **Urquiza** (T03825-423279). There are
many daily minibus services (*combis*) from
Chilecito to villages in the valley.

Western La Rioja *Colour map 1, C1.*

the wild frontier

Western La Rioja is remote and undiscovered, but you might want to base yourself
in the town of Villa Unión for Talampaya Park (see box, page 238), or to visit
the strange otherworldly landscapes of the Reserva Natural Laguna Brava. The
westernmost inhabited valley in La Rioja (also known as Valle del Bermejo) follows
the Río Vinchina, which flows along the western side of the Sierra de Famatina. The
valley can be reached from La Rioja city along Route 26 via the Parque Nacional
Talampaya, or from Chilecito by Ruta 40, via Sañogasta and the spectacular Cuesta
de Miranda. Winding its way between Sierra de Famatina and Sierra de Sañogasta,
through eroded red sandstone rocks, the road rises to 2020 m and drops again,
passing through 320 bends in 11,500 m.

Villa Unión and around

Some 92 km west of Nonogasta, Villa Unión (population 4900, altitude 1240 m) is the largest settlement in the valley and is another base for visits to the Parque Nacional Talampaya, 67 km south. North of Villa Unión, paved Route 76 heads along the arid valley to **Villa Castelli** and **Vinchina** (70 km north of Villa Unión) offering the last comfortable accommodation option before the high mountains (\$\$), **Corona del Inca** ① *T0380-442 2142,* www.coronadelinca. com.ar. For more information, see www.turismovillaunion.gob.ar.gov.ar.

On the west side of Route 76, on the northern outskirts of town is the **Estrella de Vinchina**, the only surviving star-shaped stone mosaic made by ancient settlers centuries ago. Immediately north of Vinchina, Route 76 enters the spectacular **Quebrada de la Troya**, and 36 km northwest of Vinchina it reaches **Jagüe** (1900 m), with food and basic facilities; here you will be approached by park wardens of the nearby Reserva Natural Laguna Brava (see below). This is the starting point for a 154-km route to Chile through the Andean mountain pass of **Pircas Negras** (4165 m). About every 20-30 km you'll see stone huts, built in the 19th century to shelter cattle wranglers on their way across the Andes.

Reserva Natural Laguna Brava
Route 76, 170 km northwest of Villa Union. Entry US\$2 per person.

This reserve protects Laguna Brava, a salt lake at 4271 m, that's 16 km long, 3 km wide, plus some 405,000 ha of mountains and high plateau, rising from 3800 m to 4360 m. The lake lies beyond the Portezuelo del Peñón, with superb views and some of the mightiest volcanoes on Earth in the background. From the left, these are: the perfect cone **Veladero** (6436 m), **Reclus** (6335 m), **Los Gemelos** (6130 m), **Pissis** (6882 m) the highest volcano in the world, though inactive, and **Bonete** (6759 m) which is also visible from Villa Unión and Talampaya. The park is home to thousands of flamingos and *vicuñas*, the more elegant cousins of the llama.

There are many organized 4WD tours on offer here, which take you to the high plateau, the Laguna Brava itself and, occasionally, the small lagoon Corona del Inca lying at the crater of a volcano at 5300 m (see What to do, below). The nearest settlement is Jagüe, at the western end of Route 76, and from here, 4WD vehicles or mountain bikes are essential to enter the park. The nearest accommodation is at Villa Unión. Tours are run by agencies in Villa Unión, La Rioja and Chilecito. Access is limited by summer rainfall and winter snow, so the best times for a visit are April and early May.

Listings Western La Rioja

Where to stay

Villa Unión and around

\$\$\$ Cañón de Talampaya
On Ruta 76 Km 202 (southern access), T03825-470753, www.hotelcanontalampaya.com.
Comfortable rooms in rustic style with a/c, restaurant serving some organic products, and a pool.

\$\$\$ Hotel Pircas Negras
On Ruta 76 (southern access), T03825-470611, www.hotelpircasnegras.com.

Large modern building, with comfortable rooms, a restaurant and a pool. Trips organized.

\$\$ Chakana
In Banda Florida, T03825-15-510168, www.chakana hospedajerural.blogspot.com.ar.
In rural surroundings across the river from Villa Unión, this charming little hotel is carefully run by Natalia and Martín, who also prepare excellent meals.

Parque Nacional Talampaya

Extending over 215,000 ha at an altitude of 1200 m, Talampaya is remarkable for its impressive rock formations, of which the main feature is the 4-km canyon surrounding the River Talampaya. A stroll through this vast chasm gives you the unforgettable experience of being entirely dwarfed by the landscape. Though some sections of the park are only accessible by vehicle, guided walks and cycle rides are possible.

The park and circuits

The park itself occupies a basin between the Sierra Morada to the west and the Sierras de Sañogasta to the east. This is the site of an ancient lake, where piled-up sediments have since been eroded by water and wind for the last 200 million years, forming a dramatic landscape of pale red hills named **Sierra de los Tarjados**. Numerous fossils have been found, and some 600-year-old petroglyphs can be seen not far from the access to the gorge. As in Ischigualasto, along the canyon there are extraordinarily shaped structures which have been given names such as 'the balconies', 'the lift', 'the crib' or 'the owl'. At one point, the gorge narrows to 80 m wide and rises to 143 m deep. A refreshing leafy spot in the centre of the gorge has been named 'the botanical garden' due to the amazing diversity of plants and tree specimens living here. The end of the canyon is marked by the imposing cliffs of 'the Cathedral' and the curious 'King on a camel'. 'The chessboard' and 'the monk', 53 m high, lie not far beyond the gorge, marking the end of the so-called **El Monje circuit**. Only accessible with 4WD vehicles, another circuit, **Circuito Los Cajones**, continues in the same direction up to '*los pizarrones*', an enormous wall of rock covered with petroglyphs, and then to '*los cajones*', a narrow pass between rock walls. Two additional circuits in other areas within the park are organized from an entrance on Route 76, Km 134. **Ciudad Perdida**, southeast of the gorge, accessible only with 4WD vehicles, leads to an area of high cliffs and a large number of breathtaking rock formations, and the **Arco Iris circuit** leads to a multi-coloured canyon.

Access and information

The park is reached by Route 76: turn off at Km 134 (217 km from La Rioja), 61 km north of the police checkpoint at Los Baldecitos and 55 km south of Villa Unión, onto a paved road, 14 km long. Independent access is possible, since buses or *combis* (minibuses) linking La Rioja and Villa Unión stop at the park entrance, but note that it's a long

$$ Hotel Noryanepat
JV González 150, T03825-470133,
www.hotelnoryanepat.com.ar.
Good hotel featuring small rooms with a/c.

What to do

Villa Unión and around
Runacay, *T03825-470368, www.runacay.com.*
Tours to Laguna Brava. Recommended.

(14 km), lonely and unshaded walk to the administration building. No private vehicles are allowed beyond the administration building, where you have to park, and arrange alternative transport around the park: either a park vehicle, walking or bicycle.

Accommodation
The only option inside the park is a basic campsite, next to the administration office (US$3.50 per person). The closest base for visiting the park is the small town of Villa Unión, 67 km north, see under Western La Rioja, page 237, see www.turismovillaunion.gov.ar.

Tour operators
Tour operators in La Rioja and Chilecito organize tours into the park, sometimes combining a visit with Ischigualasto, which is otherwise difficult to access. Check when you book that both the entrance fee and guides' fees are included in the cost of your tour.

Tours of the park along the **El Monje**, and **Circuito Los Cajones** circuits can be arranged at the administration office, but not for the **Ciudad Perdida** and **Arco Iris** circuits. These both take 4½ hours and cost US$33 per person each; tours start from Route 76, Km 133.5.

Guided walks, cycle rides and tours
Guides speak English.
Guided walks to Quebrada Don Eduardo, a secondary gorge, next to the canyon (about three hours, US$23 per person).
Guided bike rides (2½ hours, US$33 per person, cycle and helmet provided) follow the whole length of the *cañón* up to *'la catedral'*. A shorter journey is also on offer up to 'the botanical garden'.
Guided visits in a park vehicle for El Monje circuit (three hours, US$33 per person).

When to go
The best time to visit is in the morning, when the natural light is best, avoiding the strong winds in the afternoon.

Entry cost
US$10, September to April 0800-1930, May to August 0830-1830.

Further information
Call the park administration T03825-470356, or see www.talampaya.com (in English) or www.talampaya.gov.ar (in Spanish), for more information on excursions and for advance bookings.

Transport

Western Catamarca
Bus
Empresa Gutiérrez runs buses from Fiambalá, via Tinogasta, to **Catamarca** (connection to Buenos Aires) US$19; also Tinogasta to Catamarca with **Robledo**, 4-5 hrs, US$16. For **Belén**, change at Aimogasta.

Northwest Argentina

painted mountains, indigenous culture and colonial cities

The northwest is a different Argentina. The Andes here are wilder and less travelled, and ancient civilizations have left ruined cities sprawling over rugged mountainsides in the vast canyons at Quilmes, Purmamarca and Santa Rosa de Tastil.

Traditional Andean culture is thriving, with lively celebrations of the ancient Pachamama (Mother Earth) festivities throughout indigenous communities. The poorer province of Jujuy has even more spectacular riches in the stunning Quebrada de Humahuaca, a vast gorge of stratified rock with tiny white churches.

Landscapes here are among Argentina's most breathtaking: winding roads snake up the Quebrada del Toro with its steep gorges clad with cloudforest, through canyons dotted with giant cacti, and then streak across the high-altitude *puna*, with its shimmering salt flats and vast skies. Set off up the dramatic Cuesta del Obispo to the magical Valles Calchaquíes to find giant cacti set against snow-capped mountains, and tranquil villages at Cachi and Molinos, or sophisticated wineries at Colomé and the charming village of Cafayate, a wine-growing region to rival Mendoza.

Salta is the splendid colonial city at the heart of the region, with fine hotels in its plazas of crumbling buildings and palm trees, and vibrant *peñas* where passionate *folclore* music is sung.

Best for
Cultural festivities ▪ Hiking ▪ Horse riding

Footprint picks

★ **Los Valles Calchaquíes**,
page 256
Red rock formations are the icons of Argentina's northwestern valleys.

★ **Cafayate's bodegas**, page 257
Mendoza isn't the only destination for wine; the north produces some tasty varietals as well.

★ **Peñas in Salta city**, page 277
There's no better place to enjoy some local northern music than a *peña folklórica*.

★ **Santa Rosa de Tastil**, page 284
A splendid archaeological site featuring ruins of Northwest Argentina's oldest pre-Colombian city.

★ **Quebrada de Humahuaca**, page 295
Painted mountains rising up over colonial villages make this one of the country's must-visit sights.

★ **The journey to Iruya**, page 297
Journey to a hidden colonial town nestled deep in the mountains.

N

50 km
50 miles

BOLIVIA

CHILE

Villazón
La Quiaca
Yavi
Reserva Nacional Laguna de los Pozuelos
Parque Nacional Baritú
Abra Pampa
Aguas Blancas
Tartagal
Iruya
Casabindo
Orán
Embarcación
Tres Cruces
Coctaca
Humahuaca
JUJUY
Salinas Grandes
Uquía
Tilcara
Quebrada de Humahuaca
Paso de Jama
Susques
Huacalera
Maimará
Parque Nacional Calilegua
Purmamarca
Libertador General San Martín
Catua
San Antonio de los Cobres
San Pedro
Paso de Sico
Jujuy
Cauchari
Salar de Pocitos
Paso Abra de Acay
Santa Rosa de Tastil
Finca El Bordo de las Lanzas
Paso de Socompa
Socompa
La Poma
SALTA
Campo de Quijano
Salta
Güemes
Parque Nacional El Rey
Salar de Arizaro
Cachi
Embalse Cabra Corral
16
Seclantás
Parque Nacional los Cardones
Molinos
La Viña
Metán
Salar de Antofalla
Angastaco
68
Río Calchaquí
Rosario de la Frontera
San Carlos
Antilla
La Fragua
Antofagasta de la Sierra
Cafayate
40
Trancas
Quilmes
Amaichá
TUCUMAN
Santa María
Tafí del Valle
Santos Lugares
Paso de San Francisco
Sierra de Aconquija
Tucumán
Ojos de Salado (6882m)
Monteros
307
38
Pozo Hondo
Pissis (6882m)
Palo Blanco
CATAMARCA
Hualfín
Andalgalá
Embalse Río Hondo
Termas de Río Hondo
Bonete (6759m)
Fiambalá
Belén
La Madrid
Santiago del Estero
34
Reserva Natural Laguna Brava
Tinogasta
Londres
El Rodeo
Villa San Martín
Lavalle
Catamarca
60

Tucumán &
Santiago del Estero provinces

Two of the oldest cities in Argentina, Santiago del Estero and Tucumán, are at the start of the route to the fascinating Northwest. Both have some good museums and other sites of interest, and the subtropical climate is ideal for growing sugar, tobacco and lemons, but the summer heat may urge you to press on to the mountains. Of the two routes north to the atmospheric city of Salta, the more beautiful is via Tafí del Valle and the wine-producing town of Cafayate at the foot of the enchanting Valles Calchaquíes. Pretty towns in arid landscapes, archaeological remains and the Andes in the distance make for a memorable journey.

The quiet, provincial town of Santiago del Estero (population 383,000) makes a handy stopping point if you're heading from the flat landscape of the Chaco to explore the northwest corner of Argentina but little of the architectural heritage of Argentina's oldest city remains. There are, however, some comfortable places to stay, a couple of museums worth seeing, and the people are among Argentina's most friendly and welcoming.

Santiago was founded in 1553 and was an important base for establishing other major cities in the northwest. As the other cities grew, Santiago was left behind and the town is now a rather impoverished older neighbour. In 1993, a demonstration over unpaid wages to government employees turned into a riot in which several public buildings were destroyed. However, the city has a warm, laid-back atmosphere and the siesta here is legendary.

Sights

On the Plaza Libertad stand the **Municipalidad** and **Jefatura de Policia**, built in 1868 in the style of a colonial *cabildo*. On the west side is the **cathedral**, the fifth on the site, dating from 1877. Two blocks southeast of the plaza is the **Convento de Santo Domingo** ⓘ *Urquiza and 25 de Mayo*, containing one of two copies of the 'Turin Shroud', but otherwise unremarkable. Six blocks east of the plaza is the welcome greenery of the **Parque Francisco de Aguirre**, which stretches to the river and incorporates the town's campsite.

The best museum is the **Museo de Ciencias, Antropológicas y Naturales** ⓘ *Avellaneda 355, Mon-Fri 0900-1300, 1700-2100, free,* with a wonderfully eclectic collection of pre-Hispanic artefacts gathered by brothers Emilio and Duncan Wagner, now sadly

Essential Santiago del Estero

Finding your feet

Mal Paso airport is on the northwestern outskirts of town. From the **bus terminal** on Perú y Chacabuco a taxi into town costs US$2, and this will save you a 12-block walk. However, if you find a taxi a little further from the terminal you'll avoid being surcharged by some taxi drivers.

Weather Santiago del Estero

January	February	March	April	May	June
34°C	33°C	30°C	26°C	23°C	20°C
20°C	20°C	18°C	15°C	11°C	6°C
100mm	90mm	90mm	30mm	10mm	0mm

July	August	September	October	November	December
21°C	24°C	26°C	31°C	32°C	34°C
6°C	7°C	10°C	15°C	18°C	20°C
0mm	0mm	10mm	30mm	60mm	80mm

haphazardly presented and badly conserved. Amongst the stuffed armadillos, bone flutes, delicate spindles and board-flattened skulls is a breathtaking quantity of beautifully decorated funerary urns, some rare bronze ceremonial *hachas*, and anthropomorphic pieces. Also interesting is the **Museo Histórico Provincial** ⓘ *Urquiza 354, T0385-421 2893, Tue-Fri 0900-1400 and 1700-2100, Sat 1000-1400 and 1800-2100, Sun 1800-2100, free*. In a 200-year-old mansion, it has 18th- and 19th-century artefacts from wealthy local families. **Centro Cultural del Bicentenario de Santiago del Estero** ⓘ *Libertad 439, T0385-422 4858, Tue-Sun 0900-1400, 1700-2100, see Facebook*, acts as an umbrella organization for all cultural activities in the city.

Termas de Río Hondo *Colour map 1, B3.*

Argentina's most popular spa town (population 34,000, altitude 265 m), 65 km northwest of Santiago del Estero, is also its most dreary. It was very popular in the 1950s, but much of it remains unmodernized from that era, and the only real reason to visit is if you want to take advantage of the warm mineral-laden waters, which are piped into every hotel in the city. Older Argentines hold it in fond regard and it's a mecca for visitors with arthritic or skin conditions in July and August, when you'll need to book in advance. Out of season, it's a depressing place.

With the casino dominating the scruffy triangular plaza, the resort consists of 160 hotels interspersed with *alfajores* shops (the much-loved chocolate and flour biscuit), mostly in run-down and flaking buildings. Even in high season, there's little to make you feel better here, and another biscuit isn't likely to help.

Listings Santiago del Estero and around

Tourist information

Santiago del Estero

Tourist office
Plaza Libertad 417, in the town centre, T0385-421 4243.
See also www.sde.gov.ar.

Termas de Río Hondo

Tourist office
Caseros 268, T03858-421969, and Av Alberdi 245, T03858-421571.
Helpful staff.

Where to stay

Santiago del Estero

$$$ Carlos V
Independencia 110, T0385-424 0303, www.carlosvhotel.com.
On the corner of the plaza, this is the city's most luxurious hotel, with elegant rooms, a pool and a good restaurant. It's still good value for its category.

$$$ Centro
9 de Julio 131, T0385-421 9502, www.hotelcentro.com.ar.
Attractive decor, very comfortable, with an airy restaurant.

$$$ Libertador
Catamarca 47, T0385-421 9252, www.hotellibertadorsrl.com.ar.
Smart and relaxing place, with a spacious lounge, plain rooms, patio with pool (summer only) and an elegant restaurant. It's 5 blocks south of the plaza in the better part of town.

$$$ Savoy
Peatonal Tucumán 39, T0385-421 1234, www.savoysantiago.com.ar.
Good option, characterful, art nouveau grandeur, swirling stairwell, large airy rooms and a small pool.

$ pp Res Emaus
Av Moreno Sur 675, T0385-421 5893.
Good cheap choice, with bath and TV, helpful.

Camping

Las Casuarinas
Parque Aguirre, T0385-421 1390,
see Facebook.
Insect repellent essential.

Termas de Río Hondo
Ask the tourist office (see under
Tourist information, above)
for accommodation advice.

$$$$ Hotel de los Pinos
Maipú 201, T03858-421043,
www.lospinoshotel.com.ar.
The best option in an attractive Spanish-style
building a little removed from the centre in
a huge park, with fantastic pools and rooms
with private thermal baths. Rates are for
minimum 3-night all-inclusive stays.

$$$ El Hostal del Abuelo
Francisco Solano 168, T03858-421489,
www.elhostaldelabuelo.com.ar.
Most central in town, this spa hotel has a
huge range of facilities and comfortable
rooms but is pricey.

Restaurants

Santiago del Estero

$$ Mia Mamma
On the main plaza at 24 de Septiembre 15.
A cheery place for *parrilla* and tasty pasta,
with good salad for starters.

Termas de Río Hondo
San Cayetano ($$, see Facebook) or the
homely **Renacimiento ($$)**, both on the
main drag Sarmiento, are reasonably priced
for *parrilla*.

$ El Chorizo Loco
Alberdi and Sarmiento.
A very cheap and lively pizzeria.

Transport

Santiago del Estero
Air
The **airport** (T0385-434 3654) has flights to
Buenos Aires with **Aerolíneas Argentinas**,
24 de Septiembre 547, T0810-222 86527.

Bus
The **bus terminal** (T0385-422 7091,
www.tosde.com.ar) has toilets, a *locutorio*,
a basic café, food stalls and *kioskos*.
  To **Córdoba**, 6 hrs, US$28-35; to **Salta**,
6-6½ hrs, US$32-42; to **Tucumán**,
2 hrs, US$13; to **Catamarca**, with
Tramat US$21 4½ hrs.

Termas de Río Hondo
Bus
The **bus terminal** (Av 12 de Octubre y
25 de Mayo) is 8 blocks north of centre near
Route 9, but buses will drop you at the plaza,
on Alberdi, opposite the casino.
  To **Santiago del Estero**, 1 hr, US$5.50,
and to **Tucumán**, 2 hrs, US$7; also several
to **Buenos Aires**, 13-14 hrs, US$92-110.

The city of San Miguel de Tucumán, known simply as Tucumán (population 491,000), lies almost equidistant from Catamarca and Salta on a broad plain, just east of the massive Sierra de Aconquija. It's the largest and most important city in the province, though it suffered economically during the recession. Visually, the city lacks Salta's style or architectural splendour, despite being one of the first cities to be founded by the Spanish, and few of its colonial buildings remain. There are few attractions for visitors, and it's overwhelmingly hot in summer – the siesta is strictly observed from 1230 to 1630 – but it does have a couple of good museums and lively nightlife. It's a busy city with plenty of restaurants and a huge park designed by architect Charles Thays (see box, page 52).

Sights *Colour map 1, B3.*

Plaza Independencia in the city's commercial centre has many tall palms and mature trees that give welcome shade in the sweltering heat. At night the plaza is full of Tucumanos eating ice cream from one of the many *heladerías*. Among its attractive buildings are the ornate **Casa de Gobierno** (1910), with tall palms outside and art nouveau balconies. Next door is a typical *casa chorizo* (sausage house), **Museo Casa Padilla** ① *25 de Mayo 36, see Facebook, Tue-Fri 0830-1230, 1530-1930, Sat-Sun 1530-1930, free*, a series of skinny rooms off open patios, whose collection of china and paintings belonging to a wealthy Tucumán family gives you a flavour of 19th-century life.

Essential Tucumán city

Finding your feet

Aeropuerto Benjamín Matienzo is 10 km east of town. It's linked to the city by bus No 121, taxi (US$10) or minibus transfer either to Plaza Independencia (US$2) or to a hotel (US$7-9). There's a huge **bus** terminal at Avenida Brígido Terán, seven blocks east of Plaza Independencia, where long-distance buses arrive. Bus No 4 goes from outside the terminal to San Lorenzo y 9 de Julio in the centre. A taxi to the centre costs US$3-4. For more details, see Transport, page 250.

Getting around

Plaza Independencia is the city's heart, with busy pedestrianized shopping streets to the north and west. Tucumán is an easy place to get around on foot, but taxis are cheap and reliable. Note that local buses require rechargeable *Ciudadana* cards, sold in kiosks for US$1 or US$1.75.

When to go

The city's big festivals include **Independence Day** on 9 July, when Tucumán becomes capital of the country for the day. On 24 September, the city celebrates Belgrano's victory at the Battle of Tucumán with a huge procession. September also sees the **Tucumán Empanada Festival**; see also Festivals, page 250. Summer is best avoided because of the heat, especially January and February.

> **Tip...**
> There are several good accommodation options, but if this is a strategic stopover for you, it would be better to retreat to the cooler mountains of Tafí del Valle, as the Tucumanos do at weekends.

BACKGROUND

Tucumán city

Tucumán was an important city in Spanish colonial times. Founded in 1565 and transferred to its present site in 1685, it was a strategic stop for mule trains on the routes from Bolivia to Buenos Aires and Mendoza. With a colonial economy based on sugar, citrus fruit and tobacco, it developed an aristocracy distinct from those in Buenos Aires and Córdoba. The city was the site of an important battle during the Wars of Independence. Belgrano's victory here in 1812 over a royalist army ended the Spanish threat to restore colonial rule over the River Plate area. Tucumán's wealth was derived from sugar, and this remains the biggest industry, though lemons have also become vital exports in recent decades.

Across the road, the **Iglesia San Francisco** (1891) has a rather gloomy interior, but a picturesque façade and tiled cupola. On the south side of the plaza, the neoclassical **cathedral** (1852) has a distinctive cupola, but a disappointingly bland modern interior, the ceiling painted with rainbows and whales.

South of the plaza, on Calle Congreso 141, is the **Casa Histórica** ⓘ *T0381-431 0826, www. museocasahistorica.org.ar/contacto, daily 0900-2000, US$1; son et lumière show in garden Fri-Wed at 2030 when fine, US$2.50, tickets also from tourist office on Plaza Independencia, no seats*. Rooms are set around two attractive patios, filled with old furniture, historical documents and some fine Cuzqueño-school paintings. The highlight is the room where the Declaration of Independence was drafted, with portraits of the Congressmen lining the walls. Next to it is a room full of interesting religious artefacts.

The **Museo Folklórico General Manuel Belgrano** ⓘ *24 de Septiembre 565, see Facebook, Tue-Fri 0900-1230,1530-1930, Sat-Sun 1530-1730*, has an impressive collection of silverwork from Peru and musical instruments in an old colonial house. To see local art and sculpture, visit the **Museo de Bellas Artes Timoteo Navarro** ⓘ *9 de Julio 36, T0381-422 7300*, which has over 680 works of art set in a wonderfully restored building.

Tucumán's enormous park, **Parque Nueve de Julio**, east of the centre, is a much-used green space with many subtropical trees, designed by French landscape architect Charles Thays, who also designed the Parque Tres de Febrero in Buenos Aires. It was once the property of Bishop Colombres who played an important role in the development of the local sugar industry, and whose handsome house is now the **Museo de la Industria Azucarera** ⓘ *see Facebook, Tue-Fri 0900-1300 and 1500-1800, Sat-Sun 1000-1330 and 1430-1800, free*, with a display on sugar-making. The park also has a lake and lots of sports facilities.

Listings Tucumán city

Tourist information

Tourist office
On the plaza, 24 de Septiembre 484, T0381-422 2199/430 3644, www.tucuman turismo.gov.ar. Mon-Fri 0800-2200, Sat-Sun 0900-2100.

Very helpful. There are also offices in the bus terminal and airport; the bus station office is particularly good at finding accommodation. The municipal website is www.smt.gob.ar.

Where to stay

$$$$ Catalinas Park
Av Soldati 380, T0381-450 2250,
www.catalinaspark.com.
The city's most comfortable and luxurious
hotel, overlooking Parque 9 de Julio,
outstanding food and service, pool
(open to non-residents), sauna and gym.
Highly recommended.

$$$ Carlos V
25 de Mayo 330, T0381-431 1666,
www.hotelcarlosv.com.ar.
Centrally located, with good service
and an elegant restaurant.

$$$ Dallas
Corrientes 985, T0381-421 8500,
www.dallashotel.com.ar.
Welcoming, well-furnished large rooms
and good bathrooms. Recommended,
though it's a long way from the centre.

$$$ Mediterráneo
24 de Septiembre 364, T0381-431 0025,
www.hotelmediterraneo.com.ar.
Good rooms, TV, a/c. 20-30% discount
for Footprint owners.

$$$ Suites Garden Park
Av Soldati 330, T0381-431 0700,
www.gardenparkhotel.com.ar.
Smart, welcoming 4-star hotel, with views
over Parque 9 de Julio, pool, gym, sauna and
restaurant. Also has apartments.

$$$-$$ Miami
Junín 580, 8 blocks from plaza, T0381-431
0265, www.hotelmiamitucuman.com.ar.
Good modern hotel, with refurbished rooms
and a pool.

$$$-$$ Versailles
Crisóstomo Alvarez 481, T0381-422 9760,
www.hotelversaillestuc.com.ar.
Comfortable beds though rooms are a
bit small. Good service, price depends
on season. Recommended.

$ pp Backpacker's Tucumán
Laprida 456, T0381-430 2716,
www.backpackerstucuman.com.
Youth hostel in a restored house with a
quiet atmosphere, lovely patio, basic dorms
(US$12.50-15), English spoken, good. Plus
$$-$ double room with bath. Offers a 20%
discount to HI members.

$ pp Hostel OH!
Santa Fe 930, T0381-430 8849,
www.hostelohtucuman.com.ar.
Neat, modern hostel with shared (US$12-15
pp) or private rooms (**$$**), quiet, *parrilla*, pool,
games and a garden.

$ pp Tucumán Hostel
Buenos Aires 669, T0381-420 1584,
www.tucumanhostel.com
In a refurbished building. Large, high-ceiling
dorms (US$12-16), double room with bath
$$**, **$ without. Slightly unkempt but chilled
garden. Recommended.

Restaurants

There are many popular restaurants
and cafés along 25 de Mayo, north
from Plaza Independencia, and on
Plaza Hipólito Yrigoyen.

$$$-$$ La Leñita
San Juan 633.
Recommended for *parrilla*, with superb
salads. The charming waiting staff can be
persuaded to produce instruments and belt
out *folklórico* tunes.

$$ Il Postino
Junín 4000.
Attractive buzzing pizza place, plus
tapas and tortillas too, with stylish decor.
Recommended.

$ Sir Harris
Laprida y Mendoza.
A Tucumán institution, cosy with good
quality *tenedor libre*, some veggie dishes.
Recommended.

Cafés

Café de París
Santiago del Estero y 25 de Mayo,
see Facebook.
Tapas bar and stylish little restaurant.

Cosas del Campo
Lavalle 853 (south of centre, next to
Plaza San Martín), T0381-420 1758.
Renowned for its *empanadas*, also
for takeaway.

Panadería Villecco
Corrientes 751.
Exceptional bread, including wholemeal
(*integral*) loaves, and pastries.

Bars and clubs

Costumbres Argentinos
San Juan 666 y Maipú, see Facebook.
An intimate place with a good atmosphere
for late drinks.

Plaza de Almas
Santa Fe and Maipú, north of centre,
see Facebook.
This bar attracts young crowds in the
late evenings.

Festivals

9 Jul Independence Day
Sep Fiesta Nacional de la Empanada
3 days of baking, eating and folk music
in Famaillá, 35 km from Tucumán, usually
in 1st half of the month.
24 Sep Battle of Tucumán. Both this festival
and Independence Day are celebrated with
huge processions and parties.

Shopping

Handicrafts
Mercado del Norte, *Maipú between Mendoza*
and Córdoba. Mon-Sat 0900-1300 and 1700-
2100. Indoor market and bazaar featuring
cheap regional foods, meat and local produce.
Regionales del Jardín, *Congreso 20.* Good
selection of local jams, *alfajores*, etc.

What to do

Tour operators
Duport Turismo, *Congreso 160, T0381-422*
0000, see Facebook. Local tours, plus a circuit
of the local valleys, 6 hrs.
Montañas Tucumanas, *T0381-467 1860,*
www.montanastucumanas.com. Great
company that organizes trekking, rappelling,
horse riding, canyoning and paragliding.

Transport

Air
To **Buenos Aires** with **Aerolíneas**
Argentinas, 9 de Julio 110, T0810-222 86527,
and **LAN**, San Juan 426, T0810-9999 526.

Bicycle
Bike Shop, San Juan 984, T0381-431 3121.

Bus
Long-distance buses to all parts of the
country depart from the huge **bus terminal**
on Av Brígido Terán, T0381-430 0452, www.
terminaltuc.com. It has a shopping complex,
left luggage lockers (US$1.50), **tourist**
information office (by boletería 1, Mon-Fri
0800-2200, Sat-Sun 0900-2100), *locutorios*,
toilets and banks (with ATM).
   To **Buenos Aires**, many companies,
14-16 hrs, US$99-119. To **Salta** direct (not
via Cafayate), 4-4½ hrs, several companies
US$23-29. To **Tafí del Valle**, Aconquija (www.
transporteaconquija.com.ar), multiple daily
2½ hrs, US$7.75. To **Cafayate**, 5½ hrs US$21,
with Aconquija. To **Mendoza**, 13-14 hrs, US$65-
95, via **Catamarca**, **La Rioja** and **San Juan**. To
Córdoba, 8 hrs, US$50-57. To **Santiago del**
Estero, 2 hrs, US$10-15. To **Posadas**, 16 hrs,
US$85, with Andesmar. To **Catamarca**, 4 hrs,
US$18, with Andesmar, El Rápido and others.
To **La Quiaca** (Bolivian border), 10-11 hrs,
US$53, with El Rápido and La Veloz del Norte.

Car hire
Movil Renta, San Lorenzo 370, T0381-431
0550, www.movilrenta.com.ar, and at airport.
20% discount for **Footprint** book owners.

Train

Tucumán is one of the few places that can be reached by long-distance train from Buenos Aires. To **Buenos Aires** via **Rosario**, with **Ferrocentral** Wed, at 0920 and Sat at 1445, US$ 25 standard, US$30 pullman, US$87 sleeper, T0800-222 8736, www.sateliteferroviario.com.ar. For more information see Buenos Aires Mitre line, page 73.

Northwest Tucumán province

little-known archaeological marvels just outside the city

Tucumán has stunning mountain scenery in the west and north of the province, along the Nevados de Aconquija, where there are several attractive small towns to visit on the way to Salta. Of the two possible routes, Route 9, via Rosario de la Frontera and Güemes, is far quicker, but it would be a shame to miss one of the most spectacular routes in the whole area: along Ruta 307 and Ruta 40 towards Cafayate. The road rises up though verdant Tafí del Valle, over the massive Infiermillo pass and then runs through spectacular landscapes all the way to the archaeological site of Quilmes, with the added small town charms of Amaichá del Valle and Santa María on the way.

Tafí del Valle *Colour map 1, B3.*

The journey from Tucumán to Tafí is very satisfying. Route 307 leads northwest towards Cafayate, climbing through sugar and citrus fruit plantations, and then jungle subtropical forest, before entering the wide Valle de Tafí, surrounded by mountains densely covered in velvety vegetation. At Km 69 there is a statue to 'El Indio', with good views from the picnic area.

Tafí del Valle (population 14,933, altitude 2000 m), known as Tafí, has a cool microclimate and is a popular weekend retreat from the heat of the city for Tucumanos. It makes a good base for walking, with several peaks of the Sierra de Aconquija providing challenging day hikes. For hikes into the mountains, it's best to go with a guide, available from **La Cumbre Hostel**, see What to do, page 255. There's some excellent accommodation, especially at the upper end of the market, making this an appealing alternative to staying in Tucumán. Most shops are on the main streets, Avenida Gobernador Critto (becoming Los Faroles to the west near the plaza) and Avenida Perón. At the junction you can buy good locally made cheese and delicious bread.

Tafí's most historic building is the attractive **Capilla Jesuítica y Museo de La Banda** ① *T03867-421685, daily 0800-1800, US$1 including guided tour.* This 18th-century chapel and 19th-century estancia has a small museum with interesting finds from the valley and 18th-century religious art. Cross the bridge over Río Tafí southwest of town, and the museum is on your left after 500 m.

Within the sprawling town, you can stroll by the ríos El Churqui and Blanquito or walk 10 km south to the Parque de los Menhires, which lies in an attractive spot at the south of a reservoir, the Dique la Angostura. The *menhires* are 129 granite stones, engraved with designs of unknown significance, said by some to symbolize fertility. They are undeniably intriguing, but not quite the mystical sight the tourist brochures claim, since the stones were unearthed in various places in the valley and put here in 1977. There's a decent campsite nearby and windsurfing and sailing are available on the reservoir in summer. Five kilometres further west, **El Mollar** is another weekend village with campsites and *cabañas*, and is popular with teenage and student crowds.

Northwest of Tafí del Valle

One of Argentina's most memorable journeys is along Route 307 northwest from Tafí, climbing out of the valley up to the **Abra del Infiernillo** mountain pass (3042 m) at Km 130, on the way to Amaichá del Valle and Cafayate. There are panoramic views south over the **Cumbres de Mala Mala**, the steeply sided deep green valley below, then breathtaking vistas as you emerge over the pass, looking north over the **Cumbres Calchaquíes**, veiled purple in the distance, and finally over the dramatic Valles Calchaquíes. The road descends along hairy zig-zags to the beautiful rocky valley of the **Río de Amaichá**.

Amaichá del Valle *Colour map 1, B2.*

Claiming rather grandly to have the best climate in the world, Amaichá (population 7500, altitude 1997 m) is a lovely, tranquil little place that does indeed always seem to be sunny. There's a splendid museum, the **Complejo Museo Pachamama** ⓘ *T03892-421004, daily 0900-1800, www.museopachamama.com, US$5.50, explanations in English, guided tour in Spanish*, also known also as Casa de Piedra. The museum was designed by the Argentine sculptor Héctor Cruz, who uses the iconography of the region's pre-Columbian art with bold flair in his own ceramics and weavings. It's part gallery, part archaeological museum, and is a great place to relax for a couple of hours, with wonderful views from the mosaic cactus gardens. The shop sells an extensive range of handicrafts, and bold rugs and hangings, designed by Cruz and made by local weavers.

The road forks at Amaichá: take Route 357 north for 14 km to the junction with Ruta 40, then follow it north towards Cafayate for the turn-off to Quilmes. For Santa María and western Catamarca, head south to join Ruta 40.

Santa María *Colour map 1, B2.*

With its lively village feel, still untainted by tourism, Santa María (population 28,000, altitude 1880 m) makes a very attractive place for a stopover on the road between Cafayate, Tucumán and western Catamarca. There's a lovely plaza full of mature trees, several friendly places to stay and to eat, and a wonderful small museum. **Centro Cultural Yokavil** ⓘ *corner of plaza, daily 0900-1300, 1600-1900, donation requested*, housing a fine collection of sophisticated ceramics tracing the development of the various indigenous cultures which lived in the Calchaquí valleys. Ask the well-informed staff to show you around. In the same building is a handicrafts gallery selling weavings, wooden objects and the delicious local *patero* wine.

In January the town has handicrafts fairs and a live music festival, with the crowning of La Reina de Yokavil (the old indigenous name for Santa María). For the **Fiesta de San Roque** on 16 August, thousands of pilgrims descend on the town, and accommodation fills up fast.

There's a *locutorio* on the plaza, the only ATMs for miles around are at **Banco Nación** on Mitre and Sarmiento, taking Visa and MasterCard, and there's a post office and several service stations.

Quilmes *Colour map 1, B2.*

17 km northeast of Amaichá or 32 km north of Santa María, 5 km along a dirt road off R40 (no shade, tiring walk up hill). The site is open daily 1000-1800.

Quilmes is one of the most important archaeological sites in Argentina, sadly little known by most Argentines, who are more likely to associate the name with the country's most popular lager, see box, opposite. Located on the slopes of the Sierra de Quilmes, at an altitude of 1850 m, it has commanding views over the entire valley. The city was

BACKGROUND
Quilmes: not just a lager

Of all the indigenous peoples of Argentina, perhaps the most tragic were the inhabitants of Quilmes. This ancient city, now an intricate lacework of terraces climbing high up the mountainside, housed around 5000 people from 5000 years ago until AD 117, with a well-developed social structure and its own language, *kakán*, now extinct. The Quilmes people lived on the plains, but built the site as a defensive stronghold to retreat to in times of attack, since the whole Calchaquí valley was the site of frequent warfare between rival clans. Added to this excellent strategic position, they were hard to dominate thanks to their sophisticated weaponry: with *boleadoras* made from stones tied with llama hide thongs, and slings of plaited lamb's wool, they hurled egg-shaped stones with great accuracy over long distances. Their houses consisted of adjacent dwellings buried some way into the earth, and lined with stone walls, which also served as walkways between houses. Posts of sturdy algarrobo wood were used to support pitched roofs (now vanished), and they lived in clans or family groups. The higher social orders and those who hold shamanic or religious positions in the community occupied dwellings highest up the mountainside, closest to the gods.

They cultivated fruit, beans, potato, pumpkins and maize in the valley, using irrigation canals to redirect snow-melt from the mountain tops. Chicha was the popular, mildly alcoholic drink made from ground and fermented algarrobo seeds, and their shamans cured people using local herbs and plants, as they do today.

The Incas were the first to dominate the Quilmes clan in the late 15th century, but the Quilmes adapted and survived. It was the arrival of the Spanish in the 17th century that proved fatal. After many years of failed attacks on the Quilmes, the Spanish finally besieged them and cut off all their supplies. Their hillside position proved to be their downfall and, in 1668, the Quilmes surrendered. The community was broken up, and the largest group was made to walk for weeks to an area now known as Quilmes, near Buenos Aires.

In 1812, the last descendent died, and Argentina's most popular lager brewery was later built in the town. Few Argentines are aware that its namesake was this sophisticated civilization. The next time you have a sip of Quilmes, take a moment to think of this forgotten people.

home to 5000 Diaguitan people, who lived here peacefully for hundreds of years until the Incas and then the Spanish arrived. What remains today is an extensive network of thousands of roofless rooms bordered with low walls, mostly heavily reconstructed. Walk up to the top of the mountain and you'll see a beautiful and elaborate lacework that continues right up from the valley to the higher slopes. It's a spectacular site, especially early or late in the day, when the silvery walls are picked out against the pale green of the enormous cacti.

For a day trip to the site, take the 0600 Aconquija bus (Monday-Saturday) from Cafayate to Santa María, and after an hour get off at the stop on Ruta 40, 5 km from the site. You can also take a tour from Cafayate. Check that the site is open before going.

Tourist information

Tafí del Valle

Tourist office
Peotonal Los Farores, T0381-156 438337, opposite the park.
Basic office which has a good map of the town and the surrounding areas, and listings of accommodation options. For more information, see www.tafidelvalle.com (in Spanish).

Santa María

Tourist office
On the plaza, Belgrano and Sarmiento, T03838-421870. Mon-Fri 0800-1300 and 1600-2000.
Small but helpful office which can provide a map and a list of places to stay.

Where to stay

Tafí del Valle
Many places, including hotels, close out of season.

$$$ Hostería Tafí del Valle
Av San Martín y Gdor Campero, T03867-421027, www.soldelvalle.com.ar.
Right at the top of the town, with splendid views, good restaurant, luxurious small rooms, pool.

$$$ La Rosada
Belgrano 322, T03867-421323.
Well-decorated, spacious rooms, with plenty of hot water, comfortable, excellent breakfast included, helpful staff, lots of expeditions on offer and free use of cycles.

$$$ Lunahuana
Av Critto 540, T03867-421330, www.lunahuana.com.ar.
Stylish comfortable rooms with good views, spacious duplexes for families.

$$$ Mirador del Tafí
R 307, Km 61.2, T03867-421219, www.miradordeltafi.com.ar.
Warm attractive rooms and spacious lounge, superb restaurant, excellent views, look for midweek offers. Highly recommended.

$ pp La Cumbre
Av Perón 120, T03867-421768, www.lacumbretafidelvalle.com.
Basic, cramped rooms, but central, helpful owner is a tour operator with wide range of activities (see What to do, below).

Estancias

$$$ Estancia Las Carreras
R 325, 13 km southwest of Tafí, T03867-421473, www.estancialascarreras.com.
A fine working estancia with lodging and a restaurant serving its own produce (including cheeses). It offers many activities, such as riding, trekking, mountain biking and farm visits.

$$ Los Cuartos
Av Gob Critto y Av Juan Calchaquí s/n, T0381-15-587 4230, www.estancialoscuartos.com.
Old estancia in town, with rooms full of character, and charming hosts. Recommended. Also offer a day at the estancia, with lunch US$9.50. Delicious *té criollo* (US$6) and farm cheese can be bought here.

Amaichá del Valle

$$$ Altos de Amaicha Posada
Ruta 307 at Km 117, just outside town, T03892-421430, www.amaichadelvalle.com/hotel-altos-de-amaicha.html.
Wonderful boutique hotel with 8 well-decorated rooms, an amazing pool and a notable restaurant. Ask for a room with a view of the mountains. Recommended.

$$ pp El Portal de Amaichá
On the main road, next to the petrol station, T0381-15-464 5904, www.elportaldeamaicha.blogspot.com.
Quiet and comfortable accommodation with great views either in simple rooms, dorms or in *cabañas*.

$ pp La Rocca Camping
Ruta 337 La Puntilla, T011-15-6249 1964,
see Facebook.
Fantastic camping facility from the team
behind the popular La Rocca hostels. They
offer rented tents, mountain bikes and also
can organize trekking trips. The facilities are
modern and comfortable.

Santa María

$$ Hotel de Turismo Cielos del Oeste
San Martín 450, corner 1 de Mayo,
T03838-420240.
Occupying a block of its own, 2 blocks east
of the plaza, this large institutional place is
the best option, with several newish and very
comfortable rooms. Internet, a restaurant
and a pool surrounded by a large garden.

$ Inti-Huaico
Belgrano 146, T03838-422060, see Facebook.
A bargain, with good, clean rooms with bath,
friendly owners and lovely gardens.

$ Plaza
San Martín 258, on the plaza, T03838-420309,
see Facebook.
Small, simple and rather dark but comfy rooms
all with bath and TV, breakfast included.

Camping

Municipal campsite
At end of Sarmiento, about 6 blocks east of
the plaza, T03838-421083.
With an *albergue* ($) and restaurant.

Restaurants

Tafí del Valle
Many places along Av Perón.

$$ Parrilla Don Pepito
Av Perón 193.
Very good food, excellent *empanadas*.

Santa María
There are some good and lively places
on the plaza, including:

$ El Colonial del Valle
Serves *empanadas* and other meals, and it is
also a good *confitería*.

What to do

Tafí del Valle
Tour operators
La Cumbre, *see Where to stay, above.*
Energetic and helpful company, offering
day walks to nearby peaks, waterfalls and
ruins, or to Cerro Muñoz, with an *asado* at
the summit (4437 m). They have an open-
sided truck.

Transport

Tafí del Valle
Bus
The small but welcoming Aconquija bus
station is 2 blocks from the centre on
Av Gobernador Critto, which you might
mistake for another hotel, with café, public
phones, toilets and helpful information,
T0381-421025.
    Many daily to **Tucumán**, 2½ hrs,
US$7.75, with **Aconquija**. To **Cafayate**,
4 a day, 2½ hrs, US$11.

Amaichá del Valle
Bus
To **Tucumán**, 6 daily, 5 hrs, US$13.75, sit on
the right for best views. To **Santa María**,
15 mins, US$1, with **Gutiérrez**.

Santa María
Bus
Buses arrive and depart at Av 9 de Julio
and Maestro Argentino, 8 blocks south of
the plaza.
    To **Tucumán**, 4½-5 hrs, US$15, with
Aconquija. To **Cafayate**, daily, 2 hrs, US$6,
with **Aconquija**. To **Salta**, daily, 5-6 hrs,
US$16.50, with **El Indio**. To **Belén**, 4 hrs,
US$11, check with tourist office for current
times, with **Cayetano** and **Parra**. To **Amaichá
del Valle**, 15 mins, US$1-3, with **Gutiérrez**.
To **Catamarca**, US$15.50, with **Aconquija**.

Los Valles
Calchaquíes

★ Dramatic, constantly changing and stunningly beautiful, the Valles Calchaquíes are perhaps the most captivating part of Salta province. The River Calchaquí springs 5000 m up on the slopes of the Nevado de Acay, just south of San Antonio de los Cobres, and flows – via a series of timeless oasis villages – through a spectacularly long and broad valley to Cafayate and beyond.

Driving north on Ruta 40, the first destination in the valley is the established wine-growing centre of Cafayate, with extraordinary rock formations just to the north at Quebrada de las Flechas. Beyond, there are unspoilt villages dotted along the valley: San Carlos, Angastaco, Molinos with its lovely church, and Seclantás, with its poncho weavers, all reached by the rough *ripio* Ruta 40. The pretty town of Cachi is set against the massive Nevado de Cachi mountain range, with its hidden valley, Cachi Adentro, irrigated since pre-Inca times to produce the bright red peppers you'll see drying in the sun in April. From Cachi, a breathtaking drive up the Cuesta del Obispo and through the giant cactus park, Parque Nacional los Cardones, will take you east to Salta. Ruta 40, meanwhile, continues north to La Poma, set in wide open red rocky land, and on to San Antonio de los Cobres.

Cafayate (population 14,850, altitude 1660 m) is beautifully situated in a broad stretch of valley at the confluence of the Santa María and Calchaquí rivers. There are mountains on all sides, and the valley is filled with vineyards, which produce wine to rival Mendoza in quality, if not in quantity. Cafayate has long been a popular destination for visits to the bodegas, which open their doors to tourists with free tours and wine tastings. There are superb red grapes grown at high altitude here, and it's worth asking specifically to try the white Torrontés grape, which is grown in few places other than Argentina and flourishes in the annual 350 days of sunshine, and the cool nights.

There's lots of accommodation and one exquisite place to stay, **Patios de Cafayate** (see Where to stay, page 260), making this a good base for exploring the dramatic scenery all around or just relaxing for a couple of days. Cafayate is easy to get around on foot, with restaurants and shops located around the main plaza, but you'll need transport to reach many of the bodegas further out. Take a taxi or hire a bike, available from shops on the plaza.

Sights *Colour map 1, B2.*
Conventional sights aren't Cafayate's strong point; it's much more interesting to explore the landscape and the bodegas. The **Museo de la Vid y El Vino** ⓘ *Güemes Sur y F Perdiguero, www.museodelavidyelvino. gov.ar, Tue-Sun 1000-1930, US$2*, in a new building, contains old winemaking equipment and a display on the history of wine. The **Museo Arqueológico Rodolfo I Bravo** ⓘ *Calchaquí y Colón 191, T03868-421054, Mon-Sat 0830-1230 and 1300-1900, free*, is tiny but has some beautiful funerary urns, black ceramics from the fifth century, and Inca pieces too – well worth seeing if you haven't come across them elsewhere.

★ **Bodegas**
Cafayate's wines are sophisticated and generally of very high quality, with intense high-altitude reds (Malbec and Cabernet Sauvignon predominate) and the famous white Torrontés. This superbly fruity dry wine with delicious floral aromas is grown only in the Valles Calchaquíes and makes an excellent aperitif. There are several bodegas

Essential Los Valles Calchaquíes

Access

It's possible to reach both Cachi and Cafayate using public transport. To reach Cafayate quickly, there are several buses daily along the fast, paved Ruta Nacional 68 from Salta. There are also buses to Cafayate from Santa María (Catamarca) and Tucumán to the south. If you're short of time, there are one or two day tours from Salta to the Cafayate and Calchaquíes valleys, but they are frustratingly brief, with many hours spent cooped up in a minibus. Only a few buses each day go from Salta to Cachi and Molinos along the nail-biting Cuesta del Obispo (see page 268), which is quite an experience in itself. And from Molinos there's only one bus a week south to Angastaco, leaving you stranded for days.

The best way to see this region is to hire a car – note there is a rough stretch between Cachi and Cafayate and a 4WD is essential in summer, when rains swell the rivers.

BACKGROUND
Los Valles Calchaquíes

The whole vast Calchaquí Valley was densely populated in pre-Hispanic times by sophisticated people, often referred to as 'Diaguitan', who built stone dwellings in large organized 'cities', the impressive remains of which you can see still at Las Pailas, near Cachi, and at Quilmes, further south. Much archaeological work has yet to be done to establish more detail about their daily lives and there are currently digs at Las Pailas and La Borgata, near Cachi Adentro. The Diaguita were just one of several tribes in the valley. They left a rich legacy of ceramics, which you can see today in all the small museums throughout the region. From beautifully painted urns made to contain the bodies of their dead, to simple cooking pots and glazed black polished vessels, these artefacts speak of a population with a high degree of social organization.

After the defeat of the indigenous population in the Calchaquí Wars, the Spanish established missions and haciendas in the valley, which were run along feudal principles – some until as recently as the 1980s. During the colonial period the valley prospered, providing pasturage for mules and herds of cattle en route to the mountain passes into Chile and Alto Perú (Bolivia). After independence, lower parts of the valley became the primary wheat-growing and wine-producing area for Salta city, but the local economy declined in the late 19th century when the railway brought cheap wheat from the Pampas and wine from Mendoza. Salta's endemic racism and the feudal legacy have meant that the indigenous people in the valley are only recently coming to value their own cultural inheritance.

Rather than taking a commercial group tour from Salta, seek out local guides who will tell you about their fascinating history.

that can be visited and all are shown on the tourist office's map; the best are described below. Tours usually take around 45 minutes, most are free, and are followed by a free tasting. Ask if the guides speak English.

The most highly recommended bodega, with an informative tour, is **El Esteco** ① *at the junction of R68 and R40, T011-5198 8000, www.elesteco.com.ar, Mon-Fri, 8 tours daily 1000-1830, Sat-Sun 1000, 1100, 1200.* Visitors can learn more about the process of winemaking and tasting on one of the courses on offer. Next door is Cafayate's best accommodation: the sumptuous **Patios de Cafayate** (see Where to stay, page 260), formerly part of the bodega and now with luxury spa. It's also a great place for lunch.

Another excellent bodega is **Etchart** ① *2 km south on R40, Km 1047, T03868-421310, www.bodegasetchart.com, tours daily on demand, open Jan, Feb, Jul, closed for lunch, book in advance,* which produces high-quality wines, some of which are exported to Europe.

The diminutive **San Pedro de Yacochuya** ① *7 km behind Cafayate, T011-4313 6470, www.sanpedrodeyacochuya.com.ar, phone to arrange a tour, Mon-Fri 1000-1700, Sat-Sun 1000-1300,* is a boutique bodega, beautifully situated high up into the hills, making exquisite wines. To get there, take Ruta 40 in the direction of Cachí; after 2 km turn left on Ruta 2, then follow this for 6 km until you reach the bodega.

Once you've visited the best three, you could go to **Finca de las Nubes** ① *3 km above Cafayate, on the Camino al Divisadero, beyond Hotel Viñas de Cafayate, T03868-422129, www.bodegamounier.com.ar, guided visits are available Mon-Sat 1000-1700,*

Cafayate

To Cachi & Molinos (RN40)

N

80 metres
80 yards

To Cerro San Isidro & Bodega
San Pedro de Yacochuya

Río Chuscha

Bodega
Vasija Secreta

Bodega
El Esteco

To Salta (RN68)

Lamadrid

Buenos Aires

Bartolomé Mitre

Sevilla

Pedraza

Brachieri

ACA

Alvarado

Aconquija

Gral Güemes Norte

Salta

Córdoba

To 9

Rivadavia

Pharmacy

D de Almagro

ATM

San Martín

Q de Niño

Municipalidad

Cathedral

Toscano

Mercado
Municipal de
Artesanía

El Indio

To Cerro
Santa Teresita

Banco de
la Nación
Museo
Arqueológico
Rodolfo I Bravo

Nuestra Señora del Rosario

Belgrano

Bodega
Nanni

Calchaquí

Finca las Nubes &

Museo
de la Vid
y el Vino

Gral Güemes Sur

Colón

Hurtado

S Chavarría

Chacabuco

25 de Mayo

Bodega
Domingo
Hermanos

To 8, Bodega
Etchart, Quilmes
& Tucumán

Where to stay
Camping Luz y Fuerza **8**
El Hospedaje **2**
Hostal del Valle **12**
Hostel Ruta 40 **4**
Killa **1**
Patios de Cafayate **3**
Portal del Santo **11**
Rusty K Hostal **9**
Villa Vicuña **5**
Viñas de Cafayate **6**

Restaurants
Baco **8**
El Rancho **1**
El Terruño **2**
Helados Miranda **5**
La Carreta de
  Don Olegario **6**
La Casa de las
  Empanadas **3**

Sat 1000-1300, dramatically set against the mountains. This is a small family bodega, which produces fine wines and offers simple meals so you can sit and enjoy a bottle of wine on the terrace.

Then there are two interesting mass-production bodegas that can also be visited: **Domingo Hermanos** ① *Nuestra Sra Del Rosario s/n, T03868-421225, www.domingohermanos.com*, and **Vasija Secreta** ① *outskirts of Cafayete, next to ACA hostería, T03868-421850, www.vasijasecreta.com.*

If you only have an hour spare and don't want to wander far from the centre of town, head to **Nanni** ① *Chavarría 151, T03868-421527, www.bodegananni.com, US2.50,* which is also recommended. It's only one block from the plaza, but once you're inside, you feel you're in the outskirts of town with only vineyards and the mountains in sight. The bodega is very traditional and has been family-owned for over 100 years. They grow Malbec, Torrontés, Tannat and Cabernet Sauvignon grapes, and produce organic wines.

Around Cafayate
In addition to the Quebrada de las Conchas to the east (see below) and the Quebrada de las Flechas to the north (see below), there are lots of places to walk, cycle or drive to from the Cafayate itself. **Cerro San Isidro**, 5 km west, has cave paintings and views across the Aconquija mountains in the south and to the Nevado de Cachi in the north. Behind it, the waterfalls of **Río Colorado** are a pretty place for bathing in summer. For a stroll and a good view, take Vía Toscano west out of the centre up to **Cerro Santa Teresita**, 2 km each way.

Quebrada de las Conchas
Heading north from Cafayate towards Salta, the Ruta Nacional 68 enters the Quebrada de las Conchas (Gorge of Shells). Though no one seems to know why it has this name, it's a truly magnificent stretch of road, with huge ochre, burgundy and terracotta rocks carved into extraordinary

forms by wind and rain. These formations have been helpfully named after the things they most resemble: El Anfiteatro (the amphitheatre), Km 48; the Garganta del Diablo (devil's throat), Km 49; El Sapo (the toad), Km 35; and El Fraile (looks

Tip...
The best light for photography of the rock formations is in the early morning or late afternoon.

vaguely like a praying friar), Km 29. Take a few minutes to walk inside the Garganta del Diablo and to stop to photograph Los Castillos (the castles), Km 20.

The valley floor beside the Río de las Conchas is richly green with tipa and algarrobo trees, contrasting beautifully with the chocolate-coloured mountains and raspberry ripple strata. There's lots of birdlife to be spotted, including ñandúes (rheas). If you haven't got a car but want to experience the Quebrada, take a bus from Cafayate towards Salta and get off at Los Loros, Km 32, or at the Garganta del Diablo; walk back, and catch a return bus from Salta. Or hire a bike, take it on an El Indio bus and cycle back.

Listings Cafayate and around map page 259.

Tourist information

Tourist centre
20 de febrero, T03868-422442/422223, www.cafayate.todowebsalta.com.ar. Daily 0800-1400-1400 and 1700-2100.
Tiny but informative, located in a hut on the northeast corner of the plaza. They have a basic map with the bodegas marked, and an accommodation list. Tour operators can be found along C General Güemes (this street changes names from Norte to Sur across the plaza, and, confusingly, identical numbers can be found on both sides).

Where to stay

Accommodation is hard to find during holiday periods (Jan, Easter, late Jul), but there are many places to stay. Off season, prices are much lower. All those listed are recommended. See also www.munayhotel.com.ar.

$$$$ Patios de Cafayate
Routes 68 and 40, T0387-422 229, www.patiosdecafayate.com.
A stunning hotel, in the converted building of the old winery (now **El Esteco**, see page 258 for visits to the bodega), with beautifully designed rooms, sumptuous lounges,

and set in gorgeous gardens with a lovely pool. There are interesting wine-oriented treatments in the spa and the restaurant serves fine food, has a lovely terrace and excellent wines. Highly recommended.

$$$$-$$$ Viñas de Cafayate
R21, Camino al Divisadero, T03868-422272/282, www.cafayatewineresort.com.
On a hillside above Cafayate, colonial style, calm, welcoming with pretty, spacious bedrooms, some with views. Excellent restaurant (see Restaurants, below) and a full buffet breakfast.

$$$ Killa
Colón 47, T03868-422254, www.killacafayate.com.ar.
A delightfully restored colonial house with pleasing views. Delightful owner, who has a fascinating garden, tranquil, comfortable, good breakfasts.

$$$ Portal del Santo
Silvero Chavarria 250, T03868-422400, www.portaldelsanto.todowebsalta.com.ar.
Family-run hotel with lovely large rooms overlooking a beautiful pool and garden.

$$$ Villa Vicuña
Belgrano 76, T03868-422145, www.villavicuna.com.ar.

Half a block from the main plaza, 2 colourful patios, bright rooms, pleasant and calm. Afternoon tea with home-made pastries served on demand.

$$ Hostal del Valle
San Martín 243, T03868-421039.
Well-kept big rooms around leafy patio, charming owner. The living room at the top has superb views over the valley (as do upper floor rooms).

$ pp El Hospedaje
Quintana de Niño y Salta, T03868-421680, www.elhospedaje.todowebsalta.com.ar.
Simple but pleasant rooms in colonial-style house, wonderful pool, good value, heater in room.

$ Hostel Ruta 40
Güermes Sur 178, T03868-421689, www.hostel-ruta40.com.
Very sociable place to stay, dorms US$17, private room $$. Discount for HI members.

$ Rusty K Hostal
Rivadavia 281, T03868-422031, www.rustykhostal.todowebsalta.com.ar.
Neat, basic rooms and a great garden with barbecue. 2 blocks from the main plaza. Lots of activities to enjoy by bike.

Camping

Camping Luz y Fuerza
On R40, south of the town, T03868-421568.
More appealing than the municipal site and quieter, with pool, games, grills, showers and a buffet.

Restaurants

Cafayate has lots of lovely choices around the plaza, most of them huge and prepared for coach parties. In summer many provide live music. The following are recommended:

$$$ Viñas de Cafayate
In hotel of the same name, see Where to stay, above.

Elegant food, including local delicacies, served in simple surroundings. Lovely views from this hotel. Book ahead; open to non-residents with a reservation.

$$ Baco
Güemes Norte y Rivadavia, T0387-15 573 5831, see Facebook.
Parrilla, *pasta casera*, pizzas, regional dishes, *empanadas* and *picadas*. Seating inside and on attractive street corner, lively atmosphere. Good selection of local wines and beers.

$$ El Rancho
Toscano 4, T03868-421256.
A traditional restaurant on the plaza serving *parrilla* and good regional dishes (try the *tamales*).

$$ El Terruño
Güemes Sur 28, T03868-422460, www.terruno.todowebsalta.com.ar.
Meat and fish dishes, including local specialities, good service.

$$ La Carreta de Don Olegario
Güemes Sur 20 and Quintana de Niño, T03868-421004, www.lacarretaolegario.com.
Huge, but does good set menus for the usual meat dishes and pastas. Good wine menu.

$$-$ La Casa de Las Empanadas
Mitre 24, T03868-15-454111, www.casadelaempanada.com.ar.
Cosy place with exposed brick and wooden tables featuring local specialities, such as *humitas* and the titular *empanadas*.

Ice cream parlours

Helados Miranda
Güemes Norte 170.
Cafayate's unmissable treat is this fabulous home-made ice cream. The creative owner makes wine-flavoured ice cream as well as many other delicious flavours.

Shopping

Lots of fairly trashy souvenir shops have opened on the plaza, but there are some fine handicrafts shops to be found if you dig around. There's the **Calchaquí tapestry exhibition** of Miguel Nanni on the main plaza (Güemes 65), silver work at **Jorge Barraco** (Colón 157, T03868-421244). Local pottery, woollen goods, and more are sold in the **Mercado de Artesanos Cafayetanos** on the plaza (small, pricey).

What to do

Cycling
There are many places to hire a bike around the main plaza; compare rates before renting.

Tour operators
Turismo Cordillerano, *Güemes Sur 178, T03868-421689, www.turismocordillerano.com.* Tours, trekking, horses, bike hire.

Transport

From Salta along the fast Ruta Nacional 68 is an easy drive in a hire car, though the road is winding for the last 30 km as you enter the amazing rock formations of the Quebrada de las Conchas (see page 259). The alternative and even more scenic route from Salta is the Ruta 40 via Cachi and the Valles Calchaquíes (see below) but the road is rough *ripio* and there are very few buses between Molinos and Angastaco. There are many trips on offer from Salta to Cafayate (US$40-45, including lunch and visit to a bodega), with brief stops in the Quebrada de las Conchas. But these make for a long day, and you'll miss the chance to walk around the region.

Bus
Cafayate has 2 separate bus terminals: **El Indio** bus terminal on Belgrano, half a block from the plaza, T03868-421002; and the **Aconquija** terminal at Güemes Norte and Alvarado, T03868-421052 (open only when buses are due).

El Indio (T03868-421002) to **Santa María** (for Quilmes) daily, US$5; also to **Salta** (via the Quebrada de las Conchas), multiple daily, 3 hrs, US$14, travel in daylight to see the rock formations; to **Angastaco**, Fri 1100, US$5, 1½ hrs (note this bus does not continue to Molinos and Cachi). **Aconquija** to **Tucumán**, daily, 5½ hrs, US$21; to **Tafí del Valle**, daily, US$17, 3 hrs (more services via **Santa María**, 5½ hrs); and to **Salta,** US$21.

Cafayate to Cachi *Colour map 1, B2.*

villages lost in time

San Carlos and the Quebrada de las Flechas
San Carlos (1710 m, Km 24) is a pleasant place and was the most important village in the valley until the growth of Cafayate. The main buildings are on the pretty plaza, including the church, the largest in the valley, which was built between 1801 and 1860. Nearby, there's a small **archaeological museum** ⓘ *daily 1000-1400*, which contains superb archaeological finds from the region, including fine funerary urns. Also on the plaza are artisans' shops and workshops, and a craft market.

The highlight of your trip on this fabulous route will probably be the next stretch of road through the **Quebrada de las Flechas** (the gorge of arrows) from San Carlos. You'll find yourself surrounded by massive rocks, eroded into complex forms and massive sharp peaks, towering above you into the blue sky; all very photogenic.

Angastaco
Angastaco (population 881, altitude 1900 m) is a modern village, 2 km off Ruta 40, at Km 77, less picturesque than Cachi, but it does have an **archaeological museum** in the Centro Cívico. The church is modern, so it's worth the trek to the much older one, the **Iglesia del Carmen de Angastaco** (1800) about 8 km further north on the **Finca El Carmen**. Stop in

Angastaco to try the *vino patero*, for which the town is famous. This sweet red or white wine is traditionally made by treading the grapes in the traditional manner – hence the name (*pata* is the informal word for leg).

Molinos

From Angastaco, Ruta 40 weaves its way through some of the most exquisite scenery in the region, but the road is rough *ripio* and only manageable in a hire car as long as it hasn't rained; consider hiring a 4WD for safety. The landscape is beautiful: tiny settlements with green fields and orchards, against the constant backdrop of the rugged Andes. Some 52 km before Cachi, you come to the village of Molinos (2220 m), hidden away 1 km off Ruta 40 at Km 118. Set in a bowl of craggy mountains with a wide plaza and neat adobe houses, it's a peaceful place and an idyllic retreat for relaxing and doing very little. Founded in 1659, it has a fine church dating from 1692, with a simple gold *retablo*, containing the mummified body of the last Royalist governor of Salta, Don Nicolás Severo Isasmendi. The house he built, opposite the church, is now the **Hostal Provincial de Molinos**.

There are a couple of satisfying two-hour walks: either across the river bed (usually dry) and then up the hill opposite; or up to the Cross above the town. Both offer fine views of Molinos and the surrounding country.

Accommodation is limited in Molinos, but the nuns opposite the church have pristine little rooms to rent, and there are several families that rent rooms in the village. There are a few simple places to eat near where the bus to Cachi stops; ask around, or at the basic tourist office; see Tourist information, page 265.

Just 20 km from Molinos, along a road running west into the mountains, is the extraordinary and fabulous winery, **Colomé** ① *4 hrs from Salta, 2½ hrs from Cafayate via a short cut, 20 km west of Molinos, T0387-421 9132, www.bodegacolome.com*. Owned by charming art collector Donald Hess and his wife, Ursula, this remote retreat is more than just a swish place to stay (see page 265). As well as having a stunningly lovely setting, the bodega produces the highest-altitude wines in the world, at 2300 m. In an arid valley of red and grey rock, surrounded by mountains, there are hundreds of hectares of rare pre-Phylloxera vines, producing Malbec-heavy wines of exquisite intensity – and all grown on organic and biodynamic principles. A Spanish-style house with nine rooms provides ultra-luxurious accommodation and delicious meals, and there is great walking and riding in the extensive finca. It's impressive in terms of social responsibility too, since the Hesses have built a church, clinic and community centre for the 400 families living on their land, and take great care of their wellbeing.

Seclantás

The road continues north to Cachi on the west side of the river, via the *hostería* **Casa de Campo La Paya** (see Where to stay, page 266), 9 km from Cachi, where there are interesting archaeological ruins of an important pre-Inca town and administrative centre.

For a pretty detour to the hamlet of Seclantás (population 900), cross the river and follow signs. This is a quaint tranquil village with simple colonial-style houses and an interesting church dating from 1835. Seclantás' weavers are among the finest in the country, and they sell ponchos directly from their workshops on the side of the road; look for the looms strung up between the pillars on a porch. The quality is higher and prices are much lower than in the Cachi tourist office shop, and you have the satisfaction of knowing that the profits go directly to the weavers. Wander down the main street and ask around for *telares* (weavers), as there are few signs. There's currently nowhere great to stay in Seclantás, but a couple of places sell food and snacks and there is a camping ground.

Cachi

Cachi (population 7000, altitude 1228 m) is a beautiful, tranquil town, 180 km from Salta in a wide green valley at the foot of the majestic Nevado del Cachi, whose nine peaks are snow-covered for much of the year and whose highest summit is **San Martín** (6380 m). Founded in 1694, it had been a Diaguita settlement long before the Incas arrived in 1450, and the extensive irrigation channels they built to channel the Nevado's snow-melt are still used today to make the valley green and to grow huge fields of peppers. These are an amazing sight when harvested in April and laid out to dry in huge scarlet squares, which stand out against the arid mountains beyond.

Cachi has a pleasingly simple church, the **Iglesia de San José**, whose roof and lecterns are made of cactus wood. Next door, there's a fascinating survey of pre-colonial Calchaquí culture in the **Museo Arqueológico** ① *T03868-491080, Tue-Sun 0900-1800, US$1.25*, with impressive painted funerary urns and an intriguing cat/man petroglyph. There are panoramic views from Cachi's spectacularly sited hilltop cemetery, just 20 minutes' walk from the plaza. On the plaza you'll find an ATM, restaurants and cafés.

The town feels more like a small village and has a lively community life with fiestas throughout the year, where you can hear traditional *folclore* music as well as the *bagualas* and *coplas* from the indigenous traditions; see Festivals, page 267.

Around Cachi

With its sunny climate, Cachi is the perfect place for a few days' rest, but there are superb walks into the mountains all around. A pleasant walk will take you to **La Aguada**, 6 km southwest along the lush valley fringed with *álamo* trees and dotted with adobe farmhouses. Leave town by Calle Benjamín Zorrilla at the southwest of the plaza, and walk along the *ripio* track.

Don't miss the ancient ruins at **Las Pailas**, 16 km northwest of Cachi (via Cachi Adentro), with intriguingly complex circular dwellings, long irrigation channels and worked stone cultivation terraces. The views are breathtaking, with huge cacti set against the snow-topped Nevado de Cachi behind. To get there you can take a bus to Las Arcas from where it's a two-hour walk. The bus leaves Cachi early in the morning (check the current timetable with the tourist office) and returns in the afternoon. However, it's better to go with a guide, since Cachi has the special advantage of being one of the few original towns in the region with trained local guides.

Cerro de la Virgen is another rewarding day hike near Cachi, up through a pretty hanging valley and slopes strewn with giant boulders to a peak with wonderful views over the Calchaquí Valley beyond. The hamlet **Cachi Adentro**, on the opposite side of the valley from La Aguada, has more fine views, a school, church and dairy farm, **El Tambo**.

Serious climbers should plan to spend a week or so climbing the spectacular peaks of the Nevado de Cachi. To climb any of the peaks, you must take a mountain guide who is trained and familiar with the route; do not attempt these peaks alone. For further information, see What to do, page 267.

Tourist information

Angastaco

Tourist office
In the Municipalidad on the plaza.
Mon-Fri 0900-1400.

Molinos

Tourist office
In the Municipalidad, on the plaza at Belgrano s/n. Daily 0800-2200, low season daily 0900-1300 and 1600-2100.
No one speaks English here but they are kind and want to help.

Cachi

Tourist office
On the plaza, opposite side to the church, Av Gral Güemes s/n, T03868-491902, www. cachi.todowebsalta.com.ar. Mon-Fri 0900-2100, Sat-Sun 0900-1300 and 1700-2100.
Provides basic leaflets and maps. No one speaks English, but they are well meaning and will give advice if you're patient.

Casa de Turismo de Cachi
By the entrance to the town on the left.
A private tourist office. Local guides can be found here, and they sell crafts.

Where to stay

San Carlos and the Quebrada de las Flechas

\$\$ La Casa de Los Vientos
Las Alfareras s/n, San Carlos, T03868-495075, www.casadelosvientos.com.ar.
Comfortable accommodation in a colonial-style house built almost entirely of adobe, recreating a traditional Calchaquí residence. Just 7 rooms, and it's rustic but very welcoming with the friendly Swiss owner on hand to make your stay enjoyable. Excellent value, with breakfast included.

Camping

Municipal campsite
Rivadavia and San Martín, T03868-491123.
Well tended with plenty of shade.

Angastaco

\$\$-\$ Hostería de Angastaco
Av Libertador s/n, T03868-491123.
Breakfast included, and prices negotiable in low season. Rooms are basic but comfortable, and this place is especially recommended for its warm welcome from reception staff who are very helpful and can provide information on the region. Pool, meals on request.

Molinos

\$\$\$\$ Bodega Colomé
20 km west of Molinos, T0387-421 9132, www.bodegacolome.com.
Leave town via the vicuña farm and follow signs, or phone for directions from Cafayate. Recommended as one of the best places to stay in Argentina, this is a winery in a beautiful setting with delightful rooms. There's horse riding, tastings of excellent wines, all food is organic, and power is hydroelectric. See also Restaurants, below.

\$\$\$\$-\$\$\$ Hacienda de Molinos
A Cornejo (by the river), T03868-494094, www.haciendademolinos.com.ar.
Open all year round.
Stunning 18th-century hacienda, with rooms around a courtyard. Great attention to detail, the rooms are an oasis of calm. There's a pool with a view of the Cachi mountains.

\$ pp Hostal San Agustín
Sarmiento y A Cornejo at the Colegio Infantil, T03868-494015.
Small but spotless rooms, some with private bath, run by nuns (who don't like to advertise the place, ask around discretely for 'las monjas' and someone will come and give you a key).

Camping

Municipal campsite
In the sports complex, Alvarado and Mitre, T03868-494062.
Hot showers, electricity, also has cabins
for rent.

Seclantás

$$ Hostería El Capricho
Abrahan Cornejo s/n, T0387-421 6322,
www.elcaprichosalta.com.ar.
With 4 attractively decorated double rooms
set around a well-kept courtyard, this
hostería is the best choice in town. Rooms
are $ with shared bath. Includes breakfast.

$ Hostería La Rueda
Abrahan Cornejo and Pedro Ferreyra,
T03868-498041, see Facebook.
The small, basic rooms in this clean *hostería*
are the cheapest option. Welcoming staff
make up for the lack of luxuries.

Cachi and around

$$$$-$$$ Finca Santana
Take the road to Cachi Adentro, and
ask for the camino to Finca San Miguel,
on the right at the top, T54-9 3868 638762,
www.fincasantana.com.
2 rooms in boutique B&B in the heart of
the valley, spectacular views, and complete
sense of privacy and silence. Welcoming,
spacious living room, terrace and garden,
gourmet breakfast, trekking can be arranged.
Wonderful.

$$$ ACA Hostería Cachi
At the top of Juan Manuel Castilla, T0387-
491904, www.hosteriacachi.com.ar.
Smart modern rooms (with wheelchair
access), great views, pool, good restaurant,
non-residents can use the pool if they have
lunch here.

$$$ Casa de Campo La Paya
12 km south of Cachi at La Paya, clearly
signposted from the road, T0387-491139,
see Faecbook.

A restored 18th-century house, with a
pool, elegant rooms, excellent dinners and
hospitable atmosphere. Recommended.

$$$ Llaqta Mawk'a
Ruiz de Los Llanos s/n, up from plaza,
T0387-491016.
Traditional frontage hides modern block,
garden/terrace, view of the Nevado
de Cachi, pool. Comfy rooms, ample
breakfast, good value, popular with
tourists. Street parking.

$$ Hospedaje Don Arturo
Bustamante s/n, T0387-491087,
hospedajedonarturo.blogspot.com.
Homely, small rooms, quiet street,
charming owners.

$ Hospedaje El Nevado de Cachi
Ruiz de los Llanos y F Suárez, T0387-491912.
Impeccable small rooms around a central
courtyard, with hot water and a *comedor*.

$ Viracocha Art Hostel
Ruiz de los Llanos s/n, T03868 491713,
www.hostelcachi.com.ar.
Good central option offering bike hire,
cable TV, private and shared rooms.

Camping
Municipal campsite at Av Automóvil
Club Argentina s/n, T0387-491902.
With pool and sports complex, also
cabañas and an *albergue*.

Restaurants

Molinos

$$$-$$ Bodega Colomé
See Where to stay, above.
Good local specialities. After eating world-
class delicacies on the terrace, stay around
and try out the inviting spa. Pure luxury.

Cachi

$$$-$$ La Merced del Alto
Fuerte Alto, T03868-490030,
www.lamerceddelalto.com.

Set in luscious surroundings, this is a treat to your taste buds and your eyes. Make sure you try a local wine.

$$-$ Ashpamanta
Bustamante – Cachi 4417, T03868-15-578 2244.
Just off the main plaza, this little restaurant serves universal favourites, such as pizza and pasta, plus some regional gems such as quinoa risotto.

$ Oliver Café
Ruiz de Los Llanos 160, on the plaza.
Tiny café for ice creams, coffee, breakfasts, fruit juices, sandwiches and pizza.

Festivals

Angastaco
2nd week Dec Fiesta Patronal Virgen del Valle features processions, music, dancing, gauchos and rodeos.

Molinos
Feb La Virgen de la Candelaria, with processions, music and handicrafts.

Cachi
3rd week Jan Fiesta de la Tradición Calchaquí. This fiesta is worth seeing.
Feb Carnaval, with colourful processions.
Aug Pachamama. A celebration giving thanks to Mother Earth, or Pachamama.

Shopping

Cachi
Cachi has a great tradition in weaving, and you can buy beautiful handmade ponchos, shawls, rugs and wall hangings at the government-run **handicrafts shop** in the same room as the tourist office on the plaza. But these are more expensive than if bought directly from weavers, and they receive hardly any of the profit. Instead, go up the street to find the workshop of **Oscar Cardozo** (Juan Calchaquí, opposite the monument, T03868-491037). Oscar teaches weaving and can direct you to other weavers in his association.

What to do

Cachi
Tour operators and guides
Fernando Gamarra, *corner of Benjamín Zorrilla and Güemes, T0387-431 7305, fg_serviciosturisticos@yahoo.com.ar.* More conventional trips around Cachi with genial Fernando, who is good company: to Las Pailas, La Poma and Seclantás, including the beautiful Laguna de Brealito. Knowledgeable, and reasonably priced, especially if divided amongst a group.
Santiago Casimiro, *T03868-15-638545.*
Particularly recommended for all mountain hikes; he's a nurse trained in mountain rescue and has lived in the valley all his life. He'll take you to La Poma, Cerro de la Virgen and up the Nevado peaks, all very reasonable. Highly recommended.
Tourism Urkupiña, *Benjamin Zorrilla s/n, T03868-491317, uk_cachi@hotmail.com.* Local agency that can book tours and bus tickets.

Transport

San Carlos and the Quebrada de las Flechas
Bus
Flecha Bus has daily services to **Cafayate**, 30 mins, US$1.50.

Angastaco
Bus
To **Salta**, Mon-Fri, US$16. To **Cafayate** via San Carlos at 1100, US$5, with **Flecha Bus**.

Remise taxi
Alto Valle Remis, 12 de Octubre 233, Cachi, T03871-5502 0981.

Molinos
Bus
To **Salta** (via Cachi), **Ale** (as above), Mon, Tue, Thu, Sat 0700, Sun 1355, 2 hrs to **Cachi**, 7 hrs to **Salta,** US$12.

Cachi

Bus

To **Salta**, **Ale**, T0387-423 1811, www.alehnos. com.ar, daily, 4 hrs, US$12. Also to **Molinos**, Mon, Wed, Fri, Sun at 1130, 2 hrs, US$4.75.

Remise taxis

Los Calchaquies, T03868-491071; **San José**, T03868-491907.

Beyond Cachi

between Cachi and Salta

La Poma to San Antonio de los Cobres

From Cachi it is 61 km north to **Poma** (3015 m), whose modern adobe houses and population of 1700 sit beneath the massive Cumbre del Libertador General San Martín (6380 m). It's the most northerly village in the Calchaquí valley but not the original one, which was destroyed by an earthquake in 1930; its ruins lie 2 km north at La Poma Vieja.

North of La Poma, Ruta 40 heads towards **San Antonio de los Cobres** (see page 285) via the **Paso Abra del Acay** (4900 m, Km 282), the highest pass in South America negotiable by car. Road conditions vary depending on the weather and whether the roads have been recently cleared, so a 4WD vehicle is strongly advised. The critical part of the route is south of the pass at **Mal Paso** (Km 257), where summer rains can wash the road away. Buses do not travel on this road and anyone tempted to try it on a bicycle should think twice: there is no shade; night temperatures are several degrees below freezing, and you need to be well adapted to the altitude. Take plenty of water and an arctic sleeping bag.

Cachi to Salta

Cachi is 170 km west of Salta, along one of the most unforgettable routes in Argentina. About 11 km beyond Cachi is the small village of **Payogasta**, where you can find the Hotel Sala de Payogasta ① T03868-496754, www.saladepayogasta.com, and the **Parque Nacional Los Cardones administrative office** ① T03868-15 414365, loscardones@apn. gov.ar. The road runs east through the national park at altitudes between 2700 m and 5000 m, along a dead straight stretch known as **La Recta del Tin-Tin**, surrounded by an astonishing landscape of huge candelabra cacti. Walking amongst these giant sentinels, their arms thrust up to the cloudless sky, with a backdrop of stratified bright pink rock, is an extraordinary experience. There are occasionally *guardaparques* at Recta del Tin-Tin, but no services. Camping is officially not allowed.

Beyond the arid **Piedra del Molino Pass** (3347 m), where you'll want to stop for photos, the road (mostly *ripio*) snakes along the hairpins of the breathtaking **Cuesta del Obispo**. Take great care if you drive the Cuesta del Obispo in fog, which often hangs in the valley in the early mornings, or in rain. It is not advisable at all at night. Throughout the journey, you'll pass tiny hamlets of adobe houses shrouded in low cloud. As the cloud clears, you'll glimpse dramatic views of the vast bronze, green-velvety mountains. There are two places to stop for tea roughly halfway to Salta: **Café Margarita** serves coffee and layered *tortillas* for bus passengers, and at **El Maray** (70 km from Salta), there's a nice *confitería* in a yellow building; delicious jams and walnuts are sold opposite. You might also like to take the turn-off down to the **Valle Encantado**, an eerie, fascinating place for a picnic amongst bizarre wind-sculpted terracotta rocks.

The road enters the fertile **Quebrada de Escoipe** and heads towards the quaint little town of **Chicoana**, where you could stay the night. After Chicoana, turn left at El Carril onto Ruta Nacional 68 and head north to Salta city.

Chicoana

There's not much to do in Chicoana, but it's an interesting example of a colonial-style town, sitting amidst some of the finest tobacco-producing land in the world, and with lots of buildings dating from the 1900s. Religious festivals are celebrated with much enthusiasm; see Festivals, below.

Listings Beyond Cachi

Where to stay

La Poma to San Antonio de los Cobres

$$ Hostería La Poma
*Sarmiento and Belgrano 40, La Poma,
T03868-491003.*
Welcoming place, breakfast included,
also serves meals.

Chicoana

$$$$-$$$ Finca Los Los
T0387-683 3121. Mar-Dec.
Most welcoming and highly recommended,
beautifully situated on a hilltop with fabulous
views from the colonial-style galleried
veranda. Spacious rooms, decorated with
old furniture, and beautiful gardens with a
pool. Includes unforgettable horse riding
into the forested mountains of the huge
finca, where you will be cooked lunch in a
remote rustic lodge. Reserve in advance.

$$$-$$ Hostería de Chicoana
*On the plaza at España 45, T0387-490 7009,
www.new sendas.com.*
A pretty colonial building, now slightly
faded, but with the added advantage of
expert guide Martín Pekarek (see **New
Sendas**, under What to do, below).

Festivals

Chicoana

Feb Carnaval, with processions and music.
Mar/Apr Easter celebrations are impressive,
with the Passion re-enacted throughout
the town.
16 Jul Fiesta Patronal, recommended for
a fun day out.
23 Jul Fiesta de Tamales, a famous festival
when regional delicacies (meat and corn tied
up in corn-husk bundles) are traditionally
made on a massive scale, famous *folclore*
musicians come to sing, and gauchos
compete in Doma contests. It's roughly
equivalent to rodeo and very impressive.

What to do

Chicoana

New Sendas, *T0387-490 7009, www.new
sendas.com.* Expert guide Martín Pekarek
offers wine tours, adventure excursions and
horses for hire, English and German spoken.
Also with lodging at **Hostería de Chicoana**
(see above).
Sayta, *T0387-15-683 6565, see Facebook.*
An estancia specializing in horse riding, for
all levels of experience, good horses and
attention, great *asados*, also has lodging for
overnight stays, adventure and rural tourism.
Recommended.

Salta
& around

Salta is one of Argentina's most charismatic and historical cities; its colourful past is tangible in palm-filled plazas lined with crumbling 17th-century buildings. Its fine museums chart the city's fascinating past, including the amazing finds from an Inca burial site on remote Mount Llullaillaco. Salta's tourist agencies offer trips to the beautiful Calchaquí Valley and to the splendid wineries around Cafayate. You could take the 'train to the clouds' into the dramatic Quebrada del Toro, or explore the ancient archaeological site of Santa Rosa de Tastil. Head further west into the shimmering salt flats and the *puna* (high-altitude desert).

Salta buzzes with life in the mornings, grinds to a halt at lunchtime and comes alive again at night. Balmy evenings are perfect for wandering the streets to find live music in the local *peñas* of Calle Balcarce. Or sample the superb food, such as *locro*, *tamales*, *empanadas* and *humitas*, for which Salta is famous, accompanied by a glass or two of the area's fine 'high-altitude' wine. This region is rich in indigenous culture, and you can buy the characteristic blood-red Güemes ponchos, as well as other handicrafts, in smart shops around the main plaza, or in the Mercado Artesanal.

The countryside is on your doorstep, with lush jungle to explore on horseback in nearby San Lorenzo – also a good place for a relaxing evening.

colonial majesty in Argentina's north

Plaza 9 de Julio and around

In just a few hours you can get a feel for Salta (population 1,333,000, altitude 1190 m). At its heart is the pleasant Plaza 9 de Julio, richly planted with wonderful tall palm trees and orange trees and surrounded by colonial-style buildings. The whole area has been spruced up and three sides of it are now pedestrianized and lined with cafés.

There's an impressive **Cabildo** built in 1783, one of the few that remains intact in the whole country, and behind its pleasingly uneven arches is an impressive museum, the **Museo Histórico del Norte** ① *Caseros 549, Tue-Sat 0900-1800, US$2, free Wed.* In a series of rooms around two open courtyards, the collection charts the region's history from pre-Hispanic times, with particularly good displays on the Wars of Independence and on Güemes leading the gauchos to victory. Upstairs, among some lovely religious art, is a fine golden 18th-century pulpit and some Cuzco school paintings, while outside are carriages and an ancient wine press. It's fascinating and informative.

Opposite the museum, on the north side of the plaza, is the lovely **cathedral**, built 1858-1878, now strangely painted pastel pink, and open mornings and evenings so that you can admire a huge baroque altar (1807) and the images of the Cristo del Milagro and of the Virgin Mary. These are central to Salta's beliefs and psyche, and the focus of Salta's

Essential Salta

Finding your feet

Salta's **airport** is 12 km southwest of the city. There are minibus services, US$3.50 to the centre, or take a *remise* taxi, US$8, 15 minutes. Bus on Corredor 8A to airport from San Martín, US$0.30.

The **bus terminal** is eight blocks east of the main plaza; walk along Avenida Yrigoyen and then Caseros, or take a taxi to the centre for US$2-3. The **train station** is at 20 de Febrero and Ameghino, nine blocks north of Plaza 9 de Julio; a taxi costs US$2-3. See also Transport, page 278.

Getting around

The best way to get around Salta is on foot, allowing you to soak up the atmosphere and see the main examples of its splendid architecture, all within four blocks of the main plaza, 9 de Julio. The main area for nightlife (Thursday to Saturday) and site of a weekend handicraft market is Calle Balcarce, 10 blocks north and west of the main plaza. This is five minutes in a taxi (US$2-3), but

it's a pleasant stroll, past attractive Plaza Güemes. There is also a hop-on, hop-off bus called the BTS (Bus Turístico Salta) which does a circuit of the town. City buses charge US$0.30 (www.saetasalta.com.ar).

Useful addresses

Bolivian Consulate, Mariano Boedo 34, T0387-421 1040, coliviansalta@yahoo.com.ar. Monday-Friday 0800-1300.
Chilean Consulate, Santiago del Estero 965, T0387-431 1857. Monday-Friday 0900-1300.
Immigration office, Maipú 35, T0387-422 0438, del.salta@migraciones.gov.ar. Daily 0700-1230.

Tip...

For a grand overview of the whole city, take the cable car from the central Parque San Martín to the top of Cerro San Bernardo (or it's a 45-minute walk). At the top are impeccably manicured gardens, waterfalls and a café with an amazing view.

biggest mass ritual. In 1692 Jesuit priests were amazed to discover that two statues, of Christ and the Virgin of Rosario, had survived a severe earthquake intact. During a series of tremors they paraded them through the streets in procession, and the following day, 14 September, the tremors stopped. The **Milagro** (miracle) is now the biggest event of Salta's year, when thousands of pilgrims walk to the city from hundreds of kilometres

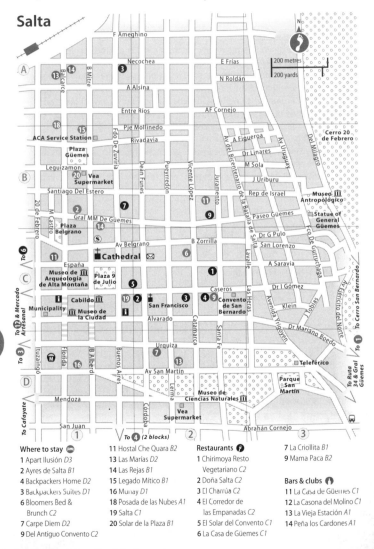

Salta

Where to stay 🛏
1 Apart Ilusión *D3*
2 Ayres de Salta *B1*
4 Backpackers Home *D2*
3 Backpackers Suites *D1*
6 Bloomers Bed & Brunch *C2*
7 Carpe Diem *D2*
9 Del Antiguo Convento *C2*

11 Hostal Che Quara *B2*
13 Las Marías *D2*
14 Las Rejas *B1*
15 Legado Mítico *B1*
16 Munay *D1*
18 Posada de las Nubes *A1*
19 Salta *C1*
20 Solar de la Plaza *B1*

Restaurants 🍴
1 Chirimoya Resto Vegetariano *C2*
2 Doña Salta *C2*
3 El Charrúa *C2*
4 El Corredor de las Empanadas *C2*
5 El Solar del Convento *C1*
6 La Casa de Güemes *C1*

7 La Criollita *B1*
9 Mama Paca *B2*

Bars & clubs 🍸
11 La Casa de Güemes *C1*
12 La Casona del Molino *C1*
13 La Vieja Estación *A1*
14 Peña los Cardones *A1*

BACKGROUND
Salta

The first Spanish expedition, led by Diego de Almagro from Cuzco (Peru), entered Argentina in 1536 and soon a busy trade route was established through the Quebrada de Humahuaca (now in Jujuy). Along this route the Spanish founded a group of towns: Santiago del Estero, Tucumán, Salta and Jujuy. Throughout the colonial period these were the centres of white settlement, and *encomiendas* were established to subdue the indigenous population. Jesuit and Franciscan missions were also attempted, but resistance was fierce, especially in the Calchaquí and Humahuaca valleys and, as a result, this is one of the few areas in Argentina that retains a rich indigenous culture.

The city of Salta was founded in 1582 and became one of the viceroyalty's most important administrative centres, governing a wide area and gaining considerable wealth from the fertile outlying land. The city also had an important role in the Wars of Independence between 1810 and 1821, when General Güemes led gaucho anti-Royalist forces to victory, utilizing their detailed knowledge of the terrain and inventing the now-famous red poncho which his men wore. Through the 19th century, Salta suffered a decline, since trade went directly to the country's new capital, Buenos Aires. Relatively little immigration and expansion allowed the city's colonial buildings to survive, boosted by neocolonial architecture in the 1930s when there was a large influx of newcomers. Today, Salta retains its old, aristocratic population but has a more affluent middle class than its neighbour, Jujuy. Tourism has taken off since devaluation in 2002 and is now the province's main source of income.

away. There is a huge procession uniting the population in an ancient communal act of superstition: parading the Christian figures that keep Salta safe from earthquakes.

Next to the cathedral is the **Museo de Arqueología de Alta Montaña (MAAM)** ① *Plaza 9 de Julio at Mitre 77, T0387-437 0592, www.maam.gob.ar, Tue-Sun 1100-1930, US$2.50, shop and café*, which houses the *Niños de Llullaillaco*. Like the Christian statues next door, these Inca deities were intended to avert earthquakes and volcanic eruptions. They were unearthed from a sacred burial site by a National Geographic expedition in 1999. Controversially, MAAM has on show the mummified remains of sacrificial children as well as many of the other fabulous objects found in the burial, with texts in English. A guided tour is included in the entry price; the guides are trained by resident archaeologist Christian Vitry. There's a fine library too. Opposite MAAM on the other side of the plaza is the interesting **Museo de Arte Contemporáneo** ① *Zuviria 90, T0387-437 3036, www.macsaltamuseo.org, Tue-Sun 0900-1900*, which is also worth a look.

Near the plaza, there are also a couple of historical houses worth visiting for a glimpse of wealthy domestic life, of which the best is **Casa de los Uriburu** ① *Caseros 417, T0387-421 8174, www.museonor.gov.ar, Tue-Fri 0900-1900, Sat Sun 0900-1330*, situated in the former mansion of the Uriburu family, the most distinguished of Salteño families, containing furniture, clothes and paintings.

A block west of the Cabildo, on one of the main pedestrian streets, are a couple of interesting museums housed in colonial mansions. The **Casa Leguizamón**, Caseros and Florida, has interesting architecture and the **Casa Arias Rengel**, next door, now houses the **Museo de Bellas Artes** ① *Belgrano 992, T0387-422 1745 (see Facebook), Tue-Sun 0900-*

1900, free, which has the city's finest collection of paintings, including superb Cuzqueño school works and small exhibitions of Salteño painters and sculptors.

Across the street is the **Museo de la Ciudad 'Casa de Hernández'** ⓘ *Florida 97 and Alvarado, T0387-437 3352, www.museociudadsalta.gov.ar, Mon-Fri 0900-1300, 1600-2030, Sat 1600-2030, free*, in a fine 18th-century mansion with a collection of old furniture, musical instruments and dull portraits, but a marvellous painting of writer Güemes.

East of Plaza 9 de Julio

Walk east from the plaza, along Caseros, an appealing street of slightly crumbling buildings. After a block, you'll come to the **Iglesia San Francisco** (1796) ⓘ *Caseros and Córdoba, daily 0900-2000*, one of the city's landmarks, with its magnificent plum-coloured façade ornately decorated with white and golden stucco scrolls, and its elegant tower (1882) rising above the low city skyline. The interior is relatively plain, but there are some remarkable statues to admire, such as the rather too realistic San Sebastián. Two blocks further east is the **Convento de San Bernardo** ⓘ *Caseros and Santa Fe*, built in colonial style in 1846, with an exquisitely carved wooden door dating from 1762. You can't enter the convent as it's still home to nuns, but they'll open up the little shop for you, with its collection of quaint handicrafts.

Continuing along Caseros for two blocks and turning right at Avenida Yrigoyen, you come to the wide open green space of **Parque San Martín**, where you'll find the **Museo de Ciencias Naturales** ⓘ *Mendoza 2, T0387-431 8086, Tue-Sun 1530-1930,* with various stuffed animals. It's not a particularly elaborate park, but there's a boating lake, and from here you can take the *teleférico* (cable car) up to **Cerro San Bernardo** (1458 m) ⓘ *daily 1000-1900, www.telefericosanbernardo.com, US$10 return, children US$5.50, under 5s free*, whose forested ridge looms over the east of the city centre. The top of the hill can be climbed in 45 minutes by a steep path (which starts beside the Museo Antropológico, see below). At the top there are lovely gardens and a great café (try the *empanadas*) with deck chairs and fabulous views. Recommended.

At the base of the hill is an impressive **statue** of General Güemes by Victor Gariño. His gaucho troops repelled seven powerful Spanish invasions from Bolivia between 1814 and 1821. The nearby **Museo Antropológico Juan M Leguizamón** ⓘ *follow Paseo Güemes behind the statue and up Av Ejército del Norte, T0387-422 2960, www.antropologico.gov.ar, Mon-Fri 0800-1900, Sat 1000-1800 closed Sun, the museum is closed for renovation in 2016,* makes a good introduction to the pre-Hispanic cultures of the region. It has a superb collection of anthropomorphic ceramics and beautifully painted funerary urns. There's also an exhibition on high-altitude burial grounds, complete with mummies, objects found at the ancient ruins of Tastil (see page 284) and, most mysteriously, skulls flattened during the owner's life by wearing boards to squash the head (thought to confer higher intelligence). It's all very accessible and well laid out.

Tourist information

For more information, see www.
turismoensalta.com (in English).

Cámara de Turismo
*Gral Güemes 15 y Av Virrey Toledo,
T0387-210698, www.saltalalinda.gov.ar
and www.saltaciudad.com.ar.*

Municipal tourist office
*Caseros 711, T0800-777 0300. Mon-Fri
0800-2100, Sat and Sun 0900-2100.*
For Salta city only, this office is small
but helpful.

National parks office
*España 366, 3rd floor, T0387-431 2683,
elrey@apn.gov.ar. Mon-Fri 0800-1500.*

Provincial tourist office
*Buenos Aires 93 (1 block from main plaza),
T0387-431 0950, www.turismosalta.gov.ar.
Mon-Fri 0800-2100, Sat and Sun 0900-2000.*
Helpful and provides free maps, both of the
city and the province, gives advice on tours
and arranges accommodation in private
houses in high season (Jul), when hotels
are fully booked. Staff speak English.

Where to stay

All hotels and hostels listed are
recommended. Book ahead in Jul
holidays and around 10-16 Sep during
celebrations of Cristo del Milagro.

$$$$ Legado Mítico
*Mitre 647, T0387-422 8786,
www.legadomitico.com.*
This small, welcoming hotel is absolutely
lovely: luxurious rooms each with its own
personality. The personalized pre-ordered
breakfasts are a fantastic way to start the day.

$$$$ Solar de la Plaza
*Juan M Leguizamon 669, T0387-431 5111,
www.solardelaplaza.com.ar.*

Elegant old former Salteño family home,
faultless service, sumptuous rooms, great
restaurant and a pool.

$$$$-$$$ Ayres de Salta
*Gral Güemes 650, T0387-422 1616,
www.ayresdesalta.com.ar.*
Spacious, central 4-star hotel near Plaza
Belgrano. Everything you would expect in
this price range: spacious rooms, heated
pool, great views from roof terrace.

$$$ Apart Ilusión (Sweet Dreams)
*José Luis Fuentes 743, Portezuelo Norte,
T0387-15 539 3198, see Facebook.*
On the slopes of Cerro San Bernardo, well-
equipped self-catering apartments for 2-4,
decorated with local handicrafts, beautiful
views. English-speaking owner, Sonia
Alvarez, is welcoming. Breakfast and parking
available, good value.

$$$ Bloomers Bed & Brunch
*Vicente López 129, T0387-422 7449,
www.bloomers-salta.com.ar.
Closed mid-May to mid-Jun.*
In a refurbished colonial house, 5 spacious
non-smoking rooms individually decorated,
and one apartment. Use of kitchen and
library. The brunch menu, different each day,
is their speciality.

$$$ Carpe Diem
*Urquiza 329, T0387-421 8736,
www.bedandbreakfastsalta.com.*
Welcoming B&B German/Italian-owned,
beautifully furnished, convenient, with
comfortable public areas. No children
under 14.

$$$ Salta
*Buenos Aires 1, on main plaza, T0387-
426 7500, www.hotelsalta.com.*
A Salta institution with neocolonial public
rooms, refurbished bedrooms, marvellous
suites overlooking plaza, *confitería* and
honorary membership of the Polo and
Golf Club.

$$ Del Antiguo Convento
Caseros 113, T0387-422 7267,
www.hoteldelconvento.com.ar.
Small, convenient, with old-fashioned
rooms around a neat patio, very helpful,
a good choice.

$$ Las Marías
Lerma 255, T0387-422 4193,
www.saltaguia.com/lasmarias.
Central hostel, $ pp in shared rooms,
close to Parque San Martín.

$$ Las Rejas
General Güemes 569, T0387-422 7959,
www.lasrejashostel.com.ar.
2 houses converted into a small B&B and a
hostel (US$15-17 pp), comfortable, central,
helpful owners.

$$ Munay
San Martín 656, T0387-422 4936,
www.munayhotel.com.ar.
Good choice, smart rooms for 2-5 with
good bathrooms, warm welcome. Also have
hotels of the same standard in Cafayate,
Humahuaca, Jujuy and La Quiaca.

$$ Posada de las Nubes
Balcarce 639, T0387-432 1776,
www.posadadelasnubes.com.ar.
Charming, small, with simply decorated
rooms around a central patio. Great location
for Balcare nightlife; might be a little too
loud at weekends.

$ Backpackers Home
Buenos Aires 930, T0387-423 5910;
Backpackers Suites, *Urquiza 1045, T0387-*
431 8944, www.backpackerssalta.com.
HI-affiliated hostels, well run, with dorms and
private rooms ($$, cheaper for HI members),
with laundry and budget travel information.
Crowded and popular.

$ Hostal Che Quara
Santiago del Estero 125, T0387-422 0392,
www.hostalquara.com.
Dorms US$13-14, also doubles with and
without bath, with heating, TV room, drinks
for sale. The helpful staff can organize tours.

Restaurants

There are lots of great *peñas* for live music,
serving good regional food at night along
the north end of C Balcarce. Salta has
delicious and distinctive cuisine: try the
locro, humitas and *tamales,* served in the
municipal market at San Martín y Florida.

$$$ El Solar del Convento
Caseros 444, half a block from plaza,
T0387-421 5124.
Elegant and not expensive, champagne
when you arrive, delicious steaks.
Recommended.

$$ Chirimoya Resto Vegetariano
España 211, T0387-431 2857, see Facebook.
Those looking to get away from the *carne*
can opt for this café located a few blocks
off the main plaza. It offers veggie twists on
pastas, sandwiches and *milanesas.* There's
even a 'raw ravioli'.

$$ Doña Salta
*Córdoba 46 (opposite San Francisco convent
library), T0387-432 1921.*
Excellent regional dishes and pleasant, rustic
atmosphere, good value.

$$ El Charrúa
Caseros 221, T0387-432222,
www.parrillaelcharrua.com.ar.
A good, brightly lit family place with a
reasonably priced and simple menu; the
parrilla is particularly recommended.

$$ La Casa de Güemes
España 730.
Popular, local dishes and *parrilla,*
traditionally cooked in the house
where General Güemes lived.

$ El Corredor de las Empanadas
Caseros 117 and Zuviría 913.
Delicious *empanadas* and tasty local dishes
in airy surroundings.

$ La Criollita
Zuviría 306.
Small and unpretentious, a traditional place
for tasty *empanadas.*

$ Mama Paca
Gral Güemes 118.
Recommended by locals, traditional restaurant for seafood from Chile and home-made pasta.

Cafés
There are lots of cafés on Plaza 9 de Julio; it's a great place to sit and people watch, although the 2 cafés outside MAAM, **Havana** and **El Palacio**, are very touristy.

Don Blas
Balcarce 401.
A lovely old corner of Balcarce serving good coffee.

Fili
Corner of Güemes and Sarmiento 299.
The best ice cream in Salta, try the *dulce de leche* with almonds or cinnamon. Heaven.

MAAM
Inside the museum, Plaza 9 de Julio.
Lovely airy café for meals and drinks.

New Time
Plaza 9 de Julio, corner with Alberdi.
Avoid the tourist cafés and go where the Salteños go. Great juice, salads and light meals.

Plaza Café
Next to Hotel Salta.
This elegant café is popular with Salteños late morning, when the centre is buzzing. A nice spot for breakfast.

★ Bars and clubs

No trip to the northwest is complete without sampling its stirring *folclore* music. You can eat *empanadas* while watching great musicians playing live in Salta's *peñas* or listening to spontaneous performers in the crowd.

Most are concentrated at the north end of C Balcarce, where you will find many *peñas* within 3 blocks, including **Los Cardones** (No 885, T0387-432 0909), which has good

food and a good nightly show, and **La Vieja Estación** (No 877, T0387-421 7727, www.la-viejaestacion.com.ar), with a great atmosphere and good food. This area also has a number of popular rock and jazz bars, such as **Macondo** or **Café del Tiempo** (both on Facebook), as well as intimate restaurants and nightclubs. The result is an entertaining and noisy mix, though there are quieter bars here too. This area is most alive Thu, Fri and Sat nights from 1900 (taxi US$1.50). **La Casa de Güemes** (España 730, close to Plaza 9 de Julio), is recommended for shows and frequented by Salteños. West of the centre (reached by taxi), **La Casona del Molino** (Luis Burela 1, T0387-434 2835, see Facebook), is the most authentic place for spontaneous *peña*, in a crumbling old colonial house, serving good food and drink.

Festivals

Feb/Mar Carnival. Salta celebrates with processions on the 4 weekends before Ash Wed at the *corsódromo*, located on Av Gato Mancha near the convention center (US$3). On **Mardi Gras** (Shrove Tue) there is a procession of decorated floats and dancers with intricate masks of feathers and mirrors. It's the custom to squirt water at passers-by and *bombas de agua* (small balloons to be filled with water) are on sale for dropping from balconies.
16-17 Jun Commemoration of the death of Martín Güemes. There's folk music in the afternoon and a gaucho parade in the morning around his statue.
6-15 Sep Cristo del Milagro. Salta's biggest event (see page 272). All accommodation is heavily booked ahead, so reserve at least a month in advance.
24 Sep Battles of Tucumán and Salta.

Shopping

The best places for shopping are the parallel pedestrianized streets of Alberdi, off Plaza 9 de Julio, and Florida, a block to the west. There are pricey but high-quality local goods on C Buenos Aires near the plaza, and in the shopping centre next to MAAM on the plaza.

Mercado Artesanal, *in the Casa El Alto Molino, San Martín 2555, on the western outskirts, T0387-434 2808. Daily 0900-2100.* If you're short of time, head straight for this lovely 18th-century mansion, selling beautiful handicrafts made by craftsmen in the surrounding areas. Perhaps a little more expensive than if you buy them from a tiny village, but superb quality and all under one roof. Look out for soft and warm llama wool socks, wonderful hand-woven ponchos, delicately carved wood and weavings. Opposite is a cheaper tourist market for similar items, but factory-made. To get there, take bus 2, 3, or 7 from Av San Martín in centre and get off where the bus crosses the railway line.

Mercado Municipal, *San Martín and Florida. Closed 1300-1700 and Sun.* Wonderful place for cheap food; great fruit and vegetables and some handicrafts.

What to do

There are many tour operators, mostly on Buenos Aires, offering adventure trips and excursions; staff give out flyers on the street. Out of season, tours often run only if there is sufficient demand; check carefully that the tour will run on the day you want. All agencies charge similar prices for tours (though some charge extra for credit card payments): city tour, US$20; Valles Calchaquíes, US$71 (2 days); Cachi, US$47; Puna and salt lakes, US$85. The tourist office gives reports on agencies and their service.

Clark Expediciones, *Mariano Moreno 1950, T0387-492 7280, www.clarkexpediciones.com.* Specialist birding tours, eco-safaris and treks. English spoken.

Dexotic, *Guemes 569, T0387-421 5971, www.dexotic.com.* Company specializing in various excursions and adventure packages including to Valle Calchaquíes, Cachi, Puna, the salt lakes and Humahuaca. Also horse

riding, rafting, bungee jumping and more. Friendly staff, professional.

Movitrack, *Caseros 468, T0387-431 6749, www.movitrack.com.ar.* Entertaining safaris in a 4WD truck to San Antonio de los Cobres, Humahuaca, Cafayate. German and English spoken. Expensive. They also have an **OxyBus** for high-altitude journeys.

Norte Trekking, *Gral Güemes 265, T0387-431 6616, www.nortetrekking.com. Mon-Fri 0900-1300, 1500-2000.* Excellent tours in 4WDs and minivans all over Salta and Jujuy, including small group tours to Iruya, over Jama Pass to San Pedro de Atacama, hiking, horse riding and trips to El Rey national park with a highly experienced guide, Federico Norte, who speaks English. Tailors tours to your interest and budget. Highly recommended.

Puna Expediciones, *Agustín Usandivaras 230, T0387-416 9313, www.punaexpeditions. com.ar.* Qualified and experienced guide Luis H Aguilar organizes treks in remote areas of Salta and Jujuy and safaris further afield. Recommended.

Socompa, *Balcarce 998, p 1, T0387-431 5974, www.socompa.com.* Excellent company specializing in trips to salt flats and volcanoes in the *puna*, 3 days to the beautiful, remote hamlet of Tolar Grande; can be extended to 12 days to include Atacama and Puna of Catamarca; 4 days to Puna of Catamarca. English and Italian spoken, knowledgeable guides. Highly recommended.

Transport

Air

The **airport** (T0387-424 3115, www.aa2000. com.ar) has a café, *locutorio* with internet, ATM and car rental companies. There's also a **Movitrack** stand, useful for information on tours as you wait for your luggage. **Tourist information** is in the main hall, next to **Avis**, but isn't always open.

Aerolíneas Argentinas/Austral, Caseros 475, T0810-2228 6527, flies to **Buenos Aires**, 2¼ hrs, also **Andes**, Caseros 459, T0387-437

3514, www.andesonline.com and **LAN**, Caseros 476, T0810-999 9526.

Bus
Local Buses to local destinations, such as **Coronel Moldes** and Cabra Corral can be caught next to the *teleférico* office on the corner of San Martín and Yrigoyen. There are hourly buses to Silleta and **Campo Quijano** (at the head of the Quebrada del Toro).

Long distance The bus terminal (information T0387-401 1143, www.terminalsalta.com) has a *confitería*, toilets, *locutorio*, café, *panadería*, kiosks, ATM and left luggage, but no internet.

To **Buenos Aires**, several companies daily, US$121-174, 20-22 hrs. To **Córdoba**, several companies daily, 12 hrs, US$66-100. To **Santiago del Estero**, 6-7 hrs, US$35-44. To **Tucumán**, 4 hrs, several companies, US$23-29. To **Mendoza** via Tucumán with **Andesmar** and **Flecha Bus** companies daily, US$106-123, 18-20 hrs. To **La Rioja**, US$55, 10-11 hrs. To **Jujuy**, frequent service, US$5-10, 2-2½ hrs.

To **Cachi,** 0700, 1330, US$6.50, 4-4½ hrs, with **Ale Hnos**, T0387-421 1588/423 181, US$8; also **Marcus Rueda**, T0387-421 4447, spectacular journey. **Ale** buses continue to **Molinos**, Mon, Wed, Fri, Sun, 6½ hrs from Salta, US$11. To **Cafayate**, US$13-21, with **Flecha Bus**, and **Aconquija**. To **Santa María**, daily, 5½ hrs, US$16. To **Rosario de la Frontera**, 2½-3 hrs, US$15. To **San Antonio de Los Cobres**, 5 hrs, **El Quebradeño**, daily, US$10-12.

International To **Paraguay**: travel to **Resistencia**, daily, 13 hrs, US$65, with **La Veloz del Norte** or **Flecha Bus,** or to **Formosa**, US$74, 16 hrs, then change to a direct bus to Asunción. To **Chile**: There are services to **Calama** and **San Pedro de Atacama**, via Jujuy and the Jama Pass, with **Andesmar**, T0387-431 0263 and **Géminis**, T0387-431 7778, 3 each a week, but check days as they change, US$56-65, 11 hrs. Géminis and Pullman offices are at booths 15 and 16 in the terminal. To **Bolivia**: To **La Quiaca**, on Bolivian border, **Balut**, **Andesmar**, **Flecha**, 7½ hrs, US$20. To **Aguas Blancas** US$21, 5 hrs, or **Pocitos** (both on the Bolivian border, see pages 310 and 310), US$30, 8 hrs, **Balut**, **La Veloz del Norte** and **Flecha** daily.

Car hire
Avis, Caseros 420, T0387-421 2181 and at the airport, Ruta 51, salta@avis.com.ar. Efficient and very helpful, recommended. **NOA**, Buenos Aires 1, T0387-431 7080, www.noarentacar.com, in **Hotel Salta**, helpful. Many others.

Train
The only train service is the **Tren a las Nubes**, which usually runs end Mar to early Dec on Sat, with extra trains in high season (Semana Santa and July) between Salta and La Polvorilla viaduct, departing 0700, arriving back in Salta 2000, weather permitting. The regular route is train to La Polvorilla and back to San Antonio de los Cobres, where passengers change to a bus arriving back in Salta by 2300. There are also several multi-day tours to the region which include the train (see website). The basic fare (train up, bus back) is US$114, US$77 for minors and seniors. Contact T0387-422 8021, www.trenalasnubes.com.ar. For more information, see box, page 284.

There are many lovely places close to Salta where Salteños go to relax: the smart leafy suburbs of San Lorenzo, 11 km to the west; jungly Campo Quijano on the way to Quebrada del Toro (see page 283), Chicoana en route to Cachi (see page 264) or the Dique Cabra Corral for fishing and water sports.

Dique Cabra Corral
Salta makes a big deal of its only big lagoon – one of the largest artificial lakes in Argentina, the Dique Cabra Corral. It's popular with locals for fishing *pejerrey*, the tasty local delicacy, and for enjoying a bit of beach life, with water-skiing, fishing, camping and restaurants also on offer. The best place to stay is the **Hotel del Dique**, on the banks of the lake; the **Finca Santa Anita** (see Where to stay, below) is nearby and also gives you ready access to the water. The nearest town is the quaint gaucho town of **Coronel Moldes**, which, though not perhaps worth a special trip, has a quiet charm all of its own, with a strong sense of community.

Listings Around Salta

Where to stay

It's worth considering staying outside Salta if you're in search of more tranquillity: at San Lorenzo (11 km); at the Dique Cabra Corral; at Campo Quijano in the Quebrada del Toro (see page 283); or at one of the many fincas within an hour of the city. See www.turismosalta.gov.ar for more information.

$$$ El Castillo
Juan Carlos Dávalos 1985, San Lorenzo, T0387-492 1052, www.hotelelcastillo.com.ar.
Stunning building in an amazing location with lots of places to hike to. High ceilings, antique furniture, a lovely pool and a nice garden to enjoy. There is a good restaurant which is open to non-guests (see below).

$$$ Hotel del Dique
Dique Cabra Corral, R47, Km 12, T0387-490 5111, www.hoteldeldique.com.
Extremely comfortable, great lakeside position, with a pool and good food.

Estancias/fincas
To experience the beautiful landscape of this region and to meet the people, stay at an estancia, or finca to use the local term. Most owners speak English, are extremely hospitable and are delighted to have guests from abroad. Stay for at least a couple of days to make the most of the facilities, which usually include horse riding, a pool and lovely places to walk. There are many fincas throughout the region, but the following are some of the most distinctive within easy access of the city. All are in the **$$$$-$$$** price range, mostly per person.

Finca El Bordo de las Lanzas
El Bordo, 45 km east of Salta, in department of General Güemes, T0387-5534 6942, www.estanciaelbordo.com.
Formal and luxurious, a taste of aristocratic life, with splendid accommodation, horse riding on the immense tobacco plantation, dining with the charming hosts. Highly recommended.

Finca Santa Anita
Coronel Moldes, 60 km from Salta, on the way to Cafayate, T0387-490 5050, www.santaanita.com.ar.
The whole family makes you welcome on this prize-winning organic farm with

superb goat's cheese, which has won 'Slow Food' prizes: great organic food and all activities included in the price. A traditional, colonial-style finca, beautiful views, swimming, guided walks to prehistoric rock paintings and horse riding in wonderful landscapes. It also houses the first tobacco museum in Argentina.

Finca Valentina
Ruta 51, Km 6, La Merced Chica, T0387-15-415 3490, www.finca-valentina.com.ar.
Italian-owned, excellent accommodation, only 5 rooms, activities include horse riding, cookery classes, massage, day visits arranged. Associated with recommended tour operator **Socompa**, below.

La Casa de los Jazmines
R51, Km 6 south towards La Silleta, T0387-497 2002, www.houseofjasmines.com.
Not exactly an estancia, but a beautiful place to unwind: old finca building redesigned to the height of luxury and good taste, perfumed with roses and jasmine, with a pool and superb spa offering a great range of treatments. Recommended.

Selva Montana
C Alfonsina Storni 2315, San Lorenzo, T0387-492 1184, www.hostal-selvamontana.com.ar.

Nestling high up in the lush leafy hills of San Lorenzo, just 15 mins by car from Salta. Complete comfort, and peace and quiet in stylish rooms, with a pool, horses, walking and birdwatching on offer. Take a taxi (US$10) or city bus No 7 from the terminal.

Restaurants

See www.sanlorenzosalta.org.ar for more information.

$$$ Castillo de San Lorenzo
Juan Carlos Daválos 1985, San Lorenzo, T0387-492 1052, www.hotelelcastillo.com.ar.
Fabulous interior in this castellated building, with delicious meals served in a stylish setting. Recommended.

$$ Lo de Andrés
Juan Carlos Dávalos y Gorritti, San Lorenzo, T0387-15 603 7042, see Facebook.
Fabulous restaurant. Great steaks and pasta.

Festivals

Dique Cabra Corral
Coronel Moldes
1 Aug Fiesta Patronal, with wonderful local processions of gauchos on the celebration days of the town's patron saints.

Northwest Salta
& the Quebrada del Toro

The landscapes of northwestern Salta province are utterly spectacular. In one unforgettable journey up the Quebrada del Toro from Salta to San Antonio de los Cobres, you'll travel through dense forest, gorges of brightly coloured rock strewn with cactus and high-altitude desert. This is the route of Argentina's famous narrow-gauge railway, Tren a las Nubes (Train to the Clouds), but it's a long, frustrating and very touristy experience. It's far better to take a minibus tour or hire a car.

You might stay a night in the forested weekend resort of Campo Quijano, and don't miss the superb ruined city of Santa Rosa de Tastil, one of Argentina's archaeological gems. Set in stunning rocky landscapes there's evidence of ancient pre-Inca and Inca civilizations.

At the top of the gorge, the quiet mining town of San Antonio de los Cobres is at its best for the Fiesta de la Pachamama in August. To offset altitude sickness, stop off for coca tea at El Mojón, and then be dazzled by the shimmering expanse of Salinas Grandes salt flats. From here drop to Purmamarca in the Quebrada de Humahuaca down the thrilling Cuesta de Lipán road. Or head west, into the *puna* to discover tranquil isolation at Tolar Grande.

Essential Northwest Salta

Tours

This part of Salta has traditionally been the sole preserve of the Tren a las Nubes, but in the last few years another tour operator, **Movitrack**, www.movitrack.com.ar, has run very successful tours along the same route which actually allow you to see far more of the impressive engineering of the train track and absorb more of the landscape. Inevitably, other tour operators followed, and along Salta's Calle Buenos Aires, you'll find plenty of tours on offer, though Movitrack is the only company to have pressurized oxygen-pumped vehicles to counter the inevitable effects of altitude.

Hiring a car will give you more time to explore the Quebrada del Toro and to visit Santa Rosa de Tastil, which few agencies include in any detail. Ask the tourist office for latest information on local guides at the

site, since there is a project to put trained locals in place.

Accommodation

There is comfortable accommodation at San Antonio de los Cobres, but very little on the way.

Cycling

If cycling, note that much of the road is *ripio*, that there is no shade, and it's extremely cold at night.

Altitude

However you travel, the effects of altitude are not to be underestimated, since you'll be climbing to nearly 4000 m. You must take time for your body to adjust if you're going to exert yourself beyond a gentle stroll. Drink plenty of water, avoid alcohol and don't overeat. Take it easy and you should feel fine.

Quebrada del Toro and Tren a las Nubes

unforgettable landscapes seen by rail or car

The route for the Train to the Clouds (see box, page 284) is the same as the road through the Quebrada del Toro. The only difference is that travelling by road gives you the chance to get out and walk around – and to examine the spectacular feat of engineering of the train track – which of course you can't see from the train itself.

You'll leave Salta's subtropical valleys via the jungle weekend retreat of **Campo Quijano**, at Km 30, which lies in a beautiful, thickly vegetated valley at the entrance to the gorge and is an attractive place for a stop. The road and track then climb along the floor of the Quebrada del Toro, fording the river repeatedly amidst densely growing Pampas grass and *ceibo*, Argentina's national flower, with its striking fringed red blossoms. At **Chorrillos**, you'll see one of several identical wooden 1920s train stations along the route, with outside ovens built to heat steel fixings during the building of the track. From here the train track zigzags as it climbs past tiny farmsteads lined with *álamo* trees, up into the dramatic **Quebrada Colorada** – so called because of its bright red, pink and green stratified rock – to Ingeniero Maury (2350 m, Km 65), where there is a police control point. From Km 96, now paved, the road climbs the **Quebrada de Tastil**, parting company from the railway which continues through the **Quebrada del Toro**. The road passes through the tiny hamlet of Santa Rosa de Tastil, where there are marvellous pre-Inca ruins, and the only accommodation before San Antonio de los Cobres.

ON THE ROAD
Train to the Clouds

The famous narrow-gauge Tren a las Nubes is an extraordinary feat of engineering, and a good way to experience the dramatic landscape up to the *puna*.

Built to enable commerce over the Andes to Chile, the track, which runs 570 km from Salta to Socompa on the Chilean border, was the outstanding achievement of Richard Maury, an engineer from Pennsylvania. Work started in 1921 and took 20 years. The track starts in Salta at 1200 m above sea level, rising to 4200 m, up through the impossibly rocky terrain of the steep Quebrada del Toro gorge, with several switchbacks and 360-degree loops to allow diesel engines to gain height over a short distance with a gentler gradient. One thousand men worked with only the most basic tools through inhospitable conditions, detonating rock and carving away at steep mountainsides through howling winds and snow. Many died in the attempt. The destination of the tourist train (passengers no longer being allowed on the weekly cargo trains) is La Polvorilla viaduct, near San Antonio de los Cobres, a delicate bridge across a mighty gorge, spanning 224 m. At 63 m high, it feels like you're travelling on air: both scary and exhilarating.

The tourist train is a comfortable ride, though a long day out. Leaving Salta at 0700 (cold and dark in winter) to the cheerful accompaniment of *folclore* singers on the platform, the train edges to the entrance of Quebrada de Toro, steep forested mountains tinged with pink as the sun rises, and a light breakfast is served. The landscape, dotted with farms and adobe houses, changes to arid red rock as you climb through the gorge, where giant cacti perch, past multi-coloured sculptural mountains to the staggeringly beautiful *puna*. The seven hours of the ascent are kept lively by chats from bilingual guides (English spoken; French and Portuguese too on request). Altitude sickness hits many people, and oxygen is on hand. At La Polvorilla viaduct, you can get out briefly to admire the construction and to buy locally made llama wool goods from the people of San Antonio. Don't bother haggling: these shawls and hats are beautifully made and are these people's only source of income. At San Antonio, the Argentine flag is raised to commemorate those who worked on the railway, and the national anthem is sung in a rather surreal ceremony.

The descent, however, is slightly tedious, despite the constant stream of entertainment from *folclore* singers and Andean bands. Consider returning by road instead to see the ruins at Santa Rosa de Tastil. For more information, see www.trenalasnubes.com.ar.

★ Santa Rosa de Tastil *Colour map 1, A2.*

This picturesque little hamlet (3080 m, Km 103) lies near the site of one of Argentina's most important pre-Hispanic settlements, which once contained well over 400 houses and over 2000 people. It is believed to have been inhabited from AD 1336 to 1439. There is a small worthwhile **museum** ① *at the side of the road, Mon 0900-1500, Tue-Sun 0900-1800, free,* which has some of the finds from this intriguing culture, among them a well-preserved mummy, delicate jewellery and a xylophone of sonorous rocks.

The remains of this ancient city are extraordinarily beautiful: a vast expanse of regular walls and roads, stretching out on an exposed hillside with views along the entire gorge.

BACKGROUND
Santa Rosa de Tastil

Spread out over 12 ha and looming 60 m over the Valle de Lerma in Salta's dry centre are the ruins of a complex pre-Inca civilization founded around AD 1336. The site is one of the most complete archaeological sites in the country, and the intricate houses (not built to any recognizable grid) sprawl haphazardly on the slope. As it hardly ever rains in this area, walls are still standing, pottery and arrow tips can still be found on the ground and erosion to the structures has been kept to a minimum (although some walls have been rebuilt).

Abandoned around AD 1439 and rediscovered in 1903 by anthropologist Eric Boman, the site was once home to over 2000 people who traded with the neighbouring Andean towns and farmed at the foot of the mountains. They were excellent weavers, bred llamas and guanacos, and made stone and rustic pottery. No one is quite sure why the highly developed site was abandoned, but we can learn about their religion and beliefs from the rock paintings they left behind. If you are in the area, consider a trip to these remote and well-preserved ruins. They are a great example of the civilizations that lived peacefully up and down the Andes until the Incas arrived.

The ruins themselves are well worth visiting, but be sure to ask for a local guide, since the site is extensive and you'll get more out of it with a little interpretation. Guides are unpaid so appreciate a tip. See also box, above.

San Antonio de los Cobres *Colour map 1, B2.*
Beyond Tastil the road climbs through green hanging valleys where cattle roam, and then up over the **Abra Blanca Pass** (4050 m) where the landscape changes dramatically, suddenly becoming vast, open and eerily empty. At the top of the pass, the road drops and runs across the *puna*, offering views of Mount Chañi (5896 m) to the right, Acay (5716 m) to the left, and Quewar (6102 m) in the far distance.

San Antonio de los Cobres is a simple, remote mining town of low adobe houses situated in a shallow hollow, at 3774 m, 168 km northwest of Salta. There's nothing much to do here but it's a good introduction to the reclusive life of the *puna*, and it does have its subtle charms. It's also one of the few places that retains authentic indigenous culture and where the **Pachamama festival** is celebrated in style every August. This is a wonderful tradition of the indigenous peoples of the entire Andean region, in which they give thanks to mother earth, La Pachamama, with offerings of drinks and food, in a fascinating ceremony that binds the whole community. Tourists are welcome at this great event, which is not to be missed. People are friendly and the handicrafts on offer are of high quality and incredibly cheap.

From San Antonio you can continue west into Chile (see below) or head south along Ruta 40 to La Poma and Cachi over the mighty Paso Abra del Acay (4900 m), see page 268. This road should only be attempted in a 4WD as it is very rough in places. Alternatively, you could head north to the fabulous salt flats at Salinas Grandes and on to Purmamarca in the Quebrada de Humahuaca – a spectacular journey, see

> **Tip...**
> Altitude sickness can strike heavily here, so avoid eating too much or drinking alcohol until you've acclimatized.

BORDER CROSSING
Argentina–Chile

Paso de Sico

The border should be open 24 hours, but check in San Antonio de los Cobres before setting out, T0387-498 2001.

Argentine immigration The offices are at the pass itself and in San Antonio de los Cobres at the other end of town from the *aduana* (customs house). There is a police checkpoint at Catúa, 26 km east of Paso de Sico and in Toconao.

Chilean customs and immigration are in San Pedro de Atacama.

Note This is a high-altitude pass, with the road reaching up to 4080 m above sea level. From Salta the road is tarmac for the first 110 km of the Ruta Nacional 51, after that it is sealed road. On the Chilean side it continues via Mina Laco and Socaire to Toconao; it may be in bad condition between these two points). See www.gendarmeria.gov.ar/pasos-chile/sico.html.

Paso de Socompa

The border is open 24 hours. From Paso de Socompa a poor road runs to Pan de Azúcar, with roads west to the Pan-American Highway, or north via the Salar de Atacama to San Pedro de Atacama. No fuel is available until San Pedro or Calama.

Note This is another high-altitude pass, with the road reaching up to 4080 m above sea level. Snow in this area is common from May to August and can reach as high as 2 m. In winter temperatures can drop to -15°C. This route is rocky, with lots of bends and uneven roads, and is not recommended.

below. Ask at the **Municipalidad** ① *Belgrano s/n, T0387-490 9045*, about minibus tours to the salt flats and Purmamarca.

San Antonio to Chile

From San Antonio there are two possible crossings to Chile. The best, closest, and most used, is the **Paso de Sico** (see box, above), due west on Route Nacional 51. (About 14 km west of San Antonio de los Cobres, there is a road that runs below the famous **La Polvorilla** railway viaduct, giving you the chance to photograph it.) Alternatively, at Caucharí, take Route Provincial 27 southwest across the giant Salar de Arizaro to the Chilean border at the **Paso de Socompa**. The road runs through very beautiful scenery including salt flats and desert, but be warned that it is extremely isolated and only for the very intrepid. There are no services whatsoever, so make sure you stock up on drinking water and fuel before setting out from San Antonio.

San Antonio to Purmamarca

The Ruta 40 continues north from San Antonio and is recommended for a taste of the extraordinary landscapes of the northwest. The road runs dead flat across the scrubby yellow *puna* – its horizons edged with pinkish mauve or bronze mountains, with the occasional flock of llamas or cows grazing. It's either wonderfully meditative or unbearably monotonous, depending on your point of view, but the salt flats, **Salinas Grandes**, which you'll reach in two hours from San Antonio, are certainly worth seeing. The huge expanses of dazzling white salt, with their geometric patterns of crusted lines, are striking and otherworldly. There are crossroads some 20 north of the salt flats, where you could head west to Susques (in Jujuy, see page 305), up to Abra Pampa or follow the spectacular road to Purmamarca in the Quebrada de Humahuaca (see page 295), down the broad slalom bends of **Cuesta de Lipán** with breathtaking views of the valley below.

Listings Quebrada del Toro and Tren a las Nubes

Where to stay

Quebrada del Toro

$$$ Hostería Punta Callejas
In Campo Quijano, R51, 30 km west of Salta, T0387-490 4086, www.puntacallejas.com.ar.
Very clean and comfortable, with a/c, pool, tennis, horse riding, trips and meals. Breakfast included.

Camping

There's a municipal campsite at the entrance to Quebrada del Toro; a lovely spot with good facilities, hot showers and bungalows.

Santa Rosa de Tastil

Basic accommodation in shared dorms is available in the village, ask at the museum.

San Antonio de los Cobres

Ask at the **Municipalidad** (Belgrano s/n, T0387-490 9045), about other lodgings (**$**).

$$$ Hostería de las Nubes
Edge of San Antonio on the Salta road, T0387-490 9059, www.hoteldelasnubes.com.
Smart, comfortable, modern and spacious. Recommended.

$$ Hostería El Palenque
Belgrano s/n, T0387-490 9019, www.hostalelpalenque.com.
Basic, hot showers, cable TV.

Transport

San Antonio de los Cobres
Bus
To **Salta city**, via Santa Rosa de Tastil, **Ale**, daily, 5 hrs, US$10.

Jujuy province

The beautiful province of Jujuy lives slightly under wealthier Salta's shadow, but it has some of the richest culture of the whole country thanks to its large population of indigenous people, who most Argentines refer to as 'los indios'. Absorb the lively street life in Jujuy city, take part in a Pachamama (Mother Earth) ceremony, or witness the vibrant festival in remotest Casabindo, and you'll feel the palpable energy of the authentic Andean culture. So, although Jujuy is less developed in terms of tourist infrastructure, it's definitely worth making the effort to explore, and as tourism brings more income to the region, bus services and hotels are opening up fast in response.

Jujuy's great attraction is the Quebrada de Humahuaca, named a World Heritage Site by UNESCO in 2003 for its spectacular beauty. Easter and Carnival are celebrated here in exuberant style, combining Christian traditions with Andean religious beliefs. Dotted along the Quebrada are pleasant towns for a few days' walking and exploring. Further north, there are beautiful, remote villages to discover along the Bolivian border.

East and west of the province are two contrasting landscapes. In Jujuy's expanse of *puna* in the west, you'll find the fascinating small villages of Susques and Casabindo, Jesuit gold mines and Laguna de los Pozuelos with its wealth of birdlife. To the east, explore the cloudforest in Calilegua National Park, accessible from Libertador General San Martín.

where Mother Earth meets city streets

Often overlooked by tourists, the capital of Jujuy province (pronounced whoo-whooey) may be Salta's poorer sister but it has plenty of life and culture to make it a good starting point for the Quebrada de Humahuaca which stretches northwest from here. Properly referred to by locals by its full name, San Salvador de Jujuy (population 300,000) it sits at 1260 m in a bowl of lushly wooded mountains, 100 km north of Salta.

Jujuy was founded in 1593, between two rivers, the Río Grande and Chico, or Xibi Xibi, but it has sprawled south supporting a growing population on dwindling industry. Wars and earthquakes have left the city with few colonial buildings, but there's some fine architecture around its plaza and from the bridge over the Río Xibi Xibi, with its brightly coloured market stalls, you have wonderful views of the dramatic purple mountains, contrasting with the thick green vegetation that fills the river bed.

Although more chaotic than Salta, Jujuy has some lively bars where you can hear the region's wonderful *folclore* music, and its history is worth exploring, with two fine churches, a packed archaeological museum and a fabulous market. All this makes a good introduction to the province's rich indigenous culture and a handy base for exploring a variety of landscapes within easy reach. The region's most accessible cloudforest park, Calilegua, is just 125 km east of here.

Sights

If you arrive in the city by bus, you will be greeted by a perfectly typical example of the usual mayhem of *boleterías* (ticket offices) for myriad bus companies, crowds waiting with huge packages to be carried to remote parts of the *puna* and people selling balloon-like plastic bags of pink popped corn. To get into town from the bus station, walk along Dorrego/Lavalle, crossing the bridge across the thickly vegetated river bed where the city teems cheerfully with life, and you'll pass the fabulous fruit and vegetable market with delicious *empanadas* and stalls selling razors and peaches, tights and herbal cures, pan pipes and plimsols.

In the eastern part of the city is the tranquil **Plaza Belgrano**, a wide square planted with tall palms and lined with orange trees, with a striking equestrian statue of Belgrano at its centre. On the south side stands the **Casa de Gobierno** ① *daily 0800-2100*, a cream French-style neoclassical building built in 1927. Inside, you can see the very flag that Belgrano gave the city in recognition of their great sacrifice in a sumptuously decorated long

Essential Jujuy city

Finding your feet

Jujuy's airport, **El Cadillal**, is 32 km southeast of the capital. Minibuses run between the airport and the **Aerolíneas Argentinas** office in town (US12, 25 minutes); a taxi costs US$25-30. The **bus terminal** is six blocks south of the main street, Belgrano, over the river at Dorrego e Iguazú. See also Transport, page 294.

Getting around

The city is pleasant to walk around and is particularly interesting around the plaza, the market opposite the bus terminal, and on the bridges. The most interesting sights are within six blocks and could comfortably be visited in a day.

BACKGROUND

Jujuy city

Jujuy has an extraordinary history. The Spanish wanted to found a city to link the chain of settlements connecting Alto Perú with Córdoba but met extreme resistance from the indigenous people, who destroyed their first two attempts in 1561 and 1575. The city was finally established in 1593 and prospered until the 18th century, but the province of Jujuy bore the brunt of fighting during the Wars of Independence when the Spanish launched 11 invasions down the Quebrada de Humahuaca from Bolivia between 1810 and 1822. Then, in August 1812, General Belgrano, who was commander of the Republican troops, demanded an incredible sacrifice from Jujuy's people when he ordered the city to be evacuated and destroyed before the advancing Royalist army. The people obeyed his orders and left the city, which was razed to the ground. The citizens of Jujuy remain proud of this event, which is marked on 22-23 August by festivities known as El Exodo Jujeño, with gaucho processions and military parades. As a tribute to the city for obeying his orders, Belgrano donated the flag, which is displayed in the lavish Casa de Gobierno in Plaza Belgrano.

Jujuy has experienced growing poverty in recent years; its traditional industries – sugar and tobacco – suffered in the economic crisis, resulting in widespread unemployment. It's one of the few Argentine cities where the population is largely indigenous, boosted in the last 20 years by considerable immigration from Bolivia. You may well find bus journeys in the region delayed en route by peaceful demonstrations of *piqueteros* blocking the road, protesting about job and benefit cuts. Tourism is the main growth industry in the area as the city is slowly waking up to its huge natural asset: the incredible beauty on its doorstep.

hall with pleasing art nouveau statues representing Justice, Liberty, Peace and Progress, by the Argentine sculptor, Lola Mora.

On the west side of the plaza is the **cathedral**, whose neoclassical façade was built in the late 19th century to replace the early 17th-century original, which was destroyed by an earthquake. It contains an exquisite gold-plated wooden pulpit, carved by indigenous tribes in the Jesuit missions. Its elegant biblical illustrations are very moving and the delicate modelling of the dove overhead and of the angels' faces is stunning. It's one of Argentina's finest colonial treasures. There are also several fine 18th-century paintings. On the north side of the plaza is the **Cabildo**, built in 1867 and now occupied by the police, with a rather dull police museum inside.

The **Iglesia de San Francisco** ① *Belgrano and Lavalle, 2 blocks west of the plaza, daily 0730-1200 and 1700-2100*, is modern but has a calm interior and contains another fine gilded colonial pulpit, with ceramic angels around it, like that at Yavi (see page 299). There are well informed guides on hand. The **Iglesia de San Bárbara** (1777), San Martín and Lamadrid, is similar in style to the colonial churches in the Quebrada de Humahuaca.

The **Museo Arqueológico Provincial** ① *Lavalle 434, T0388-422315, Mon-Fri 0800-2000, US$1*, has some superb ceramics from the pre-Inca Yavi and Humahuaca cultures, and beautifully painted funerary urns, some containing the tiny bones of children. The museum may be underfunded and poorly displayed, but it's definitely worth visiting –

particularly for a fabulous 2500-year-old sculpture of a goddess giving birth and the rather gruesomely displayed mummified infant.

If you like military portraits, you could visit the **Museo Histórico Provincial Juan Galo Lavalle** ① *Lavalle 256, T0388-4221355, Mon-Fri 0800-2000, Sat-Sun 0900-1300, 1600-2000, US$0.50,* though it's pretty dry. A whole room is dedicated to the death of General Lavalle which occurred in this house, a turning point in the civil war between Federalists and Unitarists. There are also a couple of fine Cuzco-school paintings dating from 1650.

Around Jujuy city

Termas de Reyes ① *T0388-492 2522, www.termasdereyes.com, 1 hr by bus Etap (línea 1C) from bus terminal or corner of Gorriti and Urquiza,* is a thermal resort set among magnificent mountains. It has baths and a pool plus cabins with thermal water (open only to guests), plus various treatments; there are also packages from one to seven nights. See also Where to stay, below.

Listings Jujuy city *map page 292.*

Tourist information

For more information on travelling in and around Jujuy, see www.norteargentino.gov.ar (in English). A provincial government's website, with lots of information, is www.jujuy.gob.ar (in Spanish).

Tourist office

On the plaza at Gorriti 295 and Belgrano, T0388-422 1325, www.turismo.jujuy.gov.ar (also in English). Mon-Fri 0700-2200, Sat-Sun 0900-1300 and 1600-2200.
Has a helpful accommodation leaflet and a map, but little information about the rest of the province or transport.

Where to stay

All hotels will be fully booked for the festival of **El Exodo Jujeño**, 22-23 Aug: book ahead. For a complete listing with prices, see www.turismo.jujuy.gov.ar and www.welcomeargentina.com. See also www.munayhotel.com.ar.

$$$ El Arribo
Belgrano 1263, T0388-422 2539, www.elarribo.com.
Attractive, well located *posada* set in a restored colonial house with swimming pool, smiling staff. Highly recommended.

$$$ Gregorio I
Independencia 829, T0388-424 4747, www.gregoriohotel.com.
Wonderful, small boutique hotel with 20 rooms. Smart, modern style, with local art scattered throughout. Recommended.

$$ Sumay
Otero 232, T0388-423 5065, www.sumayhotel.com.ar.
Rather dark, but clean, very central, helpful staff.

$ pp Club Hostel
San Martín 132, 2½ blocks from plaza, T0388 423 7565, www.clubhosteljujuy.com.ar.
Dorms and doubles (**$$**); with jacuzzi, patio, lots of information, welcoming, has a good travel agency.

$ pp Hostal Casa de Barro
Otero 294, T0388-423 5581, www.casadebarro.com.ar.
Lovely double, triple and quadruple rooms from US$11 pp, whitewashed with simple decorations, shared bathrooms and a fantastic area for eating and relaxing. The wonderful staff provide dinner on demand. Highly recommended.

Around Jujuy city
Although there's plenty of accommodation in Jujuy itself, you might want to head out to

Termas de Reyes or Yala for a more relaxing experience within easy reach of the city.

$$$$-$$$ Hotel Termas de Reyes
Termas de Reyes, 19 km northwest of Jujuy, T0388-492 2522, www.termasdereyes.com. 1 hr by bus from Jujuy bus terminal, US$0.75.
This sumptuous thermal spa resort with a grand neoclassical hotel is set among magnificent mountains at an altitude of 1800 m. Rates include the use of the thermal pools. No children allowed.

$$$ La Escondida
Ejército del Norte s/n, T0388-15-682 2141, www.laescondidadeyala.com.ar.
This homestead is actually in the village of Yala, which is a great alternative (if you have car) to the bustle of Jujuy as it is only 14 km away. Minimum 2-night stay, lovely doubles, and also main homestead for rent (for up to 8), and 2 bungalows (for 2-5). Impressive swimming pool set in luscious gardens.

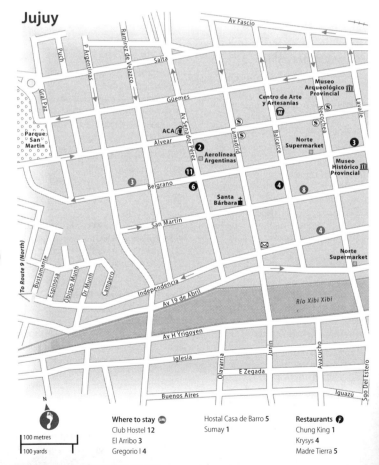

Jujuy

Where to stay
Club Hostel 12
El Arribo 3
Gregorio I 4
Hostal Casa de Barro 5
Sumay 1

Restaurants
Chung King 1
Krysys 4
Madre Tierra 5

100 metres
100 yards

$ pp Aldea Luna
Tilquiza, 20 km (1 hr) from Jujuy,
3 hrs from Salta, T0388-15-509 4602,
www.aldealuna.com.ar.
A new concept in hostelling, set in 900 ha
of lush rainforest, with native trees, rivers
and mountains in a natural reserve. The
accommodation is in solar-powered stone
cottages with bathrooms (yes, there's hot
water!). Shared cabin US$20 pp (discount
with 4-night stay), private room US$28 pp.
Spanish classes offered; volunteers welcome.

Call to arrange a pick up from Jujuy US$37 for
up to 4 people, or from Salta US$120 for up
to 4. In summer, the 4WD can't make it all the
way to the hostel, so you will have to walk
the remaining 1 km. All the food served is
vegetarian and breakfast and lunch or dinner
is included in the price.

Camping

$ pp El Refugio
R9, Km 14, Av Libertador 2327, Yala, T0388-
490 9344, www.elrefugiodeyala.com.ar.
This is the nearest campsite to the city in a
pretty spot on the banks of the river. There's
also a hostel, pool, restaurant, and trekking
and horse-riding excursions are on offer.
Highly recommended, a great place to relax.

Restaurants

There are lots of great places to eat in Jujuy.
Following Lavalle across the bridge to the
bus terminal (where it changes names to
Dorrego) there are lots of cheap places
selling *empanadas*.

$$$ Krysys
Balcarce 272.
Popular bistro-style *parrilla*, excellent steaks.

$$ Chung King
Alvear 627. Closed Sun.
Atmospheric, serving regional food for over
60 years; with pizzeria at No 631.

$$ Manos Jujeñas
Senador Pérez 381, see Facebook.
Tue-Sun 1200-1500, 2000-2330.
Regional specialities, the best *humitas*,
charming, good for the *peña* at weekends.

$$ Ruta 9
Belgrano 743 and Costa Rica 968.
Great places for regional dishes such as *locro*
and *tamales*, also a few Bolivian dishes.

$ Madre Tierra
Belgrano 619, see Facebook.
Mon-Sat 0700-1500, 1600-2230.

To Parque Nacional Calilegua

Former Railway Station

Av Urquiza

Savoy

Sarmiento

Gorriti

Cabildo

Belgrano

San Francisco

Cathedral

Plaza Belgrano

Paseo de las Artesanías

Otero

Casa de Gobierno

Argañaraz

To 12

6

Av H Yrigoyen

J Newbery

Rep. de Siria

Rep. del Libano

M Gorriti

Mercado Municipal

Campero

Urdininea

Leandro N Alem

Dorrego

L De La Torre

To Airport & RN9

To 7

Manos Jujeñas 2
Ruta 9 3
Sociedad Española 6
Tío Bigote 11

Bars & clubs
La Casa de Jeremías 7
Salamanka 8

Vegetarian café, behind a wholemeal bakery, delicious food.

$ Sociedad Española
Belgrano y Senador Pérez. Closed Sun.
Good cheap set menus with a Spanish flavour.

$ Tío Bigote
Senador Pérez y Belgrano, see Facebook. Closed Sun.
Very popular café and pizzeria.

Bars and clubs

Head for a *peña* to hear the region's passionate *folclore* music played live. All have live music and dancing at weekends, and during the week in busy holiday periods.

Popular options include **La Casa de Jeremías** (Horacio Guzmán 306, T0388-424 3531, see Facebook); and **Salamanka** (San Martín 889, see Facebook), which has resident and guest DJs, and good cocktails.

Shopping

Food
You can't beat the colourful **Municipal market** (Dorrego y Alem), near the bus terminal. Outside it, women sell home-baked *empanadas* and *tamales*, and delicious goat's cheese, as well as all kinds of herbal cures. There is a **Norte** supermarket (Belgrano 823), and a bigger branch at 19 de Abril y Necochea.

Handicrafts
Handicrafts are sold from stalls on Plaza Belgrano near the cathedral and from **Paseo de las Artesanías**, on the west side of the plaza.

What to do

Tour operators offer full-day trips from Jujuy into the *puna* and the Quebrada de Humahuaca, but if you have the time it's far better to take at least a couple of days to explore both areas properly. Jujuy is also the starting point for the cloudforest park of

Calilegua, by bus via Libertador General San Martín (see Transport, below).
Noroeste, *San Martín 155, T0388-423 7565, www.noroestevirtual.com.ar.* Trips to Quebrada de Humahuaca, salt flats, the *puna*. Also offer adventure tourism. Located at **Club Hostel** (see Where to stay, above). Recommended.

Transport

Air
Airport, T0388-491 1102. Flights to **Buenos Aires,** and **Córdoba** with **Aerolíneas Argentinas**, San Martín 96, T0388-422 2575.

Bus
Long distance The bus terminal (T0388-422 1375) serves the whole province, including all destinations north of the city and border towns with Bolivia, as well as south to **Salta** (2 hrs) and from there to most major destinations. There are direct overnight buses to **Buenos Aires** taking at least 21 hrs.

Several companies run buses almost hourly up the Quebrada de Humahuaca. To **Humahuaca**, US$5.50, 2½ hrs, several daily with **Balut**, via Tilcara 1½ hrs, US$3.50. To **Purmamarca**, take buses to Susques or to Humahuaca but check they call at Purmamarca village, off the main road. To **Susques**, **Purmamarca** and **Andes Bus**, US$10-12, 4-6½ hrs, Tue-Sun. To the Bolivian border at **La Quiaca**, 5-6 hrs, US$12, with **Balut and Panamericano**; several rigorous luggage checks en route for drugs, including coca leaves. To **Iruya** with **Panamericano de Jujuy**, US$10.50, daily at 0615

To **Salta**, hourly, 2 hrs, US$11. El Rápido, Andesmar and La Veloz del Norte to **Tucumán**, 6 hrs, US$29, and **Córdoba**, 15-16 hrs, US$79-105. To **Buenos Aires**, several daily, 21-24 hrs, US$116-139, with **Flecha Bus; La Veloz del Norte; Balut**.

To **Orán** and **Aguas Blancas** (border with Bolivia), US$14-24, daily with **Balut, Flecha Bus and La Veloz del Norte**, via San Pedro. To **Calilegua**: various companies to Libertador Gral San Martín almost every hour (eg **Balut**, US$4.50); from there take **Empresa 23 de Agosto** or **Empresa 24 de Setiembre**, leaving 0830, to **Valle Grande**, across Parque Nacional Calilegua. All **Pocitos** or **Orán** buses pass through **Libertador Gral San Martín**.

To Chile: the route via the **Jama** pass (4400 m) is taken by most traffic crossing to northern Chile, including trucks; hours 0800-2300. **Géminis** bus tickets sold at

Paisajes del Noroeste, San Martín 134, www.paisajesdelnoroeste.tur.ar.

Car hire
At the airport: **Earth Rent a Car**, T0388-491 2734; **Hertz**, T0387-424 0113, www.hertzargentina.com.ar. In town: **Sudamerics**, Belgrano 601, T0388-422 9034, www.sudamerics.com.

★ Quebrada de Humahuaca

the highlight of Jujuy Province

Since it was declared a World Heritage Site by UNESCO in 2003, the Quebrada de Humahuaca has attracted a deluge of visitors. However, while a couple of its main towns are being transformed beyond recognition by tourism, much of the area retains its ancient authentic indigenous culture.

The main route north from Jujuy city to the Bolivian border is one of the most dramatic areas of natural beauty in the country, passing through a long gorge of intensely coloured rock strata and arid mountains speckled with giant cacti. In the fertile valley floor of the Quebrada are several small historic towns, some with their neat adobe houses now mingled with modern new developments, but all centred on the characteristic squat, white 18th-century churches of the region. Tilcara is probably the best base for exploring the area, with lots of good accommodation, a lively market, a museum and the Pucará, a ruined pre-Incan fortress. Further north, Humahuaca is popular and friendly, and provides access to remote border region in the far north of the province.

Purmamarca *Colour map 1, A3.*
The first village you come to in the Quebrada, just off Ruta Nacional 9 at Km 61, is Purmamarca (population 2100, altitude 2200 m), a perfect place to rest and acclimatize to the altitude. It's a tiny, peaceful, slightly expensive village with a choice of comfortable places to stay and a stunning setting at the foot of the Cerro de los Siete Colores – a mountain striped

Essential Quebrada de Humahuaca

Getting around

Starting at the city of Jujuy, Route 9 heads north through the Quebrada to the Bolivian border. Public transport is easy to use. A number of bus companies go up and down the Quebrada from Jujuy to Humahuaca, stopping at Purmamarca, Tilcara, Maimará and Uquía. **El Quiaqueño**, **Panamericano** and **Balut** go all the way to La Quiaca on the Bolivian border.

If driving, fuel is available at Jujuy, Tilcara, Humahuaca, Abra Pampa and La Quiaca, so you might need to take a spare can if you're heading far into rural areas.

It's a good area for cycling, preferably away from the Ruta Nacional 9 where there can be a lot of traffic through the valley and there's not much shade. See also Transport, page 304.

Information

See www.turismo.jujuy.gov.ar and www.norteargentino.gov.ar.

with at least seven colours, from creamy pink to burgundy and copper to green. Once the steady trickle of tour buses has left, Purmamarca resumes its own quiet rhythm of life. There's a good market on the plaza, selling a mixture of locally made llama wool goods, but lots of alpaca spoons and weavings are imported from Bolivia.

At the top of the plaza, there's a beautiful church, **Iglesia de Santa Rosa** (1648, rebuilt in 1778), typical of those you'll see elsewhere in the Quebrada, with its squat tower, whitewashed adobe walls and simple, well-balanced construction. Inside there's a splendid time-darkened cactus roof and pulpit, and a series of exquisite paintings depicting the life of Santa Rosa. Next to the church is an algarrobo tree thought to be 500 years old.

Maimará

About 12 km from Purmamarca at Km 75, Maimará (population 5000, altitude 2383 m) is a lovely, tranquil oasis village. Its green fields of onion and garlic are set in contrast with the backdrop of richly coloured marbled rock, known as La Paleta del Pintor, to the east of the village. For an enjoyable walk in the low evening light, when the colours of the rock are at their warmest, walk along the old road to the east of Maimará; take your camera. Just off the road, 3 km south, is **La Posta de Hornillos** ⓘ *open, in theory, Wed-Mon 0830-1800, free*, one of the chain of colonial posting houses that used to extend from Buenos Aires to Lima. It was the scene of several battles and is where Belgrano stayed. Now restored, the building houses a historical **museum** with a collection of 18th- and 19th-century furniture, as well as weapons and historical documents. North of Maimará there's a huge cemetery on the hillside, brightly decorated with paper flowers at Easter.

Tilcara *Colour map 1, A3.*

Tilcara (population 11,000, altitude 2461 m) lies 22 km north of Purmamarca at Km 84. It's the liveliest Quebrada village and the best base for exploring the area, with plenty of places to stay and to eat. There's an excellent handicrafts market around its pleasant plaza, though lots of the goods are mass produced in Bolivia. For fine local weavings, visit the women's weaving co-operative, **La Flor del Cardón**, next to the **tourist office** ⓘ *Belgrano 590 (a new tourist office is being constructed at the entrance to the town but at the time of writing was not finished), T0388-495 5720, www.tilcara.com.ar, 0900-1200, 1500-2000,* which has very helpful staff. Useful websites include www.tilcarajujuy.com.ar (in Spanish).

Tilcara was the site of an important pre-Hispanic settlement, and you can visit the **Pucará** ⓘ *daily 0900-1800, US$3.75 including entry to the museum (below),* a restored hilltop fortress above the town. There are panoramic views of the gorge from its complex web of low-walled dwellings, made more splendid by mighty cacti. To get there, turn right off Belgrano where signposted; head up the hill and across the metal bridge over the Río Huasamayo. At the entrance to the Pucará, there's also a small handicrafts shop where you can get helpful information, and a small botanical garden with many species of cactus. On the plaza is a superb **Museo Arqueológico** ⓘ *Belgrano 445, daily 0900-1800, US$4 including entry to Pucará and the Jardín Botánico,* with a fine collection of pre-Columbian ceramics, masks and mummies. There are four art museums in town, of which **Museo Regional de Pintura (Museo Terry)** ⓘ *Rivadavia 352, Tue-Sat 0900-1800, Sun 0900-1200 and 1400-1800,* is worth a look, with paintings on the customs and traditions of Tilcara.

There are fiestas in Tilcara throughout the extended Carnival period, but the Easter celebrations are justifiably famous; see Festivals, page 303.

Huacalera and Uquía *Colour map 1, A3.*

Huacalera lies 2 km north of the Tropic of Capricorn; a sundial 20 m west of the road marks the exact location. The church, several times restored, has a roof made of cactus wood and a small museum. **Uquía** is one of the smaller villages along the Quebrada and is totally un-touristy with a tranquil atmosphere and a narrow main street of adobe houses. However, it also has one of the valley's finest churches, whose beautifully proportioned white tower is very striking against the deep red rock of the mountain behind. Built in 1691, **Iglesia San Francisco de Paula** contains an extraordinary collection of Cuzqueño-style paintings of angels in 17th-century battle dress, the *ángeles arcabuceros*. Painted by local indigenous artists under the tuition of Jesuits, the combination of tenderness and swagger in these winged figures, brandishing their weapons, is astonishing.

Humahuaca and around *Colour map 1, A3.*

Although Humahuaca (population 11,300, altitude 2940 m) was founded in 1591 on the site of a pre-Hispanic settlement, it was almost entirely rebuilt in the mid-19th century. It is a labyrinth of narrow streets, with low adobe houses around a small central plaza. Despite being the most popular tourist destination for Argentines along the Quebrada, it retains its own culture. Accommodation here is more limited than at Tilcara, but once the coach trips have left, it's quiet and is a useful stopping point for travelling north up to the *puna*, or to Iruya. The bus terminal has toilets and a *confitería*, and there are fruit and sandwich sellers outside.

On the tiny plaza is the church, **La Candelaria**, originally constructed in 1631, rebuilt 1873-1880, containing wonderfully gaudy gold *retablos* and 12 fine Cuzqueño-school paintings. Every day at 1200, tourists gather outside **El Cabildo**, the neocolonial town hall on the plaza, to watch a large mechanical figure of San Francisco Solano emerge to bless the town from his alcove high in the wall. You may find this kitsch rather than spiritually uplifting, but it's quite a sight. Overlooking the town and surrounded by fantastically large cacti is the **Monumento a la Independencia Argentina**, commemorating the scene of the heaviest fighting in the country during the Wars of Independence. There is a good *feria artesanal* on Avenida San Martín (on the far side of the railway line) and a fruit market at Tucumán and Belgrano.

About 10 km northeast of Humahuaca, near **Coctaca**, there's an impressive and extensive (40 ha) series of pre-colonial agricultural terraces – the largest archaeological site in Jujuy, though you'll have to go with a guide to find them. Contact **Ser Andino** ① *Jujuy 393, Humahuaca, T03887-421659, www.serandino.com.ar*, who offers two- to three-hour tours to Coctaca from Humahuaca, US$17.50 per person. Ask the tourist office about trips over the mountains to enter **Parque Nacional Calilegua** (see page 308), via the beautifully situated little hamlet of Abra Zenta.

★ Iruya *Colour map 1, A3.*

Highly recommended is a night or two at least in the peaceful hamlet of Iruya (population 5500), reached by a breathtaking (or hair-raising) three-hour bus ride. Twenty-five kilometres north of Humahuaca, a rough *ripio* road turns northeast off the Ruta Nacional 9, 8 km to Iturbe (also called Hipólito Irigoyen). The bus stops here for five minutes, giving you a chance to glimpse captivating rural life and perhaps buy a woven hat from women waiting by the bus stop. There are no facilities. The road then crosses the broad river (manageable in an ordinary car only if it hasn't rained heavily) and climbs up over the 4000-m pass, Abra del Cóndor, where you have panoramic views,

BORDER CROSSING

Argentina–Bolivia

La Quiaca

The border bridge is 10 blocks from La Quiaca bus terminal (15 minutes' walk, taxi US$2). **Argentine customs and immigration** The office is open 0700-2400. If leaving Argentina for a short stroll into Villazón (not really advised), show your passport, but do not let it be stamped by Migración, otherwise you will have to wait 24 hours before being allowed back into Argentina. Formalities on entering Argentina are usually very brief at the border but thorough customs searches are made 100 km south at Tres Cruces. Leaving Argentina is very straightforward, but travellers who need a visa to enter Bolivia (check with your embassy) are advised to get it before arriving in La Quiaca. The Bolivian consulate in La Quiaca is at 9 de Julio 100 y República Arabe Siria, T03885-422283, colivianlaquiaca@yahoo.com.ar, Monday-Friday 0700-1830 (in theory). **Transport** There are multiple buses a day from Jujuy to La Quiaca (stopping at most bigger villages in the Quebrada de Humahuaca), five to six hours, US$9, three hours from Tilcara. The bus terminal in La Quiaca, at España and Belgrano, has luggage storage available. If your bus arrives in the early morning when no restaurants are open and it is freezing cold outside, wrap up warm and stay in the terminal until daylight as the streets are unsafe in the dark.

Villazón

This is a grim place, little more than the centre of commercial activity in an otherwise remote and uninhabited area. The road from the border bridge, Avenida República de Argentina, is lined with shops and stalls selling sandals, toys, sunglasses, paper flowers, sacks of pink puffed corn and armfuls of coca leaves. Women in traditional Bolivian dress, with their enormous skirts (*cholitas*), spin wool and weave vividly coloured textiles on the pavement, and there's plenty of fresh orange juice and cheap ice cream for sale. However, there's nowhere decent to stay and no tourist information. The bus station has toilets, but they aren't pretty.

Note Argentina time is one hour ahead of Bolivia, two hours when Buenos Aires adopts daylight saving. Remember not to photograph the border area. See www.gendarmeria.gov.ar/pasos-bolivia/la-quiaca.html (in Spanish).

before dropping steeply, around an amazing slalom of many hairpin bends, into the Quebrada de Iruya.

Iruya is an idyllic small town tucked into a steep hillside, remote and hidden away, but full of warm and friendly inhabitants. In recent years, its character has started to change due to the influx of wealthier tourists staying at the *hostería* at the top of the town.

It's worth spending a few days here to lap up the tranquil atmosphere, and to go horse riding or walking in the beautiful valleys nearby. The hike to the even more remote hamlet of **San Isidro** (seven hours return) is unforgettable. At **Titiconte**, 4 km away, there are some unrestored pre Inca ruins, though you'll need to take a guide to find them. Iruya has a *locutorio* and food shops. Wander up the tiny narrow main street to find a post office, a shop selling wonderful herbal teas of all kinds and dried peaches from a local co-operative, and another selling superb woven and knitted goods. Not to be missed.

La Quiaca and into Bolivia *Colour map 1, A2.*

La Quiaca (population 25,000, altitude 3442 m) lies on the border with Bolivia, linked by a concrete bridge to **Villazón** on the Bolivian side. Neither town is appealing, but if you have to stay the night, La Quiaca is definitely preferable: there are a few decent places to stay, and if you're around here on the third weekend in October, you can see the three-day **Fiesta de la Olla**. For information on the border crossing, see box, opposite, and Transport, below.

Yavi and around *Colour map 1, A3.*

Yavi is 16 km from La Quiaca but no buses go there. A remise taxi from La Quiaca costs US$2 one way.

By far the best place to stay around here is actually in Yavi, 16 km east, which has a couple of good *hosterías*. Yavi is an intriguing *puna* village, consisting of little more than a few streets of uniformly brown adobe dwellings, most often deserted, but it has a beguiling, hidden quality. It was founded in 1667 and was the crossing point to Bolivia until rail and road connections were built through La Quiaca. The surrounding landscape is wide open, with the distinctive swooping stratified hills of the Siete Hermanos to the east. These have long been an important landmark and their stark beauty immediately catches your attention, even before you stumble across the prehistoric petroglyphs on the rocks at the foot of the hills. Ask at **Hostal de Yavi** for a tour, see page 302.

Yavi also has perhaps the finest church in the northwest, well worth the detour from La Quiaca. The **Iglesia de Nuestra Señora del Rosario y San Francisco** ① *Mon 1500-1800, Tue-Fri 0900-1200, 1500-1800, Sat-Sun 0900-1200*, was built in 1676-1690, a sturdy, white construction with buttresses and a single tower. Inside are the most magnificent gold *retablo* and pulpit, made by artisans who were brought, like the gold, from Peru. The *retablo* is adorned with a gold sculpture of an angel in 18th-century battle dress (like a three dimensional version of the paintings of Uquía) and the tabernacle is lined with mirrors to make candlelight within glow like the sun. Above the exquisite pulpit, decorated with ceramic cherubs, flies a golden dove. All this splendour is seen in the yellowy light from windows made of transparent onyx, giving the beautiful Cuzqueño paintings even more power. It's an impressive and moving sight.

Opposite the church is the 18th-century **Casa del Marqués Campero y Tojo** ① *Mon-Fri 0900-1200, 1400-1700, Sat 0900-1200*, the austere former mansion of the family that was were granted large parts of the *puna* by Philip V of Spain. It's an imposing building with empty courtyards, whose one-room museum houses a strange and eclectic collection of 18th-century bedsprings, arrowheads and candelabras. There's a small but excellent selection of handicrafts for sale inside, and some nicely carved local slate with petroglyphs on a stall outside. There is a colourful evening procession during Easter week.

For a really marvellous experience of the wild beauty and isolation of this region, make time to visit the remote town of **Nazareno**, a four-hour drive east of La Quiaca. The road crosses astonishingly bold rolling hills, before climbing and then dropping thousands of metres to find Nazareno nestled in a crown of vermillion mountains. There are some wonderful walks along old Inca roads to Cuesta Azul and to Milagro. Accommodation is with local families; the hospitality is warm and the landscapes are unforgettable. If you speak Spanish and can chat to the people living here, you'll be able to get a real taste of fascinating Andean culture.

Tourist information

Purmamarca

Tourist office
On the plaza, T0388-490 8443.
Open 0700-1800.
Tiny, helpful office which can provide
maps, information on accommodation
and bus tickets.

Humahuaca

Tourist office
Tucumán and Jujuy.
Small but helpful office on the plaza in the
lovely white Cabildo building. Ask for a map
of the area; as they are underfunded and
have no resources they will ask you to make
a small donation, but it is worth it as the map
can be very helpful.

Iruya

Tourist office
C San Martín. Open irregular hours.
See also www.iruyaonline.com (in Spanish).

Where to stay

Purmamarca

$$$$ El Manantial del Silencio
Ruta 52 Km 3.5, T0388-490 8080,
www.hotelmanantialdelsilencio.com.
Signposted from the road into Purmamarca.
Luxurious rooms, modern building, wonderful
views, spacious living rooms with huge fire,
charming hosts, includes breakfast, heating,
riding, pool, superb restaurant (guests only).

$$$ Casa de Piedra
Pantaleon Cruz 6, T0388-490 8092,
www.postadelsol.com.
Well-situated hotel made of stone and
adobe with very comfortable rooms.

$$$ La Posta
C Santa Rosa de Lima 4 blocks
up from plaza, T0388-490 8029,
www.postadepurmamarca.com.ar.
Beautiful setting by the mountain,
comfortable rooms, helpful owner.
Highly recommended.

$$ El Viejo Algarrobo
C Salta behind the church, T0388-490 8286,
www.hosteriaelviejoalgarrobo.com.
Small but pleasant rooms, cheaper with
shared bath, helpful, good value and quality
regional dishes in its restaurant ($).

$ El Pequeño Inti
C Florida 10 m from plaza, T0388-490 8089.
Small, modern rooms around a little
courtyard, breakfast, hot water, good value.
Recommended.

Maimará

$$$ La Casa del Tata
Belgrano s/n, T0388-499 7389,
www.lacasadeltata.com.ar.
Nicely decorated and welcoming *hostería*
serving great breakfasts which include
home-baked pastries. Rooms have cable TV
and good bathrooms with hot water. They
also serve a fantastic afternoon tea with
several varieties of cakes.

$$$ Posta del Sol
Martín Rodríguez y San Martín, T0388-
499 7156, www.postadelsol.com.
Comfortable *hostería* with a good
restaurant. The owner, a tourist guide,
can take you on a tour of the area and
has helpful information.

Tilcara

Book ahead during carnival and around
Easter when Tilcara is very busy. All those
listed are recommended.

$$$ Alas de Alma
Dr Padilla 437, T0388-495 5572,
www.alas.travel.
Central, relaxed atmosphere, spacious
doubles, and *cabañas* for up to 4 people.
2 mins from the main street.

$$$ Posada con los Angeles
Gorriti 156 (signposted from
access to town), T0388-495 5153,
www.posadaconlosangeles.com.ar.
A much-recommended favourite with
charming rooms, each in a different colour,
all with fireplace and door to the garden
with beautiful views.

$$$ Quinta La Paceña
Padilla 660 at Ambrosetti, T0388-495 5098,
www.quintalapacena.com.ar.
This architect-designed traditional adobe
house is a peaceful haven. The garden is
gorgeous and wonderfully kept.

$ Casa los Molles
Belgrano 155, T0388-495 5410,
www.casalosmolles.com.ar.
Not really a hostel, this affordable *casa de
campo* offers simple dorms in a friendly
atmosphere (US$10 pp), as well as a
charming double ($) and 2 comfortable
cabañas ($$ for up to 4 people). Small
and central, book in advance.

$ pp Malka
San Martín s/n, 5 blocks from plaza
up steep hill, T0388-495 5197,
www.malkahostel.com.ar.
A superb youth hostel, one of the country's
best. It has beautifully situated rustic *cabañas*
($$$ up to 8), dorms for 5 people, US$20 pp,
and doubles with bath ($$$). Catch a taxi
from town or walk for 20 mins.

$ Tilcara Hostel
Bolívar 166, T0388-15 585 5994,
see Facebook.
This hostel is welcoming with dorms
at US$8 pp. Also offer doubles and
comfortable cabins ($$).

Camping

Camping El Jardín
Access on Belgrano 700, T0388-15 484 9931,
www.eljardintilcara.com.ar.
Hot showers, also hotel and basic hostel.

Huacalera and Uquía

$$$ Solar del Trópico
T0388-154 785021, www.solardeltropico.com.
2 km from Huacalera.
Argentine/French-owned B&B offering
fusion food on request. Rustic, spacious
bedrooms, organic gardens, artist's studio;
workshops are run regularly. Tours offered.
Call to arrange a pickup beforehand.

Humahuaca and around
See also www.munayhotel.com.ar.

$$$$-$$$ Hotel Huacalera
Ruta 9 km 1790, T0388-15 581 3417,
www.hotelhuacalera.com.
Upscale resort in the *puna* offering colourful
rooms with terraces, spa, swimming pool
and nature excursions.

$$ Hostal Azul
B Medalla Milagrosa, La Banda,
T0388-421107.
Across the river, smart, welcoming, pleasant,
simple rooms, good restaurant and wine list,
parking. Recommended.

$ pp Posada El Sol
Medalla milagrosa s/n over bridge
from terminal, then 520 m, follow signs,
T0388-421466.
Quiet rural area, shared rooms or private ($$)
in a warm welcoming place, laundry, horse
riding, owner will collect from bus station if
called in advance. Recommended.

Iruya

$$$ Hostería de Iruya
San Martín 641, T03887-15 533 8482,
www.hoteliruya.com.
A special place, extremely comfortable,
with good food, and great views from the
top of the village. Highly recommended.

$$$-$$ Mirador de Iruya
La Banda s/n, T03887-427123,
www.elmiradordeiruya.com.ar.
Cross the river and climb a little to this
hostal. Doubles, triples and quads available.
Fantastic views from the terrace.

$ Hospedaje Asunta
Belgrano s/n (up the hill),
T0387-154 045113.
Friendly hostel with 28 beds. Fantastic views.
Recommended.

La Quiaca and into Bolivia

$$ Munay
Belgrano 51-61, T03885-423924,
www.munayhotel.com.ar.
In same group as Munay in Salta, rooms
with heating and fan, parking.

$ Hostel Copacabana
Pellegrini 141, T03885-423875,
www.hostelcopacabana.com.ar.
Only a few blocks from the bus terminal
and the plaza. Clean dorms and doubles
and comfortable living areas.

Camping

Camping Municipal
R5, on the route to Yavi, T03885-422645.
Very basic facilities and quite a way out
of town.

Yavi and around

$$ Hostal de Yavi
Güemes 222, www.hostaldeyavi.
blogspot.com.
Simple bedrooms with bath, and some
hostel space. Cosy sitting room, good food.

Tours also arranged: to see cave paintings;
moonlight walks; trekking; and trips to the
Laguna de los Pozuelos. Recommended.

$ La Casona
Senador Pérez y San Martín, T03887-422316.
Welcoming, with and without bath, breakfast.

Restaurants

Purmamarca

$$ El Rincón de Claudia Vilte
Libertad s/n, T0388-490 8088.
Folclore music and regional dishes served
at this pretty restaurant 1 block from the
main plaza.

$ La Posta
Rivadavia s/n, on the plaza,
www.restaurantelaposta.com.ar.
Excellent local dishes; the *humitas* and
tamales are especially recommended.
Touristy, but the service and the food are
good. A small handicrafts shop next door
sells high-quality goods.

Tilcara

$$ El Patio
Lavalle 352, T0388-495 5044.
Great range, lovely patio at the back,
popular, very good.

$ CApEC (Bar del Centro)
Belgrano 547, T0388-495 5318, see Facebook.
Small restaurant/café serving local dishes
in the patio. Not always open. Both the
restaurant and crafts shop next door sustain
an NGO that organizes free art and music
workshops for local children.

Humahuaca and around

$$-$ El Portillo
Tucumán 69, T0387-421288.
A simply decorated room, serves slightly
more elaborate regional meals than the
usual, such as llama with a fine plum sauce.

$$-$ La Cacharpaya
Jujuy 317, T0387-421016.

This brightly lit, large place lacks sophistication, but it's central and the food is good. Attracts an interesting mix of clientele.

Iruya

All hotels have their own restaurant, see Where to stay, above. They all serve regional meals (*locro, empanadas, humita, tamales*).
Hostal Federico Tercero (on the plaza at the bottom of the hill) is the most welcoming place to hang out, but the most sophisticated and elegant place to eat is the pricey **Hostería de Iruya** (at the top of the town).

$ Comedor Iruya
Lavalle and San Martín.
Basic but tasty menu serving local cuisine.

$ Comedor Margarita
Near the plaza.
Good home-made food and a menu that changes daily. The *menú del día* is always good.

La Quiaca and into Bolivia

$ Frontera
Belgrano and Siria, T03885-422269.
An atmospheric place, with a generous set menu.

Tilcara

El Cafecito de Tukuta
Rivadavia s/n, on the plaza, see Facebook.
Serves good coffee and wonderful locally grown herbal teas during the day, and has superb live *folclore* music at weekends (in season) from celebrated local musicians.

Lapeña de Carlitos
Lavalle 397, on the plaza, see Facebook.
Regional music from the charismatic and delightful Carlitos, also cheap meal-of-the-day, *empanadas* and drinks. A selection of all the typical music of the area, with bits of history and culture thrown in. Recommended.

Tilcara
Mar/Apr Easter on Holy Thursday night a gathering of thousands of pan pipe musicians follow the procession of the Virgin de Copacabana down the mountain into the town. It's an extraordinary, noisy and moving event. Book accommodation well in advance.

Humahuaca
2 Feb La Candelaria festival. Carnival is famously lively with **Jueves de Comadres**, and **Festival de las Coplas y de la Chicha**, when everyone throws flour and water at each other and gets very drunk. Book accommodation ahead.

Iruya
Mar/Apr Easter, a lively festival, when accommodation is booked up in advance.
1st Sun in Oct Rosario festival, a colourful fiesta.

La Quiaca
3rd week of Oct Fiesta de la Olla, when villagers from the far reaches of the remote *puna* arrive on donkeys and in pickups to sell their ceramic pots, sheepskins and vegetables during a colourful festival that involves a lot of dancing and drinking *chichi*.

Tilcara
Caravana de Llamas, *Alverro and Ambrosetti, T0388-15-408 8000, www.caravanadellamas. com.ar.* Hiking into the mountains while llamas carry your belongings, reviving the ancient tradition. Explore magnificent mountain landscapes, half- to 3-day trips departing daily.
Cerro Morado, *T0388-495 5117, branchesi_ guia@yahoo.com.ar.* Oscar Branchesi will take you to meet locals, giving you great insight into indigenous culture. Recommended.

Iruy
For local guides (walking and mules) in the surrounding area, ask at the **tourist office** (T03887-482001, www.iruyaonline.com). If you're short of time, however, it's probably a good idea to contract a guide in Humahuaca or Salta; **Norte Trekking** (T0387-431 6616, www.nortetrekking.com, based in Salta), is highly recommended.

Transport

Purmamarca
Buses to **Jujuy**, 1½ hrs, US$3.50 with **Empresa Evlia** (T0388-490 8141); to **Tilcara**, US$1. Buses between Salta and San Pedro de Atacama can also be boarded here.

Tilcara
Balut bus to **Jujuy**, multiple daily, US$3.50, 1½-2 hrs; to **La Quiaca** daily with **Balut**, 40-50 mins, US$2. **Jama Bus** runs between Tilcara, Humahuaca and La Quiaca.

Humahuaca and around
Buses to all places along the Quebrada depart from the terminal. To **Jujuy** with **Panamericano de Jujuy**, US$10.50 daily at 1400. To **Iruya**, Iruya SA, daily 0820, 1030 and Sun-Fri also 1600, 3-3½ hrs, US$5 one

way. To **La Quiaca**, with **Balut**, several daily, 2½ hrs, US$7.

Iruya
Tickets are available from the bus station (ticket office open 0800-1230 and1500-2100 and from the food shop round the corner from the church. Buses stop outside **Hostal de Gloria**.

To **Humahuaca**, Iruya SA, daily 1300, 1600 (also 0600 bus Mon and Sat), 3-3½ hrs, US$5.

La Quiaca and into Bolivia
Bus
There are several buses a day to **Salta**, US$19, 7½ hrs, with **Balut** and others. To **Humahuaca**, with **Balut** (more comfortable), several daily, 2½ hrs, US$7. To **Jujuy**, with **Balut**, 5-6 hrs, US$12. Take your own food, as there are sometimes long delays. Buses are stopped for routine border police controls and rigorous searches for drugs. To **Buenos Aires** (via Jujuy), 26-28 hrs with **La Veloz del Norte**, US$100-115, including meals. **Andes Norte** links several villages west of R9, including **Santa Catalina**, Mon-Fri.

Remise taxis
Remiseria Acuario, España y 25 de Mayo, s/n, T03885-423333. You can take a *remise* taxi to Yavi for US$2 each way.

Puna Jujeña
spectacularly remote and bleak place with few settlements

The Puna Jujeña (3700 m, Km 213) covers all the area to the west of the Quebrada de Humahuaca. It has extraordinary salt flats, lakes full of birdlife and plenty of history to be explored. If you have time it's definitely worth spending a few days in the area.

The *puna* is high altitude (between 3000 and 4000 m) and it's an inhospitable area to travel alone, so although you could hire a 4WD vehicle and be independent, consider trips with adventure travel company **Socompa** ⓘ *www.socompa.com*, which enable you to explore the *puna* in the company of expert guides without having to worry about the many practicalities.

There are two main areas to explore. **Salinas Grandes** and **Susques** can be reached either from San Antonio de los Cobres in Salta, or from Purmamarca in the Quebrada de Humahuaca. The second area, in the far north, is the **Monumento Natural Laguna**

BORDER CROSSING
Argentina–Chile

Paso de Jama

The border (4200 m) is open 0900-1800 and is 360 km west of Jujuy, reached by a 60-km road that branches off Route 70. This is the route taken by most passenger and truck traffic from Salta or Jujuy to San Pedro de Atacama. There is a car park, toilets and phone services but no money exchange. **Note** Even in summer it can drop to -5°C at night. See www.gendarmeria.gov.ar/pasos.

Argentine customs and immigration At Susques. On the Chilean side the road continues (unpaved) to San Pedro de Atacama (Km 514), where fuel and accommodation are available, and Calama.

Chilean immigration At San Pedro de Atacama.

de los Pozuelos, reached by turning west from Abra Pampa. You could do one round trip (now offered by **Movitrack** and other tour companies), setting off from Salta, climbing the Quebrada del Toro to San Antonio de los Cobres, and reaching the Salinas Grandes (Ruta 40), before descending via the spectacular **Cuesta de Lipán** (Route 52) to Purmamarca in the Quebrada de Humahuaca. See also Salta, What to do, page 278.

Susques and Salinas Grandes *Colour map 1, A2.*

The main crossing to Chile is via Route 52 which links Purmamarca and the Salinas with the little village of **Susques**, and on to the **Paso de Jama** (see box, above) over the awesome Abra Potrerillos pass (4170 m). Susques is the only settlement between Purmamarca and the border, lying in a hollow at the meeting of the Río Susques and Río Pastos Chicos. It has a stunning little church, dating from 1598, and one of the outstanding examples of colonial architecture in the region, with a roof of cactus-wood and thatch. Inside is an old bellows-organ. There are regular buses from Jujuy, with Andes Bus and Purmamarca (four to six hours), but it's best to hire a car or join a tour. There are a few basic places to stay and eat in Susques, see Where to stay, below.

The salt flats of Salinas Grandes are astonishing: a seemingly endless, perfectly flat expanse of white, patterned with eruptions of salt around regular shapes, like some kind of crazy paving. Against the perfectly blue sky, the light is dazzling. It's safe to walk or drive onto the surface, and you'll find men mining salt, creating neat oblong pools of turquoise water where salt has been cut away, and stacking up piles of white and brown salt blocks, ready for refining.

Casabindo *Colour map 1, A3.*

Heading north from Susques on Route 11, you'll reach the tiny hamlet of Casabindo (3500 m), founded in 1602. It can also be approached by travelling 63 km southwest from Abra Pampa – quite a trip over the *puna*. There's a magnificent church, one of the finest in the whole region, with twin towers dating from 1772. It's beautifully proportioned and contains a superb series of 16th-century paintings of *ángeles arcabuceros* (archangels in military uniforms) like those at Uquía. It's worth trying to visit on 15 August, when there's a lively celebration of **La Ascensión de la Virgen**, accompanied by the last remaining *corrida de toros* (running with bulls) in Argentina. **El Toreo de la Vincha** takes place in front of the church, where a bull defies onlookers to take the ribbon and medal it carries: a symbolic offering to the virgin rather than a gory spectacle. Most visitors come on a day trip from

Tilcara and return there to sleep at night. If you wish to stay in the village, ask at the village school where you may be able to stay.

Monumento Natural Laguna de los Pozuelos *Colour map 1, A3.*
Park office: Rivadavia 339, Abra Pampa, T03887-491349, www.parquesnacionales.gov.ar.

Monumento Natural Laguna de los Pozuelos (3650 m) is a nature reserve 50 km northwest of Abra Pampa and centred around the lake. Laguna de los Pozuelos hosts 44 species of bird and is visited by huge colonies of up to 30,000 flamingos. It's a stunning landscape, well worth exploring if you have a few days. Be warned, however, that this is high-altitude *puna*, and temperatures can drop to -25°C at night in winter; don't attempt camping unless you have high-mountain gear and all the food, warm clothing and drinking water you're likely to need, plus spare supplies. There is a ranger station at the southern end of the Laguna with a campsite nearby. At **Lagunillas**, further west, there is a smaller lagoon, which also has flamingos. There are no visitor services and no public transport. Unless you have your own car, the only real option is to go with a guide. Try **Socompa** (see page 304).

If you're keen to explore the wild *puna* further, you could head for the tiny village of **Santa Catalina**, 67 km west of La Quiaca, along *ripio* Route 5. There's a *centro artesanal*, La Negra, and a 19th-century church with a dazzling gold and red interior, and a small museum of artefacts from local history housed in the oldest building in the village.

Listings Puna Jujeña

Where to stay

Susques and Salinas Grandes

$$ El Unquillar
R52, Km 219 (1 km west of Susques), T03887-490201,www.hotelelunquillar.com.ar.
Attractive, with local weavings, good rooms. Restaurant open to public. Phone for pickup.

$$ Pastos Chicos
R52, Km 220 (at Casas Quemadas, 3 km west of Susques), T0388-423 5387, www.pastoschicos.com.ar.

A rustic building providing comfortable accommodation. Good value. Its restaurant serves delicious regional specialities and is open to non-residents. Wi-Fi and satellite TV. Phone for pickup.

$ Residencial La Vicuñita
San Martín 121, Susques, T03887-490207, see Facebook, opposite the church.
Without bath, hot water, breakfast available, simple and welcoming.

Las Yungas

In complete contrast to the *puna* and the Quebradas, the Yungas (pronounced 'shungas') are areas of cloudforest lying along the eastern edges of Salta and Jujuy provinces. These forests receive heavy rainfall and support an incredible wealth of wildlife and vegetation, together with fragile indigenous communities. Three national parks were created to protect them: Baritú and El Rey in Salta, and Calilegua in Jujuy.

All three are very much worth visiting, but you'll need to be determined. Access is restricted, and planning is required as infrastructure is still limited. If you don't have a 4WD vehicle, contact one of the few adventure tourism agencies who are allowed to operate in the parks. All three parks are difficult to access during the rainy season, January to March, when the roads are mostly impassable. For more information, see www.redyaguarete.org.ar/yungas and www.welcomeargentina.com/parques (both in English).

Parque Nacional Calilegua is 125 km northeast of Jujuy and the most accessible of the three cloudforest parks in the region. The park protects an area of mountains, subtropical valleys and cloudforest on the eastern slopes of the Serranía de Calilegua. There are some surprisingly high peaks, including Cerro Amarillo (3720 m), which you can climb in a three-day trek round trip, starting from the park entrance, and Cerro Hermoso (3200 m), which lies closer to the road, but is attempted by few visitors as you must go with a guide.

Several rivers flow southeast across the park into the Río Ledesma. The wildlife is wonderful with at least 300 species of bird, including the red-faced guan and the condor, and over 60 species of mammal. You're likely to see tapirs, otters, taruca (Andean deer) and perhaps even pumas.

   The unpaved Route 83 runs through the park climbing from southeast to northwest and affording splendid views, before reaching Valle Grande beyond the park's borders. From Valle Grande there is a basic road leading, via Aparzo, to the Quebrada de Humahuaca. Or you could hike west from the park to Humahuaca and Tilcara (allow at least four days); you'll need to take a guide.

Walks
Within the park, there are 22 km of trails for trekking, most of which are close to the Aguas Negras ranger station. There are also some roads crossing the park for cars and bikes, and horse riding is allowed. A good tourist circuit is to **Calilegua** and then on to **Aguas Calientes**, a very rural place, where there are *hosterías* and a covered pool. You can do this in a day, if it hasn't rained, and it is accessible in an ordinary vehicle.

Essential Parque Nacional Calilegua

Access
The park entrance and ranger station is at Aguas Negras, 12 km along unpaved Ruta 83, a dirt road (4WD essential when wet) that turns off Ruta 34 just north of Libertador General San Martín. From the entrance, Ruta 83 climbs through the park for 13 km to another *guardaparque* at Mesada de las Colmenas and continues to Valle Grande, 90 km from Libertador, where there's basic accommodation and shops. There are frequent buses, including **Balut**, T03886-422 2134, US4.50, from Jujuy's terminal to Libertador General San Martín (also called Ledesma). From there, buses run to the park, where you'll be met by the *guardaparque* guides. Hitching is also possible.

Park information
Contact the **park administration office**, San Lorenzo 4514, T03886-422046, calilegua@ apn.gov.ar, www.calilegua.com, in the village of Calilegua, 4 km northeast of Libertador.

When to go
The climate is subtropical with average temperatures ranging from 17°C in winter to 28°C in summer. Mean annual rainfall is 2000 mm, falling mainly in summer (November to March).

Cerro Amarillo ⓘ *3720 m.* A three-day trek starting from the entrance. Ask the *guardaparques* for advice on directions.

Alto Calilegua You could walk to an interesting shepherds' hamlet at 2700 m, starting near the base of Cerro Amarillo. It's actually outside Calilegua park but close to its northern border and only accessible on foot (eight to 10 hours each way) or on horseback (three hours each way). Mules can be hired from San Francisco (contact Luis Cruz). There are some small pre-Hispanic ruins near the hamlet, but the main point of visiting is to witness a culture that has remained isolated for centuries, in a picturesque mountainous setting. Locals will tell you they're tired of transporting everything by mules, and long for a road to be built. Visit now, before the road comes.

Listings Parque Nacional Calilegua

Where to stay

There is no accommodation inside the parks themselves, except for very basic campsites with few facilities. However, there are some recommended places to stay nearby that can arrange trips into the parks.

$$$ Finca Portal de Piedra
Villa Monte, Santa Bárbara, T03886-15-682 0564, www.ecoportaldepiedra.com.
17 km north of Libertador General San Martín. Fabulous eco-run finca in its own reserve (Las Lancitas), convenient for PNs Calilegua and El Rey. Guesthouse accommodation and self-contained cabin available, with simple food, horse riding, trekking, birdwatching and other trips. To get there from Jujuy take a bus via San Pedro and Palma Sola (which is 12 km north of the finca).

$$$ Posada del Sol
Los Ceibos 747 at Pucará, Libertador General San Martín, T03886-424900, www.posadadelsoljujuy.com.ar.
Comfortable, functional hotel, with gardens and pool, has advice on local trips.

$$ Termas de Caimancito
Aguas Calientes, east of Libertador General San Martín, T03886-15-650699, www.termasdecaimancito.com.ar.
A beautiful and tranquil place in tropical surroundings, owned by a welcoming, English-speaking family. Simple rooms with bath, a campsite, thermal pools and a small restaurant. The owner, Tony Strelkov, runs bilingual excursions and trekking into the park, just a 30-min drive from here.

Camping
There is a campsite at Aguas Negras, near the first rangers' station; you'll find it when entering Calilegua park from the R34. There is drinking water from the river nearby, and some cooking facilities and tables. To camp at Mesada de las Colmenas, ask permission at Aguas Negras.

Transport

From Libertador San Martín **Empresa 23 de Agosto** or **Empresa 24 de Setiembre** leave 0830 to **Valle Grande**, across Parque Nacional Calilegua (US$4-5, 5 hrs), returning the same day. *Remise* charges about US$7-10 from Libertador to park entrance.

From Libertador, Ruta 34 runs northeast for 244 km to the Bolivian border at Pocitos (also called Salvador Mazza) and Yacuiba in southeastern Bolvia. It passes through Embarcación and Tartagal, which has a good regional museum.

In **Pocitos**, the border town, is **Hotel Buen Gusto**, which is just tolerable. There are no *casas de cambio* here. The border is open 24 hours. From Yacuiba, across the border, buses go to Santa Cruz de la Sierra and Tarija. There is a **Bolivian consulate** ① *Av San Martín 446, T03873-471336, Mon-Fri 0800-1200, 1500-1800*. Several bus companies have services from the border to Salta and Tucumán.

An alternative route is via Aguas Blancas. At Pichanal, 85 km northeast of Libertador, Ruta 50 heads north via **Orán** (full name San Ramón de la Nueva Orán), an uninteresting place where you can refuel. Also here is the **Bolivian consulate** ① *Av San Martín 134, Orán, T03878-421969, Mon-Fri 0830-1330, 1600-1900*. **Aguas Blancas** is 53 km beyond **Orán** on the border (open 24 hours). There are restaurants, shops and fuel here but no accommodation. Nor is there anywhere to change money; note that Bolivianos are not accepted south of Aguas Blancas. Buses run from Bermejo, across the river by bridge, to Tarija, three to four hours, US$3 (US$6 by shared taxi).

Tip...
Take plenty of repellent to the Yungas because there are lots of mosquitoes all year round. The prevalence of malaria varies from year to year, so check with your doctor about medication, especially in midsummer.

Listings Routes to Bolivia

Transport

All Pocitos or Orán buses pass through Libertador San Martín. Between Aguas Blancas and **Orán** buses run every 45 mins, US$1, luggage checks on the bus. Some services from Salta and Jujuy call at **Orán** en route to **Tartagal** and **Pocitos**. Note that buses are subject to slow searches for drugs and contraband.

Parque Nacional Baritú
delicate ecosystems in a tropical paradise

Baritú is Argentina's only tropical park, lying north of the Tropic of Capricorn. It's spectacularly beautiful, covering 72,439 ha of the eastern slopes of the Andean foothills, with peaks rising to around 2000 m, mostly covered by cloudforest. Fauna is abundant and varied, including many of the same birds and animals as Calilegua but also several species that are close to extinction, such as the yaguarete which lives only in a few eco-regions of this kind and whose only rival carnivore is the puma. There are also rare plant and tree species here, making the park a great destination for serious nature lovers.

Essential Parque Nacional Baritú

Access

Although the park lies entirely within Salta province, to reach it you'll have to go into Bolivia first. Start in Orán and travel up Route 50 to Aguas Blancas. Then drive 110 km through Bolivian territory – a beautiful winding road through hills – to reach the international bridge El Condado–La Mamora. Take Route 19 south (now back in Argentina). After 14 km you'll reach the region known as Los Toldos; keep heading south for a further 26 km until you reach the northern boundary of the park.

Remember to bring your passport (with a Bolivian visa if necessary) and, if hiring a car in Argentina, warn the hire company that you plan to take it into Bolivia. Fill up with fuel in Orán or Aguas Blancas, and check the state of the roads before setting off at Salta's **tourist office** (see page 275), or by contacting the **park's officers**, T0387-15-507 4433, baritu@apn.gov.ar, www.parquesnacionales.gov.ar (follow links under 'Areas protegidas').

Facilities

There are no facilities apart from ranger posts, campsites at the entrances and rustic *cabañas*.

When to go

Baritú is the hottest of the three national parks in the Yungas, with average temperatures of 21°C in winter and 30°C in summer. Summer also brings between 900 and 1300 mm of rain, making roads completely impassable in January and February. This makes Baritú one of the most inaccessible parks in the country, and you'll have to be determined to make a visit.

Walks

There are many walks in the northeast area of the park, which allow you close contact with the many species of bird in the park. A recommended walk is to **Termas de Cayotal**, two hours' walk from the *guardaparques'* office in El Lipeo. Another is to the settlement of **Campo Grande**, where you can meet local indigenous peoples living in the park and get a glimpse of their rich culture. From here, you could also walk the seven hours to **Angosto del Río Lipeo**.

Listings Parque Nacional Baritú

What to do

Movitrack and **Clark Expediciones**, both in Salta, are authorized to take visitors into the park. Both are recommended for specializing in natural history, with 1- to 2-day trips in 4WD vehicles, camping and walking inside the park.

Parque Nacional El Rey is the closest of the three cloudforest parks in the Yungas to Salta city (196 km), though it's still not easily accessible unless you go with a special expedition, since visitors to the park are few and far between, and there's little vehicular access. Covering 44,000 ha, it was once a private estate, 'El Rey' (the king), on the eastern border of the Spanish territory, owned by Coronel Fernández Cornejo, who carried out the expulsion of the Jesuits. The remains of his 18th-century house can still be found in the park.

Its landscapes stretch from arid steppe in the east, at 750 m above sea level, to mountainous regions at over 2000 m, resulting in extremely varied vegetation. In the east, you can find Chaqueño-serrano forest, then transition jungle in the middle and high mountain forest at the most western extreme. The natural amphitheatre formation of the park's terrain is created by the horseshoe-shaped ridge of the Sierra de la Cresta del Gallo, northwest of the park, which reaches heights of around 1700 m. Rivers descend from here through lush jungle to the Río Popayán flowing below. There's abundant wildlife, much of it easily spotted. Toucans and other birdlife abound, and you might be lucky enough to spot wild cats and tapirs.

Walks

There are several good paths you can take to explore the park's varied landscape and accompanying wildlife. **Los Patitos** is a small lake, 1.5 km from the *guardaparques'* centre and a great one-hour walk for spotting aquatic birds and mammals. **Popayán River** is 10 km (a two-hour walk) from the *guardaparques'* centre. **Pozo Verde** path is 12 km

Essential Parque Nacional El Rey

Access

The park entrance is 46 km off Route 5, but no public transport reaches the park so it's best to take a tour from Salta city with one of the three operators licensed to take groups into the park: **Norte Trekking**, T0387-431 6616, www.nortetrekking.com, **Clark Expediciones**, T0387-492 7280, www.clarkexpediciones.com), and **Movitrack**, www.movitrack.com.ar. These are highly recommended, with expert guides to the interesting flora and fauna in the park, offering one- and two-day trips in 4WD vehicles with walks in the park, and camping.

Accommodation

There is a rangers' office near the entrance with a clearing where you can camp. This is a simple campsite with drinking water and bathrooms. No other accommodation is possible in the park.

Park information

There is a **park office**, España 366, 3rd floor (4400), T03487-431 2683, in Salta. More information is available on the Parques Nacionales website, www.parquesnacionales.gov.ar.

When to go

The park has a warm climate and relatively high average rainfall. The best time to visit is May to November, avoiding the very rainy season of January to March.

from the *guardaparques'* centre and challenging for the first 3 km. Part of the way there is a footpath with interpretation information called 'Los Ocultos'. **Santa Elena Field and Los Lobitos waterfall** is a challenging hike but good for seeing transition jungle; 4 km from the *guardaparques*, two hours each way; you'll need a guide. **Chorro de los Loros** is a pedestrian path of medium-high difficulty. It is 10 km long and crosses the transition jungle. It starts at the *guardaparques'* centre.

Northeast Argentina

thundering falls, ancient ruins and indigenous culture

Of all Argentina's many natural wonders, there is nothing quite as spectacular as the Iguazú Falls. With a magical setting in subtropical rainforest, alive with birdsong and the constant dancing of butterflies, the colossal Garganta del Diablo waterfall at their centre is an unforgettable sight.

Misiones province holds other delights: Jesuit missions unearthed from the jungle at San Ignacio, and the extraordinary Saltos de Moconá, 3000 m of falls more horizontal than vertical.

El Litoral's wealth of wildlife is astounding. In the vast wetlands of Esteros del Iberá, giant storks and caiman nestle between floating islands. In Mburucuyá, tall palms wave in grasslands and passion flowers thrive. In the Chaco, watch out for pumas and monkeys, while the palm forests of Entre Rios are centuries old. Stop on the lazy Paraná river either at relaxed, pretty Colón with its port or amid the faded splendour of Paraná. For more stimulation, historical Corrientes is a riot at Carnival time, and lively Rosario produces the country's finest musicians.

The northeast's rich culture stems from its indigenous peoples, the Guaraní and Wichí, who produce beautiful art. The gently meandering rivers set the pace, giving the land its lush vegetation and generating in its people a charming, laid-back warmth.

Best for
Ecological reserves ▪ Jungle trips ▪ Wildlife spotting

Footprint
picks

★ **Carnaval in
Gualeguaychú**, page 318

Just as energetic as Brazil's Carnaval and it lasts longer, too.

★ **Monumento de la Bandera, Rosario**, page 325

This imposing memorial looks out over the Río Paraná and welcomes you to Rosario.

★ **Reserva Natural de los Esteros del Iberá**, page 348

The largest expanse of wetlands outside of Brazil can be found at this nature reserve.

★ **San Ignacio**, page 359

This tranquil town is home to the ruins of the Jesuits' crowning mission: San Ignacio Miní.

★ **A boat ride under the Iguazú Falls**, page 367

Prepare to get wet as take a trip to the base of South America's most majestic waterfalls.

BRAZIL

PARAGUAY

Río Pilcomayo

Espinillo
PN Pilcomayo
Ibarreta
Clorinda
FORMOSA
81
Foz do Iguaçú   Iguazú   PN Foz do
Falls   Iguaçu
Ciudad del Este
Puerto Iguazú   PN Iguazú
Wanda
Esperanza
101

CHACO
Avia Terai
PN Chaco
16
Formosa
Río Paraguay
Eldorado
12   17

Resistencia
Itatí
Ita Ibaté
Puerto Rico   Río Alto Paraná
Capiovi
Jesús   MISIONES
Trinidad   San Ignacio
Encarnación   San Ignacio Mini
Posadas   Campo Viera   Moconá
11   Paso de
la Patria
12
Corrientes   Santa Ana   Obera   Falls
LN Alem   Río Uruguay

Empedrado
12
Mburucuyá
Reserva Natural
del Iberá
Apóstoles   5
Parque Nacional   San Miguel
Mburucuyá
Concepción   105
Garruchos
Las
Toscas
Saladas
Bella Vista
Esteros del Iberá
3   Colonia
Carlos
Pellegrini
SANTA FE
CORRIENTES
Santo Tomé
Reconquista
Santa
Lucía
123
Mercedes
BRAZIL
Vera
Goya
119
Yapeyú
Río Corrientes
Curuzú
Paso de
los Libres
Monte Caseros
San Javier
14
Santa
Elena
11
La Paz
Embalse
Salto
Grande
12
127
ENTRE RIOS
Concordia
URUGUAY
Santa Fé
6
San Salvador
Paraná
18   Ubajay
PN El Palmar
Vialle   Villaguay
Diamante   130
Colón
14   Paysandú
Victoria   Concepción
del Uruguay
San Lorenzo
2   Rosario
Gualeguaychú   1
Fray Bentos
Villa Constitución
San Nicolás
12
San Pedro   9
Ibicuy   12
Río Paraná
de las Palmas
Pergamino   8   Delta del
Zárate   Paraná
Luján

N
50 km
50 miles

Footprint
picks

1 **Carnaval in Gualeguaychú**, page 318
2 **Monumento de la Bandera, Rosario**,
   page 325
3 **Reserva Natural de los Esteros del Iberá**,
   page 348
4 **San Ignacio**, page 359
5 **A boat ride under the Iguazú Falls**, page 367

Along the
Río Uruguay

The mighty Río Uruguay, which forms Argentina's eastern boundary with Uruguay and Brazil, is over 1600 km long, and a staggering 10 km wide in places. Unless you're in a rush to reach Iguazu, you could meander northeast from Buenos Aires along the river, stopping off at some interesting towns on the Argentine side.

Gualeguaychú is so keen to party, it celebrates its carnival every weekend for two months, but you can calm down in Concepción del Uruguay, with its attractive old buildings, or Colón, with its historic port area and sandy beaches. There's a national park protecting splendid palm forests, though the reserve La Aurora del Palmar is more accessible. You can stay on colonial estancias, jungle islands, and with small communities at Irazusta and Arroyo Barú.

The first town of any size on the Ruta 12/14 north from Buenos Aires, Gualeguaychú is famous for its extended carnival. En route to Gualeguaychú, you may want to stop at Villa Paranacito, a village set in the delta islands, accessible only via a 22-km dirt road, branching off Route 12, 10 km south of Ceibas. (There are daily buses to Villa Paranacito with Nuevo Expreso from Gualeguaychú, Zárate and Buenos Aires.) Houses here are built on tall stilts and boats are the essential means of transport. It's popular with anglers in the waters of the nearby Río Uruguay (half an hour further east by boat) and anyone looking for a quiet place to stay, immersed in the islander culture. There are campsites, a hostel and *cabañas* offering boat trips, and delicious local fish at Villa Paranacito Annemarie.

Sights

Gualeguaychú is lively throughout the summer, with an attractive *costanera* on the Río Gualeguaychú, where there are several *balnearios* (bathing spots) and restaurants; it's a pleasant place for a stroll with views of the picturesque port. Carnival is celebrated at the local *corsódromo* (arena), a hugely popular event lasting well beyond the usual fortnight to fill every weekend for a couple of months. The port and *balneario municipal* are the departure points for short boat trips and city tours. About 200 m south of the port in Plazoleta de los Artesanos, local handicrafts are sold at weekends in summer.

On the *costanera* at Gervasio Méndez is **El Patio del Mate** ① *T03446-424371, www. elpatiodelmate.com.ar, daily 0830-2000 (2100 in summer)*, a workshop where dedicated craftsmen make the cups from which *mate* is drunk, varying widely from simple dyed gourds to ornate silver goblets.

On the outskirts are thermal pools at **Termas del Guaychú** ① *Ruta 14 Km 63.5, www.termas delguaychu.com.ar*, and **Termas del Gualeguaychú** ① *Ruta 42 Km 2.5, T03446-15 607620*.

Into Uruguay: Fray Bentos *Colour map 4, A6.*

Fray Bentos (population 25,047) is the main port on the east bank of Río Uruguay, a friendly little town with an attractive *costanera*. The main reason to visit is to see the meat-packing factory. The name Fray Bentos was synonymous with corned beef in Britain throughout the 20th century, and the factory (*frigorífico*) known as El Anglo, which produced Oxo for many years, has been beautifully restored as the **Museo de La Revolución Industrial** ① *T+598 4562-2918/3690, Tue-Sun 0930-1700, US$2.75 including a 1½-hr guided tour in Spanish at 1000 and 1500, leaflet in English, Tue free*. The office block in the factory has been preserved and some of the old machinery can be seen; there's also a restaurant on site.

Listings Gualeguaychú and around

Tourist office

Gualeguaychú

Tourist office
*Paseo del Puerto, T03446-423668,
www.gualeguaychuturismo.com.*

*Daily 0800-2000 (2200 in summer,
2400 Fri-Sat).*
Housed in a thatched hut. There's another
office at the terminal (open same hours).

BORDER CROSSING

Argentina–Uruguay

Puente Libertador General San Martín

Situated 33 km southeast of Gualeguaychú, the Libertador General San Martín Bridge (5.4 km long) provides the most southerly route across the Río Uruguay, to Fray Bentos. It's open 24 hours.

Customs and immigration are at opposite ends of the bridge and it's an uncomplicated crossing; formalities take about 10 minutes. Passport details are noted when booking bus tickets and passed to officials at the border, and passports are inspected on the bus. Pedestrians and cyclists can only cross in motor vehicles, though officials may arrange lifts. The vehicle toll is US$8.

There's an **Argentine consulate** in Fray Bentos at 18 de Julio 1031, T+598-4562 3510, cfben@mrecic.gov.ar, Monday-Friday 1300-1800. The **Uruguayan consulate** in Gualeguaychú is at Rivadavia 510, T03446-426168, conurugale@entrerios.net, Monday-Friday 0800-1400.

Transport From Gualeguaychú to Fray Bentos, see Transport, below.

Fray Bentos

Tourist office
25 de Mayo and Lavalleja, T+598-4562 2233. Daily 0900-1800.

Where to stay

Gualeguaychú

Accommodation is scarce during carnival. Prices are 25% higher Dec-Mar, Easter and long weekends. The tourist office can contact estate agents for short stays in private flats.

$$$ Puerto Sol
San Lorenzo 477, T03446-434017, www.hotelpuertosol.com.ar.
Good rooms next to the port, plus a small resort on a nearby island (transfer included) for a relaxing drink.

$$$ Tykuá
Luis N Palma 150, T03446-422625, www.tykuahotel.com.ar.
3 blocks from the bridge, with all services including safe.

Camping

There are several sites on the riverside, others next to the bridge and north of it.

El Ñandubaysal, on the Río Uruguay, 15 km southeast, T03446-423298, www.nandubaysal.com, is the smartest.

Restaurants

Gualeguaychú

$$ Campo Alto
San Lorenzo and Concordia, T03446-429593.
A large *quincho* (rustic place to eat) at the end of the *costanera*, serving lots of local fish such as *surubí*, *boga*, *dorado* and *patí*.

$ Dacal
Av Costanera and Andrade, T03446-427602.
A traditional restaurant, serving good food; the *surubí* is recommended.

Festivals

Gualeguaychú

Jan/Feb Carnival, is celebrated every weekend throughout Jan and Feb at the *corsódromo*, a purpose-built parade ground with grandstand, at the back of the former railway station on Piccini y Maipú. Local teams or *comparsas* compete in colourful parades to the powerful drumbeats of the *batucada*, with *carrozas* and dancers dressed in brightly coloured costumes and feathers. Tickets for adults in 2016 cost from US$7 to US$19 depending on the night; details of how to buy can be found on the websites, including www.grancarnaval.com.ar (in Spanish).

Transport

Gualeguaychú
Bus

The **bus terminal** (Blv Artigas and Blv Jurado, T03446-440688) is a 30-min walk from the centre (*remise* taxi US$3). The terminal has tourist information, a post office, phones, a small restaurant and 24-hr left luggage.

To **Concepción del Uruguay**, 1 hr, US$3.50. To **Buenos Aires**, US$20-23, 3½ hrs, several daily. Buses to **Zárate** or **Buenos Aires** stop at **Ceibas**, and there are also regular buses to **Larroque** and **Urdinarrain**, where *remise* taxis will take you to **Irazusta** and **Aldea San Antonio**. There are daily buses to **Villa Paranacito** with Nuevo Expreso.
To **Fray Bentos**, **Uruguay**, with Ciudad de Gualeguay (T03446-440555, www.ciudad degualeguay.com), 1½ hrs, US$8. To **Montevideo**, from US$58, 6½ hrs, Plus Ultra. Arrive 30 mins before departure to do the border paperwork.

Concepción del Uruguay and around *Colour map 2, C1.*

river islands and summer parties

Concepción del Uruguay lies on the western shore of the Río Uruguay, 74 km north of Gualeguaychú, with views of islands in the river opposite. Founded in 1783, it was capital of Entre Ríos province between 1813-1821 and 1860-1883, and retains some fine architecture in its public buildings. It has a distinctively lively character, thanks to a young student population.

Sights

The old town is centred on beautiful **Plaza Ramírez**, with the Italian neoclassical-style **Basílica de la Inmaculada Concepción**, containing the remains of General Urquiza on its western side. Next to it is the **Colegio Superior Justo José de Urquiza**, the first secular school in the country, although its 19th-century buildings were largely replaced in 1935. One block northeast of the plaza is **Museo Casa de Delio Panizza** ① *Galarza and Supremo Entrerriano 58, see Facebook, Mon-Fri 0900-1200 and 1600-1900, Sat-Sun 0900-1200 and 1600-2000, US$0.50*, in a mansion dating from 1793 and containing 19th-century furnishings and artefacts.

West of Concepción del Uruguay

Buses going to Paraná or Rosario del Tala will stop at El Cruce or Caseros, and from here, the palacios are 4 km and 8 km away, respectively (take a remise taxi from Caseros; Palacio San José's website recommends 2 companies). Tour operators run combis (minibuses) only in high season (check companies at tourist office, since they change every year). Basavilbaso has regular buses which link Concepción del Uruguay and Paraná or Rosario del Tala.

Palacio San José ① *32 km west of the town, www.palaciosanjose.com.ar, Mon-Fri 0800-1930, Sat-Sun 0900-1830, US$1.35, information in Spanish, French and English, free guided visits throughout the day, and night visits at Easter, Jan-Feb (on Fri) and Oct-Dec (1 Sat a month)*, is the former mansion of General Urquiza and dates from 1848. Built in Italian style with 38 rooms and a chapel, it was once the country's most luxurious residence. Now a museum with artefacts from Urquiza's life, the palace stands in a beautiful park with an artificial lake. It can be reached by taking Route 39 west and turning right after Caseros train station.

There is also a second palace, **Palacio Santa Cándida** ⓘ *www.santacandida.com*, which is another wonderfully old estancia that can be visited and which offers accommodation and lots of outdoor activities.

Basavilbaso, 68 km west, is a historical small town which in the early 20th century was an urban centre for Lucienville, inhabited by Jewish immigrants from Russia. There are three well-preserved synagogues, of which the **Tefila L Moises** has a beautifully painted wooden ceiling. It's also worth visiting the **Navibuco synagogue**, 2.5 km out of town, dating from 1895, and two Jewish cemeteries nearby. Basavilbaso used to be a busy transport hub until the last passenger train left in 1992. The station now houses a museum where the rich history of the local railway can be explored.

Listings Concepción del Uruguay and around

Tourist information

Concepción del Uruguay

Tourist office
Galarza y Supremo Entrerriano, T03442-425820. Daily 0700-2100.
There's another office at Galarza y Daniel Elías (T03442-440812, www.concepcionentrerrios. tur.ar, daily 0700-2200).

Basavilbaso

Asociación Israelita
Uchitel 367, T03445-481908.
Also offers information.

Tourist office
Lagocen and Hipólito Yrigoyen, T03445-481015, www.turismoentrerios.com/basavilbaso.

Where to stay

Concepción del Uruguay

$$$$-$$ Grand Hotel Casino
Eva Perón 114, T03442-425586, www.grandhotelcasino.com.ar.
Originally a French-style mansion with adjacent theatre. Superior rooms have a/c and TV; VIP rooms have new bathrooms.

$$$ Antigua Posta del Torreón
España y Almafuerte, T03442-432618, www.postadeltorreon.com.ar.
9 comfortable rooms in a stylish boutique hotel with a pool.

$$ Nuevo Residencial Centro
Moreno 130, 1½ blocks from the plaza, T03442-427429, see Facebook.
One of the cheapest options in town. Basic rooms, some with a/c, in a traditional 19th-century building with a lovely patio. No breakfast.

Restaurants

Concepción del Uruguay

$$$ El Conventillo de Baco
España 193, T03442-433809.
A refined choice with some outside tables and a chance to try fish from the river.

Transport

Concepción del Uruguay
Bus
The **bus terminal** (Rocamora y Los Constituyentes, T03442-422352) is 11 blocks from Plaza Ramírez (*remise* to centre, US$2). Luggage can be left at the information desk. To **Buenos Aires**, frequent, 4-4½ hrs, US$24-28. To **Colón**, 1 hr, US$2.

a slower pace on the Río Uruguay

One of the prettiest towns on the river, Colón was founded in 1863 as a port for the Swiss colony of San José, 9 km west, and it's an excellent base for visiting several interesting places nearby, including the Parque Nacional El Palmar, www.colonentrerios.com.ar/elpalmar. It is also linked by a bridge to the Uruguayan city of Paysandú; see box, opposite. Colón itself has many well-preserved early 19th-century houses and a beautiful riverbank with long sandy beaches and shady streets.

Sights
The most attractive part of town is the port district, next to the Plaza San Martín, with fine old houses on the plaza and nearby streets leading down to the riverside. At the corner of Avenida 12 de Abril and Paso is **La Casona** (1868), where there's a handicrafts exhibition and shop. North of the port, Calle Alejo Peyret gives access to the *balnearios* and their sandy beaches on the river and Calle Belgrano leads to the **Complejo Termal** ⓘ *T03447-424717, www.termasdecolon.com.ar, daily 0900-2100, US$10*, where there are 10 thermal pools (34-40°C) in an attractive setting, very popular for treating a variety of ailments. Most shops and banks can be found on Avenida 12 de Abril, with the old **Teatro Centenario**, opened in 1925.

Arroyo Barú
Some 40 km north of Villa Elisa (east of Colón) is Arroyo Barú, a village whose inhabitants have opened their houses to visitors who want to enjoy the tranquillity of this small rural community. This place, together with Irazusta (west of Gualeguaychú), are both case studies for NGO research. The village is reached via a 35-km-long dirt road, branching off Route 130, 5 km west of Villa Elisa.

Parque Nacional El Palmar *Colour map 2, C1.*
Entrance on Ruta 14, 58 km north of Colón, 6 km south of Ubajay, T03447-493053, www. pnelpalmar.com.ar. US$6.75. Buses from Colón, 1 hr, US$2, will drop you at the entrance; it may be possible to hitch the 12 km to the park administration, otherwise you have to walk. Local JoviBus services run to Ubajay, from where a remise taxi to the park administration costs about US$10; ask at Parador Gastiazoro where buses stop. Remises also go from Colón and Concordia. Otherwise take a tour.

On the west bank of the Río Uruguay km north of Colón, this park covers 8500 ha of gently undulating grassland and mature palm forest, including *yatay* palms that are hundreds of years old. These graceful trees were once found all over the Pampas, until the introduction of cattle, who found the young seedlings irresistible. Growing in *palmares*, or palm groves, mature trees may reach 12 m in height, with fronds some 2 m in length. Along the Río Uruguay, and the *arroyos* (streams) that flow into it, there are gallery forests of subtropical trees and shrubs. You'll find indigenous tombs hidden away on the edge of the Río Uruguay where there are beaches and the remains of an 18th-century quarry and port. Look out for capybaras, foxes, lizards and vizcachas as well as rheas, monk parakeets and several species of woodpecker.

At the entrance gates on Route 14, you are given a map and information on walks. From here, a *ripio* road leads to the administration centre, in the east of the park, near the Río

BORDER CROSSING
Argentina–Uruguay

Puente General José Artigas

Seven kilometres southeast of Colón, the General José Artigas Bridge gives access to the Uruguayan city of Paysandú. The crossing is open 24 hours; the toll is US$8.

The **Argentine consulate** in Paysandú is at Gómez 1034, T+598-4722 2253, open Monday-Friday 1300-1800. The **Uruguayan consulate** in Colón is at San Martín 417, T03447-421999, crou@ciudad.com.ar. Argentine and Uruguayan immigration formalities are both dealt with at the Uruguayan end of the bridge. *Migraciones* officials board the bus, but non-Argentines or Uruguayans should get off the bus to have their passports stamped. When driving you don't need to get out of your car, just present your passport and car registration details when asked.

For **transport** from Colón to Paysandú, see Transport, below.

Uruguay, with access to several viewpoints: **Mirador de La Glorieta**, **Mirador del Arroyo El Palmar**, **Mirador del Arroyo Los Loros** and to the coast of the Río Uruguay. There are walks between 300 m and 1000 m and you are free to walk around the main roads, though there's little shade. The administration centre is the departure point for guided walks and cycle tours run by **Capybara Aventura** (English spoken). Nearby there's camping (www.campingelpalmar.com.ar, US$5.50 per person) with electricity, hot water, a restaurant opposite and a small shop. Visit at any time of year, but note that the park is very popular at weekends in summer and during Easter week. In summer there are more chances of thunderstorms and very hot weather.

Refugio de Vida Silvestre La Aurora del Palmar

Opposite the Parque Nacional El Palmar, 3 km south of Ubajay, on Route 14, Km 202, T0345-490 5725, www.auroradelpalmar.com.ar, free. There are buses from Colón; ask for Ruta 14 Kilómetro 202 and tell the driver you are going to La Aurora del Palmar to avoid confusion with the national park. For transport from Ubajay, see Parque Nacional el Palmar, above.

More accessible than the national park, the wildlife reserve of La Aurora del Palmar was created to protect a similar environment. It covers 1150 ha, of which 200 are covered with a mature palm forest. There are also gallery forests and patches of *espinal*, or scrub. There's lots of birdlife, and capybaras can also be spotted along the streams. You can reach the vantage point of the *quincho panorámico* for a drink (try the *yatay* spirit), while enjoying the view of the palm forest. The administration centre is only 500 m from Route 14, and offers well-organized services for visitors. Guided trips include horse riding into the palm forest and the Arroyo de los Pájaros (1½ hours, US$13.50 per person, children half price); canoe journeys along Arroyo El Palmar (two hours, US$13.50 per person); and walks to the Mirador del Cerro de Piedra. All recommended. There's accommodation and camping available too (see Where to stay, below), but you should book in advance for lodging and to check the availability of trips.

Tourist information

Colón

Tourist information office
Av Costanera Quirós y Gouchón,
T03447-421233, www.colonturismo.tur.ar.
Daily 0700-2100.
Housed in the former passenger boat
terminal in the port area.

Where to stay

Colón

$$$ Holimasú
Belgrano 28, T03447-421305,
www.hotelholimasu.com.ar.
Good patio, a/c extra, **$$** in low season.

$$$ Hostería Restaurant del Puerto
Alejo Peyret 158, T03447-422698,
www.hosteriadecolon.com.ar.
Great value, lovely atmosphere in old house,
pool, no credit cards.

$$ La Posada de David
Alejo Peyret 97, T03447-423930.
Welcoming family house, garden,
good double rooms, great value.

Camping

There are several sites, some with cabins,
on the river bank, from US$5 pp daily.

Refugio de Vida Silvestre La Aurora del Palmar

$$$ Casona La Estación
T0345-490 5725/T03447-15-431689,
www.auroradelpalmar.com.ar.
Rooms for up to 6 people and apartments
for up to 8, with breakfast, bath, a/c, well-
suited to families. Also offers one of the
most extraordinary places to stay: train
carriages (**$$$-$$**) converted into double
rooms or dorms. Camping is also permitted
in the park's own site.

Restaurants

Colón

$$$ Chiva Chiva
Gral Urquiza y Brown.
An artist's refuge; her creativity is in evidence
in the meals, drinks and pottery on display.

$$$ La Cosquilla del Angel
San Martín 304, T03447-423711,
see Facebook.
The smartest place in town, with fish dishes,
set menu and live piano music in evenings.

$$$ Viejo Almacén
Gral Urquiza y Paso.
Cosy, very good cooking and
excellent service.

Festivals

Colón

Feb Fiesta Nacional de la Artesanía. Held
over 9 evenings in Parque Quirós, where
craftspeople display a wide variety of
handicrafts. There are also *folcore* and pop
music concerts.

Transport

Colón
Bus

The bus terminal (Paysandú and Sourigues,
T03447-421716) is 10 blocks from the
main plaza. Left luggage storage is available
at Remises Base (opposite the terminal) on
9 de Julio. Not all long-distance buses enter
Colón: buses going north from Colón will
stop at Ubajay. To **Buenos Aires**, US$28-32,
5-6 hrs. To **Mercedes** (for Iberá), several
companies, 7-8 hrs, US$23. To **Paraná**,
4-6 hrs, US$12.50. To **Paysandú** (**Uruguay**),
Copay and **Río Uruguay**, US$3.50, 1 hr;
see also box, page 323.

Río
Paraná

Running parallel to the Río Uruguay, the Río Paraná weaves its lazy course right across the northeast of Argentina, from Misiones to Buenos Aires where it forms a vast delta. If you have time for a road trip from Buenos Aires to Corrientes, there are two main routes north: the more major route north along the western banks, through the cities of Rosario and Santa Fe to Reconquista and Resistencia; or an interesting journey along the eastern banks of the river, through Paraná via small towns for wildlife spotting and fishing and onwards to Goya and Corrientes.

Rosario *Colour map 4, A5.*

big-city fun away from Buenos Aires

Rosario is Argentina's third largest city with 1.3 million inhabitants, and is renowned for its rich cultural life, since it is home to many famous artists and pop musicians, as well as being the birthplace of Che Guevara (see box, page 327). Although little visited by travellers, it has some fine buildings in its attractive centre and a well-kept *costanera* along the Paraná River. The nightlife is lively, with plenty of cafés, restaurants and nightclubs, and there are daily theatre and live music shows at venues all around the city. To recover from all that entertainment, visit the nearby islands in the river, just minutes away from the centre, where you can relax on sandy beaches. It is a fantastic place to spend the weekend.

Sights

The old city centre is on the Plaza 25 de Mayo, just a block south of the Parque a la Bandera which lies along the riverside. Around it is the cathedral, built in a somewhat eclectic style and containing the Virgen del Rosario, and the Palacio Municipal. On the north side is the **Museo de Arte Decorativo** ① *Santa Fe 748, T0341-480 2547, museo@museoestevez. gov.ar, Wed-Sun 0900-1300, in winter to 1700, US$1,* a sumptuous former family residence housing a valuable private collection of paintings, furniture, tapestries, sculptures, and silver, brought mainly from Europe. To the left of the cathedral, the **Pasaje Juramento** is the pedestrian access to the imposing ★ **Monumento a la Bandera** ① *T0341-480 2238,* *www.monumentoalabandera.gov.ar, daily 0900-1800, US$1 (tower; last entrance at 1730), free (Salón de las Banderas)*, an impressively large monument built on the site where General Belgrano raised the Argentine flag for the first time in 1812. The tower has a vantage point 70 m high with excellent panoramic views over the city and the river.

From Plaza 25 de Mayo, Calle Córdoba leads west towards Plaza San Martín and the **Paseo del Siglo**, the largest concentration of late 19th- and early 20th-century buildings in the city. The palm-lined **Boulevard Oroño** leads north to the riverside parks, the Rosario Norte railway station and south to the **Pichincha district**, popular for nightlife, and to **Parque Independencia** at the south end. This beautiful 126-ha park was designed by the landscape architect Charles Thays. It has a large lake, gardens with fountains and fine statues, shady avenues and the Newell's Old Boys football club stadium. There are also three museums in the area.

Just outside the park, the **Museo de Bellas Artes J B Castagnino** ⓘ *Av Pellegrini 2202, T0341-480 2542, www.museocastagnino.org.ar, Wed-Mon 1400-2000, US$1*, is considered one of the best fine arts museums in the country, with a large collection of European paintings, particularly French Impressionist, Italian Baroque and Flemish works, and one of the best collections of paintings and sculpture by renowned Argentine artists.

Next to the stadium is the **Museo Histórico Provincial** ⓘ *Av Pellegrini and Oroño, T0341-472 1457, www.museomarc.gob.ar, Tue-Fri 0900-1800, Sat-Sun 1400-1900, US$1*, which has a very well displayed collection of Latin American aboriginal artefacts and valuable pieces of religious art including Cuzco-school paintings and a magnificent altar covered with silver plaques, which was used by Pope John Paul II in 1987.

The riverside is lined with several parks, making it a very attractive place to walk. Eight blocks south of the Monumento a la Bandera is an open-air theatre, **Parque Urquiza** ⓘ *T0341-480 2533, shows on Sun 2000, museum open Sat-Sun 1700-1900, US$1*, and the **Complejo Astronómico Municipal** with an observatory, a planetarium and a small science museum.

Essential Rosario

Finding your feet

Fisherton Airport is located 15 km west of the centre. *Remise* taxis charge US$14-16 for the journey to town. Transfers are also arranged by airline companies. The **bus terminal** is about 30 blocks west of the Monumento de la Bandera. There are several bus lines to the centre with stops on Córdoba (eg 101, 115). *Remise* taxis charge US$4-6.

There is also the Rosario Norte railway station at Avenida del Valle 2750 and Avenida Ovidio Lagos. Also, there is the smaller Apeadero Sur railway station at San Martín 6000. For further details, see Transport, page 331.

Further north is the **Estación Fluvial** where boats leave for excursions around the islands and where you'll find the **Museo del Paraná y las Islas** ⓘ *closed in 2016 with tentative plans to reopen, T0341-440 0751, hours subject to the whims of the owner, US$1*, which gives an insight into islander culture through local art and artefacts. At the foot of the monument is the **Parque a la Bandera**, one of the most appealing parks, and the tourist office, beyond which is the **Parque de España**, a modern red-brick development which incorporates the old railway arches as an exhibition centre and offers fine views over the Río Paraná. Further up the river is the fantastic **Museo de Arte Contemporáneo** (MACRO) ⓘ *Blv Oroño on the river shore, T0341-480 4981, www.macromuseo.org.ar, Thu-Tue 1400-2000, in summer 1500-2100, US$1*. Located inside a massive old silo, this remarkable

ON THE ROAD

¡Che!

Ernesto 'Che' Guevara is one of the most recognized faces in the word, and his image can be seen on T-shirts, posters, mugs and key rings virtually everywhere you go. His is an enduring image of youthful revolutionary zeal, something he would have never predicted when he set off on his now legendary travels around South America with a friend and a beaten-up motocycle called *El Poderoso*, the powerful one.

The future revolutionary was born into a middle-class family in Rosario in 1928, but his parents soon moved with their asthmatic son to the healthier climate of the Sierras of Córdoba. The large white house at Entre Ríos y Urquiza where he lived the first two years of his life is now fronted by an insurance business. You can visit the house where the family lived in Alta Gracia (see page 153). After growing up in a small town, his eyes were soon opened to the plight of South America's poor during his famous journey around the continent documented in his book *The Motorcycle Diaries*, which is a recommended and entertaining read. Rather than pursue a career in medicine, he decided mid-trip to dedicate the rest of his life to the fight for the 'liberation of the American continent'.

In 1956 he met Fidel Castro in Mexico and together they planned to create the ideal Socialist model in Cuba, as well as establish links with other sympathetic nations. His overriding ambition had always been to spread the revolutionary word, and take the armed struggle to other parts. So he began his fight in Bolivia. After spending a little time in La Paz, he then travelled to a guerrilla base at Nanchuazú. However, the constant movements of the group aroused the suspicion of neighbours and the army were alerted. The group fled and spent several months wandering the steep valleys of eastern Bolivia. In August 1967, the small group was ambushed by Bolivian troops and Ernesto Guevara was executed, photographed and buried in an unmarked grave, aged just 39. In 1997 his body was exhumed and taken to Cuba.

The name 'Che' was given to him as a form of reverence. Che in Argentina roughly translates as 'mate' or 'buddy', and is used by friends and family.

museum is 10 levels high with one small gallery on each level, and at the top is a viewing deck. Highly recommended.

On Sunday afternoons there is a great craft, antiques and vintage clothing market along the river starting at Boulevard Oroño. It's great fun and less crowded than Buenos Aires' markets.

The most popular destinations for locals as well as visitors are the dozens of riverside resorts on the islands and sandy banks opposite Rosario. These have restaurants and bars, and most have comfortable facilities for an enjoyable day's stay, with woods, beaches and lagoons. There are campsites and *cabañas* for rent on some of them. Boats depart daily in summer from La Fluvial or from Costa Alta to the island resorts, each with its own transfer service. Weekend services run throughout the rest of the year.

BACKGROUND
Rosario

Unlike most Spanish American cities, Rosario was never officially founded. Though a fort was established in 1689 by Luis Romero de Pineda, it was just a place to export mules and tobacco throughout the 18th century. However, it grew rapidly in the late 19th century, with the opening of a railway line to Córdoba in 1870 and the increase of shipping along the Paraná: its port became a major exporter of grain and beef, while new industries were established, including breweries, grain mills and leather industries. In the late 20th century, Rosario attracted thousands of immigrants from the northern provinces of Argentina who settled on the outskirts, later forming one of the largest deprived communities in the country.

Listings Rosario *map page 329.*

Tourist information

See also www.viarosario.com (in Spanish) for the latest events information.

Tourist office
Av Belgrano y Buenos Aires, on the riverside park down from the Monumento a la Bandera, T0341-480 2230, www.rosarioturismo.com.
Very efficient staff, some of whom speak English.

Where to stay

Rosario has a good range of business hotels (including 4 in the Solans group, www.solans.com) and a number of hostels at the budget end.

$$$ Esplendor Savoy Rosario
San Lorenzo 1022, T0341-429 6000, www.esplendorsavoyrosario.com.
Early 20th-century mansion, once Rosario's best, now completely remodelled as a luxury hotel with all modern services. Gym, business centre, Wi-Fi, etc.

$$$ Majestic
San Lorenzo 980, T0341-440 5872, www.hotelmajestic.com.ar.
Modern, inviting 3-star, well designed rooms in an ornate turn-of-the-century building, stylish.

$ Cool Raul
San Lorezno 1670, T0341-679 3039, www.coolraulhostel.com.
Down the street from **La Lechuza**, this sociable party hostel has its rock'n'roll theme painted on the walls. Good for big groups.

$ Hostel Point
Catamarca 1837, T0341-440 9337, www.hostelpoint.com.ar.
Central, well-designed, brightly coloured dorms (US$10.55-11.25) and a lovely double. Recommended.

$ pp La Lechuza
San Lorenzo 1786, T0341-424 1040, www.lalechuzahostel.com.ar.
Welcoming, sociable hostel with helpful owner, dorms from US$11, private rooms **$$**, with bar, central, good meeting point. Chef makes an excellent breakfast (included) and dinner (not included). Recommended.

Restaurants

$$$ Parrilla Escauriza
Bajada Escauriza y Paseo Ribereño, La Florida, 30 mins' drive north from centre, near bridge over the Paraná, T0341 454 1777, www.escaurizaparrilla.com.ar.
Said to be the "oldest and best" fish restaurant, with terrace overlooking the river.

$$ Amarra2
Av Belgrano y Buenos Aires, T0341-447 7550, see Facebook.
Good food, including fish and seafood, quite formal, cheap set menus Mon-Fri noon. Also offers wine classes.

$$ La Estancia
Av Pellegrini 1510 y Paraguay T0341-440 7373.
Recommended by a local *asador* as the best *parrilla* in town. Very popular with locals, a few blocks east of Parque Independencia.

$$ Rock & Feller's
Blv N Oroño 106, T0341-423 4002, www.rockandfellers.com.ar.

Popular American-style restobar serving upmarket international fare including Tex-Mex options. Rock 'n' roll theme. Popular at night.

$$-$ Pizza Piazza
Santa Fe and Cafferata, T0341-437 4384, www.pizzapiazzaweb.com.ar.
Popular pizzeria with unique, regional twists on sandwiches and hot dogs.

$ New Taipei
Laprida 1121, T0341-449 8508, see Facebook.
Decent Chinese food for a change from the usual Argentine fare.

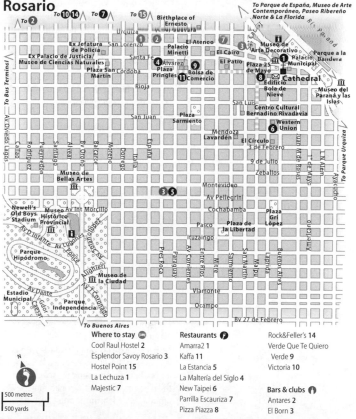

Rosario

Where to stay 🛏
Cool Raul Hostel 2
Esplendor Savoy Rosario 3
Hostel Point 15
La Lechuza 1
Majestic 7

Restaurants 🍴
Amarra2 1
Kaffa 11
La Estancia 5
La Maltería del Siglo 4
New Taipei 6
Parrilla Escauriza 7
Pizza Piazza 8

Rock&Feller's 14
Verde Que Te Quiero
Verde 9
Victoria 10

Bars & clubs 🍸
Antares 2
El Born 3

Cafés

Kaffa
Córdoba 1473.
Good coffee served inside the large bookshop **El Ateneo Yenny**.

La Maltería del Siglo
Santa Fe 1601, T0341-425-1846. Daily.
Food, drinks and background music. Livens up when major football matches are on.

Verde Que Te Quiero Verde
Córdoba 1358, T0341-530 4419.
Open 0800-2100, closed Sun.
Great vegetarian café, serving a fantastic brunch and lots of good veggie options. Recommended.

Victoria
Jujuy and Blv Oroño.
One of the oldest cafés in town and the most traditional.

Bars and clubs

There are many discos in Barrio Pichincha, with most only getting busy from 0130 onwards.

Bars

Antares
Callao 286, T0341-437 0945, see Facebook.
Daily 1830.
A good choice of own label beers, happy hour, serves good pub grub.

El Born
Pellegrini 1574, T0431-449 5196, see Facebook.
Daily from 1800 Sat-Sun.
Tapas bar, also has a clothes shop.

Entertainment

A good listings guide can be found in a section of the daily paper *Rosario 12*, as well as www.viarosario.com.

Cinema

In the centre there are cinemas in the shopping malls, **Del Siglo** (Córdoba y Presidente Roca, www.shoppingdelsiglo.com), and **Alto Rosario** (Caning y Junín, www.alto-rosario.com.ar); also **El Cairo** (Santa Fe 1120, www.elcairocinepublico.gob.ar), and **Village Cinemas** (Perón 5856, www.villagecines.com).

Cultural centres

Centro Cultural Bernardino Rivadavia, *San Martín 1080, T0341-480 2401*. A large centre holding year-round art exhibitions, video screenings, plays, music shows, seminars and puppet shows.

Centro Cultural Parque de España, *on Parque de España, T0341-426 0941, www.ccpe.org.ar*. Shows temporary art exhibitions, photography and plays at the **Teatro Príncipe de Asturias**.

Centro de Expresiones Contemporáneas, *Sargento Cabral y El Río (on the riverside, opposite Ex Aduana building), T0341-480 2245, www.cecrosario.org.ar*. A large warehouse with almost daily music, theatre and cinema events.

Theatre

De la Comedia (Cortada Ricardone y Mitre, T0341-480 2597, www.teatrolacomedia.com.ar); **El Círculo** (Laprida 1223, T0341-424 5349, www.teatro-elcirculo.com.ar); **Lavarden** (Mendoza and Sarmiento, T0341-472 1132 ext 170, www.plataformalavarden.gob.ar).

Festivals

20 Jun Día de la Bandera Nacional. It is worth going to the Monumento a la Bandera for the swearing-in ceremony made by hundreds of school pupils to the country's flag.

Nov Fiesta de las Colectividades. Every year during Nov at the Parque a la Bandera (opposite the monument) the town celebrates the diverse origins of the inhabitants, offering food, folk music and dancing.

Shopping

The main shopping street is the pedestrianized Córdoba.

Books
Balcarce, *San Nicolás 650*. A massive place for second-hand books and vinyl records.
El Ateneo, *Córdoba 1473*, *www.yenny-elateneo.com*.
Stratford, *Santa Fe 1340*. Sells English books.

Markets
Feria del Boulevard, *Blv Oroño and Rivadavia*. A weekend handicraft market.
Mercado de Pulgas, *next to the tourist office on the riverside*. Flea market at weekends.
Mercado Retro La Huella, *Av del Valle and Culluo (next to Rosario Norte railway station in Pichincha district)*. Every Sun and bank holiday there is a large flea market.

Outdoor gear
Central de Pesca, *San Juan 1089*, *T0371-424 7945, see Facebook*.
El Combatiente, *San Martín 816*, *T0341-426 1755, see Facebook*.

Shopping malls
Alto Rosario (Caning and Junín, www.alto-rosario.com.ar), an impressive mall; **Del Siglo** (Córdoba and Presidente Roca); **Palace Garden** (Córdoba 1358).

What to do

Swimming
On Laguna Setúbal, from El Espigón; at the **Club de Regatas**, next to the bridge; or from Piedras Blancas on Costanera Este.

Tour operators
For city tours check agencies at **Asociación Rosarina de Agencias de Viaje** (T0341-421 3554, www.arav.org.ar).
Barco Ciudad de Rosario, *T0341-449 8688*, *www.barcocr1.com*. A large passenger boat leaves from the pier next to Estación Fluvial for 2-hr trips on the river on weekend afternoons.

Transport

For transport from the airport and bus terminal into the centre, see box, page 326.

Air
The airport (T0341-451 3220, www.aeropuertorosario.com) has daily flights to **Buenos Aires**.

Bike hire and repair
Bike House, San Juan 973, T0341-424 5280, info@bikehouse.com.ar, see Facebook.
Speedway Bike Center, Roca 1269, T0341-426 8415, www.speedwaybikecenter.com.ar.

Bus
The bus terminal (Santa Fe and Cafferata, T0341-437 3030, www.terminalrosario.gov.ar) has an information point, post office, shops, restaurants and left luggage (open 24 hrs). From the centre to the bus terminal, catch a bus on Plaza 25 de Mayo, via C Santa Fe. Note that to use local buses you must buy a rechargeable magnetic card sold at kiosks in the centre or near bus stops (US$3 for card and 1st journey).

To **Buenos Aires**, 4 hrs, US$22. To **Córdoba**, 6 hrs, US$29. To **Santa Fe**, 2½ hrs, US$10-11.

Train
Rosario Norte railway station is operated by **Ferrocentral** (T0800 333 822, www.ferrocentralsa.com.ar). The ticket office is open Mon-Fri 0800-2200 and Sat-Sun 1600-2400. The Apeadero Sur railway station ticket office is open daily 1800-0100, and is run by **Trenes Argentinos** with limited services to Buenos Aires.

To **Buenos Aires**, leaves daily from Apeadero Sur at 0026, 7 hrs, US$14; to **Tucumán**, Mon and Fri at 1614, 7 hrs.

Santa Fe (population 500,000) is capital of its province and one of the oldest cities in the country, though there's little architectural evidence and this is not really a tourist destination. It lies near the confluence of the Santa Fe and Salado rivers in a low-lying area with lagoons and islands just west of the Río Paraná and was severely flooded in May 2003, one of Argentina's most shocking disasters. It is connected to the smaller city of Paraná, on the east bank of the river, by road bridges and a tunnel.

Sights

The city's **commercial centre** lies a few blocks southwest of the bus terminal, along the partially pedestrianized San Martín. This street leads southwards to the historic centre, around Plaza 25 de Mayo, with the oldest buildings and a few museums.

On the plaza itself is the majestic **Casa de Gobierno**, built in 1911-1917 in French style on the site of the historic Cabildo, in which the 1853 constitution was drafted. Opposite is the **cathedral**, dating from 1751 but remodelled in 1834, its twin towers capped by blue-tiled cupolas.

Across San Martín, southeast of the plaza, is the extensive Parque General Belgrano. The **Museo Histórico Provincial** ① *San Martín 1490, T0342-457 3529, all year Tue-Fri 0830-1200 and 1530-1900, Sat-Sun 0830-1200, afternoon hours change frequently, free but donations welcome*, is in a former family house dating from 1690 (one of the oldest surviving civil buildings in the country). It's worth visiting for the house itself rather than the exhibition of two 17th-century Cuzco-school paintings. About 100 m south is the **Iglesia y Convento de San Francisco** built between 1673 and 1695. The church has walls nearly 2 m thick and fine wooden ceilings, built from timber floated down the river from Paraguay, carved by indigenous craftsmen and fitted without the use of nails. The pulpit and altar are 17th-century baroque.

On the opposite side of the park is the superb **Museo Etnográfico y Colonial** ① *25 de Mayo 1470, Tue-Fri 0830-1200 and 1530-1900, Sat-Sun from 1530, 1600 or 1730 depending on season, free, but donations welcome*, with a chronologically ordered exhibition of artefacts from aboriginal inhabitants from 2000 BC to the first Spanish settlers who lived in Santa Fe la Vieja, the town's original site. The most remarkable objects are delicate zoomorphic ceramic pots, Spanish amulets and board games, and a model of both Santa Fe towns, showing that the distribution of the main buildings remained unchanged after the move.

Listings Santa Fe

Tourist information

Provincial office
San Martín 1399, T0342-458 9477,
www.turismosantafe.com.ar.

Tourist office
T0342-457 4124, www.santafeturismo.gov.ar.
Mon-Fri 0700-2000 (0800 at weekends).
There are additional information offices
opposite the **Teatro Municipal** on San Martín
2020, also at Blv Gálvez 1150 and Santiago del
Estero 3100, T0800-777 5000. All are good.

Where to stay

$$$-$$ Hostal Santa Fe de la Veracruz
San Martín 2954, T0342-455 1740,
www.hostalsf.com.
Traditional favourite, 2 types of room,
both good value, large breakfast, restaurant,
sauna (extra).

$$ Castelar
25 de Mayo 2349, T0342-456 0999,
www.castelarsantafe.com.ar.
Overlooking a small plaza, this 1930s hotel is
good value and has comfortable rooms and
a restaurant. Breakfast is included.

Restaurants

Many places in the centre close on Sun.

$$ El Quincho de Chiquito
Av Almirante Brown y Obispo Príncipe
(Costanera Oeste).
Classic fish restaurant, excellent food,
generous helpings and good value.

$$ España
San Martín 2644.
An elegant place, specializing in seafood
and fish.

$ Club Sirio Libanés
25 de Mayo 2740, see Facebook.
Excellent Middle Eastern food, popular Sun
lunch for families.

$ El Brigadier
San Martín 1670.
This colonial-style place next to the Plaza
25 de Mayo serves superb *surubí al paquete*
(stuffed fish) and many *parrilla* dishes.

Cafés

Las Delicias
Hipólito Yrigoyen and San Martín.
A well-preserved, early 20th-century café
and bakery, with beautiful decor, serving a
wide variety of coffees and sweet pastries.
Try their speciality, the *alfajor santafesino*.

Tokio
Rivadavia y Crespo (on Plaza España).
Another café with a rich history in Santa Fe.

Bars and clubs

Santa Fe has a long tradition of brewing
and is one of the few places where local
lagers can compete with the big national
monopoly, Quilmes. Beer is usually sold
in a *liso* (not a very large glass). There are
lively areas of bars and nightclubs, popular
with young crowds, all along the Costanera
Este; beyond the bridge on Laguna Setúbal;
in the Recoleta district, north of centre;
around Plaza Los Constituyentes, and next
to Blv Pellegrini and to Blv Gálvez.

Transport

Air
The airport, **Sauce Viejo** (T0342-499 5064) is
located 17 km south of the centre; a taxi to
the bus terminal costs US$8-9. Daily flights to
and from **Buenos Aires**.

Bus
The bus terminal (Belgrano 2910, T0342-457
4124) is near the centre and has luggage
lockers. To **Córdoba**, US$27-40, 5 hrs. Many
buses to **Buenos Aires**, US$35-40, 6 hrs; to
Paraná, frequent service, US$2, 50 mins.

Capital of Entre Ríos province, Paraná (population 350,000) stands on the eastern bank of a bend in the Río Paraná, opposite Santa Fe. Its centre lies on a hill offering fine views over the river, and if you're travelling up the Paraná river, it is a good place to stop on a journey north. It was founded in 1649, when Santa Fe was moved from its original spot and settlers crossed the river in search of higher ground for cultivation, and a suitable port. In the mid-19th century it gained importance as capital of the Argentine Confederation and a subsequent period of growth left some sumptuous public buildings. The city's faded splendour creates a quiet, rather melancholic atmosphere but there is an appealingly calm pace of life here.

Sights
From Plaza Alvear, Avenida Rivadavia leads to the beautiful **Parque Urquiza** and the riverside. Though nothing remains from the colonial period, the city retains many fine 19th- and 20th-century public buildings, centred on Plaza Primero de Mayo. On the east side is the impressive **cathedral**, built in 1883 in Italianate neoclassical style, with a fine dome and colonnaded portico, though the interior is plain. Also on the plaza are the **Municipalidad** (1890), with its distinctive tower, and the **Club Social** (1906), for years the elite social centre of the city. Take pedestrianized San Martín half a block west of the corner with 25 de Junio to see the fine **Teatro 3 de Febrero** (1908).

Two blocks north is the **Plaza Alvear**, and opposite one of its corners, the provincial tourist office (see above). On the same block is the mildly engaging **Museo Histórico Martiniano Leguizamón** ① *Laprida and Buenos Aires, T0343-420 7869, Tue-Fri 0800-1230 and 1500-1930, Sat 0900-1200 and 1600-1900, Sun 0900-1200, donation.*

On the west side of the plaza is the **Museo de Bellas Artes** ① *Buenos Aires 355, T0343-420 7868, Tue-Fri 0800-1300 and 1500-2000, Sat 1000-1200 and 1600-1900, Sun 1000-1200, donation*, housing a vast collection of Argentine artists, with many works by painter Cesáreo Bernaldo de Quirós. On the north side of the plaza is the **Museo de Ciencias Naturales y Antropológicas** ① *Carlos Gardel 62, T0343-420 8894, Tue-Fri 0800-1200 and 1500-1900, Sat 0830-1230 and 1500-1900, Sun 0900-1200, donation*, particularly appealing for kids, with an insect collection (see the 25-cm-wide moth), and lots of stuffed animals. Among fascinating artefacts by Guaraní people are a rare ornate urn, with red geometrical paintings, and small utensils made by groups of indigenous peoples to the north, and a rather alarming display of jars containing human foetuses, from five weeks to six months old.

From the northwestern corner of the plaza, it's a pleasant stroll along tree-lined Avenida Rivadavia, with the monumental

Essential Paraná

Finding your feet

The bus terminal is 10 blocks southeast of Plaza Primero de Mayo. Leave the small plaza on your right and take Avenida Echagüe right to the centre, or buses No 1, 4, US$0.60. A *remise* taxi will cost US$2-3.

Getting around

The city can easily be visited on foot, since the most interesting sights lie around the two main plazas, Plaza 1 de Mayo and, three blocks north, Plaza Alvear.

Escuela del Centenario (1910) ① *Av Rivadavia 168*, to reach the city's pride and joy, the **Parque Urquiza**. Extending along the low cliffs of the Paraná River, with wonderful views and many fine statues, the park is well planted with *lapachos, palos borrachos* and pines. There's an open-air theatre, and steps to the Avenida Costanera. The cobbled street **Bajada de los Vascos**, which in the 19th century gave access to the port area, is now known as **Puerto Viejo** and retains some original buildings. The **Avenida Costanera** is lively, with restaurants, sports clubs and sandy beaches on the river.

Listings Paraná

Tourist information

Paraná has 4 city **tourist offices** (all open daily 0800-2000): at the bus terminal (T0343-420 1862); at Parque Urquiza at Av Laurencena and Juan de San Martín, on the east side (T0343-420 1837); at San Martín and Urquiza in Plaza 1 de Mayo; and at the Hernandarias tunnel. For more information, see www.turismoparana.com.ar.

Where to stay

$$$ Gran Hotel Paraná
Urquiza 976, T0343-422 3900,
www.hotelesparana.com.ar.
Overlooking Plaza Primero de Mayo,
with 3 room categories, smart restaurant
La Fourchette and a gym.

$$ San Jorge
Belgrano 368, T0343-422 1685,
www.sanjorgehotel.com.ar.
Renovated house, helpful staff, clean rooms,
attractive decor, Wi-Fi in lobby only. Good
mid-range option. Recommended.

$$-$ Paraná Hostel
Andrés Pazos 159, T0343-422 8233,
www.paranahostel.com.ar.
Small, central, good living room with cable
TV and comfy sofas. Smart dorms and private
rooms available. The best budget option in
the area.

Restaurants

$$ Giovani
Urquiza 1047, T0343-423 0527.
A popular place in the centre,
good for pasta.

$$ La Fourchette
Urquiza 976, T0343-422 3900
(at Gran Hotel Paraná).
The finest restaurant in town is a small,
stylish place. Choose from a small menu of
really fine dishes. Perfect for a sophisticated,
intimate dinner.

$ Club de Pescadores
Access from Av Estrada at Puerto Viejo
(closed when river levels are too high,
usually in summer).
A good traditional fish restaurant in the old
and picturesque section of the port.

$ Coscoino
Corrientes 373, T0343-422 4120, see Facebook.
A relaxed family establishment serving good
and very filling home-made pastas, *tenedor
libre*, except Sat evenings and Sun lunchtime.

$ El Viejo Marino
Av Laurencena 341, the opposite end of
Av Costanera, T0343-431842, see Facebook.
Well-prepared fish dishes.

What to do

Tour operators
Costanera 241, *Buenos Aires 212, T0343-423*
4385, www.costanera241.com.ar. City tours
and boat trips on the Paraná river.

Transport

Bus

From Santa Fe, the road goes under the Río Paraná by the Hernandarias tunnel (toll) and then crosses a number of bridges to reach Paraná (bus service, US$24 pesos, 50 mins). In Paraná, the bus terminal (Av Ramírez 2350 T0343-422 1282) has left-luggage facilities available Mon-Fri 0700-2100, Sat-Sun 0700-1800.

To **Colón** on Río Uruguay, 4-5 hrs, US$13. To **Buenos Aires**, 7-8 hrs, US$35-45.

North of Paraná

scenic journeys north

Heading north from Paraná along the Río Paraná, you can take monotonous Route 11 to Resistencia on the western bank, or Route 12 north to Corrientes, which closely follows the eastern banks of the river through varied landscapes giving access to two attractive small towns on the coast with good fishing: Santa Elena and La Paz, and a marvellous traditional estancia, Vizcacheras.

Santa Elena

On the Río Paraná about 150 km north of the provincial capital is Santa Elena (population 23,000), a small port whose fishing attracts many anglers. Its history is closely associated with its meat-packing factory, which was run by British firms from the late 19th century until it closed down in 1993. The red-brick buildings of the *frigorífico* can still be seen in town. At the end of the *costanera* is the Paseo La Olla, with beautiful views over the river.

La Paz *Colour map 4, A5.*

Nearly 170 km north of Paraná, La Paz (population 24,716) is another small port in an area popular for fishing, where the fishing festivals **Fiesta Provincial del Surubí** and **Fiesta Provincial del Dorado** are held respectively every April and September. The undulating terrain and the cliffs above the river make a picturesque setting for the old houses still standing in the town.

There is a small history museum at the Parque Berón de Astrada, from where there are fine views, while another park, the **Parque de la Aventura**, has trails along the riverside for walking or cycling. Access is on the way to La Armonía, reached by Blv 25 de Mayo and then Yrigoyen.

Listings North of Paraná

Tourist information

Santa Elena

Tourist office
Eva Perón y 9 de Julio, T03437-481223, www.santaelena.tur.ar.

La Paz

Tourist office
Vieytes and España, T03437-422389, www.lapazentrerios.gov.ar.

Provides information on accommodation at a few nearby estancias.

Where to stay

Santa Elena

$$$$ Estancia Vizcacheras
R12, Km 554.5, T011-4719 5613 (in Buenos Aires).
South of Santa Elena, the estancia was built in the early 1900s by the Bovril company in

British colonial style with Argentine touches. The owners are extremely hospitable, making guests feel at home in luxuriously furnished bedrooms, all with their own bathroom (some with old-fashioned baths) and private verandas. Have drinks on the terrace with splendid views of the gardens and the grasslands beyond, and delicious dinner served under the stars. You'll be invited to see the daily routines of the working cattle ranch, with walking and horse riding, fishing and birdwatching also arranged. Highly recommended.

La Paz

$$ Milton
Italia 1029, T03437-422232,
www.miltonhotel.com.ar.
Central, with comfortable enough rooms. A/c and breakfast extra.

$$ Posta Surubí
España 224, T03437-421128,
www.postasurubi.com.ar.
Attractive location by the river with good rooms, fine views and a restaurant. Breakfast included.

Corrientes *Colour map 1, B6.*

colonial riverside town with a vibrant carnival

Capital of its province, Corrientes (population 400,000) lies some 30 km southwest of the meeting of the rivers Paraná and Paraguay. The city is mainly a service centre for its agricultural hinterland, which produces beef, cotton, tobacco, rice and *yerba mate*. Although Corrientes is a less important transport hub than Resistencia, it is a pleasant place for a stopover. The city centre, with its peaceful traditional streets and squares, is well preserved and its *costanera* is one of the most attractive in the country. The national capital of Carnival, the city is also famous as the location of Graham Greene's novel *The Honorary Consul*. In summer the air can be oppressively hot and humid, but in winter the climate is pleasant.

Sights

The main Plaza 25 de Mayo, one block inland from the *costanera*, is a beautiful shady space. You could take a pleasant stroll from here around the surrounding blocks, with their fine old houses and river views, and to the Avenida Costanera. On the north side of the plaza is the **Jefatura de Policía**, built in 19th-century French style. The **Museo de Artesanías** ⓘ *Quintana 905, Mon-Fri 0800-1200 and 1600-2000, Sat 0800-1300, free,* is a large old house with an exhibition of handicrafts made from the most diverse materials imaginable, by indigenous groups, as well as by contemporary urban and rural artisans. Tiny skeleton-shaped images represent San La Muerte, a popular devotion that ensures the bearer a painless death. A large room at the front is a workshop where you can watch the patient work of the local craftspeople. On the east side of the plaza are the Italianate **Casa de Gobierno** (1881-1886) and the **Ministerio de Gobierno**. On the south side is the

Essential Corrientes

Finding your feet

Dr Fernando Piragine Niveyro (Cambá Punta) Airport is 10 km east of the city and is reached by Route 12 (*remise* taxi US$12.) The **bus terminal** is 5 km southeast of the centre. Bus No 103 goes to the centre (but check with the driver as the same line has many different routes), 20 minutes, US$0.40. See Transport, page 339, for details.

Corrientes

Corrientes was founded in 1588 on the Paraná river, next to seven relatively high *puntas*, or promontories, by an expedition from Asunción, led by Juan Torres de Vera y Aragón. It became important as a port on the route between Buenos Aires and Asunción. Numerous shipyards led to the development of a naval industry that endured for centuries. The Guaraní population that inhabited the region were mainly absorbed into the Jesuit missions or became workers for the estancias. They progressively mixed with the Spanish newcomers giving the local society a distinctive character, still evident today in the faces of the inhabitants, and also in the daily use of Guaraní words and a particular accent in spoken Spanish.

church **La Merced**, where there are confessionals carved by the indigenous inhabitants of Misiones in the mid-18th century, and a colonial-style altar. The **Casa Lagraña**, a huge building with three interior patios, built in 1860 for the governor, lies one block south.

At 9 de Julio 1044 is the **Museo Histórico** ① *Mon-Fri 0800-1200, 1600-2000, free,* displaying, among other pieces, a collection of religious objects dating from the 18th and 19th centuries. Only two blocks north is the **Teatro Juan de Vera** ① *San Juan 637, T03783-442 7743,* a lively cultural centre and a beautiful building itself (1913). Across the road is the **Museo de Bellas Artes** ① *San Juan 634, www.museovidalctes.es.tl, Mon-Fri 0800-1200 and 1600-2000, Sat 0800-1200, free,* a small arts museum with temporary exhibitions and a permanent collection including valuable works by the painters Petorutti, Fader and Quinquela Martín. The quite impressive **Iglesia y Convento de San Francisco** ① *Mendoza 468,* was rebuilt in 1861 on the site of the original which dated from 1608.

Six blocks south of the Plaza 25 de Mayo is the leafy Plaza de la Cruz and opposite, the church of **La Cruz de los Milagros**, which houses the Santo Madero. This miraculous cross was placed by the founder of the city, and when the indigenous residents tried to burn it, they were allegedly killed by lightning from a cloudless sky. Near the plaza, the **Museo de Ciencias Naturales Amadeo Bonpland** ① *San Martín 850, Mon-Sat 0800-1200 and 1600-2000,* has a large archaeology collection and plants with a remarkable display of 5800 insects including a huge wasp nest.

The attractive Avenida Costanera, lined with *lapachos* and *palos borrachos*, leads along the Río Paraná from its southwestern end, next to the bridge, to **Parque Mitre**, from where there are good views of sunsets over the river.

Listings Corrientes

Tourist information

City tourist office
Carlos Pellegrini 542, T0379-442377, www.ciudaddecorrientes.gov.ar. Daily 0800-1200 and 1600-2000.
Provides a good map.

Provincial tourist office
25 de Mayo 1330, T0379-442 7200, www.corrientes.gov.ar. Mon-Fri 0800-1200 and 1600-2000.
There's another office in the bus station (hours subject to change) and on the Costanera and 9 de Julio (T0379-447 4829).

Where to stay

$$$ La Alondra
2 de Abril 827, T0379-443 0555,
www.laalondra.com.ar.
The best place to stay in town. 8 beautiful
rooms and a wonderful communal area.
Antique furniture throughout, exquisite
styling and a homely feel. There's a lovely
patio and a 12-m-long pool.

$ pp Bienvenida Golondrina
La Rioja 455, T0379-443 5316, www.
hostelbienvenidagolondrina.com.
The only hostel in the city. Half a block from
the port, in a beautifully remodelled old
building. Bright dorms, all rooms with a/c,
private rooms (**$$**), a roof-top terrace and lots
of internal patios to relax in. Also organizes
fishing and kayaking trips to Iberá.

Restaurants

$ Martha de Bianchetti
9 de Julio y Mendoza.
Smart café and bakery.

Cafés

Panambí
Junín near Córdoba.
A traditional, central *confitería* serving good
pastries and regional breads.

Festivals

Jan Chamamé Festival, this regional music
chamamé has its own festival in Corrientes at
Anfiteatro Tránsito Cocomarola, Barrio 1000
Viviendas, 10 blocks south of Av 3 de Abril.
This cheerful music is danced in couples with
the upper body close, legs far apart. Join in!
See also www.corrienteschamame.com.ar.
Feb Carnival, which has been one of the
most popular celebrations for decades in
Argentina and is celebrated on Fri and Sat
evenings throughout Feb at the Corsódromo.

This stadium lies a little distance from the
centre reached by special bus marked
'Corsódromo'. The colourful parade opens
the competition among the different
comparsas, passionately supported by the
audience as football teams. Tickets are not
sold in the stadium, but in many shops in
the centre. See also www.carnaval.com/
argentina/corrientes.

What to do

Experiencia Corrientes, *T011-15 3688 6999,*
www.experienciacorrientes.com. Experienced
guide Pablo runs fishing and kayaking trips in
Corrientes and Iberá. Enquire at **Bienvenida
Golondrina** hostel (see Where to stay, above).

Transport

Air
The airport (T0379-448 3336) has flights
to/from **Buenos Aires**.

Bus
The bus terminal is at Av Maipú 2700 (T0379-
447 7600). A left-luggage facility is available
at the Crucero del Norte office.
    To **Resistencia**, 1 hr, US$1. To **Posadas**
US$24-28, 3½-4 hrs, several companies.
To **Buenos Aires**, several companies,
11-12 hrs, US$75-100.
    Several companies run buses from
Corrientes to Asunción via Resistencia,
5-7 hrs, US$17 from Corrientes or Resistencia.
Sol, **NS de la Asunción** runs Corrientes–
Resistencia–**Asunción** (Paraguay), US$17.
Alternatively, take the bus from Clorinda
to Asunción (1 a day), or to **Puerto Falcón**,
US$1, with **Empresa Falcón** every hour from
the border, last bus to the centre of Asunción
1830. See also box, page 345.
    Note Buses don't wait for you to go
through formalities: if you cannot process
your paperwork in time, wait for the same
company's next bus and present ticket, or
buy a new ticket.

The Argentine
Chaco

Little visited by travellers, the Argentine Chaco is just part of an immense sprawling lowland some 900 km wide, covering half of Paraguay and huge areas of Bolivia and Brazil. Rising gently from east to west, it's crossed by meandering rivers, and filled in central parts with cattle and cotton fields, soya and sunflowers. Though much of the Chaco is inaccessible, with little public transport, and rough roads that become almost impassable after heavy rains, two national parks can easily be reached all year round, both hosting a rich diversity of wildlife largely uninterrupted by human activity: Parque Nacional Chaco reached from Resistencia, and Parque Nacional Río Pilcomayo reached from Formosa. These are the region's two main cities, both close to Río Paraguay; the only other settlement is Presidencia Roque Sáenz Peña, 170 km northwest of Resistencia, it's an uninspiring place though its thermal waters are among the country's finest.

The most fascinating aspect of the Chaco is its pure and extensive indigenous population. Two of the largest groups are the Qom/Toba, mainly settled in towns next to the Paraná River, and the semi-nomadic Wichí in the west, who maintain their traditions of fine weaving, woodwork and ancient fishing techniques.

BACKGROUND

The Argentine Chaco

The Chaco falls into two distinct zones along a line south of the boundary between Chaco and Formosa provinces: the Wet Chaco and the Dry Chaco. The **Wet Chaco** spreads south from the Río Pilcomayo (the border with Paraguay) and west of the Río Paraguay, and consists of fertile wetlands supporting rich farming and abundant vegetation, and marshlands with savanna and groves of *caranday* palms, hosting many species of bird. Further west, as rainfall diminishes, the **Dry Chaco** is arid and wild, with little plant or, indeed, human life. The scrub vegetation is dotted with the algarrobo trees, white quebracho, the spiny bloated trunks of palo borracho and various types of cacti. This is one of the hottest places in South America and is sometimes known as 'El Impenetrable'.

Resistencia and around *Colour map 1, B6.*

the heart of the Chaco

The hot and energetic capital of the Chaco province is Resistencia (population 430,000). Together with the port of Barranqueras, just to the south on the Río Paraná, it's the commercial centre for the Chaco region. It's a modern city, not architecturally rich, but has an impressive number of sculptures by renowned artists, earning it the title of 'city of statues'. There's also a splendid central plaza, a nature reserve and the lovely Isla del Cerrito within easy reach, making it an appealing alternative stopover to neighbouring Corrientes on the journey between Iguazú and Salta.

Sights

The large Plaza 25 de Mayo occupies four blocks in the centre of the city, with a variety of indigenous plants and palms turning it into a mini botanical garden.

Five blocks from here, there's an informal cultural centre, **Fogón de los Arrieros** (literally, 'the hearth of the muleteers') ① *Brown 350 (between López and Planes and French), T0362-442 6418, open to non-members Mon-Sat 0800-1200, Tue-Wed 2100-2300, US$1.30, free for those taking the free city tour that leaves from the Casa de Cultura on the plaza Tue-Sun at 0945.* This rather wonderful institution was formed in the late 1960s by artists who decided to make the city an open-air gallery, with public spaces filled with sculpture and murals. The centre itself still operates as a meeting place and exhibition space:

Essential Argentine Chaco

Access

From Resistencia and Formosa, parallel Routes 16 and 81 head dead straight northwest across the plains until they encounter the first hills of eastern Salta, which mark the border of this vast territory. Buses to Salta take Route 16; Route 81 has long unpaved sections west of the small town of Las Lomitas, making the journey tough going after heavy rains.

Information

For more information, see www.chaco turismo.com. For introductory articles see www.pueblos-originarios-argentnina. wikispaces.com, www.pocnolec.blogspot. co.uk and www.chacolinks.org.uk.

inspiring, and highly recommended. In the surrounding streets, you'll find more than 175 pieces of art by the country's finest artists.

Take López and Planes (later Sáenz Peña) and turn right at Juan B Justo to reach the **Museo del Hombre Chaqueño** ① *Juan B Justo 280, Mon-Fri 0800-1200 and 1500-1900, free.* This small anthropological museum covers the story of colonization in the region, with a fine exhibition of handicrafts by native Wichi, Toba and Mocoví peoples, together with a fascinating mythology section in which small statues represent the Guaraní peoples' beliefs. Many of the rituals detailed are still practised in rural areas today and are characterized by creatures of the marsh and woodland.

Isla del Cerrito

The Isla del Cerrito, a beautiful island northeast of Resistencia at the confluence of the Paraná and Paraguay rivers, has a provincial nature reserve of 12,000 ha, covered mainly with grassland and palm trees. At the eastern end of the island (51 km from Resistencia), on the Río Paraná, in Cerrito, there's an attractive tourist complex with white sand beaches, a history museum, accommodation and restaurants. It all gets very busy during the **Fiesta Nacional del Dorado**, which is held on the opposite shores in Paso de la Patria.

To get to Cerrito, follow Route 16 east and turn north 3 km before the bridge to Corrientes; from here a road, the last 20 km of which are dirt (difficult after heavy rain), leads to a bridge, from where it is 17 km further to Cerrito. **Turismo Continental** ① *T0362-452 5421*, minibuses leave for Cerrito from Ameghino 127 Monday-Friday at 1900, Saturday at 2000, one hour's journey, stopping 30 minutes there, US$2.

Parque Nacional Chaco *Colour map 1, B6.* The Chaco National Park, 115 km northwest of Resistencia, extends over 15,000 ha and protects one of the last remaining untouched areas of the Wet Chaco. There are exceptional *quebracho colorado* trees, *caranday* palms and dense riverine forests, with orchids growing along the banks of the Río Negro. It is a very good place for birdwatching, with 340 species having been sighted in the park, including the parrot *loro hablador*. You're certain to be woken in the morning by the loud screams of *carayá* monkeys, though other mammals living in the park may be less obtrusive, like the collared *peccary*, the *corzuela parda*, the puma and the *yaguarundí* cat (*Felis jaguamindi*).

At 300 m from the park's entrance there's a visitor centre and a free campsite with hot showers and electricity. Two short

---

Essential Parque Nacional Chaco

Access

To get to the park from Resistencia, follow paved Route 16 northwest; after about 60 km take Route 9 north to Colonia Elisa and Capitán Solari, which lies 5 km east of the park entrance via a dirt road. La Estrella runs daily buses between Resistencia and Capitán Solari, from where *remise* taxis make the short journey to the park, which can also be done on foot. Or, if there's a group of you, call the park in advance to be picked up at Capitán Solari. For more information contact T03725-499161, chaco@apn.gov.ar. Tour operators run day-long trips to the park from Resistencia.

Entry and opening hours

Access to the park is free and open 24 hours.

When to go

It's best visited between April and October to avoid intense summer heat and voracious mosquitoes.

footpaths, *sendero del puente colgante* and *sendero del abuelo* respectively, lead to the banks of the Río Negro and to an 800-year-old specimen of the *quebracho* tree. A vehicle road goes north 6 km up to two high *mangrullos* or viewpoints, overlooking the two lakes, Laguna Carpincho and Laguna Yacaré, where, with a bit of patience, you'll see *yacarés* (alligators). Another track, suitable only for 4WD vehicles, goes south through a forest of *quebracho* trees and, after 9 km, reaches the peaceful Laguna Panza de Cabra. There is a campsite by the lake, without facilities, where you'll often hear the rare maned wolf *(aguará guazú)* at night.

Listings Resistencia and around

Tourist information

City tourist office
Plaza 25 de Mayo, T0362-445 8289. Mon-Sat 0730-1230 and 1400-2000, Sun 1400-2000.
Helpful office on the main plaza with many maps.

Provincial tourist office
Av Sarmiento 1675, T0362-443 8880, www.chaco.travel. Mon-Sat 0730-1230 and 1400-2000, Sun 1400-2000.
You can also get information on other destinations.

Where to stay

Resistencia

$$$ Covadonga
Güemes 200, T0362-444 4444, www.hotelcovadonga.com.ar.
Comfortable, swimming pool, sauna and gym.

$$$-$$ Niyat Urban Hotel
Hipólito Yrigoyen 83, T0362-444 8451, www.niyaturban.com.ar.
The newest and best hotel in town. Modern, spacious and stylish rooms overlooking the park, efficient staff.

$$-$ Bariloche
Obligado 239, T0362-442 0685, residencialbariloche@hotmail.com.
Good budget choice, welcoming owner, decent rooms with a/c. No breakfast, but there's a nearby café at **Gran Hotel Royal**.

Restaurants

Resistencia
There is a lack of choice when it comes to good-value restaurants but these are recommended:

$$ Almacén Gourmet
Pellegrini 399, T0362-15 474 9266, www.almacengourmetweb.com.
Popular restaurant with *parrilla* and good desserts.

$ San José
Roca and Av Alberdi, Plaza 25 de Mayo, T0362 442 7008.
A popular café and *confitería* with excellent pastries (try the *medialunas*) and ice creams.

Shopping

Resistencia
Fundación Chaco Artesanal, *Carlos Pellegrini 272*. A charity selling fine handicrafts made by Toba, Wichi and Mocoví native groups in varied materials, whose profits return to those communities.

Transport

Resistencia
Air
The **airport** (T0362-444 6009) is 8 km west of town (taxi US$14-15). Flights to/from **Buenos Aires**, 1¼ hrs.

Bus
The modern bus terminal (Av Malvinas Argentinas and Av MacLean, T0362-446

1098) is on the western outskirts; bus 3 or 10 runs to/from Oro y Perón, 1 block west of plaza (20 mins, US$0.40 paid with card); *remise* US$3-4. Left luggage is open 24 hrs.

To **Buenos Aires** 12-13 hrs, US$75-100 several companies. To **Formosa** 2-2½ hrs, US$9-15. To **Iguazú**, 8-10½ hrs, US$39-55, several companies, some require change of bus in **Posadas**, 5½ hrs, US$22-29. To **Salta, FlechaBus, El Norte** and **La Veloz del Norte**, 12½ hrs, US$67-76. To **Asunción** 3 companies: **NSA, Plus Ultra** and **Godoy**, 6 hrs, US$13-22.

North of Resistencia
to the Paraguayan border

Route 11 runs north to Formosa and then onwards to the Paraguayan border near Clorinda, with the city of Asunción just over the border; see box, opposite. Crossing low-lying pastures with streams and *caranday* palms, this route offers views of the diverse birdlife of the Wet Chaco, and is beautiful in the evening.

Formosa *Colour map 2, A1.*
Formosa (population 234,354) is the capital of its province and the only Argentine port of any note on the Río Paraguay. Oppressively hot from November to March, the city is the base for boat trips along the rivers in the eastern part of the province during the winter, when the weather is mild. It's also a possible stopover on the way to the **Parque Nacional Río Pilcomayo** or the **Bañado La Estrella**, and it's close to the Paraguayan capital, Asunción. From the town's small port, boats cross the river to Alberdi (only if you have a multiple entry visa).

Parque Nacional Río Pilcomayo
Free, open 24 hrs. Administration centre, Av Pueyrredón and R86, Laguna Blanca, T03718-470045, riopilcomayo@apn.gov.ar, Mon-Fri 0700-1400. The park is best visited in winter.

This park, 162 km north of Formosa, covers 48,000 ha of Wet Chaco environment bordering Paraguay on the southern bank of the Río Pilcomayo. The lower parts may be flooded during the rainy season and the resulting lakes and *esteros*, or marshlands, create the park's most beguiling landscapes. The rest is grassland with *caranday* palm forests, where rheas can be seen, with some Chaco forest in the upper lands, habitat of three monkey species and several types of woodpecker. Due to its significance as a natural wetland, the park is a Ramsar site with diverse birdlife, including herons and three different species of stork. Anteaters, capybaras, coatis, two species of *yacaré* and *aguará guazu* are on the list of animals protected within the park.

The park has two entrances leading to different areas. The most visited and easier to reach if you are on foot is Laguna Blanca, where there's an information point and a free campsite with electricity and cold water. From there, a footpath leads to the **Laguna Blanca**, the biggest lake in the park where you'll spot alligators among the rich aquatic plant life. The lake is not recommended for swimming, since the resident piranhas have a penchant for human toes. The second entrance leads to **Estero Poí**, another information point and a campsite without facilities. Here take the 1200-m footpath, which has informative signs on the botany of the upper areas of the park. A vehicle road goes into the park up the Río Pilcomayo and the international border, but can only be used with special permission.

BORDER CROSSING
Argentina–Paraguay

Puente Loyola

The easiest crossing into Paraguay is by road via the Puente Loyola, 4 km north of Clorinda. From Puerto Falcón, at the Paraguayan end of the bridge, the road runs 40 km northeast, crossing the Río Paraguay at Puente Remanso (with a pedestrian walkway on upstream side, 20 minutes to cross) to reach Asunción.

The border is open 24 hours. Formalities for entering Argentina are dealt with at the Argentine end, at Puerto Pilcomayo, and for those leaving Argentina at the Paraguayan end at Itá Enramada, which is an easy crossing.

For **transport** to Asunción, see page 339.

To get there, from Formosa take R11 to Clorinda, and from there take R86 going west. After 47 km, a 5-km dirt road leads north to the Laguna Blanca entrance; follow R86 for a few kilometres further for the 5-km access dirt road to the Estero Poí entrance. **Godoy** buses run from Formosa or Resistencia to the small towns of Laguna Naineck, 5 km from the park (for Laguna Blanca) and Laguna Blanca, 8 km from the park (for Estero Poí). *Remise* taxis from both towns should charge no more than US$5 for these short journeys. There are police controls on the way to the park.

Listings North of Resistencia

Tourist information

Formosa

Tourist office
José M Uriburu 820 (on Plaza San Martín), T0370-442 5192, www.formosa.gob.ar/ turismo. Daily 0730-1230 and 1600-2030.
Tourism is not well developed here yet, but increasingly activities like guided tours and accommodation at estancias are offered; ask at this tourist office.

Where to stay

Formosa

$$ Colón
Belgrano 1068, T0370-442 6547, see Facebook.
Central, comfortable rooms, all usual services.

$$ Plaza
José M Uriburu 920, T0370-442 6767, plaza_formosa@hotmail.com.
On plaza, pool, very helpful, some English spoken, secure parking.

$ El Extranjero
Av Gutnisky 2660, T0370-452276.
Opposite bus terminal, OK, with a/c.

Restaurants

Formosa

$$ Baldomero
Costanera 1101.
Modern restaurant serving everything from regional dishes to sushi and paella. It's also a *heladería*.

$$ El Nuevo Fortín
Fontana 926.
A traditional place, serving good varied local fish dishes.

Festivals

Formosa
Mar/Apr The world's longest **Via Crucis** pilgrimage with 14 stops all the way along R81 (already registered in the *Guinness Book*

of Records) takes place every **Easter** week, starting in Formosa and ending at the border with the province of Salta, 501 km northwest. **31 Jul Festival de la Caña Con Ruda**. On the night of the last day of Jul, when a drink of the Paraguayan *caña* flavoured by the ruda plant is taken as a protection for the midwinter blues. The celebration is very popular and organized annually by the local authorities (ask at the tourist office about the venue). It's also a good chance to try regional dishes. **Nov Festival Provincial de Folclore**. Held at Pirané (115 km northwest), the major music festival in the northeast, attracting national stars of stirring *folclore* music.

Transport

Formosa
Air
El Pucu Airport (T0370-445 0521) is 5 km southwest (*remise* US$3). Flights to/from **Buenos Aires**, 1½ hrs.

Bus
The bus terminal (Av Gutnisky 2615, T0370-445 1766, www.terminalformosa.com.ar) is 15 blocks west of plaza San Martín (*remise* US$3). To **Asunción**, 3 hrs, US$9. To **Buenos Aires** 15-17 hrs, US$88-116.

Esteros
del Iberá

The immense and beautiful Esteros del Iberá wetlands are among the largest expanse of virgin lagoons in South America, bettered only by the far more famous Pantanal in Brazil. Fed by an expanse of freshwater the size of Belgium, the Esteros (marshes) del Iberá host an incredible diversity of bird and animal life in one of Argentina's most exquisite landscapes. The area has been loved by ornithologists for some time, and they still come here in great numbers to tick off rare species, which can't be seen elsewhere, and certainly not at such close quarters. However, the great appeal of a stay here is that you don't have to be an expert to find the varied wildlife fascinating.

Stay in one of the estancias at Colonia Carlos Pellegrini, or further south at Rincón del Socorro, and your accommodation includes at least one boat trip on the lagoons, with a guide who can tell you all about the flora and fauna. In this country of so many natural wonders, it's one of the most unforgettable experiences. Come here soon before everyone else does. For more information, see www.esterosdelibera.com (mostly in Spanish).

On the western side of the region, in an area of lowlands and higher woodlands, is the Parque Nacional Mburucuyá, where natural conditions are ideal for a close view of the local wildlife.

★ Reserva Natural del los Esteros del Iberá

sprawling wetlands and abundant wildlife

This reserve protects nearly 13,000 sq km of the Esteros del Iberá wetlands and is really only accessible to visitors from the small village of Colonia Carlos Pellegrini, from where tours depart.

Mercedes *Colour map 2, B1.*

Located 250 km southeast of Corrientes, Mercedes (population 47,425) is the most convenient access point for Colonia Carlos Pellegrini and the Esteros del Iberá, with regular overnight buses from Buenos Aires. A chirpy little town, with some quaint 1900s buildings, it has a couple of decent places to stay and a few restaurants, internet facilities and ATMs around the plaza. Both Calle Pujol and Calle San Martín lead from the bus station to the plaza, and you're likely to see gauchos hanging around here wearing the distinctive red berets of Corrientes province.

A few kilometres west of town, on the road to Corrientes, is a shrine to pagan saint **Gauchito Gil** at the place where it's said he was killed. Shrines to Gil can be seen all over the country, decorated with red flags.

Colonia Carlos Pellegrini *Colour map 2, B2. See map, page 351.*

With a remote setting on the beautiful Laguna Iberá 120 km northeast of Mercedes, the sprawling village of Pellegrini is the only base for visiting the Esteros del Iberá. A quiet, very laid-back place with only 900 inhabitants, it has just a few blocks of earth roads, and all the hotels are a few hundred metres away from each other. There are not many

Essential Esteros del Iberá

Access

Part of the magic of the Esteros del Iberá is that they are isolated. It's best not to hire a car, but rather to allow your accommodation to arrange transport from Posadas or Mercedes. The quickest way to get to the region is to fly from Buenos Aires to Posadas (daily, 1½ hours), from where the 200-km journey to Colonia Carlos Pellegrini takes four to five hours. Note that the roads are earth and gravel after the first 60 km and negotiable only in a 4WD vehicle; they are impassable after heavy rain. Another option is to take the overnight bus (*coche cama*, 9 10 hours) from Buenos Aires to Mercedes, and ask your estancia or hotel to arrange a 4WD *remise* transfer from there. Mercedes is 120 km from Pellegrini, but note that this journey takes two hours

on the gravel roads. There is a bus from Mercedes to Colonia Carlos Pelegrini but it takes forever and leaves at inconvenient times (see Transport, page 353).

Accommodation

The hotels are all near the Iberá Lagoon, the easiest lagoon to access in the Esteros, reached by boat from the sleepy little village of Colonia Carlos Pellegrini. **Estancia Rincón del Socorro** (see Where to stay, page 352) 30 km south of Pellegrini, is slightly closer to Mercedes.

When to go

Autumn, winter or spring are the best times to visit to avoid the intense heat of midsummer. There is less chance of rain and thunderstorms during these months.

restaurants or shops and no ATMs, so bring everything you may need, including extra money as few places accept credit cards. Bring a hat, mosquito repellent, plenty of sunblock, and binoculars too, if you're keen to spot the more distant birds as well as those right by your boat.

Tip...
Carry a torch at night because there are few streetlights in the village.

From the reserve visitor centre, **Aguas Brillantes** (see Tourist information, below) you can walk to see the howler monkeys in a patch of lovely jungle nearby. (Most accommodation will include or charge extra for this walk, but you can actually do it yourself.) It is clearly marked, each new species of tree is labelled and it takes about 20 minutes to complete.

Esteros del Iberá

There are several hotels and estancias around Pellergini, most very comfortable and all offering full board, or a picnic if you're out during the day. They also provide boat trips on the lake as part of your accommodation, and some estancias offer walking and horse riding too. A one-day visit allows for a two-hour boat trip (US$15 per person if not included in hotel rates), but you may want to plan to stay for three or four nights to really unwind and lap up the tranquil atmosphere.

Boat trips and walks in the reserve

Your hotel or estancia will offer at least one boat trip included in your accommodation into Laguna Iberá to visit areas where there are lots of birds, alligators and capybaras. Depending on the time of day, these usually take two to three hours, and in summer it's best to go out in the early morning or later evening, to avoid the intense heat and to stand a better chance of seeing more birds. If you're lucky, your trip will be timed to return as the sun sinks on the water – sunsets here are really spectacular, when both planes of water and sky are tinted vivid vermillion, an unforgettable sight. The boat trip is at its most exciting when you travel down narrow creeks between the *embalsados*, and when you're invited to walk on them – they are amazingly stable, but yield subtly to your feet with a pleasing springiness. In case you don't understand your guide's instructions in Spanish: if you suddenly start sinking, you're advised to

Reserva Natural de los Esteros del Iberá

The Esteros del Iberá – 'shining water' in the Guaraní language – are fed exclusively by fresh water from rain: no rivers flow into them. The marshes extend 250 km northeast to Ituzaingó on the Alto Paraná, and are some 70 km wide at their broadest. Clear waters cover 20-30% of the protected area, and there are over 60 *lagunas*, or small lakes, astonishingly no more than a few metres deep, the largest being the **Laguna Iberá** and **Laguna de la Luna**.

The area is rich in aquatic plants, including the beautiful purple *camelote*, tiny cream-coloured star-shaped flowers, *irupé* (*Victoriana cruziana*) which forms a kind of floating plate supporting animal and birdlife; when it stretches along the shoreline, it's hard to differentiate the land from the lake. The area owes its rich animal life to the profusion of *embalsados*, which sit like islands in the *lagunas*, but are just floating vegetation, dense enough to support large animals, such as the marsh deer, and sizeable trees and bushes.

Carpinchos (capybaras) make their homes along the edges, and alligators can be seen basking on any protruding clump of mud. Watch out for the ghastly but ingenious colonial spiders, weaving enormous horizontal nets for unsuspecting insects in the late afternoon. Prolific birdlife is all around. Among the some 370 species of bird, herons and egrets soar elegantly from bush to bush, swifts and kingfishers swoop low on the water, giant storks nest on the many floating islands, rich with plant life, and there are tiny bright red-headed federal birds, long-tailed flycatchers, families of southern screamers – *chajá* – with their fluffy heads and rasping cry, amongst many others.

This beautiful area at the heart of Corrientes province became a nature reserve in 1983 and has only recently opened to tourism. Previously it was a rich territory for hunters and grazing land for cattle ranchers. Several local estancias are now open to guests, keen to enjoy the perfect tranquillity here as much as the birdlife. The Esteros have yet to gain national park status, however, which would ensure their greater protection.

The Conservation Land Trust, founded by the late North American conservationist Douglas Tompkins was campaigning for this and bought up huge sections of the land from private owners, in order to rescue it from cattle farming and rice growing which pollute the pristine waters. Though Tompkins was a controversial figure, his aims were sincere: his plans are still in effect, and his widow, along with the trust, are currently working to give all the land to Argentina if it can be guaranteed national park status.

spread out your arms before the *embalsado* closes in over you. But don't worry – this is very unlikely to happen.

Do ask your hotel or estancia at the time of booking if there are guides who speak your language: many of the local guides are excellent and know the *lagunas* like the back of their hands, complete with all the resident wildlife, but speak little English. You can be guaranteed English-speaking guides at **Posada de la Laguna**, **Irupé Lodge** and **Rincón del Socorro** (see Where to stay, below).

Some estancias also offer walks to the jungle to see and hear howler monkeys swinging off the trees and roaring, especially when rain is approaching. Night safaris are fun too: mammals, vizcachas, owls and lots of capybaras running around by the light of your guide's lamp.

Tourist information

Aguas Brillantes
Mbigua and Yacare, Colonia Carlos Pellegrini,
T03773-15-459110, www.ibera.gov.ar.
Daily 0800-1200 and 1400-1800.
The rangers' office and reserve visitor
centre is just by the bridge as you come into
Colonia Carlos Pellegrini on the right. Here,
you can chat to the *guardaparques*, study
a map of the natural reserve, and get more
information on the flora and fauna. They
also sell an excellent guide to all the plants,
birds and animals you'll find here – *Iberá,*
Vida y Colour, in Spanish and English with
the Latin names noted as well – which is
indispensable if your guide on the boat trip
doesn't speak English.

Mercedes

Tourist office
Sarmiento 650, T03773-438769,
www.mercedescorrientes.gov.ar.
Small tourist office on the main square.

Colonia Carlos Pellegrini
See under Reserva Natural del los Esteros del
Iberá, above, for details of the reserve visitor
centre. For Colonia Carlos Pellegrini, see
www.coloniapellegrini.gov.ar.

Where to stay

Mercedes

$$ La Casa de China
Mitre y Fray L Beltrán, call for directions, T03773-
15-627269, lacasadechina@hotmail.com.
A delightful historical old house with clean
rooms and a lovely patio. Recommended.

Colonia Carlos Pellegrini

N

Not to scale

Where to stay ⬤
Aguapé Lodge **1**
Ecoposada del Estero **2**
Hostería Ñandé Retá **4**
Irupé Lodge **3**
Posada de la Laguna **6**

Posada Yacaré **10**
Posada Ypa Sapukai **5**
Rancho Iberá **7**
Rancho Inambú **8**
Rincón del Socorro **9**

Restaurants 🍴
Don Marcos **1**
Santa Rita **4**
Yacarú Porá **5**

$$ Sol
San Martín 519 (entre Batalla de Salta y B Mitre), T03773-420283.
Comfortable rooms around a wonderful patio with black and white tiles and lots of plants. Lovely.

Colonia Carlos Pellegrini
Rates are generally full board and include water- and/or land-based trips.

$$$$ pp Aguapé Lodge
T011-4742 3015 (Buenos Aires), www.iberawetlands.com.
On a lagoon with a garden and pool, comfortable rooms, attractive dining room. Recommended.

$$$$ pp Posada de la Laguna
T03773-499413, www.posadadelalaguna.com.
A beautiful place run by Elsa Güiraldes (grand-daughter of famous Argentine novelist, Ricardo Güiraldes) and set on the shores of the lake, in a large neat garden. It's very comfortable, and there's a swimming pool and excellent country cooking. English and some French spoken. Highly recommended.

$$$$ pp Rincón del Socorro
T03773-475114, www.rincondelsocorro.com (Conservation Land Trust).
Incredibly luxurious place, beautifully set in its own 12,000 ha 35 km south of Carlos Pellegrini. It offers 6 spacious bedrooms, each with a little sitting room, 1 double bungalow, and elegant sitting rooms and dining rooms. There's delicious home-produced organic food, bilingual guides, *asados* at lunchtime, night safaris and horse riding. It's set in gorgeous gardens, featuring a pool with superb views all around. Highly recommended.

$$$$-$$$ Ecoposada del Estero
T03773-15-443602, www. ecoposadadelestero.com.ar.
2-room bungalows and restaurant, associated with **Iberá Expediciones** (see What to do, below), which run guided treks, horse riding, 4WD trips, birdwatching, lots of information.

$$$$-$$$ Irupé Lodge
T03773-15 456730, www.ibera-argentina.com.
Rustic, simple rooms, great views of the *laguna* from dining room, offers conventional and alternative trips, camping on islands, diving and fishing. Several languages are spoken. Offers combined Iberá and Iguazú tours.

$$$ pp Hostería Ñandé Retá
T03773-499411, www.nandereta.com.
A large old wooden house in a shady grove, with a play room and home cooking. Rates are full board.

$$$ pp Posada Ypa Sapukai
Sarmiento 212, T03773-15-514212, www.posadadeibera.com.
Good value *posada* with a great atmosphere, offering private rooms and shared single rates ($ pp). Excellent staff.

$$$ Rancho Iberá
Caraguatá y Aguará, T03773-15-412661, www.posadaranchoibera.com.ar.
Designed like an old Argentine country house, a *posada* with double and triple bedrooms and a well-maintained garden. Also has a cottage for 5.

$$$ Rancho Inambú
T03773-15 401362, Yeruti, entre Aguapé y Pehuajó, www.ranchoinambu.com.ar.
Attractive rustic rooms set in a lush garden, with a lovely common area and a great bar (open to non-guests).

$$$-$$ Posada Yacaré
Curupi y Yaguareté, T03773-15-499415, www.posadaelyacare.com.
Small hostel 4 blocks from the lake, 1 from the plaza, with a restaurant and a garden.

Camping

Municipal campsite
T03773-15-432388.
With hot showers, jetty for boat trips, also riding and other guided tours.

Restaurants

Colonia Carlos Pellegrini
There aren't many restaurants here since all hotels and estancias offer full board. There are a couple of *kioskos* selling cold drinks and snacks on the road leading to the bridge; these have unreliable opening times. The following are all within walking distance of the main plaza:

$ Don Marcos
RP 40 and Guasuvirá, T03773-15 457697
Offering a variety of *empanadas* and *milanesas*, but also regional dishes such as *chastaca*, *bai pui*, *carbonada* and *locro*.

$ Santa Rita
Curupí and Tuyuyú, T03773-15-411053.
Pizza, pastries and delicious home-made desserts.

$ Yacarú Porá
Yaguarte y Cara Huata, T03773-15-413750.
Tasty barbecue, pasta, pizzas and *empanadas*. Vegetarians catered for.

What to do

Colonia Carlos Pellegrini
As part of your stay at most lodges you will have at least a few activities included but local enterprises also offer several tours, such as boat trips, horse riding and kayaking. Ask at the visitor centre for details; see Tourist information, page 351.

Iberá Expediciones, *in Ecoposada del Estero, see Where to stay, above, T03773-15-5020 4031, www.iberaexpediciones.com.* Small but professional tour agency run by the informative José Martín, who can organize boat trips, birdwatching tours, horse riding and treks. He can also help you find accommodation and is happy to help with information on the area. Recommended.
Rincón Tres Lagunas, *T03756-15-511931, www.rincontreslagunas.com.* For birdwatching, night boat trips, tours to Misiones and more. Also offers day trips to Estancia San Lorenzo.

Transport

Mercedes
Bus
To **Colonia Carlos Pellegrini**, Iberá Bus (T03773-15 462836) provides a combi service Mon-Sat 1230 (but check as times change on weekends), from the bus terminal, 4-5 hrs, US$25. Note that it spends 1 hr picking up passengers from the whole of Mercedes after leaving the office.

To **Buenos Aires**, 9-10 hrs, US$52-62, several companies. To **Corrientes**, 3 hrs, US$14, several companies. To **Puerto Iguazú,** go via Corrientes or via any important town along Ruta 14, such as Paso de los Libres, 130 km southeast.

Colonia Carlos Pellegrini
Bus
To **Mercedes**, Iberá Bus combi, daily at 0430, 3-5 hrs, US$25. The bus picks up passengers at their lodging. Booking is required before 2200 the night before; *posada* receptionists will book tickets. To **Posadas**, catch a bus back to Mercedes and on to Posadas.

The western side of Iberá, some two hours from Corrientes by road, has several access points, including Portal San Nicolás, which is on a reserve owned by the Conservation Land Trust (CLT), www.proyectoibera.org. The Trust's aim is integrate its lands into the publicly owned national reserve. San Nicolás, reached from San Miguel (160 km from Corrientes) has a *guardaparques'* post and a campsite. From the jetty it's 45 minutes by boat or a two-day, one-night ride to CLT's San Alonso lodge (see Where to stay, below). Another access point is Portal Yahaveré, southwest of San Nicolás. Between here and Corrientes is Parque Nacional Mburucuyá.

Parque Nacional Mburucuyá

12 km east of the town of Mburucuyá, national park office T03782-498022, free. See www. parquesnacionales.gov.ar. Buses go from San Antonio Corrientes daily to Mburucuyá, the journey takes 2½ hrs and costs US$4. A remise taxi from there to the park is US$15.

If you can't make it over to the Esteros del Iberá and are in Corrientes city, you might like to visit this park, which stretches north from the marshlands of the Río Santa Lucía. It's 180 km southeast of Corrientes, 12 km east of the small town of Mburucuyá (where there are several places to stay overnight), accessible by a 47-km-long road branching off at Saladas. Unpaved Route 86 (later Route 13) links Mburucuyá with the park and this sandy road leads northeast to Itá Ibaté, on Route 12, 160 km east of the provincial capital.

The land was donated by Danish botanist Troels Pedersen, whose long research had identified 1300 different plants, including some newly discovered species. There's a variety of natural environments, ranging from savanna with *yatay* palms and 'islands' of Wet Chaco forest, with *lapacho* trees (which have purple blossom in late winter) and *timbó* trees, to the aquatic vegetation of the *esteros*. You'll also see the *mburucuyá* (passion flower) that gives its name to the park. There's lots of interesting wildlife too: capybaras, the rare *aguará guazu* (maned wolf) and the *aguará pope*, similar to the North American raccoon (though these are both nocturnal animals), deer, such as *corzuela parda* (*Mazama gouazoubira*) and *ciervo de los pantanos*, foxes *aguará-í*, monkeys and many bird species, such as the lovely *yetapá de collar* (*Alectrurus risora*) or strange-tailed tyrant, with its beautiful double tail.

Provincial Route 86 (unpaved) crosses the park for 18 km, to the information centre and free campsite (hot water and electricity) at the centre of the park. From there, two footpaths branch off the access road. The **Sendero Yatay** goes south to a vantage point on Estero Santa Lucía, winding 2.5 km through gallery forests and grassland with mature palms. The Sendero Aguará Popé goes north 1.2 km, through thick vegetation and Wet Chaco forests, and near the western access to the park, the road crosses the *arroyo Portillo*, where 2-m-long *yacarés negros* alligators are often spotted.

Listings Western Iberá

Where to stay

$$$$ San Alonso Lodge
45 mins by boat from San Nicolás,
T03773-475114.

Owned and managed by the Conservation Land Trust. A 2-night programme includes rustic rooms, *criollo* food and all trips.

Misiones province
& the Jesuit missions

There are wonderfully evocative remains of several Jesuit missions in the south of picturesque Misiones province and they make a worthwhile stop on your way to or from Iguazú Falls. If you're interested in seeing more, there are the ruins of San Ignacio Miní, Santa Ana and Loreto, all within reach of the small pleasant town of San Ignacio.

Misiones' lush landscapes of red earth roads cutting through fecund green jungle and forest plantations are matched by a rich culture, generated by the mix of indigenous Guaraní and European immigrants, together with Paraguayans and Brazilians.

The fertile land produces pine forests for wood, huge plantations of tea, and most important of all, the *yerba* for *mate*, the Argentine drink without which the country would grind to a halt (see box, page 36).

It's a fairly wet region with hundreds of rivers and waterfalls, the most magnificent of which are the Iguazú Falls. But there are more falls, the Saltos de Moconá, almost as spectacular and staggeringly wide, on the southeasternmost edge of the province.

With time to spare, you could head inland to Oberá, whose 35 churches represent immigrants from an amazing 15 countries.

Posadas is the lively but unattractive capital of Misiones, set on a bend on the southern bank of the Río Paraná, with views over the river from its *costanera* (river banks). It was founded in 1814 and developed after the War of Triple Alliance as a useful strategic post. It's a modern city and there aren't any particularly remarkable sights; if you are looking for a place to stop on your way from the Esteros del Iberá to Iguazú, head up to the small town of San Ignacio instead.

Sights

The centre of the city is the Plaza 9 de Julio, with its French-style cathedral and government building, and several hotels. Banks and ATMs can be found one block west on San Martín, or one block south on Félix de Azara. Two blocks southeast there's a peaceful spot at Paseo Bosetti, a quiet plaza with mural paintings. There are a couple of rather old-fashioned museums near the Plaza, the **Museo de Ciencias Naturales e Historia 'Andrés Guaçurarí'** and the **Museo Regional de Posadas** with the obligatory collection of stuffed animals. There's also a cultural centre and arts exhibition hall at **Museo de Arte Juan Yaparí** ⓘ *Sarmiento 319, T0376-444 7375, www.museojuanyapari.misiones.gov.ar, Mon-Fri 0800-1230 and 1630-2100, Sat-Sun 0900-1230 and 1700-2100, free*, a block north of the plaza, and next door is **Mercado de Artesanías**, where Guaraní handicrafts are for sale, and the **Museo Arqueológico** ⓘ *General Paz 1865, T0376-444 7616, Mon-Fri 0900-1200 and 1600-2000, Sat 0900-1200, free.*

Posadas' main feature is the long Costanera, extending northeast of the centre alongside the broad river Paraná and a good place for a stroll. In the afternoon you'll see residents sitting on folding chairs sipping *mate* as the sun goes down. **Avenida Andrés Guaçurarí** (referred to also as Avenida Roque Pérez) is a pretty boulevard which becomes

Essential Misiones province

Access

From the region's capital, the unattractive business hub of Posadas, two parallel roads run northeast to the Iguazú Falls, but only Route 12, the northernmost one, is tarmacked and negotiable in an ordinary vehicle. The Jesuit ruins at San Ignacio are 60 km north of Posadas and the road continues, via a series of small towns such as Eldorado, to Wanda, famous for its open mines of semi-precious stones, to Puerto Iguazú, the best base for visiting the falls. The other road, Route 14, runs parallel and south along the interior of the province, via Oberá to Bernardo de Irigoyen. It's paved but there are no buses. To visit the Saltos de Moconá in the southeast, you'll need to take an even rougher road further south, Route 2, which is unpaved from Alba Posse onwards (about halfway), so you'll need a 4WD vehicle. See Transport, page 359.

When to go

Summers are incredibly hot here, with temperatures reaching 40°C from November to March, but winters are warm and sunny. Flowers and birdlife are most abundant in spring.

Information

See www.misiones.tur.ar (in Spanish and English).

BORDER CROSSING
Argentina–Paraguay

Puente San Roque

A bridge, the Puente San Roque, links Posadas with Encarnación in Paraguay. Pedestrians and cyclists are not allowed to cross the bridge; cyclists must ask officials for assistance. Argentine pesos are accepted in Encarnación, so there is no need to change them. Paraguay is one hour behind Argentina, except during the Paraguayan summer time (October-April).

The border is open 24 hours. Immigration formalities are conducted at respective ends of the bridge. The Argentine side has different offices for locals and foreigners; Paraguay has one for both.

The **Argentine consulate** is in Encarnación, at Artigas 960, T+595-(0)71-201066, cenca@mrecic.gov.ar, open Monday-Friday 0800-1300. The **Paraguayan consulate** in Posadas is at San Lorenzo 1561, T0376-442 3858, open Monday-Friday 0800-1500.

For **transport** to Encarnación from Posadas, see page 359.

livelier by night with several popular bars. A few blocks northwest is the small **Parque Paraguayo** and the **Museo Regional Aníbal Cambas** ① *Alberdi 600, T0376-444 7539, Mon-Fri 0800-1200 and 1500-1900, free.* This is Posadas' most interesting museum with a permanent exhibition of Guaraní artefacts and pieces collected from the nearby Jesuit missions, including the façade of the temple at San Ignacio Miní.

Around Posadas

There is a marvellous traditional estancia nearby, **Estancia Santa Inés** ① *R105, Km 8.5, 20 km south of Posadas, T0376-443 5771, www.estancia-santaines.com.ar, half-day activities, US$90; taxi from Posadas, US$20-22,* which covers 2000 ha and grows *yerba mate.* Activities include walking, horse riding and, between February and October, helping with *mate* cultivation.

If you're here in July, you might also like to visit the **Fiesta Nacional de la Yerba Mate** (see Festivals, below) in **Apóstoles**, a prosperous town 65 km south of Posadas, founded in 1897 by Ukrainian and Polish immigrants on the site of a Jesuit mission dating from 1633. The town is set in the heart of *yerba mate* plantations in a picturesque hilly region, reached by regular buses.

The **Museo Histórico Juan Szychowski** ① *13 km further at La Cachuera, follow the 6-km dirt road, branching off R1, 7 km south of Apóstoles,* is worth a trip if you have a car. It displays tools and machinery invented by a young Polish immigrant: mills for processing rice, corn and *yerba mate,* and hydraulic works, which can be seen in the grounds, and still amaze engineers. He was the founder of a *yerba mate* processing plant, **La Cachuera** ① *T0376-442 2077, www.yerbamanda.com.ar,* still operating, now under the brand name of **Amanda**.

You could also cross the border to Encarnación in Paraguay to visit more Jesuit missions at Trinidad and Jesús. For more on the border crossing, see box, above. For access to Esteros del Iberá, see page 348.

Tourist information

Posadas

Tourist office
2 blocks south of the Plaza 9 de Julio
at Colón 1985, T0376-444 7539,
www.turismo.misiones.gov.ar.
Mon-Fri 0800-1300 and 1500-2000.
Can provide a basic map but not much else.
There is also a small tourist office in the bus
station (Mon-Sat 0800-1200 and 1600-2000).

Where to stay

Posadas

$$$ Julio César
Entre Ríos 1951, T0376-442 7930,
www.juliocesarhotel.com.
4-star hotel, pool and gym, spacious
reasonably priced rooms, some with
river views. Recommended.

$$ City
Colón 1754, T0376-433901,
www.misionescityhotel.com.ar.
Good rooms, some overlooking plaza,
restaurant and parking.

$$ Le Petit
Santiago del Estero 1630, T0376-443 6031,
www.hotellepetit.com.ar.
Good value, small hotel, a short walk
from the centre on a quiet street.

$$ Residencial Colón
Colón 2169, T0376-442 5085,
www.residencialcolon.blogspot.com.
Small but affordable rooms, parking.
Also apartments for up to 6 people.

$ pp Hostel Posadeña Linda
Bolívar 1439, T0376-443 9238,
www.hostelposadasmisiones.com.
Central, good value, very pleasant, with all
hostel facilities and tourist information.

Restaurants

Posadas
Most places offer *espeto corrido*, eat
as much as you can *parrilla* with meat
brought to the table.

$$ La Querencia
Bolívar 1849, on Plaza 9 de Julio.
A large traditional restaurant offering
parrilla, *surubí* and pastas.

$$ Mendieta
Corrientes and Sentenario, T0376-443 3844,
see Facebook.
Popular *parrilla*.

$$ Plaza Café
Bolívar 1979, just outside the shopping centre.
Great salads and large mains.
Busy during the day and busier at night.
Highly recommended.

$ Bar Español
Bolívar 2085.
Open since 1958, this restaurant has tasty
Spanish-influenced food. Have an ice cream
for dessert next door at **Duomo**.

$ Café Vitrage
Colón y Bolívar.
Good pizzas, sandwiches and coffee,
nice view of the plaza.

Festivals

Apóstoles
Jul Fiesta Nacional de la Yerba Mate, as its
name suggests, is a celebration of *yerba mate*,
and attracts *folclore* singers to the region.

What to do

Posadas
Abra, *Salta 1848, T0376-442 2221, www.
abratours.com.ar.* Tours to San Ignacio,
including Santa Ana Jesuit ruins, also
those in Paraguay and in Brazil, plus
tours to waterfalls.

Guayrá, *San Lorenzo 2208, T0376-443 3415, www.guayra.com.ar.* Tours to Iberá, to Saltos del Moconá, to both sites in a 5-day excursion, and to other sites in Misiones, also car rental and transfers to Carlos Pellegrini (for Iberá).

Transport

Posadas
Air

General San Martín Airport (T0376-445 7413) is on Route 12, 12 km west of town, which can be reached by *remise*, US$11-12. To **Buenos Aires**, 1-2 direct daily flights, 1 hr 35 mins.

Bus
The bus terminal (Av Santa Catalina and Av Luis Quaranta, T0376-445 4888) is 3 km south of the centre on the road to Corrientes.

A *remise* to town costs US$7. For a bus into town, cross the street from the terminal and look for Nos 15, 14 21 or 8 to the centre, US$0.75. Travel agencies in the centre can book bus tickets in advance, or at designated posts in **Shopping Posadas**.

To **Buenos Aires**, 12-13 hrs, US$76-88. Frequent services to **San Ignacio Miní**, 1 hr, US$4, and **Puerto Iguazú**, US$16, 5-6 hrs.

To reach **Brazil** and the Jesuit Missions in Rio Grande do Sul, take an **Aguila Dorada** or **Horianski** bus from Posadas to **San Javier**, 124 km, then a ferry, US$2, to Porto Xavier, from where buses run to Santo Ângelo, 4 hrs. Immigration is at either end of the ferry crossing.

To **Encarnación** (Paraguay), **Servicio Internacional**, 50 mins, US$1.25, leaving at least every 30 mins from platforms 11 and 12 (lower level) of the bus station, tickets are available on the bus.

★ San Ignacio and the Miní Jesuit Mission *Colour map 2, B2.*

ruins of the first settlers

The pleasant village of San Ignacio, 63 km northeast of Posadas, is the site of the most impressive Jesuit mission in Misiones province. The site, together with the nearby Jesuit missions of Loreto and Santa Ana, was declared a World Heritage Site by UNESCO in 1984. It's a very sleepy village of only 1500 inhabitants, but is a rural and welcoming place to recharge for a few days if you have just been in, or are heading to, busy Puerto Iguazú. Only a few of the streets are paved, the rest have red dirt.

San Ignacio Miní Jesuit Mission

Like other Jesuit missions, San Ignacio Miní was constructed around a central plaza: to the north, east and west were about 30 parallel one-storey buildings, each with a wide veranda in front and each divided into four to 10 small, one-room dwellings for slaves. Guaraní communities lived in the surrounding areas. The roofs of these buildings have gone, but the massive 1-m-thick walls are still standing except where they have been destroyed by the *ibapoi* trees. The public buildings, some still 10 m high, are on the south side of the plaza; in the centre are the ruins of the church, 74 m by 24 m, finished in about 1724. To the right is the cemetery, which was divided for men and women, priests and children; to the left are the cloisters, the priests' quarters, guest rooms and the workshops for wood and metal work, gold and silver.

Sculpture was of particular significance in San Ignacio, and some of the most pleasing details are to be found in the red sandstone masonry. While the architecture is the traditional colonial baroque style found in all Jesuit public buildings, the influence of the Guaraní culture can be seen in the many natural details in bas-relief on walls and lintels: elegantly entwined grapes, fruit and flowers, together with naïve human forms and angels, so that even the buildings reveal a harmony between the Jesuit priests and their Guaraní workers. The chapel was designed by two Italian *sacerdotes*, and it took 36 years to build. Along the same stretch of terrace, you will see the remains of the music conservatory, library and kitchen. Many of the porticos and windows are elaborately carved, testimony to the highly trained workforce and high standards of aesthetics. The whole area is excellently maintained and is a most impressive sight.

Essential San Ignacio Miní Jesuit Mission

Access

Buses from Posadas and further south stop in San Ignacio on their way to the falls. Most come into town, but a few stop at the terminal on Avenida Roca/RN 12, near the junction with Avenida Sarmiento, leaving a 15-minute walk into town. San Ignacio Miní Jesuit Mission is located five blocks from Avenida Sarmiento on the northwest side of town. Keep walking and you'll find the ruins on your right. Note that the entrance on Calle Alberdi is 200 m beyond the exit, which is on Calle Rivadavia. There are plenty of restaurants and cafés along this road near the ruins.

Opening hours

Daily 0700-1800.

Entry fee and tour

US$13 with leaflet and tour (ask for English version), which leaves from the entrance every 30 minutes (tips are appreciated). You can reliably leave your luggage by the ticket office. Tickets are also valid for the Jesuit ruins at Santa Ana, Santa María La Mayor and Loreto, within a 15-day period.

When to go

Visit San Ignacio early in the day to avoid the crowds and to have the best light for pictures.

Just 40 m inside the entrance to the ruins is the **Centro de Interpretación Jesuítico-Guaraní**, with a fine model of the mission in its heyday and an exhibition that includes representations of the lives of the Guaraní before the arrival of the Spanish, displays on the work of the Jesuits and the consequences of their expulsion.

There's a daily **Son et lumière show** ⓘ *T0376-447 0186, 1930 (weather permitting), US$13.*

Other sights

Follow Avenida Sarmiento to its very end and turn right for a picturesque view of a row of wooden houses on a reddish road amidst lush vegetation. An interesting art collection is at the **Museo Provincial Miguel Nadasdy** ⓘ *Sarmiento 557, Sat 0700-1900, Sun 0900-1200 and 1500-1800*, which contains a collection of artefacts from the Guaraní and Jesuits of the missions, some beautiful examples of stone carving and a bas-relief of San Ignacio de Loyola, founder of the Jesuit order.

On the other side of the town, in the opposite direction to the ruins, there's a really delightful 20-minute walk (with little shade) along San Martín to the house of celebrated Uruguayan writer Quiroga. Walk to the end of the street, past the Gendarmería and two attractive wooden and stone houses. After 200 m the road turns left and 300 m later, a signposted narrow road branches off leading to the **Casa de Horacio Quiroga** ⓘ *daily 0700-1700, US$3 including a 40-min guided tour; ask for an English guide; phone the tourist office for details.* Quiroga (1878-1937) lived here for part of his tragic life as a farmer

BACKGROUND
San Ignacio Miní Jesuit Mission

San Ignacio Miní ('small' in comparison with San Ignacio Guazú – 'large' – on the Paraguayan side of the Río Paraná) was originally founded in 1610 near the river Paranapanema in the present Brazilian state of Paraná, but frequent attacks from the *bandeirantes* (hunting for slaves as workers) forced the San Ignacio Jesuits to lead a massive exodus south, together with the neighbouring Loreto mission. Taking their Guaraní population down the river by a series of rafts, they established San Ignacio on the river Yabebiry, not far from its present site, which was settled by 1696.

At the height of its prosperity in 1731, the mission housed 4356 people. Only two priests ran the mission: a feat of astounding organization. Latin, Spanish and Guaraní were taught in the school, and nearly 40,000 head of cattle grazed in the surrounding land, where *yerba mate* and cotton, maize and tobacco were also cultivated. The mission itself once covered around 14 ha: today you can see remains of only 6 ha, but these are still an impressive sight with the immense central plaza lined with buildings in dramatic red sandstone.

But after the expulsion of the Jesuits in 1767 by the Spanish king (see box, page 628), the mission rapidly declined. By 1784 there were only 176 Guaraní, and by 1810 none remained. In 1817, by order of the Paraguayan dictator, Rodríguez de Francia, San Ignacio was set on fire.

The ruins, like those of nearby Santa Ana and Loreto, were lost in the jungle until the late 19th century when attempts at colonization forced the founding of new towns; San Ignacio was founded near the site of the former mission. It wasn't until the 1980s that there was some attempt to give official protection to the ruins.

and carpenter between 1910 and 1916, and again in the 1930s. Many of his fantastical short stories were inspired by this subtropical region and its inhabitants. The scenery is beautiful, with river views, a garden with palms and an amazing bamboo forest planted by him. There's a replica of his first house, made for a movie set in the 1990s, while his second house is still standing, and contains an exhibition of a few of his belongings. Return to the main road, follow it down the slope amongst thick vegetation for a gorgeous riverside (25-minute) walk.

Other missions: Loreto and Santa Ana

If you have time, it's interesting to complement your visit to San Ignacio with a trip to see the ruins of two other Jesuit missions nearby. The mission of **Loreto** ① *access via a 3-km dirt road (signposted) off Route 12, 10 km south of San Ignacio, daily 0700-1800, on same ticket as San Ignacio within 15 days*, has far fewer visitors than San Ignacio, and under thick shady trees, the silence of the still air and the refreshing darkness add an attractive touch of mystery. The mission was moved to its present site in 1631, after the exodus from the former Jesuit province of Guayrá, and more than 6000 people were living here by 1733. It's thought that this was the site of the first printing press in the Americas and of an extensive library. It was also impressively productive: cattle and *yerba mate* were grown here, and ceramics were made. Little remains of this once-large establishment other than a few walls, though excavations are in progress. Note the number of old trees growing entwined with stone buttresses. There is no public transport to Loreto, but you can take a tour from San Ignacio with **Misiones Excursions** (see What to do, below) or catch one of the **Henning** buses that pass along Sarmiento starting at 0600 until 2000; ask the driver to drop you outside the mission. You can ask for help at the tourist office if your Spanish isn't up to it.

Some 16 km south of San Ignacio at **Santa Ana** ① *700 m along a path from Route 12 (signposted), daily 0700-1800, on the same ticket as San Ignacio if visited within 15 days,* are the ruins of another Jesuit mission. Founded much earlier, in 1633, they are not as extensive as San Ignacio, but reveal an interesting architectural adaptation to the terrain. Moved to its present site in 1663, Santa Ana housed the Jesuit iron foundry. In 1744 the mission was inhabited by 4331 people and covered an area of 37 ha, of which only 10 remain. The impressively high walls are still standing and there are beautiful steps leading from the church to the wide-open plaza. Regular buses stop on Route 12 near the ruins.

You could also explore the ruins of **Santa María la Mayor**, 76 km southwest, on paved Route 2 linking San Javier and Concepción de la Sierra, 9 km west of Itacaruare. They date from 1637 and were never restored. Remains of the church and a jail are still standing, and a printing press operated there in the early 18th century.

Listings San Ignacio and the Miní Jesuit Mission

Tourist information

San Ignacio

Municipal office
Independencia 605, T0376-447 0130.
There is another tourist office (daily 0600-2100) on RN12 at the entrance to town. See also What to do, below.

Where to stay

San Ignacio

$$ La Toscana
H Irigoyen y Uruguay, T0376-447 0777, see Facebook.
Family-run, 12-bedroom hotel with rustic, inviting rooms and a wonderful pool with a terrace. It's an easy 10-min walk from the tourist office and main plaza. Highly recommended.

$$ San Ignacio
San Martín 823, T0376-447 0047.
Good if dated rooms with a/c, plus self-catering apartments for 4-5 people. Breakfast extra. An interesting view of town from the reception.

$ pp Adventure Hostel
Independencia 469, T0376-447 0955, see Facebook.
Large hostel with a fantastic pool and a games area. Spacious communal areas and comfortable double rooms (**$$**). Camping available. It's a short walk to the centre of town.

$ pp Hostel El Jesuita
San Martín 1291, T0376-447 0542, www.eljesuita.hostoi.com.
Welcoming owners, spacious double rooms with their own exit to the garden, small comfortable dorm (US$10), 1½ blocks from the ruins. Lots of travel advice and they can organize tours. There's Wi-Fi throughout, laundry service and camping, US$4.50. Recommended.

Camping

Complejo Los Jesuitas
C Emilia Mayer, T0376-446 0847, www.complejolosjesuitas.com.ar.
Campsite and cabins for 4 people.

Restaurants

San Ignacio
There are several restaurants catering for tourists on the streets by the Jesuit ruins.

$$ La Carpa Azul
Rivadavia 1295, www.lacarpaazul.com.
Large restaurant near the ruins serving quality meals but you will be surrounded by tour buses.

$$ La Misionerita
Route 12 Emilia Mayer.
Another expansive restaurant serving the tourist hoards staples like pastas and river fish. Convenient location.

$ Pizzería La Aldea
San Martín 1240.
Friendly place serving good cheap pizzas, *empanadas* and other simple meals. Will make sandwiches to take away. Recommended.

What to do

San Ignacio
Misiones Excursions, *Ruta Nacional and Sarmiento, T0376-437 3448, www.misiones excursions.blogspot.com.ar.* Excellent, small company with its office in the tourist office; see Tourist information, above. Personalized tours around San Ignacio, including visits to the other ruins of Santa Ana and Loreto, local Guaraní villages and a *yerba* estancia. All cost US$20 pp. They also organize kayaking trips, cycling tours and trips to Saltos del Moconá (US$90 pp). They can arrange a full day trip into Paraguay to see the famous mission ruins of Trinidad (US$50). If you contact then in advance they can organize 2-night trips to the Esteros de Iberá, including luxury accommodation, breakfast, a boat trip on the wetlands and personal 4WD transfers, for US$130 pp. Recommended.

Transport

San Ignacio
Bus
Frequent service to **Posadas** or to **Puerto Iguazú** (US$13). To **Paraguay**, a ferry crosses the Río Paraná at **Corpus** to **Bella Vista** Mon-Fri 0800-1630, foot passengers US$2, which is a good route to the Paraguayan Jesuit missions. There are immigration and customs facilities.

Oberá *Colour map 2, B3.*

a cultural melting pot among mate plantations

With 51,400 inhabitants, Oberá is the second largest town in Misiones. It's also one of the province's biggest centres of 20th-century European immigration, and there are around 15 different nationalities here, including Japanese, Brazilian, Paraguayan and Middle Eastern communities, represented every September in the annual Fiesta Nacional del Inmigrante, held in the Parque de las Naciones. Located amongst tea and *yerba mate* plantations, local factories are open for visits.

The town has over 35 churches and temples, but there's little reason to make a special trip. There is the **Jardín de los Pájaros** ① *Italia y Venezuela, T03755-427023, Mon-Fri 0700-1800, Sat-Sun, 0900-1200 and 1400-1800, US$1.30,* an aviary which houses native birds.
　　If you're interested in tea, you could head for **Campo Viera**, 21 km north of Oberá on Route 14. The 'national capital of tea', it has about 8000 ha of tea fields and 25 processing plants. The **Fiesta Nacional del Té** is held here every September with the Queen of Tea coronation (for more information, go to the **Casita del Té**).

Tourist information

Tourist office
Plazoleta Güemes, Av Libertad 90, T03755-401808, www.obera.gov.ar. Mon-Fri 0700-1900, Sat-Sun 0800-1200 and 1500-1900.
Information on local *estancias* which are open to visitors.

Where to stay

Ask the tourist office for details of farms run by host families of different nationalities.

$$$ Cabañas del Parque
Ucrania y Tronador, T03755-426000, www.hotelcabanas.com.ar.
Situated next to the Parque de las Naciones, this is a tourist complex of several houses or rooms for 2 to 8 people. Kitchen, a/c and breakfast included. It also has a large swimming pool and a restaurant.

$$$-$$ Premier
9 de Julio 1114, T03755-407400, www.hotelpremierobera.com.
A good central option, with a/c.

$ Cuatro Pinos
Sarmiento 853, T03755-429808.
A well-located hotel.

Restaurants

$$ Del Monte
Costa Rica 334.
Great modern fare.

$$ Engüete
Cabeza de Vaca 340.
Good food and a varied menu is available.

Festivals

Sep Fiesta Nacional del Inmigrante.
Popular, vibrant festival that lasts a week around 4 Sep (Immigrants' Day). The Parque de las Naciones, with houses built in various national styles, is the attractive setting for folk dances, parades, tasting national dishes and the election of a queen.

Transport

Bus
To **Posadas**, 1½ hrs, US$6, with **Expreso Singer** and **Río Uruguay**. **Singer** also goes to **El Soberbio**, US$17.

San Ignacio to Puerto Iguazú

on the road to the falls

From San Ignacio Route 12 continues northeast, running parallel to Río Alto Paraná, towards Puerto Iguazú, through appealing landscapes of bright red soil and green vegetation; plantations of *yerba mate*, manioc and citrus fruits can be seen, as well as timber yards and *yerba mate* factories. The road passes through several small, modern, uninteresting towns, including Jardín America, Puerto Rico, Montecarlo and Eldorado. If you're driving and feel like an extra stop you could consider the Salto Capioví. Just 100 m from Route 12 in Capioví, 60 km from San Ignacio, this 7-m waterfall is immersed in a patch of jungle, with a campsite. Nearby, there's the Parque Natural Las Camelias.

One hundred kilometres south of Puerto Iguazú is **Eldorado**, a quaint, friendly and typical little Misiones town with an interesting archaeological collection at the **Museo Municipal**

① *T03751-434038, Mon-Fri 0800-1200 and 1300-1900, Sat-Sun 1300-1900, free.* The bus stops here between Puerto Iguazú and San Ignacio. If you're interested in seeing how amethyst and quartz are mined, you might like to stop off at **Wanda**, 50 km north, a famous open-cast mine, which also sells precious gems. There are daily guided tours to two mines, Tierra Colorada and Compañía Minera Wanda; contact tour operators in Eldorado or Puerto Iguazú (see page 378).

Listings San Ignacio to Puerto Iguazú

Tourist information

Eldorado

Tourist office
Ruta Nacional 12, T03751-426473.

Saltos del Mocona

stunning waterfalls off the tourist trail

While the main tourist route through Misiones runs along Route 12, if you have time, a 4WD and a spirit of adventure, you might well want to get off the beaten track and explore Misiones' hilly interior. Beautiful waterfalls are hidden away in the dense subtropical forests, and, at the furthest end of the track, you'll find the remote Saltos de Mocona. Tourist services are less well developed here, but you can stay next to the falls or in San Pedro or El Soberbio.

For a staggering 3 km, on the Argentine side of the Río Uruguay, water falls over a vast shelf of rock from 18 m up to 120 m, creating one of the most magnificent sights in the region. The rocky edge is quite easily reached on foot from the bank of the river, in an area surrounded by dense woodland, and protected by the Parque Estadual do Turvo (Brazil) and the Parque Provincial Mocona, the Reserva Provincial Esmeralda and the Reserva de la Biosfera Yabotí (Argentina). The Reserva de la Biósfera Yabotí protects one of the last major areas of Paraná forest in South America – the Selva Paranaense is more endangered than the Amazon rainforest – and tucked deep within the reserve. A few tiny communities (around 30 families in 2016) of Mbya Guaraní people survive on ancestral grounds, seriously threatened by timber exploitation.

The **Parque Provincial Mocona** covers 1000 ha, with vehicle roads and footpaths, and there's accommodation nearby where activities and trips to the falls are arranged. Note that, if the river is high (May-October), the falls may be underwater. In all three natural reserves the hilly forested landscape offers tremendous trekking, kayaking, birdwatching and exploring in 4WD vehicles. Alternative bases for exploring the area are the small towns of **El Soberbio** (70 km southwest) or **San Pedro** (92 km northwest). From the former a paved road runs to the park entrance; from the latter the road is impassable after heavy rain.

There is a regular bus service from Posadas to El Soberbio or San Pedro, and from Puerto Iguazú to San Pedro.

Where to stay

There are other lodges in the vicinity, for example: www.donenriquelodge.com.ar, www.lodgelamision.com.ar and www.posadalabonita.net.

$$$ Don Moconá Virgin Lodge
7 km from the falls, inside the Yabotí Reserve, www.donmoconavirginlodge.com.
Rustic rooms for 2-4 with shared bath, restaurant and bar. Many activities, including trekking, kayaking and zip-line, even a night bonfire. Transfer to and from San Pedro, is extra and run through a local company, Thu-Sun, 2 hrs.

$$ Hostería Puesta del Sol
C Suipacha s/n, El Soberbio, T03755-495161 (T011-4300 1377 in Buenos Aires).
A splendid vantage point overlooking town, with a swimming pool and restaurant. Comfortable rooms, full board available. They also run boat trips to the falls; see What to do, below.

What to do

Hostería Puesta del Sol, *see Where to stay, above.* Boat trips arranged to the falls, 7-8 hrs, landing and meal included, minimum 4 people. The journey to the falls is by a boat crossing to Brazil, then by vehicle to Parque do Turvo. Otherwise, a 4WD journey on the Argentine side with more chances for trekking also takes 7 hrs, with a meal included.

Iguazú
Falls

★ Any trip to Argentina should include the Iguazú Falls. They're the biggest falls in South America – half as high again as Niagara – and a spectacular experience. In all, there are 275 falls stretching over 2.7 km but the main attraction is the Garganta del Diablo (devil's throat), where walkways take you right above the falls to see the smooth river transformed in an instant into a seething torrent as the water crashes 74 m over a horseshoe-shaped precipice onto basalt rocks below, filling the air with bright spray and a deafening roar. The whole chasm is filled with billowing clouds of mist in which great dusky swifts miraculously wheel and dart, and an occasional rainbow hovers.

You can walk close to the bottom of the immensely wide Saltos Bossetti and Dos Hermanos, or take a boat trip, which speeds you beneath the falling water to get a total drenching. Viewed from below, the rush of water is unforgettably beautiful, falling through jungle filled with begonias, orchids, ferns, palms and toucans, flocks of parrots, cacique birds and myriad butterflies. There are some longer trails enabling you to enjoy the diverse flora and fauna and several excellent guides on hand.

Essential Iguazú Falls

Park information

Argentina shares the falls with Brazil and you can visit them from either side for two quite different experiences. The Brazilian side has a smaller, more restricted park and offers a panoramic view from its limited trails but you're kept at a distance from the falls themselves. If you have to choose just one, go for the Argentine side, where you can get closer to the falls, walk in the jungle and explore the rainforest.

The falls on both sides are contained within national parks, the Parque Nacional Iguazú in Argentina (see below) and the Parque Nacional Foz do Iguaçu in Brazil (see page 379). Both have well-organized free transport to take you to the waterfalls. For transport between the Argentine and Brazilian sides, see Transport in the box on page 375.

On the Argentine side you should allow at least a day and start early; the park opens at 0800 and it takes six hours to see the main attractions if you do it quickly. If you find a brisk pace exhausting in the heat of summer, you can revisit the park the next day at half the price – make sure you keep your ticket.

On the Brazilian side, the park opens at 0900 and a visit takes around two hours. Free buses take you to the start of a walkway with steps down to the falls. See also www.cataratasdoiguacu.com.br (in Portuguese and English).

Both parks have visitor centres, cafés and restaurants.

Entry fees

Both national parks charge entry fees. See box, page 370, for the Parque Nacional Iguazú in Argentina, and box, page 380, for the Parque Nacional Foz do Iguaçu in Brazil.

Tip...
Get to the park as early as you can to spot wildlife and avoid the queues.

When to go

The falls can be visited all year round. There's officially no rainy season, though it tends to rain more in March and June and there can be heavy downfalls in summer. The average temperatures are 25°C in summer and 15°C in winter. The busiest times are the Argentine holiday periods – January, Easter week and July – when you must book accommodation in advance, and on Sundays when helicopter tours over the falls from the Brazilian side are particularly popular (and noisy).

Remember that between October and March Argentina is one hour behind Brazil (daylight saving dates change each year) and, from December to March, one hour behind Paraguay.

What to take

In the rainy season, when water levels are high, waterproof coats or swimming costumes are advisable for some of the lower catwalks and for all boat trips. Wear shoes with good soles, as the walkways can be very slippery. Wear a hat, good sunscreen and sunglasses: the sun is fierce here. Bring insect repellent, bottled water and some snacks. Cameras and binoculars should be carried in a plastic bag. Take all rubbish out of the park with you, or use the bins.

Accommodation

The most pleasant place to stay is undoubtedly the laid-back Argentine town of Puerto Iguazú (see page 374), where hotels are cheaper and the streets are far safer than in the Brazilian city of Foz do Iguaçu (see page 379), where there is a serious crime problem.

Money

On either side, most establishments will accept Brazilian reais, Argentine pesos or dollars.

BACKGROUND

Iguazú Falls

Iguazú means 'big water' in the local Guaraní language (i = water, guazú = big). The first recorded European visitor to the falls was the Spaniard Alvar Núñez Cabeza de Vaca in 1542, on his search for a connection between the Brazilian coast and the Río de la Plata; he named them the Saltos de Santa María. Though the falls were well known to the Jesuit missionaries, they were unexplored until the area was covered by a Brazilian expedition sent out by the Paraguayan president, Solano López, in 1863.

In 2012 they were confirmed as one of the New 7 Wonders of Nature.

Parque Nacional Iguazú (Argentina)

natural wonders and diverse wildlife

Created in 1934, the park extends over an area of 67,000 ha of dense subtropical rainforest. There is excellent access to the falls themselves from various angles and along two further trails that wind through the forest to give you an experience of the wildlife.

Wildlife

You'll see amazingly rich wildlife whatever time you visit the park: there are more than 430 species of bird, 70 species of mammal and over 100 species of butterfly. Look out for restless and curious brown capuchin monkeys, seen in groups of around 20, howler monkeys and friendly coati with

> **Tip...**
> Come in the early morning or late afternoon to stand a good chance of seeing the more elusive species such as pumas and tapirs.

their striped tails. Toucans are ubiquitous, with their huge orange cartoon beaks, and also the curious plush crested jays, black with pale yellow breasts, which can be seen perched inquisitively around the park's restaurants. You'll also see two kinds of vultures wheeling above the falls themselves, both with fringed wing tips: the red-headed turkey vulture, and the black vulture whose wing tips are white. You should spot blue-winged parakeets, the red-rumped cacique, which builds hanging nests on *pindo* palms, and fruit-eaters like the magpie tanager and the colourful purple-throated euphonia. The butterflies are stunning: look out for electric blue *morpho* butterflies, as big as your hand, the poisonous red and black *heliconius*, and species of *Papilionidae* and *Pieridae*, with striking black and white designs. Don't feed or disturb animals and birds, or damage the flora.

Trails

Garganta del Diablo From Estación Garganta, it's a 1-km easy walk along boardwalks (fine for wheelchairs) across the wide River Iguazú to the park's centrepiece, the Garganta del Diablo falls.

Circuito Inferior and Circuito Superior **Circuito Superior** (650 m) and **Circuito Inferior** (1400 m), both taking around 1½ to two hours to complete. To reach them, get off the train at the Estación Cataratas (after a 10-minute journey) and follow signs a short distance to where the trails begin. Alternatively, you can walk from the visitor centre along

Essential Parque Nacional Iguazú (Argentina)

Access

The park lies 20 km east of the town of Puerto Iguazú along Route 12. A public **Cataratas/Waterfalls** bus runs every 30 minutes 0630-1830 from Hito Tres Fronteras with **Río Uruguay**. It stops at Puerto Iguazú bus terminal 10 minutes after departure, at the park entrance for the purchase of entry tickets, then continues to the visitor centre, US$3, journey time 45 minutes; return buses from the park run 0815-1915. You can get on or off the bus at any point en route.

Getting around

From Estación Central, just beyond the visitor centre opposite the entrance, a free natural gas-powered mini-train, the *Tren de la Selva*, whisks visitors on a 25-minute trip (2.3 km) through the jungle to Estacíon Cataratas, from where you can walk to the Sendero Verde, the Circuito Inferior and the Circuito Superior; see Trails, below. The train continues to Estación Garganta, where a 1-km-long walkway leads to the Garganta del Diablo falls. Allow at least two hours for the whole trip: train, walking, watching the falls and photos.

There are optional extra boat trips right up to the falls themselves run by **Jungle Explorer** (see What to do, page 372), including a great trip that takes you rushing right underneath the falls. You will get wet. See also www.iguazuargentina.com.

Park information

The park is open daily 0800-1800. Entry is US$24 for all foreign visitors (payable in pesos only). Entry the next day is half price with the same ticket, which you must get stamped at the end of the first day.

There's an excellent **visitor centre** (**Centro de Interpretación**) on the right after you enter, with information and photographs of the flora and fauna, and details of the history of the area from the earliest settlers. Opposite, you'll find plenty of places to eat in the **Patio de Comidas**, including a pizzeria, *parrilla* and snack bar.

As you walk towards the barriers where you pay the entry fee, there are excellent souvenir shops selling both commercial souvenirs and local Guaraní handicrafts (note that these are cheaper when bought from the Guaraní people themselves, just inside the entrance). These shops will also download digital photos to CD. Opposite are clean toilets, *locutorio* (a public phone centre) and ATMs. Further along the 'Sendero Verde' at the Estación Cataratas, towards the start of the 'Circuitos Inferior' and 'Superior' there's a great open-air café, *parrilla*, *locutorio* and toilets At the **Estación Garganta** there's another little café, toilets and shop selling postcards and water.

The **Guardería** (ranger station) is next to the Estación Cataratas, on the way to the Circuitos Inferior and Superior. The *guardaparques* are hugely knowledgeable about the park and will give you detailed information on wildlife and where to spot it, and will even accompany you if they're not too busy. They also hand out a helpful leaflet with a clear map of the park, and another in English, *Birds of Iguazú*.

There are also night-time walking tours to the falls when the moon is full; see What to do, page 373.

Recommended books

The *Laws of the Jungle*, by Santiago G de la Vega, and *Iguazú Life and Colour* are both available in English in shops throughout Puerto Iguazú. Also useful is *Birds of Southern South America and Antarctica*, by De la Peña and Rumboll, published by Harper Collins, 1998.

the Sendero Verde to the Estación Cataratas, which takes 10-15 minutes and avoids the crowds waiting for the next train.

Start with the **Circuito Superior**, a level path that takes you along the westernmost line of falls – Saltos Dos Hermanos, Bossetti, Bernabé Mendez, Mbigua (Guaraní for cormorant) and San Martín – allowing you to see these falls from above. This path is safe for those with walking difficulties, wheelchairs and pushchairs, but you should wear supportive, non-slippery shoes.

The **Circuito Inferior** takes you down to the water's edge via a series of steep stairs and walkways with superb views of both San Martín falls and the Garganta del Diablo from a distance, and then up close to Salto Bossetti. Wheelchair users, pram pushers, and those who aren't good with steps should go down by the exit route for a smooth and easy descent. There's a café on the way down and plenty of shade. You could then return to the **Estación Cataratas** to take the train to Estación Garganta, at 10 minutes and 40 minutes past the hour, and see the falls close up from above.

Isla San Martín An optional extra hour-long circuit is to take the free two-minute ferry ride (leaves every 15 minutes 0930-1530, or on demand) at the very bottom of the Circuito Inferior, which crosses to the small hilly island of Isla San Martín where two trails lead to *miradores* (viewpoints). Take the right-hand path for good close views of the San Martín Falls and straight ahead to Salto Rivadavia, or left for a longer walk to the same place. Bathing on the beach here is strictly speaking not allowed, but there are usually a few Argentines sunning themselves. Note that the paths down to the ferry and up to the *miradores* on the island are very steep and uneven. Take water to drink, as there are no services. The ferry ride may be suspended due to high waters at times; ask at the entrance.

Alternative trails The park offers two more trails through the forest which allow you to get closer to the wildlife. The **Macuco Nature Trail** (7 km return; allow six hours) allows you to see particularly superb birdlife. It starts from the path leading from the visitor centre to the Sheraton Hotel, and is a magnificent walk down to the river via a natural pool (El Pozón) fed by a slender, ice-cold, 20-m-high waterfall, **Salto Arrechea**. This is a good place for bathing (and the only permitted place in the park), and the walk is highly recommended. See the helpful leaflet in English produced by the Iguazú National Park: *Macuco Nature Trail*. The first 3 km are easy but the next 150 m are more challenging, as the path descends steeply, before the final easy 200 m; the elderly and children may find this route tough. The path is open 0800-1500, but leaving in the early morning is recommended. There are no services, so bring water and lunch and contact tour agencies for guides.

The **Sendero Yacaratía** trail starts from nearer the visitor centre and reaches the river by a different route, ending at **Puerto Macuco** trail is really for vehicles and less pleasant for walkers, so it's best visited on an organized safari. See What to do, below.

Where to stay

$$$$ Sheraton Iguazú Resort and Spa
T491800, www.sheraton.com/iguazu.
Fine position overlooking the falls, excellent
restaurant and breakfast, sports facilities and
spa. Taxi to airport available. Recommended.

What to do

Agencies arrange day trips from Puerto
Iguazú to the Argentine side of the falls,
including transfer from your hotel and
guide (request English speakers), and to
the Brazilian side with lunch in Foz, but

neither includes the park entrance fee. The
tour to the Brazilian side of the falls may
include a stop at the **Duty Free Shop**, a large,
flash indoor mall between the 2 customs
points selling perfumes and cosmetics,
electrical goods, spirits and cigarettes at
reduced prices.

Boat trips
Jungle Explorer, *T03757-421696, www.
iguazujungle.com.* Run a series of boat
trips, all highly recommended, including
Aventura Náutica, an exhilarating journey
by launch along the lower Río Iguazú, from
opposite Isla San Martín right up to the San

1 Around Iguazú Falls

→ Iguazú Falls maps
1 Around Iguazú Falls, page 372
2 Puerto Iguazú, page 376

Where to stay			
1 Camping e Pousada Internacional	2 Hostel Inn Iguazú	5 Hotel Das Cataratas	7 Pousada Evelina
	4 Hostel Natura & Paudimar Campestre	6 Posada 21 Oranges	8 Sheraton Iguazú Resort & Spa
		9 Pousada Cataratas	

Martín falls and then into the Garganta del Diablo, completely drenching passengers in the mighty spray. Great fun; not for the faint-hearted, 12 mins. On **Paseo Ecológico** you float silently for 2.5 km from Estación Garganta to appreciate the wildlife on the river banks: basking tortoises, caiman, monkeys and birdlife. A wonderful and gentle introduction to the river, 30 mins, US$9. **Gran Aventura** combines the Aventura Náutica with a longer boat trip along rapids in the lower Río Iguazú to Puerto Macuco, followed by a jeep trip along the Yacaratiá trail, 1 hr, US$38. There are other combinations at reduced prices and also tailor-made tours. Tickets are available at all embarkation points.

Full moon walks

Every month on the 5 nights of the full moon there are 1½-hr guided bilingual walks that may include a dinner before or after the walk at **Restaurant La Selva**, depending on the time of departure; US$60 with dinner, US$45 without. For information, T03757-491469, or see www.iguazuargentina.com for dates, times and an email booking form. Alternatively, you can book through tour agencies, or make reservations in person at the park.

Tour operators

Iguazú Forest, *Moreno 58, T03757-421140, www.iguazuforest.com.* Runs a half- or full-day's adventure in the jungle offering the chance to try canopying, climbing waterfalls, repelling and mountain biking. Great for kids and teenagers.

Wildlife safaris

Explorador Expediciones, *T03757-491469, www.rainforest.iguazuargentina.com.* Offers small-group safaris (Safari a la Cascada and Safari en la Selva), 3-day packages, birdwatching trips, adventure tours and trips to Moconá. Expert guides will bring the natural world alive and provide fantastic insights into the jungle. Recommended.

Puerto Iguazú (population 81,000, altitude 210 m) is a friendly, atmospheric place, its low white buildings splashed with the red dust from roads, and with bright green vegetation growing abundantly everywhere. Its houses are neat, decorated with flowers, and although the centre is slightly chaotic, the town has an appealing authentic life of its own, despite the massive daily influx of tourists on whom the economy depends. It's a pleasant place to walk around, and with several comfortable and economical places to stay, it's a much more appealing base than Foz on the Brazilian side.

Sights
The town's main street is Avenida Victoria Aguirre where, at No 66, you will find the Iguazú national park information office (see Tourist information, below). This avenue runs northwest from the entrance to the town to the little plaza at its hub, and changes names to Avenida Tres Fronteras as it turns east and heads to the spectacular viewpoint high above the meeting of rivers Paraná and Iguazú, known as the **Hito Tres Fronteras** (three borders landmark). You can also reach this point via an attractive *costanera*, running above the Río Iguazú, past the small port where boats leave for cruises along the Paraná and to Paraguay. At the Hito, there's a string of touristy souvenir stands, where children will press you to buy orchid plants and tasty little rolls of the local *chipita* bread, made from mandioc root. The views over the rivers and neighbouring Paraguay and Brazil are impressive.

Essential Puerto Iguazú

Finding your feet

The airport is some 20 km southeast of Puerto Iguazú near the falls. The **Four Tourist Travel** bus service between the airport and the bus terminal, US$4.50, will also drop off/collect you from your hotel. A taxi to town costs US$20-22. The bus terminal is at Avenida Córdoba and Avenida Misiones. See Transport, page 378, for more details.

Best hotels, lodges and posadas
Iguazú Jungle Lodge, page 376
Panoramic Grand, page 375
Posada 21 Oranges, page 376
Posada Puerto Bemberg, page 377
Yacutinga Lodge, page 377

Around Puerto Iguazú
There are a couple of interesting projects worth visiting. **La Aripuca** ① *T03757-423488, www.aripuca.com.ar, daily 0830-1830, US$5; turn off Ruta 12 at Km 4.5 just after Hotel Cataratas; or get off the bus here and walk 250 m*, is a charming centre for appreciation of the native trees of the forest. An Aripuca is a traditional Guaraní trap for birds, and a giant version of the pyramid structure that they use has been made from the fallen logs of 30 ancient trees of different species. A 30-minute guided tour (English, Spanish or German) explains all about the tree life, and then you can clamber up their trunks, or enjoy the sculpture from enormous chairs made from tree roots. Sponsor a living tree in the forest to protect it. Recommended.

Tip...
La Aripuca is a good option for families if it's raining.

BORDER CROSSING
Argentina–Brazil

Puente Tancredo Neves
This crossing is straightforward. When leaving Argentina, Argentine immigration is
at the Brazilian end of the bridge. Before setting off, check if you need a visa for Brazil.
The border is open 24 hours. Both Argentine and Brazilian officials stamp you in and
out, even if only for a day visit. Whether you are entering Brazil for the first time, or
leaving and returning after a day in Argentina, you must insist on getting off the bus
to get the required stamp and entry card. Buses also stop at the Duty Free Shop in
Puerto Iguazú. The bus does not wait for those who need stamps, so just catch the
next one, of whatever company, but often it's Río Uruguay.

The **Brazilian consulate** in Puerto Iguazú is at Avenida Córdoba 278, T03757-
420192, info.piguazu@itamaraty.gov.br. It's open Monday-Friday 0800-1400.

For **transport** from Puerto Iguazú to Foz do Iguaçu, see page 378.

Nearby, **Güira Oga** ① Casa de los Pájaros, T03757-423900, www.guiraoga.com.ar, daily
0900-1700, US$11, children 4-10 years US$6.50, under 4s free, is a sanctuary for birds that
have been injured or rescued from traffickers. Here, they are treated and reintroduced to
the wild; there are exquisite parrots and magnificent birds of prey. Endangered species
are bred here, and eagles and hawks are taught to hunt. It is an entirely self-funded family
enterprise. A 1-km-long trail from the road winds through the forest and through the
large aviaries, with families of monkeys in trees overhead. A guided visit in English or
Spanish takes 40 minutes, after which you can wander around at your leisure, and enjoy
the peace. It is inspiring and informative. To get there, turn off Ruta 12 at Hotel Orquídeas
Palace, and the entrance is 800 m further along the road from Aripuca.

Listings Puerto Iguazú and around *maps pages 372 and 376.*

Tourist information

See also www.misiones.gov.ar.

National park office
*Victoria Aguirre 66, T03757-420722, www.
iguazuargentina.com. Mon-Fri 0700-1330.*
There's another office in the park itself
(T03757-420180, daily 0700-1400 and
1430-1900).

Tourist office
*Aguirre 311, T03757-420800,
www.iguazuturismo.gob.ar.
Daily 0800-1400 and 1600-2100.*
This office and the **municipal office**
(Av Victoria Aguirre y Balbino Brañas,

T03757-423002) are useful only for the very
patient and those who speak good Spanish.
They are not always friendly but they do have
a basic map with useful phone numbers and
bus timetables.

Where to stay

Puerto Iguazú

$$$$ Panoramic Grand
*Paraguay 372, T03757-498100,
www.panoramicgrand.com.*
On a hill overlooking the river, this hotel is
stunning. There's a serene outdoor pool with
great views, large well-designed rooms and
all the usual 5-star facilities.

$$$ Iguazú Jungle Lodge
Hipólito Iyrigoyen y San Lorenzo, T03757-420600, www.iguazujunglelodge.com.
A well-designed complex of lofts and family suites, 7 blocks from the centre, by a river, with a lovely pool. Comfortable and stylish, with DVDs, great service and a restaurant. Warmly recommended.

$$$ Posada 21 Oranges
C Montecarlo y Av los Inmigrantes, T03757-494014, www.21oranges.com.
Welcoming *posada* offering 10 simple but comfortable rooms set around a pool, in a lovely, expansive garden. All rooms have stocked mini fridges, a/c and Wi-Fi. It's a US$6 taxi ride or 30-min walk to town. Recommended.

$$$ Secret Garden
Los Lapachos 623, T03757-423099, www.secretgardeniguazu.com.
Small B&B set in a fern garden, with an attentive owner and a relaxing atmosphere. Spacious rooms, good breakfast and cocktails.

$$$-$$ Hostería Casa Blanca
Guaraní 121, near bus station, T03757-421320, www.casablancaiguazu.com.ar.
Beautifully maintained family-run *hostería*, with large rooms and good showers.

$$ Petit Hotel Sí Mi Capitán
Las Guayabas 228, T03757-424012, www.petithotelsimicapitan.com.
3 blocks from the town centre, this hotel has 2 standards of room and bungalows,

2 Puerto Iguazú

➡ **Iguazú Falls maps**
1 Around Iguazú Falls, page 372
2 Puerto Iguazú, page 376

Where to stay 🛏
1 Garden Stone
2 Hostel Inn Iguazú
3 Hostería Casa Blanca
4 Iguazú Jungle Lodge
5 Marco Polo Inn
6 Noelia
7 Panoramic Grand
8 Peter Pan
9 Petit Hotel Sí Mi Capitán
10 Secret Garden

Restaurants 🍴
1 Aqva
2 El Quincho del Tío Querido
5 La Rueda
6 Pizza Boy
7 Pizza Color

Bars & clubs 🍸
8 Brook Iguazu
9 Casanova Nightclub
10 Cuba Libre

with a safe in the room. There's a swimming pool, bar and parking. They can arrange transfers, and offer packed lunches and tourist information.

$ pp Garden Stone
Av Córdoba 441, T03757-420425, www.gardenstonehostel.com.
Lovely hostel with a homely feel set in attractive gardens, with a large outdoor eating area and a swimming pool. Recommended for a tranquil stay.

$ pp Hostel Inn Iguazú
R12, Km 5, www.hiiguazu.com.
Large, well-organized hostel which used to be a casino. Huge pool, games and a range of free DVDs to watch. There's a 20% discount to HI members.

$ pp Marco Polo Inn
Av Córdoba 158, T03757-425575, www.hostel-inn.com.
The biggest and most central hostel in town, right in front of the bus station, also with a/c doubles (**$$**). Good pool, outdoor bar and cinema. Slow Wi-Fi in reception area only. Aloof staff.

$ pp Noelia
Fray Luis Beltrán 119, T03757-420729, www.hostelnoelia.com.
Cheap, well kept and helpful hostel, with a good breakfast. It's family-run and good value.

$ pp Peter Pan
Av Córdoba 267, T03757-423616, www.peterpanhostel.com.
Just down the hill from the bus station, this spotless hostel has a central pool and a large open kitchen. The doubles (**$$**) are lovely. Helpful staff.

Around Puerto Iguazú

$$$$ Posada Puerto Bemberg
Fundadores Bemberg s/n, Puerto Libertad (some 35 km south of Iguazú), T03757-496500, www.donpuertobemberglodge.com.

Wonderful luxury accommodation and gourmet cuisine in **Casa Bemberg**, dating from 1940s, surrounded by lush gardens. Huge living areas, beautifully decorated rooms and helpful staff. Good birdwatching with resident naturalist. Highly recommended.

$$$$ Yacutinga Lodge
30 km from town, pick up by jeep, www.yacutinga.com.
A beautiful lodge in the middle of the rainforest, with 2- to 4-night packages, learning about the bird and plant life and Guaraní culture. Accommodation is in rustic adobe houses in tropical gardens, with superb food and drinks included, as well as boat trips and walks.

Restaurants

Puerto Iguazú
At the end of Av Brasil is Siete Boca, a roundabout with food stalls, *parrillas* and other vendors.

$$ Aqva
Av Córdoba y Carlos Thays, T03757-422064, www.aqvarestaurant.com.
Just down from the bus station, this lovely restaurant serves dishes made with ingredients from the area.

$$ El Quincho del Tío Querido
Perón 159, T03757-420151, www.eltioquerido.com.ar.
Recommended for *parrilla* and local fish, very popular, great value.

$$ La Rueda
Córdoba 28, T03757-422531, www.larueda1975.com.ar.
Good food and prices, fish, steaks and pastas, often with mellow live music. Highly recommended.

$$ Pizza Color
Córdoba 135, T03757-420206, www.parrillapizzacolor.com.
Popular for pizza and *parrilla*.

$$-$ Pizza Boy
Misiones 294, T03757-421466, see Facebook.
A good budget options with decent
thin-crust pizza. Great-value *milanesas*
in generous portions.

Bars and clubs

Puerto Iguazú

Brook Iguazu
Tres Fronteras 350, see Facebook. Sat only.
The largest and most upscale club in the city.

Casanova Nightclub
Perito Moreno 469, see Facebook.
Wed and Fri-Sat.
One of just a few locally recommended
clubs. Multiple floors, 6 bars.

Cuba Libre
Av Brasil and Paraguay, T03757 528984,
see Facebook.
Just a block from the newly popular area of
town for eating out, this is a fun place for a
drink, or if you fancy dancing salsa. Owned
by a Cuban, the music is great and the
atmosphere lively at weekends.

What to do

Puerto Iguazú
Tour operators
Aguas Grandes, *Entre Ríos 66, T03757 425500,*
www.aguasgrandes.com. Tours to both sides
of the falls and further afield, activities in the
forest, abseiling down waterfalls, good fun.
Cabalgatas Ecológicas, *T03757-15-50942,*
www.cabalgatasecologicas.com.

Good personalized horse-riding tours
around Iguazú.
Hostel Inn and Marco Polo Inn, *see Where*
to stay, above. Run friendly and efficient travel
agencies where you can arrange trips to the
falls and surrounding area.

Transport

Puerto Iguazú
Air
Direct flights to **Buenos Aires**, 1½ hrs.
For transport from the airport to the town
centre, see box, page 374.

Bus
The bus terminal (T03757-423006) has a
phone office, a restaurant, various tour
company desks and bus company offices.
To **Buenos Aires**, 16-18 hrs, US$95-110,
various companies. To **Posadas**, direct
and some stopping at San Ignacio Miní,
frequent, 5-6 hrs, US$16-18; to **San Ignacio**
Miní, US$14.
    Direct buses to **Ciudad del Este** leave
every 40 mins, US$3, 45 mins, liable to delays
especially when crossing the Puente de la
Amistad bridge to Ciudad del Este. Buses
run daily 0600-1800 but less frequently on
Sun, no schedule; it's better to go to Foz
(see below) and change buses there.
    Buses leave for **Foz do Iguaçu** every
30 mins or so, 0730-1830, US$1.50. Taxis
between the border and Puerto Iguazú
cost US$20-25.

Taxi
T03757-15 457065. Fares in town, US$3-4.

Parque Nacional
Foz do Iguaçu (Brazil)

The Brazilian National Park was founded in 1939 and declared a World Heritage Site in 1986. The park covers 170,086 ha, extending along the north bank of the Rio Iguaçu, sweeping northwards to Santa Tereza do Oeste on the BR-277. The experience is less impressive than on the Argentine side since you are not immersed in the jungle, but it's fascinating to see the whole panorama of the falls from a distance and, because there are fewer crowds, you will see more wildlife.

Exploring the national park

a tranquil view of the waterfalls

Wildlife

Most frequently encountered are the little and red brocket deer, South American coati, white-eared opossum and brown capuchin monkey. Much harder to see are the jaguar, ocelot, puma, white-lipped peccary, bush dog and southern river otter. The endangered tegu lizard can also been seen. Over 100 species of butterfly have been identified, among them the electric blue *morpho* and the poisonous red and black *heliconius*, and the birdlife is especially rewarding for the birdwatcher. Five members of the toucan family can be seen including toco and red-breasted toucans. Never feed wild animals and keep your distance when taking photos; coatis have been known to attack visitors with food.

Trails

The shuttle bus stops first at park administration. Next is the start of the Poço Preto trail (9 km through the forest to the river, walking or by bicycle), then the Bananeiras trail and Macuco Safari (see What to do, below). After 10 km the bus stops at the start of the Cascadas Trail and the Hotel das Cataratas, and finally at the end of the road, Porta Canoas. There are Portuguese, Spanish and English announcements of the five stops.

The 1.5-km paved walk from **Hotel das Cataratas** to the falls is an easy stroll, taking you high above the Río Iguazú, giving splendid views of all the falls on the Argentine side from a series of galleries. At the end of the path, you can walk down to a viewing point, the Espaço Naipi, almost right under the powerful **Floriano Falls**, a dramatic view, since you're in the middle of the river. A boardwalk at the foot of the Floriano Falls goes almost to the middle of the river to give a good view of the **Garganta del Diablo**.

Essential Parque Nacional Foz do Iguaçu (Brazil)

Access

It is 17 km from the city of Foz do Iguaçu to the park entrance. Buses leave Foz do Iguaçu from the Terminal Urbana on Avenida Juscelino Kubitschek and República Argentina every 40 minutes starting at 0730-1800, and are clearly marked 'Parque Nacional'. You can get on or off at any point on the route past the airport and **Hotel das Cataratas**, 40 minutes US$1 one way, payable only in reais or pesos. The bus route ends at the park entrance where you purchase entry tickets (see below) and change to a park bus.

Getting around

From the entrance, shuttle buses leave every 10-15 minutes for Porto Canoas, stopping at the start of the trails mentioned below. There are Portuguese, Spanish and English announcements of the five stops.

Park information

Entry is US$17.30, payable in reais, Argentine pesos, dollars, euros or by credit card, also online by credit card, and the park is open daily 0900-1700. At the entrance is a smart modern visitor centre, with toilets, ATMs, a small café, a large souvenir shop and a Banco Itaú *câmbio* (1000-1500). An Exposição Ecológica has information about the natural history of the falls and surrounding park (included in entry fee; English texts poor). See also www.cataratasdoiguacu.com.br (in English).

When to go

Nature lovers are advised to visit first thing in the morning or late in the afternoon, preferably in low season, as crowds can significantly detract from the experience of the falls and surrounding park (at peak times, such as Semana Santa, the park receives up to 10,000 visitors a day).

From here, there are 150 steps up to the **Porto Canoas complex**, a quick and easy walk, but for those who find stairs difficult, you can take a lift, or return the way you came, and walk a little further along the road. The Porto Canoas complex consists of a big souvenir shop, toilets, a smart buffet restaurant, a café and *lanchonete*. Sit on the patio and enjoy the fantastic view of the river above the falls. Return to the visitor centre and entrance by the free shuttle bus. The visit will take you around two hours; allow extra time for lunch.

Listings Parque Nacional Foz do Iguaçu (Brazil) *map page 372.*

Tourist information

Municipal tourist office
Av das Cataratas 2330, midway between town and the turn-off to Ponte Tancredo Neves, T+55(0)45-3521 8128 or 0800-451516 (freephone 0700-2300), www.pmfi.pr.gov.br. The staff are extremely helpful and well organized, and speak English. There are also tourist offices at the **bus terminal** (open 0700-1800), the Terminal de Transporte Urbano (open 0730-1800) and at the **airport** (open 0800-2200), with map and bus information; English spoken. If you arrive without a place to stay, there are plenty of agencies to help you find a hotel and transfer you there.

Where to stay

There's a good selection of hotels and many also offer trips to the falls. The tourist office (see above) has a full list. Taxis are only good value for short distances when you have your luggage.

$$$$ Hotel das Cataratas
Directly overlooking the falls, 28 km from Foz, T+55 (0)45-2102 70, www.belmond.com/hotel-das-cataratas-iguassu-falls.
Elegant, pale pink colonial-style building with a pool in luxuriant gardens, where you might spot wildlife at night and early morning. Generally recommended, caters for lots of groups, The restaurant is open to non-residents for midday and evening buffets, also à la carte dishes and dinner with show. Member of the Belmond group (www.belmond.com). An environmental fee of about US$10 is added to the room rate.

On the road to the falls (Rodovia das Cataratas) are several expensive modern hotels with good facilities (eg **Bristol Viale Cataratas**, www.vialecataratas.com.br, **Carimã**, www.hotelcarima.com.br, **San Martin**, www.hotelsanmartin.com.br), but for budget travellers, check out:

$$ Hostel Natura
Rodovia das Cataratas Km 12.5, Remanso Grande, T+55 (0)45-3529 6949, www.hostelnatura.com.
Rustic hostel with a small pool set in fields, near the **Paudimar**. Rooms with fan, $ pp in dorm, camping, pool table, TV lounge, small kitchen, arrange visits to the falls; the website has detailed instructions for how to reach them.

$$-$ Paudimar Campestre
Av das Cataratas Km 12.5, Remanso Grande, near airport, T+55 (0)45-3529 6061, www.paudimar.com.br.
This quiet place has a pool, a football pitch and kitchen. They offer communal meals and breakfast. Tours run to either side of the falls (good value). There's a Paudimar desk at the *rodoviária*. From airport or town take Parque Nacional bus (0525-0040) and get out at Remanso Grande bus stop, by **Hotel San Juan Eco**, then take the free *alimentador* shuttle (0700-1900) to the hostel, or walk 1.2 km from main road. Camping as well ($). In high season they take HI members only. Highly recommended.

What to do

Tour operators
Macuco Safari, *Rodovia das Cataratas, Km 20, T+55-(0)45-3529 6262, www.macucosafari.com.br.* Run the **Macuco Safari Tour**, 2 hrs, US$54, which leaves from the 1st stop on the free shuttle bus service. Ride down a 1.5-km-long path through the forest in open electric jeeps, have an optional walk and then take a motor boat close to the falls themselves; similar to **Jungle Explorer** on the Argentine side (see page 372). Portuguese, English and Spanish spoken. Take insect repellent and a waterproof camera bag.

Foz do Iguaçu and around *Colour map 2, A3.*

a small, modern city

Located 28 km from the falls, Foz (population 232,000) has a wide range of accommodation and good communications by air and road with the main cities of southern Brazil and Asunción in Paraguay. It's not a particularly attractive town, and Argentina's Puerto Iguazú makes a better base, with cheaper hotels and better access to the falls. Street crime has increased in Foz in recent years, but the inhabitants are friendly and welcoming, and there are some good places to eat.

Around Foz do Iguaçu

Apart from the Parque Nacional do Iguaçu there are a couple of other attractions. The **Parque das Aves** ① *next to the visitor centre at Rodovia das Cataratas, Km 18, just before the falls, T045-3529 8282, www.parquedasaves. com.br (in English), daily 0830-1700, US$8.50,* contains Brazilian and foreign birds, many species of parrot and beautiful toucans, in huge aviaries through which you can walk, with the birds flying in formation and dive-bombing their wingless visitors. There are other birds in cages and a butterfly and hummingbird house.

The world's largest hydroelectric dam is at **Lago Itaipu** ① *12 km north on the Río Paraná, T0800-645 4645, www.itaipu.gov. br, www.turismoitaipu.com.br, there are bus tours every 30 mins 0800-1630, 2 hrs, US$8.50, full tours including the interior of the dam: 8 departures daily between 0800 and 1600, 2½ hrs, US$20 and night views, Fri-Sat 2000, US$4.75, children and seniors half price for all visits, check times with tourist office, take buses Conjunto C Norte or Conjunto C Sul from Terminal Urbano, Av JK and República Argentina, US$1.50.* It's a major feat of human achievement, an interesting contrast to the natural wonder of the falls. It was built jointly by Brazil and Paraguay and provides 80% of Paraguay's electricity and 25% of Brazil's. The main dam is 8 km long, creating a lake of 1400 sq km. A short film is shown at the visitor centre 10 minutes before each guided visit. Wear long trousers and sensible shoes. Check times with the tourist office and take your passport.

Several beaches can be visited around the lake. A large reforestation project is underway and six biological refuges have been created on the lakeshore in both countries. There is also the **Ecomuseu de Itaipu** ① *Av Tancredo Neves, Km 11, T0800-645 4645, Tue-Sun 0800-1630, US$3.25,* and **Refúgio Bela Vista** ① *Tue-Sun 0830, 1000, 1430 and 1530 from the visitor centre, 2½ hrs, US$6,* an animal rescue centre and home to the fauna displaced by the dam, both geared to educate about the preservation of the local culture and environment, or that

Essential Foz do Iguaçu

Finding your feet

Iguaçu international Airport is 13 km east of the centre and 12 km from the falls. Taxis charge US$17.50 for a trip into town. All buses marked Parque Nacional pass the airport in each direction daily 0525-0040 and cost US$1 to anywhere around town; they allow backpacks but not lots of luggage. Many hotels run minibus services for a small charge.

The long-distance *rodoviária* **bus terminal** is 4 km from the centre on the road to Curitiba. Take a bus to the centre from next to the taxis, US$0.75, taxi US$8. For transport to the falls, see page 386.

Getting around

Local buses leave from the Terminal de Transporte Urbano, TTU on Avenida Juscelino Kubitscheck and passengers can buy pre-paid cards, US$0 75 per journey (it costs more if you don't have a card). Services called *alimentador* in the suburbs are free. For transport to the falls, see box, page 380.

Safety

Tourists are warned not to stray from the main roads in town and to leave all valuables and documents in the safe in the hotel. Avenida Kubitschek and the streets south of it, towards the river, have a reputation for being unsafe at night as there is a *favela* or shanty town, nearby. Having said that, there are some good places to stay here with their own restaurants, so you shouldn't need to be out in town at night too much.

Argentina/Brazil–Paraguay

Ponte de Amizade/Puente de la Amistad (Friendship Bridge)

The ferry service from the port in Puerto Iguazú to Tres Fronteras is for locals only (and there are no immigration facilities). The Puente de la Amistad/Ponte da Amizade, a bridge over the Río Paraná 12 km north of Foz, leads straight into the heart of Ciudad del Este in Paraguay.

The border crossing is very informal but is jammed with vehicles and pedestrians all day long. No passport stamps are required to visit Ciudad del Este for the day. Motorcycle taxis (helmet provided, hang on tight) are a good option if you have no luggage. There are lots of minibuses, too. On international buses, eg from Florianópolis to Ciudad del Este and Asunción, or from Foz to Asunción, the procedure is that non-Brazilians get out at immigration for an exit stamp, then take the bus across the bridge to Paraguayan immigration where everyone gets out for an entry stamp. On buses from Asunción to Foz and beyond, non-Paraguayans get out at Paraguayan immigration for an exit stamp, then the bus takes all passengers across the river to Brazilian immigration for the entry stamp. Make sure you get all entry and exit stamps. Speak to the driver about waiting at the immigration posts at either end of the bridge. Most buses will not wait at immigration, so disembark to get your exit stamp, walk across the bridge (10 minutes) and obtain your entry stamp; keep your ticket and continue to Foz on the next bus free. Paraguayan taxis cross freely to Brazil (US$15-20), but it is cheaper and easier to walk across the bridge and then take a taxi, bargain hard. You can pay in either currency (and often in Argentine pesos). Obtain all necessary exit and entry stamps.

Direct buses to Puerto Iguazú, leave frequently from outside the Ciudad del Este bus terminal, US$2.50. If continuing into Argentina, you need to get Argentine and Paraguayan stamps (not Brazilian), but the bus usually does not stop, so ask driver if he will. Also check what stamps you need, if any, if making a day visit to Puerto Iguazú.

For transport from Puerto Iguazú to Ciudad del Este, see page 378. For transport from Foz, see page 386.

There is a friendly tourist office in the customs building on the Paraguayan side, open 24 hours. You can get out of the bus here, rather than going to the bus terminal. Taxis wait just beyond immigration, US$4-6 to most places in Ciudad del Este, but settle a price before getting in as there are reports of exorbitant fares. Remember to adjust your watch to local time (Brazil is one hour ahead). Although Paraguay observes daylight saving throughout the country, only some states in Brazil (including Paraná) do so.

The **Brazilian consulate** in Ciudad del Este at Pampliega 205 y Pa'í Pérez, T+595 (0)61-500984, consulado.deleste@itamaraty.gov.br, Monday-Friday 0800-1400, issues visas. The **Argentine Consulate** in Ciudad del Este is at Avenida Boquerón y Adrián Jara, Edificio China p 7, T+595 (0)61-500945, www.embajada-argentina.org.py/V2/consulados/consulado-gral-en-cde, Monday-Friday 0800-1300. The **Argentine consulate** in Foz do Iguaçu is at Travessa Eduardo Bianchi 26, T+55 (0)45-9113 5482, open Monday-Friday 1000-1500. The **Paraguayan consulate** in Foz is at Rua Marechal Deodoro 901, T+55 (0)45-3523 2768, open Monday-Friday 0900-1700. The **Paraguayan consulate** in Puerto Iguazú is at Perito Moreno 236, T03757-424230, open Monday-Friday 0800-1500.

part which isn't underwater. Recommended. In addition there is the **Polo Astronômico** ① *T045-3576 7203, Tue-Sun at 1000 and 1600, Fri-Sat also 1830 (1930 in summer), 2½ hrs, US$6,* a planetarium and astronomical observatory.

Listings Foz do Iguaçu and around *map page 372.*

Tourist information

For details of the Parque Nacional Foz do Iguaçu (Brazil), see Tourist information, page 380.

Where to stay

Foz do Iguaçu
Check hotels' websites for internet prices and special offers. Av Juscelino Kubitschek and the streets south of it, towards the river, are unsafe at night. There are many prostitutes around R Rebouças and Almirante Barroso. Taxis are only good value for short distances when you are carrying all your luggage.

$$$$ Suíça
Av Felipe Wandscheer 3580, T+55 (0)45-3025 3232, www.hotelsuica.com.br.
Some way out of the city, a comfortable hotel with rooms, suites and lodges, as well as attractive pools and a gym. Swiss manager, helpful with tourist information.

$$$ Best Western Tarobá
R Tarobá 1048, T+55 (0)45-2102 7700, www.hoteltaroba.com.br.
In the Best Western chain, bright and welcoming, with a small pool, attractive rooms, helpful staff and good breakfast (extra). Good value. Recommended.

$$$ Foz Presidente I
R Xavier da Silva 1000 and II at R Mcal Floriano Peixoto 1851, T+55 (0)45-3572 4450, www.foz presidentehoteis.com.br.
Good value, with decent rooms, a restaurant and a pool. No 1 is convenient for buses.

$$$ San Juan Tour
R Marechal Deodoro 1349, T+55 (0)45-2105 9100, www.sanjuanhoteis.com.br.

Comfortable, popular hotel with an excellent buffet breakfast. Good value but cheaper if booked online. Recommended. The more expensive **San Juan Eco** is on the road to the falls.

$$$-$$ Baviera
Av Jorge Schimmelpfeng 697, T+55 (0)45-3523 5995, www.hotelbavieraiguassu.com.br.
This comfortable, renovated hotel with a chalet-style exterior is on the main road and is central for bars and restaurants.

$$$-$$ Del Rey
R Tarobá 1020, T+55 (0)45-2105 7500, www.hoteldelreyfoz.com.br.
Nothing fancy, but a perennially popular hotel, with a little pool and great breakfasts.

$$$-$$ Foz Plaza
R Marechal Deodoro 1819, T+55 (0)45-3521 5500, www.foz plazahotel.com.br.
Serene and very attractive place, with a restaurant and a pool. It also has a newish annex.

$$$-$$ Luz
Av Gustavo Dobrandino da Silva 145, near the rodoviária, T+55 (0)45-4053 9434, www.luzhotel.com.br.
Buffet restaurant, pool. Recommended.

$$ Pousada Cataratas
R Parigot de Sousa 180, T+55 (0)45-3523 7841, www.pousadacataratas.com.br.
Well-maintained modern rooms with decent hot showers, small pool, good value with regular discounts and promotions through the website. Can organize tours and transfers to and from the airport and *rodoviária.*

$$ Pousada da Laura/Ziza
R Naipi 671, T+55 (0)45-3572 3374, www.pousadalauraziza.com.

A popular place to meet other travellers, this secure *pousada* has a kitchen and laundry facilities. **$** pp in a shared dorm with a good breakfast.

$$-$ Arterial
Av José Maria de Brito 2661, T+55 (0)45-3573 1859, http://hotelarterial.com.br.
Near the *rodoviária*. Good value, huge breakfast. Opposite is a 24-hr buffet restaurant.

$$-$ Pousada El Shaddai
R Rebouças 306, near Terminal Urbana, T+55 (0)45-3025 4490, www.pousadaelshaddai. com.br.
Rooms are cheaper with fan and shared bath, **$** pp in dorm, pool.

$$-$ Pousada Evelina
R Irlan Kalichewski 171, Vila Yolanda, T+55 (0)45-3029 9277, www. pousadaevelinafoz.com.br.
Good location, near **Muffato Supermarket**, and near Av Cataratas on the way to the falls. Great breakfast, lots of tourist information, and English, French, Italian, Polish and Spanish spoken. Warmly recommended.

Camping
Note Camping is not permitted by the **Hotel das Cataratas** and falls.

Camping e Pousada Internacional
R Manêncio Martins 21, 1.5 km from town, T+55 (0)45-3529 8183, www. campinginternacional.com.br.
For vehicles and tents, half price with an International Camping Card, also basic cabins (**$**), helpful staff, English, German and Spanish spoken, pool, restaurant.

Restaurants

Foz do Iguaçu

$$$ Búfalo Branco
R Rebouças 530, T+55 (0)45-3523 9744, http://bufalobranco.com.br.
Superb all-you-can-eat *churrasco*, includes filet mignon, bull's testicles, salad bar and

desert. Sophisticated surroundings and attentive service. Highly recommended.

$$$ Rafain
Av das Cataratas 1749, T+55 (0)45-3523 1177, www.rafainchurrascaria.com.br.
Closed Sun evening.
Set price for excellent buffet with folkloric music and dancing (2100-2300), touristy but very entertaining. Out of town, take a taxi or arrange with travel agency. Recommended.

$$$ Zaragoza
R Quintino Bocaiúva 882, T+55 (0)45-3028 8084, http://restaurantezaragoza.com.br.
Large and upmarket, for Spanish dishes and seafood. Recommended.

$$ Atos
Av Juscelino Kubitschek 865, T+55 (0)45-3572 2785. Lunch only.
Per kilo buffet with various meats, salads, sushi and puddings.

$$ Bier Garten
Av Jorge Schimmelpfeng 550, T+55 (0)45-3523 3700, see Facebook.
Bustling pizzeria, *churrascaria* and *choperia*.

Cafés

Marias e Maria
Av Brasil 505, T+55 (0)45-3523 5472, http://mariasemaria.com.br.
Established *confeitaria* with good savouries and sweets.

Oficina do Sorvete
Av Jorge Schimmelpfeng 244.
Daily 1100-0100.
Excellent ice creams, a popular local hang-out.

Bars and clubs

Foz do Iguaçu Bars, all doubling as restaurants, concentrated on Av Jorge Schimmelpfeng for 2 blocks from Av Brasil to R Mal Floriano Peixoto. Wed to Sun are the best nights; the crowd tends to be young.

Capitão Bar
Av Jorge Schimmelpfeng 288 and
Almte Barroso, T+55 (0)45-3572 1512,
http://capitaobar.com.
Large, loud and popular, nightclub attached.

Oba! Oba!
Av Mercosul 400, T+55 (0)45-3529 9070,
www.obaobasambashow.com.br. Daily 1200-
1530 for lunch, Mon-Sat 2000-2200.
At **Churrascaria Bottega**, with live samba
show at 2200.

Pizza Park Bar
R Almirante Barroso 993.
Specializes in vodka and whisky brands.
Wi-Fi zone.

What to do

Foz do Iguaçu
Tour operators
Lots of companies organize conventional half-
day tours to the falls, which are convenient
as they collect you from your hotel, prices do
not include the park entrance.
Guayi Travel, *Av Nacional 611, T+55-(0)45-*
3027 0043, www.guayitravel.com. Some of the
best tours to both sides of the falls, Ciudad
del Este, Itaipu and around, including options
for birders and wildlife enthusiasts. English
and Spanish spoken.
STTC Turismo, *Av das Morenitas 2250,*
Jardim das Flores, T+55 (0)45-3529 6161,
www.sttcturismo.com.br. Standard packages
to the Brazilian and Argentine side of the falls
to Ciudad del Este, Itaipu and with trips on
the river.

Transport

Foz do Iguaçu
Air
In Arrivals at the airport (T+55-(0)45-3521
4200) there are ATMs, **Caribe Tours e
Câmbio**, car rental offices, a tourist office
and an official taxi stand. For transport from

the airport, see box, page 382. There are
daily flights to **Rio de Janeiro**, **São Paulo**,
Curitiba and other Brazilian cities.

Bus
For local buses, see box, page 380. For
transport to the falls, see box, page 382.
    At the long-distance *rodoviária* bus
terminal (Av Costa e Silva, T+55-(0)45-3522
3590) there's a tourist office, **Cetreme** desk
for tourists who have lost their documents,
a *guarda municipal* (police), ATM and luggage
store. For transport from the *rodoviária* to the
centre, see box, page 382.
    To Brazil To **Curitiba**, 9-10 hrs, paved
road, US$40, with **Pluma** and **Sulamericana**.
To **Florianópolis**, 14 hrs, US$45-53; to
Porto Alegre with **Unesul** US$40-50. To
São Paulo, 16 hrs, US$34-58. To **Campo
Grande**, US$40, 20 hrs, for the Pantanal.
    To Paraguay There are 2 bus companies
which cross the international bridge
between Ciudad del Este and Foz's bus
terminals: **Pluma** (T0800-646 0300, www.
pluma.com.br) buses marked Cidade-
Ponte leave from the Terminal Urbana on
Av Juscelino Kubitschek for the Ponte de
Amizade (Friendship Bridge). From Ciudad
del Este, they operate daily 0700-1830
each way every 10 mins, 30-40 mins, US$2.
Rafagnin (in Brazil, no office in Paraguay,
T+55 (0)45-3523 1986) have buses 0800-
1900, US$3. To **Asunción**, direct from Foz do
Iguaçu, US$20-22, with **Pluma** and **Nuestra
Señora de la Asunción**. Buses are cheaper
from Ciudad del Este. See box, page 383, for
more on crossing the border.

Around Foz do Iguaçu
Bus
Take bus lines **Conjunto C Norte** or
Conjunto C Sul from Foz do Iguaçu
Terminal de Transporte Urbano to
Itaipu Dam, US$0.75.

Lake District

Trek amongst craggy snow-capped peaks flanked by glaciers and crystalline rivers running through virgin Valdivian rainforest to lakes of peppermint green and Prussian blue.

Ski down long pistes with panoramic views of lagoons below, or hike for days among remote mountain tops. Take a slow boat across fjords or a hair-raising whitewater rafting trip. Whatever you choose to do, Argentina's Lake District is spectacular and unforgettable.

Bariloche is the main tourist centre, a friendly but large town in alpine style with chocolate shops, lakeside hotels and chalet-style restaurants. Towering above is a range of peaks where you can hike, ski or cycle.

A magical road winds north from here through seven lakes and three national parks to the pretty tourist towns of Villa La Angostura and San Martín de los Andes. Retreat to Lago Huechulafquen, where perfectly conical Volcán Lanín is reflected in cobalt blue waters. North of here, it's wilder and less visited. Pehuenia is a quiet haven with forests of prehistoric monkey puzzle trees, broad lagoons and the rich culture of the native Mapuche people.

At the southern end of the lakes, El Bolsón and Esquel are wonderfully relaxed places for a few days' hiking. Take the *Old Patagonian Express*, try a Welsh tea in quaint Trevelin, and then explore the region's most unspoilt national park, Los Alerces.

Best for
Camping ▪ Skiing ▪ Trekking

Footprint picks

★ **Villa Pehuenia**, page 400

Monkey puzzle trees are in abundance at this remote lakeside retreat.

★ **Bariloche**, page 432

Ski, trek or camp in the untouched wilderness just outside this most famous of towns in the Lake District.

★ **Estancia Peuma Hue**, pages 444 and 446

A true Argentine estancia experience offering horse riding, kayaking and world-class fly-fishing.

★ **Mount Tronador**, page 452

Mountaineering at its finest, with glaciers, coihue forests and panoramic views of Lago Nahuel Huapi.

★ **Parque Nacional Los Alerces**, page 473

Patagonian steppe meets Andean forest in an area known for glassy lakes, snow-capped peaks and the famed alerce tree.

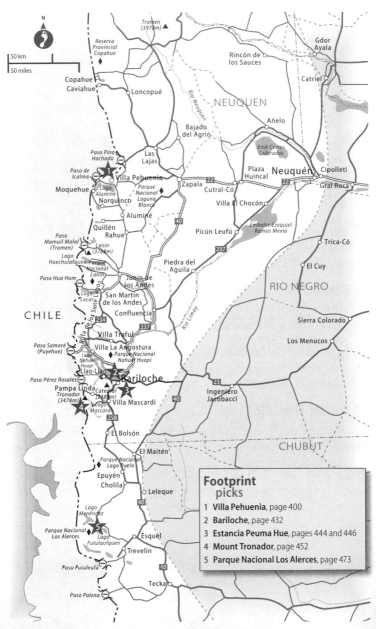

N

50 km
50 miles

Tromen (3978m)

Reserva Provincial Copahue

Rincón de los Sauces

Gdor Ayala

Catriel

Copahue
Caviahue

Loncopué

NEUQUEN

Río Neuquén

Bajado del Agrio

Añelo

Emb Cerros Colorados

Paso Pino Hachado

Las Lajas

Plaza Huincal

Neuquén

Cipolleti

Paso de Icalma

Villa Pehuenia

1

Zapala

22

Cutral-Có

22

Gral Roca

Moquehue

Lago Alumine

Norquinco

Parque Nacional Laguna Blanca

Villa El Chocón

Alumine

40

Picún Leufú

Embalse Ezequiel Ramos Mexía

Trica-Có

Quillén Rahue

237

Piedra del Aguila

El Cuy

RIO NEGRO

Paso Mamuil Malal (Tromen)

Lanín (3768m)

Lago Huechulafquen

Parque Nacional Lanín

Junín de los Andes

Paso Hua Hum

Lago Lacar

San Martín de los Andes

Confluencia

Sierra Colorada

Los Menucos

CHILE

Villa Traful

237

Río Limay

Paso Samoré (Puyehue)

Villa La Angostura

Lago Nahuel Huapi

Parque Nacional Nahuel Huapi

Llao-Llao

2 Bariloche

23

Ingeniero Jacobacci

Paso Pérez Rosales

Pampa Linda

Tronador (3478m)

Catedral (2388m)

Villa Mascardi

4

Lago Mascardi

40

258

El Bolsón

El Maitén

CHUBUT

Parque Nacional Lago Puelo

Epuyén

Cholila

Leleque

40

Lago Menéndez

Esquel

Parque Nacional Los Alerces

Lago Futulaufquen

Trevelin

Paso Futuleufu

Tecka

40

Paso Palena

Footprint picks

1 **Villa Pehuenia**, page 400
2 **Bariloche**, page 432
3 **Estancia Peuma Hue**, pages 444 and 446
4 **Mount Tronador**, page 452
5 **Parque Nacional Los Alerces**, page 473

Eastern &
central Neuquén

The northern half of the Lake District falls into the province of Neuquén, encompassing an enormous region that stretches from the border with Mendoza, beyond Copahue and Caviahue in the north, to just north of Bariloche in the south.

The provincial capital is the pleasant modern city of Neuquén, centre of an important fruit growing area, providing most of Argentina's apples, pears and grapes.

You're likely to stop off only briefly here on the way to greater adventures in the mountains further west, but it's worth making time for a brief encounter with dinosaurs at several sites easily reached from Neuquén city. There are incredibly huge dinosaur footprints and a good museum at Villa El Chocón, where you can see proof that the largest carnivores ever known actually stomped around these lands 100 million years ago. You could try a spot of excavation yourself at Valle Cretacico or see the skeleton of the largest herbivorous dinosaur on earth in Plaza Huincul. For more information, see www.neuquen.com.

Essential Lake District

Air

There are several flights daily from Buenos Aires to Neuquén, Chapelco (for Junín and San Martín de los Andes), Bariloche and Esquel (for the southern lakes), as well as flights from Santiago in Chile to Bariloche. The army airline **LADE** runs weekly flights connecting Bariloche with other Patagonian towns. If you're short on time, flying is preferable to long bus journeys, and it's inexpensive. Consider buying two singles (same price as a return), flying to San Martín de los Andes in the north and leaving from Esquel in the south, allowing you to see the whole area by hired car or bus. Book well in advance from December to March.

Bus

Long-distance buses connect Neuquén and Bariloche with Buenos Aires, other major cities in Argentina and the Chilean border. But distances are huge so it's better to fly.

Train

One of the country's few long-distance railways, the *Tren Patagónico*, runs to Bariloche from Viedma, a comfortable overnight service that also carries cars. See www.trenpatagonico-sa.com.ar.

Getting around

Bicycle

The area is fabulous for cycling. Avoid cycling in January and early February when it's busy with traffic. There are good bike shops in Bariloche and San Martín. You can also rent bikes, although they're not of the highest standard. Carry plenty of food and water.

Boat

There are lots of boat trips around Lago Nahuel Huapi. The Three Lakes Crossing to Chile from Bariloche is a good way of getting to Puerto Montt in Chile, but the bus is cheaper. For more on the Three Lakes Crossing, see box, page 448.

Bus and car

Hiring a car is the most flexible option but distances are huge. There are excellent bus services around Bariloche and regular bus services running between Junín de los Andes, San Martín de los Andes, Bariloche and El Bolsón, and on to Esquel, with less frequent services via Cholila, Lagos Puelo and Epuyen. Many big buses will take bicycles; book beforehand. The national parks are less easy to access by bus, although there is a daily bus linking Los Alerces and Esquel. Reaching Pehuenia and the dinosaur region near Neuquén is almost impossible by bus.

It's best to visit the northern lakes by car or on a tour. Car hire is easiest in Bariloche, but is also possible in San Martín de los Andes, El Bolsón, and Esquel. Tell the car rental company if you're taking a hire car into Chile.

Walking

There are plenty of *refugios* in the mountains behind Bariloche, near Pampa Linda, around El Bolsón, and in Los Alerces and Lanín national parks. Get advice from park offices or **Club Andino offices** (see page 436).

Summer (December to February) is the obvious time to come, but January is impossibly busy. In summer, *tábanos* (horseflies) are common on lakes and at lower altitudes. In March and early April there are far fewer visitors. Late spring and early summer (October to November) can be lovely, though cool, and also busy. Autumn has brilliant displays of autumn leaves in late April and early May. The ski season runs from late June to September and is busiest in July, when prices rise and Bariloche is inundated. Hotels are all more expensive in peak periods, with the highest prices in January and July.

dinosaur fossils offer a prehistoric welcome

The provincial capital is at the eastern tip of the province and is an attractive industrial town, founded in 1904, just after the arrival of the railway. It's on the opposite side of the Río Neuquén from Cipolletti, a prosperous centre of the Río Negro fruit-growing region. While it has no major tourist attractions, it's a useful stopping point for the lakes and also a good base for exploring the dinosaur finds in the area to the immediate southwest.

Sights

At the northern end of Avenida Argentina at the Parque Centenario is the **Mirador Balcón del Valle** with panoramic views over the city and the confluence of the rivers (be sure not to take the bus to Centenario industrial suburb). The city is home to the **Museo Paleontológico de la Universidad Nacional del Comahue**, but as of 2016 is closed indefinitely. Consult the tourist office (see Tourist information, page 394) about the possible reopening of the museum as well as exhibitions of dinosaur fossils found in the region. The **former railway station**, at Olascoaga and Pasaje Obligado, has been converted into a cultural centre and exhibition centre.

South of the centre there is a pleasant walk along the Río Limay. There's also the **Bodega del Fin del Mundo** ⓘ *R8, Km 9, near San Patricio de Chañar, T0299-15-580 9085, www.bodegadelfindelmundo.com, Tue-Sun 1000-1630. Free tours* take an hour and include a tasting.

Routes to the lakes

From Neuquén, there are various ways to approach the lakes. An attractive route involves continuing due west to Zapala on Ruta 22, and then south to Junín de los Andes on Ruta 40. Or from Zapala, you could continue west to Villa Pehuenia, or north to Caviahue and Copahue. For the direct route to Bariloche, take Ruta 237, via **Piedra del Aguila** and Confluencia and the astounding scenery of the **Valle Encantado**, with mountains whipped into jagged peaks. The road continues to Lago Nahuel Huapi where there are fine views over Cerros Catedral and Tronador.

Essential Neuquén city

Finding your feet

The **airport is** 7 km west of town. A taxi costs US$8-10 or take city buses No 10 or 11. The **bus terminal** is at Ruta 22 y Solalique, 4 km west of town. A taxi to the centre costs US$4-5.

Getting around

The town can easily be explored on foot in a few hours, with most hotels and restaurants around the main street Avenida Argentina, which runs north from the disused railway track running east–west across the town, just south of General San Martín. Don't get confused with the street Félix San Martín, three blocks further south. Note that city buses, **Indalo**, take rechargeable magnetic cards, sold at the bus terminal and elsewhere, from US$1.75.

Useful addresses

Chilean consulate, La Rioja 241, T0299-442 2447.

Useful websites

To plan your trip and for more information before you come, check out these sites: www. neuquentur.gob.ar (in English); www.trekbariloche.com (trekking information, in English); www.interpatagonia.com (excellent site for general information on the area in English); www.clubandino.org (for walks and mountain climbing); www.activepatagonia.com.ar (hiking and trekking expeditions); and www.revistapatagonia.com.ar (a useful magazine).

Listings Neuquén city

Tourist information

Municipal tourist office
Av Argentina y Roca 8300, T0299-15-576 4264. Mon-Fri 0700-1400 (summer), 0800-1500 (winter).
There's another tourist office at the bus terminal, T0299-449 1200 ext 4354.

Tourist office
Félix San Martín 182, T0299-442 4089, and El Ceibo 438, Barrio Alta Barda, T0299-449 1200, www.neuquentur.gob.ar, www.neuquen.com. Daily 0800-2100.
Provides helpful lists of accommodation and a map.

Where to stay

$$$$ Del Comahue
Av Argentina 377, T0299-443 2040, www.hoteldelcomahue.com.
4-star, extremely comfortable, spa, pool, good service, wine bar and excellent restaurant, **1900 Cuatro**, specializing in Patagonian fare.

$$$ Hostal del Caminante
JJ Lastra (Ruta 22, Km 1227), 13 km west of Neuquén, towards Zapala, T0299-444 0118, www.hostaldelcaminante.com.
A comfortable suburban place set among fruit plantations with garden, swimming pool and restaurant.

$$$ Royal
Av Argentina 143, T0299-448 8902, www.hotelroyal.com.ar.
Central hotel with all services, free continental breakfast, parking.

$ Hostel Punto Patagónico
Periodistas Neuquinos 94, T0299-447 9940, www.puntopatagonico.com.
A bit out of the centre, good hostel, breakfast, rustic furniture. Recommended.

Restaurants

$$$-$$ La Toscana
Lastra 176, T0299-447 3322, www.latoscanarestaurante.com.
Rustic cuisine in chic surroundings. Extensive wine list.

$$ El Ciervo
Argentina 219.
Good central option featuring an abundance of fresh seafood dishes.

What to do

Arauquen, *H Yrigoyen 720, T0299-442 5101, www.arauquen.com.* Great local agency that can organize day tours and trips further afield.

Transport

Air
Flights to **Buenos Aires** (daily) and **Comodoro Rivadavia**; LADE also flies

to **Bariloche**. Schedules change frequently. **Airport**, T0299-440 0245, www.anqn.com.ar.

Bus
The bus terminal (T0299-445 2300) is huge and modern, with lots of services and clean toilets.

Many companies to **Buenos Aires**, daily, 15-19 hrs, US$88-100. To **Zapala**, daily, 3 hrs, US$12-16. To **Junín de los Andes**, 5-6 hrs, US$23-36, with **Albus**, T0810-333 7575, www. albus.com.ar. To **San Martín de los Andes**, 7 hrs, US$25-40, **Albus**. Also **Albus** daily to **Villa Pehuenia**, 7 hrs, US$33, and **Aluminé**, 6 hrs, US$25 (less predictable in winter, when the roads are covered in snow).

To **Bariloche**, many companies, 5-6 hrs, US$25-39, sit on left. To **Mendoza**, with **Andesmar**, **Cata**, and others, daily, 12-13 hrs, US$52-75. To **Chile**: several companies, eg **Albus**, run to **Temuco**, 12-14 hrs, US$28, also from Zapala. Buy Chilean pesos before leaving. See box, page 402.

South and west of Neuquén

follow the rivers that feed the lakes

To the southwest of Neuquén lies the huge lake Embalse Ezequiel Ramos Mexía in an area that has become famous in recent years for the wealth of dinosaur fossils found here from the Cretaceous period (100 million years ago). There are a number of places where you can see the finds and even walk close to the footsteps of dinosaurs. The towns themselves are not appealing, but they make convenient stopping points along the road from Neuquén to the lakes, with a good museum at Villa El Chocón.

Villa El Chocón *Colour map 5, A3.*
For information on reaching the footprints and how they were formed, see www. interpatagonia.com/paseos/huellas (in English).

Your only reason to visit Villa El Chocón at the northern end of Lago Ezequiel Ramos Mexía, 72 km from Neuquén, is to see the remains of dinosaurs. It's a neat, rather uninspiring town, a strictly functional place built for workers on the hydroelectric dam. To see the amazing evidence of **dinosaurs**, take Route 237 towards Piedra del Aguila and turn left at Barrio Llanquén, where indicated, to the lake shore. Red sedimentary rocks have preserved, in relatively good condition, bones and even footprints of the creatures that lived in this region during the Cretaceous period about 100 million years ago. Some of the fossils can be seen in the **Museo Paleontológico Ernesto Bachmann** ① *Civic Centre, El Chocón, T0299-490 1223, www.interpatagonia.com/paseos/ernestobachmann, daily 0800-1830, US$1.50,* where there's a well laid out and informative display and guides give very good tours. Exhibits include fossils of the mighty 10-ton, 15-m-long *Gigantosaurus carolinii*, a carnivorous dinosaur larger than the famous *Tyrannosaurus rex*.

Excavation at Valle Cretácico
www.interpatagonia.com/paseos/valle_cretacico2, has information in English.

The lunar landscape around Villa El Chocón is rather amazing and contains a surprising number of dinosaur remains. So much so that an area has been named 'Cretaceous Valley'. The valley lies 18 km south of Villa El Chocón, near the Dique, and has improbably shaped pedestals of eroded pink rock coming out of the blue water. There are two walks beside the lake to see the dinosaur footprints, which are incredibly well preserved.

ON THE ROAD

Walking with dinosaurs

Few countries are as important as Argentina for palaeontologists. The relative abundance of fossils near the surface has made the country a centre for the study of dinosaur evolution. The Ischigualasto and Talampaya parks (in San Juan and La Rioja respectively) have yielded rich evidence of dinosaurs from the Triassic period (225-180 million years ago), among them, the small *Eoraptor lunensis*, 220 million years old.

Patagonia was home to Jurassic dinosaurs (180-135 million years old), with some outstanding examples found here: Cerro Cóndor in Chubut is the only site of Middle Jurassic period dinosaurs found in the Americas, and has given palaeontologists an important breakthrough in understanding the evolutionary stages of the period. The five examples of *patagosaurus* found here indicated that these dinosaurs were social creatures, perhaps uniting for mutual defence. In Santa Cruz, traces of dinosaurs from the Upper Jurassic period have been found in rocks, surprising palaeontologists with the news that dinosaurs could live and breed in arid and desert-like conditions.

The most important discoveries of dinosaurs from the Cretaceous period (135-70 million years ago) have been made in Neuquén and Chubut. Dating from the period of separation of the continents of South America and Africa, these provide evidence of the way dinosaurs began to evolve differently due to geographic isolation. The *Carnotaurus sastrie* found in Chubut has horns and small hands, for example, whereas the Patagonian dinosaurs are huge. The carnivorous *Gigantosaurus carolinii*, found near Neuquén city, was larger even than the better known *Tyranosaurus rex*, discovered in North America. You'll find dinosaur footprints, eerily well preserved, near Villa Chocón, southwest of Neuquén city. You can even take part in excavation at a site in Cretaceous Valley, and there are remains of the largest herbivorous dinosaur on earth at Plaza Huincul's famous museum.

Trelew on the Atlantic coast has the country's finest dinosaur museum, the Museo Paleontológico Egidio Feruglio (www.mef.org.ar). There's an associated site with 40 million years of history near the Welsh village of Gaiman (see page 500). In 2013, scientists led by MEF researchers discovered the remains of the largest dinosaur found to date: a 40-m-long, 80,000-kg herbivorous Titanosaur found near Trelew.

Plaza Huincul *Colour map 5, A3.*

There are more dinosaur remains at a quite impressive little museum in the otherwise rather dull town of Plaza Huincul (population 13,000). The road to Zapala, Route 22, leaves Neuquén and passes through the fruit-growing region of the Río Limay and the much duller oil-producing zone. Situated 107 km west of Neuquén, Plaza Huincul was the site of the country's first oil find in 1918. The **Museo Municipal Carmen Funes** ⓘ *on the way into Plaza Huicul, at the crossing of R22 and RP17, T0299-496 5486, Mon-Fri 0900-1900, Sat-Sun 1030-2030, US$0.75*, includes the vertebrae of *Argentinossaurus huinclulensis*, believed to have weighed over 100 tons and to have been one of the largest herbivorous dinosaurs ever to have lived, as well as a nest of fossilized dinosaur eggs. It's mainly a centre for research, and you can see the results of the fieldwork in fossils, photographs and videos, as well as the skeletons themselves. For more information, see www.plazahuincul.com.ar and www.plazahuincul.gov.ar (in Spanish).

Zapala *Colour map 5, A2.*

Zapala (population 43,000, altitude 1012 m) lies in a vast dry plain with views of snow-capped mountains to the west. It's a modern and rather unappealing place, but you'll need to stop here at the **bus terminal** ⓘ *Etcheluz y Uriburu, T02942-423191*, if you want to take buses to Pehuenia, Copahue and Caviahue, or to cross the border into Chile at the Icalma Pass; see box, page 402.

The **Museo Mineralógico Dr Juan Olsacher** ⓘ *Etcheluz 52 (by bus terminal), T02942-422928, Mon-Fri 0900-1930, free*, is one of the best fossil museums in South America; it contains over 2000 types of mineral and has the finest collection of fossils of marine reptiles and marine fauna in the country. On display is the largest turtle shell from the Jurassic period ever found and an ophthalmosaur, as well as photos of an extensive cave system being excavated nearby.

Parque Nacional Laguna Blanca
Colour map 5, A2.

Covering 11,250 ha at altitudes of between 1200 m and 1800 m, this park is one of only two reserves in the Americas created to protect swans and lies 35 km southwest of Zapala. This is a rare example of high arid steppe, and its 1700-ha lagoon is one of the most important nesting areas of the black-necked swan in Argentina. Other birdlife includes several duck species, plovers, sandpipers, grebes and Chilean flamingos, with birds of prey such as the red-backed hawk and the peregrine falcon nesting on the steep slopes of the *laguna*. The landscape is very dry, and rather bleak, with fierce winds, encouraging only the lowest and most tenacious plant life. A rough track runs round the lake, suitable for 4WD vehicles only. There's a hiking trail which takes in 10 lagoons in all.

Nearby, the **Arroyo Ñireco** has eroded the volcanic rock to form a deep gorge, and it's worth seeking out a small cave, inhabited in prehistoric times and decorated with cave paintings. Southwest of the park Route 46 continues through the spectacular Bajada de Rahue, dropping 800 m in under 20 km before reaching the town of Rahue, 120 km southwest of Zapala.

Essential Parque Nacional Laguna Blanca

Access

The park entrance is 10 km from the junction of Route 46 (which runs across the park) with Ruta 40. The *laguna* itself lies 5 km beyond this. There's no public transport, so without your own vehicle the only option is a tour from Zapala. There's a *guardería* post near the southeast corner of the *laguna*, with a **visitor centre** (daily 0900-1600, free).

When to go

The park is best visited in spring, when young can be watched at many sites around the *laguna*.

Where to stay

There's free camping by the *guardaparque*; otherwise Zapala has the nearest accommodation; see www.pnlagunablanca. com.ar or www.parquesnacionales.gov.ar.

What to take

Take drinking water and a hat for the heat.

Tourist information

Villa El Chocón

Tourist office
Ruta 237, T0299-552 0760.
Mon-Fri 0800-1500.

Zapala

Tourist office
RN 22, Km 1392, T02942-424296.
Daily 0700-2100 in summer,
closes earlier off season.

Where to stay

Villa El Chocón

$$$ La Posada del Dinosaurio
Costa del Lago, Barrio 1,
Villa El Chocón, T0299-490 1201,
www.posadadeldinosaurio.com.ar.
Comfortable, modern, all rooms have
lake view.

Plaza Huincul

$$ Hotel Tortorici
Av Olascoaga and Di Paolo, Cutral-Co,
3 km west, T0299-496 3730,
www.hoteltortorici.com.ar.
The most comfortable option is this basic
but slightly run-down hotel with neat rooms
and a restaurant. Can arrange golf on a
nearby course.

Zapala

$$$ Hue Melén
Brown 929, T02942-422407,
www.hotelhuemelen.com.ar.
Good value, decent rooms and restaurant
with the best food in town. Try your luck in
the downstairs casino.

$$ Coliqueo
Etcheluz 159, opposite bus terminal,
T02942-421308.
Convenient and a reasonable place to stay.

$$ Pehuén
Elena de la Vega y Etcheluz, 1 block from bus
terminal, T02942-423135.
Comfortable and recommended.

Restaurants

Zapala
See also Where to stay, above, for
hotel restaurants.

$$ Del Hotel Hue Melen
Brown 929.
Great value for money and has a varied menu.

$ El Chancho Rengo
Av San Martín and Etcheluz, T02942-430956.
Where all the locals hang out.

Festivals

All the towns in the valley celebrate the
Fiesta Nacional de la Manzana (apples
are the main local crop) in early Feb.

What to do

Zapala
Mali Viajes, *Alte Brown 760, T02942-432251.*
Monserrat Viajes y Turismo, *Etcheluz 101,*
T02942-422497. Both offer traditional day
tours to the surrounding area. Can help
with bus and plane tickets.

Transport

Zapala
Bus
To **San Martín de los Andes**, 4 hrs,
US$20-25, via Junín de los Andes.
To **Bariloche**, change at San Martín.

Pehuenia &
northwest Neuquén

Pehuenia is the area due west of Zapala, running along the border with Chile. It is a wonderful expanse of unspoilt wilderness, which is only now opening up to visitors, around the picturesque villages of Villa Pehuenia and Moquehue. Pehuenia is quite different from the southern lakes, thanks to its large forests of ancient *pehuén* or araucaria – monkey puzzle trees. These magnificent silent forests exert a mysterious force and give a prehistoric feel to the landscape, while the sleepy backwater feel of the villages makes them appealing for a few days' rest or gentle walking.

Further north there are two little-visited tourist centres, useful stopping points if you're heading to Mendoza: Caviahue is good for walking in rugged and unspoilt landscapes or skiing in winter, while bleaker Copahue is known for its high-quality thermal waters.

The magical and unspoilt region of Pehuenia is named after the unique forests of *pehuén* trees, which grow here in vast numbers. Covering a marvellous open mountainous landscape, these ancient, silent trees create a mystical atmosphere, especially around the lakes of Aluminé and Moquehue, where a pair of small villages provides good accommodation.

Villa Pehuenia is the best set up for tourism, with its picturesque setting on the lakeside, a cluster of upmarket *cabañas* and one exceptionally lovely boutique hotel, La Escondida ① *www.posadalaescondida.com.ar*. Moquehue is quite different in style: more sprawling and relaxed. There are more *cabañas* here, excellent hiking up La Bella Durmiente and good fly-fishing. You can approach Pehuenia from Neuquén city, or, even closer, from Temuco over the border in Chile.

★ Villa Pehuenia *Colour map 5, A2.*

This pretty village on sprawling Lago Aluminé's northern shore is beautifully set amongst steep wooded hills, and makes a lovely base for a few days' relaxation or gentle walks in the hills and forests around.

This is Mapuche land and was chosen for a settlement when the Mapuche were forcefully flushed out of Buenos Aires province in the late 19th century. It has special significance because seven volcanoes in a chain are visible from here, and because the area abounds with *pehuén* (monkey puzzle) trees, which are sacred to the Mapuche (see box, opposite).

With the rapid building of *cabaña* complexes, tourism is slowly taking off here, and at the moment you have the best of both worlds: an unspoilt feel but enough tourist infrastructure to stay in comfort, with good restaurants.

The centre of the village is just off the main road, Route 13, where you'll find a service station, *locutorios*, food and handicrafts shops, and a pharmacy. There are tour operators who can arrange trekking, boat trips on the lake and bike hire, and there is another area of restaurants and tea rooms by the lake side.

Parque de Nieve Batea Mahuida
www.cerrobateamahuida.com.

Just off the main road, a few kilometres west of town, this reserve was created to protect an area of *pehuén* trees and the majestic Volcán Mahuida (1900 m), which is regarded as sacred by the Mapuche people. The skiing and winter sports area here is one of the few businesses in the area run by Mapuche people, and is good for limited skiing in winter, with snowmobile and snowshoe walking. It's also a lovely place for walking in summer, with tremendous views of all seven volcanoes around. Delicious home-cooked food is served; contact the Mapuche Puel community at the entrance. It takes three hours to walk up here or one hour by bike.

Walk to Lago Moquehue

For walks through the araucaria forests, drive west from Villa Pehuenia towards Chile for 4 km, until you reach the end of the lake,

Tip...
Walk onto the peninsula stretching out into the lake from Villa Pehuenia for wonderful walks along the araucaria-fringed shore, and up to the Mirador del Ciprés with fabulous views.

ON THE ROAD

Monkey puzzle trees and the Mapuche

The stunningly beautiful area of Pehuenia is remarkable for its forests of araucaria, or monkey puzzle trees (*Araucaria araucana*). Growing slowly to a mighty 40 m high and living for 1200 years, the trees exert a powerful presence when seen en masse, perhaps because their forests are silent, moving little in the breeze. A true conifer, the araucaria is a descendent of the petrified pines found in Argentina's *bosques petrificados*.

For centuries the *pehuén* or araucaria have been revered by indigenous peoples, and the local Mapuche still eat its pine nuts. The custom of collecting their nuts, around which a whole array of foods and a celebratory harvest festival are based, has been the source of a bitter territory dispute in parts of the northern Lake District. The Mapuche feel that they have a natural right to harvest the fruits of their trees, and local landowners, backed by local government, clearly don't agree.

There's a growing respect for the Mapuche in the area, and they are beginning to get involved in the provision of basic tourist services. You'll see *pan casero* (home-made bread), *tortas fritas* (fried pastries) and handicrafts for sale on roadsides, as well as the winter sport centre near Villa Pehuenia, all run by the local Mapuche. These small enterprises enable them to survive financially, while retaining their traditions and customs and, with luck, access to the magnificent araucarias which they hold so sacred.

where you turn left at the *gendarmería*, following a dirt road across the bridge over a narrow strip of water, La Angostura. Follow the arrow to a campsite 50 m further on, El Puente (a delightful place, recommended). Continue past it and, when you come to a little hut and a sign to Lago Redonda, take the right fork and follow the track. Park or leave your bike at the largest of the three small *lagunas*, and take the path due south when the track comes to an end at a farmstead by a large lagoon. Climb from here to a ridge with great views, and then take the path which drops and skirts around **Lago Moquehue** – the view is awe-inspiring. You could walk to Moquehue from here, but you need a map; ask for the *Sendas y Bosque*'s map of Norte Neuquino, which shows the Pehuenia-Moquehue area, and some paths.

This whole area is the heart of the Mapuche community: many houses offer *pan casero* (home-made bread), horse riding or walking guides.

Moquehue *Colour map 5, A2.*
Another 10 km on Route 13 brings you to the sprawling village of Moquehue (population 600). It's a wilder, more remote place than Villa Pehuenia, spreading out on the shores of its lake, with a lovely wide river. Famous for fishing, this is a beautiful and utterly peaceful place to relax and walk, and it has a less cultivated feel, inspiring adventurous treks. A short stroll through araucaria forests brings you to a lovely waterfall; a longer hike to the top of Cerro Bandera (four hours return) gives wonderful views over the area, and to Volcán Llaima. There are fine camping spots and a couple of comfortable places to stay. For more information, see www.villapehuenia.org (in English).

Aluminé *Colour map 5, A2.*
In the splendid Aluminé Valley, on Route 23 between Pehuenia and Junín de los Andes, lies the area's self-proclaimed rafting capital, the small town of Aluminé (population 5000). There is indeed superb rafting (Grades II or IV to VI, depending on rainfall) nearby on Río Aluminé.

BORDER CROSSING
Argentina–Chile

Paso Pino Hachado

Paso Pino Hachado (1864 m) lies 115 km west of Zapala via Route 22, which is almost completely paved. Buses from Zapala and Neuquén to Temuco use this crossing. On the Chilean side a paved road runs northwest to Lonquimay, 63 km west of the border. Temuco lies 145 km southwest of Lonquimay.

Argentine immigration and customs 9 km east of the border, daily 0800-2000. See www.gendarmeria.gob.ar/pasos-chile/pino-hachado.html.

Chilean immigration and customs Liucura, 22 km west of the border, daily 0800-1900. Very thorough searches and two- to three-hour delays reported.

Paso de Icalma

Paso de Icalma (1303 m) lies 132 km west of Zapala and is reached by Route 13 (*ripio*). It is used as an alternative border crossing when other crossings at higher altitude are closed due to snow. On the Chilean side this road continues unpaved to Melipeuco, 53 km west of the border, and then to Temuco. See www.gendarmeria.gob.ar/pasos-chile/icalma.html.

Argentine immigration and customs 9 km east of the border, daily 0900-2000. All paperwork is carried out at the customs office, clearly signposted.

Chilean immigration and customs Daily 0800-1900.

There are places to stay, but despite the lovely setting, it's a drab place. There's a service station, the last between Villa Pehuenia and Junín de los Andes. See also What to do, page 405.

Rucachoroi

From Aluminé there is access to Lago Rucachoroi, 23 km west, inside Lanín national park. The biggest Mapuche community in the park live here, in gentle farmland surrounded by ancient *pehuén* forests. Access is by a rough *ripio* road, best in a 4WD in winter, and spectacular in autumn when the deciduous trees are a splash of orange against the bottle-green araucarias. The only accommodation is in two campsites, both offering Mapuche food and horse riding. Here too, there's a *guardería* where you can ask about a possible trek to Lago Quillén. The landscape is very beautiful and you will want to linger, but bring provisions and camping gear. Private transport is essential.

Lago Quillén

At the junction by the small town of Rahue, 16 km south of Aluminé, a road leads west to the valley of the Río Quillén and the exquisite Lago Quillén, from where there are fine views of Volcán Lanín peeping above the mountains. The lake itself is one of the region's most lovely, jade green in colour, with beaches along its low-lying northern coast. Further west, where annual rainfall is among the heaviest in the country, the slopes are thickly covered with superb Andean Patagonian forest. There's no transport, and the only accommodation (with food shop and hot showers) is at Camping Quillén ① T02942-496599, camping.ruka@gmail.com, on the lake shore. Here you can get advice about walks, and register with *guardaparques* if you plan to hike to Rucachoroi. There's another walk to the remote **Lago Hui Hui**, 6 km north from the second campsite (3½ hours return). For fishing, contact **Estancia Quillén** (see Where to stay, page 404).

Tourist information

Villa Pehuenia

Tourist kiosk
*Off the main road, by the turning
for Villa Pehuenia, T02942-498044,
www.villapehuenia.gov.ar.*
Along with most hotels, this kiosk has the
excellent free leaflet showing a detailed
map of Villa Pehuenia with all the hotels
and restaurants marked.

Aluminé

Tourist office
*C Christian Joubert 321, T02942-496001,
www.alumine.gov.ar. Daily 0800-2000.*
Very friendly.

Where to stay

Villa Pehuenia
You'll find a superb boutique hotel, and plenty
of *cabañas*, many with good views over the
lake and set in idyllic woodland. Email or ring
first for directions, since there are no road
names or numbers here. For more listings,
see www.villapehuenia.org (in English).

$$$$-$$$ La Escondida
*Western shore of the peninsula, T02942-15-
691166, www.posadalaescondida.com.ar.*
By far the best place to stay in the whole
area, this is a really special boutique hotel
with just 6 rooms in an imaginatively
designed building on the rocky lakeside.
Each room is spacious and beautifully
considered, with smart bathrooms (all with
jacuzzi), and private decks, all with gorgeous
views over the lake. The restaurant is superb
and non-residents can dine here with a
reservation. The whole place is relaxing
and welcoming. Highly recommended.

$$$ Altos de Pehuén
*T02942-15-5383 6300,
www.altosdelpehuen.com.ar.*

Comfortable *cabañas* with lovely views, and
a *hostería*.

$$$ Cabañas Caren
*T02942-15-400615, www.cabanascaren.
com.ar.*
Simple A-frame *cabañas*, but with
open views and balconies, and made
especially welcoming by the warm
friendly owner Walter.

$$$ Complejo Patagonia
*T02942-15-548787 (T011-15-5011 4470 in
Buenos Aires), www.complejopatagonia.
com.ar.*
Very comfortable indeed, these lovely
cabañas are traditionally designed and the
service is excellent. Recommended.

$$$ Complejos del Lago Aluminé
*T02942-15-665068, www.villa-pehuenia.
com.ar.*
Complejo La Serena has beautifully equipped
and designed *cabañas* for 2-6 people with
lovely uninterrupted views, gardens going
down to beach, sheltered from the wind
and furnished with rustic-style, handmade
cypress furniture, and wood stoves, all very
attractive. Also has Complejo Culle Lafquen.

$$$-$$ Cabañas Bahía Radal
*T02942-498057, www.bahiaradal.com.ar,
on the peninsula (ask the tourist office
for directions).*
Luxurious *cabañas*, with clear lake views
from its elevated position.

$$$-$$ Las Terrazas
*T02942-498036, www.lasterrazaspehuenia.
com.ar.*
The owner is an architect, who has retained
Mapuche style in his beautiful design of
these comfortable *cabañas*, which are
tasteful, warm and with perfect views over
the lake. Also with bed and breakfast. He
can direct you to magical places for walking,
and to Mapuche communities to visit.
Recommended.

$$ Puerto Malén Club de Montaña
T02942-498007 (T011-4226 8190 in Buenos Aires), www.puertomalen.com.
Well-built wooden *cabañas* with lake views from their balconies, and the highest-quality interiors. Also a luxurious *hostería* ($$$). Recommended.

Moquehue

$$ La Bella Durmiente
T02942-660993, www.bdurmientemoquehue. com.ar.
In a rustic building, rooms heated by wood fires, also camping, summer only, the welcoming owner offers good food and also trekking, horse riding, diving in the lake and mountain biking. Call for directions.

Cabañas

$$$ Cabañas Los Maitenes
T02942-15-665621, www. complejolosmaitenes.com.ar.
Right on the lake, well-equipped *cabañas*, with breakfast included and friendly owners. Recommended.

$$$ La Busqueda
T02942-15-660377, www. labusquedamoquehue.com.ar.
Just north of the lake, before you reach the head of Lago Moquehue. Interesting design in these well-equipped *cabañas* with TV, including breakfast. Recommended

Camping
Along R13, 11 km to Lago Ñorquinco, past mighty basalt cliffs with *pehuenes* all around, there's idyllic camping.

Camping Trenel
T02942 487202.
In a fabulous site elevated on the southern shore of Lago Moquehue, just beyond the **Hostería Moquehue**. Beautiful, well-kept sites in the thick of little *nirre* trees, with seats and *parrillas* overlooking the lake. Smart, hot showers, good restaurant, food shop, information and trips. Recommended.

Ecocamping Ñorquinco
T02942-496155, www.ecocamping.com.ar. Dec or Mar, Apr to Easter.
There is an amazing rustic *cabaña* right on the lake, with a café by the roadside. Great fishing, hot showers and a *provedura*. Lovely place to eat if it rains.

Los Caprichosos
On Lago Ñorquinco. Nov-Apr only.
With water and food shop.

Aluminé

$$$ Piedra Pintada
T11-4328 0145, www.piedrapintada.com.
Only 35 km from town, this is the best option. 12 rooms, stylishly fitted out, with a sauna, fantastic views over the lake and impressive restaurant.

$$ Aluminé
C Joubert 312, T02942-496174, www.hosteriaalumine.com.ar.
In the middle of town, opposite tourist information, this is a drab 1960s place, with clean, functional rooms. There's an excellent little restaurant next door, **La Posta del Rey**.

Rucachoroi
Camping
There are 2 sites, **Rucachoroi 1** and **Rucachoroi 2**, located before and after the lake (www.campingruka.blogspot.com). Open all year, but ideal only Dec-Feb. The first has more facilities, with toilets, but no hot water, some food supplies, including Mapuche home-made bread and sausages, and horse riding.

Lago Quillén

$$$ Estancia Quillén
R46 near Rahue, near the bridge crossing Río Aluminé, T02942-496196, www. interpatagonia.com/quillen. Dec-Apr.
A comfortable, traditionally furnished house, with spacious rooms and a restaurant, where you'll be welcomed by the estancia owners. Great for fishing and hunting.

Restaurants

Villa Pehuenia

$$$ La Escondida
On the western shore of the peninsula, T02942-15-691166, www.posadalaescondida.com.ar.
By far the best in town. Only open to non-residents with a reservation, this is really special cuisine. All local ingredients, imaginatively prepared and served. Highly recommended.

$$ Anhedonia
On the lakeside, T02942-15-469454.
Fondue, beef and pasta.

$$ Gnaien Chocolatería and tea room
On the lakeside, T02942-498082.
Good for tea, lovely views of the lake, chocolate delicacies, *picadas* and range of wines.

$$ La Cantina del Pescador
On the lakeslde, T02942-498086.
Fresh trout.

$ Costa Azul
On the lakeside, T02942-498 035.
Tasty local dishes and pasta; *chivito al asado* (roast kid) is the speciality of the house.

Aluminé

$ La Posta del Rey
Next to the service station, opposite the plaza, Cristian Joubert, T02942-496174, www.lapostadelrey.7p.com.
The best place by far, with friendly service, great trout, local kid, delicious pastas and sandwiches. Recommended.

Festivals

Villa Pehuenia
Mar Fiesta del Pehuén, www.villapehuenia.org (in Spanish). The harvest of the *piñones*, celebrated with riding displays and live music.

What to do

Villa Pehuenia
Los Pehuenes, *T02942-15-566 4827, www.pehuenes.com.ar.* Excellent company offering wide range of trips and adventures: trekking in the mountains; rafting (Grade IV); horse riding; visits to the local Mapuche communities, with roast kid, and local history and culture; and fishing and boat trips. Professional, helpful and friendly. Ask for Fernando. Can also arrange transfers to Pehuenia from San Martín and Neuquén.

Aluminé
Aluminé Rafting, *Villegas 610, T02942-496322, www.interpatagonia.com/aluminerafting.* Price for 3 hrs' rafting depends on difficulty, Grades II-VI, all equipment included. Options are: Circuito Abra Ancha, 2½ hrs, Grade II, 6 km, very entertaining, suitable for everyone; Circuito Aluminé Superior, 12 or 15 km run, 5-6 hrs, Grade III-IV, very technical river leaving Lago Alumine, for those who like a thrill, passing little woods of araucarias and *ñirres*; family trips Grades I and II. Also offers trekking, kayaking and biking.

Transport

Villa Pehuenia
To reach Villa Pehuenia, you could take one of the daily buses from Neuquén city, but these take a long time, and once you're here you may want to explore the area in your own transport so car rental is the best option. Hire a car in Neuquén (3½-hr drive) and drop it off in San Martín de los Andes or Bariloche afterwards. Route 13 continues to the Paso de Icalma crossing to Chile, just a few kilometres from Villa Pehuenia, with easy access to Temuco, 130 km further, on the other side. See box, page 402.

Albus (www.albus.com.ar) has daily buses to **Neuquén** via Zapala (less predictable in winter, when the roads are covered in snow), 7 hrs, US$33. Also to **Aluminé**, 1 hr, US$8.

Aluminé
Buses daily to **Neuquén** via **Zapala**, 3 hrs, with **Albus** (T02942-496672) and **Campana Dos** (T02942-496666). **Albus** also daily to **Villa Pehuenia**, 1 hr.

About 150 km north of Zapala, the Reserva Provincial Copahue covers an arid, dramatic and otherworldly landscape at whose heart is a giant volcanic crater surrounded by mountains. The park was created to protect the araucaria trees and there are some wonderful walks in unexpectedly stunning landscapes.

There's an ATM at the *municipalidad*, several restaurants and a tea room, as well as some decent accommodation.

Caviahue and around
Caviahue is by far the most attractive of the two towns in this area, with an appealing lakeside setting and opportunities for walking and horse riding; it converts into a skiing and winter sports centre from July to September and swells to a winter population of over 10,000. There are three 22 *pistas*, excellent areas for cross-country skiing, snow-shoeing and snowmobiling, all with tremendous views, and it's one of the region's cheaper resorts.

Volcán Copahue on the Chilean–Argentine border is an active volcano, with recent eruptions in 2013. In 2000 an eruption destroyed the bright blue lake in its crater, but it's still popular for horse riding, and the views of the prehistoric landscape are astounding. The most highly recommended excursion, however, is to **El Salto del Agrio**, 15 km northeast of Caviahue along Route 27. This is the climax in a series of delightful falls, approached by a road passing between tall, ancient araucaria trees poised on basalt cliffs.

Copahue and around
Copahue (1980 m) is a thermal spa resort enclosed in a gigantic amphitheatre formed by mountain walls with the best thermal waters in South America, though it's decidedly the bleaker of the two towns. A fantastic walk is to the extraordinary **Las Máquinas**, 4 km south, where sulphurous steam puffs through air holes against a panoramic backdrop, making the weirdest noises. At **El Anfiteatro**, thermal waters reach 150°C, in a semicircle of rock edged with araucaria trees. Just above Copahue, a steep climb takes you to **Cascada Escondida**, a 15-m-high waterfall surrounded by an araucaria forest; above it Lago Escondida is a magical spot.

Listings Caviahue and Copahue

Tourist information

Caviahue

Tourist office
8 de Abril, bungalows 5 and 6, T02948-495408, www.caviahue-copahue.gov.ar.

Copahue

Tourist office
On the approach road into town, Route 26.

Where to stay

Caviahue

$$$ Lago Caviahue
Costanera Quimey-Co, T02948-495110, www.hotellagocaviahue.com.
Better value than the Nevado; comfortable but dated lakeside apartments with kitchen, also a good restaurant and great views. 2 km from the ski centre.

$$$ Nevado Caviahue
*8 de Abril s/n, T02948-495053, T011-4313 7639
(Buenos Aires) www.hotelnevado.com.ar.*
Plain, modern rooms, and there's a restaurant
and cosy lounge with wood fire. Also
13 *cabañas*, well-equipped but not luxurious.

$$ Farallón
*Caviahue Base, T02948-495085,
www.hotelfarallon.com.ar.*
Neat apartments, some with kitchens.

$$ La Casona de Tito
Puesta del Sol s/n, T02948-495093.
Cabañas, excellent meals.

Hostels

$ pp Hebe's House
*Mapuche y Puesta del Sol, T02948-495138,
www.hebeshouse.com.ar.*
Lovely chalet-style building with great
communal areas and only 2 blocks from the
centre of town. Doubles (**$$**) available.

Camping

Copahue
*T02948-495111, Hueney Municipal.
Summer only.*
Basic but well maintained.

Copahue

$$$ Aldea Termal
T0299-15 504 7694, www.aldeatermal.com.
Attractively decorated chalet-style
apartments. Recommended.

$$$ Hotel Copahue
*Olascoaga y Bercovich, T0236-442 3390,
www.copahuejunin.com.ar.*
This lovely old place, where you'll be warmly
welcomed by Pocho and Moriconi, is the
most recommended place in Copahue. There
are well-built wood and stone *cabañas*.

Restaurants

Caviahue

$ Hotel Lago Caviahue
See Where to stay, above.
The most stylish place to eat with an inspired
chivo a la cerveza (kid cooked in beer),
traditional favourites and local specialities.

Copahue

$ Copahue Club Hotel
Valle del Volcán T02948 495020.
Serves good *chivito al asado* and local trout.

What to do

Caviahue
To find out about the ski centre, contact
Caviahue Base (www.caviahue.com).
Caviahue Tours, *Maipu 42, Buenos Aires,
T011-4343 1932, www.caviahuetours.com.*
Good information, including details of
thermal waters.

Transport

Caviahue
Bus
To **Neuquén**, 6 hrs via Zapala, 4 daily, with
Conosur, US$27; tickets can be booked
through **Caviahue Tours**, see above.

Parque Nacional
Lanín

Some of the most beautiful sights in the Lake District are to be found in one of the country's largest national parks, Lanín. The park's centrepiece, and its most climbed peak, is the magnificent, extinct, snow-capped Volcán Lanín. Lanín is especially superb seen from the two connected lakes in the centre of the park: Lago Huechulafquen and Lago Paimún. These lakes are the easiest part of the park to visit.

Quiet Lago Lolog further south also offers good fishing, and it's worth the drive to find two more tranquil and very pretty lakes hidden away in the mountains: Lago Curruhué Grande and Lago Chico. Further along the same road, there are thermal waters at Lahuen-Co.

The southern park can be visited easily from San Martín de los Andes, which sits at the head of picturesque Lago Lacar. Northernmost areas of the park are harder to access. But there are several Mapuche communities living in the park who organize campsites and horse riding, making this area interesting to visit.

The whole park is definitely more rewarding if you visit in your own transport, as bus services are sporadic at best, and there is a great deal of unspoilt landscape to explore, varying from lowland hills in the east to steep craggy mountains in the west, all heavily clad in native beech trees, *coihue*, *lenga* and *ñire*.

Essential Parque Nacional Lanín

Access

Bus transport into the park is tricky. There are some high season services from Junín de los Andes to Lago Paimún, and **KoKo Bus** (www.empresakoko.com.ar) usually runs a service to Lago Huechulafquen from San Martín de los Andes, although the timetable varies from year to year. To explore the park, you will need to join a tour or have your own transport.

The park has two official entrances. **Lago Huechulafquen** provides the easiest access to the beautifully situated lakes in the centre of the park. To get there, travel west on Route 61 from Junín de los Andes, a good dirt road, as far as the *guardaparque* office at the eastern end of the lake, where you can get free maps and information on hikes. The other entrance to the park is at **San Martín de los Andes**, which is the main tourist centre and gives easy access to Lago Lacar and the River Hua Hum on its western end. It is also the access point for Lago Lolog further north.

The very north of the park is hard to access, since the roads are poor, but it's possible to reach Quillén from Rahue by heading west along Route 46, which is signposted off Route 23. There's little infrastructure when you reach Quillén, but there are Mapuche communities to visit and some rural campsites. For details of this area, see page 402.

Park information

Park entry is US$10 (paid at the entry point). You're supposed to register at the **park administration**, Perito Moreno 749 y Elordi, San Martín de los Andes, T02972-427233, informeslanin@apn.gov.ar, Monday-Friday 0800-1300, before setting out on any major treks. If you don't manage this, then be sure to notify the *guardaparque* office at the Huechulafquen entrance to the park instead. Ask them about your route and if paths are open. They have two really good free leaflets: one on the park itself and another on climbing Lanín, both with sections in English. You should also check out www.parquesnacionales.gob.ar (Areas Protegidas section) or www.tresparques.com.ar/lanin.

Having a good map is essential: look out for the *Sendas y Bosques* (Walks and Forests) map for Parque Nacional Lanín, 1:200,000, which is laminated and easy to read, with a book containing English summaries of the walks, www.guiasendasybosques.com.ar.

Tip...

Always put out campfires with lots of water, not just earth because wherever you are in the park, fires are a serious hazard. Make sure you take all your rubbish away with you.

Lago Huechulafquen and around

From Lago Huechulafquen there are fabulous walks up into the hills and along the shore, and along beautiful Lago Paimún further west. Three *hosterías* and great campsites offer accommodation, and there are simple food shops and places to eat. Trips on the comfortable catamaran José Julián ① *T02972-428029, www.catamaranjosejulian.com.ar, US$32,* start at Puerto Canoa, on the northern shore of Lago Huechulafquen. This is a fantastic boat trip, offering the chance to see Lanín and the beautiful surrounding mountains from the water, and to reach the relatively inaccessible Lago Epulafquen with its impressive 6-km lava deposit.

Termas de Lahuen-Co

It's well worth getting to beautiful Lago Curruhué and the thermal pools at **Lahuen-Co** in the far west of the park. You can hike there in two days from Lago Paimún (see below), but if that's too much, they can also be accessed on Route 62, a good dirt road, starting either south of Junín, or from Lago Lolog. Route 62 heads west past Lago Curruhué Chico and Lago Grande, through ancient *pehuén* forests along the southern shores, and then passes the impressive lava field at Laguna Escorial. At the thermal baths there is a fantastic spa and eco lodge (www.lahuenco.com), which organizes tours in the area.

Trekking routes

There are some delightful walks near Lago Huechulafquen, indicated by yellow arrows; allow plenty of time to return before dark. Guides are only needed for the longer treks where paths are not marked. (For these, ask in the Junín park office or at San Martín de los Andes.) Ask the *guardaparques* for advice on routes before setting off.

El Saltillo Falls ① *2 hrs return, fabulous views*. Start from campsite **Piedra Mala** (where you can stock up on provisions) at Lago Paimún, and head west towards the Paimún *guardaparque* office. From here you can also walk on to Río Paimún, three to four hours one way, from Piedra Mala campsite.

Termas de Lahuen-Co ① *Best done over 2 days*. Start from beautiful **La Unión**, where Lago Huechulafquen meets Lago Paimún. (To cross to the other side of Lago Paimún at La Unión, there's a boat operated by the local **Mapuche** community, US$5; just ring the bell.) From here, it is an eight-hour walk along the northern shore to reach the western end of Lago Paimún, then four more to reach the Termas. You must consult the book of walks *Sendas y Bosques* for Parque Nacional Lanín, and notify *guardaparques* and the San Martín administration office before setting off. It's a beautiful walk, and you'll be rewarded by a soak in the pools at the end.

Base of Volcán Lanín ① *8 hrs return*. A satisfying walk. Start from Puerto Canoa. For other walks and the ascent of Lanín, see box, page 412.

Cerro El Chivo ① *2064 m, 8-9 hrs return*. Set off early, and register in campsite at Bahía Cañicul. This is a more challenging walk through forest. Note that heavy snow can lie till January. Potentially dangerous without a guide. See the *Sendas y Bosques* book for Parque Nacional Lanín (see Park information in the box, page 409), and notify the *guardaparques*.

Parque Nacional Lanín

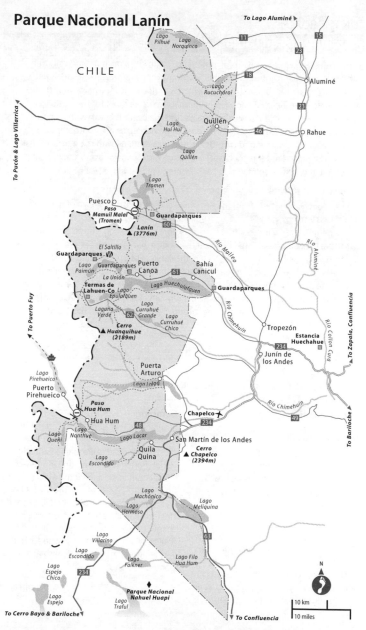

CHILE

To Lago Aluminé ▶

11 15 23

18

Lago Pilhué
Lago Norquinco

Aluminé

Lago Rucuchóroi

23

Lago Hui Hui

Quillén

46

Rahue

Lago Quillén

Lago Tramen

Puesco
Paso
Mamuil Malal
(Tromen)

Lanín
(3776m)

60

Guardaparques

To Pucón & Lago Villarrica

Río Malleo

Río Aluminé

Río Collon Cura

To Zapala, Confluencia ▶

El Saltillo
Guardaparques

Lago Paimún

Guardaparques
La Unión

Termas de
Lahuen-Co

Puerto
Canoa

61

Bahía
Canicul

Lago Huechulafquen

Guardaparques

Lago Epulafquen

Laguna
Verde

62

Lago
Currhué
Grande

Lago
Currhué
Chico

Cerro
Huanquihue
(2189m)

Río Chimehuín

Tropezón

Estancia
Huechahue

Junín de
los Andes

234

Lago
Pirehueico

Puerto
Pirehueico

Puerta
Arturo

Lago Inluq

Río Chimehuín

To Puerto Fuy

Paso
Hua Hum

Hua Hum

48

Lago
Nonthue

Lago Lacar

Lago
Queñi

Chapelco

234

49

To Bariloche ▶

San Martín de los Andes

Quila
Quina

Cerro
Chapelco
(2394m)

Lago
Escondido

Lago
Machónico

Lago
Hermoso

Lago
Meliquina

Lago
Villarino

63

Lago
Escondido

Lago
Falkner

Lago Filo
Hua Hum

Lago
Espejo
Chico

234

Parque Nacional
Nahuel Huapi

N

Lago
Espejo

Lago
Traful

To Cerro Bayo & Bariloche ▼

To Confluencia ▼

10 km
10 miles

ON THE ROAD

Climbing Volcán Lanín

One of the world's most beautiful mountains, Lanín (3776 m), is geologically one of the youngest volcanoes (though now extinct) in the Andes. It is a challenging three-day return climb to the summit, with two *refugios* at 2400 m (both without charge), sleeping 14 to 20 people. The normal departure point for the climb lies some 3 km east of the Mamuil Mamal pass. This is a beautiful spot, with a good campsite and some lovely walks: from the *guardaparque* centre, footpaths lead to a mirador (1½ hours round trip), or across a grassy prairie with magnificent clear views of Lanín and other jagged peaks, through ñirre woodland and some great araucaria trees to the point where Lago Tromen drains into Río Malleo (4 km).

Access

The ascent of Lanín starts from the Argentine customs post, 3 km east of the Mamuil Malal Pass (see box, page 417), where you must register with *guardaparques* and obtain a free permit. They will check that you are experienced enough, and also check that you have the equipment listed below. If they judge that you are not suitably prepared for the climb, they will insist that you hire the services of a trained and licensed guide. Access is all year, but best between November and April, when the weather is the most agreeable. Set off between 0800 and 1400 the first day, but 1000 is recommended. The number of climbers is limited to 60 per day, but in summer up to 120 are often allowed up. It's vital to get detailed descriptions of the ascent from the *guardaparques*, and take a detailed map.

Listings Parque Nacional Lanín *map page 411.*

Where to stay

$$$ Hostería Paimún
Ruta 61, Lago Paimún, T02972-491758, www.hosteriapaimun.com.ar.
Basic, comfortable rooms, private beach, fly-fishing guide, lake trips, cosy restaurant, stunning views all around.

$$$ Huechulafquen
Ruta 61, Km 55, Lago Huechulafquen, T02972-427598, www.hosteriahuechulafquen.com. Nov-May.
Half board, comfortable cabin-like rooms, gardens, expert fly-fishing guide, restaurant open to non-residents in high season.

Camping
Several sites in beautiful surroundings on Lagos Huechulafquen and Paimún. The most recommended are: **Bahía Cañicul** (48 km from Junín), **Camping Lafquen-co** (53 km from Junín) and **Piedra Mala** (65 km from Junín); US$4.25 pp (US$1 extra for hot water). **Mawizache**, T02972 492150, beyond **Hostería Paimún** and the picturesque little chapel, Lago Paimún. Open all year. Run by Raúl and Carmen Hernández, who are both very knowledgeable and offer fishing trips. Good restaurant.

Preparation and cautions

Because of its relative accessibility, the risks of climbing Lanín are often underestimated. An authorized guide is absolutely necessary for anyone other than the very experienced, and crampons and ice-axe are essential. Other equipment you will be required to show includes: good walking boots, an all-season sleeping bag, stove and fuel, sunglasses, torch, first-aid kit, walking sticks, helmet and VHF radio (frequency is VHF 155675). Start hydrating 24 hours before setting off and continue doing so as you climb. Take at least two litres of water with you. Eat light and frequent snacks, including bananas, raisins, cereal bars and chocolate. Bring all rubbish down with you. You will be given numbered waste bags for this purpose. On your return, it is essential to check in with the *guardaparques*, so that they can log your safe return.

Route

To climb the north face, follow the path through *lenga* forest to the base of the volcano, over Arroyo Turbio and up the Espina de Pescado (fish bone), following red and yellow marks. From here the path becomes steeper. Follow the signs to the Camino de Mulas (mule track), and then follow the red markers to reach the Nuevo Refugio Militar (new military shelter). From here keep right to the Viejo Refugio Militar (old military shelter) and the CAJA Refugio. From then on, the ascent is steep and requires ice-climbing techniques. The section to the *refugios* may be done in one day if you set out early and are mentally and physically prepared. See the excellent free leaflet produced by the Parque Nacional Lanín on the ascent, with all GPS references provided and English translation.

Mountain guiding agency

Alquimia Viajes, O'Higgins 603, Junín de los Andes, T02972-491355, www.alquimiaturismo.com.ar.

Restaurants

There are lots of places to eat on Lago Huechulafquen, with *provedurías* selling good *pan casero* at Bahía and Piedra Mala. **Mawizache** campsite (see Camping, above) has a great restaurant serving fabulous local dishes very inexpensively, plus hot chocolate and cakes.

What to do

Horse riding

You can explore much of the area on horseback, including the trek to the base of Volcán Lanín. 5 places along the lake hire horses: ask *guardaparques* for advice, or ask at the local Mapuche community where you see the signs, *cabalgatas* (horse rides).

Spas

Lahuen Co, *T02972-424709, www.lahuenco. com*. This thermal spa resort can organize trekking, kayaking, biking and fishing trips in the area, and afterwards you can relax in their thermal water pool.

Situated on the Río Chimehuin, the quiet town of Junín de los Andes (population 10,300, altitude 773 m) is justifiably known as the trout-fishing capital of Argentina. It offers some of the best fly-fishing in the country during the season from mid-November to May. Junín is also an excellent base for exploring the wonderful Parque Nacional Lanín to the west and for climbing its extinct volcano, as well as for rafting on Río Aluminé further north.

Founded in 1883, Junín is a real town, not as picturesque or tourist-orientated as its neighbour, San Martín: there are far fewer chalet-style buildings and few chocolate shops here. But it's a quiet, neat place with genuinely friendly people. The hotels are not as upmarket as San Martín, but **Estancia Huechahue** nearby (see Where to stay, page 416) is superb, and there are some decent family-run hotels here, plus a couple decent

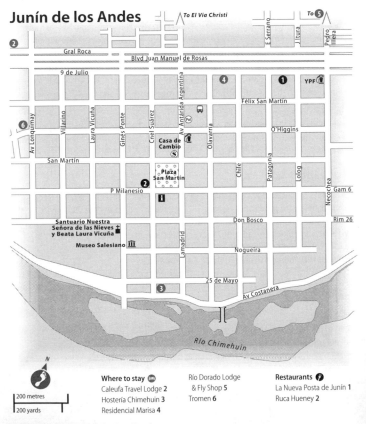

Junín de los Andes

To El Via Christi

To 5

E Serrano
Itura
Pedro Illera

Gral Roca

Blvd Juan Manuel de Rosas

9 de Julio

Av Antártida Argentina

4

1

YPF

Félix San Martín

Villarino
Laura Vicuña
Ginés Ponte
Cnel Suárez
Olavarría

O'Higgins

Av Lonquimay

6

Casa de Cambio

San Martín

Plaza San Martín

Chile
Patagonia
Lolog

P Milanesio

2

Gam 6

1

Necochea
Rim 26

Santuario Nuestra
Señora de las Nieves
y Beata Laura Vicuña

Don Bosco

Museo Salesiano

Lamadrid

Nogueira

25 de Mayo

3

Av Costanera

Río Chimehuin

N

200 metres
200 yards

Where to stay
Caleufá Travel Lodge 2
Hostería Chimehuin 3
Residencial Marisa 4

Río Dorado Lodge
& Fly Shop 5
Tromen 6

Restaurants
La Nueva Posta de Junín 1
Ruca Hueney 2

restaurants and *parrillas*, making it worth an overnight stop. Don't forget to try the celebrated local trout.

Sights

Most of what you need can be found within a couple of blocks of the central Plaza San Martín with its fine araucaria trees among mature *alerces* and cedars. The small **Museo Salesiano** ① *Ginés Ponte and Nogueira, Mon-Fri 0900-1200, 1500-2000*, has a fine collection of Mapuche weavings, instruments and arrowheads, and you can buy a whole range of excellent Mapuche handicrafts in the **Feria Artesanal** behind the tourist office.

There's an impressive religious sculpture park, **El Vía Christi**, situated among pine forest on a hillside just west of town. To get there from the plaza, walk up Avenida Antárida Argentina across the main road, Route 234, to the end. The Stations of the Cross are illustrated with touching and beautifully executed sculptures of Mapuche figures, ingeniously depicting scenes from Jesus's life together with a history of the town and the Mapuche community. It's a lovely place to walk and highly recommended. The church, **Santuario Nuestra Señora de las Nieves y Beata Laura Vicuña**, also has fine Mapuche weavings, and is a pleasing calm space.

Some 7 km away, clearly signposted, at Km 7 on Route 61 towards Lago Huechulafquen, is the **Centro Ecológico Aplicado de Neuquén** (CEAN) ① *Mon-Fri 0900-1400, free*, where trout are farmed, and ñandus and llamas can be seen; it's a good place for kids.

Fishing is undoubtedly one of the great attractions of Junín, and the best fishing is at the mouth of the Río Chimehuin, 22 km from town on the road to Lago Huechulafquen. On your way to the national park, stop off here for a moment to appreciate the heavenly turquoise water edged by a black sandy shore. In the town itself, there are pleasant places to fish and picnic along the river, and there are several fishing lodges in the area that cater for experts, with guides whose services you can hire. See also What to do, below.

Listings Junín de los Andes *map page 414.*

Tourist information

Tourist office
On the main plaza, Domingo/Padre Milanesio and C Suárez, T02972-491160. Daily 0800-2100 in summer, 0800-2000 in winter.
Fantastic office with friendly staff who can advise on accommodation and hand out maps. The **Parque Nacional Lanín office** (T02972-492748), is in the same building and is very helpful. See also www.junindelosandes.com.

Where to stay

$$$$ Río Dorado Lodge & Fly shop
Pedro Illera 378, T02972-492451, www.riodoradolodge.com.
Comfortable rooms in log cabin-style fishing lodge, big American breakfast, good fly shop, fishing excursions to many rivers and lakes, lovely gardens, attentive service.

$$$ Caleufu Travel Lodge
JA Roca 1323 (on Ruta 234), T02972-492757, www.caleufutravellodge.com.ar.
Excellent value, welcoming, very good, homely rooms, neat garden, also comfortable apartments for up to 5 people, 3- to 6-night packages and fly-fishing. Owner Jorge speaks English. Recommended.

$$ Hostería Chimehuin
Col Suárez y 25 de Mayo, T02972-491132, www.hosteriachimehuin.com.ar. Closed May.
Cosy, quaint fishing lodge by the river, fishing and mountain guides. Recommended.

$$ Residencial Marisa
JM de Rosas 360 (on Ruta 234), T02972-491175, residencialmarisa@hotmail.com.
A simple place with helpful owners, breakfast extra, very good value.

$ pp Tromen
Lonquimay 195, T02972-491498, see Facebook.
Small house with dorms and private rooms for up to 4 people. At night take a taxi from the bus station as the streets in the area have no signs or lights.

Estancias

$$$$ Estancia Huechahue
30 km east of town off R234, near Río Collon Curá and junction with Ruta 40, www.huechahue.com.
The best riding in the Lake District is at this marvellous self-sufficient, traditional Patagonian estancia, where they breed horses and cattle and welcome guests to stay in very comfortable rooms in the main house and in cabins. Other activities on offer include fishing, rafting and walking. Sauna and jacuzzi, great *asados* in the open air. Highly recommended.

Restaurants

$$$ Ruca Hueney
Col Suárez y Milanesio, T02972-491113, www.ruca-hueney.com.ar.
Good steak, trout and pasta dishes, popular, great atmosphere. The roast lamb might be the best in the country.

$ La Nueva Posta de Junín
JM de Rosas 160 (on Ruta 234), T02972-492080.
Parrilla with good service and wine list; also trout, pizza and pastas.

Festivals

Jan Agricultural show and exhibition of flowers and local crafts, at the end of the month.

Feb Fiesta Provincial de Puestero, www.fiestadelpuestero.org.ar. Mid-Feb sees the election of the queen, handicrafts, *asados* with local foods and fabulous gaucho riding. This is the most important country fiesta in the south of Argentina.
Mar Carnival.
Jul Festival of Aboriginal Arts, mid-month.
Nov Opening of the fishing season, 2nd Sat.
Dec Inauguration of the church of **Laura Vicuña**, with a special Mass on the 8th and singing to celebrate the life of Laura Vicuña.

Shopping

Patagonia Rodeo, *Padre Milanesio 562, 1st floor, T01972-492839, see Facebook.*
A traditional shop selling what real gauchos wear in the field, plus quality leather work: belts, wallets, saddlery. Look like the real thing before you turn up at the estancias.

What to do

Fishing
The season runs from 8 Nov to 1 May. For fly casting and trolling the best places are lakes Huechulafquen, Paimún, Epulaufken, Tromen and Currehue, and the rivers Chuimehuin, Malleo, Alumine and Quilquihué. Ask the helpful tourist office for more information and also see Tour operators, below.
Río Dorado Lodge, *Pedro Illera 448, T02972-492451, www.riodoradolodge.com.* The luxury fishing lodge at the end of town has a good fly shop, and organizes trips, run by experts and fishermen.

Horse riding
Estancia Huechahue, *www.huechahue.com.* Located northeast of Junín, this estancia offers unbeatable riding and hospitality. Rides into the national park enable you to reach areas that are otherwise completely inaccessible. Recommended.

BORDER CROSSING
Argentina–Chile

Paso Mamuil Malal (formerly Tromen)

Paso Mamuil Malal is 64 km northwest of Junín de los Andes and reached by *ripio* Route 60 which runs from Tropezón on Route 23, through Parque Nacional Lanín. Parts of the road are narrow and steep, so it is unsuitable for bicycles. On the Chilean side the road continues through glorious scenery, with views of the volcanoes of Villarrica and Quetrupillán to the south, to Pucón, 76 km west of the pass, on Lago Villarrica.

The border is open all year, but is closed during heavy rain or snow (phone the gendarmerie to check, T02972-427339). See www.gendarmeria.gob.ar/pasos-chile/mamuil-mamal.html.

Argentine immigration and customs Puesto Tromen, 3 km east of the pass, daily 0900-2000, co-ordinated with the Chilean side.

Chilean immigration and customs Puesco, 8 km west of the pass, daily 0800-1900.

Transport Buses San Martín run from Junín de Los Andes and San Martín de Los Andes, four to five hours, US$23.

Tour operators

Alquimia Viajes and Turismo, *O'Higgins 603, T02972-491355, www.alquimiaturismo.com.ar.* Offers fishing excursions with expert local guides among a range of adventure tourism options, including climbing Lanín, climbing in rock and ice, rafting, and transfers.
Tromen, *Lonquimay 195, T02972-491498, see Facebook.* Trips up Volcano Lanín, horse riding, mountain biking, car rental and bicycle rental.

Transport

Air

Chapelco airport is served by **Aerolíneas Argentinas** from Buenos Aires. The airport is 19 km southwest of town on the road to San Martín de los Andes, with buses to the centre. A taxi will cost around US$20.

Bus

The bus terminal is on Olavarría and Félix San Martín (don't confuse it with Gen San Martín), information T02972-492038. There's a public phone but no other facilities. To **San Martín**, with **Albus**, **Ko Ko** and others, 50 mins, US$3-4. To **Buenos Aires**, 20-21 hrs, US$130. To **Chile** (via Paso Mamuil Malal), see box, above.

San Martín de los Andes and around *Colour map 5, A2.*

Swiss style in the Argentine wilderness

San Martín de los Andes (population 30,000) is a charming upmarket tourist town in a beautiful setting on the edge of Lago Lácar, with attractive chalet-style architecture and lots of good accommodation. It's an excellent centre for exploring southern parts of the Parque Nacional Lanín including the nearby lakes Lolog and Lácar, where there are beaches for relaxing and good opportunities for rafting, canoeing, mountain biking, trekking and even diving. There is also excellent skiing at the Chapelco resort.

Sights

The main street, San Martín, runs perpendicular to the *costanera*, and here you'll find most shops and plenty of places to eat. Of the two plazas, the more interesting is Plaza San Martín, which has a sporadic crafts market. It's a pleasant 1½-hour walk north and west up the hill to **Mirador Bandurrias**, with great views. Start at the far northernmost end of the *costanera*, passing the fish trap and walk along the shore before ascending the path, 40 minutes up. Even lovelier, set off from the *costanera* up to **Mirador Arrayán**, where there's a gorgeous tea room, **La Casa de Té Arrayán**, and *hostería* with spectacular views over the lake.

The town is surrounded by lakes and mountains that are ripe for exploration. In addition to trips around Lago Lacar, the most popular trips are south along the **Seven Lakes Drive** to Lagos Traful, Meliquina, Filo Hua Hum, Hermoso, Falkner and Villarino (see page 424) and north to the thermal baths at **Termas de Lahuen-Co** (see above). Trips to the *termas* via **Lago Curruhué** are offered by tour operators, but you could also cycle or drive there along *ripio* roads from Lago Lolog. There's no public transport to these places at present.

Lago Lacar

The north shore of Lago Lacar can be explored by car along much of its length, following *ripio* Route 48 towards the Chilean border at **Paso Hua Hum**, 41 km; see box, opposite. **Río Hua Hum** has become a popular place for rafting, with some good stretches of rapids, as the river flows west towards the Pacific; take a tour from an agency in town. You can cycle or walk all the way around the lake on a rough track and also to **Lago Escondido** to the south. There are beaches at **Catrite**, 4 km south of San Martín, at **Hua Hum** and at **Quila Quina** on the southern shore, 18 km from San Martín. This is a quieter beach, with a walk to a lovely waterfall along a guided nature trail. There's also a two-hour walk from here that takes you to a tranquil Mapuche community in the hills above the lake. Both Quila Quina and Hua Hum can be reached by boat from the pier in San Martín, T02972-428427: to Quila Quina hourly, 30 minutes each way, US$21 return; to Hua Hum, US$64 return, three daily in season.

Chapelco ski and summer resort

19 km south of San Martín, www.chapelco.com.

Cerro Chapelco (2394 m) offers superb views over Lanín and many Chilean peaks. The ski resort is well organized, with 29 km of pistes for skiing and snowboarding, many of them challenging, including several black runs and a lovely long easy piste for beginners. With an overall drop of 730 m and very good slopes and snow conditions, this is a popular resort for wealthier Argentines and, increasingly, foreigners. There's also a ski school and snowboards for hire.

Essential San Martín de los Andes

Finding your feet

The nearest **airport** is Chapelco, northeast of town on Route 234 towards Junín de los Andes (see Transport, above); a transfer costs US$8.50. The **bus terminal** on Villegas y Juez del Valle is reasonably central.

Getting around

It's easy to orient yourself here as the town nestles in a valley surrounded by steep mountains at the eastern end of Lago Lacar. Beware of confusing street names: Perito Moreno runs east–west, crossing Mariano Moreno, which runs north–south, and Rudecindo Roca which is two blocks north of General Roca.

BORDER CROSSING
Argentina–Chile

Paso Hua Hum

Paso Hua Hum (659 m) lies 47 km west of San Martín de los Andes along Route 48 (*ripio*), which runs along the north shore of Lago Lacar and crosses the border to Puerto Pirehueico (very tough going for cyclists) 11 km from the crossing. From here, a boat crosses Lago Pirihueico, a long, narrow and deep lake, to Puerto Fuy at its northern end. The border is usually open all year 0800-2000 (Chile open till 1900) and is an alternative to the route via the Paso Mamuil Malal (Tromen); see page 417. See www.gendarmeria.gob.ar/pasos-chile/hua-hum.html.

Transport Ko Ko/Lafit (T02972-427422) run buses from San Martín to Puerto Pirehueico, two hours, leaving San Martín early in the morning; check with the terminal for the schedule. They connect with **Somarco** ferries across the lake to Puerto Fuy (T+56 63-228 2742/T+56 2-2322 3900, www.barcazas.cl). These run three times a day in January to February, but at 1300 only the rest of the year. Fares are US$1.30 for foot passengers, US$7.50 for motorbikes and US$25 for cars; bicycles are also taken. Buses connect Puerto Pirehueico with Panguipulli, from where transport is available to other destinations in the Chilean Lake District. For further information, contact the tourist office in Panguipulli, T+56 63-231 0436, or see www.sietelagos.cl and www.municipalidadpanguipulli.cl.

The price of a day pass varies from US$75 in high season (10-30 July). There is a daily bus in high season from San Martín to the slopes, US$8 return, with **Siete Lagos Turismo** ⓘ *T02972-427877*. Details of the resort, passes and equipment hire are available in season from the **Chapelco office** ⓘ *Moreno 859, T02972-427845, www.sanmartindelosandes.gov.ar*. At the foot of the mountain is a restaurant and base lodge, with three more restaurants on the mountain and a small café at the top.

In summer this is a good place for cycling (take your bike up on the cable car then cycle down), trekking, archery or horse riding.

Listings San Martín de los Andes and around

Tourist information

Tourist office

San Martín y J M de Rosas 790, on the main plaza, T02972-427347, www.sanmartinde losandes.gov.ar/turismo, www.sanmartinde losandes.com (in English). Daily 0800-2100. This large and helpful tourist office hands out maps and has lists of accommodation, with prices up on a big board. The staff speak English and Portuguese, but are very busy in summer, when it's advisable to go early in the day before they get stressed. Also check out www.chapelco.com.

Where to stay

There are 2 high seasons, when rates are much higher: Jan/Feb and Jul/Aug. Single rooms are expensive all year. *Cabañas* are available in 2 main areas: up Perito Moreno on the hill to the north of town, and down by the lakeside; prices for these increase in high season but they are good value for families or groups. When everywhere else is full, the tourist office will provide a list of private addresses in high season. See www.sanmartindelosandes. gov.ar for a full list of places to stay. All those listed here are recommended.

$$$$ La Casa de Eugenia
Coronel Díaz 1186, T02972-427206,
www.lacasadeeugenia.com.ar.
B&B in a beautifully renovated 1900s house, very welcoming and relaxing, cosy rooms, huge breakfast, charming hosts.

$$$$ Le Châtelet
Villegas 650, T02972-428294,
www.lechatelethotel.com.
Chic and luxurious, beautiful chalet-style hotel with excellent service to pamper you. Wood-panelled living room, gorgeous bedrooms and suites, buffet breakfast, spa and pool with massage and facial treatments. Also, a welcome glass of wine is offered on arrival.

$$$ Arco Iris
Los Cipreses 1850, T02972-428450,
www.arcoirisar.com.
Comfortable, well-equipped *cabañas* with Wi-Fi and cable TV in a quiet area of town, each has a cosy living room and spacious kitchen. Own access to the river, so you can fish before breakfast or enjoy a drink on the water side in the evening.

$$$ Hostería Bärenhaus
Los Alamos 156, Barrio Chapelco (8370),
T02972-422775, www.barenhaus.com.ar.
5 km outside town, pick-up from bus terminal and airport arranged. Welcoming young owners, very comfortable rooms with heating, English and German spoken.

$$$ Hostería Walkirias
Villegas 815, T02972-428307, www.
laswalkirias.com. Open all year.
A lovely place, smart, tasteful rooms with big bathrooms. Sauna and pool room. Buffet breakfast. Great value off season and for longer stays.

$$$ Plaza Mayor
Coronel Pérez 1199, T02972-427302,
www.hosteriaplazamayor.com.ar.
A chic and homey *hostería* in a quiet residential area, with traditional touches in the simple elegant rooms, excellent home-made breakfast, heated pool with solarium, barbecue and parking.

$$ Crismalú
Rudecindo Roca 975, T02972-427283,
www.interpatagonia.com/crismalu.
Simple rooms in attractive chalet-style converted home, good value.

$$ Hostería Las Lucarnas
Cnel Pérez 632, T02972-427085, www.
hosterialaslucarnas.com. Open all year.
Great value, centrally located, pretty place with simple comfortable rooms, English-speaking owner, breakfast included. Discounts for more than 5 nights.

$ pp Puma
A Fosbery 535 (north along Rivadavia,
2 blocks beyond bridge), T02972-422443,
www.pumahostel.com.ar.
Discount for ISIC members, small dorms with bath and a double room with view, laundry, bikes for hire, very well run by mountain guide owner, good value.

$ pp Rukalhue
Juez del Valle 682 (3 blocks from terminal),
T02972-427431, www.rukalhue.com.ar.
Large camp-style accommodation with 1 section full of dorm rooms (US$15-21) and 1 section with doubles, triples and apartments (**$$$-$$**). Also has apartments with private bath and kitchenette.

Camping

ACA Camping
Av Koessler 2175, T02972-429430,
www.interpatagonia.com/aca.
With hot water and laundry facilities, also *cabañas*.

Camping Quila Quina
T02972-411919, www.campingquilaquina.
com.ar. Summer to Easter.
Lovely site on a stream near Lago Lácar, 18 km from San Martín, with beaches, immaculate toilet blocks, restaurant and shop, access to boats and treks.

Restaurants

$$ El Regional
San Martín and Mascardi, T02972-414600,
www.elregionalpatagonia.com.ar.
Popular for regional specialities – smoked
trout, venison, wild boar, pâtés and hams,
and El Bolsón's home-made beer. Cheerful
German-style decor.

$$ La Costa del Pueblo
Costanera opposite pier, T02972-429289,
www.lacostadelpueblo.com.ar.
Overlooking the lake, huge range of pastas,
chicken and trout dishes, generous portions,
good service, cheerful.

$$ La Tasca
Mariano Moreno 866, T02972-428663.
Good for venison, trout and home-made
pastas, varied wine list.

Cafés

Beigier
Av Costanera 815.
Hidden cottage with views of the bay
serving a fantastic afternoon tea with
home-made goodies.

Vieja Deli
Villegas y Juez del Valle, T02972-428631.
Affordable place with views of the bay and
nice salads, pastas and pizzas.

Bars and clubs

Down Town Matias
San Martín 598, T02972-413386,
www.downtownmatias.com/andes.
Fantastic, welcoming building, good for a
late night drink with snacks.

Dublin South Bar
Av San Martín 599, T02972-410141.
Huge pub (with no reference to Ireland at all)
with comfy seats, great food – try the home-
made pasta – and a good atmosphere.

Shopping

A great place for shopping, with chic
little shops selling clothes and handmade
jumpers; try **La Oveja Negra** (San Martín
1025, T02972-428039, see Facebook), for
wonderful handmade scarves and jumpers,
plus esoteric crafts and interesting souvenirs.
There's also a handicraft market in summer in
Plaza San Martín. There are 2 recommended
places for chocolates: **Abuela Goye** (San
Martín 807, T02972-429409, www.abuela
goye.com), which serves excellent ice
creams and a killer hot chocolate, and
Mamusia (San Martín 601, T02972-427560,
see Facebook), which also sells home-made
jams. Lots of outdoor shops on San Martín
sell clothes for walking and skiing, including
Nomade (San Martín 881).

What to do

Canopying
Canopy, *8 km from town, T0294-15-459 6215,*
see Facebook. 1400 m of course, spread over
10 different resting stations with a height
that varies from 8 to 20 m off the ground.
Recommended.

Cycling
Many places in the centre rent mountain
and normal bikes, US$10-20 per day,
maps provided.
HG Rodados, *San Martín 1061, T02972-*
427345, hgrodados@smandes.com.ar (also
see Facebook). Arranges trips, rents mountain
bikes, also spare parts and expertise.

Fishing
For guides contact the tourist office or the
park office. A licence costs US$26 for a day,
US$78 for a week, and US$104 for a season,
with extra charges for trolling.
Hernan Zorzit, *T02972-414538, www.patagon*
fly.com. Also runs tours to Junín de los Andes.
Jorge Cardillo Pesca, *Villegas 1061,*
T02972-428372, www.jorgecardillo.com.
Sells equipment and fishing licences and
offers excursions.

Jorge Trucco, *based in Patagonia Outfitters, Pérez 662, T02972-429561, www.jorgetrucco. com.* Expert and professional trips, good advice and many years of experience.

Skiing

For details of the Chapelco resort, see page 418.

Tour operators

Prices for conventional tours, such as the Seven Lakes Drive, are similar with most agencies. Most tours operate from 2 Jan. 1 day's rafting at Hua Hum costs US$60-70.
El Claro, *Coronel Díaz 751, T02972-428876, www.elclaroturismo.com.ar.* For conventional tours, horse riding, mountain biking and trekking.
El Refugio, *Villegas 698, corner of Coronel Pérez, upstairs, T02972-425140, www.elrefugio turismo.com.ar.* Bilingual guides, conventional tours, boat trips, also mountain bike hire, rafting, horse riding and trekking. Recommended.
Lanín Turismo, *San Martín 437, oficina 3, T02972-425808, www.laninturismo.com.*

Adventure tourism and trekking in Lanín area, ascents of the volcano, Chapelco skiing packages and more.

Transport

Air

See Transport, under Junín de los Andes above. **LADE** office in bus terminal, T02972-427672.

Bus

The bus terminal, T02972-427044, has all the usual services, including a luggage store, toilets and a *locutorio*.

To **Buenos Aires**, 21-22 hrs, US$135, daily. To **Villa La Angostura**, **Albus** 2 a day, US$9. To **Bariloche** (not via 7 Lagos), 3½-4 hrs, US$14, **Vía Bariloche** and **Ko Ko**. To **Chile**: **Pucón**, **Villarrica** and **Valdivia** via **Junín de los Andes** and **Paso Mamuil Malal**, US$23, 5 hrs to Pucón with **San Martín**, heavily booked in summer (see also box, page 417). Alternatively, **Ko Ko/Lafit** (T02972-427422) run buses to **Puerto Pirehueico**, via **Paso Hua Hum**, 2 hrs; check terminal for schedule (see also box, page 419).

San Martín
to Bariloche

The journey south to Bariloche along the celebrated Seven Lakes Drive is the most famous tourist route in the Argentine Lake District. It follows Route 234 through the Lanín and Nahuel Huapi national parks and passes seven magnificent lakes, all flanked by mixed natural forest; it is particularly attractive in autumn (April to May).

The seven lakes are (from north to south): Lácar, Machónico, Falkner, Villarino, Espejo, Correntoso and Nahuel Huapi. The road is paved.

On the way from picturesque San Martín de los Andes, there are two good bases. Remote Villa Traful is tucked into a deep fold between dramatic, spired mountains, on the side of a navy blue sliver of lake. It's a peaceful place for a few days' rest, with good walks and some appealing places to stay.

Further south, on the northern side of Lake Nahuel Huapi, is the pretty, upmarket town of Villa la Angostura. Much loved by wealthier Argentines, there's no shortage of smart places to stay and eat here, such as the famous and blissful boutique hotel, Las Balsas. From Villa la Angostura you can visit the tiny national park, Los Arrayanes, which protects a rare forest of *arrayán* trees with their cinnamon-coloured bark and twisting trunks.

Leaving San Martín, the first lake you reach in the Nahuel Huapi national park is Lago Falkner, which is popular with fishermen. It's a wide and open lake, with thickly forested fjord-like mountains descending steeply into it. There's a long narrow sandy beach on the roadside, a good place for a picnic stop, and wild camping; Camping Lago Falkner nearby has facilities. To the south, there's another pretty, if exposed, free campsite (with no facilities) by the deep green Río Villarino, near Lago Villarino, and a campsite and picnic ground amidst little beech trees at Pichi Traful, at the northern tip of Lago Traful. This is a beautiful spot by the wide green banks of a river, with steeply rising mountains on all sides.

At Km 77, Route 65 branches off to the east, running along the south shore of Lago Traful through Villa Traful to meet the main Neuquén–Bariloche highway (Route 237) at Confluencia. If you have a couple of days to spare, this makes a lovely detour (see below). Continuing south, however, the drive passes gorgeous, secluded Lago Espejo ('lake mirror'), which has lovely beaches on its shore. Opposite, you'll be treated to a superb view of Lago Correntoso on the final stretch towards Villa la Angostura on Lago Nahuel Huapi.

You can see the route from the windows of a bus on a round trip from Bariloche, Villa la Angostura or San Martín, which will take about five hours, but you may prefer your own transport, so you can stop and explore. Buses will stop at campsites on the route. It's a good route for cycling, as you can really appreciate the beauty of the ever-changing landscape, though note that there's more traffic in January and February.

The alternative route to Bariloche

There's a quicker route from San Martín to Bariloche, via **Confluencia**, further east. Head south from San Martín on Route 234, but at Lago Machónico, instead of continuing southwest, take Route 63 along the tranquil shore of Lago Meliquina. Further south, you could turn off to the isolated Lago Filo-Hua-Hum at Km 54 (unpaved track). A little further on the road climbs to the **Paso de Córdoba**, Km 77 (1300 m), with fabulous views, from where it descends to the valley of the Río Traful, following it east to Confluencia. From Confluencia, you can head west along Route 65 to Villa Traful and rejoin the Seven Lakes Drive, or continue south to Bariloche on Route 237 through the astounding **Valle Encantado**, where there are bizarre rock formations including El Dedo de Dios (The Finger of God) and El Centinela del Valle (The Sentinel of the Valley).

Villa Traful

If you want to get off the beaten track, Villa Traful (population 503) is ideal. It was created after the Nahuel Huapi National Park was set up, with the aim of giving visitors the greatest possible contact with nature. Approaching from the west, along the southern shore of Lago Traful, the winding road passes through forests of lenga and tall *coihue* trees, their elegant trunks creating a woody cathedral, with idyllic spots to camp all along the shore.

The quiet pretty village sprawls alongside the narrow deep-blue sliver of

Tip...
The best time to visit Villa Traful is December or late February to March when the few restaurants aren't full of tourists.

Lago Traful, enclosed on both sides by stunning sharp-peaked mountains. There's not much to do here, but it's popular with fishermen, and there are a couple of wonderful walks and waterfalls to see, it's a pleasant place to unwind. At the heart of the village opposite the main pier is a kiosk selling basic supplies and bus tickets, and the best restaurant. Traful is prone to mercurial winds, so check the forecast if you're coming for a few days as it's miserable being stuck here in bad weather and the buses are infrequent.

Walks around Villa Traful

A 1½-hour walk from the village centre takes you to the lovely **Cascadas del Arroyo Coa Có y Blanco** waterfalls thundering down through beech forest and *cañas colihues* bamboo. Walk up the hill from the Ñancu Lahuen restaurant and take the left-hand path to the mirador over Cascada Coa Có, and from here take the right-hand path through *coihue* forest. Better still, there's a satisfying hike up to **Cerro Negro** (2000 m) five hours up, following uncertain yellow markers. Ask at the national park office to get the best advice on the route. It's a stiff climb to start with, through gorgeous *coihue* and *lenga* forest, and the views as you clear the tree line are unbelievable, with the dramatic spired peaks visible on the northern side of Lago Traful. There's a lot of scree near the summit, but the views of Lanín, Tronador and the others make it all worthwhile. Alternatively, cross the lake (15 minutes) by boat, leaving from the main pier, to reach a sand beach from where you can walk up a steep path to twin lagoons and some superbly well conserved prehistoric cave paintings nearby. Ask in the tourist office (see Tourist information, below) to see which companies are currently running trips.

Listings La Ruta de los Siete Lagos

Tourist information

Villa Traful

The national park *guardería* is opposite the pier, open only in high season, with advice on walks.

Tourist office

Ruta Provincial 65, T0294-447 9099, see www.villatraful.gov.ar or www. interpatagonia.com/villatraful.
Small but very helpful, this tourist office has information on walks, riding and fishing.

Where to stay

The alternative route to Bariloche

$$$-$$ Hostería La Gruta de las Virgenes
Confluencia, T0294-442 6138.
On a hill with views over the 2 rivers, very hospitable.

Villa Traful

$$$ Hostería Villa Traful
T0294-447 9005, www.hosteriavillatraful.com.
A cosy house with a tea room by the lake, also *cabañas* for 4-6 people, pretty gardens, good value. The owner's son, Andrés, organizes fishing and boat trips.

$$ Cabañas Aiken
T0294-447 9048, www.aiken.com.ar.
Well-decorated *cabañas* in beautiful surroundings near the lake (close to the tourist office), each with its own *parrillada*, also has a restaurant. Recommended.

$ pp Vulcanche Hostel
Ruta Provincial 61, T0294-15-469 2314, www.vulcanche.com.
Chalet-style hostel in gardens with good views, with good dorms and **$$** doubles, breakfast extra, large park for camping.

Restaurants

Villa Traful

$$ Ñancu Lahuen
T0294-447 9017.
A chocolate shop, tea room and restaurant serving local trout. Delightful and cosy, with big open fire, delicious food and reasonably priced.

Transport

Villa Traful
Bus
In high summer, a **La Araucana** bus (info@araucana.com.ar) between **Villa la Angostura** and **San Martín** stops here daily; otherwise there are buses to **Bariloche** with **Vía Bariloche**, US$4.50. **Kiosko El Ciervo**, by the YPF service station, sells tickets and has the timetable.

Villa La Angostura and around   *Colour map 5, B2.*

a tiny star in the Lake District

Villa La Angostura (population 13,285) is a delightful little town which, apart from in January when it is packed out, is an appealing place to stay, especially for those who like their nature seen from the comfort of a luxurious hotel. There are some superb restaurants here and some seriously chic hotels. *Cabaña* complexes and great hostels have mushroomed up everywhere, so there's no shortage of places to stay. And there are some good walks nearby, excellent fly-fishing, and a golf course, as well as skiing in winter.

Sights

The town is divided into several different *barrios*: around the sprawling centre, **El Cruce**; around the lakeside area of **Puerto Manzano**, and around the picturesque port, known as **La Villa**, 3 km away at the neck of the Quetrihué Peninsula, which dips into the northern end of Lago Nahuel Huapi. From La Villa it's a short trip on foot or by boat to Villa La Angostura's great attraction, the **Parque Nacional Los Arrayanes** (see box, opposite), at the end of the peninsula. Also from La Villa, a short walk leads to lovely **Laguna Verde**, an intense emerald-green lagoon surrounded by mixed *coihue* cypress and *arrayán* forests, where there's a 1-km self-guided trail, taking about an hour. There are no services in La Villa apart from a *kiosko*, a tea room in high season, and the restaurant at **Hotel Angostura**. A bus runs from the centre at El Cruce to La Villa every couple of hours, taking 15 minutes, but it's a pleasant walk.

About halfway between the two centres is a chapel (1936), designed by Bustillo, the famous architect who gave this region's buildings their distinctive style, and nearby is **El Messidor** (1942), the summer resort of Argentine presidents, where you can visit the beautiful gardens with lake views. There's also a tiny museum, **Museo Regional** ① *Blv Nahuel Huapi 2177, on the road to La Villa, museo.vla@gmail.com, Tue-Sat 1030-1700, donation*, with interesting photos of the original indigenous inhabitants.

In winter, there's good skiing at Villa La Angostura's popular ski resort **Cerro Bayo** ① *9 km north of town, T0294-449 4189, www.cerrobayoweb.com*, with 24 pistes, 20 km in total, many of them fabulously long, and all with excellent views over the lakes below. It's a great area for snowboarding. This is one of Argentina's pricier resorts: a one-day ski pass costs US$68 for adults in high season.

Parque Nacional Los Arrayanes

This park covers the Quetrihué Peninsula, which dips south from Villa La Angostura into the Lago Nahuel Huapi and lies within the Parque Nacional Nahuel Huapi. It was created to protect a rare forest of *arrayán* trees, since it's one of the few places in the world where the *arrayán* grows to full size, and some of the specimens are 300 years old. This myrtle-like tree grows near water in groves and likes to have its roots wet, since it really has no bark. The trunks are extraordinary: a smooth powdery or peeling surface, bright cinnamon in colour and cold to the touch. They have no outer bark to protect them, but the surface layer is rich in tannins that keep the tree free from disease. They have creamy white flowers in January and February, and produce blue-black fruit in March. The sight of so many of these trees together, with their twisting trunks, creates a wonderful fairy-tale scene. The most rewarding way to see the wood is to take the boat trip across the deep-blue lake, fringed with spectacular peaks, to the tip of the peninsula, and then take a leisurely walk along the wheelchair-friendly wooden walkways through the trees, waiting until the guided tour has left. Halfway along you'll see a small wooden café which serves tea and coffee and has great views of the forest. Stroll back to the port through the mixed forest, passing two pretty and secluded lakes, Laguna Patagua, and Laguna Hua Huan.

Access

The entrance to the park is a walkable 2 km south of the port area of Villa la Angostura, known as La Villa. Bus company **15 de Mayo** runs buses from El Cruce to La Villa every few hours (15 minutes) from 0830-1900 US$1. A taxi to Villa costs US$6. For information contact the Nahuel Huapi **park office** in Bariloche, San Martín 24, T0294-442 3121, www.parquesnacionales.gob.ar. You may enter the park 0900-1400 in summer, 0900-1200 in winter, US$10. You must leave the park by 1700 and 1500 respectively.

Walking and cycling

There's a clear path all the way from the tip of the Quetrihué Peninsula where the boat arrives, through the prettiest part of the *arrayán* forest, and then running the length of the peninsula back to La Villa. You can walk or cycle the whole length: three hours one-way walking; two hours cycling (for cycle hire, see page 430).

Boat trips

Two companies run catamarans from the pier in La Villa to the end of the peninsula, and take passengers on a short guided tour through the forest. Catamarán Patagonia Argentina, T0294-449 4463, www.catamaranpatagonia.com.ar, and Greenleaf Turismo, Avenida Siete Lagos 118 Piso 1 Of C, Villa La Angostura, T0294-449 4004, www.bosquelosarrayanes.com.ar; tickets, US$32 return. Boats also run from Bariloche, via Isla Victoria, with Turisur, T0294-442 6109, www.turisur.com.ar.

Walks around Villa La Angostura
Parque Nacional Los Arrayanes For an easy flat walk, take the boat to the head of the Quitrihué Peninsula and walk the 13 km back. See box, above.

National parks in the Lake District

There are five national parks covering enormous swathes of the Lake District, and these areas are generally where you'll find the best hiking, rafting and horse riding, in the most unspoilt forests and mountain landscapes you can imagine. The area's main centre, **Bariloche**, is inside **Parque Nacional Nahuel Huapi** (see box, page 436) and has a well-developed infrastructure for activities in the park. Inside this park is another tiny park, **Parque Nacional Los Arrayanes**, accessed from **Villa La Angostura**; see box, page 427.

Immediately to the north of Nahuel Huapi is **Parque Nacional Lanín**, which contains the town of **San Martín de los Andes**, and also has superb hiking, especially around **Volcán Lanín** (see box, page 412). South of Bariloche there is the tiny but beautiful **Parque Nacional Lago Puelo**, just south of **El Bolsón**. Finally, **Los Alerces** is the most pristine of all the parks, with just one road running through it, and most areas accessible only on foot. The nearest towns are **Esquel** and **Trevelin**, see pages 467 and 471.

Each park has a ranger's station, where *guardaparques* will give you a map and advise on walks in the park, as well as on accommodation and the state of the paths.

Mirador Belvedere Offers fine views of Lagos Correntoso and Nahuel Huapi. It's a 3-km drive or walk up the old road, northwest of El Cruce; and from the mirador a path to your right goes to **Cascada Inacayal**, a waterfall 50 m high, situated in an area rich in native flora and forest.

Cascada Río Bonito A delightful walk leading to a beautiful waterfall, lying 8 km east of El Cruce off Route 66. The steep path gives tremendous views, and the falls themselves are impressive, falling 35 m from a chasm in basalt cliffs to an emerald-green pool. Further along the same path, you can reach the summit of Cerro Bayo (1782 m). Alternatively, 1 km further along the road, a ski lift takes you to the platform at 1500 m, where there's a restaurant with great views, and from here, it's a short trek to the summit. The ski lift runs all year; cyclists can take bikes up in the lift and cycle down.

Listings Villa La Angostura and around

Tourist information

Tourist office
Av Arrayanes 9, T0294-449 4124, www. villalaangostura.gov.ar, near the bus terminal, Av Siete Lagos 93. High season 0800 2200, low season 0800 2000.
Helpful, with lots of information, but a madhouse in summer. English spoken.

Where to stay

$$$$ La Escondida
Av Arrayanes 7014, T0294-482 6110, www.hosterialaescondida.com.ar.
Wonderful setting, right on the lake, 14 rooms, heated pool, offers mid-week, weekend and long-stay specials. Recommended.

$$$$ La Posada
R 231, Km 64.5, Las Balsas (no number), T0294-449 4450, www.hosterialaposada.com.
In a splendid elevated position off the road with clear views over the lake, welcoming, beautifully maintained hotel in lovely gardens, with pool, spa, fine restaurant; a perfect place to relax.

$$$$ Las Balsas
on Bahía Las Balsas (signposted from Av Arrayanes), T0294-449 4308, www.lasbalsas.com.
One of the best small hotels in Argentina, with fabulous cosy rooms, warm relaxed public areas, fine cuisine, impeccable service, and a wonderfully intimate atmosphere in a great lakeside location with its own secluded beach. Lakeside heated swimming pools, spa, and trips arranged. Highly recommended.

$$$ Hostería ACA al Sur
Av Arrayanes 8 (behind the petrol station), T0294-448 8412, www.aca.tur.ar/hoteles.
Modern, attractive single-storey hotel with well-designed rooms in the centre of town. Recommended.

$$$ Hostería Le Lac
Av de los 7 Lagos 2350, T0294-448 8029, www.hosterialelac.com.ar.
3-star, 8 rooms, some with jacuzzi and DVD, gardens, lake view, can arrange lots of activities, several languages spoken by owner.

$$$ Hotel Angostura
Nahuel Huapi 1911, at La Villa, T0294-449 4224, www.hotelangostura.com.
Built in 1938, this traditional hotel has a lovely lakeside setting and a good restaurant and tea room, **Viejo Coihue**. Also has 3 cabins for 6 (**$$$$**). Boat excursions along the nearby shore are arranged.

$$ Bajo Cero
Av 7 Lagos al 1200, T0294-449 5454, www.bajocerohostel.com.
Well-situated, rooms for 2-6, can arrange trekking, cycling and other trips.

$ pp Hostel La Angostura
Barbagelata 157, 150 m up road behind tourist office, T0294-449 4834, www.hostellaangostura.com.ar.
A warm, luxurious hostel, all small dorms have bathrooms (US$21), good doubles (US$60), HI discounts, welcoming owners organize trips and rent bikes. Recommended.

$ pp Italian Hostel
Los Maquis 215 (5 blocks from terminal), T0294-449 4376. Closed Apr-Oct.
Welcoming, small, with dorms and doubles. Rustic, functional and pleasant, run by a biker. Fireplace and orchard from where you can pick berries and herbs for your meals. Recommended.

Camping

Osa Mayor
Signposted off main road, close to town, T0294-449 4304, www.campingosamayor.com.ar.
Well-designed leafy and level site, US$8-10, all facilities, also rustic *cabañas* US$140 for up to 4 people, and dorms US$140 for up to 6 people, helpful owner.

Restaurants

Plenty of places are to be found on the main Av Arrayanes, lots of them chalet-style and open all day from breakfast onwards. Prices reflect the fact that this is a popular tourist town. Don't miss out on some of the really excellent places for fine cuisine here.

$$$ Cocina Waldhaus
Av Arrayanes 6431, T0294-447 5323, see Facebook.
Highly recommended, this is 'auteur cuisine' with gorgeous local delicacies created by Chef Leo Morsea, served in a charming chalet-style building.

$$ El Esquiador
Las Retamas 146 (behind the bus terminal), T0294-449 4331, see Facebook.

Good, popular *parrilla* has an all-you-can-eat choice of cold starters, a main meal and a dessert.

$$ Los Pioneros
Av Arrayanes 267, T0294-449 5525.
Famous for fine local dishes in a chalet-style building and great Argentine steaks. Great pizza place next door run by the same owners. They also serve locally brewed beers.

$ Jardín Patagonia
Av Arrayanes 4.
Popular pizzeria and *parrilla*.

$ TemaTyCo
Ruta 231 y Mirlo, T0294-447 5211.
Chic tearoom with a wide range of teas and delicious cakes.

What to do

Boat trips
There are a few companies running catamaran trips, including the following:
Catamarán Patagonia Argentina, *Huapi 2159, T0294-449 4463, www.catamaran patagonia.com.ar.* Runs trips on a 60-passenger catamaran.
Greenleaf Turismo, *Av Siete Lagos 118, Piso 1 Of C, T0294-449 4004, www.bosquelos arrayanes.com.ar.* Runs the 105-passenger *Catamarán Futuleufu.*
Turisur, *Mitre 219 T0294-442 6109, www.turisur.com.ar.* Runs boats from Bariloche, via Isla Victoria.
Velero Luz de Luna, *T0294-449 4834.* Offers trips on sailing boats with a special meal on board, or a drink with *picadas* of smoked meat and fish.

Canopying
Canopy Villa la Angostura, *Curruhué and Melinquina, T02944 15 579071, www.canopy bariloche.com.* Runs a great trail in the forest nearby, with over 1400 m of cable to zoom along.

Climbing
Club Andino Villa La Angostura, *Cerro Bayo 295, T0294-449 4954, www.cavla.com.ar.* Excursions, maps and information.

Cycling
Expect to pay around US$15-20 per day for bike hire.
Bayo Abajo, *Av Siete Lagos 94, T0294-448 8383, bayoabajo@argentina.com.* Bike hire starting at around US$15 per day.
Taquari Bici Shop, *Av Arrayanes 259, T0294-448 8415, see Facebook.*
New bikes, knowledgeable.

Fishing
The season runs from mid-Nov to May. For permits and a list of fishing guides, ask at the tourist office.
Anglers Home Fly Shop, *Belvedere 22, T0294-449 5222.* Arranges fishing trips.
Banana Fly Shop, *Av Arrayanes 282, T0294-449 4634.* Fly shop.
PatagonFly, *www.patagonfly.com.* A fly shop and association of local fishing guides, also runs trips.

Horse riding
Cabalgatas Correntoso, *Cacique Antrao 1850, T02944-15-451 0559, see Facebook.* Offers horseback excursions in the surrounding area and to Villa Traful.

Skiing
Cerro Bayo, *www.cerrobayoweb.com.* Although smaller, this is more popular with families than the famous Cerro Catedral in Bariloche. See description, page 444.

Tour operators
Nómades de la Montaña, *Ruca Choroy 38 y Cerro Inacayal 35, T0294-15-455 1385.* Offering everything from trekking and mountain biking to rappelling, diving and fly fishing.
Rucán Turismo, *Av 7 Lagos 239, T0294-447 5263, www.rucanturismo.com.* Offers skiing, riding, mountain biking and conventional tours.

BORDER CROSSING
Argentina–Chile

Paso Samoré

Paso Samoré, formerly **Paso Puyehue** (1280 m), lies 125 km northwest of Bariloche on Route 231 at Km 122. It's a spectacular six-hour journey, with plenty of buses from Bariloche, making it a cheaper alternative to the expensive Three Lakes Crossing (see box, page 448). Cyclists should note that there are no supplies between Villa La Angostura and Entre Lagos. For more information, contact the *gendarmería* in Bariloche, T0294-442 2711 or see www.gendarmeria.gob.ar/pasos-chile/cardenal-antonio-samore.html.

Argentine customs and immigration El Rincón, Route 231, Km 105. Open daily 0900-1900 but liable to be closed after snowfalls.

Chilean immigration It's 22 km from the pass to Chilean customs at Pajarito (Km 145) in the middle of a forest, over a wonderful mountain pass. Immigration is open daily 0800-1800.

Accommodation Termas Puyehue, Route 215, Km 76, T+56-600-293 6000, www.puyehue.cl. Luxurious accommodation and excellent thermal baths at a huge complex set in beautiful open parkland, framed by mountains, with an impressive spa. There are humbler places to stay in the town of Entre Lagos at the southwestern end of Lago Puyehue.

Transport For bus services from Bariloche to Osorno, Puerto Montt and Valdivia, see page 441.

Trekking

Alma Sur, *T0294-456 4724/T0294-15-456 4724*, *www.almasur.com*. Great trips in the local area and further afield, with bilingual, knowledgeable Anthony Hawes. A trained guide of Nahuel Huapi National Park, he creates really imaginative walks, which can include boats, climbing and hiking way off the beaten track. Recommended.

Transport

Bus

The small bus terminal at the junction of Av 7 Lagos and Av Arrayanes is opposite the ACA service station and offers a left-luggage service. Urban buses, run by **15 de Mayo**, US$1, link El Cruce (main bus stop on main road, 50 m from tourist office), La Villa, Correntoso and Puerto Manzano, and go up to Lago Espejo and Cerro Bayo in high season.

To **Bariloche**, 1 hr 15 mins, US$5, several companies. Buses from Bariloche to **Osorno** in Chile will pick you up in La Angostura by arrangement. For transport to Chile from Bariloche, see page 441.

Bariloche
& around

★ Beautifully situated on the steep and wooded southern shore of Lago Nahuel Huapi, surrounded by high peaks, San Carlos de Bariloche (its official name) is an ideal base for exploring the Lake District. It's right in the middle of Nahuel Huapi National Park.

The town was founded in 1902 but really took off in the 1930s when the national park was created. The chalet-style architecture was established at this time by early German and Swiss settlers.

Bariloche is well set up for tourism with the main street, Mitre, bustling with tour operators, outdoor clothing shops and chocolate makers. There are plenty of hotels and restaurants in the town centre, but the best places are sprinkled along the shore of Lake Nahuel Huapi, towards Llao Llao, where Argentina's most famous hotel enjoys a spectacularly beautiful setting.

To the immediate south of Bariloche there are fabulous walks in the mountains, and up giant Mount Tronador, reached from Pampa Linda further west. On the way are two gorgeous lakes: Gutiérrez and Mascardi. Ski resort Cerro Catedral is arguably the best in South America and makes a great base for trekking in summer.

Essential Bariloche and around

Finding your feet

The **airport** is 15 km east of town; bus service 72 runs to the town centre, as do *colectivos* and taxis (US$18-20). If you're staying on the road to Llao Llao, west of town, expect to pay more for transport to your hotel.

The **bus station** and the **train station** are both 3 km east of the centre. A taxi into town costs US$15-18. Otherwise, there are urban bus companies that run *colectivos*: **Santa De** and **Grottoes**. These lines travel between the bus station and the centre: 20, 21, 22 and 10. Buy a rechargeable card, US$2.50, before travelling; *colectivos* don't accept cash. See also Transport, page 441.

Best hotels

Premier, page 438
Tres Reyes, page 438
Hotel Llao Llao, page 445
Tunquelén, page 445

Getting around

Bariloche is an easy city to walk around. Avenida Bustillo (see Orientation, below) is a viable place to stay even if you haven't got a car since frequent local buses, run by **3 de Mayo**, run along its length. Take No 20 to Llao Llao, for lakeside hotels and restaurants and Puerto Pañuelo; No 10 to Colonia Suiza and Bahía López for trekking; No 50 to Lago Gutiérrez, via the base for the cable car to Cerro Otto; and the bus labelled 'Catedral' for Cerro Cathedral.

Orientation

It's straightforward to orient yourself in the city, since the lake lies to the north and the mountains to the south. The main street is Mitre, running east to west, and unmistakable with its souvenir and chocolate shops. Here you'll find all the tour operators, *locutorios* and internet cafés, as well as banks and some food shops. The tourist information office (see Listings, below) is in the distinctive chalet-style Centro Cívico, with an open space giving good views onto the lake, and most hotels and restaurants are gathered within three or four blocks from here, with cheaper accommodation and hostels tending to be a few blocks further south on the upper slopes of town. More upmarket hotels and many restaurants are spread out along Avenida Bustillo, the road running beside the southern shore of Lago Nahuel Huapi for some 25 km, as far as the famous **Hotel Llao Llao**, and in an area known as Colonial Suiza.

When to go

Bariloche is busiest in the school holidays (January and July), but it's also the destination for all graduating secondary school students in August, September and January, though these groups are now confined to special hotels (not listed here), and rarely stray beyond the city's bars and nightclubs for their inevitable rites of passage. Accommodation is cheaper outside the peak periods, but the weather becomes unpredictable at the end of April. For skiing, July and August are best, though hotels are packed with mass tourism from Chile and Brazil. Try June or September instead, and always book well ahead.

Useful addresses

Chilean Consulate, España 275, T0294-442 3050. Monday-Friday 0900-1300 (office), 1400-1700 (phone and email). Helpful.
Immigration office, Libertad 191, T0294-442 3043. Monday-Friday 0800-1600.
Police, T0294-442 2772, or 101.

Best camping

El Yeti, page 445
Petunia, page 445
Selva Negra, page 445

Parque Nacional Nahuel Huapi

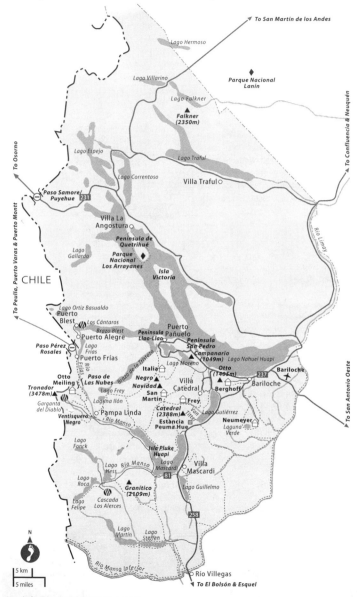

To San Martín de los Andes

Lago Hermoso

Lago Villarino

Parque Nacional Lanín

Lago Falkner

Falkner (2350m)

To Osorno

Lago Espejo

Lago Trafúl

Lago Correntoso

Villa Traful

To Confluencia & Neuquén

Río Limay

Paso Samore/ Puyehue 231

To Peulla, Puerto Varas & Puerto Montt

Villa La Angostura

Península de Quetrihué

Lago Gallardo

Parque Nacional Los Arrayanes

Isla Victoria

CHILE

Lago Ortiz Basualdo

Puerto Blest

Los Cántaros

Brazo Blest

Puerto Alegre

Paso Pérez Rosales

Lago Frías

Puerto Frías

Puerto Pañuelo

Península Llao-Llao

Península San Pedro

Campanario (1049m)

Lago Nahuel Huapi

Bariloche

Río Elías

Otto Meiling

Paso de Las Nubes

Italia

Lago Moreno

Otto (1405m)

Bariloche

237

To San Antonio Oeste

Tronador (3478m)

Negro

Brazo de la Tristeza

Villa Catedral

Berghoff

Garganta del Diablo

Lago Frey

Navidad

San Martín

Frey

Ventisquero Negro

Laguna Ilón

Pampa Linda

Río Manso

Catedral (2388m)

Estancia Peuma Hue

Lago Gutiérrez

Neumeyer

Laguna Verde

Lago Fonck

Isla Pluke Huapi

Lago Hess

Lago Roca

Río Manso

Lago Mascardi

Villa Mascardi

81

Granítico (2109m)

Lago Guillermo

Cascada Los Alerces

Lago Felipe

258

Lago Martín

Lago Steffen

N

5 km
5 miles

Río Manso Interior

Río Villegas

To El Bolsón & Esquel

The famous Hotel Llao Llao (www.llaollao.com) and the civic centre, at the heart of Bariloche (population 120,000), were designed by major Argentine architect Bustillo, who set the trend for 'Bariloche Alpine style', with local stone, brightly varnished wood and carved gable ends, now ubiquitous throughout the region.

The Centro Cívico is set on an attractive plaza above the lake, where there's also a small museum, **Museo de la Patagonia** ① *T0294-442 2309, www.museodelapatagonia.nahuel huapi.gov.ar, Tue-Fri 1000-1230 and 1400-1900, Saturday 1000-1700, entry by donation*, with some indigenous artefacts and material from the lives of the first white settlers. Mitre is the main commercial area, and here all the chocolate shops are clustered – a sight in themselves, and not to be missed: Abuela Goye and Mamushka are most highly recommended. The cathedral, built in 1946, lies south of Mitre; opposite is a huge rock left in this spot by a glacier during the last glacial period.

On the lakeshore is the **Museo Paleontológico** ① *12 de Octubre and Sarmiento, T0294-15-461 1210, Mon-Sat 1500-1800, US$2.25*, which has displays of fossils mainly from Patagonia including an ichthyosaur and replicas of a giant spider and shark's jaws.

Bariloche's real sights are the mountains themselves; don't miss a cable car trip up to either **Cerro Campanario** (page 442) or **Cerro Otto** (page 443) to see lakes and mountains stretching out in front as far as the eye can see.

➡ **Bariloche maps**
1 Bariloche, page 435
2 Bariloche – the road to Llao Llao, page 442

N
200 metres
200 yards

Where to stay 🛏
1 41 Below *A1*
2 Antiguo Solar *B2*
5 Hostel Inn Bariloche *A1*
6 Hostería Güemes *B1*
7 La Bolsa *B2*
8 Penthouse 1004 *A1*
9 Periko's *B1*
10 Premier *A2*
11 Pudu *A1*
12 Ruca Hueney *B2*
13 Tres Reyes *A2*

Restaurants 🍴
1 Chez Philippe *B1*
2 Covita *A3*
3 Días de Zapata *B2*
4 El Boliche de Alberto *B2*
5 El Vegetariano *B1*
6 Huang Ji Zhong *A2*
7 Jauja *B2*
8 La Alpina *A2*

Bars & clubs 🍸
11 Cerebro *A1*
12 Wilkenny *A1*

Parque Nacional Nahuel Huapi

Nahuel Huapi is the national park you're most likely to visit since Bariloche is right at its heart. It stretches along the Andes for over 130 km, from south of Lago Mascardi to north of Villa Traful, and so there are no official entry points like most of the other national parks. It was Argentina's first ever national park, created in 1934 from a donation made to the country by naturalist Francisco 'Perito' Moreno of 7500 ha of land around Puerto Blest. Extending across some of Argentina's most dramatic mountains, the park contains lakes, rivers, glaciers, waterfalls, torrents, rapids, valleys, forest, bare mountains and snow-clad peaks. Among those you can climb are Tronador (3478 m), Catedral Sur (2388 m), Falkner (2350 m), Cuyín Manzano (2220 m), López (2076 m), Otto (1405 m) and Campanario (1052 m). The outstanding feature is the splendour of the lakes and the pristine nature of the virgin forests.

Park information

To enter the park costs US$10. There are many centres within the park, at Villa la Angostura and at Villa Traful, for example, but Bariloche (see page 432) is the usual first port of call for park activities, and here you can equip yourself with information on transport, walks and maps. The National Park Intendencia, San Martín 24, Bariloche, T0294-442 3111, www.nahuelhuapi.gov.ar, daily 0800-1600, is fairly unhelpful, with little hard information. Much better information on walks, *refugios* and buses is available from the trained guides and mountaineers at Club Andino Bariloche (CAB), see Tourist information, below. Ask for the Sendas y Bosques (walks and forests) series, which are 1:200,000, laminated and easy to read, with good books containing English summaries of the walks, www.guiasendasybosques.com.ar. Also recommended is the Active Patagonia map, with fabulous detail, and the Carta de Refugios, Senderos y Picadas for Bariloche. CAB can also tell you about transport: services: these vary from year to year and between high and low season, so it's best to check.

Flora and fauna

Vegetation varies with altitude and climate, but you're most likely to see large expanses of southern beech forest – the magnificent *coihue* trees (small-leaved evergreen

Listings Bariloche *map page 435.*

Tourist information

Nahuel Huapi National Park intendencia
San Martín 24, T0294-442 3111,
www.nahuelhuapi.gov.ar.
Daily 0800-1600, Sat 1000-1600.
Pretty unhelpful; it's far better to go straight to **Club Andino Bariloche (CAB)** (just above the Centro Cívico, 20 de Febrero No 30, T0294-442 2266, www.clubandino.org, Mon-

Fri 0900-1330, 1500-1930) for information on walks, hikes, mountain climbs, *refugios* and buses to reach all the local areas for walking. They sell excellent maps and books for walks, including *Carta de Refugios, Senderos y Picadas* maps for Bariloche and the book *Infotrekking de la Patagonia*, which gives great detail on all the possible walks, times, distances and *refugios* where you can stay, with satellite-based maps to guide you. All Club Andino

beeches) – many over 450 years old, and near the Chilean border where rainfall is highest, there are areas of magnificent virgin rainforest. Here you will see an alerce tree over 1000 years old, with the ancient species of bamboo cane *caña colihue* growing.

Eastern parts of the park are more steppe-like with arid land, supporting only low shrubs and bushes. Wildlife includes the small pudu deer, the endangered huemul and river otter, as well as foxes, cougars and guanacos. Among the birds, scarlet-headed Magellan woodpeckers and green austral parakeets are easily spotted as well as large flocks of swans, geese and ducks.

Around the park

The centrepiece of the park is its largest lake, Lago Nahuel Huapi, which measures a huge 531 sq km and is 460 m deep in places. It is particularly magnificent to explore by boat since the lake is very irregular in shape and long fjord-like arms of water, or *brazos*, stretch far into the west towards Chile, where there is superb virgin Valdivian rainforest. There are many islands, the largest of which is Isla Victoria, which has a luxurious hotel (www.islavictoria.com). On the northern shores of the lake is the Parque Nacional Los Arrayanes (see box, page 427), which contains a rare woodland of exquisite *arrayán* trees, with their bright cinnamon-coloured flaky bark. Access to this park within a park is from the small, upmarket village of Villa La Angostura at the southern end of the famous Seven Lakes Drive (see page 423). The northernmost stretch of this drive and three of its lakes are in Parque Nacional Lanín (see page 408), but Lagos Correntoso and Espejo near Villa Angostura are both within Nahuel Huapi and offer stunning scenery and tranquil places to stay and walk. Another tiny centre, Villa Traful (see page 424), lies on the shore of navy blue Lago Traful, with fishing, camping and walking.

The tourist town of Bariloche (see page 432) on the southern shore of Lago Nahuel Huapi is the main tourist centre in the national park. It has plentiful accommodation and opportunities for hiking, rafting, tours and boat trips. West of Bariloche, there are glaciers and waterfalls near Pampa Linda, the base for climbing Mount Tronador and starting point for the trek through Paso de las Nubes to Lago Frías. South of Lago Nahuel Huapi, Lagos Mascardi, Guillelmo and Gutiérrez have even grander scenery, offering horse riding, trekking and rafting along the Río Manso.

staff know the mountains well and some of them speak English, French or German.

Tourist office

Centro Cívico, Mitre and Reconquista, T0294-442 9850, www.barilocheturismo.gob.ar. Daily 0800-2100.
Helpful staff speak English (all), French, German and Portuguese (some), and have maps showing the town and whole area, with bus routes marked. They can also help with accommodation and campsites in the area.

Where to stay

Prices rise in 2 peak seasons: Jul-Aug for skiing, and mid-Dec to Mar for summer holidays. If you arrive in the high season without a reservation, consult the listing published by the tourist office (address above). This selection gives lake-view and high-season prices where applicable. In low season you pay half of these prices in most cases. All those listed are recommended.

$$$ Premier
Rolando 263, T0294-442 6168,
www.hotelpremier.com.
Good central choice (very good value in
low season), small 'classic' rooms and larger
superior rooms, English spoken.

$$$ Tres Reyes
12 de Octubre 135, T0294-442 6121,
www.hotel3reyes.com.ar.
Traditional lakeside hotel with spacious
rooms, splendid views, all services, gardens.

$$ Antiguo Solar
A Gallardo 360, T0294-440 0337,
www.antiguosolar.com.
Not far from the centre, this pleasant, simple
B&B on the upper level of an attractive
residential building has parking. Breakfast
includes fresh biscuits and local jams.

$$ Hostería Güemes
Güemes 715, T0294-442 4785,
www.hosteriaguemes.com.ar.
Lovely, quiet, lots of space in living areas,
very pleasant, big breakfast included, owner
is a fishing expert and very knowledgeable
about the area.

$ pp 41 Below
Pasaje Juramento 94, T0294-443 6433,
www.hostel41below.com.
Central, quiet, relaxing atmosphere, good
light rooms for 4-6 (US$18-22) and a double
with lake view (US$72 in high season).

$ pp Hostel Inn Bariloche
Salta 308, T0294-442 6084,
www.hostelbariloche.com.
Large, well-designed hostel with great
views of the lake from the communal areas
and rooms. Comfortable beds, in dorm
(from US$10 pp); also doubles (from US$35),
discount for HI members. The best feature
is the great deck with a view in the garden.
Neighbouring **Marco Polo Inn** (T0294-440
0105), is in the same group.

$ pp La Bolsa
Palacios 405 y Elflein, T0294-442 3529,
www.labolsadeldeporte.com.ar.

Relaxed atmosphere, rustic rooms with
duvets, 1 double with bath, some rooms
with views, deck to sit out on.

$ pp Penthouse 1004
San Martín 127, 10th floor, T0294-443 2228,
www.penthouse1004.com.ar.
Welcoming hostel at the top of a block of
apartments with amazing views. Helpful
staff, cosy rooms, dorms US$18-19, doubles
US$48-50. Big communal area for chilling
and watching the sunset.

$ pp Periko's
Morales 555, T0294-452 2326,
www.perikos.com.
Welcoming, quiet, nice atmosphere, dorms.
US$13-15, and doubles US$38-44 (depending
on season), breakfast included, washing
machine. Arranges tours, including to Ruta
40. Reserve in advance by email.

$ pp Pudu
Salta 459, T0294-442 9738,
www.hostelpudu.com.
"A gem". Irish/Argentine-run, dorms US$21-
25 and doubles US$65 with spectacular lake
views, downstairs is a small garden and a bar.
Long-term rates available.

$ pp Ruca Hueney
Elflein 396, T0294-443 3986,
www.rucahueney.com.
Lovely and calm, comfortable beds with
duvets, rooms for 2 to 6 people, great view,
very kind owners.

Restaurants

Bariloche is blessed with superb food, much
of it locally produced, including smoked trout
and salmon, wild boar and other delicacies,
not least fine chocolate and, in season,
delicious berries. There are many good delis.

$$$ Chez Philippe
Primera Junta 1080, T0294 442 7291,
see Facebook.
Delicious local delicacies and fondue, fine
French-influenced cuisine. Intimate and
secluded, away from the centre.

$$$ Jauja
Elflein 148, T0294-442 2952,
www.restaurantejauja.com.ar.
Recommended for delicious local dishes,
quiet and welcoming, good value.

$$$-$$ Días de Zapata
T0294-442 3128.
Mediocre Mexican, but a welcome change
from all the grilled meat.

$$ Covita
Rolando 172, T0294-442 1708.
Mon-Sat for lunch, Thu-Sat for dinner.
Vegetarian restaurant (also serves fish),
offering curries, masalas and pastas.

$$ El Boliche de Alberto
Villegas 347, T0294-443 1433,
www.elbolichedealberto.com.
Very good pasta, huge portions, popular
after 2000 (queues in summer). There is a
second location at Bustillo Km 8800 that
specializes in grilled meats.

$$ El Vegetariano
20 de Febrero 730, T0294-442 1820.
Also fish, excellent food, beautifully served,
warm atmosphere, takeaway available.
Highly recommended.

$ Huang Ji Zhong
Rolando 268, T0294-442 8168.
Good Chinese, next to a bowling alley.

Cafés

La Alpina
Moreno 98.
Old-fashioned café serving delicious cakes,
good for tea, Wi-Fi, charming.

Bars and clubs

Cerebro
JM de Rosas 406, www.cerebro.com.ar.
Jun-Dec.
The party starts at 0130, Fri is the best night.

Wilkenny
San Martín 435, T0294-442 4444.
Lively Irish pub with expensive food but it
really gets busy around 2400. Great place to
watch sports on TV.

Shopping

The main shopping area is on Mitre between
the Centro Civíco and Beschtedt, also on San
Martín. Local chocolate is excellent, and wines
from the Alto Río Negro are also good buys.

Chocolate
Several shops on Mitre.
Abuela Goye, *Mitre 252, www.abuelagoye.
com.* First-rate chocolatier and café (5 other
branches and outlets nationwide).
Fenoglio, *Av Bustillo 1200, www.museo
chocolate.com.ar.* Chocolate museum
and production facility with tastings and
a good shop.
Mamuschka, *Mitre y Rolando, www.
mamuschka.com.* Considered the best
chocolate here, also with café.

Handicrafts
Feria Artesanal Municipal, *Moreno y Villegas.*

What to do

Adventure tours
Canopy, *Colonia Suiza, Cerro López, T0294-
445 8585, www.canopybariloche.com.* Zip-line
adventure in the forest, including 4WD ride
to get there and night descents.
Eco Family, *20 de Junio 728, T0294-442 8995,*
www.eco-family.com. Riding, walking,
skiing, other adventures, bilingual guides.
Highly recommended.
Senza Limiti Adventures, *J Cortázar 5050,*
T0294-452 0597, www.slimiti.com.
Adventure travel company, including
kayaking, mountain-biking, hut-to-hut
treks and much more, licensed by National
Parks Administration.
Tronador Turismo, *Quaglia 283, T0294-
442 5644, www.tronadorturismo.com.ar.*
Conventional tours, trekking and rafting. Also

to Refugio Neumeyer, and to Chilean border. Great adventurous wintersports options.

Climbing

Note that at higher levels, winter snow storms can begin as early as Apr, making climbing dangerous. Contact **Club Andino Bariloche** (see page 436) for mountain guides and information.

Cycling

Bikes can be hired at many places in high season.
Circuito Chico, *Av Bustillo 18300, T0294-459 5608, www.circuitochicobikes.com.* Rents mountain bikes, with road assistance service, and kayaks.
Dirty Bikes, *Lonquimay 3908, T0294-444 2743, www.dirtybikes.com.ar.* Very helpful for repairs, tours and bike rentals (US$20-45 per day).

Fishing

Martín Pescador, *Rolando 257, T0294-442 2275, see Facebook.* Fishing, camping and skiing equipment.

Horse riding

Ariane Patagonia, *T0294-441 3468, www.arianepatagonia.com.ar.* Horse-riding trips, visits to farms and estancias, personalized service.
Bastión del Manso, *Av Bustillo 13491, T0294-445 6111, www.bastiondelmanso.com.* Relaxed place with tuition and full-day's riding offered, including rafting and longer treks. See also **Estancia Peuma Hue**, page 446.

Kayaking and rafting

Aguas Blancas, *Morales 564, T0294-443 2799, www.aguasblancas.com.ar.* Rafting on the Río Manso, all grades, with expert guides, and all equipment provided, also 'duckies' – inflatable kayaks for beginners.
Patagonia Infinita, *T0294-15-455 3954, www.patagoniainfinita.com.ar.* Kayaking

and trekking trips in Parque Nacional Nahuel Huapi.
Pura Vida Patagonia, *T0294-15-441 4053, www.puravidapatagonia.com.* Informative, attentive guides, good-value trips from 1-9 days in Nahuel Huapi.

Language schools

Academia Bariloche, *Mitre 17-2A, T0294-442 9307, www.academiabariloche.com.* Offers Spanish classes and cultural activities.
ILEE, *www.argentinailee.com.* Arranges classes and home stays.
La Montaña, *Elflein 251, T0294-452 4212, www.lamontana.com.* Spanish courses, family lodging, activities and volunteering.

Paragliding

There are several paragliding schools. Take-offs are usually from Cerro Otto, but there are other starting points, 10- to 40-min tandem flights.

Skiing

Cerros Otto and **Catedral**, *see pages 443 and 444.*

Tours

Check what your tour includes; cable cars and chair lifts are usually extra. Tours get booked up in season. Most travel agencies will pick you up from your hotel, and charge roughly the same prices: Circuito Chico half day, US$17; Isla Victoria and Bosque de Arrayanes, full-day boat trip from Puerto Pañuelo, US$50, or US$30 from other departure points (park entry, US$10, not included); Tronador, Ventisquero Negro and Pampa Linda, US$45 plus National Park entry via Lago Mascardi by boat; El Bolsón US$45, full-day, including Lago Puelo; several other tours.
Turisur, *Mitre 219, T0294-442 6109, www.turisur.com.ar.* Boat trips to Bosque de Arrayanes, Isla Victoria on a 1937 ship and to Tronador via Lago Mascardi. Licensee for the Cruce Andino trip to Puerto Montt. Always reserve 1 day ahead.

Trekking

For further information, contact **Club Andino Bariloche** (see page 436).

Active Patagonia, *20 de Febrero 30, T0294-452 9875, www.activepatagonia.com.ar.* As well as trekking to Tronador and Refugio Frey, also offers kayaking, rafting, horse riding, mountain biking and climbing.

Andescross, *T0294-15-463 3581, www. andescross.com.* Expert guides, all included. Trekking to Chile across the Andes, via Pampa Linda, Lago Frías, Peulla.

Transport

Air

The airport (T0294-440 5016) has car rental agencies, internet, exchange, ATM and a café. Many flights a day to **Buenos Aires**. AR also flies to **El Calafate** in summer only. **LADE** flies to **Buenos Aires**, **Comodoro Rivadavia** (with connections to **El Calafate**) and several other destinations in Patagonia.

Boat

For boat trips, see page 447. For the route by boat and bus to Chile, see box, page 448.

Bus

The bus terminal (T0294-443 2860) has toilets, small *confitería*, *kiosko*, *locutorio* with internet, left luggage and a tourist information desk.

Tickets can be bought at the bus company offices in town or at terminal: **Vía Bariloche**, Mitre 321, T0810-333 7575 and at the terminal; **Chevallier/Flechabus**, Moreno 107, T0294-442 3090. **Andesmar**, at terminal, T0294-443 0211; **Ko Ko**, at terminal, T0294-443 1135.

Local To **Llao Llao**, bus No 20 from Moreno y Rolando, US$1.50, 45 mins. To **Villa Catedral**, bus 'Catedral' from the bus terminal or Moreno y Palacios, every 90 mins, US$1.50, 35 mins.

Long distance To **Buenos Aires**, 7 companies daily, 19-22 hrs, US$120-140. To **Bahía Blanca**, with **Andesmar**, 14 hrs, US$75-85. To **Mendoza**, US$80-113, with **Andesmar** and Cata, 17-19 hrs. **Marga** to **El Bolsón**, US$8, 2 hrs, and on to **Esquel**, 4-5 hrs, US$21, heavily, even over, booked in high season. To **San Martín de los Andes** (not via 7 Lagos), 3½-4 hrs, US$15-19, with **Vía Bariloche**. To **Villa La Angostura**, 1 hr, US$5, several companies. To **Comodoro Rivadavia**, US$64-73, **Andesmar**, 14 hrs, **Marga/TAQSA** (T0800-333 1188, www.taqsa.com.ar). **To El Bolsón** with **Vía Bariloche**, US$6.50, 2 hrs. It's also possible to take **Chaltén Travel**'s (www.chaltentravel.com) 3-day trip on Ruta 40 down to **El Chaltén**, **El Calafate** and **Ushuaia**, depart 0745 on odd-numbered days from 20 de Febrero 30, at Club Andino Bariloche. Operates from Nov-Apr only.

To Chile: Vía Bariloche runs daily services via Samoré pass to **Osorno**, 5 hrs, US$36, and **Puerto Montt**, 6-7½ hrs, same fare; **Andesmar** goes to **Valdivia** via Osorno, US$43-52, not daily. Take your passport when booking. Sit on the left side for the best views.

Car hire

Rates are from US$40, up to US$120 per day, depending on the size of the vehicle. Larger companies may permit hiring in one town and returning to another for an extra charge (price depends on distance and type of vehicle). **Lagos**, Mitre 83, T0294-442 8880, www.lagosrentacar.com.ar, among many others. To enter Chile, a permit is necessary; it's generally included in the price but you should state your intention of driving to Chile when booking the car, allow 24 hrs.

Train

Train station, T0294-442 2450. See Essential box, page 433, for **Tren Patagónico** service to **Viedma**, www.trenpatagonico-sa.com.ar.

Llao Llao and the Circuito Chico

To really appreciate the splendid setting of Bariloche, you need to get out of town and head 25 km west towards the area known as **Llao Llao**. Named after one of Argentina's most famous hotels, this is a charming area that offers lovely walking and gorgeous views. It's at the end of Avenida Bustillo, which runs along Lago Nahuel Huapi to the port (Puerto Pañuelo), from where boat trips depart. Frequent buses run along this road, so it's easy to explore even without your own transport. (Bus No 20 departs from the big bus stop at Moreno y Rolando for a lovely 45-minute ride, US$1.50.) There's easy access to the mountains above Avenida Bustillo and parallel **Avenida de los Pioneros**: just get off the bus at the kilometre stop you want. The free tourist office map *Circuito Chico* shows the stops clearly.

The Circuito Chico is a classic old Argentine tour: you sit in the car and gaze at the view. These days, you're more likely to want to stop, hike, take photos and find somewhere to eat, so the tour as offered by tour operators can be a frustrating experience. To really enjoy this great introduction to the area, drive or cycle instead. This is a satisfying all-day cycle ride, but beware that Avenida Bustillo is a busy road, and drivers will show you no mercy, expecting you to pull over onto the gravel verges as they pass.

Start by travelling along Avenida Bustillo. At Km 17.5, a **chairlift** ① *T0294-442 7274, www.cerrocampanario.com.ar, daily 0900-1730, 7 mins, US$11 return, extended opening in summer;* bus No 10, 20 or 22, goes up to **Cerro Campanario** (1049 m). There is a restaurant and bar

② Bariloche – the road to Llao Llao

Where to stay
1 Alaska
2 Aldebaran
3 Departamentos Bellevue
5 El Yeti
6 Gringos Patagonia
7 Hostería Santa Rita
8 La Caleta
9 Llao Llao
10 Petunia
11 Selva Negra
12 Tunquelén

at the top with fabulous views of the lake, edged with mountains, as well as of the San Pedro peninsula below and Lago Moreno.

Tip...
Hotel Llao Llao is a good place for tea on the terrace, with stunning views.

Back on Avenida Bustillo, turn off at Km 18.3 to go around Lago Moreno Oeste, past Punto Panorámico (with really great views) and continue around **Bahía López**, through the Parque Municipal Llao Llao. Covering a small peninsula that juts into the lake, the park offers superb walks in beautiful virgin forest that is rich in wildlife. There's a small hill to climb and a little beach, **Villa Tacul**, both offering good views. **Hotel Llao Llao** and **Puerto Pañuelo** are located just east of the park.

Hotel Llao Llao (see Where to stay, page 445) is one of Argentina's finest hotels and worth the extortionate rates for its view, spa and restaurant. Superbly situated on a hill, it has incredible views over the lake. The hotel was designed by Bustillo and opened in 1937. Originally almost entirely a wooden construction, it burned down within a few months of opening and was rebuilt using local stone.

You could extend the circuit by returning via **Colonia Suiza** and the ski resort of **Cerro Catedral** (2388 m), both of which are possible starting points for longer treks (see Trekking, page 441).

Cerro Otto

A free bus service runs from Mitre y Villegas or Pagano y San Martín, daily from 1000 in high season, to Km 5 on Avenida de los Pioneros, from where a **cable car** (*teleférico*) ⓘ *T0294-444 1035, www.telefericobariloche.com.ar, daily 1000-1730 (last descent at 1900),*

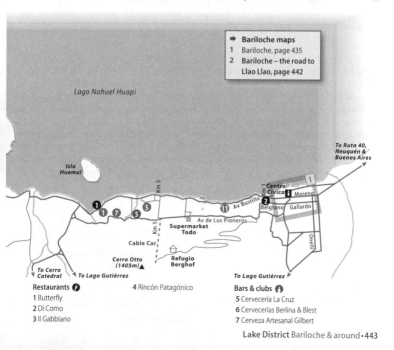

Bariloche maps
1 Bariloche, page 435
2 Bariloche – the road to Llao Llao, page 442

Restaurants 🍴
1 Butterfly
2 Di Como
3 Il Gabbiano
4 Rincón Patagónico

Bars & clubs 🍸
5 Cervecería La Cruz
6 Cervecerías Berlina & Blest
7 Cerveza Artesanal Gilbert

US$22 return, goes up to Cerro Otto (1405 m) with its revolving restaurant and really wonderful views over the lakes and mountains all around. Alternatively, 20 minutes' walk away on the summit at **Refugio Berghof** is a *confitería* belonging to Club Andino Bariloche. Highly recommended. Urban buses 50 and 51 also go to the cable car station, or by car, take Avenida de los Pioneros, then the signposted dirt track 1 km out of town.

To climb Cerro Otto on foot (two to three hours), turn off Avenida de los Pioneros at Km 4.6, then follow the trail past **Refugio Berghof**, with splendid views. This is not recommended alone, as paths can be confusing.

Cerro Catedral

T0294-440 9000, www.catedralaltapatagonia.com. Slopes are open from mid-Jun to end of Sep and are busiest 15 Jun-15 Aug (school holidays). Ski lifts daily 0900-1700 (last ascent 1615); adult passes US$55-77 per day depending on season.

Cerro Catedral (2338 m), 21 km southwest of Bariloche, is one of the major ski resorts in Argentina and is extremely well organized with a great range of slopes for all abilities. There are 120 km of slopes of all grades, allowing a total drop of 1010 m, starting at 2000 m, and 52 km of cross-country skiing routes, all with utterly spectacular views. There are also snowboarding areas and a well-equipped base with hotels, restaurants, equipment hire, ski schools and nursery care for children. As a summer resort, there's a cable car to take you further into the hills, useful for starting walks to **Refugio Lynch** (from where you can walk on to Laguna Jakob) and **Refugio Frey**, or for cycling down to Lago Gutiérrez.

To get to Cerro Catedral, take the bus marked 'Catedral' from the bus terminal or the bus stop on Moreno y Palacios to the ski station base (known as Villa Catedral). The bus leaves every 90 minutes, takes 35 minutes and costs US$1.50; taxis cost US$20-25. The **cable car** from Villa Catedral is US$20 return.

Lago Gutiérrez

Easily accessible by bus from Bariloche, Lago Gutiérrez feels like a fjord, with mountains dropping steeply into its western side and spectacular views all around. There are many ways to access the lake and it can be explored on foot or bike almost all the way round. There are several campsites, a hostel and fine hotels at its northern end, or a fabulous comfortable estancia, ★ **Peuma Hue** ⓘ *www.peuma-hue.com, see page 446*, on the southern lakeshore, offering great trekking and horse riding.

For an adventurous approach, you could hike down from **Refugio Frey** or walk or cycle down the stony track from Cerro Catedral (see above). Or just get off any bus heading from Bariloche to El Bolsón to explore either end of the lake. Water sports can be practised on the lake in summer, and there's a golf course at Arelauken on the northern shore.

Listings Around Bariloche *map page 442.*

Where to stay

The road to Llao Llao

There are lots of great places to stay along the shore of Lago Nahuel Huapi, many of them very close to the centre. All can be reached by buses which run every 20-30 mins.

$$$$ Aldebaran
On Península San Pedro, reached from Av Bustillo Km 20.4, T0294-444 8678, www.aldebaranpatagonia.com.
Not in chalet style, but tasteful rooms in this modern boutique hotel on the lake shore, superb views. Rustic-style restaurant, sauna and spa with outdoor pool, so you can bask

under the stars. Great service from helpful bilingual staff.

$$$$ Llao Llao
Av Bustillo Km 25, T0294-444 5700/8530,
www.llaollao.com.
Deservedly famous, superb location, complete luxury, golf course, pool, spa, water sports, restaurant.

$$$$ Tunquelén
Av Bustillo, Km 24.5, T0294-444 8400/8600,
www.tunquelen.com.
4-star, comfortable, splendid views, feels quite secluded, superb restaurant, attentive service.

$$$ Departamentos Bellevue
Av Bustillo, Km 24.6, T0294-444 8389,
www.bellevue.com.ar. Open year-round.
A famous tea room with beautiful views also offers accommodation with high-quality furnishings, very comfortable, well-equipped self-catering *cabañas*, delicious breakfast included. Access to beaches on Lake Moreno, lovely gardens.

$$$ Gringos Patagonia
Av Bustillo, Km 24.3, T0294-444 8023,
www.gringospatagonia.com.
Delightful, peaceful garden full of flowers, charming Slovenian family Kastelic (also half-board, **$$$$**). Also offers adventure tourism.

$$$ Hostería Santa Rita
Av Bustillo, Km 7.2, T0294-446 1028,
www.santarita.com.ar.
Bus 10, 20/21 to Km 7.5.Peaceful lakeside views, comfortable, lovely terrace, great service.

$$$ La Caleta
Av Bustillo, Km 1.95, T0294-444 3444,
www.bungalows-bariloche.com.ar.
Cabañas sleep 4, open fire, excellent value. Also owns **San Isidro** *cabañas* at Km 5.7, further west.

$ pp Alaska
Lilinquen 328 (buses 10, 20, 21, get off at La Florida, Av Bustillo Km 7.5), T0294-446 1564,
www.alaskahostelbariloche.com.

Well run, cosy with shared rustic rooms for 4, US$14 pp, also doubles US$43 (cheaper without bath), nice garden, washing machine, organizes horse riding and rafting, rents mountain bikes. Recommended.

Camping
A list of sites is available from the tourist office. Shops and restaurants on most sites; these are closed outside Jan-Mar. These are recommended among the many along Bustillo:

El Yeti
Km 5.7, T0294-444 2073.
All facilities, *cabañas*.

Petunia
Km 13.5, T0294-446 1969,
www.campingpetunia.com.
A lovely shady site going down to lakeside with all facilities.

Selva Negra
Km 2.95, T0294-444 1013,
www.campingselvanegra.com.ar.
Very good, discounts for long stay.

Cerro Catedral

$$$$ Pire-Hue
Villa Catedral, T011-4782 0322 (Buenos Aires),
www.pire-hue.com.ar. Prices rise in Jul/Aug and fall in Jun/Sep.
Exclusive 5-star hotel with beautifully decorated rooms and all the facilities.

Lago Gutiérrez

$$$$ El Retorno
Villa Los Coihues, on the shore of Lago Gutiérrez, T0294-446 7333, www.hosteria elretorno.com (closed for major renovation until early 2017).
Stunning lakeside position, comfortable hunting lodge style, family-run, with a beach, tennis, very comfortable rooms (**$$$** in low season) and self-catering apartments (Bus 50, follow signs off the road to El Bolsón).

$$$$ Estancia Peuma Hue
Ruta 40, Km 2014, T0294-15-450 1030,
www.peuma-hue.com.
Best comfort in a homely environment, on the southern shores of Lago Gutiérrez, below Cerro Catedral Sur. Charming owner Evelyn Hoter and dedicated staff make it all work perfectly: tasty home-made food, superb horse riding and other activities, health treatments, yoga, meditation, etc, candlelit concerts. All inclusive, varied accommodation. Highly recommended.

Camping

Villa los Coihues
Lago Gutiérrez, T0294-446 7481,
www.campingloscoihues.com.ar.
Well-equipped and beautifully situated. Camping from US$8.50 and dorm rooms from US$22. Take bus No 50 or take the track down to Gutiérrez from Cerro Catedral (4WD advisable) or the road to El Bolsón (Ruta 258), and follow signs.

Restaurants

The road to Llao Llao

$$$ Butterfly
Hua Huan 7831, just off Av Bustillo Km 7.9, T0294-446 1441, www.butterflypatagonia. com.ar.
2 seatings: 1945 and 2130. German/ Argentine/Irish owned, an elite dining experience, tasting menus using only local ingredients, carefully selected wines, art exhibitions, only 8 tables. Reserve in advance and discuss the menu with the chef.

$$$ Il Gabbiano
Av Bustillo Km 24.3, T0294-444 8346. Closed Tue.
Delicious Italian lunches and dinners. Booking essential (no credit cards).

$$$ Rincón Patagónico
Av Bustillo, Km 14, Paraje Laguna Fantasma, T0294-446 3063, www.rinconpatagonico.com.
Traditional *parrilla* with Patagonian lamb cooked *al palo*. Huge menu but service can be minimal at busy times.

$$ Di Como
Av Bustillo, Km 0.8, T0294-452 2118.
A 10-min walk from town. Good pizza and pasta, terrace and great views of the lake.

Bars and clubs

Cervecería Berlina
Ruta 79 y F Goye, T0294-445 4393, www.cervezaberlina.com. Open 1200 until around 2400.
3 good brews. They have a diverse menu ($$) at their restaurant at Av Bustillo Km 11.750, with a deck for watching the sunset.

Cervecería Blest
Av Bustillo Km 11.6, T0294-446 1026, www.cervezablest.com.ar.
Wonderful brewery with delicious beers, serving imaginative local and German dishes and steak and kidney pie ($$$-$$).

Cervecería La Cruz
Nilpi 789, T0294-444 2634, www.cervecerialacruz.com.ar.
Great brewpub with many local beers on tap. Also delicious bar food such as burgers and thin-crust pizzas. Good place to kick back and imbibe with ski bums.

Cerveza Artesanal Gilbert
Km 24, Barrio Las Cartas, Circuito Chico, T0294-445 4292, www.cerveceriagilbert. com.ar. Daily 1200-1900.
Popular beers and simple meals ($$).

What to do

Lago Gutiérrez
Horse riding
From **Estancia Peuma Hue** on Lago Gutiérrez (see Where to stay, above), you can ride into the mountains and over to Pampa Linda. Riding is also available from **Los Baqueanos** (signposted from R258, on the eastern shore of Lago Gutiérrez, T0294 423 0556, www.complejobaqueanos.com.ar).

Isla Victoria and Bosque de Arrayanes

There are popular trips from Puerto Pañuelo (bus No 10, 11 or 20 to get there) and other departure points to Isla Victoria and on to Parque Nacional Los Arrayanes, on the Quetrihué Peninsula (see box, page 427). Park entry (US$10) is not included in the tour price.

Puerto Blest

The other great boat trip in the area is the all-day excursion to Puerto Blest, **Cascada de los Cántaros**, at the western end of Lago Nahuel Huapi, and **Lago Frías**, visiting native forest and Valdivian rainforest – highly recommended. This is usually done as a nine-hour trip from Bariloche, leaving at 0900 from Puerto Pañuelo

> **Tip...**
> Visit the national park by boat or on foot from Villa La Angostura, which allows you more time in the forest and a good 13-km hike back.

(Km 25.5), and sailing down to fjord-like Puerto Blest, where there's a good *hostería* and restaurant at the end of the lake. *Coihue*-clad mountains drop steeply into Prussian blue water, and it's usually raining, but very atmospheric. The tour then continues by short bus ride to **Puerto Alegre** on Lago Frías, and you cross the still, peppermint-green lake by launch. From Puerto Blest, the walk through beautiful forest to the **Cascada de los Cántaros** (one hour) is superb. If you set off while the rest of the party stops for lunch, you'll have time for your picnic by the splendid falls before the crowd arrives by boat. Or walk beyond them up to quiet **Lago de los Cántaros**, enclosed by vertical granite cliffs.

Boat trips run by Turisur depart Puerto Pañuelo at 1000. They cost US$49, plus an extra US$11 for a bus transfer to Puerto Pañuelo; it's cheaper to take a bus before 0800 from the centre of town. Boats are comfortable but be aware that they fill up entirely in high season; they are much more pleasant in December and March. There's a good (but expensive) *cafetería* on board and set lunch is available at **Hostería Blest**; cheaper sandwiches are available from the snack bar next door or you should stock up on picnic provisions before you go. The **Hotel y Restaurant Puerto Blest ($$$)** is a small cosy hotel built in 1904, with homely rather than luxurious rooms. It's worth staying a night if you want to try any of the treks from here, or fish for trout, and the only other option is camping *libre* with no facilities. The *guardaparques* at Puerto Blest can advise on the many walks from here (and their state), but the seven-hour, 15-km trek to **Lago Ortiz Basualdo** is recommended (mid-December to March only). For information on the Three Lakes Crossing into Chile, see box, page 448.

Walks around Bariloche

hiking, trekking, or a quick stroll

There are many superb walks in this area. A network of paths in the mountains and several *refugios* allow for treks over several days. *Refugios* are leased by Club Andino Bariloche, who charge US$10-20 per night, plus US$8-20 for food. Take a good sleeping bag.

Below is just a small selection of walks of various grades of difficulty, recommended for the surrounding natural beauty: There's not space here to give detailed descriptions or instructions, so for all walks contact **Club Andino Bariloche** (see page 436) for advice,

BORDER CROSSING
Argentina–Chile

Three Lakes Crossing
This popular route to Puerto Varas in Chile, with ferries across Lago Nahuel Huapi, Lago Frías and Lago Todos Los Santos, is outstandingly beautiful whatever the season, though the mountains are often obscured by rain and heavy cloud. It's a long journey, however, and is not recommended in really heavy rain. Book well ahead in high season (you can reserve online), and take your passport when booking in person. No cars are carried on the boats on this route.

The route is Bariloche to Puerto Pañuelo by road (30 minutes, departure from hotel at 0830), Puerto Pañuelo to Puerto Blest by boat (one hour at 1000), Puerto Blest to Puerto Alegre on Lago Frías by bus (15 minutes), cross the lake to Puerto Frías by boat (20 minutes) for Argentine immigration, then two hours by road to Peulla (lunch is not included in the price). Leave for Petrohué at 1600 by boat (one hour 40 minutes), cross Lago Todos Los Santos, passing the Osorno volcano and other peaks, then by bus to Puerto Varas (two hours, arrive 1900).

If you take two days over the journey, you spend the first afternoon and second morning in Peulla, staying overnight in either the **Hotel Peulla** (T+56-(0)65-297 2288, www.hotelpeulla.cl) or the **Hotel Natura Patagonia** (T+56-(0)65-297 2289, www. hotelnatura.cl); breakfast is included, but supper, lodging and the second day's lunch are not. Nor are the prices of any excursions you may choose to do in Peulla, such as horse riding, canopy, boat trips or kayaking.

The mid-2016 season price was US$280 one way in high season (US$230 in low season), 50% on return ticket; check the website before booking as prices alter with the season. **Cruce Andino** (www.cruceandino.com) has the monopoly on this crossing. In Bariloche bookings are handled by **Turisur** (Mitre 219, T0294-442 6109, www.turisur.com.ar), although tickets are sold by various operators. The trip runs every day except 1 May.

Paso Pérez Rosales
The Three Lakes Crossing enters Chile via the Paso Pérez Rosales; see www.gendarmeria.gob.ar/pasos-chile/perez-rosales.html.
Argentine immigration and customs At Puerto Frías, open daily.
Chilean immigration and customs At Peulla, open daily 0900-2000.
Chilean currency can be bought at Peulla customs at a reasonable rate.

maps and to check paths are open before you set off: crucial in spring when snow may not have cleared the upper slopes. You could also consider contacting a trekking company to take you on guided hikes rather than setting off alone.

Around Llao Llao There are several easy and very satisfying walks from Llao Llao: a delightful easy circuit in Valdivian (temperate) rainforest in the Parque Municipal Llao Llao (turn left off the road, just past the golf course, two hours); the small hill Cerrito Llao Llao (900 m) for wonderful views (turn right off the road and follow signs – one to two hours), or a 3-km trail through to Brazo de la Tristeza (turn right off the road opposite

Puerto Varas

This beauty spot was the southern port for shipping on Lago Llanquihue in the 19th century and now makes a good base for trips around the lake, although many places close in the off-season. North and east of the **Gran Hotel Puerto Varas** (1934) are German-style mansions dating from the early 20th century. On the south shore, two of the best beaches are Playa Hermosa (Km 7) and Playa Niklitschek (Km 8, entry fee charged). La Poza, at Km 16, is a little lake to the south of Lago Llanquihue reached through narrow channels overhung with vegetation. Isla Loreley, an island on La Poza, is very beautiful (frequent boat trips, US$3.50); a concealed channel leads to yet another lake, the Laguna Encantada. Just past the village of Nueva Braunau, 9 km west of Puerto Varas, is the remarkable **Museo Antonio Felmer** (T+56 9 9449 8130, www.museoaleman.cl, summer daily 1100-2000, otherwise Saturday and Sunday 1100-1300, 1500-1800 or by appointment, US$3.50), a huge private collection of machinery, tools and household items used by the first Austrian immigrants to the area, some with English descriptions. There's a municipal tourist office at Del Salvador 320 (T+56 65-236 1194, www.ptovaras.cl). **Pullman** and **ETM** are the only long-distance bus company to have terminals in the town centre (Diego Portales). Other companies have ticket offices dotted around the centre but buses leave from the outskirts of town. Minibuses to Puerto Montt (**Thaebus, Suyai, Puerto Varas Express** and **Full Express**) leave from San Bernardo y Walker Martínez every five minutes, US$1.30, 30 minutes.

Puerto Montt

South of Puerto Varas, Puerto Montt is a less appealing, but still popular centre for trips to the Chilean Lake District and is the departure point for boats to Puerto Chacabuco and Puerto Natales (if operating). A paved road runs 55 km southwest to Pargua, where there is a ferry service to the island of Chiloé. The little fishing port of Angelmó, 2 km west, has become a tourist centre with many seafood restaurants and handicraft shops (reached by **Costanera** bus along Portales and by *colectivo* Nos 2, 3, 4, 22 or 33 from the centre). For information and town maps, the **Sernatur** office is just southwest of the Plaza de Armas at Antonio Varas 415 y San Martín (T+56 (0)65-222 3016, turismopuertomontt@gmail.com, daily 0900-2100 in high season; Monday-Friday 0830-1300, 1500-1730 in low season). There are information desks at the airport and the bus station (daily 0830-1600); see also www.puertomonttchile.cl.

the *guardebosque*), via tiny Lago Escondido, with magical views. Bus No 20 to Llao Llao leaves from the terminal every 20 minutes from 0540.

Refugio López ⓘ *2076 m, 5-7 hrs return*. This is a great hike with some of the most wonderful views of the whole area. Starting from the southeastern tip of Lago Moreno, go up alongside Arroyo López, and then along a ridge to the distinctive rose-coloured **Refugio López**, with its fabulous views. Refugio López is the only *refugio* that is privately owned and not part of CAB's chain. The owners may charge you to use the paths. From Refugio López, you could do some climbing, or continue to make this a three- to four-day trek: head south to **Refugio Italia**, which is on the shores of the incredibly calm Laguna Negra at the foot of Cerro Negro. Then from here, you could hike on via Cerro Navidad to Laguna Jakob and **Refugio San Martín**. But

Tip...
On treks to *refugios* remember to also allow for the costs of ski lifts and buses.

note that this section is poorly signposted, and advisable only for very experienced walkers who are well equipped and can use a compass proficiently. Take a trekking guide if in any doubt, and always ask at CAB for the conditions of the paths. Bus No 10 or 11 to Colonia Suiza and Arroyo López (check return times).

Refugio Frey ⓘ *1700 m*. From the ski station at **Villa Catedral**, there are two ways up: 1) Walk up to Refugio Frey, or take the cable car to **Refugio Lynch** (check before you set off, as precise cable-car routes change each year) and from here walk along the ridge of Cerro Catedral to Refugio Frey, which occupies a beautiful setting on a small lake (two to four hours one-way, experience necessary); or 2) from Villa Catedral, walk south and up alongside the Arroyo Van Titter to **Refugio Piedritas**, a very basic emergency shelter with no services, to reach Refugio Frey (three to six hours to climb one-way). The area around **Refugio Frey** is the best area for climbing in the whole region, with innumerable options in the granite walls around. From Refugio Frey there are several possibilities: walk on to Refugio Piedritas (four hours each way), and then down the Arroyo Van Titter to reach Lago Gutiérrez. Once you reach the lake, you could either walk around its southern head to join the Route 258, which runs from Bariloche to El Bolsón, or ask **Estancia Peuma Hue** (see Where to stay, page 446) to collect you at the start of a few night's stay there. (The same is also possible in reverse.)

Lago Gutiérrez This grand lake southwest of Bariloche has the relaxing ★ **Estancia Peuma Hue** on its shores with excellent horse riding (see Where to stay, page 446). You can reach the lake by walking 2 km downhill from the ski base at Cerro Catedral and along the northern lake shore, reaching the El Bolsón road (Route 258) where you can take a bus back to Bariloche (six hours). Or arrange with **Estancia Peuma Hue** to collect you by boat from the shore of Lake Gutiérrez and stay a couple of nights at the estancia for more great walks.

Refugio Neumayer ⓘ *Has an office in town: Diversidad, 20 de Junio 728, T0294-442 8995, www.eco-family.com*. Some 12 km south of Bariloche, this makes a really charming centre for exploring the area, with eight paths to walk, information and guides on offer. Two are particularly recommended, to **Laguna Verde**, and to a mirador through Magellanic forest at **Valle de los Perdidos**. This is a cosy, friendly *refugio*, very well set up for walkers and families, and offering a wonderful range of activities. There is also superb cross-country skiing (also called Nordic skiing) around here, with bilingual guides and equipment available for hire. Great fun.

Bariloche
to El Bolsón

Some of Argentina's most spectacular and unspoilt scenery lies south of Bariloche, where there is a wilder, more relaxed feel to the landscape. Route 258, the road south from Bariloche to El Bolsón, is breathtaking, passing the picturesque lakes of Gutiérrez and Mascardi, lying below a massive jagged range of mountains. There are some fabulous, peaceful places to stay here and wonderful hikes and horse riding. From Villa Mascardi, a road leads to glorious Pampa Linda, where there is excellent trekking, including access to climb Mount Tronador. Further south, Río Manso Medio has become famous for whitewater rafting, and at Lago Hess there is the lovely Cascadas Los Alerces.

El Bolsón is a pretty and relaxed town, sprawled out between two mountain ranges, with superb hikes nearby and beautiful rivers, waterfalls and mountains to explore. Several microbreweries here convert local hops into fine handmade beers, and craftsmen supply the local market with wood and leather work, as well as delicious jams from the abundant soft fruits in summer.

Further south, Lago Puelo is a tiny national park, offering great fishing, some good walks and a boat trip to the Chilean border. As you head south, Cholila might attract Butch Cassidy fans, but though it feels authentically like the Wild West, there's little appeal here now.

Lago Mascardi Colour map 5, B2.

At the southern end of Lago Mascardi (Km 35), **Villa Mascardi** is a small village from where the *ripio* Route 81 runs towards Lago Hess and Cascada Los Alerces. This road operates a one-way system: going west 1000-1400, east 1600-1800, two-way 1900-0900; times may vary, check with the Bariloche tourist office (see page 437). Along Lago Mascardi, there are several beautifully situated places to stay, all easily reached by car, or bus when the service is running in summer. Shortly after the lovely straight beach of Playa Negro, handy for launching boats and fishing, the road forks, with the left-hand branch following the crystalline Río Manso Medio to Lago Hess. The **Río Manso** is popular for rafting (arranged through tour operators in Bariloche, see page 440). The right fork of the road, meanwhile, follows a narrow arm of Lago Mascardi northwest, with a viewpoint in lovely woodland to see Isla Piuke Huapi in the centre of the lake. A few kilometres further on is the lakeside paradise of **Hotel Tronador** before reaching Pampa Linda and Mount Tronador at the end of the road. For further information, see Where to stay, page 453.

Pampa Linda

Pampa Linda lies 40 km west of Villa Mascardi in the most blissfully isolated location, with spectacular views of Cerro Tronador towering above. There's a ranger station with very helpful *guardaparques* who can advise on walks, and whom you must consult about the state of the paths and register your name before setting out. From Pampa Linda, a lovely track (*ripio*) continues to **Ventisquero Negro** (Black Glacier), which hangs over a fantastically murky pool in which grey 'icebergs' float. The colour is due to sediment, and while not exactly attractive, the whole scene is very atmospheric. The road ends at the awesome **Garganta del Diablo**, one of the natural amphitheatres formed by the lower slopes of Mount Tronador. A beautiful walk (90 minutes' walk there and back) from the car park through beach forest takes you to a more pristine glacier, and up to the head of the gorge, where thin torrents of ice melt from the hanging glacier above and fall in columns like sifted sugar. Another pleasant walk is to tranquil **Laguna Ilon** (5½ hours each way), with bathing on the shore in summer.

A day tour to Pampa Linda from Bariloche will usually include both **Ventisquero Negro** and the falls at **Garganta del Diablo**, as well as the beautiful lakes Gutiérrez and Mascardi en route, but will not allow much time for walking. A good way to make the most of the area is to take a tour with an agency, and then stay on at Pampa Linda for trekking, returning with the minibus service run by **Transitando lo Natural** ① *20 de Febrero 25, T0294-442 3250*. Alternatively, buses to Pampa Linda run daily in season (December-15 April) from outside **Club Andino Bariloche** ① *transitando1@hotmail.com, US$18*. There's a great simple *hostería* at Pampa Linda, offering lunch.

★ Mount Tronador Colour map 5, B2.

The highest peak around is the mighty Mount Tronador ('The Thunderer', 3478 m). From Pampa Linda two other paths lead up **the mountain**: the first is 15 km long and leads to **Refugio Otto Meiling** (2000 m), in itself a wonderful walk (five hours each way), situated on the edge of the eastern glacier. Another hour from the *refugio*, a path takes you to a view over Tronador and the lakes and mountains of **Parque Nacional Nahuel Huapi**. The other path leads to a *refugio* on the south side of the mountain. Otto Meiling is a good base camp for the ascent, with lots of facilities and activities, including trekking and ice climbing; always ask the *guardaparques* in Pampa Linda if there's space (capacity 60); dinner is available (let them know in advance if you're vegetarian). The lower sections of these paths are great for mountain biking in the forest,

Paso de los Nubes

Pampa Linda is the starting point for a 22-km walk over Paso de los Nubes (1335 m) to **Laguna Frías** and **Puerto Frías** on the Chilean border. Allow at least two days; start the walk at Pampa Linda, rather than the other way around, as there's a gentler rise to the pass this way. There is camping at **Campamento Alerce** (after four hours) or **Campamento Glacier Frías** (after seven hours); from here it's another five hours to Puerto Frías. You'll see a spectacular glacial landscape, formed relatively recently (11,000 years ago), and the pass lies on the continental divide, with water flowing north to the Atlantic, and south to the Pacific. Views from the Río Frías valley are tremendous, and from Glacier Frías you enter Valdivian rainforest. Boats cross Lago Frías at 1600, but check this before leaving Bariloche. From Puerto Frías a 30-km road leads to Peulla on the shore of Chilean Lago Todos Los Santos. Or you can take a boat back to Bariloche – highly recommended.

You must register with *guardaparques* at Pampa Linda before setting out, and check with them about conditions. The route is not always well marked and should only be attempted if there is no snow on the pass (it's normally passable only between December and February) or if the path is not excessively boggy. Do not cross rivers on fallen bridges or trees. Buy the map produced by Infotrekking for Mount Tronador/Paso de las Nubes before you leave Bariloche (available from **Club Andino Bariloche**, see page 436) and also see the excellent leaflet for *Paso de las Nubes* produced by Parque Nacional Nahuel Huapi, all found online at www.nahuelhuapi.gov.ar.

Río Manso Medio and Lago Hess

Some 9 km west of Villa Mascardi, a road runs 18 km through the beautiful valley of the Río Manso Medio to Lago Hess and on to the nearby **Cascada Los Alerces**. This is the starting point for trekking trips in a more remote area of small lakes and forested mountains, including the lakes Fonck, Roca, Felipe, and Cerros Granito and Fortaleza. Check with *guardaparques* at Lago Hess about the conditions of the paths. There is also wonderful rafting here, but you have to take an organized trip from Bariloche. Note that there is also rafting on the **Río Manso Inferior**, further south (see below). For further information, see What to do, opposite.

Lago Steffen and Lago Martín

About 20 km south of Villa Mascardi, another one-way dirt road leads to Lago Steffen, where a footpath runs along both northern and southern shores (of Lago Steffen) to Lago Martín. Both lakes are quite outstandingly lovely, fringed with beech and *álamo* trees, with far-off mountains in the distance and pretty beaches where you can sit at the water's edge. There's also great fishing here. The *guardería* is at Lago Steffen and wild camping is possible further north on the lake shore. To the south, a road leads west from Villegas along the Río Manso Inferior towards Chile. The river here is ideal for wilder rafting and for the trip to the Chilean border, run by rafting companies in Bariloche (see page 440).

Listings Bariloche to El Bolsón

Where to stay

Lago Mascardi

\$\$\$ pp Hotel Tronador
*T0294-4449 0556, www.hoteltronador.com.
Nov-Apr.*

60 km from Bariloche, on the narrow road between Villa Mascardi and Pampa Linda. A lakeside paradise, offering lovely rooms with views of Lago Mascardi, beautiful gardens, charming owner, also riding, fishing and lake trips. Full board.

Camping

Camping La Querencia
R81 towards Pampa Linda, Km 5, T0294-15-461 6300, www.campinglaquerencia.com.ar. Camping US$11 for adults.
A pretty and peaceful spot on the side of the river and the banks of the lake, opposite Playa Negro.

Camping Las Carpitas
Lago Mascardi, at Km 33, T0294-449 0527, www.campinglascarpitas.com.ar. Camping from US$7 and dorms from US$11.
Set in a great lakeside position, summer only, with *cabañas* and restaurant.

Camping Los Rápidos
R258, Km 37, T0294-15-431 7028, www.losrapidos.com.ar.
Attractive shaded site going down to the lake, with *confitería*, food store and all facilities, US$10 per person. Also bunk beds in a basic *albergue* for US$19 per person (sleeping bag needed). Friendly owners organize trekking, kayaking, fishing and mountain biking.

Pampa Linda

$$$ Hostería Pampa Linda
T0294-449 0517, www.hosteriapampalinda.com.ar.
A comfortable, peaceful base for climbing Tronador and many other treks (plus horse riding, trekking and climbing courses), simple rooms, all with stunning views, restaurant, full board optional, packed lunches available for hikes. Charming owners, Sebastián de la Cruz is one of the area's most experienced mountaineers. Highly recommended.

Camping

Los Vuriloches
Pampa Linda, T0294-446 2131, pampalindatere@hotmail.com.
Idyllic spacious lakeside site, with a *confitería* serving good meals and food shop. Excellent service, run by the Club Andino Bariloche.

Río Manso Medio and Lago Hess

$$$$ Río Manso Lodge
T0294-492 2961, www.riomansolodge.com.
Spectacularly set on the bank of the Río Manso in beautiful mountainous scenery, this is a top-class fishing lodge, with lovely rooms with great views from their large windows, fine food and great fishing. Loved by experts. Transfers organized.

What to do

Río Manso Medio and Lago Hess
Rafting
Rafting on the Río Manso is arranged through operators in Bariloche; see page 440.

Transport

Lago Mascardi
Bus
Services from Bariloche to **El Bolsón** pass through **Villa Mascardi**. Buses to **Los Rápidos** run from the terminal in Bariloche between 0800-0930 daily in summer. Check with **Vía Bariloche/El Valle** for times.

Pampa Linda and Mount Tronador
Bus
A bus from Bariloche leaves at 0830 daily and returns at 1700 in summer only; contact **Transitando lo Natural**, 20 de Febrero 25, Bariloche, T0294-442 3250, transitando1@hotmail.com. From Pampa Linda you can also often get a lift with a trip returning to **Bariloche**, if there's room.

El Bolsón is a very seductive little place of 16,000 with a laid-back atmosphere, sprawled out in a broad fertile valley 130 km south of Bariloche. It is contained within huge mountain ranges on either side (hence its name 'the big bag'), and it makes a great base for relaxing for a few days and for hiking in the tempting peaks around. The great serrated ridge of Cerro Piltriquitrón (2284 m) dominates the town, apparently emitting healthy positive ions, which might be why you feel so relaxed while you're here. Certainly it's a magical setting, and it's not surprising that it inspired thousands of hippies to create an ideological community here in the 1970s.

What remains is a young, friendly place where the locals make lots of handicrafts. With the sparkling Río Azul running close by and a warm sunny microclimate, you're likely to want to stay for a few days to try the home-brewed beers and fruit for which the town is famous.

Nearby there are many beautiful mountain walks, a couple of waterfalls and rafting on the Río Azul. The small national park of Lago Puelo is within easy reach, 18 km south of town, and there's a small family-orientated ski centre in the winter at Centro de Ski Perito Moreno.

Around El Bolsón

El Bolsón's great attraction – apart from the pleasure of being in the town itself – is the superb hiking up to the mountains west of the town (see page 457). These start from the other side of turquoise Río Azul, where there are lovely places to sunbathe, camp and picnic. East of town, a pleasant hour-long walk will take you to the top of Cerro Amigo, with lovely views. Follow Calle General Roca east until it becomes Islas Malvinas and continue

Essential El Bolsón

Finding your feet

Note there is not a central bus terminal. Different bus companies stop at different places. Buses from Bariloche and Esquel arrive off the main street at Via Bariloche's offices at Sarmiento and General Roca.

Orientation

El Bolsón sprawls out from the spine of Avenida San Martín which runs through the town, where you'll find places to eat. There are lots of places to stay dotted around the town, though the prettiest cabañas are in Villa Turismo up the hill.

Getting around

There are buses to Lago Puelo, but buses to other sites are infrequent and geared to locals rather than tourists. However, El Bolsón is a lovely place to walk around; you can hire bikes, and there are plenty of cheap remises (taxis).

When to go

Summer is obviously the best time to visit, when you can take full advantage of the blissful rivers and mountains, and there's a lively atmosphere on the plaza with music at nights. But it's very busy here in January, so try to come in February or March, or even in April, when autumn turns the trees brilliant yellow and orange, and there are sunny days but cold nights. Winter is very rainy and best avoided, though there is a basic ski resort at Cerro Perito Moreno.

up the hill. Better still are the panoramic views from **Cerro Piltriquitrón**, the jagged peak looming over El Bolsón to the east. Drive, join a tour or take a taxi 10 km (US$30 for up to four people) up winding earth roads. Then it's an hour's walk to the **Bosque Tallado**, where sculptures have been carved from fallen trees by local craftspeople; from the mirador there are fabulous views over the valley to the Andes beyond. It's a six- to seven-hour round trip walking all the way. Food and shelter are available at the *refugio* (1400 m),

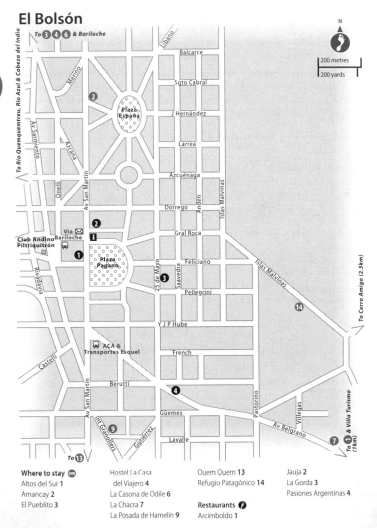

El Bolsón

To ③ ④ ⑥ & Bariloche

To Río Quemquemtreu, Río Azul & Cabeza del Indio

N

200 metres
200 yards

Balcarce

Libano

Sgto Cabral

Merino

J Hernández

Plaza España

②

Av Sarmiento

Azcuénaga

Larrea

Av San Martín

Azcuénaga

Onelli

Dorrego

Andén

Islas Malvinas

Gral Roca

Vía Bariloche ②

Club Andino Piltriquitrón

❶

Plaza Pagano

Feliciano

25 de Mayo

Saavedra

❸

Rivadavia

Pellegrini

Islas Malvinas

To Cerro Amigo (2.5km)

Y J P Hube

Castelli

ACA & Transportes Esquel

French

Berutti

⑭

❹

Av San Martín

Int Cordolas

Güemes

Pastorino

Villegas

❾

Gutiérrez

Lavalle

Av Belgrano

To ⑬

❼ To & Villa Turismo (1km)

Where to stay 🛏
Altos del Sur **1**
Amancay **2**
El Pueblito **3**

Hostel La Casa
del Viajero **4**
La Casona de Odile **6**
La Chacra **7**
La Posada de Hamelin **9**

Ouem Ouem **13**
Refugio Patagónico **14**

Restaurants 🍴
Arcimboldo **1**

Jauja **2**
La Gorda **3**
Pasiones Argentinas **4**

and from there it's three hours' walk to the summit. You can also do paragliding from here. See What to do, page 460.

There are also good views from **Cabeza del Indio**, so called because the rock's profile resembles a face, a good 6-km drive or bike ride from the centre. Take Calle Azcuénaga west to cross the bridge over Río Quemquemtreu and follow signs to Cabeza del Indio. From here, there's a waymarked walk north to **Cascada Escondida**. This impressive sweep of waterfalls, 10 km northwest of El Bolsón, is a good place for a picnic, with a botanical garden in woods reached from winding gravel roads. This area is also worth visiting for the good rustic *parrilla* **El Quincho** ⓘ *open summer only*, which serves local lamb and other great meat dishes (vegetarians: don't even think about it). There are rather less exciting falls at **Cataratas Mallín Ahogado**, a little further north, but it's still a pleasant spot for a stop. **La Golondrina** runs daily buses Monday to Saturday from the plaza to the loop around Mallin Ahogado, but extra walking is required to reach both falls. See the tourist office map for details.

There are many microbreweries dotted around town; **Cervecería El Bolsón** ⓘ *R258, Km 123.9, just north of town, www.cervezaselbolson.com*, is particularly worth a visit, with a brief guided tour, a restaurant and no fewer than 16 different beers on offer, including options for coeliacs. You could also ask at the tourist office for the *Agroturismo* leaflet, which details the *chacras* (fruit farms) throughout El Bolsón and El Hoyo that you can visit in summer for delicious, freshly picked soft fruits and berries, jams and other delights.

The famous narrow-gauge railway **La Trochita** ⓘ *www.patagoniaexpress.com/el_trochita.htm*, also known as the *Old Patagonian Express,* is a novel way of seeing the landscape and catching a glimpse into Patagonia's past. As well as the better-known route from Esquel, there's another journey from El Maitén, near El Bolsón, where you can see the fascinating steam railway workshops too. See What to do, page 460.

El Bolsón benefits from a gentle microclimate which means it's warmer than much of the Lake District, even in winter. However, there is a ski centre, **Centro de Ski Perito Moreno** (www.bolsonweb.com/aventura/ski.htm), on the upper slopes of Cerro Perito Moreno (2216 m). With good snow and no wind, its 720 skiable metres are good for families, but there are three ski lifts and ski instructors too. It's a newish centre and the only place to stay at the moment is the **Refugio Perito Moreno** ⓘ *T0294-448 3433*, with 30 beds. Ask the tourist office for more information. Leave town by Route 258, and take the left-hand turn to Río Azul. Follow signs to Refugio Perito Moreno.

Walks For Parque Nacional Lago Puelo, see page 461.
There are wonderful treks in the mountains west of the town. For all walks, get the *Sendas y Bosques* (Walks and Forests) map and book for El Bolsón, Lago Puelo and Los Alerces. Maps are 1:200,000, laminated and easy to read, and the book is full of great walks, with English summaries. Register for all walks before setting off at the Oficina de Informes de Montaña; see Tourist information in Listings, below). There are some 14 *refugios* (shelters) which offer basic accommodation (US$22 per night, bed linen included), some meals (US$14.50), hearty breakfasts (U$$10.50), basic supplies (such as home-baked bread and home-brewed beer), camping and hot showers.

Cerro Lindo Due west of town, there's a great hike up Arroyo Lali to Cerro Lindo (2105 m), in one of the most beautiful mountain landscapes of the whole area, with **Refugio Cerro Lindo** halfway up, after a five-hour walk. From here, you can reach an ancient glacier and climb onwards to several viewpoints. You'll need a map, and you should check the route before setting off. The altitude difference is pretty extreme here, so you're advised to go slowly and steadily.

Cerro Hielo Azul This is a more serious and demanding hike up to Cerro Hielo Azul (2255 m); it's steep and takes six hours one-way. You can stay at comfortable **Refugio Cerro Azul** at 1300 m, from where you can also walk to the glacier on the slopes of Cerro Hielo Azul (three hours return), or on to Cerro Barda Negra. It's often suggested that you could walk from here via **Refugio Natación** to **Refugio Cajón de Azul**, but this is really not to be recommended without a local guide. The path can be confusing in places, the area remains marshy well into the summer months, and people have got lost, with dangerous consequences. Ask in the **Oficina de Informes de Montaña** for advice (see Tourist information, below).

Cajón de Azul One of the loveliest and most accessible walks can be done in a day, although once you reach the delightful *refugio* (600 m) at Cajón de Azul, you're going to wish you could stay at least a night. It's a fabulous four-hour walk up the Río Azul which flows from a deep canyon. There's a well-marked path and bridges crossing the river. It's worth it for a dip in the sparkling turquoise water on the way down. Set off early to allow for a leisurely lunch at the top, or spend the night in the *refugio* in the company of Atilio and friends, who make a fine dinner with produce from the lovely garden. To get to the start of the walk, take a *traffic* (minibus) from El Bolsón at 0900. You'll be collected by the *traffic* at 2000.

Refugio Los Laguitos This wonderful four-day walk takes you right into the deepest part of the Andes Cordillera, almost to the border with Chile, and through outstanding alerce forests. Allow four hours to **Refugio Cajón de Azul**, another three hours to the Mallín de los Chanchos, and another four hours on from there to reach the basic **Refugio Los Laguitos** in a beautiful spot on the shore of Lago Lahuán. A map and guidebook are absolutely essential; seek advice before setting out.

Listings El Bolsón *map page 456.*

Tourist information

For more information, see www.elbolson.com.

Oficina de Informes de Montaña
Sarmiento and Roca, T0294-445 5810, cerroselbolson@hotmail.com. Mon-Fri 0800-2000 (until 2200 in summer).
All walkers must register here before setting off. They have detailed advice on mountain walking.

Tourist office
San Martín and Roca opposite the big post office, on the side of the semi-circular plaza, T0294-449 2604, www.turismoelbolson. gob.ar. Daily 0800-2200.

Staff are helpful and friendly (with plenty of English speakers). They'll give you an excellent map of the town and the area, and suggest places to stay. They can also give limited advice on hikes and sell useful maps, including *Sendas y Bosques El Bolsón* and *Los Alerces*.

Where to stay

It's difficult to find accommodation in the high season: book ahead.

$$$ Amancay
Av San Martín 3207, T0294-449 2222.
Good, comfortable and light rooms, though small and a bit old-fashioned. Breakfast included.

$$$ La Posada de Hamelin
Int Granollers 2179, T0294-449 2030,
www.posadadehamelin.com.ar.
Charming rooms, welcoming atmosphere,
huge breakfasts with home-made jams and
cakes, German spoken. Highly recommended.

$$ La Casona de Odile
Barrio Luján, T0294-449 2753,
www.odile.com.ar.
Private rooms and 3- to 6-bed dorms
(US$12.50 pp) by stream, delicious home
cooking, bicycle rental. Recommended.

$ pp Altos del Sur
Villa Turismo, T0294-449 8730,
www.altosdelsur.bolsonweb.com.
Peaceful hostel in a lovely setting, shared
rooms and private doubles, dinner available,
will collect from bus station if you call ahead.
Recommended.

$ pp El Pueblito
4 km north in Barrio Luján, 1 km off Ruta 40
(take bus "El Lujancito" from Plaza Principal),
T0294-449 3560, www.elpueblitohostel.
com.ar.
Wooden building in open country, dorms
from US$16 depending on season, also has
cabins (**$$**), laundry facilities, shop, open fire.
Recommended.

$ pp Hostel La Casa del Viajero
Libertdad y Las Flores, Barrio Usina, T0294-
449 3092, www.lacasadelviajero.com.ar.
A little out of the centre in a beautiful setting,
surrounded by organic gardens. Simple,
comfortable rooms (dorms US$18, and
private US$22). Call them for pick up from
the centre of town.

$ pp Refugio Patagónico
Islas Malvinas y Pastorino, T0294-448 3628,
www.refugiopatagonico.com.
Basic hostel, with small dorms (US$18) and
doubles (US$43), in a spacious house set in
open fields, views of Piltriquitrón, 5 blocks
from the plaza.

Camping
There are many *cabañas* in picturesque
settings with lovely views in the Villa
Turismo, about US$60-100 for 2 people.

Camping La Cascada
At Mallín Ahogado, near La Cascada
Escondida, north of El Bolsón, T0294-483
5304, see Facebook.
On the edge of a botanical garden and a
forest reserve. Spacious, tranquil, lovely view
of the Valley of the Arroyo del Medio and
the snow-capped mountains beyond. The
helpful owner Pablo Panomarenko has good
contacts with the *refugios* and businesses
in Bolsón. Has *cabañas*, a great club house,
home-grown organic vegetables available,
home-made bread and beer for sale,
delicious mountain spring water from the
tap, swimming in the brook that feeds the
waterfall. Recommended.

La Chacra
Av Belgrano 1128, T0294-449 2111,
www.lachacracamping.com.ar.
15 mins' walk from town, well shaded, good
facilities, lively atmosphere in season.

Quem-Quem
On Río Quemquemtreu, T0294-449 3550.
Lovely site, hot showers, good walks, free
pick-up from town.

Restaurants

$$$ Pasiones Argentinas
Av Belgrano y Berutti, T0294-448 3616,
see Facebook.
Traditional Argentine food in a wonderful
cosy setting.

$$$-$$ La Gorda
25 de Mayo 2709, T0294-472 0559.
Hugely popular *parrilla* with portions
as grandiose as its reputation.

$$ Arcimbaldo
Av San Martín 2790, T0294-449 2137.
Good value *tenedor libre*, smoked fish
and draft beer, open for breakfast.

$$ Jauja
Av San Martín 2867, T0294-449 2448,
www.restaurantejauja.com.ar.
The best restaurant in town is a great meeting
place, serving delicious fish and pasta. It also
makes outstanding ice cream from organic
milk and local berries: there are 11 varieties of
chocolate alone. English spoken.

Cafés

Cerveza El Bolsón
RN 258, Km 123.9, T0294-449 2595,
www.cervezaselbolson.com.
Microbrewery where you can see how the
beer is made and sample the 16 varieties.
Picadas are served with beer, and you can sit
outside in the gardens. Highly recommended.

Festivals

Jan Fiesta de la Fruta Fina (Berry Festival)
at nearby El Hoyo.
Feb Fiesta del Lúpulo (Hop Festival), at the
end of the month.

Shopping

The handicraft and food market is on Tue,
Thu, Sat and Sun 1000-1600 in season
around the main plaza. Some fine leather
and jewellery, carved wood and delicious
organic produce.

Granja Larix, *R40, Km 1923, T0294-449
8466, alejandra@bariloche.com.ar.* Fabulous
smoked trout and home-made jams.
**La Casa de la Historia y la Cultura del
Bicentenario (Cultural House)**, *Av San
Martín 2219, T0294-445 5322. Mon-Fri
0800-1400 and 1600-1900.* Centre for
cultural offerings such as music and locally
made fabrics and textiles. Also operates
occasionally as a cinema and lecture hall.

Monte Viejo, *San Martín y Hube, T0294-449
1735.* Excellent selection of high quality
handicrafts from all over Argentina.
Museo de Piedras Patagónicas, *Laten K'Aike,
13 km from El Bolsón, T0294-449 1969,
www.museodepiedraspatagonicas.blogspot.
com.ar. Daily 1100-1800.* For exquisite semi-
precious stones.
Verde Menta Almacén Naturista, *Av San
Martín 2137, T0294-449 3576, see Facebook.*
Good supplier of dried foods, fruits and cereals.

What to do

Tour operators
Grado 42, *Av Belgrano 406, on the corner with
Av San Martín, T0294-449 3124, www.grado42.
com.* Excellent company offering wide range
of tours, including *La Trochita*'s lesser-known
trip from El Maitén, where there is a superb
steam railway workshop and you can learn
all about how the trains work. Also rafting
on the Río Manso; horse riding in glorious
countryside at Cajón de Azul; wonderful
fishing in Lago Puelo; paragliding from
Piltriquitrón. Recommended.

Transport

Bus
Several daily to **Bariloche** and **Esquel**,
with **Marga**, Via TAC **Andesmar**, **Don Otto**
and **Vía Bariloche** (T0800-333 7575, www.
viabariloche.com.ar). Very busy, even
overbooked in high season; to **Bariloche**,
US$7-8.50, 2 hrs; to **Esquel**, US$10-14,
2½-3 hrs. Other destinations are accessible
from these towns. Buses to **Lago Puelo**
with **Vía Bariloche** every couple of hours
from 0915 to 1915, 30 mins, US$0.85. To
Parque Nacional Los Alerces (a highly
recommended route), with **Transportes
Esquel**, departing from the information point
at Lago Puelo for Parque Nacional Los Alerces
every Wed, Sat and Sun at 1530, US$11.

Parque Nacional Lago Puelo *Colour map 5, B2.*

off-season paradise

This lovely green and wooded national park is centred around the deep turquoise-coloured Lago Puelo, 15 km south of El Bolsón on the Chilean border, surrounded by southern beech forest and framed by the spiky peaks of snow-dusted far-off mountains. It's a blissful spot out of the busy holiday season. With relatively low altitude (200 m) and high rainfall, the forest is rich in tree species, particularly the cinnamon-bark *arrayán* and the *pitra, coihues* (evergreen beech) and cypresses. There's lots of wildlife, including the huemul, pudu and foxes, and the lake is known for its good fishing for trout and salmon. There are gentle walks on marked paths around the northern shore area, boat trips across the lake and canoes for rent. *Guardaparques* at the park entrance can advise on these and provide a basic map.

Walks

For all walks, get the *Sendas y Bosques* (Walks and Forests) map and book for El Bolsón, Lago Puelo and Los Alerces, www.guiasendasybosques.com.ar.

Bosque de las Sombras (Forest of the Shadows). An easy 400-m walk on wooden walkways, through delightful overgrown forest on the way to the shingle beach at 'La Playita', with guided trails and signs telling you what trees you're passing.

Essential Parque Nacional Lago Puelo

Access

The main entrance is along a pretty road south from El Bolsón, through *chacras* (small farms) growing walnuts, hops and fruit, to Villa Lago Puelo, 3 km north of the park, where there are shops, plenty of accommodation and fuel. From here the road is unpaved. Entry is also possible at El Desemboque, on the eastern side of the park: take the bus from El Bolsón to Esquel, alight at El Hoyo, then walk 14 km to El Desemboque. There are hourly buses (US$1-2) from Avenida San Martín and Dorrego in El Bolsón to the lake via Villa Lago Puelo.

Entry fees

US$10.

Park information

The **Intendencia** (500 m north of the lake, T0294-449 9232, lagopuelo@apn.gov.ar, Monday-Friday 0800-1500, with a booth at the pier in summer) can provide a helpful leaflet and advice on walks. Register here before embarking on long hikes, and register your return. In the town of Lago Puelo there's a **tourist office** (Avenida 2 de Abril and Los Notros, T0294-449 9591, www.lagopuelo. gob.ar, daily 0900-2100 in summer, 0900-1900 in winter) on the roundabout as you enter town. Staff are helpful, English-speaking and can advise on accommodation.

When to go

It's best to visit between November and April, though the northern shore can get crowded in January and February. The lake is glorious in April, when trees turn yellow.

Senda los Hitos A 14-km (five hours each way) walk through marvellous woods to the rapids at Río Puelo on the Chilean border (passport required). There is some wild camping on the way at **Camping de Gendarmería**, after two hours.

Cerro Motoco There's a tremendous two-day hike up Cerro Motoco, with **Refugio Motoco** at the top of the path. Leave Lago Puelo heading north and cross the hanging bridge to access Río Motoco. It's 25 km altogether, and could be done in seven hours, one way, but you'll want to stay at the top. Take the walks book with you.

Cerro Plataforma From the east of the lake, you can hike to **El Turbio** and Cerro Plataforma, crossing the lake first by boat to El Desemboque (or taking the bus and walking 14 km). At Cerro Plataforma, there's a tremendous amount of marine life in evidence, as this was a beach in the ice age. It's about seven hours to Río Turbio, where there's a *guardaparque*, and then 12 hours to Cerro Plataforma; allow three days for the whole trip. There's also a three-day trek through magnificent scenery to **Glaciar y Cerro Aguaja Sur**: get advice and directions from the *guardaparques*.

Other activities

There is wonderful **fly-fishing** in the park, thanks to the fact that this is the lowest crossing in the whole of the Andes region (at only 190 m). The lack of snow and the mild, warm summers mean that Pacific salmon come here in large numbers. Contact fishing guides through the park *guardería*. There are boat trips across Lago Puelo with **Juana de Arco** (T0294-449 8946, www.interpatagonia.com/juanadearco) and others, as well as kayaking. For further information, see What to do, page 460.

Listings Parque Nacional Lago Puelo

Where to stay

Apart from wild camping, there's no accommodation in the park itself, but plenty in Villa Lago Puelo, just outside, with *cabañas*, restaurants and campsites spread out along R16 through the little village.

Cabañas

$$$ Frontera
Ruta Nacional 40, 9 km from Lago Puelo, isolated in woodland, off the main road heading for Esquel, T0294-447 3092, www.frontera-patagonia.com.ar.
Cabañas for 4 and *hostería*, in native forest, furnished to a very high standard, delicious breakfasts and dinner if required.

$$$ Lodge Casa Puelo
R16, km 10, T0294-449 9539, www.casapuelo.com.ar.

Beautifully designed rooms and self-catering cabins right against forested mountains where you can go walking. Good service, English-speaking owner Miguel knows the local area intimately. Very comfortable, dinner offered. *Cabañas* for up to 6. Recommended.

$$$-$$ La Granja
20 m from Río Azul, T02944-499 265, www.interpatagonia.com/lagranja.
Traditional chalet-style *cabañas* with simple furnishings, nothing out of this world, but there's a pool, and these are good value.

$$$-$$ La Yoica
Just off R16, Km 5, T0294-449 9200, www.layoica.com.
Charming Scottish/Argentine owners make you feel at home in these traditional *cabañas* set in lovely countryside with great views. Price for up to 4 people.

$$ San Jorge
A block from the main street, on Plaza Ilia, Perito Moreno 2985, T02944-491313, www.sanjorgepatagonico.com.
Excellent value, neat but dated self-catering apartments in a pretty garden, with friendly, helpful owners.

$ pp La Pasarela
2 km from town, T0294-449 9061, www.lpuelo.com.ar.
Dorms (US$16 pp), cabins (us$69) and camping US$8.50, shops, fuel.

Camping
There are 2 free sites in the park itself, on Lago Puelo, of which **Camping del Lago** is most highly recommended; it offers all facilities, plus rafting, fishing and trekking.

Outside the park there are many good sites with all facilities; these are recommended: **Ailin Co** (Km 15, T02944-499078, www.ailinco.com.ar); **Los Quinchos** (Km 13).

Restaurants

$$ Familia von Fürstenberg
R16 on the way to the national park, T0294-449 9392, www.vonfuerstenberg.com.ar.
In a delightful, perfectly decorated Swiss-style chalet, try the beautifully presented traditional waffles and home-made cakes. Sumptuous. Also *cabañas* (**$$$**) to rent.

Transport

Transportes Esquel, www.transportes esquel.com.ar, run daily buses connecting Lago Puelo with **Cholila**, **PN Los Alerces** and **Esquel**.

South of El Bolsón *Colour map 5, B2.*

remote outposts and outlaw havens

Epuyén
Some 40 km southeast of El Bolsón on Route 258, the little settlement of Epuyén (pronounced epooSHEN, population 2500) is relatively undeveloped, with nothing much to do except stroll around Lago Epuyén. Buses between El Bolsón and Esquel stop (briefly) at Lago Epuyén, though some don't enter the village itself. There's a simple *hostería*, which also has rustic *cabañas* with meals on request. Good picnic grounds with facilities (no camping) and a Centro Cultural overlook the lake. The centre sells *artesanía* and exhibits wood carving. A fire destroyed some trees some years ago, making the area less attractive for walks, but there's a good trek around the lakeside and fishing in the lake.

Cholila
Cholila (population 3000) lies 76 km south of El Bolsón on Route 71, which branches off Route 258 at Km 179. It is a real Patagonian settlement that one day will make a great place to stay, thanks to its lovely setting in broad open landscape with superb views of Lago Cholila, crowned by ranges of mountains all around. For the moment, there's excellent fishing, canoeing and kayaking on rivers nearby, but very little tourist infrastructure; the accommodation is extremely limited, and there's little information.

You might have heard that the reason to visit Cholila is to see the wooden cabins where **Butch Cassidy**, the **Sundance Kid** and **Etta Place** lived between 1901 and 1905 (see box, page 464). You can understand why they hid out here for so long: Cholila still feels remote and untouched, and the views from their land are breathtaking. The cabins themselves were rather evocative, falling to pieces, patched up with bits of wood and with a lichen-stained slatted roof, but, in 2006, the owner of the land started to 'renovate' them, by replacing the tattered timbers with brand new bright orange beams, doors and window

ON THE ROAD

Butch Cassidy and the Sundance Kid

Near Cholila, south of El Bolsón, is a wooden cabin which was home to infamous US bank robbers Butch Cassidy (Robert LeRoy Parker) and the Sundance Kid (Harry Longabaugh) immortalized by Paul Newman and Robert Redford in the 1969 film. In America in the late 1890s, the two were part of a loosely organized gang, known variously as the Train Robbers' Syndicate, the Hole in the Wall Gang and the Wild Bunch, which carried out hold-ups on railway payrolls and banks in the borders of Utah, Colorado and Wyoming. In 1900, the gang celebrated the wedding of one of their colleagues by having their photo taken: a big mistake. The photo was recognized by a Wells Fargo detective, and with their faces decorating Wanted posters across the land, Cassidy, Sundance and his girlfriend Etta Place escaped to Argentina in February 1901.

Using the names Santiago Ryan and Harry Place, the outlaws settled on government land near Cholila and applied to buy it, but Pinkerton detectives hot on their trail soon tracked them down and informed the Argentine authorities. The three lay low in their idyllic rural retreat until 1905, when, needing money to start up elsewhere, the gang raided banks in Villa Mercedes and a particularly audacious job in Río Gallegos. Posing as ranching company agents, they opened a bank account with US$7000, spent two weeks at the best hotels and socialized with the city's high society, and then entered the bank to close their accounts and empty the safe before escaping to Chile. Then Etta returned to the United States, and disappeared from the history books.

Butch and Sundance moved to Bolivia, and worked at the Concordia tin mine, disappearing every now and then to carry out the occasional hold-up. Lack of capital to settle as respectable ranchers was, however, their undoing. In 1908, near Tupiza in southern Bolivia, they seized an Aramayo mining company payroll, but gained only a fraction of the loot they expected. With military patrols in pursuit and the Argentine and Chilean forces alerted, they rode into the village of San Vicente and were recognized. Besieged, they did not, as in the film, run into the awaiting gunfire. Their deaths were not widely reported in the United States until the 1930s, and rumours abounded: Butch was said to have become a businessman, a rancher, a trapper and a Hollywood movie extra, while Sundance had run guns in the Mexican Revolution, migrated to Europe, fought for the Arabs against the Turks in the First World War, sold mineral water, founded a religious cult, and still found time to marry Etta.

frames. As a result, little remains of the authentic cabins where Butch and Sundance lived, and, unless you're a true fan, it might not be worth the considerable effort required to visit them. To get there make a detour from Route 258 heading south from El Bolsón, towards Los Alerces National Park's northern entrance; 13 km north of Cholila along Route 71, look out for a sign on the right; park by the little kiosk and walk 400 m to the cabins. Entry is free.

There is a good walk around **Lago Mosquito**: continue down the road from El Trébol past the lake then take a path to the left, following the river. Cross the river on the farm bridge and continue to the base of the hills to a second bridge. Follow the path to the lake and walk between the lake and the hills, crossing the river via a suspension bridge just past El Trébol – six hours.

Leleque

Ruta 40 (paved) is a faster way to get from El Bolsón to Esquel than Route 71 via Cholila, and this is the route the bus takes. You could stop off at Leleque to see the **Museum of Patagonia (Museo Leleque)** ① *off the R40, Km 1440, 90 km from Esquel and 80 km from El Bolsón, www.benetton.com/patagonia/inglese/index-net.html, Thu-Tue 1100-1700 Mar-Dec, 1100-1900 Jan-Feb, closed May, Jun and Sep, US$3.50*, on the estate owned by Carlo and Luciano **Benetton**, of Italian knitwear fame. There's a beautifully designed exhibition on the lives of indigenous peoples, with dwellings reconstructed of animal skins, using the original techniques, a huge collection of delicate arrowheads and the *boleadoras* for catching cattle. Other moving exhibits focus on the first pioneers in Patagonia, especially the Welsh. There's an attractive café in a reconstructed *boliche* (provisions shop and bar).

Listings South of El Bolsón

Where to stay

Epuyén

$$ El Refugio del Lago
T02945-499025, www.elrefugiodellago. com.ar.
Transfers available on request. Relaxed, comfortable rooms in a lovely wooden house a short walk from the lakeshore, also cabins, dorms (US$23), with breakfast, good meals. Camping US$7 pp in high season. Recommended.

Camping

Puerto Patriada
25 km south of El Bolsón, access through El Hoyo.
Free and paying pitches on the shore of Lago Epuyén, also has *cabañas*.

Cholila

$$$-$$ Cabañas Cerro La Momia
Ruta 71, Villa Lago Rivadavia, T02945-1569 6161, www.cabanascerrolamomia.com.ar.
Very good *cabañas* for up to 6, picturesque setting among fruit orchards and wooded slopes. Restaurant, trips arranged.

Restaurants

Cholila

La Casa de Piedra
R71 outside village, T02945-498056.
Welsh tea room, chocolate cake recommended.

Southern
Lake District

This southernmost area of the lakes is the most Patagonian in feel, with pioneer towns Esquel and Trevelin caught between the wild open steppe to the east and the dramatic mountains of the Andes to the west. Esquel retains the quiet charm of an ordinary country town but has one very famous attraction: it's the starting point for the narrow-gauge railway known as *La Trochita*, an atmospheric way to see the surrounding landscape. The town also has a family ski resort and a few places to trek and mountain bike. Far more tranquil is the village of Trevelin, which still bears signs of its origins as a Welsh colony.

Both towns make good bases for exploring the most unspoilt national park in the Lake District: Los Alerces. With just one road running through it, the park has pristine forested mountains and several stunning lakes, and is best enjoyed on foot. There are wonderful hikes, boat trips to see ancient alerce trees, and some unforgettable views, like Río Arrayanes and Lago Verde. Since this area is less developed for tourism than the rest of the lakes, it's best to hire a car to see it independently if you don't want to do a full-day tour.

One of the most authentic towns in the Lake District, Esquel (population 32,234) is a pleasant, breezy place that still feels like a pioneer outpost, set where the steppe meets the mountains. It's a typical Patagonian country town, with many buildings dating from the early 1900s and battered pickups filling the streets in the late-morning bustle when local farmers come into town. There are few tourist sights, but it's all the more appealing for that. It is the starting point for the narrow-gauge railway, *La Trochita*, made famous by Paul Theroux as the *Old Patagonian Express* and is the best base for visiting the Parque Nacional Los Alerces and for skiing at La Hoya in winter. The tranquil village of Trevelin, where the Welsh heritage is more in evidence, is just 25 km away.

Sights

The main point of visiting Esquel is to get to Los Alerces, or Trevelin, but it's a pleasant place to walk around. There aren't any sights as such, although there is the **Museo Lituano Olgbrun** ① *Calle Los Ñires 1038, T02945-450536, see Facebook*, a few kilometres south of town, near the road to Trevelin. This is a Lithuanian museum with a well-stocked gift shop. All the food shops and services you need are contained within a few blocks east of Avenida Alvear, between Mitre and the wide Avenida Fontana.

La Trochita

Estación Viejo Expreso Patagónico, 6 blocks north of the town centre at the corner of Brun and Roggero, T02945-451403 in Esquel, T02945-495190 in El Maitén, www.patagoniaexpress. com/el_trochita.htm. Schedules change frequently. It's best to check the website schedules before embarking. The train runs twice daily Mon-Sat in Jan and much less frequently in winter, US$42, under 5s free; tour operators in town sell tickets.

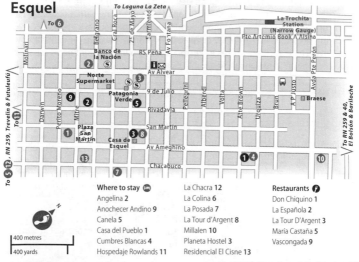

Esquel

To Laguna La Zeta

To **6**

To **11**

RN 259, Trevelin & Futuleufú

To **5 12**, RN 259, Trevelin & Futuleufú

To RN 259 & 40, El Bolsón & Bariloche

La Trochita Station (Narrow Gauge)
Pte Artemio Rook A Alsina

Banco de la Nación
RS Peña
Av Alvear
Norte Supermarket
Patagonia Verde
9 de Julio
Rivadavia
San Martín
Av Ameghino
Chacabuco
Plaza San Martín
Casa de Esquel
Braese

400 metres
400 yards

Where to stay		Restaurants
Angelina 2	La Chacra 12	Don Chiquino 1
Anochecer Andino 9	La Colina 6	La Española 2
Canela 5	La Posada 7	La Tour D'Argent 3
Casa del Pueblo 1	La Tour d'Argent 8	María Castaña 5
Cumbres Blancas 4	Millalen 10	Vascongada 9
Hospedaje Rowlands 11	Planeta Hostel 3	
	Residencial El Cisne 13	

The famous narrow-gauge railway, *La Trochita* (*Old Patagonian Express*), also known in Spanish as *El Viejo Expreso Patagónico*, chugs off into the steppe from a pretty old station north of town. While it's obviously a tourist experience, this is a thoroughly enjoyable trip, and as the steam train rumbles across the lovely valleys and mountains of the *precordillera* on tracks just 75 cm wide, you'll find yourself wanting to know how it works. There's Spanish and English commentary along the way. The quaint carriages each have little wood stoves, and there's a small tea room on board, but it's worth waiting for the home-made cakes (and handicrafts) for sale at the wild and remote Mapuche hamlet of **Nahuel Pan**, where the train stops, and where you'll hear an interesting explanation of how the engine works. Recommended.

In high season a service also runs from El Maitén at the northernmost end of the line to Desvío Thomae (55 km) three days a week in July (once or twice a week in other months), US$42.

La Hoya
15 km north of Esquel, information from Club Andino Esquel, Pellegrini 787, T02945-453248, see Facebook, www.skilahoya.com, www.cerrolahoya.com.

There's good skiing on high-quality powder snow over a long season at this low-key family resort. It is popular with Argentines, since it's one of cheapest and friendliest. There are 22 km of pistes, many of them suitable for kids or beginners, with good challenging pistes too, and seven ski lifts. There are daily buses to La Hoya from Esquel leaving at 0900, 0930 and returning at 1730, US$11.50. A skipass costs US$36 per day in high season, with reductions for a week or longer. Equipment can be rented.

Walks around Esquel
There are some challenging walks and mountain bike trails in the surrounding mountains. See the map *Sendas y Bosques* (Walks and Forests) for El Bolsón, Lago Puelo and Los Alerces, which has the trails clearly marked. It's an easy climb along a clear path to **Laguna La Zeta**, 5 km from the centre of town, with good views and a lake with birdlife. From there, head further north up the Río Percey or towards Cañadón Huemul. The path is signposted from the end of Avenida La Fontana. Another good hike, with spectacular views, is to **Cerro La Cruz**, five hours return; walk from the centre of town signposted from the end of the street 25 de Mayo. There are longer hikes to **Cerro Veinte Uno** (five to eight hours return) and the pointy cone of Cerro Nahual Pan (eight hours return).

Listings Esquel *map page 467.*

Tourist information

For information on Los Alerces and the whole area, see www.patagoniaexpress.com.

Tourist office
In a little hut on the corner of Av Alvear and Sarmiento, T02945-451927, www.esquel.tur.ar. Mon-Fri 0800-2000 Sat-Sun 0900-2000.
Friendly enough, but doesn't seem to have much information. They do hand out a useful town map, however, and another leaflet with a yellow map of Los Alerces National Park showing all access and accommodation in the park, as well as the crossing to Chile via Paso Futaleufú. You might have to press them patiently for bus timetables.

Where to stay

Ask at tourist office for lodgings in private houses.

$$$ Angelina
Av Alvear 758, T02945-452763, www.
hosteriaangelina.com.ar. High season only.
Good value, welcoming, big breakfast,
English and Italian spoken.

$$$ Canela
Los Notros y Los Radales, Villa Ayelén,
on road to Trevelin, T02945-453890,
www.canelaesquel.com.
Bed and breakfast and tea room in a lovely,
quiet residential area, English spoken, owner
knowledgeable about Patagonia.

$$$ Cumbres Blancas
Av Ameghino 1683, T02945-455100,
www.cumbresblancas.com.ar.
Attractive modern building, a little out of the
centre, very comfortable, spacious rooms,
sauna, gym, airy restaurant. Recommended.

$$$-$$ La Chacra
Km 5 on Ruta 259 towards Trevelin, T02945-
452802, www.lachacrapatagonia.com.
Relaxing, spacious rooms, huge breakfast,
Welsh and English spoken.

$$ La Posada
Chacabuco 905, T02945-454095,
www.laposadaesquel.blogspot.com.ar.
Tasteful B&B in quiet part of town, lovely
lounge, very comfortable, excellent value.

$$ La Tour D'Argent
San Martín 1063, T02945-454612,
www.latourdargent.com.ar.
Bright, comfortable, family-run,
very good value.

$ pp Anochecer Andino
Av Ameghino 482, 4 blocks from
the commercial centre and 2 from
the mountains, T02945-450498.
Basic, helpful, can organize ski passes
and trips. They also can provide dinner
and have a bar.

$ pp Casa del Pueblo
San Martín 661, T02945-450581,
www.esquelcasadelpueblo.com.ar.

Smallish rooms but good atmosphere
(**$$** double), laundry, organizes
adventure activities.

$ pp Hospedaje Rowlands
Behind Rivadavia 330, T02945-452578,
gales01@hotmail.com.
Warm family welcome, Welsh spoken,
breakfast extra, basic rooms with shared
bath and a double with bath (**$**), good value.

$ pp Planeta Hostel
Alvear 1021, T02945-456846,
www.planetahostel.com.
4- to 6-bed dorms (US$20-22), doubles **$$$**,
shared bath, specialize in snowboarding,
climbing and mountain biking, English spoken.

$ Residencial El Cisne
Chacabuco 778, T02945-452256.
Basic small rooms, hot water, quiet,
well kept, good value, breakfast extra.

Camping

La Colina
Darwin 1400, T02945-455264,
www.lacolinaesquel.com.ar.
Complex a little out of the centre with
cramped dorms (US$14.50 pp), doubles
US$43 and shady camping, US$7.50 per tent
or vehicle.

Millalen
Av Ameghino 2063 (5 blocks from bus
terminal), T02945-456164.
Good services and cabins.

Restaurants

$$ Don Chiquino
Behind Av Ameghino 1641, T02945-450035,
see Facebook.
Delicious pasta served in a fun atmosphere
with plenty of games brought to the tables
by magician owner Tito. Recommended.

$$ La Española
Rivadavia 740, T02945-451509.
Excellent beef, salad bar and tasty pasta.
Recommended.

$$ Vascongada
9 de Julio 655, T02945-452229.
Traditional style, trout and other
local specialities.

$ La Tour D'Argent
San Martín 1063, T02945-454612,
www.latourdargent.com.ar.
Delicious local specialities, good-value set
meals and a warm ambience in this popular,
traditional restaurant.

Cafés

María Castaña
Rivadavia y 25 de Mayo, T02945 451 752,
see Facebook.
Popular, good coffee.

Shopping

Braese, *9 de Julio 1540, T02945-451014,*
www.braese.com.ar. Home-made chocolates
and other regional specialities.
Casa de Esquel, *25 de Mayo 415.* A range of
rare books on Patagonia, also souvenirs.

What to do

The tourist office (see Tourist information,
above) has a list of fishing guides and
companies hiring out equipment. For details
of skiing at **La Hoya**, 15 km north, see above.

Tour operators
Aucan Travel, *Alsina 1632, T02945-1552 5052,*
www.aucantravel.com.ar. Recommended
operator that runs trips to Los Alerces and
Lago Puelo, among others.
Frontera Sur, *Sarmiento 784, T02945-450505,*
www.fronterasur.net. Good company offering
adventure tourism of all sorts, as well as more
traditional trips, ski equipment and trekking.
Patagonia Verde, *9 de Julio 926, T02945-*
454396, www.patagonia-verde.com.ar. Boat
trips to El Alerzal on Lago Menéndez, rafting
on Río Corcovado, tickets for *La Trochita*

and for Ruta 40 to El Calafate. Also range of
adventure activities, horse riding, short local
excursions and ski passes. Ask about lodging
at **Lago Verde**. English spoken. Excellent
company, very professional.

Transport

Air
The airport (T02945-451676) is 20 km east
of town by paved road, US$15-18 by taxi,
US$14 by bus. There are direct flights to
Buenos Aires with **Aerolíneas Argentinas**.

Bus
There's a smart modern bus terminal at
Av Alvear 1871, T02945-451584, 6 blocks
from the main commercial centre (US$2-3
by taxi). It has toilets, a *kiosko*, *locutorio* with
internet, café, tourist information desk and
left luggage.
  To **Buenos Aires** with **Rápido Argentina**
(T800-333 1970), 25 hrs, US$142, otherwise
connect in Bariloche. To **Bariloche** (via
El Bolsón, 2½ hrs), 4-5 hrs, US$19-24, with
Andesmar, **Rápido Argentina** and others.
To **Trelew**, US$44-73, 8-9 hrs overnight, with
Don Otto. To **Río Gallegos** (for connections
to El Calafate or Ushuaia), take a bus to Trelew
and change there. To **Trevelin** with **Jacobsen**
(T02945-454676, www.transportejacobsen.
com.ar), Mon-Fri hourly 0600-2300, less
frequent on weekends, US$1. To **Río Pico**,
via Tecka and Gobernador Costa, Mon, Wed
and Fri at 0900, 4½ hrs, with **Jacobsen**. To
Comodoro Rivadavia, daily at 1200 and
2100 with **ETAP**.

Car hire
Los Alerces, Sarmiento 763, T02945-456008,
www.losalercesrentacar.com.ar. Good value,
good cars, top service.

Train
See page 467.

The pretty village of Trevelin, 25 km southwest of Esquel, was once an offshoot of the Welsh colony of Gaiman on the Atlantic coast (see page 500), founded when the Welsh travelled west to find further lands for growing corn. The name means Town (*tre*) of the Mill (*velin*) in Welsh. You can still hear Welsh spoken here, and there is plenty of evidence of Welsh heritage in several good little museums around the town. With a backdrop of snow-capped mountains, the village is an appealing place to rest for a few days, to go fishing and rafting on nearby Río Futuleufu, or to see the beautiful waterfalls at the reserve of Nant-y-fall.

Sights

Trevelin remains a quiet village of 9123 inhabitants with a strong sense of community, and its history is manifest in several sights. The Welsh chapel (1910), **La Capilla Bethel**, can be visited, with a guided tour to fill you in on a bit of history. A fine old flour mill (1918) houses the **Museo Histórico Regional** ① *Molino Viejo 488, T02945-480545, daily 1100-2000, US$4*, which has fascinating artefacts from the Welsh colony. The **Museo Cartref Taid** ① *El Malacara s/n, ask for directions in the tourist office, T02945-480108, Mon-Fri 1100-2000, Sat-Sun 1400-1830, US$4.25*, is another great place for exploring the Welsh pioneer past. It's the house of John Evans, one of Trevelin's first settlers, and filled with his belongings. There's another extraordinary and touching relic of his life in **La Tumba del Caballo Malacara** ① *200 m from main plaza, guided tours are available, US$4.25*, a private garden containing the grave of his horse, Malacara, who once saved his life.

Eisteddfods are still held here every year in October, and you'll be relieved to hear that **Té Galés**, that other apparently traditional Welsh ritual, is alive and well in several tea rooms, which offer a ridiculous excess of delicious cakes. Extensive research has established that **Nain Maggie** is, in fact, the town's best. There are good day walks in idyllic scenery around the town; get directions on routes from the tourist office. It's also a good area for horse riding or mountain biking. For more on the history of Welsh emigration to the region, see box, page 499.

Around Trevelin

For a gentle outing with quite the best insight into the Welsh history in Patagonia, visit the rural flour mill **Molino Nant Fach** ① *Route 259, T02945-15-698058, entry US$4.25*, 22 km southwest towards the Chilean border. This beautiful flour mill was built by Merfyn Evans, descendant of the town's founder, Thomas Dalar Evans, as an exact replica of the first mill built in the town in 1899. Merfyn's fascinating tour (in Spanish, but English booklet available to read) recounts a now familiar tale of the Argentine government's persistent mismanagement of natural resources and industry, through the suppression of the Welsh prize-winning wheat industry. It's a beautiful spot, and Merfyn tells the rather tragic story in a wonderfully entertaining way. Highly recommended.

Before you reach Molino Nant Fach, look out for the **Nant-y-fall Falls** on the same road (Route 259), 17 km southwest of Trevelin, heading to the Chilean border. These are a series of spectacular waterfalls reached by an easy 1½-hour walk along a trail through lovely forest. There's an entry charge of US$4 per person (reductions for children and local residents). Guides will take you to all seven falls.

Route 259 continues to the Chilean border at the spectacularly beautiful Paso Futaleufú. For further details, see box, page 477.

Fishing is popular in many local rivers and lakes, most commonly in Río Futuleufú, and Corintos, and Lagos Rosario and Corcovado. The season runs from the end of November to mid-April, and the tourist office (see Tourist information, below) can advise on guides and where to go.

Listings Trevelin

Tourist information

Tourist office
Central octagonal plaza, T02945-480120, www.trevelin.gob.ar. Mon-Fri 0800-2200, Sat and Sun 0900-2200.
The enthusiastic and helpful staff speak English and can provide maps and advice on accommodation and fishing.

Where to stay

$$$ Casa de Piedra
Almirante Brown 244, T02945-480357, www.casadepiedratrevelin.com.
Stone and wood cottage in the suburbs. King-size beds, heating and a charming common area, popular.

$$ Pezzi
Sarmiento 351, T02945-480146, see Facebook.
Charming family house with a beautiful garden, English spoken. Recommended.

Camping
Many sites, especially on the road to Futaleufú and Chile; also many *cabañas*; ask for full list at the tourist office, see Tourist information, above.

Restaurants

$$ Parrilla Oregón
Av San Martín y JM Thomas, T02945-480408.
Large meals (particularly breakfasts), set menus based on *parrilla* and pastas.

$ Nain Maggie
Perito Moreno 179, T02945-480232, www.nainmaggie.guiapatagonia.net.
Tea room, offering *té galés* and *torta negra*, expensive but good.

What to do

Gales al Sur, *Patagonia 186, T02945-453379, www.galesalsur.com.ar.* Tours to Chilean border; Los Alerces National Park and Futaleufú dam; *La Trochita.* Recommended for their rafting, trekking, biking, 4WD and horse-riding trips. Friendly and English spoken.

Transport

Bus
To **Esquel**, Jacobsen (T02945-454676, www.transportejacobsen.com.ar), Mon-Fri hourly from 0645 (last at 2345), Sat and Sun less frequent, US$1. To **Paso Futaleufú** (Chilean border) with **Jacobsen**, Jan and Feb daily, Mar-Dec Mon, Wed and Fri.

emerald waters and ancient forests

One of the most magnificent and untouched expanses of wilderness in the whole Andes region, this national park was established to protect the stately alerce trees (*Fitzroya cupressoides*). The alerce is among the longest-living tree species in the world, and there are some specimens in the park that are over 4000 years old. They grow deep in the Valdivian rainforest that carpets these mountains a rich velvety green, beside vivid blue Lago Futalaufquen and emerald Lago Verde. There are several good hikes, plus rafting and fishing, in the park, and idyllic lakeside campsites and *hosterías*, making this a great place to spend a few days.

The park is enormous at over 200,000 ha, and it remains the most virgin park in the whole Lake District, since much of it is only accessible on foot. There are four large lakes: navy-blue **Lago Futalaufquen**, with fine fishing; **Lago Menéndez**, which can be crossed by boat to visit the ancient *alerce* trees; the exquisite green **Lago Verde**; and the almost inaccessible **Lago Amutui Quimei**. In order to protect this fragile environment, access by car is possible only to the eastern side of the park, via *ripio* Route 71, which runs between Cholila and Trevelin alongside the eastern side of Lagos Futalaufquen, Verde and Rivadavia. The western side of the park, where rainfall is highest, has areas of Valdivian forest, and can only be accessed by boat or by hiking to Lago Krügger.

Walks

For all walks, get the *Sendas y Bosques* (Walks and Forests) map and book for El Bolsón, Lago Puelo and Los Alerces. Maps are 1:200,000, laminated and easy to read, and the book is full of great walks, with English summaries and detailed directions in Spanish (www.guiasendasybosques.com.ar). The park office Intendencia also has leaflets listing the walks, but these have insufficient detail.

Essential Parque Nacional Los Alerces

Access

There are two main entrances to the park, both off Route 71: one is at the northern end of Lago Rivadavia (south of Cholila), and the other is 12 km south of Lago Futulaufquen. Head from this entrance to the southern tip of the lake, 52 km west of Esquel, to reach the Intendencia (park office) with a **visitor centre** (T02945-471015, www.parquesnacionales.gob.ar, see also www.losalercesparquenacional.blogspot.com). Helpful *guardaparques* give out maps and advise on walks.

Right by the Intendencia, and less than 2 km from Route 71, **Villa Futulaufquen** is a little hamlet with a petrol station, *locutorio*, food shops and a restaurant, **El Abuelo Monje**. Fishing licences can be obtained at the the Intendencia.

Entry fees

Park entrance costs US$10.

Getting around

A daily bus runs along Route 71 in each direction, picking up and dropping off passengers at lakeside campsites and *hosterías*, and also at the petrol station opposite the Intendencia. Ask at the petrol station for bus times, or contact the visitor centre in Villa Futalaufquen, above. See Transport, page 476.

Cave paintings There are *pinturas rupestres* to be found just 40 minutes' stroll from the park Intendencia (Km 1). You'll also pass a waterfall and a mirador with panoramic views over Lago Futulaufquen.

Cascada Arroyo This is a satisfying and easy four-hour walk south of Villa Futalaufquen to see waterfalls, passing various miradors.

Pasarella Lago Verde Signposted off Route 71 at Km 34.3. The most beautiful walk in the whole park and unmissable, no matter how little time you have, is across the

Parque Nacional Los Alerces

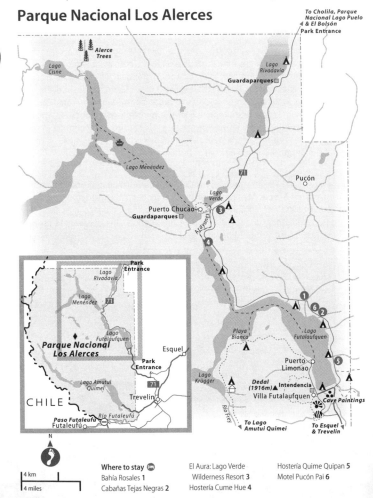

suspension bridge over Río Arrayanes to heavenly Lago Verde. A self-guided trail leads around a peninsula to Puerto Chucao on Lago Menéndez, where boat trips begin (see below). Go in the early evening to see all kinds of birdlife from the beach by Lago Verde, including swifts and swallows darting all around you. While you're in the area, take a quick 20-minute stroll up to **Mirador Lago Verde** for gorgeous views up and down the whole valley. From here you can appreciate the string of lakes, running from Lago Futulaufquen in the south to Lago Rivadavia in the north.

Cerro Dedal For a great day hike, there is a longer trek up Cerro Dedal (1916 m). This is a circular walk, at least eight hours return, with a steep climb from the Intendencia and wonderful views over the lake and mountains further west. Register with *guardaparques* and get detailed instructions. You're required to register between 0800-1000. Carry plenty of water. The path up Cerro Dedal was closed due to a fire in early 2016. It may or may not reopen by the time this book is published.

Lago Krügger There is also a long but rewarding two- to three-day (12- to 14-hour) hike though *coihue* forest to the southernmost tip of **Lago Krügger**, where there is a *refugio* (open only in January and February) and campsite, as well as a *guardaparques'* office. Here you can take a boat back to Puerto Limonao on Lago Futalaufquen, but check when the boat is running before you set off and always register with the park's Intendencia. From Lago Krügger, you could walk south along the course of Río Frey, though there is no *refugio* here.

Boat trips
Boat trips leave from Puerto Limonao at the southwestern end of Lago Futalaufquen: follow signs up the western side of the lake, just for a few kilometres. They cross Lago Futalaufquen and travel along the pea-green Río Arrayanes, which is lined with the extraordinary cinnamon-barked *arrayán* trees. Even more spectacular are the trips from Puerto Chucao, which is reached from the suspension bridge crossing Lago Verde, halfway along Route 71. These cross Lago Menéndez (1½ hours) where you land, and walk a short distance to see a majestic 2600-year-old alerce tree, known as 'el abuelo' (the grandfather). From here you walk to the hidden and silent jade-green Lago Cisne and then back past the rushing whitewaters of Río Cisne: an unforgettable experience. Boats also go from Puerto Limonao to Lago Krügger, or you can trek there and take the boat back (see above), but check the boat times before you set off. Boats sail in summer only.

Listings Parque Nacional Los Alerces *map page 474.*

Where to stay

$$$$ El Aura: Lago Verde Wilderness Resort
T011-4813 4340 (Buenos Aires),
www.elaurapatagonia.com.
Exquisite taste in these 3 stone cabins and a guesthouse on the shore of Lago Verde. Luxury in every respect, attention to detail, eco-friendly. Impressive place.

$$$ Hostería Quime Quipan
East side of Lago Futalaufquen, T02945-425423, www.hosteriaquimequipan.com.ar.
Comfortable rooms with lake views, dinner included. Recommended.

$$ Bahía Rosales
Northeast side of Lago Futalaufquen, T02945-15-403413, www.bahiarosales.com.
Comfortable *cabaña* for 6 with kitchenette and bath, **$** pp in small basic cabin without

bath, and camping in open ground, hot showers, restaurant, all recommended. There are also plans to add dome tents.

$$ Cabañas Tejas Negras
East side Lago Futalaufquen, T02945-471046, www.tejasnegras.com.
Really comfortable *cabañas* for 4, also good camp site, and tea room.

$$ Motel Pucón Pai
Next to Tejas Negras, T02945-451425.
Slightly spartan rooms, but good restaurant, recommended for fishing; basic campsite with hot showers.

Camping
Several campsites at Villa Futalaufquen and on the shores of lakes Futalaufquen, Rivadavia, Verde and Río Arrayanes.

What to do

Agencies in Esquel or Trevelin run tours including the boat trip across Lago Menéndez to the alerce trees. For short guided trips, ask at the Intendencia in Villa Futalaufquen. Lago Futalaufquen has some of the best fishing in this part of Argentina (the season runs end Nov to mid-Apr); local guides offer fishing trips and boat transport. Ask in the Intendencia or at **Hostería Cume Hue**.

Transport

Bus
Transportes Esquel, Alvear 1871 (Esquel) T02945-453529, www.transportesesquel. com.ar, runs from Esquel bus terminal daily at 0800 along the east side of Lago Futalaufquen, US$4.50, and ending at **Lago Puelo**, US$11.50.

South of Esquel
where wilderness meets emptiness

The iconic Ruta 40 continues (paved) south from Esquel across very deserted landscapes that give you a taste for the full experience of Patagonia. It's a tricky section for travel by public transport, since there are few settlements or services along this section of road until you reach the small town of Perito Moreno (about 14 hours' drive).

At Tecka, Km 101, Route 62 (paved) branches off east and follows the valley of the Río Chubut to Trelew: another lonely road. (West of Tecka is the Paso Palena border with Chile, see box, opposite.) Ruta 40 continues south to Gobernador Costa, a small service centre for the estancias in this area on the Río Genoa at Km 183. Buses go up and down Ruta 40 to the town of Perito Moreno, and from here you can take a daily service on to El Chaltén or El Calafate; ask in Esquel's bus terminal.

Río Pico *Colour map 5, C2.*
Río Pico (population 1000) lies in a wide green valley close to the Andes and has become quietly known among trout-fishing circles as a very desirable place to fish. Permits are available from the *municipalidad* in Gobernador Costa. Río Pico is the site of an early 20th-century German settlement and some old houses remain from that period. Nearby are several lakes that are good for fishing and free camping; ask locals for hitching advice.

The northern shore of Lago Tres, 23 km west of town, is a peaceful and remote place, with a rich birdlife and wild strawberries at the end of January. Some 30 km north of Río Pico lies the huge Lago Vintter, reached by Route 44. There are also smaller lakes good for trout fishing.

BORDER CROSSING
Argentina–Chile

There are two border crossings south of Esquel, the spectacularly beautiful Paso Futaleufú and Paso Palena. On the Chilean side roads from these crossings both link up to the route to Chaitén.

Paso Futaleufú
Paso Futaleufú is 70 km southwest of Esquel via Trevelin and is reached by Route 259 (*ripio* from Trevelin). The border is crossed by a bridge over the Río Futaleufú, and formalities should take no longer than an hour. See www.gendarmeria.gov.ar.
Argentine immigration and customs On the Argentine side of the bridge, open 0900-2100.
Chilean immigration and customs In Futaleufú, 9 km west of the border, open 0800-2000.
Transport There are regular buses to Paso Futaleufú from Esquel and Trevelin (see Transport, page 472). From the border, Futaleufú (T+56 65-272 1458) runs a connecting bus service three times a week December-March; two days a week the rest of the year) to Futuleufú and on to Chaitén. From Chaitén there are services to Coyhaique. Cars must have special papers and the registration number etched into all windows: advise your hire company when booking.

Paso Palena
Paso Palena, or Río Encuentro, lies 120 km southeast of Esquel and is reached by Route 17 from Trevelin, which runs to Corcovado, 75 km east of Tecka (reached by *ripio* road). From Corcovado it is 26 km west to the border.
Argentine immigration and customs At the border, open daily 0900-2100.
Chilean immigration At Palena, 11 km west of border, open 0800-2000.
Fronteras del Sur buses run between Palena and Futaleufú (T+56 (0)65-272 1360).

South of Gobernador Costa

At Km 221, Ruta 40 (poor *ripio*) forks southwest through the town of **Alto Río Senguer** from which visits can be made to the relatively unexplored Lago Fontana and Lago La Plata. Provincial Route 20 (paved) heads almost directly south for 81 km, before turning east towards Sarmiento and Comodoro Rivadavia. At La Puerta del Diablo, in the valley of the lower Río Senguer, Route 20 intersects provincial Route 22, which joins with Ruta 40 at the town of Río Mayo (see page 521). This latter route is completely paved and preferable to Ruta 40 for those travelling long distance.

Listings South of Esquel

Transport

Bus
To **Esquel** via **Gobernador Costa** and **Tecka**, Mon, Wed and Fri at 1400, 4½ hrs, with **Jacobsen** (T02945-454676, www.transportejacobsen.com.ar).

Patagonia

Earth's natural wonders converge on rugged steppe

Patagonia has earned an almost mythic status as a travel destination, and for good reason. Its windswept landscapes are cinematic in their beauty, and its immensity and sprawling emptiness are at once liberating and lonely.

No wonder it has attracted pioneers and runaways from the modern world. From Welsh settlers to Butch and Sundance; from Bruce Chatwin to Ernesto 'Che' Guevara riding the Ruta 40, Patagonia invites adventure.

East of the Andes, Patagonia makes up the whole southernmost cone of the Americas: a vast expanse of treeless steppe, dotted with the occasional sheep estancia. At its edges whales bask and sea lions cavort at Península Valdés, and descendants of the Welsh still live in Gaiman. Thousands of handprints are testimony to Stone Age life at Cueva de las Manos, and there are two petrified forests of mighty fallen monkey puzzle trees.

Take the Ruta 40 south, and you'll travel hundreds of kilometres without seeing a soul, until the magnificent granite towers of Mount Fitz Roy rise up from the flat plains: a trekking mecca. El Calafate is the base for boat trips to the Perito Moreno Glacier: put on your crampons to walk its sculpted turquoise curves, or escape to splendidly isolated Estancia Cristina. Once you've seen Upsala Glacier stretching out into a milky Prussian-blue lake, silent and pristine, you'll be addicted.

Best for
Glaciers ▪ Trekking ▪ Wildlife

Footprint picks

★ **Península Valdés**, page 493

The greatest concentration of marine life can be found on this peninsula near Puerto Madryn.

★ **Travelling along Ruta 40**, page 519

Lose yourself on Ruta 40, where the highways stretches endlessly out to the horizon, and there's nothing but the steppe and wind to keep you company.

★ **Staying at a Patagonian estancia**, page 536

Live, if only briefly, the rugged life of a gaucho on the windswept plains of Patagonia.

★ **Perito Moreno and Upsala glaciers**, pages 541 and 542

Seeing these majestic walls of ice calve into the turquoise waters below is a natural phenomenon not to be missed.

★ **Trekking around Cerro Fitz Roy**, page 543

Some of the best trekking in the world is found amid the twin granite peaks of Fitz Roy.

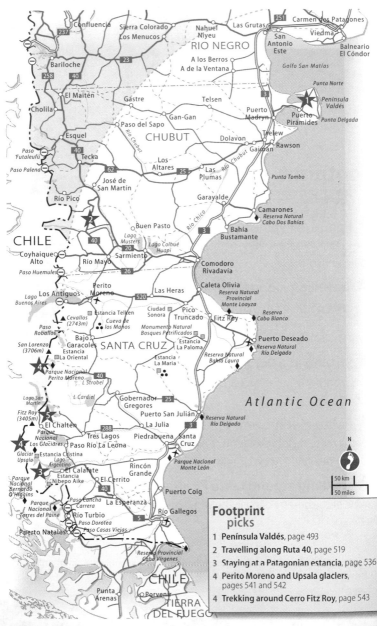

Footprint picks

1 **Península Valdés**, page 493
2 **Travelling along Ruta 40**, page 519
3 **Staying at a Patagonian estancia**, page 536
4 **Perito Moreno and Upsala glaciers**, pages 541 and 542
4 **Trekking around Cerro Fitz Roy**, page 543

Northern
Atlantic Coast
& Puerto Madryn

The sight of a mother and baby whale basking in quiet waters just a few metres from your boat is an unforgettably moving sight. Not, perhaps, what you expected to see after travelling for days through the wild, unpopulated, open plains of Patagonia. But the whole Atlantic coast hosts huge colonies of marine life, and there is no region quite as spectacular as Península Valdés. This wide splay of land stretching into the Atlantic from a narrow isthmus enclosing a gulf of protected water attracts an astonishing array of animals which come to breed here each spring, most famously the southern right whales, who can be seen from September to November.

The small breezy town of Puerto Madryn is the best base for exploring the peninsula, though there are estancias on Valdés itself. Just to the south, Trelew is worth a visit for its superb palaeontological museum, and as a base to reach the old Welsh pioneer villages of Gaiman and Dolavon further west. If you're heading south by road, consider stopping off at historic Carmen de Patagones, a quaint Patagonian town. Patagonia's fine estancias start here, with riding and sheep mustering at La Luisa.

Essential Patagonia

Finding your feet

Strictly speaking, Patagonia is the whole southern cone of South America, combining all parts of Argentina and Chile, south of the Río Colorado, which runs from west to east, just north of Viedma. It includes the Andes, running north–south (marking the Chilean border) and therefore the Lake District, which has been given its own chapter in this book, see pages 388-477. The Patagonia chapter includes all of Argentine Patagonia apart from the Lake District and Tierra del Fuego, the island at the very bottom, which also has its own chapter, see pages 588-621.

The main centres, with good accommodation and services, are Puerto Madryn for the northern Atlantic coast, El Calafate on the edge of Parque Nacional Los Glaciares, Río Gallegos for the southern Atlantic coast (these all have airports) and El Chaltén for Cerro (Mount) Fitz Roy.

Access

Fortunately Patagonia is served by good public transport. There are daily flights from Buenos Aires to Viedma, Puerto Madryn (in high season), Trelew, Comodoro Rivadavia, Río Gallegos, El Calafate's airport Lago Argentino and also to Ushuaia. **Aerolíneas Argentinas** and **LADE** fly these routes, and flights fill up very quickly, so it's vital that you book in advance in the summer (December to March) and during the winter ski season for Ushuaia (July and August). At other times of the year, flights can be booked with just a few days' warning. The Chilean airline, **Lan Chile**, also flies to Ushuaia from Argentine destinations as well as from Santiago in Chile.

Getting around

Patagonia is vast, and it's no surprise that getting around takes some organization.

Air

Flying between the main towns in Patagonia is complicated and may involve flying all the way back to Buenos Aires, since connecting flights within Patagonia are only provided by the army airline **LADE**. Instead, to get between Puerto Madryn and Ushuaia or El Calafate, for example, your best bet is an overnight bus.

Road

Long-distance buses cover the whole of Argentina and are very comfortable – if you choose *coche-cama* (bed seat) – and reasonably cheap. There are several daily services between all the towns in Patagonia, though tourist routes book up quickly. There are two main routes south: Ruta 3 along the Atlantic coast and Ruta 40 (made famous by Ernesto 'Che' Guevara on his motorcycle) running along the Argentine side of the Andes. This road is notoriously bleak and empty, mostly unsurfaced, and there is very little traffic, but a number of bus companies run daily services in summer for tourists between the lovely oasis of Los Antiguos on Lago Buenos Aires and El Chaltén. From Los Antiguos you can reach Chile and the Lago General Carrera, and from El Chaltén there are frequent services to El Calafate. Some buses stop over at Cueva de las Manos, and if you have the time (14 hours) it's a great way to get a feel for Patagonia, with fine views of the Andes and plenty of wildlife to be spotted.

Hiring a car isn't recommended if you're travelling alone because the elements are harsh, distances are enormous and it's not a place to be stranded alone. However, hire companies will now let you rent a car in one place and drop it off in another for a rather large but worthwhile fee, so you could consider combining flying with driving.

Driving and cycling in Patagonia require care and patience. Most of the roads are *ripio* (gravel) limiting driving speeds to 60 kph, or slower where surfaces are poor, and it's worth driving your hire car very carefully, as there are huge fines for dents or turning them over. Carry spare fuel, as service stations may be as much as 300 km apart, carry warm clothing in case of breakdown at night, and make sure your car has antifreeze. There are lots of cattle grids (watch out for signs saying *guardaganados*) to be crossed with care. Hitchhiking is difficult, even on Ruta 3 in the tourist season, and hitching along Ruta 40 is only possible with a lot of luck and a little assistance from locals; it helps to speak good Spanish.

The Ruta 40 has become a long-distance favourite among hardy cyclists, and it is an amazing experience. But do your research first: winds are fierce; there are few places to get food and water and a complete absence of shade. A tent is essential, with camping allowed pretty much everywhere, but very few *hosterías* or places to stay.

Train

One of the country's few long-distance railways, the **Tren Patagónico** (www.trenpatagonico-sa.com.ar), runs between Bariloche in the Lake District and Viedma on the east coast, a comfortable overnight service that also carries cars. Check in advance if the service is running.

When to go

The summer months from December to mid-April are best for trekking. However, January should be avoided everywhere but the most remote places if possible, as this is when most Argentines go on holiday, and

transport and accommodation are both heavily booked. Most hotels close from mid-April until mid-November, and many bus services don't operate. This is because temperatures in the south plummet to -20°C, making it very inhospitable. For Península Valdés, the season for spotting whales is between September and November, when all services are open.

Money

Traveller's cheques are hard to change throughout Patagonia; depending on the state of the Argentine economy, it's easier and safer to use credit or debit cards to withdraw cash. There are ATMs in all the main towns in Patagonia.

Tourist information

There are tourist offices in even small towns, although the best ones are inevitably in El Calafate and El Chaltén, with excellent information centres in Puerto Madryn, Trelew and Río Gallegos. Many have good websites, some with links to hotels for booking accommodation: **Puerto Madryn** and **Península Valdés**, www.madryn.gov.ar; **Chubut province** (northern half of Patagonia), www.chubut.gov.ar; **Santa Cruz province** (southern half of Patagonia), www.santacruz.gov.ar; **El Chaltén**, www.elchalten.com; **El Calafate**, www.elcalafate.gov.ar. Also see the national parks site, www.parquesnacionales.gov.ar. For further information on towns and tourist services, see www.interpatagonia.com.

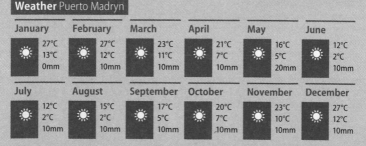

Weather Puerto Madryn					
January ☀ 27°C 13°C 0mm	**February** ☀ 27°C 12°C 10mm	**March** ☀ 23°C 11°C 10mm	**April** ☀ 21°C 7°C 10mm	**May** ☀ 16°C 5°C 20mm	**June** ☀ 12°C 2°C 10mm
July ☀ 12°C 2°C 10mm	**August** ☀ 15°C 2°C 10mm	**September** ☀ 17°C 5°C 10mm	**October** ☀ 20°C 7°C 10mm	**November** ☀ 23°C 10°C 10mm	**December** ☀ 27°C 12°C 10mm

These two towns straddle the broad sweep of the Río Negro, about 250 km south of Bahía Blanca, and while neither has any real tourist attractions, you could stop off here on the way south and find warm hospitality and a couple of decent places to stay. The two towns face each other and share a river, but little else.

Capital of Río Negro province, Viedma, on the south bank, was founded as Mercedes de Patagonia in 1779 but was destroyed almost immediately by floods, after which Carmen de Patagones was founded on higher ground on the north bank later that same year. The little town prospered for many years by shipping salt to Buenos Aires. However, in 1827, it was the site of an extraordinary battle and was destroyed. Poor old Viedma was rebuilt, but destroyed again by floods in 1899.

Now, it's a rather dull place, rather less attractive than Patagones, and serves as the administrative centre for the province of Río Negro. Patagones (as it's called by the locals) has more tangible history, with the towers of a handsome church thrusting above charming streets of 19th-century adobe houses near the river, where the tiny ferry takes you across to Viedma, and there's a fabulous little museum.

Viedma

Viedma (population 60,000) is quite different in character from Carmen de Patagones: it's the provincial administrative centre, rather than the home of farmers and landowners. An attractive *costanera* runs by the river, with large grassy banks shaded by willow trees, and the river water is pleasantly warm in summer and clean, good for swimming. On a calm summer's evening, when groups gather to sip *mate*, the scene resembles Seurat's painting of bathers.

There are two plazas. The cathedral, built by the Salesians (1912), is on the west of Plaza Alsina, with a former convent next door. This was the first chapel built by the Salesians (1887) in the area and is now a cultural centre housing the **Museo del Agua y del Suelo** and the **Museo Cardenal Cagliero**, which has ecclesiastical artefacts. Two blocks east, on Plaza San Martín, is the French-style **Casa de Gobierno** (1926). Most diverting, though, is the **Museo Gardeliano** ① *Rivadavia y Colón (1st floor), Mon-Fri 0930-1230*, a fabulous collection of biographical artefacts of tango singer Carlos Gardel; see box, page 48. It also has a space for cultural events.

Along the attractive *costanera*, the **Centro Cultural**, opposite Calle 7 de Marzo, houses a small **Mercado Artesanal** selling beautifully made Mapuche weavings and woodwork.

Carmen de Patagones

Carmen de Patagones (population 40,000) is the more dynamic of the two towns (which isn't saying much), with a feeling of bustle on the main street on weekday mornings. The town centre, just east of the river, lies around the Plaza 7 de Mayo, and just west is the **Iglesia del Carmen**, built by the Salesians in 1880. Take a stroll down the pretty streets winding down to the river to find many early pioneer buildings along the riverside: the **Torre del Fuerte**, tower of the stone fortress built in 1780 against indigenous attacks; the **Casa de la Tahona**, a disused 18th-century flour mill now housing the **Casa de la Cultura**; and another late-colonial building, **La Carlota**, one block east.

Nearby there's the fascinating **Museo Histórico Regional 'Emma Nozzi'** ① *JJ Biedma 64, T02920-462729, Mon-Fri 1000-1200, 1500-1700, Sat-Sun and bank holidays 1700-1900*, which

BACKGROUND
Patagonia

Patagonia was inhabited by various groups of indigenous peoples from thousands of years ago until colonization by the Europeans. The region gets its name from early Spanish settlers' first impressions of these native people: big feet (*pata* being the informal word for leg). The first European visitor to the coast of Patagonia was the Portuguese explorer Fernão Magalhães in 1519, who gave his name to the Magellan straits. This sea passage afforded ships a safer route through the southern extreme of the continent, going north of the island of Tierra del Fuego, rather than heading south on the perilous route around Cape Horn. The first to traverse Patagonia from south to north was the English sailor, Carder, who survived a shipwreck in 1578 in the Strait of Magellan, walked north to the Río de la Plata and arrived in London nine years later.

For several centuries, European attempts to settle along the coast were deterred by isolation, lack of food and water, and the harsh climate, as well as understandable resistance from the indigenous peoples. Sadly, the indigenous population was almost wiped out in the bloody war known as the Conquest of the Desert in 1879-1883 (see box, page 88). Before this there had been a European colony at Carmen de Patagones, which shipped salt to Buenos Aires, and a Welsh settlement in the Chubut Valley from 1865.

After the Conquest of the Desert, colonization was rapid. Welsh, Scots and English farmers were among the biggest groups of immigrants; others included sheep farmers from Las Malvinas/Falkland Islands and Chilean sheep farmers from Punta Arenas moving eastwards into Santa Cruz. The discovery of large oil reserves in many areas of southern Patagonia brought wealth to Chubut and Santa Cruz provinces in the 1900s. However, when President Menem privatized the national oil company YPF in the 1990s, much of that wealth immediately diminished. One of the few people to gain from it all was the former president, Néstor Kirchner (deceased husband of Argentina's president from 2007-2015, Christina Kirchner), who had been governor of Santa Cruz province while it was rich and influential within the country.

gives a great insight into early pioneer life. There are Tehuelche arrowheads, stone *boleadoras*, silver gaucho stirrups and great early photos (one of a baptism by Salesians of a 100-year-old Tehuelche man in a field), next to delicate tea cups. There are guided tours too. The **Museo de la Prefectura Naval** ① *Mitre s/n y Costanera, T02920-461742, Mon-Fri 0800-1300, Sat-Sun 1500-1900,* is also worth a look if you're into ships; it's housed in a building dating from 1886 and contains a marine history of the area.

Patagones is linked to Viedma by two bridges and a very small ferry which takes four minutes and leaves every 15 minutes, US$0.40.

South of Viedma and Carmen de Patagones
This whole stretch of coast is great for shore fishing, with *pejerrey, variada* and even shark among the many other species. Equipment is available in Viedma (see Shopping, below). There's a well-established little fishing resort at **Bahía San Blas**, 100 km east of Patagones, an area renowned for its shark fishing, with plentiful accommodation. For more information, see www.vivesanblas.com.ar.

At **El Cóndor**, 30 km south of Viedma (six buses daily in summer), there is a beautiful beach (also known as La Boca), with the oldest lighthouse in the country, dating from 1887. Facilities include a hotel, restaurants and shops (most facilities have reduced hours or are close entirely after January or February). There's free camping on a beach 2 km south.

Playa Bonita, 12 km further southwest is known as a good fishing spot, and offers more good beaches.

Ask the tourist office in Viedma (see Tourist information, below) for their leaflet about the *Lobería Punta Bermeja*, 60 km west of Viedma. This sea lion colony is visited by some 2500 sea lions in summer, which you can see at close range (daily bus in summer; but hitching is easy). There's also an impressive visitor centre (with toilets).

Listings Viedma and Carmen de Patagones

Tourist information

Viedma

Municipal tourist office
Av Francisco de Viedma 51, T02920-427171, www.viedma.gov.ar. Daily 0900-2100.
Helpful staff.

Provincial tourist office
Av Caseros 1425, T02920-422150, www.rionegrotur.gob.ar (Spanish only). Mon-Fri 0700-1400, 1800-2000.

Carmen de Patagones

Tourist office
Mitre 84, T02920-464819, www.patagones. gov.ar. Mon-Fri 0800-2000, Sat-Sun 0930-1330 and 1530-1930.
Helpful and dynamic tourist office.

El Cóndor

Tourist office
T02920-497148. Mon-Fri 0900-1900, Sat-Sun 1130-1835.

Where to stay

Viedma
The best places to stay are in Viedma.

$$$ Nijar
Mitre 490, T02920-422833, www.hotelnijar.com.
Comfortable, smart, modern, good service.

$$$ Peumayen
Buenos Aires 334, T02920-425222, www.hotelpeumayen.com.ar.
Old-fashioned friendly place on the plaza.

$$ Residencial Roca
Roca 347, T02920-431241.
A cheap option with comfortable beds, helpful staff, breakfast included.

Camping
At the sea lion colony, **Trenitos** (T02920-497098), has good facilities.

Restaurants

$$ La Balsa
On the river at Colón and Villarino, T02920-431974.
By far the best restaurant, inexpensive with a pleasant atmosphere. Delicious seafood accompanied a bottle of superb Río Negro wine, Humberto Canale Merlot, is highly recommended.

Festivals

Carmen de Patagones
Mar Fiesta de 7 de Marzo, www.maragato. com.ar, when the whole town is packed out for the celebration of the victory at the Battle of Patagones. It's a week of music and handicrafts, fine food, a huge procession, gaucho horse-riding displays and lots of

meat on the *asados*. It's great fun but make sure you book accommodation in advance.

Shopping

Viedma
Patagonia Out Doors Life (25 de Mayo 340), and **Tiburón** (Zatti 250), both stock fishing equipment.

What to do

Viedma
Tour operators
Mona Tour, *San Martín 225, T02920-422933, www.monatour. com.ar.* Sells flights as well as tickets for the train to Bariloche, www. trenpatagonico-sa.com.ar (check first to see if train is in service).

Transport

Air
LADE (Saavedra 576, T02920-424420, www. lade.com.ar) flies to **Buenos Aires**, **Mar del Plata**, **Bahía Blanca**, **Comodoro Rivadavia** and other Patagonian destinations.

Viedma
Bus
The **bus terminal** (Av Pte Perón and Guido, www.terminalpatagonia.com.ar) is 15 blocks from the plaza; a taxi to town costs around US$3.

To **Buenos Aires**, 13 hrs, daily, US$80-100, with **Don Otto** and others. To **Bahía Blanca**, 4 hrs, many daily, US$15-25. To **Puerto Madryn**, 6½ hrs, several daily, US$35-40, with **Don Otto** and others.

Train
A comfortable sleeper train, which also carries cars, normally goes from Viedma to **Bariloche** overnight. For information on the current state of the service, as well as schedules, T02920-422130, www.trenpatagonico-sa.com.ar.

Puerto Madryn   *Colour map 5, B5.*

number one destination on Patagonia's Atlantic coast

The undoubted highlight of the whole Atlantic Coast in Patagonia is the splendid array of marine wildlife on Península Valdés, best visited from Puerto Madryn (population 100,000). This seaside town has a grand setting on the wide bay of Golfo Nuevo and is the perfect base for setting off to Valdés to the east, as there are plenty of hotels and reliable tour operators running trips to the peninsula, including boat trips to see the whales. Puerto Madryn itself is a good place to enjoy the sea for a couple of days, with lots of beachfront restaurants selling superb locally caught seafood.

The town is a modern, relaxed and friendly place. It hasn't been ruined by its popularity as a tourist resort with a large workforce occupied by its other main industry: a huge aluminium plant, which you can visit by arrangement through the tourist office (see under Tourist information in Listings, page 489); best during summer.

Puerto Madryn was the site of the first Welsh landing in 1865 and is named after the Welsh home of the colonist, Jones Parry. However, it wasn't officially founded until 1889, when the railway was built connecting the town with Trelew to enable the Welsh living in the Chubut Valley to export their produce.

Essential Puerto Madryn

Finding your feet

El Tehuelche Airport is 8 km west of the centre and can be reached by taxi, US$10-13. More frequent flights serve Trelew airport (see page 503), some 60 km south, with buses to Puerto Madryn that meet all flights, US$4; the journey takes one hour. The **bus terminal** is on Avenida Dr Avila, entre Necochea e Independencia.

Getting around

The city centre is easy to get around on foot, with many restaurants and hotels lined up along the seafront at Avenida Roca, and most shops and tour companies on the streets around 28 de Julio, which runs perpendicular to the sea and past the town's neat little plaza, all contained within four or five blocks.

Sights

You're most likely to be visiting the town to take a trip to Península Valdés (see page 493), but there are other tourist sights closer to hand. In the town itself, the real pleasure is the sea, and it's a pleasant first day's stroll along the long stretch of beach to **El Indio**, a statue on the road at the southeastern end of the bay, marking the gratitude of the Welsh to the native Tehuelche people whose shared expertise ensured their survival. As the road curves up the cliff here, don't miss the splendid **EcoCentro** ① *Julio Verne 3784, T0280-488 3173, www.ecocentro.org.ar, Wed-Mon 1500-2000 (2100 high season), US$9.50.* This interactive sea life information centre combines an art gallery, café and fabulous reading room with comfy sofas at the top of a turret. The whole place has fantastic views of the bay.

Just a little closer to town, perched on the cliff, is the tiny **Centro de Exposición de Punta Cuevas** ① *daily 1700-2100, www.puntacuevas.org.ar, US$2.50, temporarily closed at the time of writing,* of interest if you're tracing the history of the Welsh in Patagonia. It's little more than a couple of rooms of relics near the caves and basic huts on the cliffs where the settlers first lived, but enthusiastic guides make the visit worthwhile. A more conventional museum, with displays on local flora and fauna, is the **Museo de Ciencias Naturales y Oceanográfico** ① *Domecq García y J Menéndez, T02965-445 1139, Mon-Fri 1000-1800, Sat 1500-1900, US$0.75,* which is informative and worth a visit.

Around Puerto Madryn

During the right season, you can spot whales at the long beach of **Playa El Doradillo**, 16 km northeast of town, along the *ripio* road closest to the coast. There are also sea lions at the **Punta Loma Reserve** ① *daily 0800-2000, US$7.50, child US$3.75, many companies offer tours,* 15 km southeast of Puerto Madryn and best visited at low tide in December and January. Access is via the coastal road from town.

Puerto Madryn is Patagonia's **diving** capital, with dives to see wildlife and many off-shore wrecked ships, together with all kinds of courses from beginners' dives to the week-long PADI course on offer from tour operators, such as **Puerto Madryn Buceo**. You can also hire mountain bikes and windsurfing boards here, from many places along the beachfront. For more information, see What to do, page 492.

Tip...
A great bike ride is from the town to the Punta Loma Reserve along the coastal road; allow 1½ hours to get there. The road to the north of town is another good ride to do.

Tourist information

Tourist information centre
Av Roca 223, just off 28 de Julio, T0280-445 3504, www.madryn.travel. Mar-Nov daily 0700-2100, Dec-Feb daily 0800-2100.
Efficient and friendly office on the seafront, next to the shopping complex; there's another branch at the **bus station** (daily

0800-2100). The staff are extremely well organized and speak English. They have leaflets on Península Valdés and accommodation, and can advise on tours.

Where to stay

Accommodation is generally of a high standard, but can be pricey. This is one of several tourist centres in Argentina

Puerto Madryn

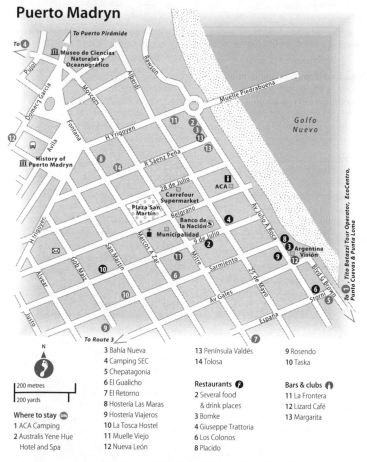

Where to stay 🛏
1 ACA Camping
2 Australis Yene Hue
  Hotel and Spa
3 Bahía Nueva
4 Camping SEC
5 Chepatagonia
6 El Gualicho
7 El Retorno
8 Hostería Las Maras
9 Hostería Viajeros
10 La Tosca Hostel
11 Muelle Viejo
12 Nueva León
13 Península Valdés
14 Tolosa

Restaurants 🍴
2 Several food
  & drink places
3 Bomke
4 Giuseppe Trattoria
6 Los Colonos
8 Placido

9 Rosendo
10 Taska

Bars & clubs 🍸
11 La Frontera
12 Lizard Café
13 Margarita

where higher rates apply for foreigners than Argentines for hotel rooms and some entrance fees; it's hopeless to argue. Book ahead in summer and during whale-watching season.

$$$$ Australis Yene Hue Hotel and Spa
Roca 33, T0280-445 2937,
www.hotelesaustralis.com.ar.
Luxury hotel on the beachfront with a small spa, modern rooms, and a good buffet breakfast. Ask for a room with a view.

$$$$-$$$ Península Valdés
Av Roca 155, T0280-447 1292,
www.hotel peninsula.com.ar.
Luxurious seafront hotel with great views. Spa, sauna, gym.

$$$ Bahía Nueva
Av Roca 67, T0280-445 1677,
www.bahianueva.com.ar.
One of the best seafront hotels, quite small but comfortable rooms, professional staff, cheaper in low season.

$$$ Hostería Las Maras
Marcos A Zar 64, T0280-445 3215,
http://lasmarashotel.com.ar.
Appealing modern place, offering well-decorated rooms with large beds, cheaper with fan. Parking.

$$$ Tolosa
Roque Sáenz Peña 253, T0280-447 1850,
www.hoteltolosa.com.ar.
Extremely comfortable, modern place, with great breakfasts. Disabled access.

$$ Hostería Viajeros
Gob Maíz 545, T0280-445 6457,
www.hostelviajeros.com.ar.
Rooms for 2, 3 and 4 people, big kitchen/dining room, lawn, parking, new superior rooms on 2nd floor (**$$$**), helpful, family-run.

$$ Muelle Viejo
H Yrigoyen 38, T0280-447 1284,
www.muelleviejo.com.
Ask for the comfortable modernized rooms in this funny old place. Rooms for 4 are excellent value.

$$ Nueva León
D García 365, T0280-447 4125,
www.nuevaleon.com.ar.
Good-value bungalows for up to 6 people located 2 blocks from the beach. Each *cabaña* comes equipped with cable TV.

$ pp Chepatagonia
Alfonsina Storni 16, T0280-445 5783,
www.chepatagonia hostel.com.ar.
Good view of the beach (and whales in season), helpful owners, mixed and single dorms, doubles with shared bath (**$$**), lockers, bicycle hire and many other services. A good choice.

$ pp El Gualicho
Marcos A Zar 480, T0280-445 4163,
www.elgualicho.com.ar.
Decent budget option, some double rooms (**$$**), HI discounts, enthusiastic owner, English-speaking staff, heating, free pick up from bus terminal, *parrilla*, garden, bikes for hire, runs tours, parking, pool table. Recommended.

$ El Retorno
Bartomolmé Mitre 798, T0280-445 6044,
www.elretornohostel.com.ar.
3 blocks from beach, hot water, lockers, cosy common area, free bus terminal pick-up. Double rooms available (**$$**). Also rents apartments with sea view (**$$$**).

$ pp La Tosca Hostel
Sarmiento 437, T0280-445 6133,
www.latoscahostel.com.
This hostel was renovated in 2015 to add lovely new doubles, triples and quadruples (**$$**). Each has a private bath and is equipped with all mod cons. There are also dorms with bathrooms. Free pick up from bus station. Organizes tours and provides advice about the area. The kitchen with *parrilla* is open 24 hrs; a stay includes a big breakfast. Welcoming, helpful vibe. Highly recommended.

Camping

ACA
Blv Brown 3869, 4 km south of town centre (at Punta Cuevas), T0280-488 3485, www.acamadryn.com.ar. Open year-round.
Hot showers, café, shop, also duplexes for 4-6, no kitchen facilities, shady trees, close to the sea. US$10 per night; cheaper rates Apr-Nov.

Camping SEC
Río Mayo 800, 5 km from the town centre, T0280-447 3015.
Basic campsite from US$6 per night.

Restaurants

One of the unmissable pleasures of Puerto Madryn is its great seafood. While you're here, try at least one plate of *arroz con mariscos* (rice with a whole selection of squid, prawns, mussels and clams). Most restaurants are mid-range and charge around the same price, but differ widely in quality. The block of 9 de Julio between 25 de Mayo and Mitre has an interesting mix of food and drink places, including a wine bar, a craft beer pub and several restaurants.

$$$ Placido
Av Roca 506, T0280-445 5991, www.placido.com.ar.
On the beach, great location and service, but food can be hit and miss. Seafood and vegetarian options, also cheaper pasta dishes.

$$$ Taska
9 de Julio 461, T0280-447 4003.
Excellent food with a Basque influence; book ahead. Highly recommended.

$$ Giuseppe Trattoria
25 de Mayo 388, T0280-456 891.
With its red-checked tablecloths and cosy family vibe, this pizza and pasta restaurant is quite popular with locals. The large portions certainly don't hurt.

$$ Los Colonos
Av Roca y A Storni, T0280-445 8486.
Quirky, cosy restaurant built into the wooden hull of a boat, plenty of maritime heritage, *parrilla*, seafood and pasta.

$ Rosendo
Av Roca 549, 1st floor, T0280-445 0062. Open lunchtime and evenings in high season, from 1700 in low season.
Snack bar/café overlooking the main street. Excellent home-made *empanadas*, snacks, cocktails and wines. Reading and games room. Recommended.

Cafés

Bomke
Av Roca 540, T0280-447 4094, www.bomke.com.ar. Open late.
Popular ice cream place with outdoor seating at the back. Excellent ice creams. Recommended.

Bars and clubs

La Frontera
9 de Julio 254, T0280-472-2232, see Facebook. Closes at 0500 Thu-Sat.
Popular with locals, this nightclub only really gets busy in the small hours.

Lizard Café
Av Roca y Av Galés, near the seafront, T0280-472 2232.
Lively funky place with friendly people. Good for generous pizzas or late-night drinks.

Margarita
RS Peña 15, T0280-447 2659, see Facebook.
Late-night bar for drinks and live music, serves expensive but tasty food.

Shopping

You'll find clothes, T-shirts, high-quality Patagonian handicrafts and leather goods, and artesanal *alfajores* and cakes for sale on 28 de Julio and Av Roca. For fishing tackle, guns and camping gear, try **Nayfer** (25 de

Mayo 366). For diving gear, there's **Pino Sub** (Yrigoyen 200, www.pinosub.com).
Cardon, *Shopping El Portal de Madryn, Av JA Roca and 28 de Julio*. Recommended for regional goods and leather bags.
Portal de Madryn, *28 de Julio and Av Roca, www.portaldemadryn.com*. The indoor shopping centre has all the smart clothes shops, a café on the ground floor, and a kids' games area with a fast-food place, **Mostaza**, on the top floor (not cheap).

What to do

Diving

Puerto Madryn is a diving centre, with several shipwrecked boats in the Golfo Nuevo. A first dive ('bautismo') for beginners costs about US$70 pp.
Aquatours, *Av Roca 550, T0280-445 1954, www.aquatours.com.ar*. A variety of options, including PADI courses, good value.
Lobo Larsen, *Roca 885, loc 2 (also Blv Brown 860), T0280-447 0277, www.lobolarsen.com*. Friendly company that specializes in diving with the sea lion colony at Punta Lomas. Wide variety of courses offered.
Scuba Duba, *Blv Brown 893, T0280-445 2699, www.scubaduba.com.ar*. Professional and good fun, diving with sea lions at Punta Loma, pick up from hotel, offer a hot drink and warm clothes after the dive, good equipment, instructor Javier A Crespi is very responsible.

Horse riding

Carlo Bonomi, *T0280-432 2541, www.cb.fofuente.org*. Equestrian trainer rents horses for US$20 an hour.
Huellas y Costas, *Blv Brown 1900, T0280-447 0143, www.huellasycostas.com*. Also whale watching.

Mountain bike hire

El Gualicho, *Marcos A Zar 480, T0280-445 4163*. From US$10.

Tour operators

Many agencies do similar 7- and 9-hr tours to the Península Valdés, about US$50-60 pp, plus the entrance to the Peninsula. They include the interpretation centre, Puerto Pirámides (the boat trip is US$70 extra), Punta Delgada and Caleta Valdés. Most tour companies stay about 1 hr on location. Shop around to find out how long you'll spend at each place, how big the group is and whether your guide speaks English. On all tours take binoculars. Tours do not run after heavy rain in the low season. Tours to see the penguins at Punta Tombo and the Welsh villages are better from Trelew (see page 503). Many of the agencies below now also have offices at the bus terminal (Dr Avila 350); all are recommended for Península Valdés:
Alora Viaggio, *Av Roca 27, T0280-445 5106, www.aloraviaggio.com*. Helpful company, also has an office in Buenos Aires (T011-4827 1591, daily 0800-1300).
Argentina Visión, *Av Roca 536, T0280-445 5888, www.argentinavision.com*. Also 4WD adventure trips and estancia accommodation, English and French spoken.
Chaltén Travel, *Av Roca 115, T0280-445 4906, www.chaltentravel.com*. Runs a tourist bus service to Perito Moreno on Ruta 40, for connections north to Bariloche and south to El Chaltén and El Calafate.
Cuyun Có, *Av Roca 165, T0280-445 1845, www.cuyunco.com.ar*. Offers a friendly, personal service and a huge range of conventional and more imaginative tours: guided walks with local experts, 4WD expeditions, and can arrange estancia accommodation. Bilingual guides.
Tito Botazzi, *Blv Brown y Martín Fierro, T0280-447 4110, www.titobottazzi.com*, and at Puerto Pirámides (T0280-449 5050). Particularly recommended for its small groups and well-informed bilingual guides; very popular for whale watching.

Transport

Air

There are daily flights to **Buenos Aires** in high season from the town's airport (T0280-445 6774). Also limited **LADE** (Roca 119, T0280-445 1256) flights to **Buenos Aires**, **Bahía Blanca**, **Viedma**, **Trelew**, **Comodoro Rivadavia** and other Patagonian airports. More frequent flights from Bariloche, Buenos Aires, Ushuaia and El Calafate serve Trelew airport (see page 503), with buses to Puerto Madryn that meet all flights.

Bus

The bus terminal (T0280-445 1789) has a café, toilets, *locutorio* and a small but helpful tourist office.

To **Buenos Aires**, 18-19 hrs, several companies, US$150. To **Bahía Blanca**, 9½ hrs with **Don Otto** and **Andes Mar**, US$80. To **Comodoro Rivadavia**, 6 hrs, US$45 with **Don Otto** and **Andes Mar**. To **Río Gallegos**, 18 hrs; US$130, with **Andes Mar**. To **Trelew**,

1 hr, every hour, US$5 with **28 de Julio/Mar y Valle**. To **Puerto Pirámides**, Mar y Valle, Mon-Fri 0630, 0945, 1600, returns 0815, 1300, 1800 (1 departure Sat-Sun at 0945) US$7 each way, 1½ hrs.

Car hire

This is expensive, US$100 per day, and note large excess for turning the car over. Drive slowly on unpaved *ripio* (gravel) roads; it's best to hire 4WD. There are many agencies on Av Roca, including **Dubrovnik**, Av Roca 19, T0280-445 0030, www.rentacar dubrovnik.com. Reliable company with offices in El Calafate and Bariloche. **Wild Skies**, Morgan 2274, p 1, Depto 6 B Sur, T0280-15-467 6233, www.wildskies.com.ar. Efficient service, English spoken. Recommended.

Taxi

Taxis can be found outside the bus terminal, T0280-445 2966/447 4177, and on the main plaza.

★ Península Valdés *Colour map 5, B5.*

a haven for threatened species

Whatever time of year you visit Península Valdés you'll find a wonderful array of marine life, birds and a profusion of Patagonian wildlife such as guanacos, rheas, Patagonian hares and armadillos. But in spring (September-November), this treeless splay of land is host to a quite spectacular numbers of whales, penguins and seals, who come to breed in the sheltered waters south of the narrow Ameghino isthmus and on beaches at the foot of the peninsula's chalky cliffs.

The land is almost flat, though greener than much of Patagonia, and at the heart of the peninsula are large salt flats, one of which, **Salina Grande**, is 42 m below sea level. The peninsula is privately owned – many of its estancias offering comfortable and wonderfully remote places to stay in the middle of the wild beauty – but it is also a nature reserve and was declared a World Heritage Site by UNESCO in 1999. The beach along the entire coast is out of bounds and this is strictly enforced.

The main tourist centre on the peninsula is **Puerto Pirámides**, on the southern side, which has a few good hotels and hostels, places to camp and a handful of restaurants.

Around the peninsula *The following are the main marine wildlife colonies.*
The entrance to the reserve is about 45 km northeast of Puerto Madryn, in the **interpretation centre** ⓘ *administration T0280-447 0197, www.peninsulavaldes.org.ar, daily 0800-2100 (2000 in low season), US$21.75 for foreigners, children US$11*, where you buy

Essential Península Valdés

Access

Península Valdés can most easily be visited by taking one of the many well-organized full-day tours from Puerto Madryn (see Tour operators, page 492). These usually include a whale-watching boat trip, which departs from Puerto Pirámides (see below), together with a stop or two on the eastern coastline to see sea lions, penguins and other wildlife at close hand. Minibus travel, the boat trip and transfers to your hotel are included, but not lunch or entrance to the peninsula.

Getting around

You can hire a car relatively inexpensively for a group of four, and then take a boat trip to see the whales (June to December) from Puerto Pirámides. Note that distances are long on the peninsula, and roads beyond Puerto Pirámides are *ripio*, so take your time – hire companies charge a heavy excess if you damage the car.

A cheaper option is the daily bus to Puerto Pirámides with **Mar y Valle**, leaving Puerto Madryn's terminal daily at 0630, 0945 and 1600, and returning at 0815, 0945 and 1800, 1½ hours, US$5.50 each way (on Saturday and Sunday there is only one daily bus to Península Valdés, leaving at 0945). This would only allow you to see the whales though, since there is no public transport to other areas of the peninsula. To explore the peninsula in more detail and gain closer contact with nature, a stay one of the peninsula's estancias is recommended.

When to go

Much of Península Valdés' wildlife can be enjoyed throughout the year, with sea lions, elephant seals, dolphins and many species of bird permanently resident. The bull elephant seals can be seen fighting for females from September to early November, and killer whales can sometimes be sighted off the coast at this time too, staying until April. Penguins can be seen from September to March, and the stars of the show, the southern right whales, come to these waters to breed in spring (September to November).

---

the ticket for visiting all the sites on the peninsula. Twenty kilometres beyond, on the isthmus, there's an interesting **interpretation centre** with stuffed examples of the local fauna, many fossils and a wonderful whale skeleton, which makes a great complement to seeing the real thing gracefully soaring through the water. Ask for the informative bilingual leaflet on southern right whales.

Isla de los Pájaros, is in the Golfo San José, 5 km from the interpretation centre. Its seabirds can be viewed through fixed telescopes (at 400 m distance), since only recognized ornithologists can get permission to visit the island itself. Between September and April you can spot wading birds, herons, cormorants and terns.

Caleta Valdés, 45 km south of Punta Norte in the middle of the eastern shore, has huge colonies of elephant seals which can be seen at close quarters. In the breeding season, from September to October, you'll see the rather unappealing blubbery masses of bull seals hauling themselves up the beach to make advances to one of the many females in their harem. During the first half of August the bull seals arrive to claim their territory, and can be seen at low tide engaging in bloody battles over the females. At **Punta Cantor**, just south of here, you'll find a good café and clean toilets. There are also three marked walks, ranging from 45 minutes to two hours. **Estancia La Elvira** is a short distance inland from here, and is clearly signposted.

Punta Delgada, at the southeastern end of the peninsula, 110 km from the entrance, is where elephant seals and sea lions can be seen from the high cliffs in such large numbers that they seem to stretch out like a velvety bronze tide line on the beautiful beach below. It's mesmerizing to watch as the young frolic in the shallow water and the bulls lever themselves around the females. There's a hotel nearby, **Faro Punta Delgada** (see Where to stay, below), which is a good base for exploring this beautiful area further.

Punta Norte, at the northern end of the peninsula, 97 km from the entrance, is not often visited by tour companies, but it has colonies of elephant seals and sea lions. Killer whales (orca) have also been seen here, feeding on sea lion pups at low tide in March and April. **Estancia San Lorenzo** is nearby.

★ Estancias

There are several estancias on the peninsula which allow you to really appreciate the space and natural beauty of the land, and give you much more access to some of the most remote places, with great wildlife to observe. Ask the tourist office for advice. Day trips to the estancias can also be arranged, which might include wildlife trips, an *asado* and perhaps horse riding. For further details, see Where to stay, below.

Whale watching from Puerto Pirámides *Colour map 5, B5.*

Puerto Pirámides (population 429), 107 km east of Puerto Madryn, is the departure point for whale-watching boat trips, which leave from its broad sandy beach. Every year, between June and December, 400 to 500 southern right whales migrate to the Golfo Nuevo to mate and give birth. It is without doubt one of the best places in the world to watch these beautiful animals, since in many cases the whales come within just a few metres of the coast. From Puerto Pirámides, boat trips take you gently close to basking whales; if you're lucky, you may find yourself next to a mother and baby. Sailings are controlled by the Prefectura (Naval Police), according to weather and sea conditions.

On land, a 3-km track (beware of the incoming tide), or a 15-km *ripio* road go to a *mirador* at Punta Pardelas where you can see the whales. The prevailing currents may throw smelly carcasses of the young whales that didn't make it onto the beach. Camping is allowed, but there are no services or drinking water.

> **Tip...**
> If you're prone to sea sickness, think twice before setting off on a whale-watching trip on a windy day.

Listings Península Valdés

Tourist information

In addition to the tourist office below, information is also available from the tourist office in Puerto Madryn (see page 489) and from the interpretation centre on the peninsula (see above).

Puerto Pirámides

Tourist office
1ra Bajada al Mar, near the beach, T0280-449 5048, www.puertopiramides.gov.ar.
Offers useful information for hikes and driving tours.

Where to stay

The following are all in Puerto Pirámides; hotels are packed out in Jan and Feb.

$$$$-$$$ Las Restingas
1ra Bajada al Mar, T0280-449 5101, www.lasrestingas.com.
Exclusive, 8 rooms with sea views, very comfortable, with sophisticated regional restaurant. Good deals available in low season.

$$$ ACA Motel
Julio A Roca s/n, T0280-449 5004, www.motelacapiramides.com.
Welcoming, handy for the beach, with good seafood restaurant (you might spot whales from its terrace). There is also an ACA service station (open daily) with a good café and shop.

$$$ Cabañas en el Mar
Av de las Ballenas y 1ra Bajada al Mar, T0280-449 5044, www.piramides.net.
Comfortable, well-equipped 2- to 6-bed *cabañas* with sea view.

$$$ Del Nómade
Av de las Ballenas s/n, T0280-449 5044, www.ecohosteria.com.ar.
Eco lodge using solar power and water recycling, buffet breakfast, heating, café, specializes in wildlife watching, nature and underwater photography, kayaking, scuba diving, adventure sports, courses offered. Discounts via their website.

$$$ The Paradise
2da Bajada al Mar, T0280-449 5030, www.hosteriaparadise.com.ar.
Large comfortable rooms, suites with jacuzzis, fine seafood restaurant.

$$ La Nube del Angel
2da Bajada al Mar, T0280-449 5070, www.lanubedelangel.com.ar. Open all year.
Lovely owners, small *cabañas* for 2-6 people, quiet, 5 mins' walk from the beach.

Camping
Municipal campsite by the black-sand beach, T0280-154202760. Hot showers in evening, good, get there early to secure a place, US$6 per night. Do not camp on the beach: people have been swept away by the incoming tide.

Estancias
For more estancias in Patagonia, see www.interpatagonia.com/estancias.

$$$$ El Pedral
Punta Ninfas, T0280-154572551, www.elpedral.com.ar.
By a pebble beach, with lots of wildlife-watching opportunities, farm activities, horse riding, zodiac trips (extra), guesthouse with en suite rooms, restaurant and bar, swimming pool.

$$$$ Faro Punta Delgada
Punta Delgada, T0280-445 8444, www.puntadelgada.com.
Next to a lighthouse, amazing setting, half and full board, excellent food, very helpful. Recommended; book in advance, no credit cards.

$$$ La Elvira
Caleta Valdés, near Punta Cantor, T0280-445 8444 (contact Gonzalo Hernández), www.laelvira.com.ar.
Traditional Patagonian dishes and comfortable accommodation (B&B, half and full board available).

$$$ San Lorenzo
On RP3, 20 km southwest of Punta Norte, T0280-445 8444 (contact through Argentina Visión in Puerto Madryn, see Tour operators, page 492).
Great for day trips to a beautiful stretch of coast to see penguins, fossils, birdwatching and horse treks.

Restaurants

There are many restaurants on the main street in Puerto Pirámides and reasonably priced ones at Punta Norte, Punta Cantor and the Faro in Punta Delgada. These recommendations are on the beach:

$$$ Las Restingas
1ra Bajada on the beach, Puerto Pirámides, T0280-4495101, www.lasrestingas.com.
Perfect for a romantic dinner, sea views and tranquillity. An imaginative menu combines quality local produce with a touch of sophistication.

$$ Quimey Quipan
1ra Bajada opposite Las Restingas, Puerto Pirámides, T0280-445 8609.
By the beach and next to **Tito Bottazzi**, this family-run place specializes in delicious seafood with rice and has a cheap set menu. It's always open for lunch, ring to reserve for dinner. Recommended.

$$ The Paradise
Av de las Bellenas y 2da Bajada, T0280-4495030, www.hosteriatheparadise.com.ar.
Just off the beach, good atmosphere and great seafood. Also offers lamb and a few vegetarian choices.

$ Towanda
1ra Bajada al Mar s/n, Puerto Pirámides, T0280-422 1460.
Quirky café and snack bar with outside seating overlooking the main street and beach. Friendly staff, recommended.

What to do

Tour operators
Hydrosport, *1ra Bajada al Mar, Puerto Pirámides, T0280-449 5065, www.hydrosport. com.ar.* Rents scuba equipment and boats, and organizes land and sea wildlife tours to see whales and dolphins.
Whales Argentina, *1ra Bajada al Mar, T0280-449 5015, www.whalesargentina.com.ar.* Recommended for whale watching.

Trelew and the Chubut Valley

outlaw hideouts and Welsh tea houses

The Río Chubut is one of the most important rivers in Patagonia, flowing a massive 820 km from the eastern foothills of the Andes into the Atlantic at Bahía Engaño. It's thanks to the Río Chubut that the Welsh pioneers came to this part of the world in 1865, and their irrigation of the arid land around it enabled them to survive and prosper. You can trace their history west along the valley from the pleasant airy town of Trelew to the quiet little village of Gaiman, which has a wonderful museum and cafés serving traditional Welsh afternoon tea. Further west, past little brick chapels sitting amidst lush green fields, is the quieter settlement of Dolavon.

If you're keen to investigate further into the past, there's a marvellous museum full of dinosaurs in Trelew and some ancient fossils in the Parque Palaeontológico Bryn-Gwyn near Gaiman. From Trelew you could also visit South America's largest single colony of Magellanic penguins on the coast at Punta Tombo.

Trelew *Colour map 5, B5.*
Some 70 km south of Puerto Madryn, Trelew (population 110,000) is the largest town in the Chubut Valley. Founded in 1884, it was named in honour of Lewis Jones, an early settler, and the Welsh colonization is still evident in a few remaining chapels in the town's modern centre. It's a cheerful place with a quietly busy street life, certainly more appealing than the industrial town of Rawson, 20 km east on the coast. Trelew has a splendid paleontological museum, a great tourist office and a couple of fabulous cafés.

Sights There's the lovely shady **Plaza Independencia** in the town centre, packed with mature trees, and hosting a small **handicraft market** ⓘ *every Sat 0900-1800.* Nearby is the **Capilla Tabernacle**, on Belgrano between San Martín and 25 de Mayo, a red-brick Welsh chapel dating from 1889. Heading east, rather more impressive is the **Salon San David** ⓘ *Mon-Fri 0900-1300, extended hours during Sep-Oct*, a Welsh meeting hall first used for the Eisteddfod of 1913. It has a mini-museum of objects donated by descendants of the Welsh settlers and also organizes Welsh language and dance classes. On the road to Rawson, 3 km south, you'll find one of the oldest standing Welsh chapels, **Capilla Moriah**. Built in 1880, it has a simple interior and a cemetery with the graves of many original settlers, including the first white woman born in the Welsh colony.

Back in Trelew itself, not the oldest but quite the most wonderful building is the 1920s **Hotel Touring Club** ⓘ *Fontana 240, www.touringpatagonia.com.ar.* This was the town's grandest hotel in its heyday. Politicians and travellers met in its glorious high-ceilinged mirrored bar, which is now full of old photographs and relics. You can eat lunch here and there's simple accommodation available. Butch Cassidy once called this hotel home when he was on the run from representatives of the Pinkerton detective agency. Ask the friendly owner, Luis, if you can see the elegant 1920s meeting room at the back. Wanted posters of Butch himself adorn the walls.

The town's best museum – and indeed one of the finest in Argentina – is the **Museo Paleontológico Egidio Feruglio** ⓘ *Fontana 140, T0280-442 0012, www.mef.org.ar, Sep-Mar daily 0900-1900, Apr-Aug Mon-Fri 1000-1800, Sat-Sun 1000-1900, US$7.50, full disabled access, guides for the blind.* Imaginatively designed and beautifully presented, the

Trelew

Where to stay 🛏
1 Galicia
2 Libertador
3 Rayentray
4 Rivadavia
5 Touring Club

Restaurants 🍴
2 Café de mi Ciudad
3 Café Verdi
5 La Bodeguita
6 La Casona
7 Miguel Angel

BACKGROUND

Welsh Patagonia

Among the tales of early pioneers to Argentina, the story of Welsh emigration, in search of religious freedom, is one of the most impressive. The first 165 settlers arrived in Patagonia in July 1865. Landing on the bay where Puerto Madryn now stands, they went south in search of drinking water to the valley of the Chubut river, where they found cultivatable land and settled.

The settlement was partly inspired by Michael D Jones, a non-conformist minister whose aim was to create a 'little Wales beyond Wales', far from the intruding influence of the English restrictions on Welsh religious beliefs. He provided much of the early finance and took particular care to gather people with useful skills, such as farmers and craftsmen, recruiting settlers through the Welsh language press and through the chapels. Between 1865 and 1915, the colony was reinforced by another 3000 settlers from Wales. The early years brought persistent drought, and the Welsh only survived through creating a network of irrigation channels. Early settlers were allocated 100 ha of land and when, by 1885, all irrigable land had been allocated, the settlement expanded westwards along the valley to the town of Trevelin in the foothills of the Andes.

The Welsh colony was tremendously successful, partly due to the creation of its own cooperative society, which sold their excellent produce and bought necessities in Buenos Aires. Early settlers were organized into chapel-based communities of 200 to 300 people, which were largely self-governing and organized social and cultural activities. The colony thrived after 1880, producing wheat from the arid Chubut Valley which won prizes all over the world. However, the depression of the 1930s drove wheat prices down, and poor management by the Argentine government resulted in the downfall of the Welsh wheat business. Many of the Welsh stayed, however; most of the owners of Gaiman's extraordinary Welsh tea rooms are descendants of the original settlers. The Welsh language is kept alive in both Gaiman and Trevelin, and Gaiman's festival of the arts – Eisteddfod – is held every October.

museum traces the origins of life through the geological ages, displaying dynamically poised dinosaur skeletons, with plentiful information in Spanish. Tours are free and are available in English, German and Italian. There's also a reasonably cheap café and a shop. It's highly recommended and great for kids. For details of the **Geoparque Bryn Gwyn** near Gaiman, see below.

The **Museo Regional Pueblo de Luis** ⓘ *Fontana and Lewis Jones 9100, T0280-442 4062, Mon-Fri 0800-2000, US$2.50,* is appropriately housed in the old railway station, built in 1889, since it was Lewis Jones who founded the town and started the railways that exported Welsh produce so successfully. It has interesting displays on indigenous societies, on failed Spanish attempts at settlement, and on Welsh colonization.

Next to the tourist office is the **Museo Municipal de Artes Visuales (MMAV)** ⓘ *Mitre 350, T0280-443 3774, Mon-Fri 0800-1900, Sat-Sun 1400-1900, US$1,* located in an attractive wooden building. Recommended.

South of Trelew

There is a lovely rock and sand beach at **Playa Isla Escondida**, 55 km south of Trelew along unpaved Ruta 1, which is a possible route to Punta Tombo. It's a favourite spot for sports fishermen, and you can see sea elephants, sea lions and birds here. There's secluded camping but

Tip...
Visit the Reserva Natural Punta Tombo in the afternoon when it's quieter because noisy colonies of tourists dominate the place in the morning.

no facilities. The main destination to the south, however, is the **Reserva Natural Punta Tombo** ① *www.puntatombo.com, daily 0800-1800 in high season, US$14, children US$7*, which is the largest breeding ground for Magellanic penguins in Patagonia and the largest single penguin colony on the South American continent. The nature reserve is best visited from September to March, when huge numbers of Magellanic penguins come here to breed. Chicks can be seen from mid-November and they waddle to the water in January or February. It's fascinating to see these creatures up close and you'll see guanacos, hares and rheas on the way.

To reach the reserve follow Ruta 1 for 100 km south towards Camarones; this is a *ripio* road best attempted in a high clearance vehicle. Alternatively, take paved Ruta 3 south and then turn onto Ruta Provincial 75 until it reaches Ruta 1, a total distance of 122 km. Tours from Trelew and Puerto Madryn cost US$70, allow 45 minutes at the site and usually include a stop at Gaiman.

Gaiman *Colour map 5, B5.*

The quaint village of Gaiman lies west of Trelew, in the floodplain of the Río Chubut, and was made beautifully green and fertile thanks to careful irrigation of these lands by Welsh settlers. After travelling for a few days (or even hours) on the arid Patagonian steppe, it will strike you as a lush green oasis, testimony to the tireless hard work of those hardy Welsh emigrants. Gaiman is the first village you come to on Route 25, which heads west past Dolavon before continuing through attractive scenery to Esquel (see page 467) and the other Welsh colony of Trevelin in the Andes (see page 471). On the way, you'll find old Welsh chapels tucked away amongst the poplars in this green valley.

Gaiman is a pretty little place with old brick houses, which retains the Welsh pioneer feel despite the constant influx of tourists It has several tea rooms, many of them run by descendants of the original pioneers, serving delicious Welsh teas and cakes. Before you fill up on those, gain an insight into the spartan lives of those idealistic pioneers by visiting the **old railway station** (1909), which now houses the wonderful, tiny **Museo Histórico Regional Galés** ① *Sarmiento and 28 de Julio, T0280-154569372, daily 1500-1900, US$1.* This has an impressive collection of Welsh artefacts, objects and photographs that serve as an evocative and moving testimony to extraordinary lives in harsh conditions. It is a great resource if you're looking for books on the subject or trying to trace your emigrant relatives.

Many other older buildings remain, among them the low stone first house, **Primera Casa** (1874) ① *corner of main street, Av Tello y Evans, daily 1100-1800, US$1.* Other notable buildings include the old hotel (1899), at Tello and 9 de Julio; and the Ty Nain tea room (1890), on the Plaza at Yrigoyen 283. Cross the bridge to the south side of the river, and then take the first right to find two old chapels: pretty Capilla Bethel (1913) and the Capilla Vieja.

Some 8 km south of town there are fossil beds dating back 40 million years at the **Geoparque Bryn Gwyn** ① *T0280-442 0012, www.mef.org.ar, Tue-Sun 1000-1600, US$3, US$1.50 children, taxi from Gaiman US$5.* This is a mind-boggling expanse of time brought to life by a good guided tour. It takes two hours to do the circuit, with fossils to see, as well as a visitor centre where you can try some fieldwork in palaeontology.

Dolavon *Colour map 5, B4.*

Founded in 1919, Dolavon (population 2500) is the most westerly Welsh settlement in the valley and not quite as inviting as Gaiman, though its quiet streets are rather atmospheric, and on a short stroll you can find a few buildings reminiscent of the Welsh past. The main street, Avenida Roca, runs parallel to the irrigation canal built by the settlers, where willow trees now trail into the swiftly flowing water; there's a Welsh chapel, **Capilla Carmel**, at its quieter end. The old **flour mill** ① *Maipú and Roca, Tue-Sun 1100-1600, US$2*, dates from 1927 and can be visited. There's **Autoservicio Belgrano** at the far end of San Martín for food supplies, but there is only one tea room, **El Molienda** ① *Maipú 61, T0280-449 2290, www.molinoharinerodedolavon.com, US$7.50*, and nowhere really to stay apart from the municipal campsite two blocks north of the river which is free and has good facilities.

If you're in your own transport, it's worth driving from Dolavon back towards Gaiman via the neat squared fields in this beautiful irrigated valley, where you'll see more Welsh chapels tucked away among poplar trees and silver birches. Follow the main road that leads south through Dolavon, and then turn left and take the next right, signposted to Iglesia Anglicana. The **San David Chapel** (1917) is a beautifully preserved brick construction, with an elegant bell tower and sturdy oak-studded door, in a quiet spot surrounded by birches. Further on you'll cross the raised irrigation canals the Welsh built, next to small orchards of apple trees and tidy fields bordered by *álamo* trees.

West of Dolavon

West from Dolavon, paved Ruta 25 runs to the upper Chubut Valley, passing near the **Florentino Ameghino** dam, 120 km west of Trelew, which is a leafy spot for a picnic. The road from Ameghino to Tecka (on the junction with Ruta 40 south of Trevelín) is one of the most beautiful routes across Patagonia to the Andes, with lots of wildlife to see. It goes through Las Plumas (mind the bridge if driving), reaching Los Altares at Km 321, which has an ACA motel (**$$**) with restaurant and bar, a basic campsite 400 m behind the service station, fuel and some shops. Beyond, Route 25 continues via Paso de Indios.

Listings Trelew and the Chubut Valley *map page 498.*

Tourist information

Trelew

Useful websites include www.trelew turismo.wordpress.com (in Spanish only) and www.trelewpatagonia.gov.ar.

Tourist office
Mitre 387, on the main plaza, T0280-442 0139. Mon-Fri 0800-2000, Sat-Sun 0900-2100.
Very helpful office. There's another office at bus station (same opening times) and at the airport when flights arrive. They'll give you an excellent map, directing you to the town's older buildings.

Gaiman

Tourist office
Av Belgrano 574, on the main plaza, T0280-449 1571, www.gaiman.gov.ar. Daily 0900-1900, Sun 1100-1800 (shorter hours in low season).

Where to stay

Trelew

$$$$-$$$ La Casona del Río
Chacra 105, Capitán Murga, T0280-443 8343, www.lacasonadelrio.com.ar.

5 km from town, pick-up arranged, attractive, family-run B&B with heating, TV, meals available, bicycles, massage, laundry, tennis and bowls, English and French spoken. Higher prices Feb-Jul.

$$$ Galicia
9 de Julio 214, T0280-443 3802,
www.hotelgalicia.com.ar.
Central, grand entrance, comfortable rooms, excellent value. Recommended.

$$$ Libertador
Rivadavia 31, T0280-442 0220,
www.hotellibertadortw.com.ar.
Modern hotel, highly recommended for service and comfortable bedrooms.

$$$ Rayentray
Belgrano 397, cnr San Martín, T0280-443 4702, www.cadena rayentray.com.ar.
Large, modern, comfortable rooms, professional staff, pool, Wi-Fi.

$$ Rivadavia
Rivadavia 55, T0280-443 4472.
Simple, comfortable rooms, breakfast extra.

$$ Touring Club
Fontana 240, Peatonal Luis Gazín, T0280-443 3997, www.touringpatagonia. com.ar.
Gorgeous 1920s bar, faded elegance, simple rooms, great value, breakfast included. Open from breakfast until 1230 at night for sandwiches and drinks. Wi-Fi in rooms and bar. Butch Cassidy himself endorsed the place.

Camping

Camping Sero
Playa Unión, 25 km from Trelew, T0280-449 6982.
Located in the quaint seaside village of Playa Unión, this campsite offers lodging from US$7.50 per night.

Gaiman

$$$$-$$$ Posada Los Mimbres
Chacra 211, 6 km west of Gaiman, T0280-449 1299, www.posadalosmimbres.com.ar. Cheaper Apr-Aug.
Rooms in the old farmhouse or in modern building, good food, very relaxing.

$$$-$$ Ty Gwyn
9 de Julio 111, T0280-449 1009,
tygwyn@tygwyn.com.ar.
Neat, comfortable, above the tea rooms, excellent value.

$$ Hostería Ty'r Haul
Sarmiento 121, T0280-449 1880.
Historic building, rooms are comfortable and well lit. Recommended.

$$ Plas y Coed
Yrigoyen 320, T02965-449 1133,
www.plasycoed.com.ar.
Ana Rees' delightful tea shop has double and twin rooms in an annex next door. Highly recommended.

Camping
Camping de los Bomberos is the municipal site.

Restaurants

Trelew

$$ La Bodeguita
Belgrano 374, T0280-443 7777.
Delicious pasta and pizzas. Reasonable wine list. Recommended.

$$ La Casona
Pasaje Jujuy and Lewis Jones, near Plaza Centenario, T0280-443-4026, www.lacasonatrelew.blogspot.com.
Patagonian lamb, *parrilla*, good lunchtime venue.

$$ Miguel Ángel
Fontana 246, next door to Touring Club (see Where to stay, above), in Peatonal Luis Gazín, Av Fontana.
Good standard fare of meat and pasta dishes.

Cafés

Café de mi Ciudad
Belgrano 394.
Smart café serving great coffee; read the
papers here. Also has Wi-Fi.

Café Verdi
*Attached to Teatro Verdi, Bulevú, San Martín
412, T0280-443 6601, see Facebook.*
Cosy café featuring an array of healthy
dishes including sandwiches, salads and
fresh juices. Mouth-watering bakery. Great
for vegetarians.

Gaiman
Welsh teas
You're unlikely to be able to resist the Welsh
teas for which Gaiman has become famous,
though quite how the tradition sprung up
remains a mystery. It's hard to imagine the
residents' abstemious ancestors tucking
into vast plates filled with 7 kinds of cake
and scones at one sitting. Tea is served from
1400-1900; all the tea rooms charge US$15-20
and include the most well-known of the
'Welsh' cakes, *torta negra* – a delicious dense
fruit cake.

Casa de Té Gaiman
*Av Yrigoyen 738, T0280-449 1633,
amaliaj51@hotmail.com.*
One of the few remaining tea houses
in Gaiman still run by the original
Welsh descendants.

Plas Y Coed
See Where to stay, above.
The best, and oldest; owner Ana Rees
learned how to cook at the feet of Marta
Rees, her grandmother and one of the best
cooks in Gaiman.

Ty Gwyn
*9 de Julio 111, T0280-449 1009,
tygwyn@tygwyn.com.ar. Opens 1400.*
Large tea room, more modern than some,
welcoming; generous teas.

Festivals

Gaiman
Sep Eisteddfod (Welsh Festival of Arts).

Shopping

Trelew
The main shopping area is around San Martín
and from the plaza to Belgrano. Though
Trelew can't compare with Puerto Madryn
for souvenirs, it has a good little handicrafts
market on the plaza. There is a **Norte**
supermarket, Rivadavia y 9 de Julio.

What to do

Trelew
Tour operators
Agencies run tours to Punta Tombo, Chubut
Valley (half- and full-day). Tours to Península
Valdés are best done from Puerto Madryn.
Explore Patagonia, *Roca 94, T0280-443
7860, www.explore-patagonia.com.ar.*
A competing operator offering similar tour
packages to **Nieve Mar**. Also has an office
in Puerto Madryn.
Nieve Mar, *Italia 20, T0280-443 4114, www.
nievemartours.com.ar.* Trips to Punta Tombo
and Valdés, bilingual guides (reserve ahead),
organized and efficient. Has a branch in
Puerto Madryn (Av Roca 493).

Transport

Trelew
Air
The airport is 5 km north of centre. A taxi
costs US$7 and local buses to/from Puerto
Madryn will stop at the airport entrance
if asked.
   Aerolíneas Argentinas (Rivadavia 548,
T0810-222 86527) has flights to/from **Buenos
Aires**, **Bariloche**, **El Calafate** and **Ushuaia**.
LADE (Italia 170, T0280-443 5740) flies to
Patagonian airports.

Bus
Local **28 de Julio/Mar y Valle** go frequently
to **Gaiman**, 30-45 mins, US$1; to **Dolavon**

1 hr, US$3.50; to **Puerto Madryn** (via **Trelew airport**), 1 hr, US$3; to **Puerto Pirámides**, 2½ hrs, US$7, daily.

Long distance The bus terminal is on the east side of Plaza Centenario at Urquiza y Lewis Jones, T0280-442 0121. To **Buenos Aires**, daily, 19-20 hrs, US$100-140, several companies; to **Comodoro Rivadavia**, 5 hrs, US$30-37, many departures; to **Río Gallegos**, 17 hrs; US$90-105 (with connections to **El Calafate**, **Puerto Natales**, **Punta Arenas**), many companies. To **Esquel**, 9-10 hrs, US$45-50, **Don Otto**.

Car hire
Car hire desks at the airport are staffed only at flight arrival times and cars are taken quickly. All have offices in town: **AVIS**, airport, T0280-15425997; **Fiorasi**, Urquiza 310, T0280-443 5344; **Hertz**, at the airport, T0280-442 4421.

Gaiman
Bus
To **Trelew** every 30 mins, US$1, **Don Otto**.

Dolavon
Bus
To **Trelew**, several a day, 1 hr, US$1.50, with **28 de Julio**.

Southern
Atlantic Coast

Quieter, and much less visited by tourists than Puerto Madryn and Península Valdés, the southern stretch of the Atlantic coastline from Camarones to Río Gallegos is extremely rich in marine life of all kinds. There are several wonderful reserves protecting a wide variety of species of bird and mammal, and a few good bases for exploring them at the coastal towns of Camarones, Puerto Deseado and Puerto San Julián, with decent services and accommodation. If you have your own transport, you could head out to the only national park on the coast, Monte León, where you can walk the shore for miles and stay in a remote but comfortable *hostería*. And on the last spit of land before Tierra del Fuego, there's ancient history to explore near the coast at Cabo Vírgenes.

There are two cities in this huge region, of which the most appealing is the southernmost town on the Argentine mainland, Río Gallegos. It's a small, pleasant place, with fair accommodation and tours offered to penguin colonies, though there's little else to draw you here unless you're changing buses. The other city, Comodoro Rivadavia, is probably best avoided, unless you're keen to see the petroleum museum.

Aside from coastal attractions, this region also has the country's finest petrified forest, the Monumento Natural Bosques Petrificados.

Camarones and around *Colour map 5, C4.*

Camarones (population 2000) is a quiet fishing port on Bahía Camarones, south of Trelew, whose main industry is harvesting seaweed. This is also prime sheep-rearing land, and Camarones wool is world-renowned for its quality. Aside from the salmon festival in early or mid-February, the only real attraction is a penguin colony, which you can walk to from the town.

There's another well-known penguin colony with lots more species of marine life, 35 km southeast at **Reserva Natural Cabo Dos Bahías** ① *open daily, free; there are buses to the reserve from Trelew, see page 497.* This is a small reserve at the southern end of the bay, reached by a dirt road. It protects a large colony of some 100,000 penguins, which you can see close up; there are also seals and sea lions all year round, and whales from March to November; killer whales might be spotted from October to April. On land there are rheas, guanacos and maras.

Bahía Bustamante

Some 90 km south of Camarones along the coast is Bahía Bustamante, a settlement of seaweed harvesters and sheep ranchers on Golfo San Jorge (180 km north of Comodoro Rivadavia). Its main attractions are the coastal and steppe landscapes of the surrounding Patagonia Austral Marine national park, which offers exceptional opportunities to see birds (including 100,000 penguins), marine and land mammals.

Comodoro Rivadavia and around *Colour map 5, C4.*

Situated at the end of the Bioceanic Corridor, a fast road to Chile, Comodoro is the hub for terrestrial transport and a bus nexus from all areas of Patagonia. You're most likely to end up here if you need to change buses, and there's little to make you want to stay (certainly not the high prices). With a population of 350,000, Comodoro Rivadavia is the largest city in the province of Chubut.

It was established primarily as a sheep-exporting port, and early settlers included Boer immigrants fleeing British rule in southern Africa. The city began to flourish suddenly when oil was discovered here in 1907, bringing in many international companies. However, since the petrol industry was privatized by President Menem in the 1990s, there's been consequent unemployment and now the town has a slightly sad, rather unkempt feel.

Around Comodoro Rivadavia There's a good view of the city from **Cerro Chenque**, 212 m high, a dun-coloured hill, unattractively adorned with radar masts, whose cliffs give the town its drab backdrop. It's interesting to take a taxi up there, if you don't feel like the walk, to see the first pioneers' homes, now dilapidated, but with panoramic views of the bay.

If you're really stuck for something to do, you could also visit the **Museo Nacional del Petróleo** ① *San Lorenzo 250, 3 km north of the centre, T0297-455 9558, Mon-Fri 0900-1700, Sat-Sun 1500-1800, US$4,* for a good history of local oil exploitation.

There's a good beach at the resort of **Rada Tilly**, 8 km south, where you can walk along the beach at low tide to see sea lions. **Expreso Rada Tilly** runs buses every 30 minutes, US$1; they're packed in summer.

You could use Comodoro Rivadavia as a base for exploring a petrified forest, the **Bosque Petrificado José Ormachea**, but the little town of **Sarmiento**, some 140 km west, is far more pleasant. For information on getting to Sarmiento, see Transport, below.

Tourist information

Comodoro Rivadavia

Tourist office
Dr Scocco and Abasolo, T0297-444 0664,
www.comodoroturismo.gob.ar.
Very helpful and English is spoken.
There's another office at the bus terminal;
see Transport, below.

Where to stay

Camarones

For other lodgings see www.argentina
turismo.com.ar/camarones.

$$$-$$ Complejo Indalo Inn
Sarmiento and Roca, T0297-496 3004,
www.indaloinn.com.ar.
Simple but clean, doubles and singles with
en suite. Good food, and the owner runs trips
to the penguin colony. Recommended.

$$$-$$ El Faro
Brown s/n, T0297-414 5510,
www.elfaro-patagonia.com.ar.
2-person private rooms with sea views.
Also rents beachside houses for up to
5 people. Cash only. Under the same
ownership as **Bahía Bustamante**.

Bahía Bustamante

Bahía Bustamante
T011-4156 7788/T0297-480 1000, www.
bahiabustamante.com. Closed Apr-Sep.
An award-winning resort offering full-board
and self-catering accommodation, plus
hiking, cycling, riding and kayaking; guides
are on hand. Electricity 1900 to 2400. If you
don't have your own transport, you can
phone or email in advance to be picked up
from the ACA station in Garayalde, or there
are regular buses from Trelew.

Comodoro Rivadavia

$$$ Lucania Palazzo
Moreno 676, T0297-449 9300,
www.lucania-palazzo.com.
Most luxurious business hotel, superb rooms,
sea views, good value, huge American
breakfast, sauna and gym included.
Recommended.

$$ Azul
Sarmiento 724, T0297-446 7539,
info@hotelazul.com.ar.
Breakfast extra, quiet old place with
lovely bright rooms, kind, great views
from the *confitería*.

$$ Hospedaje Cari Hue
Belgrano 563, T0297-447 2946, see Facebook.
Sweet rooms, with separate bathrooms,
indifferent owner, breakfast extra. Probably
the cheapest place to stay that's halfway safe.

Camping

Camping Municipal
Rada Tilly, T445 2689, www.radatilly.com.ar.
Open in high season only.
Reached by **Expreso Rada Tilly** bus from
town. Hot showers.

San Carlos
37 km north on R3, T0297-486 3122.
Open all year.
Covers 20 ha.

Restaurants

Comodoro Rivadavia

$$ Cayo Coco
Rivadavia 102, T0297-4097 3033.
Bistro with excellent pizzas, good service.
Also Cayo Coco del Mar, Av Costanera 1051.

$$ Maldito Peperoni
Sarmiento 581, T0297-446 9683.
Cheerful, modern, pastas.

Transport

Camarones
Bus

To **Trelew**, Mon, Wed, Fri at 0800, 2½ hrs, US$17, with **Transportes El Ñandu SRL**.

Comodoro Rivadavia
Air

The **airport** is 13 km north of town and bus No 6 leaves hourly for the bus terminal, 45 mins, US$0.50. A taxi from the airport costs US$17.

Aerolíneas Argentinas (Rivadavia 156, T0810-222 86527) and **LAN** (www.lan.com) have regular flights to **Buenos Aires** and **Bariloche** (Aerolíneas Argentinas also flies to **Esquel**). **LADE** (Rivadavia 360, T0297-447 0585) flies to all Patagonian destinations.

Bus

The bus terminal (Pellegrini 730, T0297-446 7305) is convenient for the town centre. It has a luggage store, a good *confitería* upstairs and toilets. There's a tourist information office (open Mon-Fri from 0800 to 2000, Sat 0900-2000, Sun 1000-2000). In summer buses usually arrive full, so book ahead.

To **Buenos Aires**, several daily, 24-28 hrs, US$135-155. To **Bariloche**, 14½ hrs, US$57-77, with **Don Otto** (T0297-447 0450), **Marga** and **Andesmar** (T0297-446 8894). To **Esquel** (paved road), 9 hrs direct with **EETAP**, T0297-447 4841, and **Don Otto**, US$45-50. To **Río Gallegos**, daily, several companies 10-12 hrs, US$60-70. To **Puerto Madryn**, US$33-40. To **Trelew**, daily, 5 hrs, US$28-35, several companies including **Don Otto**. To **Caleta Olivia**, 1 hr, US$5-8. To **Sarmiento**, 4 daily, 2½ hrs, US$11. To **Puerto Deseado**, **Sportman**, 2 a day, US$25.

Car rental

Avis, Moreno 725 (in the Hotel Austral lobby), T0297-4464828; **Patagonia Sur Car**, Rawson 1190, T0297-446 6768.

South of Comodoro Rivadavia

towards Tierra del Fuego

Caleta Olivia *Colour map 5, C4.*
Caleta Olivia (population 51,733) lies on the Bahía San Jorge, 74 km south of Comodoro Rivadavia. Founded in 1901, it became the centre for exporting wool from the estancias of Santa Cruz. It boomed with the discovery of oil in 1944 but has suffered since the petroleum industry was privatized in the 1990s and is now a rather sad place with high unemployment and a reputation for petty crime. However, there's a lovely 70-km stretch of pebbly beach, popular with locals for bathing, and lots of fishing nearby.

At **Pico Truncado**, some 50 km southwest, there's the gas field that feeds the pipeline to Buenos Aires. There's a daily bus service from Caleta Oliva, and Pico Truncado has a few simple hotels, a campsite, and **tourist information** ⓘ *T0297-499 2202*.

Monumento Natural Bosques Petrificados
256 km west of Puerto Deseado; access is via Route 49 which branches off the R3 at Km 2063, 86 km south of Fitz Roy. Daily 1000-2000, donations welcome.

Extending over 10,000 ha in a bizarre, wind-wracked lunar landscape surrounding the **Laguna Grande**, this park contains much older petrified trees than the forests further north around Sarmiento. The trunks, mainly of giant araucaria trees, are up to 35 m long and 150 cm in diameter.

Tip...
Bring your own food and drink as there are no facilities, services or water sources in the park.

They were petrified in the Jurassic period 140 million years ago by intense volcanic activity in the Andes cordillera which blew ash over the entire area. It was the silicates in this volcanic ash that petrified the trunks of fallen trees and created these strange jasper-like hulks, which were only revealed when other organic matter around them eroded. The place is more eerie than beautiful, but it does exert a strange fascination, especially when you consider that the fossils of marine animals that you see on the site are a mere 40 million years old, belonging to a sea that covered the land long after the trees had turned to stone. There is a small visitor centre and museum, and a well-documented 1-km trail that takes you past the most impressive specimens. You may be very tempted to take away your own personal souvenir: don't.

The only way to visit the park, unless you have your own transport, is with a tour: try **Los Vikingos** based in Puerto Deseado. For further information, see What to do, page 511.

Listings South of Comodoro Rivadavia

Tourist information

Caleta Olivia

Tourist office
San Martín y Güemes, T0297 485 0088, turismocaletaolivia on Facebook.
The municipal website is www.caletaolivia.gov.ar.

Where to stay

Caleta Olivia

$$$ Patagonia Hotel
Av Eva Perón 1873, T0297-483 0517, www.patagoniahotelco.com.ar.
Welcoming, slightly dated hotel with clean bright rooms and views of the ocean.

$$ pp Hotel Robert
San Martín 2152, T0297-485 1452, www.hotelrobert.com.ar.
Comfortable option. All rooms have bathroom, and breakfast is included.

$ Grand Hotel
Mosconi and Chubut, T0297-485 1393.
Reasonably comfortable rooms.

Camping

Camping Gerald
Route 3, 5 km south of Caleta Oliva, T0297 485 0613.
Also *cabañas*.

Monumento Natural Bosques Petrificados

There is no accommodation in the area, apart from camping at **Estancia La Paloma** (on Ruta 49, 25 km away, T0297-444 3503). Note that camping is not allowed in the park.

Transport

Caleta Olivia
Bus

To **Río Gallegos**, with **Andesmar**, **Sportman** and others, US$54-71, 9½ hrs. Many buses to/from **Comodoro Rivadavia**, 1 hr, US$5-8, and 2 daily to **Puerto Deseado**, 2½-3 hrs, US$18, with **Sportman**. To **Perito Moreno** 5-6 hrs, US$24, 3 a day **Sportman** and **Marga**; to **Los Antiguos** 3-5 hrs, US$29, 3 a day.

Puerto Deseado (population 20,000) is a pleasant fishing port on the estuary of the Río Deseado, which drains, curiously, into Lago Buenos Aires in the west. It's a stunning stretch of coastline, rich in wildlife: the estuary encompasses a wonderful reserve, and there are more reserves within reach, protecting sea lions and penguins. In fact, Puerto Deseado offers an abundance of marine life in much the same vein as Puerty Madryn, but at a fraction of the cost of visiting that tourist hotspot.

The **Museo Regional Mario Brozoski** ⓘ *Belgrano (9050) and Colón, see Facebook, Mon-Fri 0900-1600, Sat-Sun 1500-1800*, has remains of an 18th-century ship that sank off the coast here in 1770, as well as some evocative photos. Outside the former railway station, a rather fine old building in vaguely English medieval style, is the **Vagón Histórico** ⓘ *San Martín and Almirate Brown, www.deseado.gov.ar*, an 1898 carriage now used as the tourist office.

Reserva Natural Ría Deseado
The submerged estuary (*ría*) of the Río Deseado, 42 km long, is an important nature reserve and a stunning area to visit. The crumbling chalky cliffs in mauve and ochre are splattered with *guano* (droppings) from many varieties of seabird. There's a colony of Magellanic penguins and five species of cormorant, including the unique red-legged cormorant, most appealing with their smart dinner-jacketed appearance. These birds nest from October to April on four islands offshore. The reserve is also a breeding ground for Commerson's dolphins, beautiful creatures that frolic playfully around your boat. Excellent tours run from the pier in Puerto Deseado; they last about two hours and are best in early morning or late evening (see What to do, below).

Other reserves round Puerto Deseado
There are several other nature reserves within easy reach if you have transport, and all offer good places to walk. North of Puerto Deseado, some 90 km on the northern shore of the peninsula, is **Cabo Blanco**, the site of the largest fur seal colony in Patagonia. It's another magnificent area, a rocky peninsula bursting out from flat lands, with one of the oldest lighthouses on the coast perched on top and thousands of seals on the rocks below. The breeding season is December to January.

A little further west, you should also visit Cañadón de Duraznillo and Monte Loayza, which combine to form the **Reserva Natural Provincial Monte Loayza** ⓘ *www. monteloayza.com.ar*. Cañadón de Duraznillo is an area of Patagonian steppe, while Monte Loayza is a strip of coastal and marine habitat. Here you'll see lots of guanacos, *ñandues*, foxes and birds, as well as the largest seal colony in the province on spectacular unspoilt beaches.

The visitor centre is at Estancia La Madrugada, which is 83 km from Puerto Deseado; the reserve is 18 km further west, towards Jaramillo. Visits are limited to groups of 10 or less from November to March and must be accompanied by a specialist guide; if you arrive without a guide you will only be allowed in to the visitor centre.

South of Puerto Deseado are two more reserves: **Isla Pingüino**, an offshore island with a colony of Magellanic penguins, as well as cormorants and steamer ducks, and the **Reserva Natural Bahía Laura**, an uninhabited bay where black-necked cormorants, ducks and other seabirds can be found in abundance. Isla Pingüino can be reached by boat, and Bahía Laura by *ripio* and dirt roads. For further information, see What to do, below.

The **Gruta de Lourdes**, 24 km west, is a cave which attracts pilgrims to see the Virgen de Lourdes. Further south along the same road is the **Cañadón del Puerto**, a mirador offering fine views over the estuary.

Where to stay

Puerto Deseado

$$ Isla Chaffers
San Martín y Mariano Moreno,
T0297-487 2246, administracion@
hotelislachaffers.com.ar.
Modern, central.

$$ Los Acantilados
Pueyrredón y España, T0297-487 2167,
reservas.losacantilados@gmail.com.
Beautifully located, good breakfast.
Travellers report some rooms run down
and dingy.

Camping
Camping Cañadón de Giménez (4 km
away on R281, T0297-487 2135); **Camping
Municipal** (Av Lotufo, on the seafront).
Lovely locations but the sites are a bit
run down.

Restaurants

Puerto Deseado

$$ Puerto Cristal
España 1698, T0297-487 0387.
Panoramic views of the port, a great place
for Patagonian lamb, *parrilla* and seafood.

What to do

Puerto Deseado
Darwin Expediciones, *España 2551, T0297-15-
624 7554, www.darwin-expeditions.com.* Boat
trips to Ría Deseado reserve and tours to the
Monumento Natural Bosques Petrificados.
Los Vikingos, *Prefectura Naval s/n, T0297-
15-624 5141/0297-487 0020, www.losvikingos.
com.ar.* Boat trips to Ría Deseado reserve and
Reserva Provincial Isla Pingüino, bilingual
guides, customized tours.

Transport

Puerto Deseado
Bus
To **Caleta Olivia**, daily, US$17, with **Sportman**.

Puerto San Julián and further south *Colour map 6, A2.*

an oasis between remote outposts

Puerto San Julián
The quiet port town of Puerto San Julián (population 6200), lying on a peninsula overlooking the Bahía San Julián 268 km south of Fitz Roy, is the best place for breaking the 834-km run from Comodoro Rivadavia to Río Gallegos. It has a fascinating history, although little of it is in evidence today.

The first Mass in Argentina was held here in 1520 after the Portuguese explorer Magellan had executed a member of his mutinous crew. Then, in 1578, Francis Drake also put in here to behead Thomas Doughty, after amiably dining with him. In 1780, Antonio Viedma attempted to found

> **Tip...**
> The best time to visit the Reserva Natural San Julián is in December to see dolphins and cormorants, though there's plenty to see from December to April.

a colony here, but it failed due to scurvy. (You can visit the ruins of the site at **Florida Blanca**, 10 km west.) The current town was founded in 1901 as a port to serve the sheep estancias of this part of Santa Cruz.

The small **Museo Regional** at Rivadavia and Vieytes houses the amazingly well-preserved dinosaur footprint found in the town. There's plenty of wildlife to be seen in the area, especially in the coastal **Reserva Natural San Julián**, which is very accessible; ask about the superb tours at the **tourist office** (see Tourist information, below) and in the bus station. The reserve, on the shores of Bahía San Julián, includes the islands **Banco Cormorán** and **Banco Justicia**, thought to be the site of the 16th-century executions; there is a colony of Magellanic penguins and nesting areas for several species of cormorant and other birds. You're also very likely to spot Commerson's dolphins. It's a lovely location and the concentration of marine life is stunning.

There are 30 km of spectacular coastline north of San Julián, including **Cabo Curiosa**, 15 km north, which has fine beaches; it's a popular bathing place for the whole of the region. It's also worth visiting **Estancia La María**, 150 km west, which has one of the main archaeological sites in Patagonia: a huge canyon with 87 caves full of paintings including human hands and guanacos, 4000-12,000 years old. The estancia offers transport and accommodation (see Where to stay, below).

Piedrabuena *Colour map 6, B2.*

Known officially as Comandante Luis Piedrabuena, the quiet town of Piedrabuena (population 6405) is named after the famous Argentine explorer and sailor, Piedra Buena, who built his home on Isla Pavón, an island in the river Santa Cruz, in 1859. On this small mound in the deep emerald green fast-flowing river you can visit the **Casa Histórica Luis Piedra Buena**, a reconstruction of the original building where he carried on a peaceful trade with local indigenous groups. However, the island has become most popular as a weekend resort for those fishing steelhead trout and it's a world-renowned fishing spot.

Piedrabuena is a good base for exploring the Parque Nacional Monte León, which protects 40 km of coastline and steppe, 30 km south.

Essential Parque Nacional Monte León

Access

It's difficult to reach the park unless you have a 4WD; access is along 23 km of poor *ripio* road which branches off Route 3, 36 km south of Piedrabuena. Or fly from Buenos Aires to Río Gallegos and take a taxi from the airport (two hours, US$120-140 for up to four passengers). Further information is available from the **park office**, Belgrano y 9 de Julio, Puerto de Santa Cruz, T02962-489184, monteleon@apn.gov.ar, www.parquesnacionales.gob.ar, www.vidasilvestre.org.ar.

Parque Nacional Monte León and around

The only national park on Argentina's long Atlantic coastline, Monte León is a beautiful stretch of steppe and shore, south of Piedrabuena. It includes 40 km of coastline, with many caves and little bays, as well as the tiny island Monte León, an important breeding area for cormorants and terns. In addition, there's the world's fourth largest colony of penguins and several colonies of sea lions. It was acquired for the Argentine nation by deceased North American billionaire Douglas Tompkins (whose foundation also owns Parque Pumalín in Chile, and Rincón del Socorro in Los Esteros del Iberá), and was looked after by the organization **Vida Silvestre**, before being made a national park in 2004.

ON THE ROAD

National parks and nature reserves

Parque Nacional Los Glaciares is the most famous park in Patagonia. At the northern end the main centre is El Chaltén for trekking around **Mount Fitz Roy** and at the southern end are the glaciers, reached from El Calafate. Both have *guardaparques'* offices where staff speak English and other languages, hand out maps and can advise on where to walk and camp. See www.parquesnacionales.gov.ar (in Spanish) for more information.

    Parque Nacional Perito Moreno is also spectacular, and well worth the considerable effort involved in reaching its remote lakes and mountains. Access is via the Ruta 40, but there is almost no infrastructure whatsoever and little information for visitors. The best way to see the park is to stay at an estancia, such as **La Maipú**, and ride horses into the park.

    Marine life abounds on the Atlantic coast in Península Valdés, reached by organized tour or hire car from Puerto Madryn. Although it's not a national park, this is a well-organized area for visits, with several estancias on the peninsula where you can stay in great comfort. Further south, **Parque Nacional Monte León** is reached by Ruta 3, you'll need your own transport, but there is a comfortable *hostería*. There are many other colonies of penguins and other sea life reserves along the Atlantic coast. Unless you have your own transport it's best to take an organized tour to reach these, as services are few at the sites themselves.

It's not easy to access the park, but your efforts to get here will be rewarded by wonderful walks along wide isolated beaches with their extraordinary rock formations, and cliffs dotted with vast caverns, fabulous at low tide. The park also protects an important habitat of seashore steppe, which is home to pumas and wolves as well as guanacos and choiques. The old house at the heart of the park has been converted into a *hostería*; staying here is by far the best way to enjoy the surroundings in comfort (see Where to stay, below). Plans for the national park include improving access and turning the old shearing shed into a visitor centre.

Listings Puerto San Julián and further south

Tourist information

Puerto San Julián

Tourist office
*Av San Martín entre Rivadavia y M Moreno,
T02962-452009, www.sanjulian.gov.ar.*

Piedrabuena

Tourist office
*Av G Ibáñez 157 (bus station),
T02962-1557 3065.*

Where to stay

Puerto San Julián

$$$ Bahía
*San Martín 1075, T02962-453144,
www.hotelbahiasanjulian.com.ar.*
Modern, comfortable, good value.
Recommended.

$$ Municipal Costanera
*25 de Mayo y Urquiza, T02962-452300,
www.costanerahotel.com.*

Attractive, well-run place with good-value rooms, but no restaurant.

Estancias

$$$ Estancia La María
150 km northwest of Puerto San Julián; office in San Julián, Saavedra 1163, T02962-452328, see Facebook.
Offers transport, lodging, meals and trips to cave paintings that are less visited than Cueva de las Manos (see page 523).

Camping
Good **municipal campsite** (Magallanes 650, T02962-454506). Repeatedly recommended, all facilities.

Parque Nacional Monte León

$$$$ Hostería Estancia Monte León
R3, Km 2399, T011-15-6155 1220 (Buenos Aires), www.monteleon-patagonia.com. Nov-Apr.
4 tasteful rooms, all decorated with Douglas Tompkins' considerable style. There's a good library, living room and even a small museum. Fishing is good here, too. It's a fantastic place to stay.

Restaurants

Puerto San Julián

$$ La Rural
Ameghino 811.
Good, but not before 2100.

Festivals

Piedrabuena
Mar National trout festival.

What to do

Puerto San Julián
Excursiones Pinocho, *Av Costanera between San Martín and Mitre, T02962-454600, www. pinochoexcursiones.com.ar.* Excellent Zodiac boat trips, lasting 90 mins, into Reserva Natural San Julián.

Transport

Puerto San Julián
Bus
Many companies to both **Comodoro Rivadavia**, US$30-40, and **Río Gallegos**, 6 hrs, US$21-29.

Río Gallegos *Colour map 6, B2. See map, page 516.*

the southernmost city in Patagonia

The capital of Santa Cruz province, Río Gallegos (pronounced rio ga-shay-gos, population 120,000) lies on the estuary of the Gallegos river, which is famous for its excellent brown trout fishing. It's a pleasant, airy town, founded in 1885 as a centre for the trade in wool and sheepskins, and is by far the most appealing of the main centres on Patagonia's southern Atlantic coast (which isn't saying a great deal). It has always been a major transport hub, but receives fewer visitors since the airport opened at El Calafate. However, if you come here to change buses, you could visit the penguin reserve at Cabo Vírgenes some 130 km south, or Monte León National Park 210 km north. The town itself has a couple of museums and a few smart shops and restaurants.

Sights
The tidy, leafy Plaza San Martín, two blocks south of the main street, Avenida Roca, has an interesting collection of trees, many planted by the early pioneers, and a diminutive corrugated-iron **cathedral**, with a wood-panelled ceiling in the chancel and stained-glass windows.

The best of the town's museums is the small **Museo de los Pioneros** ⓘ *Elcano y Alberdi, T02966-437763, daily 1000-1700, free*. Set in a house built in England and shipped here in 1890, there are interesting photographs and artefacts telling the story of the first Scottish settlers, who came here in 1884 from the Falklands/Malvinas Islands enticed by government grants of land. There's an interesting tour given by the English-speaking owner, a descendent of the Scottish pioneers, and great photos of those first sheep-farming settlers. There's work by local artists at **Museo de Arte Eduardo Minichelli** ⓘ *Maipú 13, T02966-436323 Mon 0800-1500, Tue-Fri 0800-1900, Sat-Sun 1500-1900*. **Museo Regional Provincial Padre Jesús Molina** ⓘ *El Cano and Alberdi, T02966-423290, Mon-Fri 1100-1900, Sat-Sun*

Essential Río Gallegos

Finding your feet

The **airport** is 10 km from the centre; a *remise* taxi should cost US$10-12. The bus terminal is inconveniently 3 km from the centre, at the corner of Route 3 and Avenida Eva Perón. Public transport **Montecristo SRL** runs to the centre, US$0.75, or take a taxi for US$4-5.

Useful addresses

Chilean Consulate, Mariano Moreno 148, T02966-422364. Monday-Friday 0800-1300 and 1400-1700, www.chile.gob.cl/rio-gallegos.

1100-1800, has some dull rocks and fossils and a couple of dusty dinosaur skeletons. **Museo Malvinas Argentinas** ⓘ *Pasteur 72, T02966-437618, Mon-Fri 1100-1600, Sat-Sun 1000-1700*, is quite stimulating. It aims to inform visitors why the Malvinas are Argentine.

Around Río Gallegos Laguna Azul, 62 km south near the Monte Aymond border crossing, is nothing more than a perfect royal-blue lagoon in the crater of an extinct volcano, but it does have a certain atmosphere, set in an arid lunar landscape, and it's a good place for a walk. Take a tour, or get off the bus along Route 3, which stops on the main road.

Reserva Provincial Cabo Vírgenes ⓘ *134 km south of Río Gallegos via Ruta 3 and Ruta 1 (ripio), 3½ hrs, free entry; tours with tour operators US$60*, is a nature reserve protecting the second largest colony of Magellanic penguins in Patagonia. There's an informative self-guided walk to see their nests amongst the *calafate* and fragrant *mata verde* bushes. It's good to visit from November to January, when chicks are born and there are nests under every bush: fascinating for anyone and wonderful for children. You can climb the **Cabo Vírgenes lighthouse** (owned by the Argentine Navy) for wonderful views. There's a *confitería* close by for snacks and souvenirs. Both the reserve and the lighthouse are usually included in tours from Río Gallegos or you could stay at **Estancia Monte Dinero** (see Where to stay, below) 13 km north of Cabo Vírgenes, which is a wonderful base for visiting the reserve. It is a working sheep farm, where the English-speaking Fenton family offers accommodation, food and trips (US$60 for a day visit); all excellent.

South of Cabo Vírgenes are the ruins of **Nombre de Jesús**, one of the two settlements founded by Pedro Sarmiento de Gamboa in 1584 and where, tragically, all its settlers died.

Tourist information

Carretón Municipal
Kirchner y San Martín. High season only, Mon-Fri 1100-1800, Sat-Sun 0900-2100.
An information caravan with helpful staff who speak English; they have a list of estancias and will phone round hotels for you.

Municipal tourist office
Av Beccar 126, T02966-436920, www.turismo.mrg.gov.ar.
There's also a small information desk at the **bus terminal** (T02966-442159, Mon-Fri 0700-2000, Sat-Sun 0800-1300 and 1500-2000).

Provincial tourist office
Av Pres Kirchner 863, T02966-437412, www.santacruzpatagonia.gob.ar. Mon-Fri 0800-1600.

Where to stay

Most hotels are situated within a few blocks of the main street, Av Roca, running northwest to southeast. Do not confuse the street Comodoro Rivadavia with (nearby) Bernardino Rivadavia.

$$$ Santa Cruz
Kirchner 701, T02966-420601, www.hotelsantacruzrgl.com.ar.

Río Gallegos

Where to stay 🛏
2 Comercio
3 Covadonga
5 Oviedo
6 París
7 Punta Arenas

8 Santa Cruz
9 Sehuen

Restaurants 🍴
1 Buffalo Grill House
2 El Chino

3 El Club Británico & Café Central
4 La Casa del Sushi

Good value, spacious rooms with good beds, full buffet breakfast. Recommended.

$$$ Sehuen
Rawson 160, T02966-425683, www.hotelsehuen.com.
Good, cosy, helpful.

$$ Comercio
Kirchner 1302, T02966-420209, www.hotelcomercio.com.ar.
Good value, including breakfast, attractive design, comfortable, cheap *confitería*.

$$ Covadonga
Kirchner 1244, T02966-420190, www.hotel-alonso.com.ar.
Small rooms, attractive old building, breakfast extra. Same owners as the **Hotel Alonso** at Corrientes 33.

$$ París
Kirchner 1040, T02966-420111, www.hotelparisrg.com.ar.
Simple rooms, shared bath, good value.

$$ Punta Arenas
F Sphur 55, T02966-427743, www.hotelpuntaarenas.com.
Rooms with shared bath cheaper. Smart, rooms in new wing cost more. **Something Café** attached.

$ Oviedo
Libertad 746, T02966-420118, www.hoteloviedo.com.ar.
A cheaper budget option, breakfast extra, laundry facilities, café, parking.

Around Río Gallegos
Estancias

$$$$ Monte Dinero
120 km south of Río Gallegos, near Cabo Vírgenes, T02966-428922, www.montedinero.com.ar.
Comfortable accommodation on a working sheep farm. The house is lined with wood rescued from ships wrecked off the coast, and the food is delicious and home-grown. Highly recommended.

Camping

Club Pescazaike
Paraje Guer Aike, Ruta 3, 30 km west, T02966-423442, info@pescazaike.com.ar.
Also *quincho* and restaurant.

Restaurants

$$ Buffalo Grill House
Lista 198, T02966-439 511.
Popular chowdown spot. Somehow manages to mix North American, Mexican and Argentine cuisine.

$$ El Club Británico
Kirchner 935, T02966-432668.
Good value, excellent steaks.

$$ La Casa del Sushi
Libertad 398, T02966-15 590604, www.lacasadelsushi.com.
Sushi and Chilean sandwiches.

$ El Chino
9 de Julio 27.
Varied *tenedor libre.*

Cafés

Café Central
Kirchner 923.
Smart and popular.

What to do

Fishing
The southern fishing zone includes rivers Gallegos, Grande, Fuego, Ewan, San Pablo and Lago Fagnano, near Ushuaia. It is famous for runs of sea trout. Ask the tourist office for fishing guides and information on permits.

Tour operators
Maca Tobiano Turismo, *Av San Martín 1093, T02966-422466, macatobiano@macatobiano. com.* Air tickets and tours to Pingüinero Cabo Vírgenes and to Estancia Monte León, as well as tickets to El Calafate and Ushuaia. Recommended.

Air

Aerolíneas Argentinas (San Martín 545, T0810-222 86527) have regular flights to/ from **Buenos Aires**, **Ushuaia** and **Río Grande** direct. **LADE** (Fagnano 53, T02966-422316, closed in low season) flies to many Patagonian destinations between **Buenos Aires** and **Ushuaia**, including **El Calafate** and **Comodoro Rivadavia**, but not daily. Book as far in advance as possible.

Bus

The **terminal** (T02966-442159) is small and crowded; there's no left luggage, but many transport companies will store bags by the hour. There is a *confitería*, toilets and some kiosks. For all long-distance trips, turn up with ticket 30 mins before departure. Take your passport when buying ticket; for buses to Chile some companies give out immigration and customs forms.

To **El Calafate**, 4-5 hrs, US$28, with **Marga**, **Sportman** and **Taqsa** (T02966-442194, and at airport, www.taqsa.com.ar). To **Comodoro Rivadavia**, with **Andesmar**, **Don Otto/ Transportadora Patagónica**, **Sportman** and others, 10-12 hrs, US$49-63. To **Bariloche**, with **Marga**, daily, 24 hrs, US$130, change in Comodoro Rivadavia.

To **Buenos Aires**, 36 hrs, several daily with **Andesmar**, US$200-240. To **Río Grande** US$43, 9 hrs, with **Marga** and **Tecni Austral**; also to **Ushuaia**, US$55.

To Chile: **Puerto Natales**, with **Pacheco** (T02966-442765, www.busespacheco.com) and **Bus Sur** (T02966-457047, www.bus-sur.cl), 4-5 weekly, 4½ hrs, US$121. To **Punta Arenas**, with **Ghisoni** (T02966-457047, www.busesbarria.cl), 5 a week leaving at 1200, 5½ hrs, US$21.

Car

To Chile Make sure your car papers are in order: go first to tourist office for necessary documents, then to the customs office at the port, at the end of San Martín, very uncomplicated.

Avis at the airport. **Cristina**, Libertad 123, T02966-425709. **Localiza**, Sarmiento 245, T02966-436717. Essential to book rental in advance in season.

Taxi

Hiring a taxi for group trips may be the same price as a tour bus. Taxi ranks are plentiful; rates are controlled, *remises* are slightly cheaper. *Remise* meters show metres travelled, refer to card for price; taxi meters show cost in pesos. Also consider hiring a car with driver from **Todo Transfer Patagonia** (www.interpatagonia.com/todotransfer/).

Ruta 40

★ The Ruta 40 – known in Argentina simply as 'La Cuarenta' – is one of the wildest and least travelled roads on the planet. It runs the whole length of Argentina, from La Quiaca on the border with Bolivia in the north, all the way down to El Chaltén and Río Gallegos in the south. Ernesto 'Che' Guevara travelled along much of it on his famous motorcycle jaunts and his experience helped form his revolutionary spirit. You can get a flavour of the toughest parts by travelling this stretch through Patagonia.

In the 14 hours it takes to go from Los Antiguos to El Chaltén, you're likely to see no more than a few cars; you'll also spot condors wheeling high above the Andes, the occasional Patagonian fox, and not much else apart from the clouds, whipped into amazing shapes by the ubiquitous winds.

Essential Ruta 40

Access

There are several logical places to start your journey along the Ruta 40 through Patagonia. Travelling from the Atlantic coast, you can reach Río Mayo from Comodoro Rivadavia, with regular buses along the Route 26. There are also daily buses from Esquel, at the southernmost end of the Lake District. Those travelling south along the Carretera Austral in Chile can take the ferry across Lago General Carrera/Lago Buenos Aires, from south of Coyhaique to Chile Chico, and cross the border into Argentina at Los Antiguos before continuing the journey south along the Ruta 40.

Getting around

Travelling along the Ruta 40 is quite an experience, and unless you're taking the bus, it's one that requires careful planning. Travelling south, the road is paved as far as Perito Moreno, and then is good *ripio*, improving greatly after Las Horquetas. From Río Mayo to El Calafate, the wide stony *ripio* track of the Ruta 40 zigzags its way across windswept desolate land. Every few hundred kilometres or so, there will be a small, improbable signpost to an estancia, somewhere off the road unseen; many are just ordinary sheep farms and do not accept paying guests.

For travel information on the Ruta 40, see www.rutanacional40.com (in Spanish with good maps).

Bus The most efficient way to travel this stretch is by making use of the bus services offered by two companies. **Chaltén Travel** (www.chaltentravel.com) runs a service every other day in each direction between Bariloche and El Calafate, via Los Antiguos and El Chaltén. This service operates from November to Semana Santa. Alternatively a year-round no-frills service is run by **Taqsa** (www.taqsa.com.ar), departing daily in summer and twice a week for the rest of the year between El Calafate and Bariloche.

Car/motorbike/bike Hiring a car in one town and dropping it off in another is possible and allows great flexibility. But it can be expensive and is only fun if you're not travelling alone. Make sure you know exactly where the next petrol station is, as they can easily be 300 km apart, carry spare fuel and allow more time than you think to reach your destination before nightfall. There are only a few service stations for fuel along the whole stretch and few places offering accommodation (see below). It's not advisable to travel faster than 60 kph on *ripio* roads. Take warm clothes, liquids and a blanket, in case you become stranded at night. If cycling, note that food and water stops are scarce, the wind is fierce, and there is no shade whatsoever. Hitching along this road is virtually impossible and isn't recommended, as you could be stranded for days.

Accommodation

Be warned that there are few decent places to stay along this entire route. The best bases for accommodation after Esquel in the north are the pretty little town of Los Antiguos, near the border with Chile, and Perito Moreno. After that, there are only remote rural estancias and some very bleak one-horse towns until you reach the tourist haven of El Chaltén. Take a tent if you're on a bike. To get to the estancias, you'll need to have booked in advance and to have your own transport. Various companies organize tours along the route, with estancia stays and travel included.

When to go

The best time to go is between October and April. Outside these months travel is still possible, but accommodation and transport is harder to find, and the winter is deadly cold.

The vital east–west road link between Chile and the Atlantic is Route 26, also known as the Bioceanic Corridor, which runs east from the Chilean towns of Coyhaique and Puerto Aisén, over the Chilean border in the Andes and across the steppe, dotted with oil wells, to Comodoro Rivadavia. Mainly used by lorries, it gives access to two petrified araucaria forests at José Ormachea and Héctor Szlapelis, both within easy reach of the small town of Sarmiento.

Sarmiento and the petrified forests *Colour map 5, C3.*

Sarmiento (population 18,000) is reached by Ruta 20, which brances off Ruta 26 110 km west of Comodoro Rivadavia. (Beyond Sarmiento Ruta 20 joins Ruta 22 towards Río Mayo.) Just to the north of town are two great lakes, **Lago Musters** and **Lago Colhué Huapi**, both of which offer good fishing in summer.

Sarmiento is a quiet and relaxed place, sitting in fertile, well irrigated land on the Río Senguer, and it's little visited by tourists. Founded in 1897 and formally known as Colonia Sarmiento, it was first settled by Welsh, Lithuanians and Boers.

Most accessible of the petrified forests is the **Bosque Petrificado José Ormachea** ① *30 km south of Sarmiento on a good ripio road, warden T0297-489 8282/0297-15 464 0659 (Ivan), Apr-Sep daily 1000-1800, Oct-Mar daily 0800-2000, free.* Less easy to reach is the rather bleaker **Bosque Petrificado Héctor Szlápelis**, some 40 km further southwest along the same road (follow signposts). These forests of fallen araucaria trees, nearly 3 m in circumference and 15-20 m long, are 60 million years old and are a remarkable sight, best visited in summer as the winters are very cold. There are *guardaparques* (rangers) at both sites, who can give tours and information.

Río Mayo *Colour map 5, C2.*

Set in beautifully bleak landscape by the meandering Mayo river, the rural little town of Río Mayo (population 3800) has little of tourist interest, but it's an important junction at the intersection of routes 40 and 26, so you're likely to find yourself here to change buses or pick up fuel. In January, it is the site for an extraordinary display of dexterity at the **Fiesta Nacional de la Esquila** (national sheep-shearing competition); see Festivals, below.

From Río Mayo, Ruta 26 runs west 140 km to the Chilean border at Coyhaique Alto (see box, page 524). South of Río Mayo Ruta 40 is unpaved as far as Perito Moreno (124 km, high-clearance advised).

Listings Along Ruta 26

Tourist information

Sarmiento

Tourist office
Av Regimiento de Infantería 25 y Pietrobelli, T0297-489 2105, www.sarmientochubut. gov.ar. High season 0700-1100, low season 1100-1900.

Very helpful, staff speak English, and they have a map of the town. They can also provide information about transport to the petrified forests. There's another office in the bus terminal (Av San Martín y 12 de Octubre, T0297-489 3401).

Río Mayo

Tourist office
Av Argentino s/n, T02903-420058,
www.turismoriomayo.gob.ar.
Daily 0800-1200 and 1500-1800.

Where to stay

There are some superb estancias in
this region. They are tricky to get to
without your own transport but offer
an unforgettable experience of
Patagonian life.

Sarmiento and the petrified forests

$$$ Chacra Labrador
10 km from Sarmiento, T0297-489 3329,
agna@coopsar.com.ar.
Excellent small estancia, breakfast included,
other meals extra and available for non-
residents, English and Dutch spoken, runs
tours to petrified forests at good prices, will
collect guests from Sarmiento (same price
as taxi).

$$ El Molle
Roca337, T0297-489 3637, www.
elmollehotelboutique.com.
Private bathroom, Wi-Fi, laundry service,
breakfast included. Good central option.

$ Colón
Perito Moreno 645, T0297-489 4212.
One of the better cheap places in town.

$ Los Lagos
Roca y Alberdi, T0297-489 3046.
Good, heating, restaurant.

Camping

Puente Traverso
T0297-489 5038. Río Senguer 1 km from
centre, on the left where the road branches
off at the river, T0297-489 8482.

SGPCH
T0297-489 7112, Río Senger, 1 km from centre,
on the right where the road branches off at
the river.

Río Mayo

$$$$ Estancia Don José
3 km west of Río Mayo, T02903-420015 or
T0297-15-624 9155, www.turismoguenguel.
com.ar.
Excellent estancia, with superb food, 2 rooms
and 1 cabin. The family business involves
sustainable production of guanaco fibre.

$$ Hotel Aka-Ta
San Martín 640, T02903-420054,
hotelacata@gmail.com.
One of a couple hotels in town that could
pass for a chalet in Normandy. Cosy, well-
furnished rooms, friendly owners, great vibe.
Restaurant open in high season.

$$-$ El Viejo Covadonga
San Martín 573, T02903-420020,
elviejocovadonga@hotmail.com.
The other chalet-style lodging, this option
has a beautiful, expansive reception area.
Run for years by 2 helpful and friendly
sisters, all rooms have hot water and Wi-Fi.
Recommended.

$$-$ San Martín
San Martín S/N, T02903-420066.
Decent hotel noteworthy mostly for its
good restaurant.

Camping

There is a free campsite on the northern
outskirts, near the river.

Camping Río Mayo
On the west side of town.

Festivals

Sarmiento and the petrified forests
**2nd week in Feb Festival Interprovincial de
Doma y Folclore**, a 3-day festival featuring
music, gaucho parades and products made
by local artisans.

Río Mayo
**3rd weekend in Jan Fiesta Nacional
de la Esquila** (national sheep-shearing
competition), where teams of 5-6 *esquiladores,*

who travel around Patagonia from farm to farm in shearing season, compete to shear as many sheep as possible: a good shearer might get through 10 in an hour.

What to do

Sarmiento and the petrified forests
Santa Teresita Turismo, *Roca 490, T0297-489 3238, www.agenciasantateresita@gmail.com, Mon-Sat 1000-1200 and 1700-2000.* Tours to the petrified forest and the lakes.

Transport

Sarmiento and the petrified forests
Bus
Overnight services to **Esquel**, Sun-Fri, with **Etap**, T0297-489 3058, US$35-40; take food for the journey, as cafés are expensive. Frequent buses to **Comodoro Rivadavia**, US$10 with **Etap**.

Río Mayo
Bus
To **Sarmiento** once a day (1900) with **Etap**, US$11, 2 hrs. To **Perito Moreno**, 3 weekly (2100) with **Etap**, US$11.

Perito Moreno and around   *Colour map 5, C2.*

ancient art preserved on cave walls

Not to be confused with the famous glacier of the same name near El Calafate, nor with Parque Nacional Perito Moreno (see page 528), this Perito Moreno is a spruce little town of 10,000 inhabitants, 25 km west of Lago Buenos Aires. The town has no sights as such, apart from the pleasure of watching a rural community go about its business. It's the nearest but not the most attractive base for exploring the mysterious cave paintings at the Cueva de las Manos to the south.

Around Perito Moreno
Southwest of the town is **Parque Laguna**, where you can see varied birdlife, including flamingos and black-necked swans, and go fishing. You could also walk to the crater of **Volcán Cerro**, from a path 12 km outside Perito Moreno; ask at the tourist office (see Tourist information, page 525) for directions.

Cueva de las Manos
Access is via a 28-km road which branches east off Ruta 40, 88 km south of Perito Moreno; another 46-km access road, branches off Ruta 40 at Km 124, 3 km north of Bazjo Caracoles. The road can be difficult after rain. Compulsory guided tours with rangers Nov-Apr 0900-1900, May-Oct 1000-1800, US$9, under-12s free.

Situated 47 km northeast of Bajo Caracoles, the stunning canyon of the **Río Pinturas** contains outstanding examples of handprints and cave paintings, estimated to be between 9500 and 13,000 years old. It is one of the major cultural and archaeological sites in South America, declared a World Heritage Site by UNESCO in 1999, and definitely one of the highlights of any trip to Patagonia.

In the cave's four galleries are over 800 paintings by the Toldense peoples of human hands, all but 31 of which are of left hands, as well as images of guanacos and rheas, and various geometrical designs.

Tip...
Come to Cueva de las Manos in the morning in summer to beat the crowds.

BORDER CROSSING
Argentina–Chile

Paso Huemules
From Río Mayo, there are two roads crossing the border into Chile to take you to Coyhaique, the main town for visiting the southern part of the Carretera Austral. The more southerly of the two, via Paso Huemules, has better roads and is the crossing used by buses between Comodoro Rivadavia and Coyhaique. It is reached by a road that branches off Ruta 40 some 31 km south of Río Mayo and runs west 105 km via Lago Blanco (small petrol station), where there is an estancia community, 30 km from the border. There's no hotel here but the police are friendly and may permit camping at the police post. The border is open 0800-2200 in summer, 0900-2000 in winter. The road continues from Balmaceda on the Chilean side of the border to Coyhaique. See www.gendarmeria.gov.ar.

Coyhaique Alto
This border crossing is reached by a 133-km road (87 km *ripio*, then dirt) that branches off Ruta 40 about 7 km north of Río Mayo. On the Chilean side this road continues to Coyhaique, 50 km west of the border. **Chilean immigration** is 6 km west of the border, April to November daily 0800-2000, December to April daily 0800-2200.

Los Antiguos
The main reason to enter Chile here is either to explore the beautiful southern shore of Lago General Carrera, or to take the ferry over the lake north to Puerto Ibáñez which has minibus connections on to Coyhaique.
Transport Four bus companies cross the border by the bridge to the village of Chile Chico, 8 km west, US$4, 45 minutes. If crossing from Chile Chico to Los Antiguos, there are buses daily in summer, taking one hour, US$4; company offices are at B O'Higgins 426, and at Santiago Ericksen 150.

Paso Roballos
From Bajo Caracoles Route 41 (unpaved) goes 99 km northwest to the Paso Roballos border with Chile. On the Chilean side this road continues 201 km to Cochrane, Km 177. Though passable in summer, it is often flooded in spring (September to November). There's no public transport available here.

The red, orange, black, white and green pigments were derived from earth and calafate berries, and fixed with a varnish of guanaco fat and urine. They are mysterious and rather beautiful, albeit indecipherable. The canyon itself is also worth seeing: 270 m deep and 480 m wide, it has strata of vivid red and green rocks that are especially beautiful in the early morning or evening light. *Guardaparques* living at the site give helpful information and a tour. See Transport, page 527.

Los Antiguos and border with Chile
Though there are two crossings to Chile west of Perito Moreno, the easiest and most commonly used is via the pretty little village of Los Antiguos (population 7000), which lies just 2 km east of the border. The town lies on the southern shore of Lago Buenos Aires,

the second largest lake in South America, extending into Chile as Lago General Carrera, where the landscape is very beautiful and unspoilt. The Río Baker, which flows from the lake, is world-renowned for excellent trout fishing. For further information on crossing the border here, see box, opposite.

Los Antiguos is a sleepy little place, but it has a pleasant atmosphere, thanks largely to its warm microclimate, and it's a much better place to stay than Chile Chico or Perito Moreno. Modern hotels have been built, and there are countless services, including restaurants, internet cafés and a newish bus terminal on Avenida Tehuelches with a large café/restaurant and free Wi-Fi. Minibuses from Chile arrive at this terminal. It is a good place to stay for two days or longer and to stock up on basics before continuing the journey. The **Parque Municipal** at the east end of the town is a pleasant place to walk, along the bank of the river, with birdlife to look at, and two blocks down, there's a superb campsite. This is a rich fruit-growing area and there are 12 local *chacras* (small farms) worth visiting. You can walk to one of them, **Don Neno** from the main street, where there are strawberries growing and jam for sale. You'd have to drive, or take a taxi, though, to the idyllic **Chacra el Paraíso**, where the charming owners make delicious jams and chutney.

Listings Perito Moreno and around

Tourist information

Perito Moreno

Tourist office
Av San Martín 2005, http://peritomoreno.tur.ar. Daily 0700-1200.
The friendly staff can advise on tours to the cave and *estancias*.

Los Antiguos

Tourist office
*Buenos Aires 59, T02963-491261, www.losantiguous.tur.ar.
Dec-Easter daily 0800-2400,
Easter-Nov daily 0800-2000.*
New modern office.

Where to stay

Perito Moreno and around

$$$-$$ Americano
San Martín 1327, T02963-432074, www.hotelamericanoweb.com.ar.
19 pleasant rooms, some superior, decent restaurant.

$$ Belgrano
San Martín 1001, T02963-432019.

This hotel is often booked by Ruta 40 long-distance bus companies, basic, not always clean, 1 key fits all rooms, helpful owner, breakfast extra, excellent restaurant.

$$ Hotel El Austral
San Martín 1381, T02963-432605, hotelaustral@speedy.com.ar.
Similar to others on the main street, but clean.

$ Hospedaje Las Formoseñas
O'Higgins 943, T02963-432123.
The only true budget hostel in town. Bunks with thin mattresses from US$10 per night. Still, the owner is friendly and you stand to save hundreds of pesos by lodging here than at other hotels.

$ Hotel Santa Cruz
Belgrano 1530, T02963-432133.
Simple rooms.

Camping

Municipal site at Paseo Roca y Mariano Moreno, near Laguna de los Cisnes, T02963-432130.
Also 2 *cabaña* places near the river on Ruta 43: **Cabañas Las Moras** (T02963-15 400 7549), and **Turístico Río Fénix** (T02963-432458).

Estancias

$$$ Hostería Cueva de Las Manos
20 km from the cave at Estancia Los Toldos,
60 km south, 7 km off the road to Perito
Moreno, T02963-432207 or T0297-15-623 8811
(mobile), www.cuevadelasmanos.net.
1 Nov-5 Apr, closed Christmas and New Year.
Private rooms and dorms, runs tours
to the caves, horse riding, meals extra
and expensive.

$$ Estancia Turística Casa de Piedra
80 km south of Perito Moreno on Ruta 40,
in Perito Moreno ask for Sr Sabella,
Av Perón 941, T02963-432199.
Price is for rooms, camping, hot showers,
home-made bread, use of kitchen, trips to
Cueva de las Manos and volcanoes by car
or horse.

Los Antiguos

$$$ Antigua Patagonia
Ruta 43, T02963-491055, www.
antiguapatagonia.com.ar.
Luxurious rooms with beautiful views,
excellent restaurant. Tours to Cueva de
las Manos and nearby Monte Zevallos.

$$$-$ Mora
Av Costanera 1064, T02963-15-540 2444,
www.hotelmorapatagonia.com.
Rooms range from dorms to first class
with private bath. Parking, lake views.

$$ Sol de Mayo
Av 11 de Julio 1300, T02963-491232,
chacrasoldemayo@hotmail.com.
Basic rooms with shared bath, kitchen,
central, also has cabins for rent.

$ pp Albergue Padilla
San Martín 44 (just off main street),
T02963-491140.
Comfortable dorms, doubles (**$$**);
quincho and garden. Also camping.
El Chaltén travel tickets.

Camping

Camping Municipal
2 km from centre on Ruta Provincial 43,
T02963-491265.
An outstanding site, with hot showers,
US$4 pp, also has cabins for 4 (no linen).

Restaurants

Perito Moreno
The restaurant in **Hotel Americano** is
highly recommended.

El Viejo Bar
San Martín 991, T02963-432538.
Good *parrilla* that also rents rooms.

Los Antiguos
There are several other places in town.

Viva El Viento
11 de Julio 477, T02963-491109,
www.vivaelviento.com.
Daily 0900-2100 in high season.
Dutch-owned, great vibe, food and coffee,
also has Wi-Fi, lots of information about the
area. Live music Tue. Recommended.

Festivals

Los Antiguos
Early Jan Fiesta Nacional de la Cereza,
a popular cherry festival that attracts
national *folclore* stars.

What to do

Perito Moreno
Tour operators
Las Loicas, *Transporte Lago Posadas, T02963-490272, www.lasloicas.com.* Offers an all-day
tour with the option of collecting passengers
from Bajo Caracoles. Also does the Circuito
Grande Comarca Noroeste, one of the
highlights of Santa Cruz, taking in some of
the province's scenery.
Zoyen Turismo, *San Martín near Saavedra,*
T02963-432207, T0297-15 623 8811,
www.zoyenturismo.com.ar. The friendly

staff can help with R40 connections and estancia visits.

Los Antiguos
Tour operators
Chelenco Turs, *11 de Julio 548, T02963-491198, www.chelencoturs.com.ar.* Can arrange trips to the Cueva de las Manos, Monte Zeballos, Lago Posadas and Capilla Mármol in Chile.

Transport

Perito Moreno
Air
The airport is 7 km east of town and the only way to get there is by taxi.

Bus
The bus terminal (T02963-432177) is on the edge of town next to the EG3 service station. It is open only when buses arrive or depart.

Many long-distance buses with **Transporte Ruca** (transporte.ruca@yahoo.com.ar): Bariloche 850 km US$100 El Chaltén 530 km, US$92 El Calafate 620 km US$123; **Esquel** 500 km, US$70; **Cueva de Los Manos** US$23 it is nearly impossible to hitchhike between Perito Moreno and El Calafate as there's hardly any traffic and few services. To **Los Antiguos** border crossing, 2 buses daily in summer, 1 hr, US$7, with **Sportman**, T02963-432177. To **El Chaltén** and **El Calafate**, **Chaltén Travel** (www.chaltentravel.com) at 0700. **Chaltén Travel** also runs a tourist service to **Puerto Madryn** at 0630 every other day from **Hotel Belgrano**.

Car
Several mechanics on C Rivadavia and Av San Martín, good for repairs.

Taxi
Parada El Turista, Av San Martín y Rivadavia, T02963-432592.

Los Antiguos
Bus
To **Comodoro Rivadavia**, with **ETAP** (at the terminal, T0297-491078) and **Sportman** (at the terminal, T0297-442983) daily, US$34; to **Caleta Olivia** with **Taqsa** (at the terminal T02966-15-419615), **Andesmar** (at the terminal, T0297-15 623 4882) and **Sportman**, daily US$30. **Chaltén Travel** (open only in high season, www.chaltentravel.com) runs to **El Chaltén** (10 hrs) and **El Calafate** (12 hrs), via Perito Moreno, every other (even) day at 0800; also north to **Bariloche**, every even day, mid-Nov to mid-Apr.

Bajo Caracoles and south to Tres Lagos *Colour map 6, A1.*

remote settlements in Patagonia

After hours of spectacular emptiness, even tiny Bajo Caracoles (population 100) is a relief. It's nothing more than a few houses with an expensive grocery store and very expensive fuel. From Bajo Caracoles Route 41 (unpaved) goes 99 km northwest to the Paso Roballos border with Chile (see box, page 524), passing Lago Ghio and Lago Columna. Route 39, meanwhile, heads southwest from Bajo Caracoles, reaching Lago Posadas and Lago Pueyrredón after 72 km. These two beautiful lakes with contrasting blue and turquoise waters are separated by a narrow isthmus. Guanacos and rheas can be seen and there are sites of archaeological interest.

South to Tres Lagos
South of Bajo Caracoles Ruta 40 crosses the Pampa del Asador and then, near Las Horquetas, Km 371, swings southeast to follow the Río Chico. Some 92 km south of Bajo Caracoles is the turn-off west to Lago Belgrano and Parque Nacional Perito

Moreno (see below). From the Parque Moreno junction to Tres Lagos, Ruta 40 improves considerably. About 23 km east of the turn-off, along Route 521 is **Tamel Aike**, Km 393, where there is a police station and water but little else.

At Km 464, Route 25 branches off to **Puerto San Julián** via **Gobernador Gregores**, 72 km southeast, where there is fuel and a good mechanic. (This is the only place with fuel before Tres Lagos, so carry extra if you want to avoid the 72-km detour.) The Ruta 40, meanwhile, continues southwest towards Tres Lagos. At Km 531, a road heads west to Lago Cardiel, a very saline lake with no outlet and good salmon fishing.

Tres Lagos, at Km 645, is a solitary village with a minimarket, restaurant and fuel at the junction with Route 288. A road also turns off northwest here to Lago San Martín, which straddles the Chilean border (the Chilean part is Lago O'Higgins). From Tres Lagos, Ruta 40 deteriorates rapidly and remains very rugged until after the turn-off to the Fitz Roy sector of Parque Nacional Los Glaciares (see page 531). Twenty-one kilometres beyond this turn-off is the bridge over Río La Leona, where delightful **Hotel La Leona** serves good cakes.

Listings Bajo Caracoles and south to Tres Lagos

Where to stay

Bajo Caracoles and south to Tres Lagos

$$ Hotel Bajo Caracoles
Bajo Caracloes, T02963-490100.
Old-fashioned but hospitable, meals.

Estancias

$$$ pp La Angostura
55 km from Gobernador Gregores, T02962-491501, www.estancialaangostura.com.ar.

Offers horse riding, trekking and fishing. Recommended.

Camping
The campsite is in the middle of Bajo Caracoles. Rooms ($ pp) are also available. A simple and welcoming place, also runs trips to Cueva de las Manos, 10 km by vehicle then 1½-2 hrs' walk, and to nearby volcanoes by car or horse. Ask for **Señor Sabella** (Av Perón 941, Perito Moreno, T02963-432199).

Parque Nacional Perito Moreno Colour map 6, A1.
untamed wilds within a national park

Situated southwest of Bajo Caracoles on the Chilean border, this is one of the wildest and most remote parks in Argentina. It encompasses a large, interconnected system of lakes, lying between glaciated peaks of astonishing beauty, and has good trekking and abundant wildlife. However, since much of the park is dedicated to scientific study, it's largely inaccessible.

Around the park

Lago Belgrano, in the park's centre, is the biggest in the chain of lakes; its vivid turquoise waters contrast with the surrounding mountains which are streaked with a mass of differing colours, and you might find ammonite fossils on its shores. Just outside the park, but towering over it to the north, is **Cerro San Lorenzo** (3706 m), the highest peak in southern Patagonia. Between the lakes are other peaks, permanently snow-covered, the highest of which is Cerro Herros (2770 m). The vivid hues of Sierra Colorada run across the northeast of the park: the erosion of these coloured rocks has given the lakes their differing colours. At the foot of Cerro Casa de Piedra is a network of caves containing cave paintings, accessible only with a guide. Wildlife in the park includes guanacos, foxes and one of the most important surviving populations of the rare huemul deer. Birds include flamingos, ñandus, steamer ducks, grebes, black-necked swans, Patagonian woodpeckers, eagles and condors. The lakes and rivers are unusual for Argentina in that only native species of fish are found here.

Hiking

Several good hikes are possible from here. There are also longer walks of up to five days. Ask the *guardaparques* for details, and see the website. You should always inform *guardaparques* before setting out on a hike.

Lago Belgrano ① *1-2 hrs*. Follow the Senda Natural Península Belgrano to the peninsula of the lake, 8 km, where there are fine views of Cerro Herros and an experience of transition landscape from steppe to forest. **Lago Burmeister** ① *Via Cerro Casa de Piedra, 16 km*. The trail follows the northern shore and offers nice views of the lake. There is free camping (no fires permitted). It is hard to find the official trail in parts, but if in doubt, follow the shore. **Cerro León** ① *4 hrs*. Start at **Estancia La Oriental**. This walk has fabulous panoramic views over the park and offers the chance to see condors in flight.

Essential Parque Nacional Perito Moreno

Access

Access to the park is via the park entrance, a turn-off the paved Ruta 40, 100 km south of Bajo Caracoles, onto 90 km of unpaved road (see above). There is no public transport into the park. Much of the park is closed to visitors. The most accessible part is around Lago Belgrano, 12 km from the entrance. What is accessible is open 0900-2100, free.

Park information

The **park office**, 9 de Julio 610, T02962-491477, www.parquesnacionales.gov.ar or www.turismoruta40.com.ar/pnperitomoreno.html, is 220 km away in Gobernador Gregores; get information here before reaching the park itself. The *guardaparques'* office is 10 km beyond the park entrance (see Access, above) and has maps and leaflets on walks and wildlife.

It's essential to get detailed maps here and to ask advice about hikes and paths.

What to take

Make sure you carry all fuel you need because there is nowhere to buy it inside the park, unless you're staying at one of the estancias. Cyclists should bring water, as there is no source along the 90-km branch road. Bring an all-season sleeping bag and plenty of warm clothing.

When to go

The best time to visit is in summer (December to February). The access road may be blocked by snow at other times.

Accommodation

There is an estancia inside the park boundaries: **Estancia La Oriental**. There are also several good sites for camping (free). For more information, see Where to stay, below.

BACKGROUND

Exploring Argentina

Francisco 'Perito' Moreno was one of Argentina's most prolific explorers. He played a leading role in defending Argentine rights in Patagonia and was pivotal in creating Argentina's first national park. Born in Buenos Aires in 1852, by the age of 14 he had created his first collection of specimens, which would go on to form the basis of the famous La Plata History Museum. When he was 20 he embarked on a series of expeditions for the Argentine Scientific Society. By 1876 he had reached Lake Nahuel Huapi in the Lake District. On the same trip, he 'discovered' El Chaltén in the south and named Cerro Fitz Roy. His second expedition was, however, decidedly more dangerous as he was captured by an unfriendly Tehuelche tribe and taken prisoner, before managing to escape. After several more expeditions, namely to claim Patagonian land for Argentina, he was given the name 'Perito' (expert) in 1902. For his exploring efforts the government gave him land in the Lake District, which he subsequently donated in order to create the country's first national park, Parque Nacional Nahuel Huapi. Ironically, Perito Moreno never set eyes on the famed Perito Moreno Glacier; it was simply named after him because he had extensively explored the surrounding lakes and mountains.

Listings Parque Nacional Perito Moreno

Where to stay

$$$ Estancia La Oriental
T02962-407197, laorientalpatagonia@ yahoo.com.ar. Nov-Mar. Full board.

Splendid setting, with comfortable rooms, horse riding, trekking.

Parque Nacional
Los Glaciares

Of all Argentina's impressive landscapes, the sight of these immense glaciers stretching out infinitely before you may stay with you longest. This is the second largest national park in Argentina, extending along the Chilean border for over 170 km, almost half of it covered by the 370-km-long Southern Ice Cap. From it, 13 major glaciers descend into two great lakes: Lago Argentino and Lago Viedma. At the southern end, the spectacular glaciers can be visited from El Calafate. At the northern end, reached from El Chaltén, there is superb trekking around the dramatic Fitz Roy massif and ice climbing on glaciers. The central section, between Lago Argentino and Lago Viedma, is composed of the ice cap on the western side. East of the ice fields, there's plentiful southern beech forest, but further east still, the land flattens to the typical wind-blasted Patagonian steppe, with sparse vegetation.

Birdlife is surprisingly prolific, and you'll spot the scarlet-headed Magellanic woodpecker, black-necked swans, and perhaps even the torrent duck, diving for food in the streams and rivers. Guanacos, grey foxes, skunks and rheas can be seen on the steppe, while the rare huemul inhabits the forest. The entire national park is a UNESCO World Heritage Site.

Essential Parque Nacional Los Glaciares

Access

Access to the park is very straightforward at both El Calafate and El Chaltén, although all transport gets heavily booked in the summer months of January and February. There are direct flights to El Calafate from Buenos Aires and Ushuaia, as well as charter flights from Puerto Natales in Chile. There are regular bus services into the park from El Calafate, as well as many tourist excursions, combining bus access with boat trips, walking and even ice trekking on Glaciar Perito Moreno. From El Chaltén you can hike directly into the park, with a well-established network of trails leading to summits, lakes and glaciers around Mount Fitz Roy, with many campsites. There are several buses daily to El Chaltén from El Calafate.

Park information

There is a **park office**, Av del Libertador 1302, T02901-491005, www.losglaciares.com, Monday-Friday 0800-1600, in El Calafate. The **El Chaltén park office**, T02962-493004, same opening hours, is across the bridge at the entrance to town. Both hand out helpful trekking maps of the area, with paths and campsites marked, distances and walking times. Note that the hotel, restaurant and transport situation in this region changes greatly between high and low season. For more information, see www.losglaciares.com.

Opening hours

The park is open daily 0800-2100 January-February, 0800-2000 March to Easter, 0800-1600 Easter to 31 July, 0800-1800 August-30 October, 0800-1900 in November, 0800-2000 in December.

Entry fees

US$21.75, payable at the gates of the park, 50 km west of El Calafate.

When to go

Although this part of Patagonia is generally cold, there is a milder microclimate around Lago Viedma and Lago Argentino, which means that summers can be reasonably pleasant, with average summer temperatures between 5°C and 22°C, though strong winds blow constantly at the foot of the Cordillera. Precipitation on the Hielo Sur, up to 5000 mm annually, falls mainly as snow. In the forested area, rainfall is heavier and falls mainly between March and late May. In winter, the whole area is inhospitably cold, and most tourist facilities are closed, although El Calafate and the Perito Moreno Glaciar are open all year round. The best time to visit is between November and April, avoiding January and early February, when Argentines take their holidays, campsites are crowded and accommodation is hard to find.

Parque Nacional Los Glaciares

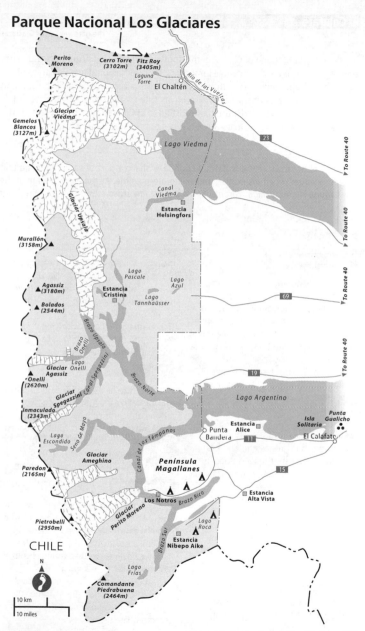

El Calafate (population 8000) sits on the south shore of Lago Argentino and exists almost entirely as a tourist centre for visiting Parque Nacional los Glaciares, 50 km west. Though the town was founded in 1927, it grew very slowly until the opening of the road to the Perito Moreno Glacier in the 1960s, since which time it has expanded rapidly as a tourist town. Almost all of El Calafate's inhabitants, as is the case with El Chaltén, came from Buenos Aires or other large provincial capitals.

Sights

Just west of the town centre is **Bahía Redonda**, a shallow part of Lago Argentino that freezes in winter, when ice-skating and skiing are possible. At the eastern edge of the bay, **Laguna Nímez** ① *high season daily 0900-2000, low season 0900-1800, US$7,* is a bird

Essential El Calafate

Finding your feet

The airport, **Lago Argentino**, is 23 km east of town. A minibus service run by **Transpatagonia Expeditions**, T02902-494355, runs between the town and airport, US$7 (US$8.50 from the airport) for an open return. A taxi (T02902-491850/491745) costs US$18. Buses from Río Gallegos arrive in the town centre. The **bus terminal** is centrally located on Julio A Roca 1004, up a steep flight of steps from the main street, Avenida del Libertador.

Orientation

El Calafate's shops, restaurants and tour operators can mostly be found along its main street, Avenida del Libertador, running east to west, with hotels lying within two blocks north and south and smaller *hosterías* scattered through the residential areas sprawling up the hill and north of centre, across the river. There are many estancias on the way to the national park, and also campsites.

Getting around

A small municipal public transport system carries people from one end of the city to the other, which is useful if you are staying at some of the hotels on the edge of town. Bus travel and tour trips to the Perito Moreno glaciers are well organized, although they can be more difficult to arrange out of season. The cheapest method is with a regular bus service (US$32 return), but tours can be informative and some include a boat trip.

Money

El Calafate can be expensive. At the moment in El Calafate many ATMS do not accept newer bank cards with smart chips. Only two ATMs in El Calafate accept them: **Banco Patagonia** on Avenida del Libertador 1355 and in the airport. There are no *casas de cambio*, but some hotels may change money.

When to go

It's best to come in March or April if you can. The town is empty and quiet all winter, when it can be extremely cold, and most tourist services close down. If you can brave the weather, however, you can visit the Perito Moreno Glacier all year round.

Bear in mind that it's essential to book ahead in January and February, when the hotels, hostels and *cabañas* can't quite accommodate the hordes.

reserve where there are flamingos, black-necked swans and ducks; the 2.5-km self-guided trail with multilingual leaflets is recommended for an hour's stroll either early morning or late afternoon. To get there from the **Intendencia del Parque** ⓘ *Av del Libertador 1302*, follow Calle Bustillo up the road to cross the bridge. Keep heading north across a pleasant new residential area: the *laguna* is signposted.

On the way back, you can stop by the **Centro de Interpretación Histórica** ⓘ *Av Brown and Bonarelli, T02902-492799, US$7; half price for children*, a small well-run centre housing an educational exhibition created by an anthropologist and a historian with pictures and bilingual texts about the region. There's also a relaxing café and library. The **Glaciarium** ⓘ *6 km from town on R11, www.glaciarium.com, daily 0900-2000, US$16, free for under-5s, free bus from provincial tourist office hourly*, is a modern museum dedicated to Patagonian ice and glaciers. It has an **ice bar** ⓘ *daily 1130-1700, US$13, under 16s US$9.50, cash only, entry is for 25 mins, includes drink*, café and shop.

El Calafate

N

200 metres
200 yards

Where to stay 🛏
1 Albergue y Hostal Lago Argentino
2 Alto Verde
3 América del Sur
4 Ariel
5 Cabañas Nevis
6 Calafate Hostel & Hostería
7 Camping AMSA
8 El Ovejero
10 El Quijote
11 Hostel Buenos Aires
12 Hostel del Glaciar 'Libertador'
13 Hostel del Glaciar 'Pioneros'
15 i Keu Ken Hostel
16 Kau Yatún
17 Kosten Aike
18 Los Alamos
19 Marcopolo Inn Calafate
20 Michelangelo
21 Patagonia Rebelde
23 Vientos del Sur

Restaurants 🍴
1 Borges y Alvarez
2 Casablanca
4 Heladería Aquarela
5 La Lechuza
6 La Tablita
7 La Vaca Atada
8 Mi Viejo
9 Pura Vida
10 Rick's Restaurante
11 Viva la Pepa

Bars & clubs 🍸
12 Elba'r

Around El Calafate

From El Calafate you can visit Glaciar Perito Moreno by bus and boat, and even go trekking on its surface. Alternatively, travel by boat along the western arms of Lago Argentino, between stately floating icebergs, to see the glaciers of Spegazzini and Upsala. Best of all, take the long-day excursion by boat to **Estancia Cristina**, which gives you the chance to trek or ride horses up to a spectacular viewpoint above the Upsala glacier. All these trips are breathtakingly beautiful and an unforgettable part of your visit to Patagonia. For details, see page 539. However, El Calafate has a number of other attractions, worth considering if you're here for a few days, including some good places for trekking, horse riding and exploring by 4WD.

At **Punta Gualicho** (or Walichu) on the shores of Lago Argentino, 7 km east of town, there are cave paintings. Though they're rather badly deteriorated, a visit is worthwhile. Some tour operators run trips to the top of nearby hills for views of the southern end of the Andes, **Bahía Redonda** and Isla Solitaria on Lago Argentino. An easy five-hour walk (or horse ride with **Cabalgata en Patagonia**, T02902-493 278) is possible to the top of Cerro Calafate for panoramic views too; ask for directions at the **Hostel del Glaciar Pioneros**. Trekking, 4WD or horse-riding trips to the top of Cerro Frías (1030 m) for fantastic views of Mount Fitz Roy, Paine and Lago Argentino are organized by **Cerro Frías** ⓘ *Libertador 1857, T02902-492808, www.cerrofrias.com*, for around US$63 per person, including lunch (US$41 without lunch).

★ Several estancias are within reach, offering a day on a working farm, a lunch of Patagonian lamb, cooked *asado al palo* (speared on a metal structure over an open fire), and activities such as trekking, birdwatching and horse riding. **Estancia Alice** ⓘ *T02902-497503, www.elgalpondelglaciar.com.ar*, also known as 'El Galpón del Glaciar', 21 km west, is a lovely house with views of Lago Argentino. It offers 'El Día de Campo', including tea with home-made cakes, walks through a bird sanctuary where 43 species of bird have been identified, displays of sheep shearing, *asado* and music shows, all for US$64 per person (including transfer to and from hotels); English spoken. See also Where to stay, below. At **Estancia Quien Sabe**, near the airport, strawberries and walnuts are grown, and you can see beehives and sheep shearing, and eat an *asado* lunch; contact **Turismo Leutz**, www.leutzturismo.com.ar.

Lago Roca, 40 km southwest of El Calafate, is set in beautiful open landscape, with hills above offering panoramic views, perfect for lots of activities, such as trout and salmon fishing, climbing, walking. There are estancias here too, such as the beautifully set **Estancia Nibepo Aike** ⓘ *on Brazo Sur of Lago Argentino in the national park, 55 km southwest (book at Av Libertador 1215 p 1A, T02902-492797; Buenos Aires T011-5272 0341, www.nibepoaike.com.ar)*, where you can watch typical farm activities, such as the branding of cattle in summer. There is good camping in a wooded area and a restaurant.

Listings El Calafate map page 535.

Tourist information

El Calafate

For more information on El Calafate, see www.losglaciares.com and www.todocalafate.com.

Tourist office
In the bus station, T02902-491476, www. elcalafate.tur.ar, and at Bajada Palma 44, T02902-491090, and another in the Amphitheatre del Rosque at Libertador 1400, T02902-496 497. Daily 0800-2000. Friendly staff have folders of helpful information that you can browse.

Where to stay

Prepare to pay more for accommodation here than elsewhere in Argentina. El Calafate is very popular in Jan-Feb, so book all transport and accommodation in advance. Many hotels are open only from Sep/Oct to Apr/May.

$$$$ El Quijote
Gob Gregores 1191, T02902-491017, www.quijotehotel.com.ar.
A very good hotel, spacious, well designed with traditional touches, tasteful rooms with TV, restaurant, stylish lobby bar, English and Italian spoken.

$$$$ Kau Yatún
Estancia 25 de Mayo (10 blocks from the centre, east of Arroyo Calafate), T02902-491059, www.kauyatun.com. Closed in low season.
Renovated main house of a former estancia, well-kept grounds, 2 excellent restaurants, half board or all-inclusive packages that include trips in the national park.

$$$$ Kosten Aike
Gob Moyano 1243, T02902-492424, www. kostenaike.com.ar. Open year-round.
Relaxed yet stylish, elegant spacious rooms (some superior), jacuzzi, gym, excellent restaurant, **Ariskaiken** (open to non-residents), cosy bar, garden, English spoken. Recommended.

$$$$ Los Alamos
Guatti 1135, T02902-491144, www.posada losalamos.com. Cheaper in low season.
Very comfortable, charming rooms, good service, lovely gardens, good bar and without doubt the best restaurant in town, **La Posta**.

$$$ Alto Verde
Zupic 138, T02902-491326, www.welcome argentina.com/altoverde. **$$** *in low season.*
Top quality, spotless, spacious, helpful, also with apartments for 4.

$$$ Cabañas Nevis
Av del Libertador 1696, T02902-493180, www.cabanasnevis.com.ar.

Owner Mr Patterson offers good cabins for 5 and 8 (price quoted is for 5), some with lake view, great value.

$$$ Michelangelo
Espora y Gob Moyano, T02902-491045, www.michelangelocalafate.com.
Lovely, quiet, welcoming, restaurant.

$$$ Patagonia Rebelde
José Haro 442, T02902-494495 (in Buenos Aires T015-5890 1276), www.patagoniarebelde.com.
Charming building in traditional Patagonian style, like an old inn with rustic decor, good comfort with well-heated bedrooms and comfy sitting rooms.

$$$ Vientos del Sur
up the hill at Río Santa Cruz 2317, T02902-493563, www.vientosdelsur.com.
Very hospitable, calm, comfortable, good views, kind family attention.

$$$-$$ Ariel
Av Libertador 1693, T493131, www.hotelariel.com.ar.
Modern, functional, well maintained. Breakfast included.

$$ Hostel Buenos Aires
Buenos Aires 296, 200 m from terminal, T02902-491147.
Quiet, kind owner, helpful, comfortable with doubles, cheaper without bath, good hot showers, laundry service, luggage store, bikes for hire.

$$-$ pp Albergue y Hostal Lago Argentino
Campaña del Desierto 1050-61 (near bus terminal), T02902-491423, www.lagoargentinohostel.com.ar.
$ pp shared dorms, too few showers when full, pleasant atmosphere, good flats, *cabañas* and **$$** doubles on a neat garden and also in building on opposite side of road.

$$-$ pp Calafate Hostel & Hostería
Gob Moyano 1226, T02902-492450, www.calafatehostels.com.

A huge log cabin with good rooms: dorms with or without bath, breakfast extra, **$$** doubles with bath and breakfast. Book a month ahead for Jan-Feb, HI discounts, travel agency, **Always Glacier** and restaurant **Isabel** on premises.

$$-$ pp Marcopolo Inn Calafate
Los Lagos 82, T02902-493899,
www.marcopoloinncalafate.com.
Part of Hostelling International. **$** pp in dorms. Laundry facilities, various activities and tours on offer.

$ pp América del Sur
Puerto Deseado 153, T02902-493525,
www.americahostel.com.ar.
Panoramic views from this comfortable, relaxed hostel, welcoming, well-heated rooms (dorms for 4, **$$** doubles with views, 1 room adapted for wheelchair users), chill-out area, fireplace. Warmly recommended, but can be noisy.

$ pp Hostel del Glaciar 'Libertador'
Av del Libertador 587 (next to the bridge),
T02902-492492, www.glaciar.com. Sep-Apr.
Smaller and pricier than **Pioneros**, rooms are good and well-heated, all with private bath and safe boxes (**$$$-$$** doubles), breakfast included for private rooms. Laundry service. Owners run **Patagonia Backpackers** (see What to do, below). Low energy usage; owners are environmentally minded.

$ pp Hostel del Glaciar 'Pioneros'
Los Pioneros 255, T02902-491243,
www.glaciar.com. 1 Nov 1-end of Feb.
Accommodation for all budgets: standard **$$** doubles (also for 3 and 4) with bath and safe boxes, superior **$$$**, shared dorms up to 4 beds, US$17 pp. Many languages spoken, lots of bathrooms, breakfast is separate, only for guests in private rooms, laundry service, Wi-Fi. Arranges tours to glaciers, as well **NaviMag** boat trips in Chile. Very popular, so book well in advance.

$ pp i Keu Ken Hostel
FM Pontoriero 171, T02902-495482,
www.patagoniaikeuken.com.ar.
On a hill, very helpful, flexible staff, hot water, heating, luggage store, good.

Camping
Ferretería Chuar (Los Pioneros 539, T02902-491513) sells camping gas.

AMSA
Olavarría 65 (50 m off the main road, turning south at the fire station), T02902-492247.
Open in summer.
Hot water, US$7 pp.

El Ovejero
José Pantín 64, near the river, T02902-493422,
www.campingelovejero.com.ar.
Also has dorm (**$$**)

$$ La Lechuza
Av del Libertador 1301, see Facebook.
Good-quality pizzas, pasta, salad and meat dishes. Excellent wine list. Has another branch up the road at No 935.

$$ La Tablita
Cnel Rosales 28 (near the bridge),
www.la-tablita.com.ar.
Typical *parrilla*, serving generous portions and quality beef. Recommended.

$$ La Vaca Atada
Av del Libertador 1176.
Good home-made pastas and more elaborate and expensive dishes based on salmon and king crab.

$$ Mi Viejo
Av del Libertador 1111. Closed Tue.
Popular *parrilla*.

$$ Pura Vida
Av Libertador 1876, near C 17, see Facebook.
Open 1930-2330 only, closed Wed.
Comfortable sofas, home-made Argentine food, vegetarian options, lovely atmosphere, lake view (reserve table). Recommended.

$$ Rick's Restaurante
Av del Libertador 1091.
Lively *parrilla* with a good atmosphere.

$$ Viva la Pepa
Emilio Amado 833, see Facebook.
Mon-Sat 1200-2100.
A mainly vegetarian café with great sandwiches and crêpes. Wi-Fi, craft beers. Child-friendly.

Cafés

Borges y Alvarez
Av del Libertador 1015, 1st floor, Galería de los Gnomos, T02902-491 464. Daily till 0200.
Cosy, wooden café-bar with huge windows looking out over the shopping street below. Affordable, with delicious lunch and dinner options, as well as live music and books for sale. Excellent place to hang out. Recommended.

Casablanca
25 de Mayo y Av del Libertador.
Jolly place for omelettes, burgers, vegetarian, 30 varieties of pizza.

Heladería Aquarela
Av del Libertador 1197.
The best ice cream – try the *calafate*. Also home-made chocolates and local produce.

Bars and clubs

Elba'r
9 de Julio 57, T02902-493594, see Facebook.
Just off the main street, this café/bar serves hard-to-find waffles and juices, as well as home-made beer and sandwiches.

Festivals

14 Feb Lago Argentino Day. Live music, dancing and *asados*.
10 Nov Día de la Tradición. Displays of horsemanship and *asados*.

Shopping

There are plenty of touristy shops along the main street, Av del Libertador.

Estancia El Tranquilo, *Av del Libertador 935, www.eltranquilo.com.ar.* Recommended for home-made local produce, especially Patagonian fruit teas, sweets and liqueurs.

What to do

Most agencies charge the same rates for similar trips: minibus tours to the Perito Moreno glacier (park entry not included), US$31; mini-trekking tours (transport plus a 2½-hr walk on the glacier), US$105. Note that in winter boat trips can be limited or cancelled due to bad weather.

Calafate Mountain Park, *Av del Libertador 1037, T02902-491446, www.calafate mountainpark.com.* Trips in 4WDs to panoramic views, 3-6 hrs. Summer and winter experiences including kayaking, quad biking, skiing and more.
Chaltén Travel, *Av del Libertador 1174, T02902-492212, also Av Güemes 7, T493092, El Chaltén, www.chaltentravel.com.* Huge range of tours (it has a monopoly on some): glaciers, estancias, trekking and bus to El Chaltén. English spoken. Also sells tickets along the Ruta 40 to Perito Moreno, Los Antiguos and Bariloche (see Transport, below).
Hielo y Aventura, *Av del Libertador 935, T02902-492205, www.hieloyaventura.com.* Mini-trekking includes walk through forests and 2½-hr trek on Moreno glacier (crampons included); Big Ice full-day tour includes a 4-hr trek on the glacier. Also half-day boat excursion to Brazo Sur for a view of stunning glaciers, including Moreno. Recommended.
Lago San Martín, *Av del Libertad 1215, p 1 A, T02902-492858, www.lagosanmartin.com.* Operates with **Estancias Turísticas de Santa Cruz**, specializing in arranging estancia visits, helpful.
Mar Patag, *Libertador 1319 loc. 7, T02902-492118, www.crucerosmarpatag.com.* Exclusive 2-day boat tour to Upsala, Spegazzini and Moreno glaciers, with full board. Also does a shorter full-day cruise with gourmet lunch included.

Mundo Austral, *Libertador 1080 piso 1, T02902-492365, www.mundoaustral.com.ar*. For all bus travel and cheaper trips to the glaciers, helpful bilingual guides.
Patagonia Backpackers, *at Hosteles del Glaciar, T02902-492492, www.patagonia-backpackers.com*. Alternative Glacier tour takes a more scenic route and is the only one that treks off the tourist trail on the south side of the glacier, entertaining, informative, includes walking, park entrance not included, US$52. Recommended constantly.
Solo Patagonia, *Av del Libertador 867, T02902-491155, www.solopatagonia.com*. This company runs 2 7-hr trips taking in Upsala, Onelli and Spegazzini glaciers, US$92.

Transport

Air
The airport (T02902-491220) has daily flights to/from **Buenos Aires**. There are many more flights in summer to **Bariloche**, **Ushuaia** and **Trelew**. **LADE** (J Mermoz 160, T02902-491262) flies to **Ushuaia**, **Comodoro Rivadavia**, **Río Gallegos** and other Patagonian airports). Note that a boarding fee of US$20.50, not included in the airline ticket price, has to be paid at El Calafate.

Bus
Buses from Río Gallegos (where you can connect with buses to Ushuaia) arrive in the centre of town. The bus terminal (T02902-491476) is open daily 0800-2000, A terminal fee of US$0.35 is always included in the bus ticket price. Some bus companies will store luggage for a fee.

To **Perito Moreno** glacier, with **Taqsa**, US$32 return. Many agencies in El Calafate also run minibus tours (see What to do, above). Out of season trips to the glacier may be difficult to arrange.

To **Puerto Madryn** with **Red Patagonia** (T02902-491250) 2 per day at 0300 and 1330, US$112; to **Río Gallegos** daily, 4-5 hrs, US$28-33, with **Taqsa** (T02902-491843). To **El Chaltén** daily with **Taqsa**, US$30, **Chaltén**

Travel (T02902-492212, at 0800, 1300, 1800) and **Cal-Tur** (T02902-491368, www.caltur.com.ar, who run many other services and tours), 3 hrs, US$30. To **Bariloche**, via **Los Antiguos** and **Perito Moreno**, 36 hrs, with **Chaltén Travel**, departs mid-Nov to Apr 2000 on odd-numbered days from El Chaltén with an overnight stop in Perito Moreno (it's cheaper to book your own accommodation); also **Cal-Tur** and **Taqsa** to **Bariloche** via **Los Antiguos** (Ruta 3 every day in high season; Ruta 40 frequency depends on demand). To **Ushuaia**, take a bus to Río Gallegos for connections US$83.

To **Puerto Natales** (Chile, for Torres del Paine), daily in summer with **Cootra** (T02902-491444), via **Río Turbio**, 8½ hrs US$32, daily at 0830, or with **Turismo Zaahj** (T02902-491631), 3 a week, fewer off-season, 5 hrs, US$32 (advance booking recommended, take your passport when booking, tedious customs check at border). **Note** Argentine pesos cannot be exchanged in Torres del Paine.

Bike hire
Patagonia Shop, Av del Libertador 995, also at 9 de Julio 29.

Car hire
Average price around US$65 per day for small car with insurance but usually only 200 km are free. **Avis**, Av del Libertador 1078, T02902-492 877, www.avis.com.ar, **Localiza**, Av del Libertador 687, T02902-491398, www.localiza.com.ar, or **Nunatak**, Gregores 1075, T02902-491 987, www.nunatakrentacar.com. All vehicles have a permit for crossing to Chile included in the fee, but cars are in poor condition.

Taxi
Taxis charge about US$90 for 4 passengers round trip to Perito Moreno glacier including wait of 3-4 hrs. Reliable providers include **El Tehuelche**, I02902-491850, **La Terminal** T02902-490 933, and **Calafate** T02902-492 005. There is a small taxi stand outside the bus terminal.

walls of living ice advancing on the shore

★ Glaciar Perito Moreno

The sight of this expanse of ice, like a frozen sea, its waves sculpted by wind and time into beautiful turquoise folds and crevices, is unforgettable. You'll watch in awed silence, until suddenly a mighty roar announces the fall of another hunk of ice into the milky turquoise water below. Glaciar Moreno is one of the few accessible glaciers in the world that you can see visibly advancing. Some 30 km long, it reaches the water at a narrow point in one of the fjords, **Brazo Rico**, opposite Península Magallanes. At this point the glacier is 5 km across and 60 m high. It occasionally advances across Brazo Rico, blocking the fjord, but, in recent decades, as the water pressure builds up behind it, the ice has broken, reopening the channel and sending giant icebergs (*témpanos*) rushing down the appropriately named **Canal de los Témpanos**. This happened in 1988, 2004, 2006, 2008, 2013 and March 2016. Walking on the ice itself is a wonderful way to experience the glacier: what appear from a distance to be vertical fish scales, turn out to be huge peaks; climb their steep curves and look down into mysterious chasms below, lit by refracted bluish light.

Essential Glaciar Perito Moreno

Access

There are various ways to approach the glacier. Tour companies in El Calafate offer all of these or some in combination. The regular bus service and all excursions not involving boat trips will take you straight to the car park that is situated 77 km west of El Calafate (around 30 km beyond the gates of the park). From here you begin the descent along a series of extensive wooden walkways (*pasarelas*) to see the glacier slightly from above, and then, as you get lower, directly head-on. There are several wide viewing areas, where crowds wait expectantly in summer, cameras poised, for another hunk of ice to fall with a mighty roar from the vertical blue walls at the glacier's front into the milky turquoise lake below. There is a large and fairly inexpensive café at the site with clean bathrooms.

You could also approach the glacier on a boat trip from two different piers.

To survey the glacier from the south (and for trekking on the glacier), boats leave from Bajo de las Sombras pier (7 km east of the glacier). To approach from the north, boats leave regularly from Perito Moreno pier (1 km north of the glacier, where there is a restaurant). This latter service is offered as an extra (US$17.50 pp) when you book your standard trip to the glacier or it can be booked directly at the pier.

To get closer still, there are guided treks on the ice itself, known as Big Ice and Mini-trekking, which allow you to walk along the crevices and frozen wave crests in crampons (provided). The latter is not technically demanding and is possible for anyone with a reasonable level of fitness. The glacier is approached by a lovely walk through lenga forest, and there's a place to eat your lunch outside, with wonderful views; but bring your own food and drink. See What to do, page 539.

★ Glaciar Upsala

The fjords at the northwestern end of Lago Argentino are fed by four other glaciers. The largest is the Upsala Glacier, named after the Swedish university that commissioned the first survey of this area in 1908. It's a stunning expanse of untouched beauty, three times the area of the Perito Moreno Glacier and the longest glacier flowing off the Southern Patagonian icefield. However, Upsala is suffering tremendously from the effects of global warming. Unusually, it ends in two separate frontages, each about 4 km wide and 60 m high, although only one frontage can be seen on the lake excursion by motorboat from Punta Bandera on Lago Argentino, 50 km west of Calafate. The trip also goes to other, much smaller, glaciers: **Spegazzini**, which has a frontage 1.5 km wide and 130 m high, and **Agassiz** and **Onelli** glaciers, both of which feed into **Lago Onelli**. This is a quiet and very beautiful lake, full of icebergs of every size and sculpted shape, surrounded by beech forests on one side and ice-covered mountains on the other.

The best way to see Upsala Glacier is to visit the remote Estancia Cristina ⓘ *see Where to stay, below*, which lies in a lonely spot on the northern shores of Lago Argentina, not far from the glacier. It's beautiful, utterly wild and yet is an unbeatably comfortable base for exploring the region. Accommodation is available, or you can come on a full-day visit offering various trips, including hiking tours lasting 2½ to five hours, as well as horse riding or driving in sturdy 4WD vehicles to a vantage point high above the lake. You'll walk through incredible ancient landscapes, alongside massive rocks polished smooth by the path of glaciers, to see Upsala Glacier from above. This is an overwhelmingly beautiful sight, stretching apparently endlessly away from you, with the deep, still Prussian-blue lake below, and rocks the colour of fire all around. Boat trips and day visits to **Estancia Cristina** are run by the estancia itself; see the website for details.

Listings Lago Argentino

Where to stay

$$$$ Estancia Cristina
Office at 9 de Julio 69, El Calafate, T02902-491133 (T011-4218 2333 ext 106/107 in Buenos Aires), www.estanciacristina.com.

On the northern tip of Lago Argentina, this estancia offers unrivalled access to the Upsala glacier and its surroundings. 20 comfortable rooms available in 5 lodges. Boat transfers from El Calafate are included. See also Glaciar Upsala, above.

one of the most magnificent mountains in the world

The soaring granite towers of Mount Fitz Roy rise up from the smooth baize of the flat steppe, more like a ziggurat than a mountain, surrounded by a consort of jagged snow-clad spires, with a stack of spun-cotton clouds hanging constantly above them. Cerro Fitz Roy (3405 m) towers above the nearby peaks, its polished granite sides too steep for snow to settle. Its Tehuelche name was El Chaltén ('smoking mountain' or 'volcano'), perhaps because at sunrise the pink towers are briefly lit up bright red for a few seconds, the *amanecer de fuego* ('sunrise of fire').

Perito Moreno named the peak after the captain of the *Beagle,* who saw it from afar in 1833, and it was first climbed by a French expedition in 1952. It stands in the northern section of Parque Nacional Los Glaciares, at the western end of Lago Viedma, 230 km north of El Calafate. Around it are other high peaks, lakes and glaciers that make marvellous trekking country, every bit as satisfying as Torres del Paine across the border.

El Chaltén

The small modern town of El Chaltén (population 1000) is set in a wonderful position at the foot of Cerro Fitz Roy and at the mouth of the valley of the Río de las Vueltas. The village was founded very recently, in 1985, in order to settle the area and pre-empt Chilean territorial claims. However, it has grown very rapidly, along with its popularity as a centre for trekking and climbing in summer, and for cross-country skiing in winter. It can be an expensive and not particularly attractive place, especially when the harsh wind blows. But its visitors create a cheerful atmosphere, there are some great bars, and from

Esssential Cerro Fitz Roy

Access

The base for walking and climbing around Fitz Roy is the tiny town of El Chaltén. The quickest way to reach the town is by flying to El Calafate's airport, 220 km away. There are frequent bus connections from El Calafate (four hours), and regular bus services in summer from Ruta 40 in the north, useful if you've come from the Lake District in either Argentina or Chile.

Walking

Most paths are very clear and well worn, but a map is essential, even on short walks. The **park information centre** provides helpful maps of treks, but the best are published by *Zagier and Urruty*, www.patagoniashop.net, regularly updated and available in various scales (1:50,000;

1:250,000; 1:350,000), US$10-13. They are sold in shops in El Calafate and El Chaltén. Do not stray from the paths. Always wear sunscreen (factor 30 at least) and be prepared for bad weather. See Lago del Desierto, page 546, for minibus services from El Chaltén.

When to go

Walking here is only viable from mid-October to April, with the best months usually March to early April when the weather is stable and not very cold, and the autumn colours of the beech forest are stunning. Midsummer (December and January) and spring (September to October) are very windy. In December and January the campsites can be full to bursting, with many walkers on the paths. Outside of these months most accommodation and many services close.

its concrete and tin dwellings you can walk directly into breathtaking landscapes. There is a small chapel, the **Capilla Tomás Egger**, named after an Austrian climber killed on Fitz Roy and built entirely from materials brought from Austria.

There are two ATMs in town – one in the bus station and the other a block away at **Banco de la Nación** (Monday-Friday 0800-1300). Many ATMS do not accept newer bank cards with smart chips. Luckily credit cards are accepted in all major hotels and most

The Fitz Roy area

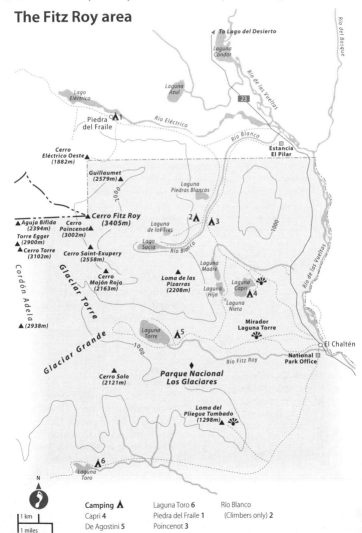

Camping **Λ**
Capri **4**
De Agostini **5**

Laguna Toro **6**
Piedra del Fraile **1**
Poincenot **3**

Río Blanco
(Climbers only) **2**

El Chaltén

Where to stay 🛏
Albergue
  Patagonia 1
Albergue Rancho
  Grande 15
Camping
  del Lago 11
Cóndor de
  los Andes 3
Estancia La Quinta 12
Hospedaje
  La Base 16
Hostería El Puma 5
Los Cerros 10
Lunajuim 7
Nothofagus 9
Senderos 17

Restaurants 🍴
Ahonikenk Chaltén 3
B&B Burger Joint 7
Domo Blanco 2
Estepa 9
Fuegia 6
Josh Aike 1
Pangea 4
Patagonicus 5

Bars & clubs 🍸
La Cervecería
  Artesanal
  El Chaltén 8

Not to scale

restaurants. Accommodation is available and ranges from camping and hostels to not-quite-luxurious *hosterías* and some top hotels, all overpriced in high season. Food is expensive too, though there is an increasing amount of choice.

Trekking

The main attraction here is the trekking around the Fitz Roy or Torre cordons. Always ask at your accommodation, at the tourist office or with the *guardaparques* for up-to-date information on trails and weather conditions.

Laguna Torre For a dramatic approach to Cerro Torre, take the path to Laguna Torre (three hours each way). After 1½ hours you'll come to Mirador Laguna Torre, with views of Cerro Torre and Cerro Fitz Roy, and after another 1¼ hours, to Camping De Agostini; see Where to stay, below.

Laguna de los Tres For closer views of Cerro Fitz Roy, take the path to Laguna de los Tres (four hours each way). Walk up to Camping Capri (just under two hours), with great views of Fitz Roy, then another hour to Camping Poincenot. Just beyond it is Camping Río Blanco (only for climbers, previous registration at park office required). From Río Blanco you can walk another hour, though it's very steep, to Laguna de los Tres where you'll get a spectacular view (although not if it's cloudy). In bad weather, you're better off walking an hour to Piedras Blancas (four hours total from El Chaltén). You can connect the two walks (to Laguna Torre and Laguna de los Tres) by taking a transverse path (two hours) from a point northwest of Laguna Capri to east of Camping De Agostini (see Where to

Tip...
The best day walks are Laguna Capri and Mirador Laguna Torre, both of which have great views.

stay, below), passing two lakes, Laguna Madre and then Laguna Hija; but note that this alternative can take more than one day.

Loma del Pliegue Tumbado A recommended day walk is to the Loma del Pliegue Tumbado viewpoint (four hours each way) where you can see both *cordones* and Lago Viedma. There's a marked path from the *guardería* with excellent panoramic views, best in clear weather. The onward trek to **Laguna Toro**, a glacial lake on the route across the ice cap (seven hours each way) is for more experienced trekkers.

Piedra del Fraile The trek up Río Blanco to Piedra del Fraile (seven hours each way) is beautiful. It starts at Campamento Río Blanco running north along the Río Blanco and west along the Río Eléctrico via Piedra del Fraile (four hours) to Lago Eléctrico. Piedra del Fraile can be reached more easily from the road to Lago del Desierto in about two hours. At Piedra del Fraile, just outside the park, there are *cabañas* ($$ per person, hot showers) and a campsite ($$$); see Where to stay, below. From here a path leads south, up Cerro Eléctrico Oeste (1882 m) towards the north face of Fitz Roy (two hours); it's tough going but offers spectacular views. You should take a guide for this last bit.

Climbing
Base camp for Fitz Roy (3405 m) is Campamento Río Blanco. Other peaks include Cerro Torre (3102 m), Torre Egger (2900 m), Cerro Solo (2121 m), Poincenot (3002 m), Guillaumet (2579 m), Saint-Exupery (2558 m), Aguja Bífida (2394 m) and Cordón Adela (2938 m): most of these are for very experienced climbers. The best time to climb is generally mid-February to late March; November and December are very windy; January is fair; winter (May to July) is extremely cold, but the weather is unpredictable and it all depends on the specific route being climbed. Permits for climbing are available at the national park information office in El Chaltén. Guides are also available in El Chaltén, see What to do, page 549. **Fitz Roy Expediciones**, www.fitzroyexpediciones.com.ar, are recommended.

Lago Viedma
Lago Viedma to the south of El Chaltén can be explored by boat. The trips usually pass Glaciar Viedma, with the possibility of ice trekking too. Contact **Fitz Roy Expediciones** (see What to do, page 549) for circuits that connect Lago Viedma and Lago San Martín.

Lago del Desierto and around
There is stunning virgin landscape to explore around **Lago del Desierto**, 37 km (one hour) north of El Chaltén. The long skinny lake is fjord-like and surrounded by forests. It's reached by unpaved Route 23, which leads north along the Río de las Vueltas. After about 30 minutes' drive, there is a one-hour hike along a marked path to Chorillo del Salto, a small but pristine waterfall. Route 23 continues via **Laguna Cóndor**, where flamingos can be seen, to Lago del Desierto. A short walk to a mirador at the end of the road gives fine views. There is a campsite at the southern end of the lake (sometimes no food, although there is a kiosk that sells drinks, beer and *choripán*), and a path runs along the east side of the lake to its northern tip (4½ hours), where there is a *refugio*. From here a trail leads west along the valley of the Río Diablo to Laguna Diablo.

Estancia El Pilar is the best place to stay on the way to Lago del Desierto; it's in a stunning position and has views of Fitz Roy. Use it as an excellent base for trekking up Río Blanco or Río Eléctrico, with a multi-activity adventure circuit. In summer **Transporte Las Lengas** in El Chaltén (www.transportelaslengas.com; see also page 550) runs a minibus twice daily to Lago del Desierto (US$30), stopping at **El Pilar** (US$13), and three times a day to Río Eléctrico (US$8.50). Highly recommended. There are also excursions with **Chaltén Travel** daily in summer to connect with boats across the lake (see What to do, page 549).

From December to April, it is possible to travel on foot, horseback and boat from Lago del Desierto to **Villa O'Higgins** in Chile, the southernmost town on the Carretera Austral. Take the Las Lengas minibus to Lago del Desierto, then either take a boat (45 minutes, US$32) to the northern end, or walk up the eastern shore (4½ hours). From there you can trek or go on horseback (with a guide, US$45 per horse), 5 km to the border. Hans Silva in Villa O'Higgins (T+56-67-243 1821) offers horses and a 4WD service from the Chilean border to Puerto Candelario Mancilla (14 km, US$22, US$15 for luggage only, reserve in advance) on Lago O'Higgins. Spend the night at Candelario Mancilla (Tito and Ricardo have lodging as well as 4WD and horses) and then, the next day, take a boat to Bahía Bahamóndez (three hours, US$66.50), followed by a bus to Villa O'Higgins, 7 km, US$3.75. For further information on dates, tours and boat availability, see www.villaohiggins.com. Note that the border is closed from May to November.

Listings Cerro Fitz Roy and around *maps pages 544 and 545.*

Tourist information

El Chaltén
There is also an excellent private website with accommodation listed, www.elchalten.com.

National park office
Across the bridge, right at the entrance to the town, T02962-493004, www.parquesnacionales.gov.ar.
Visitors are met by the friendly *guardaparques* (some speak English), who have advice on trekking and climbing.

Tourist office
In the bus station, T02962-493370. Daily 0800-2200 high season.
Helpful and efficient, with plenty of maps on offer. The staff hand out trekking maps of the area that show paths, campsites, distances and walking times. There's another tourist office at the bus station.

Where to stay

Cerro Fitz Roy area
Camping
A gas/alcohol stove is essential for camping as open fires are prohibited in the national park. Take plenty of warm clothes and a good sleeping bag. It is possible to rent equipment in El Chaltén; ask at the park office or Rancho Grande. There are campsites at Poincenot, Capri, Laguna Toro and Laguna Torre (Camping De Agostini, see below). None have services, but there are very basic public bathrooms. All river water is drinkable, so do not wash within 70 m of rivers. Pack up all rubbish and take it back to town.

Camping De Agostini
Next to Laguna Torre.
With fantastic views of the Cordón Torre.

Camping Los Troncos/Piedra del Fraile
On Río Eléctrico beyond the park boundary.
It is privately owned and has facilities.

El Chaltén
In high season places are full: you must book ahead. Most places close in low season.

$$$$ Hostería El Puma
Lionel Terray 212, T02962-493095, www.hosteriaelpuma.com.ar.
A little apart, splendid views, lounge with log fire, tasteful stylish furnishings, comfortable, transfers and big American breakfast included. Recommended.

$$$$ Los Cerros
Av San Martín 260, T02962-493182,
www.loscerrosdelchalten.com.
Stylish and sophisticated, in a stunning
setting with mountain views, sauna,
whirlpool and massage. Half-board and all-
inclusive packages with trips available.

$$$$ Senderos
Perito Moreno 35, T02962-493336,
www.senderoshosteria.com.ar.
4 types of room and suite in a new, wood-
framed structure, comfortable, warm, can
arrange tours, excellent restaurant.

$$$ Estancia La Quinta
On R23, 2 km south of El Chaltén, T02962-
493012, www.estancialaquinta.com.ar.
Oct-Apr.
A spacious pioneer house with renovated
rooms surrounded by beautiful gardens, very
comfortable, has Wi-Fi. A superb breakfast
is included and the restaurant is also open
for lunch and dinner. Transfer to and from
El Chaltén bus terminals is included.

$$$ Lunajuim
Trevisán 45, T02962-493047,
www.lunajuim.com.
Stylish yet relaxed, comfortable (duvets
on the beds), lounge with wood fire.
Recommended.

$$$ Nothofagus
Hensen y Riquelme, T02962-493087, www.
nothofagusbb.com.ar. Oct and Apr ($$).
Cosy bed and breakfast, simple rooms,
cheaper without bath and in low season,
good value. Recommended.

$$ Hospedaje La Base
C 10 N 16, T02962-493031, see Facebook.
Good rooms for 2, 3 and 4, tiny kitchen,
self-service breakfast, great video lounge.
Recommended.

$ pp Albergue Patagonia
Av San Martín 493, T02962-493019, www.
patagoniahostel.com.ar. Closed Jun-Sep.
HI-affiliated, cheaper for members, small and
cosy with rooms for 2 with own bath ($$)

or for 2 ($$), 4, 5 or 6 with shared bath, also
has cabins, video room, bike hire, laundry,
luggage store and lockers, restaurant, very
welcoming. Helpful information on Chaltén,
also run trips to Lago del Desierto.

$ pp Albergue Rancho Grande
San Martín 724, T02962-493005,
www.ranchograndehostel.com.
In a great position at the end of town with
good open views and attractive restaurant
and lounge, rooms for 4, with shared
bath, breakfast extra. Also $$ doubles,
breakfast extra. Helpful, English spoken.
Recommended. Reservations in Calafate at
Hostel/Chaltén Travel.

$ pp Cóndor de los Andes
Av Río de las Vueltas y Halvorsen, T02962-
493101, www.condordelosandes.com.
Nice little rooms for up to 6 with bath, sheets
included, breakfast extra, also doubles with
bath ($$$-$$), laundry service, library, quiet,
HI affiliated.

Camping

Camping del Lago
Lago del Desierto 135, T02962-493245.
Centrally located with hot showers.
Several others.

Lago Viedma

$$$$ Estancia Helsingfors
73 km northwest of La Leona, on Lago
Viedma, T011-5277 0195 (Buenos Aires),
reservations T02966-675753,
www.helsingfors.com.ar. Nov-Apr.
Fabulous place in a splendid position on
Lago Viedma, stylish rooms, welcoming
lounge, delicious food (full board), and
excursions directly to glaciers and to Laguna
Azul, by horse or trekking, plus boat trips.

Lago del Desierto and around

$$$ Aguas Arriba Lodge
RP23, Km 130, T011-4152 5697,
www.aguasarribalodge.com.

Comfortable wooden lodge on the eastern shore, reached only by boat, 15 mins, or by a 2- to 3-hr walk with guide (luggage goes by boat). Great views and trekking opportunities.

$$$ El Pilar
RP23, Km 17, T02962-493002, www.hosteriaelpilar.com.ar.
Country house in a spectacular setting at the meeting of Ríos Blanco and de las Vueltas, with clear views of Fitz Roy. A chance to sample the simple life with access to the less-visited northern part of the park. Simple comfortable rooms, great food, breakfast and return transfers included.

Restaurants

El Chaltén

$$ Estepa
Cerro Solo y Antonio Rojo, www.esteparestobar.com.
Small, intimate place with good, varied meals, friendly staff.

$$ Fuegia
San Martín 342. Dinner only.
Pastas, trout, meat and vegetarian dishes.

$$ Josh Aike
Lago de Desierto 105.
Excellent *chocolatería*, home-made food, beautiful building. Recommended.

$$ Pangea
Lago del Desierto 330 y San Martín. Lunch and dinner, drinks and coffee.
Tranquil atmosphere, with good music and a varied menu. Recommended.

$$ Patagonicus
Güemes y Madsen. Midday to midnight.
Lovely warm place with salads, *pastas caseras* and fabulous pizzas for 2, US$3-8. Recommended.

$$-$ Ahonikenk Chaltén
Av Martín M de Güemes 23, T02962-493070.
Restaurant and pizzeria, good home-made pasta.

$$-$ B&B Burger Joint
San Martín between C 6 and Terray.
Great burgers, microbrews and pub grub.

$ Domo Blanco
San Martín 164.
Delicious ice cream.

Bars and clubs

El Chaltén

La Cervecería Artesanal El Chaltén
San Martín 564, T02962-493109.
Brews its own excellent beer, also local dishes and pizzas, coffee and cakes, English spoken. Recommended.

Laguna de Los Tres
Trevisán 45, see Facebook.
Newer bar, live music, craft beer, sandwiches and pizzas. Free salsa classes on Thu.

Shopping

El Chaltén
Several outdoor shops. Also supermarkets, although these are all expensive, with little fresh food available. Fuel is available next to the bridge.

What to do

El Chaltén
Casa De Guías, *Av San Martín s/n, T02962-493118, www.casadeguias.com.ar.*
Experienced climbers who lead groups to nearby peaks, to the Campo de Hielo Continental and on easier treks.
Chaltén Travel, *Av Güemes 7, T02962-493092, www.chaltentravel.com.* Huge range of tours (see under El Calafate, page 539).
El Relincho, *San Martín s/n, T02962-493007, www.elrelinchopatagonia.com.ar.* For trekking on horseback with guides, also trekking, accommodation and rural activities.
Fitz Roy Expediciones, *San Martín 56, T02962-493178, www.fitzroyexpediciones. com.ar.* Organizes trekking and adventure trips including on the Campo de Hielo Continental, ice-climbing schools, and

fabulous longer trips. Climbers must be fit, but no technical experience required; equipment provided. Email with lots of notice to reserve. Also has an eco-camp with 8 wilderness cabins. Highly recommended.
Patagonia Aventura, *San Martín 56, T02962-493110, www.patagonia-aventura.com.* Has various ice trekking and other tours to Lago and Glaciar Viedma, also to Lago del Desierto.
Transporte Las Lengas, *Viedma 95, T02962-493023; also at the bus station, T02962-493227, www.transportelaslengas.com.* Transfers from El Calafate airport, plus minibuses to Lago del Desierto and Río Eléctrico.

Transport
El Chaltén
Bus
A tax of US$1.15 is charged at the terminal. In summer, buses fill quickly, so book ahead; there are fewer services off season. Daily buses to **El Calafate**, 3 hrs (most also stop at El Calafate airport), with **Taqsa** (T02962-493 130), US$30, **Chaltén Travel** (T02962-493092), **Los Glaciares** and **Cal-Tur** (T02962-493150). **Chaltén Travel** also go to **Los Antiguos** (1000) in high season daily at 2000 and **Bariloche** (2020), mid-Nov to Apr on odd-numbered days at 2000. To **Piedrabuena** on Ruta 3 (connect in El Calafate and Río Gallegos) with **Taqsa**, 3 daily in high seasons (1050), **Transporte Las Lengas** (T02962 493 023, www.transportelaslengas.com.ar) has a service to **El Calafate airport** 6 times a day in high season, 3 hrs, US$28, reserve in advance.

Taxi
Taxi/rent Oxalis, T02962-493343.

El Calafate to Chile
on the road to Torres del Paine

If travelling from El Calafate to Torres del Paine in Chile by car or bike, you can take the paved combination of Route 11, Route 40 and Route 5 to La Esperanza (165 km), where there's fuel, a campsite and a large but expensive *confitería* (accommodation $$ with bath). From La Esperanza, paved Route 7 heads west along the valley of the Río Coyle. A shorter but rougher route (closed in winter), missing Esperanza, goes via El Cerrito and joins Route 7 at Estancia Tapi Aike. Route 7 continues to the border, crossing at Cancha Carrera (see box, opposite) and then meets the good *ripio* road between Torres del Paine and Puerto Natales (63 km). For bus services along this route, see Transport, below.

Río Turbio *Colour map 6, B1.*
Located near the border, 250 km south of El Calafate, Río Turbio (population 8814) is a charmless place you're most likely to visit en route to or from Torres del Paine in Chile. For information on crossing the border near Río Turbio at Paso Mino Uno, see box, opposite.

Río Turbio has a cargo railway connecting it with Punta Loyola, and visitors can see Mina 1, where the first mine was opened, but the site of Argentina's largest coalfield hasn't really recovered from the depression that hit the industry in the 1990s. There's a small ski centre nearby, **Valdelén**, which has six pistes and is ideal for beginners; there is also scope for cross-country skiing between early June and late September.

BORDER CROSSING
Argentina–Chile

All crossings may have different hours in winter; see www.gendarmeria.gov.ar. For the crossing from Lago del Desierto to Villa O'Higgins (on foot, on horseback or by bike only), see page 547.

Paso Río Don Guillermo/Cancha Carrera

The Paso Río Don Guillermo or Cancha Carrera, 129 km west of La Esperanza and 48 km north of Río Turbio is open all year, and is the most convenient crossing to reach Parque Nacional Torres del Paine in Chile. The fast and friendly **Argentine customs and immigration** (daily 0900-2300) are at Cancha Carrera, 2 km east of the border. On the Chilean side the road continues to Cerro Castillo (with **Chilean immigration,** daily 0800-2200), where it meets the road between Puerto Natales, 65 km south, and the national park.

Paso Mina Uno/Dorotea

Paso Mina Uno/Dorotea is 5 km south of Río Turbio and is open all year, daily 0900-2300. On the Chilean side this road runs south to join the main Puerto Natales–Punta Arenas road. This is the crossing used by buses from Río Turbio to Puerto Natales.

Paso Casas Viejas/Laurita

Paso Casas Viejas is 33 km south of Río Turbio via 28 de Noviembre and is open all year, daily 0900-0100. It runs west on the Chilean side to join the Puerto Natales–Punta Arenas road. It runs west on the Chilean side to join the Puerto Natales–Punta Arenas road; see box, page 577.

Listings El Calafate to Chile

Tourist information

Río Turbio
Tourist office
Plazoleta Agustín del Castillo,
T02902-421950. Also see www.
welcomeargentina.com/rioturbio.

Where to stay

Río Turbio
Hotels here are almost always full.

$$ Nazó
Gob Moyano 464, T02902-421800,
www.hotelnazo.com.ar.
Modern building, rooms for 2-4, laundry service, restaurant and bar.

$ Hostería Capipe
Paraje Julia Dufour, 9 km from town,
T02902-482935, see Facebook.
Simple, with restaurant.

Transport

Río Turbio
Bus
To **Puerto Natales**, daily at 1530, 2 hrs, US$8, hourly with **Buses Pacheco** (www.busespacheco.com) and other companies. To **El Calafate** via **La Esperanza**, with **Taqsa,** 4 hrs, US$17-20. To **Río Gallegos**, 5 hrs, US$28, with **Taqsa/Marga** (T02902-421422).

Chilean Patagonia

A spectacular land of fragmenting glaciers and teetering icy peaks, southern Patagonia feels like nowhere else on earth.

Although Chileans posted here will often say that they are a 'long way from Chile', this is the country's most popular destination for visitors.

The jewel in the crown is the Parque Nacional Torres del Paine, a natural magnet for travellers from all over the world. The 'towers', three massif-like fingers after which the park is named, point vertically upwards from the Paine, surrounded by glaciers, turquoise-coloured lakes and thick forests of native trees.

Puerto Natales is the base for exploration of Torres del Paine and for boat trips to the glaciers in the Parque Nacional Bernardo O'Higgins. It also provides access to El Calafate and the Parque Nacional Los Glaciares in Argentina.

Further south, Punta Arenas is a European-style city with a lively Chilote community and remnants of earlier English and Croatian influences.

Best for
Camping ▪ Glacier walks ▪ Horse riding ▪ Trekking

Footprint
picks

★ Museo Regional Salesiano Maggiorino, page 558

Let this must-visit regional museum be your introduction to all
things Patagonian.

★ A cruise to Tierra del Fuego, page 564

Pamper yourself with a southern cruise replete with excellent scenery,
from Punta Arenas to Ushuaia.

★ Penguins at Seno Otway, page 567

Walk alongside thousands of Magellanic penguins and snap photos from
viewing stations.

★ Visiting glaciers in Bernardo O'Higgins National Park,
page 578

Take a Zodiac boat up Río Tyndall and visit the majestic Glacier Balmaceda.

★ Trekking in Parque Nacional Torres del Paine, page 579

No trekker's appetite is sated until they've completed the 'W' circuit at
this magnificent national park.

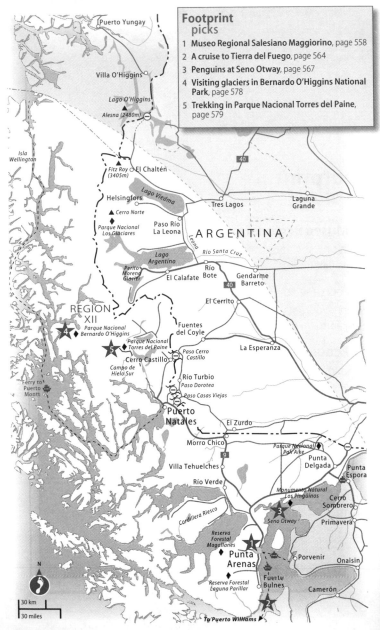

Puerto Yungay

Villa O'Higgins

Lago O'Higgins
Alesna (2480m)

Isla Wellington

Fitz Roy (3405m)   El Chaltén
Lago Viedma
Helsingfors
Cerro Norte   Paso Río La Leona   Tres Lagos   Laguna Grande
Parque Nacional Los Glaciares   ARGENTINA
Río Santa Cruz
Lago Argentino   Leona
Perito Moreno Glacier   Río Bote   Gendarme Barreto
El Calafate
40
El Cerrito

REGIÓN XII
Parque Nacional Bernardo O'Higgins   Fuentes del Coyle
Parque Nacional Torres del Paine   La Esperanza
Paso Cerro Castillo
Cerro Castillo
Campo de Hielo Sur   Río Turbio
Paso Dorotea
Ferry to Puerto Montt   Paso Casas Viejas
Puerto Natales
El Zurdo
Morro Chico   Parque Nacional Pali Aike
9   Punta Delgada
Villa Tehuelches   Punta Espora
Río Verde   Monumento Natural Los Pingüinos   Cerro Sombrero
Cordillera Riesco   Seno Otway   Primavera
Reserva Forestal Magallanes   Punta Arenas   Porvenir   Onaisin
Reserva Forestal Laguna Parillar   Fuerte Bulnes   Camerón

N

30 km
30 miles

To Puerto Williams

Punta Arenas
& around

Capital of Región XII, Punta Arenas lies 2140 km due south of Santiago. The city was originally named 'Sandy Point' by the English, but adopted the Hispanic equivalent under Chilean colonization. A centre for natural gas production, sheep farming and the fishing industry as well as an important military base, it is also the home of Polar Austral, one of the most southerly breweries in the world.

Although Punta Arenas has expanded rapidly, it remains a tranquil and pleasant city. The climate and architecture give it a distinctively northern European atmosphere, quite unlike anywhere else in Chile.

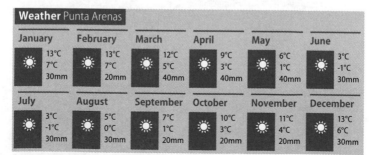

Weather Punta Arenas

January	February	March	April	May	June
13°C	13°C	12°C	9°C	6°C	3°C
7°C	7°C	5°C	3°C	1°C	-1°C
30mm	20mm	40mm	40mm	40mm	30mm

July	August	September	October	November	December
3°C	5°C	7°C	10°C	11°C	13°C
-1°C	0°C	1°C	3°C	4°C	6°C
30mm	30mm	20mm	20mm	20mm	30mm

Around the attractive Plaza Muñoz Gamero in Punta Arenas (population 160,000) are a number of mansions that once belonged to the great sheep-ranching families of the late 19th century.

A good example is the **Palacio Sara Braun** ⓘ *Mon 1000-1300, Tue-Sat 1000-1300 and 1600-1930, US$1.50*, built between 1894 and 1905 with materials from Europe. The Palacio has several elegantly decorated rooms open to the public and also houses the **Hotel José Nogueira**. In the centre of the plaza is a statue of Magellan with a mermaid and two indigenous Fuegians at his feet. According to local wisdom, those who rub or kiss the big toe of one of the Fuegians will return to Punta Arenas.

Just north of the plaza is the fascinating **Museo Regional de Magallanes** ⓘ *Palacio Braun Menéndez, Magallanes 949, T61-224 2049, www.museodemagallanes.cl, Wed-Mon 1030-1700 (May-Sep closes 1400), free*, the opulent former mansion of Mauricio Braun, built in 1905. A visit is recommended. Part of the museum is set out as a room-by-room regional history; the rest of the house has been left with its original furniture. Guided tours are in Spanish only, but an information sheet written in butchered English is also available. In the basement there is a permanent exhibition dedicated to the indigenous people of southern Patagonia, somewhat ironic considering the leading part the Braun Menéndez family played in their demise.

Essential Punta Arenas

Access

Punta Arenas is cut off from the rest of Chile. Puerto Natales, 247 km north, is easily reached on a paved road, with many buses daily, but other than that the only road connections are via the Argentine towns of Comodoro Rivadavia and Río Gallegos, either from Coyhaique on the Carretera Austral (20 hours; buses weekly in summer) or from Puerto Montt via Bariloche (36 hours, daily buses in summer); it is quicker, and often cheaper, therefore to take one of the many daily flights to/from Puerto Montt or Santiago instead.

Finding your feet

Carlos Ibáñez del Campo Airport is 20 km north of town. A minibus service is run by **Transfer Austral**, Av Cólon and Magallanes, T61-224 5811, www.transferaustral.com, US$4. Alternatively, a taxi costs US$11 to the city. Note that in most taxis much of the luggage space is taken up by natural gas fuel tanks. Buses from Puerto Natales to Punta Arenas will only stop at the airport if they are scheduled to drop passengers there.

Getting around

Punta Arenas is not a huge city and walking about is a pleasant way of getting to know it. Buses and *colectivos* are plentiful and cheap (around US$0.50; US$0.60 at night and Sundays): a taxi is only really necessary for out-of-town trips. For further details, see Transport, page 565.

Useful addresses

Argentine Consulate, 21 de Mayo 1878, T61-226 0600. Monday-Friday 1000-1500. Visas take 24 hours.

BACKGROUND
Southern Patagonia

Southern Patagonia was inhabited from the end of the Ice Age, mainly by the Tehuelche people, who roamed from the Atlantic coast to the mountains (see box, page 558). When Magellan sailed through the Straits in 1520, the strategic importance was quickly recognized. The route became less important after 1616 when Dutch sailors discovered a quicker route into the Pacific round Cape Horn.

At independence, Chile claimed the far southern territories along the Pacific coast but little was done to carry out this claim until 1843 when, concerned at British activities in the area, President Bulnes ordered the preparation of a secret mission. The expedition, on board the vessel *Ancud*, established Fuerte Bulnes; the fort was abandoned in 1848 in favour of a new settlement 56 km north, called Punta Arenas.

The development of sheep farming in Patagonia and on Tierra del Fuego (with the help of arrivals from the nearby Falkland Islands), and the renewed importance of the Magellan Straits with the advent of steam shipping, led to the rapid expansion of Punta Arenas in the late 19th century.

Sheep farming remains vital to the local economy, although wool exports have dropped in recent years. Forestry has become more important, but is controversial, as native forests are used for woodchips to export. This is especially serious on Tierra del Fuego. Although oil production has declined, large quantities of natural gas are now produced and Riesco Island contains Chile's largest reserves of coal. Tourism is growing rapidly, making an increasingly important contribution to the local economy.

Geography and climate

Chilean southern Patagonia stretches south from the icefields of the Campo de Hielos Sur to the Estrecho de Magallanes (Straits of Magellan), which separate continental South America from Tierra del Fuego. The coastline is heavily indented by fjords; offshore are numerous islands, few of which are inhabited. The remnants of the Andes stretch along the coast, seldom rising above 1500 m, although the Cordillera del Paine has several peaks over 2600 m and Cerro Balmaceda is 2035 m. Most of the western coast is covered by thick rainforest but further east is grassland, stretching into the arid Patagonian plateau across the Argentine border. Together with the Chilean part of Tierra del Fuego, Isla Navarino and Chilean Antarctica, this part of Chile is administered as Región XII (Magallanes); the capital is Punta Arenas. The region covers 17.5% of Chilean territory, but the population is only around 150,000, less than 1% of the Chilean total.

People from Punta Arenas say they often have four seasons in one day. Frequently, however, the only season appears to be winter. Cold winds, often exceeding 100 kph, blow during the summer bringing heavy rain to coastal areas. Further east, the winds are drier; annual rainfall at Punta Dungeness at the east end of the Straits is only 250 mm compared to over 4000 mm on the offshore islands. Coastal temperatures seldom rise above 15°C in summer. In winter, snow covers the whole region, except near the sea, making many roads impassable. There is little wind in the winter months, meaning tourism remains possible for most of the year.

ON THE ROAD
The original big foots

The original wanderers of the dry Patagonian plateau were one principal indigenous group, the Tehuelches, who inhabited the eastern side of the Andes, as far north as modern-day Bariloche. They were hunter-gatherers, subsisting on guanaco and rheas. In the 18th century, they began to domesticate the wild horses of the region and sailed down the Patagonian rivers to reach the Atlantic coast.

The Tehuelches were very large, almost mythically so. It is said that when the Spanish first arrived in this area, they discovered Tehuelche footprints in the sand, exclaiming '*qué patagón*' ('what a large foot'), hence the name Patagonia.

In the 18th and early 19th centuries, the Tehuelche interacted with European whalers and were patronizingly described as 'semi-civilized'. The granting by the Chilean government of large land concessions in the late 19th century, combined with Argentine President Julio Roca's wars of extermination against Patagonian native peoples in the 1870s, spelled the end for the Tehuelches. They were hunted and persecuted by settlers and only a few survived diseases and the radical change of lifestyle.

Towards the end of the 20th century, a belated sense of moral guilt arose among the colonizers, but it was too late to preserve the Tehuelche way of life. Today, only a few isolated groups remain in Argentine Patagonia.

For details of the indigenous groups further south and in the Patagonian fjords, see box, page 598.

Three blocks east of the plaza, the **Museo Naval y Marítimo** ⓘ *Pedro Montt 981, T61-224 5987, www.museonaval.cl, Tue-Sat, 0930-1230, 1400-1700, US$1.50,* houses an exhibition of local and national maritime history with sections on naval instruments, cartography, meteorology, and shipwrecks. There is a video in Spanish and an information sheet in English.

West of the Plaza Muñoz Gamero on Waldo Seguel are two reminders of British influence in the city: the **British School** and **St James's Anglican Church** next door. Nearby on Calle Fagnano is the **Mirador Cerro de La Cruz** offering a view over the city and the Magellan Straits complete with its various shipwrecks.

Three blocks further west is the **Museo Militar** ⓘ *Zenteno y Balmaceda, T61-222 5240, Tue-Sun, 1000-1200, and 1400-1730, free, closed at the time of writing but due to reopen in 2017,* at the Regimiento Pudeto. Lots of knives guns, flags and other military memorabilia are displayed here plus many items brought from Fuerte Bulnes. There are explanatory notes in excruciating English.

North of the centre along Bulnes is the ★ **Museo Regional Salesiano Maggiorino Borgatello** ⓘ *Colegio Salesiano, Av Bulnes 336, entrance next to church, T61-222 1001, see Facebook, Tue-Sun 1000-1230 and 1500-1730, hours change frequently, US$4,* an excellent introduction to Patagonia and easily the most complete and fascinating regional museum in Chile. It covers the interesting history of the indigenous peoples and their education by the Salesian missions, alongside an array of stuffed birds and gas extraction machinery. The Italian priest, Alberto D'Agostini, who arrived in 1909 and presided over the missions, took wonderful photographs of the region and his 70-minute film can be seen on video (just ask to see it).

Three blocks further on, the **cemetery** ① *Av Bulnes 029, daily 0730-2000 in summer, 0800-1800 in winter US$5*, is one of the most interesting places in the city, with cypress avenues, gravestones in many languages that bear testimony to the cosmopolitan provenance of Patagonian pioneers, and many mausolea and memorials to pioneer

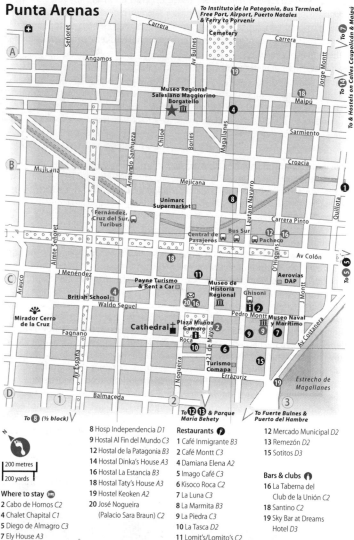

Punta Arenas

Where to stay
2 Cabo de Hornos C2
4 Chalet Chapital C1
5 Diego de Almagro C3
7 Ely House A3
8 Hosp Independencia D1
9 Hostal Al Fin del Mundo C3
12 Hostal de la Patagonia B3
14 Hostal Dinka's House A3
16 Hostal La Estancia B3
18 Hostal Taty's House A3
19 Hostel Keoken A2
20 José Nogueira
  (Palacio Sara Braun) C2

Restaurants
1 Café Inmigrante B3
2 Café Montt C3
4 Damiana Elena A2
5 Imago Café C3
6 Kiosco Roca C2
7 La Luna C3
8 La Marmita B3
9 La Piedra C3
10 La Tasca D2
11 Lomit's/Lomito's C2
12 Mercado Municipal D2
13 Remezón D2
15 Sotitos D3

Bars & clubs
16 La Taberna del
  Club de la Unión C2
18 Santino C2
19 Sky Bar at Dreams
  Hotel D3

BACKGROUND
Punta Arenas

After its foundation in 1848, Punta Arenas became a penal colony modelled on Australia. In 1867, it was opened to foreign settlers and given free-port status. From the 1880s, it prospered as a refuelling and provisioning centre for steam ships and whaling vessels. It also became a centre for the new sheep estancias as it afforded the best harbour facilities. The city's importance was reduced overnight by the opening of the Panama Canal in 1914.

Although immigrants from Britain and Croatia were central in the growth of Punta Arenas (their influence can be seen to this day), most of those who came to work in the estancias were from Chiloé; many people in the city have relatives in Chiloé and feel an affinity with the island (the barrios on either side of the upper reaches of Independencia are known as Chilote areas); the Chilotes who returned north took Patagonian customs with them, hence the number of *mate* drinkers on Chiloé.

families and victims of shipping disasters. Look out for the statue of Indicito, the 'little Indian', on the northwest side, which is now an object of reverence, bedecked with flowers.

Further north still, the **Instituto de la Patagonia** houses the **Museo del Recuerdo** ⓘ *Av Bulnes 1890, Km 4 northeast (opposite the university), T61-220 7051, outdoor exhibits, Mon-Sat 0830-1700, US$2.75*, an open-air museum with 3000 artefacts used by the early settlers, pioneer homes and botanical gardens. Opposite is the Zona Franca with a mall and ice rink (see Shopping, page 563).

On 21 de Mayo, south of Independencia, is a small ornate Hindu temple, one of only two in Chile, while further along the same street, on the southern outskirts of the city, the wooded **Parque María Behety** features a scale model of Fuerte Bulnes, popular for Sunday picnics. In winter, there is an ice rink here.

Reserva Nacional Magallanes ⓘ *9 km west of town, US$2.50, taxi US$5.50*, known locally as the Parque Japonés, extends over 13,500 ha and rises to 600 m. Although getting there by taxi is the easiest option, it can also be reached on foot or by bike: follow Independencia up the hill and take a right for Río de las Minas, about 3 km from the edge of town; the entrance to the reserve is 2 km beyond. Here you will find a self-guided nature trail through lenga and coigue trees. The road continues through the woods for 14 km passing several picnic sites. From the top end of the road a short path leads to a lookout over the **Garganta del Diablo** (Devil's Throat), a gorge with views over Punta Arenas and Tierra del Fuego. From here a slippery path leads down to the Río de las Minas Valley and then back to Punta Arenas.

Within the reserve, 8 km west of Punta Arenas, Cerro Mirador is one of the few places in the world where you can ski with a sea view. In summer there is a good two-hour walk on the hill, with labelled flora; contact **Club Andino** ⓘ *T61-224 1479, www.clubandino.cl*.

Tourist information

CONAF office
Av Bulnes 0309, p 4, T61-223 8554,
magallanes.oirs@conaf.cl.
For information on national parks
and other protected areas.

Municipal tourist information
Opposite Centro Español in the Plaza de
Armas, T61-220 0610, www.puntaarenas.cl.
High season Mon-Fri 0800-1900, Sat-Sun
0900-1700; Mon-Fri 0800-1700.
Helpful staff. There is also a kiosk in the plaza
with experienced, English-speaking staff and
a good town map with all hotels marked.

Sernatur
Lautaro Navarro 999 y Pedro Montt,
T61-222 5385, www.patagonia-chile.com.
High season Mon-Fri 0830-2000, Sat-Sun
1000-1800; in low season Mon-Fri 0830-1800,
Sat-Sun 1000-1800.

Where to stay

Hotel prices are lower during winter
months (Apr-Sep). A few streets, in
particular Caupolicán and Maipú, some
10-15 mins' walk from the centre have
become are packed with hostels, most
of them with similar facilities and similar
prices (**$$**). These include Ely House, Maipú
Street and Hostal Dinka's House; the
latter is painted bright-red and run by the
indomitable Dinka herself. The area is also
full of car repair places, which can make
it noisy during the day and occasionally
at night. For accommodation in private
houses, usually **$** pp, ask at the tourist
office. There are no campsites in or near
the city, except in certain hostels.

$$$$-$$$ Cabo de Hornos
Plaza Muñoz Gamero 1039, T61-271 5000,
www.hoteles-australis.com.

4-star, comfy, bright and spacious rooms,
with good views from 4th floor up.

$$$$-$$$ Diego de Almagro
Av Colón 1290, T61-220 8800,
www.dahotelespuntaarenas.com.
Very modern, good international standard,
on waterfront, many rooms with view,
heated pool, sauna, small gym, big bright
rooms, good value.

$$$$-$$$ José Nogueira
Plaza de Armas, Bories 967 y P Montt,
in former Palacio Sara Braun, T61-
271 1000, www.hotelnogueira.com.
Best in town, stylish rooms, warm
atmosphere, excellent service. Smart
restaurant in the beautiful *loggia.* A few
original rooms now a 'small museum'.

$$$ Chalet Chapital
Sanhueza 974, T61-273 0100,
www.hotelchaletchapital.cl.
Small well-run hotel, smallish rooms, helpful
staff, a good choice in this price range.

$$$ Hostal de la Patagonia
O'Higgins 730, T61-224 9970,
www.ecotourpatagonia.com.
Rooms with heating, good services, dining
room, 10 mins' walk from centre. Organizes
a variety of tours, including fly-fishing.

$$ Hostal Al Fin del Mundo
O'Higgins 1026, T61-271 0185,
www.alfindelmundo.hostel.com.
Rooms and dorms, bright, cosy, shared baths,
central, helpful, pool table, English spoken.

$$ Hostal La Estancia
O'Higgins 765, T61-224 9130, www.estancia.cl.
Simple but comfortable rooms, some with
bath. **$** pp in dorms. English spoken, small
shop attached, music and games room.

$$ Hostal Taty's House
Maipu 1070, T61-224 1525,
www.hostaltatyshouse.cl.

Nice rooms with good beds, decent choice in this price bracket, basic English spoken.

$$ Hostel Keoken
Magallanes 209, T61-224 4086/6376, www.hostelkeoken.cl.
Light, wooden, spacious building on 3 floors each with its own entrance up rickety outside staircases. Some rooms with small bath. Good value, some info. Top-floor rooms with shared bathroom have paper thin walls. Recently expanded into an even bigger, rambling place.

$ Hospedaje Independencia
Independencia 374, T61-222 7572, www.hostalindependencia.es.tl.
Private rooms, dorms (3-4 beds) and camping with use of kitchen and bathroom. Trekking equipment rental, parking, fishing and other tours, lots of information; very knowledgeable owners. Discount without breakfast. Recommended.

Restaurants

Many eating places close on Sun. There are seasonal bans on *centolla* (king crab) fishing to protect dwindling stocks; out of season *centolla* served in restaurants will probably be frozen. Note that *centolla* is caught illegally by some fishermen using dolphin, porpoise and penguin as live bait. If there is an infestation of red tide (*marea roja*), a disease which is fatal to humans, bivalve shellfish must not be eaten. Mussels should not be picked along the shore because of pollution and the *marea roja*. Sernatur and the Centros de Salud have leaflets.

$$$ Remezón
21 de Mayo 1469, T61-224 1029, see Facebook.
Regional specialities such as krill. Very good, but should be, given the prices.

$$$-$$ Damiana Elena
Magallanes 341, T61-222 2818. Mon-Sat from 2000-2400, see Facebook.

Stylish restaurant serving Mediterranean food with a Patagonian touch, popular with locals, book ahead at weekends.

$$$-$$ La Tasca
Plaza Muñoz Gamero 771, in Casa Español.
Large helpings, limited selection, decent set lunch, views over the plaza.

$$$-$$ Sotitos
O'Higgins 1138, T61-224 3565, see Facebook. Daily lunch and dinner, Sun 1200-1500 only.
An institution, famous for seafood in elegant surroundings, excellent. Book ahead in season. 2nd floor serving local specialities and Italian food.

$$ La Luna
O'Higgins 1017, T61-222 8555, www.laluna.cl.
Fish, shellfish and local specialities, huge pisco sours, popular, reasonable. Quirky decor, friendly staff. Recommended.

$$ La Marmita
Plaza Sampiao 678, T61-222 2056, www.marmitamaga.cl. Mon-Sat 1230-1500 and 1830-2330, Sun 1830-2330.
Regional dishes with international twist, vegetarian options, good sized portions, prettily presented, chatty owner, generally very good.

$$-$ La Piedra
Lautaro Navarro 1087, T9-665 1439. Mon-Sat 1200-2300.
Meat dishes, fish, soups, salads, good burgers and sandwiches, daily lunch specials, housed over 2 floors.

$ Kiosco Roca
Roca 875. Mon-Fri 0700-1900, Sat 0800-1300.
Unassuming sandwich bar, voted the best in Punta Arenas; it's always packed. Also serves breakfast and brunch. Takeaway or there are a few seats available at the counter.

$ Lomit's/Lomito's
Menéndez 722.
A fast-food institution with bar attached, cheap snacks and drinks (local beers are

good), open when the others are closed, good food.

$ Mercado Municipal
21 de Mayo 1465. Daily 1000-2000.
Wide range of *cocinerías* offering cheap *empanadas* and seafood on the upper floor of the municipal market.

Cafés

Café Inmigrante
Quillota 599, esq Mejicana, T61-222 2205, www.inmigrante.cl. Daily afternoons and evenings.
Hugely popular café run by 3rd generation Croatian expats. Beautifully prepared sandwiches, daily changing cake menu, huge portions, family history on menus. Quirky and popular. Book in advance if possible. Highly recommended.

Café Montt
Pedro Montt 976, T61-222 0381, www.cafemontt.cl.
Coffees, teas, cakes, pastries and snacks, Wi-Fi. Cosy, friendly. Recommended.

Imago Café
Costanera y Colón.
Tiny, laid-back café hidden away in a beachfront bunker overlooking the straits. Live music occasionally.

Bars and clubs

La Taberna del Club de la Unión
In the Sara Braun mansion.
Atmospheric bar, good for evening drinks.

Santino
Colón 657, T61-271 0882, www.santino.cl. Open 1800-0300.
Also serves pizzas and other snacks, large bar, good service, live music Sat.

Sky Bar
O'Higgins 1235.
Bar with panoramic views on the top floor of the luxury **Dreams** hotel and spa.

Entertainment

There is a single-screen **cinema** (Mejicana 777, www.cinesalaestrella.cl). The **casino** (www.mundodreams.com), is at O'Higgins 1235, just north of the port.

Festivals

Late Jul Carnaval de invierno The winter solstice is marked by a carnival on 23-24 Jul.

Shopping

Punta Arenas has free-port facilities: **Zona Franca**, 4 km north of the centre, opposite Museo del Recuerdo (Instituto de la Patagonia), is cheaper than elsewhere. The complex has over 100 shops and is open daily 1000-2100 (www.zonaustral.cl); take bus No 8 or catch *colectivo* 15 or 20; taxi US$5.

Handicrafts
Chile Típico, *Carrera Pinto 1015, T61-222 5827, Mon-Sat 0900-2130, Sun 1000-2000.* Beautiful knitwear and woollen ponchos.
Mercado Municipal *(see Restaurants, above).* Excellent handicrafts and souvenirs.

What to do

Skiing
Cerro Mirador in the Reserva Nacional Magallanes has skiing Jun-Sep, weather and snow permitting. Midway lodge with food, drink and equipment rental. Taxi US$7.

Tour operators
Most organize trips to Torres del Paine, the *pingüineras* on Isla Magdalena and Otway Sound, and Tierra del Fuego; shop around.
Adventure Network International, *T+1-801 266 4876, www.adventure-network.com.* Antarctic experiences of a lifetime, operating out of Punta Arenas, flying to the interior of the Antarctic Continent. Flights to the South Pole, guided mountain climbing and fully guided skiing expeditions. Camping with emperor penguins in Nov.

★ A cruise at the end of the world

From September to April, Australis have two vessels running cruises between Punta Arenas and Ushuaia, the *Vía Australis* and the *Stella Australis*. *Vía Australis* has capacity for 136 passengers, while *Stella Australis* can accommodate 210. (For the 2017-2018 season, the *Vía Australis* will be replaced by the *Ventus Australis*, similar to *Stella Australis*.) Passengers sail in comfort, treated to fine food and expert service, through the Straits of Magellan and the channels and fjords between Tierra del Fuego and the islands that cling to its southern shore. These were the waters fished by the Yámana and Kawéskar people and surveyed by Robert Fitzroy and his crew.

The cruise takes four nights from Punta Arenas to Ushuaia (three nights the opposite way). Each includes a visit to Cape Horn where, sea conditions permitting, you can land to see the monuments and to sign the visitors' book in the lighthouse, manned by a Chilean naval officer and his family. The landing follows a rigorous procedure: everyone is togged up in waterproofs and lifejackets, and is transferred from ship to Zodiac, before disembarking with the aid of crew standing in the surf. From the shore, 160 wooden steps lead up the cliff to wooden walkways. On a relatively benign day – sunny, with an icy breeze – it's hard to imagine the tragedies of so many mariners lost, to remember the many souls that, according to legend, have become albatrosses, and to accept that this is the last piece of terra firma before Antarctica.

Other shore trips are followed by a whisky or hot chocolate. You need the sustenance, especially after a visit to Piloto and Nena glaciers in the Chico fjord. The blue ice of Piloto calves into the water, while Nena is scarred by rocky debris. All around water pours off the mountains; sleet and rain drive into your face as the Zodiac powers away.

En route from Ushuaia to Punta Arenas (the itinerary varies according to the route and the weather), there are other landings. At Wulaia Bay on Isla Navarino two walks are available, up a hill or along the shore to look for birds and flora. An information centre, in an old radio station, tells the history of the place. It was here that one of Fitzroy's Fuegians, Jemmy Button, who was briefly a celebrity in England in the 1830s, was reportedly present at the massacre of missionaries in 1859. Another visit is to Isla Magdalena, just off Punta Arenas. Here, between November and January, 60,000 pairs of Magellanic penguins breed in burrows.

At all times the ship is accompanied by giant petrels, black-browed albatross and king cormorants. Occasionally, dolphins ride the wake. If it is too cold on deck, you can go onto the bridge and be entertained by the navigator. The bar is open until midnight; stewards and guides are on hand at any hour; and there are lectures and films, visits to the engine room and cookery lessons to fill the hours at sea. Everything runs like clockwork thanks to clear instructions for safety and fine-tuned organization: when the captain says you'll dock at 1100, dock at 1100 you will.

For more information on these cruises, see www.australis.com, and Australis, at Turismo Comapa, Lautaro Navarro 1112, T61-220 0200 (in Santiago: Avenida El Bosque Norte 0440, p 11, T2-2840 0100; in Buenos Aires: T011-5128 4632; in USA: T01-877 678 3772; in Europe: T34-93-497-0484).

Arka Patagonia, *Manuel Señoret 1597, T61-224 8167, www.arkapatagonia.com.* All types of tours, whale watching, trekking, Cape Horn.
Go Patagonia, *Lautaro Navarro 1013, T61-237 1074, www.gopatagoniachile.com.* Tours to Torres del Paine, Tierra del Fuego and Seno Otway.
Solo Expediciones, *Nogueira 1255, T61-271 0219, www.soloexpediciones.com.* Operate their own service to Monumento Natural Los Pingüinos on a small fast boat, also passing by Isla Marta, half-day tour, mornings only.
Turismo Aventour, *Soto 2876, T9-7827 9479, www.aventourpatagonia.cl.* Specialize in fishing trips, organize tours to Tierra del Fuego, helpful, English spoken.
Turismo Comapa, *Lautaro Navarro 1112, T61-220 0200, www.comapa.com.* Tours to Torres del Paine (responsible, well-informed guides), Tierra del Fuego and to see penguins at Isla Magdalena. Agents for **Australis** cruises (see opposite).
Turismo Laguna Azul, *21 de Mayo 1011, T61-222 5200, www.turismolagunaazul.com.* Full-day trips to a colony of king penguins on Tierra del Fuego. Trips run all year round. Also city tours, trips to glaciers and others.
Turismo Yamana, *T61-222 2061, www.yamana.cl.* Conventional and deluxe tours, trekking in Torres del Paine, kayaking the fjords of Parque Nacional Alberto de Agostini (Tierra del Fuego), multilingual guides.
Whale Sound, *Lautaro Navarro 1191, T9-9887 9814, www.whalesound.com.* Whale-watching trips in the Magellan Straits.

Transport

Most transport is heavily booked from Christmas to Mar so book in advance.

There is a daily ferry service on the **Melinka** from Punta Arenas and Porvenir on Tierra del Fuego, but buses to Tierra del Fuego use the more northerly ferry crossing at Punta Delgada (many daily) to Puerto Espora.

Air
To **Santiago**, LAN and **Sky**, direct, many daily. To **Porvenir**, Aerovías DAP (O'Higgins 891, T61-261 6100, www.aeroviasdap.cl), 3 times daily Mon-Fri (0815, 1230, 1700), 2 on Sat (0815, 1230), 9 passengers, 12 mins. To **Puerto Williams**, daily except Sun, 1¼ hrs (book a week in advance for Porvenir, 2 in advance for Puerto Williams).

To **Ushuaia**, private charter with **DAP**. Take passport when booking tickets to Argentina. To **Falkland Islands/Islas Malvinas**, with **LAN**, once a week on Sun; for information contact **International Tours & Travel Ltd**, PO Box 408, 1 Dean St, Stanley, Falkland Islands, T+500 22041, www.falklandislands. travel, Mon-Fri 0800-1700, Sat 1000-1200, who are the Falkland Islands agents for LAN. They also handle inbound tourist bookings, book FIGAS flights and arrange tours.

Bus
The bus terminal is at the northern edge of town by the Zona Franca. To book all tickets visit the **Central de Pasajeros**, Colón y Magallanes, T61-224 5811, also *cambio* and tour operator. At the time of writing, bus companies were maintaining their own offices in the city centre: **Cruz del Sur, Fernández**, and **Turibus**, Sanhueza 745, T61-224 2313/222 1429, www.busesfernandez. com; **Pacheco**, Colón 900, T61-224 2174, www.busespacheco.com; **Pullman**, Colón 568, T61-222 3359, www.pullman.cl, tickets for all Chile; **Bus Sur**, Colón 842, T61-222 2938, www.bussur.com; **Ghisoni** and **Tecni Austral (also tours)**, Lautaro Navarro 975, T61-261 3420, www.turismoghisoni.com.

To **Puerto Natales**, 3-3½ hrs, **Fernández, Bus Sur** and **Pacheco**, up to 8 daily, last departure 2100, US$8.50, look out for special offers and connections to Torres del Paine. Buses may pick up at the airport with advance booking and payment. To **Otway Sound**, with **Fernández** daily 1500, return 1900, US$9.

To **Tierra del Fuego** via Punta Delgada (see Essential Tierra del Fuego, page 591;

no buses via Porvenir) **Pacheco**, **Sur**, **Tecni-Austral**, **Pullman** and others (check with companies for schedules); to **Río Grande** Mon-Fri 0900, 8 hrs, US$28, heavily booked; to **Ushuaia**, 12 hrs, US$42-50; some services have to change in Río Grande for Ushuaia, others are direct; book well in advance in Jan-Feb.

To **Río Gallegos** (Argentina), via Route 255, **Pacheco**, Sun, Mon, Tue, Fri; **Barria/Ghisoni** (www.busesbarria.com), Mon, Wed, Thu, Fri, Sat, Sun, **Bus Sur** Mon, Wed, Thu, Fri, Sat; fares US$20, 5-8 hrs, depending on customs: 15 mins on Chilean side, up to 2 hrs on Argentine side (see also box, page 569).

To **Puerto Montt** with **Bus Sur** and **Pullman**, Mon, Wed, Fri, 0800 US$63, 34 hrs, also **Osorno**, US$63, 30 hrs.

Car hire

Note that you need a hire company's authorization to take a car into Argentina. This takes 24 hrs (not Sat or Sun) and involves mandatory international insurance for US$100, plus notary fees. In addition to the multinationals, there are some local companies: **EMSA**, Kuzma Slavic 706, T61-261 4378, www.emsarentacar.cl; **Payne**, Menéndez 631, T61-224 0852, www.payne.cl, also tours, treks, birdwatching, etc.

Ferry and cruise services

To Tierra del Fuego The ferry dock is 5 km north of Punta Arenas centre, at Tres Puentes. For all ferry services to the island, see box, page 591.

To **Puerto Montt** Contact **Navimag**, Navarro 1225, 1st floor, T61-220 0200, www.navimag.com. For **Australis**, see box, page 564.

To **Antarctica** Most cruise ships leave from Ushuaia, but a few operators are based in Punta Arenas. Try **Adventure Network International** (see above) or **Antarctica XXI**, O'Higgins 1170, T61-261 4100, www.antarcticaxxi.com, for flight/cruise packages. Otherwise, another possibility is with the Chilean Navy vessels *Galvarino* and *Lautaro* (around US$50, 1 month; enquire at the Tercera Zona Naval, Lautaro 1150, T61-220 5599), which sail regularly (no schedule; see www.armada.cl). Note that the navy does not encourage passengers, so you must approach the captain direct. Present yourself as a professional or student as opposed to a tourist. Spanish is essential.

Taxi

Ordinary taxis have yellow roofs. *Colectivos* (all black) run on fixed routes and pick up from taxi stands around town, US$0.50 flat fee.

Reserva Nacional Laguna Parrillar

About 25 km south of Punta Arenas, there is a fork in the road to the right; 21 km further on is the very peaceful Parrillar reserve, covering 18,814 ha and surrounded by snow-capped hills. It has older forest than the Magallanes Reserve and sphagnum bogs, and offers excellent salmon and trout fishing. There is a three-hour walk to the treeline (and others along poorly marked, boggy paths) and fine views from the mirador. There are CONAF-administered campsites and picnic sites. Note that there is no public transport to the reserve and hitching is virtually impossible; a radio taxi will cost about US$55.

Fuerte Bulnes and further south

Some 56 km south of Punta Arenas, **Fuerte Bulnes** ① *US$17, US$8.50 children*, is a replica of the wooden fort erected in 1843 by the crew of the Chilean vessel *Ancud*. Built in the 1940s and originally designed to house a museum, nearly all the interesting exhibits and artefacts were moved to museums in Punta Arenas and Santiago in 1986 and now only the empty shells of the various buildings remain. Several agencies run half-day tours to here, but hitching is not difficult at weekends or in summer, as there are many holiday camps in the area.

Nearby is **Puerto Hambre**, where there are ruins of the church built by Sarmiento de Gamboa's colonists in 1584 (see box, page 568). The views towards the towering ice mountains near Pico Sarmiento cut an impressive scene; it was of Puerto Hambre that Darwin wrote: "looking due southward … the distant channels between the mountains appeared from their gloominess to lead beyond the confines of this world". Southern dolphins can often be seen in the straits around this point.

At the intersection of the roads to Puerto Hambre and Fuerte Bulnes, 51 km south of Punta Arenas, is a small monolith marking the **Centro Geográfico de Chile**, the midway point between Arica and the South Pole. Bypassing Fuerte Bulnes, the road continues past a memorial to Captain Pringle Stokes, Captain of the *Beagle*, who committed suicide here in 1829, being replaced as captain by Fitz Roy. The road carries on, past San Juan to the lighthouse at San Isidro. The last part of this journey can only be done in summer in a high-clearance vehicle and at low tide, as it involves crossing an estuary at the mouth of the Río San Pedro. Alternatively, leave your vehicle on the north side of the estuary, ford the river (at low tide) and walk 2½ hours to San Isidro. From here, it is a day hike to **Cape Froward**, the southernmost point of the continent of South America, marked by a 24-m-high cross. There is no path, and a guide is essential (this can be arranged by the hostería at San Isidro with advance notice).

Some 70 km west of Cape Froward along the Magellan Straits is *Isla Carlos III*, a popular base for humpback whale watching.

North of Punta Arenas

Some 70 km north of Punta Arenas, ★ **Seno Otway** ① *Oct to mid-Mar, US$10.50*, is the site of a colony of thousands of Magellanic penguins that can be viewed from walkways and bird hides; rheas, skunks and foxes can also be seen. There are beautiful views across the sound to the mountains to

Tip...

It is best to go to Seno Otway early in the day. Try to avoid going at the same time as the large cruise ship tours; it is not much fun having to wait behind 200 people for your turn at the viewing stations.

ON THE ROAD

Port Famine (Puerto Hambre)

In 1582, Felipe II of Spain, alarmed by Drake's passage through the Straits of Magellan, decided to establish a Spanish presence on the Straits. A fleet of 15 ships and 4000 men, commanded by Pedro Sarmiento de Gamboa, was despatched in 1584. Before the ships had left the Bay of Biscay, a storm arose and scattered the fleet, sinking seven ships and killing 800 people. Further depleted by disease, the fleet of three remaining ships at length arrived at the Straits, with just 300 men on board. Led by Sarmiento this small force founded two cities: Nombre de Jesús on Punta Dungeness at the eastern entrance to the Straits and Rey Don Felipe near Puerto Hambre.

Disaster struck when their only remaining vessel broke its anchorage in a storm near Nombre de Jesús; the ship, with Sarmiento on board, was blown into the Atlantic, leaving many of Sarmiento's men stranded on land. After vain attempts to re-enter the Straits, Sarmiento set sail for Río de Janeiro where he organized two rescue missions: the first ended in shipwreck, the second in mutiny. Captured by English corsairs, Sarmiento was taken to England where he was imprisoned. On his release by Elizabeth I, he tried to return to Spain via France, but was jailed again. Until his death in 1608, Sarmiento besieged Felipe II with letters urging him to rescue the men stranded in the Straits.

When the English corsair Thomas Cavendish sailed through the Straits in 1587 he found only 18 survivors at Rey Don Felipe. With the English and Spanish at war, only one – Tomé Hernández – would trust Cavendish when he first arrived. A sudden spell of fine weather arose, and Cavendish set sail, leaving the rest of the men to die. He named the place Port Famine as a reminder of their grisly fate.

the north, and it is also becoming a popular area for sea kayaking and other adventure sports. Several agencies offer trips to the colony lasting five hours (US$14 plus entry fees at peak season); if you wish to visit independently, a taxi from Punta Arenas will cost US$80 return or there are daily buses with Fernández. Access to the colony is via a private road where a toll of US$2 per person is charged.

A small island, 30 km northeast, **Isla Magdalena** is the location of the **Monumento Natural Los Pingüinos** ① *US$7, free for children*, a colony of 80,000 pairs of Megallanic penguins, administered by **CONAF**. Deserted apart from during the breeding season from November to early February, Magdalena is one of a group of three islands visited by Drake (the others are Marta and Isabel), whose men killed 3000 penguins for food. Boat trips to the island are run by **Comapa** and **Solo Expediciones**, while the **Australis** cruise ships also call here (see box, page 564). Take a hat, coat and gloves.

Beyond, Route 255 heads northeast towards the Argentine border (see box, opposite), passing **Kamiri Aike** where a road branches southeast towards Punta Delgada for ferries to Tierra del Fuego (see box, page 591).

There is also a turn-off north along a *ripio* road for 26 km to **Parque Nacional Pali Aike** ① *managed by CONAF, T61-223 8554, magallanes.oirs@conaf.cl, US$1.50; children free*, a fantastic volcanic landscape dotted with small cones and craters. It's one of the oldest archaeological sites in Patagonia, with evidence of aboriginal occupation from 10,000-12,000 years ago. (Pali Aike means 'desolate place of bad spirits' in Tehuelche.) There are five easy, marked trails, all of which can be done in a day. Tour operators offer full-day trips, US$47.

BORDER CROSSING
Chile–Argentina

Integración Austral
The border is located 30 km north of Kamiri Aike via Route 255 (190 km from Punta Arenas) and is open daily 24 hours in summer and 0900-2300 from 1 April to 3 October. On the Argentine side the road continues as Route 3 for 67 km northeast to Río Gallegos. For bus passengers the border crossing is easy, although you have about a 30-minute wait at each border post as luggage is checked and documents are stamped. Hire cars from Argentina need special documents in order to cross the border. For more information see www.gendarmeria.gob.ar/pasos-chile/integracion-austral.html.

Listings Around Punta Arenas

Where to stay

Fuerte Bulnes and further south

$$$$ Hostería Faro San Isidro
75 km south of Punta Arenas, booking office Lautaro Navarro 1163, Punta Arenas, T9-934 93862, www.hosteriafarosanisidro.cl.

The southernmost lodging on the American continent and within striking distance of Cape Froward. Trips offered.

Puerto Natales
& around

From Punta Arenas, a good paved road runs 247 km north to Puerto Natales through forests of southern beech and prime pastureland; this is the best area for cattle- and sheep-raising in Chile. Ñandúes and guanacos can often be seen en route. Puerto Natales lies between Cerro Dorotea (which rises behind the town) and the eastern shore of the Seno Ultima Esperanza (Last Hope Sound), over which there are fine views, weather permitting, to the Península Antonio Varas and the jagged peaks and receding glaciers of the Parque Nacional Bernardo O'Higgins beyond.

Founded in 1911, the town grew as an industrial centre and, until recent years, the town's prosperity was based upon employment in the coal mines of Río Turbio, Argentina. Today, Puerto Natales is the starting point for trips to the magnificent O'Higgins and Torres del Paine national parks, and tourism is one of its most important industries; the town centre has a prosperous if somewhat touristy atmosphere.

Essential Puerto Natales

Finding your feet

The **Aerodromo Teniente Julio Gallardo** is 7 km north of town. All buses use the bus terminal 20 minutes outside town at Avenida España 1455. *Colectivos* to/from the centre cost US$0.55 (US$0.65 at night and Sun); taxis charge a flat fee of US$1.75 (US$2 at night and Sun) throughout Puerto Natales.

Getting around

Puerto Natales itself is small, so taxis are only needed for journeys out of town. For further details, see Transport, page 576.

Tip...
If driving between Punta Arenas and Puerto Natales, make sure you have enough fuel.

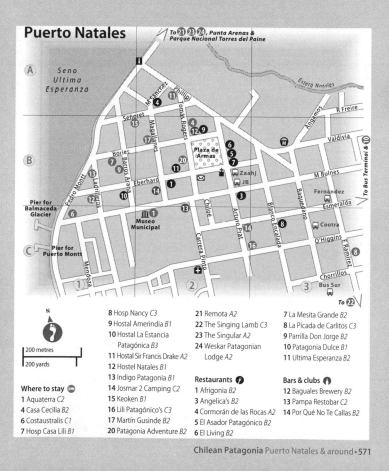

Puerto Natales

To (21) (23) (24), Punta Arenas & Parque Nacional Torres del Paine

Seno Ultima Esperanza

Estero Natales

Pier for Balmaceda Glacier

Pier for Puerto Montt

Museo Municipal

Plaza de Armas

To Bus Terminal & (10)

To (22) Bus Sur

200 metres
200 yards

Where to stay
1 Aquaterra C2
4 Casa Cecilia B2
6 Costaustralis C1
7 Hosp Casa Lili B1

8 Hosp Nancy C3
9 Hostal Amerindia B1
10 Hostal La Estancia Patagónica B3
11 Hostal Sir Francis Drake A2
12 Hostel Natales B1
13 Indigo Patagonia B1
14 Josmar 2 Camping C2
15 Keoken B1
16 Lili Patagónico's C3
17 Martín Gusinde B2
20 Patagonia Adventure B2

21 Remota A2
22 The Singing Lamb C3
23 The Singular A2
24 Weskar Patagonian Lodge A2

Restaurants
1 Afrigonia B2
2 Angelica's B2
4 Cormorán de las Rocas A2
5 El Asador Patagónico B2
6 El Living B2

7 La Mesita Grande B2
8 La Picada de Carlitos C3
9 Parrilla Don Jorge B2
10 Patagonia Dulce B1
11 Ultima Esperanza B2

Bars & clubs
12 Baguales Brewery B2
13 Pampa Restobar C2
14 Por Qué No Te Callas B2

Puerto Natales *Colour map 6, B1.*

In Puerto Natales (population 19,000) the **Museo Histórico Municipal** ① *Bulnes 285, T61-241 1263, Nov-Apr, Mon-Fri 0800-1900, May-Oct, 0800-1700, Sat-Sun 1000-1300 and 1500-1900, US$2,* houses a small collection of archaeological and native artefacts as well as exhibits on late 19th-century European colonization, with reasonable descriptions in English.

The colourful old steam train in the main square was once used to take workers to the **meat-packing factory** ① *daily 0930-1300 and 1500-1830, US$7, 45 mins,* at **Puerto Bories**, 5 km north of town. It is a pleasant hour-long walk along the shore to Bories with glimpses of the Balmaceda Glacier across the sound. In its heyday the plant was the biggest of its kind in Chile with a capacity for 250,000 sheep. Bankrupted in the early 1990s, much of the plant was dismantled in 1993. Belatedly the plant was given National Monument status and in 2013 it was restored. The remaining buildings and machine rooms can be visited. It's also the site of **The Singular Hotel** (see Where to stay, below).

The slab-like **Cerro Dorotea** dominates the town, with superb views of the whole Seno Ultima Esperanza. It can be reached on foot or by any Río Turbio bus or taxi (recommended, as the hill is further away than it seems). The trail entrance is marked by a sign that reads 'Mirador Cerro Dorotea'. Expect to be charged US$7 in one of the local houses. It is a 1½-hour trek up to the 600-m lookout along a well-marked trail. In theory you can continue along the top of the hill to get better views to the north, but the incredibly strong winds often make this dangerous.

Listings Puerto Natales *map page 571.*

Tourist information

CONAF
Baquedano 847, T61-241 1438, patricio.salinas@conaf.cl.
For information on national parks and other protected areas.

Municipal tourist office
At the bus station, Av España 1455. Open all year 0600-1200.

Sernatur office
On the waterfront, Av Pedro Montt 19, T61-241 2125, infonatales@sernatur.cl. Oct-Mar Mon-Fri 0830-2000, Sat-Sun 0900-1300 and 1500-1800, Apr-Sep Mon-Fri 0830-1800, Sat 1000-1600.
Good leaflets in English on Puerto Natales and Torres del Paine, as well as bus and boat information.

Where to stay

In season cheaper accommodation fills up quickly. Hotels in the countryside are often open only in the summer months. Good deals in upper-range hotels may be available, out of season especially, when prices may be 50% lower.

$$$$ Costaustralis
Pedro Montt 262, T61-241 2000, www.hoteles-australis.com.
Very comfortable, tranquil, lovely views (but not from inland-facing rooms), lift, English spoken, waterfront restaurant **Paine** serves international and local seafood.

$$$$ Indigo Patagonia
Ladrilleros 105, T2-2432 6800, www.indigopatagonia.cl.
Relaxed atmosphere, on the water front, great views, a boutique hotel with roof-top spa, rooms and suites, café/restaurant serves good seafood and vegetarian dishes. Tours organized.

$$$$ Remota
Ruta 9 Norte, Km 1.5, Huerto 279,
T61-241 4040, www.remota.cl.
Modernist design with big windows, lots
of trips, activities and treks offered, spa, all-
inclusive packages, good food, first-class.

$$$$ The Singular
Km 5 Norte, Puerto Bories, T61-272 2030,
www.thesingular.com.
Luxury hotel in converted warehouses
a short distance from the town centre,
in a scenic spot overlooking the Ultima
Esperanza Sound. Spa, gourmet restaurant
and varied trips offered.

$$$$-$$$ Martín Gusinde
Bories 278, T61-271 2100, www.
hotelmartingusinde.com.
Modern 3-star standard, smart, parking,
laundry service, excursions organized.

$$$$-$$$ Weskar Patagonian Lodge
Ruta 9, Km 05, T61-241 4168, www.weskar.cl.
Quiet lodge overlooking the fjord, standard
or deluxe rooms with good views, 3-course
dinners served, lunch boxes prepared for
excursions, many activities offered, helpful.

$$$ Aquaterra
Bulnes 299, T61-241 2239,
www.aquaterrapatagonia.com.
Good restaurant with vegetarian options,
'resto-bar' downstairs, spa, warm and
comfortable but not cheap, very helpful
staff. Trips and tours.

$$$ Hostal Sir Francis Drake
Phillipi 383, T61-241 1553,
www.hostalfrancisdrake.com.
Calm and welcoming, tastefully
decorated, smallish rooms, good views.

$$$ Keoken
Señoret 267, T61-241 3670,
www.keokenpatagonia.com.
Cosy, upmarket B&B, spacious living room,
some rooms with views. All rooms have
bathroom but not all are en suite, English
spoken, helpful staff, tours.

$$$-$$ Hostel Natales
Ladrilleros 209, T61-241 4731,
www.hostelnatales.cl.
Private rooms or dorms in this high-end
hostel, comfortable, minibar and lockboxes.

$$ Casa Cecilia
Tomás Rogers 60, T61-241 2698,
www.casaceciliahostal.com.
Welcoming, popular, with small simple
rooms, private or shared bath. English,
French and German spoken, rents camping
and trekking gear, tour agency and
information for Torres del Paine.

$$ Hospedaje Nancy
Ramírez 540, T61-241 0022,
www.nataleslodge.cl.
Warm and hospitable, information, tours,
equipment rental.

$$ Lili Patagónico's
Prat 479, T61-241 4063,
www.lilipatagonicos.com.
$ pp in dorms. Small but pleasant heated
rooms, helpful staff. Lots of information,
good-quality equipment rented. Tours
offered. Indoor climbing wall.

$$ Patagonia Adventure
Tomás Rogers 179, T61-241 1028,
www.apatagonia.com.
Lovely old house, bohemian feel, shared
bath, $ pp in dorms, equipment hire, bike
and kayak tours and tour arrangements for
Torres del Paine.

$$-$ Hostel Amerindia
Arana 135, T61-241 1945,
www.hostelamerindia.com.
Central option near restaurants as well
as the plaza. Dorms and private rooms.
Breakfast included and served in the
popular café, which also serves sundry
and artisanal products.

$$-$ pp The Singing Lamb
Arauco 779, T61-241 0958,
www.thesinginglamb.com.
Very hospitable New Zealand-run
backpackers, dorm accommodation

only but no bunks. Home-from-home feel. Good information.

$ Hospedaje Casa Lili
Bories153, T61-241 4039, lilipatagonia@gmail.com.
Dorms or private rooms, small, family-run, rents equipment and can arrange tickets to Paine. Free bag storage.

$ Hostal La Estancia Patagónica
Juan MacLean 567, T9-9224 8601, hostallaestanciapatagonica@gmail.com.
Friendly, family-run *hostal* near the bus terminal. Private rooms (**$$**) and 4-bed dorms. Breakfast included. Thin walls, great showers.

Camping

Josmar 2
McLean 367, T61-241 1685, www.josmar.cl.
Family-run, convenient, hot showers, parking, barbecues, electricity, café, tent site (US$9.50) or shared room (US$9.50).

Vaiora
Kruger 233, T61-241 1737, see Facebook.
Camping and *hospedaje* option in centre. US11, **$** per night.

Restaurants

$$$ Afrigonia
Eberhard 343, T61-241 2877.
An unexpected mixture of Patagonia meets East Africa in this Kenyan/Chilean-owned fusion restaurant, considered by many to be the best, and certainly the most innovative, in town.

$$$ Angelica's
Bulnes 501, T61-241 0007.
Elegant Mediterranean style, well-prepared pricey food with quality ingredients.

$$$-$$ Cormorán de las Rocas
Miguel Sánchez 72, T61-261 5131-2, www.cormorandelasrocas.com.
Patagonian specialities with an innovative twist, wide variety of well-prepared dishes, pisco sours, good service and attention to detail, incomparable views.

$$$-$$ El Asador Patagónico
Prat 158 on the Plaza, T61-241 3553, www.elasadorpatagonico.cl.
Spit-roast lamb, salads, home-made puddings.

$$$-$$ Parrilla Don Jorge
Bories 430, on Plaza, T61-241 0999, reservas@parrilladonjorge.cl.
Also specializes in spit-roast lamb, but serves fish too, good service.

$$ La Mesita Grande
Prat 196 on the Plaza, T61-241 1571, www.mesitagrande.cl.
Fresh pizzas from the wood-burning oven, also pasta and desserts. Poor service but good food. Wildly popular.

$$ Ultima Esperanza
Eberhard 354, T61-241 1391, www. restaurantuesperanza.galeon.com.
One of the town's classic seafood restaurants.

$$-$ El Living
Prat 156, Plaza de Armas, www.el-living.com. Mon-Sat in high season.
Comfy sofas, good tea, magazines in all languages, book exchange, good music, delicious vegetarian food, British-run, popular, Wi-Fi. Recommended.

$$-$ La Picada de Carlitos
Esmeralda and Encalada, T61-241 4885, Blanco Encalada y Esmeralda.
Good, cheap traditional Chilean food, popular with locals at lunchtime, when service can be slow.

$ Artimaña
Bories 349, T61-241 4856, see Facebook.
Newer café/restaurant offering fresh salads, sandwiches, juices and desserts. Bright, intimate surroundings; Wi-Fi.

Cafés

Amerindia
See Hostal Amerindia in Where to stay, above.
Located in a hostel and recommended for
coffee and hot chocolate. Fun vibe; also sells
artisan sundry and baked goods.

Patagonia Dulce
Barros Arana 233, T61-241 5285.
Tue-Sun 1400-2100.
For the best hot chocolate in town,
good coffee and chocolates.

Bars and clubs

Baguales Brewery
Bories 430, on the plaza,
www.cervezabaguales.cl.
Sep-Mar Mon-Sat 1300-0200. Pub with
microbrewery attached. Also serves
hamburgers and other snacks. Great
lunch specials.

Pampa Resto Bar
Bulnes 371, T95-32236, see Facebook.
Fun vibe with live music on Tue nights. Good
spot for meeting both travellers and locals.
In high season expect to pay premium prices
for what is merely decent bar food.

Por Qué No Te Callas
Magallanes 247, T61-241 4942.
Neighbourhood bar with beer, pizza and
Chilean favourites like *chorillana* on the
menu. Live music various nights.

Shopping

Casa Cecilia, **Lili Patagónico's**, **Sendero
Aventura** and **Erratic Rock** (see Where
to stay, above, and What to do, below)
all hire out camping equipment (deposit
required). Always check the equipment
and the prices carefully. Camping gas is
widely available in hardware stores. There
are several supermarkets in town and the
town markets are also good.

What to do

It is better to book tours direct with
operators in Puerto Natales than through
agents in Punta Arenas or Santiago. There
are many agencies along Arturo Prat. Several
offer single-day tours to the Perito Moreno
glacier in Argentina, US$70-80 for a 14-hr trip,
including 2 hrs at the glacier, excluding food
or park entry fee; reserve 1 day in advance.
You can then leave the tour in Calafate to
continue your travels in Argentina.
Baguales Group, *Encalada 353, T9-5168 8447,*
www.baguealesgroup.com. Specialists in the
route from Torres del Paine back to Puerto
Natales. Tailor-made multi-activity tours that
can incorporate zodiacs, horse riding, kayaking
and trekking, mostly off the beaten track.
Blue Green Adventures, *Galavarino 618,*
T61-241 1800, www.bluegreenadventures.com.
Adventure tour specialist and travel agent,
with trekking, riding, kayaking, fishing and
multi-activity options, estancia, whale
watching, wine and yoga programmes.
Also caters for families.
Chile Nativo Travel, *Eberhard 230, T2-2717*
5961, T1-800 649 8776 (toll-free in US and
Canada), www.chilenativo.travel. Specializes
in 'W' trek, Paine circuit trek, horse riding,
multi-sport options and tailor-made tours.
Comapa, *Bulnes 541, T61-241 4300, www.*
comapa.com. Large regional operator
offering decent day tours to Torres del Paine.
Erratic Rock, *Baquedano 719 and Zamora 732,*
T61-241 4317, www.erraticrock.com. Trekking
experts offering interesting expeditions from
half a day to 2 weeks. Also hostel (walk-ins
only), good-quality equipment hire and daily
trekking seminar at 1500.
Estancia Travel, *Casa 13-b, Puerto Boris,*
T61-241 2221, www.estanciatravel.com. Based
at the Estancia Puerto Consuelo, 5 km north
of Puerto Natales, offers horse-riding trips
from 1 to 12 days around southern Patagonia
and Torres del Paine, with accommodation
at traditional estancias. Also kayaking trips,
British/Chilean-run, bilingual, professional
guides, at the top of the price range.

Kayak in Patagonia, *Rogers 235, T61-261 3395, www.kayakenpatagonia.com*. Specializes in half-day, full-day and multi-day kayaking trips around Cisne Bay and the Serrano and Gray rivers. Also runs **Hello Patagonia**.

Punta Alta, *Blanco Encalada 244, T61-241 0115, www.puntaalta.cl*. Sailings in a fast boat to the Balmaceda glacier and the possibility to continue by zodiac to Pueblito Serrano at the southern edge of Torres del Paine national park (from US$180 one way). You can return to Natales on the same day by minibus along the southern access road, thus avoiding Torres del Paine entry fees. Also offers car hire.

Sendero Aventura, *T9-6171 3080, www.senderoaventura.com*. Adventure tours by land rover, bike or kayak.

Skorpios Cruises, *Augusto Leguía Norte 118, Santiago, T2-2477 1900 (and the the terminal in Puerto Bories) www.skorpios.cl*. The *Skorpios 3* sails from Puerto Natales to Glaciar Amalia and Fiordo Calvo in the Campo de Hielo Sur, 4 days, fares from US$1400 pp, double cabin. An optional first day includes a visit to Torres del Paine or the Cueva del Milodón. No office in Puerto Natales; book online or through an agency.

Turismo 21 de Mayo, *Eberhard 560, T61-614420, www.turismo21demayo.com*. Sailings to the Balmaceda glacier and the possibility to continue by zodiac to Pueblito Serrano at the southern edge of Torres del Paine national park (from US$144 one way from Puerto Natales, includes lunch).

Transport

Air Starting in 2017 **LAN** and **Sky** will operate direct flights to **Santiago** all year. There are also charter services from **Punta Arenas** and onward connections to Argentina with **Aerovías DAP**. Other airlines use Punta Arenas airport, see page 556.

Bicycle repairs El Rey de la Bicicleta, Galvarino 544, 161-241 1905. Good, helpful.

Bus In summer book ahead. All buses leave from the bus terminal 20 mins outside town at Av España 1455, but tickets can be bought at the individual company offices in town: **Bus Fernández**, E Ramírez 399, T61-241 1111, www.busesfernandez.com; **Pacheco**, only in the terminal, T61-241 4800, www.busespacheco.com; **Bus Sur**, Baquedano 668, T61-241 0784, www.bussur.com; **Zaahj**, Prat 236, T61-241 2260, www.turismozaahj.co.cl. For transport from the bus terminal, see box, page 571.

To **Punta Arenas**, several daily, 3-3½ hrs, US$7-9, with **Fernández**, **Pacheco**, **Bus Sur** and others. In theory buses from Punta Arenas to Puerto Natales will also pick passengers up at Punta Arenas airport (US$8) as long as reservations and payment have been made in advance through **Buses Pacheco** (T61-241 4800); in practice, though, they are often unreliable.

For buses to **Torres del Paine**, see page 587.

To Argentina To **Río Gallegos** direct, with **Bus Sur**, 2-3 weekly each, US$28, 4-5 hrs. To **Río Turbio**, hourly with **Cootra**, Pacheco and others, US$8, 2 hrs (depending on customs at Paso Dorotea; change bus at border; see box, opposite). To **El Calafate** daily 0830 and 1800, US$20, with **Cootra** daily, 5 hrs; or with **Zaahj**, daily 0700-1630, 5 hrs; otherwise travel agencies run several times a week depending on demand (see above). To **Ushuaia**, with **Bus Sur**, Oct-Apr Mon, Wed, Fri Sat at 0700, 13 hrs, US$56.

To **Ushuaia** with **Pacheco**, Tue, Thu, Sun direct at 0730, US$55 15 hrs. Note that buses from Argentina invariably arrive late.

Car hire Hire agents can arrange permission to drive into **Argentina**; it takes 24 hrs to arrange and extra insurance is required. Try **EMSA**, Arana 118, T61-261 4388, www.emsarentacar.com, or **Punta Alta**, Blanco Encalada 244, T61-241 0115, www.puntaalta.cl.

Ferry The town is the terminus of the *Navimag* ship to Puerto Montt. **Navimag**, In the bus terminal, T61-241 1421, www.navimag.com, runs ferries to/from **Puerto Montt**; for details, see page 571.

BORDER CROSSING
Chile–Argentina

There are three crossing points east of Puerto Natales. For further information, see www.pasosfronterizos.gov.cl and www.gendarmeria.gov.ar, which gives details of all three crossings in its Santa Cruz section. Information on these sites is generally up to date.

Paso Casas Viejas/Laurita
This crossing, 16 km east of Puerto Natales, is reached by turning off Route 9 (towards Punta Arenas) at Km 14. For the Argentine side see box, page 551.

Paso Dorotea/Mina Uno
This crossing is reached by branching off Route 9 (towards Punta Arenas) 9 km east of Puerto Natales and continuing north for a further 11 km. For the Argentine side see box, page 551.

Paso Río Cerro Castillo/Paso Río Don Guillermo
Chilean immigration is 7 km west of the border in the small settlement of Cerro Castillo, which lies 65 km north of Puerto Natales on the road to Torres del Paine. Cerro Castillo is well-equipped with toilets, ATM, tourist information, souvenir shop, several *cafeterías* and *hospedajes*, including $ pp **Hospedaje Mate Amargo**, Santiago Bueras, s/n, T9-536 1966, which offers rooms for four, Wi-Fi and luggage storage. There's sheep shearing in December, and a rodeo and rural festival in January. For **Argentine immigration** at Cancha Carrera, a few kilometres east of the border, where there are few facilities; see box, page 551. All buses between Puerto Natales and El Calafate go via Cerro Castillo, making it the most convenient route for visiting the Parque Nacional Los Glaciares from Chile. Travelling into Chile, it is possible to stop in Cerro Castillo and transfer to a bus passing from Puerto Natales to Torres del Paine.

Around Puerto Natales *Colour map 6, B2.*
prehistoric relics, windswept landscapes and the best trekking in the world

Monumento Nacional Cueva Milodón
25 km north, in high season daily 0800-1900 (0830-1800 in low season), www.cuevadelmilodon.cl. US$5.50 (US$2.75 in low season), getting there: regular bus from Prat 297, T61-241 5891 (Huellas del Milodón), leaves 0900, 1500, returns 1300 and 1900, US$21 (includes guide); taxi US$27 return, 20 mins each way; the taxi driver waits 1 hr.

This is the end point of Bruce Chatwin's travelogue *In Patagonia*. The cave, a massive 70 m wide, 220 m deep and 30 m high, contains a plastic model of the prehistoric ground sloth whose remains were found there in 1895. The remains are now in London. Evidence has also been found here of occupation by Patagonians some 11,000 years ago. Nearby, a visitor centre has summaries in English. There's also a handicraft shop.

★ Parque Nacional Bernardo O'Higgins

US$7, only accessible by boat from Puerto Natales summer daily 0800, returning 1730 (Sun only in winter), US$100-130, minimum 10 passengers, heavily booked in high season; book through a tour operator, see page 575.

Often referred to as the **Parque Nacional Monte Balmaceda**, this park covers much of the Campo de Hielo Sur, plus the fjords and offshore islands further west. A three-hour boat trip from Puerto Natales up the Seno de Ultima Esperanza takes you to the southernmost section, passing the Balmaceda Glacier, which drops from the eastern slopes of **Monte Balmaceda** (2035 m). The glacier is retreating; in 1986 its foot was at sea level. The boat docks further north at **Puerto Toro**, from where it is 1-km walk to the base of the Serrano Glacier on the north slope of Monte Balmaceda. On the trip, dolphins, sea lions (in season), black-necked swans, flightless steamer ducks and cormorants can often be seen. Take warm clothes, including a hat and gloves.

There is a route from Puerto Toro on the eastern side of the Río Serrano for 35 km to the Torres del Paine administration office (see page 580); guided tours are available on foot or on horseback. It is also possible to continue to the southern edge of Torres del Paine by boat or zodiac. For further details, see What to do, page 575.

Listings Around Puerto Natales

Where to stay

$$$$ Hostería Monte Balmaceda
Parque Nacional Bernardo O'Higgins; contact Turismo 21 de Mayo (see Puerto Natales Tour operators, above).
Although the park is uninhabited, guest accommodation is available in the southern section by the mouth of the Serrano river.

$$$$-$$$ Estancia Tres Pasos
40 km north of town, T9-9644 5862, www.hotel3pasos.cl.

Simple and beautiful lodge between Puerto Natales and Torres del Paine. Horse-riding trips offered.

$$$ Cabañas Kotenk Aike
2 km north of town, T61-241 2581, www.kotenkaike.cl.
Sleeps 4, modern, very comfortable, great location.

$$$ Hostería Llanuras de Diana
Ruta 9, Km 215 (30 km south of Puerto Natales), T61-241 0661.
Hidden from road, beautifully situated. Recommended.

Parque Nacional
Torres del Paine

★ Covering 242,242 ha, 145 km northwest of Puerto Natales, this national park is a UNESCO Biosphere Reserve and a trekker's mecca for its diverse wildlife and spectacular surroundings. Taking its name from the Tehuelche word 'Paine', meaning 'blue', the park encompasses stunning scenery, with constantly changing views of peaks, glaciers and icebergs, vividly coloured lakes of turquoise, ultramarine and grey, and quiet green valleys filled with wild flowers. In the centre of the park is one of the most impressive mountain areas on earth, a granite massif from which rise oddly shaped peaks of over 2600 m, known as the 'Torres' (towers) and 'Cuernos' (horns) of Paine.

Landscape and wildlife *Colour map 6, B1.*
volcanic peaks, expansive ice fields and rugged terrain

There are 15 peaks above 2000 m, of which the highest is Cerro Paine Grande (3050 m). Few places can compare to its steep, forested talus slopes topped by 1000-m vertical shafts of basalt with conical caps; these are the remains of frozen magma in ancient volcanic throats, everything else having been eroded. On the western edge of the park is the enormous Campo de Hielo Sur icefield. Four main *ventisqueros* (glaciers) – Grey, Dickson, Zapata and Tyndall – branch off it, their meltwater forming a complex series of lakes and streams, which lead into fjords extending to the sea. Two other glaciers, Francés and Los Perros, descend on the western side of the central massif.

A microclimate exists that is especially favourable to plants and wildlife. Over 200 species of plant have been identified and, although few trees reach great size, several valleys are thickly forested and little light penetrates. The grassland here is distinct from the monotony of the pampa and dispersed sclerophyl forest. Some 105 species of bird call the park home, including 18 species of waterfowl and 11 birds of prey. Particularly noteworthy

Essential Parque Nacional Torres del Paine

Access

The most practical way to get to Torres del Paine is with one of the many bus or tour companies that leave Puerto Natales daily. Hiring a pickup truck is another option. There are two *ripio* roads to the park from Puerto Natales. The old road goes via Cerro Castillo and Lago Sarmiento, entering the park at Laguna Amarga and continuing through the park to the **administration office** on Lago del Toro, 147 km northwest of Puerto Natales (3½ hours); this is the route taken by public buses. The other road, 85 km, links Natales to the south side of the park via the Pueblito Serrano. While it is a more direct route – total journey time to the administration is around 1½ hours – the road is narrow with lots of blind corners and sudden gusts of wind and can be rough in patches. An alternative way to access the park is on a three-hour zodiac trip up the Río Serrano from Parque Nacional Bernardo O'Higgins, see page 578.

There are entrances at Laguna Azul in the northeast, Laguna Amarga and Lago Sarmiento in the east and at the Puente Serrano in the south. See also Transport, page 587.

Entry fees

Park entrance fees are US$25 (low season US$21) for foreigners, payable in Chilean pesos, euros and dollars; only pesos in low season. You are also required to register and show your passport when entering the park, since rangers (*guardaparques*) keep a check on the whereabouts of all visitors. If you are based outside the park and plan on entering and leaving several times, explain this to the rangers in order to be given a multiple-entry stamp valid for three consecutive days.

Getting around

The park is well set up for tourism, with frequent bus services from Puerto Natales running through the park to pick up and drop off walkers at various hotels and trailheads and to connect with boat trips (see Transport, page 587). In season there are also boats and minibus connections within the park itself: from Laguna Amarga to **Hotel Las Torres**, US$4, and from the administration centre to **Hostería Lago Grey**, US$14. Other than these routes, getting around the park without your own transport is difficult and expensive. When public services are reduced, travel agencies run buses subject to demand; arrange your return date with the driver and try to coincide with other groups to keep costs down.

When to go

Do not underestimate the severity of the weather here. The park is open all year round, although snow may prevent access to some areas in the winter. The warmest time is December to March, but this is when the weather is the most unstable: strong winds often blow off the glaciers, and rainfall can be heavy. The park is most crowded in the summer holiday season January to mid-February, less so in December or March. October and November are recommended for wild flowers. Visiting in winter (April to September) is becoming increasingly popular as, although the temperature is low, there can be stable conditions with little wind, allowing well-equipped hikers to do some good walking. However, some treks may be closed and boats may not be running.

Time required

Allow a week to 10 days to see the park properly.

Torres tips

Torres del Paine has become increasingly popular, receiving over 100,000 visitors a year and the impact is showing. Try to ensure your visit does not have a negative effect on this unique landscape. See also Equipment, below.

- The summer months (January and February) should be avoided due to overcrowding. Try to visit in late November/early December or mid-April.
- When trekking, keep to the trails.
- Set out early to catch the sunrise, and to arrive early at the next campsite.
- Stay at less popular campsites.

- Most campsites are riddled with field mice so string up all your food in plastic bags, and hang it from a tree.
- Take all your rubbish out of the park, including toilet paper.
- Forest fires are a serious hazard. Open fires are prohibited throughout the park.

are condors, black-necked swans, kelp geese, ibis, flamingos and austral parakeets. The park is also one of the best places on the continent for viewing rheas and guanacos. Apart from the 3500 guanacos, 24 other species of mammal can be seen here, including hare, fox, skunk, huemul and puma (the last two only very rarely).

Trekking

for the novice as well as the seasoned pro

There are about 250 km of well-marked trails. Visitors must keep to the trails: cross-country trekking is not permitted. Some paths are confusingly marked and it is all too easy to end up on precipices with glaciers or churning rivers waiting below; be particularly careful to follow the path at the Paso John Gardner on El Circuito (see below). In addition to those mentioned below there are also plenty of shorter walks in the park; see www.torresdelpaine.com for details.

Equipment

It is essential to be properly equipped against the cold, wind and rain. A strong, streamlined, waterproof tent is essential if doing El Circuito (although you can hire camping equipment for a single night at the *refugios* on the 'W'). Also essential are protective clothing, strong waterproof footwear, hat, sunscreen, compass, good sleeping bag and sleeping mat. In summer also take shorts. Do not rely on availability of food at the *refugios* within the park; the small shops at the *refugios* (see below) and at the Posada Río Serrano are expensive and have a limited selection. You are strongly advised to bring all necessary equipment and your own food from Puerto Natales, although all running water within the park is fine to drink. You are not allowed to make open fires in the park, so take a camping stove but only cook in designated areas. A decent map is provided with your park entrance ticket (also available in the CONAF office); other maps (US$4) are obtainable in many places Puerto Natales but most have one or two mistakes. The map produced by Patagonia Interactiva has been recommended as more accurate.

El Circuito

The park's most emblematic trek is a circuit round the Torres and Cuernos del Paine. Although most people start at the *guardería* at **Laguna Amarga**, it is probably best done anticlockwise starting from Lodge Paine Grande at the western edge of Lago Pehoé.

Parque Nacional Torres del Paine

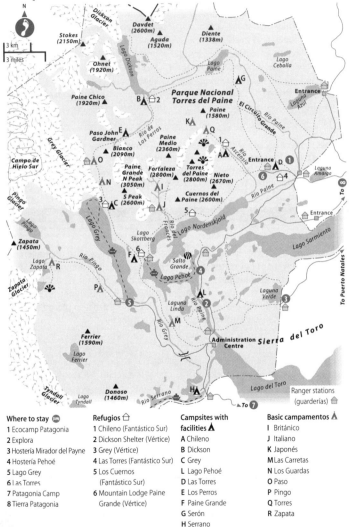

Where to stay 🛈
1 Ecocamp Patagonia
2 Explora
3 Hostería Mirador del Payne
4 Hostería Pehoé
5 Lago Grey
6 Las Torres
7 Patagonia Camp
8 Tierra Patagonia

Refugios ⌂
1 Chileno (Fantástico Sur)
2 Dickson Shelter (Vértice)
3 Grey (Vértice)
4 Las Torres (Fantástico Sur)
5 Los Cuernos (Fantástico Sur)
6 Mountain Lodge Paine Grande (Vértice)

Campsites with facilities 🛆
A Chileno
B Dickson
C Grey
D Las Torres
E Los Perros
F Paine Grande
G Serón
H Serrano

Basic campamentos 🛆
I Británico
J Italiano
K Japonés
M Las Carretas
N Los Guardas
O Paso
P Pingo
Q Torres
R Zapata

Safety

It is vital to be aware of the unpredictability of the weather (which can change in a few minutes). Rain and snowfall are heavier the further west you go and bad weather sweeps off the Campo de Hielo Sur without warning. The only means of rescue are on horseback or by boat; the nearest helicopter is in Punta Arenas and high winds usually prevent its operation in the park. Four visitors have died since 2013 due to accidents in the park. Report your route to staff and don't be tempted to stray off the marked trails. Mobile phone coverage is erratic. See also When to go, page 580.

Some walkers advise doing the route clockwise so that you climb to Paso John Gardner with the wind behind you. The route normally takes between seven and 10 days. The circuit is often closed in winter because of snow; major rivers are crossed by footbridges, but these are occasionally washed away.

From Laguna Amarga the route is north along the western side of the Río Paine to **Lago Paine**, before turning west to follow the pastures of the valley of the Río Paine to the southern end of **Lago Dickson** (it is possible to add a journey to the *campamento* by the Torres on day one of this route); the *refugio* at Lago Dickson lies in a breathtaking position in front of the icy white lake with mountains beyond. From Lago Dickson the path runs along the wooded valley of the **Río de los Perros**, past the Glaciar de los Perros, before climbing through bogs and up scree to **Paso John Gardner** (1241 m, the highest point on the route), then dropping steeply through forest to follow the Grey Glacier southeast to **Lago Grey**, continuing to **Lago Pehoé** and the administration centre. There are superb views en route, particularly from the top of Paso John Gardner.

The longest stretch is between Refugio Laguna Amarga and Refugio Dickson (30 km, 10 hours in good weather; there is camping on the way at Serón and a food preparation area at Cairon), but the most difficult section is the very steep, slippery slope from Paso John Gardner down to the Campamento Paso; the path is not well signed at the top of the pass, and some hikers have got dangerously lost. Camping gear must be carried, as many of the campsites do not have *refugios*.

The 'W'

A more popular alternative to El Circuito, this four- to five-day route can be completed without camping equipment as there is accommodation in *refugios* en route. In summer this route is very crowded and far from being the solitary Patagonian experience many people expect. It combines several of the hikes described separately below. From Refugio Laguna Amarga the first stage runs west via **Hostería Las Torres** and up the valley of the **Río Ascensio** via Refugio Chileno to the base of the **Torres del Paine** (see below). From here return to the **Hostería Las Torres** and then walk along the northern shore of **Lago Nordenskjold** via Refugio Los Cuernos to **Campamento Italiano**. From here climb the **Valley of the Río del Francés** (see below) before continuing to Lodge Paine Grande. From here you can complete the third part of the 'W' by walking west along the northern shore of **Lago Grey** to Refugio Grey and the Grey Glacier before returning to **Lodge Paine Grande** and the boat back across the lake to the **Guardería Pudeto**.

To the base of the Torres del Paine

From Refugio Laguna Amarga, this six-hour route follows the road west to Hostería Las Torres (1½ hours), before climbing along the western side of the Río Ascensio via Refugio Chileno (two hours) and Campamento Chileno to Campamento Las Torres (two hours), close to the base of the Torres del Paine (be careful when crossing the suspension bridge over the Río Ascensio near Hostería Las Torres, as the path is poorly marked and you can end up on the wrong side of the ravine). The path alongside the Río Ascensio is well marked, and the Campamento Las Torres is in an attractive wood (no *refugio*). A further 30 minutes or more up the moraine (the last bit involves a hard scramble over rocks at a near-vertical grade) takes you to a lake at the base of the towers themselves; they seem so close that you almost feel you could touch them. To see the Torres lit by sunrise (spectacular but you must have good weather), it's well worth carrying your camping gear up to Campamento Torres and spending the night. One hour beyond Campamento Torres is Campamento Japonés, another good campsite (only for climbers; non-climbers need to arrive with guide).

Valley of the Río del Francés

From Lodge Paine Grande this route leads north across undulating country along the western edge of Lago Skottberg to Campamento Italiano and then follows the valley of the Río del Francés, which climbs between Cerro Paine Grande and the Ventisquero del Francés (to the west) and the Cuernos del Paine (to the east) to Campamento Británico; the views from the mirador, a half-hour's walk above Campamento Británico, are superb. Allow 2½ hours from Lodge Paine Grande to Campamento Italiano, 2½ hours further to Campamento Británico.

Treks from Guardería Grey

Guardería Grey, 18 km west by road from the administration centre, is the starting point for a five-hour trek to Lago Pingo, recommended if you want to get away from the crowds, and one of the best routes in the park for birdwatching. It can only be undertaken with a certified private guide (check with CONAF for available guides). To reach the lake from the *guardería*, follow the Río Pingo, via Refugio Pingo and Refugio Zapata (four hours), with views south over Ventisquero Zapata; look out for plenty of wildlife and for icebergs in the lake. Ventisquero Pingo can be seen 3 km away over the lake. Note the bridge over a river here, marked on many maps, has been washed away. The river can be forded when it is low, however, allowing access to the glacier.

Two short signposted walks from Guardería Grey have also been suggested: one is a steep climb up the hill behind the ranger post to Mirador Ferrier, from where there are fine views; the other is via a suspension bridge across the Río Pingo to the peninsula at the southern end of Lago Grey, from where there are good views of the icebergs on the lakes.

To Laguna Verde

From the administration centre follow the road north 2 km, before taking the path east over the Sierra del Toro and then along the southern side of Laguna Verde to the Guardería Laguna Verde. Allow four hours. This is one of the easiest walks in the park and may be a good first hike.

To Laguna Azul and Lago Paine

This route runs north from Laguna Amarga to the western tip of Laguna Azul, from where it continues across the sheltered Río Paine valley past Laguna Cebolla to the Refugio Lago Paine at the eastern end of Lago Paine. Allow 8½ hours. Good birdwatching opportunities.

Tourist information

See also www.parquetorresdelpaine.cl.

CONAF administration centre
In the southeast of the park, at the northwest end of Lago del Toro, T61-2360 496, magallanes.oirs@conaf.cl. Summer daily 0800-1900, winter daily 0800-1800.
Has interesting videos and exhibitions, as well as the latest weather forecast. There are 13 ranger stations (*guarderías*) staffed by rangers, who offer help and advice. The outlying *guarderías* are open Oct-Apr only. Luggage can be stored for US$3 per day. On payment of the park entry fees (proceeds are shared between all Chilean national parks) you will receive a reasonable trail map to take with you (not waterproof). Climbing the peaks requires 2 permits, first from **DIFROL** (can be obtained free online, www.difrol.cl; takes 2 weeks to receive permit), then from **CONAF** in the park itself (take passports, **DIFROL** permit, insurance and route plan). See also www.torresdelpaine.com.

Where to stay

Accommodation is available on 3 levels: hotels, which are expensive, not to say overpriced (over US$300 for a double room per night); privately run *refugios*, which are generally well equipped and staffed, offering meals and free hot water for tea, soup, etc; and campsites with amenities, and basic *campamentos*. All options fill up quickly in Jan and Feb, so plan your trip and book in advance. Pay in dollars to avoid IVA (VAT). Agencies in Puerto Natales offer accommodation and transfers or car hire.

$$$$ Ecocamp Patagonia
reservations T2-2923 5950, www.ecocamp.travel.
Luxurious, all-inclusive accommodation is provided in geodesic domes, powered by renewable energy. This is the only environmental sustainability-certified hotel in Chile. Offers 4- to 10-day hiking, wildlife-watching and multi-sport trips, meals included. Their partner, **Cascada Expediciones** (www.cascada.travel/en), offers eco-friendly tours and custom trips to Torres del Paine and other destinations.

$$$$ Explora (Hotel Salto Chico Lodge)
T61-241 1247 (reservations: Av Américo Vespucci Sur 80, p 5, Santiago, T2-2395 2800, www.explora.com).
The park's priciest and most exclusive place is nestled into a nook at Salto Chico on edge of Lago Pehoé, superb views. It's all included: pool, gym, horse riding, boat trips, tours. Arrange packages from Punta Arenas.

$$$$ Hostería Mirador del Payne
Estancia Lazo, 52 km from Sarmiento entrance, reservations from Fagnano 585, Punta Arenas, T9-9640 2490, miradordelpayne@gmail.com.
Comfortable, meals extra, riding, hiking, birdwatching. Lovely location on Laguna Verde on east edge of the park, but inconvenient for most of the park. Private transport essential, or hike there from the park.

$$$$ Hostería Pehoé
T61-296 1238, 5 km south of Pehoé ranger station, 11 km north of park administration.
Beautifully situated on an island with spectacular view across Lago Pehoé, restaurant.

$$$$ Hotel Lago Grey
Head office Lautaro Navarro 1077, Punta Arenas, T61-2360280, www.turismolagogrey.com.
Great views over Lago Grey, superior rooms worth the extra, glacier walks.

$$$$ Hotel Las Torres
T61-261 7450, www.lastorres.com.
Comfortable rooms, beautiful lounge with wood fire and great views of the Macizo,

good service, horse riding, transport from Laguna Amarga ranger station, spa, disabled access. Visitor centre and *confitería* open to non-residents.

$$$$ Patagonia Camp
Reservations from Eberhard 230, Puerto Natales, T61-241 5149, www.patagonia camp.com.
Luxury yurts outside the park at Lago Toro, 15 km south of the administration.

$$$$ Tierra Patagonia
T2-2207 8861, www.tierrapatagonia.com.
Excellent, environmentally sensitive luxury hotel with spa, pool and outdoor jacuzzi on the edge of the national park overlooking Lago Sarmiento. Full- and half-day guided trips by minibus, on foot or on horseback. Gourmet dining in panorama restaurant overlooking the lake and mountains. Highly recommended.

Refugios
2 companies, **Fantástico Sur** and **Vértice Refugios**, between them run the *refugios* in the park, which provide comfortable dormitory or *cabaña* accommodation with hot showers; bring your own sleeping bag, or hire sheets for US$8-10 per night. Prices start from US$45pp bed only and go up to US$200 pp in a *cabaña* with full board. Meals can be bought individually (**$$**) and restaurants are open to non-residents. Kitchen facilities are available in some Vértice Refugios but Fantástico Sur will not let you prepare your own hot food unless you are camping. *Refugios* also have space for camping (**$**) per night (book in advance for Vértice Refugios as they have very few tents available). Most close in winter, although 1 or 2 may stay open, depending on the weather. Advance booking essential in high season.

Fantástico Sur Book through agencies in Puerto Natales or direct at Esmeralda 661, Puerto Natales, T61-261 4184, www. fslodges.com.

Refugio El Chileno, in the valley of Río Ascencio, at the foot of the Torres.
Refugio Las Torres (Torre Central, Torre Norte), 2 *refugios* next to the Hotel Las Torres (see above), good facilities, especially in the newer **Torre Central**.
Refugio Los Cuernos, on the northern shore of Lago Nordenskjold. Also has 8 cabins (**$$$$**).

Vértice Refugios Book through agencies in Puerto Natales, or direct at Bulnes 100, Puerto Natales, T61-241 2742, www.verticepatagonia.com.
Mountain Lodges Paine Grande, on the northwest tip of Lago Pehoé, with kitchen facilities and internet.
Vértice Grey, on the northeast shore of Lago Grey.
Vértice Dickson Shelter, southern end of Lago Dickson. Basic.

Camping
Equipment is available to hire in Puerto Natales (see above). The wind tends to rise in the evening so pitch your tent early. Mice can be a problem; do not leave food in packs on the ground. Fires may only be lit at organized campsites, not at *campamentos*. The *guardaparques* expect people to have a stove if camping.
There are 4 sites run by
Vértice Patagonia: **Camping Los Perros**, **Paine Grande**, **Dickson** and **Grey** (from US$11 pp).
Camping Chileno, **Serón** and **Las Torres** (by the **Refugio Las Torres**) are run by **Fantástico Sur** (US$11), hot showers.

Lago Pehoé
www.campingpehoe.com.
US$14 pp, tent rental US$24 for 2 including sleeping mat, also pre-pitched dome tents, hot showers, shop, restaurant.

Camping Río Serrano
Just outside the park's southern entrance.
On a working estancia, also has horse rides and hikes.

Free camping is permitted in 9 other locations including Torres, Italiano and Paso, Las Carretas (see map, page 582) in the park: these sites are known as *campamentos* and are generally extremely basic.

What to do

See under Puerto Natales, What to do, page 575 for Tour operators. Before booking a tour, check the details carefully and get them in writing.

Transport

Boat Catamarán Hielos Patagónicos, Los Arrieros 1517, Puerto Natales (also in bus terminal, 2nd floor, T61-241 1133, info@hielospatagonicos.com, runs boats from Guardería Pudeto to **Refugio Paine Grande**, 30 mins, US$20 one way with 1 backpack (US$7 for extra backpacks), US$33 return, leaving Pudeto at 0930, 1200, 1800, returning from Paine Grande 1000, 1230, 1830; reserve in advance. Services are reduced off season with only 1 sailing from Pudeto at at 1200 and Lago Payne Grande at 1230 1 Apr-15 Nov. At all times check in advance that boats are running. There are also boats from **Hotel Lago Grey** (booked through **Hotel Martín Gusinde**) to the face of the glacier, 2-4 times daily, 3½ hrs, US$55 return, and from the hotel via the glacier face to/from Refugio Grey for US$48 one-way.

Bus After mid-Mar there is little public transport and trucks are irregular. **Bus Gómez** (in terminal, T61-241 5700), **JB** (Prat 258, T61-241 0242) and **Trans Vía Paine** (in terminal, T61-2411 927) run daily services into the park, leaving **Puerto Natales** in high season between 0630 and 0800, and again at 1430, using the old road, with a 15-min stop at Cerro Castillo (see box, page 577), then

Laguna Amarga, 3 hrs to **Guardería Pudeto** and 4 hrs to the administration centre, all charge US$11 one way, US$20 open return (return tickets are not interchangeable between different companies). Buses will stop anywhere en route, but all stop at Laguna Amarga entrance, Salto Grande del Paine and the administration centre. Return buses to Puerto Natales stop at Laguna Amarga from 1430 to 2000. In high season the buses fill quickly. Depending on route, for the return trip to Puerto Natales it's best to catch the bus for the return trip at Laguna Amarga if you are coming from Mirador Los Torres; take a bus at Pudeto if you are coming from Glaciar Grey; or take a bus from administration if you don't have a boat pass. All buses wait at Guardería Pudeto until the boat from **Refugio Paine Grande** arrives.

To **El Calafate** (Argentina) Either return to Puerto Natales for onward connections (see page 570), or take a bus from the park to **Cerro Castillo** (106 km east of the administration centre) then catch a direct service to Calafate. **Zaahj** (in terminal and Prat 236, T61-249 1631) has a very comfortable **Super Pullman** service Cerro Castillo–El Calafate, US$20. Beware that the border crossing can take up to several hours in peak season (see box, page 577).

Car hire Hiring a pick-up in Punta Arenas is an economical proposition for a group (up to 9 people): US$400-450 for 4 days. A more economical car can cope with the roads if you go carefully; ask the rental agency's advice. If driving to the park yourself, note that the shorter road from Puerto Natales is narrow with lots of blind corners and sudden gusts of wind and can be rough in patches. In the park, the roads are also narrow and winding with blind corners: use your horn a lot. Always fill up with fuel in Puerto Natales.

Tierra del Fuego

confronting nature at the end of the world

The island of Tierra del Fuego is the most captivating part of all Patagonia. This is America's last remaining wilderness and an indispensable part of any trip to the south.

At the very foot of the South American continent and separated from the mainland by the intricate waterways of the Straits of Magellan, the island is divided between Argentina and Chile by a north–south line that grants Argentina the Atlantic and southern coasts and gives Chile an expanse of wilderness to the west, where the tail of the Andes sweeps east in the form of the mighty Darwin range.

The Chilean side is largely inaccessible, apart from the small town of Porvenir, though expeditions can be organized from Punta Arenas to take you hiking and trout fishing. On the Argentine side, glaciers and jagged peaks offer a dramatic backdrop to the city of Ushuaia, the island's main centre, set in a serene natural harbour on the Beagle Channel, with views of the Dientes de Navarino mountains on the Chilean island of Navarino opposite.

Sail from Ushuaia along the channel to the pioneer home of Harberton; to Cape Horn; or even to Antarctica. Head into the small but picturesque Parque Nacional Tierra del Fuego for strolls around Bahía Lapataia and for steep climbs with magnificent views out along the channel.

Best for
Sailing the Beagle Channel ▪ Skiing ▪ Trekking ▪ Wildlife

Footprint picks

★ Dientes de Navarino, page 597

These jagged peaks let you know that you've reached the end of the world.

★ Fishing around Río Grande, page 603

Trout run the waters and make for some of the best fly-fishing in the region.

★ Museums in Ushuaia, page 608

Discover the history of Tierra del Fuego's indigenous people in the city's fine museums.

★ Estancia Harberton, pages 617 and 618

The site where missionary Thomas Bridges all but invented Ushuaia in the 1800s, and which is still a working estancia today.

★ A boat trip on the Beagle Channel, page 618

Sail the same waters as Darwin, when he was riding the *HMS Beagle* nearly two centuries ago.

★ Parque Nacional Tierra del Fuego, page 620

A number of good walks are a great way to experience Patagonian forests, and the end of the Andes.

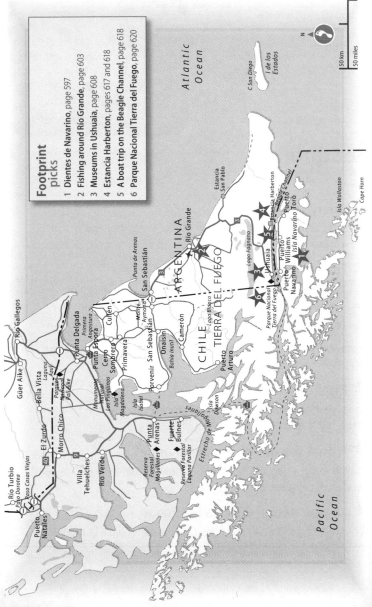

50 km
50 miles

N

Atlantic Ocean

Pacific Ocean

CHILE

ARGENTINA

TIERRA DEL FUEGO

Cape Horn

Essential Tierra del Fuego

Access

Argentine Tierra del Fuego is easy to reach with several flights daily from Buenos Aires to Río Grande and Ushuaia, and less frequent flights from El Calafate, and some other towns in Patagonia. Flights are heavily booked in advance in summer (December to February). **Chilean Tierra del Fuego** is only reached by plane from Punta Arenas to Porvenir, daily, and to Puerto Williams on Isla Navarino, Monday to Saturday (but always check for seasonal variations).

There are no road or ferry crossings between the Argentine mainland and Argentine Tierra del Fuego. You have to go through Chilean territory.

From Río Gallegos, Route 3 reaches the Integración Austral border at Monte Aymond, after 67 km, passing Laguna Azul (see box, page 515). The road continues beyond the border as Chilean Route 255, reaching Kamiri Aike after 30 km. Take Route 257 for 16 km east of here to reach the dock at Punta Delgada for the 20-minute Straits of Magellan ferry crossing over the Primera Angostura (First Narrows) to Bahía Azul in Chilean Tierra del Fuego. For more on this crossing, see page 596. From Bahía Azul, the road is paved to Cerro Sombrero, from where *ripio* roads run southeast to Chilean San Sebastián (130-140 km from ferry, depending on the route taken). It's 15 km east, across the border (see box, page 596), to Argentine San Sebastián. From here the road is paved to Río Grande (see below) and Ushuaia.

The second main ferry crossing is Punta Arenas to Porvenir. The ferry dock is 5 km north of Punta Arenas centre, at Tres Puentes. The ferry crosses to Bahía Chilota,

Tip...
It's essential to book ahead. Accommodation is sparse, and planes and buses fill up quickly from November to March.

5 km west of Porvenir. From Porvenir a 234-km *ripio* road runs east to Río Grande (six hours, no public transport) via San Sebastián. Note that fruit and meat may not be taken onto the island, nor between Argentina and Chile.

There is also a weekly ferry service on the **Yaghan** (also www.tabsa.cl) from Punta Arenas to Puerto Williams on Isla Navarino. For more details of the Punta Arenas–Porvenir ferry, see page 596 and for Punta Arenas–Puerto Williams ferries, see Transport, page 601.

Getting around

There are good bus links from Punta Arenas to Río Grande in Argentina, with an option of going via Porvenir, along the decent loop of road on the Chilean side. From Porvenir your options are limited to a *ripio* road around Bahía Inútil to near Lago Blanco, though there's no public transport here. Argentine Tierra del Fuego is much easier to get around, via Route 3 between Río Grande and Ushuaia with several buses a day. A fan of roads spreads out south and west from Río Grande to the estancias on the Argentine side, but these are unpaved and best attempted in a 4WD vehicle. A good *ripio* road leads east of Ushuaia along the south coast, and another goes part of the way along the north coast to Estancia Cabo San Pablo; there is no public transport here either.

Chilean
Tierra del Fuego

The Chilean half of Tierra del Fuego is in two sections: the western half of Isla Grande (the main island) and the whole of Isla Navarino, to the south of the main island. Much less developed than the Argentine side of Tierra del Fuego, it has just two small towns where Chile's Fuegians are mostly concentrated: Porvenir on Isla Grande, easily reached by ferry from Punta Arenas; and Puerto Williams on Isla Navarino, which can be reached by a flight from Punta Arenas, a twice-weekly ferry also from Punta Arenas and by boat from Ushuaia.

The northern part of Isla Grande is flat steppe, but the south is dominated by the Darwin range of mountains, which provide a dramatic visual backdrop, even if you can't easily get to them.

Tourism on Chilean territory is limited, but it's possible to organize trekking tours from Punta Arenas, and there are fishing lodges offering magnificent trout fishing, particularly on the Río Grande.

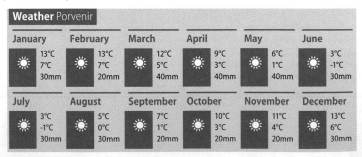

Weather Porvenir

January	February	March	April	May	June
13°C	13°C	12°C	9°C	6°C	3°C
7°C	7°C	5°C	3°C	1°C	-1°C
30mm	20mm	40mm	40mm	40mm	30mm

July	August	September	October	November	December
3°C	5°C	7°C	10°C	11°C	13°C
-1°C	0°C	1°C	3°C	4°C	6°C
30mm	30mm	20mm	20mm	20mm	30mm

virgin wilderness and treasures of natural history

Puerto Porvenir

Chilean Tierra del Fuego has a population of around 8000, with 5600 living in the small town of Porvenir, the only town on the Chilean half of the main island. Founded in 1894 during the gold boom, when many people came seeking fortunes from Croatia and Chiloé, Porvenir is a quiet place with a wide open pioneer feel, streets of neat, brightly painted houses of corrugated zinc and quaint, tall-domed trees lining the main avenue.

There is a small museum, the **Museo Fernando Cordero Rusque** ① *Zavattaro 402, on the plaza, T61-258 1800, Mon-Thu 0800-1730, Fri 0900-1600, Sat-Sun 1030-1330 and 1500-1700, US$1*, with archaeological and photographic displays on the Onas, and good displays on natural history and the early gold diggers and sheep farmers. There's little else to do here, but you could stroll around the plaza, with its **Iglesia San Francisco de Sales**, and down to the shoreside promenade, where there's a strange collection of 19th-century farm machinery and a striking wooden monument to the Selk'nam.

Beyond Porvenir

Beyond Porvenir there is wonderfully wild virgin territory to explore. However, if you want an adventure, your best bet is to arrange a trip through tour operators in Punta Arenas (such as **Go Patagonia**, www.gopatagoniachile.com, or see page 565), since there's still very little infrastructure

> **Tip...**
> Cabo Boquerón, the headland at the start of Bahía Inútil, has great views on a clear day, as far as Cabo Froward, Isla Dawson and the distant Cordillera Darwin's snow peaks.

on the Chilean side of the island. All roads are good *ripio* except a paved section from Bahía Chilota to Porvenir and in Porvenir itself. For tour operators, see page 563.

North of Porvenir, 6 km, is the **Monumento Natural Laguna de los Cisnes**. Access is across private land; the owner will give permission. Another place to see wildfowl, including black-necked swans from December, is **Laguna Santa María**, not far from Porvenir on the road to **Bahía Inútil**, a wonderful windswept bay.

Driving east along the bay you pass Los Canelos, with trees, a rare sight, and then the junction for the Cordón Baquedano, on the **Circuito de Oro**. This is a recommended tour, on which you can see gold panning using the same techniques that have been employed since mining began in 1881; it's a four-hour, 115-km round trip.

Camerón and further south

About 90 km east of Porvenir, roads head east to San Sebastián and south to Camerón via Onaisin (99 km from Porvenir). Camerón is a large farm settlement and the only other community of any size on the Chilean part of the island. It is 149 km from Porvenir on the opposite shore of Bahía Inútil. This wonderful windswept bay, with views of distant hills and the snow-capped Darwin range all along the southern horizon, was named 'useless' by British engineers making a hydrographic survey here in 1827 because it has no useful port. Nevertheless, as you near Camerón, the road passes secluded canyons and bays, interspersed with a few farms, and the palpable sense of isolation drowns out civilization, leaving nothing but the sound of wind and the wild silence of nature.

Other options are sailing from Porvenir to **Río Cóndor** across Bahía Inútil, south of Camerón, and trekking or riding from Camerón to **Seno Almirantazgo**, a beautiful, wild and treeless place, where mountains sink into blue fjords with icebergs.

ON THE ROAD

Shipwrecked in the Magellan Straits

The Estrecho de Magallanes, 534 km long, is a treacherous sea passage linking the Atlantic and the Pacific oceans. The eastern entrance to the straits is between Punta Dúngeness on the Argentine mainland and Cabo del Espíritu Santo on Tierra del Fuego. From here the route heads west and then south, past Punta Arenas and Fuerte Bulnes, before negotiating the channels and islands of southern Chile. The straits have a long history of claiming victims, and the hostile conditions are eloquently conveyed in the words of Sir John Narborough: "horrible like the ruins of a world destroyed by terrific earthquakes".

From the Atlantic, the first navigational problem facing sailors is simply the difficulty of entering the straits against the fierce westerly gales that prevail. Once in the straits the dangers are far from over: many ships have fallen victim to the notorious *Williwaws*, winds with the ferocity of tornados that spring up from nowhere; no less vicious are the *Pamperos*, which blow off the land with enough force to capsize a vessel.

Although in 1520 Magellan succeeded in passing through the straits that bear his name, few others managed to do so in the years that followed; of the 17 ships that attempted the passage in the early 16th century, only one, the *Victoria*, succeeded in reaching the Pacific and returning to Europe. Twelve were lost near the eastern entrance and four returned in failure. The reason these early navigators chose to attempt the dangerous voyage was the lure of a short route between Europe and the spices of the East. Even when it became clear that there was no such short route, the straits still provided a useful means for Europeans to reach the rich Pacific ports of Peru and Chile without disembarking to cross Mexico or Panama overland.

Even with the development of advanced navigation techniques in the 19th century, losses continued: in 1869, the *Santiago*, an iron paddle-steamer built in Glasgow and owned by the Pacific Mail line, went down off Isla Desolación at the western end of the straits with a cargo of gold and silver. While the Panama Canal now provides a shorter route between the Atlantic and Pacific Oceans, the size of modern ships means that the straits are still a busy shipping route. The most common cargo is now oil; casualties still occur but now, of course, with the added risk of environmental disaster from oil spillage.

A large part of the peninsula between Bahía Inútil and Seno Almirantazgo is covered by the **Karukinka nature reserve** ⓘ *search for Karukinka on www.wcs.org*. From Camerón a road runs southeast past an airfield and into the hills, through woods where guanacos hoot and run off into glades, and the banks are covered with red and purple moss. The north shores of **Lago Blanco** can be reached by cutting east through the woods from Sección Río Grande, with superb views of the mountains surrounding the lake and the snows in the south.

Meanwhile, the rough road continues as far south as Estancia Lago Fagnano on Lago Fagnano, four hours from Onaisin. The government is hoping to complete the road to **Yendegaia** on the Beagle Channel with a view to having a summer route, including ferry, to Puerto Navarino. This would traverse the **Parque Nacional Yendegaia**, which was created in 2013 and which adjoins the Parque Nacional Tierra del Fuego in Argentina. They hope to finish the project in 2020. It's essential to organize any trip to this area through a reliable tour operator with solid infrastructure.

Tourist information

Tourist information is available at the **Museo Fernando Cordero Rusque** (the best option; see above), on notice boards outside the Municipalidad, on the seafront and elsewhere, and from a handicrafts stall in a kiosk on the seafront (opposite **Comercial Tuto**, No 588). See also www.patagonia-chile.com.

Where to stay

Puerto Porvenir

$$$ Hostería Yendegaia
Croacia 702, T61-258 1919.
Comfortable, family-run inn with good facilities and helpful staff. English-speaking owner runs birdwatching tours and to the king penguins.

$$ Central
Phillipi 298, T61-258 0077, opposite Rosas, see below.
All rooms with bath.

$$ España
Croacia 698, T61-258 0540, www.hotelespana.cl.
Comfortable, well equipped, light and spacious rooms, helpful and friendly. Good restaurant with food all day.

$$ Rosas
Phillippi 269, T61-258 0088.
Heating, restaurant and bar.

$ pp Hostal Kawi
Pedro Silva 144, T61-258 1570.
Comfortable, rooms for 3, meals available, offers fly-fishing trips.

Beyond Porvenir

If you get stuck in the wilds, note that it is almost always possible to camp or bed down in a barn at an estancia.

$$$-$$ Hostería Tunkelen
Arturo Prat Chacón 101, Cerro Sombrero, T61-221 2757, www.hosteriatunkelen.cl.
3 buildings with rooms of different standards: some with private bathrooms, shared bathrooms or backpacker dorms. Restaurant. Good for groups.

$$-$ Hostería de la Frontera
San Sebastián, T61-269 6004.
Where some buses stop for meals and cakes, cosy, with bath (the annex is much more basic), good food.

Restaurants

Puerto Porvenir

There are many lobster fishing camps nearby, where fishermen prepare lobster on the spot.

$$ Club Croata
Señoret entre Phillippi y Muñoz Gamero, next to the bus stop on the waterfront.
A lively place with good food.

$$-$ El Chispa
Señoret 202, T61-258 0054.
Good restaurant for seafood and other Chilean dishes.

What to do

Puerto Porvenir

For adventure tourism and trekking activities contact tour operators in Punta Arenas (see What to do, page 563).

Transport

For details of how to get to Tierra del Fuego, see box, page 591, and Boat, below.

Puerto Porvenir

Air To **Punta Arenas** (weather and bookings permitting), with **Aerovías DAP**, Señoret s/n, T61-258 0089, www.aerovias dap.cl. Heavily booked so make sure you have your return reservation confirmed.

BORDER CROSSING

Chile–Argentina

San Sebastián

This is the border between the Chilean and Argentine sides of Tierra del Fuego. Chilean San Sebastián is located 130 km southeast of the ferry dock at Bahía Azul, via Cerro Sombrero. It consists of just a few houses with **Hostería La Frontera** 500 m from the border. Argentine San Sebastián is 15 km further east, across the border. It has a seven-room ACA hostería (T02961-15-405834) and a service station, open 0700-2300. For further details, see www.gendarmeria.gob.ar/pasos-chile/san-sebastian.html and www.pasosfronterizos.gov.cl/cf_sansebastian.html.

Boat For information on getting to Tierra del Fuego by boat, see also box, page 591.

To Argentina At **Punta Delgada** is the **Hostería El Faro** where you can get food and drink. There are 3 boats working continuously to cross Bahía Azul, each with a café, lounge and toilets on board. Buses can wait up to 90 mins to board and the boats run every 40 mins 0830-0100, US$21 per vehicle, foot passengers US$2.50. See www.tabsa.cl for more information.

Ferries to **Punta Arenas** operate Tue-Sun taking 2 hrs 20 mins, US$65 per vehicle, motorcycles US$18.50, foot passengers US$10. **Transportadora Austral Broom** (www.tabsa.cl) publishes a timetable a month in advance but this is dependent on tides and subject to change, so check in advance. Reservations are essential, especially in summer.

Bus The only public transport on Chilean Tierra del Fuego is Jorge Bastián's minibus Porvenir–**Cerro Sombrero**, T61-234 5406, jorgebastian@hotmail.com, or axelvig20@hotmail.com, which leaves Sombrero at 0830 on Mon, Wed and Fri; returns from Porvenir Municipalidad, 2 hrs, US$3.

Isla Navarino *Colour map 6, C3.*

jagged peaks, exotic animals and ancient archaeological finds

Situated on the southern shore of the Beagle Channel, Isla Navarino is totally unspoilt and beautiful, offering great geographical diversity, thanks to the Dientes de Navarino range of mountains, with peaks over 1000 m, covered with southern beech forest up to 500 m, and south of that, great plains covered with peat bogs, with many lagoons abundant in flora.

The island was the centre of the indigenous Yaganes (Yámana) culture, and there are 500 archaeological sites, the oldest dated as 3000 years old. Guanacos and condors can be seen inland, as well as large numbers of beavers, which were introduced to the island and have done considerable damage. The flight from Punta Arenas is beautiful, with superb views of Tierra del Fuego, the Cordillera Darwin, the Beagle Channel and the islands stretching south to Cape Horn.

Puerto Williams

The only settlement of any size on the island is Puerto Williams (population 2500), a Chilean naval base situated about 50 km east of Ushuaia on Argentine seas across the Beagle Channel. Puerto Williams is the southernmost permanently inhabited town in the

Essential Isla Navarino

Access

Ushuaia Boating travels from Ushuaia to Puerto Williams, US$125 each way, which includes a 40-minute crossing in a semi-rigid boat to Puerto Navarino. Then it's a one-hour ride in a combi on a lovely *ripio* road to Williams; make sure you are clear about transport arrangements for your return. Fernández Campbell (www.fernandezcampbell.com) has a 1½-hour crossing from Ushuaia, on Friday, Saturday and Sunday at 1000, returning at 1500. Tickets (US$125 for foreigners) are sold at Naviera RFC in Puerto Williams and Zenit Explorer, Juana Fadul 126, in Ushuaia, T02901-433232.

world; 50 km east-southeast is Puerto Toro, the southernmost permanently inhabited settlement on earth. Some maps mistakenly mark a road from Puerto Williams to Puerto Toro, but it officially doesn't exist (although the military travels frequently along the route); access is only by sea.

Due to past border disputes with Argentina, the Chilean navy maintains a heavy presence in Puerto Williams. Outside the naval headquarters, you can see the bow section of the *Yelcho*, the tug chartered by Shackleton to rescue men stranded on Elephant Island.

Your main purpose for visiting the island is likely to be the trekking on the Dientes de Navarino. But you should also take time to explore the indigenous heritage here too. It's beautifully documented in the Museo Martín Gusinde ① *Aragay 1, T61-262 1043, www.museomartingusinde.cl, 1 Nov to late Mar Tue-Fri 0930-1300 and 1500-1800, Sat-Sun 1430-1830; 1 Apr-30 Oct Tue-Fri 0930-1800 and 1500-1800, Sat 1430-1830, free,* known as the Museo del Fin del Mundo (End of the World Museum), which is full of information about vanished indigenous tribes, local wildlife and the famous voyages by Charles Darwin and Fitzroy of the *Beagle*. A visit is highly recommended.

One kilometre west of the town is the yacht club (one of Puerto Williams' two nightspots), whose wharf is made from a sunken 1930s Chilean warship. The town has a bank, supermarkets and a hospital.

Exploring the island

For superb views climb Cerro Bandera which is reached by a path from the dam 4 km west of the town (it's a steep, three- to four-hour round trip, take warm clothes). There is excellent trekking around the ★ Dientes de Navarino range, the southernmost trail in the world, through impressive mountain landscapes, frozen lagoons and snowy peaks, resulting in superb views over the Beagle Channel. It's a challenging hike, over a distance of 53 km in five days, possible only from December to March, and a good level of fitness is needed. One highlight is hiking to Lago Windhond and searching the guestbook at the entrance to the reserve. Inside you'll find previously unknown routes imparted by former trekkers. Some of these even lead to Windhond Bay, which offers views of Cape Horn.

There is no equipment rental on the island. Ask for information in the tourist office at Puerto Williams, but it's best to go with an organized expedition from Punta Arenas.

Travellers can also visit Omora Ethnobotanical Park, an NGO dedicated to conservation and biological research in the Cape Horn Region. The park offers three different circuit tours between one to two hours each. Entrance is US$50 (with a guide) and can be booked through Lakutaia Lodge in Puerto Williams (see Where to stay, page 599).

Beyond Cerro Bandera, a road leads 56 km west of Puerto Williams to Puerto Navarino, where there is a jetty, the Alcaldía del Mar and four more houses, plus a few horses and

BACKGROUND
Tierra del Fuego

Tierra del Fuego has been inhabited by indigenous groups for some 10,000 years. The most populous of these groups, the Onas (also known as the Selk'nam), were hunter-gatherers in the north, living mainly on guanaco. The southeastern corner of the island was inhabited by the Haus or Hausch, also hunter-gatherers. The Yaganes or Yámana lived along the Beagle Channel and were seafaring people surviving on seafood, fish and birds. The fourth group, the Alacalufe, lived in the west of Tierra del Fuego as well as on the Chonos Archipelago, surviving by fishing and hunting seals.

The first Europeans to visit the island came with the Portuguese navigator Fernão Magalhães (Magellan), who, in 1520, sailed through the channel that now bears his name. Magellan named the island 'Land of Fire' when he saw the smoke from many fires lit along the shoreline by local inhabitants. The indigenous population were left undisturbed for three centuries.

Fitzroy and Darwin's scientific visits in 1832 and 1833 recorded some fascinating interaction with the indigenous peoples. Fitzroy and Darwin's visits were a precursor to attempts to convert the indigenous groups to Christianity so that the island could be used by white settlers without fear of attack. Several disastrous missions followed, encountering stiff resistance from the inhabitants.

In 1884, Reverend Thomas Bridges founded a mission at Ushuaia. He was the first European to learn the Yámana language, and he compiled a Yámana-English dictionary. He soon realized that his original task was a destructive one. The purpose of the missionary work had been to facilitate lucrative sheep farming on the island, but the Ona were attracted to the 'white guanacos' on their land and took to hunting sheep, easier than catching the fast-footed guanaco. In response, the colonists offered two sheep for each Ona that was killed (proof was provided by a pair of Ona ears). The indigenous groups were further ravaged by epidemics of European diseases. In a desperate attempt to save the Ona, Salesian missionaries founded three missions in the Straits of Magellan in the early 20th century, but, stripped of their land, the Ona lost the will to live, and the last Ona died in 1999. The Hausch also died out. The last of the Yámana, a woman called Cristina Calderón, presently survives near Puerto Williams. She is 89 years old.

Imprecision in the original colonial land division and the greed of the rush southwards led to border disputes between Argentina and Chile, which have mostly been quelled despite the underlying tension. The initial settlement of the dispute in 1883 was followed by a desire by both governments to populate the area by allocating large expanses of land for sheep farming.

For many years, the main economic activity of the northern part of the island was sheep farming, but Argentine government tax incentives to companies in the 1970s led to the establishment of new industries in Río Grande and Ushuaia and a rapid growth in the population of both cities. Tourism is increasingly important in Ushuaia.

cows. There is little or no traffic on this route and it is very beautiful, with forests of lengas stretching right down to the water's edge. You can also visit **Villa Ukika**, 2 km east of town, the place where the last descendants of the Yámana people live, relocated from their original homes at Caleta Mejillones, which was the last indigenous reservation in the province, inhabited by hundreds of Yámana descendants. At **Mejillones**, 32 km from Puerto Williams, is a graveyard and memorial to the Yámana people.

Just before Estancia Santa Rosa (10 km further on), a path is said to cross the forest, lakes and beaver dams to Wulaia (10 km, one to two days), where the *Beagle* anchored in 1833; however, even the farmer at Wulaia gets lost following this track.

Cape Horn

It is possible to catch a boat south from Isla Navarino (enquire at the yacht club) to Cape Horn (the most southerly piece of land on earth apart from Antarctica). There is one pebbly beach on the north side of the island; boats anchor in the bay and passengers are taken ashore by motorized dinghy. A stairway climbs the cliff above the beach, up to the building which houses the naval post. A path leads from here to the impressive monument of an albatross overlooking the wild, churning waters of the Drake Passage below. See also box, page 568.

Listings Isla Navarino

Tourist information

Puerto Williams

Tourist office
Municipalidad de Cabos de Hornos, corner of Arturo Pratt and Piloto Pardo, T61-262 1018 extension 25, www.ptowilliams.cl/turismo. html. Mon-Thu 0800-1300 and 1430-1700, Fri 0800-1300 and 1400-1600, closed in winter. For maps and details on hiking.

Where to stay

Puerto Williams

$$$$ Lakutaia
2 km west of town, T61-261 4108 (Santiago: T9-6226 8448), www.lakutaia.cl.
A 'base camp' for a range of activities and packages (horse riding, trekking, birdwatching, boating, kayaking, flight tours. Book 48 hrs in advance. 24 double rooms in simple but attractive style, lovely views from spacious public areas, free bike rental, 3 golf 'holes' – most southerly in world!

$$$-$$ Hostal Beagle
Presidente Ibañez 147, T9-7765 9554, contacto.hostalbeagle@gmail.com.
Pleasant self-service *hostal*. No dorms, but doubles and triples.

$$ Hostal Akainij
Austral 22, T61-262 1173, www.turismoakainij.cl.
Comfortable rooms, very helpful, excellent, filling meals, basic English spoken, adventure tours and transfers.

$$ Hostal Cabo de Ornos
Maragaño 146, T61-262 1849.
Decent central option above Plaza O'Higgins. Above the *hostal* is a good restaurant run by the same owners (see Restaurants, below).

$$ Hostal Coirón
Maragaño 168, T61-262 1227.
Double rooms or dorms, shared and private bath, helpful, good food, relaxed, quite basic, but OK.

$$ Hostal Miramar
Muñoz 155, T61-262 1372, aibanjou@hotmail.com.

Small, family-run *hostal*, comfortable living spaces, good food upon request.

$$ Hostal Pusaki
Piloto Pardo 222, T61-262 1116,
pattypusaki@yahoo.es.
Double room or dorms, good meals available, owner Patty is helpful and fun.

$$ Refugio El Padrino
Costanera 276, T61-262 1136,
ceciliamancillao@yahoo.com.ar.
The vivacious Cecilia Mancilla is great fun. Good food served, and musical instruments are on hand. Also offers camping. Recommended.

Restaurants

Puerto Williams
There are several grocery stores; prices are very high because of the remoteness. **Simón & Simón** and **Temuco** are opposite each other on Piloto Pardo, junction Condell. The former seems to be the reference point in town. Most hotels and hostels will offer food.

$$-$ Resto del Sur
Maragaño 146, T61-262 1849.
Located above **Hostal Cabo de Ornos**, this restaurant has more food options than other places, including all-you-can-eat pizza on Fri nights.

$ Los Dientes de Navarino
Centro Comercial Sur.
Open until 0400 on weekends.
Colombian owner Yamilla incorporated much of her native flavour into this popular eatery, down to the Caldas rum stocking the shelves and Romeo Santos playing on the TV. Good, hearty fare. Set menu.

Cafés

Puerto Luisa
Costanera 317, T9-9934 0849, see Facebook.
Mon-Fri 1200-2000, Sat 0830-1800.
Owner Valeria welcomes people with espressos, hot chocolate, teas and home-made cakes and pastries.

What to do

Puerto Williams
Boat trips
Note No tour companies in Puerto Williams go to Cape Horn. It's possible to enquire at the yacht club about boat hire, but it all depends on the owner.
Navarino Travel, *Centro Comercial (in the Fio Fio souvenir shop), T9-6629 9201, navarinotravel@gmail.com.* Knowledgeable owner Maurice offers boat trips to different destinations around the island, including glaciers.
Wulaia Expeditions, *Yelcho 224, T9-9832 6412, wulaiaexpediciones@gmail.com.* Runs all-day boat tours and fishing trips from Puerto Williams to Wulaia Cove. Lunch included. Around US$700 per trip for parties of 2 people; it's better value with parties of 4-6.

Estancias
Estancia Santa Rosa, *Piloto Pardo s/n, T9-8464 2053, fcofilgueira29@gmail.com.* Francisco offers day tours at the oldest estancia on the island. Activities include kayaking in Bahía Santa, horse riding, trekking and a traditional Chilean barbecue. US$100 for the day.

Tour operators
Akainij, *see Where to stay, above.*
Navarino Beaver, *T9-9548 7365, barberjorge@ gmail.com.* Hunters Miguel and Jorge run beaver-watching tours (including trips to a tannery), beaver hunting, beaver meat sampling. Pretty much everything beaver.
Shila, *O'Higgins 322 (a hut at entrance to Centro Comercial), T(569)-7897 2005, www. turismoshila.cl.* Luis Tiznado González is an adventure expert offering trekking and fishing, plus equipment hire (bikes, tents, sleeping bags, stoves, and more). Lots of trekking information, sells maps.

Trekking

You must register first with *carabineros* on C Piloto Pardo, near Brito. Tell them when you get back, too.

Transport

Puerto Williams

Air To **Punta Arenas** with **DAP** (details under Punta Arenas). Book well in advance; there are long waiting lists (be persistent). The flight is beautiful (sit on right from Punta Arenas) with superb views of Tierra del Fuego, the Cordillera Darwin, the Beagle Channel, and the islands stretching south to Cape Horn. Also army flights are available (they are cheaper), but the ticket has to be bought through DAP. The airport is in town.

Boat See box, page 591, for details of the **Yaghan** ferry of Broom, www.tabsa.cl. For boat services between Puerto Navarino and Ushuaia, see box, page 597. The *Isla Navarino* to **Punta Arenas** is a 30- to 34-hr trip through beautiful channels. It takes 65 passengers, US$142 for a pullman seat, US$200 for sofa-bed seat.

Argentine
Tierra del Fuego

The Argentine half of Tierra del Fuego is much easier to visit than the Chilean half and more rewarding. The northern half of the island is windswept steppe, and its only town, Río Grande, once rich in oil, is now very faded.

But before you head straight for Ushuaia pause to visit two splendid estancias. Viamonte (www.estanciavia monte.com) was built by Lucas Bridges to protect the indigenous Ona people and is an evocative place to stay, while Estancia María Behety (see www.maribety.com.ar) is world famous for its brown trout fishing. The landscape turns to hills as you head south, and there's a lovely silent lake, Lago Fagnano, ideal for a picnic.

Ushuaia is the island's centre, beautifully set on the Beagle Channel, with a backdrop of steep mountains. With a picturesque national park on its doorstep, boat trips up the Beagle Channel to the Bridges' other superb estancia, Harberton, and a ski centre at Cerro Castor, there's plenty to keep you here. Huskies will draw your sledge in winter, and in summer you can walk around Bahía Lapataia and contemplate the serenity of the end of the world.

Río Grande (population 100,000) is a sprawling modern coastal town, the centre for a rural sheep-farming community. It's a friendly place which you are most likely to visit in order to change buses. There are a couple of good places to stay, however, and a small museum worth seeing.

Río Grande grew rapidly in the 1970s, with government tax incentives for sheep farming. The new population was stranded when incentives were withdrawn, but revival came with expansion into mobile phone and white goods assembly. This in turn declined when Argentina relaxed import restrictions and currently the town is benefitting from the exploitation of oil and gas in the vicinity.

Sights

The city's architecture is a chaotic mix of smart nouveau-riche houses and humble wooden and tin constructions. It was founded by Fagnano's Salesian mission in 1893, and you can visit the original building, **La Candelaria** ① *11 km north, T02964-421642, Mon-Sat 1400-1900, US$6.75, getting there: taxi US$8 with wait*, whose museum has displays of natural history and indigenous artefacts, with strawberry plantations, piglets and an aviary. The **Museo Virginia Choquintel** ① *Alberdi 555, T02964-430647, see Facebook, Mon-Fri 1000-1900, Sat 1500-1900,* is recommended for its history of the Selk'nam, the pioneers, missions and oil. Next door is a handicraft shop called **Kren** ('sun' in Selk'nam), which sells good local products.

★ Around Río Grande

The **fly-fishing** in this area is becoming world-renowned and it's now possible to stay in several comfortable lodges in Río Grande and at Lago Escondido. This area is rich in brown trout, sea run brook trout and steelheads, weighing 2-14 kg; you could expect to catch an average of eight trout a day in season. Contact specialist fly-fishing tour operators. The season runs from 15 October to 14 April, with the best fishing from January to April.

Estancia María Behety, 15 km from town, built by the millionaire José Menéndez, has a vast sheep-shearing shed and is heaven for brown trout fishing. **Estancia Viamonte**, on the coast, 40 km south of town, is a working sheep farm with a fascinating history. Here, Lucas Bridges, son of Tierra del Fuego's first settler, built a home to protect the large tribe of indigenous Onas, who were fast dying out. The estancia is still inhabited by his descendants, who will take you riding and show you life on the farm. There is also a house to rent and superb accommodation, highly recommended.

Tourist information

Provincial tourist office
*Av Belgrano 319, T02964-422887, infuerg1@
tierradelfuego.org.ar. Mon-Fri 0800-1600.*

Tourist office
*Rosales 350, T02964-430516, www.tierradel
fuego.org.ar. Mon-Fri 0900-2000.*
In the blue-roofed hut on the plaza is this
small but helpful tourist office.

Where to stay

Book ahead, as there are few decent
choices. Several estancias offer full board
and some, mainly on the northern rivers,
have expensive fishing lodges; others offer
horse riding.

$$$ Grande Hotel
Echelaine 251, T02964-436500.
Modern hotel with standard rooms,
executive suites and lofts, spa services and
a pool fit for a debauched Roman emperor.
Also has a highly regarded restaurant
featuring Argentine and Patagonian dishes.

$$$ Posada de los Sauces
*Elcano 839, T02964-432895,
www.posadadelossauces.com.*
The best by far, with breakfast, beautifully
decorated, comfortable, good restaurant
(trout recommended), cosy bar, very
helpful staff.

$$$ Villa
*Av San Martín 281, T02964-424998,
hotelvilla@live.com.*
Central, modern, restaurant/*confitería*,
parking, discount given for cash.

Estancias

$$$$ Estancia María Behety
*16.5 km from Río Grande, T02964-424215
reservations at The Fly Shop (www.theflyshop.
com), www.maribety.com.ar.*

Established in 1897 on a 40-km stretch
of the river that has become legendary
for brown trout fishing, this estancia has
accommodation for 18 anglers, and good
food. It is one of the country's priciest
fishing lodges, deservedly so. Guides and
equipment included.

$$$$ pp Estancia Viamonte
*40 km southeast on the coast, T02964-
430861, www.estanciaviamonte.com.*
For an authentic experience of Tierra
del Fuego, built in 1902 by pioneer Lucas
Bridges, writer of *Uttermost Part of the Earth*,
to protect the Selk'nam/Ona people, this
working estancia has simple and beautifully
furnished rooms in a spacious cottage.
Price is for full board and all activities:
riding and trekking; cheaper for dinner,
bed and breakfast only. Delicious meals.
Book a week ahead.

Camping

Club Náutico Ioshlelk-Oten
Montilla 1047, T02964-420536, see Facebook.
Situated 2 km from town on the river.
Clean, cooking facilities, heated building
available in cold weather. YPF petrol station
has hot showers.

Restaurants

The restaurants in Hotel Villa and
Hotel Grande have good reputations.

$$ Don Peppone
*Perito Moreno 247, T02964-432066,
see Facebook.*
For pizzas, pastas, *empanadas* and
sandwiches. One of the most popular
spots in town.

Cafés

El Roca
*Espora 643, ½ block from the plaza,
T02964-430693, see Facebook.*

A *confitería* and bar in historic premises (the original cinema), good and popular.

Tío Willy
Alberdi 279.
Serves *cerveza artesanal* (microbrewery).

Festivals

Jan Sheep Shearing Festival. Definitely worth seeing if you're in the area.
Feb Rural Exhibition. Exhibition with handicrafts in 2nd week.
Mar Shepherd's Day. An impressive sheep-dog display during the 1st week.
20-22 Jun Winter solstice. The longest night. Fireworks and ice-skating contests; this is a very inhospitable time of year.

Transport

Book ahead in summer as buses and planes fill up fast. Take your passport when buying ticket.

Air There is an **airport** (T02964-420699), 4 km west of town. A taxi to the centre costs US$7. To **Buenos Aires**, daily, 3½ hrs direct. **LADE** flies to **Río Gallegos**.

Bus To **Punta Arenas**, Chile, via Punta Delgada, 7-9 hrs, with **Pacheco** (Perito Moreno 647, T02964-421554, Mon-Sat) and **Tecni Austral** (Moyano 516, T02964-432885), US$40. To **Río Gallegos**, with **Tecni Austral**, Mon-Sat 0500, 8 hrs; with **Marga/Taqsa** (Mackinley 545, T02964-434316), daily 0700, US$55, connection to El Calafate and Comodoro Rivadavia. To **Ushuaia**, 3½-4 hrs, with **Montiel** (25 de Mayo 712, T02964-420997) and **Líder** (Perito Moreno 635, T02964-420003, www.lidertdf.com.ar), US$22; both use small buses and have frequent departures; they stop en route at **Tolhuin**, US$15; also with **Marga**.

From Río Grande, several roads fan out southwest to the heart of the island, though this area is little inhabited. The paved road south, Route 3, continues across wonderfully open land, more forested than the expanses of Patagonian steppe further north and increasingly hilly as you near Ushuaia. After around 160 km, you could turn left along a track to the coast to Cabo San Pablo. There are also other trips to places of interest within reach. Route 3 then climbs up above Lago Fagnano and Tolhuin.

Tolhuin and around

This is a friendly, small settlement close to the shore of Lago Fagnano, a large expanse of water, right at the heart of Tierra del Fuego. The village has a stretch of beach nearby and is a favourite Sunday afternoon destination for day trippers from Ushuaia. There's a YPF service station just off the main road, but it's worth driving into the village itself for the famous bakery **La Unión** (see Restaurants, page 606), where you can buy delicious bread, *empanadas* and fresh *facturas* (pastries). It's also a good source of information. Handicrafts, including fine leather goods, are available at El Encuentro half a block from the tourist information office (see Tourist information, below). From the village a road leads down to the tranquil lakeshore, where there are a couple of good places to stay.

Further along Route 3, 50 km from Ushuaia, a road to the right swoops down to **Lago Escondido**, a fjord-like lake with steep, deep-green mountains descending into the water. After Lago Escondido, the road crosses the cordillera at Paso Garibaldi. It then descends to the Cerro Castor winter-sports complex and the Tierra Mayor Recreation area (see What to do, page 615). There is a police control just as you enter Ushuaia city limits; passports may be checked.

Listings Río Grande to Ushuaia

Tourist information

Tolhuin and around

Tourist office
Av de los Shelknam 80, T02901-492125, tolhuinturismo@tierradelfuego.org.ar. Daily 0900-1500.
Tiny, friendly office with very helpful staff.

Where to stay

Tolhuin and around

$$$ Cabañas Khami
on Lago Fagnano, 8 km from Tolhuin, T02964-15-611243, www.cabaniaskhami.com.ar.
Well-equipped, rustic cabins, good value with linen. Price given for 6 people, 3-night weekend rates available.

$$ Terrazas del Lago
R3, Km 2938, T02964-422710, www.lasterrazasdellago.com.ar.
A little way from the shore, smart wooden *cabañas*, well decorated, and also a *confitería* and *parrilla*.

Camping

Camping Hain del Lago
T02964-1560 3606, robertoberbel@hotmail.com.

Lovely views, fireplaces, hot showers, and a *quincho* for when it rains.

Camping Rural La Correntina
See Facebook, T02964 15-612518 137, 17 km from Tolhuin.
In woodland, with bathrooms, and horses for hire.

Restaurants

Tolhuin and around

La Posada de los Ramírez
Av de los Shelknam 411, T02901-492382, see Facebook. Open weekends only, lunch and dinner.
A cosy restaurant and *rotisería*.

Panadería La Unión
Jeujepen 450, T02901-492202, www.panaderialaunion.com. Daily 0600-2400.
Deservedly famous bakery.

What to do

Tolhuin and around
Sendero del Indio, *T02901-15-476803, see Facebook.* For horse riding.

Ushuaia *Colour map 6, C2.*

the last town before the edge of the world

The most southerly town in the world, Ushuaia's setting is spectacular. Its brightly coloured houses look like toys against the dramatic backdrop of vast jagged mountains. Opposite are the forbidding peaks of Isla Navarino, and between flows the serene green Beagle Channel. Sailing those waters you can just imagine how it was for Darwin, arriving here in 1832, and for those early settlers, the Bridges, in 1871.

Though the town has expanded in recent years, its population of 55,000 sprawling untidily along the coast, Ushuaia still retains the feel of a pioneer town, isolated and expectant. There are lots of places to stay, which fill up entirely in January, a fine museum and some great fish and crab restaurants.

There is spectacular landscape to be explored in all directions, with good treks in the accessible **Parque Nacional Tierra del Fuego** (see page 620), just to the west of the city, and more adventurous expeditions offered into the wild heart of the island, trekking, climbing or riding. There's splendid cross-country skiing and downhill skiing nearby at **Cerro Castor** ⓘ www.cerrocastor.com.

And to the east, along a beautiful stretch of coastline is the historic estancia of Harberton, which you can reach by a boat trip along the Beagle Channel. Ushuaia is also the starting point for expeditions to Antarctica; for more information, see www.dna.gov.ar. For more about Ushuaia, see www.e-ushuaia.com.

Essential Ushuaia

Finding your feet

The airport, **Aeropuerto Internacional Malvinas Argentinas**, T02901-431232, www.aeropuertoushuaia.com, is 4 km from town on a peninsula in the Beagle Channel. A taxi to or from the airport costs US$10-15 (there is no bus). Buses and minibuses from Río Grande arrive at their respective offices around town. See Transport, page 615.

Getting around

It's easy to walk around the town in a morning, since all its sights are close together. You'll find banks, restaurants, hotels and shops along San Martín, which runs parallel to the shore, a block north of the coast road, Avenida Maipú. Ushuaia is very well organized for tourism, and there are good local buses to the national park and other sights, as well as many boat trips. Urban buses run from west to east across town; most stop along Maipú, US$0.50 (it can be a bit of a wait to catch a bus).

The tourist office provides a list of minibus companies that run daily to nearby attractions; most of these use the bus stop at the junction of Maipú and Fadul (see map).

Boat trips leave from the Muelle Turístico (tourist pier) by a small plaza, 25 de Mayo on the seafront.

When to go

Ushuaia is at its most beautiful in autumn (March to May), when the dense forests all around are turned a rich red and yellow, and there are many bright days with clear azure skies. Summer (December to February) is best for trekking, when maximum temperatures are around 15°C, but try to avoid January, when the city is swamped with tourists. Late February is much better. The ski season is mid-June to October, when temperatures are around zero, but the wind drops.

Money

Banks are open 1000-1500 in summer. ATMs are plentiful all along San Martín; using credit cards is easiest (but machines can be empty on Saturdays, Sundays and holidays). **Agencia de Cambio Thaler**, San Martín 209, T02901-421911, Monday-Friday 1000-1500 (extended hours in high season).

Useful addresses

Biblioteca Popular Sarmiento, San Martín 1589, T02901-423103. **Monday-Friday** 1000-2000, www.bpsarmientoush.com.ar. Library with a good range of books about the area. **Chilean Consulate**, Jainén 50, T02901-430909, Monday-Friday 0900-1300 (telephone 0900-1700). **Dirección Nacional de Migraciones**, Fuegia Basket 187, T02901-422334.

★ Sights

There are several museums worth visiting if bad weather forces you indoors, and the most fascinating is **Museo del Fin del Mundo** ① *along the seafront at Maipú y Rivadavia, T02901-421863, Mon-Fri 1000-1900, Sat, Sun and bank holidays 1400-2000, US$9, guided tours at 1100, 1400 and 1700, fewer in winter*. Located in the 1912 bank building, it tells the history of the town through a small collection of carefully chosen exhibits on the indigenous groups, missionaries, pioneers and shipwrecks, together with nearly all the birds of Tierra del Fuego (stuffed), and you can get an 'end of the world museum' stamp in your passport. There are helpful and informed staff, and also an extensive reference library. Recommended.

Further east, the old prison, Presidio, at the back of the naval base, houses the **Museo Marítimo** ① *Yaganes y Gobernador Paz, www.museomaritimo.com, daily 0900-2000 (1000-2000 in winter), excellent guided tours in Spanish at 1130, 1630 and 1830 (1130 and 1630 in winter), US$13.50, ticket valid 24 hrs*, with models and artefacts from seafaring days. The cells of most of the five wings of the huge building also house the **Museo Penitenciario**, which details the history of the prison. Guided visits also include a tour of the lighthouse (a life-size replica of the original) that inspired Jules Verne's novel, *Around the World in Eighty Days*. Recommended. Much smaller but also interesting is **Museo Yámana** ① *Rivadavia 56, T02901-422874, museoyamana@gmail.com, see Facebook), daily 1000-2000, US$7.50*, which has interesting scale models showing scenes of everyday life of Yámana people and the geological evolution of the island.

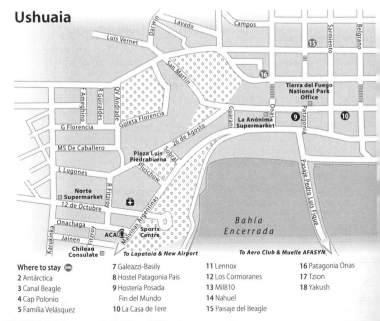

Ushuaia

Where to stay 🛏
2 Antártica
3 Canal Beagle
4 Cap Polonio
5 Familia Velásquez
7 Galeazzi-Basily
8 Hostel Patagonia Pais
9 Hostería Posada
  Fin del Mundo
10 La Casa de Tere
11 Lennox
12 Los Cormoranes
13 Mil810
14 Nahuel
15 Paisaje del Beagle
16 Patagonia Onas
17 Tzion
18 Yakush

BACKGROUND
Ushuaia

Founded in 1884 after missionary Thomas Bridges had established his mission in these inhospitable lands, Ushuaia attracted many pioneers in search of gold. Keen to populate its new territory, the government set up a penal colony on nearby Staten Island, which moved to the town in 1902, and the town developed rapidly. Immigration was largely Croatian and Spanish, together with those shipwrecked on the shores, but the town remained isolated until planes arrived in 1935. As the prison closed, a naval base opened and in the 1970s there was a further influx, attracted by job opportunities in assemblage plants of electronic equipment that flourished thanks to reduced taxes.

Now the city is capital of Argentina's most southerly province, and though fishing is still a traditional economic activity, Ushuaia has become an important tourist centre, particularly as the departure point for voyages to Antarctica.

The most recently opened museum is the **Galería Temática** ① *San Martín 152, PB, 1er y 2do pisos, T02901-422245, www.historiafueguina.com, Mon-Sat 1100-2000, US$10*, where numerous life-sized displays take you through an informative history of Tierra del Fuego with a useful audioguide in different languages. There is also a themed garden at the back, reached through a huge souvenir shop with good knitwear and other goods.

Restaurants 🍴	6 Chicho's	13 Martinica	19 Tante Sara
1 137 Pizza & Pasta	8 El Bambú	14 Moustacchio	20 Tía Elvira
2 Bodegón Fueguino	9 El Turco	16 Parrilla La Rueda	21 Volver
3 Café Bar Banana	10 Gadget Café	17 Ramos Generales	
5 Café Tante Sara	12 Laguna Negra	18 Sandwichería Kami	

Tierra del Fuego Argentine Tierra del Fuego • 609

Tourist information

Oficina Antártica
At entrance to the port, near the main tourist office at the pier (Muelle Turístico), T02901-430015, antartida@tierradelfuego.org.ar. Mon-Fri 0900-1700.
Information on Antarctica and a small library with navigational charts.

Provincial tourist office
Maipú 505, T02901-423423, info@tierradelfuego.org.ar.

Tierra del Fuego tourist office
San Martín 1395, T02901-421315.
Can provide a basic map of the park.

Tourist office
Prefectura Naval 470, at the Pier (Muelle Turístico), T02901-432000, www.turismo ushuaia.com. Mon-Fri 0800-2100, Sat-Sun 0900-2000.
One of the best in Argentina. The helpful staff speak several languages. They have a map and a series of leaflets about all the things to see and do, and can provide bus and boat times. Another tourist office is at the airport (T02901-423970, open at flight times only).

Where to stay

The tourist office (see above) has a comprehensive list of all officially registered accommodation and will help with rooms in private homes, campsites, etc. An excellent choice is to stay with Ushuaia families on a B&B basis. The range of lodging is growing at all budget levels, from the very chic, to *cabañas*, to basic B&Bs in the centre and the suburbs. There are too many to list here. You must book in advance in high season.

$$$$ Canal Beagle
Maipú y 25 de Mayo, T02901-432303, www.hotelcanalbeagle.com.ar.
ACA hotel (discounts for members), Apr-Oct, comfortable and well-attended, with a small pool, gym, spa, business centre, some rooms with channel views (others overlook the container dock), good restaurant.

$$$$ Cap Polonio
San Martín 746, T02901-422140, www.hotelcappolonio.com.ar.
Smart, central, modern, comfortable, popular restaurant/café **Marcopolo**.

$$$$ Lennox
San Martín 776, T02901-436430, www.lennoxhotels.com.
Boutique hotel on the main street, with breakfast, services include hydromassage, minibar, restaurant and *confitería* on 4th floor. Laundry service.

$$$$ Mil810
25 de Mayo 245, T02901-437710, www.hotel1810.com.
City hotel with 30 standard rooms, 1 with disabled access, no restaurant but breakfast and *confitería* (0700-1000, 1700-2000), all rooms with minibar, safe, quite small but cosy, calm colours, good views, business centre and multiple use room where you can hang out while waiting for flight.

$$$ Galeazzi-Basily
G Gob Valdez 323, T02901-423213, www.avesdelsur.com.ar.
Among the best, beautiful family home, incredible welcome, in pleasant area 5 blocks from centre, 4 rooms with shared bath. Also excellent *cabañas* ($$$) in the garden. Highly recommended.

$$$ Hostería Posada Fin del Mundo
Rivadavia 610, T02901-437345, www.posadafindelmundo.com.ar.
Family atmosphere, comfortable rooms, good value, has character.

$$$ Paisaje del Beagle
Gob Paz 1347, T421214, www.paisajedelbeagle.com.ar.

Family-run, quiet, with a cosy dining area for good breakfast, laundry service. Recommended.

$$$ Tzion
Gob Valdez 468, T02901-432290,
tzion_byb@hotmail.com.
B&B with 3 rooms, 1 with bath, high above town, 10 mins' walk from centre, nice family atmosphere, cheaper low season, laundry service, English and French spoken, great views. Highly recommended.

$$ pp La Casa de Tere
Rivadavia 620, T02901-422312,
www.lacasadetere.com.ar.
Shared or private bath, use of kitchen facilities, freshly baked bread, open fire, singles, doubles and triples, hot water, helpful owner.

$$ Nahuel
25 de Mayo 440, T02901-423068,
see Facebook.
Charming Sra Navarrete has a comfortable B&B with channel views from the upper rooms and the terrace, good value, but noisy street.

$$-$ Familia Velásquez
Juana Fadul 361, T02901-421719,
losnokis_figueroa@hotmail.com.
Cosy, welcoming house of a pioneer, with basic rooms, breakfast, cooking and laundry facilities, good.

$ pp Antártica
Antártida Argentina 270, T02901-435774,
www.antarcticahostel.com.
Central, welcoming, spacious chill-out room, excellent 24-hr bar, dorms for 6 and large doubles, breakfast included, game night Thu with good prizes. Recommended.

$ pp Los Cormoranes
Kamshén 788 y Alem, T02901-423459,
www.loscormoranes.com.
Large hostel, with good views, cosy rooms with lockers, OK bathrooms, *parrilla*. Doubles ($$) available. They can book tours. HI members can still receive discount.

$ Patagonia Onas
Onas 176, T0291-433389,
www.patagoniaonas.com.
Owned by the same husband and wife who run **Patagonia Pais**, see below. This tranquil option is more central, and less of a party hostel. Also has doubles with shared bath ($$). Breakfast is included.

$ Patagonia Pais
Alem 152, T0291-431886,
www.patagoniapais.com.
Just above the centre, this welcoming, family-run hostel is a good meeting point. Dorms from US$17, laundry service, *parrilla*, breakfast included, information on tours and trips. Be sure to say hi to Gordita ("little fat one"), the hostel's canine mascot. Highly recommended.

$ pp Yakush
Piedrabuena 118 y San Martín, T02901-435807.
Very well run, central with spacious dorms, also doubles ($$, cheaper without bath), book exchange and library, dining room, steep garden with views. Information centre has details on various tours. Recommended.

Camping

La Pista del Andino
Leandro N Alem 2873, T02901-435890.
Set in the Club Andino ski premises in a woodland area, it has wonderful views over the channel. Electricity, hot showers, tea room and grocery store, very helpful. Recommended.

Restaurants

There are lots of restaurants along San Martín and Maipú. Most are open 1200-1500 and again from 1900 at the earliest. Several cafés are open all the time. Ask around for currently available seafood, especially *centolla* (king crab) and *cholga* (giant mussels). It's much cheaper if you prepare your own meal. But note that *centolla* may not be fished Nov-Dec. Beer drinkers should try the handcrafted brews of the Cape Horn brewery: Pilsen, Pale Ale and Stout.

$$$ Bodegón Fueguino
San Martín 859, T02901-431972,
www.tierradehumos.com/bodegon.
Snacks, home-made pastas and good roast
lamb with varied sauces in a renovated 1896
casa de pioneros.

$$$ Tía Elvira
Maipú 349, T02901-424705.
Mon-Sat 1200-1500, 1900-2300.
Excellent seafood.

$$$ Volver
Maipú 37, T02901-423907.
Delicious seafood and fish in atmospheric
1896 house, with ancient newspaper all
over the walls. Recommended.

$$$-$$ Moustacchio
San Martín 298, T02901-430548,
www.moustacchio.com.ar.
Long established, good for seafood and meat.

$$$-$$ Parrilla La Rueda
San Martín y Rivadavia, T02901-436540.
Good *tenedor libre* for beef, lamb and great
salads. Recommended for freshness.

$$ 137 Pizza & Pasta
San Martín 137, T02901-435005.
Tasty filling versions of exactly what the
name says, plus excellent *empanadas,*
elegant decor.

$$ Chicho's
Rivadavia 72, T02901-423469.
Bright, cheerful place just off the main street,
friendly staff, kitchen open to view. Fish,
meat and chicken dishes, pastas, wide range
of *entradas.* Also recommended for *centolla.*

$$ El Turco
San Martín 1410.
A very popular place, serving generous
milanesas, pastas, pizzas, seafood and meat.
Very tasty *empanadas.*

$$-$ Martinica
*San Martín 68 (between Antártida Argentina
and Yaganes).*
Cheap, small, busy, sit at the bar facing the
parrilla and point to your favourite beef cut.

Takeaway (T02901-432134) and good meals
of the day, also pizzas and *empanadas.*

Cafés

Café Bar Banana
San Martín 273, T02901-424021, see Facebook.
Quite small, always busy, pool table, offers
good fast food, such as burgers, small pizzas,
puddings, breakfasts and an all-day menu
for **$$.**

Café Tante Sara
*San Martín 701, opposite the tourist office,
T02901-423912, www.tantesara.com.*
Very good, smart, good coffee, tasty
sandwiches, always busy, open late. Also
has a restaurant and *panadería* at San
Martín 175 called **Tante Sara,** selling breads,
sandwiches, chocolates, *empanadas* and
snacks, coffee, lots of choice.

El Bambú
Piedrabuena 276, T02901-437028.
Daily 1100-1700.
One of few purely vegetarian places in town,
takeaway only, home-made food, delicious
and good value.

Gadget Café
San Martín 1256, T0800-999 0223,
www.gadgettugelateria.com.ar.
The best ice cream parlour in town, multiple
flavours, friendly. Recommended.

Laguna Negra
San Martín 513, T02901-431144,
www.lagunanegra.com.ar.
Mainly a shop selling chocolate and other
fine produce, catering to the cruise ship
passengers, but has a good little café at
the back for hot chocolate and coffee. Also
has a bigger branch at Libertador 1250,
El Calafate. Sells postcards and stamps, too.

Ramos Generales
*Maipú 749, T02901-424317, www.ramos
generalesush.com.ar. Daily 0900-2400
in high season.*
An old warehouse with wooden floors and
a collection of historic objects. Sells breads,

pastries, wines and drinks, also cold cuts, sandwiches, salads, ice cream, Argentine *mate* and coffee. Not cheap but atmospheric.

Sandwichería Kami
San Martín 54, T02901-430870. Daily until 2100.
Friendly, simple sandwich shop, selling rolls, baguettes and *pan de miga*.

Bars and clubs

Bar Ideal
San Martín 393, T02901-437860, www.elbarideal.com.
Funky corner backpacker bar with a solid drink menu. Also serves food.

Dublin Bar Irlandés
9 de Julio 168, T02901-434704. Daily 2100-0400.
A favourite with locals and tourists.

Küar
Av Perito Moreno 2232, east of town, T02901-437396, www.kuaronline.com. Daily for lunch from 1230 and dinner from 1800.
Great setting by the sea, restaurant, bar and brewery.

Festivals

20-22 Jun Winter solstice. The longest night. Torch-lit procession and fireworks.
Aug Dog Sled Race. Held annually.
Aug Marcha Blanca. www.marchablanca. com. A ski trek from Lago Escondido to Tierra Mayor valley.
Oct Classical Music Festival, www.festivaldeushuaia.com.

Shopping

Ushuaia's tax-free status doesn't produce as many bargains as you might hope. Lots of souvenir shops on San Martín offer good-quality leather and silver ware. The **Pasaje de Artesanías** (by the Muelle Turístico), sells local arts and crafts.

Atlántico Sur, *San Martín 627*. The (not especially cheap) duty free shop.

Boutique del Libro, *San Martín 1120, T02901-424750, www.boutiquedellibro.com.ar. Mon-Sat 1000-1300 and 1530-2030*. An excellent selection of books, including several in English and other languages on Tierra del Fuego. CDs and DVDs upstairs.

What to do

Boat trips and sea cruises
Sightseeing trips All short boat trips leave from the Muelle Turístico. Take your time to choose the size and style of boat you want. Representatives from the offices are polite and helpful. All have a morning and afternoon sailing and include Isla de los Lobos, Isla de los Pájaros and Les Eclaireurs lighthouse, with guides and some form of refreshment. Note that weather conditions may affect sailings, prices can change and that port tax is not included. See also **Rumbo Sur** and **Tolkeyen** under Tour operators, below.
Canoero, *T02901-433893, www.catamaran escanoero.com.ar.* Runs 2 catamarans (one can accommodate 138 passengers), 2½- to 3-hr trips to the 3 main sites, US$53. They also have a 4½-hr trip almost daily to the Pingüinera on Isla Martillo near Estancia Harberton (Oct-Mar only), boats stay for 1 hr, but you cannot land on Martillo, US$75 (US$112 including Harberton – entry extra). Also longer tours to Estancia Harberton and Lapataia Bay.
Patagonia Adventure Explorer, *T02901-15-465842, www.patagoniaadvent.com.ar.* Has a sailing boat (US$60 plus US$1.50 port tax) and motor boats for the standard trip, plus Isla Bridges. Good guides.
Pira-Tour, *San Martín 847, T02901-435557, www.piratour.com.ar.* Runs 2 buses a day to Harberton, from where a boat goes to the Pingüinera on Isla Martillo: 20 people allowed to land (maximum 4 groups per day; the only company licensed to do this). US$110 plus US$20 for entrance to Harberton. Also offers various trekking and Beagle Channel tours.
Tres Marías, *T02901-436416, www.tres mariasweb.com.* The only company licensed

to visit Isla H, which has archaeological sites, cormorants, other birds and plants. 2 departures 1000 and 1500, 4 hrs. Also has a sailing boat for no more than 10 passengers; specialist guide, café on board. Trip costs US$70. Highly recommended.

To Antarctica From Oct to Mar, Ushuaia is the starting point, or the last stop en route, for cruises to Antarctica. These usually sail for 9 to 21 days along the western shores of the Antarctic peninsula and the South Shetland Islands. Other trips include stops at Falkland/Malvinas archipelago and at South Georgia. Go to the **Oficina Antártica** for advice (see page 610). Agencies sell 'last-minute tickets', but the price is entirely dependent on demand. Coordinator for trips is **Turismo Ushuaia**, Gob Paz 865, T02901-436003, www.ushuaiaturismoevt.com.ar, which operates with IAATO members only. See the website for prices for the upcoming season. Port tax is US$1.50 per passenger and an exit tax of US$10 is also charged. **Freestyle Adventure Travel**, Gob Paz 866, T02901-15-609792, www.freestyleadventure travel.com. Organizes 7- to 22-day cruises to Antarctica, particularly good for last-minute deals. Wide variety of itineraries. Cape Horn expeditions also available. **Polar Latitudes**, T(1) 802 698 8479 (US) sales@polar-latitudes.com, www.polar-latitudes.com. Antarctic cruises aboard small expedition vessels, some itineraries take in the Falklands/Malvinas and South Georgia. All-suite accommodation onboard.

To Chile You can ask at **Muelle AFASYN** (near the old airport, T02901-437842), about possible crossings with a club member to Puerto Williams, about 4 hrs; from Puerto Williams a ferry goes once a week to Punta Arenas. There may also be foreign sailing boats going to Cabo de Hornos or Antarctica. **Australis**, www.australis.com. Operates 2 luxury cruise ships between Ushuaia and **Punta Arenas**, with a visit to Cape Horn, highly recommended. Full details are given in the box, page 556. Check-in at **Comapa** (see below). **Fernández Campbell**, www.fernandez campbell.com. Has a 1½-hr crossing to **Puerto Williams**, Fri-Sun 1000, return 1500, US$125 for foreigners, tickets sold at **Zenit Explorer**, Juana Fadul 126, Ushuaia, T02901-433232, and **Naviera RFC** in Puerto Williams. **Ushuaia Boating**, Gob Paz 233, T02901-436193 (or at the Muelle Turístico). Operates a channel crossing to Puerto Navarino (Isla Navarino) all year round, 30-90 mins depending on weather, and then bus to Puerto Williams, 1 hr, US$125 one way, not including taxes.

Fishing
Trout season is Nov to mid-Apr, licenses US$19 per day (an extra fee is charged for some rivers and lakes). **Asociación de Caza y Pesca**, Maipú 822, T02901-423168, www.cazaypescaushuaia.org. Mon-Fri 1600-2000. Sells licences and has a list on the door of other places that sell them.

Hiking and climbing
The winter sports resorts along Ruta 3 (see below) are an excellent base for summer trekking and many arrange trips. **Antartur**, 25 de Mayo 296, T02901-430329, www.antartur.com.ar. Organizes treks, canoeing, mountain biking and 4WD trips to Lagos Escondido and Fagnano. Good winter trips. **Club Andino**, Alem 2873, T02901-440732, www.clubandinoushuaia.com.ar. Mon-Fri 1000-1300 and 1500-2000. Sells maps and trekking guidebooks; sports programmes like skiing, snowboarding, ice hockey and mountain climbing.

Horse riding
Centro Hípico, Ruta 3, Km 3021, T02901-15-569099, www.horseridingtierradelfuego.com. Rides through woods, on Monte Susana, along coast and through river, 2 hrs, US$48; 4-hr ride with light lunch, US$96; 7-hr ride with asado, US$144. Also offers a 10-day

expedition on Península Mitre with a stay in an estancia, food included, US$3600. Gentle horses, which are well-cared for; all guides have first-aid training. Very friendly and helpful. All rides include transfer from town and insurance. Hats provided for children; works with disabled children.

Tour operators

Lots of companies offer imaginative adventure tourism expeditions. All agencies charge the same fees for trips; ask the tourist office for a complete list: Tierra del Fuego National Park, 4½ hrs, US$40 (entry fee US$9.50 extra, valid for 48 hrs); Lagos Escondido and Fagnano, 7 hrs, US$60 without lunch. With 3 or 4 people it might be worth hiring a *remise* taxi.

All Patagonia, *Juana Fadul 58, T02901-433622, www.allpatagonia.com.* Trekking, ice climbing, and tours; trips to Cabo de Hornos and Antarctica.

Canal, *Roca 136, T02901-435777, www.canalfun.com.* Huge range of activities, trekking, canoeing, riding, 4WD excursions. Recommended.

Comapa, *San Martín 409, T02901-430727, www.comapa.tur.ar.* Conventional tours and adventure tourism, bus tickets to Punta Arenas and Puerto Natales, trips to Antarctica, agents for **Australis**. Recommended.

Compañía de Guías de Patagonia, *Godoy 193B, T02901-437753, www.companiadeguias.com.ar.* The best agency for walking guides, expeditions for all levels, rock and ice climbing (training provided), also diving, sailing, riding, 7-day crossing of Tierra del Fuego on foot and conventional tours. Recommended.

Rumbo Sur, *San Martín 350, T02901-421139, www.rumbosur.com.ar.* Flights, buses, conventional tours on land and sea, including to Harberton, plus Antarctic expeditions, mid-Nov to mid-Mar, English spoken.

Tolkar, *Roca 157, T02901-431412, www.tolkarturismo.com.ar.* Flights, bus tickets to Argentina and Punta Arenas/Puerto

Natales, conventional and adventure tourism, canoeing and mountain biking to Lago Fagnano.

Tolkeyen, *San Martín 1267, T02901-437073, www.tolkeyenpatagonia.com.* Bus and flight tickets, catamaran trips (50-300 passengers), including to Harberton (Tue, Thu, Sat in summer; itineraries vary in winter, US$101) and Parque Nacional, large company.

Travel Lab, *San Martín 1444, T02901-436555, www.travellab.com.ar.* Conventional and unconventional tours, mountain biking, trekking, etc, English and French spoken, helpful.

Winter sports

Ushuaia is popular as a winter resort with 11 centres for skiing, snowboarding and husky sledging. Cerro Castor is the only centre for Alpine skiing, but the other centres along Ruta 3, 18-36 km east of Ushuaia, offer excellent cross-country skiing and alternative activities in summer.

Cerro Castor, *Ruta 3, Km 26, T02901-499301, www.cerrocastor.com.* 31 *pistas* including a vertical drop of 800 m and powder snow. It's an attractive centre with complete equipment rental, also for snowboarding and snowshoeing.

Llanos del Castor, *Ruta 3, Km 3033, www.llanosdelcastor.com.ar.* Wide range of activities throughout the year (plus a *refugio* and restaurant), but in winter they focus on dog-sledging expeditions.

Tierra Mayor, *20 km from town, T02901-437454.* The largest and most recommended. Lies in a beautiful wide valley between steep-sided mountains. It offers half- and full-day excursions on sledges with huskies, as well as cross-country skiing and snowshoeing. Equipment hire and restaurant.

Transport

Air Book ahead in summer; flights fill up fast. In winter flights are often delayed. Schedules tend to change from season to season.

To **Buenos Aires** (Aeroparque or Ezeiza), daily, 3½ hrs. Frequent flights to **El Calafate**, 1 hr 20 mins, and **Río Gallegos**, 1 hr; also to **Río Grande**, 1 hr, several a week (but check with agents). The **Aeroclub de Ushuaia** flies to **Puerto Williams** and organizes flight tours of Tierra del Fuego from the downtown airport (US$155 pp, 30 mins), www.aeroclubushuaia.com.

Boat See What to do, above.

Local bus To **Parque Nacional Tierra del Fuego**, in summer buses and minibuses leave hourly from 0900 from the bus stop on Maipú at the bottom of Fadul, including **Transporte Santa Lucía** (www.transportesantalucia.com), 3 a day each, last return 1900, US$21 return. From same bus stop, many *colectivos* go to the **Tren del Fin del Mundo** (0900 and 1400, return 1145 and 1745, US$10.50 return), **Lago Escondido**, **Lago Fagnano** (1000 and 1400 return at 1400 and 1800), US$50 pp, minimum 6 people) and **Glaciar Martial** (1000 and 1200, return 1400 and 1600, US$10.50). For **Harberton**, check the notice boards at Maipú y Fadul. The only regular bus is run by **Pira-Tur**, see What to do, above.

Long-distance bus Passport needed when booking international bus tickets. Buses always booked up Nov-Mar; buy your ticket to leave as soon as you arrive. To **Río Grande**, 3½-4 hrs, combis run by **Líder** (Gob Paz 921, T02901-436421, www.lidertdf.com.ar), and **Montiel** (Gob Paz 605, T02901-421366), US$25, also buses en route to Río Gallegos and Punta Arenas. To **Río Gallegos**, with **Tecni Austral**, 0500, and **Marga/Taqsa** (Gob Godoy 41), 0700, 13 hrs, US$55 (book through Tolkar; see Tour operators). To **Punta Arenas**, US$55, with **Tecni Austral**, Mon, Wed, Fri 0500, 11-12 hrs (book through Tolkar); with **Pacheco**, 0700 Mon, Wed, Fri, 12-13 hrs (book through Tolkeyen, see above), with **Bus Sur** (at Comapa) Tue, Thu, Sat, Sun 0800; Bus Sur also goes to **Puerto Natales**, US$67, Tue, Sat 0800.

Car hire Most companies charge minimum US$60-70 per day, including insurance and 200 km per day, special promotions available. **Localiza**, Sarmiento 81, T02901-437780, www.localizadietrich.com. Cars can be hired in Ushuaia to be driven through Chile and then left in any Localiza office in Argentina, but you must buy a one-off customs document for US$107 to use as many times as you like to cross borders. Must reserve well in advance and pay a drop-off fee. **Budget**, Godoy 49, T02901-437373.

Taxi Cheaper than *remises*, Maipú at Lasserre, T02901-422007, T02901-422400. Taxi stand by the Muelle Turístico. **Remises Carlitos y Bahía Hermosa**, San Martín y Rosas, T02901-422222.

For exhilarating views along the Beagle Channel and to Isla Navarino opposite, visit Cerro Martial, 7 km from town, there is a chairlift (*aerosilla*) up the *cerro*, but it has been out of service since 2014, and now the only option is trekking.

To reach the base, follow Magallanes out of town; allow 1½ hours. Several companies run sporadic minibus services in summer from the corner of Maipú and Fadul, but they are more expensive than taxis. Taxis charge US$7-9 (up to four people) to the base, from where you can walk all the way back. There are several marked trails, ranging from 600 m to 1 km, including to a viewpoint and to Glaciar Martial itself.

There is a splendid **tea shop** ① *0900-2030*, at the Cumbres de Martial *cabañas* at the base, and a basic *refugio* with no electricity up at the *cerro*. Also by the lower platform is the **Canopy** ① *T02901-15-510307, www.canopyushuaia.com.ar, US$35, US$25 for a shorter run, US$32 and US$22 under 12s, daily 1000-1700*, a series of zip-lines and bridges in the trees. All visitors are accompanied by staff; it's safe and good fun. The café at the entrance, Refugio de Montaña, serves hot chocolate, coffee, cakes, pizzas and has a warm stove.

Parque Nacional Tierra del Fuego (see page 620), just outside Ushuaia, is easily accessible by bus and offers superb walks for all levels of fitness. Another way to get to the park is on the **Tren del Fin del Mundo** ① *T02901-431600, www.trendelfindelmundo.com.ar, 3 departures daily, US$36.50 (US$7.50 for children aged 5-15), US$58.50 1st class return, US$75.50 premium and US$720 VIP special (up to 6 people, includes private bath, kitchenette, food, park entrance fees, unlimited drinks, souvenirs), cheaper in winter, plus US$10 park entrance*. This is the world's southernmost steam train, running new locomotives and carriages on track first laid by prisoners to carry wood to Ushuaia. It's a totally touristy experience with commentary in English and Spanish. Sit on the left side on the outbound journey to get the views. See Transport, below, for buses to the train station.

The ★ **Estancia Harberton** ① *T02901-422742, open 1 Oct to mid-Apr daily 0930-1900, except 25 Dec, 1 Jan and Easter, US$13 (see box, page 618)*, 85 km from Ushuaia, is the oldest estancia on the island and is still run by descendants (currently the fifth generation) of the British missionary Thomas Bridges. It's a beautiful place, with the attractive wood-framed house that Thomas built sitting in quiet contemplation on a tranquil bay.

The impressive **Museo Akatushún** ① *phone as above, 1 Oct to mid-Apr daily 0930-1900, except 25 Dec, 1 Jan and Easter, 8 tours a day, entrance fee is included in the estancia admission price*, has skeletons of South American sea mammals, the result of more than 35 years' scientific investigation in Tierra del Fuego, with excellent tours in English.

You can camp for free with permission from the owners, or stay in cottages or one of the original remodelled farm buildings; see Where to stay, below. Access is along a good unpaved road (Route 33, ex 'J') that branches off Route 3, 40 km east of Ushuaia and runs about 45 km through forest and then through the open country around Harberton with marvellous views; it takes about an hour and a half, and there's no petrol outside Ushuaia and Tolhuin. See What to do and Transport, below, for trips to Harberton with Pira-Tur and bus services (irregular). For boat trips to Harberton, see below.

Trips can be made to Lagos Fagnano and Escondido: agencies run seven-hour tours for US$60 per person without lunch; US$140 for nine hours including canoe rides, or check the list of cheaper but rather unreliable minibuses that go there, which is available at the tourist office. Tour agencies offer many good packages, which include trekking, canoeing,

ON THE ROAD

Estancia Harberton

In a land of extremes and superlatives, Harberton stands out as special. The oldest estancia in Tierra del Fuego, it was built in 1886 on a narrow peninsula overlooking the Beagle Channel. Its founder, the missionary Thomas Bridges, was granted land by President Roca for his work amongst the indigenous people and for his help in rescuing victims of numerous shipwrecks in the channels.

Harberton is named after the Devonshire village where his wife Mary was born. The English connection is evident in the neat lawns, shrubs and trees between the jetty and the farmhouse. Behind the buildings is a large vegetable garden, a real rarity on the island, and there's noticeably more wildlife here than in the Tierra del Fuego National Park, probably owing to its remoteness.

Still operating as a working farm, mainly with cattle and sheep, Harberton is run by Thomas Goodall, great-grandson of the founder, whose wife Natalie has created an impressive museum of the area's rich marine life with a thriving research centre. Visitors receive a bilingual guided tour of the museum, or of farm buildings and grounds with reconstructions of the Yámana dwellings. Tea or lunch (if you reserve ahead) are served in the tea room overlooking the bay, and you may well be tempted to rent one of the two simple cottages on the shore. There are wonderful walks along the coast, and nowhere in Argentina has quite the feeling of peace you'll find here.

birdwatching and horse riding in landscape accessible only by 4WDs. See the tourist office's list of trips, indicating which companies go where.

Boat trips

All these trips are highly recommended, but note that the ★ **Beagle Channel** can be very rough. Food and drink on all boats is pricey. Trips can be booked through most agencies, or at the Muelle Turístico where boat companies have their ticket offices; most boats leave from the Muelle Turístico, with a few trips leaving from Muelle AFASYN (next to the old airport). All passengers must pay US$1.40 port tax; this is not included in tickets.

Most popular excursions visit the small islands southeast of Ushuaia in 2½ to three hours, all year round, passing next to the sea lion colony at Isla de los Lobos, Isla de los Pájaros and Les Eclaireurs lighthouse. Alternatively, they add an hour or so for a landing on Bridges Island. Prices vary depending on whether trips are made on big catamarans or on more exclusive sailing boats. A few pricier services include lunch on board; otherwise a light snack or a coffee is served. Summer options add more to the itinerary, with some trips going further east past the Isla Martillo penguin colony and on to Estancia Harberton. Note that Harberton is included only on a few trips, and you should check that your tour actually visits the estancia and not just the bay, as some do. A few trips also go west to the national park in about 5½ hours. See What to do, page 613, for companies and prices.

Where to stay

$$$$ Cabañas del Beagle
Las Aljabas 375, T02901-432785,
www.cabanasdel beagle.com.
3 rustic-style cabins 1.3 km above the
city, kitchen, hydromassage, fireplace,
heating, phone, self-service breakfast,
very comfortable, personal attention.

$$$$ Cumbres del Martial
Luis F Martial 3560, 7 km from town, T02901-
424779, www.cumbresdelmartial.com.ar.
At the foot of the *aerosilla* to Glaciar Martial,
4 *cabañas* and 6 rooms, beautifully set in the
woods, charming, very comfortable, cabins
have whirlpool baths. Small spa (massage
extra) with saunas and gym. The tearoom,
with disabled access, is open all year,
restaurant with traditional fondues.

$$$$ Las Hayas
Luis Martial 1651 (road to Glaciar Martial),
T02901-442000, www.lashayashotel.com.
4 standards of room, all very good with
TV, jacuzzi, safe, 3 types of view, channel,
mountains or forest. Restaurant and bar.
Everything is included in room price
(including breakfast), except massages
and hairdresser. A fine hotel. Just beyond
and run by the same family company is:

$$$$ Los Acebos
Luis F Martial 1911, T02901-442200,
www.losacebos.com.ar.
All rooms with channel view, safe, games
room. Golf days organized. Very comfy,
as expected, but less characterful than
Las Hayas.

$$$$ Los Cauquenes
At Bahía Cauquen, De La Ermita 3462,
T02901-441300, www.loscauquenes.com.
High-quality 5-star hotel overlooking
Beagle Channel, price varies according
to size and view, spa, very tastefully
decorated, prize-winning restaurant,
regional food on dinner menu, wine
bar with over 100 Argentine wines.

$$$$ Los Yámanas
Costa de los Yámanas 2850, western suburbs,
T02901-446809, www.hotelyamanas.com.ar.
All rooms with Channel view, spacious, well-
decorated, hydromassage, fitness centre, spa
outside in wooded grounds, shuttle to town.
Very pleasant.

$$$$ Tierra de Leyendas
Tierra de Vientos 2448, T02901-446565,
www.tierradeleyendas.com.ar.
In the western suburbs. 5 very comfortable
rooms with safe, views of the Beagle Channel,
or the mountains at the back, 1 room with
jacuzzi, all others with shower, excellent
restaurant serving regional specialities. No
cable TV, but DVDs, living room with games,
library, deck overlooking Río Pipo's outflow.
Wi-Fi. Only for non-smokers. Recommended
and award-winning.

$$$ pp Estancia Harberton
T02901-422742. 1 Oct to mid-Apr.
Restored buildings on the estancia (see
above), very simple rooms, wonderful views,
heating. Price includes walking tour and
entry to museum; 2 rooms with bath, 1 room
with 2 beds, shared bath, 1 room with bunks,
shared bath. There is also a guest-house
with 2 triple rooms, and a *hostal* (**$$**) with
3 private rooms with shared bathroom.
Kitchenette for tea and coffee. Lunch and
dinner extra. Offers half and full-board
options. No credit cards. See opposite.

easy hikes through nature's splendour

Covering 63,000 ha of mountains, lakes, rivers and deep valleys, this small but beautiful park stretches west to the Chilean border and north to Lago Fagnano, though large areas have been closed to tourists to protect the environment. All walks are best early morning or afternoon to avoid the tour buses. You'll see lots of geese, the beautiful torrent duck, Magellanic woodpeckers and austral parakeets.

Walks

Senda Costera ① *8 km, 3 hrs each way.* This lovely easy walk along the shore gives you the essence of the park, its rocky coastline, edged with a rich forest of beech trees and glorious views of the low islands with a backdrop of steep mountains. Start at Bahía Ensenada (where boat trips can be taken around the bay, and where the bus can drop you off). Walk along a well-marked path along the shoreline, and then rejoin the road briefly to cross Río Lapataia (ignoring signs to Lago Acigami to your right). After crossing the broad green river and a second stretch of water (where there's a small camping spot and the *gendarmería*), it's a pleasant stroll inland to the beautifully tranquil **Bahía Lapataia**, an idyllic spot, with views across the sound.

Senda Hito XXIV ① *Along Lago Acigami (Roca), 3.5 km, 90 mins one way.* Another easy walk beside this peaceful lake, with lovely pebble beaches, and through dense forest at times, with lots of birdlife. This is especially recommended in the evening. Get off the bus at the junction for Lago Acigami, turn right along the road to the car park (passing the *guardaparques*' house) and follow the lake side.

Parque Nacional Tierra del Fuego

🚌 Bus stop

Essential Parque Nacional Tierra del Fuego

Access

The park entrance is 12 km west of Ushuaia, on the main road west signposted from the town centre, where you'll be given a basic map with marked walks. The **park administration**, San Martín 1395, T02901-421315, tierradelfuego@apn.gov.ar, Monday-Friday 0900-1600, is in Ushuaia.

Entry fees

US$14.

Tourist information

Ask at the tourist office for bus details (see also Transport, below) and a map of the park, with walks. There are no legal crossing points from the park to Chile. There's a helpful *guardaparque* (ranger) at Lago Acigami (formerly known as Roca).

What to take

Wear warm, waterproof clothing: in winter the temperature drops to as low as -12°C, and although it can reach 25°C in summer, evenings can be chilly.

Cerro Guanaco ① *4 km, 4 hrs one way.* A challenging hike up through the very steep forest to a mirador at the top of a hill (970 m) with splendid views over Lago Acigami, the Beagle Channel and mountains. The ground is slippery after rain; take care and don't rush. Allow plenty of time to return while it's light, especially in winter. The path branches off Senda Hito XXIV (see above) after crossing Arroyo Guanaco.

Listings Parque Nacional Tierra del Fuego *map page 620.*

Where to stay

Camping Lago Roca
T02901-422748, 21 km from Ushuaia, by forested shore of Lago Acigami (Roca), a beautiful site with good facilities, reached by bus Jan-Feb.
It has a backpackers' *refugio*, toilets, showers, restaurant and *confitería*, expensive small shop; camping equipment for hire.

There are also campsites with facilities at **Río Pipo**, 16 km from Ushuaia, and at **Laguna Verde**, 20 km, near Lapataia, and at **Bahía Ensenada**, with no facilities.

What to do

For a really rich experience, go with guides who know the territory well and can tell you about the wildlife. Inexpensive trips for all levels are available with the highly recommended **Compañía de Guías de Patagonia** (www.companiadeguias.com.ar).

Background

History

Much of Argentina's fascinating history is visible on a visit to the country today, not only in colonial architecture and the 19th-century artefacts which fill the museums but in the culture and customs of everyday life. Many towns in the Pampas of Buenos Aires province are just as they were in the 19th century, such as San Antonio de Areco and Chascomús, where the traditions of a lively gaucho culture are still maintained. The lives of early pioneers can be explored in the Welsh towns of Gaiman and Trevelin in Patagonia and in the more remote estancias throughout the country. Córdoba's history of Jesuit occupation is visible in many buildings in the city itself and estancias in the province.

And in the northwest of Argentina you'll find the richest evidence of the country's history. This is where the Spanish first arrived in the 16th century and before them the Incas in the early 15th century, and both have left their mark in colonial architecture and intriguing archaeological evidence. Long before these invasions, the present day provinces of Salta, Catamarca, Tucumán and Jujuy were inhabited by many sophisticated indigenous cultures whose ruined cities can be visited at Santa Rosa de Tastil, Tilcara and Quilmes, and whose beautiful ceramics fill the area's many museums. This is the most rewarding part of the country to visit if you're interested in exploring Argentina's past.

Archaeology and prehistory

Earliest origins

It used to be generally accepted that the earliest settlers in South America were related to people who had crossed the Bering Straits from Asia and drifted through the Americas from about 13,000 years ago (the Clovis model). In recent years, however, a growing number of discoveries from earlier dates in North and South America have raised doubts about this. In South America these include: a coastal site in southern Chile called Monte Verde from 14,800 years ago; stone tools from the Serra da Capivara in northeastern Brazil from some 22,000 years ago, and paleontological evidence from Uruguay from earlier still. If nothing else, these finds question the theory of a single migration into South America from the north. Other early evidence of human presence has been found at various sites: in the Central Andes (with a radiocarbon date between 12,000 and 9000 BC), in northern Venezuela (11,000 BC), in southeast Brazil, and in south-central Chile and Argentine Patagonia (from at least 10,000 BC). After the Pleistocene Ice Age (8000-7000 BC), rising sea levels and climatic changes introduced new conditions, as many mammal species became extinct and coastlands were drowned. A wide range of crops were brought into cultivation, and camelids and guinea pigs were domesticated. It seems that people lived nomadically in small groups, mainly hunting and gathering but also cultivating some plants seasonally, until villages with effective agriculture began to appear, it was originally thought, between 2500 and 1500 BC. The earliest ceramic-making in the western hemisphere was thought to have come from what is now Colombia and Ecuador, around 4000 BC, but fragments of painted pottery were found near Santarém, Brazil, in 1991, dating from 6000-5000 BC.

Northwest Argentina

Argentina has a rich history of pre-Hispanic indigenous civilizations, with the most important archaeological sites situated in the northwest and west areas of the most highly developed cultures south of the central Andes. Along a migratory path which followed the Andes, this region became a meeting place for established settlers from northern Chile, the central Andes, the Chaco and the hunter-gatherers of the south. Cave paintings and petroglyphs engraved on rocks remain from 13,000 to 10,000 years ago, made by cave dwellers who lived by hunting vizcacha, guanaco, vicuña and birds, some painted with pigments derived from minerals mixed with gesso. Their lines, dots and geometrical forms belong to a symbolic system impossible to interpret today. The extraordinary quantity of handprints visible in the Cueva de las Manos in Patagonia were made as long ago as 10,000 years, and again, their purpose and origin remains a mystery.

By about 1000 to 500 BC, the nomadic groups had grown in size and were too large to subsist on hunting alone. So they started early attempts at agriculture, growing potatoes and maize, among other staples. A mummy found from this period (displayed in Cachi's archaeological museum) with a few artefacts and belongings suggests that these peoples had a developed system of beliefs. By 2000 years ago, small communities had started to gather on the alluvial plains, living on agriculture and herding llamas. In many of the area's museums, you'll see large grinding stones made of granite used to grind maize, as well as arrowheads and pipes used for smoking tobacco. Weaving began around this time, and there are some fine fabrics found at Santa Rosa Tastil.

There were three distinct periods in the cultural development of the northwest. The Early Period (500 BC to AD 650) witnessed the beginnings of agriculture, as well as pottery and metalworking, with the remains of terraces near Humahuaca in Jujuy. The Middle Period (AD 650-850) was marked by the influence of the great culture of Tiahuanaco in present-day Bolivia. Fine metal objects, some of them of gold and silver, were made and new plant varieties were introduced. You'll find stone vessels, anthropomorphic clay pieces, and ornate ceramics from this period all over the Northwest.

In the Later Period (AD 850-1480), known as the Period of Regional Development, small groups of settlers formed communities with individual dwellings, usually based on circular stone walls, next to water sources. Both ritual and functional ceramics were made by people known as the Santamariana or Diaguita culture. Although there was no system of writing, their language, Kakán, survived until the Inca invasion in the late 15th century. These cultures made large, beautifully painted funerary urns, thought to bury the bones of children, since the infant mortality rate was high. The predominant religious beliefs centred on worship of the mother earth goddess, the Pachamama, and she's still worshipped in rural communities all over the Northwest today, with lively festivals on 1 August.

The Incas first arrived in the Calchaquíes valleys area between 1410 and 1430, incorporating the area into the part of their empire known as Kollasuyo. They built two parallel roads along the length of the Andes and along the Pacific shore: busy trade routes linking their communities with the rest of the Inca Empire. The Incas made Quechua the official language, punished the chiefs of any groups whose members transgressed, and absorbed the local cult of the earth goddess Pachamama into their own system of worship of the sun. The Incas also brought with them their own sacrificial burial customs. The bodies of three children found at the summit of Cerro Llullaillaco on the Salta/Chile border indicate young humans were killed as offerings. These three, aged between four and 13, were taken to the summit, dressed in special garments, adorned with feather headdresses and jewellery, and put to sleep forever. Latest evidence suggests that they were given alcohol and drugs for a long period before their sacrifice. It's thought that they were offered as a sacrifice to the gods in the belief that to gain life, life has also to be sacrificed. It's also possible that their death sealed some kind of political alliance between the Inca and the chief of a new colony. The teenager's peaceful face shows no sign of distress so it's likely that she died painlessly within minutes. The fate of the younger girl and boy is less clear, but it appears that they were not as well treated. Salta's MAAM museum (see page 273) has a fascinating display of photographs and an extraordinary array of the artefacts buried with the children. The Calchaquíes valleys were the site of bloody battles when the Spanish attempted to dominate in the 16th century and many indigenous groups were wiped out, but fortunately, in the northwest of Argentina, there are living descendants from many of the original inhabitants, keeping their customs and beliefs alive.

Central and southern Argentina

The Comechingones, who inhabited what are now the provinces of Córdoba and San Luis, lived in settlements of pit-dwellings and used irrigation to produce a range of crops. In the far northeast on the eastern edge of the Chaco were the Guaraní; organized into loose confederations, they lived in rudimentary villages and practised slash-and-burn agriculture to grow maize, sweet potatoes, manioc and beans. They also produced textiles and ceramics.

Further south, the Pampas and Patagonia were much more sparsely populated than the northwest and most groups were nomadic long after the arrival of the Spanish. One of the most important groups were the Querandí, who eked out a living by hunting guanaco and rheas with *boleadoras*, three balls of stone tied with thong and hurled at the legs of a running animal. Patagonia was inhabited by scattered nomadic groups, including the Pampa, the Chonik and the Kaingang, who managed to avoid contact with white settlers until the 19th century. In the steppes of Patagonia, the Tehuelche and Puelche lived as nomadic hunters living off guanaco, foxes and game. In the far south, in southern Patagonia and Tierra del Fuego, there were four indigenous groups: the land-based Selk'nam (or Ona) and Haush (Manekenk), who hunted foxes and guanaco, wearing their hides and constructing temporary dwellings of branches covered loosely with skins; and the sea-based Yáman (Yaghan) and Alacaluf (Kaweskar), who made canoes, paddles, bailers and mooring rope, catching fish with spears or by hand, though seals were their main source of food. These peoples survived until the late 19th century and were befriended and protected by the son of Tierra del Fuego's first settler and missionary. Lucas Bridges' account in the book *Uttermost Part of the Earth* gives an extraordinary insight into the customs and hunting practices of the Selk'nam/Ona and Yámana. Within 50 years of the arrival of white sheep-farmers, many had been shot or coerced into religious missions where they could be controlled. President Roca's genocidal Conquest of the Wilderness (1879-1880) exterminated any indigenous tribes who resisted the influence of the new settlers in the Pampas and Patagonia. Today no single descendant remains of these tribes, which is why you may see that every statue of Roca is permanently disfigured and has graffiti.

European exploration and settlement

At the time of the arrival of the first Europeans, the land that is now Argentina was sparsely populated with about two-thirds of the indigenous population living in the northwest. European exploration began in the Río de la Plata estuary when in 1516 Juan de Solís, a Portuguese navigator employed by the Spanish crown, landed on the shore – though his men were soon killed by indigenous Querandí. Four years later he was followed by Fernão de Magalhães (Ferdinand Magellan) who explored the Río de la Plata, before turning south to make his way into the Pacific via the straits north of Tierra del Fuego, now named after him. In 1527 both Sebastián Cabot and his rival Diego García sailed into the estuary and up the Río Paraná and the Río Paraguay. Cabot founded a small fort, Sancti Spiritus, not far from the modern city of Rosario, but it was wiped out by indigenous inhabitants about two years later. Despite these difficulties Cabot took back to Spain stories of a great Indian kingdom beyond the Plata estuary, rich in precious metals, giving the Río de la Plata its misleading name: a translation would be 'river of silver'. A Portuguese expedition to the estuary, led by Affonso de Souza, returned with similar tales, and this led to a race between the two Iberian powers. In 1535, Pedro de Mendoza set out with 16 ships and a well-equipped force of 1600 men and founded a settlement at Buenos Aires (actually he settled closer to San Isidro along the coast), which he gave its present name, originally Puerto Nuestra Señora Santa María de Buen Ayre. The indigenous inhabitants soon made life too difficult; the settlement was abandoned and Mendoza returned home, but not before sending Juan de Ayolas with a small force up the Río Paraná in search of the Indian kingdom. In 1537 this force founded Asunción, in Paraguay, where the locals were friendly.

After 1535 the attention of the Spanish crown switched to Peru, where Pizarro was engaged in the successful conquest of the Inca Empire, where there was instant wealth in gold and silver and a malleable workforce in the enormous indigenous population. The small settlement at Asunción remained an isolated outpost until 1573, when a force from there travelled south to establish the city of Santa Fe. Seven years later Juan de Garay refounded Buenos Aires (the city's first ever street bears his name, it is in San Telmo), but it was only under his successor, Hernando Arias de Saavedra (1592-1614), that the new settlement became secure, benefiting both from back-up in Asunción and from the many cattle brought over by Mendoza which had increased and multiplied meanwhile.

However, before the time of Mendoza's expedition to the Plata estuary, Spanish expeditions were already exploring northern parts of present-day Argentina. In 1535 Diego de Almagro led a party from Peru, which crossed northwest into Argentina, and in 1543 the Spanish Viceroyalty of Peru was made administrative capital of southern South America. There was greatly increased motivation for exploring the region, however, when silver deposits were found in Potosí (now in Bolivia), and the Governorship of Tucumán was set up as an administrative centre as a halfway point between Bolivia and the port of Buenos Aires. Explorations set forth from Chile and Peru to find trade routes and a source of cheap labour to work the mines, and so the oldest towns in Argentina were founded: Santiago del Estero (1553), Mendoza (1561), San Juan (1562), Córdoba (1573), Salta (1582), La Rioja (1591), and Jujuy (1593). A total of 25 cities were founded in present-day Argentina in the 16th century, 15 of which survived, at a time when the total Spanish population was under 2000.

Colonial rule

Throughout the colonial period the Argentine territories were an outlying part of the Spanish Empire and of minor importance since Spanish colonial settlement and government was based in Peru, busy exploiting the vast mineral wealth of Potosí in Alto Perú (and large supplies of forced indigenous labour). Argentine lands offered only sparse population and little mineral wealth by comparison. Also, the nomadic nature of many indigenous groups made any attempt at control difficult, whereas in Peru, Spanish rule was more readily superimposed on the centralized administration of the defeated Incas.

Buenos Aires failed to become an important port because apart from the fact that the port wasn't deep enough to welcome large ships, from 1543 all the Spanish territories in South America were governed from Lima, the Vice-Regal capital, and trade with Spain was routed via Lima, Panama and the Caribbean. Trading through Buenos Aires was prohibited. However, the Paraná delta north of the city near Tigre provided ample opportunity for smuggling British and Portuguese goods into the city, and it rapidly expanded as a centre for contraband. By 1776 the city's population was 24,000, double the size of any of the cities of the interior. However, the Governorship of Tucumán was more important as a centre, due to the success of the *encomienda* system, in which lands belonging to indigenous peoples were seized and redistributed to Spanish settlers. The idea was that the *encomenderos* in charge would exchange work done for religious education, but in reality the majority of these men were ruthless exploiters of slave labour and offered little in the way of spiritual enlightenment or even food. In the Valles Calchaquíes the substantial indigenous population resisted conversion by Jesuit missionaries, and was effectively almost wiped out when they rose up against the Spanish landowners. Settlers in the northeast of the country also had their conflicts with the indigenous population. The Pampas and Buenos Aires province were dangerous areas for white settlement, since in these lands wild cattle had long been hunted for their hides by Tehuelches and Mapuches. They drove cattle to Chile over the Andes for trade, and their violent armies, or *malones,* clashed regularly with newly arrived settlers. Around the early 18th century, the figure of the gaucho emerged, nomadic men of mixed *criollo* (early Argentine settlers) and indigenous origin, who roamed free on horseback, living off cattle. Once the Argentine state started to control land boundaries, these characters became emblematic of freedom and were romanticized in important fictional works, *Martín Fierro* and *Don Segundo Sombra.* The gaucho is still a much admired figure all over Argentina today, though less wild and certainly no longer an outcast.

Jesuits came to 'civilize' the indigenous population under the protection of the Spanish crown in the late 16th century. They quickly set up missions, which employed the reasonably pliant Guaraní residents of the upper Paraná in highly organized societies, with a militant component, equipped to resist the frequent raids by Portuguese in search of slaves. The Guaraní were compelled to comply with their educators since this exempted them from working in the silver mines, and as many as 4000 Guaraní lived in some missions, also producing *yerba mate* and tobacco as successful Jesuit businesses. The Jesuits and their faith were, however, expelled from Argentina by King Charles III of Spain in 1767, as they had grown rich and powerful. The remains of their handsome architecture can be admired in Córdoba city and province, as well as at San Ignacio Miní and neighbouring sites in Misiones. For more on the Jesuit missions, see box, page 628.

Buenos Aires at last gained some considerable power when the new viceroyalty of the River Plate was created in 1776, with the rapidly growing city as head of the large area and now able to trade with Spain and her other ports. However, as the trade of contraband into the city increased, flooding the market with cheaper European-produced goods, conflict increased between those advocating free trade, such as Manuel Belgrano, and those who wanted to retain a monopoly. The population of Buenos Aires increased enormously with the viceroyalty, along with its economy, as estancias sprang up to farm and export cattle, instead of rounding up the wild beasts, with great success.

BACKGROUND
The Jesuit missions

Jesuits were the religious force that accompanied the Spanish conquest of much of northern Argentina, and though their impact on indigenous culture was far more positive, their rule remains controversial. Were they pioneers of a primitive socialism or merely exploiting the local Guaraní in the name of religious enlightenment?

Between 1609, when they built their first *reducción* or mission, in present-day Brazil, and 1767 when they were expelled by the Spanish King, the Jesuits founded about 50 missions around the upper reaches of the rivers Paraná, Paraguay and Uruguay.

In 1627, they were forced to flee southwards, when their northern missions were attacked by slave-hunting *bandeirantes*. The priests led some 1000 converts down the Parapanema River into the Paraná on 700 rafts, only to find their route blocked by the Guaíra Falls. They pushed on for eight long days through dense virgin forest, built new boats below the falls and continued their journey. Some 725 km from their old homes, they re-established their missions, and trained militias to protect them from further attacks.

The missions prospered on agricultural produce, which raised profits to fund religious teaching. The Guaraní grew traditional crops such as manioc (the local root vegetable), sweet potatoes and maize, plants imported from Europe, such as wheat and oranges, and they also kept horses and herds of cattle and sheep. The missions became major producers of *yerba mate* (see page 36), favoured by the Jesuits as an alternative to alcohol. Apart from common lands the Guaraní also farmed their own individual plots. Due to their growing wealth, they became a powerful force in the Americas and in time they were considered a threat to Spanish rule in the area. The population of the missions grew in size from a population of 28,000 in 1647 to 141,000 in 1732.

The decision by Carlos III to expel the Jesuits from South America in 1767 was made under the conditions of highest secrecy: sealed orders were sent out to the colonies with strict instructions that they should not be opened in advance. On the appointed date, over 2000 members of the order were removed by force and put on ships for Italy. Jesuit property was auctioned, schools and colleges were taken over by the Franciscans and Dominicans, and many missions fell into disuse, or were destroyed.

The Jesuits had attracted many enemies since their wealth and economic power angered landowners and traders, and their control over the Guaraní irritated farmers short of labour. Rumours circulated that the missions contained mines and hordes of precious metals, which gold diggers still look for today. In fact, when building the new bridge just outside of San Ignacio government workers found 60 kg of Jesuit gold! The Jesuits may have exploited their manpower of the Guaraní, but they certainly defended the Guaraní from enslavement by the Spanish and Portuguese, and many feel their societies were a vanished arcadia.

Only four of the missions retain their former splendour: San Ignacio Miní in Argentina, Jesús and Trinidad in Paraguay, and São Miguel in Brazil. The first three can be visited with ease from San Ignacio, along with several others, including Santa Ana and Loreto, which are a short bus ride away.

The Wars of Independence

The drive for independence in Argentina was partly a response to events in Europe, where Spain was initially allied to Napoleonic France. In 1806 and 1807 the British, at war with Napoleon and attracted by what they thought were revolutionary tensions in Buenos Aires, made two attempts to seize the city but were defeated. In 1808 Napoleon invaded Spain, deposing King Ferdinand VII, and provoking widespread resistance from Spanish guerrilla armies. Throughout Spanish America the colonial elites debated where their loyalties lay: with Napoleon's brother Joseph, now officially king; with Ferdinand, now in a French prison; with the Viceroy; or with the Spanish resistance parliament in Cadiz.

On 25 May 1810, the *cabildo* of Buenos Aires deposed the viceroy and established a *junta* to govern on behalf of King Ferdinand VII, when the city's people gathered in front of the *cabildo* (which you can still see today) wearing pale blue and white ribbons, soon to become the colours of the Argentine flag. This move provoked resistance in outlying areas of the viceroyalty, Paraguay, Uruguay and Upper Peru (Bolivia) breaking away from the rule of Buenos Aires. Factional rivalry within the junta between supporters of independence and their opponents added to the confusion and instability. Six years later in July 1816, when Buenos Aires was threatened by invasion from Peru and blockaded by a Spanish fleet in the Río de la Plata, a national congress held at Tucumán declared independence. The declaration was given reality by the genius and devotion of José de San Martín, who boldly marched an Argentine army across the Andes to free Chile, and embarked his forces for Peru, where he captured Lima, the first step towards liberation. San Martín was aided by an extraordinary feat from a local *caudillo* in the north, Martín Miguel de Güemes, whose army of gauchos was later to liberate Salta. *Caudillos* were local warlords who governed areas far larger than today's provinces, organizing their own armies of local indigenous groups and gauchos. The *caudillos* did not recognize the Tucumán declaration, but so it was on 9 July 1816 that the United Provinces of the River Plate came into being.

Since independence

The 19th century

Much of the current rift between Buenos Aires and the rest of Argentina has its roots in a long-standing conflict, which emerged in the early 19th century. The achievement of independence brought neither stability nor unity, since the new junta was divided between Federalists and Unitarists, a conflict that was to rage for over 40 years. The Unitarists, found mainly in the city of Buenos Aires, advocated strong central government, free trade, education and white immigration, looking to Europe for their inspiration. The Federalists, backed by the provincial elites and many of the great *estancieros* of Buenos Aires province, resisted, defending local autonomy and traditional values. Behind the struggle were also economic interests: Buenos Aires and the coastal areas benefited from trade with Europe; the interior provinces did not. As the conflict raged, the territory, known officially as the United Provinces of the Río de la Plata, had none of the features of a modern state: there was no central government, nor an army, capital city or constitution.

Order, of a sort, was established after 1829 by Juan Manuel de Rosas, a powerful *caudillo* and governor of Buenos Aires. In 1833, he attempted to gain widespread support from local *caudillos* with his Campaign of the Desert, which claimed vast areas of land from indigenous groups, granted to Rosas' allies. However, his overthrow in 1852 unleashed another round of battles between Unitarists and Federalists and between

Buenos Aires and the provinces. In 1853 a constitution establishing a federal system of government was finally drafted but the Buenos Aires province refused to join the new Argentine Confederation, which had its capital at Paraná, and set up its own separate republic. Conflict between the two states erupted over the attempt by Buenos Aires to control and tax commerce on the Río Paraná but the victory of Buenos Aires at Pavón (1861) opened the way to a solution: the city became the seat of the federal government. Bartolomé Mitre, former governor of Buenos Aires became the first president of Argentina. There was another political flare-up of the old quarrel in 1880, ending in the humiliation of the city of Buenos Aires, which was separated from its province and made into a special federal territory.

Although there was resistance to the new constitution from some of the western provinces, the institutions of a modern state were created in the two decades after 1861 by Mitre's important period of government. He set up a national bank, bureaucracy, a postal service and an army. The building of railways across the Pampas did most to create national unity, breaking the power of the *caudillos* by enabling the federal government to send in troops quickly. The new army was quickly employed to defeat Francisco Solano López of Paraguay in the War of the Triple Alliance (1865-1870). They were used again in President Roca's genocidal Conquest of the Wilderness (1879-1880), which exterminated the indigenous tribes of the Pampas and Patagonia.

In the last quarter of the 19th century Argentina was transformed: the newly acquired stability encouraged foreign investment; the Pampas were fenced, ploughed up and turned over to commercial export agriculture; railways and port facilities were built. The presidency of Domingo Sarmiento had been keen on widespread immigration from Europe, which transformed the character of Buenos Aires and other cities around the Plata estuary, where the population grew from 200,000 in 1870 to two million in 1920. Sarmiento also sought to Europeanize the country, and his impressive educational policy included the importing of teachers from North America. Political power, however, remained in the hands of a small group of large landowners, who had been granted territories after the Conquest of the Desert, and their urban allies. Few Argentines had the vote, and the opposition Unión Cívica Radical, excluded from power, conspired with dissidents in the army in attempts to overthrow the government.

The 20th century

As the British-built railways stretched across the country, the sheep industry flourished, making Argentina's fortune through exporting both wool and meat. Refrigerator ships were invented in the 1870s, enabling meat to be shipped in bulk to the expanding industrial countries of Britain and Europe. One of the landmarks of modern Argentine history was the 1912 Sáenz Peña law, which established universal manhood suffrage, since until then power had been centralized in the hands of the elite, with no votes for the working classes. Sáenz Peña, president between 1910 and 1916, sought to bring the middle and working classes into politics, gambling that the Conservatives could reorganize themselves and attract their votes. The gamble failed: the Conservatives failed to gain a mass following and the Radicals came to power. The Unión Cívica Radical was created in 1890, but Radical presidents Hipólito Yrigoyen (1916-1922 and 1928-1930) and Marcelo T de Alvear (1922-1928) found themselves trapped between the demands of an increasingly militant urban labour movement and the opposition of the Conservatives, still powerful in the provinces and with allies in the armed forces. Through the 1920s, Argentina was the 'breadbasket of the world' and its sixth richest nation.

Fifty years later, the country had become practically Third World, a fall from grace that still haunts the Argentine consciousness. The world depression following the Wall Street Crash of 1929 devastated export markets, but the military coup that overthrew Yrigoyen in 1930 was a significant turning point: the armed forces returned to government for the first time in over 50 years and were to continue to play a major political role until 1983. Through the 1930s a series of military backed governments, dominated by the Conservatives, held power. The Radicals were outlawed and elections were so fraudulent that frequently more people voted than were on the register. Yet the armed forces themselves were disunited: while most officers supported the Conservatives and the landholding elites, a minority of ultra-nationalist officers, inspired by developments in Europe, supported industrialization and the creation of a one-party dictatorship along Fascist lines. The outbreak of war in Europe increased these tensions and a series of military coups in 1943-1944 led to the rise of Colonel Juan Domingo Perón. When the military allowed a return to civilian rule in 1946, Perón swept into power winning the presidential elections. His government is chiefly remembered by many Argentines for improving the living conditions of the workers through the introduction of paid holidays and welfare measures in his *justicialismo:* social justice. Perón was an authoritarian and charismatic leader, and especially in its early years the government was strongly nationalistic, taking control over the British-owned railways in 1948 by buying them back at a staggering £150 million. Opposition parties were harassed and independent newspapers taken over since Perón wasn't at all interested in free press. Perón is also well known for his famous second-wife, Eva (Evita) Perón, who became the darling of the country, helping her husband's popularity no-end. Although Perón was easily re-elected in 1951, his government soon ran into trouble when economic problems led to the introduction of a wage freeze, which upset the labour unions which were the heart of Peronist support. The early and tragic death of Evita in 1952 was another blow; and a dispute with the church in 1954-1955 also added to Perón's problems. In September 1955 a military coup unseated Perón who went into exile, in Paraguay, Panama, Venezuela, the Dominican Republic and, from 1961 to 1973, in Spain.

Perón's legacy dominated Argentina for the next two decades. No attempt was made to destroy his social and economic reforms but the armed forces determined to exclude the Peronists from power. Argentine society was bitterly divided between Peronists and anti-Peronists and the economy struggled, partly as a result of Perón's measures against the economic elite and in favour of the workers. Between 1955 and 1966 there was an uneasy alternation of military and civilian regimes. The military officers who seized power in 1966 announced their intention to carry out a Nationalist Revolution, with austerity measures to try to gain control of a spiralling economy, but they were quickly discredited by a deteriorating economic situation. The Cordobazo, a left-wing student and workers uprising in Córdoba in 1969, was followed by the emergence of several guerrilla groups such as the Montoneros and the People's Revolutionary Army (ERP), as well as the growth of political violence. As Argentina became more ungovernable, Perón, from his exile, refused to denounce those guerrilla groups, which called themselves Peronist.

In 1971 General Alejandro Lanusse seized power, promising a return to civilian rule and calculating that the only way to control the situation was to allow Perón to return. When the military bowed out in 1973, elections were won by the Peronist candidate, Hector Campora. Perón returned from exile in Madrid to resume as president in October 1973, but died on 1 July 1974, leaving the presidency to his widow, Vice-President María Estela Martínez de Perón, his third wife, known as 'Isabelita'. Perón's death unleashed

BACKGROUND
Dirty War

The 'Dirty War', unleashed by the armed forces after 1976, is one of the most violent incidents in modern South American history, and hardly a month goes by without this grim episode provoking further controversy in the Argentine press.

Guerrilla groups started emerging in Argentina after 1969, in angry response to military rule, among them the Monteneros and the People's Revolutionary Army (Ejército Revolucionario del Pueblo or ERP). The middle-class educated Monteneros, inspired by a mixture of Peronism, Catholicism and Marxism, proclaimed allegiance to the exiled Perón, and wanted to liberate the working classes from the evils of capitalism. The ERP, by contrast drawing their inspiration from Trotsky and Ernesto Guevara, argued that political violence would push the military government towards increased repression which would ignite working-class opposition and lead to civil war and socialist revolution.

If Peronists and non-Peronists disagreed over their aims, their methods were similar: kidnappings and bank robberies raised money and gained publicity; army and police officers were assassinated along with right-wing Peronists; and wealthy Argentine families and multinational companies were forced to distribute food and other goods to the poor to obtain the release of kidnap victims. Head of the Argentine military, General Jorge Videla retaliated by quashing any uprising before it had a chance to establish: pop concerts were banned, as was any gathering of the young. Far more terrifying, Videla initiated a plan called The Process of National Reorganization, El Proceso. The military carried out their own kidnappings of anyone they deemed likely to be dangerous. Anyone with left-wing tendencies might be taken without warning, tortured in one of over 340 detention centres, and then,

chaos: hyperinflation, resumed guerrilla warfare and the operation of right-wing death squads who abducted people suspected of left-wing sympathies. In March 1976, to nobody's surprise, the military overthrew Isabelita and replaced her with a junta led by General Jorge Videla.

The new government closed Congress, outlawed political parties, placed trade unions and universities under military control and unleashed the so-called 'Dirty War', a brutal assault on the guerrilla groups and anyone else who manifested opposition. The military leaders were not at all interested in trying to convict those they suspected of being dissidents. They started a campaign of violence against anyone remotely troublesome as well as anyone Jewish or Marxist, and journalists, intellectuals, psychologists and anyone, according to President General Videla, who was 'spreading ideas contrary to Western Christian civilization'. As many as 30,000 people are thought to have 'disappeared' during this period, removed by violent squads who would take them to clandestine detention centres to be raped, tortured or brutally killed. This is one of Argentina's bleakest memories. In order that the disappeared should never be forgotten, the Madres de la Plaza de Mayo still parade around the plaza in Buenos Aires with photographs of their lost children pinned to their chests (see box, above) looking for answers.

Videla's nominated successor, General Roberto Viola, took over for three years in March 1981 but was overthrown by General Leopoldo Galtieri in December 1981, who mysteriously, 'disappeared'. All three armed services operated their own death squads and camps in a campaign of indiscriminate violence. By 1978-1979 both the ERP and the Monteneros had ceased to function, and in the process, tens of thousands of people disappeared: although an official report produced after the return to civilian rule put their number at 8960, some 15,000 cases have been documented and human rights groups now estimate the total at some 30,000. They are still remembered by the Madres de la Plaza de Mayo (Mothers of the Plaza de Mayo), a human-rights group made up of relatives, who march anti-clockwise around the Plaza de Mayo in central Buenos Aires every Thursday at 1530, with photos of their 'disappeared' loved ones pinned to their chests, demanding information.

On 24 March 2006, the 30th anniversary of the military junta was marked with a national day of awareness and demonstrations in Buenos Aires, suggesting that the scars of the Dirty War have yet to heal. Videla, along with other military leaders, was charged with human rights abuse. After serving only five years in prison, he was pardoned by President Carlos Menem in 1990, but was arrested again in 1998 and transferred to house arrest. In 2010 Videla was sentenced to life imprisonment for the torture and death of 31 dissidents. He and eight other defendants were sentenced to further prison terms in 2012 for the theft of babies from political prisoners. Videla died in May 2013. He was by no means the sole recipient of justice for human rights abuses and crimes, a process which continues to this day. This was evident even in 2016, when, for the Dirty War's 40th anniversary, Argentine President Mauricio Macri led US President Barack Obama on a tour of the Parque de la Memoria (Memory Park), www.parquedelamemoria.org.ar, a Dirty War memorial on the banks of the Río Plata. For more information visit the Madres de Plaza de Mayo organization, Hipólito Yrigoyen 1584, T011-4382 3261, http://madresfundadoras.blogspot.co.uk and www. abuelas.org.ar. For a clear explanation in English, see www.yendor.com/vanished.

failed to keep a grasp on a plummeting economy and an increasingly discontent public. Attempting to win the crowds, Galtieri's decision to invade the Falkland/Malvinas Islands in April 1982 backfired when the British retaliated by sending a fleet to the south Atlantic, subsequently forcing the Argentines to flee. This loss is still felt in every town in Argentina today. There are monuments to the dead and parades every year commemorating the battles. Many Argentines still consider the Malvinas as Argentine property. After the war was lost in June 1982 General Reynaldo Bignone took over, and promptly created a law giving amnesty to all human rights abusers in the military.

Elections in October 1983 were won by Raúl Alfonsín and his Unión Cívica Radical (UCR) and during 1985 Generals Videla, Viola and Galtieri were sentenced to long terms of imprisonment for their parts in the dictatorship. While Alfonsín's government struggled to deal with the legacy of the past, it was overwhelmed by continuing economic problems, the most obvious of which was hyperinflation. Workers rushed to the shops once they'd been paid to spend their earnings before prices rose, and supermarkets announced price increases over the loudspeaker since they were so unstable. When the Radicals were defeated by Carlos Menem, the Peronist (Justicialist) presidential candidate, Alfonsín, stepped down early because of economic instability. Strained relations between the Peronist government and the military led to several rebellions, which Menem attempted to appease by pardoning the imprisoned generals. His popularity among civilians declined,

BACKGROUND
The Falklands/Malvinas conflict

The dispute between Britain and Argentina over the Falkland Islands/Islas Malvinas has a long history. Dutch sailor Sebald de Weert made the first generally acknowledged sighting of the islands in 1598. In 1764, France established a small colony there, while the British built an outpost on the northern tip. But when the French government sold Port Louis to Spain in 1766, the British were expelled. In 1811, following the outbreak of the Wars of Independence, Spain withdrew her forces from the islands. And after British warships expelled a force from Buenos Aires in 1833, the islands came under British rule, an act that has angered Argentines ever since.

Around 100 years, President Juan Perón was quick to exploit the disputed status of the islands as part of an appeal to Argentine nationalism during his first administration (1946-1955). In 1965, the United Nations called on Britain and Argentina to resolve their differences peacefully, and talks took place but were complicated by the hostility of the islanders themselves towards any change in their status.

In 1982, when the British government reduced its forces in the area, the Argentine military regime seized its chance. President General Galtieri had huge economic problems and thought a successful invasion would unite the population behind him. An Argentine force of 5000 men landed in South Georgia on 2 April 1982, quickly overwhelming the small British garrison without loss of life. The British military and civilian authorities were expelled from the Falklands/Malvinas and the islands' inhabitants placed under an Argentine military governor. Though most Latin American states sympathized with Argentina over the sovereignty issue, many were unhappy with the use of force. Backed by a United Nations resolution and the crucial logistical support of the United States, the British government launched a naval force to regain the islands.

but from 1991 to 1992 the economy minister, Domingo Cavallo, succeeded in restoring economic confidence and the government as a whole with his Plan de Convertabilidad. This, the symbol of his stability, was the introduction of a new currency pegged to the United States dollar. The central bank was prevented from printing money that could not be backed up by the cash in reserve. After triumphing in the October 1993 congressional elections at the expense of the UCR, the Peronists themselves lost some ground in the April 1994 elections to a constituent assembly. The party to gain most, especially in Buenos Aires, was Frente Grande, a broad coalition of left-wing groups and disaffected Peronists. Behind the loss of confidence of these dissident Peronists was unrestrained corruption and a pact in December 1993 between Menem and Alfonsín pledging UCR support for constitutional changes, which included re-election of the president for a second term of four years.

By the 1995 elections, the majority of the electorate favoured stability over constitutional concerns and returned President Menem.

In November 1998 Alianza Democrática chose the Radical Fernando de la Rúa as its candidate for the October 1999 presidential election. Moves from Menem supporters to

The British reoccupation of the islands began on 21 May. They met stiff resistance from Argentine defensive positions around Stanley (Puerto Argentino), but most of the Argentine troops were conscripts, poorly trained, ill-equipped and in the end no match for British forces. On 14 June Argentine forces surrendered. Argentines to this day have never forgotten the fierceness of the fighting. One event is particularly sensitive: the sinking of the *General Belgrano*. The Argentine cruiser had apparently drifted accidently into enemy waters and, while retreating, British forces attacked and sank the cruiser with a huge loss of life. It resulted in nearly a third of the deaths of the entire conflict: over 300 personnel, out of total Argentine casualties of 746 and compared with 256 British soldiers.

The consequences of the war for Argentina were that the military government was discredited: perhaps less by defeat than by its obvious misjudgement, and by the accounts given by returning troops of incompetent leadership and lack of supplies. General Galtieri was replaced as president, and in 1983, Argentina returned to civilian rule. It was such a traumatic event in Argentina's recent history that almost every town and village has a monument to the war, and every year in Rosario the war is remembered in a large parade of veterans. In Buenos Aires the Malvinas monument is located at the base of Parque San Martín, almost at Retiro. In 2010, President Cristina Kirchner spoke of reclaiming the Malvinas, even going as far as seeking 'support' from China and other nations. In her second term in office, President Kirchner raised the issue on several occasions, including writing to Prime Minister David Cameron in January 2013, calling on Britain to relinquish the islands. She also asked Pope Francis to mediate in the dispute in March that year. In the same month, the islanders voted in a referendum on whether to stay a British overseas territory. Almost 100% of those eligible to vote chose to remain so.

The political fervour seems to have slightly subsided in recent times. As of 2016, new president Mauricio Macri, while not abandoning claims to sovereignty, has made overtures that Argentina is willing to further open diplomatic relations with Britain regarding the islands and the potential for oil exploration in the area.

put forward Menem for a further (constitutionally dubious) term of office helped delay the Peronist choice of candidate until July 1999 when Eduardo Duhalde received the backing of Menem. Although Alianza Democrática offered little change in economic policy, the Peronists were harmed by the corruption scandals surrounding the Menem administration and the continuing rivalry between Menem and Duhalde, enabling De La Rúa to win the presidency and take office in December 1999.

The 21st century

Facing recession and impossible debts with the IMF, President De La Rúa implemented austerity measures, but these were not enough to save the peso, nor the many jobs which were lost in late 2000. Young people started to leave the country in massive numbers, looking for work elsewhere, taking their savings with them. In an attempt to keep these reserves of cash within the country, De la Rúa started the *corralito* (meaning 'little pen'), a law determining that individuals could only withdraw 250 pesos from their accounts per week, and converting savings to government bonds. People literally lost their savings. In December 2001, the people of Buenos Aires and other large cities took to the streets in an unprecedented display both of violent rioting, and peaceful pot bashing by furious middle-class housewives, the *cacerolazos*. The country went through five presidents in a period of a couple of months, but nothing could prevent devaluation, and in January 2002 the peso lost its parity with the dollar. Suddenly Argentina plummeted from being a first world nation on a par with the United States, to being a third world state, with a weak currency, and little hope of bolstering the economy. Huge numbers of Argentines lost their jobs, and many were forced into poverty and homelessness. The blow to the Argentine psyche has been severe. Duhalde was the last of the quick succession of presidents, and he attempted to impose some order, appeasing the IMF by sacking a large number of public employees who were a considerable drain on public spending. However, corruption remained and street crime increased, with an alarming fashion for express kidnappings of members of the wealthier Buenos Aires families. Elections held in May 2003 threatened to return Menem to power, in a brief rush of nostalgia for the days of apparent prosperity. But fearing defeat, before a second election could be held Menem stepped down, and ex-governor of Santa Cruz province, Néstor Kirchner, came to power with a meagre 24% of the country's votes. He was not much liked throughout the country, particularly by landowners and farmers, since he raised taxes on exports to an absurd degree. While unemployment remained rife in Argentina, many criticized Kirchner for maintaining a dependency on Plan Trabajar, the government handout to the unemployed, which some feared was eroding the culture of work.

By October 2005, Kirchner had gained sufficient popular support to win a substantial majority in mid-term congressional elections. At the same time, the economy recovered from a decline of 11% in 2002 to growth of over 8% between 2003 and 2007. Kirchner decided not to run for the presidency in 2007, but his wife, Cristina Fernández de Kirchner, was nominated as a candidate. Her landslide victory may have indicated a desire for continuity among the electorate, but many people saw the move as a way of extending Néstor's chance of holding on to power. In certain media outlets Cristina was labelled a puppet, offering only a continuation of her husband's presidency. At any rate, she was the first elected female president in Argentina, and she has her own webpage, www.cristina. com.ar. Her first years in office were confrontational. An increase in taxes on agricultural exports, for instance, in order to redistribute income from high soya, wheat and corn prices, led to strikes and blockades which caused food shortages, adding to problems of energy shortages and general price rises. In mid-term elections in June 2009 Fernández de Kirchner's party lost its majorities in both houses of Congress.

By 2011, though, the picture had changed significantly. Néstor Kirchner died of a heart attack in October 2010, but his widow was not prepared to relinquish power. With the opposition fragmented, she won a big majority in presidential elections in October 2011. Her victory was helped greatly by a thriving economy, which was registering growth of just under 10% a year on the back of healthy commodity prices, with high government spending, falling rates of poverty and unemployment, a significant rise in the minimum wage and a consumer boom. Inflation remained a problem, though (10.6% officially in 2013, unofficially put at three times that) while investment from abroad remained low, deterred by the nationalization of key industries. Other economic factors in 2012, such as a fall in GDP growth to 1.9%, began to accentuate the deep polarization of Argentine society, between those who supported the ruling party's policies and those who did not. Many low income and rural workers were in favour, but the middle classes, for example, grew more antagonistic over rising prices, the severe restriction of the sale of dollars at the official exchange rate in order to limit the use of international reserves to pay off national debts, and levels of crime. Government disputes with the media, especially the Clarín group, intensified.

Following the 30th anniversary of the 1982 Falklands/Malvinas conflict, diplomatic relations with the UK were very strained and remained so into 2013, although as of 2016, current President Mauricio Macri has signalled a possible thawing of tensions. Soon after Jorge Bergoglio, former archbishop of Buenos Aires, was elected Pope Francis I in March 2013, President Fernández asked him to mediate in the dispute. Francis, the first Latin American pope, had previously had a difficult relationship with the governments of Fernández de Kirchner and her husband, partly because of his dealings with opposition politicians, but also because of disagreements over policy towards abortion and homosexuality (gay marriage, for instance, was legalized in 2010, but the Pope remains opposed).

Mid-term congressional elections in October 2013 highlighted the divisions as Fernández' Frente para la Victoria (FPV) party struggled to maintain its majority in both houses of congress. In key Buenos Aires province polling, FPV lost to Frente Renovador, a dissident Peronist movement led by Sergio Massa, formerly Fernández' cabinet chief. FPV also lost in five other large voting districts and in Fernández's home province of Santa Cruz. Fernández herself was forced to abandon campaigning in October when she was admitted to hospital for brain surgery, from which she had recovered by the end of the year.

Confidence in the economy continued at a low ebb into 2014. Pressure on the peso from inflation, declining international reserves and savers seeking to buy dollars on the unofficial 'blue market' rather than keep their funds in the national currency, forced a devaluation of 15% in January 2014. Less than a year previously the president had vowed that this would never happen. Likewise, restrictions on buying foreign currency were lifted. In May 2014, the government renegotiated its debt to the Paris Club group of creditor countries, an issue dating back to the 2001-2002 crisis, which should allow the country to raise new loans on international markets.

Ultimately economic uncertainty and its political and social ramifications dominated the final months of Cristina Fernández's presidential term, and when she left office the country was burdened with a 25% inflation rate. On 22 November 2015, the founder of the conservative political party Propuesta Republicana, Mauricio Macri, a wealthy businessman and former president of the Boca Juniors football club, as well as an ex-mayor of Buenos Aires, defeated Néstor Kirchner's former Vice President Daniel Scioli in a run-off election. Despite being the reform candidate and a conservative free market proponent, his election to office (with a narrow 51% of the vote) was more a repudiation of Kirchnerismo than it was any great enthusiasm for Macri. Still, one of his first acts as president was to follow up on a campaign promise, and in December 2015 he lifted the currency controls favoured by Cristina Fernández, allowing the peso to float freely. The move all but eliminated the blue market for dollars, but it also caused an abrupt 30% devaluation of the peso. It also did nothing to curb inflation, which is projected to top 40% by the end of 2016. Whether Macri's particular brand of US-inspired conservatism (he's a graduate of Columbia Business School in New York), is the right countermeasure to the populist Kirchner governments remains to be seen. What is certain is that he has got off to an inauspicious start.

Population
With an estimated population of 43,900,000 (2016), the third largest in South America after Brazil and Colombia, Argentina is one of the least densely populated countries on the continent. Forty five per cent of the population lives in the Federal Capital and Province of Buenos Aires, leaving most of Patagonia, for example, with 2 sq km per inhabitant.

In the province of Buenos Aires, people are mainly of European origin and the classic Argentine background is of Spanish and Italian immigrants. In Patagonia and the Lake District there's a considerable number of Scottish, Welsh, French, German and Swiss inhabitants, with Eastern Europeans to be found in the northeast of the country. In the northwestern provinces, at least half the population are indigenous, or of indigenous descent, mixed with a long line of *criollo* stock. Although *mestizos* (of mixed Spanish and indigenous origin) form about 15% of the population of the whole country, the existence of different ethnic groups wasn't recognized until the mid-1990s. There are 13 indigenous groups, totalling between 300,000 and 500,000 people, many living in communities in the northwest, and scattered throughout the country. The largest minorities are the Toba (20%), the Wichí (10%), the Mapuche (10%) and the Guaraní (10%). Several of the smaller groups are in danger of extinction: in 1987 the Minority Rights Group reported the death of the last Selk'nam/Ona in Tierra del Fuego and noted that the 100 remaining **Tehuelches** were living on a reservation in southern Patagonia.

Immigration

The city of Buenos Aires and the surrounding province was transformed through immigration in the 19th century into a society of predominantly European origin. White immigration was encouraged by the 1853 Constitution and the new political stability after 1862 encouraged a great wave of settlers from Europe. Between 1857 and 1930 total immigration was over 6,000,000, almost all from Europe. About 55% of these were Italians, followed by Spaniards (26%), and then, far behind, groups of other Europeans and Latin Americans. British and North Americans generally came as stockbreeders, technicians and business executives. By 1895, 25% of the population of 4,000,000 were immigrants. Over 1,300,000 Italians settled in Argentina between 1876 and 1914. Their influence can be seen in the country's food, its urban architecture and its language, especially in Buenos Aires where the local vocabulary has incorporated *lunfardo*, a colourful slang of largely Italian origin, which started out as the language of thieves. Today it is estimated that 12.8% of the population are foreign born. The large influence on immigration nowadays comes from Bolivia, Peru and Paraguay.

Culture

Religion

Throughout Spanish America the Catholic Church played an important role in the conquest. From the start of the colonial period, Spanish control in South America was authorized by the Papacy; in return the colonial powers were to support the conversion of the indigenous population to Catholicism. This close identification of Church and state helps to explain why the main centres of Church power and activity were usually (though not always) close to the main centres of Spanish settlement. While present-day Argentina, a border territory on the outskirts of empire, was therefore of relatively minor importance to the Church hierarchy, it became a focus for work by missionary orders, particularly the Jesuits. Jesuit activity in Argentina was centred in two areas: around Córdoba, where they established a training college for the priesthood, and in Misiones and adjoining areas of present-day Paraguay and Brazil, where an extensive network of *reducciones* was set up to convert and 'protect' the indigenous population.

As in much of Spanish America, the Church lost most of its formal political power at independence. Although today over 90% of Argentines are officially Roman Catholics, the Church's political and social influence is much less significant than in neighbouring Chile or in most other South American countries. One reason for this is the introduction of a system of non-religious state schools in the 19th century. The great waves of immigration in the late 19th and early 20th centuries also affected the position of the Church; while the majority of immigrants were Catholics, significant minorities were not, including the large numbers of East European Jews and the Arab immigrants from Lebanon and Syria. Both of these communities have a strong presence especially in Buenos Aires; the largest mosque in South America was opened in the capital in September 2000 and there are estimated to be 800,000 Muslims in the country. Buenos Aires also has the eighth largest Jewish population in the world.

Yet the Catholic Church's power and influence should not be underestimated. The support of the Church hierarchy was important in bringing Perón to power in 1946 and the rift with the Church played a key role in the overthrow of the latter in 1955. The strongly conservative nature of the Catholic hierarchy became particularly apparent during the 1976-1983 military dictatorship; unlike its Chilean counterpart, the Argentine hierarchy was silent on the issue of human-rights violations and gave little support to relatives of the disappeared. According to *Nunca Más*, the official report on the disappeared, military chaplains attended some torture sessions and even assisted in the torture.

The lingering influence of the Church can be seen in several ways: the continuing legal ban on abortion (divorce was finally legalized in 1986; gay marriage in 2010), and in the constitutional provision (removed in the 1994 amendments) that required the president to be a Catholic (and which necessitated President Carlos Menem's conversion).

As in some other parts of Latin America, this close identification of the Catholic Church with the state has, in recent years, provided opportunities for evangelical churches, including the Baptists and Mormons, to recruit followers, particularly among newcomers to the large cities.

Arts and crafts

All over Argentina you'll find fine handicrafts made by local indigenous groups, which vary widely all over the country, or by the continuing tradition of gaucho craftsmen, who make fine pieces associated with rural life.

Gaucho crafts

There's a strong tradition of working precious metals, such as silver, into fine belts and buckles, since the gaucho's way of carrying his wealth with him was originally in the ornate silver *rastras* and buckles which are still used today over leather belts, or to tie *fajas* (woven cloth belts). Silver spurs, stirrups and the fine silver decoration on saddles are all extraordinary examples of traditions dating from the early 18th century. The gaucho *facón*, an all-purpose knife used especially for cutting his *asado*, is made with an elaborately wrought silver handle, and the *mate* (the vessel itself, rather than the drink) which is often just a hollowed out gourd, can also be an exquisitely worked piece of silver which you'd probably rather display than use. Associated objects with the same fine silverwork today include earrings, belt buckles and scarf rings. Leather was always important for making all the items associated with horses, and obviously widely available, and the complexity of the traditional bridles, belts and straps is impressive. Long thin strips of leather are woven into wide plaits, or *trensas*, and used still for all parts of horse bridlery, as well as more decorative pieces. The *mate* itself is made most traditionally from the gourd, but also from wood, tin, llama (a type of material that looks like silver) or silver, with attractive examples made by artisans in the Lake District at El Bolsón, for example.

Indigenous crafts

Argentina's many indigenous groups produce fine handicrafts, and in the northeast, the Guaraní produce woodwork, much of it inspired by the rich animal and bird life all around them. Delicate fabric for bags is woven from the tough fibrous strands of tree creepers, and there are necklaces made from seeds.

Handicrafts are richest in the northwest, particularly the Valles Calchaquíes, near the *puna* and along the Quebrada de Humahuaca, where there is abundant llama wool and vicuña, which is woven into *ponchos*, or knitted into jumpers, socks, scarves and hats. Brightly coloured woven textiles from Bolivia can also be found at many markets. The ubiquitous pan pipes are the most available examples of instruments from the rich Andean musical tradition, and can be found in abundance at Tilcara and Purmamarca markets. Ponchos are woven throughout the northwest but particularly fine examples can be found in the Valles Calchaquíes and around Salta, where the red ponchos of Güemes are made, and in western Catamarca province, where the finest ponchos of woven vicuña are made. You can also find beautiful woven wall hangings in the Valles Calchaquíes, often depicting scenes of churches in the valleys, and the local symbol, the ostrich-like *suri*. Wood from the giant *cardón* cactus is used for carving distinctive small objects and furniture, with the spines of the cactus leaving attractive slits in the wood.

In the Chaco region, bags are made from textile woven from *chaguar* fibre by Wichí, Toba, and other indigenous groups of the area, as they have done for hundreds of years. The Wichí also make fine wooden objects, animals mainly, from *palo santo*, a greenish scented wood, also used extensively in wood carving by communities that live along the Río Pilcomayo, which forms the border with Paraguay. In northeastern Salta, painted wooden masks are made by the Chané culture for use in traditional agricultural ceremonies. Isolated indigenous groups of Toba, Chané and Mataco in the lowlands to the east of the province produce exquisite carvings of birds and animals, using a variety of local woods. Cow bones are used to make the beaks and feet, as well as an inlay to decorate spoons and other utilitarian items. And *palo santo* is also used for *mate* vessels, replacing the traditional gourd. Throughout the south, there are superb Mapuche weavings in natural wool colours with bold geometric designs.

Fine art and sculpture

Colonial art

Argentina (along with neighbouring Uruguay) is arguably the most European of Latin American cultures. Mass immigration and the 19th-century extermination of the few remaining indigenous people have created a mainstream culture, which defines itself largely in relation to Europe. The exception to this is in the northwest of the country, where Andean civilizations struggle to retain their identity against the irresistible tide of westernization and the tourist industry.

As the region, which is now Argentina, was initially of little importance to the Spanish, there is relatively little colonial art or architecture in most of the country. However, in the northern regions of Salta, Jujuy and Misiones, there are some impressive colonial buildings and some good examples of colonial painting, especially the remarkable portraits of archangels in military uniform in the churches at Uquía and Casabindo, as well as some exquisite golden retables and pulpits in the churches of the Quebrada de Humahuaca. Yavi, at the very north, is the most remarkable of all these, with a golden sculpture of an angel in military uniform, and beautiful ceramic cherubs on the golden pulpit. Fine colonial art can be seen at the Museo de Arte Hispanoamericano Isaac Fernández Blanco in Buenos Aires. In Misiones, there are several sites with remains of Jesuits missions – particularly impressive is that at San Ignacio. Córdoba province too has remains of Jesuit churches and residences at Santa Catalina and Jesús María.

The 19th century

In the 19th century, as Argentina gained independence and consolidated itself as a modern nation, the ruling elite of the country were determined to make Argentine culture as close to European as possible, against what they saw as the 'barbarism' of indigenous customs. The prosperous Buenos Aires bourgeoisie commissioned European architects to build their mansions and collected European fine and decorative arts to decorate them. Rich Argentines travelled to Europe to buy paintings, and gradually began to demand that European painters come to Argentina to depict the wealth and elegance of the ruling class through portraits and landscapes. The most famous foreign artist was Carlos Enrique Pellegrini, whose fine society portraits can be seen in the Museo Nacional de Bellas Artes in Buenos Aires.

By the middle of the century, as Argentina became more politically stable, a new generation of Argentine-trained artists appeared in Buenos Aires. They absorbed some of the techniques and interests of the European artists who were the first to depict their country, but they also discovered a new interest in Romanticism and Realism. Most famous in this period was Prilidiano Pueyrredón (1823-1870), whom many Argentines consider to be their first national painter. Of more obvious appeal is the rather eccentric Cándido López (1839-1902) whose work has only recently been re-evaluated. López followed the Argentine army to the north of the country during the wars with Paraguay and Uruguay, where he depicted the great battles in a characteristic naïve style. López left behind a remarkable series of paintings, which are often displayed in the Museo Nacional de Bellas Artes in Buenos Aires. By the end of the century, many artists who had been through the National Art School were working in Argentina. Generally speaking, they absorbed European movements decades after they appeared in their original forms. Benito Quinquela Martín's work celebrated the workers in the dockyards of La Boca, in a colourful naïve style, and his paintings can be seen in the gallery bearing his name in La Boca.

The 20th century to the present

In the 20th century, Argentina really found its artistic expression; the dynamism, size and mix of nationalities in the capital created a complex urban society in which artists and intellectuals have prospered. Some of the Bohemian attraction of Buenos Aires can still be felt in its more intellectual cafés and districts. This cultural effervescence has been at the expense of the regions; the capital totally dominates the country, and most artists are forced to move there to have any chance of success.

The first avant-garde artistic movement in Buenos Aires emerged in 1924 with the formation of a group which called itself 'Martín Fierro', in homage to the national epic poem of the same name. This group brought together a small number of upper-class intellectuals, the most famous of which was the writer Jorge Luis Borges. The most important visual artist was Xul Solar (1887-1963), who illustrated many of Borges' texts. Solar was one of the 20th century's most eccentric and engaging artists. He had a great interest in mysticism and the occult, and tried to create an artistic system to express his complex beliefs, mostly small-scale watercolours in which a sometimes-bizarre visionary world is depicted. Many of them are covered in inscriptions in one of the languages he himself created: Neo-Creole or Pan-Lengua. During the final decades of his life Solar lived in a house on the Paraná Delta near Tigre, where he created a total environment in accordance with his fantastic world, even inventing a new game of chess with rules based on astrology. There is now a Xul Solar Museum in the house where he was born in Buenos Aires and where many of his watercolours and objects are displayed.

Intellectual life in the 1920s was divided into two factions, each named after districts in the city. The elegant Calle Florida gave its name to the Martín Fierro set, which belonged to the elite. Several blocks away, the working-class Boedo district gave its name to a school of working-class socialist artists who rejected the rarefied atmosphere of Florida in favour of socially critical paintings in a grim realistic style. Possibly the most important artist associated with this group was Antonio Berni (1905-1981), whose colourful paintings give a vivid impression of Buenos Aires working-class life, and are in the Museo de Bellas Artes and MALBA in Buenos Aires.

In the 1940s, with the political crisis provoked by the Second World War, a new avant-garde movement emerged to overtake the Martín Fierro group. In the mid-1940s, a group of young artists founded an abstract art movement called 'Madí' which attempted to combine sophisticated abstract art inspired by Russian Constructivism with a more chaotic sense of fun. Madí works are characterized by blocks of bright colours within an irregular frame often incorporating physical movement within the structure of the work. As such, they are somewhere between painting and sculpture. For the first time in Argentina, Madí developed artistic principles (such as the irregular frame, or the use of neon gas) before the rest of the world.

Madí was a short-lived adventure plagued by infighting amongst its members and political divisions. The cultural climate under Perón (1946-1955) rejected this type of 'decadent' art in favour of a form of watered-down populism. It was not until the 1960s that cultural life regained its momentum.

The 1960s were a golden age for the arts in Argentina. As in many countries, the decade brought new freedom to young people, and the art scene responded vigorously. Artistic activity was focused around the centre of Buenos Aires between Plaza San Martín and Avenida Córdoba, an area known as the 'manzana loca' (crazy block). This area contained a huge number of galleries and cafés, and most importantly the Di Tella Institute, a privately funded art centre that was at the cutting edge of visual arts. Artistic movements of the time ranged from a raw expressionism called 'Nueva Figuración' to very sophisticated conceptual art. The most provocative form of art during this period took the form of 'happenings', one of the most famous of which (by Marta Minujín) consisted of a replica of the Buenos Aires obelisk made in sweet bread, which was then eaten by passers-by.

After the military coup of 1966 the authorities began to question the activities of these young artists and even tried to censor some exhibitions. The Di Tella Institute closed, leaving the 'manzana loca' without a heart, and making it more dangerous for alternative young artists to live without harassment (often for little more than having long hair). During the 'leaden years' of the military government during the 1970s, there was little space for alternative art and many left-wing artists abandoned art in favour of direct political action. However, one space in Buenos Aires continued to show politically challenging art: the Centro de Arte y Comunicación (or CAYC), often through works that were so heavily coded that the authorities would not pick up the message.

Since the restoration of democracy in 1983, Argentina has been coming to terms with the destruction or inefficiency of many of its cultural institutions over recent decades. The last few years have seen a rebirth of activity, with improvements in the National Museum of Fine Arts and the creation of the important Centro Cultural Recoleta and more recently the Centro Cultural Jorge Luis Borges and many others. There are important alternative art centres, especially the Ricardo Rojas Centre and the Klemm Foundation, which show some of the most interesting young artists. The art scene in Buenos Aires is very vibrant, with myriad conflicting and apparently contradictory styles and tendencies. For information on exhibitions and local artists see www.arteba.org, an art fair with information on artists and galleries (in English) and www.wanderarti.com, a global travel/art site with information on Buenos Aires galleries (in English).

Literature

Modern Argentina has an extremely high literacy rate, around 98%, and even in small country towns there are good bookshops, and some really splendid librerías in Buenos Aires. Correspondingly, the country has produced some great writers, quite apart from the wonderful Borges, and it is well worth reading some of their work before you come, or seeking out a few novels to bring on your travels.

With an urban culture derived almost entirely from European immigrants, Argentina's literary development was heavily influenced by European writers in the 19th century, the works of Smith, Locke, Voltaire and Rousseau among others being inspiration for the small literate elite of young intellectuals, such as Mariano Moreno (1778-1811), one of the architects of the independence movement. The great theme was how to adapt European forms to American realities, first in the form of political tracts and later in early nationalist poetry. Outside the cities, popular culture thrived on storytelling and the music of the gauchos, whose famous payadores are superbly evocative. They recount lively and dramatic stories of love, death and the land, in poetic couplets to a musical background, with an ornate and inventive use of words (see Music, below). Gaucho poets, like medieval *troubadours*, would travel from settlement to settlement, to country fairs and cattle round-ups, singing of the events of the day and of the encroaching political constraints that would soon bring restrictions to their traditional way of life.

The theme of Argentine identity has been a constant through the country's development and remains a burning issue today. While many writers looked to Europe for inspiration, others were keen to distance themselves from the lands they had come from and to create a new literature, reflecting Argentina's own concerns. The extremes within the country further challenge attempts at creating a single unified identity: the vast stretches of inhospitable and uninhabited land, the vast variety of landscapes and peoples, and the huge concentration of population in a capital that little resembles any other part of the country. These conflicts were clearly expressed in 1845 by politician Domingo Faustino Sarmiento (1811-1888): *Facundo: Civilization and Barbarism*. This was the most important tract of the generation, and became one of the key texts of Argentine cultural history. Strongly opposed to the Federalist Rosas, Sarmiento's allegorical biography of gaucho *Facundo* laments the ungovernably large size of the country which allows *caudillos* like Quiroga and Rosas to dominate. For Sarmiento, the only solution was education and he looked to what he perceived to be the democracy of North America for inspiration.

With the attempt to consolidate the nation state in the aftermath of independence Esteban Echeverría (1805-1851) played a leading role in these debates through literary salons, in poetry and in short fiction. Other memorable protest literature against the Rosas regime included Echeverría's *El Matadero* (The Slaughterhouse, published posthumously in 1871) and José Mármol's melodramatic novel of star-crossed lovers battling against the cut-throat hordes of Rosas, *Amalia* (1855).

The consolidation of Argentina along the lines advocated by Sarmiento and the growth of the export economy in alliance with British capital and technology may have benefited the great landowners of the Littoral provinces. But those who did not fit into this dream of modernity – in particular the gaucho groups turned off the land and forced to work as rural labourers – found their protest articulated by a provincial landowner, José Hernández (1834-1886). He wrote the famous gaucho epic poems *El Gaucho Martín Fierro* (1872) and its sequel, *La Vuelta de Martín Fierro* (The Return of Martín Fierro, 1879). The first part of *Martín Fierro* is most definitely the most famous Argentine literary work and is a genuine shout of rage against the despotic *caudillos* and corrupt authorities, which disrupt local communities and traditional ways of life. Framed as a gauchesque song, chanted by the appealing hero and dispossessed outlaw, it became one of the most popular works of literature, and *Martín Fierro* came to symbolize the spirit of the Argentine nation.

As a small group of families led the great export boom, the 'gentleman' politicians of the 'Generation of 1880' wrote their memoirs, none better than Sarmiento's *Recuerdos de Provincia* (Memoirs of Provincial Life, 1850). As Buenos Aires grew into a dynamic modern city, the gentleman memorialist soon gave way to the professional writer. The key poet in this respect was the Nicaraguan Rubén Darío (1867-1916), who lived for an important period of his creative life in Buenos Aires and led a movement called *modernismo* which asserted the separateness of poetry as a craft, removed from the dictates of national panegyric or political necessity. It was Darío who would give inspiration to the poet Leopoldo Lugones (1874-1938), famous also for his prose writings on nationalist gauchesque themes. Lugones's evocation of the gaucho as a national symbol would be

Jorge Luis Borges

More than any writer, Borges has most vividly captured the spirit of Buenos Aires. Born in the city in 1899, he was obsessed with the myths and realities of Argentina and its culture, and by the wealth of literature from world classics. His entirely original blend of these two different worlds has made him the most influential figure in Argentine literary culture, with a worldwide reputation. In 1914, Borges travelled with his family to live in Switzerland and Spain, where he added Latin, French and German to his already fluent English (he had an English grandmother). He started to write, and became involved with the *Ultraísmo* literary movement, which scorned the mannerism and opulence of *Modernismo* for a style that embraced shocking imagery and free verse, which Borges described as 'avoiding ornamental artefacts'. Borges became an active member of the literary avant garde when he returned to Buenos Aires in 1921, and in the following few years, he contributed regularly to literary magazines, publishing seven books of poetry and essays that established his lifelong obsessions: a view of life from the margins, and a fascination with authorship and individual consciousness.

From 1933, Borges was Literary Editor of the Newspaper *Crítica*, where he published his *Historia Universal de la Infamia* (A Universal History of Infamy) in 1935, establishing a style somewhere between the non-fictional essay and the fictional short story. In the late 1930s he published a series of significant essays and short stories collections, including *El Jardín de Senderos que se Bifurcan* (The Garden of Forking Paths), in 1931, with one of his most famous stories, *El Sur* (The South). In 1944 Borges published arguably the most important series of stories in the history of Latin American literature, the great *Ficciones* (Fictions), which overturned conventions of realism while exploring the nature of literature itself, together with philosophy and metaphysics. *El Aleph* followed in 1949, and his most important essays, *Otras Inquisiciones* (Other Inquisitions) in 1952. A masterful storyteller, Borges never wrote more than a few pages, and was never tempted by the novel form, insisting that more could be explored in a few elliptical, highly suggestive and poetic lines than in hundred of pages of dull realist prose.

The late 1940s brought him almost total blindness due to glaucoma, and a running dispute with the Perón regime. Borges' work was overlooked in Europe and the USA until the late 1960s, by which time he was completely blind, and wrote mainly poetry, a form that he could compose in his head. The worldwide popularity of his fiction led him to publish two further books of short stories later in life, *El Informe de Brodie* (Dr Brodie's Report, 1970), and *El Libro de Arena* (The Book of Sand, 1975). In his final years, he travelled the world with his companion María Kodama, whom he married. He died in Geneva, of liver cancer, in June 1986.

developed in the novel *Don Segundo Sombra* by Ricardo Güiraldes (1886-1927), the story of a boy taught the skills for life by a gaucho mentor.

The early 20th century

The complex urban societies evolving in Argentina by the turn of the century created a rich cultural life. In the 1920s a strong vanguard movement developed which questioned the dominant literary orthodoxies of the day. Little magazines such as *Martín Fierro* (another appropriation of the ubiquitous national symbol) proclaimed novelty in poetry and attacked the dull social-realist writings of their rivals the Boedo group. Argentina's most famous writer, Jorge Luis Borges (1899-1986; see box, page 645) began his literary life as an avant-garde poet in the company of writers such as Oliverio Girondo (1891-1967) and Norah Lange (1906-1972). Many of these poets were interested in expressing the dynamism and changing shape of their urban landscape, Buenos Aires, this Paris on the periphery. The city tourist office offers a free tour, the 'Borges Circuit', which covers the capital's landmarks that feature prominently in the life of the master, as well as his favourite haunts. Roberto Arlt also caught the dreams and nightmares of the urban underclasses in novels such as *El Juguete Rabioso* (The Rabid Toy, 1926) and *Los Siete Locos* (The Seven Madmen, 1929).

Much of the most interesting literature of the 1930s and 1940s was first published in the literary journal *Sur*, founded by the aristocratic writer, Victoria Ocampo. By far the most important group to publish in its pages were Borges and his close friends Silvina Ocampo (1903-1993), Victoria's sister, and Silvina's husband, Adolfo Bioy Casares (1914-1999) who, from the late 1930s, in a series of short fictions and essays, transformed the literary world. They had recurrent concerns: an indirect style, a rejection of realism and nationalist symbols, the use of the purified motifs and techniques of detective fiction and fantastic literature, the quest for knowledge to be found in elusive books, the acknowledgement of literary criticism as the purest form of detective fiction and the emphasis on the importance of the reader rather than the writer.

Peronism and literature

In the 10-year period of Perón's first two presidencies, 1946-1955, there was a deliberate assault on the aristocratic, liberal values that had guided Argentina since 1880. Claiming to be a new synthesis of democracy, nationalism, anti-imperialism and industrial development, Peronism attacked the undemocratic, dependent Argentine elite (personified in such literary figures as Victoria Ocampo or Adolfo Bioy Casares). This period was seen by most intellectuals and writers as an era of cultural darkness. Some writers such as Julio Cortázar (1914-1984) – a writer of elegant fantastic and realist stories – chose voluntary exile rather than remain in Perón's Argentina. The much-loved novelist, Ernesto Sábato (1911-2011) who later confronted the *Proceso,* set his best novel *Sobre Héroes y Tumbas* (On Heroes and Tombs, 1961) partly in the final moments of the Peronist regime, when the tensions of the populist alliance were beginning to become manifest. (His novella *El Túnel* is also an interesting read). But Perón was not much interested in the small circulation of literature and concentrated his attention on mass forms of communication such as radio and cinema. This period saw further mature work from the poets Enrique Molina (1910-1997), Olga Orozco (1922-1999) and Alberto Girri (1919-1991), whose austere, introspective verse was an antidote to the populist abuse of language in the public sphere. The literary field was to be further stimulated after the downfall of Perón with the development of publishing houses and the 'boom' of Latin American literature of the 1960s.

The 1960s

In Argentina the 1960s was a decade of great literary and cultural effervescence. The novel to capture this mood was Cortázar's *Rayuela* (Hopscotch, 1963), which served as a Baedeker of the new, with its comments on literature, philosophy, new sexual freedoms and its open, experimental structure. It was promoted in a weekly journal *Primera Plana*, which also acted as a guide to expansive modernity. Thousands of copies of *Rayuela* were sold to an expanded middle-class readership in Argentina and throughout Latin America. Other novelists and writers benefited from these conditions, the most significant being the Colombian Gabriel García Márquez (1928-2014), who published what would later become one of the best-selling novels of the 20th century, *Cien Años de Soledad* (One Hundred Years of Solitude, 1967), with an Argentine publishing house. Significant numbers of women writers helped to break the male monopoly of literary production, including the novelists Beatriz Guido (1922-1988) and Marta Lynch (1925-1985) and the poet Alejandra Pizarnik (1936-1972).

Literature and dictatorship

The 'swinging' sixties were curtailed by a military coup in 1966. In the years that followed, Argentine political life descended into anarchy, violence and repression. As a result, virtually all forms of cultural activity were silenced and well known writers, including Haroldo Conti (1925-1976) and Rodolfo Walsh (1927-1977), 'disappeared'. Many more had to seek exile including the poet Juan Gelman, whose son and daughter-in-law counted among the disappeared.

Understandably this nightmare world provided the dominant themes of the literary output of these years. The return in old age of Perón, acclaimed by all shades of the political spectrum, was savagely lampooned in Osvaldo Soriano's (1943-1998) novel *No Habrá Más Penas ni Olvido* (A Funny, Dirty Little War, completed in 1975 but only published in 1982). The world of the sombre designs of the ultra-right wing López Rega, Isabel Perón's Minister of Social Welfare, is portrayed in Luisa Valenzuela's (1938-) terrifying, grotesque novel *Cola de lagartija* (The Lizard's Tail, 1983). Of the narrative accounts of those black years, none is more harrowing than Miguel Bonasso's (1940-) fictional documentary of the treatment of the Montoneros guerrilla group in prison and in exile: *Recuerdo de la Muerte* (Memory of Death, 1984). Other writers in exile chose more indirect ways of dealing with the terror and dislocation of those years. Daniel Moyano (1928-1992), in exile for many years in Spain, wrote elegant allegories such as *El Vuelo del Tigre* (The Flight of the Tiger, 1981), which tells of the military-style takeover of an Andean village by a group of percussionists who bring cacophony.

Within Argentina, critical discussion was kept alive in literary journals such as *Punto de Vista* (1978) and certain novels alluded to the current political climate within densely structured narratives. Ricardo Piglia's (1941-) *Respiración Artificial* (Artificial Respiration, 1980) has disappearance and exile as central themes, alongside bravura discussions of the links between fiction and history and between Argentina and Europe.

The return to civilian rule

Following Alfonsín's election victory in 1983, the whole intellectual and cultural field responded to the new freedoms. Certain narratives depicted in harsh realism the brutalities of the 'Dirty War' waged by the military and it was the novelist, Ernesto Sábato, who headed the Commission set up to investigate the disappearances. He wrote in the prologue to the Commission's report *Nunca más* (Never Again, 1984): "We are convinced that the recent military dictatorship brought about the greatest and most savage tragedy in the history of Argentina".

Current literature echoes the famous lines by Borges in the essay *The Argentine Writer and Tradition* (1951): "I believe that we Argentines ... can handle all European themes, handle them without superstition, with an irreverence which can have, and already does have, fortunate consequences." While many of the writers that first brought modernity to Argentine letters have died – Borges, Victoria and Silvina Ocampo, Girri, Cortázar, Puig – the later generations have assimilated their lessons. Juan Carlos Martini (1944-) wrote stylish thrillers, blending high and low culture. Juan José Saer (1937-2005), from his self-imposed exile in Paris, recreated his fictional world, Colastiné, in the city of Santa Fe, in narratives that are complex, poetic discussions on memory and language. The most successful novel of recent years is Tomás Eloy Martínez's (1934-2010) *Santa Evita* (1995) which tells/reinvents the macabre story of what happened to Evita's embalmed body between 1952 and the mid-1970s. The narrative skilfully discusses themes that are at the heart of all writing and critical activity. The critic, like the embalmer of Evita's body, "seeks to fix a life or a body in the pose that eternity should remember it by". But what this critic, like the narrator of Eloy Martínez's novel, realizes is that a corpus of literature cannot be fixed in that way, for literature escapes such neat pigeonholes. Instead, glossing Oscar Wilde, the narrator states "that the only duty that we have to history is to rewrite it". The ending of the novel makes the point about the impossibility of endings: "Since then, I have rowed with words, carrying Santa Evita in my boat, from one shore of the blind world to the other. I don't know where in the story I am. In the middle, I believe. I've been here in the middle for a long time. Now I must write again". (*Santa Evita*, New York and London, 1996, page 661.) See also Books, page 661.

Music

Tango is the country's most prominent and most exported musical form, but by no means its only genre of musical expression. The traditional music which binds almost the whole country is *folclore* (pronounced *folc-LAW-ray*), whose stirring rhythms and passionate singing can be found in varying forms throughout the northern half of the country. Superb music is produced in the north, in the Andean region of Salta and Jujuy. And home-grown Rock Nacional is the country's main strand of pop music, successfully fending off North American and European competition throughout the 1980s and 1990s to form a distinctive sound.

Tango

If your trip to Argentina includes any time in Buenos Aires, you'll undoubtedly see some tango – probably danced on the streets of Florida or San Telmo, though it's much more than a tourist attraction. Testimony to the enduring success of the music among Argentines are the radio stations that only play tango, and the *milongas* (dance clubs) filled with young people learning the old steps.

Although also sung and played, the tango was born as a dance just before the turn of the 20th century. The exact moment of birth was not recorded by any contemporary observer and continues to be a matter of debate, though the roots can be traced. The name 'tango' predates the dance and was given to the carnivals (and dances) of the local inhabitants of the Río de la Plata in the early 19th century, elements of this tradition being taken over by settlers as the local population declined. However, the name 'tango Americano' was also given to the *habanera* (a Cuban descendant of the English country dance) which became all the rage in Spain and bounced back into the Río de la Plata in the middle of the 19th century, not only as a fashionable dance together with the polka, mazurka, waltz and cuadrille but also as a song form in the very popular 'zarzuelas', or Spanish operettas. However, the Habanera led not a double, but a triple life, by also infiltrating the lowest levels of society directly from Cuba via sailors who arrived in the ports of Montevideo and Buenos Aires. Here it encountered the milonga, originally a gaucho song style, but by 1880 a dance, especially popular with the so-called 'compadritos' and 'orilleros', who frequented the port area and its brothels, whence the

Argentine Tango emerged around the turn of the century to dazzle the populace with its brilliant, personalized footwork, which could not be accomplished without the partners staying glued together.

As a dance tango became exceedingly popular and, as the infant recording industry grew in leaps and bounds, it also became popular as a song and an instrumental genre, with the original violins and flutes being eclipsed by the *bandoneón* button accordion, then being imported from Germany. In 1911 the new dance took Paris by storm, thanks to the performance of the dance in a Paris salon by Argentine writer Ricardo Güiraldes, one of a group of aristocrats who enjoyed frequenting the dives where tango was popular. As soon as it was the fashion in Paris, it returned triumphant to Buenos Aires, achieving both respectability and notoriety, and becoming a global phenomenon after the First World War. Actor Rudolph Valentino helped the image of the dance, when his 1926 movie *The Four Horsemen of the Apocalypse* included a tango scene.

But it was Carlos Gardel (1887-1935), Argentina's most loved tango legend, whose mellifluous voice brought popularity to the music of tango, and whose poor background made him a hero for the working classes too. Tango has always been an expression of the poor and of social and political developments in the country. Incredibly, Gardel recorded over 900 songs and was a huge success in many movies. *The Tango on Broadway* (1934) was his biggest success. Today you will still see his image on everything from posters to ice-cream shops, and people still dance to his voice. After Gardel's tragic death in 1935, tango slumped a little, frowned upon by the military regime who considered it subversive. Its resurgence in the 1940s was assisted by Perón's decree that 50% of all music played on the radio must be Argentine. Great stars of this era include the brilliant *bandoneón* player Aníbal Troilo, whose passionate and tender playing made him much loved among a wide audience. In the 1950s, tango again declined, replaced in popularity by rock'n'roll. It had become increasingly the preserve of middle class and intellectual circles, with the emphasis on nostalgia in its themes. But its next innovator and star was Astor Piazzolla (1921-1992), who had played with Troilo's orchestra, and who went on to fuse tango with jazz to create a tango for listening, as well as dancing. Threatened by the military government in the 1970s Piazzollla escaped to Paris, but his success was already international, and his experimental arrangements opened up the possibilities for other fusions.

However, in the past thirty years it has made a resurgence and is once again popular with young people in Argentine bars and cafés and it has become a popular dance throughout the rest of the world. A new genre of tango music has arisen which mixes traditional themes with electronica, and groups like the Gotan Project (www.gotanproject.com) are now world-renowned. All over Buenos Aires, and all over the province, you can find dance classes where the classic moves are taught, followed by a dance or milonga where couples, young and old, breathe life into the steps. Part of its attraction, perhaps, is that in the world of tango, men are allowed to be macho and seductive, while their women are required to be sensitive to the subtlety of their next move. Unlike salsa, for example, tango is a dance of repressed passion. Try a class, at least once, while you're in Argentina, to get a feel for the dance from the inside. And then, if you can afford it, see the expert dancers' dextrous footwork at a show such as *El Viejo Almácen* in San Telmo.

Folclore

Beyond Buenos Aires, the dominant musical traditions can be broadly described as *folclore*. This takes various forms over the north of the country, with the finest examples in

Salta, but all the northern provinces have a very rich and attractive heritage of folk dances, mainly for couples, with arms held out and fingers clicked or handkerchiefs waved, with the 'Paso Valseado' as the basic step. The slow and stately *zamba* is descended from the Zamacueca, and therefore a cousin of the Chilean *cueca* and Peruvian *marinera*, where the handkerchief is used to greatest effect. Equally popular throughout most of the country are the faster *gato*, *chacarera* and *escondido*. These are the dances of the gaucho and their rhythm evokes that of a cantering horse with wonderfully stirring syncopation. Guitar and the *bombo* provide the accompaniment. Particularly spectacular is the *malambo*, where the gaucho shows off his dextrous footwork, creating a complex rhythm using the heels of his boots, alternating with percussion created by whirling the hard balls of the *boleadoras* into the ground, with the spurs of his boots adding a steely note to the rhythm.

Different regions of the country have their own specialities. The music of *cuyo* in the west is sentimental and very similar to that of neighbouring Chile, with its *cuecas* for dance and *tonadas* for song. The northwest on the other hand is Andean, with its musical culture closer to that of Bolivia, particularly on the *puna*, where the indigenous groups play haunting wind instruments, the *quena*, and sound mournful notes on the great long *erke*, evocative of huge mountain landscapes. Here the dances are Bailecitos and Carnavalitos, depending on the time of year. Exquisitely beautiful and mournful songs – the extraordinary high-pitched *bagualas* – are sung to the banging of a simple drum. And everyone, from children to grandmothers, can quote you a *copla*: two lines of rhymed verse expressing love or a witty joke. Tomás Lipan's music is worth seeking out, especially his *Cautivo de Amor*. Andean bands use the *sikus* (pan pipes) and *charango* (miniature guitar) to create ethereal and festive music which reflects the seasons of the rural calendar. In the northeast provinces of Corrientes and Misiones, the music shares cultural similarities with Paraguay. The *polca* and *galopa* are danced and the local *chamamé* is sung, to the accordion or the harp, in sentimental style. Santiago del Estero has exerted the strongest influence on Argentine folk music as a result of the work of Andres Chazarreta: it is the heartland of the Chacarera and the lyrics are often part-Spanish and part-Quichua, a local dialect of the Andean Quechua language. Listen, too, to Los Caravajal, and Los Hermanos Abalos. Down in the province of Buenos Aires you are more likely to hear the gauchos singing their milongas, *estilos* and *cifras* and challenging each other to a *payada* or rhymed duel – protest songs and wonderfully romantic and witty stories to guitar accompaniment. Seek out Atahualpa Yupangui's *El Payador Persguido*. Argentina experienced a great *folclore* revival in the 1950s and 1960s and some of the most celebrated groups are still drawing enthusiastic audiences today. These groups include Los Chalchaleros and Los Fronterizos, the perennial virtuoso singer and guitarist, Eduardo Falú and, more recently, León Gieco from Santa Fe. Most famous of all, though, is the superb Mercedes Sosa, whose rich voice articulated much of the sorrow and joy of the last 30 years in a brilliant series of albums, which also include the most popular *folclore* songs. Start with *The Best of Mercedes Sosa*. Also listen to Ariel Ramírez, a famous singer and pianist whose moving *Misa Criolla* is among his best known work. The *cuartetos* of Córdoba, popular since the 1940s with the characteristic dance in a huge circle, can best be sampled in the much-loved records of Carlos 'La Mona' Jiménez.

Rock Nacional

The great stars of Rock Nacional are still much listened to. The movement started in the 1960s with successful bands Los Gatos and Almendra, whose songwriter Luis Alberto Spinetta later became a successful solo artist. But the Rock Nacional found its real strength in expressing unspeakable protests during the military dictatorship from 1976-1983. Charly García, who was a member of the enormously successful band Sui Generis, captured popular feeling with his song *No Te Dejes Desanimar* (Don't be Discouraged), which roused mass opposition amongst young people against the atrocities of the *Proceso*. Inevitably, the military regime cottoned on to this form of subversive behaviour and stopped rock concerts, so that many bands had given up performing by the end of the 1970s. However, the rock movement survived, and the cynical lyrics of Fito Páez in *Tiempos Difíciles* and Charly García in *Dinosaurios* remain as testimonies to that time, and guaranteed them subsequent success. Once democracy had returned, lightweight music became more popular, with likeable output from Los Abuelos de la Nada and Patricio Rey y sus Redonditos de Ricota, Soda Stereo (one of the most significant bands of the 1980s and they are still popular today) and also the work of Fito Páez who has continued to record and whose album *El Amor Después del Amor* was a success across Latin America. Los Fabulosis Cadillacs and Andrés Calamaro also made some great records, and Charly García continues, undiminished in popularity. The 1980s also saw the rise of punk music in Argentina, with notable acts, such as Los Violadores and Sumo, spearheading a musical scene that continues to this day.

Cinema

Argentina's cinema is one of its liveliest art forms and it has enjoyed a recent renaissance with some brilliant films being made, more in the European or *auteur* tradition, than in Hollywood style. With a couple of worldwide successes and an Oscar for Best Foreign Film with *El Secreto de Tus Ojos* (The Secret of Your Eyes, 2009), Argentine cinema has made its mark on the world stage.

In 1922, Buenos Aires had some 27,000,000 film-goers each year and 128 movie theatres, the largest being the Grand Splendid which seated 1350 people. By 1933 there were 1608 cinemas throughout Argentina, with 199 in the capital. However, the taste of the cinema-going public was for Hollywood movies. Hollywood has dominated the screens in Latin America for the first hundred years of film history, averaging some 90% of viewing time in Argentina.

However, in the 1950s, New Argentine Cinema started as a movement of independent films which offered a far more honest and accurate reflection of life in the country. Film clubs and journals created a climate of awareness of film as an art form and the tenets of Italian neo-realism and the 'politique des auteurs' of *Cahiers du Cinéma* provided alternatives to the studio-based Hollywood system. In Argentina, Leopoldo Torre Nilsson (1924-1978) explored aristocratic decadence and his early film *La Casa del Angel* (The House of the Angel, 1957) was greeted with praise all over the world. Fernando Birri (1925-) used neo-realist principles to explore the hidden realities of Argentina. His film school in Santa Fe made an important documentary about young shanty town children, *Tire Dié* (Throw us a Dime, 1957) and helped pioneer a more flexible, socially committed, cinema.

Younger film makers of the 1960s like Manuel Antín (1926-), David Kohon (1929-2004) and Leonardo Favio (1938-2012) explored themes such as middle-class alienation or the sexual rites of the youth, set in the cafés and streets of Buenos Aires. Meanwhile, the growing climate of revolutionary sentiment of the late 1960s was reflected in Solanas's *La Hora de los Hornos* (The Hour of the Furnaces, 1966-1968), a key work of populist radicalism.

After a brief spell of radical optimism in the late 1960s and early 1970s, reflected in a number of other nationalist-populist movies, the dream of the second coming of Perón turned into the nightmare that led to the brutal military takeover in March 1976. The spiralling violence affected film-makers as much as artists in any other sector and saw key industry figures threatened and, in some cases, forced into exile. Heavily censored imports, limp comedies and musicals became the norm, the only beneficiaries being foreign producers and distributors. Film-makers such as Solanas, who went into exile, found it difficult to adapt to the new conditions and remained in a cultural wilderness. Within Argentina, the tight military control began to slacken in the early 1980s and some important films were made, including María Luisa Bemberg's (1922-1995) *Señora de Nadie* (Nobody's Woman, 1982) which premiered the day before the invasion of the Falklands/Malvinas.

With the return to civilian rule in 1983, the Radical government abolished censorship and put two well known film-makers in charge of the National Film Institute, Manuel Antín and Ricardo Wullicher (1948-). Antín's granting of credits to young and established directors and his internationalist strategy had an immediate effect. For several years there was a great flowering of talent, a development that would only be halted temporarily by the economic difficulties of the late 1980s. The trade paper *Variety* (25 March 1987) commented on this new effervescence: "Never before has there been such a mass of tangible approval as in the years since democratic rule returned at the end of 1983". In 1986, the Hollywood Academy granted the first Oscar for an Argentine picture, *La Historia Oficial* (The Official History) directed by Luis Puenzo (1946-), which dealt with the recent traumas of the disappearances of the 'Dirty War', but in rather sentimental Hollywood terms. This followed the massive box office success of Bemberg's *Camila*, which commented by analogy on the same subject. Solanas' two films about exile and the return to democracy, *Tangos, el Exilio de Gardel* (Tangos: the Exile of Gardel, 1985) and *Sur* (South, 1988), both offer interesting insights in Solanas' idiosyncratic poetic style. Puenzo, Bemberg and Solanas remained the most visible directors in the 1980s and 1990s, but dozens of other directors made movies in a range of different styles. Lita Stantic made perhaps the most complex film about the 'Dirty War' of the military regime, the superb *Un Muro de Silencio* (A Wall of Silence, 1993). This was a success with the critics, but was ignored by the public who preferred to view politics and repression through a gauze of melodrama and rock music, as in Marcelo Piñeyro's *Tango Feroz* (1993).

Argentine cinema has undergone a revival in recent years, but the hard economic fact remains that by far the vast majority of screens in the country show Hollywood films, and home-grown movies have to compete in very commercial terms. However, prior to *El Secreto de Tus Ojos* (see above), the Oscar nomination of Argentine film *El Hijo de la Novia* (Son of the Bride) in 2002 had boosted national self-confidence, and was a big success within Argentina. Its anti-hero Ricardo Darín also starred in Fabiano Belinski's sophisticated heist movie *Neuve Reinas* (Nine Queens, 2000), which through a labyrinth of tricks and scams neatly articulates a Buenos Aires where no one can trust anyone. It was a huge success worldwide as well as in the country, and the death of Bielinsky following his second film, *El Aura*, was a tragic loss to Argentine cinema.

Successes of the new Argentine cinema included a return to cinema with a social conscience in Adrián Gaetano's *Bolivia*, addressing the sorry plight of an illegal Bolivian worker in urban Argentina, and his *Un Oso Rojo* (Red Bear, 2002) charting the fate of a newly released prisoner trying to reclaim the affection of his daughter from his wife's new boyfriend. Pablo Trapero's *Mundo Grúa* (1999) is a stark but touching portrayal of the life of a crane driver, while his more recent *Elefante Blanco* (2012), confronts the issues of life in a deprived barrio of Buenos Aires, and Lisandro Alonso's astonishing *Libertad* shows with utter honesty the life of a peon on an estancia. In Luis Ortega's charming *Caja Negra* (2004) a young woman's relationship with her outcast father and eccentric ancient grandmother is explored with great humour and compassion, while Carlos Sorin's *Bonbón El Perro* (2004), set in Patagonia, introduces a mechanic who dreams of a different life after his adopted puppy wins first prize at a local dog show.

Two other striking films are *Pizza, Birra, Faso* (Pizza, Beer, Cigarettes, 1998) by Stagnaro and Gaetano, and *No Quiero Volver a Casa* (I Don't Want to Return Home, 2001) by Albertina Carri. Lucrecia Martel showed an original voice in her disturbing *La Cienaga* (The Swamp, 2001), a vivid portrayal of a divided family's unhappy summer in their country house. Highly allegorical and rich in atmospheric detail, it's a wonderful contemporary portrait. Her *La Niña Santa* (Holy Girl, 2004) was less successful.

Although most cinemas in the country show Hollywood movies, the larger cities have an art house cinema, and if you happen to be around during any of the film festivals, you can usually catch a few recent Argentine releases: Mar del Plata Film Festival in mid-March; Buenos Aires film festival in mid-April; and Salta's film festival in the first week of December.

Spectator sports

It is said that sport came to Argentina through the port of Buenos Aires, brought first by British sailors, who played football on vacant lots near the port watched by curious locals who would later make it their national passion.

Football is out on its own, both in terms of participation and as a spectator sport, with the country being passionately divided between fans of River Plate and Boca Juniors and reaching fever pitch when the national team reached the 2014 FIFA World Cup final. In second place comes motor racing. The legend of Juan Manuel Fangio in the 1950s is still very much alive and well. Tennis is increasingly popular, especially since there are several successful Argentine tennis players, headed up by Cordobian David Nalbandian and Juan del Potro, both from Tandil. Basketball and volleyball are both popular participation sports among young people, with strong teams in many sizeable towns, and basketball attracts fans since Argentine players play for the NBA in the States.

Although the best **polo** in the world is played in Argentina, it's only accessible to an elite class, due to its cost (although you can watch it without it costing you an arm and a leg). Despite being played throughout the country and all year round, the top Argentine players, who now play all over the world, return only for the high handicap season between September and November. This consists of tournaments, played on the outskirts of Buenos Aires, followed by the Argentine Open, which takes place on Palermo's polo field, known as the 'cathedral of polo'.

Rugby was brought to Argentina by the British over a hundred years ago and is played throughout the country. The national team, Los Pumas, reached the semi-finals of the 2007 Rugby World Cup, and in 2012 they became the fourth team in the Rugby Championship (formerly Tri Nations). They were the fourth and third teams in the 2014 and 2015 Championships, respectively. Locally, the most popular teams both come from San Isidro, north of the capital.

Argentina's native sports include the squash-like *pelota paleta* and *pato*, a cross between polo and basketball. Originally played between large bands of gauchos, today, it is played by teams of four horsemen and a football with handles, and is one sport which is unique to Argentina.

Land &
environment

Argentina is the second largest country in South America in area, extending across the continent some 1580 km from east to west and 3460 km from north to south. Its northern-most point is at latitude 22°S (just within the tropics); at Tierra del Fuego and Isla de los Estados it extends south of 54°S (the latitude of Scotland or Labrador). The coast of this territory, which extends over 2000 km, runs wholly along the Atlantic apart from the north coast of the Beagle Channel linking the Atlantic and the Pacific. The western border with Chile follows the crest of the Andes, but below 46°S, the drainage is complex and border disputes have arisen ever since the Treaty of 1881 when the principle that the border should follow the watershed was established.

Geology and landscape

Together with Brazil, Paraguay and Uruguay, Argentina is the visible part of the South American Plate which has been moving for the past 125 million years away from its former union with Africa. The submerged part of this plate forms a broad continental shelf under the Atlantic Ocean; in the south this extends over 1000 km east and includes the Falkland Islands/Islas Malvinas. Since the 'break' between the plates, there have been numerous invasions and withdrawals of the sea over this part of the South American continent, but the Andean mountain building from the end of the Cretaceous period (65 million years ago) to the present day dominates the surface geology. Of the many climatic fluctuations, the Pleistocene Ice Age up to 10,000 BC has done most to mould the current landscape. At its maximum, ice covered all the land over 2000 m and most of Patagonia. In the mountains, ice created virtually all the present-day lakes and glaciers, and moraine deposits can be found everywhere. However, the special feature of the heartland of Argentina is the fine soil of the Pampas, the result of ice and water erosion and the unique wind systems of the southern cone of the continent.

The Northwest

Northern and western Argentina are dominated by the satellite ranges of the Andes. Between the mountains of the far northwest is the *puna*, a high plateau rising to 3400-4000 m, on which are situated salt flats or *salares*, some of which are of interest for their wildlife. East of this is the *prepuna*, the gorges and slopes ranging in altitude from 1700 m to 3400 m which connect the *puna* with the plains. On the fringe of the Andes are a string of important settlements including Salta, Tucumán and Mendoza. Though the climate of this region is hot and dry, there is sufficient water to support maize and pasture and a thriving wine industry, mostly relying on irrigation. East of the Andes lies several ranges of hills, the most important of which are the Sierras de Córdoba and the Sierras de San Luis. These are mostly of ancient Precambrian rocks.

The Paraná Basin

The vast Paraná Basin stretches from the borders with Brazil and Paraguay to the Atlantic at Buenos Aires. In the northeast it mainly consists of geologically recent deposits. The easternmost part of this basin, between the Ríos Paraná and Uruguay, is the wettest part of the country. Known as Mesopotamia and consisting of the provinces of Entre Ríos, Corrientes and Misiones, it is structurally part of the Brazilian plateau of old crystalline rocks, the 'heart' of the South American Plate. Here there are undulating grassy hills and marshy or forested lowlands, among them the Esteros del Iberá, an extensive area of flooded forest similar to the Pantanal in Brazil. The horizontal stratum of the rocks in this area is dramatically evident in the river gorges to the north and the spectacular Iguazú Falls shared with Brazil.

The Chaco

Northwest of Mesopotamia and stretching from the Paraná and Paraguay rivers west to the Andean foothills and north into Paraguay and Bolivia lies the Gran Chaco, a vast plain that covers the provinces of Formosa, Chaco and Santiago del Estero, as well as parts of Santa Fe and Córdoba. It is crossed from west to east by three rivers, the Teuco-Bermejo, the Salado and the Pilcomayo. Annual rainfall ranges from 450-500 mm in the western or Dry Chaco, a semi-desert mainly used for cattle ranching, to 800-1200 mm in the eastern or Wet Chaco, where periodic floods alternate with long periods of drought.

The Pampas

South of 33°S, the latitude of Mendoza and Rosario, is a great flat plain known as the Pampas. Extending almost 1000 km from north to south and a similar distance from east to west, the Pampas cover some 650,000 sq km, including most of Buenos Aires province, southern Córdoba, Santa Fe and Entre Ríos, north eastern La Pampa and a small part of San Luís. This area is crossed by meandering rivers and streams, and there are many lakes, lagoons and marshes. Geologically the Pampas are similar to the Chaco, basic crystalline and granite rocks almost completely overlain with recent deposits, often hundreds of metres thick. Prevailing winds from the southeast and southwest help to create the fine loess-type soils which make this one of the richest farming areas in the world, ideal for grasslands and cattle ranching. Being comparatively close to the ocean, extremes of temperature are rare, another favourable feature.

A distinction is often made between the 'wet' Pampa and the 'dry' Pampa. The former, inland from Rosario and Buenos Aires, is the centre of wheat, maize and other cereal production; the latter, west of 64°W, is where cattle ranching predominates.

The Patagonian steppe

Patagonia extends from the Río Colorado (39°S) south to the Straits of Magellan and covers some 780,000 sq km. Most of this area consists of a series of tablelands and terraces, which drop in altitude from west to east. The basic rocks are ancient, some classified as Precambrian, but the surface has been subjected to endless erosion. Rainfall is lighter and the winds stronger than in the Pampas frequently stripping the surface of cover and filling the air with dust. Only where rivers have scored deep valleys in the rock base can soil accumulate, allowing more than extensive sheep farming.

From the Straits of Magellan north to Lago Argentino (46°S) and beyond, a geological depression separates the edge of the South American Plate from the Andes. Most of Patagonia was under ice during the Quaternary Ice Age and has been rising since the ice receded. This area was presumably the last to be uncovered. However, considerable volcanic activity associated with the uplift of the Andes has taken place along the depression which is transversely divided into basins by lava flows. Alluvial and glacial deposits have created relatively fertile soils in some areas, useful for sheep and producing attractive wooded landscapes in the lake regions in contrast to the general desolation of Patagonia.

The Andes

Geographically the Isla de los Estados forms the southernmost extent of the Andes, which then swing north to become the border between Chile and Argentina just north of the Paine mountains. The 350-km section north of Paine is one of the most dramatic stretches of the Andes. The crest lies under the Southern Patagonian ice cap, with glaciers reaching down to the valleys on both the Argentine and Chilean sides. On the Argentine side this has created the spectacular range of glaciers found in the Parque Nacional Los Glaciares, the most famous of which, the Perito Moreno Glacier, is one of the highlights for many travellers to Argentina. The northern end of this section is Cerro Fitz Roy, which, along with the Torres del Paine (in Chile) at the southern end, is among the most spectacular hiking and climbing centres in South America.

Further north between 46°S and 47°S there is another ice cap, the North Patagonian ice cap, centred on Monte San Valentín on the Chilean side of the border. North of this lies 1500 km of mountain ranges rarely exceeding 4000 m; on the east side of these are a series of attractive lakes, formed by a mixture of glacial and volcanic activity. The high section of the Andes begins at 35°S and includes Aconcagua (6960 m), the highest peak outside the Himalayas. For a further 1000 km northwards, the ranges continue to the border with Bolivia with many peaks over 6000 m, the Argentine side becoming progressively drier and more inhospitable.

Climate

Climate ranges from subtropical in the northeast to cold temperate in Tierra del Fuego, but is temperate and quite healthy for much of the year in the densely populated central zone. Between December and the end of February, Buenos Aires can be oppressively hot and humid. The Andes have a dramatic effect on the climate of the south: although on the Chilean side of the mountains there is adequate rainfall from Santiago southwards, very little of this moisture reaches the Argentine side. Furthermore, the prevailing winds in Patagonia are southwest to northeast from the Pacific. The result is a temperate climate with some mist and fog near the coast, but not much rain. Further inland, the westerlies, having deposited their moisture on the Andes, add strength to the southerly airstream, creating the strong dry wind (*El Pampero*) characteristic of the Pampas. Only when these systems meet humid maritime air in the northeast of the country does rainfall significantly increase, often with violent thunderstorms, and the heaviest precipitation is in Mesopotamia where the summer months are particularly wet.

The highest temperatures are found in the northeast where the distance from the sea and the continuous daytime sunshine produce the only frequently recorded air temperatures over 45°C anywhere in South America. The northwest is cooler due to the effects of altitude, rainfall here occurring largely in the summer months.

Vegetation

Few countries offer as wide a range of natural environments as Argentina; its varied vegetation supports equally diverse wildlife. The main types of vegetation are described below. Details of some of the animals to be seen are given where appropriate in the text; to avoid repetition they are not described here. There are 10 main vegetation types:

Llanura pampeana

Extensive cattle grazing and arable farming have altered the original vegetation of the Pampas, notably through the introduction of tree species such as the eucalyptus for shelter. The least altered areas of the Pampas are the coastal lowlands, the Paraná delta and the southern sierras. The sandy soils of the coastal lowlands, including marshes and estuaries, are home to Pampas grass or *cortadera*. In the marshy parts of the Paraná delta there are tall grasses with *espinillo* and *ñandubay* (*Prosopis*) woods in the higher areas. Willows and alisos grow along the riverbanks while the ceibo, the national flower of Argentina, grows in the nearby woodlands.

Espinal

These are open woodlands and savannahs which extend in an arc around the Pampas covering southern Corrientes, northern Entre Ríos, central Santa Fe, large parts of Córdoba and San Luis and the centre-west of La Pampa. In these areas xerophitic and thorny woods of prosopis and acacia predominate. The major prosopis species are the *ñandubay*; the white algarrobo; the black algarrobo and the caldén. The *ñandubay is* found in Entre Ríos and parts of Corrientes, along with the white *quebracho*, *tala*, *espinillo* and, on sandy soils, *yatay* palms. The white algarrobo and black algarrobo are found in areas of Santa Fe, Córdoba and San Luis which have been heavily affected by farming. The caldén appears across large areas of La Pampa, southern San Luis and southern Buenos Aires, along with bushes such as the alpataco and the creosote bush (*Larrea*).

Monte

Monte is a bushy steppe with a few patches of trees, in areas with rainfall from 80 mm to 250 mm. Covering large areas of San Juan, Mendoza, La Pampa and Río Negro, it can be found as far north as Salta and as far south as Chubut. Vegetation includes different species of the creosote bush, which have small resinous leaves and yellow flowers, as well as thorny bushes from the cacti family and bushes such as *brea*, *retamo* and *jume*. In the northern areas of *monte* the white algarrobo and sweet algarrobo can be found, while the native willow grows along the riverbanks as far south as the Río Chubut.

Puna and prepuna

Low rainfall, intense radiation and poor soils inhibit vegetation in the *puna*, the major species being adapted by having deep root systems and small leaves; many plants have thorny leaves to deter herbivores. These include species of cactus, which store water in their tissue, and the *yareta*, a cushion-shaped plant, which has been over-exploited for firewood, as well as the *tolilla*, the *chijua* and the *tola*. The *queñoa*, which grows to over 5 m high in the sheltered gorges and valleys of the *prepuna*, is the highest growing tree in Argentina. These valleys also support bushes from the Leguminosae family such as the *churqui*, and species of cactus, such as the cardoon and the *airampu*, with its colourful blossom.

High Andean grasslands

Extending from Jujuy to Neuquén, and then in discontinuous fashion south to Tierra del Fuego, these areas range in altitude from 4200 m in Jujuy to 500 m in Tierra del Fuego. Grasses adapted to the cold include *iros*, *poa* and *stipa* as well as some endemic species.

Subtropical cloudforest

Often known as *yungas*, this extends into Argentina from Bolivia and covers parts of the sub-Andean sierras. It is found in eastern Jujuy, central Salta and Tucumán and eastern Catamarca. Its eastern sides receive the humidity of the winds which cross the Chaco from the Atlantic. Winters are dry but temperature, rainfall and humidity vary with changes in latitude and altitude. These forests are important regulators of the water cycle, preventing erosion and floods. It is best seen in three national parks: Baritú, Calilegua and El Rey.

Vegetation changes with altitude. Along the edge of the Chaco at the foot of the hills and rising to 500 m, where there is annual rainfall up to 1000 m, is a transition zone with mainly deciduous trees such as the *palo blanco*, the *lapacho rosado* and *lapacho amarillo* (pink and yellow tabebuia); the *palo borracho* (Chorisia bottle tree), the *tipa blanca* and the huge *timbo colorado* or black eared tree. Higher and reaching from 500 to 800 m in altitude, where there is greater humidity, are montane or laurel forests. Predominant tree species here are the laurel, the jacaranda and the *tipa;* epiphytes (orchids, bromeliads, ferns, lichens, mosses) and climbers are abundant. Above 800 m and rising to 1300-1700 m annual rainfall reaches some 3000 mm, concentrated between November and March. Here myrtle forest predominates, with a great diversity of species, including great trees such as the *horco molle*, a wide range of epiphytes, and, in some areas such as Baritu, tree ferns. Higher still, the evergreen trees are replaced by deciduous species including the mountain pine (*Podocarpus*), the only conifer native to the northwest, the walnut and the alder. Above these are clumps of *queñoa* and, higher still, mountain meadow grasslands.

The Chaco

The eastern or Wet Chaco is covered by marshlands and ponds with savannah and caranday palm groves, as well as the characteristic red *quebracho,* a hardwood tree overexploited in the past for tannin. The Dry Chaco, further west, is the land of the white *quebracho* as well as cacti such as the quimil (*opuntia*) and the palo borracho (*Chorisia*). Similar climatic conditions and vegetation to those in the Dry Chaco are also found in northern San Luis, Córdoba and Santa Fe and eastern Tucumán, Catamarca, Salta, Jujuy, La Rioja and San Juan.

Subtropical rainforest

This is found mainly in Misiones, extending southwards along the banks of the Ríos Paraná and Uruguay. The wet climate, with annual rainfall of up to 2000 mm, and high temperatures produce rapid decomposition of organic material. The red soils of this area contain a thin fertile soil layer which is easily eroded.

This area offers the widest variety of flora in Argentina. There of over 2000 known species of vascular plants, about 10% of which are trees. Forest vegetation rises to different strata: the giant trees such as the *palo rosa*, the Misiones cedar, *incienso* and the *guatambú* rise to over 30 m high. The forest canopy includes species such as strangler figs and the pindo palm, while the intermediate strata includes the fast growing *ambay* (*Cecropia*), tree-ferns, the *yerba mate* and bamboos. Llianas, vines and epiphytes such as orchids and bromeliads as well as ferns and even cacti compete in the struggle for sunlight.

In the hills of northwestern Misiones there are remnants of forests of Paraná pine (*Araucaria angustifolia*).

Sub-Antarctic forest

This grows along the eastern edges of the southern Andes, from Neuquén in the north to Tierra del Fuego and Isla de los Estados in the south. These are cool temperate forests including evergreen and deciduous trees. Species of *nothofagus* predominate, the most common being *lenga* (low deciduous beech), *ñire* (high deciduous beech), *coihue* and *guindo*. The *pehuén* or monkey puzzle tree (*Araucaria araucana*), is found in northwestern and north-central Neuquén. The fungus *llao llao* and the hemiparasitic *Misodendron* are also frequent. Flowering bushes include the *notro* (firebush), the *calafate* (*Burberis boxifolis*) and the *chaura* (prickly heath).

Areas of the Lake District with annual rainfall of over 1500 mm are covered by Valdivian forest and a wider range of species. The *coihue* (southern beech) is the predominant species of *nothofagus*, reaching as far south as Lago Buenos Aires. Below colihue canes form a dense undergrowth; flowers include the *amancay* (alstromeria), mutisias, and near streams, the fuschia. *Arrayán* trees also grow near water, while the Andean Cypress and the *Maiten* grow in the transition zone with the Patagonian steppe. In areas where annual rainfall reaches over 3000 mm, there is a wider range of trees as well as epyphites, ferns, and lichens such as Old Man's Beard. The *alerce* (larch) is the giant of these forests, rising to over 60 m and, in some cases over 3000 years old.

Magallanic forest, found from Lago Buenos Aires south to Tierra del Fuego, is dominated by the *guindo* (evergreen beech) as well as the *lenga*, the *ñire* and the *canelo* (winter bark). There are also large areas of peatbog with sphagnum mosses, and even the carnivorous *Drosera uniflora*.

Patagonian steppe

Plant life in this area has adapted to severe climatic conditions: strong westerly winds, the heavy winter snowfall that occurs in some years, high evaporation in summer, low annual rainfall and sandy soils with a thin fertile layer on top. The northwest of this area is covered by bushy scrublands: species include the *quilembai, molle*, the *algarrobo patagónico*, the *colpiche*, as well as *coiron* grasses. Further south are shrubs such as the *mata negra* and species of *calafate*. Nearer the mountain ranges the climate is less severe and the soil more fertile: here there is a herbaceous steppe that includes *coiron blanco* and shrubs such as the *neneo*. Overgrazing by sheep has produced serious desertification in many parts of the Patagonian steppe.

National parks

Fortunately in a country so rich in natural beauty, Argentina has an extensive network of reserves and protected areas, the most important of which are designated as national parks. The history of Argentine national parks is a long one, dating from the donation by Francisco 'Perito' Moreno of 7500 ha of land in the Lake District to the state. This grant formed the basis for the establishment of the first national park, Nahuel Huapi, in 1934.

There are 33 national parks stretching from Parque Nacional Baritú on the northern border with Bolivia to Parque Nacional Tierra del Fuego in the far south. Additional areas have been designated as natural monuments and natural reserves and there are also provincial parks and reserves. The largest national parks are all in western Argentina; these include a string of eight parks in the Andean foothills in the Lake District and Patagonia. These make ideal bases for trekking, with *guardaparque* (rangers) offices at main entrances where you can get advice and maps. Argentina has poor maps for trekking and climbing. Those available from the Instituto Geografico Militar in Buenos Aires are badly out of date and do not show all paths and refuges. Before you travel, therefore, it's a good idea to buy a good basic map of the land you want to explore and to search the national parks website for more information (sadly only available in Spanish). Access to the more remote national parks can be tricky without your own transport and you should allow a couple of extra days, especially for the cloudforest parks in the northwest, and for Parque Nacional Perito Moreno (not the one with the Glaciar Perito Moreno in it). Once you reach the parks, you'll find *guardaparques* very knowledgeable and helpful, and many are happy to take time to explain the wildlife and recommend good walks. The main national parks and other protected areas are shown on the map and further details of all of these are given in the text. See also www.parquesnacionales.gov.ar.

The main administration office of the Argentine National Parks authority is at Santa Fe 680, near the Plaza San Martín in central Buenos Aires. Leaflets are available on some of the parks. For more information, see Essentials A-Z, page 681.

Books

See also Literature, page 643.

Borges, Jorge Luis *Collected Fiction, Penguin, UK*. Strange, wonderful and sometimes a little off-the-wall, Argentina's most celebrated modern author still captivates.

Chatwin, Bruce *In Patagonia, Vintage/Penguin*. The classic travel book. A little outdated and old fashioned but this book inspired a generation of travellers to head to Argentina.

Cortázar, Julio *Rayuela (Hopscotch, 1963)*. A novel which typifies the philosophy and freedom of the 1960s.

Figueras, Marcelo *Kamchatka (2003)*. A coming-of-age novel set in the coup of 1976, by a writer, journalist and film-maker.

Guevara, Ernesto 'Che' *The Motorcycle Diaries, Verso, UK*. Funny, thoughtful and a ripping read, Guevara's diaries are great to sink into whilst travelling in Argentina.

Güiraldes, Ricardo *Don Segundo Sombra*. A 2nd great gaucho work (see Hernández, below), further cementing the figure of the gaucho as national hero.

Granado, Alberto *Travelling with Che: The Making of a Revolutionary, Newmarket Press, US*. Ernesto Guevara's travelling partner tells his version of their journey together.

Hernández, José *El gaucho Martín Fierro (1872)*. An epic poem about the disruption of local communities by the march of progress; the eponymous hero and dispossessed outlaw came to symbolize Argentine nationhood.

Hudson, W H *Far Away and Long Ago and Idle Days in Patagonia*. These books deal with this English writer's early life in the countryside.

Lucas Bridges, E *Uttermost Part of the Earth*. About the early colonization of Tierra del Fuego.

Martínez, Tomás Eloy *Santa Evita (1995) and La novela de Perón (The Perón Novel, 1985)*. 2 highly acclaimed novels on Argentina's enduring 20th-century figures. Other famous novels of his are *El cantor de tango* (The Tango Singer, 2004) and *Purgatorio* (Purgatory, 2008).

McEwan, Colin, ed *Patagonia: Natural History, Prehistory and Ethnography at the Uttermost Part of the Earth, British Museum Press*. The indigenous cultures of Patagonia and their destruction in the early 20th century. Illustrated, well-written essays.

Palmer, Marina *Kiss and Tell, William Morrow, US*. The story of a girl falling in love with tango and a tango dancer in the *milongas* of Buenos Aires.

Puig, Manuel *El beso de la mujer araña (The Kiss of the Spider Woman, 1976 – made into a renowned film)*. A novel about mass culture, gender roles and the banal as art.

Soriano, Osvaldo *No habrá más penas ni olvido (A Funny, Dirty Little War, 1982)*. About dictatorship and the 'dirty war'.

Traba, Marta (1930-1982) *Conversación al sur (Mothers and Shadows in English, 1981)*.

Valenzuela, Luisa (1938-) *Cola de lagartija (The Lizard's Tail, 1983)*.

Practicalities

Getting there

Air

Flights from Europe

There are flights to Buenos Aires from London, Amsterdam, Barcelona, Madrid, Frankfurt, Paris, Milan, Rome and Zurich with **Aerolíneas Argentinas** ① *T0871-644 4453 or 0800-0969 747, www.aerolineas.com.ar*, and other European carriers. From Britain, only **British Airways** goes direct to Buenos Aires, and has been repeatedly recommended for comfort and service. **Air Europa** ① *T087 1423 0717, www.aireuropa.com*, specializes in flights to Argentina and elsewhere in Latin America from European airports.

Flights from North America and Canada

Aerolíneas Argentinas and other South American and North American airlines fly from Miami, New York, Washington, Los Angeles, San Francisco, Atlanta, Dallas and Chicago. **Air Canada, Copa** and **LATAM** fly from Toronto and Montreal.

Flights from Australasia and South Africa

Aerolíneas Argentinas, LATAM and **Qantas** fly from Sydney (Australia), via Auckland (New Zealand) or Santiago (Chile), several times a week. **South African Airways** fly four times a week from Johannesburg, via Sao Paulo.

Flights from Latin America

Aerolíneas Argentinas and other carriers fly between Buenos Aires and all the South American capitals, plus Santa Cruz and Cochabamba in Bolivia and Guayaquil in Ecuador. Several flights between Buenos Aires, Rio de Janeiro and São Paulo stopover in Porto Alegre, Florianópolis and Curitiba. There are also flights from Belo Horizonte, Salvador, Recife and Fortaleza, Havana, Mexico City and Cancún.

General tips

Check your baggage allowance as airlines vary widely. The limit is usually between 20 and 32 kg per person for economy class, strictly enforced with high charges for excess baggage. You must check with your airline for its rules. For internal flights in Argentina, the baggage limit with **Aerolíneas Argentinas** is 15 kg (23 kg for international flights), and they are extremely inflexible, also charging wildly for excess. This means you will either have to leave some things in your hotel in Buenos Aires, or consider limiting your baggage to 15 kg when you leave home.

Airport information

All flights from outside Argentina, apart from those from neighbouring countries, arrive at Ezeiza International Airport (officially known as Ministro Pistarini), situated 35 km southwest of Buenos Aires (for detailed information including transport to Buenos Aires, see page 44). All internal flights as well as some flights to or from neighbouring countries come to Jorge Newbery Airport, generally known as Aeroparque, situated 4 km north of the centre of Buenos Aires on the bank of the Río de la Plata (see page 44 for details). Most provincial airports have a desk offering tourist information, banking facilities and a *confitería* (cafeteria) as well as car hire. There are usually minibus services into the city and taxis are available. For details of airport tax, see page 681.

Packing for Argentina

You'll be able to buy most things you're likely to need once you're in Argentina, and at cheaper prices than at home in most cases (except imported goods, which are prohibitively expensive). Scan all documents, your passport and flight ticket, and email them to yourself and a friend in case there's an emergency. Carry a photocopy of your passport at all times.

Rather than keeping your digital photos on a massive memory card, use an online cloud storage service to save them, such as Dropbox, Google Drive or One Drive.

Along with your usual clothes, camera and diary, consider bringing: a light waterproof jacket, comfortable walking shoes or boots, a lightweight fleece top, a smartish set of clothes (for the occasional night at a good hotel or restaurant), a money pouch (worn under your clothes, particularly in Buenos Aires), sun cream, insect repellent, sunglasses, a torch/flashlight (useful for walking around remote, unlit villages at night) and a folding knife (handy for picnics, but remember not to carry it in hand luggage on the plane). Carry tissues for use in bus toilets. If you're planning to stay in youth hostels bring a padlock, cutlery, pillow case, sleeping bag liner and indelible pen to mark food containers in the kitchen. See page 23 for a list of trekking equipment.

Entry fee

Argentina charges entry fees for citizens of those countries that require Argentines to obtain a visa and pay an entry fee, namely Australia (US$100, valid one year), Canada (CAD$100, valid 10 years) and the US (US$160, valid 10 years). However, in 2016 the Argentine government suspended the entry fee for US citizens (but the fee still applies to Canadian and Australian citizens). This fee is only payable by credit card online before arrival. You must print the receipt and present it to immigration wherever you enter the country. Go to www.migraciones.gov.ar or www.provinciapagos.com.ar for instructions. US citizens can visit www.embassyofargentina.us to see if the suspension still stands at time of travel.

Prices and discounts

Fares vary considerably from airline to airline, so it's worth checking with an agency for the best deal for when you want to travel. The cheap-seat allocation will sell out quickly in holiday periods. The busiest seasons for travelling to Argentina are 7 December to 15 January, Easter, and 1 July to 10 September, when you should book as far ahead as possible. There might be special offers available from February to May and September to November.

Road

There are many entry points from neighbouring countries, and with good long-distance bus services, this is a convenient way of entering Argentina if you're travelling around. The main routes are as follows:

In the west from Santiago (Chile) via the Puente del Inca to Mendoza (see box, page 201).

In the northwest from Villazón (Bolivia) to Jujuy and Salta (see box, page 298).

In the northeast from Paraguay, either from Asunción to Resistencia in Argentina via Puente Loyola (see box, page 345), or from Encarnación to Posadas (see box, page 357).

From Foz do Iguazú (Brazil) to Puerto Iguazú via la Puente de la Amistad (see box, page 383).

In the Lake District by boat and bus from Puerto Montt (Chile) to Bariloche (see box, page 448).

In Patagonia by road from Puerto Natales (Chile) to El Calafate or by road and ferry crossings from Tierra del Fuego to Río Gallegos and El Calafate (see box, page 577).

There are also three road crossings from Uruguay via bridges over the Río Uruguay, as well several ferry crossings, the most important of which are from Montevideo and Colonia de Sacramento to Buenos Aires; see boxes on pages 319 and 323.

For more information on border crossings, see the boxes in individual chapters.

Sea

It's possible to cruise to Argentina and there are some luxurious options available, as well as more basic freight travel options. Contact a specialist agency, such as **Strand Travel** ① *www.strandtravelltd.co.uk*, in London, which has information on all cruise lines.

Getting around

Air

Internal air services are run by **Aerolíneas Argentinas (AR)** ⓘ *T0810-222 86527, www.aerolineas.com.ar*, **Austral** (part of AR), **LATAM** (formerly **LAN**, before its merger with Brazilian carrier **TAM** Airlines, in 2016) ⓘ *T0810-999 9526, within Chile T600-526 2000, www.latam.com*, and the army airline **LADE** (in Patagonia, Buenos Aires, Córdoba and Paraná) ⓘ *T0810-810 5233, www.lade.com.ar*; its flights are booked up ahead of time. **Andes** ⓘ *T0810-777-26337, www.andesonline.com*, based in Salta, flies between Buenos Aires and Salta, Jujuy and Puerto Madryn.

All internal flights are fully booked way in advance for travel in December and January. Outside busy periods, it's usually possible to book internal flights with just a few days' notice, though note that flights to Ushuaia are always heavily booked. It's wise to leave some flexibility in your schedule to allow for bad weather, which may delay flights in the south, at El Calafate and Ushuaia. Meals are rarely served on internal flights, though you'll get a hot drink and a snack.

Air passes

Air passes allow you to pre-book between three to six internal flights at a discount, as long as your international flight is also with that company. **Aerolíneas Argentinas** (as well as **Austral**) has a Visite Argentina internal air pass which offers domestic flights at cheaper rates than those bought individually. Details can be found on **www.aerolineas.com.ar**: go to the 'Cheap flights' menu. You can buy from three to 12 coupons for a maximum of 90 days. Coupon prices vary depending on arrival/departure cities. It is unwise to set too tight a schedule because of delays caused by bad weather, or flight cancellations or postponements. Air passes are no longer the cheapest way of getting around, and can be very restricting since you have to book all dates when you book your international ticket. You'll probably find it easier to book internal flights separately. But check with the airlines directly, in case they have a promotion.

Road

Bus

This enormous country is connected by a network of efficient long-distance buses, which are by far the cheapest way of getting around, as well as being more environmentally friendly than plane travel. They are safe and comfortable, and long journeys are travelled overnight, which saves time, as long as you can sleep.

There are three levels of service: *común*, which offers little comfort for overnight buses, and with lots of stops (*intermedio*); *semi-cama*, with a slightly reclining seat; and *coche-cama*, where seats recline (some almost completely flat) and there are few stops. On *semi-cama* and *coche-cama* services videos will be shown (usually action movies, very loud, just as you're about to go to sleep), and meals will be provided. This might be anything from a *sandwich de miga* (very soft white bread with a slice of cheese and ham) to a full meal, with wine and a pudding. Ask the bus company to order you a vegetarian meal, if you want one, at least 24 hours before the scheduled departure. There will also be a toilet on board (of dubious cleanliness), and the bus will usually stop somewhere en route for toilets and food. The difference in price between the services is often small, and *coche-cama* is most definitely worth the extra for a good night's sleep.

On long bus journeys it's a good idea to bring: water, both to drink and for brushing your teeth, as the water in the toilet usually runs out; tissues or toilet roll; toothbrush and toothpaste; fruit or snacks, and a sandwich. Avoid being downstairs because although the larger seats are down there, they are right next to the toilet and the main door both of which are in constant use throughout the night.

Local buses are to be recommended too: since many Argentines rely on public transport, buses run to small villages and places in mountains, steppe or *puna*. Services are less frequent, but worth waiting for, to get off the beaten track and completely away from other tourists. Information on frequency and prices is given in the text where possible, but services may change, so it's worth ringing the bus terminal to check.

Bus companies may give a 20% discount if you show an international student card (or ISIC card), and this may also be available to teachers and university professors if they provide proof of employment. Note that discounts aren't usually available December to March. You can request the seat you want when you book; on old buses, seats at the back can be intolerably noisy with air conditioning (take a jumper in summer, since the air conditioning can be fierce). Make sure your seat number is on your ticket. Luggage is safely stored in a large hold at the back of the bus, and you'll be given a numbered ticket to reclaim it on arrival. It's always a good idea to lock your bags. *Maleteros* take the bags off the bus, and expect a small tip; a couple pesos is fine (many Argentines refuse to pay).

Bus company websites www.andesmar.com.ar and www.viabariloche.com.ar are useful for route planning across Argentina. Another great site to help you plan your journey is www.plataforma10.com. You can check bus prices and times, and can also book tickets for buses all over Argentina.

Car

Just over 30% of Argentina's roads are paved. Most main roads are rather narrow but roadside services are good. To avoid flying stones on gravel and dirt roads, don't follow trucks too closely, overtake with plenty of room, and pull over and slow down for oncoming vehicles. You'll find that most people won't use their indicator or brakes regularly, and the horn frequently. Most main roads have private tolls about every 100 km, US$0.20-3. Public secondary roads are generally poor. Internal checkpoints prevent food, vegetable and meat products from entering Patagonia, Mendoza, San Juan, Catamarca, Tucumán, Salta and Jujuy provinces.

All motorists are required to carry two warning triangles, a fire extinguisher, a tow rope or chain, and a first-aid kit. The handbrake must be fully operative and seat belts must be worn. Headlights must be on during the day in Buenos Aires province.

Full car documentation must be carried (including an invoice for the most recently paid insurance premium) together with your international driving licence.

Petrol/gasoline (*nafta*) costs on average US$1 a litre and US$0.75 for diesel. Cars are being converted to *gas natural comprimido* (GNC), which costs around 25% cheaper than *nafta* but filling stations are further away.

Automóvil Club Argentino (ACA) ⓘ *Av Libertador1850, Buenos Aires, T011-4808 4040 or T0800-888 3777, www.aca.org.ar,* has a travel documents service, car service facilities and road maps. Foreign automobile clubs with reciprocity with **ACA** are allowed to use facilities and discounts (with a membership card). **ACA** accommodation comprises: Motel,

Hostería, Hotel and Unidad Turística, and they also organize campsites. All have meal facilities of some kind.

Car hire You'll need a credit card to hire a car, since companies take a print of the card as their guarantee, instead of a deposit. You'll be required to show a drivers' licence (just the plastic bit of a British licence) and minimum age for renting is 25 (private arrangements may be possible). You must ensure that the renting agency gives you ownership papers of the vehicle, which have to be shown at police and military checks, and if you plan to take the car over a border into Chile or Bolivia, for example, you must let the hire company know, as they'll need to arrange special papers for you to show, and the car must have the number plate etched on its windows. Prices range from US$50 to over US$100 a day, with the highest prices in Patagonia. In tourist centres such as Salta, Bariloche or Mendoza it may be easier and cheaper to hire a taxi for the day. The multinational car hire companies (**Hertz, Avis**) are represented all over Argentina, along with Brazilian company **Localiza**, who are very reliable. Local companies may be cheaper, but check the vehicles carefully. Details of car hire companies are given in the Transport sections throughout the book.

Security Car theft has become common in Buenos Aires, much less so in the rest of the country, but park the car in busy well-lit places where possible throughout the country. Always remove all belongings and leave the empty glove compartment open when the car is unattended to reduce temptation. In tourist areas, street children will offer to guard your car, or outside restaurant areas in cities, there may be someone guarding cars for around US$3. It's worth paying, though it doesn't guarantee anything.

Cycling

If you have the time, cycling offers you one of the most rewarding ways to explore Argentina. You can get to all of the out-of-the-way places and enjoy some exhilarating rides, especially in the Andes – anywhere from Salta to El Calafate, with some breathtaking and hair-raising rides in the Lake District in between. Travelling by bike gives you the chance to travel at your own pace and meet people who are not normally in contact with tourists. There's little traffic on the roads in much of the country, which are wide enough to let trucks pass with ease in most places. The challenges are the enormous distances, the fact that there are few places to stop for food and drink in much of the country, and the lack of shade.

Main roads are paved, apart from the famous Ruta 40 in its southern half, and many roads into rural areas, which are gravel. For these, a mountain bike is advisable. Bring a comprehensive tool kit and spares. Bike shops are few and far between, although there are excellent shops in the Lake District, for example. Consider hiring bikes here if you just want some gentle riding for a few days or so. It goes without saying that you'll need tough waterproof panniers and clothing.

Useful tips Wind, not hills, will be your biggest enemy when cycling in Argentina. Try to make the best use of the mornings when wind speeds are lowest. In parts of Patagonia there can be gusting winds of 80 kph around the clock at some times of year, whereas in other areas there can be none. Take care to avoid dehydration by drinking regularly, and carry the basic food staples (sugar, salt, dried milk, tea, coffee, porridge oats, raisins, dried soups, etc) and supplement these with whatever local foods can be found in the markets.

Always camp out of sight of a road. Remember that thieves are attracted to towns and cities, so when sightseeing, try to leave your bicycle with someone, such as a café owner. However, don't take unnecessary risks; always see that your bicycle is secure (most hotels will allow bikes to be kept in rooms). All over Argentina, the dogs are famous for barking at bikes and some can be vicious; carry a stick or some small stones to frighten them off. There's little traffic on most roads, but make yourself conspicuous by wearing bright clothing, and for protection, wear a helmet.

Train

The British built a fine network of railways all over the country, which gradually fell into decline through the second half of the 20th century and were dealt the final blow when control was handed over to the provinces in 1994. Few provinces had the resources to run trains and now the few tracks operating run freight trains only.

The only passenger services are within the area of Gran Buenos Aires, to Tigre with **Tren de la Costa** ① *T011-3220 6300*, see page 75. There's also a service from Buenos Aires Constitución station south through the Pampas to the coast: via Chascomús to Mar del Plata, Necochea and Tandil, run by **Ferrobaires** ① *T0180-666 8736 (although services were suspended in 2016)*. **Ferroviario** runs a long-distance train line from Buenos Aires to Tucumán, which is uncomfortable and not recommended. The only other train services are the tourist **Tren a las Nubes** ① *www.trenalasnubes.com.ar*, which runs from Salta up to San Antonio de los Cobres in the *puna* (see box, page 284), and the narrow-gauge railway from Esquel in Patagonia, **La Trochita** ① *www.patagoniaexpress.com/el_trochita.htm*, made famous by Paul Theroux as the *Old Patagonian Express*; see page 457.

Maps

Several road maps are available, including those of the **ACA** (the most up to date), the **Firestone** road atlas and the **Automapa** ① *www.automapa.com.ar* (regional maps, Michelin-style, high quality). Most cities in Argentina have been added to Google Maps, so this will help with directions, though remember to ask a local as well, to make sure you are heading through a safe part of town.

Topographical maps are issued by the **Instituto Geográfico Militar** ① *Av Cabildo 381, Buenos Aires, T011-45765545 (1 block from Subte Ministro Carranza, Line D, or take bus 152), Mon-Fri 0800-1300, www.ign.gob.ar.* 1:500,000 sheets cost US$3 each; there's better coverage on 1:100,000 and 1:250,000 sheets, but no city plans. For walkers, the *Sendas y Bosques* (Walks and Forests) series are recommended. They're at 1:200,000 scale, laminated and easy to read, with good books containing English summaries, www.guiasendasybosques.com.ar.

Essentials A-Z

Accident and emergency

Police T101 and 911 (*31416 from a mobile).
Medical T107.

If robbed or attacked, call the tourist police, **Comisaría del Turista**, Av Corrientes 436, Buenos Aires, T011-4346 5748 (24 hrs) or T0800-999 5000 (English spoken), turista@policiafederal.gov.ar. Note that you will most likely not get your stolen goods back, but a police report is essential for your insurance claim.

Begging

There is increasingly more begging in larger cities, where you will be asked for '*una moneda*' (some change). On trains and sometimes buses you'll see and hear people telling their stories and asking for help. Although not all Argentines give to beggars, they are universally polite and apologetic to them. So whether you decide to give or not, make sure you are just as polite as the Argentines in your conduct.

Children

Travel with children will most definitely bring you into closer contact with Argentine families and individuals, and you may find officials tend to be more amenable where children are concerned. Everyone will be delighted if your child knows a little Spanish.

Travelling with children in Argentina is potentially safe, easy and a great adventure. The country is full of wonders that children can enjoy, and Argentine people are extremely affectionate to children. There's a real feeling here that children are part of society, not to be sent to be bed at 2000, and are often seen running around restaurants at 2300, or out with their parents in the evenings. This means that many family restaurants have play zones for kids with a climbing frame or soft play area, usually within sight of your table. And if you'd rather dine without your children, more expensive hotels provide a babysitter service.

Accommodation
Hotel accommodation in Argentina is good value for families; most places have rooms for 3, 4 or even 5 people, or 2 rooms with a connecting door. Many quite modest hotels have a suite, with 2 rooms and a bathroom, for families. If you're happy to be self-catering, look out for *cabañas* all over rural areas, like the Lake District.

Food
Food is easy in Argentina, since most dishes aren't strongly seasoned, and easy meals like pasta, pizza and salads are of a high standard and available everywhere. The meat is lean and portions are huge, so that if you order a steak in a restaurant there will generally be enough for you and a child (or 2 hungry children). However, children's meals are offered at most restaurants, and many establishments have high chairs. Argentine children tend to drink fizzy drinks, but freshly squeezed orange juice is widely available, and it's best to order mineral water. If your children have special dietary needs, it's worth learning the Spanish words to explain.

Transport
For most tourist attractions, there are cheaper prices for children. However, on all long-distance buses you pay a fare for each seat, and there are no half-fares if the children occupy a seat each. For shorter trips it is cheaper, if less comfortable, to seat small children on your knee. For long bus journeys, it's a good idea to bring water, fruit and biscuits, since the food provided may not be to your children's taste. There are toilets

on all long-distance buses, and these are definitely improving, but they may not be clean or have water and toilet paper, so bring tissues. All bus stations have a *kiosko*, selling drinks, snacks and tissues. Bring games and perhaps music for them to listen to as the videos shown on most buses are generally action movies, not suitable for under 12s. On sightseeing tours you could try and bargain for a family rate – often children can go free. All civil airlines charge half for children under 12 but some military services don't have half-fares, or have younger age limits.

Customs and duty free

You can buy duty-free goods on arrival at Ezeiza Airport, though the shops are small and pricey, and you can also buy products on the boats to Uruguay.

No duties are charged on clothing, personal effects or toiletries. Cameras, laptops, binoculars, MP3 players and other things that a tourist normally carries are duty-free if they have been used and only 1 of each article is carried. This is also true of scientific and professional instruments for personal use. Travellers may only bring in new personal goods up to a value of US$300 (US$100 from neighbouring countries). The duty and tax payable amounts to 50% of the item's cost. At the airport, make sure you have the baggage claim tag (usually stuck to your ticket or boarding card), as these are inspected at the exit from the customs inspection area. 2 litres of alcoholic drink, 400 cigarettes and 50 cigars are also allowed in duty-free. For tourists originating from neighbouring countries the quantities allowed are 1 litre of alcoholic drink, 200 cigarettes and 25 cigars.

If you have packages sent to Argentina, the green customs label should not be used unless the contents are of real value and you expect to pay duty. For such things as books or samples use the white label if available. A heavy tax is imposed on packages sent to Argentina by courier.

Global Refund

Some products give you the option to get the tax back on them, see page 24. The IVA (VAT) is usually 13.70% of the product's cost. For further information see **Global Blue Argentina**, T011-5238 1970, www.globalblue.com.

Disabled travellers

Facilities for the disabled in Argentina are sorely lacking. Wheelchair users won't find many ramps or even lowered curbs, although this is improving in Buenos Aires where the revamped BRT system is greatly improving bus travel for disabled travellers. Elsewhere, pavements tend to be shoddy and broken even in big cities. Only a few upmarket hotels have been fully adapted for wheelchair use, although many more modern hotels are fine for those with limited mobility. The best way to assess this is to ring or email the hotel in advance. Argentines generally go out of their way to help you, making up for poor facilities with kindness and generosity.

Tourist sites aren't generally well adapted for disabled visitors, with limited access for the physically disabled, particularly at archaeological sites. However, many museums have ramps or lifts, and some offer special guided tours for the visually impaired, and signed tours for the hearing impaired. Iguazú Falls has good access for wheelchair users or those with walking difficulties, along sturdy modern walkways with no steps, right up to the falls. Getting close to Glaciar Perito Moreno is not easy. Speaking Spanish is obviously a great help, and travelling with a companion is advisable.

Some travel companies specialize in holidays tailor-made for the individual's level of disability.

Books

You might like to read *Nothing Ventured* by Alison Walsh (Harper Collins), which gives personal accounts of worldwide journeys by disabled travellers, plus advice and listings.

Contacts

Other useful contacts include **Directions Unlimited**, New York, T914-241 1700; and **Mobility International USA**, T541-343 1284.

Websites

Disability Action Group, www.disabilityaction.org. Information on independent travel.
Global Access Disabled Network, www.globalaccessnews.com.
Royal Association for Disability and Rehabilitation, www.radar.org.uk.
Society for Accessible Travel and Hospitality, www.sath.org. Lots of advice on how to travel with specific disabilities.

Other useful sites include www.gimponthego.com and www.makoa.org/travel.htm.

Dress

Argentines of whatever class tend to dress neatly and take care to be clean and tidy so it's much appreciated if you do the same. Buying clothing locally can help you to look less like a tourist – clothes are cheap in Argentina in comparison with Western Europe and America.

Drugs

Users of drugs without medical prescription should be particularly careful, as Argentina imposes heavy penalties – up to 10 years' imprisonment – for even possession of such substances. The planting of drugs on travellers by traffickers or the police is not unknown. If offered drugs on the street, make no response at all and keep walking. Although the possession of cannabis has been decriminalized, it remains illegal to buy it, possess it or transport it.

Note that people who roll their own cigarettes are often suspected of carrying drugs and can be subjected to intensive searches. It is advisable to stick to commercial brands of cigarettes.

Electricity

220 volts AC (and 110 too in some hotels), 50 cycles. European Continental-type plugs in old buildings, Australian 3-pin flat-type in the new. Adaptors can be purchased locally for either type (ie from new 3-pin to old 2-pin and vice versa). Best to bring a universal adapter for British 3-pin plugs, as these are not available in Argentina.

Embassies and consulates

For all Argentine embassies and consulates abroad and for all foreign embassies and consulates in Argentina, see http://embassy.goabroad.com.

Gay and lesbian travellers

Argentina is fast becoming one of the most popular gay destinations in the world and there is enough happening in the capital to keep you busy for a few weeks. New gay hotels are opening, gay clubs are booming and there is a range of gay-orientated travel agencies to help you plan your stay, including **BA Gay Travel**, T011-2058 7297, www.bagaytravel.com. However, in the interior of the country, away from Buenos Aires, you might encounter homophobia; being openly demonstrative in public will certainly raise eyebrows everywhere apart from the hipper places in Buenos Aires. The tourist office produces a handy leaflet with a map showing gay friendly bars, pubs, saunas, health centres and wine bars, and change is gradually reaching government levels as well. Discrimination on the grounds of sexual orientation was banned in 1996, and in 2005 Argentina was the first South American country to legalize same-sex marriages.

Accommodation

There are plenty of gay-friendly hotels, see www.Gmaps360.com, for recommendations in Buenos Aires and Mar del Plata. For exclusively gay accommodation we recommend the **Lugar Gay de Buenos Aires**, in the San Telmo area of Buenos Aires, see page 59.

Clubs
There are many gay-friendly and gay-exclusive clubs. See www.theronda.com.ar, for more details, and page 65 for listings.

Publications
The 2 best publications are bi-monthly: *Gmaps* (www.Gmaps360.com) and the *Ronda* (www.theronda.com.ar), both found in coffee shops, hotels and gyms around the city. *Gmaps* also produce a free **G-Card** which gives you discounts, free passes, and extra services in a range of places. Order one and have it sent to your hotel.

Useful websites
www.gaytravel.com Excellent site with information on gay travel.
www.nexo.org A useful site for gay information within Argentina (Spanish only).
www.purpleroofs.com/southamerica/argentina.html For help in planning your trip.
www.thegayguide.com.ar For travel tips on bars in Buenos Aires.

Greetings

Argentines are extremely courteous and friendly people, and start every interaction, no matter how small, with a greeting. You'll be welcomed in shops and ticket offices too. Take the time to respond with a smile and a *buenos días* or *hola* in return. Argentines are sociable people, and haven't yet lost the art of passing the time of day – you'll be considered a bit abrupt if you don't too. As you leave, say *chau* (bye) or *hasta luego* (see you later). Strangers are generally treated with great kindness and generosity and your warmth in return will be greatly appreciated.

If you're introduced to new people or friends, you'll be kissed, once, on the right cheek as you say hello and goodbye. This sometimes goes for men to men too, if

they're friends (although it's more of a touching of cheeks than a kiss). In a business or official context, Argentines tend to be formal and very polite.

Health

See your GP or travel clinic at least 6 weeks before departure for general advice on travel risks and vaccinations. Try phoning a specialist travel clinic if your own doctor is unfamiliar with health conditions in Argentina. Make sure you have sufficient medical travel insurance, get a dental check, know your own blood group and if you suffer a long-term condition such as diabetes or epilepsy, obtain a Medic Alert bracelet/necklace (www.medicalert.org.uk). If you wear glasses, take a copy of your prescription.

Vaccinations and anti-malarials
Vaccinations for hepatitis A, tetanus, typhoid and, following the 2009 outbreak, influenza A (H1N1) are commonly recommended for Argentina. Sometimes advised are vaccines for hepatitis B and rabies. The final decision, however, should be based on a consultation with your GP or travel clinic. You should also confirm your primary courses and boosters are up to date.

Malaria is a substantial risk in parts of north and northeastern Argentina. Specialist advice should be taken on the best anti-malarials to use.

Health risks
The most common cause of travellers' **diarrhoea** is from eating contaminated food. Be wary of salads (what were they washed in, who handled them), re-heated foods or food that has been left out in the sun having been cooked earlier in the day. There is a simple adage that says wash it, peel it, boil it or forget it. It is also standard advice to be careful with water and ice. Ask yourself where the water came from. If you have any doubts then boil it or filter and treat it. Tap water in the major cities, especially

in Buenos Aires, is in theory safe to drink but it may be advisable to err on the side of caution and drink only bottled or boiled water. Avoid having ice in drinks unless you trust that it is from a reliable source. There are many filter/treatment devices now available on the market. Swimming in sea or river water that has been contaminated by sewage can also be a cause; ask locally if it is safe. Diarrhoea may be also caused by viruses, bacteria (such as E-coli), protozoal (such as giardia), salmonella and cholera. It may be accompanied by vomiting or by severe abdominal pain. Any kind of diarrhoea responds well to the replacement of water and salts. Sachets of rehydration salts can be bought in most chemists and can be dissolved in boiled water. If the symptoms persist, consult a doctor.

Travelling in high altitudes can bring on **altitude sickness**. On reaching heights above 3000 m, the heart may start pounding and the traveller may experience shortness of breath. Smokers and those with underlying heart or lung disease are often hardest hit. Take it easy for the first few days, rest and drink plenty of water – you will feel better soon. It is essential to get acclimatized before undertaking long treks or arduous activities.

Mosquitoes are more of a nuisance than a serious hazard but some, of course, are carriers of serious diseases such as **malaria** and **dengue**, so it is sensible to avoid being bitten as much as possible. Cases of the **Zika virus**, similarly spread, have been reported in Argentina in 2016. Sleep off the ground and use a mosquito net and some kind of insecticide. Mosquito coils release insecticide as they burn and are available in many shops, as are tablets of insecticide, which are placed on a heated mat plugged into a wall socket.

If you get sick
Contact your embassy or consulate for a list of doctors and dentists who speak your language, or at least some English. Doctors and health facilities in major

cities are also listed below. Good-quality healthcare is available in the larger centres of Argentina but it can be expensive, especially hospitalization. Make sure you have adequate insurance (see below).

Medical facilities
Bariloche
Hospital Zonal, Moreno 601, T0294-442 6119, www.hospitalbariloche.com.ar.

Buenos Aires
Urgent medical service: for free municipal ambulance service to an emergency hospital department (day and night) **Casualty ward**, **Sala de guardia**, T107, or T011-4923 1051/58 (SAME).
Inoculations: Hospital Rivadavia, Av Las Heras 2670, T011-4809 2000, Mon-Fri 0700-1200 (bus Nos 10, 37, 59, 60, 62, 92, 93 or 102 from Plaza Constitución), or **Dirección de Sanidad de Fronteras y Terminales de Transporte**, Ing Huergo 690, T011-4343 1190, Mon-Fri 1100-1500, bus No 20 from Retiro, no appointment required (yellow fever only; free injection; take passport). If not provided, buy the vaccines in **Laboratorio Biol**, Uriburu 153, T011-4953 7215, biol.com. ar, or in larger chemists. Many chemists have signs indicating that they give injections. Any hospital with an infectology department will give hepatitis A. **Centros Médicos Stamboulian**, 25 de Mayo 464, T011-4515 3000, Pacheco de Melo 2941, also in Belgrano, Villa Crespo, Villa Urquiza and Flores, www. stamboulian.com.ar. Private health advice for travellers and inoculations centre.
Public hospitals: Hospital Argerich, Almte Brown esq Py y Margall 750, T011-4121 0700. **Hospital Juan A Fernández**, Cerviño y Bulnes, T011-4808 2600, www.hospital fernandez.org. Probably the best free medical attention in the city. **British Hospital**, Perdriel 74, T011-4309 6400, emergencies T011-4309 6633/4 www.hospitalbritanico.org. ar. **German Hospital**, Av Pueyrredón 1640, between Beruti and Juncal, T011-4827 7000, www.hospitalaleman.com.ar. Both have first-

aid centres (*centros asistenciales*) as do other main hospitals.

Dental treatment: there's an excellent dental treatment centre at **Croid**, Vuelta de Obligado 1551 (Belgrano), T011-4781 9037, www.croid.com.ar. **Dental Argentina**, Laprida 1621, p 2 B, T011-4828 0821, www. dental-argentina.com.ar.

Córdoba
Hospital Córdoba, Libertad 2051, T0351-434 9013, see Facebook. **Hospital Clínicas**, Santa Rosa 1564, T0351-433 7014. For both, www.fcm.unc.edu.ar.

Corrientes
Hospital Escuela General San Martín, Rivadavia 1250, T03783-441 3113; **Sanatorio del Norte**, Carlos Pellegrini 1354, T0370-441 0410.

Formosa
Hospital Central, Salta 550, T0370-42 6194; **Hospital de la Madre y el Niño** (for children), Ayacucho 1150, T0370-442 6519.

Los Antiguos
Hospital Patagonia, Argentina 68, T02963-491303. **Farmacia Rossi Abatedaga**, Av 11 Julio 231, T02963-491204.

Mendoza city
Central hospital near bus terminal at Alem y Salta, T0261-449 0684; **Lagomaggiore**, public general hospital (with good reputation) at Timoteo Gordillo s/n, T0261-413 4600; **Children's Hospital Notti**, Bandera de los Andes 2603 (Guaymallén), T0261-413 2500.

Paraná
Hospital San Martín, Perón 450, T0343-4234545.

Posadas
Hospital Dr Ramón Madariaga, Av Marconi 3736, T0376-444 3700.

Puerto Iguazú
Hospital SAMIC, Victoria Aguirre s/n, T03757-420288.

Puerto Madryn
SEP, Sarmiento 125, T02965-445 4445.

Punta Arenas
Hospital Clínico Magallanes, 'Dr Lautaro Navarro Avaria', Av Los Flamencos 1364, T61-229 3000, www.hospitalclinico magallanes.cl. Public hospital, for emergency room ask for Urgencias. **Clínica Magallanes**, Bulnes 01448, T61-220 7200, www.clinicamagallanes.cl. Private clinic, medical staff the same as in the hospital but fancier surroundings and more expensive.

Resistencia
Hospital Pediátrico (Children's Hospital), 9 de Julio and Velez Sarfield, T0362-444 1477; **Hospital Perrando**, Av 9 de Julio 1101, T0362-442 5050.

Rosario
Hospital de Emergencias Clemente Alvarez (HECA), T0341-480811.

Salta
Hospital San Bernardo, Tobias 69, T0387-432 0300, www.hospitalsanbernardo.com.ar.

San Martín de los Andes
Hospital Ramón Carrillo, San Martín y Coronel Rodhe, T02972-427211.

Villa La Angostura
Hospital Rural Arraiz, Copello 311 (at Barrio Pinar), T02944-494170.

Useful websites
www.bgtha.org British Global Travel Health Association.
www.cdc.gov US government site that gives excellent advice on travel health and details of disease outbreaks.

www.fco.gov.uk British Foreign and Commonwealth Office travel site has useful information on each country, people, climate and a list of UK embassies/consulates. **www.fitfortravel.scot.nhs.uk** A-Z of vaccine/health advice for each country.

Insurance

Insurance is strongly recommended and policies are very reasonable. If you have financial restraints the most important aspect of any insurance policy is medical care and repatriation. Ideally you want to make sure you are covered for personal items too. Read the small print *before* heading off so you are aware of what is covered and what is not, what is required to submit a claim and what to do in the event of an emergency.

Internet

The best way to keep in touch is undoubtedly online. Broadband is widely available even in small towns, and most hotels and hostels have Wi-Fi. Telephone is expensive in Argentina so all Argentines have adapted rapidly to internet. Most *locutorios* (phone centres) also have internet, and there are dedicated centres on almost every block in town. Prices vary.

Language

See page 690 for a list of useful words and phrases, and page 32 for a menu reader.

Your experience in Argentina will be completely transformed if you can learn even a little of the language before you arrive. Spanish is the first language, with a few variations and a distinctive pronunciation. In areas popular with tourists, you'll find some people speak English and perhaps French or Italian, but since much of the pleasure of Argentina is in getting off the beaten track, you'll often find yourself in situations where only Spanish is spoken. Argentines are welcoming and curious, and they're very likely to strike up conversation on a bus, shop or in a queue for the cinema. They're also incredibly hospitable and your attempts to speak Spanish will be enormously appreciated.

If you have a few weeks before you arrive, try and learn a few basic phrases, useful verbs and numbers. If you're reading this on the plane, it's not too late to get a grasp of basic introductions, food and directions.

Language schools

Large cities all offer Spanish-language classes; see Language schools under What to do in the Listings sections of individual

Learn to speak Spanish!

Recommended by travellers since 2004. Courses on all levels starting every Monday, year-round. City combinations using the same materials and level system.

Buenos Aires
Montevideo
Bariloche

Instituto Cervantes
Centro Acreditado

www.academiabuenosaires.com www.academiabariloche.com www.academiauruguay.com

towns and cities. If you would like to arrange your classes before you arrive, as well as your accommodation, try one of the following organizations:

Amerispan, *T0800-511 0179, www. amerispan.com*. North American company offering Spanish immersion programmes, educational tours, and volunteer and internship positions in Buenos Aires, Córdoba and Mendoza. Also programmes for younger people.

Expanish, *25 de Mayo 457, 4th floor, T011-5252 3040, www.expanish.com*. Buenos Aires-based agency that can organize packages including accommodation, trips and classes in Buenos Aires, and Patagonia in Argentina, as well as in Peru, Ecuador and Chile. Highly recommended.

Spanish Abroad, *T1-888-722 7623, www.spanishabroad.com*. Spanish classes in Buenos Aires and Córdoba.

Media

Newspapers

The national daily papers are *La Nación*, a broadsheet, intelligent and well written (www.lanacion.com.ar); and *Clarín*, more accessible, also a broadsheet (www.clarin.com.ar). Both these papers have good websites and excellent Sunday papers with informative travel sections. Other daily national papers are *La Prensa* (www.laprensa.com.ar), *La Razón* (www.larazon.com.ar), and the left wing *Página-12* (www.pagina12.com.ar), always refreshing for a different perspective. There's a daily paper in English, the *Buenos Aires Herald* (www.buenosairesherald.com), which gives a brief digest of world news, as well as Argentine news. Magazines you might like to look at include: *Noticias*, news and culture; *Gente*, a kind of *Hello!* for Argentina; *El Gráfico*, a good sports magazine; and particularly *Lugares*. This glossy monthly travel magazine has superb photography and is a very useful resource for travel tips and ideas of where to go, often with English translation at the back.

Issues are themed; the northwest, the lakes, etc, and previous issues are often available from *kioskos* too. For information in English on what is going on around the country, see www.argentinaindependent.com

Few foreign-language newspapers are available outside Buenos Aires, but to keep in touch with world news, websites of your own favourite newspaper are invaluable. Many hotels have cable TV in the rooms, and occasionally have English news channels such as CNN and/or Bloomberg.

Money

US$1=AR$15.30, £1=AR$18.70, €1=AR$16.64, AUS$1=AR$11.70 (Nov 2016).

Currency

The unit of currency is the Argentine peso (AR$), divided into 100 centavos. Peso notes in circulation are 2, 5, 10, 20, 50 and 100, with 200- and 500-peso bills to be released in 2016, as well as a 1000-peso note to be released in 2017. Coins in circulation are 5, 10, 25 and 50 centavos, 1 peso and 2 pesos. For many years, restrictions on Argentines buying US dollars created a free, or "blue", market rate for dollars (*mercado azul*). Before Jan 2014, the official rate was devalued to AR$8=US$1, and by Sep 2014 the blue rate was valued at AR$14=US$1. However, on taking office in 2015, President Macri lifted the price controls put in place by the previous Kirchner administration. The result was a free-floating peso that all but eliminated the blue market. For the time being the official bank rate is the normal rate of exchange.

Still, it's often wiser to change large amounts of money at an exchange house rather than pay the transaction fees for multiple ATM withdrawals. You can also find decent rates by wiring US dollars from a US bank account via www.xoom.com, which allows transfers to its Argentine outlet, More Argentina (www.moreargentina.com), for a single fee for up to a US$2000 transfer.

Note The exchange rate tends to change on a daily basis and inflation is high, so prices fluctuate. Prices given in this edition are calculated at the official exchange rate at the time of research. Always pay the exact amount of a bill as small change is in short supply. Fake notes circulate; see Safety below.

Cost of travelling

Argentina's economy has picked up since the 2001 economic crisis, but prices have risen steeply, particularly for hotels and tourist services. Nevertheless, you'll still find Argentina a very economical country to travel around.

You can find comfortable accommodation with a private bathroom and breakfast for around US$45-60 for 2 people, while a good dinner in the average restaurant will be around US$12-20 per person. Prices are much cheaper away from the main touristy areas: El Calafate, Ushuaia and Buenos Aires can be particularly pricey. For travellers on a budget, hostels usually cost US$10-20 per person in a shared dorm. Cheap breakfasts can be found in any ordinary café for around US$4-5, and there are cheap set lunches at many restaurants, costing around US$7, US$10 in Buenos Aires. Camping costs vary widely, but expect to pay no more than US$3-6 per tent – usually less. Long-distance bus travel on major routes is very cheap, and it's well worth splashing out an extra 20% for *coche-cama* service on overnight journeys.

Credit, debit and currency cards

The easiest way to get cash while you're in Argentina is to use a credit card at an ATM (*cajero automático*). These can be found in every town or city and most accept all major cards, with **MasterCard** and **Visa** being the most widely accepted in small places. They are usually **Banelco** or **Link**, accepting international cards, but they dispense only pesos, impose withdrawal and daily limits and a charge per transaction (limits change,

check on arrival). You will also have to add any commission imposed by your card's issuing company. Note that many Argentine ATMs give you your cash and receipt before the card is returned: don't walk away without the card. Transactions at ATMs (known as *cajeros automáticos*), as at exchange houses (*casas de cambio*) and banks, are at the official rate. If you withdraw cash from the bank counter with a card and when making a purchase with a credit card, you will also have to show your passport. It's a good idea to carry cash to pay in cheaper shops, restaurants and hotels, and some places will give a discount for cash. **MasterCard** emergency number is T0800-627 8372 and **Visa** is T0800-666 0171

Traveller's cheques

There's little point in carrying traveller's cheques (TCs) in Argentina since there are exchange facilities only in big towns, and commission is very high: usually 10%. A passport is essential and you may have to show proof of purchase, so transactions can take a long time.

Opening hours

Business hours Banks, government offices and businesses are usually open Mon-Fri 0800-1300 in summer, and Mon-Fri 1000-1500 in winter. Some businesses open again in the evening, 1700-2000. **Cafés and restaurants**: cafés are busy from 2400. Restaurants are open for lunch 1230-1500, dinner 2100-2400. **Nightclubs**: open at 2400, but usually only get busy around 0200. **Post offices**: often open *corrido* – don't close for lunch or siesta. **Shops**: in Buenos Aires most are open 0900-1800. Elsewhere, everything closes for siesta 1300-1700.

Police

Whereas Europeans and North Americans are accustomed to law enforcement on a systematic basis, enforcement in Argentina is more of a sporadic affair. Many people feel that the police are corrupt and unreliable due to incredibly low pay, and there are reports that they sometimes work with local thieves to turn a blind eye to muggings. In fact, they are usually courteous and will be helpful to tourists. When reporting an incident police will invariably ask for identification, so be sure to always have your passport (or a copy of it) with you.

Post

Be aware that mail sent to Argentina may not arrive or may arrive late. Sending mail home is not a problem, it is cheap and efficient. Letters from Argentina take 10-14 days to get to Europe and the USA. Rates for letters up to 20 g to Europe and USA, up to 150 g. Post can be sent from the *correo* (post office) or from private postal service *Oca*, through any shop displaying the purple sign. The post service is reliable, but for assured delivery, register everything.

Small parcels of up to 2 kg can be sent from all post offices. Larger parcels must be sent from the town's main post office, where your parcel will be examined by customs to make sure that the contents are as stated on your customs form, and taken to *Encomiendas Internacionales* for posting. Any local *correo* can tell you where to go. Customs usually open in the morning only. Having parcels sent to Argentina incurs a customs tax, which depends on the value of the package, and all incoming packages are opened by customs. If when you are in Buenos Aires you are sent anything large or electronic, it will get stopped at Ezeiza International Airport Customs, you will then have to go there (or to the international post office in Retiro, near the bus station), wade through paperwork for about 2 hrs and then possibly pay a duty tax. Try to avoid being sent anything really valuable. Poste restante is available in every town's main post office, fee US$2.

Public holidays

1 Jan New Year's Day (public holiday).
Mar/Apr Good Friday and **Easter** weekend (public holiday).
1 May Labour Day (public holiday).
25 May May Revolution of 1810 (public holiday).
10 Jun Malvinas Day (public holiday). Best not to announce it if you are British around this day.
20 Jun Flag Day (public holiday).
9 Jul Independence Day (public holiday).
17 Aug Anniversary of San Martín's death (public holiday).
12 Oct Columbus Day (public holiday).
10 Nov Día de la Tradición. There are gaucho parades throughout Argentina on the days leading up to this festival, with fabulous displays of horsemanship, gaucho games, enormous *asados* and traditional music. It's worth seeing the festivities in any small town.
25 Dec Christmas Day. Banks are closed and there are limited bus services on 25 and 31 Dec.
30 Dec (not 31 because so many offices in centre are closed). There is a ticker-tape tradition in downtown Buenos Aires.

Safety

Relatively speaking, Buenos Aires is one of the safest cities in South America, and Argentina as a whole is an easy and safe place to travel, but that doesn't mean you need to drop your guard altogether. There are a few simple things you can do to avoid being a victim of crime.

Fake money

There is a big problem with fake notes in Argentina. The best way to tell if your money is not a fake is to look for the following 3 things: the green numbers showing the value of the note (on the top left-hand corner) should shimmer; if you hold the note up to the sky you should see a watermark;

lastly there should be a continuous line from the top of the note to the bottom about ¾ of the way along (also when held up to the light). The most common fake notes are $100 pesos, $20 pesos and $10 pesos. Some taxi drivers reportedly circulate fakes late at night with drunk passengers, or you may be given them back in change in markets and fairs. Check the notes thoroughly before walking away. Try to break large notes in hostels/hotels or supermarkets to avoid being given a fake in change. US dollar bills are often scanned electronically for forgeries.

Places to avoid
In most towns the train and bus stations should be avoided late at night and early in the morning. If you arrive at that time, try to arrange for your hotel or hostel to pick you up. If you can, in Buenos Aires and when you are travelling, visit the bus station to buy your tickets the day before so you can find out where the platform is and where you need to go. Also watch your belongings being stowed in the boot of the bus, and keep the ticket you'll be given since you'll need it to claim your luggage on arrival.

Precautions
Some general tips are: don't walk along the street with your map or guidebook in hand – check where you are going beforehand and duck into shops to have a quick look at your map. In cafés make sure you have your handbag on your lap or your backpack strap around your ankles. Try not to wear clothes that stand out, and certainly don't wear expensive rings, watches or jewellery that shines. Remember that the people around you don't know that you bought that watch for US$10 second hand – to them it looks expensive. Always catch Radio Taxis ask at your hostel/hotel the best taxi company to use and their direct number. When in a taxi, if possible lock the doors, or ask the driver to.

And finally, just remember the golden rules: store your money and credit cards in small amounts in different places in your

luggage; if carrying a wallet, keep it in a front rather than a back pocket; scan and email yourself copies of your passport, visas and insurance forms; and keep an eye on the news or newspapers to be aware of what is happening in the country that you are travelling in.

If you are the victim of a **sexual assault**, you are advised in the first instance to contact a doctor (this can be your home doctor if you prefer). You will need tests to determine whether you have contracted any sexually transmitted diseases; you may also need advice on post-coital contraception. You should also contact your embassy, where consular staff are very willing to help in cases of assault. For more advice see www.dailystrength.org and www.rapecrisis.org.uk.

Scams
Be aware of scams. There are 2 favoured scams in use. One is that someone will discreetly spill a liquid on you, then a 'helpful stranger' will draw your attention to it and offer to help you clean it off. Meanwhile someone else has raided your pockets or run off with your bags. If someone does point out something on your clothes, keep walking until you see a coffee shop and clean up there. The second scam involves someone driving past you on a motorbike, ripping your bag off your shoulders, or smartphone right out of your hand, and driving away off into the sunset. To avoid this, wear your bag with the strap over your head and one shoulder and keep your bag on the opposite side of your body to the street. Also, try to avoid talking on your mobile when walking along busy streets on the main thoroughfares. If travelling with a laptop, don't use a computer bag. Buy a satchel or handbag big enough to carry it in.

Taxis
Always take Radio Taxis. Ask your hostel or hotel for a reputable company and call them whenever you need a taxi. They generally take only around 10 mins to come. Always

lock the doors in the taxi as taxi doors have reportedly been opened at traffic intersections when the car is stationary.

Student travellers

If you're in full-time education, you're entitled to an International Student Identity Card (ISIC), www.isic.org, available from student travel offices and agencies. This gives you special prices on transport, cultural events and a variety of other concessions and services. All student cards must carry a photograph. Some hostel chains also give ISIC card discounts.

Almundo, Florida 835, p 3, oficina 320 (with many branches in BA and around the country), T0810-4328 7907, www.almundo.com.ar. Mon-Fri 0900-2000, Sat 0900-1500. Helpful Argentine Youth and Student Travel Organization, runs a Student Flight Centre Booking for flights hotels and travel; information for all South America, notice board for travellers, sells ISIC cards; English and French spoken

TIJE, San Martín 601, Buenos Aires, T011-5272 8453, www.tije.com, and at STB (STA representative), Viamonte 577, p 3, Buenos Aires, T011-5217 2727. Cheap fares.

YMCA (Central), Reconquista 439, Buenos Aires, T011-4311 4785.

YWCA, Humberto Iº 2360, T011-4941 3776, www.ywca.org.ar.

Tax

Airport tax

By law airport taxes must be included in the price of your air ticket. When in transit from one international flight to another, you may be obliged to pass through immigration and customs, have your passport stamped. There is a 5% tax on the purchase of air tickets. There is now an entry fee (suspended for US citizens) for Argentina, see page 664.

VAT

21%; VAT is not levied on medicines, books and some foodstuffs.

Telephone *Country code +54.*

Ringing: equal tones with long pauses. Engaged: equal tones with equal pauses.

Phoning in Argentina is made very easy by the abundance of *locutorios* – phone centres with private booths where you can talk for as long as you like, and pay afterwards, the price appearing on a small screen in your booth. There's no need for change or phonecards, and *locutorios* often have internet, photocopying and fax services.

An alternative to *locutorios* is to buy a phonecard and use it with your mobile. Many *kioskos* and *locutorios* sell mobile phone cards offered by Argentina's largest communications providers, like **Movistar** and **Claro**, for around US$2.

Otherwise VoIP providers, such as Skype, Viber or WhatsApp, are the cheapest ways to keep in touch.

Time

GMT -3.

Tipping

10% in restaurants and cafés. Porters and ushers are usually tipped. Tipping isn't obligatory, but it is appreciated.

Tourist information

There are tourist information offices in all provincial capitals, in major tourist destinations and many bus terminals/ airports in popular destinations. Infrastructure varies across the country, but they can usually give you a town map and sometimes a list of accommodation, as well as the tours, sights and festivals in the area. Staff in more popular tourist areas usually speak at least some English (and sometimes French, German, Italian) and are usually helpful. Opening hours are long – typically 0800-2000 in summer but they may close at weekends. All bus terminals have an office (often signed *Informes*) with bus information.

Wanderlust Publications Ltd, T01753-620426, www.wanderlust.co.uk. A magazine for independent-minded travellers.

Useful organizations
Administración de Parques Nacionales, Santa Fe 690, opposite Plaza San Martín, Buenos Aires, T011-4311 0303, www.parquesnacionales.gob.ar. Mon-Fri 1000-2000. Has leaflets on national parks.
Aves Argentinas/AOP (a BirdLife International partner), Matheu 1246/8, Buenos Aires, T011-4943 7216, Mon-Fri 1030-1330, 1430-2030. Information on birdwatching and specialist tours, good library.

Tourist offices
Loads of information on Argentina is now available on the internet, much of it reasonably up-to-date and in English. Most provinces in Argentina have their own website (see Tourist information sections in individual towns and cities) and it's useful to have a look before you travel for inspiration and information. Each province has a tourist office, **Casa de Provincia**, in Buenos Aires, Mon-Fri 0900-1700. For bookings for cheap accommodation and youth hostels, contact **Almundo**, see Student travellers, page 681.

Useful websites
www.alojar.com.ar Accommodation search engine and tourist information in Spanish.

www.buenosairesherald.com *Buenos Aires Herald*, English-language daily.
www.baexpats.org
www.getsouth.com A fantastic site filled with accommodation and tour recommendations, as well as discounts and travel advice. Highly recommended.
www.infobae.com An Argentine online newspaper, in Spanish.
www.mercotour.com Information on travel and other matters in Argentina, Uruguay, Chile and Brazil, in Spanish, English and Portuguese.
www.responsibletravel.org
www.streema.com Site that enables you to listen to radio stations all over the world.
www.tageblatt.com.ar *Argentinisches Tageblatt*, German-language weekly, very informative.
www.welcomeargentina.com

Tour operators

If the choices available in Argentina are overwhelming, and you have little time to spend, or if you're not keen on travelling alone, it's worth considering booking a package with a specialist tour operator. Whether you choose an adventurous expedition, or a more sedate trip; a bespoke journey just for you, or a group holiday, these companies work with agents on the ground who will book all your transport and accommodation, so that you can just enjoy the experience. UK and Australian travellers

Chimu The Latin America and Antarctica Specialists

Expedition cruises to Antarctica & customised itineraries to Latin America

phone: 020 7403 8265
email: uk@chimuadventures.com

www.chimuadventures.com

Breathtaking & Unique

...Live for today

are advised to choose a tour operator from **LATA**, the Latin American Travel Association, www.lata.org, which is also a useful source of country information.

In the UK

Abercrombie and Kent, T01242-547 760, www.abercrombiekent.co.uk. Upmarket tailor-made travel.

Audley Travel, T01993-838 000, www.audleytravel.com. High-quality tailor-made travel, including the Northwest, Lake District and Patagonia. Good on the ground knowledge. Recommended.

Chimu Adventures, T020-7403 8265, www.chimuadventures.com. Provide tours, treks, active adventures and accommodation throughout South America and the Antarctic.

Explore, T01252-883 509, www.explore.co.uk. Quality small-group trips, especially in Patagonia. Also offers family adventures, or with a focus on culture, wildlife or trekking.

Journey Latin America, T020-8747 8315, www.journeylatinamerica.co.uk. Deservedly well regarded, this excellent long-established company runs adventure tours, escorted groups and tailor-made tours to Argentina and other destinations in South America. Also offers cheap flights and expert advice. Well organized and very professional. Recommended.

Last Frontiers, T01296-653000, www.lastfrontiers.com. Excellent company

offering top-quality tailor-made trips all over Argentina, including superb wine tours, trips combining Iguazú and Salta, trips to the Esteros del Iberá, and horse riding in Patagonia and Córdoba. By far the best company for estancia stays; a real in-depth knowledge of Argentina. Highly recommended.

Select Latin America, T020-7407 1478, www.selectlatinamerica.co.uk. Specializing in tailor-made and small-group tours with a cultural or natural history emphasis, this is a friendly small company with some good itineraries, including birdwatching in the Los Esteros del Iberá, Antarctica and the R40.

Steppes Travel, T02185 601 781, www.steppestravel.co.uk. Tailor-made and group itineraries throughout Argentina and Latin America.

The South America Specialists, T01525-306555, www.thesouthamericaspecialists.com. A luxury travel site for those interested in travel to South America with hotel reviews, photos and HD videos.

Specialist tour operators

There are many more specialized tour operators, offering specialist trips for birdwatching and horse riding. Below is just a selection.

Adventures Abroad, T1-800-665 3998, www.adventures-abroad.com. Impressive

DISCOVER ARGENTINA

Specialising in tailor-made and escorted tours to Latin America, Galapagos and Antarctica for more than 29 years.
ATOL protected 3760

Select LATIN AMERICA   020 7407 1478   info@selectlatinamerica.co.uk
www.selectlatinamerica.co.uk

company running superb and imaginative tours for small groups to Patagonia, Iguazú and Puerto Madryn, the glaciers and Ushuaia. Great itineraries.

Exodus, T0203 811 3155, www.exodus.co.uk. Excellent, well-run trekking and climbing tours of Patagonia and Chile, including Torres del Paine, cycling in the Lake District, Antarctica and a great tour following in Shackleton's footsteps.

Naturetrek, T01962-733051, www.naturetrek.co.uk. Small group birdwatching tours, fixed departure.

STA Travel, offices worldwide, www.statravel.co.uk/.com. Cheap flights, and sell Dragoman's trip which includes Argentina.

Trailfinders, 194 Kensington High St, London, W8 7RG, T020-7938 3939, www.trailfinders.com. Reliable for cheap flights and tours.

In North America
Argentina for Less, T1-817-230 4971, www.argentinaforless.com. Progressive tourism company with a focus solely on Latin America. US-based but with local offices and operations.
Worldwide Horseback Riding Adventures, toll free T0800-545 0019, www.ridingtours.com. US-based horse-riding company.

In South America
Class Adventure Travel, T877-240 4770, www.classadventuretravel.com. With offices throughout South America, they specialize in quality, budget adventure tours.
Say Hueque, T+54 11-5258 8740, www.sayhueque.com. Recommended Argentine travel agency with offices in Buenos Aires and friendly English-speaking staff. They offer good-value tours aimed at independent travellers. Specialize in tours to Patagonia, Iguazú and Mendoza.

The South America Specialists

We are experts in designing luxury travel itineraries throughout South America and Antarctica, offering first hand reviews, one-on-one service and on the ground back up. We are fully ATOL bonded and, with over 10 years of expertise, we can match and beat any price on the market.

Contact us now for a tailored quote
W: thesouthamericaspecialists.com
T: +44 (0)1525 306 555
E: info@thesouthamericaspecialists.com

SOUTH AMERICA

Vaccinations

No vaccination certificates are required for entry. For further details, see Health, page 673.

Visas and immigration

Visas on entry

Passports are not required by citizens of neighbouring countries who hold identity cards issued by their own governments. Visas are not necessary for US citizens, British citizens, citizens of EU countries, nationals of Central American countries and nationals of some Caribbean countries (Jamaica), plus Australia, Canada, Hong Kong, Israel, Japan, Malaysia, New Zealand, Russia, Singapore, South Africa and Turkey. Visitors from these countries are given a tourist card on entry and may stay for 3 months. For visitors from all other countries, there are 3 types of visa: a tourist visa (multiple entry, valid for 3 months; onward ticket and proof of adequate funds must be provided; fees vary depending on the country of origin; can be extended by 90 days), a business visa and a transit visa.

Visa extensions and renewals

All visitors can renew their tourist visas for another 3 months by going in person to the **National Directorate of Migration**, Antártida Argentina 1365, Buenos Aires, T011-4317 0200, Mon-Fri 0800-1400, or to any other delegation of the Dirección Nacional de Migraciones (www.migraciones.gov.ar) and paying a fee of US$40: ask for *Prórrogas de Permanencia*. No renewals are given after the expiry date. Alternatively, for a 90-day extension of your stay in Argentina, just leave the country at any land border, and you'll get another 3-month tourist visa stamped

Web Site/ www.sayhueque.com
Email / travel@sayhueque.com
Facebook/ ArgeninaTours.SayHueque
Twitter/ SayHuequeTravel

SAY HUEQUE
ARGENTINA JOURNEYS

Recommended by the most important **Travel Guides**

Time Out · lonely planet · The New York Times · Frommer's TRAVEL · Budget Travel
USA TODAY TRAVEL · routard · TRAVEL+LEISURE · ROUGH GUIDES · footprint

Palermo Soho: Thames 2062 - Tel: (+5411) 52588740
San Telmo: Chile 557 - Tel: (+5411) 43073451

Evyt Leg: 11320 Res: 111

in your passport on return. Alternatively, you can forego all the paperwork by paying a US$40 fine at a border immigration post (queues are shorter than in Buenos Aires, but still allow 30 mins). The most popular way of renewing your visa from Buenos Aires is to spend the day in Uruguay, which is only 45 mins away by boat.

Advice and tips

All visitors are advised to carry their passports at all times, and it is illegal not to have identification handy. In practice, though, this is not advisable. Photocopy your passport twice, carry 1 copy, and scan your passport and email it to yourself for emergencies. You'll often be asked for your passport number, when checking into hotels and if paying by credit card, so learn it off by heart. The police like searching backpackers at border points: remain calm – this is a normal procedure. If you are staying in the country for several weeks, it may be worthwhile registering at your embassy or consulate. This will help if your passport is stolen as the process of replacing it is simplified and speeded up.

Weights and measures

The metric system is used in Argentina.

Women travellers

Single women might attract surprise – *¿Estás sola?* Are you travelling alone? – but this is rather because Argentines are such sociable people and love to travel in groups, than because it's dangerous. Argentine men can't seem to help paying women attention, and you may hear the traditional *piropo* as you walk past: a compliment, usually rather unimaginative, and nothing to cause offence. Just ignore it and walk on. Men are generally respectful of a woman travelling alone, and won't make improper suggestions, but just in case here are some tips: Wear a ring on your wedding finger, and carry a photograph of '*mi marido*', your

'husband'. By saying that your 'husband' is close at hand, you may dissuade an aspiring suitor. Argentine men are famously charming and persistent chatters up, so firmly discourage any unwanted contact and be aware of any signals that might be interpreted as encouragement. If politeness fails, don't feel bad about showing offence and leaving.

Do not walk alone around Buenos Aires in quiet areas or at night. When accepting a social invitation, make sure that someone knows the address you're going to and the time you left. And if you don't know your hosts well, a good ploy is to ask if you can bring a friend, even if you've no intention of doing so, to check the intentions of whoever's inviting you. Wherever you are, try to act with confidence, and walk as though you know where you are going, even if you don't. Someone who looks lost is more likely to attract unwanted attention. Do not disclose to strangers where you are staying. When you set out, err on the side of caution until your instincts have adjusted to the customs of a new culture. Always ask the hotel, the restaurant or your hosts to call you a **Radio Taxi** as these are usually much safer and regulated closely.

Book accommodation ahead so that when you arrive in a new town you can take a taxi straight to your hotel or hostel and avoid looking lost and vulnerable at bus stations. Many hotels or hostels are open 24 hrs, but if you arrive in the early morning, it's safest to wait in the bus station *confitería*, where there are usually people around, than to venture into the centre.

Women should be aware that tampons are quite hard to find in Argentina and it may be best to bring a supply. In most chemists and supermarkets tampons are generally held behind the counter and you'll need to ask for them (pronounced, roughly the same in Spanish, *tampón*). Tampons and towels must never be flushed, whether in a private home or hotel. Carry a supply of plastic bags in case bins aren't provided.

For more advice for women travellers see www.womenstravelclub.com.

Working in Argentina

Foreigners can't work in Argentina without a work permit which you'll only get with an official job (or if you are from New Zealand as you can apply for a 12-month working visa). At a time of high unemployment, it's hard to find work and you might consider it unfair to take work away from Argentines. The exception to this is teaching English, and it's possible to pick up work with a school, even if you don't have any qualifications. But you will be paid more if you have a TEFL certificate (Teaching English as a Foreign Language) and experience. Otherwise, private lessons are always an option, but they pay very poorly. Jobs in schools are advertised in the English-language newspaper, the *Buenos Aires Herald*; www.craigslist.com; the South American Explorers free newsletter, www.saexplorers.org; and in the schools themselves.

EBC, www.ebc-tefl-course.com, offer a comprehensive 4-week TEFL training course that is highly recommended. Most graduates walk away with a job already organized.

If you are intent on trying to obtain a work visa speak to **Immigration**, Antártida Argentina 1365, Buenos Aires, T011-4317 0200, www.migraciones.gov.ar. A good level of Spanish is essential.

Footnotes

Basic Spanish for travellers

Learning Spanish is a useful part of the preparation for a trip to Latin America and no volumes of dictionaries, phrase books or word lists will provide the same enjoyment as being able to communicate directly with the people of the country you are visiting. It is a good idea to make an effort to grasp the basics before you go. As you travel you will pick up more of the language and the more you know, the more you will benefit from your stay.

General pronunciation

Whether you have been taught the 'Castilian' pronunciation (*z* and *c* followed by *i* or *e* are pronounced as the *th* in think) or the 'American' pronunciation (they are pronounced as *s*), you will encounter little difficulty in understanding either. Regional accents and usages vary, but the basic language is essentially the same everywhere.

Argentine Spanish sounds like no other. The main difference is that in words with 'll' and 'y', the sound is pronounced like a soft 'j' sound, as in 'beige'. The 'd' sound is usually omitted in words ending in 'd' or '-ado', and 's' sounds are often omitted altogether at the ends of words. And in the north and west of the country, you'll hear the normal rolled 'r' sound replaced by a hybrid 'r j' put together. Grammatically, the big change is that the Spanish '*tú*' is replaced by '*vos*' which is also used almost universally instead of '*usted*', unless you're speaking to someone much older or higher in status. In the conjunction of verbs, the accent is on the last syllable (eg *vos, tenés, podés*). In the north and northwest, though, the Spanish is more akin to that spoken in the rest of Latin America. In Buenos Aires, you might hear the odd word of *lunfardo*, Italian-oriented slang.

Vowels

a	as in English *cat*
e	as in English *best*
i	as the *ee* in English *feet*
o	as in English *shop*
u	as the *oo* in English *food*
ai	as the *i* in English *ride*
ei	as *ey* in English *they*
oi	as *oy* in English *toy*

Consonants

Most consonants can be pronounced more or less as they are in English. The exceptions are:

g	before *e* or *i* is the same as *j*
h	is always silent (except in *ch* as in *chair*)
j	as the *ch* in Scottish *loch*
ll	as the *y* in *yellow*
ñ	as the *ni* in English *onion*
rr	trilled much more than in English
x	depending on its location, pronounced *x, s, sh* or *j*

Spanish words and phrases

Greetings, courtesies

hello	*hola*	I speak Spanish	*hablo español*
good morning	*buenos días*	I don't speak Spanish	*no hablo español*
good afternoon/	*buenas tardes/*	do you speak English?	*¿habla inglés?*
evening/night	*noches*	I don't understand	*no entiendo/*
goodbye	*adiós/chao*		*no comprendo*
pleased to meet you	*mucho gusto*	please speak slowly	*hable despacio*
see you later	*hasta luego*		*por favor*
how are you?	*¿cómo está?*	I am very sorry	*lo siento mucho/*
	¿cómo estás?		*disculpe*
I'm fine, thanks	*estoy muy bien,*	what do you want?	*¿qué quiere?*
	gracias		*¿qué quieres?*
I'm called...	*me llamo...*	I want	*quiero*
what is your name?	*¿cómo se llama?*	I don't want it	*no lo quiero*
	¿cómo te llamas?	leave me alone	*déjeme en paz/*
yes/no	*sí/no*		*no me moleste*
please	*por favor*	good/bad	*bueno/malo*
thank you (very much)	*(muchas) gracias*		

Questions and requests

Have you got a room for two people?
 ¿Tiene una habitación para dos personas?
How do I get to_? *¿Cómo llego a_?*
How much does it cost?
 ¿Cuánto cuesta? ¿cuánto es?
I'd like to make a long-distance phone call
 Quisiera hacer una llamada de larga distancia
Is service included?
 ¿Está incluido el servicio?

Is tax included?
 ¿Están incluidos los impuestos?
When does the bus leave (arrive)?
 ¿A qué hora sale (llega) el autobús?
When? *¿cuándo?*
Where is_? *¿dónde está_?*
Where can I buy tickets?
 ¿Dónde puedo comprar boletos?
Where is the nearest petrol station?
 ¿Dónde está la gasolinera más cercana?
Why? *¿por qué?*

Basics

bank	*el banco*	expensive	*caro/a*
bathroom/toilet	*el baño*	market	*el mercado*
bill	*la factura/*	note/coin	*le billete/*
	la cuenta		*la moneda*
cash	*el efectivo*	police (policeman)	*la policía*
cheap	*barato/a*		*(el policía)*
credit card	*la tarjeta*	post office	*el correo*
	de crédito	public telephone	*el teléfono público*
exchange house	*la casa de cambio*	supermarket	*el supermercado*
exchange rate	*el tipo de cambio*	ticket office	*la taquilla*

Getting around

aeroplane	*el avión*	insured person	*el/la asegurado/a*
airport	*el aeropuerto*	to insure yourself against	*asegurarse contra*
arrival/departure	*la llegada/salida*	luggage	*el equipaje*
avenue	*la avenida*	motorway, freeway	*el autopista/ la carretera*
block	*la cuadra*		
border	*la frontera*	north, south,	*norte, sur,*
bus station	*la terminal de autobuses/ camiones*	east, west	*este (oriente), oeste (occidente)*
bus	*el bus/el autobús/ el camión*	oil	*el aceite*
		to park	*estacionarse*
collective/ fixed-route taxi	*el colectivo*	passport	*el pasaporte*
		petrol/gasoline	*la gasolina*
corner	*la esquina*	puncture	*el pinchazo/ la ponchadura*
customs	*la aduana*		
first/second class	*primera/segunda clase*	street	*la calle*
		that way	*por allí/por allá*
left/right	*izquierda/derecha*	this way	*por aquí/por acá*
ticket	*el boleto*	tourist card/visa	*la tarjeta de turista*
empty/full	*vacío/lleno*	tyre	*la llanta*
highway, main road	*la carretera*	unleaded	*sin plomo*
immigration	*la inmigración*	to walk	*caminar/andar*
insurance	*el seguro*		

Accommodation

air conditioning	*el aire acondicionado*	power cut	*el apagón/corte*
		restaurant	*el restaurante*
all-inclusive	*todo incluido*	room/bedroom	*el cuarto/ la habitación*
bathroom, private	*el baño privado*		
bed, double/single	*la cama matrimonial/ sencilla*	sheets	*las sábanas*
		shower	*la ducha/regadera*
		soap	*el jabón*
blankets	*las cobijas/mantas*	toilet	*el sanitario/ excusado*
to clean	*limpiar*		
dining room	*el comedor*	toilet paper	*el papel higiénico*
guesthouse	*la casa de huéspedes*	towels, clean/dirty	*las toallas limpias/ sucias*
hotel	*el hotel*	water, hot/cold	*el agua caliente/ fría*
noisy	*ruidoso*		
pillows	*las almohadas*		

Health

aspirin	*la aspirina*	diarrhoea	*la diarrea*
blood	*la sangre*	doctor	*el médico*
chemist	*la farmacia*	fever/sweat	*la fiebre/el sudor*
condoms	*los preservativos, los condones*	pain	*el dolor*
		head	*la cabeza*
contact lenses	*los lentes de contacto*	period/sanitary towels	*la regla/las toallas femeninas*
contraceptives	*los anticonceptivos*	stomach	*el estómago*
contraceptive pill	*la píldora anti-conceptiva*	altitude sickness	*el soroche*

Family

family	*la familia*	husband/wife	*el esposo (marido)/ la esposa*
friend	*el amigo/la amiga*		
brother/sister	*el hermano/ la hermana*	boyfriend/girlfriend	*el novio/la novia*
		married	*casado/a*
daughter/son	*la hija/el hijo*	single/unmarried	*soltero/a*
father/mother	*el padre/la madre*		

Months, days and time

January	*enero*	Friday	*viernes*
February	*febrero*	Saturday	*sábado*
March	*marzo*	Sunday	*domingo*
April	*abril*		
May	*mayo*	at one o'clock	*a la una*
June	*junio*	at half past two	*a las dos y media*
July	*julio*	at a quarter to three	*a cuarto para las*
August	*agosto*		*tres/a las tres*
September	*septiembre*		*menos quince*
October	*octubre*	it's one o'clock	*es la una*
November	*noviembre*	it's seven o'clock	*son las siete*
December	*diciembre*	it's six twenty	*son las seis y veinte*
		it's five to nine	*son las nueve*
Monday	*lunes*		*menos cinco*
Tuesday	*martes*	in ten minutes	*en diez minutos*
Wednesday	*miércoles*	five hours	*cinco horas*
Thursday	*jueves*	does it take long?	*¿tarda mucho?*

Numbers

one	*uno/una*	ten	*diez*
two	*dos*	eleven	*once*
three	*tres*	twelve	*doce*
four	*cuatro*	thirteen	*trece*
five	*cinco*	fourteen	*catorce*
six	*seis*	fifteen	*quince*
seven	*siete*	sixteen	*dieciséis*
eight	*ocho*	seventeen	*diecisiete*
nine	*nueve*	eighteen	*dieciocho*

nineteen	*diecinueve*	sixty	*sesenta*
twenty	*veinte*	seventy	*setenta*
twenty-one	*veintiuno*	eighty	*ochenta*
thirty	*treinta*	ninety	*noventa*
forty	*cuarenta*	hundred	*cien/ciento*
fifty	*cincuenta*	thousand	*mil*

Key verbs

to go	**ir**
I go	*voy*
you go (familiar)	*vas*
he, she, it goes,	
you (formal) go	*va*
we go	*vamos*
they, you (plural) go	*van*

to be	**ser**	**estar**
I am	soy	estoy
you are	eres	estás
he, she, it is,		
you (formal) are	es	está
we are	somos	estamos
they, you (plural) are	son	están

(*ser* is used to denote a permanent state, whereas *estar* is used to denote a positional or temporary state)

to have (possess)	**tener**
I have	*tengo*
you (familiar) have	*tienes*
he, she, it,	
you (formal) have	*tiene*
we have	*tenemos*
they, you (plural) have	*tienen*
there is/are	*hay*
there isn't/aren't	*no hay*

This section has been assembled on the basis of glossaries compiled by André de Mendonça and David Gilmour of South American Experience, London, and the Latin American Travel Advisor, No 9, March 1996.

Index

*Entries in **bold** refer to maps*

Advertisers' index

FOOTPRINT

Features

About the author

Chris Wallace has been travelling through, and writing about, Central and South America since 2004. He has lived in Colombia, Argentina, Chile, Brazil and Peru. He has tailored travel and tourism content for entrepreneurs and publishers alike, and, more than 10 years in, feels he's barely scratched the surface of what the South American continent has to offer.

Acknowledgements

Here are some of the folks in Argentina instrumental in helping me complete this book, and they have my everlasting thanks: Marcos Torres, Danny Feldman, Myrta Rojas, AnaLaura Rodríguez Esquercia, Patricia from Yo Amo el Norte Argentino, Cony and the staff at the BA Stop Hostel, Remy at Posada 21 Oranges, Juan from La Lechuza Hostel and all the helpful people at the tourist offces throughout Argentina.

Credits

Footprint credits
Editor: Jo Williams
Production and layout: Emma Bryers
Maps: Kevin Feeney
Colour section: Angus Dawson

Publisher: Felicity Laughton
Patrick Dawson
Marketing: Kirsty Holmes
Sales: Diane McEntee
Advertising and content partnerships:
Debbie Wylde

Photography credits
Front cover: Anibal Trejo/Shutterstock.com
Back cover top: Curioso/Shutterstock.com
Back cover bottom: Pola Damonte/
Shutterstock.com

Colour section
Page 1: Milosz Maslanka/Shutterstock.com.
Page 2: buenaventura/Shutterstock.com. **Page 4**:
T photography/Shutterstock.com, Michael Runkel/
Superstock.com. **Page 5**: Christian Kober/Superstock.
com, Guillermo Caffarini/Shutterstock.com, Pablo
Sebastian Rodriguez/Shutterstock.com. **Page 6**:
Prisma/Superstock.com, Pichugin Dmitry/Shutterstock.
com, robertharding/Superstock.com. **Page 7**: Eduardo
Rivero/Shutterstock.com, elnavegante/Shutterstock.
com, imageBROKER/Superstock.com, Jefferson
Bernardes/Shutterstock.com. **Page 9**: Seth Resnick/
Superstock.com. **Page 10**: sharptoyou/Shutterstock.
com. **Page 11**: Kobby Dagan/Shutterstock.com.
Page 12: Chris Howey/Shutterstock.com. **Page 13**:
Eduardo Rivero/Shutterstock.com, sunsinger/
Shutterstock.com. **Page 14**: Hugo Brizard –
YouGoPhoto/Shutterstock.com, javarman/Shutterstock.
com. **Page 15**: Yongyut Kumsri/Shutterstock.com.
Page 16: T photography/Shutterstock.com.

Duotones
Page 40: DSBfoto/Shutterstock.com. **Page 76**: kavram/
Shutterstock.com. **Page 126**: amybbb/Shutterstock.
com. **Page 176**: Stefano Oppo/Superstock.com.
Page 240: Nicolás Durán/Superstock.com. **Page 314**:
Aleksandra H. Kossowska/Shutterstock.com.
Page 388: saiko3p/Shutterstock.com. **Page 478**:
jorisvo/Shutterstock.com. **Page 552**: Pichugin Dmitry/
Shutterstock.com. **Page 588**: Andreea Dragomir/
Shutterstock.com.

Publishing information
Footprint Argentina
8th edition
© Footprint Handbooks Ltd
February 2017

ISBN: 978 1 911082 09 5
CIP DATA: A catalogue record for this book
is available from the British Library

® Footprint Handbooks and the
Footprint mark are a registered
trademark of Footprint Handbooks Ltd

Published by Footprint
5 Riverside Court
Lower Bristol Road
Bath BA2 3DZ, UK
T +44 (0)1225 469141
footprinttravelguides.com

Distributed in the USA by
National Book Network, Inc.

Printed in India by Replika Press Pvt Ltd

Every effort has been made to ensure that
the facts in this guidebook are accurate.
However, travellers should still obtain advice
from consulates, airlines, etc about travel
and visa requirements before travelling.
The authors and publishers cannot
accept responsibility for any loss, injury
or inconvenience however caused.

All rights reserved. No part of this
publication may be reproduced, stored
in a retrieval system, or transmitted, in
any form or by any means, electronic,
mechanical, photocopying, recording,
or otherwise without the prior permission
of Footprint Handbooks Ltd.

Colour map index

Footprint Mini Atlas
Argentina

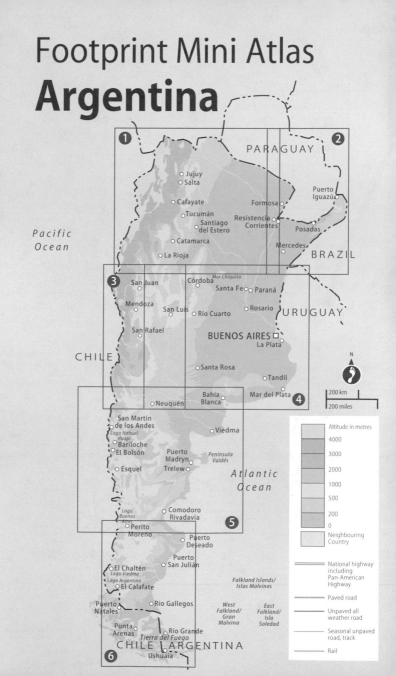

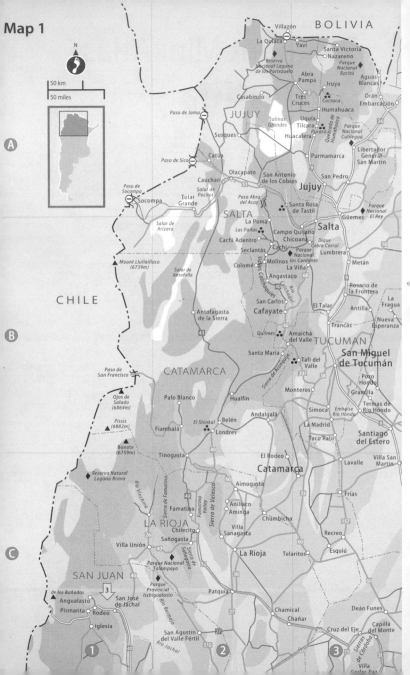

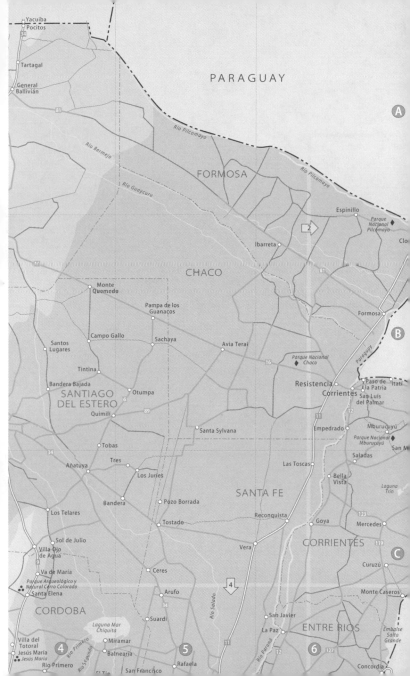

Map 2

Rio Pilcomayo

PARAGUAY

FORMOSA

Espinillo

Parque
Nacional
Pilcomayo

Clorinda

A ← 1

Paraguay

BRAZIL

Foz do Iguaçu
Iguazú Falls   Parque
Ciudad del Este   Nacional
Puerto Iguazú   Foz do
Iguaçu
Parque
Nacional
Iguazú

Formosa

Wanda
Esperanza

81

Bernardo
de Irigoyen

Rio Alto Paraná

Eldorado   Tobuna
San Pedro

101

Parque
Nacional
Chaco

Puerto Rico   MISIONES

Resistencia   11

Itatí

Paso de
la Patria

Corrientes   San Luis
del Palmar

San Cosmé
y Damián

12

Jesús   Corpus   Capioví   Reserva
Trinidad   Dos de   Natural San
Encarnación   Jardín América   Mayo   Antonio
San Ignacio
Posadas   San Ignacio Miní   Campo Viera   El Sobierbo
Candelaria   Santa Ana   Mocoñá
LN Alem   Santa Ana   Falls
Oberá   105

Ituzaingó

Empedrado   Mburucuyá

105   Alba
Posse

Rio Uruguay

San Miguel   San Javier

B   Parque Nacional
Mburucuyá

Las Toscas

Saladas

Apóstoles

Azara

Bella Vista   Esteros del Iberá   Garruchos

Laguna
Iberá

BRAZIL

Laguna
Trin   Laguna
Fernández

Colonia
Carlos   Santo Tomé
Pellegrini

CORRIENTES

123

quista

Goya   Mercedes

119   Yapeyú

Paso de
los Libres

Curuzú

4   Monte Caseros

14

ENTRE RIOS

Embalse
Salto
Grande

127

C   Concordia

San Salvador

Rio Uruguay

URUGUAY   N

Ubajay
Villaguay   Parque
Nacional
El Palmar

50 km

130   Colón   Paysandú

50 miles

Concepción
del Uruguay

1   2   3

aleguay   Gualeguaychú

Fray Bentos

Map 3

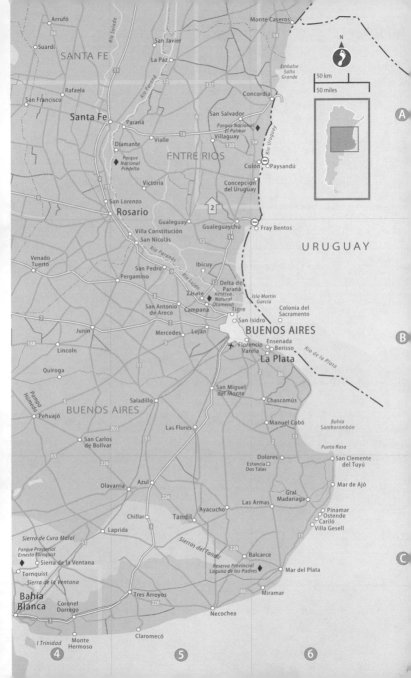

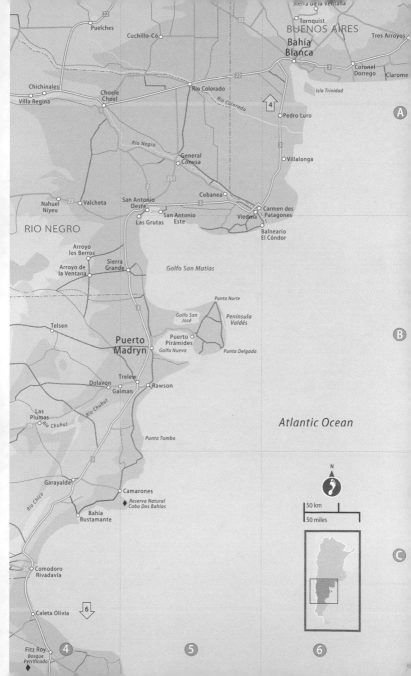

Wanderlust is the ultimate travel magazine for curious, independent-minded travellers

FOOTPRINT
SPECIAL SUBSCRIPTION OFFER
SAVE 75%

www.wanderlust.co.uk

BUY NOW
WanderlustOffer.co.uk/Footprint
Or call: 01753 620426 and quote **Footprint**

Distance chart

Buenos Aires
1121 Catamarca
689 432 Córdoba
939 836 894 Corrientes
1525 565 878 873 Jujuy
1142 156 453 992 721 La Rioja
1042 730 675 1443 1296 580 Mendoza
1161 1469 1167 1911 2045 1319 834 Neuquén
1005 1158 1207 322 1175 1314 1759 2085 Posadas
1019 820 874 19 857 970 1436 1896 341 Resistencia
2504 3015 2583 3326 3461 3036 2728 1874 3476 3292 Río Gallegos
1497 537 850 845 120 693 1268 2017 1147 829 3419 Salta
1110 623 585 1435 1164 449 168 1002 1763 1419 2799 1136 San Juan
791 685 412 1192 1229 535 255 784 1510 1185 2461 1201 323 San Luis
485 773 342 557 1105 795 903 1357 866 537 2773 1069 927 652 Santa Fe
1352 1863 1431 2174 2319 1884 1576 722 2338 2154 1140 2281 1647 1313 1621 Trelew
1193 233 546 748 332 389 964 1713 1070 732 3129 304 832 918 743 1977 Tucumán
3090 3601 3169 3912 4047 3622 3314 2460 4062 3878 586 4019 3385 3061 3359 1726 3715 Ushuaia
911 1621 1191 1802 2069 1644 1336 567 1897 1717 1640 2041 1407 1083 1184 508 1737 2226 Viedma

Distances in kilometres   1 kilometre = 0.62 miles

Discover Argentina with Air Europa, the Latin American specialist.

Fly from LONDON Gatwick to:

Buenos Aires
Daily flights on board our new 787 Dreamliner

And to Cordoba
In any of our 4 weekly services

All flights are via Madrid.
Cordoba via Madrid and Asuncion.

Œ AirEuropa

For more information call: 0871 423 0717 or visit us at: www.aireuropaexperts.com